Frommer's®

China

2nd Edition

Glenda

by Jen Lin-Liu, Dinny McMahon,
Paul Mooney, Sharon Owyang,
Beth Reiber, Graeme Smith,
and Christopher D. Winnan

Here's what the critics say about Frommer's:

"Amazingly easy to use. Very portable, very complete."
—*Booklist*

"Detailed, accurate, and easy-to-read information for all price ranges."
—*Glamour Magazine*

"Hotel information is close to encyclopedic."
—*Des Moines Sunday Register*

"Frommer's Guides have a way of giving you a real feel for a place."
—*Knight Ridder Newspapers*

WILEY
Wiley Publishing, Inc.

Published by:

Wiley Publishing, Inc.

111 River St.
Hoboken, NJ 07030-5774

ISBN-13: 978-0-7645-9743-5
ISBN-10: 0-7645-9743-4

Editor: Lorraine Festa
With special thanks to Ann Feng
Production Editor: Ian Skinnari
Cartographers: Tim Lohnes and Bart Wright
Photo Editor: Richard Fox
Production by Wiley Indianapolis Composition Services

Front cover photo: Fisherman on the Lí River, Guǎngxī Province
Back cover photo: Section of the Great Wall

For information on our other products and services or to obtain technical support, please contact our Customer Care Department within the U.S. at 800/762-2974, outside the U.S. at 317/572-3993 or fax 317/572-4002.

Wiley also publishes its books in a variety of electronic formats. Some content that appears in print may not be available in electronic formats.

Contents

(4) Běijīng & Héběi   76

by Graeme Smith

(5) The Northeast   155

by Paul Mooney

(6) Along the Yellow River   207

by Jen Lin-Liu

(7) The Silk Routes   247

by Jen Lin-Liu

8 Eastern Central China   323

by Jen Lin-Liu

9 Shànghǎi   411

by Sharon Owyang

10 The Southeast   459

by Christopher D. Winnan

11 Hong Kong   537

by Beth Reiber

12 The Southwest: Mountains & Minorities   584

by Christopher D. Winnan

13 Yángzǐ & Beyond   667

by Dinny McMahon

14 The Tibetan World   731

by Jen Lin-Liu

Appendix A: The Chinese Language   780

Appendix B: The Chinese Menu   803

Index   824

List of Maps

About the Authors

Jen Lin-Liu has worked as a freelance journalist based in China for five years. She has written for the Associated Press, the *Chronicle of Higher Education, Newsweek,* and the *Wall Street Journal,* among other publications. Though born in Chicago, she was raised in Southern California and studied at Columbia University. She is currently writing a book about how and what modern China eats. She would like to thank Wang Xin, Sherrise Pham, Hyeon-Ju Rho, and Matt Flynn for their much-needed help in traveling to far-flung places.

Dinny McMahon recently settled in Shànghǎi to work for Dow Jones Newswires, the culmination of years of studying in China, interspersing an undergraduate degree in his hometown of Sydney, Australia. During his studies, Dinny lived in Běijīng, and, most recently, Nánjīng where he studied economics and politics at the Johns Hopkins Center for Chinese and American studies.

Sharon Owyang, born in Singapore and a graduate of Harvard University, divides her time between film and television productions in the U.S. and China, and freelance travel writing. She is the author of *Frommer's Shànghǎi,* 3rd Edition, and also contributed to the 1st edition of *Frommer's China.* She has also written about Shànghǎi, China, Vietnam, and San Diego for Insight Guides, Compact Guides, the *Los Angeles Times,* and several websites. She speaks Mandarin, Cantonese, and enough Shanghainese to be a curiosity to the locals. When she's not traveling, she pays her dues in Los Angeles, California.

Before she could even read, **Beth Reiber** couldn't wait to go to her grandparents' house so she could pour through their latest *National Geographic.* After living several years in Germany as a freelance travel writer writing for major U.S. newspapers and in Tokyo as editor of the *Far East Traveler,* she authored several Frommer's guides, including *Frommer's Japan, Frommer's Tokyo,* and *Frommer's Hong Kong.* She also contributes to *Frommer's Europe from $85 a Day, Frommer's Europe by Rail,* and *Frommer's USA* and writes a monthly column on Japan. When not sleeping in far-flung hotels, she resides in Lawrence, Kansas, with her two sons, a dog, and a cat.

Graeme Smith previously wrote the Tibetan World and Silk Routes chapters of *Frommer's China,* 1st Edition, and most of the 3rd edition of *Frommer's Běijīng.* He was lured away from the comforts of academic life and a substantial contract with the South Coogee Wanderers Football Club to contribute to this edition. Although he spent 2 years at Peking and Tsinghua universities, Graeme attributes most of his language skills to an incurable love of local soap operas. While not sampling the pleasures of the capital, he divides his time between a research position at the Contemporary China Centre of the Australian National University and conducting agricultural research in rural Ānhuī (www.cedpa.org.cn).

Christopher D. Winnan's love/hate relationship with the continent currently known as China has lasted more than a decade. He has lived and worked in Běijīng, Shànghǎi, and Guǎngzhōu, and, unable to keep his comments to himself, has written extensively in both English and Chinese, most recently for *Time Out* and *Intercontinental Press.* Last year he bought a retirement house in Thailand, but even that cannot seem to keep him away from China, and he is currently residing in Dàlǐ, Yúnnán Province.

An Invitation to the Reader

In researching this book, we discovered many wonderful places—hotels, restaurants, shops, and more. We're sure you'll find others. Please tell us about them, so we can share the information with your fellow travelers in upcoming editions. If you were disappointed with a recommendation, we'd love to know that, too. Please write to:

Frommer's China, 2nd Edition
Wiley Publishing, Inc. • 111 River St. • Hoboken, NJ 07030-5774

An Additional Note

Please be advised that travel information is subject to change at any time—and this is especially true of prices. We therefore suggest that you write or call ahead for confirmation when making your travel plans. The authors, editors, and publisher cannot be held responsible for the experiences of readers while traveling. Your safety is important to us, however, so we encourage you to stay alert and be aware of your surroundings. Keep a close eye on cameras, purses, and wallets, all favorite targets of thieves and pickpockets.

Other Great Guides for Your Trip:

Frommer's Běijīng
Frommer's Shànghǎi
Frommer's Hong Kong
Suzy Gershman's Born to Shop Hong Kong, Shànghǎi & Běijīng

Frommer's Star Ratings, Icons & Abbreviations

Every hotel, restaurant, and attraction listing in this guide has been ranked for quality, value, service, amenities, and special features using a **star-rating system.** In country, state, and regional guides, we also rate towns and regions to help you narrow down your choices and budget your time accordingly. Hotels and restaurants are rated on a scale of zero (recommended) to three stars (exceptional). Attractions, shopping, nightlife, towns, and regions are rated according to the following scale: zero stars (recommended), one star (highly recommended), two stars (very highly recommended), and three stars (must-see).

In addition to the star-rating system, we also use **seven feature icons** that point you to the great deals, in-the-know advice, and unique experiences that separate travelers from tourists. Throughout the book, look for:

Finds	Special finds—those places only insiders know about
Fun Fact	Fun facts—details that make travelers more informed and their trips more fun
Kids	Best bets for kids and advice for the whole family
Moments	Special moments—those experiences that memories are made of
Overrated	Places or experiences not worth your time or money
Tips	Insider tips—great ways to save time and money
Value	Great values—where to get the best deals

The following **abbreviations** are used for credit cards:

AE	American Express	DISC Discover	V Visa
DC	Diners Club	MC MasterCard	

Frommers.com

Now that you have the guidebook to a great trip, visit our website at **www.frommers.com** for travel information on more than 3,000 destinations. With features updated regularly, we give you instant access to the most current trip-planning information available. At Frommers.com, you'll also find the best prices on airfares, accommodations, and car rentals—and you can even book travel online through our travel booking partners. At Frommers.com, you'll also find the following:

- Online updates to our most popular guidebooks
- Vacation sweepstakes and contest giveaways
- Newsletter highlighting the hottest travel trends
- Online travel message boards with featured travel discussions

What's New in China

China recently broke the 100-million mark for international visitors, ranking it fourth in the world, leaving Italy in fifth place and snapping at the heels of France, Spain, and the U.S. Official predictions are very optimistic, especially with the 2008 Olympics looming closer.

In reality, it looks as though this upward trend has occurred despite the authorities rather than because of them. Scandals over the fudging of official statistics emerged in May 2005 and the Golden Week policy that proved so profitable for price gougers is quickly losing popularity with the ordinary travelers who have to bear the brunt of the transportation chaos and ridiculous price hikes that the shortsighted policy created. Undeterred, the National Tourism Office announced 2005 as The Year of Red Tourism, designating "100 Classic Red Tourism Sites" and vowing to "reap capitalist gains from communist landmarks." Here's more news by region.

BĚIJĪNG & HÉBĚI There are now 19 brand-new **Z** (*zhídá*; direct) **trains** connecting with other cities, which depart at night and arrive early the following morning. Cities served are: Chángchūn, Chángshā, Harbin, Hángzhōu, Héféi, Nánjīng, Shànghǎi, Sūzhōu, Wǔhàn, Xī'ān, and the newly opened railway station in Yángzhōu. **Metro Line 5,** which will run past the east side of the Temple of Heaven, up to Dōng Dān, Dōng Sì, Lama Temple, and farther north to the east side of Yàyùn Cūn (Asian Games Village), will open in late 2006.

New hotel arrivals include the excellent **Holiday Inn Central Plaza,** Càiyuán Jiē 1 (© 010/8397-0088), offering great value for money in the south of town, and the less spectacular **Crowne Plaza Park View Wǔzhōu,** Běi Sì Huán Lù 4 (© 010/ 8498-2288). Many upscale properties are due to open during the life of this book, including **Park Hyatt, Hyatt Regency, Westin, Four Seasons, Ritz-Carlton,** and a new **Marco Polo** in Yàyùn Cūn.

Some newly renovated sections of the **Forbidden City** formerly closed to the public will open in 2005. These include the **Wǔyīng Diàn (Hall of Valiance and Heroism)** and the **Jiànfú Gōng Huāyuán (Garden of the Palace of Building Happiness)** in the western section of the palace. In the northeast section of the palace, the magnificent private theater of the Qiánlóng emperor, **Juànqín Zhāi,** will open in late 2006. The future of Běijīng's largest money-losing **Friendship Store** looks doubtful, although one announcement of its demise has already proven premature.

The **Great Wall** finally boasts respectable lodgings, allowing you to appreciate its ancient ramparts at sunset and sunrise. If expense is no object, treat yourself to the **Red Capital Ranch** (© 010/8401-8886), a boutique resort styled after a Manchurian hunting lodge, set in a river valley near **Mùtiányù.** Those on a budget will find adequate lodgings at the friendly **Sīmǎtái Youth Hostel.**

THE NORTHEAST   Construction has started on a new commercial airport in **Chángchūn,** scheduled to open by the time this book is published. That means that flights that used to land at a shabbier military field are now being redirected to a shiny new runway.

Yóutài Xīn Huìtáng, an old Jewish Synagogue, was recently renovated and opened to the public in Harbin. The elegantly restored house of worship holds contemporary art exhibitions of Russian and Jewish artists.

The Russian border town of **Mǎnzhōulǐ** recently opened its own airport, with daily flights to and from Běijīng and Harbin and three weekly flights to and from Hohhot.

ALONG THE YELLOW RIVER   The long-delayed **Dàtóng airport,** already 2 years behind schedule, was finally set for completion at press time, and promises to provide more convenient air connections to Běijīng, Shànghǎi, Guǎngzhōu, Chéngdū, and Shěnyáng.

Dàtóng has also seen the construction of several new hotels, providing a wider, and much improved, choice of places to stay.

One of the more curious new additions to tourism in Dàtóng is an arranged visit to one of Shānxī's many **coal mines.** Visitors are outfitted in a coal miner's outfit, complete with light-equipped helmet, for the short descent to a work site.

Visitors to **Píngyáo** must now purchase a 2-day pass for ¥120 ($15) that allows entrance to the small town's best 20 sights.

THE SILK ROUTES   The outskirts of **Xī'ān's Great Goose Pagoda (Dà Yàn Tǎ)** have been remodeled into a giant public square featuring a nightly light-and-water fountain show.

The **City Wall (Chéngqiáng)** of Xī'ān has been reconnected so that you can circle the entire perimeter of the wall by foot, bicycle, or golf cart.

Lánzhōu's Provincial Museum (Shěng Bówùguǎn) expects to complete an extensive renovation in 2006 and its treasures will be housed in a brand-new building.

Buddhist caves in Tuyoq, about 50km (31 miles) from Tǔlǔfān, were recently opened but there's not much to see here as all the relics have been removed by archaeologists; a few cave paintings remain.

Kuqa recently opened its airport to commercial flights, and now has two daily flights to and from Ürümqi.

The old town in **Kashgar,** absurdly enough, has also been handed over to a private Hàn company, which has set up a ticket booth at the front of certain neighborhoods, charging anyone who looks like a tourist ¥30 ($3.80). That same company has also begun charging those who want to enter Lake Karakul via Karakorum Highway ¥50 ($6.25).

EASTERN CENTRAL CHINA Qīngdǎo's World of Tsingtao Beer, a recently opened tourist attraction, has become a must-see for most visitors to Qīngdǎo, as the beer factory was only recently opened to the public. Speaking of beer, Qīngdǎo's **annual beer festival,** which takes place for 2 weeks each August, has expanded to a second location, at the Huìquán Guǎngchǎng, which offers a slightly more sanitized, calmer experience than the original site.

When construction ends on **Nánjīng's railway station** sometime in 2006, it will be linked to Nánjīng's subway, which opened in fall 2005.

SHÀNGHǍI   New overnight, dedicated soft-sleeper **express trains** (train numbers starting with "Z") now travel between Běijīng and Shànghǎi in 12 hours. The old **Shíliùpǔ Wharf** is no longer a working dock and is being transformed into a marina, park, and commercial complex.

Metro fares have increased and now start from ¥3 (35¢). **Metro line 4,** tracing a southern ring around downtown and extending into Pŭdōng, is anticipated to be operational in early 2006.

Since the last edition, several new **five-star hotels** as well as several refurbished midrange hotels have appeared on the Shànghǎi accommodations scene; the best of the bunch is the five-star **JW Marriott,** Nánjīng Xī Lù 399 (© **800/228-9290**).

Since the last edition, nowhere have the changes in Shànghǎi been more apparent than in the explosion of dining options in a town that now boasts some of the finest international cuisine in the world as well as some creatively reimagined local food. Leading the pack are two Bund-situated French restaurants: Jean-Georges Vongerichten's **Jean Georges,** Three on the Bund (© 021/6321-7733); and French twins Jacques and Laurent Pourcel's **Sens & Bund,** Bund 18 (021/6323-9898). Other dazzlers include **Laris,** Three on the Bund (© 021/6321-9922); **Mesa,** Jùlù Lù 748 (© 021/6289-9108); **La Villa Rouge,** Héngshān Lù 811 (© 021/6431-9811); and **Whampoa Club,** Three on the Bund (© 021/6321-3737).

With Shànghǎi's goal of housing more than 100 museums by the **World Expo of 2010,** there has been a proliferation of many small museums, housing everything from traditional Chinese musical instruments to folk crafts to navy ships, many too specialized to warrant listing here.

THE SOUTHEAST In trying to lure more free-spending tourists, two cities in particular are approaching almost cutthroat competition. While **Xiàmén** has always had a reputation as an attractive coastal city, **Quánzhōu** has in recent times been little more that a large industrial park, churning out limitless quantities of plastic footwear. The authorities in Quánzhōu are out to change this perception and have invested all their sweatshop profits into new museums, attractions, and luxury hotels. In retaliation, Xiàmén has kept up its frenetic pace of development, focusing on annual events such as a marathon, rather than simple infrastructure. Stay tuned.

The meteoric financial rise of **Wēnzhōu** has seen communications within the area mushroom in the last few years so that coastal highways have gouged out immense tunnels in the landscape and concreted over vast acres of what used to be rice paddy.

Flush with the profits of a major container port and manufacturing base in **Níngbō,** the authorities are playing catch-up in order to draw as many tourists as businessmen to the region. A brand-new tourism office plus a daunting amount of infrastructure investment in the town itself has opened up whole new tourist areas that many would have never even considered before. This is thanks mainly due the growing amount of Shanghainese desperate to escape the pressure and stress of China's 21st-century megalopolis.

HONG KONG A new **TurboJET Sea Express ferry service** now operates directly from Hong Kong International Airport to both Macau and Shēnzhèn (with a bus shuttle connecting to the Shēnzhèn airport). Travelers who wish to take advantage of this great convenience should check into the Air/Sea Transfer Desk *before* passing through Customs.

The **Hong Kong Tourist Board** has moved from its former inconvenient location on Hong Kong Island to the Causeway Bay MTR station near Exit F.

The new **KCR East Tsimshatsui Station,** which opened at the end of 2004 at the tip of Kowloon in Tsimshatsui East, provides a convenient link between the MTR subway system and the KCR **East Rail** with service to the New Territories and China.

Among the best new arrivals on the dining scene is **Hutong,** 1 Peking Rd., Tsimshatsui (© **852/3428 8342**), serving creative North Chinese fare in a dark dining hall that spotlights the stunning views from its 28th-floor perch.

Hong Kong Disneyland opened its newest, 125-hectare (310-acre) theme park September 2005 on Lantau island.

THE SOUTHWEST: MOUNTAINS AND MINORITIES In the last few years, **Guìzhōu Province** has seen almost as many new highways as the provinces on the coast. Apart from the main sights such as the caves and the falls, which are now swarming with sheeplike gànbù, the province can still be very hard travel, and is favored mainly by Europeans with an interest in ethnography.

Most overseas tourists to Guǎngxī head straight for **Yángshuò,** and these days they are much better rewarded than before. Small private enterprises are transforming the karst countryside with all kinds of attractions popping up for the active vacationer. And with more foreigners (including ex–tour guides) setting up shop, we are now seeing hotels and restaurants catering to international tastes.

Long famous for its **foreigners' street,** a rather tacky imitation of West Street in Yángshuò, where visiting foreigners are the main attraction for streams of gawking local tourists, **Dàlǐ** is now building a second foreigners' street. A **huge bypass** is now being built just outside the old city to take some of the stress of **Bó'ài Lù,** which used to be home to many of the early bars and cafes but is now being partly demolished to make way for even more new shops and travel agencies.

The new Hàn town of **Zhōngdiàn,** in Yúnnán Province, is a long thin line of some of the ugliest white-tile buildings seen in the country, made even worse by the fact that the surrounding countryside is so stunningly beautiful. At one end, the old town is being further gentrified to give it the mass tourist appeal of **Lì Jiāng,** the quaint old town that is now often more busy than Sānlǐtún on a Saturday night.

YÁNGZǏ & BEYOND Hóngsè Niándài (Red Generation) nightclub was once a highlight of any trip to **Chéngdū,** with its completely red interior and roster of apolitical rock bands playing most nights. Sadly, the march of modernization has seen the red give way to the globally homogenous and the rock banks replaced with unimpressed-looking beer girls. Tragically, the name remains the same—don't be fooled.

Chóngqìng Shì Bówùguǎn (Chóngqìng Municipal Museum) has moved to new premises near Rénmín Guǎngchǎng (People's Square). Whilst the new facility wasn't open at the time of writing, it promises to be a much grander affair with a sexier name: the **Three Gorges Museum** (Sānxiá Bówùguǎn).

Once the hopping on/off point for **Three Gorges cruises,** Wǔhàn has been stricken from most itineraries in favor of Yíchāng, a fairly uninspiring town just downstream from the Three Gorges dam. A new expressway linking Wǔhàn to Yíchāng takes about 4 hours and reduces your cruising experience by a day. But don't worry, most travelers tend to regard the stretch of the Yángzǐ into Wǔhàn as a little uninspiring.

THE TIBETAN WORLD The recently opened **Qīnghǎi Province Museum (Qīnghǎi Shěng Bówùguǎn)** is worth a visit for its vast collection of relics.

From Lhasa, there is a **new direct bus to Kathmandu** leaving every Friday for ¥580 ($73), and the ride should take 20 to 30 hours, depending on road conditions.

1

The Best of China

With a landmass of almost 10 million sq. km (4 million sq. miles), plus a further 5 million sq. km (2 million sq. miles) of water, no other single country can even come close to offering such a vast choice of destinations as the unimaginable vastness that is currently known as China.

The world's foremost authority on China, Harvard professor John King Fairbank, declared that "our libraries are filled with writers who know all about China, but could not see how much they did not know." We concede that we have barely scratched the surface, especially when we consider that human history in this area stretches back almost two million years, much further than the much-vaunted "5,000 years of Chinese civilization," yet even this is hardly a smudge on the far longer geologic record. In many parts, the People's Republic has only recently been opened to visitors, and so we have only had a few decades to unlock some of this enormous realm's secrets. While we certainly do not claim to have uncovered everything, we have been truly inspired by this huge treasure house, and have included here what we have been able to find out so far, starting with what we think is some of China's very best.

1 The Best China Experiences

- **Strolling Past the Old Russian Architecture in Harbin:** At the heart of the Russian-built city, Zhōngyāng Dàjiē's unexpected cupola-topped Art Nouveau mansions are reminders of the 1920s and 1930s, when Harbin was the liveliest stop on the eastern leg of the Trans-Siberian Railroad. See chapter 5.

- **Exploring the Forbidden City's Forgotten Corners** (Běijīng): No one fails to be impressed by the grandeur of the Forbidden City's central axis, which is all most visitors see. But the quieter maze of pavilions, gardens, courtyards, and theaters to either side have the greater charm. See chapter 4.

- **Dining on Shànghǎi's Bund:** China's most famous waterfront street of colonial architecture, the Bund, has recently become the toniest address in town, with the redevelopment of a few formerly stodgy old buildings into some of the city's finest shopping and dining establishments. These rooftop restaurants serve up unsurpassed views of Shànghǎi, old and new. See chapter 9.

- **Cycling the City Wall in Xī'ān:** The largest city walls in China have been much pierced for modern purposes and can be tackled in a modern way, too, with a breezy, traffic-light-free ride above the rooftops on rented bicycles and tandems. Behold views of remnants of vernacular architecture, clustered around small temples. See chapter 7.

- **Exploring Lì Jiāng's Old Town:** Built over 800 years ago and partly rebuilt after a massive 1996 earthquake, Lì Jiāng's old town, with its maze of cobblestone streets, gurgling streams, and original and reconstructed traditional Nàxī houses, is one of the most atmospheric places in China, hordes of tourists notwithstanding. Rise before the sun, then watch its golden rays filter through the gray winding streets, lighting up the dark wooden houses. See chapter 12.

- **Walking on the Great Wall from Jīnshānlǐng to Sīmǎtái** (Běijīng): The Great Wall, winding snakelike through the mountains, was meant to be walked. This magnificent 3-hour hike follows China's greatest monument through various states of repair, from freshly restored to thoroughly crumbling, over steep peaks and gentle flats, and through patches of wilderness and rugged farmland, with over two dozen watchtowers along the way. See chapter 4.

- **Riding the Star Ferry** (Hong Kong): There's no better way to acquaint yourself with Hong Kong than to ride the cheapest cruise in China. The century-old green-and-white Star ferries weave between tugs, junks, and ocean-going vessels in a 5-minute harbor crossing. See chapter 11.

- **Cruising the Lí River** (Guìlín): One of the most popular attractions in China, the cruise along the Lí River between Guìlín and Yángshuò is overexposed and overpriced, but the scenery along the way is still some of the most memorable in the world. The tongue of the Lí River flicks lazily past islands as it courses through serried hills like dragon's teeth. See chapter 12.

- **Unwinding in a Sìchuān Teahouse:** One of the great pleasures of being in Sìchuān is drinking tea at a neighborhood teahouse. On any given afternoon at Qīngyáng Gōng in Chéngdū, for instance, seniors can be found playing mahjong with friends while

their caged songbirds sit in nearby trees providing ambient music. As patrons eat watermelon seeds, nuts, dried squid, or beef jerky, attendants appear at regular intervals to refill their cups from copper kettles. For an afternoon of perfect relaxation, bring a friend and a deck of cards, or postcards to write, and forget about sightseeing for a few hours. See chapter 13.

- **Gazing at the Sea of Terra-Cotta Warriors at the Tomb of Qín Shǐ Huáng** (Xī'ān): The first sight of the tomb, situated in a hangarlike building, leaves many visitors stunned and awed. This destination is at the top of almost every visitor's list, and it does not disappoint. See p. 257.

- **Strolling in Shànghǎi's French Concession:** The domain of the French community up until 1949 was colonial Shànghǎi's trendiest area, and it remains full of tree-lined boulevards, colonial mansions, and numerous Art Deco masterpieces, now bundled up with phone lines and pole-hung washing. Some of the city's best shopping is also here. Just beyond the former concession is one of modern Shànghǎi's trendiest areas, the mega-development of restaurants and shops known as **Xīn Tiāndì**. See chapter 9.

- **Getting Lost in the Lanes Around Běijīng's Back Lakes:** No other city in the world has anything quite like the *hútòng*, narrow lanes once "as numberless as the hairs on an ox." Now rapidly vanishing, the best-preserved *hútòng* are found around a pair of man-made lakes in the city center. This section of the city is almost the last repository of Old Běijīng's gritty, low-rise charm, dotted with tiny temples, hole-in-the-wall noodle shops, and quiet courtyard houses whose older residents can still be seen walking around in Máo suits. See the walking tour, "The Back Lakes," on p. 121.

- **Strolling the Old Neighborhoods of Kashgar:** The dusty alleys, colorful residential doorways, and mud-brick walls remain as they have been for decades. Kids with henna-dyed feet and fingernails will approach you speaking a few words of Chinese and English; men with donkey carts trudge down narrow passages; bakers arrange round large slabs of nan in coal ovens built into the ground. Spending hours watching how citizens of Kashgar live is one of the most rewarding experiences along the Silk Road. See p. 307.

- **Taking a "Peapod" Boat on Shén-nóng Stream** (Yángzǐ River): Best of the Three Gorges cruise excursions, this 2-hour journey through a long, narrow canyon takes passengers to one of the famous suspended coffins of the Bā people, then returns them downstream in a fraction of the time. Along the way, howler monkeys can sometimes be spotted swinging through the trees, small waterfalls appear from the rocks, and swallows and other small birds flit about. The water in this small tributary is surprisingly clear, and the scenery and silence are thoroughly calming. See chapter 13.

2 The Best Small Towns

- **Xià Hé** (Gānsù): This delightful monastery town nestles in a mountain valley at an elevation of 2,900m (9,500 ft.). It's divided into two sections, primarily Huí (Muslim) and Hàn Chinese at its eastern end, changing abruptly to a Tibetan town as you climb westward to the gorgeous gilded roofs of the vast Labrang Monastery. Bent and walnut-visaged Tibetan pilgrims make you welcome on the 3km (2-mile) circuit around the monastery's perimeter. See chapter 7.

- **Mǎnzhōulǐ** (Inner Mongolia): A tiny town of 50,000 on the Russian border, lost in a sea of grass, Mǎnzhōulǐ is the East-meets-Wild-West frontier outpost David Carradine should have used as the backdrop to the TV series *Kung Fu*. It stands on the edge of the Hulun Buir, an emerald expanse of grassland shot through with radiant patches of wildflowers. See p. 204.

- **Dàlǐ** (Yúnnán): This home of the Bái people, a backpacker's mecca for over a decade and recently gentrified for large numbers of tourists, remains a retreat from the world. You can hike part of the impressive 19-peak Green Mountains (Cāng Shān) to the west, sail on the cerulean Ěr Hǎi Lake to the east, and take a bike ride into any of the nearby Bái villages. See p. 630.

- **Dūnhuáng** (Gānsù): Surrounded by barren deserts, this oasis town beckons with sand dunes, camel treks, and the Buddhist cave art of Mògāo. Its tree-lined streets and backpacker cafes give it a laid-back feeling that is hard to find elsewhere in China. See p. 284.

- **Yángshuò** (Guǎngxī): Some decry it for being overcommercialized, but this small town on the Lí River, nestled in a cluster of spiny pinnacles, has retained enough of its laid-back charm to be a delightful alternative to Guìlín. Fortunately, rather than being over-developed, Yángshuò is at the cutting edge of Chinese tourism and features some of its best innovations as well as some of its worst. See p. 594.

- **Shàoxīng** (Zhèjiāng): The gondolas of this relaxed "Venice" are narrow craft with arched, black-painted woven bamboo awnings, propelled by wiry boatmen acrobatically using both hands and feet to work the oars. The inevitable rebuilding of the city center has at least showed some sense of scale and left intact a few areas of ancient housing, through which the boatmen cruise, passing under Míng-era bridges. See p. 461.

3 The Best Countryside Trips

- **Jiǔzhài Gōu** (Sìchuān): This national park has dense forest, green meadows, rivers, rapids, ribbon lakes in various shades of blue and green, chalky shoals, and waterfalls of every kind—long and narrow, short and wide, terraced, rushing, and cascading. Of cultural interest are six Tibetan villages of the original nine from which this valley gets its name. See p. 692.

- **Bayan Bulak** (Xīnjiāng): This tiny Mongolian hamlet surrounded by breathtaking grasslands is reached by a spectacular journey through pine forests, waterfalls, and wildflowers. It's also close to vast **Swan Lake,** a breeding ground for elegant black swans. See p. 305.

- **Cháng Bái Shān** (Jílín): This long-dormant 2,600m-high (8,500-ft.) volcano is home to Tiān Chí, a deep, pure, mist-enshrouded crater lake that straddles the China–North Korea border and is sacred to both Koreans and Manchurians. The northern approach to the lake, with its trail that climbs alongside the thundering Chángbái Waterfall, is best in the fall. The western approach is ideal in early summer, when its vast fields of vibrant wildflowers are in full bloom. See p. 189.

- **The Bridges of Tàishùn County** (Zhèjiāng): Within living memory, this mountainous area above Wēnzhōu had no highways other than the winding paths and steep, stone-flagged staircases slithering down slopes to cross fast-moving rivers at extraordinary "centipede bridges"—photogenic hump-backed and often two-story constructions, with mid-stream shrines and topped with writhing ceramic dragons. Tàishùn still has many unpaved roads, and as you follow the original paths through the lush countryside to find some hidden bridge, you pass water buffalo pulling plows. See p. 480.

- **Lángmù Sì** (Gānsù): This Tibetan monastic center is largely unknown to Chinese tourists, and the tranquil mountain village is reminiscent of Lìjiāng before it was "discovered." The town is home to two major Tibetan monasteries, housing around 1,000 monks whose chanting of the scriptures may be heard throughout the day. Ramble through narrow ravines and moraine valleys crowded with wildflowers, or take a horse trek up Flower Cap Mountain to obtain stunning views as far as the holy mountain of Amnye Machen. See p. 277.

- **Amnye Machen** (Qīnghǎi): The route around this holy mountain, for a while believed to be the world's highest, must be clockwise—turning back is sacrilegious. So once you start on the 3-day horse trek, or the 7- to 10-day walk with the aid of a baggage-carrying yak, there's no turning back. But the scenery around the 6,282m (20,605-ft.) peak, and the company of sometimes entire villages of Tibetans, make the trek well worthwhile. See p. 748.

- **Around Lìjiāng** (Yúnnán): This area offers a wide variety of countryside experiences, from riding a chairlift up to the glacier park of the magnificent, snowcapped **Jade Dragon Snow Mountain,** to hiking the sheer-sided **Tiger Leaping Gorge** while the Yángzǐ River rages below, to being rowed in a "pig-trough" boat across the pristine **Lúgū Lake**—China's answer to Lake Tahoe. See p. 649.

- **Karakul Lake** (Xīnjiāng): On the highway between Kashgar and Tashkurgan lie stark, jagged mountains surrounded by a pristine lake at an altitude over 4,000m (13,120 ft.). Come here for some peace and quiet and a change of scenery from the dusty Uighur towns along the Silk Road. See p. 315.

- **Wǔ Líng Yuán & Zhāng Jiā Jiè** (Húnán): This scenic area is made up of three adjoining subtropical parklands, with quartzite sandstone peaks and pillars to rival Guìlín's scenery. There are plentiful rare plants and insects, swarms of butterflies, a large cave with calcite deposits, and stunning views through bamboo, pine, and oak forest. See p. 726.

- **Everest Base Camp** (Tibet): Whether by 3-hour drive from the village of Pelbar, or by a 3- to 4-day trek from Tingri, the trip to the tented base camp (at 5,150m/16,890 ft.) or to rooms in Rongbuk Monastery (at 4,980m/16,330 ft.) offers unbeatable vistas of the world's toothiest snowcaps set against a startling cobalt sky. See chapter 14.

- **Hulun Buir Grasslands** (Inner Mongolia): Located just outside the remote border town of Mǎnzhōulǐ, the Hulun Buir's grasslands are the most pristine in China. This expanse of gentle emerald hills, perfectly punctuated with small streams and rocky outcrops, is all the more attractive for how difficult it is to reach. See chapter 5.

- **Eastern Qīng Tombs** (Héběi): This rural tomb complex offers more to the visitor than the better-known Míng Tombs, but sees a fraction of the visitors. Undeniably difficult to reach, the effort is rewarded many times over by the Qiánlóng emperor's breathtakingly beautiful tomb chamber, **Yù Líng,** and an (unintentionally) drop-dead funny photo exhibit of the much-maligned dowager empress Cíxǐ. See chapter 4.

- **The Leaning Towers of Kāipíng** (Guǎngdōng): This county is littered with extraordinary towers called *diāolóu*—some of them squat brick fortresses dating from the 17th century; others bizarre, alien watchtowers mostly built by Chinese who traveled out through the treaty ports and returned wealthy enough to build fortified residences. Up to nine stories high, the towers sprout turrets and loopholes, balconies and cupolas, borrowed from half-understood European styles encountered anywhere from Macau to Manila. *Diāolóu* tower over almost every village and rice paddy in the county. See chapter 10.

- **Rice Terraces** (Guǎngxī): Some of southwest China's most spectacular vistas are of its terraced rice fields—golden yellow in the fall and sparkling silver in the spring—painstakingly hewn over hundreds of years by various minority groups. See chapter 12.

- **Huáng Shān** (Ānhuī): The most famous mountain in China for scenic beauty, actually a group of 72 peaks, is known for its sea of clouds, strangely shaped rocks, unusual pine trees, and bubbling hot springs—four features that have inspired countless painters and poets for over 1,500 years. See p. 643.

4 The Best Mansions & Palaces

- **Wáng Jiā Dàyuàn** (Píngyáo): It took a century for this vast mansion to grow to 123 courtyards and 1,118 houses; the decorative lattice screens and windows, shaped openings between rooms and courtyards, and undulating walls are exquisite examples of Míng and Qīng vernacular architecture. See p. 236.

- **Potala Palace** (Lhasa): A monastery, a palace, and a prison, the Potala symbolizes the fusion of secular and religious power in Tibet in a vast, slab-sided, red-and-white agglomeration on a hilltop dominating central Lhasa. Despite the ruination of its surroundings, there's no more haunting sight within China's modern political boundaries, and nothing else that speaks so clearly of the otherness of Tibet. See p. 757.

- **The Forbidden City** (Běijīng): Preeminent among the surviving complexes of ancient buildings in China, the former residence of the emperors needs far more time than most tours give it. See "The Best China Experiences," earlier in this chapter, and p. 107.

- **Wěi Huánggōng** (Chángchūn): Also known as the Puppet Emperor's Palace and best known in the west as the setting for part of Bernardo Bertolucci's film *The Last Emperor*, this impressive palace complex, opened to visitors after an admirable full-scale restoration in 2002, was the residence of Henry Pǔyí, China's last emperor and subsequently puppet ruler of Japanese-controlled Manchukuo. See p. 180.

- **Wáng Jiā Dàyuàn** (Héběi): With investment from a Běijīng entrepreneur, part of a traditional courtyard mansion which once housed Shān-hǎiguān's wealthiest burgher has been magnificently restored and is expected to expand farther south. Set in the heart of the old walled town, it also boasts a folk museum crammed with curiosities. Four of the rooms are available for overnight stays, although you'll have to be out before the next day's visitors arrive. See p. 146.

- **Qiáo Jiā Dàyuàn** (Píngyáo): One of the loveliest of the several merchant family mansions of this area, this was the set for the film *Raise the Red Lantern*. With six large courtyards, 313 houses, and fine craftsmanship of lattices, lintels, carvings, wooden balustrades, and chimneys throughout, the 18th-century manse takes hours to explore. See p. 235.

- **Bìshǔ Shānzhuāng** (Chéngdé): The imperial summer resort and its surrounding Eight Outer Temples form another of the greatest ancient architectural complexes of China, arranged around a green valley. The temples have bizarre borrowings from a number of minority architectural traditions, and both temples and palace have 18th-century replicas of buildings of which the country is most proud. See p. 140.

5 The Best Museums

- **Hong Kong Museum of History** (Hong Kong): A life-size diorama of a Neolithic settlement, replicas of fishing boats and traditional houses, ethnic clothing, displays of colorful festivals, and whole streets of old shop frontages with their interiors removed piece by piece and rebuilt here, make this the most entertaining museum in China. See p. 562.

- **Shǎnxī Lìshǐ Bówùguǎn** (Xī'ān): If you can visit only one museum in

China, this should be it. An unrivaled collection of treasures, many demonstrating Xī'ān's international contacts via the Silk Routes, is more professionally displayed here than almost anywhere else in the mainland. See p. 256.

- **Sānxīng Duī Bówùguǎn** (Chéngdū): An attractive and well-laid-out museum housing items from a group of sacrificial pits, this is one of the most significant finds in 20th-century China. See p. 674.
- **Shànghǎi Bówùguǎn** (Shànghǎi): In terms of display and English labeling, this ultra-modern museum (lights fade as you approach cabinets), loaded with stunning antiquities, is China's most modern and inviting. See p. 439.
- **Nánjīng Dàtúshā Jìniànguǎn** (Nánjīng): The deaths of over 300,000 Chinese, killed over the course of 6 weeks during the 1937 Japanese invasion of Nánjīng, are commemorated here. Photographs and artifacts documenting the Japanese onslaught, the atrocities suffered, and the aftermath, are sobering, grisly, and shockingly effective. See p. 381.
- **Wáng Āntíng Xiǎoxiǎo Zhǎnlǎnguǎn** (Chéngdū): Located in a narrow lane west of the main town square, this small, one-of-a-kind museum contains tens of thousands of Máo pins, Cultural Revolution memorabilia, and vintage photographs. The museum occupies the living room of its devoted proprietor. See p. 675.
- **Maritime Museum (Hǎiwài Jiāotōng Shǐ Bówùguǎn)** (Quánzhōu): Hidden away on the second floor, visitors will find a unique collection of painstakingly hand-crafted, scale models that trace the entire history of Chinese seafaring from its very beginnings. See p. 497.

6 The Best Temples

- **Kǒng Miào** (Qūfù): One of China's greatest classical architectural complexes, this spectacular temple in Confucius's hometown is the largest and most magnificent of the hundreds of temples around the country honoring the sage. Greatly enlarged since it was originally built in 478 B.C., it has a series of gates and buildings aligned on a north–south axis and decorated with imperial flourishes like yellow-tiled roofs and dragon-entwined pillars. See p. 358.
- **Màijī Shān Shíkū** (Tiānshuǐ): This haystack-shaped mountain of soft red rock, covered in brilliant green foliage, is China's prettiest cave-temple site, and the only one where statuary has been added to the cave walls rather than carved out of them. Views from the stairs and walkways lacing the cliffs are spectacular (including those straight down). See p. 266.
- **Zhèngdìng** (Héběi): Neither the most spectacular nor the best known of temple groups, but within a short walking distance of each other, are some of China's oldest surviving unimproved temple buildings (one of which houses a 30m-high/90-ft. multi-armed bronze of Guānyīn), and a collection of ancient pagodas so varied it's almost as if they've been set out specifically to surprise you. See p. 147.
- **Jokhang Temple** (Lhasa): The spiritual heart of Tibetan Buddhism, this

temple should be visited twice: once to see the intense devotion of pilgrims circumnavigating it by prostrating themselves repeatedly across cobblestones made slippery by centuries of burning yak-butter lamps, and rubbing their foreheads against the statuary in the dim, smoky interior; and a second time in the afternoon for a closer look at the ancient images they venerate. See p. 757.

- **Mògāo Caves** (Dūnhuáng): Here is the biggest, best-preserved, and most significant site of Buddhist statuary and frescoes in all of China—and one of the best-curated attractions, too. The guides, who all have bachelor's degrees, are excellent, sometimes going well beyond the script. See p. 287.

- **Temple of Heaven** (Běijīng): The circular Hall of Prayer for Good Harvests, one of the finest achievements of Míng architecture, is almost as well known as a symbol of Běijīng as the Tiān'ān Mén, but the three-tiered sacrificial altar of plain stone is thought by many to be the most sublime object of beauty in China. See p. 115.

- **Dragon Gate Grottoes** (Luòyáng): The grottoes go well beyond just the identity of a temple, as these caves are considered one of the best sculptural treasure troves in China. The site comprises a mind-boggling 2,300 caves and niches with more than 2,800 inscriptions and over 100,000 Buddhist statues. See p. 335.

- **Sakya Monastery** (Sàjiā Sì) (Sakya): The massive 35m (115-ft.) windowless gray walls of Lhakhang Chenmo tower above the village and fields on the southern bank of the Trum Chu. Completed in 1274, this monastery fort was largely funded by Kublai Khan, and unlike the older temples of north Sakya, it survived the Cultural Revolution. See p. 772.

- **Yōnghé Gōng** (Běijīng): After the Qīng Yōngzhèng emperor moved into the Forbidden City, his personal residence was converted into this temple. Several impressive incense burners are scattered throughout the golden-roofed complex, also known as the Lama Temple. A 20m-tall (60-ft.) sandalwood statue of Maitreya, the future Buddha, fills the last building. See p. 118

- **Bǎodǐng Shān** (Dàzú): Artistically among the subtlest and most sophisticated of China's Buddhist grottoes, these Sòng dynasty caves are situated around a horseshoe-shaped cove, at the center of which is lush forest. See p. 703

- **Yúngǎng Shíkū** (Shānxī): These are the earliest Buddhist caves carved in China. Most were hollowed out over a 65-year period between 460 and 524. Viewed as a whole, they show a movement from Indian and central Asian artistic models to greater reliance on Chinese traditions. See p. 210.

See also Chéngdé's Bìshǔ Shānzhuāng and its Eight Outer Temples, in "The Best Mansions & Palaces," above.

7 The Best Markets

- **Kashgar Sunday Bazaar:** The bazaar is now split in two and not quite what it was, but the livestock part of the market, southeast of town, is still well worth visiting. Bearded Uighur men in traditional blue-and-white garb sharpen their knives and trim their sheep, small boys wearing Inter Milan strip gorge themselves on Hami melons, Kyrgyz in dark fur hats pick up and drop dozens of lambs to test their weight and meatiness before settling deals with vigorous and protracted handshakes. See p. 312.

- **Pānjiāyuán Jiùhuò Shìchǎng** (Běijīng): A vast outdoor market held on weekends, Pānjiāyuán teems with what is very likely the world's best selection of things Chinese: row upon row of everything from reproduction Míng furniture to minority clothing to Máo memorabilia. Most of the antiques are fakes, although experts have made some surprising finds in the bedlam. See p. 132.

- **Kāifēng Night Market** (Kāifēng): Visitors overnight in Kāifēng just so they can attend this famous and festive night market whose mainstay is the wide variety of delicious local snacks on offer, such as five-spice roasted bread, sesame soup, and spicy lamb kabob. See p. 345.

- **Khotan Sunday Market:** This is everything the Kashgar Market once was. Jewelers pore over gemstones, blacksmiths busy themselves shoeing horses and repairing farm tools, blanket makers beat cotton balls, rat-poison sellers proudly demonstrate the efficacy of their products—the sights and smells are overwhelming. Don't miss the horse-riding enclosure toward the north side of the melee, where buyers test the road-worthiness of both beast and attached cart, with frequent spectacular tumbles. See p. 318.

- **Temple Street Night Market** (Hong Kong): Prices here are outrageous compared to those at China's other markets, but the scene at this night market is very entertaining, especially the fortune-tellers and street-side performers singing Chinese opera. See p. 571.

- **Dǒngjiādù Fabric Market** (Shànghǎi): Bales and bales of fabric (silk, cotton, linen, wool, and cashmere) are sold here at ridiculously low prices. Many stalls have their own in-house tailors who can stitch you a suit, or anything else you want, at rates that are less than half what you'd pay at retail outlets. See p. 449.

- **Hǎizhū Square Wholesale Market** (Guǎngzhōu): With so many markets to choose from in a city whose very raison d'être is commerce, it is difficult to know which one to choose first. This is one of the most colorful. If it was made in China then there is a very good chance that you will find it around here somewhere. See p. 524.

8 The Best Festivals

For dates and contact information, see also the "China Calendar of Events" on p. 30.

- **Saka Dawa,** held throughout the Tibetan world, celebrates the Buddha passing away and thus attaining nirvana. It's held on the 8th to 15th days of the fourth lunar month, with religious dancing, mass chanting and "sunning the Buddha"—the public display of giant sanctified silk portraits. See chapter 14.

- **Ice and Snow Festival** (Harbin): Not so much a festival as an extended citywide exhibition, Harbin's Ice and Snow Festival runs from December to March every year and is without doubt the northeast's top winter attraction. The festival centers around hundreds of elaborate ice and snow sculptures, frosty reproductions of everything from Tiān'ān Mén to Elvis. See chapter 5.

- **Sānyuè Jié** (Dàlǐ): This once-religious festival celebrated by the Bái people in mid-April/early May now features 5 days and nights of considerably more secular singing, dancing, wrestling, horse-racing, and large-scale trading. This is a rare opportunity to see not only the Bái, but a number of Yún-nán's other minorities, gathering together in one of the most beautiful and serene settings in the foothills of the Green Mountains (Cāng Shān). See chapter 12.

- **Kurban Bairam** (Kashgar): Celebrations are held in Muslim communities across China, but in Kashgar they involve feats of tightrope-walking in the main square and wild dancing outside the Idkah Mosque. The 4-day festival is held 70 days after the breaking of the fast of Ramadan, on the 10th day of the 12th month (Dhul-Hijjah) in the Islamic calendar. It falls on January 13, 2006, and annually shifts backward by 12 days. See chapter 2.

- **Miáo New Year Festival** (Xījiāng, Lángdé): The Miáo celebrate many festivals, but one of the biggest blowouts is the occasion of the Miáo New Year, usually around December. The celebration features songs, dances, bullfights, and *lúshēng* competitions, not to mention Miáo women gorgeously bedecked in silver headdresses engaging in various courtship rituals. See chapter 12.

9 The Best Up-and-Coming Destinations

- **Yǒngdìng** (Fújiàn): The magnificent multistory circular **fortresses** of the Hakka minority, known as "earth buildings" and home to hundreds (usually all with the same family name), are the largest and most striking examples of surviving domestic architecture in China. See chapter 10.

- **Yùshù** (Qīnghǎi): Khampa areas within the Tibet "Autonomous Regions" are closed to the individual traveler, but here these fiercely proud Tibetan warriors trade in a traditional market town beneath a stern gray-and-red monastery. See chapter 14.

- **Yánbiān** (Jílín): A lush, achingly pretty hilly region perched on China's border with North Korea, parts of which have only recently been opened to tourism, Yánbiān is home to the largest population of ethnic Koreans outside the peninsula itself. Independent-minded travelers have the opportunity to explore one of the few truly bicultural societies in China. See chapter 5.

- **Téngchōng** (Yúnnán): This charming overlooked town on the ancient southern Silk Route is poised to become an important tourist destination in the coming years as tourist authorities gear up to promote travel along the ancient trade route. For now, Téngchōng is still a laid-back, friendly town with a surprisingly large number of attractions that include hot springs, volcanoes, waterfalls, temples, and some absolutely delightful traditional Chinese villages just outside it. See chapter 12.

- **Píngyáo** (Shānxī): Chinese tourists have discovered Píngyáo, but the numbers of Western tourists are still relatively few at what is one of the best-preserved Míng and Qīng towns in China. An intact Míng city wall surrounds clusters of elegant high-walled courtyard residences, some of which are also guesthouses. See chapter 6.

- **Quánzhōu** (Fújiàn): An overnight ferry from Hong Kong, a few days in Xiàmén, and a short bus trip to Quánzhōu combine to make the perfect less-traveled start to a China trip. The laid-back town has plenty of interest to see, at a human scale and pace. See chapter 10.

- **Níngbō** (Zhèjiāng): With a new tourist office and lots of colorful brochures, the authorities here are determined to make Níngbō more than a container port. Here is an opportunity to discover new beaches, forests, temples, and mountain ranges that many Chinese have never even heard of. See chapter 10.

10 The Best Local Accommodations

- **Dūnhuáng Shānzhuāng** (Dūnhuáng): The finest hotel on the Silk Routes, with views of the Míngshā Shān Dunes, this imposing fortress is surrounded by stylishly renovated courtyard houses. See p. 289.
- **Lǎsōng Yuán Bīnguǎn:** Of all Běijīng's traditional courtyard-style hotels, this former imperial residence has the most character, recalling the opulence of China's "feudal" era, but with a more lived-in feel than you'll find elsewhere. See p. 95.
- **Lóngmén Guìbīn Lóu** (Harbin): Built by the Russian-controlled Chinese Eastern Railroad in 1901, the Lóngmén has served as a hospital, the Russian embassy, and a cheap hostel for migrant workers. In the 1930s and 1940s, it was part of the illustrious Japanese-owned Yamato Hotel chain. The Chinese Railway Bureau renovated the building in 1996, preserving the original Russian woodwork and restoring much of its turn-of-the-20th-century atmosphere. Rooms are palatial and decorated with period furniture. See p. 200.
- **Sèmǎn Bīnguǎn** (Kashgar): Set on the grounds of the former Russian consulate, this has merely two government-issued stars and poor service, but standard rooms and suites in the original and beautifully decorated consulate buildings, with their high ceilings and dramatic oil paintings, can be bargained down to low prices. This is the nearest you'll get to experiencing some "Great Game" ambience. See p. 313.
- **Déjū Yuán & Tiān Yuán Kuí** (Píngyáo): These are the top two courtyard guesthouses in a town full of ancient architecture. The Déjū Yuán has rooms decorated with calligraphy and furnished with dark wooden Míng-style tables and chairs and traditional heated brick beds. The Tiān Yuán Kuí also offers occasional opera performances on hot summer nights when the guesthouse is full and the performers available. See p. 236.
- **Yè Bǎihé Bīnguǎn (Night Lily Guest House)** (Gǔlàng Yǔ): One of the latest, and certainly one of the most successful conversions of early colonial architecture. A fascinating combination of Qīng dynasty furniture and modern interior-design styles, although the antique beds have been causing a few problems for very tall foreign visitors whom they were definitely not designed for in the first place. See p. 512.
- **The Peninsula** (Hong Kong): Built in 1928 and retaining the atmosphere of its colonial past, The Peninsula has long been the grand old hotel of Hong Kong. It boasts an ornate lobby popular for people-watching, some of Hong Kong's best restaurants, and gorgeous rooms with sweeping views of Victoria Harbour. See p. 548.
- **Yángshuò Shèngdì (Mountain Retreat)** (Yángshuò): Situated in one of the area's most picturesque settings, this small hotel is a world away from the usual trials and tribulations of traveling in China. This is the kind of place where you will want to

extend your holiday indefinitely. See p. 602.

The **Peace Hotel,** the best of Shànghǎi's historic hotels—built in 1929 as the Cathay Hotel—features a lobby that is an Art Deco masterpiece, and splendid public areas. Rooms have been modernized, but the service has lapsed. Go for lunch or a drink. See also **Yǒngdìng** in "The Best Up-and-Coming Destinations," above. A night in a several-hundred-year-old earthen fortress is as authentic as it gets, but don't expect luxuries (or even necessities).

11 The Best Buys

- **Chén Lú** (Shǎnxī): Seventeen small factories turn out different styles of pottery, and their showrooms have starting prices so low you'll volunteer to pay more. You can also buy original works in the houses of individual artisans. See p. 263.
- **Zhōng Běi Jiùhuò Shìchǎng** (Xī'ān): There are fakes aplenty, as everywhere else, but this bustling antiques market, fed by continuous new discoveries in the surrounding plain, is geared to locals, so asking prices are not as absurd as elsewhere. See p. 258.
- **Jatson School** (Lhasa): High-quality Tibetan handicrafts, including traditional Tibetan clothing, paper, incense, mandala *thangkas,* yak-hide boots, ceramic dolls, door hangings, bags, and cowboy hats, are all made on-site, and sold at very fair prices. Your money goes to support poor, orphaned, and children with disabilities. See p. 760.
- **Name-Brand Clothing & Accessories:** Adequate to near-perfect imitations of items by North Face, Louis Vuitton, Prada, and just about any other expensive label you can think of can be had for a song at several markets in China, especially at Běijīng's Silk Street and Hóngqiáo markets, Shànghǎi's Xiāngyáng Lù market, and Shēnzhèn's Luó Hú Commercial City (not quite as cheaply). See chapters 4, 9, and 10.

- **Factory 798** (Běijīng): We left 798 out of the first edition, reasoning that an ad hoc gathering of designers, painters, and sculptors selling avant-garde art in a former military complex wasn't something the regime would tolerate for long. We were wrong. Market rents are now charged, so don't expect to pick up a bargain, but the Dàshānzi art district makes for a thoroughly enjoyable afternoon of gallery- and cafe-hopping. See p. 119.
- **Khawachen Carpet and Wool Handicraft Co. Ltd** (Lhasa): This U.S.-Tibetan factory's carpets have rich but tasteful shades woven into delightful traditional patterns. Carpets can also be made to order. You'll pay much less here than in New York or even Běijīng. See p. 760.
- **Qípáo:** Tailors in Běijīng and Shànghǎi will cut a custom-fit *qípáo,* the tight-fitting traditional dress better known by its Cantonese name *cheongsam,* sometimes for hundreds of dollars less than in Hong Kong and the West. A quality tailored dress, lined with silk and finished with handmade buttons, typically costs between $100 and $200. Slightly less fancy versions go for as little as $50. See chapters 4 and 9.

Note: Pearls, antiques, jade, jewelry in general, and objets d'art are fakes or are not worth the asking price (usually both). Unless you are an expert or are happy to have a fake, do not buy these things.

2

Planning Your Trip to China

by Christopher D. Winnan

Travel in China isn't as hard as you think. If you can manage Paris by yourself without speaking French, you can manage Běijīng without Mandarin. Tens of thousands of visitors travel in China independently each year, making their arrangements as they go, and without more than a guidebook and a phrase book to help them. You can certainly arrange various levels of assistance, either upon arrival or from home, but you can also travel just as freely as you would elsewhere, perhaps using agents to get your tickets, and picking up the odd day tour.

But whether you plan to travel at random, with a preplanned, prebooked route, or with a fully escorted tour, it's *vital* that you read this chapter carefully. The way you're used to traveling, even in many other developing nations, doesn't apply in China. Much of the advice out there on travel in China is far from wise. What's good advice in the rest of the world can be the worst advice in China, and without absorbing what's below, some of the rest of this guide may seem inscrutable.

So put down your preconceptions and read on.

1 The Regions in Brief

BĚIJĪNG, TIĀNJĪN & HÉBĚI

While there's much talk of getting to the Three Gorges on the Yángzǐ River before the area's partial disappearance, the real urgency is to see what little of the old Běijīng is left before preparations for the 2008 Olympics deliver the final coup de grâce to what remains of its ancient housing and original Míng dynasty street plan. Whole city blocks can vanish at once, not gradually drowned over a period of years, but felled in the space of a few days, sometimes taking ancient, long-forgotten temples with them (although some of these are occasionally restored and reopened to public view).

But while Běijīng suffers from being communism's showpiece for the outside world and victim of ersatz modernization, it still has far more to offer than several other Chinese cities put together, including some of China's most extravagant monuments, such as the **Forbidden City.** In addition, there's easy access to the surrounding province of **Héběi** with its sinuous sections of the **Great Wall** and vast **tomb complexes.**

THE NORTHEAST

Even if the Chinese no longer believe civilization ends at the Great Wall, most tourists still do. The frigid lands to the northeast, once known as Tartary or Manchuria, represent one of the least-visited and most challenging regions in China, and its last great travel frontier.

Despite industrialization, the provinces of **Liáoníng, Jílín,** and **Hēilóng Jiāng,** and the northern section of **Inner Mongolia,** still claim China's largest **natural forest,** its most **pristine grasslands,** and one of its most celebrated lakes (**Tiān**

Chí). What makes the region unique, however, are the architectural remnants of the last 350 years—early **Qīng palaces and tombs,** incongruous **Russian cupolas,** and eerie structures left over from Japan's wartime occupation.

AROUND THE YELLOW RIVER

As covered in this book, this region comprises an area of northern China that includes **Shānxī, Níngxià,** parts of **Shǎnxī** (sometimes spelled Shaanxi), and **Inner Mongolia,** roughly following the central loop of the Yellow River north of Xī'ān.

One of China's "cradles of civilization," the area lays claim to most of the country's oldest surviving **timber-frame buildings** and its oldest carved **Buddhist grottoes,** as well as **Píngyáo,** one of its best-preserved **walled cities.**

THE SILK ROUTES

From the ancient former capital of **Xī'ān,** famed for the modern rediscovery of the **Terra-Cotta Warriors,** trade routes ran in all directions, but most famously (because they were given a clever name in the 19th c.) west and northwest through **Gānsù** and **Xīnjiāng,** and on through the Middle East. Under the control of Tibetan, Mongol, Indo-European, and Turkic peoples more than of Chinese, these regions are still populated with Uighurs, Tajiks, Kazakhs, Tibetans, and others, some in tiny oasis communities on the rim of the **Taklamakan Desert,** which seem completely remote from China. The Silk Routes are littered with alien monuments and tombs, and with magnificent cave-temple sights such as **Dūnhuáng,** which demonstrate China's import of foreign religions and aesthetics as much as the wealth generated by its exports of silk.

EASTERN CENTRAL CHINA

Eastern central China, between the Yellow River (Huáng Hé) and the Yángzǐ River (Cháng Jiāng), is an area covering the provinces of **Hénán, Shāndōng, Jiāngsū,** and **Ānhuī.** It is the area in which Chinese culture developed and flourished with little dilution or outside influence. **Luòyáng** was the capital of nine dynasties, **Kāifēng** capital of six, and **Nánjīng** capital of eight. The hometown of China's most important philosopher, Confucius, is here, along with several of China's holiest mountains, notably **Tài Shān** and **Huáng Shān,** as well as that watery equivalent of the Great Wall, the **Grand Canal.**

SHÀNGHǍI

Shànghǎi is the city China boosters love to cite as representing the country as a whole, but it in fact represents nothing except itself—the country's wealthiest city, and with (if the government's figures are to be believed) the highest per-capita income. Look closer and you'll see that many of its shiny new towers are incomplete or unoccupied. But the sweep of 19th- and early-20th-century architecture along **The Bund,** which looks as if the town halls of two dozen provincial British cities have been transported to a more exotic setting, and the maze of Art Deco masterpieces in the **French Concession** behind the Bund, make Shànghǎi the mainland's top East-meets-West destination, with the restaurants and a more relaxed and open-minded atmosphere to match. Nearby **Hángzhōu** and **Sūzhōu** offer some of China's most famous scenery.

THE SOUTHEAST

South of Shànghǎi and the Yángzǐ River, the coastal provinces of **Zhèjiāng, Fújiàn,** and **Guǎngdōng** have always been China's most outward-looking. These towns, which boomed under the relatively open Táng dynasty and which were forced to reopen as "treaty ports" by the guns of the first multinationals in the 19th century, are also those most prosperous under the current "reform and opening" policy. But in between the famous names, smaller **Shàoxīng** and **Quánzhōu** have managed to preserve some of their charm. **Xiàmén**, connected to Hong Kong by sea, has a treasure trove of colonial-era shop-houses, and an island covered in foreign-style mansions. A short distance inland, rural life continues much as it did back in the Táng dynasty, and extraordinary collections of **fortress-mansions, corridor bridges,** and **watchtowers** have survived the destruction of the Cultural Revolution. A little farther inland, the impoverished pottery-producing province of **Jiāngxī** shows the two-speed nature of China's growth.

HONG KONG & MACAU

Two sets of pencil-slim towers jostle for position on either side of a harbor, close as bristles on a brush. Between them, ponderous ocean-going vessels slide past puttering junks, and century-old ferries waddle and weave across their paths. The mixture of Asia's finest hotels, territory-wide duty-free shopping, incense-filled working temples, and British double-decker buses makes this city-state worth flying to Asia to see in its own right. **Macau,** a little bit of misplaced Mediterranean, is a short ferry ride away.

THE SOUTHWEST

Encompassing the provinces of **Yúnnán, Guìzhōu, Guǎngxī,** and **Hǎinán Island,** this region is home to some of China's most spectacular mountain scenery and three of Asia's mightiest rivers, resulting in some of the most breathtaking gorges and lush river valleys in the country.

Even more appealing is the fact that this region is easily the most ethnically diverse in China. Twenty-six of China's 56 officially recognized ethnic groups can be found in the southwest, from the Mosu in **Lúgū Lake** to the Dǎi in **Xīshuāngbǎnnà,** from the Miáo around

Kǎilǐ to the Dòng in **Sānjiāng,** each with different architecture, dress, traditions, and colorful festivals.

THE YÁNGZǏ RIVER

In addition to shared borders, the land-locked provinces of **Sìchuān, Húběi,** and **Húnán** and the municipality of **Chóngqìng** have in common the world's third-longest river, the Cháng Jiāng ("Long River," aka Yángzǐ or Yangtze). The home of five holy Buddhist and/or Daoist mountains, this area contains some of China's most beautiful scenery, particularly in northern Sìchuān and northern Húnán.

Sìchuān deserves exploration using **Chéngdū** as a base, and the Húnán should be explored from **Chángshā.** If you're taking the **Three Gorges cruise** (available indefinitely despite what you may have heard), try to at least leave yourself a few days on either end to explore **Chóngqìng** and **Wǔhàn.** And a day trip from Chóngqìng to the Buddhist grottoes at **Dàzú** is well worth the time.

THE TIBETAN WORLD

The Tibetan plateau is roughly the size of western Europe, with an average elevation of 4,700m (15,400 ft.). Ringed by vast mountain ranges such as the **Kunlun range** to the north and the **Himalayas,** the region offers towering scenic splendors as well as some of the richest minority culture within modern China's borders. **Lhasa,** former seat of the Dalai Lamas, is dominated physically by the vast **Potala Palace,** and emotionally by the fervor of the pilgrims to the **Jokhang Temple.** Fewer than half of the world's Tibetans now live in what is called Tibet—much Tibetan territory has now been allocated to neighboring Chinese provinces and particularly in **Qīnghǎi,** where the authorities are less watchful and the atmosphere in both monasteries and on the streets more relaxed.

2 Visitor Information

The mainland travel industry is, in general, a quagmire of deception, and provides no truly reliable official sources of information either within China or via its overseas operations. The branches of the China National Tourism Administration in foreign countries are called China National Tourist Offices. Nominally nonprofit, they used to be little more than agents for the state-owned China International Travel Service (CITS), but they now offer links to a variety of operators. Don't expect them to be accurate about even the most basic visa or Customs regulations, or to update their websites, which sometimes give conflicting information and can't even get the names of tour operators right.

Hong Kong and Macau have their own tourism agencies, which are vastly more professional. The Hong Kong Tourism Board is a source of endless quantities of free literature, maps, and helpful advice, and its website is comprehensive, accurate, and up-to-date. The Macau Government Tourism Office is the same on a smaller scale.

CHINA NATIONAL TOURIST OFFICE (WWW.CNTO.ORG)

In the United States   New York office: 350 Fifth Ave., Suite 6413, Empire State Building, New York, NY 10118 (© 212/ 760-8218; fax 212/760-8809; ny@cnto. gov.cn). California office: 600 W. Broadway, Suite 320, Glendale, CA 91204 (© 818/545-7507; fax 818/545-7506; la@cnto.gov.cn).

In Canada   480 University Ave., Suite 806, Toronto, ON M5G 1V2 (© 416/ 599-6636; fax 416/599-6382; www. tourismchina-ca.com).

In the U.K.   4 Glentworth St., London NW1 5PG (© 020/7935-9787; fax 020/ 7487-5842; london@cnta.gov.cn).

In Australia   Level 19, 44 Market St., Sydney, NSW 2000 (© 02/9299-4057; fax 02/9290-1958; sydney@cnta.gov.cn).

HONG KONG TOURISM BOARD (WWW.DISCOVERHONGKONG.COM)

In the United States   New York office: 115 E. 54th St., 2nd floor, New York, NY 10022-4512 (© 212/421-3382; fax 212/ 421-8428; nycwwo@hktb.com). California office: 10940 Wilshire Blvd., Suite 2050, Los Angeles, CA 90024-3915 (© 310/208-4582; fax 310/208-2398; jeffs@hktb.com).

In Canada   3rd floor, 9 Temperance St., Toronto, ON M5H 1Y6 (© 416/366-2389; fax 416/366-1098; yyzwwo@hktb. com).

In the U.K.   6 Grafton St., London W1S 4EQ (© 020/7533-7100; fax 020/ 7533-7111; lonwwo@hktb.com).

In Australia   Level 4, Hong Kong House, 80 Druitt St., Sydney, NSW 2000 (© 02/9283-3083; fax 02/9283-3383; sydwwo@hktb.com).

MACAU GOVERNMENT TOURISM OFFICE (WWW.MACAU TOURISM.GOV.MO)

In the United States   501 Fifth Ave., Suite 1101, New York. NY10017 (© 646/ 277-0690; fax 646/366-8170; macau@ myriadmarketing.com).

In the U.K.   11 Blades Court, 121 Deodar Rd., London SW15 2NU (© 44/ 20-8877-4517; fax 44/20-8874-4219; sharon@representationplus.co.uk).

In Australia   Level 17, Town Hall House, 456 Kent St., Sydney, NSW 2000 (© 02/9264-1488; fax 02/9267-7717; macau@worldtradetravel.com).

In New Zealand   Level 5, Ballantyne House, 101 Customs St. E., P.O. Box 3779, Auckland (© 09/308-5206; fax 09/ 308-5207; macau@aviationandtourism. co.nz).

3 Entry Requirements & Customs

ENTRY REQUIREMENTS
MAINLAND CHINA VISAS

All visitors to mainland China must acquire a **visa** in advance. In general, visas are not granted at the border. Visitors to mainland China must have a valid **passport** with at least 6 months' validity and two blank pages remaining (you *may* get away with just one blank page). Visa applications typically take 3 to 5 working days to process, although this can be sped up with the payment of extra fees to as little as 1 day if you apply in person. "L" (tourist) visas are valid for between 1 and 3 months. Usually 1 month is granted unless you request more, which you may or may not get according to events in China at the time. Double-entry tourist visas are also available.

At home you should apply to your nearest consulate, although it's possible to pick up Chinese visas in other countries while on an extended trip. It varies, but typically your visit must *begin* within 90 days of the date of issue. Note that although postal addresses are given below, some consulates (including all those in the U.S. and Canada) will only accept applications in person, and applications by post or courier must go through an agent, with further fees to be paid. Telephone numbers are given, but many systems are automated, and getting a human to speak to can be next to impossible; faxes and e-mail rarely get a reply, and websites are often out of date.

Applying for a visa requires completion of an application form that can be downloaded from many consular websites or acquired by mail. Visas are valid for the whole country, although some small areas require an extra permit from the local police. Temporary restrictions may also be placed, sometimes for years at a time, on areas where there is unrest, and a further permit may be required. This is currently the case with Tibet where, until recently, travelers were required to form groups before entering the region, and to pay a huge price for a tour (but they were not required to actually join it on arrival). For details of Tibet permits, see chapter 14. In general, do not mention Tibet or Xīnjiāng on your visa application, or it may be turned down flat.

Some consulates indicate that sight of an airline ticket or itinerary is required, or that you give proof of sufficient funds, or that you must be traveling with a group, while they happily carry on business with individuals who have none of this supporting documentation. Such statements do provide a face-saving excuse for refusing a visa should there be unrest or political difficulties, or should Tibet or Xīnjiāng appear on the application.

One passport photograph is required, as well as one for any child traveling on a parent's passport.

The visa fees quoted below by country are the current rates for *nationals of that country,* and can change at any time. U.S. citizens applying for a double-entry visa in the U.K., for instance, are charged more than British citizens, but other nationals are charged less. Regulations may also vary: U.S. citizens applying in Australia must submit *two* forms and *two* photos; everyone else just one of each. In addition to the visa fees quoted, there may be supplementary fees for postage, and higher fees can often be paid for speedier service. Payment must always be in cash or by money order.

Once you're inside China, *single-entry tourist visas only* can usually be extended once for a maximum of 30 days at the Aliens Entry-Exit department of the Public Security Bureau (PSB) in most towns and cities. U.S. citizens pay ¥125 ($16), U.K. citizens ¥160 (£12), Canadians ¥165 (C$28), and Australians ¥100 (A$18).

Extensions within China now typically take 5 working days to process, although you may sometimes be able to cajole offices into faster service.

Consulates in the United States

Single-entry visas are $50; double-entry $75. Visit **www.china-embassy.org**, which has links to all U.S. consular sites and a downloadable application form. Applications must be delivered and collected by hand, or sent via a visa agency. In **Washington, D.C.** (for residents of Delaware, Idaho, Kentucky, Maryland, Montana, Nebraska, North Carolina, North Dakota, South Carolina, South Dakota, Tennessee, Utah, Virginia, West Virginia, and Wyoming): Room 110, 2201 Wisconsin Ave. NW, Washington, DC 20007 (② **202/338-6688;** fax 202/588-9760; faxback 202/265-9809; chnvisa@bellatlantic.net). In **Chicago** (for Colorado, Illinois, Indiana, Iowa, Kansas, Michigan, Missouri, and Wisconsin): 100 W. Erie St., Chicago, IL 60610 (② **312/803-0098;** fax 312/803-0112). In **Houston** (for Alabama, Arkansas, Florida, Georgia, Louisiana, Mississippi, Oklahoma, and Texas): 3417 Montrose Blvd., Houston, TX 77066 (② **713/524-4311;** fax 713/524-7656; automated FAQ 713/524-4311; visa@chinahouston.org); however, its temporary location is at 3400 Montrose Blvd., 7th floor. In **Los Angeles** (for Arizona, Southern California, Hawaii, New Mexico, and Pacific Islands): 443 Shatto Place, Los Angeles, CA 90020 (② **213/807-8088;** fax 213/380-1961). In **New York** (for Connecticut, Maine, Massachusetts, New Hampshire, New Jersey, New York, Ohio, Pennsylvania, Rhode Island, and Vermont): 520 12th Ave., New York, NY 10036 (② **212/868-7752;** fax 212/502-0245). In **San Francisco** (for Alaska, Northern California, Nevada, Oregon, and Washington): 1450 Laguna St., San Francisco, CA 94115 (② **415/674-2900;** fax 415/563-0494).

Consulates in Canada

Single-entry visas are C$50; double-entry C$75. Visit **www.chinaembassycanada.org** for an application form. Applications must be delivered and collected by hand, or sent via a visa agency. **Ottawa** (for residents of the Ottawa region, Quebec, Newfoundland and Labrador, New Brunswick, Nova Scotia, and Prince Edward Island): 515 St. Patrick St., Ottawa K1N 5H3 (② **613/789-9608;** fax 613/789-1414). **Toronto** (for Ontario and Manitoba): 240 St. George St., Toronto M5R 2P4 (② **416/964-7260;** fax 416/324-9010). **Vancouver** (for British Columbia and Yukon Territory): 3380 Granville St., Vancouver (② **604/736-5188;** fax 604/737-0154). **Calgary** (for Alberta, Saskatchewan, and Northwest Territory): 1011 6th Ave. SW, Suite 100, T2P 0W1 (② **403/264-3322;** fax 403/264-6656).

Consulates in the United Kingdom

Single-entry visas are £30; double-entry £45. There's a supplementary charge of £20 for each package dealt with by mail. Visit **www.chinese-embassy.org.uk** for an application. **London:** 31 Portland Place, London, W1B 1QD (② **0207/631-1430** 2–4pm phone service; 24-hr. information at premium rate ② 0900/188-0808). **Manchester:** Denison House, 49 Denison Rd., Rusholme, Manchester, M14 5RX (② **0161/224-8672**). **Edinburgh:** 55 Corstorphine Rd., Edinburgh, EH12 5QJ (② **0131/337-3220;** fax 0131/337-1790).

Consulates in Australia

Single-entry visas are A$30; double-entry A$45. Add A$10 per package dealt with by mail or courier, and a pre-paid return envelope. **Canberra:** 15 Coronation Dr., Yarralumla, ACT 2600 (② **02/6273-7443** or 02/6273-4780, ext. 218 or 258; fax 02/6273-9615; www.chinaembassy.org.au). Canberra now only accepts applications from ACT, NT, SA, and QLD. Applications from NSW, VIC/TAS, and WA should go to Sydney, Melbourne, and Perth. **Sydney:** 30 Dunblane St., Camperdown, NSW 2050 (© **02/8595-8000;** fax 02/8595-8021; www.sydney.chineseconsulate.org). **Melbourne:** 75–77 Irving Rd., Toorak, VIC 3142 (© **03/9822-0604;** fax 03/9824-6340; www.chineseconsulatemel.org). **Perth:** 45 Brown St., East Perth, WA 60004 (© **08/9222-0302;** fax 08/9221-6144).

Consulates in New Zealand

Single-entry visas are NZ$60; double-entry NZ$90. Add NZ$15 per package dealt with by mail or courier, and a pre-paid return envelope. **Wellington:** 2–6 Glenmore St., P.O. Box 17257, Karori (© **04/472-1382,** ext. 600; fax 04/474-9632; www.chinaembassy.org.nz). **Auckland** (for Auckland-area residents only): 588 Great South Rd., Greelane; postal address P.O. Box 17123, Greelane, Auckland (© **09/525-1785,** ext. 710 or 707; fax 09/525-0733; www.chinaconsulate.org.nz).

Consulates Elsewhere

A complete list of all Chinese embassies and consulates can be found at the Chinese foreign ministry's website: www.fmprc.gov.cn/eng (or various mirror sites around the world). Click on "Missions Overseas."

Buying Visas in Countries Bordering China

Note that the Chinese Consulate in Kathmandu, Nepal, will not sell visas to individual travelers wanting to enter Tibet overland, or they may stamp the visa to prohibit overland entry via the Friendship Highway. The consulate in Bishkek, Kyrgyzstan, will usually refuse visas to those not holding a fax or telex from a Chinese state-registered travel agency, or they will stamp the visa to prohibit overland entry via the Torugart Pass. Obtaining visas at the consulate in Almaty can also sometimes be difficult for nonresidents of Kazakhstan.

Buying Visas in Hong Kong

The easiest place to apply for a mainland visa is Hong Kong, where there are several China visa options. Single-entry tourist "L" visas valid for 3 months are easily obtainable, as is the (unextendable) double-entry version. Multiple-entry "F" visas are also easy to obtain via visa agents and without the letter of invitation required to obtain them at home. Single-entry visas bought through HK agents typically cost HK$220 to HK$250 (US$25–US$30), multiple-entry "F" visas around HK$550 (US$65). Offices located just a few minutes' walk from the main tourist areas charge less still. See chapter 11, "Hong Kong," for recommendations.

Entering the Mainland from Hong Kong & Macau

It is possible for all but British citizens to buy a permit at the Lo Wu border crossing from Hong Kong to Shēnzhèn, valid for 72 hours of travel in the Shēnzhèn Special Economic Zone *only*. According to the Guǎngzhōu PSB, tourist visas can be purchased on arrival at Guǎngzhōu East station by direct express railway from Hong Kong, but this has not been tested. It is possible to buy a 3-month "L" visa or 6-month "F" visa from a branch of China Travel Service on the mainland side of the crossing from Macau to Zhūhǎi. See chapter 11 for more details.

HONG KONG VISAS

U.S., Canadian, Australian, and New Zealand citizens, and those of most other developed nations, are granted 90-day stays free on arrival. British citizens are granted 180 days. Passports should be valid for 1 month longer than the planned return date. In theory, proof of sufficient funds and an onward ticket may be demanded, but this request is almost unheard of.

> **Tips** **A Pocketful of Miracles**
>
> As I've mentioned, travel in China is a different ballgame than travel elsewhere. That's why I always pack a few extra items, for different reasons, to make me feel more at home.
>
> - Instant coffee and packet sugar. Every hotel has hot water but I tire of green tea quickly.
> - Binoculars. China is such a vast country that no way can you see it all—so every little bit helps.
> - Playing cards. Incredibly useful on long train journeys. (A few snapshots of home can also provide entertainment.)
> - Eye mask and earplugs. Sleep is easier to come by if you come well prepared. These items cost little but are worth their weight in gold in China. And if you wear glasses, don't forget a good hard case for storing them—and bring an extra pair while you're at it.

MACAU VISAS

U.S., Canadian, Australian, and New Zealand citizens are granted 30-day stays free on arrival. British and most other E.U. nationals can stay up to 90 days without a visa. Passports should have at least 30 days of remaining validity upon your arrival.

CUSTOMS
WHAT YOU CAN BRING INTO CHINA

Generally, you can bring into China anything for personal use that you plan to take away with you when you leave, with the usual exceptions of arms and drugs, or plant materials, animals, and foods from diseased areas. There are no problems with cameras or video recorders, GPS equipment, laptops, or any other standard electronic equipment. Two unusual prohibitions are "old/used garments" and "printed matter, magnetic media, films, or photographs which are deemed to be detrimental to the political, economic, cultural and moral interests of China," as the regulations put it. Large quantities of religious literature, overtly political materials, or books on Tibet might cause you difficulties (having a pile of pictures of the Dalai Lama certainly

will, if discovered), but in general, small amounts of personal reading matter in non-Chinese languages do not present problems. Customs officers are for the most part easygoing, and foreign visitors are very rarely searched. Customs declaration forms have now vanished from all major points of entry, but if you are importing more than $5,000 in cash, you should declare it, or theoretically you could face difficulties at the time of departure, although once again, this would be highly unlikely. Importing or exporting more than ¥6,000 ($750) in *yuán* is also theoretically prohibited, but again, it's never checked. Chinese currency is anyway best obtained within China (or in Hong Kong), and is of no use once you leave.

WHAT YOU CAN TAKE HOME FROM CHINA

An official seal must be attached to any item created between 1795 and 1949 that is taken out of China; older items cannot be exported. But in fact you are highly unlikely to find any genuine antiques, so this is a moot point (and if the antiques dealer is genuine, then he'll know all about how to get the seal). There are no such prohibitions on exporting items from Hong Kong, which is where you can find reliable dealers with authentic pieces and a willingness to allow thermoluminescence testing to prove it.

Almost everybody is amazed at the number of cheap DVDs on sale in China. They are extremely tempting, especially compared to the ridiculous prices at home. Know that the producers of these discs are often the same gangsters that smuggle illegal immigrants in containers and sell females into sexual slavery; don't give them your money.

CURRENCY
MAINLAND CHINA

For most destinations it's usually a good idea to exchange at least some money—just enough to cover airport incidentals and transportation to your hotel—before you leave home so you can avoid the less-favorable rates you'll get at airport currency-exchange desks. **Mainland China** is different. **Yuán,** also known as **RMB (Rénmínbì,** or "People's Money"), are not easily obtainable overseas, and rates are worse when they can be found, although rates at *back street* money-changers away from Hong Kong's main shopping areas are often better than in mainland China.

There is no legal private money-changing in mainland China, and rates are fixed to be the same at all outlets nationwide on a daily basis. So change at the airport when you arrive, and then at larger branches of the Bank of China, or at desks administered by the bank in your hotel or at major department stores in larger cities. If you find a shop offering to change your money at other than a formal Bank of China exchange counter, they are doing so illegally, and you open yourself to shenanigans with rates and fake bills, which are fairly common. Even the meanest hole-in-the-wall restaurant has an ultraviolet note tester. *Do not deal with black-market money-changers.*

Hotel exchange desks will only change money for their guests, but they are open very long hours 7 days a week. **Bank hours** vary from province to province. In some provinces they operate the same hours every day; in others, the exchange counter is open during hours different from those of the rest of the bank and not on weekends; in still others, banks are completely closed on weekends. See "Banks, Foreign Exchange & ATMs," in the "Fast Facts" section of each destination.

In a bid to avert a trade war with the U.S., China allowed a 2% appreciation of the yuán in 2005. It is no longer pegged solely to the U.S. dollar, but rather a basket of currencies, in an arrangement known as a "crawling peg." The U.S. dollar has recently been trading around ¥8.10, the pound sterling at ¥14.90, and the euro at ¥10.05. For this edition, we have taken ¥8 to the U.S. dollar as an approximate conversion, as major appreciation of the yuán seems unlikely. The latest rates can be found at **www.xe.com/ucc**.

There are notes for ¥100, ¥50, ¥20, ¥10, ¥5, ¥2, and ¥1, which also appears as a coin. The word *yuán* is rarely spoken, and sums are usually referred to as *kuài qián,* "pieces of money," usually shortened to just *kuài. Sān kuài* is ¥3. Notes carry Arabic numerals as well as numbers in Chinese characters, so there's no fear of confusion. The next unit down, the *jiǎo* (¥.10), is spoken of as the *máo.* There are notes of a smaller size for ¥.50, ¥.20, and ¥.10, as well as coins for these values. The smallest and almost worthless unit is the *fēn* (both written and spoken) or cent and, unbelievably, when you change money you may be given tiny notes or lightweight coins for ¥.05, ¥.02, and ¥.01, but this is the only time you'll see them except in the bowls of beggars or donation boxes in temples. The most useful note is the ¥10 ($1.25), so keep a good stock. Street stalls, convenience stores, and taxis are often not happy with ¥100 ($13) notes.

Keep receipts when you exchange money, and you can **reconvert** excess

¥RMB into hard currency when you leave China, although sometimes not more than half the total sum for which you can produce receipts, and sometimes these receipts must be not more than 3 months old.

HONG KONG & MACAU

In **Hong Kong** the currency is the **Hong Kong dollar** (HK$), whose notes are issued by a variety of banks, although all coins look the same. It is pegged to the U.S. dollar at around HK$7.80 to US$1. Keep foreign exchange to a minimum at the airport (use the ATMs at departures level) or at other points of entry. Do not change in hotels or banks, but with money-changers, and choose money-changers away from the main streets for a significantly better rate. Banks have limited weekend hours, but money-changers are open every day.

Macau's official currency is the **pataca** (MOP$), pegged to the Hong Kong dollar (and thus to the U.S. dollar) at a rate of MOP$103.20 to HK$100—about MOP$8 to US$1. Hong Kong dollars are accepted everywhere, including both coins and notes (even on buses), but at par. If you arrive in Macau from Hong Kong for a short stay, there's little point in changing money beforehand. But your change will invariably be in patacas, which are useless in Hong Kong or mainland China.

ATMS

There are many ATMs in China, but with few exceptions as yet, only a selection of Bank of China machines accept foreign cards. Check the back of your ATM card for the logos of the **Cirrus** (www.mastercard.com), **PLUS** (www.visa.com), and **Aeon** (www.americanexpress.com), systems, and then contact the relevant company for a list of working ATM locations in China. Běijīng and Shànghǎi are both fairly well served, and have additional Citibank and Hongkong and Shanghai Bank machines which take just about any card ever invented. But even some provincial capitals and some major tourist destinations often have no machines accepting foreign cards, even if their screens say they do. Nevertheless, it is possible, as long as you plan ahead, to travel in China relying on ATMs, but be sure to replenish your supplies of cash long before they run out, and have a couple of hundred U.S. dollars in cash as a backup. These can be exchanged in almost any branch of any bank. Some machines have a limit of ¥2,500 ($310) per transaction, but often allow a second transaction the same day. In **Hong Kong** and **Macau** there are ATMs everywhere which are friendly to foreign cards.

TRAVELER'S CHECKS

Traveler's checks are only accepted at selected branches of the Bank of China, at foreign exchange desks in hotels, at international gateways, and at some department stores in the largest cities. In the most popular destinations, checks in any hard currency and from any major company are welcome, but elsewhere, currencies of the larger economies are preferred, and hotels may direct all check-holders to the local head office of the Bank of China. U.S. dollars cash, in contrast, may be exchanged at most branches of almost any Chinese bank, so even if you plan to bring checks, having a few U.S. dollars cash (in good condition) for emergencies is a good idea. Checks attract a marginally better exchange rate than cash, but the .75% commission makes the result slightly worse (worse still if you paid commission when buying them). Occasionally, if the signature you write in front of the teller varies from the one you made when you bought the check, it may be rejected. In **Hong Kong** and **Macau,** checks are accepted at banks and money-changers in the usual way.

CREDIT CARDS

Although Visa and MasterCard signs abound, credit cards are of limited use in China—in most cases only the Chinese versions of the cards are accepted. Otherwise, an establishment will accept all of them—American Express, Diners Club, MasterCard, and Visa—or none at all. Many hotels accept foreign cards, but only the most upmarket restaurants outside hotels do so, as do those souvenir shops where you are already paying well over the odds—in fact, if a shop accepts foreign credit cards, that's a good reason to look elsewhere.

You can also obtain cash advances on your MasterCard, Visa, Diners Club, or Amex card from major branches of the Bank of China, with a minimum withdrawal of ¥1,200 ($150) and 4% commission, plus whatever your card issuer charges—a very expensive way to withdraw cash, and for emergencies only. If you do plan to use your card while in China, it's a good idea to call your card issuer and let it know in advance.

All major credit cards are widely accepted in **Hong Kong** and **Macau.**

EMERGENCY CASH

American Express also runs an **emergency check cashing system,** which allows you to use one of your own checks or a counter check (more expensive) to draw money in the currency of your choice from selected banks. This works well in major cities but it can cause confusion in less-visited spots, and the rules on withdrawal limits vary according to the country in which your card was issued. Consult American Express for a list of participating banks before you leave home.

If you're stuck in a province where banks are closed on weekends, you can have money wired from **Western Union** (© 800/325-6000; www.westernunion. com) to many post offices and branches of the Agricultural Bank of China across China, including 49 in Běijīng alone, and 18 in Hong Kong. You must present valid ID to pick up the cash at the Western Union office. In most countries, you can pick up a money transfer even if you don't have valid identification, as long as you can answer a test question provided by the sender. This should work in Hong Kong but might cause difficulties in mainland China. Let the sender know in advance that you don't have ID.

4 When to Go

Weather details are given below, but a far bigger factor in your calculations should be the movement of domestic tourists who, during the longer public holidays, take to the road in the tens or even hundreds of millions, crowding all forms of transportation, booking out hotels, and turning even the quietest tourist sights into litter-strewn bedlam.

PEAK TRAVEL SEASONS

Chinese New Year (Spring Festival): Like many Chinese festivals, this one operates on the lunar calendar. Solar equivalents for the next few years are January 29, 2006; February 18, 2007; February 7, 2008; and January 26, 2009. The effects of this holiday are felt from 2 weeks before the date until 2 weeks after, when anyone who's away from home attempts to get back, including an estimated 150 million migrant workers. Although tens of thousands of extra bus and train services are added, tickets for land transport are very difficult to get, and can command high prices on the black market (official prices also rise on some routes, and on ferries between Hong Kong and the mainland). Air tickets are usually obtainable and may even still be discounted. In the few days immediately around the new year, traffic on long-distance rail and bus services may be light, but local services may dry up altogether. Most tourist sights stay open, although some shut on the holiday itself or have limited holiday hours.

Labor Day & National Day: In a policy known as "holiday economics," the May 1 and October 1 holidays have now been expanded to 7 days each (including one weekend—most people are expected to work through the weekend prior to the holiday to exchange for two weekdays, which are added to the official 3 days of holiday). The aim is to draw out some of China's vast savings and get it sloshing around the economy on leisure spending, a policy which has been spectacularly successful. These two holidays now mark the beginning and end of the domestic travel season, and mark the twin peaks of leisure travel, with the remainder of May, early June, and September also busy. Most Chinese avoid traveling in the summer except specifically to cooler high ground or an offshore island, usually on a weekend. The exact dates of each holiday are not given out until around 2 weeks before each takes place, but it's best, if you're traveling independently, to arrive at a larger destination before the holiday starts, and move on in the middle or after the end. The disposable income to fund travel is more often found in the larger cities, so these tend to become quieter, easier to get around, and less polluted. Noted tourist destinations around the country will be extremely busy, however. In **Hong Kong** and **Macau,** these are only 1- or 2-day holidays introduced in 1997 and 1999 respectively.

University Holidays: Exact term dates are rarely announced far in advance, but train tickets can be difficult to obtain as the student populace moves between home and college. Terms run for 18 weeks with 2 weeks of exams, from the beginning of September to just before

Spring Festival, and from just after the Spring Festival to the end of June.

Local Difficulties: China's main international trade fair occupies the last 2 weeks of April and October, and drives up hotel prices in **Guǎngzhōu,** where it's held, and as far away as Hong Kong. In the summer, pleasant temperatures in the **northeast** (slightly cooler than the rest of China) draw students on summer vacation (which makes train tickets hard to acquire), as well as large Chinese tour groups who trample all before them; it may not be the best time for your visit. The northeast's Dàlián is also overbooked during the International Fashion Festival in September (see later in this chapter). Across China, **midweek travel** is always better than weekend travel, particularly true at destinations easily tackled in a weekend, such as Wǔtái Shān and Píngyáo (see chapter 6, "Along the Yellow River"). Government-imposed travel restrictions in **Tibet** tend to increase around the Monlam Festival (sometime mid-Jan to mid-Feb), Saka Dawa Festival (mid-May to mid-June), and around the present Dalai Lama's birthday (July 6). The border crossing between Hong Kong and the mainland at **Lo Wu** can take a couple of hours at holiday periods.

CLIMATE

China is the third-biggest country in the world, with the second-lowest inland depression (Turpan) and some of its highest peaks (Everest and K2 are both partly in China). Its far northeast shares the same weather patterns as Siberia, and its far southwest the same subtropical climate as northern Thailand.

In the **north,** early spring and late autumn are the best times to travel, both offering warm, dry days and cool, dry evenings. During March and April winds blow away the pollution but sometimes bring sand from the Gobi and topsoil from high ground to the northeast of

Běijīng, increasingly desiccated by the mismanagement of water resources. The sky can at times turn a vivid yellow.

In the **south,** November to February brings a welcome drop both in temperature and in all-pervasive humidity, although in Hong Kong all public interiors and many private houses are air-conditioned to cryogenic temperatures year-round.

Central China, lacking the sea breezes that moderate the coast's summers and make its winters more temperate, has some of the country's most searing summer temperatures and bitterest winters, but it also escapes the worst of the humidity. **Tibet** has springlike days in the summer but far milder winters than most people expect, at least in Lhasa, made endurable by the dryness of the climate. The **northwest** has perhaps the greatest range of temperatures, with severe summers and winters alike, but it is also largely dry.

Average Temperature (Celsius/Fahrenheit)

	Běijīng	Shànghǎi	Hong Kong	Xī'ān	Lhasa
Jan	–3/26	4/40	16/62	0/32	–2/28
Feb	0/31	5/42	17/63	2/35	0/33
Mar	6/43	8/48	19/67	8/48	3/38
Apr	13/57	15/59	22/73	14/57	8/47
May	20/68	20/68	26/79	19/66	11/53
June	24/76	23/75	28/83	25/77	15/60
July	26/79	28/83	29/85	27/80	15/60
Aug	25/77	27/82	29/85	25/77	14/59
Sept	20/69	23/75	28/83	19/66	13/56
Oct	13/57	18/66	26/79	14/57	8/48
Nov	5/41	12/55	22/72	7/44	2/37
Dec	–1/30	6/44	18/65	1/33	–1/30

Average Precipitation (centimeters/inches)

	Běijīng	Shànghǎi	Hong Kong	Xī'ān	Lhasa
Jan	0/0.2	4/1.8	2/1.1	0/0.3	0/0.1
Feb	0/0.2	6/2.4	4/1.7	1/0.4	1/0.5
Mar	0/0.3	8/3.3	7/2.9	2/0.9	0/0.3
Apr	1/0.7	9/3.7	13/5.5	4/1.8	0/0.2
May	3/1.3	10/4.1	28/11.2	6/2.4	2/1
June	7/3.1	17/6.8	39/15.7	5/2.1	6/2.5
July	22/8.8	14/5.7	36/14.3	9/3.8	12/4.8
Aug	17/6.7	13/5.4	37/14.8	8/3.4	8/3.5
Sept	5/2.3	13/5.4	29/11.7	10/4.2	6/2.6
Oct	1/0.7	6/2.7	11/4.7	5/2.3	1/0.5
Nov	1/0.4	5/2.1	3/1.5	2/1	0/0.1
Dec	0/0.1	3/1.5	2/1	0/0.2	0/0

HOLIDAYS

Public holidays and their effects vary widely between mainland China and the two Special Administrative Regions, Hong Kong and Macau.

Mainland China

A few years ago the Chinese were finally granted a 2-day weekend. Offices close, but stores, restaurants, post offices, transportation, sights and, in some areas, banks, all operate the same services 7 days a week. Most sights, shops, and restaurants are also open on public holidays, but all offices and anything government-related take as much time off as they can. Although China switched to the Gregorian calendar in 1911, some public holidays (and many festivals—see below) are based on a lunar cycle, their solar dates varying from year to year. Holidays are **New Year's Day** (Jan 1), **Spring Festival** (Chinese New Year and the 2 days following it—see "Peak Travel Seasons," above, for exact dates in coming years), **Labor Day** (May 1 plus up to 4 more weekdays and a weekend), **National Day** (Oct 1 plus extra days, as with Labor Day, above).

Hong Kong

Saturday is officially a working day in Hong Kong, although many offices in fact take the day off or only open for reduced hours. Weekend ferry sailings and other transport may vary, particularly on Sunday, when many shops are closed and opening hours for attractions may also vary. Hong Kong gets many British holidays, traditional Chinese holidays, plus modern political ones added after 1997, but in shorter forms. Banks, schools, offices, and government departments are all closed on these dates, as are many museums: **New Year's Day** (Jan 1), **Lunar New Year's Day** (for the mainland Spring Festival, but in Hong Kong the day itself plus 2 more, and an extra Fri or Mon if 1 day falls on a Sun); **Ching**

Ming Festival (Apr 5), **Good Friday** (usually early Apr, plus the following Sat and **Easter Monday**), **Labor Day** (May 1), **Buddha's Birthday** (1 day in May), **Tuen Ng** (Dragon Boat Festival, 1 day in June), **Hong Kong SAR Establishment Day** (July 1), **Mid-Autumn Festival** (1 day in Sept, usually moved to the nearest Fri or Mon to make a long weekend), **National Day** (Oct 1), **Chung Yeung Festival** (1 day in Oct), **Christmas Day** and **Boxing Day** (Dec 25, and the next weekday if the 26th is a Sat or Sun).

Macau

Macau has the same holidays as Hong Kong except for SAR Establishment Day, and with similar consequences, but with the following variations: **National Day** is 2 days (Oct 1–2), **All Souls' Day** (Nov 2), **Feast of the Immaculate Conception** (Dec 8), **Macau SAR Establishment Day** (Dec 20), **Winter Solstice** (Dec 22), and **Christmas Eve** and **Christmas Day** (Dec 24–25).

CHINA CALENDAR OF EVENTS

China's festivals follow the traditional lunar calendar, and to increase confusion, some minority calendars operate according to different traditions. For conversion to solar/Gregorian calendar dates, try the websites www.est-direct.com/china/lunarcal.php or www.mandarintools.com.

The Chinese tourism industry is increasingly inventing festivals to try to boost business. Unless indicated below, be wary of any festival with the word *tourism* in its name, for instance.

January

Spring Festival (Chūn Jié), or Chinese New Year, is still the occasion for large lion dances and other celebrations in Hong Kong, Macau, and Chinatowns worldwide, but in mainland China it's mainly a time for everyone to return to his or her ancestral home and feast. Fireworks are now banned in larger cities. Temple fairs have been revived in Běijīng, but are mostly fairly low-key shopping opportunities without the color or professional entertainers of old. But in the countryside there's been a gradual revival of stilt-walking and masked processions. Spring Festival is on the day of the first new moon after January 21, and can be no later than February 20.

Monlam Festival is held throughout the Tibetan world (including at Xià Hé and Lángmù Sì). Monasteries are open to all, and there are religious dancing, the offering of *torma* (butter sculptures), and the "sunning of the Buddha" when a silk painting *(thangka)* is consecrated and becomes the living Buddha in the minds of believers. Typically, the festival culminates in the parading of the Maitreya Buddha through the town. Fourth to 16th days of the first lunar month (Feb 1–14, 2006; Feb 21–Mar 5, 2007). Check dates with Qīnghǎi Mountaineering Association (✆ **0971/823-8922**). In Tibet check with **FIT** (✆ **0891/634-4397**; www.tibet-travel.com).

Kurban Bairam (Gǔ'ěrbāng Jié), also known as the Festival of Sacrifice, is celebrated by Muslims throughout China. It marks the willingness of the prophet Abraham to sacrifice everything to God, even his son Ishmael. Celebrations in Kashgar involve feats of tightrope-walking in the main square and wild dancing outside the Idkah Mosque. The 4-day festival is held 70 days after the breaking of the fast of Ramadan, on the 10th day of the 12th month (Dhul-Hijjah) in the Islamic calendar. It falls on January 13, 2006, and annually shifts backwards by 12 days.

February

The **Lantern Festival (Dēng Jié)** perhaps reached its peak in the late Qīng dynasty, when temples, stores, and other public places were hung with fantastically shaped and decorated lanterns, some with figures animated by ingenious mechanisms involving the flow of sand. Many people paraded through the streets with lightweight lanterns in the shapes of fish, sheep, and so on, and hung lanterns outside their houses, often decorated with riddles. There are some signs of the festival's revival, including at Píngyáo in Shānxī Province, and at Quánzhōu in Fújiàn. The festival always falls 15 days after Spring Festival.

March

Hong Kong Sevens Rugby Tournament, Hong Kong. Known as "The Sevens," this is one of Hong Kong's most popular and one of Asia's largest sporting events, with more than 20 teams from around the world competing for the Cup Championship. A 3-day pass costs HK$750 (US$97). Contact the **Hong Kong Rugby Football Union** at ✆ **852/2504 8311** or www.hksevens.com.hk. Fourth weekend in March.

April

Tomb-Sweeping Festival (Qīngmíng) is still a public holiday in Hong Kong and Macau, frequently observed in Chinese communities overseas, and celebrated in more rural areas of China, as a family outing on a free day near the festival date. It's a day to honor ancestors by visiting and tidying their graves and making offerings of snacks and alcohol, which often turns into a picnic. April 5.

Sisters' Meal Festival (Zǐmèifàn Jié), Táijiāng, Shīdòng (Guìzhōu). Celebrated with *lúshēng* (wind-instrument music) dances and antiphonal singing, this is one of the prime occasions for young Miáo men and women to socialize and find marriage partners. Elaborately dressed Miáo women prepare packets of berry-stained glutinous rice to present to suitors. For exact dates, check with **CITS** Kǎilǐ (© **0855/822-2506;** www.qdncits.com). Fifteenth day of the third lunar month (usually Apr).

Water-Splashing Festival (Pōshuǐ Jié), Jǐnghóng, Xīshuāngbǎnnà. Extremely popular with Chinese tourists, the festive Dǎi New Year is ushered in with a large market on the first day, dragon-boat races on the second, and copious amounts of water-splashing on the third. Be prepared to get doused, but take heart because the wetter you are, the more luck you'll have. April 13 to April 15.

Luòyáng Peony Festival, Luòyáng. Over 300 varieties of China's best peonies, first cultivated in Luòyáng 1,400 years ago, are on display at the Wángchéng Park (Wángchéng Gōngyuán), which is awash in a riot of colors from red to violet and every shade in between. April 15 to April 25.

Wéifāng International Kite Festival, Wéifāng. The kite capital of the world hosts the largest kite-flying gala in China, as hundreds of thousands of kite lovers from around the world take over the town for several days of competition and demonstrations. April 20.

Hong Kong International Film Festival, Hong Kong. More than 200 films from more than 40 countries are featured at this 2-week event, including new releases, documentaries, and archival films. Tickets cost HK$55 (US$7.15). For more information, call © **852/2734 2903** or 852/2734 9009; or visit www.hkiff.org.hk. Two weeks in April.

Sānyuè Jié (Third Month Fair), Dàlǐ. This biggest festival of the Bái people had its origins over a thousand years ago when Buddhist monks and adherents gathered to celebrate the appearance of Guānyīn (the Goddess of

Mercy) to the Bái. Today's festival has become more secular as the Bái and other minorities from elsewhere in Yúnnán gather in the foothills of the Green Mountains (Cāng Shān) for 5 days and nights of singing, dancing, wrestling, horse racing, and large-scale trading. Ask **CITS** for more information on the precise dates (© **0872/219-1985**). Fifteenth day of the third lunar month (usually mid-Apr or early May).

Cheung Chau Bun Festival, Hong Kong. This weeklong affair on Cheung Chau island is thought to appease restless ghosts and spirits. Originally held to placate the unfortunate souls of those murdered by pirates, it features a street parade of lions and dragons and Chinese opera, as well as floats with children seemingly suspended in the air, held up by cleverly concealed wires. The end of the festival is heralded by three bun-covered scaffolds erected in front of the Pak Tai Temple. These buns supposedly bring good luck to those who receive them. **HKTB** organizes tours of the parade; call © **852/2508 1234.** Usually late April or early May, but the exact date is chosen by divination.

May

Saka Dawa festival is held throughout the Tibetan world, celebrating the Buddha passing away and thus attaining nirvana. *Koras* (circuits) of holy lakes, mountains, and buildings are undertaken by the faithful. See the contact info for the Monlam Festival (Jan), above. Eighth to 15th days of the fourth lunar month (June 11–27, 2006).

Western Journey Festival (Xīqiān Jié) marks the day in 1764 when the Qiánlóng emperor forced the Xībó people to move from their homeland in Manchuria to Qapqal County (southwest of Yīníng). Celebrations are marked by the devouring of a whole sheep cooked with coriander, preserved vegetables, and onions. Wrestling, horse riding, and archery contests evoke the Xībó's warrior ancestry. The festival is held on the 18th day of the fourth lunar month (late May to mid-June).

June

Dragon Boat Festival (Lóngzhōu Jié), Shīdòng. With over 40,000 celebrants, this Miáo minority festival, which bears no relation to the Hàn Dragon Boat Festival, commemorates the killing of a dragon whose body was divided among several Miáo villages. Over the course of 3 days, dragon boat races are held in Shīdòng and nearby Píngzhāi and Tánglóng. For exact dates, check with **CITS** Kǎilǐ (© **0855/ 822-2506;** www.qdncits.com). Twenty-fourth to 27th day of the fifth lunar month (usually June or early July).

Dragon Boat Races (Tuen Ng Festival), Hong Kong. Races of long, narrow boats, gaily painted and powered by oarsmen who row to the beat of drums, originated in ancient China, where legend held that Qū Yuán, an imperial adviser, drowned himself in a Húnán river to protest government corruption. His faithful followers, wishing to recover his body, supposedly raced out into the river in boats, beating their paddles on the surface of the water and throwing rice to distract water creatures from his body. There are two different races: The biggest is an international competition with approximately 30 teams, held along the waterfront in Tsimshatsui East; the following weekend, approximately 500 local Hong Kong teams compete, with races held at Stanley, Aberdeen, Chai Wan, Yaumatei, Tai Po, and outlying islands. Contact **HKTB** at © **852/ 2508 1234.** Fifth day of the fifth

moon (May 31, 2006; June 19, 2007; June 08, 2008) for international races. On the **mainland,** the festival is still celebrated at places connected with Qū Yuán, such as Zǐguī, Yíchāng, and Chángshā.

July

Jyekundo Horse Festival, south of Yùshù, Qīnghǎi. Khampa nomads gather for a spectacular 10-day celebration involving racing, exhibitions of equestrian skill, and horse trading. Starts on July 25.

International Motorcycle Tourism Festival, Yínchuān. People from China and abroad ride/transport their motorcycles to Yínchuān. Motorcycle stunts and contests, exhibitions, and tourism activities (beware the last) make up the core activities of the festival. Visit www. ycmtf.org/english/about_us.htm for details. Held between June and August.

Lurol Festival, Tóngrén (Repkong). This marks the Sino-Tibetan peace treaty, signed in A.D. 822, with fertility dances and body piercing in honor of a local mountain deity, and has a pagan feel. Check with **Qīnghǎi Mountaineering Association,** © **0971/823- 8922.** The 16th day of the sixth lunar month (July 11, 2006; July 29, 2007).

August

Naadam, across Inner Mongolia, including Hohhot (at the racetrack, Sàimǎ Chǎng, and the Hulun Buir Grasslands, outside Mǎnzhōulǐ). The festival features Mongolian wrestling, archery, and horse and camel racing, and occurs when the grasslands turn green. That's usually mid-August, but can be as early as July. Dates differ from place to place, and they don't coincide with (the People's Republic of) Mongolia's Naadam festival, which is tied to their National Day and always occurs from July 11 to July 13. For exact locations and dates outside

Mǎnzhōulǐ, call **CITS** (© **0470/622-2988**).

Qīngdǎo International Beer Festival, Qīngdǎo. Over a million visitors descend on this seaside resort for its famous annual Bavarian bacchanal, which features everything from beer tasting and drinking contests for adults, to amusement-park rides for kids, to go-karting for the kid in the adult. Last 2 weeks of August (proceeding to the first Sun in Sept).

September

Formula One Racing, Shànghǎi. Every fall until 2010, motor-sport fans can now catch their favorite Formula One drivers zooming around a state-of-the-art track in the Shànghǎi suburb of Āntíng. September to October.

International Shàolín Martial Arts Festival, Sōng Shān. Some patience, Grasshopper, may be necessary to negotiate the crowds of serious pugilists and Bruce Lee–wannabes who show up to trade fists and demonstrate some truly jaw-dropping, gravity-defying martial arts skills. For details, call **CITS** (© **0371/288-3442**). Second week of September.

Mid-Autumn Festival (Tuányuán Jié) is widely celebrated in Hong Kong, Macau, and Chinese communities overseas, but in mainland China the last remnant of the festival except among literary-minded students is the giving and eating of *yuèbǐng* (moon cakes), circular pies with sweet and extremely fattening fillings. Traditionally it's a time to sit and read poetry under the full moon, but pollution in many areas has made the moon largely invisible. The 15th day of the eighth lunar month (usually Sept).

International Fashion Festival, Dàlián. China's most famous fashion event is the Dàlián Guójì Fúzhuāng Jié. The 2-week gathering of mostly Asian garment producers offers an opening parade, a series of glamorous fashion shows held in the city's best hotels, and the sight of leggy models strutting downtown streets, making it worthwhile for nonindustry visitors, too. Mid-September.

Confucius's Birthday, Qūfù. China's Great Sage is honored with parades, exhibitions, and musical and dance performances that reenact some of the rites mentioned in the *Analects (Lún Yǔ)*. If you wish to stay over during this time, book your hotel well in advance; decent accommodations are hard to come by then. September 28.

October

Tsongkapa's birthday is celebrated throughout the Tibetan world. The birthplace of the founder of the Geluk order of Tibetan Buddhism, **Kumbum Tǎ'ěr Sì** (south of **Xīníng**) sees the liveliest festival. Religious dancing, mass chanting, and "sunning the Buddha" can be seen. Check with Kumbum (Tǎ'ěr Sì; © **0971/223-1357**). Twentieth to 26th days of the ninth lunar month (late Oct to early Nov).

November

International Festival of Folk Songs and Folk Arts, Nánníng. Many of Guǎngxī's minorities, including the Zhuàng, the Miáo, and the Dòng, gather for a colorful week of ethnic song and dance performances that some have criticized as being mere "urban reenactments." A visit to a village to see the minorities in their own environment is highly recommended, but if you're short on time, this explosion of song and dance will have to suffice. Check with **CITS** (© **0851/690-1660;** fax 0851/690-1600; gzcits@ china.com) for exact dates. First half of November.

Rozi Heyt (Ròuzī Jié or **Kāizhāi Jié)** marks the end of the monthlong Fast of Ramadan, and believers are keen for a feast. Presents are exchanged and alms are given to the poor. In Kazakh and Tajik areas this is often celebrated with a "lamb snatching" competition. A dead lamb is contested by two teams mounted on horses or yaks; the winning team succeeds in spiriting the lamb out of reach of their rivals. The festival is held for 4 days after the first sighting of the new moon in the 10th month (Shawwal) of the Islamic calendar. November 25 in 2006, moving backward by 11 days each year (Oct 13, 2007; Oct 2, 2008).

December

Miáo New Year Festival, Xīnjiāng, Lángdé (Guìzhōu). The Miáo New Year is celebrated with songs, dances, bullfights, and *lúshēng* competitions. For exact dates check with **CITS** Kǎilǐ (© **0855/822-2506;** www.qdncits. com). End of the 10th lunar month (usually Dec).

Ice and Snow Festival, Harbin. Every year, tens of thousands of people travel from as far south as Guǎngdōng and brave freezing cold to see the Hā'ěrbīn Bīngxuě Jié. The city's streets come alive with elaborate ice sculptures equipped with internal wires that blaze to life at night. Most impressive is the Ice and Snow Palace, a life-size frozen-water mansion with multiple levels erected every year on the banks of the Sungari River. From late December to whenever the ice begins to melt (usually late Feb).

5 Travel Insurance

Check your existing insurance policies and credit card coverage before you buy travel insurance. You may already be covered for lost luggage, canceled tickets, or medical expenses. The cost of travel insurance varies widely, depending on the cost and length of your trip, your age, your health, and the type of trip you're taking.

Purchase insurance from a broker, or directly from an online or telephone-based insurer, as it is invariably considerably cheaper than that sold by travel agents, banks, foreign exchange operations, or insurers at the airport.

TRIP-CANCELLATION INSURANCE Trip-cancellation insurance helps you get your money back if you have to back out of a trip, if you have to go home early, or if your travel supplier goes bankrupt. Acceptable reasons for cancellation can range from sickness to natural disasters to a government department declaring your destination unsafe for travel. Insurers usually won't cover vague fears, though, and in 2003 SARS wrong-footed many travelers.

MEDICAL INSURANCE For China, purchase travel insurance with air ambulance or scheduled airline repatriation built in. Be clear on the terms and conditions—is repatriation limited to life-threatening illnesses, for instance? While there are advanced facilities staffed by foreign doctors in Běijīng and Shànghǎi, and excellent facilities in Hong Kong, in most of China a hospital visit is to be avoided, if possible. Foreigners unfortunate enough to end up in provincial facilities do tend to get special treatment, but you are unlikely to consider it special enough. You may also face a substantial bill, and you will not be allowed to leave until you pay it *in cash*. You must claim back the expense when you return home, so make sure you have adequate proof of payment.

LOST-LUGGAGE INSURANCE On U.S. domestic flights, checked baggage is covered up to $2,500 per ticketed passenger. On international flights (including U.S. portions of international trips), baggage is limited to approximately $9 per pound, up to approximately $635 per checked bag. If you plan to check items more valuable than the standard liability, see if your valuables are covered by your homeowner's policy, or get baggage insurance as part of your comprehensive travel-insurance package. Read the policy carefully—some valuables are effectively uninsurable, and others have such high excess charges that the insurance is not worth buying.

If your luggage is lost, immediately file a lost-luggage claim at the airport. For most airlines, you must report delayed, damaged, or lost baggage within 4 hours of arrival. The airlines are required to deliver your luggage, once it's found, directly to your house or destination free of charge, although don't expect that necessarily to work with domestic Chinese airlines.

6 Health & Safety

STAYING HEALTHY
GREATEST RISKS
The greatest risk to the enjoyment of a holiday in China is one of **stomach upsets** or more serious illnesses arising from low hygiene standards. Keep your hands frequently washed and away from your mouth. Only eat freshly cooked hot food, and fruit you can peel yourself. Avoid touching the part to be eaten once it's been peeled. Drink only boiled or bottled water. *Never* drink from the tap. Use bottled water for brushing your teeth.

The second most common cause of discomfort is the upper respiratory tract infection or cold- or flulike symptoms in fact caused by **heavy pollution.** Many standard Western remedies or sources of relief (and occasionally fake versions of these) are available over the counter, but bring a supply of whatever you are used to. If you have sensitive eyes, you may wish to bring an eye bath and solution.

If you regularly take a nonprescription medication, bring a plentiful supply with you and don't rely on finding it in China. Feminine hygiene products such as feminine napkins are widely available, but tampons are found mainly in Hong Kong.

GENERAL AVAILABILITY
OF HEALTH CARE
While the names and addresses of reliable (and very expensive) clinics with up-to-date equipment and English-speaking foreign doctors are given in this guide

where available, in most cases they are not. So should you begin to feel unwell in China, your first contact should be with your hotel reception. Many major hotels have doctors on staff who will give a first diagnosis and treatment for minor problems, and who will be aware of the best place to send foreigners for further treatment.

Be very cautious about what is prescribed for you. Doctors are poorly paid, and many earn kickbacks from pharmaceutical companies for prescribing expensive medicines. Antibiotics are handed out like candy, and indeed, dangerous and powerful drugs of all kinds can be bought over the counter at pharmacies. Mis-prescription is now a significant cause of death in China, including the habit of prescribing a combination of Western drugs and Chinese traditional "medicines," which react badly with each other. In general, the best policy is to stay as far away from Chinese health care as possible. Much of it is not good for your health.

BEFORE YOU LEAVE
Plan well ahead. While a trip to Hong Kong or Macau can be made with little extra protection, a trip to mainland China, depending on its duration and time spent outside larger cities, may require a few new inoculations, especially if you haven't traveled much in the less developed world before. Some of these

are expensive, some need multiple shots separated by a month or two, and some should not be given at the same time. So start work on this 3 or 4 months before your trip.

For the latest information on infectious diseases and travel risks, and particularly on the constantly changing situation with malaria, consult the **World Heath Organization** (www.who.int) and the **Centers for Disease Control** in Atlanta (www.cdc.gov). Look in particular for the latest information on SARS, which may continue long after the media has become bored with reporting it. Note that family doctors are rarely up-to-date with vaccination requirements, so when looking for advice at home, contact a specialist travel clinic.

To begin with, your standard inoculations, typically for **polio, diphtheria,** and **tetanus,** should be up-to-date. You may also need inoculations against **typhoid fever, meningococcal meningitis, cholera, hepatitis A and B,** and **Japanese B encephalitis.** If you will be arriving in mainland China from a country with **yellow fever,** you may be asked for proof of vaccination, although border health inspections are cursory at best. See also advice on **malaria,** below.

WHILE YOU ARE THERE

Mosquito-born **malaria** comes in various forms, and you may need to take two different prophylactic drugs, depending upon the time you travel, whether you venture into rural areas, and which areas they are. You must begin to take these drugs 1 week *before* you enter an affected area, and *for 4 weeks after you leave it, sometimes longer.* For urban tours, prophylaxis is usually unnecessary.

If you visit Tibet, you may be at risk from **altitude sickness,** usually marked by throbbing headache, loss of appetite, shortness of breath, and overwhelming lethargy. Other than retreating to a lower altitude, avoiding alcohol, and drinking plenty of water, many find a drug called Diamox (acetazolamide) to be effective, and used with caution. For most, one sleepless night is all you will have to endure.

Standard precautions should be taken against exposure to **strong summer sun,** its brightness often dimmed by pollution but its power to burn undiminished.

The Chinese are phenomenally ignorant about **sexually transmitted diseases,** which are rife. As with the respiratory disease SARS, the government denied there was any AIDS problem in China until it grew too large to be contained, and it still issues estimates of the spread of infection that are highly conservative. In short, even more than at home, you should not undertake intimate activities without protection. Condoms are widely available, including Western brands in bigger cities.

STAYING SAFE

China is one of Asia's safest destinations. You must still be cautious about theft in the same places as anywhere else in the world—crowded markets, popular tourist sights, bus and railway stations, and airports. The main danger of walking the ill-lit streets at night is of falling down an uncovered manhole or walking into a phone or power wire strung at neck height. Take standard precautions against pickpockets (distribute your valuables around your person, and wear a money belt inside your clothes). There's no need to be concerned about dressing down or not flashing valuables—it's automatically assumed that all foreigners are astonishingly rich anyway, even the scruffiest backpackers, and the average Chinese cannot tell a Cartier from any other shiny watch. If you are a victim of theft, make a police report (go to the same addresses given for visa extensions in each city, where you are most likely to find an English-speaking policeman). But don't necessarily expect sympathy, cooperation, or action. The main purpose is to get a theft report to give to your insurers for compensation.

Street crime increases in the period leading up to Chinese New Year as migrants from the country become more desperate to find ways to fund their journeys home. Be especially vigilant at this time of year.

Harassment of **solo female travelers** is slightly more likely if they appear to be of Chinese descent, but is very rare.

Traffic is a major hazard for the cautious and incautious alike. In Hong Kong and Macau, driving is on the left, and road signs and traffic lights are obeyed. In mainland China, driving is on the right, at least occasionally. The rules of the road are routinely overridden by one rule: "I'm bigger than you, so get out of my way," and pedestrians are at the bottom of the pecking order. Cyclists ride along the sidewalks, and cars also mount sidewalks right in front of you and park across your path as if you don't exist. Watch out for loose paving slabs caused by these selfish SUV drivers; usually they only spurt up dirty water, but twisted ankles sometimes occur, too. Cyclists go in both directions along the bike lane at the side of the road, which is also invaded by cars looking to park. The edges of the main lanes also usually have cyclists going in both directions. The vehicle drivers are gladiators, competing for any way to move into the space ahead, constantly changing lanes, and crossing each others' paths. Pedestrians are matadors pausing between lanes as cars sweep by to either side of them. In cities they tend to group together and edge out into the traffic together, causing it to swing ever farther out away from them, often into the path of oncoming vehicles, until eventually the traffic parts and flows to either side, and the process is repeated for the next lane. Whether it's more hair-raising to be in the vehicle or on the street is an open question. Driving

tests are laughable, and even though China only has 2% of the world's cars, it already has 20% of all traffic-accident fatalities. The latest scourges to watch out for are rechargeable electric bicycles, which silently whiz along the sidewalk catching many pedestrians completely unawares.

Visitors should be cautious of various **scams,** especially in areas of high tourist traffic, and of Chinese who approach and speak in English: "Hello friend! Welcome to China!" or similar. Those who want to practice their English and who suggest moving to some local haunt may leave you with a bill that has two zeros more on it than it should, and there's trouble should you decline to pay. "Art students" are a pest: They approach you with a story about raising funds for a show overseas, but in fact are merely enticing you into a shop where you will be lied to extravagantly about the authenticity, uniqueness, originality, and true cost of various paintings, which you will be pressured into buying for dozens of times their actual value. The man who is foolish enough to accept an invitation from pretty girls to sing karaoke deserves all the hot water in which he will find himself, up to being forced by large, well-muscled gentlemen to visit an ATM and withdraw large sums to pay for services not actually provided.

DEALING WITH DISCRIMINATION

In mainland China, in casual encounters, non-Chinese are treated as something between a cute pet and a bull in a china shop, and sometimes with pitying condescension because they are too stupid to speak Chinese. At some sights, out-of-town Chinese tourists may ask to have their picture taken with you, which will be fun to show friends in their foreigner-free hometowns. ("Look! Here's me with the Elephant Man!") Unless you are of Chinese descent, your foreignness is constantly thrust in your face with catcalls of *"lǎowài,"* (or *"gweillo"* in Cantonese areas) a not particularly courteous term for "foreigner," and a bit like shouting "Chinky" at every Chinese you encounter at home. Mocking, and usually falsetto, calls of "Helloooooo" are not greetings but similar to saying "Pretty Polly!" to a parrot. Whether acknowledged or not (and all this is best just ignored), these calls are usually followed by giggles. But there's little other overt discrimination, other than persistent overcharging wherever it can possibly be arranged. Indeed, in general, foreigners get better treatment from Chinese, both officials and the general public, than the Chinese give each other, once some sort of communication is established. People with darker skin do have a harder time than whites, but those with no Mandarin will probably not notice. Hong Kong and Macau are both more tolerant, although souvenir shops and markets will overcharge wherever possible. Hong Kongers married to foreigners know to leave their spouses at home when they shop for dinner.

7 Specialized Travel Resources

TRAVELERS WITH DISABILITIES

China should not be your first choice of destination, and if it is, you should travel in a specialist group (although such tours to China are very rare) or with those who are fully familiar with giving you whatever assistance you may need.

China is difficult for those with limited mobility. The sidewalks are very uneven, and there are almost always stairs to public buildings, sights, and hotels with no alternative ramps. In theory, some major hotels in the largest cities have wheelchair-accessible rooms, but rarely are they properly executed—the door to the bathroom may be wider, or the bathroom suite lower, but not both, and other switches and controls may be out of reach. Metro stations do not have lifts, and any escalators are most usually up only.

GAY & LESBIAN TRAVELERS

China is still in denial. Even Běijīng boasts only a single gay bar of any note, but it is not permitted to describe it in print as such, and there's less still for lesbians. You don't travel to China for the gay scene any more than you'd travel to Mexico for the icebergs. Only Hong Kong and Macau are well supplied with openly gay bars and clubs. Other Asian countries have much more to offer. Even **The International Gay & Lesbian Travel Association** **(IGLTA;** © **800/448-8550** or 954/776-2626; www.iglta.org) lists no gay-friendly organizations dealing with in-bound visitors to China. *Out and About* (© **800/929-2268** or 415/644-8044; www.outandabout.com), which offers gay guidebooks, has a Hong Kong title ("No other city is better equipped for the #1 gay sport: shopping!"), but nothing for the mainland.

SENIOR TRAVEL

There are no special arrangements or discounts for seniors in China, with the exception of some familiar foreign brand-name hotels that may offer senior rates if you book in advance (although you'll usually beat those prices simply by showing up in person, if there are rooms available).

FAMILY TRAVEL

China accepts children traveling on a parent's passport, although the child's photo must be submitted along with the parent's when a visa application is made.

Mainland China, however, is not the place to make your first experiment in traveling with small children, unless you are already very familiar with Third World travel or with China in particular. Your biggest challenges will be the long journeys between destinations (certainly if you travel by land), the lack of services or entertainment aimed at children, the lack of familiar foods (unless your children have been brought up with Chinese food), and hygiene.

In general, the Chinese will be fascinated by your child, especially if he or she has anything other than black hair and is not of Asian descent. Some children find Chinese strangers a little too hands-on, and may tire of forced encounters (and photo sessions) with Chinese children met on the street. But the Chinese put their children firmly first, and stand up on buses while the children sit.

Only a very few companies organize family trips to China but two of the most promising are **Pacific Delight World Tours** (www.pacificdelighttours.com) and **Rascals**

in Paradise (www.rascalsinparadise.com). Pacific's 15-day "Family Yangtze River Escapade" includes the Chéngdū Research Base of Giant Panda Breeding, home of the Giant Panda while San Francisco–based Rascals offers tours stretching from Běijīng all the way down to Yángshuò.

STUDENTS

There are no particular benefits or discounts available to foreign students traveling in China unless you're registered at a Chinese educational institution (and then not many), but an International Student Identity Card can occasionally be useful in Hong Kong, mostly for reduced-price museum entrance.

8 Planning Your Trip Online

SURFING FOR AIRFARES

The "big three" online travel agencies, **Expedia.com, Travelocity.com,** and **Orbitz.com,** sell most of the air tickets bought on the Internet. (Canadian travelers should try expedia.ca and Travelocity. ca; U.K. residents try expedia.co.uk and opodo.co.uk.) Also remember to check **airline websites** for Web-only specials. For the websites of airlines that fly to and from your destination, check "Getting There," later in this chapter. For last-minute trips, **site59.com** in the U.S. and **lastminute.com** in Europe often have better deals than the big-name sites. Do *not*

buy domestic travel online from English-language sites. Markups are horrendous.

SURFING FOR HOTELS

Booking hotel rooms online in China is not a good idea, unless money is no object, or unless you absolutely must stay at a specific hotel at a very busy time of the year. There are no online services offering Chinese hotel rooms at discounts lower than you can get for yourself, whatever they may tell you. See "Saving on Your Hotel Room," under "Tips on Accommodations," later in this chapter.

9 The 21st-Century Traveler

INTERNET ACCESS AWAY FROM HOME

Despite highly publicized clamp-downs on Internet cafes, monitoring of traffic, and blocking of websites, China remains one of the easiest countries in the world in which to get online.

WITHOUT YOUR OWN COMPUTER

Almost any hotel with a business center, right down to Chinese government–rated

two-star level, offers expensive Internet access, and almost every town has a few Internet cafes *(wǎngbā)*, with rates typically ¥2 to ¥3 (25¢–40¢) per hour, many open 24 hours a day. Locations of cafes are given for most cities in this guide, but they come and go very rapidly. Keep your eyes open for the *wǎngbā* characters given in "Appendix A: The Chinese Language." In **Hong Kong** many coffee bars have a free terminal or two.

Thanks to ADSL (Asymmetric Digital Subscriber Lines) many progressive bars and guesthouses are now offering free Internet on the mainland, too. Note that many Internet bars are dark, dirty places; you will usually find that the local library is a much cleaner, often cheaper alternative.

Many media websites and those with financial information or any data whatsoever on China that disagrees with the usually mendacious party line are blocked from mainland China, as are even some search engines.

WITH YOUR OWN COMPUTER

It's just possible that your ISP has a low-cost local access number in China, but that's unlikely. Never mind, because there's free, **anonymous dial-up access** across most of China. When, in the "Fast Facts" section of a city in this book, you see "Dial-up is . . . ," you can connect by using the number we've provided, and by making the account name and password the same as the dial-up number. Speeds vary but are usually fine for checking e-mail directly, although they're variable for checking mail via a Web interface. The service is paid for through a tiny increment in the low cost of a local phone call. Many hotels advertising "free Internet" simply mean that they don't charge you at all for calls to these numbers.

Another option in larger cities is to buy an **Internet access card** *(wǎngkǎ)*. These are on sale at newspaper kiosks, phone stores, convenience stores, and department stores, and usually allow more rapid connection speeds. The back of the card (always bought for less than its face value—bargain the price well down) has instructions in English. Scratch off the panel on the back of the card, call the administration number provided, and give the card number, a contact phone number (any hotel will do), and your passport number; English is usually spoken but get hotel desk staff to assist just

in case. Use the dial-up number and account number on the back of the card, and the password from behind the scratch-off panel. Online time usually costs well under ¥1 (15¢) an hour. **Warning:** Many cards are only usable in the city where they are purchased.

Mainland China uses the standard U.S.-style RJ11 telephone jack also used as the port for laptops worldwide. Cables with RJ11 jacks at both ends can be picked up for around $1 in department stores and electrical shops without difficulty. In Hong Kong and Macau, however, phone connections are often to U.K. standards, although in better hotels an RJ11 socket is provided. Standard electrical voltage across China is 220v, 50Hz, which most laptops can deal with, but North American users in particular should check. For power socket information, see "Fast Facts: China," later in this chapter.

Those with on-board Ethernet can take advantage of broadband services in major hotels in China, which are sometimes free. Ethernet cables are often provided but it's best to bring your own. Details are given under each hotel listing. Occasionally Internet access is provided via the TV and a keyboard with an infrared link, but this is slow and clumsy. At least one Běijīng hotel (the Kempinski) and some Hong Kong hotels now have wireless access in public areas for those with a wireless card installed.

USING A CELLPHONE IN CHINA

All Europeans, most Australians, and many North Americans use GSM (Global System for Mobiles). But while everyone else can take a regular GSM phone to China, North Americans, who operate on a different frequency, need to have a more expensive triband model.

International roaming charges can be horrendously expensive. It's far cheaper to buy a prepaid chip with a new number in

China or Hong Kong (but you'll need a different chip for each destination). You may need to call your cellular operator to "unlock" your phone in order to use it with a local provider.

Renting a phone is an expensive alternative, best done from home, since such services are not widely available in China. That way you can give out your new number, and make sure the phone works. You'll usually pay $40 to $50 per week, plus air-time fees of at least $1 a minute. In the U.S., two good wireless rental companies are **InTouch USA** (© 800/ 872-7626; www.intouchglobal.com) and **RoadPost** (© 888/290-1606 or 905/ 272-5665; www.roadpost.com).

In mainland China, **buying a phone** is the best option. Last year's now unfashionable model can be bought, with chip and ¥100 ($13) of prepaid air time, for often around ¥800 ($100), less if a Chinese model is chosen. Europeans taking their GSM phones, and North Americans with triband phones, can buy chips *(quánqiútōng)* for about ¥100 ($13). Mainland chips do not work in Hong Kong, or vice versa. Recharge cards *(shénzhōuxíng)* are available at post offices and the mobile-phone shops, which seem to occupy about 50% of all retail space. Call rates are very low, although those receiving calls pay part of the cost; and if the phone is taken to another province,

Online Traveler's Toolbox

- **On-line Chinese Tools** (www.mandarintools.com). Dictionaries for Mac and Windows, facilities for finding yourself a Chinese name, Chinese calendars for conversion between the solar and lunar calendars (on which most Chinese festivals are based), and more.

- **Ctrip** (www.english.ctrip.com). Yet another Chinese hotel booking site, but this one has a great deal of useful travel information in English as well as a very convenient map of China interface.

- **Zhongwen.com** (www.zhongwen.com). Online dictionary with look-up of English and Chinese and explanations of Chinese etymology using a system of family trees.

- **Xianzai.com** (www.xianzai.com). Order free e-mail bulletins of entertainment listings for Běijīng, Shànghǎi, Guǎngdōng, and Dàlián, which include special offers for hotels and air tickets from China.

- **Visa ATM Locator** (www.visa.com), for locations of PLUS ATMs worldwide; or **MasterCard ATM Locator** (www.mastercard.com), for locations of Cirrus ATMs worldwide.

- **Weatherbase** (www.weatherbase.com) gives month-by-month averages for temperature and rainfall in individual cities in China. **Intellicast** (www.intellicast.com) and **Weather.com** (www.weather.com) give weather forecasts for cities around the world.

- **Universal Currency Converter** (www.xe.com/ucc). Latest exchange rates of any currency against the ¥RMB, HK$, and MOP$.

- **Travel Warnings.** See http://travel.state.gov/travel_warnings.html, www.fco.gov.uk/travel, www.voyage.gc.ca, or www.dfat.gov.au/consular/advice.

that cost increases, making the use of ordinary phones a better deal for dialing out. In **Hong Kong** recharge cards are widely available at convenience stores and mobile-phone shops, and chips are included free with the cost of initial charge value.

10 Getting There

BY PLANE

On direct, nonstop flights, China's own international airlines always offer rates slightly lower than those of foreign carriers. Cabin staff try to be helpful but are never quite sure how, and the in-flight movies may be 40 years old. Air China only recently suffered its first and only fatal accident, and it should not be confused with China Airlines from Táiwān, at quite the other end of the scale.

Cathay Pacific Airlines, Hong Kong's main international carrier, is effortlessly superior to North American airlines in service standards, and should be the first choice for direct flights to Hong Kong where available.

In recent years, a program of building and modernization has left even the airports of small provincial towns often shinier, more modern, and more efficient than those of similar-size cities in North America or Europe. Flying indirectly with the airlines of other Asian nations opens up a choice of other smaller, less-crowded mainland gateways, whose airports may be much closer to the center of town and which provide a gentler introduction to China.

Note that when you leave the country there's a **departure tax,** currently ¥100 ($13), payable only in cash. Departure tax on domestic flights is ¥50 ($6.25), but note that flights between the mainland and Hong Kong and Macau are treated *as international flights.* **Hong Kong's** taxes and fees are usually included in ticket prices, but **Macau's** are not. See the chapter on Hong Kong and Macau.

FROM NORTH AMERICA Among North American airlines, **Air Canada** (www.aircanada.com) flies to Běijīng and Shànghǎi, **Northwest Airlines** (www.nwa.com) to Běijīng via Tokyo, and **United Airlines** (www.ual.com) to Běijīng and Shànghǎi.

Japan Airlines (www.jal.co.jp) flies via Tokyo to Běijīng and Shànghǎi, but also to Dàlián, Qīngdǎo, and Xiàmén. **All Nippon Airways** (www.ana.co.jp) flies to Běijīng, Dàlián, Qīngdǎo, Shànghǎi, Shěnyáng, Tiānjīn, and Xiàmén. **Korean Air** (www.koreanair.com) flies via Seoul to Běijīng, Qīngdǎo, and Shěnyáng; and **Asiana Airlines** (us.flyasiana.com) flies via Seoul to Běijīng, Chángchūn, Chéngdū, Chóngqìng, Guǎngzhōu, Guìlín, Harbin, Nánjīng, Shànghǎi, Xī'ān, and Yāntái.

Hong Kong is served by Air Canada (www.aircanada.com), American Airlines (www.aa.com), Continental Airlines (www.continental.com), Delta Airlines (www.delta.com), Northwest Airlines (www.nwa.com), US Airways (www.usairways.com), and United Airlines (www.ual.com), as well as Hong Kong's Cathay Pacific Airlines (www.cathaypacific.com). Indirect routes are offered by All Nippon Airways (www.ana.co.jp), Asiana Airlines (us.flyasiana.com), China Airlines (via Taipei; www.china-airlines.com), Eva Airways (excellent value, also via Taipei; www.evaair.com.tw), Korean Air (www.koreanair.com), and Japan Airlines (www.jal.co.jp).

FROM THE UNITED KINGDOM

British Airways (www.britishairways.com) flies to Běijīng and Hong Kong, and Virgin Airlines to Shànghǎi and Hong Kong (www.virgin-atlantic.com). Cathay Pacific (www.cathaypacific.com) also flies directly to Hong Kong. Fares with KLM Royal Dutch Airlines (www.

klm.com) via Amsterdam, with Lufthansa (www.lufthansa.com) via Frankfurt, and with Finnair (www.finnair.com) via Helsinki, can often be considerably cheaper. Fares with eastern European airlines such as Tarom Romanian Air Transport (www.tarom.ru) via Bucharest, and with Aeroflot (www.aeroflot.com) via Moscow, or with Asian airlines such as Pakistan International Airlines (www.piac.com.hk) via Islamabad or Karachi, Malaysia Airlines (www.mas.com.my) via Kuala Lumpur, or Singapore Airlines (www.singaporeair.com) via Singapore, can be cheaper still. There are even more creative route possibilities via Ethiopia or the Persian Gulf States.

FROM AUSTRALASIA There's not much choice to the mainland from down under, although Sydney is served by China Eastern and Air China to Běijīng and Shànghǎi, and by Air China and China Southern to Guǎngzhōu. Qantas (www.qantas.com.au) and Air New Zealand (www.airnewzealand.com) fly to Hong Kong, and there are possible indirect routes with Philippine Airlines (www.pal.com.ph) via Manila, and with Garuda Indonesia (www.garuda-indonesia.com) via Jakarta. Hong Kong's Cathay Pacific (www.cathaypacific.com) flies directly from six Australian cities and Auckland.

FLYING FOR LESS: TIPS FOR GETTING THE BEST AIRFARE

Passengers sharing the same airplane cabin rarely pay the same fare. Travelers who need to purchase tickets at the last minute, change their itinerary at a moment's notice, or fly one-way, often get stuck paying the premium rate. Here are some ways to keep your airfare costs down.

- Passengers who can book their ticket **long in advance,** who **stay over Saturday night,** or who **fly midweek** or at **less-trafficked hours** will pay less.

If your schedule is flexible, say so, and ask if you can secure a cheaper fare by changing your flight plans.

- Fly via an **intermediate country** rather than direct. In Europe, considerable discounts can be obtained just by using even a neighboring nation's airline and changing planes once. But North Americans can save by changing planes in Tokyo, Seoul, or Taipei, and Europeans save even more by picking eastern European airlines or those of intermediate Asian nations such as Malaysia, India, and Pakistan. Stopovers in one direction are often free or allowable at minimum cost, giving you a chance to see two nations for the price of one ticket.

- Fly with one of **China's carriers,** such as Air China, China Eastern, or China Southern. These undercut the prices of your own country's airlines.

- Fly with a carrier such as Japan Airlines, serving **smaller regional airports.**

- Search the **Internet** for cheap fares (see "Planning Your Trip Online," earlier in this chapter).

- **Consolidators,** also known as bucket shops, are the best sources for international tickets. Start by looking in Sunday newspaper travel sections and in "what's on" magazines. Small travel agents in your local Chinatown often have the best deals. *Beware:* Bucket shop tickets are usually nonrefundable or rigged with stiff cancellation penalties. Several reliable consolidators are worldwide and available on the Net. **STA Travel** (www.sta.com) offers competitive fares for travelers of all ages, as does **TravelCUTS** of Canada and the U.K. (www.travelcuts.com). **Flight Centre** guarantees to beat the lowest written quote you can get elsewhere, and has offices all over Australia, Canada, New Zealand, South Africa, the U.K, and the U.S. (www.flightcentre.com).

BY ROAD

Foreign visitors are not freely permitted to drive their own vehicles into China, unless arrangements are made far in advance with a state-recognized travel agency for a specific itinerary. The agency will provide a guide who will travel in your vehicle and make sure you stick to the itinerary, or who will travel in a second vehicle with a driver. You will have to cover all the (marked-up) costs of guide, driver, and extra vehicle if needed, and of Chinese plates for your vehicle. The agency will book and overcharge you for all your hotels and as many excursions as it can. Forget it.

There are **bus services** between Sost in Pakistan and Kashgar, between Almaty in Kazakhstan and Ürümqi, and between Hong Kong and Macau and various points in the mainland. The Torugart Pass between Bishkek in Kyrgyzstan and Kashgar can be crossed if prearranged transport is waiting to collect you on the Chinese side. It's also possible to cross various borders on foot, including from Mongolia on the route from Ulaan Baatar to Běijīng, from Vietnam to Yúnnán and Guǎngxī provinces, from Laos to Yúnnán, and from Macau and Hong Kong to Guǎngdōng Province.

BY TRAIN

From Hung Hom station in Kowloon (Hong Kong), expresses run directly to Guǎngzhōu, Běijīng, and Shànghǎi (see www.kcrc.com for schedules and fares). From Hanoi in Vietnam, there are trains to Kūnmíng in Yúnnán Province, Nánníng in Guǎngxī Province, and on via Guìlín to Běijīng (see www.vr.com.vn/English/banggiotau_lveng.htm for an English timetable). From Almaty in Kazakhstan there are trains to Ürümqi in Xīnjiāng. From Moscow there are trains via Ulaan Baatar in Mongolia to Běijīng, and via a more easterly route directly to Harbin in China's northeast and down to Běijīng. There are also services which start in Ulaan Baatar and run via Dàtóng to Běijīng. There is a service between Běijīng and Pyongyang in North Korea.

BY SHIP

There are ferry connections from Incheon in South Korea and from Shimonoseki and Kobe (www.celkobe.co.jp) in Japan to Tiānjīn; from Incheon and Shimonoseki (www.orientferry.co.jp) to Qīngdǎo; from Incheon to Wēihǎi; from Incheon to Dàlián; from Osaka and Kobe in Japan to Shànghǎi (www.fune.co.jp/chinjif and www.shanghai-ferry.co.jp); from Incheon and Busan in Korea to Yāntái; and from Hong Kong and Macau to various points around Guǎngzhōu (www.turbocat.com and www.cksp.com.hk) and Fújiàn provinces, notably Xiàmén (www.cruise-ferries.com.hk). For details of service between China and South Korea, see http://english.tour2korea.com/coming/getting/bysea.asp.

11 Packages for the Independent Traveler

Since China reopened to foreign tourism in the early 1980s, all foreign tour operators have been required to use official state-registered travel companies as ground handlers. All arrangements in China were usually put together by one of three companies: China International Travel Service (CITS), China Travel Service (CTS), or China Youth Travel Service (CYTS). Controls are now loosening, foreign tour companies are now allowed some limited activities in China, and the range of possible Chinese partners has increased, but in effect, CITS and the like are the only companies with nationwide networks of offices, and most foreign tour companies still turn to them. They work out the schedule at the highest possible prices and send the costs to the foreign package company, which then adds its own administration charges and profit margins and hands the resulting quote to you. You could get the same price yourself by dealing with CITS (which has many offices overseas) directly. But you can get far better prices by organizing things yourself as you go along so, other than convenience, there's little benefit and a great deal of unnecessary cost to buying a package. Just about any tour operator will offer to tailor an itinerary to your needs, which means it will usually simply pass on the request to one of the state monoliths, and pass the result back to you. The benefit of dealing with the Chinese travel company directly is that you cut out the middleman, but if things go wrong, you will be unlikely to obtain any compensation whatsoever. If you book through a home tour operator, you can expect to obtain refunds and compensation if this becomes appropriate. In general, however, when organized through CITS, rail or air tickets for your next leg are reliably delivered to each hotel as you go. *Never book directly over the Web with a China-based travel service or "private" tour guide.* Many are not licensed to do business with foreigners, have not been licensed as guides, or will hugely overcharge and frequently mislead you (in the most charming way possible), and you will have no recourse at all.

If money is no object, then start with the list of tour companies below, nearly all of whom will arrange individual itineraries; or contact the **CNTO** (addresses on p. 20, earlier in this chapter) to find properly registered Chinese agencies who may help you. The **Hong Kong Tourism Board** and the **Macau Government Tourism Office,** in whose territories the tourism industry is well regulated, can point you towards reputable operators and talented licensed private guides.

12 Escorted General-Interest Tours

Escorted tours are structured group tours with a group leader. The price usually includes everything from airfare to hotels, meals, tours, admission costs, and local transportation, but usually not domestic or international departure taxes.

Again, due to the distorted nature of the Chinese industry, escorted tours do not usually represent savings, but rather a significant increase in costs over what you can arrange for yourself. Foreign tour companies are for now required to work with state-owned ground handlers, although some do book as much as they can directly, and some work discreetly with private operators they trust. But even as markets become freer, most deals will continue to be made with the official state operators, if only for convenience. Tours are very attractive if you wish to see a large amount of the country very swiftly. Please read the brochures with as much skepticism as you would read a realtor's (one man's "scenic splendor" is another's "heavily polluted"), and read the following notes carefully.

Most tour companies peddle the same list of mainstream "must-sees"—not all of which can hope to live up to the towering hype—featuring Běijīng, Xī'ān, Shànghǎi, Guìlín, and the Yángzǐ River, with some alternative trips to Tibet, Yúnnán Province, or the Silk Routes.

As with package tours, the arrangements within China itself are almost always managed by a handful of local companies, whose cupidity often induces them to lead both you and your tour company astray. Various costs, which should be included in the tour fee, can appear as extras; itineraries are altered to suit the pocket of the ground handler (local operator); and there are all sorts of shenanigans to separate the hapless tourist from extra cash at every turn, usually at whatever point the tour staff appears to be most helpful. (The driver has bottles of water for sale on the bus each day? You're paying three times the shop price.)

When choosing a tour company for China, you must, of course, consider cost, what's included, the itinerary, the likely age and interests of other tour group members, the physical ability required, and the payment and cancellation policies, as you would for any other destination. But you should also investigate the following:

SHOPPING STOPS These are the bane of any tour in China, designed to line the pockets of tour guides, drivers, and sometimes the ground handling company itself. A stop at the Great Wall may be limited to only an hour so as to allow an hour at a cloisonné factory. In some cases the local government owns the shop in question and makes a regulation requiring all tours to stop there. The better foreign tour operators design their own itineraries and have instituted strict contractual controls to keep these stops to a minimum, but they are often unable to do away with them altogether, and tour guides will introduce extra stops whenever they think they can get away with it. Other companies, particularly those companies that do not specialize in China, just take the package from the Chinese ground handler, put it together with flights, and pass it on uncritically. At shopping stops, you should never ask or accept your tour guide's advice on what is the "right price." You are shopping at the wrong place to start with, where prices will often be 10 to 15 times higher than they should be. Your driver gets a tip, and your guide gets 40% of sales. The "discount" card you are given marks you for yet higher initial prices and tells the seller to which guide commission is owed. So ask your tour company how many of these stops are included, and simply sit out those you cannot avoid.

TIPPING There is *no* tipping in mainland China. If your tour company advises you to bring payments for guides and drivers, some costs that should be included in your total tour cost are being passed on to you through the back door. Ask what the company's tipping policy is and add that sum to the tour price to make true comparisons. Some tour guides make as much as *400 times* what an ordinary factory worker or shop assistant makes, mostly from kickbacks from sights, restaurants, and shops, all at your expense, and from misguided tipping. Some tour operators say that if they cut out the shopping stops, they have to find other ways to pad the tour guides' income or there would be no tour guide. Shopping-free trips are nearly always accompanied by a higher price or a higher tip recommendation (which is the same thing). The guides are doing so well now that in some cases, rather than receive a salary from the ground handling company, they have to *pay* for the privilege of fleecing you. The best tour companies know how China works, make what arrangements they find unavoidable, and leave you out of it. Some take the middle path of collecting a small sum from each tour member, putting it into a central kitty, and disbursing as they must, but only for truly exceptional service, and at a proper local scale which short-time visitors from developed nations are incapable of assessing. Foreign tour leaders can be tipped according to the customs of their country of origin, and most companies issue guidelines for this.

GUIDES Another problem with mainland guides is that they rarely know what they are talking about, although they won't miss a beat while answering your questions. What they will have on the tip of their tongue is an impressive array of unverifiable statistics, little stories of dubious authenticity but which will amuse you, and a detailed knowledge of the official history of a place that may bear only the faintest resemblance to the truth. The guides' main concern is to tell foreigners what they want to hear, and to impress them with the greatness of China. So you may be told that the Great Wall can be seen from outer space (silly), that China has 5,000 years of culture (what does this actually mean?), that one million people worked on building the Forbidden City (it was only 100,000 on last year's trip), and that the little old lady you've just met in a village has never seen a foreigner before or heard of the United States (she tells every group the same thing).

Ask your tour company if it will be sending a guide or tour manager from your home country to accompany the trip members all the way through and to supplement local guides. This is worth paying more for, as it ensures a smoother trip all around, and it helps you get more authoritative information. Otherwise, you're better off bringing background reading from home written by independent authorities. Guides in **Hong Kong** and **Macau,** however, are often extremely knowledgeable and both objective and accurate with their histories.

TOUR COMPANIES

Between them, the following tour companies (a tiny selection of what's available) cater to just about all budgets and interests (contact them directly for specific itineraries and pricing). The companies are from the U.S., Canada, the U.K., and Australia, but many have representatives globally, and you can anyway just buy the ground portion and fly in from wherever you like.

Abercrombie & Kent (U.S.): Group size is typically 12 to 18 participants (with a maximum of 28 persons), ranging in age from 35 to 70 (although "China: A Family Adventure" can accommodate children ages 8 and older). The company maintains offices in Hong Kong and Běijīng and Shànghǎi, has its own guides, and books many services directly. Tour leaders include Mandarin-speaking Westerners and Chinese, and local specialist guides. There are no compulsory shopping stops, but assistance is given to those who wish to shop on their own in their free time. Tipping is included in prices, with the exception of tips for the main tour escort, who typically receives $10 to $15 per person per day. Tours have a historical and cultural focus and are upmarket, using China's very best hotels and direct contact with local artists, archaeologists, and colorful personalities. In the United States (group tours and custom private tours): ✆ **800/323-7308;** fax 630/954-3324; www.abercrombiekent. com). In the U.K. (custom private tours): ✆ **08450/0700615;** fax 08450/0700608).

Academic Travel Abroad (U.S.): Groups are typically of 20 to 30 people, in their 40s to 70s (one Yángzǐ River trip requires 100 participants so that an entire cruise ship can be chartered for a special itinerary). The company works with local non-CITS ground handlers. A subsidiary maintains offices in Běijīng and Harbin. Tour leaders are Mandarin-speaking Americans, with additional specialty study leaders. There is one noncompulsory shopping stop per city (on some tours none at all), and those not interested are taken to their hotel. All tips are included in the tour price. The company has been operating tours to China since 1979, with seven Mandarin speakers in the office and more in China, and operates educational and cultural tours in China for The Smithsonian (educational, cultural) and National Geographic Expeditions (natural history, soft adventure) on fairly mainstream itineraries, but with some surprises. For more information, check the website at www.academic-travel.com, but book through individual sponsors. The Smithsonian: ✆ **877/ EDU-TOUR;** fax 202/633-9250; http://

smithsonianjourneys.org. National Geographic: ☎ **888/966-8687;** fax 202/342-0317; www.nationalgeographic.org/ng expeditions.

Adventure Center (U.S.): The maximum group size is 18 (typically 12), consisting of travelers of all ages. Local ground handlers with an understanding of small-group adventure travel are selected, and some services are contracted directly by regional managers based in China. Both foreign and local tour leaders are used, as well as local guides. The company favors local shopping over organized tourist stops, with only one or two brief stops in a 15-day trip. The company offers a range of trip styles from more affordable grassroots-style trips designed for younger participants to more inclusive trips using upgraded accommodations for those wanting to combine adventure and comfort. Itineraries are a little more adventurous than the mainstream, and include walks on stretches of the Great Wall, the Eastern Qīng Tombs, and Chéngdé. The choice to tip or not is up to the individual traveler: ☎ **800/227-8747** in the U.S., or 888/456-3522 in Canada. Representatives can also be contacted in Australia and New Zealand. See www.adventure center.com.

China Focus (U.S.): Group sizes are between 6 and 50 persons (typically about 30); most participants are over 40 years old. Ground handling service companies are hand-picked in each region. Groups of 10 or more are accompanied by a Chinese national throughout the tour, which will include four to five shopping stops in 15 days. Tipping is recommended at $4 per day. Itineraries (such as "Tibet and the Best of China") deal mostly with mainstream sights, covering a lot of ground quickly. They're very competitively priced, but you pay in other ways: ☎ **800/868-8660** or 415/788-8660; fax 415/788-8665; www. chinafocustravel.com.

Elderhostel (U.S.): Group size ranges from 33 to 40 participants in their 50s to 80s, with an average age of 72. Tours are developed in cooperation with Chinese educational institutions, and partly based in them. Excursions and activities supplement the educational theme of each course, not shopping. Gratuities are included in program costs. Elderhostel has been operating its educational programs in China since 1986, which include working holidays, and an opportunity to teach English in Xī'ān: ☎ **877/426-8056;** www.elderhostel.org.

Gecko's Adventures (Australia): Gecko's tours are aimed at a younger crowd (typically, 20–40-year-olds) and group sizes are 6 to 14 participants (typically 10). The ground handler is a small local company. Tour leaders are locals with Gecko's training. Shopping tours are avoided (not least because tours use public transport as much as possible), but one in 15 days may be unavoidable. A tipping kitty is organized for local guides, and a tip of $1 per person per day for the tour leader is recommended. Itineraries stick mainly but not entirely to the highlights, but these are more down-to-earth budget tours using smaller guesthouses, local restaurants, and public transport. Branches across Australia: ☎ **03/9662-2700;** fax 03/9662-2422; and now in the U.K. too (☎ **01/635872300;** geckosadventures.co.uk). For representatives worldwide, see www.geckosadventures. com.

Intrepid Travel (Australia): Tour groups are limited to a maximum of 12 people drawn from all over the world; ages range from 17 to 75. These trips are for more adventurous travelers. CITS is used for ticketing, but smaller local operators are used wherever possible. A directly employed tour leader accompanies all groups; some are Chinese nationals. Shopping stops are specifically avoided. Tipping is encouraged but is entirely left to each traveler's discretion.

Trips are graded for physical requirements and culture shock, ranging from relaxed holidays to those requiring more strenuous effort. Small local guesthouses are used rather than big hotels. Itineraries are a deft mix of popular destinations and the less visited. There's also an interesting route from Hong Kong to Hanoi, and a gourmet tour: ⓒ **1300/360-887** in Australia, or 61 3/9473-2626; ⓒ **613/9478-2626** or 877/448-1616 in the U.S., or 0800/917-6456 or 44(0)20/7354-6170 in the U.K.; fax 613/9419-4426; www.intrepidtravel.com.

Laurus Travel (Canada): Group sizes range from 10 to 20 people with some departures limited to 16; ages range from 40 to 70. Ground handlers are personally known to the owners and hand picked from smaller operations. The company maintains an office in China and directly books its own hotels and local airfares. Most of the local guides are hand picked by the owners (one of the owners used to be a tour guide in China) because the owners understand that the priorities of many tour guides are misplaced. A tour leader accompanies the tour from Canadian departure or from arrival in China. Currently, shopping stops are restricted to three per trip but the company's goal is to eliminate such stops entirely. Tips for local guides and drivers are included; $5 per day is recommended for the tour leader. Laurus is a China-only specialist, but itineraries are mainstream: ⓒ **877/507-1177** in the U.S. and Canada, or 604/438-7718; fax 604/438-7715; www.laurustravel.com).

Pacific Delight Tours (U.S.): Four grades of tours offer group sizes of up to 16, 25, or 32 people. On longer tours, the age is over 45, but shorter tours have a broader range of ages. There are special tours for families with children and tours can be modified or extended to meet client needs. Ground handling is by Pacific Delight's own Běijīng office. Top-range tours are accompanied by a bilingual tour manager from the West Coast onward (most having 15–20 years of experience); midrange tours have a guide throughout China, and some other tours are locally hosted. There are typically four shopping stops in 15 days, with no more than one stop allowed per city. Recommended tipping is $6 to $9 per person per day, plus $4 to $7 for the American tour director. Pacific Delight was the first U.S. company to offer tours to China after the normalization of relations, and is the largest U.S. travel company in volume to China. It offers a large variety of mainstream trips, with endless permutations for different time scales and budgets, but with a heavy Yángzǐ River content, including one of the longest river trips. Pacific Delight also has the lowest airfares and most space with the key U.S. airlines serving China, which include Northwest, United, and Continental, which works with Pacific Delight exclusively, as well as Cathay Pacific, Korean Airlines, and Air China: ⓒ **800/221-7179;** www.pacificdelighttours.com.

Peregrine Adventures (Australia): Group sizes range from 4 to 15 people (typically 10–12). The company designs its own programs and uses closely monitored major ground handlers to book them. Tour leaders are locals, selected and trained by the company. Shopping stops are kept to a minimum: typically two in 15 days. A tipping kitty is recommended, running to no more than $1 to $2 per participant per day in total, which is disbursed by the tour leader to local guides, drivers, and consultants. Trips include visits to private houses and smaller restaurants frequented by locals, and can include walks and bike rides. But good-quality, centrally located accommodations are used. This is the slightly more upmarket version of Gecko's: ⓒ **800/227-8747** in the U.S., or 03/9663-8611; fax 03/9663-8618; www.peregrineadventures.com.

R. Crusoe & Son (U.S.): Tour groups never have more than 24 participants (typically 18). The company uses a local Hong Kong operator with incentive travel experience and the CITS head office in order to get special access. Groups are accompanied by a Hong Kong Chinese or occasionally by a hand-picked Chinese national, joined by local guides at each stop. Time is left at museums, for instance, for optional browsing in their shops, but factory shopping stops are kept to a minimum and are limited to 45 minutes. A sample 19-day tour includes only two shopping trips, and one optional evening shopping trip. Tours include extras such as a visit to an area of the Forbidden City that is usually closed to the public, a cooking demonstration dinner in Shànghǎi, and a view of Xī'ān's Terra-Cotta Warriors at eye level, rather than just from the viewing gallery: ✆ **888/490-8045**; www.rcrusoe.com.

Ritz Tours (U.S.): Groups range in size from 10 to 40 people, and ages range widely; parents often bring children. Ritz's own Shànghǎi office organizes the selection of local ground handlers—a mixture of large and small companies, with a preference for those providing good English-speaking guides. Tour leaders are Chinese nationals. Shopping stops are limited to one in each city. Tipping consists of $2 per day for the guide accompanying the group throughout the tour, $1 per day for local guides, and $1 per day for the driver. Ritz is the number-one U.S. tour operator to China in terms of volume. It maintains offices in Shànghǎi and Hong Kong. Itineraries are mainstream, with a concentration on the Yángzǐ River: ✆ **800/900-2446**; www.ritztours.com.

Steppes Travel (U.K.): Group size is usually no more than 16 persons, and participants are ages 45 to 80. Ground handlers are hand-picked operations with decent pan-China networks. Tour groups are accompanied from the U.K. by a British tour leader. There are no shopping stops, but leaders are happy to advise those who want to use free time to shop. The company regards tipping as now unavoidable, and simply gives guests a guideline, with an emphasis on not over-tipping. Tours are organized to very high standards, and most business is from referrals by previous satisfied clients. The company's is strong on the Silk Routes and Tibet, and specializes in multicountry itineraries that include China but can be combined with Vietnam, central Asia, Russia, and Mongolia, usually along the Trans-Mongolian railway: ✆ **01285/651010**; fax 01285/8858888; www.steppestravel.co.uk.

13 Special-Interest Trips

Audubon Nature Odysseys (U.S.): The Audubon Society has just started to experiment with **bird-watching tours** in China, and works through a specialist U.S. company with a Sino-American operator based in Kūnmíng. The tour leader is a bird specialist from overseas, the tour is joined by local birding experts, and the local operator provides a bilingual guide. The only shopping stop is at Stanley Market in Hong Kong. Tips are included in the program cost. The itinerary is a clever combination of mainstream sightseeing and visits to out-of-the-way bird-watching areas from mountainous Yúnnán Province to coastal migratory areas in Héběi: ✆ **800/967-7425**; www.audubon.org.

See MacKinnon and Phillipps's *Field Guide to the Birds of China* (Oxford) for a sample of what you might see. Bird-watchers visiting **Hong Kong** should see the Hong Kong Bird-Watching Society site at **www.hkbws.org.hk**, and First Step Nature Tours at **www.firststepnt.com**.

Bike China Adventures, Inc. (U.S.-based, with an office in China): Cycling group sizes range from one to eight participants, who have ranged in age from 18 to 86. The company is based in Chéngdū and organizes its own ground handling, sometimes using local owner-operator transportation. Tours are accompanied by a bilingual local or foreign guide. Shopping stops only occur if especially requested, and there is no tipping. Tours operate both around the company's Sìchuān base, in neighboring provinces, and as faraway as Héběi and Xīnjiāng, always using local hotels, guesthouses, and restaurants so there's no camping or cooking. There are trips for beginners as well as for the obsessed cyclist: **www.bikechina.com**.

Mongol Global Tour Co. (U.S.): Specializing in personalized service and customized travel, Mongol Global tour can arrange travel for a variety of interests. Custom tours are created for artists, choirs, business groups, and more and can be designed around drama, traditional costume, fashion, photography, team-building—you name it. Their tours offer many sites and experiences not generally found on standard tours and tours can be designed with economy in mind or in all-out luxe. Groups vary widely in age range; tours typically have 10 to 15 participants but they do offer large tours (25, 50-plus) for organizations. The company has offices in Southern California as well as Běijīng, Ulaan Baatar, Siem Reap, and Danang. There are local guides in each city and a national guide accompanies tours of ten or more people. For specialty groups there is often an international guide as well. Obligatory shopping stops are limited and are not allowed to interfere with time at main tour sites: ⓒ 866/225-0577 or 714/220-2579; www.mongolglobaltours.com or www.mgtourco.com.

Myths and Mountains (U.S.): Tours focus on **cultures, crafts, religious and pilgrimage sites, natural healing** and **traditional medicines,** and the **environment** and how people interact with it. Group sizes are of no more than 15 participants. Ground handling is by hand-picked local operators with an interest in a tour's theme. Tour leaders are local hand-picked specialists, often from ethnic minority groups. There are no shopping stops unless specifically requested, but for small groups the recommended tip is $10 per day for the guide, and $5 to $7 per day for the driver. The company is particularly strong on Yúnnán and Tibet: ⓒ **800/670-6894** or 775/832-5454; fax 775/832-4454; www.mythsandmountains.com.

Nomadic Expeditions (U.S./Mongolia): Groups range in size from 6 to 15 people. Participants tend to be over 40, but travelers of any age, even children, can be accommodated. Nomadic specializes in tours of Mongolia, but also offers trips that explore Tibet, Bhutan, China, and other nearby regions. The "Ancient Empires of the Khans" package tours China and Mongolia. The friendly and expert English-speaking, local Mongolian guides is happy to design custom itineraries from Běijīng. Traveling with this company is a (relatively speaking) luxurious, unique, and memorable experience. Nomadic handles all domestic air travel, land transport, and meals: ⓒ **800/998-6634** or 609/860-9008 in the U.S., or 976-11/325-786 or 976-11/313-396 in Mongolia; www.nomadicexpeditions.com.

Trains Unlimited, Tours (U.S.): Group sizes vary, and ages range from 25 to 85. CITS is the ground handler, particularly the Jílín branch which is practically run by **Railfans.** Tours are escorted from the U.S. by an American expert guide and joined by two Chinese guides who speak both Mandarin and local dialects. A little general sightseeing is squeezed between steam locomotive–related activities, along with about 10 shopping stops, in a 15-day tour. The company advises against tipping directly. Steam will probably die out in China in 2006, and the last steam-worked main line before that. Much tour time is spent in steelyards, at mines, and at workshops, in admiration of these doomed engines: ✆ **800/359-4870** in the U.S., 800/752-1836 in Canada, or 0161/928-9410 in the U.K.; fax 530/836-1748 in the U.S., or 0161/941-6101 in the U.K.; www.trainsunltdtours.com.

While many still prefer to book their trips at home, others might want to consider **www.wildchina.com**, one of the few online booking agencies I'd recommend for travel in China. Run by a returnee ABC (American Born Chinese) from Harvard, Wild China acts as a clearinghouse for specialized China tours. Great attention is paid to comfort and yet the destinations, such as a section of the Great Wall currently under renovation, are a little different from the usual spots. The site's collection of press articles is particularly encouraging.

14 Getting Around

The first thing to do upon arrival at any Chinese destination is to buy a **map** for ¥5 (65¢) or less. Even though few of these are bilingual, and most are inaccurate, they're essential for navigation. Your hotel staff can mark on them where you want to go, and you can show the characters to the taxi driver or bus conductor. Although building numbers are given in this book, they're useless for directions. Everyone navigates by street names and landmarks.

BY PLANE
In 2003 the announcement by the Civil Aviation Administration of China (CAAC) that it would allow the permitted maximum discount on airline tickets to reach 40% was greeted with derision by Chinese travelers, who had been obtaining such discounts, and greater, for some time.

Booking domestic flights before you arrive in China is expensive and unnecessary. The only Chinese airlines offering flights on internationally accessible ticketing systems are those that also have international routes: principally China Southern, China Eastern, and Air China. The only way to book domestic tickets before you leave home is through CITS offices (other agencies will go to CITS, too), or through online websites. In either case, you'll usually be asked to pay full fare (or more), which might be, for example, ¥1,200 ($150) one-way plus perhaps a booking fee on the Běijīng-to-Shànghǎi route. Yet you could pay ¥800 ($100) or less with no booking fee by buying over the counter from an agent in China, depending on seasonal demand. Some ticketing websites even have full fares on their English pages and discounted fares on their Chinese-language ones. So avoid them.

Much flying in China is on a walk-in basis, especially on the most popular routes. It makes sense to book a few days ahead to get the best price, but for most of the time, on most routes, there is an oversupply of seats.

While you can buy tickets between any two destinations served by Air China at any Air China office, you'll usually get a much better price from agents in the town from which you plan to depart. Prices are always better from agents than from the airline, even if they are next door to each other, and you can and should bargain for a lower price, and shop around. No agent with an online terminal connected to the Chinese domestic aviation system charges a booking fee. Agents sitting in four- and five-star hotels will not offer you the discounts they could, however. You need to look out in the street away from your hotel.

You usually *cannot* get a refund on an unused ticket from anywhere except the agent where you bought it.

BY TRAIN

Take the frequencies and timings given in this book as general guidelines, but expect any changes to be for the better.

Though in backwater areas, slow trains can be primitive, intercity trains are universally air-conditioned and mostly kept very clean. Nor is the system in general backward, with a computerized signaling system and a good safety record. There are 200kmph (125-mph) trains between Shēnzhèn and Guǎngzhōu, 300kmph (188-mph) trains and tilting trains using British technology under trial; the world's highest line is under construction to Lhasa; and the world's first commercial maglev (magnetic levitation) line runs from Shànghǎi to the Pǔdōng airport.

SEAT CLASSES   Given China's size, most intercity services are overnight (or sometimes over 2 nights), so sleeper accommodations are the most common. The best choice is **soft sleeper** *(ruǎn wò)*, consisting of four beds in a lockable compartment, the two upper berths slightly cheaper than the lower ones. Berths have individual reading lights and there's a volume control for the PA system. **Hard sleeper** *(yìng wò)* has couchettes, separated into groups of six by partitions, but open to the corridor. Berths are provided in columns of three and are cheaper as they get farther from the floor. Lights go off at about 10pm and on again at 6am. Thermoses of boiled water are in each compartment and group of berths, refilled either by the attendants or by yourself from a boiler at the end of each car. Compartments often have cups, but it's best to take your own. Bed linens are provided in both classes. More modern trains have a mixture of Western and Chinese squat toilets. Washing facilities are limited, and except on the highest quality trains, there's cold water only (and this may sometimes run out). On the very best trains there's hot water, free toothbrush and toothpaste hotel-style, and even electric hand dryers and shaver sockets. But this is rare. A tiny handful of trains have deluxe soft sleeper *(gāojí ruǎn wò)*, with two berths in a compartment (Kowloon-Shànghǎi and Kowloon-Běijīng, for instance), and in the case of some trains on the Běijīng-to-Shànghǎi run, these compartments have private bathrooms.

Almost all trains also have a **hard seat** class *(yìng zuò)*, which on many major routes is now far from hard, although sometimes still benchlike and not the way to spend the night. **Soft seat** *(ruǎn zuò)* appears on daytime expresses only, is less crowded, and is now often in two-deck form, giving excellent views.

REFRESHMENTS   Attendants push carts with soft drinks, beer, mineral water, instant-noodle packages, and occasional instant coffee through all classes at regular intervals. Separate trolleys bring through *kuài cān* (fast food) in cardboard boxes. This is usually dreadful, and costs ¥15 ($1.90). Licensed carts on platforms often sell freshly cooked local dishes which are slightly better, and they also offer fresh fruit in season. All overnight trains have dining cars, but the food is usually overpriced and very poor in quality. It's best to bring a supply of what pleases you, bought in convenience stores, supermarkets, and bakeries.

TYPES OF TRAIN   Where possible, choose a train with a T prefix. These *tèkuài* (especially fast) trains are the expresses, and come with the highest levels of accommodations and service. Staff may be uniformed and coiffed like flight attendants, willing and helpful. K trains *(kuàisù*—"quick speed") are more common, and nearly as good. Occasionally Y trains *(lǚyóu,* services for tourists) and L trains *(línshí,* temporary additional services, particularly at Spring Festival), can be found. The remaining services with no letter prefixes vary widely in quality across the country, from accommodations as good as that on K trains but at slower speeds, to doddering rolling stock on winding, out-of-the-way lines and with cockroaches and mice for company (no extra charge).

TIMETABLE A national railway timetable can be found on sale at stations in larger cities, updated twice a year, and some regional bureaus produce their own, or smaller summaries of the most important trains. All are in Chinese only, and most are so poorly organized that they are initially incomprehensible even to most Chinese. Rail enthusiast Duncan Peattie produces an annual **English translation** of the October edition of the national timetable. Originally aimed at rail fans, it doesn't include every single train or every station of interest to the ordinary visitor, but it covers all major services and reorders them into an easy-to-follow format. At $15 for the PDF format (more for a bound version), it costs 15 times the Chinese version, but it will be more than 15 times as helpful to many travelers, especially those sketching out a route for themselves before leaving home. Write **chinatt@eudoramail.com** for more information.

Timetables for a particular station are posted in its ticket office, and can be read by comparing the characters for a destination given in this book with what's on the wall.

TICKETS Rail ticket prices are fixed by a complicated formula involving a tiny sum per kilometer, and supplements for air-conditioning, speed, and higher classes of berth (soft sleepers are typically 50% more expensive than hard sleepers). Prices, samples of which are given throughout this book, are not open to negotiation. Round-trip tickets are available only between a handful of destinations.

Ticket offices always have a separate entrance from the main railway station entrance. In a few larger cities, there are separate offices for VIPs and foreign guests, or just for booking sleepers. Payment is only in cash. In most cases bookings can be made only 4 days in advance, including the day of travel. But increasingly in larger cities, this is expanding to as many as 12 days, and the same or longer for advance telephone bookings (in Mandarin only, like almost every other telephone service in China).

Most seats on an individual train are sold at its point of departure, with only limited allocations kept for intermediate stops depending on their size and importance. Your best choice of train is always one that is setting off from where you are. If you can only obtain a hard sleeper ticket but want soft sleeper, you can attempt to upgrade on the train. There is a desk for this purpose in the middle of the train, usually around car nos. 10 to 12.

The simplest way to book tickets is via a travel agent. The few with terminals accessing the railway system charge ¥5 (65¢) commission. Most others charge around ¥20 ($2.50), which should include delivery to your hotel. Agents within hotels often try to charge more. It's best to give agents a choice of trains and berth. You pay upfront, but the exact ticket price, printed clearly on the ticket, will depend on the train and berth obtained.

With the exception of public holidays, tickets are now rarely difficult to obtain. Ticket prices are hiked on some routes during Spring Festival.

Advance booking from overseas is possible through CITS and some other agents at large markups, and so are not advised. Contact your local China National Tourist Office to find agents (see "Visitor Information," earlier in this chapter) if you must. In **Hong Kong,** China Travel Service sells tickets for the expresses from Kowloon to Guǎngzhōu, Běijīng, and Shànghǎi with no commission, and tickets for a selection of trains between other Chinese cities for a reasonable markup. Never use online agents, either Hong Kong or mainland based, as they charge up to *70% more* than they should.

You'll need your ticket to get to the platform, which will only open a few minutes before or after the train's arrival (if you buy a soft sleeper ticket, you can use the VIP *guì bīn* waiting room and board first). On the train, the attendant will swap your ticket for a token with your berth number. Shortly before arrival, she will return to reexchange it (you never miss your stop in China). Keep the ticket ready, as it will be checked again as you leave the station.

BY BUS

China's highway system, nonexistent 20 years ago, is growing rapidly, and journey times by road between many cities have been dramatically cut to the point where on a few routes, buses are now faster than trains. Although most buses are fairly battered, in some areas they offer a remarkable level of luxury—particularly on the east coast, where there are the funds to pay for a higher quality of travel. Some buses even have on-board toilets and free bottled water.

Many bus stations now offer a variety of services. At the top end are *kōngtiáo* (air-conditioned) *gāosù* (high-speed, usually meaning that toll expressways are used) *háohuá* (luxury) buses, on which smoking is usually forbidden and that rule is largely enforced. These tickets are usually easy to obtain at the bus station, and prices are clearly displayed and written on the ticket. There are no extra charges for baggage, which in smaller and older buses is typically piled up on the cover over the engine next to the driver. It's worth booking a day ahead to get a

seat at the front, which may have more legroom and better views.

Buses usually depart punctually, pause at a checking station where the number of passengers is compared with the number of tickets sold in advance, then dither while empty seats are filled with groups waiting at the roadside who bargain for a lower fare.

Sleeper buses, although cheaper, should generally be avoided when an overnight train is an alternative. Usually they have three rows of two-tier berths, which are extremely narrow and do not recline fully.

Transport can vary widely in quality in rural and remoter areas, but it is usually dirty and decrepit, and may be shared with livestock.

BY CAR (TAXI)

While foreign residents of China go through the necessary paperwork, with the exception of one hire operation at Běijīng's Capital Airport, self-drive for foreign visitors is not possible, and without previous experience, the no-holds-barred driving style of China is nothing you want to tackle. Renting a vehicle is nevertheless commonplace, but it comes with a driver. **Hong Kong** and **Macau** are so small that there's simply no point in hiring a car and facing navigational and parking difficulties, when there are plentiful, well-regulated taxis available.

All larger mainland hotels have transport departments, but book a vehicle from a five-star Běijīng hotel to take you to the Eastern Qīng Tombs, for instance, and you may be asked for ¥1,200 ($150). Walk outside and flag down a taxi (not those waiting outside), and you can achieve the same thing by taxi for around ¥300 ($37). Branches of CITS and other travel agencies will also be happy to arrange cars for you, but at a hugely marked-up price.

Despite the language barrier, bargaining with taxi drivers is more straightforward

Ten Rules for Taking Taxis Around Town

1. *Never* go with a driver who approaches you at an airport. Leave the building and head for the stand. As they are everywhere else in the world, airport taxis are the most likely to cause trouble, but drivers who approach you are usually *hēi chē*—illegal and meterless "black cabs."

2. Cabs waiting for business outside major tourist sights, especially those with drivers who call out to foreigners, should generally be avoided, as should cabs whose drivers ask you where you want to go even before you get in. Always flag down a passing cab, and 9 times in 10 the precautions listed here will be unnecessary.

3. If you're staying in an upmarket hotel, do not go with taxis called by the doorman or waiting in line outside. Even at some famous hotels, drivers pay kickbacks to the doormen to allow them to join the line on the forecourt. Some cabs are merely waiting because many guests, Chinese and foreign alike, will be out-of-town people who can be easily misled. Instead, just walk out of the hotel and flag down a passing cab for yourself. Take the hotel's business card to show to a taxi driver when you want to get back.

4. Better hotels give you a piece of paper with the taxi registration number on it as you board or alight, so that you can complain if something goes wrong. Often you won't know if it has, of course, and there's no guarantee that anything will happen if you complain to the hotel.

5. Look to see if the supervision card, usually with a photo of the driver and a telephone number, is prominently displayed. If it isn't, you may have problems. Choose another cab.

6. Can you clearly see the meter? If it's recessed behind the gear stick, partly hidden by the artfully folded face cloth on top, choose another cab.

7. Always make sure you see the meter reset. If you didn't actually see the flag pushed down, which shouldn't happen until you actually move off, then you may end up paying for the time the cab was in the rank.

8. If you are by yourself, sit in the front seat. Have a map with you and look as if you know where you are going (even if you don't).

9. Rates per kilometer are usually clearly posted on the side of the cab. They vary widely from place to place, as well as by vehicle type. Flag-fall, not usually more than ¥10 ($1.25), includes a few kilometers; then the standard kilometer rate begins. But in most towns, after a few more kilometers, the rate jumps by 50% if the driver has pushed a button on the front of the meter. This is for one-way trips out of town, and the button usually should not be pushed, but it always is. As a result, it's rarely worthwhile to have a cab wait for you and take you back.

10. Pay what's on the meter, and don't tip—the driver will insist on giving change. Always ask for a receipt. Should you leave something in a cab, there's a remarkably high success rate at getting even valuable items back if the number on the receipt is called, and the details on it provided.

than you might expect. In most areas there are far more taxis than there is business, and half- and full-day hires are very welcome. To take Běijīng as an example, about 67,500 taxis are cruising around empty for much of the time, the drivers typically taking in around ¥300 ($37) for a 12-hour day (the drivers of cheaper taxis earn more, not less); most are glad to have a change and a day's guaranteed employment. Start flagging down cabs the day before you want to travel, and negotiate an all-in price, using characters from this book (for your destination), those written down for you by your hotel receptionist (times, pickup point, and other details), and a pen and paper (or calculator) to bargain prices.

Avoid giving an exact kilometer distance, since if you overrun it (and with China's poor road signage and the drivers' lack of experience outside their own town centers, you're bound to get lost at least once), there will be attempts to renegotiate. For the same reason, it's best to avoid being precise to the minute about a return time, but note that especially in big cities drivers sometimes have to be back in time to hand the car to the man who will drive it through the night. Be prepared to pay road tolls, and ensure that the driver gets lunch. If you find a driver who is pleasant and helpful, take his mobile phone number and employ him on subsequent days and for any airport trip.

15 Tips on Accommodations

CHOOSING A HOTEL IN CHINA

China is not a resort or honeymoon destination, at least not for the average romantic. Mainland China still has very few hotels so special that they are worth flying all that way to sample (although Hong Kong and Macau do).

There are two types of hotel in mainland China: the **Sino-foreign joint-venture** hotels with familiar brand-names, and **Chinese-owned and -managed** hotels. At the government-issued four- and five-star Chinese properties, they want you to think that they are at the same level as the joint-ventures; at lower levels, the accommodations can range from indescribably battered and grubby, to friendly and comfortable.

Your **first choice** at the four- or five-star level should be a familiar brand name or a property from one of the Asian luxury chains. In most cases the buildings are Chinese-owned, and the foreign part of the venture is the management company, which provides senior management and trains the staff, ensures conformity with their standards (never entirely possible), does worldwide marketing, and generally provides up to 90% of what you'd

expect from the same brand at home. There are Grand Hyatts in Běijīng and Shànghǎi. The Starwood group's St. Regis, Sheraton, and Westin brands are here, as well as Six Continents' Crowne Plaza and Holiday Inn; so are Hilton, Marriott, Ramada, Best Western, and more, although all are concentrated in China's largest cities. The Hong Kong Shangri-La group's hotels are among China's best, and they are notably successful in extracting the best from local staff. The Marco Polo and Harbour Plaza luxury brands are also in China (the Běijīng Marco Polo in particular should not be overlooked). The Palace Hotel in Běijīng is managed by the same company that manages the legendary Peninsula Hotel in Hong Kong (also Bangkok, New York, and other cities).

Your **second choice** should be a wholly Chinese hotel with foreigners in senior management, whose main purpose is simply to be there and make sure that things actually happen. But in this type of hotel and in the joint-venture, the general manager may be ignorant as to what's actually going on—such as the transport department using hotel vehicles for private hires or the doormen charging taxis to be allowed to wait in the rank.

Entirely **Chinese-owned and -operated** hotels at government-issued four- and five-star levels usually have one thing in common with their counterparts—they charge the same (or, at least, attempt to), but you certainly won't get value for your money. At four-star level and below, the best choice is almost always the newest—teething troubles aside, most things will work, staff will be eager to please (if not quite sure how), rooms will be spotless, and rates will be easily bargained down, since few hotels spend any money on advertising their existence. The aim is to find sweetly inept but willing service rather than the sour leftovers of the *tiě fànwǎn* (iron rice bowl) era of guaranteed employment, for whom everything is too much effort.

A drawback for all hoteliers is that the government requires them to employ far more people than they need, and it's nearly impossible to obtain staff with any experience in hotel work. The joint-venture hotels are the training institutions for the rest of the Chinese hotel industry, which steals their local staff as soon as possible. Lower-level hotels are run on half-understood rules, with which there's half-compliance, half the time. You may stay in a three-star that has perhaps a dozen foreign guests a year, but whenever they knock on a door, housekeeping staff may announce themselves in English ("Housekeeping!") although that's the only English word they know, and 99% of their guests won't know even that. But it's written down in a manual somewhere. A hotel may have designated nonsmoking rooms, but that doesn't mean they don't have ashtrays.

Until recently throughout China, only hotels with **special licenses** were allowed to take foreign guests. This requirement has already vanished in Yúnnán and Běijīng, and may eventually disappear elsewhere. In theory, all hotels with such licenses have at least one English speaker, usually of modest ability, shouted for by nervous, giggling staff as soon as you walk in.

The **Chinese star-rating system** is meaningless. Five-star ratings are awarded from Běijīng authorities, but four-star and lower depend upon provincial concerns. In some areas a four-star hotel must have a pool, in others a bowling alley, and in others a tennis court. The Jacuzzi may have more rings than a sequoia, the bowling alley be permanently out of order, and the tennis court be used for barbecues (because although it's a required feature, China simply doesn't have enough tennis players), but the hotel will retain its four stars, as long as it banquets the inspectors adequately. In general, Chinese hotels receive almost no maintenance once they open. There are "five-star" hotels in Běijīng that have gone a decade without proper redecoration or refurbishment. Foreign managements force the issue with building owners, but it's rare elsewhere that standards are maintained. A new three-star will usually be better than an old four-star.

Outside of joint-venture hotels, don't rely on the **extras,** many of which we do not even list, and even if we do, it's no guarantee that you'll find them fit to use. Salons, massage rooms, nightclubs, and karaoke rooms are often merely bases for other kinds of illegal entertainment (for men). Fitness equipment may be broken and inadequately supervised, and pool hygiene poor, so proceed with care.

You may receive unexpected **phone calls.** If you are female, the phone may be put down without anything being said, as it may be if you are male and answer in English. But if the caller persists and is female, and you hear the word *ànmó* (massage), then what is being offered probably needs no further explanation, but a massage is only the beginning. Unplug the phone when you go to sleep.

Almost all rooms in China, however basic, have the following: a telephone whose line can usually be unplugged for use in a laptop; air-conditioning, which is either central with a wall-mounted control, or individual to the room with a remote control, and which may double as a heater; a television, usually with no English channels except CCTV 9 (to which no buttons may be tuned) and possibly an in-house movie channel using pirated DVDs or VCDs; and a thermos of boiled water or a kettle to boil your own, usually with cups (which you should wash before using) and free bags of green tea. In a cupboard somewhere there will be a quilt. Between the beds (most rooms still have twin beds) will be an array of switches, which may or may not actually control what they say they control. In the bathroom there are free soap and shampoo, and in better hotels a shower cap, and toothbrush/toothpaste package (but bring your own).

Ordinary Chinese hotels usually speak of a *biāozhǔn jiān*, or **standard room,** which usually means a room with twin beds, occasionally with a double bed, and with a private bathroom. Often double beds have only recently been installed in a few rooms, which are now referred to as *dānrén jiān* or single rooms. Nevertheless, two people can stay there, but the price is lower than that of a twin room. In older hotels, genuine single rooms are available, and in many hotels below four-star level there are triple rooms and quads, which can also serve as dorms shared with strangers.

Foreign **credit cards** are increasingly accepted in three-star hotels upwards, but never rely on this. Most hotels accepting foreigners have foreign exchange facilities on the premises, although some may send you elsewhere to exchange checks. Almost all require **payment in advance,** plus a deposit (*yājīn*), which is refundable when you leave. Keep all receipts you are given, as you may need to show one to floor staff

to get your key, and you may in fact need to hand the key back and retrieve the receipt again before you can leave. To get your deposit back, you'll need to hand over the receipt for that when you check out, and since staff occasionally forget to enter payments in computer or ledger, you may need receipts to prevent yourself from being charged twice.

To **check in,** you'll need your passport and you'll have to complete a registration form (which will usually be in English). Always inspect the room before checking in. You'll be asked how many nights you want to stay, and you should always say just 1, because if you say 4, you'll be asked for the 4 nights' fee in advance (plus a deposit), and because it may turn out that the hot water isn't hot enough, the karaoke rooms are over your head, or a building site behind the hotel starts work at 8am sharp. Once you've tried 1 night, you can pay for more.

When you **check out,** the floor staff will be called to make sure you haven't stolen anything; this may not happen speedily, so allow a little extra time.

Children 12 and under stay for free in their parent's room. Hotels will add an extra bed to your room for a small charge, which you can negotiate.

SAVING ON YOUR HOTEL ROOM

The **rack rate** is the maximum rate that a hotel charges for a room. In China these rates are nothing more than the first bid in a bargaining discussion, designed to keep the final price you will actually pay as high as possible. You'll almost never pay more than 90%, usually not more than 70%, frequently not more than 50%, and sometimes as little as 30% of this first asking price. Guidelines on discounts are given for each city. Here are some tips to lower the cost of your room:

- **Do not book ahead.** Just show up and bargain. In China this applies as much to the top-class joint-venture names as to all the others. The best price is available over the counter, as long as there's room. For most of the year, across China, there are far more rooms than customers at every level. For ordinary Chinese hotels you may well pay double by booking ahead, and there's no guarantee your reservation will be honored if the hotel fills up or if someone else arrives before you, cash in hand. E-mail is almost never replied to, and faxes get ignored. Most Chinese just show up and bargain.

- **Book online.** If you want to be absolutely certain of a particular joint-venture hotel at a busy period, look at its website for rates. Major hotel chains operating in China often have their best *published* rate on their own websites. However, these rates fluctuate constantly according to demand, and are sometimes directly linked to computerized inventory which alters prices at frequent intervals, sometimes hourly. Prices for any time of year booked a long way ahead will always look uninviting. They'll be much cheaper nearer the time, unless some major event is taking place. Ordinary hotels, if they have a website at all, will just quote rack rates.

- **Dial any central booking number.** Contrary to popular wisdom, as the better hotels manage their rates with increasing care, the central booking number is likely to have a rate as good as or better than the rate you can get by calling the hotel directly, and the call is usually toll-free.

- **Avoid Chinese online agencies.** Avoid booking through Chinese hotel agencies and websites specializing in Chinese hotels. The discounts they offer are precisely what you can get for yourself, and you can in fact beat them because you won't be paying their markup. Many of these have no allocations at all, and simply jump on the phone to book a room as soon as they hear from you.

IN HONG KONG & MACAU
Hong Kong in particular is well stocked with hotels that regularly make their way onto lists of the world's best. Service is second to none, and they are worth flying halfway around the world to stay in. None of what's said about mainland hotels above applies.

16 Tips on Dining

See "Appendix B: The Chinese Menu," for hints on dining, and a city-by-city list of recommended dishes, complete with the characters to help you order them.

17 Recommended Reading

There's enough entertaining reading on China to fill a library, so here are just a few pointers to get you started:

Readable modern novelists easily purchased in translation at home include Ha Jin, whose stories tend to be remarkably inconclusive and so all the more true to life, derived from his experiences living in the northeast. *Ocean of Words* (Vintage, 2000), *Waiting* (Vintage, 2001), and the collection of short stories *The Bridegroom* (Vintage, 2001), lift the lids on many things not obvious to the casual visitor. *Soul Mountain* (Harper Collins, 2000), by Gāo Xíngjiàn, China's first winner of the Nobel Prize for Literature (although the Chinese populace is kept in ignorance of this), is the tale of a man who embarks on a journey through the wilds of Sìchuān and Yúnnán in search of his own elusive *líng shān* (soul mountain). *The Republic of Wine* (Arcade, 2001), Mò

Yán's graphic satire about a doomed detective investigating a case of gourmand-officials eating human baby tenderloin, is at once entertaining and disturbing. His *Garlic Ballads* (Viking, 1995) is an unsettling epic of family conflict, doomed love, and government corruption in a small town dependent on the garlic market.

First-class travel books include Peter Fleming's *News from Tartary* (Northwestern University Press, 1999), originally published in 1936, and still the best travel book ever written about China. Fleming's perceptive account of a hazardous expedition along the southern Silk Route, from Běijīng to northern India, is a masterpiece of dry wit.

For good general background reading, there are a few authors and publishers who turn out so much excellent and readable work that you should start by having a look at what they've done recently. Jonathan Spence writes the most readable histories of China, not just the weighty *Search for Modern China* (W.W. Norton, 2001), but gripping and very personal histories such as *The Memory Palace of Matteo Ricci* (Viking, 1994) on the clever self-marketing of the first Jesuit to be allowed to reside in Běijīng, *God's Chinese Son* (W.W. Norton, 1997) on the leader of the Tàipíng Rebellion who thought he was the younger brother of Jesus Christ, and *The Question of Hu* (Vintage, 1989) on the misfortunes of an early Chinese visitor to Europe.

Dover Publications (http://store.dover publications.com) reprints handy guides to Chinese history and culture, as well as oddities such as Robert Van Gulik's versions of 18th-century Chinese detective stories featuring a Táng dynasty detective-judge, such as *The Haunted Monastery and the Chinese Maze Murders* (1977). Dover's two-volume reprint of the 1903 edition of *The Travels of Marco Polo* (1993) is the only edition to have—more than half is footnotes from famous explorers and geographers trying to make sense of Polo's route, corroborating his observations or puzzling why he goes so astray, and providing fascinating trivia about China far more interesting than the original account.

For more recent China watching, anything by the Italian diplomat Tizanio Terzani is a good place to start, but *Behind the Forbidden Door* is particularly compelling. While many books do their best to present the country in a favorable light, Nicholas D. Kristof and Sheryl Wudunn present a very realistic picture in *China Wakes*. Perhaps the most recent author to address the subject realistically is Gordon C. Chang in *The Coming Collapse of China*.

These next two recommendations barely mention China, but explain the problems that the country faces more clearly than any other recent writer. *The Breakdown of Nations* (Chelsea Green Publishing, 2001), by Leopold Kohr, examines why the largest nations always face the largest problems. *Small Is Beautiful*, by E. F. Schumacher, focuses on the problems a nation faces when it tries to move from an agrarian to an industrial economy; this book is out of print, but you can probably find a copy online. Truly enlightening books to have with you as you travel around the world's most populous nation.

FAST FACTS: China

American Express Běijīng: Room 2101, China World Tower, China World Trade Center; ✆ 010/6505-2639. Shànghǎi: Room 206, Retail Plaza, Shànghǎi Centre; ✆ 021/6279-8082. Guǎngzhōu: Room 806, GITIC Plaza Hotel; ✆ 020/8331-1771.

Xiàmén: Room 212, Holiday Inn Crowne Plaza; ✆ 0592/212-0268. Amex offices are open Monday through Friday from 9:30am to 5:30pm. After hours: U.S. hot line ✆ 001336/393-1111; HK hot line ✆ 00852/2885-9377. Emergency card replacement: ✆ 00852/2277-1010. Stolen checks: ✆ 010800/610-0276, toll-free.

ATM Networks See "ATMs," under "Entry Requirements & Customs," earlier in this chapter.

Business Hours Offices are generally open from 9am to 6pm but are closed Saturday and Sunday. All shops, sights, restaurants, and transport systems offer the same service 7 days a week. Shops are typically open at least from 8am to 8pm. Bank opening hours vary widely (see "Currency," earlier in this chapter, and the "Fast Facts" sections for individual destinations). In **Hong Kong** most offices are open Monday through Friday from 9am to 5pm, with lunch hour from 1 to 2pm; Saturday business hours are generally 9am to 1pm. Most Hong Kong shops are open 7 days a week, from 10am to at least 7pm.

Car Rentals Rental is only possible with a Chinese driver, except in Hong Kong and Macau. See "Getting Around," earlier in this chapter.

Currency See p. 25.

Doctors & Dentists Many hotels have medical clinics with registered nurses, as well as doctors on duty at specified hours or on call 24 hours. Otherwise, your concierge or consulate can refer you to a doctor or dentist. If it's an emergency, get a Mandarin speaker to dial ✆ **120** in mainland China, or dial ✆ 999 in Hong Kong or Macau.

Driving Rules "I'm bigger than you, so get out of my way," sums it up. But you won't be driving anyway. When you cross a road, assume that the drivers are all out to get you. Driving is on the right. **Hong Kong** and **Macau** are far more law-abiding, and driving is on the left. See "Getting Around," earlier in this chapter.

Drugstores Bring supplies of your favorite over-the-counter medicines with you, since supplies of well-known Western brands are unreliable and sometimes fake. All familiar brands are available in **Hong Kong.**

Electricity The electricity used in all parts of China is 220 volts, alternating current (AC), 50 cycles. Most devices from North America, therefore, cannot be used without a transformer. The most common outlet takes the North American two-flat-pin plug (but not the three-pin version, or those with one pin broader than the other). Nearly as common are outlets for the two-round-pin plugs common in Europe. Outlets for the three-flat-pin (two pins at an angle) used in Australia, for instance, are also frequently seen. Most hotel rooms have all three, and indeed many outlets are designed to take all three plugs. Adapters are available for only ¥8 to ¥16 ($1–$2) in department stores. Shaver sockets are common in bathrooms of hotels from three stars upwards. In **Hong Kong** and **Macau,** the British-style three-chunky-pin plugs are standard, and these also often appear in mainland joint-venture hotels built with Hong Kong assistance.

Embassies & Consulates Most countries maintain embassies in Běijīng and consulates in Hong Kong. Australia also has consulates in Guǎngzhōu and Shànghǎi;

Canada and the U.K. in Chóngqìng, Guǎngzhōu, and Shànghǎi; New Zealand in Shànghǎi; and the U.S. in Chéngdū, Guǎngzhōu, Shànghǎi, and Shěnyáng.

Emergencies No one speaks English at emergency numbers in China, although your best bet will be ☎ 110. Find help nearer at hand. In **Hong Kong** dial ☎ 999 for police, fire, or ambulance. In **Macau** dial ☎ 999 for medical emergencies, ☎ 573-333 for the police, and ☎ 572-222 for the fire department.

Holidays See "China Calendar of Events," earlier in this chapter.

Hot Lines Hot lines and all kinds of telephone booking and information numbers are given throughout this guide. But in almost no cases whatsoever will English be spoken at the other end. Ask English-speaking staff at your hotel to find answers to your queries and to make any necessary calls on your behalf.

Information See "Visitor Information," earlier in this chapter.

Internet Access Internet access through anonymous dial-up is widely available, as are Internet cafes. See "The 21st-Century Traveler," earlier in this chapter.

Language English is widely spoken in Hong Kong, fairly common in Macau, and rare in the mainland, although there will be someone who speaks a little English at your hotel. Ask that person to help you with phone calls and bookings. Almost no information, booking, complaint, or emergency lines in the mainland have anyone who speaks English.

Legal Aid If you get on the wrong side of what passes for the law in China, contact your consulate immediately.

Liquor Laws With the exception of some minor local regulations, there are no liquor laws in China. Alcohol can be bought in any convenience store, supermarket, restaurant, bar, hotel, or club, 7 days a week, and may be drunk anywhere you feel like drinking it. If the shop is open 24 hours, then the alcohol is available 24 hours, too. Closing times for bars and clubs vary according to demand, but typically it's all over by 3am. In **Hong Kong,** liquor laws largely follow the U.K. model; restaurants, bars, and clubs must obtain licenses to sell alcohol for consumption on the premises, and shops must have licenses to sell it for consumption off the premises. In either case, licenses prohibit sale of alcohol to persons under 18. Licensing hours vary from area to area.

Lost & Found Be sure to alert all of your credit card companies the minute you discover your wallet has been lost or stolen. Your credit card company or insurer may require a police report number or record of the loss, although many Public Security Bureau offices (police stations) will be reluctant to do anything as energetic as lift a pen. Most credit card companies have an emergency toll-free number to call if your card is lost or stolen: In **mainland China,** Visa's emergency number is ☎ 010/800-440-0027; American Express cardholders and traveler's check holders should call ☎ 010/800-610-0277; MasterCard holders should call ☎ 010/800-110-7309; and Diners Club members should call Hong Kong at ☎ 852/2860-1800, or call the U.S. collect at ☎ 416/369-6313. From within **Hong Kong,** Visa's telephone number is ☎ 800/900 872, MasterCard's ☎ 800/966 677, Diners Club's ☎ 2860 1888, and Amex's ☎ 800/962 403. Visa also has a phone number for within **Macau:** ☎ 300-28561. Keeping a separate list of the serial numbers of your traveler's checks will speed up their replacement.

Also see "Emergency Cash," under "Entry Requirements & Customs," earlier in this chapter.

Mail Sending mail from China is remarkably reliable, although sending it to private addresses within China is not. Take the mail to post offices rather than use mailboxes. Some larger hotels have postal services on-site. It helps if mail sent out of the country has its country of destination written in characters, but this is not essential, although hotel staff will often help. Letters and cards written in red ink will occasionally be rejected, as this carries extremely negative overtones. Overseas mail: **postcards** ¥4.20 (50¢), **letters under 10 grams** ¥5.40 (70¢), **letters under 20 grams** ¥6.50 (80¢). EMS (**express parcels** under 500g): to the U.S.: ¥180 to ¥240 ($23–$30); to Europe ¥220 to ¥280 ($28–$35); to Australia ¥160 to ¥210 ($20–$26). **Normal parcels** up to 1 kilogram (2¼ lb.): to the **U.S.** by air ¥95 to ¥159 ($12–$20), by sea ¥20 to ¥84 ($2.50–$14); to the **U.K.** by air ¥77 to ¥162 ($9.50–$20), by sea ¥22 to ¥108 ($11–$14); to **Australia** by air ¥70 to ¥144 ($8.75–$18), by sea ¥15 to ¥89 ($1.90–$11). Letters and parcels can be registered for a small extra charge. Registration forms and Customs declaration forms are in Chinese and French. The post offices of **Hong Kong** and **Macau** are entirely reliable, but both have their own stamps and rates.

Maps Purchasing city maps as you go is absolutely essential, even though few are bilingual. These are available at bus and railway stations and at airports for under ¥5 (65¢). Get your hotel staff to circle the characters of your hotel and the main sights you plan to see, and note which is which. Now you can jump in a taxi at any point, show the driver the characters for where you want to go, and keep an eye on the route he takes. Map keys in this book have Chinese characters for the same purpose, as do "Selected Destinations by City" in appendix A. The tourist boards of **Hong Kong** and **Macau** are liberal with bilingual and trilingual free maps.

Newspapers & Magazines Sino-foreign joint-venture hotels in the bigger cities have a selection of foreign newspapers and magazines available, but these are otherwise not on sale. The government distributes a propaganda sheet called *China Daily,* usually free at hotels, and there are occasional local variations. Cities with larger populations support a number of self-censoring entertainment magazines usually produced by resident foreigners and only slightly more bland when produced by Chinese aiming at the same market. Nevertheless, these do have intermittently accurate entertainment listings and restaurant reviews. A vast range of English publications is easily available in **Hong Kong** and **Macau,** as well as local newspapers such as the *South China Morning Post.*

Police Known to foreigners as the **PSB (Public Security Bureau,** *gōng'ān jú*), although these represent only one of several different types of officer in mainland China, the police (*jǐngchá*) are quite simply best avoided. Since they are keen to avoid doing any work, you have the same interests at heart. If you must see them for some reason, then approach your hotel for assistance first, and visit the PSB offices listed in this guide as dealing with visa extensions, since these are almost the only places you are likely to find an English speaker of sorts. In **Hong Kong** and **Macau,** however, you can usually ask policemen for directions and expect them to be generally helpful.

Restrooms Street-level public toilets in China are common, many detectable by the nose before they are seen. There's often an entrance fee of ¥.20 (3¢), but not necessarily running water. In many cases you merely squat over a trough. So, use the standard Western equipment in your hotel room, in department stores and malls, and in branches of foreign fast-food chains. In Hong Kong and Macau, facilities are far more hygienic.

Safety See the sections on "Travel Insurance" and "Health & Safety," earlier in this chapter.

Smoking The government of China is the world's biggest cigarette manufacturer. China is home to 20% of the world's population but 30% of the world's cigarettes. About one million people a year in China die of smoking-related illnesses. In the mainland, nonsmoking tables in restaurants are almost unheard of, and nonsmoking signs are favorite places beneath which to sit and smoke. Smokers are generally sent to the spaces between the cars on trains, but they won't bother to do so if no one protests. Similarly on air-conditioned buses, where some will light up to see if they can get away with it (but usually they'll be told to put it out).

Taxes In **mainland China,** occasional bed taxes are added to hotel bills, but these are minor and usually included in the room rate. Service charges appear mostly in joint-venture hotels, and range from 10% to 15%. Many Chinese hotels list service charges in their literature, but few have the nerve to add them to room rates unless the hotel is very full. However, restaurants may add the service charge. Departure taxes must be paid in cash at the airport before flying: domestic ¥50 ($6.25), international (including flights to Hong Kong and Macau) ¥90 ($11). There are also lesser taxes for international ferry departures at some ports. In **Hong Kong,** better hotels will add a 10% service charge and a 3% government tax to your bill. Better restaurants and bars will automatically add a 10% service charge. Included in your ticket price are an airport departure tax of HK$80 (US$10) for adults and children older than 12, or a marine departure tax if you depart by sea. In **Macau,** better hotels charge 10% for service as well as a 5% tax. Marine departure taxes are included in ticket prices. Airport passenger tax for flights to China are MOP$80 (US$10) adults and MOP$50 (US$6.25) children ages 2 to 12; for other destinations the tax is MOP$130 (US$16) adults and MOP$80 (US$10) for children. Transit passengers who continue their journey within 24 hours of arrival are exempted from passenger tax.

Telephone The international country code for mainland China is 86, for Hong Kong 852, and for Macau 853.

To call China, Hong Kong, or Macau:

1. Dial the international access code: (011 in the U.S., 00 in the U.K).
2. Dial the country code: 86 for China, 852 for Hong Kong, 853 for Macau.
3. For China, dial the city code, omitting the leading zero, and then the number. Hong Kong and Macau have no city codes, so after the country code, simply dial the remainder of the number.

To call within China: For calls within the same city, omit the city code, which always begins with a zero when used (010 for Běijīng, 020 for Guǎngzhōu, and so on). All hotel phones have direct dialing, and most have international dialing.

Hotels are only allowed to add a service charge of up to 15% to the cost of the call, and even long-distance rates within China are very low. To use a public telephone you'll need an IC (integrated circuit) card *(àisēi kǎ)*, available in values from ¥20 ($2.50). You can buy them at post offices, convenience stores, street stalls, or wherever you can make out the letters "IC" among the Chinese characters. A brief local call is typically ¥.30 (5¢). Phones show you the value remaining on the card when you insert it, and count down as you talk. **To call within Hong Kong:** In Hong Kong, local calls made from homes, offices, shops, and other establishments are free, so don't feel shy about asking to use the phone. From hotel lobbies and public phone booths, a local call costs HK$1 (US15¢) for each 5 minutes; from hotel rooms, about HK$4 to HK$5 (US50¢–US65¢). **To call within Macau:** Local calls from private phones are free, and from call boxes cost MOP$1 (10¢).

To make international calls: From **mainland China** or **Macau,** first dial 00 and then the country code (U.S. or Canada 1, U.K. 44, Ireland 353, Australia 61, New Zealand 64). Next, dial the area or city code, omitting any leading zero, and then the number. For example, if you want to call the British Embassy in Washington, D.C., you would dial ✆ 00-1-202/588-7800. Forget taking access numbers for your local phone company with you—you can call internationally for a fraction of the cost by using an IP (Internet protocol) card, *àipì kǎ,* purchased from department stores and other establishments—wherever you see the letters "IP." Instructions for use are on the back, but you simply dial the access number given, choose English from the menu, and follow the instructions to dial in the number behind a scratch-off panel. Depending on where you call, ¥50 ($6.25) can give you an hour of talking, but you should bargain to pay less than the face value of the card—as little as ¥70 ($8.75) for a ¥100 ($13) card from street vendors. To use a public phone, you'll need an IC card (see above) to make the local call. In emergencies, dial 108 to negotiate a collect call, but again, in most towns you'll need help from a Mandarin speaker. From **Hong Kong** dial 001, 0080, or 009, depending on which of several competing phone companies you are using. Follow with the country code and continue as for calling from China or Macau. It's much cheaper to use one of several competing phone cards, such as *Talk Talk,* which come in denominations ranging from HK$50 to HK$300 (US$6.50–US$39) and are available at HKTB information offices, convenience stores, and other places.

For directory assistance: In **mainland China** dial 114. No English is spoken, and only local numbers are available. If you want other cities, dial the city code followed by 114—a long-distance call. In **Hong Kong** dial 1081 for a local number, and 10013 for international ones. In **Macau** dial 181 for domestic numbers, and 101 for international ones.

For operator assistance: If in **mainland China** if you need operator assistance in making a call, just ask for help at your hotel. In Hong Kong dial 10010 for domestic assistance, 10013 for international assistance.

Toll-free numbers: Numbers beginning with 800 within China are toll-free, but calling a 1-800 number in the States from China is a full-tariff international call, as is calling one in Hong Kong from mainland China, or vice versa.

Time Zone The whole of China is on Běijīng time—8 hours ahead of GMT (and therefore of London), 13 hours ahead of New York, 14 hours ahead of Chicago, and 16 hours ahead of Los Angeles. There's no daylight saving time (summer time), so subtract 1 hour in the summer.

Tipping In **mainland China,** as in many other countries, there is **no tipping,** despite what tour companies may tell you (although if you have a tour leader who accompanies you from home, home rules apply). Until recently, tipping was expressly forbidden, and some hotels still carry signs requesting you not to tip. Foreigners, especially those on tours, are overcharged at every turn, and it bemuses Chinese that they hand out free money in addition. Chinese never do it themselves; in fact, if a bellhop or other hotel employee hints that a tip would be welcome, he or she is likely to be fired.

In **Hong Kong** and **Macau,** even though restaurants and bars will automatically add a 10% service charge to your bill, you're still expected to leave small change for the waiter, up to a few dollars in the very best restaurants. You're also expected to tip taxi drivers, bellhops, barbers, and beauticians. For taxi drivers, simply round up your bill to the nearest HK$1 or add a HK$1 (US15¢) tip. Tip people who cut your hair 5% or 10%, and give bellhops HK$10 to HK$20 (US$1.30–US$2.60), depending on the number of your bags. If you use a public restroom that has an attendant, you may be expected to leave a small gratuity—HK$2 (US25¢) should be enough.

Television The propaganda machine known as the Communist Party quickly realized the potential of TV very early on, and has made sure that nearly everybody now has access to its broadcasts. No visitor should leave the PRC without sampling some of the world's most bizarre programming. In Guǎngdōng, the Hong Kong news channels are frequently blocked, with censors on the mainland manually replacing unfavorable news items with public service broadcasts. On the mainland, there are hundreds of channels to choose from, but the best to look out for are the huge, party glorification concerts where loyal masses sing hymnlike praises to the party with lyrics like "Without the Communist Party, there would be no new China."

Water Tap water in mainland China is not drinkable, and should not even be used for brushing your teeth. Use bottled water, widely available on every street, and provided for free in all the better hotels. Tap water is drinkable in Hong Kong, but bottled water tastes better.

3

Suggested Itineraries

by Christopher D. Winnan

Mainstream tour companies almost all tackle Běijīng, Xī'ān, Shànghǎi, Guìlín, and the overrated Yángzǐ River cruise. Here are a few suggestions, most of which are not too far off the main routes, that you can do on your own.

China's huge size limits the number of practical ways to get around the country. While the number of cars in urban areas is exploding, I still try to choose Chinese-style three-wheeler taxis where possible. Private car ownership is still comparatively rare so most people choose long-distance buses when traveling between cities. A very nascent car-rental industry combined with highways in poor condition, substandard driving tests, and still some areas closed to foreigners mean that visitors should seek alternatives to the automobile.

Trains by comparison are cheap, reliable, and the mainstay of the middle class. On the downside, they can be very slow (especially over very long distances or mountainous terrain) and the network is declining as industry seeks greater profits from the burgeoning auto industry.

For travel between provinces, **air travel** is probably the best choice but bear in mind that local airlines do not have the same service levels as the Asian flag carriers. Fortunately what they lack in comfort they make up for in convenience. A trip from Kūnmíng to the Burmese border, for example, can take up to 4 days via intercity buses but can be cut down to a couple of hours by hopping on a plane.

Tip: The most important advice I can give you is to avoid the Golden Week Holidays (first week of May and first week of Oct) and the Chinese New Year at all costs. All forms of transport are booked solid and the popular destinations quickly become chaotic. Needless to say, the industry makes the most of this opportunity by hiking prices to unbelievable levels.

1 China in 1 Week: Or, China at the Speed of Light

Only a week in the Middle Kingdom is a tall order when most people could spend 10 years exploring China, and still only scratch the surface. Because of the vast distances involved (both getting to China from the West, and moving around within the country), if you have just 1 week, stick to the two main centers of change, Běijīng and Shànghǎi, and their environs.

Day ❶: Arrive in Shànghǎi

Arrive at the flashy new Pǔdōng International Airport and enter China's latest and gaudiest development zone at 430kmph (267 mph) on the **maglev** (p. 413). Climb to the 88th-floor observation deck of the **Jīn Mào Tower** ✦✦ (p. 447) to get your bearings and then cross the Huángpǔ River using the equally bizarre **Bund Sight-Seeing Tunnel** (p. 417). Finish the day with an evening stroll along the Bund and dinner at the **M on the Bund** ✦✦✦. See p. 432.

Day ➋: Shànghǎi Museum ✦✦✦ and Yù Yuán Gardens ✦✦✦

The **Shànghǎi Museum's** (p. 446) bizarre shape could make this museum China's answer to the Guggenheim; its unique architecture and many galleries inside deserve at least a morning's exploration, though you may find yourself wanting more. After exploring the museum, wander around **Yù Yuán Gardens** (p. 439); it makes for an interesting afternoon, especially when combined with souvenir shopping in the surrounding bazaar, and then a relaxing pot of green tea in the floating teahouse. If you have any shoe leather left, try an after-dinner stroll along one of Shànghǎi's main shopping arteries (it used to be the top one), **Nánjīng Road** (p. 448), where very few places close before 10pm.

Day ➌: Shànghǎi's French Concession ✦✦✦

The **French Concession area** (p. 414) is one of China's best preserved collections of colonial buildings, but is also full of modern surprises, such as the ambitious new **Xīn Tiāndì** (p. 433), a mega restaurant and retail development, which makes a great stop for lunch. The nearby **Huáihǎi Zhōng Lù** (p. 448) is where the fashionable now spend their *yuán* at imported department stores and designer boutiques.

Day ➍: Transit Day

Allowing a full day to transfer from Shànghǎi to Běijīng will make the process far easier and more relaxed. Once in Běijīng you can decompress in your hotel room for a bit before exploring the nearby surroundings.

Day ➎: The Forbidden City & Tiān'ān Mén

Plan at least a morning to explore the hidden corners of the **Forbidden City** (p. 107), Běijīng's premier attraction, and an afternoon to see the nearby sights, such as **Tiān'ān Mén Square** (p. 112). An evening of roast duck and Chinese opera makes an excellent introductory evening to the capital.

Day ➏: Exploring the Back Lakes

Check out Frommer's walking tour that takes you among the fascinating, winding **Back Lakes** *hútòng* (p. 120). In the afternoon visit the **Summer Palace** (p. 116), the grandest imperial playground in all of China. It's already a big day, but try to leave some room in the evening for an **acrobatic performance** (p. 134).

Day ➐: The Great Wall

Finish your whistle-stop tour of the Middle Kingdom literally on a high. The views from atop the Great Wall at Bādálǐng (p. 125) are tremendous; if you're after a challenge, considering navigating Sīmǎtái ✦✦ (p. 126) as well.

2 China in 2 Weeks: A Fortnight Crammed with Culture

An extra week allows a visitor to head deep into the ancestral heartland of imperial China, and spend some extra time in its two largest cities.

Days ➑–➒: Extra Time in Shànghǎi & Běijīng

A week's extension allows you to spend an extra day in each of the cities. In Shànghǎi this would allow for a day trip to the **Master of the Nets Garden** ✦✦✦ in Sūzhō (p. 453). In Běijīng, an extra day touring temples would be time well spent. While most would visit the **Temple of Heaven** (p. 115), instead head over to **Lama Temple** ✦✦ (p. 118) in the morning, and follow it up with a stroll

Suggested Itineraries

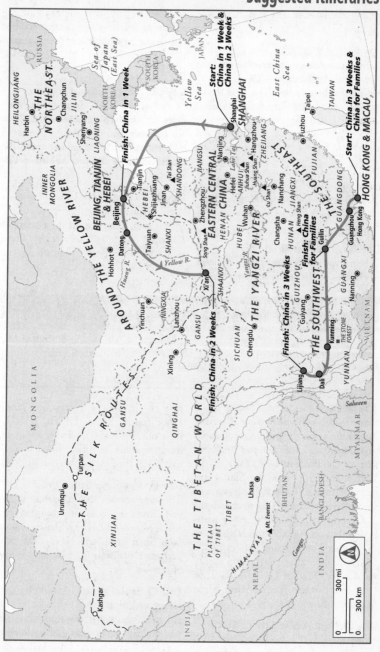

among the lakes in **Běi Hǎi Park** ✻✻ (p. 118).

Day ⑩: The Wild Wall
Another day means more face time with the Great Wall. **Jīnshānlǐng** ✻✻✻ (p. 127) is still one of the very best hikes, and shows the Wall in a very different perspective to the circus at **Bādálǐng.**

Day ⑪: Yúngǎng Caves & the Hanging Temple
Dàtóng is conveniently served by train and plane, and so the **Yúngǎng Caves** ✻✻✻ (p. 210) and the amazing **Hanging Temple** (p. 212) are now well within reach of Běijīng.

Day ⑫: Arrival in Xī'ān
Whether you decide to continue your journey by plane or by rail there is ample to see in **Xī'ān** (p. 250) that will easily fill the remaining 4 days. In fact the first point of call should be China's very best museum, the **Shǎnxī History Museum** ✻✻✻ (p. 256).

Day ⑬: China's Ancient History
Marvel at the 6,000 **Terra-Cotta Warriors** at **Bīngmǎyǒng** ✻✻✻ (p. 257) in the morning, and then if your interest in archaeology has been ignited, spend the afternoon at the **Bànpō Neolithic Village** (p. 258).

Day ⑭: The Potters of Chén Lú ✻✻
After so much time at heavily populated tourist sites, a day trip to the **Potters of Chén Lú** (p. 263) makes a far less strenuous way to wind down your trip.

3 China in 3 Weeks: The Mountains Are High & the Emperor Is Far Away

If you are fortunate enough to have 3 weeks to spend in China, you can sufficiently explore the side of China that focuses more on its timeless, natural beauty than its somewhat more temporary, cultural splendor.

Day ❶: Arrive in Hong Kong
Start the trip off with a bang by taking some time to see the bustling metropolis of Hong Kong. Whether you decide to stay at the **Peninsula** (p. 548) or the **YMCA** (p. 551), take the **Star Ferry** (p. 545) over to Central for lunch and spend the afternoon trying to absorb the 21st-century atmosphere of Asia's number-one city, as this will quickly disappear the farther you venture into mainland China. Round off the day with a visit to the **Ladies' Market** (p. 571) on Tung Choi Street or the **Temple Street Night Market** in Kowloon (p. 571).

Day ❷: Hong Kong: City of Culture
Hong Kong has far too many interesting attractions to be granted only 1 day. But if museums are too stuffy for you, check in with the very well organized Hong Kong Tourist Board (HKTB, p. 537); their offerings cater to almost any taste, from harbor dinner cruises to the innovative "Meet the People" program (p. 564).

Day ❸: Sampling Guǎngzhōu
The express train to Guǎngzhōu is fast and convenient, so an early-morning start will leave you much of the day to explore both **Shāmiàn Island** ✻ (p. 523) and perhaps **Huādìwān** (p. 524) later in the afternoon.

Day ❹: Exploring the Commercial Heart of China
An overnight train later tonight, leaves you the day free in Guǎngzhōu, which is a good chance to see what makes this commercial metropolis tick in and around **Hǎizhū Square** (p. 524); just

make sure you are at the old station for the 6:30pm sleeper train to **Guìlín** (p. 587).

Day ⑤: Yángshuò
An early-morning arrival means that you will not have to rush down to Yángshuò, but can take your time getting to one of China's most charming small towns. Once there, spend the day wandering **Xī Jiē (West Street,** p. 596), relaxing at a few of the cafes; consider Hong Kong, now a world away. Take this time to make some trip and travel arrangements for the next few days.

Day ⑥: Liú Gōng & Liú Sānjiě
A boat trip down to **Liú Gōng** (p. 599) for lunch with a gentle bike ride back through **Fúlì** (p. 599) in the afternoon should leave time to see the Zhāng Yìmóu grand waterborne epic **"Impression, Sānjiě Liú"** (p. 602) in the evening.

Day ⑦: The Yùlóng Hé (Jade Dragon River)
Time to move out of the town, to one of the quieter accommodations such as **Yángshuò Shèngdì (Mountain Retreat)** (p. 502). Here the day can be spent biking or swimming but wherever you end up, take time to soak in the magnificent sunset.

Day ⑧: China's Most Scenic Countryside
A late-morning dip followed by a hearty breakfast may be in order in the summer months, and this can be followed by a trip to one of the many local caves, to further escape the heat.

Day ⑨: In & around Yángshuò
It is difficult to pull yourself away from scenery as spectacular as this, so why not relax here for just one more day and try your hand at Chinese cooking, tai chi, or a little calligraphy. The **Chinese Culture and Art Promotion Workshop** (p. 597) and other organizations around town can help you get started.

Day ⑩: Transit from Guìlín to Kūnmíng
Even though you have 3 weeks, you're time is not unlimited; it might be wiser to avoid some of the more remote areas where transportation can be unreliable. For this reason, I recommend you taxi back up to Guìlín airport and fly straight to Kūnmíng.

Day ⑪: Green Lake
Kūnmíng city center might seem a little threatening after the sublime beauty of the Yùlóng River, so head up to the **Green Lake area** (p. 622) and spend your first day in the city acclimatizing.

Day ⑫: Stone Forest (Shí Lín)
Spend the day at the **Stone Forest** (p. 628)—visit by organized tour or on your own by train—or, even better, at the much quieter **Black Pine Stone Forest** (p. 629), which predates the Stone Forest by about 2 million years. Take plenty of supplies in case you decide not to emerge for lunch.

Day ⑬: Discovering Dàlǐ
Night trains to **Dàlǐ** are notoriously difficult to book so grab the earliest bus possible instead and spend the rest of the day exploring the cobbled streets and streams of Dàlǐ. See p. 630.

Day ⑭: Climbing the Cāng Shān
Take the cable car up to the **Cāng Shān (Green Mountains,** p. 637) and follow the paths as they wind in and out of the surflike clouds.

Day ⑮: Cycling around Ěr Hǎi Lake
The view from the mountain makes **Ěr Hǎi Lake** (p. 638) irresistible; spending a day cycling along the shore or visiting some of the islands such as **Jīnsuō Dǎo** (p. 638), filled with caves and caverns, is a must.

Day ⑯: Yúnnán Markets
Organized trips are numerous but those planning an independent visit to one of

the weekly markets such as **Shāpíng** (p. 635) should get there early to see the local minorities descending from the surrounding mountains, either on horse or on foot, resplendent in their traditional costumes. A trip to some of the batik workshops in **Zhōu Chéng** (p. 638) would round the afternoon off nicely.

Day ⑰: Transit to Lì Jiāng ✵✵✵
Spend the morning at a local **Dàlǐ market** (p. 635), stocking up on provisions ranging from papaya and pomegranates to chocolate chip cookies, and hop aboard the 2pm bus arriving in Lì Jiāng just in time for a fabulous, 36-course Nàxī slap up banquet at **Lì Jiāng Gǔchéng Jiǔlóu** (p. 645) in the old town.

Day ⑱: Lì Jiāng's Old Town ✵✵
A day spent exploring the attractions of the **old town** (p. 643) will hardly seem to be enough, but take advantage of some of the best tourist facilities in China. Food lovers are especially well catered to with everything from four-cheese pizza to frog-skin fungus to tempt the appetite.

Day ⑲: Tiger Leaping Gorge ✵
Tiger Leaping Gorge (p. 648) and the mountains surrounding it mark a suitably impressive point at which to conclude your first visit to China. But do not worry, as you will undoubtedly be back.

Day ⑳: Relax in Shù Hé ✵✵
A day in a nearby village such as **Shù Hé** (p. 647) retains the Chinese "old world" feeling of Lì Jiāng without the accompanying crowds, and is a great place to relax and catch up on things before the long journey home.

Day ㉑: Transit Day
Plan on spending your last day getting back to Kūnmíng, where you can connect to Hong Kong or maybe even Bangkok if you prefer. Take a long hard look at the magnificent 13 peaks of the Jade Dragon Snow Mountain and start planning your next trip.

4 China for Families: A 1-Week Tour

While many people will question your sanity for taking children on holiday to China (many guidebooks sternly warn against it) taking the entire tribe to China can be a uniquely rewarding experience. Here is a short venture into the south of the country to give you a taste of China.

Day ❶: Arrive in Hong Kong
Depending on how much of the day you have left once you finally touch down at **Hong Kong International Airport**, head downtown and let your kids explore all the hands-on, interactive exhibits at the **Hong Kong Science Museum,** 2 Science Museum Rd., Tsim Shat Sui East, Kowloon (© **852/2732 3232;** www.lcsd.gov.hk/CE/Museum/Science/eabout.htm). A jaunt aboard the **Star Ferry** (p. 545) across the harbor to Hong Kong Island is still one of the best and certainly one of the most inexpensive experiences that that city has to offer, and it's great for a family. Once on Hong Kong Island take the world's longest escalator and continue up to **Victoria Peak** (p. 561), where a world-class selection of amusements awaits.

Day ❷: A Snapshot of Big City Life in Guǎngzhōu
Take advantage of the fast, reliable KCR train service and jump on an early-morning **Guǎngzhōu express** and arrive in plenty of time for lunch. Spend the afternoon wandering around **Zhuàng Yuán Fǎng** (p. 524), comparing the appearance and attitudes of Chinese youngsters with

their Western counterparts, and perhaps even look in on the **White Swan Hotel** (p. 530) to see the culture that has sprung up around the adoption and export of orphans, an interesting contrast for those bringing children to China. Jump on an early-evening sleeper to **Guìlín** (p. 587) and see how easy it is to make friends on Chinese public transport.

Day ❸: Arrival in Paradise

Avoid the claptrap minibuses and arrange for your **Yángshuò** ✿✿✿ hotel to send a car to fetch you. Spend the first day acclimatizing to **West Street**'s **Xī Jiē** (p. 596) laid-back atmosphere and great cafe food. Invest a little time in arranging a few activities for the next few days. That evening take in the local show **"Impression, Sānjiě Liú"** (p. 602) and marvel at the magical landscape.

Day ❹: The Family That Plays Together . . .

With Yángshuò as your base, prepare to be spoiled with choices for the next few days in this little town. Activities include **biking, rafting, climbing,** and **caving,** and the list continues to grow all the time. Wind down your busy day at **Yángshuò Shèngdì (Mountain Retreat)** ✿✿✿ (p. 602), certainly one of the quietest accommodations in China and a well-deserved rest from the bustle of West Street.

Day ❺: More Fun in the Great Outdoors

After an early-morning swim, followed by a delicious breakfast, take a leisurely bike ride out to **Liú Gōng Pavilion** (p. 599) for lunch and then head back up stream slowly, getting up close and personal with some of the most spectacular scenery China has to offer. Spend the evening souvenir shopping in town before heading back out to **Gāotián** (p. 595) for a good night's sleep.

Day ❻: Venturing Deep into the Dragon's Belly

By now, you are all probably sunburned from too much biking or hiking, so head indoors (sort of) and explore the psychedelic **Silver Cave** (p. 600) just south of town. If the kids enjoy their introduction to speleology, try the recommended **water cave** (p. 600) where they can splash about in primordial ooze to their hearts' content.

Day ❼: The Fast Track Home

While the trains are comfortable and efficient, the restrictions of having only 7 days probably means that it is wiser to fly back from Guìlín to catch your connection flight home. Everybody feels the pangs of sadness as they drive away from those strange geological formations but don't worry: They have a strange magnetic quality that will likely lure you back.

4

Běijīng & Héběi

by Graeme Smith

Běijīng strikes most first-time visitors as ugly. Its rivers of concrete and rows of tenements, its pollution, its homely populace, and its oppressive grayness are not what anyone would expect at the heart of such an otherwise vivid nation. And yet, no other city in the nation attracts more travelers.

Visitors accept Běijīng's pallor because it is China's political and cultural capital, and because it offers the country's most staggering array of attractions. Best known among these are the Forbidden City, the Temple of Heaven, Tiān'ān Mén Square, and the Great Wall—bedazzling and symbolic structures without which no trip to the country would be complete.

But grandiose emblems are not the only reason to visit Běijīng. Scattered through the city's sprawl are a number of temples, museums, gardens, and other attractions that only grow in charm as they decrease in size. This principle culminates in the *hútòng*, narrow lanes that twist through older sections and form an open-air museum where you can happily wander for hours without aim.

Běijīng lies 120km (70 miles) west of the Bó Hǎi (sea), on a sandblasted plain that once separated Hàn Chinese–dominated territory in the south from the non-Chinese "barbarian" lands to the north. Human settlement in the area dates from the Zhōu period (1066 B.C.–221 B.C.), but the first of the four capitals to occupy space here did not appear until A.D. 936, when the Mongolian-speaking Khitan

built Yānjīng (Capital of Swallows), southern base of power for the Liáo Empire (907–1125).

The city's grid pattern and original walls were first laid down in the 13th century, when it was called Khanbalik ("Dàdū" in Mandarin) and served as eastern capital of the Mongolian Empire, referred to in China as the Yuán dynasty (1279–1368). The city was razed, rebuilt, and renamed Běijīng by Hàn Chinese rulers of the subsequent Míng dynasty (1368–1644), who added the Forbidden City and several other of the city's most impressive structures. Manchurian horsemen of the final Qīng dynasty (1636–1912) skirted the Great Wall and established themselves in the Forbidden City in 1644. Despite their nomadic origins, Qīng leaders found the Chinese system of bureaucratic rule useful in managing their new empire, a strategy mirrored in the relatively few changes they made to the city.

Some of the greatest damage to Běijīng has occurred in the last 150 years. Invasions by foreign armies, rebellions, war with Japan, and the struggle between Communists and Nationalists in the 1930s and 1940s have altered the face of the city more than any events since the 14th century. Particularly severe was the ruin that took place in the decade after the Communist victory in 1949, when Máo, in a desire to put the stamp of his own dynasty on Běijīng, leveled the city walls and the old Imperial Way and paved over both.

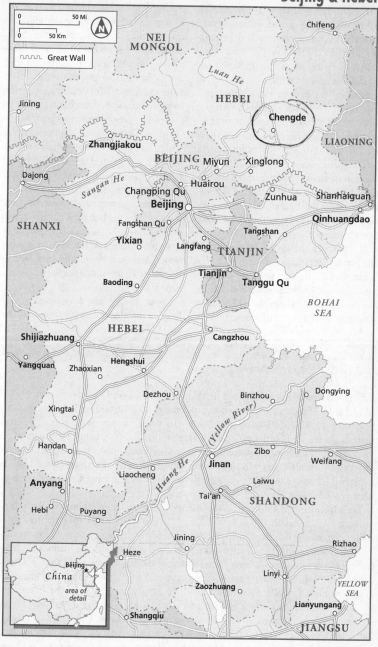

Present-day Běijīng is a vast municipality with a population of roughly 15 million. Economic reform and preparations for the 2008 Olympics have accelerated the pace and scale of change and outfitted the city with a semblance of modernity (or at least the Chinese perception of it). Roads that once swarmed with bicycles have been taken over by automobiles. Swaths of *hútòng* have been leveled to make way for office towers. And children whose parents hid tapes of Beethoven during the Cultural Revolution now have easy access to DVDs, iPods, double-tall lattes, plastic surgery, and other previously unthinkable bourgeois luxuries.

It is easy, however, to overemphasize the transformations of the past few decades in a city with so many centuries under its belt. To many observers, Běijīng has hardly changed at all. The gaze of government looms as large now as it did during the Míng. Outsiders are still Philistines. People smoke in elevators, spit in the streets (despite the SARS scare), fly kites, and practice tai chi *(tàijíquán)* in the mornings, just as they always have. And perhaps most important, the Great Wall continues to snake along the city's northern border while the Forbidden City gleams at its center.

Běijīng shares the same latitude as New York (roughly 40°N) and suffers the same weather: hot, humid summers and bitter winters. Fall, typically mid-September to mid-November, is the nicest season, with mild temperatures and relatively clear skies—by far the best time to visit. Spring brings thoroughly unpleasant sandstorms that blow down from the Mongolian steppe and coat everything in a layer of fine dust. There is little precipitation, and even less of late.

Note: Unless noted otherwise, hours listed in this chapter are the same every day.

1 Orientation

GETTING THERE & AWAY
BY PLANE

Běijīng's **Capital Airport** (Shǒudū Jīchǎng; © 010/962-580 for information, or 010/6457-1666, Mandarin only; domestic ticketing: © **010/6601-3336;** international ticketing: © **010/6601-6667**), is 25km (16 miles) northeast of the city center. Arrivals are on the first floor; departures are on the second. Change money at one of the handful of **exchange counters** on either floor upon arrival (open 24 hr.), as taxi drivers and shuttle buses will not accept foreign currency. There are also ATM and automatic exchange machines on both floors. Rates are the same across China, so get what you need now.

Taxis queue outside the international arrivals gate and take 30 minutes to an hour to reach the city center (¥80–¥100/$10–$12, including ¥10/$1 toll), depending on traffic. Bypass any drivers who approach you inside the airport, and head for the rank instead. Insist on using the meter. Air-conditioned **airport shuttle buses,** the cheapest way to get into the city, leave from in front of the domestic arrivals area. The most useful, Line 2, runs 24 hours a day (departs every 15 min., 8am–10pm; less frequently at other times; ¥16/$2). Destinations include Sān Yuán Qiáo (near the Hilton and Sheraton hotels), the Dōng Zhī Mén and Dōng Sì Shí Tiáo metro stations, Běijīng Railway Station, and the CAAC ticket office in Xī Dān. Lines 1 to 4 all pass through Sān Yuán Qiáo, but only Line 2 lets off passengers at a location convenient for picking up taxis to continue to other destinations. The new Line 5 connects with the university district in the northwest, via Yàyùn Cūn and the North Fourth Ring Road.

Tickets for domestic flights and international flights on Chinese airlines are best purchased either through a reliable agent (see below) or in one of two main ticketing halls: the Aviation Building (Mínháng Dàlóu; © **010/6601-7755;** fax 010/6601-7585; 24 hr.) at Xī Cháng'ān Jiē 15, just east of the Xī Dān metro station; or at the Airlines Ticketing Hall (Mínháng Yíngyè Dàtīng; © **010/8402-8198;** fax 010/6401-5307; 8am–5pm), opposite the north end of Wángfǔjǐng Dàjiē at Dōng Sì Xī Dàjiē 155. Both accept credit cards and offer discounts similar to those you'll get with an agent. There are daily direct flights from the Capital Airport to nearly every major Chinese city, including Shànghǎi, Guǎngzhōu, Xī'ān, Chéngdū, and Lhasa.

Most hotels can arrange tickets for flights on **foreign airlines,** but they tend to levy hefty service fees. Reliable booking agents, such as **Airtrans** (next to the Jiànguó Hotel; © **010/6595-2255**), are often the cheapest option, but also check directly with the airlines themselves, if only to get an idea of standard prices. Most major international airlines have offices in Běijīng; check websites for contact information.

BY TRAIN

Běijīng's two most important railway stations are the Soviet-style Běijīng Zhàn, southeast of Tiān'ān Mén Square, and the newer Xī Kè Zhàn (West Station), between the western Second and Third ring roads. Tickets can be purchased at both stations for any train leaving Běijīng up to 4 days in advance. It is now possible to buy **round-trip tickets** (*fǎnchéng piào*) to major destinations like Shànghǎi or Xī'ān up to 12 days in advance, subject to availability. There are now 19 brand new Z (direct) trains connecting with other cities, which depart at night and arrive early the following morning. Cities served are: Chángchūn, Chángshā, Harbin, Hángzhōu, Héféi, Nánjīng, Shànghǎi (five trains), Sūzhōu, Wǔhàn (four trains), Xī'ān, and the newly-opened railway station in Yángzhōu. Tickets for Z trains may be purchased 20 days in advance.

Satellite ticket offices (*tiělù shòupiào chù*) scattered throughout the city charge a negligible ¥5 (65¢) service fee; convenient branches are just inside the southern entrance to Gōngměi Dàshà ("Artistic Mansion") at Wángfǔjǐng Dàjiē 200 (9am–9pm; © **010/6523-8747**); at the *Shātān shòupiào chù* (ticket sales office) farther north at Píng'ān Dàdào 45, west of Jiāodàokǒu Nán Dàjiē (8am–6pm; © **010/6403-6803**); and in Sānlǐtún on Gōngtǐ Běi Lù (7:30am–8:30pm; © **010/6416-6001**).

Běijīng Zhàn (Běijīng Railway Station; © **010/5182-1114**) is the easiest to reach of Běijīng's two major stations, close to the city center and with its own metro station. The best place to pick up tickets is at the "ticket office for foreigners" inside the soft-berth waiting room on the ground floor of the main hall, in the far left corner (5:30am–11pm). This is the station for trains to Shànghǎi and cities in the northeast. Tickets for both versions of the Trans-Siberian, the Russian K19 via Manchuria (Sat 10:56pm) and the Chinese K3 via Mongolia (Wed 7:40am), must be purchased from the CITS international railway ticket office inside the International Hotel (Mon–Fri 8:30am–noon and 1:30–5pm; weekends 9am–noon and 1:30–4pm; © **010/6512-0507**) 10 minutes' walk north of the station on Jiànguó Mén Nèi Dàjiē (metro: Dōng Dān). Both trains travel to Moscow (¥2,512/$314 soft sleeper), but only the K3 passes through Mongolia and stops in Ulaan Baatar (¥845/$105). There is a separate train, the K23, which goes to Ulaan Baatar (Sat 7:40am). The International Hotel is also the nearest spot for picking up the **airport shuttle bus** (see above).

At the **West Station (Xī Kè Zhàn;** © **010/5182-6253** schedule information), the best ticket outlet is not the main ticket hall but a second office inside the main building, on the second floor to the left of the elevators (signposted in English); this is also where you go to purchase tickets for the T97 express to Kowloon/Jiǔlóng (10:06am; 27 hr.; ¥1,028/$129 soft sleeper, ¥662/$83 hard). The West Station is also the starting point for trains to Hanoi, but you have to buy tickets (Thurs and Sun; ¥1,163/$145 soft sleeper only) at a "travel service" booth (9am–4:30pm; ⓒ 010/6398-9485) inside the Construction Bank on the east side of the station complex. The nearest airport shuttle stops at the Aviation Building in Xī Dān (see above), reachable by bus no. 52 from the station's east side. The taxi rank is on the second floor. Trains leave from here for Guǎngzhōu, Xī'ān, and other points west.

BY BUS

There is no central station here but rather a series of region-specific stations spread around the outskirts. The airportlike **Lìzé Qiáo Chángtú Kèyùn Zhàn** (ⓒ 010/6347-0828), on the southwest corner of the Third Ring Road (Gōngzhǔfén metro, then bus no. 201 to terminus) has air-conditioned services to **Tàiyuán** (6 hr.; ¥111/$14); **Zhèngzhōu** (9 hr.; ¥129/$16); and comfortable minibuses to **Shíjiāzhuāng** (3½ hr.; ¥51/$6). The **Xīzhí Mén Chángtú Qìchē Kèyùn Zhàn** (ⓒ 010/6217-3556), northwest of the Xīzhí Mén metro stop on Gāoliang Qiáo Lù (walk past Line 13 station, take first right), is the best choice for luxury buses to **Chéngdé** (every 20 min.; 3½ hr.; ¥31/$4), **Shěnyáng** (8 hr.; ¥189/$24), and **Qínhuángdǎo** (twice daily; 3½ hr.; ¥60/$7.50). Numerous buses from other cities arrive at the **Dōngzhí Mén Chángtú Qìchē Zhàn** (ⓒ 010/6467-4995), next to the Dōngzhí Mén metro station, but few are useful to visitors except the occasional Chéngdé service.

VISITOR INFORMATION

For the most current information on life in Běijīng, particularly nightlife, see listings in the free English-language monthlies *Time Out* and *that's Beijing,* available in hotel lobbies and at bars in the major drinking districts (see "Běijīng After Dark," p. 134). Online, *City Weekend* manages to update its website (www.cityweekend.com) regularly. The e-mail newsletter *Xiànzài Běijīng* (see www.xianzai.com for more information) provides a weekly list of events, plus special hotel, air ticket, and restaurant offers.

The Běijīng Tourism Administration (BTA) maintains a **tourist information hot line** (some English spoken) at ⓒ 010/6513-0828. More likely to be of help are the new BTA-managed **Běijīng Tourist Information Centers (Běijīng Shì Lǚyóu Zīxún Fúwù Zhōngxīn)** located in each district and all marked with aqua-blue signs. The most competent branch is in Cháoyáng District, on Gōngtǐ Běi Lù across from the City Hotel and next to the KFC (9am–5pm; ⓒ 010/6417-6627; fax 010/6417-6656; chaoyang@bta.gov.cn). Free simple maps are available at the door, and staff will sometimes make phone calls for you. Ignore their extortionist travel service.

CITY LAYOUT

Běijīng is bordered to the north and west by mountains, the closest of which are occasionally visible through the haze. The city center, known to foreigners in the Qīng period (1644–1911) as The Tartar City, was originally surrounded by a complex of walls and gates destroyed in 1958 to make way for the **Second Ring Road (Èr Huán).** The city center is organized along a grid with major streets running to the compass points. The Third, Fourth, Fifth, and Sixth ring roads (Sān Huán, Sì Huán, Wǔ Huán, and Liù Huán respectively) run concentrically ever wider out. At the center of all this is the seldom-referred-to First Ring Road (encircling Tiān'ān Mén Sq.) and the **Forbidden City,** its own internal grid a miniature of the sprawl that surrounds it.

MAJOR STREETS

Streets in Běijīng change names like high-school students change identities. Be sure to pick up a city map on arrival (see "Fast Facts: Běijīng," p. 82). The best example of this is the city's main east–west artery. **Cháng'ān Dàjiē,** which runs between Tiān'ān Mén Square and the Forbidden City, is known (east to west) as Jiànguó Mén Wài Dàjiē, Jiànguó Mén Nèi Dàjiē, Dōng (East) Cháng'ān Dàjiē, Xī (West) Cháng'ān Dàjiē, Fùxīng Mén Nèi Dàjiē, and Fùxīng Mén Wài Dàjiē. **Píng'ān Dàdào,** a major avenue to the north that runs across the back of Běi Hǎi Park, has a similar diversity of monikers. Among important north–south streets, **Wángfǔjǐng Dàjiē** (2 long blocks east of the Forbidden City) is the Běijīng consumer equivalent of Chicago's Magnificent Mile. **Qián Mén Dàjiē** extends down from the southern end of Tiān'ān Mén Square.

NEIGHBORHOODS IN BRIEF

Citywide architectural uniformity means Běijīng's neighborhoods are defined more by feel than by appearance. In many cases, but not all, they correspond to districts *(qū).*

Dóng Chéng District Dóng Chéng (East City) occupies the eastern half of the city center, generally defined as everything inside the Second Ring Road and north of Cháng'ān Dàjiē. This is where Tiān'ān Mén Square, the Forbidden City, Wángfǔjǐng Dàjiē, Jǐng Shān Gōngyuán, and Yōnghé Gōng (the Lama Temple) are located.

Xī Chéng District The western half of the city center is home to Zhōng Nán Hǎi, the off-limits central government compound otherwise known as the new Forbidden City, Běi Hǎi Gōngyuán, and Bái Tǎ Sì (White Dagoba Temple).

The Back Lakes (Shíchà Hǎi) & Dì'ān Mén This area, with its sublime public lakes and well-preserved *hútòng,* is where the last fading ghosts of Old (pre-1949) Běijīng reside. It's popular among writers, musicians, English-language teachers, and other hipsters in the expatriate community, and their presence has helped spawn a bevy of bars and cafes (see "Běijīng After Dark," later in this chapter). Several minor sights here provide excuses for a nice day of wandering (see "Walking Tour: The Back Lakes," p. 121).

Cháoyáng District A gargantuan district that encompasses almost all of eastern and northeastern Běijīng outside the Second Ring Road, Cháoyáng is home to the two main diplomatic areas, the Sānlǐtún and Cháoyáng drinking districts, and the Central Business District (CBD) around the China World Trade Center. This is the richest district in Běijīng, the result, according to some, of the district's good *fēngshuǐ.*

The South If Cháoyáng has Běijīng's best *fēngshuǐ,* the south part of the city—composed of Chóngwén, Xuānwǔ, and Fēngtái districts—has the worst. Squalid since the city's founding, this is where you'll find the city's grittiest *hútòng* and some of its best bargains on fake antiques. This is also where you'll find the Temple of Heaven (Tiān Tán).

Hǎidiàn District & Yàyùn Cūn Occupying the northwest, Hǎidiàn is the university and high-tech district, optimistically referred to in local media as "China's Silicon Valley." There is hiking in the hills in more distant parts. Yàyùn Cūn, which will host most of the Olympic events, is home to Běijīng's best new Chinese restaurants.

2 Getting Around

BY METRO   The Běijīng Metro is the easiest and often fastest way to move around. Trains run from 5am to 11pm on two underground lines *(dìtiě)* and one new light-rail line *(chéngtiě)*. **Line 1** runs east–west past Tiān'ān Mén and the Forbidden City. **Line 8** extends Line 1 into the eastern suburbs. **Line 2,** or the Loop Line, is a closed circle that roughly follows the path of the old Tartar City wall. The light-rail **Line 13,** connected to Line 2 at Xīzhí Mén (201) and Dōngzhí Mén (214) stations, swings far into the northern suburbs. Several additional lines, such as north–south Line 5, and one to the airport, will be completed by 2008.

At present, paper **tickets,** purchased at booths in each station, cost ¥3 (45¢) for a ride to anywhere along lines 1 and 2 (free interchange). A combined ticket *(huànchéng piào)* for lines 2 and 13 costs ¥5 (60¢); ¥4 (50¢) for Line 8. The system is said to be changing to machine-readable tickets, but no one can say when. The involvement of the Hong Kong–based MTR Corporation in Line 4 should speed things along. See Metro map on the inside back cover.

BY TAXI   Fùkāng (Citroën), Xiàndài (Hyundai), and VW Jettas cost ¥10/$1.25 for the first 3km/2 miles, then ¥1.60/20¢ per kilometer, followed by full-size VW Santanas and foreign imports (¥12/$1.40 for the 1st 3km/2 miles, then ¥2/25¢ per kilometer). Rates per kilometer jump by 50% after 15km (9 miles). Always insist on using the meter unless negotiating for journeys out of town, in which case be clear about the price beforehand and withhold payment until your return.

BY BUS   This is how the vast majority of the city's residents move around, and riding with them is as close (literally shoulder-to-chest) as you can get to understanding the authentic Běijīng. City buses and trolleys (nos. less than 124) charge a flat fare of ¥1 (15¢). Longer rides on air-conditioned coaches (nos. 800–900) can cost ¥4 (50¢) or more. Most buses run between 5am and 11pm (specific times are posted at the stops).

BY BICYCLE   A bike is the best way to stay in touch with the city between sights, and faster than a taxi when traffic is bad, but you'll have to pay attention to the cars and other riders, both of which pose risks to the unwary. Simple bikes are available for rent at a number of hotels, usually for between ¥10 ($1) and ¥30 ($4) per day. *Warning:* Avoid the three-wheel pedicabs *(sānlúnchē)*—a ride almost always ends in an argument over price, and there's no such thing as a good deal.

ON FOOT   Běijīng is no friend of the pedestrian. The city's sights are scattered and most of its roads are broad rivers of unlovely gray with few channels for safe crossing. Use pedestrian underpasses and footbridges wherever available. Traffic turning right at lights does not give way to pedestrians, nor does any other traffic unless forced to do so by large groups of people bunching up to cross the road. The only parts of the city where walking is enjoyable are the few remaining *hútòng* neighborhoods, where the stroll is the point. Otherwise, use a vehicle.

FAST FACTS: Běijīng

American Express   Emergency check-cashing is available to American Express cardholders at major branches of the Bank of China (including one in the basement of Tower 2 at the China World Trade Center) and at the CITIC Industrial

Bank inside the CITIC building (Guójì Dàshà) on Jiànguó Mén Wài Dàjiē, west of the Friendship Store. For a full list of check-cashing banks, and for emergency card replacement, visit the American Express office at the China World Trade Center, Běijīng: room 2313-14, China World Tower 1, China World Trade Center; ✆ **010/6505-2838. After hours:** U.S. hot line 001336/393-1111. Emergency card replacement: 00852/2277-1010. Stolen traveler's checks: 010800/610-0276 (toll-free).

Banks, Foreign Exchange & ATMs Larger branches of the **Bank of China** typically exchange cash and traveler's checks on weekdays only, from 9am to 4pm, occasionally with a break for lunch (11:30am–1:30pm). Most central is the branch at the bottom of Wángfǔjǐng Dàjiē, next to the Oriental Plaza, with forex and credit card cash advances handled at windows 5 to 11 (until 5pm). Other useful branches include those at Fùchéng Mén Nèi Dàjiē 410; on Jiànguó Mén Wài Dàjiē, west of the Scitech Building; in the Lufthansa Center, next to the Kempinski Hotel; and in Tower 1 of the China World Trade Center. One other bank that offers forex is the **CITIC Industrial Bank** (see "American Express," above). Outside the airport, Bank of China **ATMs** accepting international cards include those outside the Wángfǔjǐng Dàjiē branch mentioned above. Others exist farther north on Wángfǔjǐng Dàjiē, outside the Xīn (Sun) Dōng'ān Plaza (24 hr.); on the left just inside the Pacific Century Plaza on Gōngtǐ Běi Lù east of Sānlǐtún (9am–9pm); and adjacent to the Bank of China branch next to the Scitech Building (see above; also 24 hr.). The Citibank ATM east of the International Hotel and the HSBC machine at the entrance to COFCO Plaza, roughly opposite each other on Jiànguó Mén Nèi Dàjiē, are useful. There are also six ATMs at the airport.

Doctors & Dentists For comprehensive care, the best choice is **Běijīng United Family Hospital** (Hémùjiā Yīyuàn; ✆ **010/6433-3960**) at Jiāngtái Lù (2 blocks southeast of the Holiday Inn Lido); it is open 24 hours, is staffed with foreign-trained doctors, and has a pharmacy, dental clinic, in- and outpatient care, and ambulance service. Other reputable health-service providers, both with 24-hour ambulance services, are the **International Medical Center** (✆ **010/6465-1561**), inside the Lufthansa Center; and the **International SOS Clinic and Alarm Center** (✆ **010/6492-9111**), in building C of the BITIC Leasing Center.

Embassies & Consulates Běijīng has two main embassy areas—one surrounding Rì Tán Gōngyuán north of Jiànguó Mén Wài Dàjiē, and another in Sānlǐtún north of Gōngtǐ Běi Lù. A third district, future home of the new U.S. Embassy, has sprouted up next to the Hilton Hotel outside the north section of the East Third Ring Road. Embassies are typically open Monday through Friday from 9am to between 4 and 5pm, with a lunch break from noon to 1:30pm. The **U.S. Embassy** is due to move in 2008, but for now it's in Rì Tán at Xiùshuǐ Dōng Jiē 2 (✆ **010/6532-3431** or, after hours, 010/6532-1910; fax 010/6532-4153). The **Canadian Embassy** is at Dōngzhí Mén Wài Dàjiē 19 (✆ **010/6532-3536**; bejing-cs@international.gc.ca). The **British Embassy** consular section is in Rìtán at Floor 21, North Tower, Kerry Centre, Guānghuá Lù 1 (✆ **010/8529-6600**, ext. 3363; fax 010/8529-6081). The **Australian Embassy** is in Sānlǐtún at Dōngzhí Mén Wài Dàjiē 21

(© 010/5140-4111; fax 010/6532-4605). The **New Zealand Embassy** is in Rì Tán at Dōng Èr Jiē 1 (© 010/6532-2731, ext. 220; fax 010/6532-4317).

For onward visas: the **Cambodian Embassy** (in Sānlǐtún at Dōngzhí Mén Wài Dàjiē; © 010/6532-2790) offers 1-month visas for ¥250 ($31), processed in 4 days (¥400/$50 for 1 day); the **Laotian Embassy** (in Sānlǐtún at Dōng Sì Jiē 11; © 010/6532-1224) charges U.S. citizens ¥291 ($35) and Canadian citizens ¥349 (C$50) for a 30-day visa, processed in 3 days; the **Mongolian Embassy** (in Rì Tán at Xiùshuǐ Běi Jiē 2; © 010/6532-1203) charges U.S. citizens ¥240 ($30) for a 1-month visa (¥485/$61 for other nationals), processed in 4 days; and the **Vietnamese Embassy** (in Rì Tán at Guānghuá Lù 32; © 010/6532-1155) charges ¥350 ($44) for a single-entry 1-month visa and ¥400 ($50) for a 3-month visa, both taking 4 days to process. Obtaining a visa at the **Russian Embassy** (in Sānlǐtún at Dōngzhí Mén Běi Zhōng Jiē 4; © 010/6532-1381) is notoriously difficult; they claim you must have a "voucher" from a travel agency (*not* a hotel) in order to be granted a 1-month tourist visa (¥560/$70 for U.S. citizens; ¥600/$75 for Australians; ¥400/$50 for everyone else; 5 days to process). Also, in retaliation for new U.S. immigration policies, U.S. citizens have to fill out an interrogation-style form when applying. If you have problems, contact the Běijīng office of **Aeroflot** (first floor Jīnglún Hotel; © 010/6500-2412) for help.

Emergencies   For medical emergencies and ambulance service 24 hours a day, call the United Family Health Center emergency number at © **010/6433-2345** or the International SOS Alarm Center (© **010/6492-9100**).

Internet Access   Internet bars in Běijīng are subject to numerous regulations (no one under 18, no smoking) and are restricted in number. The best bet for Internet access is any of the city's various **youth hostels;** the cost is usually ¥10 ($1) per hour. There are two conveniently located Internet bars on the third floor of the Lǎo Chēzhàn (Old Train Station) shopping center next to Qián Mén. **Qiányì Wǎngluò Kāfēiwū** (© 010/6705-1722) is open from 9:30am to 11pm and charges ¥20 ($2.50) per hour in a cafe setting with a full coffee menu. A simpler, nameless place next door, open from 9am to midnight, charges ¥6 (80¢) per hour. **Moko Internet Café** (Mòkè Wǎngbā; © 010/6252-3712) on Dōng Sì Dàjiē, just south of the Dōng Sì Mosque, is open from 8am to midnight. Rates are ¥10 ($1.25) per hour downstairs, ¥4 (50¢) upstairs, or free for the first hour if you spend ¥12 ($1.50) in the cafe. The basement of East Gate Plaza, just south of Oriental Kenzo on Dōng Zhōng Jiē (metro: Dōngzhí Mén, exit C) houses **Yúntiān Wǎngluò** (© 010/6418-5815) open 8am to 10pm, ¥4 (50¢) per hour. The fastest in-room **dial-up** service is © 95962 (user name and password 263).

Maps & Books   Maps with Chinese characters, English, and/or Pinyin can be purchased cheaply (¥5/60¢) from vendors near major sights and in hotel lobbies and bookstores. The best selection can be found inside and immediately to the left at the **Wángfǔjǐng Bookstore** (9am–9pm) at Wángfǔjǐng Dàjiē 218, north of the Oriental Plaza's west entrance. English-language newspapers and magazines can be found at most five-star hotels; a newsdealer on the first floor of the **Kempinski Hotel** at Liàngmǎ Qiáo Lù 50 is well stocked.

The best selection of English-language books in Běijīng can be found at the clearly marked **Foreign Languages Bookstore** (Wàiwén Shūdiàn; 9am–8:30pm) at Wángfǔjǐng Dàjiē 235, opposite the Xīn (Sun) Dōng'ān Plaza. Look on the right side of the first floor for China-related nonfiction, glossy *hútòng* photo books, cookbooks, and the full range of Asiapac's cartoon renditions of Chinese classics. Cheap paperback versions of a huge chunk of the English canon, as well as a number of contemporary works, are sold on the third floor. A more daring collection of fiction is carried by **The Bookworm** (p. 137), which also boasts a substantial library.

Pharmacies Simple Western remedies are most likely to be found in the lobbies of international five-star hotels and at branches of **Watson's** (on the first floor of Full Link Plaza at Cháoyáng Mén Wài Dàjiē 19, and in the basement of the Oriental Plaza at the bottom of Wángfǔjǐng Dàjiē 1; 10am–9pm). For more specific drugs, try the pharmacy in the Běijīng United Family Hospital (see "Doctors & Dentists," above).

Post Office There are numerous post offices across the city, including one a long block north of the Jiànguó Mén metro station on the east side of Jiànguó Mén Běi Dàjiē (8am–6:30pm), one inside the Landmark Tower (next to the Great Wall Sheraton), one next to the Friendship Store on Jiànguó Mén Wài Dàjiē, one on Gōngtǐ Běi Lù (opposite the Worker's Stadium), and the EMS Post Office (Běijīng Yóuzhèng Sùdì Jú) at the corner of Qián Mén Dōng Dàjiē and Zhèngyì Lù. There is a **FedEx** office in Oriental Plaza, room 107, No. 1 Office Building. **DHL** has branches in the China World Center and COFCO Plaza, and **UPS-Sinotrans** has a useful branch in the Scitech Building at Jiànguó Mén Wài Dàjiē 22.

Visa Extensions One-time 30-day extensions of tourist visas are available at the **PSB Exit/Entry Division office** (© 010/8401-5292) on the south side of the eastern North Third Ring Road, just east of Xiǎojiē Qiáo (open Mon–Sat 8:30am–4:30pm). Extensions take 4 working days to process; bring your passport and two passport photos (these can be taken at the office for ¥30/$4).

Weather For daily weather forecasts, check *China Daily* or CCTV 9, China Central Television's English channel (broadcast in most hotels). There is also a weather hot line (© 121); dial 6 after a minute or so for the report in English (¥3/45¢ per minute).

3 Where to Stay

No other city in mainland China offers the range of accommodations Běijīng does. And with the municipal government's decision to scrap the antiquated foreigner-approved hotel system, the range has expanded even further. The high season in Běijīng is not well defined, but you should generally expect lower availability and higher rates from mid-May to National Day (Oct 1) and around Chinese New Year (usually late Jan or early Feb). It is usually possible to wrangle discounts of anywhere between 10% and 50% off the rack rate even at these times, although some of the new boutique hotels located in *hútòng* courtyards *(sìhéyuàn)* will refuse to bargain except in the dead of winter.

On short visits the best option is to stay within walking distance of the Forbidden City and Tiān'ān Mén Square, on Wángfǔjǐng Dàjiē or nearby. The greatest luxury

Běijīng Accommodations, Dining & Nightlife

China

Běijīng

To Summer Palace

Bei Sanhuan Xi Lu

DA ZHONG SI 1302

Bei Sanhuan Zhong Lu

Madian Qiao

XiZhi Men Bei Dajie

Da Liushu Lu

Sidaokou Lu

Xueyuan Nan Lu

Zhongguancun Nan Dajie

Gaoliangqiao Lu

Xueyuan Nan Lu

Wenhuiyuan Jie

Xinjiekouwai Dajie

Desheng Men Wai Dajie

Zizhuyuan Lu

1

Zizhuyuan Park

Xi Sanhuan Bei Lu

Beijing North Railway Station

XI ZHI MEN 1301

Beijing Zoo

Desheng Men Xi Dajie

Desheng Men

JISHUITAN 218

Xi Hai

Xinjiekou Bei Dajie

Desheng Men NeiDajie

13

HAIDIAN

Xi Zhi Men Wai Dajie

XI ZHI MEN 201

XI ZHI MEN

Xizhimen Nan Dajie

Xi Zhi Men Nei Dajie

Xinjiekou Nan Dajie

3

Xi Sanhuan Zhong Lu

Chegongzhuang Xi Lu

Chegongzhuang Dajie

Ping'anli Xi Dajie

Ping 'an Dadao

Xisi Bei Dajie

Di'an Men Xi Dajie

XI SI

2

San Li He Lu

Zhanlanguan Lu

CHEGONGZHUANG 202

Dengshi Xi Kou

Fucheng Lu

Fucheng Men Wai Dajie

5

Fucheng Men Nei Dajie

Tai Ping Qiao Dajie

Xi'an Men Dajie

Fuyou Jie

Yuyuan Tan Park

Yuyuan Tan

San Li He Lu

FUCHENG MEN 203

XI CHENG

Xidan Bei Dajie

XI DAN

Yuetan Nan Jie

Picai Hutong

GONGZHUFEN 110

JUNSHI BOWUGUAN 111

FUXING MEN 114/204

Fuxing Lu

Fuxing Men Wai Dajie

Fuxing Men Nei Dajie

Xi Chang'an Jie

WANSHOU LU 109

Yangfangdian Lu

Bei Fengwo Lu

MUXIDI 112

6

Fuxing Men Wai Dajie

NAN LISHI LU 113

Bayun Lu

XI DAN 115

HEPING MEN 207

10

Lianhuachi Dong Lu

XUANWU MEN 206

9

Xuanwu Men Xi Dajie

Xuanwu Men Dong Dajie

Beijing West Railway Station

Lianhua

Changchun Jie

CHANGCHUN JIE 205

Guang'an Men Wai Dajie

Guang'an Men Nei Dajie

Xuanwu Men Wai Dajie

8

Guang'an Dajie

Luomashi Dajie

Nan Xinhua Jie

Beijing-Shijiazhuang Expressway

Maliandao Lu

Lianhua

Caiyuan Jie

7

Zaolin Qian Jie

Nanheng Dong Jie

Caishikou Dajie

Taoranting Lu

Third Ring Road

Second Ring Road

Niu Jie

Baizhifang Xi Jie

Baizhifang Dong Jie

Taoranting Park

XUANWU

Lize Lu

You'an Men Xi Bin He Lu

Tong Hui

You'an Men Dong Bin He Lu

Metro & Station

MUXIDI 112

0   1 Mi

0   1 Km

Beijing South Railway Station

FENGTAI

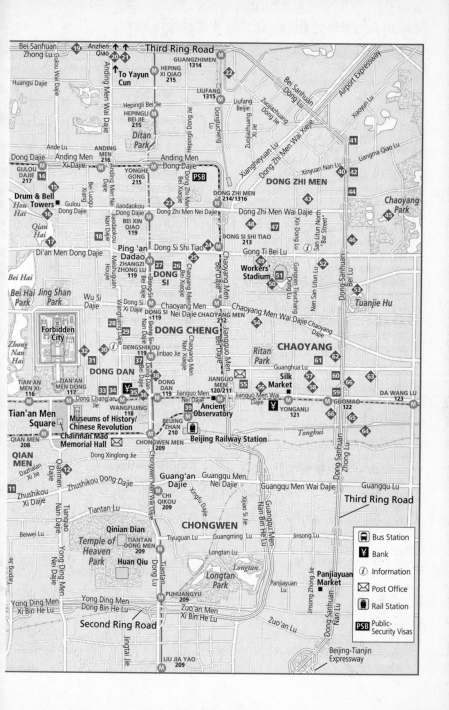

Běijīng Accommodations, Dining & Nightlife Key

ACCOMMODATIONS

Bamboo Garden Hotel
(Zhú Yuán Bīnguǎn) **14**
竹园宾馆

Běijīng Hotel
(Běijīng Fàndiàn) **34**
北京饭店

Běijīng Marriott West
(Běijīng Jīnyù Wànháo Jiǔdiàn) **2**
北京金域万豪酒店

China World Hotel
(Zhōngguó Dàfàndiàn) **59**
中国大饭店

City Central Youth Hostel
(Chéngshì Qīngnián Jiǔdiàn) **39**
城市青年酒店

Crowne Plaza Běijīng
(Guójì Yìyuàn Huángguān Fàndiàn) **29**
国际艺苑皇冠饭店

Crowne Plaza Park View Wǔzhōu
(Wǔzhōu Huángguān Jiàrì Jiǔdiàn) **20**
五洲皇冠假日酒店

Cuìmíng Zhuāng Bīnguǎn **31**
翠明庄宾馆

Far East Youth Hostel
(Yuǎn Dōng Qīngnián Lǚshè) **11**
远东青年旅社

Gōngtǐ Youth Hostel
(Gōngtǐ Qīngnián Lǚshè) **51**
工体青年旅社

Grand Hotel
(Běijīng Guìbīnlóu Fàndiàn) **33**
北京贵宾楼饭店

Grand Hyatt
(Běijīng
Dōngfāng Jūnyuè) **35**
北京东方君悦大酒店

Great Wall Sheraton
(Chángchéng Fàndiàn) **44**
长城饭店

Hilton Běijīng
(Běijīng
Xīěrdùn Fàndiàn) **41**
希尔顿饭店

Holiday Inn Central Plaza
(Zhōnghuán Jiàrì Jiǔdiàn) **7**
中环假日酒店

International Exchange Center
(Wàijiāo Xuéyuàn Guójì
Jiāoliú Zhōngxīn) **5**
外交学院国际交流中心

Kempinski Hotel
(Kǎibīnsījī Fàndiàn) **42**
凯宾斯基饭店

Kerry Centre Hotel
(Běijīng Jiālǐ
Zhōngxīn Fàndiàn) **61**
北京嘉里中心饭店

Lǚsōng Yuán Bīnguǎn **18**
吕松园宾馆

The Marco Polo
(Mǎgē Bóluó Jiǔdiàn) **10**
马哥孛罗酒店

Peninsula Palace Hotel
(Wángfǔ Fàndiàn) **37**
王府饭店

Red Capital Residence **26**
东四六条9号

Red House
(Ruìxiù Bīnguǎn) **47**
瑞秀宾馆

Shangri-La Běijīng Hotel
(Xiānggélǐlā Fàndiàn) **1**
香格里拉饭店

St. Regis Běijīng
(Běijīng Guójì Jùlèbù Fàndiàn) **55**
北京国际俱乐部饭店

Traders Hotel Běijīng
(Guómào Fàndiàn) **60**
国贸饭店

Wángfǔjǐng Grand
(Wángfǔjǐng Dàjiǔdiàn) **28**
王府井大酒店

Zhònggòng Běijīng Shì Wěi
Bàn Jīguān Zhāodàisuǒ **27**
中国北京市委办机关招待所

DINING

and highest standards of service can be found in the Cháoyáng District. For budget travelers, the obvious choice is the expanding range of comfortable but affordable hostels buried in the labyrinth of *hútòng* south and west of Qián Mén, with convenient metro and bus access.

NEAR THE FORBIDDEN CITY & QIÁN MÉN
VERY EXPENSIVE
Běijīng Hotel (Běijīng Fàndiàn) *Overrated*   This patchwork behemoth at the bottom of Wángfǔjǐng Dàjiē claims a history of over 100 years, but the main structure wasn't built until 1974, and all charm died with a modern renovation in 2000. The old rooms have now been replaced with spacious but lackluster units offering the same bland variety of luxury found in most government-affiliated hotels. You can get better value for your money up the street at the Grand Hotel.

Dōng Cháng'ān Dàjiē 33, Dōng Chéng Qū. ☎ **010/6513-7766.** Fax 010/6523-2395. www.chinabeijinghotel.com.cn. 891 units. ¥2,656 ($332) standard room (summer discounts ¥1,250/$156), plus 15% service charge. AE, DC, MC, V. Metro: Wángfǔjǐng (118, exit A). **Amenities:** 4 restaurants; bar; cafe; indoor pool; indoor and outdoor tennis courts; exercise room; Jacuzzi; sauna; concierge; tour desk; business center; shopping arcade; salon; 24-hr. room service; same-day dry-cleaning/laundry service; executive-level rooms; currency exchange; squash courts. *In room:* A/C, satellite TV, dataport, minibar, hair dryer, safe.

Grand Hotel (Běijīng Guìbīnlóu Fàndiàn)   The Grand Hotel is a separately managed 10-story 1990 addition to the west end of the Běijīng Hotel complex with better service and a pleasant central atrium. Decently sized rooms on the west side offer good views of the Forbidden City, surpassed only by the panorama from the rooftop bar. The location is tough to beat, but your money is still better spent elsewhere.

Dōng Cháng'ān Dàjiē 35, Dōng Chéng Qū (at Nán Héyàn). ☎ **010/6513-7788.** Fax 010/6513-0048. www.grand hotelbeijing.com.cn. 217 units. ¥2,300–¥2,500 ($288–$312) standard room (summer discounts ¥1,500/$188), plus 15% service charge. AE, DC, MC, V. Metro: Wángfǔjǐng (118, exit A). **Amenities:** 4 restaurants; 2 bars; indoor pool; exercise room; Jacuzzi; sauna; concierge; tour desk; business center; shopping arcade; salon; 24-hr. room service; dry-cleaning/laundry service; executive-level rooms; currency exchange. *In room:* A/C, satellite TV, broadband Internet access, fax, minibar, hair dryer, safe.

Grand Hyatt (Běijīng Dōngfāng Jūnyuè) ★★ *Kids*   The Hyatt has an excellent location directly over the Wángfǔjǐng metro station, at the foot of the capital's most famous shopping street, and within walking distance of the Forbidden City. Rooms have the signature Grand Hyatt comfortable modernity, with convenient desktop dataports and free broadband Internet access. Well-equipped bathrooms have separate shower cubicles. Kids and adults alike will have fun with the vast un-Hyatt-like swimming pool, buried among mock-tropical decor under a ceiling of electric stars.

Dōng Cháng'ān Jiē 1, Dōng Chéng Qū (within the Oriental Plaza complex). ☎ **010/8518-1234.** Fax 010/8518-0000. beijing.grand.hyatt.com. 782 units. $367 standard room (summer discounts around ¥1,440 ($180), plus 15% service charge. AE, DC, MC, V. Metro: Wángfǔjǐng (118, exit A). **Amenities:** 4 restaurants; bar; cafe; indoor resort-style pool (50m/165 ft.); fitness center with latest equipment; Jacuzzi; sauna; solarium; children's pool; airport limousine pickup; business center; shopping arcade; 24-hr. room service; massage; jogging path. *In room:* A/C, satellite TV, broadband Internet access, minibar, hair dryer, safe.

Peninsula Palace Hotel (Wángfǔ Fàndiàn) ★★★   The range of accommodations choices in Běijīng are now so vast that no hotel can claim to be the absolute best, but if a choice had to be made, it would be the Peninsula. Many in-room features—free wireless Internet, 42-inch plasma TVs, and silent, direct-line fax machines—are simply unavailable elsewhere. A 4-year renovation program was completed in March

2005, and no corner of the hotel was left untouched. Service is impeccable, and helpful touches abound: Braille on all signs; a user-friendly bedside control panel that displays the outside temperature and humidity; and trilevel mood lighting. In the exclusive shopping arcade sits Jīng, one of the city's best fusion restaurants.

Jīnyú Hútòng 8, Dōng Chéng District (at intersection with Dōng Dān Běi Dàjiē). ✆ 010/6512-8899. Fax 010/6512-9050. www.peninsula.com. 530 units. ¥2,560 ($340) standard room (discount rates around ¥1,160/$145), plus 15% service charge. AE, DC, MC, V. **Amenities:** 3 restaurants; bar; indoor pool; fully equipped fitness center; sauna; concierge; tour desk; business center; forex; extensive shopping arcade; 24-hr. room service; same-day dry cleaning/laundry; nonsmoking rooms; executive-level rooms. *In room:* A/C, satellite TV, dataport, minibar, hair dryer, safe.

EXPENSIVE

Crowne Plaza Běijīng (Guójì Yìyuàn Huángguān Fàndiàn)   The Crowne Plaza was closed for renovations during my visit, so I was unable to review the hotel for this edition; it was scheduled to reopen, however, at press time. The location, close to, but sheltered from the bustle of Wángfǔjǐng, is ideal, and the makeover should reinstate the Crowne Plaza as one of the finest hotels in Běijīng.

Wángfǔjǐng Dàjiē 48, Dōng Chéng Qū (corner of Dēngshìkǒu Dàjiē). ✆ 010/6513-3388. Fax 010/6513-2513. www.sixcontinentshotels.com. 358 units. $200 standard room, plus 15% service charge. AE, DC, MC, V. **Amenities:** 2 restaurants; bar; indoor pool; small health club; Jacuzzi, sauna, and solarium; concierge; tour desk; business center; salon; 24-hr. room service; babysitting; dry-cleaning/laundry service. *In room:* A/C, satellite TV, broadband Internet access, minibar, hair dryer, safe, iron.

Red Capital Residence 🌸🌸   Art Deco furnishings steal the show at this Cultural Revolution–themed *sìhéyuàn,* set around a tiny central courtyard that conceals a homemade bomb shelter, now converted into a wine bar. It may be a tad museum-like, pretentious even, but if you can't resist the chance to curl up with a book in stuffed armchairs once used by Premier Zhōu Ēnlái, then this boutique hotel is worth the outlay. The two Concubine's Private Courtyards, fitted with ornate Qīng dynasty beds, are the most romantic rooms in the capital. Book well in advance.

Dōng Sì Liù Tiáo 9 (walk 1 long block west from metro [Dōng Sì Shí Tiáo; 213; exit D], turn left into Cháo Nèi Běi Xiǎojiē, take 4th turn on right), Dōng Chéng Qū. ✆ 010/8403-5308. Fax 010/6402-7153. www.redcapitalclub.com. 5 units. $150 single; $190 standard room, plus 15% service charge. AE, DC, MC, V. **Amenities:** Cigar lounge; wine bar; laundry service. *In room:* A/C, satellite TV, safe.

Wángfǔjǐng Grand (Wángfǔjǐng Dàjiǔdiàn) 🌸   This is one of the better city-center hotels at this price level, with views of the Forbidden City and fresh "superior"-level rooms available for roughly the same rate as a standard room at the Crowne Plaza. Prices are the same on both sides of the hotel; ask for a west-facing unit on one of the higher floors if you want to see the Forbidden City. Standard rooms are usually only ¥80 ($10) cheaper and less recently refurbished. Go for the upgrade.

Wángfǔjǐng Dàjiē 57, Dōng Chéng Qū (south of Cháoyáng Mén Nèi Dàjiē intersection). ✆ 010/6522-1188. Fax 010/6522-3816. www.wangfujinghotel.com. 405 units. ¥2,328 ($280) superior rooms (summer discounts ¥830/$104), plus 15% service charge. AE, DC, MC, V. **Amenities:** 3 restaurants; bar; small indoor pool; exercise room; simple sauna; concierge; tour desk; business center; salon; 24-hr. room service; same-day dry-cleaning/laundry service; executive-level rooms; currency exchange. *In room:* A/C, satellite TV, broadband Internet access, minibar, hair dryer, safe.

MODERATE

Cuìmíng Zhuāng Bīnguǎn   This sleepy little three-star, built inside a Republican-era government complex west of Wángfǔjǐng Dàjiē, is just a 10-minute walk east of the Forbidden City. Rooms are smallish, simply but comfortably furnished, and kept very clean. Staff is kinder than in other state-run hotels of this kind.

Finds **In the Red Lantern District**

Southwest of Qián Mén, past the mercantile madness of Dà Zhàlán in the *hútòng* that never dreamed of pedicab tour salvation, is where you'll find the **Shǎnxī Xiàng Dì'èr Bīnguǎn** (🕐 010/6303-4609)—one of Běijīng's most luridly compelling budget hotels. The hotel sits at the north end of Shǎnxī Xiàng (a poorly marked and malodorous lane once at the center of the city's brothel district), and was formerly one of several houses where men of means would go to taste the pleasures of "clouds and rain" prior to 1949. Rooms are arranged on two floors around a central covered courtyard, restored to its original appearance with red columns and walls supporting colorfully painted banisters and roof beams, the latter hung with traditional lanterns. The rooms themselves are tiny and windowless, as befits their original purpose, but they now have air-conditioning, TVs, and bathrooms at a rate of ¥100 ($12) per night. To reach the hotel, walk east from Far East Youth Hostel (see above) and turn left down the second *hútòng* on the right.

Nán Héyàn 1, Dōng Chéng Qū (at intersection with Dōng'ān Mén Jiē). 🕐 **010/6513-6622.** Fax 010/6526-1516. www.cuimingzhuanghotel.com.cn. 133 units. ¥600 ($75) standard room (summer discounts ¥480/$60). AE, DC, MC, V. **Amenities:** Restaurant; bar; small exercise room; business center; tour desk; laundry service; currency exchange. *In room:* A/C, satellite TV, fridge, safe.   .

INEXPENSIVE

Far East Youth Hostel (Yuǎn Dōng Qīngnián Lǚshè) ✱   Buried deep inside one of the city's most interesting *hútòng* neighborhoods, and a short walk from both the Hépíng Mén and Qián Mén metro stations, the Far East offers comfortable rooms at competitive rates. Even the hallways—partly adorned with faux brick and latticed, dark wood panels—are pleasant. The hostel maintains cheaper dorms behind a courtyard house across the street, but those in the main building are far better. The Far East is a good choice even if you usually stay at midrange places.

Tiěshù Xié Jiē 113, Xuānwǔ Qū (follow Dà Zhàlán Jiē west, left at fork). 🕐 **010/6301-8811,** ext. 3118. Fax 010/6301-8233. 110 units. ¥298 ($37) standard room (often discounted to ¥200/$25); ¥60–¥75 ($8–$10) dorm bed. No credit cards. Metro: Hépíng Mén (207), Qián Mén (208). **Amenities:** Restaurant; bike rental; tour desk; cheap coin-op laundry; self-catering kitchen; Internet access. *In room:* AC, TV, fridge.

CHÁOYÁNG DISTRICT (EMBASSY AREAS)

VERY EXPENSIVE

China World Hotel (Zhōngguó Dàfàndiàn) ✱✱✱   Long the city's top business hotel, China World now aims to be the best Běijīng hotel altogether. Praised for its comfort and sterling service, the hotel, managed by Shangri-La, has used its most recent face-lift to add several up-to-date luxuries and comfortably elegant Aria (p. 101) serves the city's finest Continental cuisine. The attached China World shopping complex boasts a well-stocked supermarket, an ice rink, and a specialist wine store. A metro stop connected to the shopping area means quick (15 min.) access to the city center. Even-numbered rooms are preferred: south-facing rooms are sunnier and less affected by construction noise.

Jiànguó Mén Wài Dàjiē 1, Cháoyáng Qū (at intersection with E. Third Ring Rd.). Metro: Guómào (122, exit A). 🕐 **010/6505-2266.** Fax 010/6505-0828. www.shangri-la.com. 716 units. $350 standard room (discount rates down to

$175), plus 15% service charge. AE, DC, MC, V. **Amenities:** 4 restaurants plus several more in attached mall; indoor pool (25m/82 ft.); golf simulator; 3 indoor tennis courts; full-service health club; separate spa with aromatherapy; concierge; business center; shopping complex; salon; 24-hr. room service; same-day dry-cleaning/laundry service; executive-level rooms; nonsmoking rooms; currency exchange; wireless Internet access in executive rooms. *In room:* A/C, satellite TV, broadband Internet access, minibar, hair dryer, safe.

Kempinski Hotel (Kǎibīnsījī Fàndiàn) ⚔ The Kempinski's plain but large and very comfortable rooms have been refurbished to a high standard. Some of the staff could stand renovation, too. Last time I visited, the coffee failed to materialize at breakfast not once, but twice. Aside from this glitch, response time to requests is the most rapid in Běijīng and its position in the Lufthansa Centre means every facility imaginable is at hand, including a wine store, airline offices and ticket agents, medical and dental clinics with Western staff, restaurants, a supermarket, a bookshop, and a department store.

Liàngmǎ Qiáo Lù 50, Cháoyáng Qū (east of N. Third Ring Rd., near airport expressway junction); see map p. 86. 𝄞 010/6465-3388. Fax 010/6465-3366. www.kempinski-beijing.com. 526 units. ¥2,480 ($310) standard room (discount rates around ¥1,592/$199), plus 15% service charge. AE, DC, MC, V. **Amenities:** 7 restaurants; indoor pool; outdoor tennis court; fitness center; Jacuzzi; sauna; concierge; free shuttle to airport and city center; business center; shopping complex; 24-hr. room service; same-day dry-cleaning/laundry service; executive-level rooms; 6 nonsmoking floors; currency exchange; squash courts. *In room:* A/C, satellite TV, broadband Internet access, minibar, hair dryer, safe.

Kerry Centre Hotel (Běijīng Jiālì Zhōngxīn Fàndiàn) ⚔⚔ *Kids* The latest addition to the Shangri-La–managed properties in the city, the Kerry Centre is also the most chic, with a clean, modern design to its warm, curvaceous, and unusually high-ceilinged rooms. Full facilities, such as separate shower cubicles in bathrooms, in-room air fresheners and humidifiers (a godsend in winter), and free in-room broadband Internet access, have all helped make it one of Běijīng's most successful hotels. Executive-floor rooms have luxuries such as CD players and wireless Internet access. The Kerry Centre complex has several noteworthy restaurants and also what's hailed by many expatriates as the city's hottest bar, Centro.

Guānghuá Lù 1, Cháoyáng Qū (on west side of Kerry Centre complex, north of Guómào metro). Metro: Guómào (122, exit A). 𝄞 010/8529-6999. Fax 010/8529-6333. www.shangri-la.com. 487 units. ¥3,000 ($375) standard room (summer discounts around ¥1,500/$188), plus 15% service charge. AE, DC, MC, V. **Amenities:** 2 restaurants; bar; indoor pool; indoor basketball/tennis/badminton courts; fitness center; children's play area; concierge; tour desk; business center; shopping arcade; 24-hr. room service; same-day dry-cleaning/laundry service; executive-level rooms; 5 nonsmoking floors; currency exchange; roof-top track for running and in-line skating; sun deck. *In room:* A/C, satellite TV, broadband Internet access, minibar, hair dryer, safe.

St. Regis Běijīng (Běijīng Guójì Jùlèbù Fàndiàn) ⚔⚔⚔ No hotel in Běijīng can rival the on-call personalized butler service of the St. Regis, which boasts the highest staff-to-guest ratio in China. Almost unnerving attention is paid to your individual needs, down to what side of the bed you sleep on for turndown service. The health club is world class, with a spa drawing waters from a mile underground. If there's a complaint, it's the smallness of the rooms, but all are beautifully appointed with traditional Chinese furniture, Běijīng's deepest bathtubs, and a full range of extras.

Jiànguó Mén Wài Dàjiē 21, Cháoyáng Qū (southwest side of Rì Tán Park). 𝄞 010/6460–6688. Fax 010/6460-3299. www.stregis.com/beijing. 273 units. ¥2,720 ($340) standard room (summer discount rates ¥1,400 – ¥1,600/ $180–$200), plus 15% service charge. AE, DC, MC, V. Metro: Jiànguó Mén (120/211, exit B, 1 block away). **Amenities:** 5 restaurants; bar; indoor pool; putting green and driving area; exercise room; spa; billiards room; concierge; business center; salon; 24-hr. room service; same-day dry-cleaning/laundry service; nonsmoking rooms; cigar and wine-tasting rooms; currency exchange; 24-hr. butler service; squash courts. *In room:* A/C, satellite TV, DVD player, broadband Internet access, minibar, hair dryer, safe.

EXPENSIVE

Great Wall Sheraton (Chángchéng Fàndiàn) 🌟

The Great Wall was the city's first international five-star when it opened in 1984, and the building is starting to look its age; fortunately it has begun extensive renovations. During the lifetime of this book, there will be a substantial reduction in the number of rooms, complete remodeling of the lobby, and the opening of two new restaurants and an international-level spa. Executive-floor rooms will be renovated first; they should be your first choice if your budget allows.

Běi Sān Huán 10, Cháoyáng Qū (south of Lufthansa Centre). © 010/6590–5566. Fax 010/6590–5938. www.starwood. com. 1,007 units. ¥2,675 ($334) standard room (summer discounts to around ¥1,300/$160); ¥2,940 ($367) executive room, plus 15% service charge. AE, DC, MC, V. **Amenities:** 3 restaurants; bar; small indoor pool with sun deck; 2 outdoor tennis courts; exercise room; Jacuzzi; sauna; concierge; tour desk; business center; salon; 24-hr. room service; same-day dry-cleaning/laundry service; executive-level rooms; currency exchange. *In room:* A/C, satellite TV, broadband Internet access, minibar, hair dryer, safe.

Hilton Běijīng (Běijīng Xīěrdùn Fàndiàn) 🌟

What a difference a renovation can make. Once saddled with some of the most tired guest rooms in the capital, Hilton's newly overhauled rooms now sport attractive carpets, stylish and functional glass desks, and ultracomfortable beds. More, major changes will occur during the life of this book, including a refit of the bathroom-tiled exterior and the opening of an atrium bar and two new restaurants (the American-Cajun restaurant Louisiana will be staying put).

Dōngfāng Lù 1, Dōng Sān Huán Běi Lù, Cháoyáng Qū (east side of N. Third Ring Rd., north of Xiāoyún Lù). © 010/ 5865-5000. Fax 010/5865-5800. www.beijing.hilton.com. 375 units. $165 standard room, plus 15% service charge. AE, DC, MC, V. **Amenities:** 3 restaurants; bar; indoor pool; small outdoor tennis court; fitness club; Jacuzzi; sauna; bike rental; concierge; tour desk; business center; salon; 24-hr. room service; in-room massage; babysitting; same-day dry-cleaning/laundry service; 2 squash courts; valet. *In room:* A/C, satellite TV, broadband Internet access, minibar, hair dryer, safe.

Traders Hotel Běijīng (Guómào Fàndiàn) 🌟

The greatest advantage to staying in this Shangri-La four-star hotel is access to the five-star health club facilities in the China World Hotel next door. Otherwise, Traders is a straightforward business hotel, with slightly small and plain but nicely outfitted rooms, unobtrusive service, and easy access to the metro. The only major drawback is the tiny bathrooms, but this is compensated for by reasonably low (after-discount) room rates. The West Wing has the slightly nicer (and more expensive) rooms, renovated in 2004.

Jiànguó Mén Wài Dàjiē 1, Cháoyáng Qū (behind China World Hotel); see map p. 86. © 010/6505-2277. Fax 010/ 6505-0818. www.shangri-la.com. 570 units. ¥2,240 ($280) standard room (discount rates around ¥1,550/$194), plus 15% service charge. AE, DC, MC, V. Metro: Guómào (122). **Amenities:** 2 restaurants; bar; small exercise room; Jacuzzi; sauna; concierge; business center; shopping complex; salon; 24-hr. room service; same-day dry-cleaning/laundry service; executive-level rooms; nonsmoking rooms; currency exchange. *In room:* A/C, satellite TV, broadband Internet access, minibar, hair dryer, safe.

INEXPENSIVE

Gōngtǐ Youth Hostel (Gōngtǐ Qīngnián Lǚshè)

Located inside the Workers Stadium, in the heart of the Sānlǐtún bar area, this well-run YHA offers a quiet location above a three-star hotel (The Sports Inn), a view over pleasant gardens and a lake, and relatively new facilities. The fourth-floor rooms (not ideal if you have lots of luggage) are agreeably curved, and all face southeast. If you crave privacy, there are single rooms.

Gōngrén Tǐyùchǎng 9 Tái, Cháoyáng Qū; see map p. 86. Metro: Dōng Sì Shí Tiáo (213, exit B), 3 long blocks east. © 010/6552-4800. Fax 010/6552-4860. 38 units (communal bathrooms/showers). Dorm beds from ¥60 ($7.50);

¥120 ($15) single room. Discounts for YHA members. No credit cards. **Amenities:** Bike rental; travel service; self-serv-ice kitchen and laundry; Internet access; reading room. *In room:* A/C, TV, no phone.

AROUND THE BACK LAKES
MODERATE
Bamboo Garden Hotel (Zhú Yuán Bīnguǎn)   Said to be the former residence of the infamous Qīng dynasty eunuch, Lǐ Liányīng, Bamboo Garden was the first major courtyard-style hotel in Běijīng and is among the most beautiful. It's slightly more lux-urious than the Lǔsōng Yuán (see below), but with less character. Rooms border three different-size courtyards; each filled with rock gardens, clusters of bamboo, and cov-ered corridors. Standard rooms in two multistory buildings at opposite ends of the complex are decorated with Míng-style furniture and traditional lamps that cast pleas-ant shadows on the high ceilings.

Xiǎoshí Qiáo Hútòng 24, Xī Chéng Qū (6th *hútòng* on left walking north on Jiù Gǔlóu Dàjiē, west of Drum Tower); see map p. 86. ✆ 010/6403-2229. Fax 010/6401-2633. 44 units. ¥580–¥680 ($72–$85) standard room (discounts rare). AE, DC, MC, V. **Amenities:** Restaurant; bar; concierge; travel service; business center; salon; laundry service; cur-rency exchange. *In room:* A/C, satellite TV, fridge.

Lǔsōng Yuán Bīnguǎn 🏵🏵   Set on the site of a Qīng dynasty general's residence down a quaint *hútòng* north of Píng'ān Dàdào and nicely renovated in 2001, is this thoroughly charming courtyard hotel. Smaller and more intimate than the Bamboo Garden, with more traditional rooms, it wins with the details—bright paneled hall-way ceilings, faux rotary phones in-room, and Chinese-style wall-mounted lamps over the beds. A few rooms open directly onto quiet, semiprivate courtyards. Avoid the air-less dorms in the basement.

Bǎnchǎng Hútòng 22, Dōng Chéng Qū (walking north from Dì'ān Mén Dōng Dàjiē on Jiāodàokǒu Nán Dàjiē, 2nd *hútòng* on left). ✆ 010/6404-0436. Fax 010/6403-0418. www.the-silk-road.com. 59 units. ¥638 ($80) standard room (summer discounts rare, 40% discounts in winter). AE, DC, MC, V. **Amenities:** Restaurant; laundry service; lim-ited currency exchange; Internet access. *In room:* AC, TV.

Zhōnggòng Běijīng Shì Wěi Bàn Jīguān Zhāodàisuǒ *Finds*   Normally you should give a wide berth to any venture with the words *zhōnggòng* (Chinese Commu-nist Party) and *jīguān* (government organ) in the name, but this new hotel is an excep-tion. The impressive twin-courtyard residence formerly housed Wú Dé, the mayor of Běijīng during the Cultural Revolution, who wasn't included in the Gang of Four, but assuredly made the shortlist. Staff are surprisingly friendly, the smallish rooms are packed with amenities, and the location, in one of Běijīng's best-preserved *hútòng*, is hard to top.

Dōng Sì Liù Tiáo 71, Dōng Chéng Qū. ✆ 010/6401-8823, ext. 8100. Fax 010/6401-8823 ext. 8200. 16 units (13 with shower only). ¥320–¥800 ($40–$100) standard room (20%–30% summer discounts). No credit cards. **Amenities:** Restaurant; bike rental. *In room:* A/C, TV, fridge, safe, washing machine.

WEST SECOND RING & BEYOND
EXPENSIVE
Běijīng Marriott West (Běijīng Jīnyù Wànháo Jiǔdiàn) 🏵   This is the first full-fledged Marriott in Běijīng, the second in China after the Shěnyáng Marriott, and both are among the country's most opulent hotels. An apartment building before the Marriott Group took over, rooms are immense, furnished with sumptuous beds and overstuffed chairs, and 80% of them have Jacuzzi tubs. Guests also have free access to the attached Bally fitness center, but this hotel is far from the major sights.

Xī Sān Huán Běi Lù 98, Hǎidiàn Qū (in Jǐnyù Dàshà, at intersection with Fùchéng Lù). ☎ 010/6872-6699. Fax 010/ 6872-7302. www.marriotthotels.com/bjsmc. 155 units. ¥2,080 ($260) standard room (summer discounts ¥1,090/$136), plus 15% service charge. AE, DC, MC, V. **Amenities:** Restaurant; bar; health club with indoor pool and tennis courts; concierge; business center; salon; 24-hr. room service; same-day dry cleaning/laundry; executive-level rooms; nonsmoking rooms; bowling center; currency exchange. *In room:* A/C, satellite TV, dataport, minibar, hair dryer, iron, safe.

Crowne Plaza Park View Wǔzhōu (Wǔzhōu Huángguān Jiàrì Jiǔdiàn) *Kids*

Far from the expatriate ghettoes, the surrounding area has considerable appeal: Yàyùn Cūn is a pedestrian-friendly residential area that boasts some of Běijīng's best Chinese restaurants. Within the striking white edifice, you'll find a very North American brand of luxury, with *USA Today* delivered to your door daily; it's comfortable enough, but a bit bland. Little luxuries are lacking and service can be indifferent. It's worth upgrading to a "luxury" (*háohuá*) room, as bathrooms in the "superior" (*gāojí*) rooms are a bit pokey.

Běi Sì Huán Lù 4, Cháoyáng Qū (northwest of Ānhuì Qiáo on the N. Fourth Ring Rd.). ☎ 010/8498-2288. Fax 010/ 8499-2933. www.crowneplaza.com. 478 units. Luxury rooms ¥2,300 ($288), plus 15% service charge. AE, DC, MC, V. Bus: no. 803 from Āndìng Mén metro (216, exit B). **Amenities:** 3 restaurants; bar; indoor pool; exercise room; Jacuzzi; sauna; concierge; business center; 24-hr. room service; massage; same-day laundry/dry cleaning; executive-level rooms; currency exchange. *In room:* A/C, satellite TV, broadband Internet access, minibar, hair dryer, iron, safe.

Shangri-La Běijīng Hotel (Xiānggélǐlā Fàndiàn) *✦*

The hotel has expanded continuously since its 1987 opening, and a new building, which will house the second Chi Spa in China, will open during the life of this book. Currently, rooms are a good size and comfortably furnished, if less imaginative than rooms at other Běijīng hotels in this chain. Cafe Cha, on the first floor, offers Běijīng's finest buffet breakfast. Off by itself in the northwest, the hotel has space for a large and lush garden, easy access to the Summer Palaces and the Western Hills, and quick routes around Běijīng via the Third and Fourth ring roads.

Zǐzhú Yuàn Lù 29, Hǎidiàn Qū (northwest corner of Third Ring Road). ☎ 010/6841-2211. Fax 010/6841-8002. www. shangri-la.com. 528 units. ¥2,000 ($240) standard room (summer discounts ¥1,050/$131), plus 15% service charge. AE, DC, MC, V. **Amenities:** 3 restaurants; bar; indoor pool; health club w/sauna, solarium, exercise room; concierge; tour desk; business center; 24-hr. room service; same-day dry-cleaning/laundry service; executive-level rooms; nonsmoking rooms; currency exchange. *In room:* A/C, satellite TV, broadband Internet access, minibar, hair dryer, safe.

INEXPENSIVE

International Exchange Center (Wàijiāo Xuéyuàn Guójì Jiāoliú Zhōngxīn) *Finds*

This seldom-exploited international students' building on the Foreign Affairs College campus offers freshly refurbished dorm-style twins and large apartments at reasonable daily rates. The apartments have kitchens and washing machines, and regular rooms come with sparkling private bathrooms. There's a well-equipped self-catering kitchen on each floor. The building is located on several useful bus routes.

Zhǎnlǎnguǎn Lù 24, Xī Chéng District (in newish gray concrete apt structure behind main campus building). ☎ 010/ 6832-3000. Fax 010/6832-2900. faciec@mx.cei.gov.cn. 170 units. ¥195 ($24) standard room; ¥500 ($63) large apt (discounts for long stay). No credit cards. *In room:* A/C, satellite TV, fridge upon request.

BĚIJĪNG STATION & SOUTH

EXPENSIVE

Holiday Inn Central Plaza (Zhōnghuán Jiàrì Jiǔdiàn) *✦✦*

This site was right in the middle of things during the Jīn dynasty (1122–1215), but there's nothing central about the location of this stylish hotel. However, if you're visiting Běijīng to be amongst Chinese people, rather than pampered expatriates, I strongly recommend this hotel. Credit must be given to the local designer, who has achieved the architectural Holy

Grail: minimalism without coldness. Service is equally to the point. Set in a residential area, Běijīng's Muslim quarter is a short walk to the east, a lively strip of restaurants near Bàoguó Sì (p. 684) lie to the north, and it's also handy to both of Běijīng's main railway stations.

Càiyuán Jiē 1, Xuānwǔ Qū. ⓒ 010/8397-0088. Fax 010/8355-6688. 322 units. Standard room ¥1,660 ($208), plus 15% service charge (summer discounts ¥803/$100 all inclusive). AE, DC, MC, V. Bus: no. 395 from Chángchūn Jiē metro (205; exit Á). **Amenities:** 2 restaurants; cafe; bar; indoor pool; well-equipped exercise room; yoga room; concierge; tour desk; business center; 24-hr. room service; same-day dry cleaning/laundry; executive-level rooms; currency exchange. *In room:* A/C, satellite TV, broadband Internet access, minibar, hair dryer, safe.

The Marco Polo (Mǎgē Bóluó Jiǔdiàn) ⓐ *Value* Although not among the main clusters of foreign hotels, The Marco Polo is as close to the center of things as any of them, and is quieter and better connected than most. (The location—just south of the No. 1 Line's Xī Dān station and north of the Circle Line's Xuānwǔ Mén station—enables guests to get in and out during the worst of rush hour.) The medium-size rooms are well appointed, although bathrooms are somewhat cramped.

Xuānwǔ Mén Nèi Dàjiē 6, Xuānwǔ Qū (just south of Xī Dān metro stop). ⓒ 010/6603-6688. Fax 010/6603-1488. www.marcopolohotels.com. 296 units. ¥2,080 ($260) standard room (summer discounts up to 70%), plus 15% service charge. AE, DC, MC, V. Metro: Xī Dān (115, exit E). **Amenities:** 2 restaurants; bar; indoor pool; fitness center; concierge; tour desk; business center; salon; 24-hr. room service; dry-cleaning/laundry service; executive-level rooms; currency exchange. *In room:* A/C, satellite TV, broadband Internet access, minibar, hair dryer, safe.

MODERATE

City Central Youth Hostel (Chéngshì Qīngnián Jiǔdiàn) ⓐⓐ *Value* Housed in the old post office building, this newly opened hostel cum hotel has an unbeatable location directly opposite Běijīng railway station. The manager was inspired by a visit to Sydney Central YHA, and has attempted to create a replica here. Standard rooms on the fifth and sixth floors are minimalist and clean, with none of the sleaze associated with other railway hotels, and at a fraction of the expense. Ask for a room on the north side, facing away from the railway station square. Dorm rooms on the fourth floor have double-glazed windows and comfortable bunk beds, but squat toilets are a surprise for the less limber.

Běijīng Zhàn Qián Jiē 1, Dōng Chéng Qū. ⓒ 010/6525-8066. Fax 010/6525-9066. www.centralhostel.com. ¥268 ($33) standard room; dorm beds from ¥60 ($7.50). Discounts on dorm beds for YHA members. AE, DC, MC, V. Metro: Běijīng Zhàn (210, exit A). **Amenities:** Bar; billiards and movie room; bike rental; tour desk; self-service laundry and kitchen; supermarket; Internet access. *In room:* A/C, TV, broadband Internet access.

Airport Hotels

There are plenty of options here, all with free shuttle services. The most pleasant choice is the **Sino-Swiss Hotel** ⓐ (Guódū Dàfàndiàn; ⓒ 010/6456-5588; fax 010/6456-1588; www.sino-swisshotel.com), formerly a Mövenpick, with large rooms and queen-size beds for around ¥830 ($104) after discount. Guests have free access to a pleasant resort-style pool complex, and regular shuttles go the airport (10 min.) and downtown. Just south of the airport and almost within walking distance is the very basic **Air China Hotel** (Guóháng Bīnguǎn; ⓒ 010/6456-3440; standard twins ¥260–¥320/$33–$40). The **Kempinski Hotel** (p. 93), near the Third Ring Road, also has free shuttle service to the airport.

4 Where to Dine

Too many of Běijīng's restaurants open and close in any given month to offer an accurate count, but it is difficult to imagine a city with more eateries per square mile, or a more exhaustive variety of Chinese cuisines. The short life span of the average restaurant in Běijīng can create headaches (for guidebook writers, in particular), but the upside is a dynamic culinary environment where establishments that manage to stick around have generally earned the right to exist.

Food trends sweep through the city like tornadoes through Kansas. A few years ago it was Cultural Revolution nostalgia dishes, then fish and sweet sauces from Shànghǎi, and now yuppified minority food from Yúnnán. Tomorrow it will be something else. See the expatriate periodicals—*Time Out* and *that's Beijing*—for notes on the latest craze.

Proper foreign food is now widely available at generally reasonable prices, so there's no reason to rely on your hotel for something non-Chinese. Foreign **fast food** and other well-known food and beverage chains, most of them American, blanket the city (if you're desperately hungry and too tired to find anything else). KFC and McDonald's are ubiquitous, and a stable of Délifrance outlets (one each in Xīn Dōng'ān Plaza and Lufthansa Center) are convenient for breakfast. For cheap sandwiches, there are numerous Subway chains and Schlotsky's Deli (in the China World Trade Center). Among sit-down options are Pizza Hut, Sizzlers, TGI Friday's, Henry J. Beans, and the Běijīng Hard Rock Cafe (check *that's Beijing* for location details).

You can buy basic **groceries** and Chinese-style **snacks** at local markets and at the *xiǎomàibù* ("little-things-to-buy units") found nearly everywhere. Several fully stocked **supermarkets** and a handful of smaller grocers now carry imported wine and cheese, junk food, Newcastle Brown Ale, and just about anything else you could want, albeit at inflated prices. Supermarkets include one in the basement of the Lufthansa Center, the CRC in the basement of the China World Trade Center, and Oriental Kenzo, above Dōngzhí Mén metro. April Gourmet, opposite On/Off in Sānlítún, has sliced meats, rare Western vegetables, and a full selection of familiar breakfast cereals; much the same can be found at Jenny Lou's near Cháoyáng Park west gate. Among **delis and bakeries,** one of the best is the Kempi Deli (inside the Lufthansa Center) with good crusty-bread sandwiches, and Charlotte's Butchery and Delicatessen, at the west gate of Cháoyáng Park.

Tour groups and those visiting expat friends tend to get trotted to restaurants with absurd prices and unappetizing food, such as those supposedly specializing in "imperial" cuisine. Fresher, better choices are set out below, but information on the showpiece eateries (Fǎngshàn, Lì Family Restaurant) can be found in the expat magazines. For restaurant locations, see the map on p. 86.

AROUND WÁNGFǓJǏNG DÀJIĒ
VERY EXPENSIVE

The Courtyard (Sìhéyuàn) ✿✿ FUSION   The Courtyard wins points for its setting in a restored courtyard-style house next to the Forbidden City, with a bright modern interior that doubles as an art gallery. Fois gras brûlée, cashew-crusted lamb chop, and black cod with tomato marmalade are longtime favorites, and the tender grilled chicken breast in lemon grass and coconut curry is superb. The wine list is the most comprehensive this side of Hong Kong, and there's an intimate cigar lounge upstairs, with views across the Forbidden City moat.

Value **Chinese on the Cheap**

Affordable Chinese food is everywhere in Běijīng, and not all of the places that provide it are an offense to Western hygiene standards. Adequately clean **Chinese fast-food** restaurants include Yǒnghé Dàwáng (with KFC-style sign) and Mǎlán noodle outlets (marked with a Chicago Bulls–style graphic). A better option is the **point-to-order food courts** on the top or bottom floor of almost every large shopping center. For late-night dining, a favorite Běijīng pastime, try one of the **night markets** at Dōnghuá Mén (just off Wángfǔjǐng Dàjiē opposite the Xīn Dōng'ān Plaza) and on Lóngfú Sì Jiē (north of Wángfǔjǐng Dàjiē next to the Airlines Ticketing Hall). The famous 24-hour food street on Dōngzhí Mén Nèi Dàjiē, locally known as **Ghost Street (Guǐ Jiē)**, is now much reduced, but dozens of eateries still offer hot pot, *málà lóngxiā* (spicy crayfish), and home-style fare through the lantern-lit night.

Dōnghuá Mén Lù 95 (10-min. walk, on north side of street). ✆ 010/6526-8883. Reservations essential. Meal for 2 ¥145–¥245 ($18–$31). AE, DC, MC, V. 6–10pm. Metro: Tiān'ān Mén East (117, exit B); east side of Forbidden City.

RBL 🐟🐟🐟 FUSION   Handel Lee's latest venture is run by a team whose credits read like a food critic's naughty dream: Nobu, Megu, Sushi Yasuda, and Tetsuya's. An unmarked opaque glass door opens into a stunning minimalist lounge, then on to the main event, the Japanese fusion restaurant. Two tasting menus are offered with recommended wine pairings. Not every creation hits the spot, but many are sublime, particularly the sakura smoked duck sushi, yukke marinated wagyu beef, and crème brûlée with orange marmalade. A genuinely international dining experience is rounded off with R&B in the Icehouse, connected by underground passageway (p. 135).

Dōng'ān Mén Dàjiē 53, (just west of Dōng'ān Mén night market). ✆ 010/6522-1389. Meal for 2 ¥160–¥375 ($20–$47). AE, DC, MC, V. 5–11pm.

EXPENSIVE

Quánjùdé *(Overrated)* BĚIJĪNG   Běijīng's most famous purveyor of roast duck opened in 1864, and it must have been good at one time to survive so long. Every important state guest from Castro to Yanni has been dragged here, but regular visitors can find better, cheaper duck elsewhere (see Běijīng Dàdǒng Kǎoyā Diàn, below). Whatever you do, avoid the awful carryout fast-food duck now dispensed at the front.

Qián Mén Dàjiē 32. ✆ 010/6511-2418. Duck sets (with pancakes, condiments, and soup) ¥168 ($21) and up. No credit cards. 11am–1:30pm and 4:45–8pm.

MODERATE

Be There or Be Square (Bújiàn Búsàn) HONG KONG   This trendy Hong Kong–style cafe with hip warehouse-style decor serves all the Westernized Cantonese classics—barbecue pork with rice, black bean spare ribs, beef with rice noodles, and many others—plus a selection of vaguely Western breakfast items.

Branches in basement of Oriental Plaza (at eastern end). ✆ 010/8518-6518. Open 24 hrs. Metro: Dōng Dān (119, exit A); and Level B1, Capital Epoch Plaza; ✆ 010/8391-4078. 9:30am–9:30pm. Metro: Xī Dān (115, exit E). Main courses: ¥20–¥50 ($3–$6). No credit cards.

Otto's Restaurant (Rìchāng Chácāntīng) 🐟 HONG KONG   Otto's is authentic Hong Kong proletarian dining, down to the shouts, smoke, and indecipherable wall-mounted menu. The environment may be jarring and the staff too busy to care, but the food is tremendous, especially the range of *bāozǎi* (clay pot) rice dishes; try the *làwèi huáji bāozǎifàn*, a mix of salty-sweet sausage and chicken. Also good, but messy, are the *suànxiāng jǐchì* (paper-wrapped garlic chicken wings). New branches are sprouting all over town—notably a 24-hour branch just east of the north entrance to Běi Hǎi Park.

Dōng Dān Dàjiē 72. ⑦ 010/6525-1783. Meal for 2 ¥60–¥80 ($8–$10). No credit cards. 9am–4am. English menu. Metro: Dōng Dān (119, exit A); walk north several blocks.

CHÁOYÁNG DISTRICT (NORTH)
EXPENSIVE
Bellagio's (Lù Gǎng Xiǎozhèn) TÁIWĀN Taiwanese food, characterized by sweet flavors and subtle use of ginger, is one of the most appealing to Western palates. Don't miss the delicate *shāchá niúròu*, mustard greens combined perfectly with thinly-sliced beef strips. *Táiwān dòufu bāo*, a tofu clay-pot seasoned with shallots, onion, chili, and black beans is also remarkable, as is the signature dish, *sānbēi jī* (chicken reduced in rice wine, sesame oil, and soy sauce). Běijīng's best pearl milk tea *(zhēnzhū nǎichá)* comes with the tapioca balls served separately. In summer, don't miss the enormous shaved-ice desserts.

Branches at Xiāoyún Lù 35 (opposite Renaissance Hotel). ⑦ 010/8451-9988; and at Gōngtǐ Xī Lù 6, (south of Gōngtǐ 100 bowling center), ⑦ 010/6551-3533. Meal for 2 ¥120–¥200 ($15–$25). AE, DC, MC, V. 11am–4am.

Flo (Fú Lóu) ⊛ (Value) FRENCH Flo occupies the front of a rather flashy building, all balustrades and staircases, with an (inaudible) nightclub at the rear. The menu is straightforward French favorites all done well: smoked salmon salad with poached egg, pan-fried rib short-loin veal with mushrooms, and the chef's specialty, hot gooseliver with apple. This place is reliable and offers good value.

Dōng Sān Huán Běi Lù 12 (south of Great Wall Sheraton). ⑦ 010/6595-5139. Meal for 2 ¥90–¥230 ($11–$29); prix-fixe lunch ¥158 ($20). AE, DC, MC, V. 11:30am–2:30pm and 6–11pm.

Serve the People (Wèi Rénmín Fúwù) THAI In the heart of the Sānlǐtún diplomatic quarter, you'll find Běijīng's finest Thai food at very reasonable prices. The grilled beef salad and green chicken curry are highly recommended, and the *pad thai* (rice noodles with seafood in peanut sauce) is done to perfection.

Sānlǐtún Xī Wǔ Jiē 1 (behind German embassy). ⑦ 010/8454-4580. Meal for 2 ¥150–¥200 ($19–$25). AE, DC, MC, V. 10am–10:30pm. Metro: Dōngzhí Mén (214/1316, exit B); walk east 4 blocks, left at Xīn Dōng Lù, then 1st right.

MODERATE
Annie's Café (Ānnī Yìdàlì Cāntīng) ⊛ (Value) ITALIAN Casual, cozy, and tremendously welcoming, Annie's is the hands-down favorite for affordable Italian fare in Běijīng. Wood-fired pizzas are the most popular item, but also try the baked *gnocchi gratinate* with tomato and broccoli, or the chicken ravioli. The staff is the city's friendliest.

Cháoyáng Gōngyuán Xī Mén (west gate of Cháoyáng Park). ⑦ 010/6591-1931. Meal for 2 ¥35–¥118 ($4.60–$15). AE, DC, MC, V. 11am–11pm.

Běijīng Dàdǒng Kǎoyā Diàn ⊛⊛ BĚIJĪNG This restaurant claims to use a special method to reduce the amount of fat in its birds, although it seems unlikely that duck this flavorful could possibly be good for you. Whole (¥98/$12) and half (¥49/$5) ducks both come with a nice plain broth soup made from the parts you don't eat. The place is clean and classy, and has a separate nonsmoking room.

Tuánjié Hú Běikǒu 3 (on east side of E. Third Ring Rd., north of Tuánjié Hú Park). *©* **010/6582-2892.** Reservations essential. Meal for 2 (including half-duck) ¥80–¥100 ($10–$12). No credit cards. 11am–10pm.

INEXPENSIVE

Ǎndiē Ǎnniáng *(finds)* HOME-STYLE This charming little restaurant is justifiably famous for its immense *bāozi* (stuffed buns): Try the *zhūròu báicài bāozi* (pork and cabbage filling) and pair it with some of the infused vinegar *(làbā cù)* from the pots of preserved garlic that line the walls. The meat pies *(ròudīng báicài xiànbǐng)* are also worth a try.

Cháoyáng Gōngyuán Xī Mén (next to Cháoyáng Park ticket booth). *©* **010/6591-0231.** Meal for 2 ¥40–¥60 ($5–$8). No credit cards. 10am–4am.

Dào Jiā Cháng *☞* BĚIJĪNG The clanging dishes and shouting staff are too theatrical for this to be authentic Běijīng dining, but it's as close as you'll get. Servers rush about like madmen, pouring tea and clearing tables with a controlled, smiling fury. The kitchen produces a fine version of local favorite *jǐngjiàng ròusī* (shredded pork rolled in tofu skin with scallion) and slightly sweet *jiāoliū wánzi* (crisp-fried pork balls). They also serve traditional dishes like the pungent *yángròu mádòufu*, mashed tofu and whole soybeans drizzled in "lamb oil," and *zhá guàncháng* (taro chips with garlic sauce).

Guāngxī Mén Běi Lǐ 20, in Xībà Hé area northeast of the Chóngqìng Fàndiàn. *©* **010/6422-1078.** Meal for 2 ¥40–¥60 ($5–$8). No credit cards. 9am–9:30pm.

CHÁOYÁNG DISTRICT (SOUTH)
VERY EXPENSIVE

Aria (Ālìyà) *☞☞☞* FUSION This is one of the most thoroughly satisfying dining experiences in Běijīng, from *amuse-bouche* to dessert. The dining room, reached by spiral wooden staircase from a bustling bar, has a comforting clubby atmosphere. All courses come with convenient suggestions for accompanying wines, available by the glass. Highly recommended specialties include a melt-in-the-mouth seafood tapas and pan-fried wild halibut served on pistou whipped potato, clam and fennel escabèche and olive tapenade, perfectly paired with a nicely chilled Chateau Timberlay Bordeaux Superior Blanc.

Jiànguó Mén Wài Dàjiē (inside China World Hotel). *©* **010/6505-2266,** ext. 36. Reservations recommended. Meal for 2 ¥145–¥255 ($18–$32). AE, DC, MC, V. 11:30am–midnight.

Shànghǎi Fēngwèi Cāntīng *☞☞* SHÀNGHǍI This is one of the most authentic and lavish Shànghǎi restaurants in Běijīng, set inside an elaborate faux-forest interior with waterfalls and private dining nooks. The chef specializes in hairy crab (July–Dec) and light, flavorful stir-fried vegetables. Dishes aren't really worth the price, but the setting is. Book a table downstairs well in advance.

Xīnyuán Nán Lù 2 (inside the Kūnlún Hotel, block west of E. Third Ring Rd.). *©* **010/6590-3388,** ext. 5620. Reservations essential. Meal for 2 ¥400–¥480 ($50–$60). AE, DC, MC, V. 9am–2pm and 5:30–9:30pm.

EXPENSIVE

Hatsune (Yīnquán) *☞* JAPANESE Hatsune is sushi sacrilege via Northern California, with stylish glass-and-sand decor and a list of innovative rolls long and elaborate enough to drive serious raw fish traditionalists to ritual suicide. Nearly every roll is a delight, particularly the 119 Roll—spicy-sweet with bright red tuna inside and out. Avoid the Běijīng Roll, a roast duck and "special" sauce gimmick.

Guānghuá Dōng Lù, Héqiáo Dàshà C (4 blocks east of Kerry Centre, opposite Petro China building). ✆ **010/6581-3939.** Meal for 2 ¥200–¥250 ($25–$31). Mon–Fri lunch set meals ¥65 ($8); weekend lunch buffet ¥150 ($19). No credit cards. 11:30am–2pm and 5–10pm.

Horizon (Hǎitiān Gé) *Value* CANTONESE Horizon is one of the finest and more sumptuously decorated Cantonese restaurants in Běijīng, with surprisingly reasonable prices and the city's best deal on dim sum. Shark's fin is available for those looking to impress business partners, but there are many cheaper and tastier dishes. Recommended are the stewed beef and tofu in XO sauce, a nicely presented fried mandarin fish, and battered king prawns with mustard. The weekend all-you-can-eat dim sum lunch is ¥128 ($16) for two.

Inside Kerry Centre Mall, near rear entrance of Kerry Centre Hotel. ✆ **010/8529-6999.** Meal for 2 ¥200–¥300 ($25–$38). AE, DC, MC, V. 11:30am–2:30pm and 5:30–10pm.

Huángchéng Lǎomā ★ HOT POT This is among Běijīng's largest and most agreeably decorated hot pot restaurants, and the only one that can reasonably charge such upmarket rates. Their special ingredient is "Lǎomā's beef," a magical meat that stays tender no matter how long you boil it. Order the split *yuānyang* pot, with both spicy broth and mild *wǔyútáng* (five-fish soup) in different compartments, or risk overheating your tongue.

Dàběiyáo Nán Qìngfēngzhá Hòu Jiē 39, south of China World Trade Center and Motorola building (walk south along E. Third Ring Rd. and turn left after crossing river). ✆ **010/6779-8801.** English menu. Meal for 2 ¥180–¥200 ($22–$25). No credit cards. 11am–10:30pm.

Le Café Igosso ★★ ITALIAN A flight of stairs just north of an ugly flyover leads to Běijīng's finest Italian restaurant. Start with an aperitif on the second-floor bar, before heading up to the small, intimate dining area, with dark wooden floors and furnishings. Service is unobtrusive, quite an achievement in such a small space. Seafood dishes are compelling, particularly the appetizers. The sea bream carpaccio marinated in seaweed has a liquid freshness, and the mustard roast duck is excellent. The crab and olive spaghetti is competently delivered, and rosemary chicken is the pick of the mains. The wine list is adventurous, with a handful available by the glass.

Dōng Sān Huán Zhōng Lù (360m/1,200 ft. south of Guómào Bridge on E. Third Ring Rd.), see map p. 86. ✆ **010/8771-7013.** Weekend reservations essential. Meal for 2 ¥38–¥120 ($5–$12). AE, DC, MC, V. 11:30am–2am. Metro: Guómào (122, exit C).

MODERATE

Dǐng Dǐng Xiāng *Finds* HOT POT This Mongolian-style mutton hot pot restaurant is tremendously and justifiably popular for its dipping sauce *(jīnpái tiáoliào),* a flavorful sesame sauce so thick they have to dish it out with ice-cream scoops. Large plates of fresh sliced lamb *(yángròu)* are surprisingly cheap; other options include beef *(niúròu),* spinach *(bōcài),* and sliced winter melon *(dōngguā piàn).*

Dōngzhí Mén Wài Dōng Jiē 14, opposite Dōnghuán Guǎngchǎng (in alley across from Guǎngdōng Development Bank). ✆ **010/6417-2546.** Meal for 2 ¥80–¥100 ($10–$12). No credit cards. 11am–10pm.

Sān Gè Guìzhōurén GUÌZHŌU Southern China's Guìzhōu Province is one of the country's poorest regions, which lends a certain irony to this restaurant's hip minimalist setting and rich-artist clientele. The menu offers a stylish take on the province's Miáo minority food with dishes that tend to be spicy, colorful, and slightly rough. Both table-top hot pots—the Miáo-style peppermint lamb and the cilantro-heavy dry beef—are highly recommended, as is the flavorsome but fatty *juébā chǎo làròu* (bacon stir-fried with brake leaves) *Note:* Items listed on the menu as "vegetarian" are not.

Branches at Guānghuá Xī Lù 3 (walk north on Dōng Dà Qiáo Lù from Yǒng'ānlǐ metro [121], turn down alley north of Mexican Wave, look for blue sign). ✆ 010/6507-4761; and building 7 Jiànwài SOHO (south of Guomao metro [exit C]), ✆ 010/5869-0598. Meal for 2 ¥80–¥120 ($10–$15). AE, DC, MC, V. 11am–2:30pm and 5:30–10pm.

Sìhéxuān BĚIJĪNG/SHĀNXĪ This cluttered little restaurant has a slightly more than token Old Běijīng interior and a wide, constantly changing range of typical Běijīng snacks. Some items are listed on the English menu, while others are rolled through the restaurant dim sum–style on a cart. This is the best way to sample street food without fretting over hygiene.

Jiànguó Mén Wài Dàjiē 3, 4th floor of Jīnglún Hotel. ✆ 010/6500-2266, ext. 8116. Meal for 2 ¥50–¥100 ($6–$12). AE, DC, MC, V. 11:30am–2pm and 5:30–10pm.

Steak & Eggs (Xi Lái Zhōng) AMERICAN If its home comforts you crave, this restaurant, run by a former navy cook, delivers authentic American diner fare. Servings are enormous, cups of coffee are bottomless, and many of the cakes (particularly the carrot cake) are superb. The jumbo breakfast is an unbeatable value, and they even have grits.

Xiùshuǐ Nán Jiē 5 (behind Friendship Store); see map p. 86. ✆ 010/6592-8088. Reservations recommended on weekends. Meal for 2 ¥35–¥99 ($4–$12). No credit cards. Mon–Fri 7:30am–10:30pm; Sat–Sun 7:30am–midnight.

Yúnténg Bīnguǎn *(Finds)* YÚNNÁN Although Yúnnán is one of the poorest provinces in China, the Yúnnán provincial government (which owns the restaurant) has ingredients flown in several times a week. The decor exudes less warmth than a hospital waiting room, but friendly waitstaff compensate. The signature dish, *guòqiáo mǐxiàn* (crossing-the-bridge rice noodles) is worth the trip in itself, a delicious blend of ham, chicken, chrysanthemum petals, chives, tofu skin, and a tiny egg, all blended at your table with rice noodles in chicken broth. *Zhúsūn qìguō Jī* (mushroom and mountain herbs chicken soup) is ideal comfort food, and *zhútǒng páigǔ* (spicy stewed pork with mint), has hearty flavors.

Dōnghuā Shì Běi Lǐ Dōng Qū 7, Chóngwén Qū (follow Jiànguó Mén Nán Dàjiē south for 10 min.; on the south side of overpass). ✆ 010/6713-6439. Meal for 2 ¥80–¥140 ($10–$17). AE, DC, MC, V. 11am–1:30pm and 5–10pm. Metro: Jiànguó Mén (exit C).

Yúxiāng Rénjiā SÌCHUĀN This chain of busy restaurants has a mock-village decor and a comprehensive selection of real Sìchuān dishes, slightly heavy on the oil but as flavorful as anything found outside Sìchuān itself. Spicy familiars are all here and all nicely done, but also try at least one of the chain's worthwhile signatures—smoked duck *(zhāngchá yā)* or "stewed chicken with Grandma's sauce" *(lǎogānmā shāo jī).*

Branches: Jiànwài SOHO building 4 (south of Guómào metro stop [exit C]), ✆ 010/5869-0653, 11am–3pm and 5:30–10:30pm; and at Cháoyáng Mén Wài Dàjiē 20, on 5th floor of Liánhé Dàshà, behind Foreign Ministry Building just off East Second Ring Rd. (✆ 010/6588-3841; 11am–10:30pm). Meal for 2 ¥80–¥120 ($10–$15). AE, DC, MC, V.

BACK LAKES & DŌNG CHÉNG
EXPENSIVE
Cafe Sambal *(★★)* MALAYSIAN Sambal embraces and surpasses all the clichés of a chic Běijīng eatery—a cozy courtyard house decorated with antique and modern furnishings, a sophisticated boss, relaxed service, and a well-balanced wine list. Try the fried four-sided bean with cashew nut sauce, the divinely creamy king prawn with yellow

sauce, or the special lamb curry served in a thick, spicy coconut sauce. The signature dish, Kapitan chicken, a mildly spicy dish with a nutty aftertaste, is said to have been invented when Chinese migrants reached Penang during the Míng dynasty.

Dòufu Chí Hútòng 43, Xī Chéng Qū (walk south along Jiù Gǔ Lóu Dàjiē, near the corner of the 5th street on left, marked by a red lantern). ✆ 010/6400-4875. Reservations recommended. Meal for 2 ¥250–¥400 ($31–$50). AE, DC, MC, V. 12:30pm till late. Metro: Gǔ Lóu (exit B).

Nuage (Qìng Yún Lóu) VIETNAMESE   Lake views from this restaurant's upstairs windows are matched only by its hallucinatory Hanoi-inspired interior, with red lanterns, reed curtains, and a long silver dragon snaking up the rear staircase. Views from the rooftop are peerless, and the food is almost as impressive: The grilled la lop leaf beef *(yè niúròu juǎn)* is exquisite; and the phô (Vietnamese beef noodles in soup) has a smooth, flavorful broth.

Qián Hǎi Dōng Yàn 22 (east of Yíndìng Bridge; northeast of Qián Hǎi; see map p. 86.). ✆ 010/6401-9591. Reservations required. Meal for 2 ¥200–¥300 ($25–$38). AE, DC, MC, V. 11am–2pm and 5:30–10pm.

MODERATE

Huājiā Yíyuán HOME-STYLE   The chef-owner behind this popular courtyard restaurant claims to have created a new supercuisine from the best regional cooking styles. Whether "Huācài" will ever spread remains to be seen, but the long menu is one of the city's most impressive. The new restaurant is less raucous than the recently demolished original, but locals still crowd around tables at night to devour heaped plates of spicy crayfish *(málà lóngxiā)* and drink green "good for health" beer. Try the *làròu dòuyá juǎnbǐng*, a mix of spicy bacon and bean sprouts rolled in pancakes roast duck–style.

Dōngzhí Mén Nèi Dàjiē 235. ✆ 010/6403-0677. Meal for 2 ¥100–¥120 ($12–$15). AE, DC, MC, V. 10:30am–6:30am. Metro: Dōngzhí Mén (exit A).

Kèjiā Cài HAKKA   The best choice of the three restaurants whose art-rustic interiors and deft kitchens have taken a traditionally marginal cuisine and made it the center of food fashion in Běijīng. Hakka cuisine is hard to define vis-à-vis other styles, but ask regular patrons of these restaurants to explain the difference and most will give a quick answer: It's better. The *yán Jú xiā* (shrimp skewers served in rock salt) and *lǎncài sìjìdòu* (diced green beans with ground pork) are both divine. The one dish you'll find on every table is *mìzhì zhǐbāo lúyú*, "secret recipe paper-wrapped fish"—tender and nearly boneless, in a sweet sauce you'll want to drink.

East bank of Qián Hǎi, 50m (165 ft.) north of Běi Hǎi Park north entrance. ✆ 010/6404-2259. Meal for 2 ¥80–¥100 ($10–$12). AE, DC, MC, V. 11am–2pm and 5–10pm.

Kǒng Yǐjǐ Jiǔlóu HUÁIYÁNG   This extremely popular restaurant is named for the alcoholic scholar-bum protagonist of a Lǔ Xùn short story (see Shàoxīng, p. 461). It's set in a traditional space pleasingly outfitted with calligraphy scrolls, traditional bookshelves, and other trappings of Chinese scholarship. Highly recommended are the *mìzhì lúyú*, paper-wrapped fish, and *yóutiáo niúròu*, savory slices of beef mixed with pieces of fried dough. Fans of Lǔ's story will appreciate the wide selection of *huángjiǔ*, a sweet "yellow" rice wine aged for several years and traditionally served warm.

Déshèng Mén Nèi Dàjiē (next to the octagonal Teahouse of Family Fù on the northwest bank of Hòu Hǎi). ✆ 010/6618-4917. Reservations essential. Meal for 2 ¥100–¥140 ($12–$18). AE, DC, MC, V. 10:30am–2pm and 4:30–10:30pm.

WESTERN BĚIJĪNG & YÀYÙN CŪN

Bǎihé Sùshí (Lily Vegetarian Restaurant) ✿✿ VEGETARIAN Ch tarian restaurants often get bogged down torturing meaty flavors out of gluten, but at this ultraclean and friendly restaurant you'll find delectable dishes with high-quality ingredients. Start with the hearty *shānyào gēng* (yam broth with mushrooms) and the slightly fruity *liángbàn zǐ lúsǔn* (purple asparagus salad), followed by *rúyì hǎitái juǎn* (vegetarian sushi rolls) and the excellent *huángdì sǔn shāo wánzi* (imperial bamboo shoots and vegetarian meatballs). When in season, their vegetables are sourced from an organic farm west of Běijīng, so ask if they have any organic vegetables *(yǒujī shūcài)*. Monks dine for free, so you're likely to meet a few.

Běi Sān Huán Jìmén Qiáo, Jìmén Fàndiàn (273m/895 ft. north of N. Third Ring Rd., attached to Jìmén Hotel; walk east from metro on Zhīchūn Lù, turn right at Xuéyuàn Lù). ✆ 010/6202-5284. Meal for 2 ¥80–¥140 ($10–$17). No credit cards. 11am–10pm. Metro: Zhīchūn Lù (1303).

Dōngběi Hǔ ✿ NORTHEASTERN Běijīng's best Dōngběi cuisine. Welcoming staff usher you upstairs past an open kitchen with whole cuts of meat and huge jars of wine on display. Start with the refreshing cold noodle dish, *dà lāpí*, served in sesame and vinegar sauce. Your table will groan under the weight of the signature dish, *shǒuzhuā yáng pái* (lamb chops roasted with cumin and chili). Filling snacks, such as *sānxiān làohé* (seafood and garlic-chive buns), are delicious, as is the sweet-and-sour battered eggplant *(cuìpí qiézi).*

Ānhuì Lǐ Èr Qū Yī Lóu, Yàyùn Cūn (300m/984 ft. east of intersection with Ānlì Lù). ✆ 010/6498-5015. Meal for 2 ¥50–¥80 ($6–$10). No credit cards. 10am–10pm.

Jiǔhuā Shān BĚIJĪNG Another fine roast duck eatery, this place is not quite as pleasant as the Běijīng Dàdǒng Kǎoyā Diàn (p. 100), but it's more conveniently located for people staying on the west side of the city. Whole crispy ducks, relatively low on fat, are reasonable at ¥88 ($11). Sesame buns make a nice alternative to traditional pancakes. They only roast 200 birds a day, so get there early. A new branch, with the same state-run ambience, is located inside the Worker's Stadium.

Branches at Zhèngguāng Lù 55 (behind the Zǐyù Hotel). ✆ 010/6848-3481; and east side of the Worker's Stadium, ✆ 010/6508-5830. Meal for 2 (including half duck) ¥100–¥140 ($12–$18). AE, DC, MC, V. 11am–2pm and 5–9pm.

Moments Candlelit Dinner on the Lakes

For roughly ¥400 ($50) plus the cost of food, Běijīng's ancient roasted meats restaurant, Kǎoròujì, now arranges one of the most completely enjoyable dining experiences in the city: a meal for up to eight people served aboard a narrow **canopied flat-bottom boat** ✿✿, staffed by a lone oarsman who guides the craft in a gentle arc around the man-made serenity of Qián Hǎi and Hòu Hǎi. The entire trip takes roughly 2 hours. A few extra *yuán* buy live music and the opportunity to float candles in the lakes after dark falls—doomed to become a cliché, but who cares? The restaurant is located next to Nuage (see above) at Qián Hǎi Dōng Yàn 14 (11am–2pm and 5–9pm; meal for 2: ¥120–¥160/$15–$20). To make boat arrangements, call ✆ 010/6612-5717 or 010/6404-2554. *Note:* Boat rental prices vary from season to season, and will probably increase.

Málà Yòuhuò ✿✿ SÌCHUĀN   At Běijīng's most popular Sìchuān restaurant, service is surprisingly friendly and the mock-village decor is cheesy but fun. The signature dish, *shǔzhǔ yú* (boiled fish with chili and numbing hot peppers), comes in three different varieties: grass carp *(cǎoyú)*, catfish *(niányú)*, and blackfish *(hēiyú)*. We still prefer the traditional grass carp, but blackfish makes a nice change. Adventurous diners should try *málà tiánluó*, field snails stewed in chili and Sìchuān pepper. Skewers are provided to extract the flesh from the sizable mollusks. Leave the innermost black part to the side, unless you want a tummy ache. A nice antidote to all the spice is a clear soup with seasonal leafy greens, *tǔtāng shícài*. A second branch recently opened northeast of Dà Zhōng Sì.

Branches at Guǎng'ān Mén Nèi Dàjiē 81, Xuānwǔ Qū (just south of Bàoguó Si). ✆ 010/6304-0426. Metro: Chángchūn Jiē (205, exit D1); walk south on Chángchūn Jiē then turn right (west) at first major road; and Dà Zhōng Sì Tàiyáng Yuán, ✆ 010/8211-9966. Meal for 2 ¥80–¥140 ($10–$17). AE, DC, MC, V. 11:30am–10:30pm.

Tàipó Tiānfǔ Shānzhēn ✿✿ MUSHROOM HOT POT   The broth for this mouthwatering hot pot is made by stewing a whole black-skinned chicken with 32 different kinds of mushrooms and letting the mixture reduce for hours. Already a fine meal on its own, it gets even better as you add ingredients—lamb *(yángròu)*, beef *(niúròu)*, lotus root *(ǒupiàn)*, spinach *(bōcài)* or, best of all, more mushrooms.

At south end of Èrqī Jùchǎng Lù, behind the east side of the Cháng'ān Shāngchǎng (4 blocks west of the Fùxīng Mén metro stop). ✆ 010/6801-9641. Meal for 2 ¥120–¥140 ($15–$18). No credit cards. 11am–11pm.

Tiānjīn Bǎijiǎoyuán JIǍOZI   No restaurant has managed to fill the vacuum left by the inexplicable closing of Gold Cat, but Tiānjīn Bǎijiǎoyuán comes closest. The clichéd red-and-gold interior can't match Gold Cat's old courtyard setting, but the *jiǎozi* are just as delicious. The *xièsānxiān shuǐjiǎo* (dumplings with shrimp, crab, and mushroom filling) and *niúròu wán shuǐjiǎo* (beef ball dumplings) are treasures, best accompanied by a steaming pot of *chénpí lǎoyā shānzhēn bāo* (duck, mandarin orange peel, and mushroom potage).

Xīn Wénhuà Jiē 12A, in alley opposite The Marco Polo (see earlier in this chapter). ✆ 010/6605-9371. Photo menu. Meal for 2 ¥30–¥60 ($4–$8). No credit cards. 10am–2:30pm and 4:30–9:30pm.

Xīběi Yóumiàn Cūn ✿✿ *Kids* NORTHWESTERN   Worth the trip out to Yàyùn Cūn in itself. Friendly staff, and bright, faux-rural decor make this the best "family restaurant" in Běijīng. The signature dish is *yóumiàn wōwo* (steamed oatmeal noodles) served with mushroom *(sùshíjūn rètāng)* or lamb *(yángròu rètāng)* broth, with coriander and chili on the side. Familiar *yángròu chuàn'r* (mutton skewers with cumin) and yogurt *(suānnǎi)* with honey make excellent side dishes, while the house salad *(Xīběi dà bàncài)*, crammed with unusual ingredients, is a meal in itself. The one dish you must try is *zhǐjīcǎo kǎo niúpái* (lotus leaf-wrapped roast beef with mountain herbs).

Yàyùn Cūn Ānyuán 8 Lóu, Cháoyáng Qū (corner of Ānhuì Běi Lǐ and Huìzhōng Běi Lù). ✆ 010/6489-0256. Meal for 2 ¥120–¥200 ($15–$25). AE, DC, MC, V. 10am–1:50pm and 5–9pm.

Xīyù Shífǔ ✿✿ UIGHUR   The best Uighur food this side of Turfan. The decor is a nouveaux riche fantasy of arches, Romanesque gold light fittings, and pictures of desert scenes hanging from marble walls, but it's spotless and welcoming. The *dà pán jī* (diced chicken, pepper, potatoes, and thick noodles in tomato sauce) is spicy, so when they ask if you like it hot, be honest. The piping-hot *nan* (flat bread) is perfect for sopping up the delicious sauce, and the *shǒu zhuā fàn* (rice with lamb and carrot) and spicy mutton skewers with cumin and chili *(yángròu chuàn)* are as tasty as anything you'll find in Kashgar.

Corner of Běichén Dōng Lù and Dàtún Lù, opp. Olympic Park, Yàyùn Cūn. ✆ 010/6486-2555. Meal for 2 ¥70–¥100 ($9–$12). No credit cards. 7:30am–8:30pm.

Zhāng Shēng Jì Jiǔdiàn ✿ HUÁIYÁNG   It may lack the ambience of Kǒng Yǐjǐ Jiǔlóu, but this branch of Hángzhōu's most successful restaurant delivers more consistent Huáiyáng fare. Service is no-fuss, there's a pleasing amount of space between tables with a high ceiling and plenty of light. For starters, try the flavorsome *jiǔxiāng yúgān* (dried fish in wine sauce). The recently added *mǎtí niúliǔ* (stir-fried beef with broccoli, water chestnuts, and tofu rolls) is excellent, and nearly every table carries the signature *sǔngān lǎoyā bāo* (stewed duck with dried bamboo shoots and ham) which has complex, hearty flavors.

Běi Sān Huán, Zhèjiāng Dàshà, Cháoyáng Qū (west of Ānzhēn Qiáo on N. Third Ring Rd.). ✆ 010/6442-0006. Meal for 2 ¥100–¥180 ($13–$23). AE, DC, MC, V. 11am–2:30pm and 5–9pm.

5 Exploring Běijīng

No other city in China, and few other cities in the world, offers so many must-see attractions, or such a likelihood of missed opportunity. It is technically possible to see the big names—the Forbidden City, Temple of Heaven, Summer Palace, and Great Wall—in as little as 3 days, but you'll need at least a week to get any feel for the city. People spend years here and still fail to see everything they should.

Note: Most major sights now charge admission according to the season. The summer high season officially runs from April 1 to October 31 and the winter low season from November 1 to March 31.

THE FORBIDDEN CITY (GÙ GŌNG)

The universally accepted symbol for the length and grandeur of Chinese civilization is undoubtedly the Great Wall, but the Forbidden City is more immediately impressive. A 720,000-sq.-m (7.75-million-sq.-ft.) complex of red-walled buildings and pavilions topped by a sea of glazed vermilion tile, it dwarfs nearby Tiān'ān Mén Square and is by far the largest and most intricate imperial palace in China. The palace receives more visitors than any other attraction in the country (over seven million a year, the government says), and has been praised in Western travel literature ever since the first Europeans laid eyes on it in the late 1500s. Yet despite the flood of superlatives and exaggerated statistics that inevitably go into its description, it is impervious to an excess of hype and is large and compelling enough to draw repeat visits from even the most jaded travelers. Make more time for it than you think you'll need.

ESSENTIALS

The palace, most commonly referred to in Chinese as Gù Gōng (short for Palace Museum), is on the north side of Tiān'ān Mén Square across Cháng'ān Dàjiē (✆ 010/6513-2255; www.dpm.org.cn). It is best approached on foot or via metro (Tiān'ān Mén East, 117), as taxis are not allowed to stop in front. The palace is open from 8:30am to 5pm during summer and from 8:30am to 4:30pm in winter. Regular admission *(mén piào)* in summer costs ¥60 ($8), dropping to ¥40 ($5) in winter; last tickets are sold 1 hour before the doors close. Various exhibition halls and gardens inside the palace charge an additional ¥10 ($1). All-inclusive tickets *(lián piào)* have been discontinued, perhaps in an effort to increase revenues (see "The Big Makeover," below), but it's always possible these will be reinstated.

Běijīng Attractions

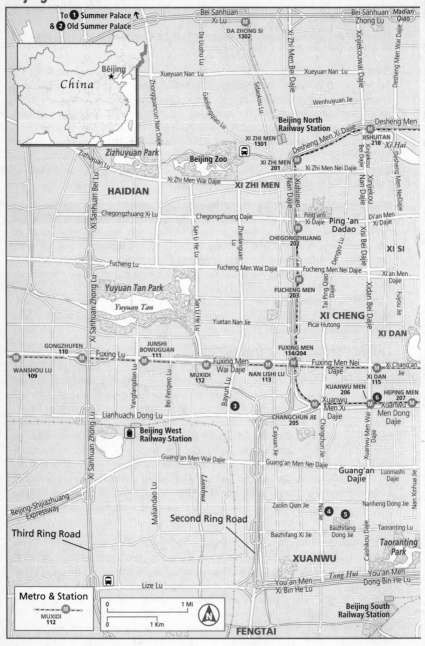

To ❶ Summer Palace ↑
& ❷ Old Summer Palace

China

Běijīng ★

Bei Sanhuan Xi Lu

Bei Sanhuan Zhong Lu

Madian Qiao

DA ZHONG SI 1302

Da Liushu Lu

Xueyuan Nan Lu

Zhongguancun Nan Dajie

Gaoliangqiao Lu

Sidaokou Lu

Xi Zhi Men Bei Dajie

Xueyuan Nan Lu

Xinjiekouwai Dajie

Desheng Men Wai Dajie

Wenhuiyuan Jie

Beijing North Railway Station

Desheng Men

Zizhuyuan Lu

Zizhuyuan Park

XI ZHI MEN 1301

JISHUITAN 218

Xi Hai

Desheng Men Xi Dajie

Xinjiekou Bei Dajie

Xinjiekou Nan Dajie

Desheng Men Nei Dajie

Beijing Zoo

Xi Zhi Men Wai Dajie

XI ZHI MEN

XI ZHI MEN 201

Xi Zhi Men Nei Dajie

Xizhimen Nan Dajie

HAIDIAN

Chegongzhuang Xi Lu

Chegongzhuang Dajie

Ping'anli Xi Dajie

Ping 'an Dadao

Di'an Men Xi Dajie

XI SI

Xi-Sanhuan Bei Lu

San li He Lu

Zhanlanguan Lu

CHEGONGZHUANG 202

Xisi Bei Dajie

Xi'an Men Dajie

Fucheng Lu

Fucheng Men Wai Dajie

Fucheng Men Nei Dajie

Dengju Lu

Tai Ping Qiao

Fuyou Jie

Yuyuan Tan Park

Yuyuan Tan

San Li He Lu

FUCHENG MEN 203

XI CHENG

Xidan Bei Dajie

Yuetan Nan Jie

Picai Hutong

XI DAN

Xi-Sanhuan Zhong Lu

GONGZHUFEN 110

JUNSHI BOWUGUAN 111

FUXING MEN 114/204

Fuxing Lu

Yangfangdian Lu

Bei Fengwo Lu

Fuxing Men Wai Dajie

MUXIDI 112

Bayun Lu

NAN LISHI LU 113

Fuxing Men Nei Dajie

Xi Chang'an

WANSHOU LU 109

❸

XUANWU MEN 206

XI DAN 115

HEPING MEN 207

Lianhuachi Dong Lu

CHANGCHUN JIE 205

Xuanwu Men Xi Dajie

❻

Xuanwu Men Dong Dajie

Beijing West Railway Station

Caiyuan Jie

Changchun Jie

Xuanwu Men Wai Dajie

Guang'an Men Wai Dajie

Guang'an Men Nei Dajie

Guang'an Dajie

Luomashi Dajie

Beijing-Shijiazhuang Expressway

Maliandao Lu

Lianhua

Zaolin Qian Jie

Niu Jie

❹ ❺

Nanheng Dong Jie

Nan Xinhua Jie

Second Ring Road

Baizhifang Xi Jie

Baizhifang Dong Jie

Taoranting Lu

Taoranting Park

Third Ring Road

Caishikou Dajie

XUANWU

Tong Hui

You'an Men Dong Bin He Lu

Lize Lu

You'an Men Xi Bin He Lu

Beijing South Railway Station

Metro & Station

MUXIDI 112

0 —— 1 Mi

0 —— 1 Km

FENGTAI

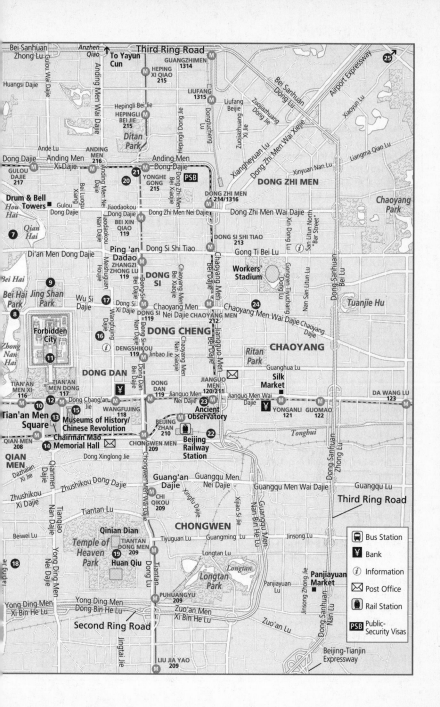

Běijīng Attractions Key

Ancient Observatory
   (Gù Guānxiàng Tái) 23
   故观象台

Báiyún Guàn (White Cloud Temple) 3
   白云观

Běi Hǎi Park (Běi Hǎi Gōngyuán) 8
   北海公园

Chairman Máo's Mausoleum
   (Máo Zhǔxi Jìniàn Guǎn) 13
   毛主席纪念馆

China National Art Gallery
   (Zhōngguó Měishùguǎn) 17
   中国美术馆

Dōngyuè Miào 24
   东岳庙

Factory 798
   (Qījiǔbā Gōngchǎng) 25
   七九八工厂

Fǎyuán Sì
   (Source of Dharma Temple) 5
   法原寺

Forbidden City (Gù Gōng) 11
   故宫

Former Residence of Lǎo Shě
   (Lǎo Shě Jìnìanguǎn) 16
   老舍纪念馆

Great Hall of the People
   (Rénmín Dàhùi Táng) 10
   人民大会堂

Gǔdài Jiànzhù Bówùguǎn
   (Museum of Ancient Architecture) 18
   古代建筑博物馆

Guó Zǐ Ǔiàn and Kǒng Miáo 20
   国子监和北京孔庙

Jīng Shān Park (Jīng Shān Gōngyuán) 9
   景山公园

Míng Chéng Qiáng Gōngyuán
   (Míng City Wall Park) 22
   明城墙公园

Museums of Chinese History
   and Revolution (Zhōngguó Lìshǐ
   Gémíng Bówùguǎn) 15
   中国历史革命博物馆

Ox Street Mosque
   (Niú Jiē Qīngzhēnsì) 4
   牛街清真寺

Prince Gong's Mansion
   (Gǒng Wáng Fǔ) 7
   恭王府

Qián Mén 14
   前门

Summer Palace (Yíhé Yuán) 1
   颐和园

South Cathedral (Nán Táng) 6
   南堂

Temple of Heaven (Tiān Tán) 19
   天坛

Tiān'an Mén
   (Gate of Heavenly Peace) 12
   天安门

Yōnghé Gōng (Lama Temple) 21
   雍和宫

Yuán Míng Yuán
   (Old Summer Palace) 2
   圆明园

OTHER ATTRACTIONS (not on map)

Eastern Qīng Tombs
   (Qīng Dōng Líng)
   青东陵

Great Wall at Bādálǐng
   (Bādálǐng Chángchéng)
   八达岭长城

Great Wall at Mùtiányù
   (Mùtiányù Chángchéng)
   幕田峪长城

Great Wall at Sīmǎtái
   (Sīmǎtái Chángchéng)
   司马台长城

Jiétái Sì (Temple of the
   Ordination Platform)
   结台寺

Míng Tombs (Shísāng Líng)
   十三陵

Tánzhè Sí (Temple of the Pool
   and Wild Mulberry)
   潭柘寺

Western Qīng Tombs (Qīng Xī Líng)
   青西陵

The Big Makeover

An immense **$75-million renovation of the Forbidden City,** the largest in 90 years, will be completed in two phases (the first by 2008, the second by 2020). Work started on halls and gardens in the closed western sections of the palace in 2002, with the most effort concentrated on opening the **Wǔyīng Diàn (Hall of Valiance and Heroism)** in the southwest corner of the palace, followed by **Cíníng Huāyuán (Garden of Love and Tranquillity)** next to the Tàihé Diàn. Wǔyīng Diàn, formerly the site of the imperial printing press, should be open by the time you arrive, displaying a collection of Buddhist sutras, palace records, and calligraphy. Cíníng Huāyuán is scheduled to open in 2008. Plans also call for the construction of new temperature-controlled buildings to house and exhibit what is claimed to be a collection of **930,000 Míng and Qīng imperial relics,** most now stored underground.

On the other side of the palace, within the northern section of the Níng-shòu Gōng Huāyuán, a remarkable building is undergoing restoration with assistance from the World Cultural Heritage Foundation. Qiánlóng commissioned the European Jesuit painters in his employ to create large-scale *trompe l'oeil* paintings, which were used both in the Forbidden City as well as in the Yuán Míng Yuán (p. 119). **Juànqín Zhāi,** an elaborately-constructed private opera house, houses the best remaining examples of these paintings, including a stunning image of a wisteria trellis, almost certainly painted by Italian master Castiglione. It is due to open in 2006.

Enter through the Wǔ Mén (Meridian Gate), a short walk north of Cháng'ān Dàjiē via Tiān'ān Mén (see below). Ticket counters are clearly marked on either side as you approach. *Tip:* If you have a little more time, it is highly recommended that you approach the entrance at Wǔ Mén (Meridian Gate) via Tài Miào to the east, and avoid the gauntlet of touts and souvenir stalls. **Audio tours** in several languages, including English (¥40/$5 plus ¥500/$63 deposit), are available at the gate itself, through the door to the right. Those looking to spend more money can hire **"English"-speaking tour guides** on the other side of the gate (¥200–¥350/$25–$44 per person, depending on length of tour). The tour guide booth also rents **wheelchairs** and **strollers** at reasonable rates. *Note:* Only the central route through the palace is wheelchair-accessible, and steeply so.

BACKGROUND & LAYOUT

Sourcing of materials for the original palace buildings began in 1406, during the reign of the Yǒnglè emperor, and construction was completed in 1420. Much of it was designed by a eunuch from Annam, Nguyen An. Without improvements to the Grand Canal, construction would have been impossible—timber came from as far away as Sìchuān, and logs took up to 4 years to reach the capital. The Yuán palace was demolished to make way for the Forbidden City, but the lakes excavated during the Jīn (1122–1215) were retained and expanded. Between 1420 and 1923, the palace was home to 24 emperors of the Míng and Qīng dynasties. The last was Aisin-Gioro Pǔyí (see chapter 5), who abdicated in 1912 but lived in the palace until 1924.

The Forbidden City is arranged along the compass points, with most major halls opening to the south (the direction associated with imperial rule). Farthest south and in the center is the perfectly symmetrical **outer court,** dominated by the immense ceremonial halls where the emperor conducted official business. Beyond the outer court and on both sides is the **inner court,** a series of smaller buildings and gardens that served as living quarters.

The palace has been ransacked and parts destroyed by fire several times over the centuries, so most of the existing buildings date from the Qīng rather than the Míng. Many of the roofs are trimmed in blue or green tile, which some scholars say reminded the Qīng's Manchu rulers of the grasslands and fertile fields they had left behind. Only half of the complex is open to visitors (expected to increase to 70% after repairs are completed in 2020; see "The Big Makeover," above), but this still leaves plenty to see.

Tiān'ān Mén (Gate of Heavenly Peace) 🕉🕉 This gate is the largest in what was once known as the Imperial City and the most emblematic of Chinese government grandeur. Above the central door, once reserved almost exclusively for the emperor, now hangs the famous **portrait of Máo,** flanked by inscriptions that read: LONG LIVE THE PEOPLE'S REPUBLIC OF CHINA (left) and LONG LIVE THE GREAT UNITY OF THE PEOPLES OF THE WORLD (right). Máo declared the founding of the People's Republic from atop the gate on October 1, 1949. There is no charge to walk through the gate, but tickets are required if you want to ascend to **the upper platform** for worthwhile views of Tiān'ān Mén Square. The ticket office is in the second of two small red shacks, on the left after you pass through.

North of Tiān'ān Mén Sq.; ticket office to left as you enter. Admission ¥20 ($3) in summer, ¥15 ($2) in winter. Summer 8am–4:30pm; winter 8:30am–4pm. Mandatory bag storage (¥2–¥6/30¢–75¢) behind and to left of ticket booth; cameras allowed.

The Outer Court The intimidating **Wǔ Mén (Meridian Gate),** built in 1420 and last restored in 1801, is the actual entrance to the Forbidden City. The emperor would come here to receive prisoners of war, issue proclamations, and supervise the punishment of troublesome officials. Beyond the gate, across a vast stone-paved courtyard bisected by the balustraded Jīn Shuǐ (Golden River), is the **Tàihé Mén (Gate of Supreme Harmony),** which marks the official beginning of the outer court.

The first of the outer courts' "Three Great Halls" (Sān Dà Diàn) is the **Tàihé Diàn (Hall of Supreme Harmony)** 🕉. Located beyond the Tàihé Mén and across an even grander stone courtyard, it is an imposing double-roofed structure mounted atop a three-tiered marble terrace with elaborately carved balustrades. This is the largest wooden hall in China, and the most elaborate and prestigious of the palaces' throne halls; it was therefore rarely used. Emperors came here to mark the new year and winter solstice.

Immediately behind it is the **Zhōnghé Diàn (Hall of Perfect Harmony),** and farther on lies the **Bǎohé Diàn (Hall of Preserving Harmony).** This last hall, supported by only a few columns, is where the highest levels of imperial examinations were held. At the rear of the hall is a carved marble slab weighing over 200 tons; 20,000 men supposedly spent 28 days dragging it to this position from a mountain roughly 50km (31 miles) away.

The Inner Court Only the emperor, his family, his concubines, and the palace eunuchs (who numbered 1,500 at the end of the Qīng dynasty) were allowed in this section, sometimes described as the truly forbidden city. It begins with the **Qiánqīng**

Mén (Gate of Heavenly Purity), directly north of the Bǎohé Diàn, beyond which are three palaces designed to mirror the three halls of the outer court.

The first of these is the **Qiánqīng Gōng (Palace of Heavenly Purity),** where the emperors lived until Yōngzhèng decided to move to another part of the city in the 1720s. Beyond are the rather boring **Jiāotài Diàn (Hall of Union),** containing the throne of the empress; and the rather more interesting **Kūnníng Gōng (Palace of Earthly Tranquillity),** a Manchu-style bed chamber where a nervous Pǔyí (China's last emperor, see p. 180) was expected to spend his wedding night before he fled to more comfortable rooms elsewhere.

At the rear of the inner court is the elaborate **Yù Huāyuán (Imperial Garden)** ⊛, a marvelous scattering of ancient conifers, rockeries, and pavilions said to be largely unchanged since it was built in the Míng dynasty. Pǔyí's famous British tutor, Reginald Fleming Johnston, lived in the **Yǎngxīn Zhāi,** the first building on the west side of the garden (now a tea shop).

From behind the mountain, you can exit the palace through the **Shénwǔ Mén (Gate of Martial Spirit)** and continue on to Jǐng Shān and/or Běi Hǎi Park. Those with time to spare, however, should explore less-visited sections on either side of the central path.

Western Axis   Most of this area is in a state of heavy disrepair, but a few buildings have been restored and are open to visitors. Most notable among these is the **Yǎngxīn Diàn (Hall of Mental Cultivation),** southwest of the Imperial Garden. The reviled Empress Dowager Cíxǐ, who ruled China for much of the late Qīng period, made decisions on behalf of her infant nephew Guāngxù from behind a screen in the east room. This is also where emperors lived after Yōngzhèng moved out of the Qiánqīng Gōng.

Eastern Axis ⊛   This side tends to be peaceful and quiet even when other sections are teeming. Entrance costs ¥10 ($1) and requires purchase of essentially useless overshoe slippers for ¥2 (30¢). The most convenient ticket booth is a 5-minute walk southwest of the Qiánqīng Mén, opposite the **Jiǔlóng Bì (Nine Dragon Screen),** a 3.5m-high (12-ft.) wall covered in striking glazed-tile dragons depicted frolicking above a frothing sea.

The Qīng dynasty Qiánlóng emperor (reign 1736–95) abdicated at the age of 85, and this section was built for his retirement, although he never really moved in, continuing to "mentor" his son while living in the Yǎngxīn Diàn, a practice later adopted by Empress Dowager Cíxǐ, who also partially took up residence here in 1894. One of the highlights here is the secluded **Níngshòu Gōng Huāyuán** ⊛⊛⊛, behind the Zhēnbǎo Guǎn (Hall of Jewelry) north of the ticket booth. The Qiánlóng emperor composed poems and drinking from cups of wine he floated in a snake-like water-filled trough carved in the floor of the main pavilion. Qiánlóng's personal compendium of verse ran to a modest 50,000 poems; he was seldom short of words. East of the garden is the **Chàngyīn Gé,** sometimes called Cíxǐ's Theater, an elaborate three-tiered structure with trapdoors and hidden passageways to allow movement between stages. In the far northeastern corner is the **Zhēnfēi Jǐng (Well of the Pearl Concubine),** a narrow hole covered by a large circle of stone, slightly askance. The Pearl Concubine, one of the Guāngxù emperor's favorites, was 25 when Cíxǐ had her stuffed down the well as they were fleeing in the aftermath of the Boxer Rebellion. According to most accounts, Cíxǐ was miffed at the girl's insistence that Guāngxù stay and take responsibility for the imperial family's support of the Boxers.

Also worth seeing is the **Hall of Clocks (Zhōngbiǎo Guǎn),** a collection of elaborate timepieces, many of them gifts to the emperors from European envoys. The exhibit costs ¥10 ($1) and at press time was temporarily relocated in a hall to the right (east) of the Bǎohé Diàn while the original Hall of Clocks is restored.

TIĀN'ĀN MÉN SQUARE (TIĀN'ĀN MÉN GUĂNGCHĂNG)

This is the world's largest public square, the size of 90 American football fields (40 hectares/99 acres), with standing room for 300,000. It is surrounded by the Forbidden City to the north, the Great Hall of the People to the west, and the museums of Chinese History and Chinese Revolution to the east. In the center of the square stands the **Monument to the People's Heroes (Rénmín Yīngxióng Jìniàn Bēi),** a 37m (124-ft.) granite obelisk engraved with scenes from famous uprisings and bearing a central inscription (in Máo's handwriting): THE PEOPLE'S HEROES ARE IMMORTAL.

The area on which the obelisk stands was originally occupied by the **Imperial Way**—a central road that stretched from the Gate of Heavenly Peace south to Qián Mén, the still extant main entrance to The Tartar City (see below). This road, lined on either side with imperial government ministries, was the site of the pivotal May Fourth movement (1919), in which thousands of university students gathered to protest the weakness and corruption of China's then Republican government. Máo ordered destruction of the old ministries and paved over the rubble in 1959, replacing them with the vast but largely empty **Great Hall of the People** to the west and the equally vast but unimpressive **museums** to the east, as part of a spate of construction to celebrate 10 years of Communist rule. But the site has remained a magnet for politically charged assemblies. The most famous of these was the gathering of **student prodemocracy protestors** in late spring of 1989. That movement and the government's violent suppression of it still define the square in most minds, Chinese as well as foreign. All physical traces of the crackdown disappeared after the square received a face-lift in 1999, just in time to celebrate the 50th anniversary of the founding of the People's Republic, but reminders remain in the stiff-backed soldiers and video cameras since put in place to ensure order is maintained.

There isn't much to do in the square, but early risers can line up in front of Tiān'ān Mén at dawn to watch the **flag-raising ceremony,** a unique suffocation-in-the-throng experience on National Day (Oct 1), when what seems like the entire Chinese population arrives to jostle for the best view.

Chairman Máo's Mausoleum (Máo Zhǔxí Jìniàn Guǎn) This is one of the eeriest experiences in Běijīng. The decision to preserve Máo's body was made hours after his death in 1976. Panicked and inexperienced, his doctors reportedly pumped him so full of formaldehyde that his face and body swelled almost beyond recognition. They drained the corpse and managed to get it back into acceptable shape, but they also created a wax model of the Great Helmsman just in case. There's no telling which version is on display at any given time. The mausoleum itself was built in 1977, near the center of Tiān'ān Mén Square. However much Máo may be mocked outside his tomb (earnest arguments about whether he was 70% right or 60% right are perhaps the biggest joke), he still commands a terrifying sort of respect inside it. This is not quite the kitsch experience some expect. The tour is free and fast, with no stopping or photos and no bags allowed inside.

South end of Tiān'ān Mén Sq. Free admission. Mon–Sat 8–11:30am, sometimes also 2–4pm (usually Tues, Thurs). Bag storage across the street, directly west: ¥10 ($1) per piece. Metro: Qián Mén (208).

Qián Mén   The phrase Qián Mén (Front Gate) is actually a reference to two separate towers on the south side of the square which together formed the main entrance to the Tartar (or Inner) City. The southernmost Arrow Tower (Jiàn Lóu) is no longer open to the public. You can, however, still climb the interior of the rear building (Zhèngyáng Mén), where a photo exhibition depicts life in Běijīng's pre-1949 markets, temples, and *hútòng*.

Tiān'ān Mén Sq. Admission ¥10 ($1.25). 8:30am–4pm. Metro: Qián Mén (208).

National Theatre   The controversial National Theatre, designed by Paul Andreu, is due to open west of the Great Hall of the People within the lifetime of this book. Andreu was awarded the project in 2000, and Beijingers have nicknamed it *jǐdànké'r* (The Eggshell). Although the project has been downsized, it still features a dazzling titanium-and-glass dome perched on a lake, and encasing three auditoriums. Patrons descend on escalators through the waters of the lake.

West of Tiān'ān Mén Sq. and the Great Hall of the People. Metro: Qián Mén (208).

THE TEMPLE OF HEAVEN (TIĀN TÁN)

At the same time Yǒnglè built the Forbidden City, he also oversaw construction of this enormous park and altar to heaven to the south. Each winter solstice, the Míng and Qīng emperors would lead a procession here to perform rites and make sacrifices designed to promote the next year's crops and curry favor from heaven for the general health of the empire. The park is square (symbolizing Earth) in the south and rounded (Heaven) in the north. *Note:* Qǐnián Diàn, the main reason for visiting, is closed until October 2006.

ESSENTIALS

Temple of Heaven Park (Tiān Tán Gōngyuán; ✆ **010/6702-8866**) is south of Tiān'ān Mén Square, on the east side of Qián Mén Dàjiē. It's open from 6am to 9pm (6am–8pm in winter), but the ticket offices and major sights are only open from 8:30am to 4:30pm. All-inclusive tickets *(lián piào)* cost ¥35 ($4.50) (¥30/$4 in winter); simple park admission costs ¥15 ($2). The east gate *(dōng mén)* is easily accessed by public transport; take the no. 807 or no. 812 bus from just north of the Chóngwén Mén metro stop (209, exit B) to Fǎhuá Sì. However, the best approach is from the south gate *(nán mén)*, the natural starting point for a walk that culminates in the magnificent Hall of Prayer for Good Harvests.

HIGHLIGHTS

Circular Altar (Yuán Qiū)   This three-tiered marble terrace is the first major structure you'll see if you're coming from the south. It was built in 1530 and enlarged in 1749, with all of its stones and balustrades organized in multiples of nine (considered a lucky number by northern Chinese).

Imperial Vault of Heaven (Huáng Qióng Yǔ)   Directly north of the Circular Altar, this smaller version of the Hall of Prayer was built to store ceremonial stone tablets. The vault is surrounded by the circular **Echo Wall (Huíyīn Bì).** In years past, when crowds were smaller and before the railing was installed, it was possible for two people on opposite sides of the enclosure to send whispered messages to each other along the wall with remarkable clarity.

Hall of Prayer for Good Harvests (Qǐnián Diàn) 👁👁   This circular wooden hall, with its triple-eaved cylindrical blue-tiled roof, is perhaps the most recognizable emblem of Chinese imperial architecture outside the Forbidden City. Completed in 1420, the original hall burned to the ground in 1889, but a near-perfect replica (this one) was built the following year. It stands 38m (125 ft.) high and is 29m (98 ft.) in diameter, and is constructed without a single nail. The 28 massive pillars inside, made of fir imported from Oregon, are arranged to symbolize divisions of time: The central 4 represent the seasons, the next 12 represent the months of the year, and the outer 12 represent traditional divisions of a single day. The hall's most striking feature is its ceiling, a kaleidoscope of painted brackets and gilded panels as intricate as anything in the country.

THE SUMMER PALACE (YÍHÉ YUÁN)

This expanse of elaborate Qīng-style pavilions, bridges, walkways, and gardens, scattered along the shores of immense Kūnmíng Lake, is the grandest imperial playground in China; it was constructed from 1749 to 1764. Between 1860 and 1903, it was twice leveled by foreign armies and rebuilt. The palace is most often associated with the empress dowager Cíxǐ, who made it her full-time residence.

ESSENTIALS

The **Summer Palace** (𝄞 010/6288-1144) is located 12km (7 miles) northwest of the city center in Hǎidiàn. Take **bus no. 726** from just west of Wǔdàokǒu light rail station (1304, exit A); or take a 30- to 40-minute **taxi** ride (¥60/$8) from the center of town. A more pleasant option is to travel here by **boat** along the renovated canal system; slightly rusty "imperial yachts" leave from the Běizhàn Hòuhú Mǎtóu (𝄞 010/8836-3576), behind the Běijīng Exhibition Center just south of the Běijīng Aquarium (50-min. trip; ¥40/$5 one-way; ¥70/$9 round-trip; ¥100/$13 includes round-trip travel and the entrance ticket), docking at Nán Rúyì Mén in the south of the park. The gates open at 6am; no tickets are sold after 6pm in summer and 4pm in winter. Admission is ¥30 ($4) for entry to the grounds or ¥50 ($6) for the all-inclusive *lián piào*, reduced to ¥20 ($2.50) and ¥40 ($5) respectively in winter (Nov–Mar). The most convenient entrance is Dōng Gōng Mén (East Gate). Go early and allow at least 4 hours for touring the major sites on your own. Overpriced **imperial-style food** in a pleasant setting is available at the Tīnglí Guǎn Restaurant, at the western end of the Long Corridor. Spots around the lake are perfect for picnics, and Kūnmíng Lake is ideal for skating in the depths of winter.

EXPLORING THE SUMMER PALACE

This park covers roughly 290 hectares (716 acres), with **Kūnmíng Lake** in the south and **Longevity Hill (Wànshòu Shān)** in the north. The lake's northern shore boasts most of the buildings and other attractions and is the most popular area for strolls, although it is more pleasant to walk around the smaller lakes behind Longevity Hill. The hill itself has a number of temples as well as **Bǎoyún Gé (Precious Clouds Pavilion),** one of the few structures in the palace to escape destruction by foreign forces. There are dozens of pavilions and a number of bridges on all sides of the lake, enough to make a full day of exploration, if you so choose.

Rénshòu Diàn (Hall of Benevolence and Longevity)   Located directly across the courtyard from the east gate entrance, Rénshòu Diàn is the palace's main hall. This is where the empress dowager received members of the court, first from behind a screen and later from the Dragon Throne itself. North of the hall is Cíxǐ's private theater, now a museum that contains an old Mercedes-Benz—the first car imported into China.

Long Corridor (Cháng Láng) ✿ Among the more memorable attractions in Běijīng, this covered wooden promenade stretches 700m (nearly half a mile) along the northern shore of Kūnmíng Lake. Each crossbeam, ceiling, and pillar is painted with a different scene taken from Chinese history, literature, myth, and geography (roughly 10,000 in all).

Seventeen-Arch Bridge (Shíqī Kǒng Qiáo) ✿ This 150m-long (490-ft.) marble bridge connects South Lake Island (Nán Hú Dǎo) to the east shore of Kūnmíng Lake. There is a rather striking life-size bronze ox near the eastern foot of the bridge.

OTHER SIGHTS IN BĚIJĪNG
TEMPLES, MOSQUES & CHURCHES

Báiyún Guàn If the incense here smells authentic, it's because this sprawling complex, said to have been built in 739, is the most active of Běijīng's Daoist temples. Chinese visitors seem intent on actual worship rather than on tourism, and the blue-frocked monks wear their hair in the rarely seen traditional manner—long and tied in a bun at the top of the head. One notable structure is the Láolǚ Táng, a large hall in the third courtyard built in 1228, now used for teaching and ceremonies.

On Báiyún Guàn Lù, east of the intersection with Báiyún Lù (1st right north of Báiyún Qiáo, directly across from Báiyún Guàn bus stop), Hǎidiàn Qū. ☎ 010/6346-3531. Admission ¥10 ($1.25). 8:30am–4:30pm. Bus: no. 727 from Mùxīdì metro (112, exit D2) to Báiyún Guàn.

Dōngyuè Miào ✿ This Daoist temple, built in 1322 and beautifully restored a few years ago, is most famous for a series of 76 stalls ("heavenly departments") that surround its main courtyard. Garishly painted divine judges in each stall can offer relief from practically every ill—for a price. The most popular stall, not surprisingly, is the Department of Bestowing Material Happiness. English signs explain each department's function.

Cháoyáng Mén Wài Dàjiē 141, Cháoyáng Qū (10-min. walk east on the north side). ☎ 010/6551-0151. Admission ¥10 ($1.25); free during festivals. Tues–Sun 8am–4:30pm. Metro: Cháoyáng Mén (212, exit B).

Fǎyuán Sì (Source of Dharma Temple) *(finds)* Despite guides droning on about a long and glorious history, most of Běijīng's sights are relatively new, dating from within the last 600 years. This temple, constructed in 645 in what was then the southeast corner of town, retains both an air of antiquity and the feel of a genuine Buddhist monastery. Orange-robed monks, housed in the adjacent Buddhist College, go about their business in earnest. The ancient *hútòng* immediately surrounding the temple are "protected" and well worth a wander.

Fǎyuán Sì Qián Jiē 7, Xuānwǔ Qū. Admission ¥5 (60¢). Thurs–Tues 8:30–11am and 1:30–4pm. Metro: Xuānwǔ Mén (206, exit D1).

Guó Zǐ Jiàn and Kǒng Miào This classic temple-school compound, buried down a tree-shaded street east of the Lama Temple (see below), is still in use. The Kǒng Miào, China's second-largest Confucian Temple, is on the right, and the Guó Zǐ Jiàn (the Imperial College) is on the left, both originally built in 1306. The front courtyard of the temple contains several dozen stelae inscribed with the names of the last successful candidates in the *jìnshì* (highest level) imperial examinations. The college, imperial China's highest educational institution, contains a striking glazed-tile gate with elaborately carved stone arches.

Kǒng Miào at Guó Zǐ Jiàn Jiē 13 (walk south from station along west side of Lama Temple, turn right onto street marked with arch), Dōng Chéng Qū. ☎ 010/8401-1977. Admission ¥10 ($1.25). 8:30am–4:30pm. Guó Zǐ Jiàn next door: admission ¥6 (75¢); 9am–5pm. Metro: Yōnghé Gōng/Lama Temple (215, exit C).

Ox Street Mosque (Niú Jiē Qīngzhēnsì)   This is Běijīng's largest mosque and the spiritual center for the city's estimated 200,000 Muslims. Built in 996, the complex looks more Eastern than Middle Eastern, with sloping tile roofs similar to those found on Buddhist temples. Halls are noticeably free of idols, however. A small courtyard on the south side contains the tombs and original gravestones of two Arab imams who lived here in the late 13th century.

Niú Jiē 88 (on east side of street), Xuānwǔ Qū. (C) 010/6353-2564. Admission ¥10 ($1.25) for non-Muslims. 8am–7pm. Bus: no. 61 to Lǐbàisì from Chángchūn Jiē metro (205, exit D1).

Yōnghé Gōng (Lama Temple) 𝕒𝕩   If you visit only one temple after the Temple of Heaven, this should be it. A complex of progressively larger buildings topped with ornate yellow-tiled roofs, Yōnghé Gōng was built in 1694 and originally belonged to the Qīng prince who would become the Yōngzhèng emperor. As was the custom, the complex was converted to a temple after Yōngzhèng's move to the Forbidden City in 1744. The temple is home to several beautiful **incense burners,** including a particularly ornate one in the second courtyard that dates back to 1746. The Fǎlún Diàn (Hall of the Wheel of Law), second to last of the major buildings, contains a 6m (20-ft.) tall bronze statue of Tsongkapa (1357–1419), the first Dalai Lama and founder of the Yellow Hat sect of Tibetan Buddhism. The final of the five central halls, the Wànfú Gé (Tower of Ten Thousand Happinesses), houses the temple's prize possession—an ominous Tibetan-style **statue of Maitreya** (the future Buddha), 18m (60 ft.) tall, carved from a single piece of white sandalwood.

Yōnghé Gōng Dàjiē 12, south of the N. Second Ring Rd. (entrance on the south end of the complex). (C) 010/6404-3769. Admission ¥25 ($3); audio tours in English additional ¥25 ($3). 9am–4pm. Metro: Yōnghé Gōng/Lama Temple (215, exit C).

PARKS & GARDENS
Běi Hǎi Park (Běi Hǎi Gōngyuán) 𝕒𝕩   This is Běijīng's oldest imperial garden, roughly 800 years old, and the one city park you should not miss. Most of the park is actually a man-made lake, **Běi Hǎi (North Sea),** part of a series of lakes that run north along the eastern edge of the Forbidden City. The central feature is a 36m (118-ft.) Tibetan-style **White Dagoba (Bái Tǎ),** similar to the one at Bái Tǎ Sì, built in 1651 to commemorate a visit by the Dalai Lama. The pagoda stands atop the artificial hill that dominates Qiónghuá Dǎo, also known as the **Jade Islet.** A hike around the island, and around the shore of Běi Hǎi, will take you past several beautiful pavilions and gardens. The **Round City (Tuán Chéng),** located just outside the south entrance of the park, stands on the site where Kublai Khan built his palace after establishing the Yuán dynasty (1279–1368). It contains a massive jade bowl that once belonged to him, and a 3m (10-ft.) Buddha of white jade.

Wénjīn Jiē 1, Xī Chéng Qū (south entrance is just west of the north gate of the Forbidden City; east entrance is opposite the west entrance of Jǐng Shān Park). (C) 010/6404-0610. Admission: summer ¥10 ($1.25); winter ¥5 (60¢); ¥10 ($1.25) extra for Yǒng'ān Sì; ¥1 (10¢) extra for Tuán Chéng. 6am–9pm. Bus: no. 812 from Dōng Dān metro stop (119, exit A) to Běi Hǎi.

Jǐng Shān Park (Jǐng Shān Gōngyuán)   If you want a clear aerial view of the Forbidden City, this is where you'll find it. The park's central hill—known both as Jǐng Shān (Prospect Hill) and Méi Shān (Coal Hill)—was created using earth left over from the digging of the imperial moat and was the highest point in the city during the Míng dynasty. A locust tree on the east side of the hill marks the spot where the last

Míng dynasty Chóngzhēn emperor hanged himself in 1644, just before Manchu and rebel armies overran the city.

Jǐng Shān Qián Jiē 1 (opposite Forbidden City north gate), Dōng Chéng Qū. © 010/6404-4071. Admission ¥2 (20¢). Summer 6am–10pm; winter 6:30am–8pm.

Yuán Míng Yuán 🌟 (Kids   An amalgamation of three separate imperial gardens, these ruins create a ghostly and oddly enjoyable scene, beloved as a picnic spot. Established by the Kāngxī emperor in 1707, Yuán Míng Yuán is a more recent construction than the New Summer Palace to the west, but it is misleadingly called the Old Summer Palace because it was never rebuilt after troops looted and razed it during the Second Opium War of 1860. Ironically, some of the buildings were filled with European furnishings and art. Two Jesuit priests, Italian painter Castiglione and French scientist Benoist, were commissioned by Qiánlóng to design the 30-hectare (75-acre) **Xīyáng Lóu (Western Mansions)** in the northeast section of the park. Inaccurate models suggest that the structures were entirely European in style, but they were curious hybrids, featuring imperial-style vermillion walls and yellow-tiled roofs. Recently, the park has been the center of environmental controversy: Park management decided to line the lakes (an integral part of Běijīng's water ecology) with plastic sheeting to save on water bills and raise the water levels to allow for a duck-boat business.

Qīnghuá Xī Lù 28 (north of Peking University), Hǎidiàn Qū. © 010/6262-8501. Admission ¥10 ($1.25), ¥15 ($2) to enter Xīyáng Lóu. 7am–7pm (to 5:30pm in winter). Bus: no. 743 from east of Wǔdàokǒu metro stop (1304) to Yuán Míng Yuán.

MORE MUSEUMS & OTHER CURIOSITIES

Ancient Observatory (Gǔ Guānxiàng Tái) (Kids   Most of the large bronze astronomical instruments on display here—mystifying combinations of hoops, slides, and rulers stylishly embellished with dragons and clouds—were built by the Jesuits in the 17th and 18th centuries. You can play with reproductions in the courtyard below.

Jiànguó Mén Dōng Biǎobèi 2 (southwest side of Jiànguó Mén intersection), Dōng Chéng Qū. © 010/6512-8923. Admission ¥10 ($1.25). 9am–4:30pm. Metro: Jiànguó Mén (120/211, exit C).

Factory 798 (Qījiǔbā Gōngchǎng) 🌟🌟   Optimistically billed as Běijīng's SoHo district, this Soviet-designed former weapons factory is a center for local art and fashion, but its long-term survival is uncertain. Purchase a map (¥2/25¢) on arrival. Establishments worth your time include the **Hart Gallery**, which holds regular screenings of alternative films, **798 Space**, still covered with slogans offering praise to Máo and **798 Photo**, immediately opposite, and **Beijing Tokyo Art Projects** (www.tokyo-gallery.com), which boasts a formidable stable of local and international artists. **At Cafe** (**Àitè Kāfēi**; © 010/6438-7264) is the best of Dàshānzi's middling cafes.

Jiǔxiān Qiáo Lù 4, Cháoyáng Qū (north of Dàshānzi Huándǎo). Some galleries closed Mon. Bus: no. 813 east from Cháoyáng Mén metro (212, exit A) to Wángyé Fén

Former Residence of Lǎo Shě (Lǎo Shě Jìniànguǎn)   Lǎo Shě (1899–1966) was one of China's greatest 20th-century writers, lauded by early Communists for his use of satire in novels like *Teahouse* and *Rickshaw Boy* (or *Camel Xiángzi*) and persecuted for the same books during the Cultural Revolution. He is said to have committed suicide but might instead have been murdered by Red Guards. The rooms contain photos, copies of his books, and his own library (Hemingway, Dickens, Graham Greene). Most interesting is his study, supposedly preserved the way he left it, with a game of solitaire laid out on the bed and the calendar turned to August 24, 1966—the day he disappeared.

Fēngfù Hútòng 19, Dōng Chéng Qū (from Wángfǔjǐng Dàjiē, turn left at the Crowne Plaza along Dēngshìkǒu Xī Jiē to the 2nd *hútòng* on your right). (𝐶 010/6514-2612. Admission ¥10 ($1.25). 9am–5pm. Metro: Wángfǔjǐng (118, exit A).

Gǔdài Jiànzhù Bówùguǎn (Museum of Ancient Architecture) 𝄞𝄞 This exhibition, a mixture of models of China's most famous architecture and fragments of buildings long disappeared, is housed in halls as dramatic as those on the central axis of the Forbidden City. These were once part of the **Xiān Nóng Tán,** or Altar of Agriculture, now as obscure as its neighbor, Tiān Tán, the Temple (properly Altar) of Heaven, is famous. From about 1410, emperors came to this once-extensive site to perform rituals in which they started the agricultural cycle by playing farmer and plowing the first furrows. Models of significant buildings around Běijīng can help you select what to see in the capital during the remainder of your trip.

Dōng Jīng Lù 21, Xuānwǔ Qū; (from bus stop, take first right into Nán Wěi Lù and walk for 5 min., look out for an archway down a street on the left). (𝐶 010/6301-7620. Admission ¥15 ($2). 9am–4pm. Bus: no. 803 from just south of Qián Mén (208) metro stops to Tiān Qiáo Shāngchǎng.

National Museum of China (Guójiā Bówùguǎn) 𝄞 The Museum of the Chinese Revolution and the Museum of History have been united in a single building, but renovations won't be completed until 2008. Until then, a series of exhibits emphasizing the greatness of the Chinese civilization will be shown. Some effort has been made to spruce things up, and English captions have been added to a number of the displays, although they are lacking from the hilarious wax figure hall. In the past, interest centered on omissions from Chinese history; now it focuses on inclusions. Former unpersons such as Máo's ill-fated heirs apparent, Liú Shàoqí and Lín Biāo, are displayed alongside their tormentors, but the Party line is scrupulously followed. Lín, the only man to outdo Zhōu Ēnlái in his relentless obsequiousness to Máo, is still said to have plotted to seize power from the Great Helmsman.

East side of Tiān'ān Mén Sq., Dōng Chéng Qū. (𝐶 010/6512-8901. www.nmch.gov.cn. Admission ¥30 ($4) for *tōng piào,* or ¥10–¥20 ($1–$3) for each exhibit. English audio tours ¥30 ($4). 9am–3:30pm. Metro: Tiān'ān Mén East (117, exit D).

Prince Gōng's Mansion (Gōng Wáng Fǔ) 𝄞 This imperial residence belonged to several people, including the sixth son of the Guāngxù emperor (Prince Gōng), and is thought to have been the inspiration behind the lushly described mansion in Cáo Xuěqín's canonical 18th-century work, *Dream of the Red Chamber.* Only the garden is open to visitors, but its labyrinthine combination of rockeries and pavilions offers plenty to see.

Liǔyīn Jiē 17 (signposted in English at top of Qián Hǎi Xī Dàjiē running north off Píng'ān Dàdào opposite north gate of Běi Hǎi Park; turn left at sign and follow alley past large parking lot. Entrance marked with huge red lanterns). (𝐶 010/6618-0573. Admission ¥20 ($2.50); ¥60 ($7.50) including guide and opera performance. 8:30am–4:30pm.

THE HÚTÒNG

As distinct as Běijīng's palaces, temples, and parks may be, it is the *hútòng* that ultimately set the city apart. Prior to the 20th century, when cars and the Communist love of grandeur made them impractical, these narrow and often winding lanes were the city's dominant passageways. Old maps of Běijīng show the city to be an immense and intricate maze composed almost entirely of *hútòng,* most no wider than 10m (30 ft.) and some as narrow as 50 centimeters (20 in.).

  Běijīng's other famous feature is the *sìhéyuàn* (courtyard house)—traditional dwellings typically composed of four single-story rectangular buildings arranged around a central courtyard with a door at one corner (ideally facing south). Originally designed to house a single family, each one now houses up to five or six families. Until recently, as much as half of Běijīng's population lived in some form of *sìhéyuàn*, but large-scale bulldozing of the *hútòng* has resulted in significant migration into modern apartment buildings. Foreign visitors charmed by the quaintness of the old houses often assume this migration is forced, and it often is. But many who move do so willingly, eager for central heating and indoor plumbing (both rare in the *hútòng* neighborhoods).

The *hútòng* are being leveled so rapidly that the term "fast-disappearing" is now a permanent part of their description. The best-preserved *hútòng*, and the ones most likely to survive because of their popularity with tourists, are those found in the Back Lakes (Shíchà Hǎi) and nearby Dì'ān Mén. But even these may not be safe, as reports claim that the city plans to demolish a swath of nearby "protected" *hútòng* to make way for an expansion of Qián Hǎi. Pedicab tour companies offer to bike you around this area and take you inside a couple of courtyards, but they all charge absurd rates. It's much cheaper, and far more enjoyable, to walk around on your own (see "Walking Tour: The Back Lakes," below). If you must, the **Běijīng Hútòng Tourist Agency** (© **010/6615-9097**) offers tours in English.

WALKING TOUR	THE BACK LAKES

Start:	Drum Tower (Gǔ Lóu), north end of Dì'ān Mén Wài Dàjiē
Finish:	Prince Gōng's Palace (Gōng Wáng Fǔ), west side of Qián Hǎi
Time:	Approximately 3 hours
Best Times:	Morning (9am) or just after lunch, no later than 1:30pm (or you risk getting locked out of Prince Gōng's Palace).

There is, quite simply, no finer place to walk in Běijīng. The Back Lakes area (Shíchà Hǎi) is composed of two idyllic lakes—Qián Hǎi (Front Sea) and Hòu Hǎi (Back Sea)—and the tree-shaded neighborhoods that surround them. Combined with other man-made pools to the south, these lakes were once part of a system used to transport grain by barge from the Grand Canal to the Forbidden City. Prior to 1911, this was an exclusive area, and only people with connections to the imperial family were permitted to maintain houses here (a situation that seems destined to return). A profusion of bars and cafes has sprung up around the lakes in recent years, providing ample opportunities to take breaks from your walk.

Beyond the lakes, stretching out in all directions, is the city's best-maintained network of *hútòng*. Many families have lived in these lanes for generations, their insular communities a last link to Old Běijīng.

Begin at a park just outside the Jīshuǐ Tán metro station (exit B) along the south side of the busy Second Ring Road at:

❶ Huìtōng Cí

This ancestral hall–cum–Buddhist temple dates from the Míng dynasty, but little of antiquity remains. The point of visiting is to climb to the top for a view of the road ahead. The nearest lake is Xī Hǎi, followed by Hòu Hǎi and the spires of the Bell Tower (to the left) and Drum Tower.

Retrace your steps, turn left as you exit the park, and then left again to follow Bǎn Qiáo Tóu Tiáo as it snakes around the side of Xī Hǎi. Cross busy Déshèng Mén Nèi Dàjiē (set to be transformed

Walking Tour—The Back Lakes

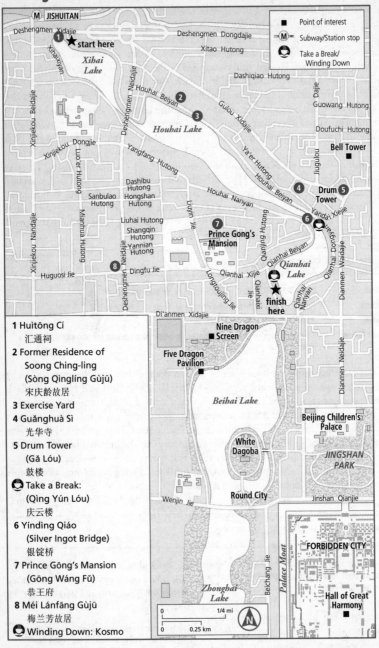

M JISHUITAN

Deshengmen Xidajie

★ **start here**

Deshengmen Dongdajie

Xitao Hutong

Xihai Lake

Dashiqiao Hutong

Xinjiekou Beidajie

Xinjiekou Dongjie

Deshengmen Neidajie

Houhai Beiyan

Gulou Xidajie

Guowang Hutong

Doufuchi Hutong

Xinjiekou

Luo'er Hutong

Yangfang Hutong

Houhai Lake

Ya'er Hutong

Houhai Beiyan

Dajie

Gulou Dongdajie

Bell Tower ■

Dashibu Hutong

Sanbulao Hutong

Hongshan Hutong

Mianhua Hutong

Xinjiekou Nandajie

Liuhai Hutong

Shangqin Hutong

Yannian Hutong

Deshengmen Neidajie

Liuyin Jie

Houhai Nanyan

Drum Tower

Yandai Xiejie

⑦ **Prince Gong's Mansion**

Qianfing Hutong

Qianhai Beiyan

Dingfu Jie

Huguosi Jie

⑧

Qianhai Lake

Qianhai Xijie

Longtoujing Jie

Qianhai Xijie

Qianhaixi Jie

Qianhai Nanyan

Qianhai Waidajie

Dianmen Waidajie

★ **finish here**

Di'anmen Xidajie

Nine Dragon Screen ■

Five Dragon Pavilion

Beihai Lake

Dianmen Neidajie

Beijing Children's Palace

White Dagoba

JINGSHAN PARK

Round City

Wenjin Jie

Jinshan Qianjie

Zhonghai Lake

Beichang Jie

Palace Moat

FORBIDDEN CITY

Hall of Great Harmony ■

0 ——— 1/4 mi
0 ——— 0.25 km

Legend:
■ Point of interest
M Subway/Station stop
☺ Take a Break/Winding Down

1 Huìtōng Cí
汇通祠

2 Former Residence of Soong Ching-ling (Sòng Qìnglíng Gùjū)
宋庆龄故居

3 Exercise Yard

4 Guǎnghuà Sì
光华寺

5 Drum Tower (Gǔ Lóu)
鼓楼

☺ Take a Break: (Qìng Yún Lóu)
庆云楼

6 Yíndìng Qiáo (Silver Ingot Bridge)
银锭桥

7 Prince Gōng's Mansion (Gōng Wáng Fǔ)
恭王府

8 Méi Lánfāng Gùjū
梅兰芳故居

☺ Winding Down: Kosmo

into a 50m-wide (164-ft.) thoroughfare during the life of this book), and take the next left turn to follow the north side of Hòu Hǎi to:

② Former Residence of Soong Ching-ling (Sòng Qìnglíng Gùjū)

Located at Hòu Hǎi Běi Yàn 46, this former imperial palace is where Soong Ching-ling (1892–1981), middle daughter of famous Bible salesman Charlie Soong and wife of Sun Yat-sen, spent most of her later life. While her family became leading supporters of the Guómíndǎng (Nationalists), Soong Ching-ling steered a neutral course, displaying some measure of sympathy for the Communists only after her husband's death in 1925. Máo later rewarded her with this house (admission ¥20/$2.50; open 9am–4:30pm).

Turn left and continue southeast along Hòu Hǎi Běi Yàn to the:

③ Exercise Yard

On the right-hand side of the road, stretch your limbs and meet some locals. There's table tennis on offer, and Běijīng's hardiest swimmers take the plunge from here—year-round! Joining the swimmers is not recommended. Just south of here is a picturesque former royal residence, **Chún Qīnwáng Fǔ.**

Continue along the lakeshore, take the second left, and immediately turn right into Yǎ'ér Hútòng. On your left is:

④ Guǎnghuà Sì

A Buddhist temple dating from the Yuán dynasty (1279–1368), this complex originally comprised over 20 buildings. Only a few of the buildings remain. China's last known eunuch, Sūn Yàotíng, was caretaker of the temple for 2 decades, and died here in 1996. Admission is allowed on the 1st and 15th days of the lunar month, when the temple is filled with locals praying for the success of their business ventures.

At this point you can make an optional detour eastward to the:

⑤ Drum Tower (Gǔ Lóu)

This vaguely trapezoidal building (admission ¥20/$2.50; open 9am–4:30pm)

with its bright yellow tile roof is the most conspicuous structure north of the old Imperial City. Skip the "free Tibetan Culture Exhibit" on the first floor (essentially an overpriced fake antiques market) and go around back to the steep set of stairs that leads to the upper chamber. From here you can survey the Back Lakes and take in tremendous views of the old Tartar City, set against the jagged-tooth backdrop of urban Běijīng.

Walk south on Dì'ān Mén Wài Dàjiē and take the first right onto Yāndài Xiéjiē, home to some of Běijīng's trendiest bars and cafes. Bear left until you approach the Yíndìng Qiáo (Silver Ingot Bridge); but before crossing the bridge, take a break for lunch.

TAKE A BREAK
Turn left before you cross the bridge, immediately on your left is an impressive four-story structure. This is **Nuage** (p. 104), which delivers pricey but delicious Vietnamese cuisine amid delightful colonial ambience. If the weather is fine, aim for a seat on the rooftop.

If you're not sufficiently rested, turn left as you exit and hire a rowboat or a "duck boat" (yāzi chuán) and go for a paddle around the lake for about ¥50 ($6) per hour. In winter, pull on a pair of ice skates for only ¥20 ($2.50).

Cross the bridge and turn right. Take the winding road along the southwest shore of Hòu Hǎi past a jumble of cafes, bars, and shops, and stop for a peek at:

⑥ Yíndìng Qiáo (Silver Ingot Bridge)

This white marble bridge, which marks the boundary between Hòu Hǎi and Qián Hǎi, has stood here for centuries, although the latest version is the work of modern masons (1984). Standing on this bridge in the 18th century, the Qiánlóng emperor could see as far as the Western Hills, and he deemed it one of the Eight Great Views of Běijīng. Air quality has dropped since.

Cross the bridge and turn right. Continue northwest as the road leaves the lakeshore, taking a sharp left turn at a wide intersection into Liŭyīn Jiē. Keep to the left side and you'll soon come to:

⑦ Prince Gōng's Mansion (Gōng Wáng Fǔ)

The most lavish of the all the Back Lakes courtyard residences is located at Liŭyīn Jiē 17 (admission ¥20/$2.50; open 8:30am–4:30pm). Inside is one of the city's most spectacular gardens, a combination of pavilions and rockeries perfectly arranged to make it all seem larger than it really is.

Turn left as you exit, continue past the touts to turn right at a T-junction. On your right, you'll soon pass another prince's mansion, Qìng Wáng Fǔ. This spectacular residence is occupied by the army, so there's no chance of admission. Cross Déshèng Mén Nèi Dàjiē, and on your right is:

⑧ Méi Lánfāng Gùjū

This is the superbly preserved courtyard residence of Běijīng opera's most eminent star, Méi Lánfāng. Most intriguing is the photo exhibition of postures and hand gestures that Méi produced while at the height of his powers in 1935. Specific postures and hand gestures to convey shyness and mild surprise hint at the intricacies of the art form.

>
> **WINDING DOWN**
> Turn left as you exit, and continue straight to rejoin the lakes at Qián Hǎi. On your right is Lotus Lane, which sports Starbucks and bars with silly names like Sex and Da City. Fortunately, there's also a branch of **Kosmo**, which serves sandwiches and freshly squeezed juices.

TOURS

Several companies offer guided group tours of Běijīng for English speakers, but these are overpriced, often incomplete, and best thought of as an emergency measure when time is short. The most popular operators are **Dragon Bus** (© 010/8563-9959; www.dragontour.com.cn) and **Panda Tours** (© 010/6522-2991), both with offices scattered through the four- and five-star hotels. City-highlight tours by air-conditioned bus typically cost around ¥300 ($38) per person for a half-day and around ¥500 ($60) for a full day with a mediocre lunch. **China International Travel Service (CITS)** (© 010/6515-8566; www.cits.net) offers tours that are more customizable, but at a much higher fee. Instead, consider the **Chinese Culture Club** (© 010/8462-2081; www.chinesecultureclub.org), which organizes outings, lectures, and film screenings for expatriates with an interest in Chinese culture. Events are often led by prominent lecturers, discussions go well beyond the "5,000 years of history" palaver that CITS will subject you to, and they are constantly on the lookout for new attractions. A smaller operation with a similar philosophy is **Cycle China** (© 010/6424-5913; www.cyclechina.com).

6 Side Trips from Běijīng

THE GREAT WALL

Even after you dispense with the myths that it is a single continuous structure and that it can be seen from space, China's best-known attraction is still a mind-boggling achievement. Referred to in Mandarin as the Wànlǐ Chángchéng (10,000-Lǐ Long Wall) or just Chángchéng for short, the Great Wall begins at Shānhǎiguān on the Bó Hǎi (sea) (p. 144) and snakes west to a fort at Jiāyù Guān in the Gobi Desert (p. 279). Its origins date from the Warring States Period (453–221 B.C.), when rival kingdoms began building defensive walls to thwart each other's armies. The king of Qín, who eventually conquered the other states to become the first emperor of a unified China, conscripted around 300,000 laborers to combine the walls into a more or less uninterrupted rampart. During the Hàn dynasty (206 B.C.–A.D. 220), the Wall was extended farther west, with subsequent dynasties adding their own bits and branches, which makes it difficult to pin down the Wall's precise length. It is at least 10,000km (6,200 miles) long by common estimates, but some guesses go as high as 50,000km (31,000 miles).

Most sections of the Great Wall visible north of Běijīng were reconstructed by the Míng dynasty (1368–1644) in an (ultimately vain) effort to defend against attack by Manchus and Mongols from the north. The four most easily visited sections are **Bādálǐng, Mùtiányù, Jūyōngguǎn,** and the vertiginous **Sīmǎtái.**

Bādálǐng   The first section of the Great Wall opened to tourists, the portion at **Bādálǐng** remains the most popular. In 1957 it was fully restored to its original Míng appearance—although the reconstruction was sloppier than subsequent efforts at Mùtiányù, Jīnshānlǐng, and Sīmǎtái, where efforts were taken to preserve a sense of antiquity. Although it is one of the most dramatic sections of the Great Wall, the sheer number of visitors is overwhelming: You might not be able to see Bādálǐng from space, but there's some chance of smelling its toilets. Set in a steep, forested mountain range, it offers tremendous views and, for those willing to travel beyond the restored sections, some worthwhile hiking. The ticket office at Bādálǐng is open from 6:30am to 7pm. Admission is ¥45 ($6) in summer, ¥40 ($5) in winter; round-trip cable-car transportation is ¥50 ($6) per person.

Bādálǐng is roughly 70km (43 miles) northwest of Běijīng. **Group tours** organized through hotel travel desks are typically combined with a trip to the Míng Tombs and cost around ¥400 ($50) per person. A cheaper but still comfortable option is to take one of the air-conditioned, city-sponsored **tourist (yóu) buses** (© **010/6779-7546**): *Yóu* no. 1 leaves from the northeast side of Qián Mén (every 20 min.; 6am–noon), and *yóu* no. 2 leaves from Dōngzhí Mén and the Běijīng Railway Station (every 30 min.; 6:30–10am); both charge ¥50 ($6), a price that includes Jūyōngguǎn (see below) and the Míng Tombs. The cheapest way to get to Bādálǐng is on the red-and-yellow striped (air-conditioned) version of **bus no. 919** (6am–6pm; 1 hr.; ¥10/$1), which leaves from the east side of Déshèng Mén. A round-trip **taxi** should cost less than ¥300 ($38).

On the Wild Wall

Sections of the Great Wall listed below are easy to reach and suitably stunning, but they represent only a part of what the Wall has to offer. People with time and inclination to explore beyond these sections are strongly encouraged to join one of the excellent, usually multiday "Wild Wall" trips to the crumbling **"unofficial" sections of the Wall** that snake through more remote areas north of Běijīng. Most weekend trips cost around ¥1,600 ($200) and are based at one of two **modernized farmhouses** (one better outfitted than the other). The fee includes guided hikes, accommodations, and excellent home cooking (transportation to the farmhouse is an extra $65). Details and booking information about weekend trips, day hikes, and "Extreme" treks can be found on the Wild Wall website at **www.wildwall.com.**

Mùtiányù The Great Wall at Bādálǐng proved so popular that authorities restored a second section of the Wall to the east in 1986. Mùtiányù is a bit rougher and slightly less crowded than Bādálǐng, but it does have its own traffic jams in summer. As at Bādálǐng, cable-car transportation is available. Sadly, a fence prevents you from walking onto the tempting unrestored sections. The ticket office is open 24 hours. Admission is ¥35 ($4) and the cable car costs ¥50 ($6) round-trip.

Mùtiányù is 90km (56 miles) north of Běijīng, and somewhat harder to reach. Once again, most hotels can arrange **guided group tours** for around ¥250 ($31). The *yóu* no. 6 combines the trip to Mùtiányù with visits to a temple and a lake for ¥50 ($6); it leaves from the northeast side of the Xuānwǔ Mén metro station every 30 minutes from 6:30 to 8am. A **taxi** will cost between ¥350 ($43).

Tip: In a quiet river valley close to Mùtiányù lies Běijīng's most appealing Great Wall resort, **Red Capital Ranch** ✿✿ (© 010/8401-8886); ¥1,520/$190 including breakfast, plus 15% service charge; Apr–Nov). Similar to its sister property, Red Capital Residence (p. 91), all 10 rooms are decorated with antique furnishings. Fishing, bike riding, hiking on the Wall, and even a Tibetan essential oil massage are offered. A shuttle connects with the Red Capital Residence.

Jūyōngguān This is the most recently restored section of the Great Wall, and the closest to Běijīng (55km/34 miles northwest, on the road to Bādálǐng). The restoration is crisp and the sense of history rather distant. But there are fewer tour groups here, and a number of impressive Buddhist bas-relief carvings on the separate and genuinely old Yún Tái (Cloud Platform) built in 1342. The ticket office is open from 8am to dusk. Admission is ¥40 ($5) in summer, ¥35 ($4.40) in winter.

The **tourist** *(yóu)* and **public buses** that go to Bādálǐng also stop here. A round-trip **taxi** ride should cost less than ¥300 ($27).

Sīmǎtái ✿✿ Somewhat tamed after a series of deaths led to the closing of its most dangerous stretch, Sīmǎtái nevertheless remains one of the best options for those who want more of a challenge from the Great Wall. The most harrowing portion, steep and unrestored, is on the east side of the Mìyún Reservoir. Several gravel-strewn spots here require all four limbs to navigate. The endpoint is Wàngjīng Tǎ, the 12th watchtower from the bottom. Beyond this is the appropriately named **Tiān Qiáo (Heavenly Bridge),** a thin, tilted ridge where the Wall narrows to only a few feet—this section is now off-limits. Despite the danger, this part of the Wall can get crowded on weekends, especially since the cable car was installed. Souvenir vendors can also be a nuisance. The round-trip hike to Tiān Qiáo takes roughly 3 hours at a moderate pace. The section of Sīmǎtái west of the reservoir is better restored (in the beginning at least) and connects to another section of the Great Wall, Jīnshānlǐng, in Héběi Province. The ticket office is in a small village 10 minutes' walk south of the reservoir; it's open from 8am to 10pm in summer (8am–6pm in winter). Admission is ¥30 ($4). The cable car runs only from April to November; a round-trip ride to the No. 8 Tower costs ¥50 ($6).

Sīmǎtái is 110km (68 miles) northeast of Běijīng. The best no-hassle option is to go there with one of the **Youth Hostel** tours (© 010/8188-9323). These tours typically leave the Běijīng's YHAs between 7am and 8am and cost ¥90 ($11) for simple transportation. The *yóu* no. 12 travels to Sīmǎtái from northeast of the Xuānwǔ Mén (206) metro stop (Apr to mid-Oct Sat–Sun 6:30–8:30am, every 30 min; ¥70/$9); you get about 3 hours at the site. A round-trip **taxi** ride should cost less than ¥400 ($50).

Responding to the popularity of the Jīnshānlǐng to Sīmǎtái hike (see above), the **Sīmǎtái YHA** (© 010/8188-9323; standard room ¥260/$33) opened in 2004.

A Great Hike on the Great Wall

Jīnshānlǐng ✿✿✿ (© 010/8402-4647; ¥30/$4) is one of the all-time Great Wall hikes. It's not as steep as Sīmátái and is more heavily restored, but with fewer visitors. The hike from here east to the Mìyún Reservoir is roughly 10km (6 miles) and takes 3 to 4 hours. The middle part of the hike, as the people fall away and the Wall begins to crumble, can be truly sublime. A number of hostels provide transportation for this hike. Otherwise, you can take an air-conditioned bus from the Xī Zhí Mén long-distance bus station to Mìyún (every 30 min.; 6am–4pm; ¥15/$2), then hire a minivan *(miàndī)* to drop you off at Jīnshānlǐng and pick you up at Sīmátái for around ¥100 ($13)—make sure you withhold payment until after you're picked up.

Courtyard-style rooms are basic, but the coffee is superb, and the view of the Wall from the patio is wonderful.

OTHER SIGHTS OUTSIDE BĚIJĪNG
THE MÍNG TOMBS

Of the 16 emperors who ruled China during the Míng dynasty (1368–1644), 13 are buried in this valley north of Běijīng (hence the Chinese name Shísān Líng, the 13 Tombs). The Yǒnglè emperor, who also oversaw construction of the Forbidden City, consulted geomancers before choosing this site, considered advantageous because it is bounded to the north by a range of protective mountains. The geography of the valley is mirrored in the tombs themselves, with each emperor buried beneath a tumulus protected from the rear by a mountain. Only three of the Míng Tombs—**Dìng Líng**, **Cháng Líng**, and **Zhāo Líng**—have been restored, and only one (Dìng Líng) has been fully excavated. Many of the buildings mirror Míng palaces found in the city. Because of this, the sight can be boring to people who've already had their fill of imperial architecture. However, several attractions, particularly the **Shén Dào (Spirit Way)**, make the trip worthwhile for those who have the time.

The valley is 48km (30 miles) north of Běijīng, on the same road that goes to Bādálǐng. Many **tours** to Bādálǐng also come here, but if you want time to explore some of the unrestored tombs (highly recommended), you'll have to make a separate trip. A **taxi** hired in Běijīng should cost less than ¥400 ($50). The most comfortable form of public transport is the air-conditioned **bus no. 845** from Xī Zhí Mén (a 10-min. walk south of the metro station) to Zhèngfǎ Dàxué in Chāngpíng (1½ hr.; ¥9/$1). Then cross the street and take bus no. 314 to the Dà Gōng Mén stop (15 min; ¥1/15¢). It is also possible to take the green-and-white *zhī* (express) version of **bus no. 919** to Zhèngfǎ Dàxué from Déshèng Mén (1 hr.; ¥4/50¢).

Shén Dào (Spirit Way) ✿ The main entrance to the valley is the **Dà Hóng Mén (Great Red Gate)**, remarkably similar to gates found in the Forbidden City, beyond which is a pavilion housing China's largest memorial stele, and beyond that the Spirit Way. The path, slightly curved to fool evil spirits, is lined on either side with willows and remarkable **carved stone animals** and human figures, considered among the best in China and far better than those found at the Qīng Tombs. Not be missed.

Ticket office north of stele pavilion. Admission ¥30 ($4) in summer, ¥20 ($3) in winter. 8am–6pm (to 5:30pm in winter). Simple bilingual maps available here for ¥3 (40¢).

Cháng Líng   This tomb, home to the remains of the Yǒnglè emperor, is the largest and best preserved of the 13. It is essentially a Forbidden City in miniature, and perhaps disappointing if you've seen the palace already. Most striking is the **Líng'ēn Diàn,** an immense hall in which the interior columns and brackets have been left unpainted, creating an eye-catching contrast with the green ceiling panels.

4km (2½ miles) due north of the Shén Dào. Admission ¥45 ($6) summer, ¥30 ($4) winter. 7am–4:30pm. Bus: no. 314 or 22 to Cháng Líng stop from lighted intersection just beyond north end of Spirit Way.

Dìng Líng   The 4,000-sq.-m (13,000-sq.-ft.) **Underground Palace** discovered here in 1956 was the burial place of the Wànlì emperor, his wife, and his favorite concubine. The "palace" is a plain marble vault, buried 27m (88 ft.) underground and divided into five large chambers. It's all a bit disappointing. The corpses have been removed, their red coffins replaced with replicas, and burial objects moved to aboveground display rooms. The original marble thrones are still here, though, now covered in a small fortune of *rénmínbì* notes tossed by Chinese visitors in hopes of bribing the emperor's ghost. Outside, behind the ticket office, is the respectable **Shísān Líng Bówùguǎn (Míng Tombs Museum).**

Admission ¥60/$7.50 summer, ¥40/$5 winter; 8:30am–5pm. On west side of valley; walk south from Cháng Líng, take 1st right, and walk west 20 min.

EASTERN QĪNG TOMBS ✦✦

The Qīng Dōng Líng have been open for more than 20 years but they are still little visited, despite offering considerably more to visitors than those of the Míng. Altogether, five emperors, 15 empresses, 136 concubines, three princes, and two princesses are buried in 15 tombs here. The first to be buried was Shùnzhì—the first Qīng emperor to reign from Běijīng—in 1663, and the last was an imperial concubine in 1935. The tomb chambers of four imperial tombs, the **Xiào Líng** (the Shùnzhì emperor), **Jǐng Líng** (Kāngxī), **Yù Líng** (Qiánlóng), and **Dìng Líng** (Xiánfēng), are open, as well as the twin **Dìng Dōng Líng** tombs (the Cíxǐ dowager empress and the Cí'ān empress). Also of interest is a group site for the Qiánlóng emperor's concubines.

The tombs are in Zūnhuà County, Héběi Province, 125km (78 miles) east of Běijīng. They are open from 8am to 5:30pm in summer, 9am to 4:30pm in winter. The *tōng piào,* which offers access to all the tombs, costs ¥90 ($11). A special Qīng Dōng Líng tourist bus leaves at 7:30am from northeast of the Xuānwǔ Mén (206) metro stop and allows you about 3 hours on-site before beginning the return journey If you want to explore at your own pace, you'll have to hire a cab or take a rickety local bus to Zūnhuà. The local bus is found just east of the Dàwàng Lù (123) metro station (exit C) (6:30am–4:30pm; 3½ hr.; ¥24/$3). After you get off the bus, hire a *miàndì* (minivan) to take you the rest of the way for about ¥20 ($3). An assortment of three-wheelers will offer their services to take you around the site, with an initial asking price of ¥10 ($1.25).

The **Xiào Líng** was the first tomb on the site, and a model for others both here and at the Western Qīng Tombs, although few others are so elaborate. Each tomb has an approach road or Spirit Way, which may have guardian figures. The entrance to the tomb itself is usually preceded by a large stele pavilion and marble bridges over a stream. To the right, the buildings used for preparation of sacrifices are now usually the residences of the staff, and hung with washing. Inside the gate, halls to the left and right were for enrobing and other preparations, and now house exhibitions, as usually does each **Hall of Eminent Favor,** at the rear, where ceremonies in honor of the deceased took place. Behind, if open, a doorway allows access past a stone altar to a steep ramp leading to the base of a **soul tower.** Through a passageway beneath, stairs to either side lead to a walkway encircling the mound, giving views across the countryside. If the tomb chamber is open, a ramp from beneath the soul tower leads down to a series of chambers.

The twin **Dìng Dōng Líng** tombs have nearly identical exteriors, but empress dowager Cíxǐ had hers rebuilt in 1895, 14 years after empress Cí'ān's death (in which she is suspected of having had a hand), using far more expensive materials. Everywhere are reminders of the Forbidden City, such as the terrace-corner spouts carved as water-loving dragons *(chē).* The interior has motifs strikingly painted in gold on dark wood, recalling the buildings where the empress spent her last years. There are walls of carved and gilded brick, and columns writhing with superbly fearsome wooden dragons. After this, the other tombs seem gaudy.

The enclosure of the **Yù Fēi Yuán Qǐn (Garden of Rest)** contains moss-covered tumuli for 35 of the Qiánlóng emperor's concubines. Another is buried in a proper tomb chamber, along with an empress whom Qiánlóng had grown to dislike.

The **Yù Líng** has the finest tomb chamber, a series of rooms separated by solid marble doors, with walls and arched ceilings engraved with Buddha figures and more than 30,000 words of Tibetan scripture. The 3-ton doors themselves have reliefs of bodhisattvas (beings on the road to enlightenment) and the four protective kings usually found at temple entrances. This tomb is worth the trip in its own right. The **Jǐng Líng** is the tomb of Qiánlóng's grandfather, the Kāngxī emperor. It's surprisingly modest given that he was possibly the greatest emperor the Chinese ever had, but that's in keeping with what is known of his character. The Spirit Way leading to the tomb has an elegant five-arch bridge; the guardian figures are placed at an unusual curve in the way, quite close to the tomb itself, and are more decorated than those at earlier tombs.

WESTERN QĪNG TOMBS ★★

The Yōngzhèng emperor broke with tradition and ordered his tomb to be constructed here, away from his father (the Kāngxī emperor). His son, the Qiánlóng emperor, decided to be buried near his grandfather and that thereafter burials should alternate between the eastern (see above) and western sites, although this was not followed consistently. The first tomb, the **Tài Líng,** was completed in 1737, 2 years after the Yōngzhèng reign. The last imperial interment was in 1998, when the ashes of Aisin-Gioro Henry Pǔyí, the last emperor, were moved to a commercial cemetery here. He and two consorts were added to four emperors, four empresses, four princes, two princesses, and 57 concubines. The site is rural, with the tombs lapped by orchards and agriculture, and with chickens, goats, and the odd rabbit to be encountered.

Chāng Líng (the Jiāqìng emperor's tomb), and **Chóng Líng** (Guāngxù) are also open, as well as **Chāng Xī Líng,** with the extraordinary sonic effects of its **Huíyīn Bì**—an echo wall where, as the only visitors, you'll actually be able to try out the special effects available only in theory at the Temple of Heaven.

The **Qīng Xī Líng** are located 140km (87 miles) southwest of Bĕijīng, outside Yì Xiàn in Hébĕi Province. The ticket office is open from 8am to 5pm; a *tōng piào* (good for access to all the tombs) costs ¥90 ($11) and is good for 2 days. There's no access by tourist bus, but that is part of the appeal for most visitors. To get there, take a bus to Yì Xiàn from the Lìzé Qiáo long-distance bus station (departs every 15 min, 6:50am–5pm; 3 hr.; ¥20/$3; last bus returns at 4pm.). Then switch to a minivan *(miàndī)* for the 15km (9-mile) ride to the tombs; the fare is around ¥20 ($3). Unless you make a very early start, you may want to spend the night at the modest, Manchu-themed **Bā Jiǎo Lóu Mǎnzú Zhuāngyuán,** just east of Tài Líng (© **0312/826-0828; ¥100/$13 standard room). Xíng Gōng Bīnguǎn,** near Yǒngfú Sì on the eastern side of the tomb complex (© **0312/471-0038;** standard room ¥150/$19 after discount), was where Manchu rulers stayed when they came to pay their respects, and the room constructed in 1748 to house the Qiánlóng emperor is now rented out as two suites (¥660/$82 after discount).

The **Dà Bēi Lóu,** a pavilion containing two vast stelae, is on the curved route to the **Tài Líng.** The general plan of the major tombs follows that of the Eastern Tombs, above. In fact, the **Chāng Líng,** slightly to the west, is almost identical, brick for brick, to the Tài Líng, although the rear section with soul tower and tomb mound is not open. The Jiāqìng empress is buried just to the west in the **Chāng Xī Líng,** on a far smaller scale, the tomb mound a brick drum. But the perfectly semicircular rear wall offers the whispering-gallery effects found at some domed European cathedrals; clapping while standing on marked stones at the center of the site produces multiple echoes, while speech is amazingly amplified. The empress can't get much peace.

Jiāqìng's son, the Dàoguāng emperor, was meant to be buried at Qīng Dōng Líng, but his tomb there was flooded. The relocated **Mù Líng** appears much more modest than those of his predecessors. No stele pavilion or Spirit Way, largely unpainted, and the tomb mound is a modest brick-wall drum, but this is the most expensive tomb: wood used to construct the exquisite main hall is fragrant *nánmù,* sourced from as far away as Myanmar. The Guǎngxù emperor was the last to complete his reign (although his aunt, Cíxǐ, is again suspected of shortening it), and his **Chóng Líng,** which uses more modern materials than other tombs, wasn't completed until 1915, well after the last emperor's abdication.

Several other tombs are open, and more are being restored. The recently opened **Tài Líng Fēi Yuán Qǐn** is a rather battered group of concubine tumuli, individually labeled with the years in which each concubine entered the Yōngzhèng emperor's service, and their grades in the complex harem hierarchy.

The ashes of **Pǔyí** (properly known as the Xuāntǒng emperor) lie buried on the eastern end of the site, up a slope behind a brand-new Qīng-style memorial arch *(páilóu),* and behind a shoddy modern carved balustrade. Neighboring plots are available for the right price.

WESTERN TEMPLES

Buried in the hills west of Běijīng, **Tánzhè Sì (Temple of the Pool and Wild Mulberry)** and **Jiètái Sì (Temple of the Ordination Platform)** are the tranquil kinds of Chinese temples people imagine before they actually come to China. Foreign travelers seldom visit them, but the effort to come out here is worth it, if only to escape the noise and dust of the city center.

Both are easily accessible by taking **bus no. 931** from the Píngguǒyuán metro station (103) at the far western end of Line 1. Take a right out of exit D and continue straight a few minutes to the bus station (be sure to take the plain red-and-beige, rather than the red-and-yellow *zhī,* version of the bus). Tánzhè Sì is the last stop on this line; the trip takes 1 hour and costs ¥2.50 (40¢). Basic but acceptable **accommodations** are available at both temples, for those who want (or need) to spend more time in quietude.

Tánzhè Sì 🐾🐾 This peaceful complex dates back to the Western Jìn dynasty (265–316), well before Běijīng was founded. In the main courtyard on the central axis is a pair of 30m (100-ft.) ginkgo trees, supposedly planted in the Táng dynasty (618–907), as well as several apricot trees, cypresses, peonies, and purple jade orchids. The **Guānyīn Diàn,** at the top of the western axis, was favored by Princess Miào Yán, a daughter of Kublai Khan; she is said to have prayed so fervently she left footprints in one of the floor stones (now stored in a box to the left).

48km (29 miles) west of Běijīng. Admission ¥35 ($4). 8am–5:30pm. Bus: no. 931. Get off at last stop and hike up stone path at end of parking lot.

Jiètái Sì 🐾 The **ordination platform** here, China's largest, is a three-tiered circular structure with 113 statues of the God of Ordination placed in niches around the base. It is located in the Jiètái Diàn, in the far-right corner of the temple. Ceremonies conducted on this platform to commemorate the ascension of a devotee to full monkhood required permission from the emperor. Other courtyards have ancient, twisted pines, as venerable as the temple itself.

13km (8 miles) east of Tánzhè Sì. Admission ¥35 ($4). 8am–6pm. Bus: no. 931 from Tánzhè Sì. The stop is marked with a huge sign pointing the way to the temple.

7 Shopping

Stores and markets in Běijīng sell everything from cashmere and silk to knockoff designer-label clothing to athletic wear, antiques, traditional art, cloisonné, lacquerware, Míng furniture, Máo memorabilia, and enough miscellaneous Chinesey doodads to stuff Christmas stockings from now until eternity. Prices are reasonable (certainly lower than in the Asian-goods boutiques back home), though increasingly less so. Cheap one-time-use luggage is widely available for hauling your booty if you get carried away.

Before you rush to the ATM, however, it is important to remember that not all that is green and gleams in Běijīng is jade. Indeed, the majority of it is colored glass. The same principle holds for pearls (see below), famous-brand clothing, antiques, and just about everything else. Shoppers who plan to make big purchases should educate themselves about quality and price well beforehand.

You should also be leery of any English-speaking youngsters who claim to be **art students** and offer to take you to a special exhibit of their work. This is a scam. The art, which you will be compelled to buy, almost always consists of assembly-line reproductions of famous (or not-so-famous) paintings offered at prices several dozen times higher than their actual value.

TOP SHOPPING AREAS

The grandest shopping area in Běijīng is on and around **Wángfǔjǐng Dàjiē,** east of the Forbidden City. The street was overhauled in 1999, the south section turned into a pedestrian-only commercial avenue lined with shops, fast-food restaurants, and the city's top two malls—the Sun (Xīn) Dōng Ān Plaza and the Oriental Plaza (Dōngfāng Guǎngchǎng). **Dōng Dān Běi Dàjiē,** a long block east, is a strip of clothing boutiques and CD shops popular among fashionable Běijīng youth.

Other major Westernized shopping areas include the section of **Jiànguó Mén Wài Dàjiē** between the Friendship Store and the China World Trade Center, and the neighborhood outside the **Northeast Third Ring Road North,** southeast of Sānyuán Qiáo around the new embassy district.

Běijīng's liveliest shopping zone, the one most beloved of tourists for its atmosphere and Chinese-style goods, is the centuries-old commercial district southwest of Qián Mén. **Liúlichǎng** is an almost too-quaint collection of art, book, tea, and antiques shops lining a polished-for-tourists, Old Běijīng–style *hútòng* running east–west 2 blocks south of the Hépíng Mén (207) metro station. The street is good for window-shopping strolls and small purchases—like the unavoidable **chop** (*túzhāng;* stone or jade stamp), carved with your name—but beware large purchases: Almost everything here is fake and overpriced. In a similar setting but infinitely more raucous, **Dà Zhàlán** (pronounced Dà Shílànr in the Běijīng dialect) is the prole alternative to Wángfǔjǐng Dàjiē; located in a pedestrian-only *hútòng* 2 blocks due south of Qián Mén, it is jammed on either side with cheap clothing outlets, cheap restaurants, and cheap luggage shops.

MARKETS

Although malls and shopping centers are becoming more popular, the majority of Běijīng residents still shop in markets. Whether indoors or out, these markets are inexpensive, chaotic and, for the visitor, tremendously interesting. Payment is in cash, bargaining is universal, and pickpockets are plentiful.

Hóngqiáo Jímào Shìchǎng ✿ An outlet for cheap jewelry better known as the **Pearl Market,** Hóngqiáo Market is just northeast of the Temple of Heaven at Hóngqiáo Lù 16. The first floor smells awful (there's a seafood market in the basement), but the upper floors have cheap Western clothing, luggage, old Chinese curios and, of course, pearls (third floor). The prices here are good and the bargaining fierce. The market is open from 8:30am to 7pm.

Pānjiāyuán Jiùhuò Shìchǎng ✿✿✿ Eureka! Also known as the Dirt or Ghost Market, this is the Chinese shopping experience of dreams: row upon crowded row of calligraphy, jewelry, ceramics, teapots, ethnic clothing, Buddha statues, paper lanterns, Cultural Revolution memorabilia, PLA belts, little wooden boxes, Míng- and Qīng-style furniture, old pipes, opium scales, and painted human skulls. There are some real

---

Tips Buying Pearls

Most of the pearls on sale at Hóngqiáo Market are genuine, although of too low a quality to be sold in Western jewelry shops, but there are some fakes floating around. To test if the pearls you want to buy are real, try any one of the following:

- Nick the surface with a sharp blade (the color should be uniform within and without)
- Rub the pearl across your teeth (this should make a grating sound)
- Scrape the pearl on a piece of glass (real pearls leave a mark)
- Pass it through a flame (fake pearls turn black, real ones don't)

Strange as it may feel to do these tests, vendors are generally willing to let you carry them out and might even help, albeit with bemused faces. If you'd rather not bother (and most don't), just assume the worst, shop for fun, and spend modestly.

antiques scattered among the junk, but you'd have to be an expert to pick them out. Locals arrive Saturday and Sunday mornings at dawn or shortly afterward (hence the "Ghost" label) to find the best stuff; vendors start to leave around 4pm. Initial prices given to foreigners are always absurdly high—Máo clocks, for instance, should cost less than ¥40 ($5) rather than the ¥400 ($50) you'll likely be asked to pay. The market is located on the south side of Pānjiāyuán Lù, just inside the southeast corner of the Third Ring Road.

Yǎxiù Fúzhuāng Shìchǎng ✦   Whatever you may think of their business practices, Běijīng's clothing vendors are nimble: Here you'll find refugees from two outdoor markets, Yǎbǎo Lù and Sānlǐtún. Opened in 2002, the market occupies the old Kylin Plaza building (Qílín Dàshà). The fourth floor is a fine hunting ground for souvenirs and gifts—there are kites from Wéifāng in Shāndōng, calligraphy materials, army surplus gear, tea sets, and farmer's paintings from Xī'ān. The basement and the first two floors house a predictable but comprehensive collection of imitation and pilfered brand-name clothing, shoes, and luggage. The market has been "discovered" by fashion-conscious locals, and starting prices are ridiculous. The market is west of Sānlǐtún Jiǔbā Jiē, at Gōngtǐ Běi Lù 58 (© 010/6415-1726), and is open from 9:30am to 8pm.

MORE MARKETS

Similar to the Yǎxiù but more fashionable and located outdoors is **Nǚrén Jiē (Girl Street),** next to the new embassy district outside the Northeast Third Ring Road (northeast of the Lufthansa Center). **Rì Tán Shāngwù Lóu** (© 010/8561-9556), at Guānghuá Lù 15A, (just east of the south gate of Rì Tán Park) is not as cheap as Yǎxiù, but is far less nasty. From outside, it looks like an uninspiring office building, inside is shopping nirvana: more than 70 shops stocking high-quality women's clothing, footwear, and accessories. There is a smattering of shops for the chaps, too. Open 10am till 8pm.

DEPARTMENT STORES

Friendship Store (Yǒuyì Shāngchǎng)   This is a dinosaur from the days when foreigners used a separate kind of money and couldn't shop anywhere else. Everything's here and everything's viciously overpriced. A good source of Western periodicals, the store is open from 9am to 8:30pm. Jiànguó Mén Dàjiē 17.

Xī Dān Bǎihuò Shāngchǎng   Crowded and chaotic, this is an old-school four-story department store selling everything from cosmetics to appliances, with good deals on denim and shoes. Open 9am to 8pm. East side of Xī Dān Běi Dàjiē (north of Xī Dān metro stop).

MALLS & SHOPPING PLAZAS

Lufthansa Center (Yānshā Yǒuyì Shāngchǎng)   Connected to the Kempinski Hotel, this is the most comprehensive but also most expensive shopping center in northeast Běijīng (open 9am–8:30pm), with a range of upscale specialty shops, boutiques, restaurants, and international airline ticketing offices. Liàngmǎ Qiáo Lù 50 (east side of the Northeast Third Ring Rd.).

Oriental Plaza (Dōngfāng Guǎngchǎng)   Asia's largest shopping/office/apartment/hotel complex covers 4 city blocks of prime real estate from Wángfǔjǐng Dàjiē to Dōng Dān Běi Dàjiē. Offering fun for the kids are a Sony ExploraScience museum, Starbucks, McDonald's, and more. Hours are from 9am to 10pm. Dōng Cháng'ān Dàjiē. Metro: Wángfǔjǐng (118).

Sun Dong An Plaza (Xīn Dōng'ān Shìchǎng)   Běijīng's most successful mall is one of its most fully stocked. The "Old Běijīng Street" in the basement is a cheap ploy to overcharge tourists. Open Monday through Thursday from 9am to 9pm; Friday through Sunday from 9am to 10pm. Wángfǔjǐng Dàjiē 138.

8 Běijīng After Dark

It wasn't so long ago that the after-dark options available to foreigners in Běijīng were limited to a short list of tourist-approved activities: Běijīng opera, acrobatics, and wandering listlessly around the hotel in search of a drink to make sleep come faster. Now opera and acrobatics are still available, but in more interesting venues, and to them have been added a range of other worthwhile cultural events: teahouse theater, puppet shows, traditional music concerts, and even the occasional subtitled film. Beyond such edification, Běijīng has China's most diverse stable of bars, clubs, discos, and cafes, cheaper and often more interesting than those of Hong Kong or Shànghǎi. For locations, see the map on p. 86.

PERFORMING ARTS
BĚIJĪNG OPERA

A relatively young opera form dating back only 300 years to the early Qīng dynasty, Běijīng Opera (Jīngjù) dazzles as much as it grates. Performances are loud and long, with dialogue sung on a screeching five-note scale and accompanied by a cacophony of gongs, cymbals, drums, and strings. This leaves most first-timers exhausted, but the exquisite costumes, elaborate face paint, and martial arts–inspired movements ultimately make it worthwhile. Several theaters now offer shortened programs more amenable to the foreign attention span, sometimes with English subtitles and plot summaries.

Most tourists on tours are taken to the bland, cinema-style **Líyuán Theater (Líyuán Jùchǎng)** inside the Qián Mén Hotel, where nightly performances at 7:30pm cost ¥30 to ¥200 ($3–$25). The venues below offer essentially the same performances in much better traditional settings.

Húguǎng Guild House (Húguǎng Huìguǎn Xìlóu)   This combination museum-theater was originally built in 1807. The theater is a riot of color, with a beautifully adorned traditional stage and gallery seating. It is currently Běijīng's best opera venue. Nightly performances take place at 7:30pm. Hǔfáng Lù 3, at intersection with Luomashì Dàjiē. © 010/6351-8284. Tickets ¥150–¥580 ($19–$72). Metro: Hépíng Mén (207, exit D1); walk south 10 min.

Zhèngyǐcí Xìlóu   Rumors that this 300-year-old theater had gone under are untrue, but funding problems and its position at the center of a massive urban reconstruction project have limited the number of performances. The theater is similar to the Húguǎng Guild House but less ostentatious, with a more local feel. Shows are held most nights at 7:30pm (call to check). This is the first choice of venue for Běijīng Opera when it's open. Pray it survives. Qián Mén Xī Héyán Jiē 220 (walk south of the Hépíng Mén Quánjùdé, take 1st left). © 010/8315-1650. Tickets ¥150–¥280 ($19–$35). Metro: Hépíng Mén (207, exit C2).

ACROBATICS

China's acrobats are justifiably famous, and probably just a little bit insane. This was the only traditional Chinese art form to receive Máo's explicit approval (back flips, apparently, don't count as counterrevolution). Not culturally stimulating, it's highly recommended nonetheless.

The city's best acrobatics venue is the **Wànshèng Jùchǎng** on the north side of Běi Wěi Lù, just off Qián Mén Dàjiē (west side of the Temple of Heaven; ✆ **010/6303-7449**). The fairly famous Běijīng Acrobatics Troupe performs nightly shows here at 7:15pm. Tickets cost ¥100 to ¥200 ($12–$25). The acrobats of **Cháoyáng Jùchǎng** (✆ **010/6507-2421**) at Dōng Sān Huán Běi Lù 36 are slightly clumsier. Nightly shows at 7:15pm cost ¥120 to ¥300 ($15–$37).

TEAHOUSE THEATER

Snippets of Běijīng opera, cross-talk (stand-up) comedy, acrobatics, traditional music, singing, and dancing flow across the stage as you sip tea and nibble snacks. If you don't have time to see these kinds of performances individually, the teahouse is a perfect solution.

Lǎo Shě Teahouse (Lǎo Shě Cháguǎn)   Performances change nightly at this somewhat garishly decorated teahouse but always include opera and acrobatics. It pays to buy the more expensive tickets, as rear views are obscured. Nightly shows take place at 7:50pm. Qiánmén Xī Dàjiē 3, west of Qián Mén on street's south side. ✆ 010/6303-6830. Tickets ¥40–¥130 ($5–$16).

PUPPETS

Puppet shows (*mù ǒu xì*) have been performed in China since the Hàn dynasty (206 B.C.–A.D. 220). Most theatrical performances, including weekend matinees, are held at the **China Puppet Art Theater (Zhōngguó Mù'ǒu Jùyuàn)**, in Ānhuá Xīlǐ near the North Third Ring Road (✆ **010/6424-3698**). Tickets cost ¥20 to ¥25 ($2–$3).

SMALL LIVE-MUSIC VENUES

CD Jazz Cafe (Sēndì Juéshì)   After much upheaval, this amalgamation of CD Cafe and the short-lived Treelounge is the best place to see local jazz and blues acts in Běijīng. If it's a special act, get there early. Open 4pm till very late. Dōng Sān Huán, south of the Agricultural Exhibition Center (Nóngzhǎn Guǎn) main gate (down small path behind trees that line sidewalk). ✆ 010/6506-8288. Cover ¥30 ($4).

The Icehouse (Kù Bīng)   Set in a warehouse that once stored the ice for the Forbidden City, Icehouse is the "B" in RBL (p. 99). Currently, a respectable blues band from Australia headlines, and the proprietors have the means to attract top-notch international acts. Open 6pm till 2am. Dōng'ān Mén Dàjiē Xīpèi Lóu 53 (connected to RBL by an underground passageway). ✆ 010/6522-1389.

New Get Lucky Bar (Xīn Háoyùn Jiǔbā)   This odd bar is the best venue to take in one of Běijīng's much-documented punk shows, often featuring the talents of Brain Failure and Hanging on the Box. If you value your eardrums, don't get too close to the speakers. In Nǚrén Jiē area, inside Oriental Qīcǎi World. ✆ 010/8448-3335. Shows ¥20–¥30 ($3–$4).

Sānwèi Bookstore (Sānwèi Shūwū)   This tiny bookshop has a teahouse upstairs that hosts intimate concerts on the weekends. On Friday it's jazz and on Saturday it's classical Chinese, usually with a minority twist. Tea and snacks, too. Performances are held at 8:30pm. Fùxīng Mén Nèi Dàjiē 60, opposite the Minorities Palace (Mínzú Gōng). ✆ 010/6601-3204. Tickets ¥30 ($4).

Yú Gōng Yí Shān   This wonderful performance space is the best live music venue in Běijīng, period. The sound isn't perfect, it can get plenty stuffy in summer, and its location in the middle of a parking lot–cum–bus depot lends it a certain seediness, but the owners have a knack for turning up the best local acts. Run by the owners of the now defunct Loup Chante, the diverse lineup—from punk to Mongolian mouth music—means you can visit night after night. It's open from 2pm to 2am. Gōngtǐ Běi Lù 1, just north of the Bus Bar. ✆ 010/6415-0687. Cover varies for performances.

OTHER PERFORMING-ARTS VENUES

Běijīng hosts a growing number of international music and theater events every year, and its own increasingly respectable troupes—including the Běijīng Symphony Orchestra—give frequent performances. Among the most popular venues for this sort of thing is the **Běijīng Concert Hall (Běijīng Yīnyuè Tīng;** ✆ 010/6605-5812), at Běi Xīnhuá Jiē in Liùbùkǒu (Xuānwǔ District). For information on other venues and the shows they're hosting, check one of the expatriate magazines (see "Visitor Information," at the beginning of this chapter).

BARS & CLUBS

Běijīng's oldest and still most popular drinking district is **Sānlǐtún.** The name comes from Sānlǐtún Lù, a north–south strip of drinking establishments east of the Workers' Stadium between the East Second and Third ring roads that at one time contained practically all of the city's bars. Now known as North Bar Street (Sānlǐtún Jiǔbā Jiē), it has been joined by other bars in the Xīngfú Cūn area to the west, and scattered around the stadium area. Bars here are rowdy and raunchy, and are packed to overflowing on weekends.

Popular clubs in this district include the very proud **Destination (Mùdìdì),** located in an alley south of the west gate of the Workers' Stadium (✆ 010/6416-1077 or 010/6417-7791); and **The Den (Dūnhuáng;** ✆ 010/6592-6290), at the intersection of Gōngtǐ Dōng Lù 4A, next to the City Hotel (Chéngshì Bīnguǎn). Bars include the sports bar **ClubFootball (Wànguó Qúnxīng Zúqiú),** Chūnxiù Lù 10, attached to the Red House (✆ 010/6417-0497); **The Tree (Yǐnbì de Shù),** with the city's best selection of Belgian beer, located west of North Bar Street, behind the eminently missable Poachers (✆ 010/6415-1954); the classy **First Cafe (Dìyī Kāfēi),** which produces the city's finest martinis, found on Nán Sānlǐtún Lù, 100m (330 ft.) south of the giant beer mug, on the east side of the street (✆ 010/6501-8812).

Similar bars surround the south and west gates of **Cháoyáng Gōngyuán** (park) to the east, an area the government has tried to promote as the new drinking district because it has fewer residential buildings. Worth checking out are Souk (✆ 010/6506-7309), with excellent Middle Eastern cuisine and fruity hookas to puff on, located just behind Annie's Café; and the seedy **World of Suzie Wong (Sūxī Huáng),** the see-and-be-seen venue for nouveau riche Chinese and new expatriates. It's located just south of the west gate of Cháoyáng Park (above Mirch Masala; ✆ 010/6593-6049).

The fastest-growing spot for late-night drinking is the **Back Lakes (Shíchà Hǎi or Hòu Hǎi),** a previously serene spot with a few discreetly fashionable bars which now threatens to explode into a riot of hip. Neon has become a common sight, and several dance clubs are in the works, but for now this remains the finest place in the city for a quiet drink. Good bars here include supercool **Bed (Chuáng Bā),** where you can enjoy an excellent caipirinha or mojito in a delightful courtyard setting, at Zhāngwàng Hútòng 17, northwest of the Drum Tower (✆ 010/8400-1554); and **Pass-by Bar (Guòkè Jiǔbā),** which also serves good Italian food, at Nán Luógǔ Xiàng 108 (alley to the left/west of the Muslim restaurant on the north side of Píng'ān Dàdào; walk north 150m/492 ft.; ✆ 010/8403-8004). Finally, there is **Hǎidiàn,** the city's university district to the northwest. Bars and clubs are congregated around gates of several universities and cater to a crowd of film students, English-language majoi ing writers.

Outside of the districts, one club worth checking out is **Banana (Bānàna)**, jiangue Mén Wài Dàjiē 22, in front of Scitech Hotel (© **010/6528-3636**).

GAY & LESBIAN BARS

Běijīng is a quiet scene for lesbians, somewhat less so for gay men. The first openly gay club in Běijīng is the recently opened **Club 70** (© **010/6508-9799**) at Cháoyáng Gōngyuán Xī Mén, ironically right by the ultimate heterosexual meat market, Suzie Wong's (see "Bars & Clubs," above). The beats are about right, but it's still in search of a comfortable vibe, a problem you won't face at **Destination. On/Off** (Shàng Xià Xiàn; © **010/6415-8083**), at Xìngfú Yī Cūn Xī Lǐ 5, is one of Běijīng's longest standing "alternative" venues. Things have turned a tad seedy in recent times, but the crowds still flock to this venue, which now boasts a bar, a restaurant, and even an Internet cafe. For the gals, it's a slow-developing scene: Aside from Thursday nights at Destination, try the Fēng Bar, just east of the south gate of the Worker's Stadium on Saturday nights.

CAFES & TEAHOUSES

Starbucks arrived at the end of the 1990s and quickly spread to all the places Běijīng's wealthy and/or hip congregate, including next to the Friendship Store, in the China World Trade Center, at the Oriental Plaza and, yes, inside the Forbidden City. More interesting alternatives include, **Tasty Taste (Tàidí Dàisī)** at Gōngtǐ Běi Mén on the southwest corner of Gōngtǐ Běi Lù and Gōngtǐ Xī Lù, which delivers the finest coffee in town and a fine cheesecake to go with it (© **010/6551-1822**); or the more stylishly decorated **Café de Niro (Nílóu Kāfēi)** at Sānlǐtún Jiǔbā Běi Jiē Tónglǐ Yī Céng, just west of Sānlǐtún North Bar Street (and north of Aperitivo), which also has wireless Internet and reasonably priced set lunches (© **010/6416-9400**). The best spot to curl up with a book for the afternoon is **The Bookworm,** whose library of 6,000 English-language books was relocating to new premises just east of Nán Sānlǐtún Lù at press time (© **010/6586-9507**). **Sculpting in Time (Diāokè Shíguāng),** Běijīng's original cafe/film establishment, is now at the Běijīng Institute of Technology (Wèigōngcūn Xī Kǒu 7 [Lǐgōng Dàxué Nán Mén]; © **010/6894-6825; 9am–1am**), just to the left of the university's south gate. A second branch is in the Western Hills (© **010/8529-0040**), south of Fragrant Hills Park. **The Teahouse of Family Fù (Chá Jiā Fù),** located at Hòu Hǎi Nán Àn, next to Kǒng Yǐjǐ (© **010/6616-0725**), is a unique and quiet teahouse, with semiprivate rooms. It's open from 11am to midnight.

9 Chéngdé ⋆⋆

Héběi Province, 233km (146 miles) NE of Běijīng

If you can do only one overnight side trip from Běijīng, make it Chéngdé—the summer camp of the Qīng emperors. Here, in a walled enclosure containing numerous palaces, pavilions, and pagodas as well as a vast hunting park, they escaped Běijīng's blazing summer temperatures, entertained delegations from home and abroad, and practiced the mounted military skills which had originally gained them their empire. The design of the resort, built between 1703 and 1794, was shaped by its varied diplomatic functions. Some buildings are plain and undecorated to show visiting tribesmen that the emperors had not lost touch with their roots or been too softened by luxury;

others were copies of some of China's most famous and elegant buildings; and some were giant edifices with hints of minority architecture, intended both to show the emperor's sympathy for the traditions of tributary and border-dwelling peoples, and to overawe their emissaries.

In 1794 Britain's Lord Macartney arrived on a mission from George III, and not finding the Qiánlóng emperor at home in Běijīng, followed him up to Chéngdé. He was impressed by the resort's vast scale, and was shown around by people who anticipated modern guides' hyperbole by telling him that the gilded bronze roof tiles of the Potala Temple were of solid gold.

The Jiāqìng emperor died here in 1820, as did the Xiánfēng emperor in 1861, having signed the "unequal" treaties which marked the close of the Second Opium War. The place came to be viewed as unlucky, and was already decaying by the fall of the Qīng in 1911. But the **Mountain Retreat for Escaping the Heat,** along with the remaining **Eight Outer Temples** around its perimeter, still form one of the greatest concentrations of ancient buildings in China. It's an 18th-century version of a "Splendid China" theme park (as seen in Florida and Shēnzhèn), but with oversize buildings rather than the miniatures offered there.

Ordinary Běijīngrén now follow imperial tradition by flocking here to escape the baking summer heat. You can hurry around the main sights by spending 1 night here, but you might want to spend 2.

ESSENTIALS

GETTING THERE   Chéngdé has no airport, and although it's an easy side trip from Běijīng, it's not well-connected to anywhere else except the northeast. A convenient morning all-seater **train** from Běijīng Zhàn, the N211, departs at 7:20am, arriving in Chéngdé at 11:18am. It returns to Běijīng as the N212, leaving Chéngdé at 2:40pm, arriving in Běijīng at 6:38pm. Soft seat costs ¥61 ($7.60), hard seat ¥41 ($5.10). The railway station is just south of the city center, and bus no. 5 from outside to your right runs to several hotels and to the Mountain Resort. The ticket office (up the stairs and to the right) is open from 5am to 10:50pm with brief breaks. There are also limited services to Shěnyáng and Shíjiāzhuāng.

The soft-seat waiting room is through a door at the far left-hand end of the main hall as you enter, while luggage storage is on the right-hand side. On the train both to and from Běijīng, enterprising staff sell tea for ¥3 (40¢), instant coffee for ¥5 (65¢), maps, and hotel reservations (do *not* book with them). About 1¼ hours after you leave Běijīng, you'll see a crumbling stretch of the Great Wall.

At least until construction of a new road/rail interchange station at Dōngzhí Mén is complete, **bus** departures for Chéngdé from Běijīng are more frequent from Xī Zhí Mén. The 233km (144-mile) trip costs ¥46 ($5.75) for an Iveco or similar, with departures about every 20 minutes from 6am to 5:30pm. The current journey takes about 3½ hours, but a new highway (due for completion in 2007) should cut journey times to around 2½ hours, while increasing prices. At the moment it's possible to alight and see the Great Wall at Jīnshānlíng en route, and subsequently flag down a passing bus to finish the trip. Express buses from Běijīng run to and from the forecourt of Chéngdé railway station. Escape the pestering of touts by dodging into a branch of the Sìchuān restaurant Dōngpō Fànzhuāng, opposite and to the left (south) where you alight, and if you're ready for a quick lunch, have it here. The main long-distance bus station has been demolished to make way for an extension of the Shèng

Eight Outer Temples

Shuxiang Temple

Putuozongcheng Temple

Puning Temple

Puyou Temple

Shizi Gou Lu

Xumifushou Temple

Puning Si Lu

Chicheng Gong Lu

Northwest Gate

Anyuan Temple

Bei Xinglong Jie

Bus Station
Bank
Post Office
Rail Station
Police

MOUNTAIN RESORT FOR ESCAPING THE HEAT

He Dong Lu

Pule Temple

Shan Zhuang Dong Lu

Bifeng Gate

Palace

Dehui Men Gate

Xi Daijie

Lizheng Men Dajie

Qingfeng Dong Jie

Dong Dajie

Wulie Lu

Yingzi Dajie

Zhong Xing Lu

Xinhua Lu

Chezhan Lu

Chengde Station

ATTRACTIONS ●

Ānyuǎn Miào (Temple of Distant Peace) **6**
安远庙

Bìshǔ Shānhuāng (Mountain Resort for Escaping the Heat) **11**
避暑山庄

Pǔlè Sì (Temple of Universal Joy) **8**
普乐寺

Pǔníng Sì (Temple of Universal Peace) **3**
普宁寺

Pǔtuózōngchèng Zhī Miào (Potala Temple) **1**
普陀宗乘之庙

Pǔyòu Sì **4**
普佑寺

Qìngchuí Fēng (Hammer Rock) **7**
磬锤峰

Xūmífúshòu Miào (Temple of Happiness and Longevity at Mount Sumeru) **2**
须弥福寿庙

ACCOMMODATIONS ■ & DINING ◆

Dōngpō Fànzhuāng **15**
东坡饭庄

Pǔníng Sì Shàngkètáng Dàjiǔdiàn **5**
普宁寺上客堂大酒店

Qiányáng Dàjiǔdiàn **9**
乾阳大酒店

Qī Wàng Lóu Bīnguǎn **10**
绮望楼宾馆

Shānzhuāng Bīnguǎn (Mountain Villa Hotel) **12**
山庄宾馆

Shèng Huá Dàjiǔdiàn **14**
盛华大酒店

Xīn Qiánlóng Dàjiǔdiàn **13**
新乾隆大酒店

0   1 Mi
0   1 Km

To Bus Station (10km) ↘

Huá Dàjiŭdiàn, and most buses now depart from the **Qìchē Dōng Zhàn** (© **0341/ 212-3588**), a ¥20 ($2.50) taxi ride south, or take bus no. 118, which passes Yíngzi Dàjiē and the Mountain Resort. The ticket office is open from 5am to 10pm. There are four services to Shíjiāzhuāng (8 hr.; ¥80/$10), with seven buses connecting with Qínhuángdǎo (6 hr.; ¥65/$8). Buses to Běijīng run every 20 minutes, but it's easier to flag an Iveco from outside the railway station.

GETTING AROUND   **Taxi** meters are generally not used. The fare is ¥5 (65¢) in town, or ¥10 ($1.25) to the outer temples. If the meter is started, ¥5 (65¢) flagfall includes 1km; then ¥1.40 (20¢) per kilometer, jumping 50% after 8km (5 miles). **Buses** usually charge ¥1 (15¢).

VISITOR INFORMATION   For tourist complaints, call © **0341/202-4549.**

FAST FACTS

Banks, Foreign Exchange & ATMs   The main foreign exchange branch of the **Bank of China** (open 8am–noon and 2–5:30pm [to 6pm in summer]) is at the junction of Dōng Dàjiē and Lìzhèng Mén Dàjiē. Another convenient branch is at Lìzhèng Mén Dàjiē 19, just east of the Mountain Villa Hotel. Both have ATMs that accept foreign cards, as does a branch on the corner of Nán Yíngzi Dàjiē and Xīnhuá Lù.

Internet Access   Dial-up © **163** works, but Internet cafes are few and mostly far from the usual visitor areas. Follow Nán Yíngzi Dàjiē south until you cross the railway line, turn right into Shǎnxī Yíng to find a cluster of Internet bars (open 8am–midnight) on the first corner, which charge ¥1.50 (20¢) per hour.

Post Office   The post office is on Yíngzi Dàjiē at its junction with Dōng Dàjiē. It's open from 8am to 6:30pm (to 6pm in winter).

Visa Extensions   Walking south along Nán Yíngzi Dàjiē, turn right after the Xīnhuá Bookstore into Xiǎo Tóng Gōu Jiē, then take the first left. Next to a branch of CITS you'll find a sign that reads ALIENS EXIT-ENTRY DEPARTMENT. Open 9am to noon and 2:30 to 5pm.

RELAXING WITH THE EMPERORS

Bìshǔ Shānzhuāng (Mountain Resort for Escaping the Heat) ⚔   While the "Winter Palace," as Běijīng's Forbidden City was sometimes called, was the creation of the indigenous Míng dynasty, the summer palace at Chéngdé was entirely the creation of the Manchu Qīng, and lay beyond the Great Wall in the direction of their homelands. Here the emperor and the Manchu nobility would play at the equestrian and military talents, which had won them China in the first place, both with formal contests in archery and with hunting in the well-stocked park. The lakes and their many pavilions, stuffed with treasures, provided the emperor and his consorts with more refined diversions.

There's a half day of wandering here, although many of the buildings shown as lying within the park have long since vanished. The most important remaining is the **Zhèng Gōng (Main Palace).** The message here is one of simplicity and frugality (the beams and columns are very plain, although actually made of hardwoods brought long distances at great expense), with a pleasing elegance in great contrast to the usual Qīng gaudiness. The palace now serves as a museum, displaying ancient military equipment in the front rooms and period furnishings and antiquities at the rear.

Straight north, up the west side of lakes dotted with pavilions and crossed by many bridges, lies the **Wénjīn Gé (Pavilion of Literary Delight),** a ripple-roofed southern-style building reached through a rockery, which is a copy of a famous library building from Níngbō (p. 471).

A little farther northeast, the handsome **Liù Hé Tǎ (Pagoda of the Six Harmonies)** is the most striking building in the park. Its nine brick stories have green- or yellow-tiled eaves hung with bells and topped by a golden knob.

The pagoda is near the east entrance of the park, close to which the retired and unemployed can be found enjoying a game of croquet. If you've already examined the gaudy pavilions around the lakes, it's possible to leave this way to walk or catch a bus to the Eight Outer Temples.

Main entrance (Zhèng Mén) in Lìzhèng Mén Dàjiē. Admission ¥90 ($11), ¥60 ($7.50) winter. 5:30am–6:30pm (to 6pm in winter).

WÀI BĀ MIÀO (EIGHT OUTER TEMPLES) 🐦🐦

There were originally 12 temples, built between 1713 and 1780, and not all of those that remain are open to the public. Summer hours are May 1 to October 15; outside these times, some lesser temples may be shut. Several temples have features unique to Chéngdé. Most are extremely grand and suitably impressive (their purpose, after all), with successive halls on rising ground.

Tip: Pǔníng Sì and the other northern temples are on morning itineraries for tour groups, followed by Pǔlè Sì and the eastern temples in the afternoon. If you're traveling independently, work the other way around. You can also buy a *tào piào* (¥80/$10) which includes entry to Xūmífúshòu Miào, the Potala Temple, Pǔlè Sì, and Ānyuán Miào.

Bus no. 118, from Yíngzi Dàjiē or the Mountain Resort main entrance, will take you to the northern group of temples.

Xūmífúshòu Miào (Temple of Happiness and Longevity at Mount Sumeru)

Partly inspired by Tashilhunpo in Tibet (p. 767), this temple was constructed to make the Panchen Lama, number two in the Tibetan religious hierarchy, feel at home during a visit in 1780.

Shīzi Gōu Lù. Admission: summer ¥30 ($4), winter ¥20 ($2.50). 8am–5:30pm (to 4:30pm in winter). Bus: no. 118 to Xūmífúshòu Zhī Miào.

Pǔtuózōngchéng Zhī Miào (Potala Temple)

Five minutes' walk west, the Potala Temple, its tapering windows and slab-sided walls obviously influenced by Tibet, is in no way "a copy of the Potala Temple in Lhasa" (p. 751), as local guides like to say. Many windows are blind, and several outbuildings are solid, just intended to add to the massy splendor of the whole. Items on display in the surrounding galleries include two nine-story sandalwood pagodas climbing through holes cut in the floors, young girls' skulls fused with silver and once used as drinking vessels, and anatomically detailed esoteric statuary of sexual acts.

Shīzi Gōu Lù. Admission: summer ¥40 ($5), winter ¥30 ($4). 8am–5pm (to 4pm in winter). Bus: no. 118 to Pǔtuózōngchéng Zhī Miào.

Pǔníng Sì (Temple of Universal Peace)

The main Hall of Mahayana is impressive—story upon story of red walls and yellow roofs, topped with a gold knob surrounded by four mini-pagoda-like points. More impressive still is its contents, a giant copper-colored wooden Guānyīn figure more than 22m (73 ft.) high, the largest of its kind in the world. It's possible to climb three levels of interior galleries to look the figure in the eye, as she sits in dusty gloom. While other sights in Chéngdé are managed by the sleepy local tourism bureau, this temple is run by an entrepreneurial group of monks: The temple now sports a hotel (see below) and a tacky but entertaining recreation of a Qīng market, and offers an evening show promising blessings and exorcisms by "real Tibetan lamas."

Off Pǔníng Sì Lù. Admission ¥50 ($6), ¥10 ($1.25) to climb the Hall of Mahayana. 7:30am–5:30pm (to 4:30pm in winter). Bus: no. 6 or 118 to Pǔníng Sì.

Pǔyòu Sì Next door to Pǔníng Sì, this temple was closed for renovations when I last visited. The point of entering is to see the remainder of a collection of statues of the 500 arhats (the first followers of the Sakyamuni Buddha). Many of these were destroyed in 1937 during the Japanese occupation, but the remainder have a lively jollity, and are hung with scarves placed by respectful devotees.

Admission ¥10 ($1.25). 8:30am–5:30pm (to 4:30pm in winter).

Pǔlè Sì (Temple of Universal Joy) Tibetan advisors were employed in the design of this temple, built to receive annual tributary visits from defeated Mongol tribes. But the most striking element is the copy at the rear of the circular Hall of Prayer for Good Harvests from the Temple of Heaven. Shady benches around the quiet courtyards make perfect picnic stops.

Off Hédōng Lù. Admission: Summer ¥30 ($4), winter ¥20 ($2.50). 8am–5:30pm (to 4:30pm in winter). Bus: no. 10 from Wǔliè Lù to terminus. Taxi: a short ride from Pǔníng Sì.

Qīngchuí Fēng (Hammer Rock) Bus no. 10's terminus is actually the cableway to Hammer Rock. The characters specifically mean a kind of hammer for striking a Buddhist musical instrument, but the shape of this clublike column will inevitably remind all who see it of something completely different. It reminds the Chinese of that, too—they're just being polite. Pleasant strolls across the hills and sweeping views of the valley await those who ascend.

Admission ¥25 ($3). 24 hrs. Cable car ¥25 ($3) one-way; ¥40 ($5) round-trip. Runs Apr 1–Oct 30, 7:30am–6pm.

Ānyuán Miào (Temple of Distant Peace) Built in 1764, this is another example of architectural diplomacy, built in imitation of a temple (now long-vanished) in Yīníng on China's remote western borders (p. 320) to please Mongol tribes who were resettled around Chéngdé. You'll almost certainly be the only visitor.

Admission ¥10 ($1.25). Summer only, 8am–5pm. A 15-min. walk north of Pǔlè Sì.

SHOPPING

A lively **market** takes over the upper part of Yíngzi Dàjiē at night, interesting for its color rather than for what's on sale. The street also has several department stores with ground-floor supermarkets. Towards the post office there's a couple of bakeries where you can pick up snacks for the onward journey.

WHERE TO STAY

From the first week of May to the first week of October the town is busy, weekends particularly so, but only during the weeklong national holidays should it be difficult to find a room. Otherwise, the town has an excess of accommodations and, even in peak season, all hotels will have 20% discounts, rising to as much as 70% in the off season for the gently persuasive bargainer who just shows up. A 50% discount is taken for granted; you work down from there.

EXPENSIVE

Pǔníng Sì Shàngkètáng Dàjiǔdiàn (Finds) 🍸🍸

Run by the market-savvy monks of Pǔníng Sì, this newly opened hotel offers cozy accommodations within the west wing of the temple. Rooms are tastefully decorated with dark wood furniture and hand-made paper lamps and are set around eight tranquil courtyards, which boast rock gardens and ponds. Buddhist touches are in evidence: There's a large (if overpriced) vegetarian selection in the main restaurant, the proscription against soft beds is enforced, and there's little chance of sleeping in—the temple bells peal at 7:30am.

Pǔníng Sì. 100 units. ¥580 ($72) standard room. 50% summer discounts offered. AE, DC, MC, V. **Amenities:** 2 restaurants; indoor pool; exercise room; large game room; tour desk; business center; next-day laundry. *In room:* A/C, TV, fridge, safe.

Shèng Huá Dàjiǔdiàn

Opened in 2003, the four-star Shèng Huá is Chéngdé's best hotel in terms of furnishings. Rooms are spacious; luxury twin (standard) rooms even come equipped with their own computer. Bathrooms are well furbished and come with elaborate massage-jet showers. A new wing, located on the site of the old bus station, is due to open in 2006. It will house a pool and fitness center. Staff is helpful with inquiries, and speaks English and French.

Wǔliè Lù 22. ✆ **0341/227-1188.** Fax 0341/227-1112. 114 units. ¥700–¥980 ($87–$122) standard room; ¥1,500–¥5,800 ($187–$725) suite. 30%–40% summer discounts offered. AE, DC, MC, V. **Amenities:** 2 restaurants; teahouse; business center (Internet access ¥30/$4 per hour); forex; next-day dry cleaning/laundry. *In room:* A/C, TV, broadband Internet access, fridge, hair dryer, safe.

MODERATE

Qī Wàng Lóu Bīnguǎn 🍸

Once good enough for the Qiánlóng emperor, it's now good enough for party luminaries, though it's less expensive than this would suggest. Peacocks roam the gardens of this courtyard-style hotel, doubtless more relaxed than they were during Qiánlóng's time. Standard hotel interiors have been recently renovated, and there are yet higher standards in a new building, opened in 2004. Inexpensive bike rental is offered, an excellent way to explore the town. Avoid the diabolical Western breakfast.

Bì Fēng Mén Dōng Lù 1 (a narrow street running up the west side of the park). ✆ 0314/202-4385. Fax 0314/202-1904. 84 units. ¥500–¥800 ($63–$100) standard room; from ¥400 ($50) 3-bed basement room in new building; ¥1,000–¥4,000 ($125–$600) suite. Typical 50% discount off season. No credit cards. Bus: no. 5 from railway station to Bìshǔ Shānzhuāng. **Amenities:** Restaurant; bar; teahouse; bike rental (¥30/$4 per day). *In room:* A/C, TV.

Shānzhuāng Bīnguǎn (Mountain Villa Hotel)

Once the only hotel in town, this six-building monster directly opposite the Mountain Resort is undergoing a full renovation, which should be completed by the time you visit. They promise to retain a variety of simpler, cheaper rooms with common bathrooms for budget travelers. Usually these longer-standing hotels should be your last choice, but here a real effort has been made to stay in competition with the newer hotels.

Xiǎo Nán Mén Jiē 11 (opposite main entrance to Mountain Resort). ✆ 0314/209-1188. Fax 0314/203-4143. mvhotel @cs-user.he.cninfo.net. 370 units. ¥210 ($26) triple, ¥280 ($35) single, both with common bathroom; ¥480–¥580 ($60–$73) standard room; ¥880–¥2,000 ($110–$250) suite. AE, DC, MC, V. Bus: no. 5 from railway station to Bìshǔ Shānzhuāng. **Amenities:** 2 restaurants; fitness room; tour desk; bike rental (¥60/$7.50 per day); business center (Internet access ¥1.10/15¢ per minute); forex. *In room:* A/C, TV, broadband Internet access on request, hair dryer, safe.

WHERE TO DINE

The **night market** on Yíngzi Dàjiē runs through the heart of town. Stalls sell kabobs (¥1/15¢) and a wide assortment of other Chinese fast food, eaten at tables behind each stall.

As befits a former hunting ground, Chéngdé's specialty is game. The town is almost like a remote outpost of Guǎngdōng, of whose residents other Chinese say, "They eat anything with legs except a table, and anything with wings except an airplane." Donkey, dog, and scorpion are on menus. But so are deer, *shān jī* ("mountain chicken"—pheasant), and wild boar—often as unfamiliar ingredients cooked in familiar styles. Stir-frying makes venison tough, but wild boar softens up nicely while retaining its gamey flavor.

The best restaurants are in larger hotels such as the **Qiányáng Dàjiǔdiàn.** Try *lùròu chǎo zhēnmó* (venison stir-fried with hazel mushrooms) and *quèchǎo shānjī piàn* ("Sparrow's nest" pheasant slices). The **Xīn Qiánlóng Dàjiǔdiàn,** just south of the Shèng Huá Dàjiǔdiàn on Xīnhuá Lù (© **0314/207-2222**), open from 10am to 9pm, has attentive service, good portions, and a picture menu. Plump dumplings stuffed with donkey meat and onions are called *lǘròu dàcōng shuǐjiǎo*; 200 grams or four *liǎng* (*sì liǎng*) should be enough per person. *Cōng shāo yězhūròu* (wild boar cooked with onions) and *zhēnmó shānjī dīng* (nuggets of pheasant with local mushrooms) are both good. As long as you don't venture into scorpion or roe deer backbone marrow, a meal costs around ¥80 ($10) for two. There's an older branch at Zhōng Xīng Lù 2. **Dōngpō Fànzhuāng** offers authentic Sìchuān cuisine, and now runs four outlets, all staffed with natives of Chéngdū. Convenient branches are located opposite the railway station and at Xiǎo Nán Mén (© **0314/210-6315**), a 5-minute walk east from the main entrance to the Mountain Resort. Open 10am to 10pm, English menu.

10 Shānhǎiguān ⟨★⟩

Héběi Province, on the Bó Hǎi coast, 439km (274 miles) E of Běijīng

Eventually the Great Wall gives up its mad zigzagging from high point to high point and plunges spectacularly down a mountainside to run across a small plain and into the sea. On its way it briefly doubles as the eastern city wall of the garrison town of Shānhǎiguān (Pass Between Mountains and Sea), built during the Míng dynasty to prevent the easy passage of mounted invaders from the northeast.

The Wall was never an effective defense mechanism, and Shānhǎiguān became irrelevant after 1644 when, following the overthrow of the Míng dynasty by peasant rebellions, the dismayed defenders here allowed Qīng forces through. Once the enemy was within the gates, the Wall became pointless, lying as it did within Qīng territory, and it was allowed to fall into ruin until the imperatives of tourism rebuilt parts of it.

Each year large quantities of material are still carted away for incorporation in domestic buildings, and local governments breach the Wall when it suits them. At Shānhǎiguān a local vegetable wholesaler was made to rebuild a section of the Wall when he pulled it down to expand his warehouse. The local government then plowed a new expressway straight through it and permitted the display of advertising on its side, to ". . . rejuvenate the national industry that will face increased competition after China's entry into the World Trade Organization," according to *China Daily*.

Entrance prices to attractions in Shānhǎiguān are in constant flux, and off season may be as low as half the high-season rates quoted here, although that fact isn't often posted. Whatever the season, always ask for a discount.

ESSENTIALS

GETTING THERE Qínhuángdǎo **airport** is just outside town to the south, reached by taxi, with infrequent flights from Tàiyuán, Harbin, Chángchūn, Dàlián, and Shànghǎi. **Train** services from major cities in the northeast pass through Shānhǎiguān on their way to many southern destinations, but **Qínhuángdǎo** is better served from Běijīng—take the T509 at 7:30am, arriving in Qínhuángdǎo at 10:24am. This is an all soft-seat train that marks the return of class designations to Chinese trains—imagine the embalmed Máo a-spin. *Yī děng* (first class) is ¥97 ($12). Outside the Qínhuángdǎo railway station, cross the road and turn left to find bus no. 33. It reaches Shānhǎiguān in about 30 minutes, for a fare of ¥2 (25¢). The bus drops you at the south gate of the old city walls (Nán Mén). Trains directly to Shānhǎiguān from Běijīng tend to be slower or ill-timed, although the T11 departing at 10:22am and arriving at 3:15pm is a possibility. Shānhǎiguān's new railway station (© 0335/ 794-2242) is a few minutes' walk southeast of the south gate. The T12 returns to Běijīng at 1:29pm, arriving at 6:17pm, and the speedier T94, which departs at 7:05pm, arrives at 9:54pm. Tickets are set aside for both trains, but unless you're fortunate, you'll probably have to buy a seatless ticket and upgrade on the train. It's safer to return to Qínhuángdǎo, where the T510 at 1:50pm reaches Běijīng Station at 4:59pm.

For **bus** services it's again better to return to Qínhuángdǎo, with twice-daily connections to Běijīng's Xī Zhí Mén bus station and others to Běijīng Railway Station, for ¥60 ($7.50). Bus no. 33 to Qínhuángdǎo Railway Station runs every 2 to 5 minutes from 6:20am to 7pm.

GETTING AROUND   **Buses** have conductors and cost ¥1 (15¢). A **tourist shuttle service** runs from Nán Mén (South Gate) to the Tiānxià Dìyī Guān and Jiǎo Shān at 8:30am, 11am, and 3:30pm, summer only. Most **taxis** have a flagfall of ¥8 ($1), which includes 2km (1¼ miles), then charge ¥1.20 (15¢) per kilometer up to 8km (5 miles), then ¥1.80 (25¢) per kilometer thereafter. Use one taxi to see all the sights. Insist that the "one-way" button is not pushed, and then this should be about 32km (20 miles), and cost less than ¥50 ($6.25), including waiting time. There's also an assortment of meterless rickety three-wheelers with extravagant ideas about the depth of foreigners' pockets. A better choice is to rent a **bicycle** from one of the cluster of stores on Nán Dàjiē. **Battle Cycles** (Bāngdéfú Shìdá Zìxíngchē) at Nán Dàjiē 112 (© 0335/506-7800) is open from 7am to 7pm (6pm in winter) and rents mountain bikes for ¥15 ($2) per day.

FAST FACTS

Banks, Foreign Exchange & ATMs   The main **Bank of China** (8am–12:30pm and 2–5pm) is just inside the city wall's southeast corner at Dìyī Guān Lù 60. Money exchange is offered Monday through Friday only. There is no ATM.

Internet Access   The **Língshí Wǎngbā,** between the post office and the Friendly Cooperate Hotel, charges ¥2 (25¢) per hour. Dial-up is © 163.

Post Office   The post office is on Nán Guān Dàjiē, right next to the Friendly Cooperate Hotel. Hours are from 8am to 6pm.

INSPECTING CHINA'S DEFENSES

Tiānxià Dìyī Guān   The "First Pass Under Heaven" is the east gate of the city's walls and a gate through the Great Wall itself, originally defended by towers overlooking a large walled enclosure, most of which still stands. The only entrance was from the south, and would have required a sharp left turn to reach the main gate while coming under attack from all sides. To the north and south the Wall is heavily restored, the odd reconstructed tower holding either a small exhibition or a shop. It was once possible to walk north to Jiǎo Shān; the way is now barred by a metal door.

Admission ¥40 ($5). 7:30am–6pm (to 5:30pm in winter). From the south gate, walk north up Nán Dàjiē and turn right at Dōng Dàjiē, or walk west outside the walls and turn left up Dìyī Guān Lù inside the east wall—also the route any taxi will take. Alternatively, enter the south gate and simply zigzag through the back streets—worthwhile in itself; because there's no way through the walls once you're inside; you can't get lost.

Jiǎo Shān   The rebuilt Wall plunges spectacularly down the mountainside, so your climb up it is consequently steep. There are handrails to assist you, and ladders up the sides of watchtowers, or the alternative of a chair lift for ¥15 ($1.90) one-way, ¥20 ($2.50) round-trip. The towers are certainly worth scaling for the views of the Wall wriggling down the hillside and running away to the sea. Higher up, the Wall becomes more attractively decayed but still safely passable, and those with the stamina (and a picnic) can travel some distance.

Admission ¥15 ($2). Open 24 hr. 3km (2 miles) north of Shānhǎiguān, and best reached by taxi.

Lǎo Lóng Tóu   A few years ago the "Old Dragon's Head" was just rubble, with the odd stone sticking out of the sea. The Great Wall's final kilometer was re-created in 1992, and it runs past a brand-new "old barracks area" (with shops) and a final tower before it expires in the sea. Stand at the Wall's end, look back, try to see beyond the tawdry desperation for the tourist dollar, and view the Wall as the beginning of a vast drama, ending thousands of kilometers away in Gānsù Province. It's the culmination of a Míng dynasty arms race, the "Star Wars" project of its time, which nearly sank the national economy and which turned out to be pointless since scruffy little men on ponies armed with bows and arrows, the "terrorists" of their day, regularly got through it.

Stairs to the right lead down to a beach where Chinese, most of whom live a very long way from the sea, paddle in search of pebbles and shells. Beyond lies a small temple to the Sea God, rebuilt in 1989, an excellent vantage point for photography of the "Old Dragon's Head" itself.

Admission ¥50 ($6). Open daylight hours. Bus: no. 13 south down Nán Hǎi Xī Lù (everyone knows where you want to get off, at a point where the road forks); or bus no. 23 (which terminates here).

Mèngjiāngnǚ Miào   This temple, a reminder of the Great Wall's human cost, is linked to a myth that crops up repeatedly around China, where compulsory labor on vast civil engineering projects led to the deaths of tens of thousands: Husband goes off to imperial construction project, and nothing more is heard. Eventually wife goes to look for husband, discovers that he has died during his labors, and the Wall crumbles under the weight of her tears to reveal his bones. She subsequently chooses suicide in preference to becoming an imperial concubine.

Such was the fate of the probably mythical Mèngjiāngnǚ. Her temple is on a lookout point up a steep flight of stairs, called "Looking for Husband Rock," and consists of some remarkably battered halls and oddly shaped rocks, labeled opportunistically as her bed, dressing table, and so on.

Admission ¥25 ($3). 6am–7pm (to 6pm in winter). 8km (5 miles) east of town.

Wáng Jiā Dàyuàn ★★   This small but fascinating folk museum provides a clue as to what the Cultural Relics Bureau could achieve if it were properly funded and had some marketing savvy. With investment from a Běijīng entrepreneur, part of a courtyard mansion that once housed Shānhǎiguān's wealthiest burgher has been sensitively renovated and is slated to expand farther south. Exhibits are crammed with curiosities: a mustache comb, a portable barber's chair, sepia pictures of the former residents, and an impressive collection of shadow puppets and ceramics. Four of the rooms are available for overnight stays (¥298–¥398/$37–$50), with meals included.

Dōng Sān Tiáo 29. www.wjdy.com.cn. Admission ¥30 ($3.75). Includes English-speaking guide. Open daylight hours. From Nán Mén, walk north up Nán Dàjiē, take the 5th turn on the right.

WHERE TO STAY

A single night in Shānhǎiguān is enough. Few hotels take foreigners, and most are fairly modest. The town's coastal position makes May to August its busiest months, with visitors from Běijīng escaping the city heat. There are one or two resort hotels which are rather far-flung, inconvenient, overpriced, and of two minds about taking foreigners. The **Jīguān Zhāodàisuǒ,** Dōng Sì Tiáo Hútòng 17 (make a right turn about 4 blocks north of the south gate; ℂ **0335/505-1938;** fax 0335/505-1490), is an acceptable choice, plus it provides a rare chance to stay in something approaching traditional Chinese housing, an old courtyard residence in the Shānhǎiguān back streets that's been refurbished. Opened as a hotel in 2002, its rooms (¥80/$10 dorm bed with foul common bathroom; ¥180/$23 standard room; no credit cards), which open on to courtyards are bright, cheerful, and simply furnished.

WHERE TO DINE

Close to the Jīguān Zhāodàisuǒ on Nán Dàjiē is the friendly **Sì Tiáo Bāoziguǎn,** which boasts an English-speaking staff member. Smock-clad ladies roll the dumplings in an open kitchen while locals queue out the door for dumpling heaven. Perfect for an early start, they're open 6am to 6:30pm. Shānhǎiguān's locals wistfully recall a time when they dined on unfarmed fish, but despite the depletion in fish stocks, Shānhǎiguān is still renowned for its seafood. The bustling **Wàng Yáng Lóu Fànzhuāng** (ℂ **0335/505-2264**), just outside the southwest corner of the city wall, is the best choice. There's no English menu, but there's a display case to the left as you enter, with the raw ingredients of most dishes on show (not always to their advantage). Open 11am to 2pm, 5 to 8pm. Bus no. 33 from Nán Mén to Wénhuà Gōng.

11 Shíjiāzhuāng

Héběi Province, 269km (168 miles) SW of Běijīng

Héběi's nondescript capital is one of the few places in China where the intention to rebuild everything from scratch in only 20 years is actually improving the city. Down-at-heel Shíjiāzhuāng is an accident arising from the crossing of major north–south and east–west railway lines—here X really does mark the spot. It's grown from village to provincial capital in 100 years.

Even that status is a hand-me-down from Tiānjīn, after the metropolis gained the right to report directly to Běijīng rather than through the provincial government. As a result there's little of glamour here. But the city has a decent infrastructure for visitors and provides a base for exploring marvelous sights in the surrounding countryside, including **Zhèngdìng** 🌸🌸, about 15km (10 miles) northeast. It was an important town for centuries before anyone had heard of Shíjiāzhuāng. Today it is still home to **Lóngxīng Sì** 🌸🌸, one of the oldest, most atmospheric, and (luckily) least "restored" Chinese temples. Zhèngdìng is also home to a number of pagodas so different from each other it's hard to believe they were produced by the same culture.

Zhào Xiàn, 42km (26 miles) southeast, has an important example of religious revival in the large Zen (Chán) Buddhist temple, the **Bǎilín Sì.** It also has the elegant **Zhàozhōu Qiáo** ✧—the first bridge of its kind in the world. Roughly 80km (50 miles) southwest, **Cāngyán Shān** has the bridge-top temple featured in the closing scenes of *Crouching Tiger, Hidden Dragon*. *Note:* Please turn to appendix A for Chinese translation of key locations in this section.

ESSENTIALS

GETTING THERE   The **airport** is 33km (20 miles) to the northeast. A shuttle bus (¥20/$2.50) meets flights and runs to the CAAC ticket office at Zhōngshān Dōng Lù 471, on the east side of town at the terminus of bus no. 5 to the center. **CAAC,** (open 8am–8pm) has a 24-hour flight-booking line (© **0311/8505-4084**). Buy in town from agents such as the **Hébĕi Oversea Tour Aviation Ticket Center** (Hébĕi Hǎiwài Lǚyóu Hángkōng Piàowù Zhōngxīn), inside the Tiědào Dàshà, Zhōngshān Dōng Lù 97 (© **0311/8607-7777**) on the corner of Píng'ān Bĕi Dàjiē. They also have a branch inside the Hébĕi Century Hotel. There are air connections to most provincial capitals, including daily flights to and from Bĕijīng, Hohhot, Shànghǎi, and Xī'ān.

Since Shíjiāzhuāng's prosperity, such as it is, originates with its railway connections, it's right that the **railway station** is in the center of town. Getting there from **Bĕijīng West** couldn't be easier, with six daily express trains taking 2 hours and 40 minutes, tickets (¥50/$6.25 soft seat [sometimes ¥40/$5 the other way]) can be bought outside waiting room 3 or on the train itself. These are all-seat double-decker trains with snack service. Taking the T511 from Bĕijīng at 7:35am and returning by the T514 at 5:58pm can make Shíjiāzhuāng a possible day trip. Shíjiāzhuāng is also a stop on the T97/98 run between Bĕijīng West and Kowloon (¥965/$120 soft sleeper; ¥609/$76 hard sleeper), arriving at 3:29pm from Kowloon and leaving at 12:49pm headed south. You will need your passport to book this ticket. Most south- and southwest-bound trains from Bĕijīng stop at Shíjiāzhuāng, offering connections to Tàiyuán, Xī'ān, and points as far flung as Ürümqi. **Rail tickets** can be booked by telephone (© **8699-5426;** 8am–6pm) for a ¥10 ($1.25) commission. The railway station has been renovated, and boasts 17 windows from which tickets can be purchased. Window 1 is for soft-seat tickets only, windows 8 through 19 are normal ticket windows, 20 through 24 are for 10-day advance purchases. There's even a screen displaying the availability of tickets.

Shíjiāzhuāng is littered with **bus stations.** The most important of them, **Chángtú Kèyùn Zhàn,** is a 5-minute walk south of the railway station on Zhàn Qián Lù. Destinations served include Jǐ'nán (241km/149 miles; ¥55/$7), Tài'ān (281km/174 miles; ¥60/$7.50), Zhèngzhōu (437km/271 miles; ¥45/$5.60), and Qínhuángdǎo (480km/298 miles; ¥105/$13). There are frequent connections to several Bĕijīng bus stations, including Lìzé Qiáo (7am–5:30pm) and Liánhuā Chí (6:30am–4pm; 3½ hr). But the real competition with the rail link to Bĕijīng is just to the right at the **Kèyùn Zǒng Zhàn,** where the Alsa company runs luxury coaches to Bĕijīng Liù Lǐ Qiáo (roughly every 25 min. 6am–12:15pm; returning 12:30–7:30pm; ¥70/$8.75). In addition, twice-daily super luxury buses have large, airline-style tiltable seats, only three across the bus (¥90/$11), departing at 8:55 and 10:25am, returning at 3:10pm and 4:40pm. For service from Bĕijīng call © **010/6386-1263;** from Shíjiāzhuāng call © **0311/8611-3886.** They also run two morning services to Jǐ'nán and Zhèngzhōu, with afternoon returns.

GETTING AROUND   Taxis are mostly Jettas and Fùkāng, and cost ¥1.40 (20¢) per kilometer. Xiàlì cost ¥1.20 (15¢) per kilometer. Flagfall of ¥5 (65¢) includes 2km. Add 50% after 6km (3¾ miles), and 20% from 11pm to 5am.

VISITOR INFORMATION   CITS, at Dōnggǎng Lù 26, quotes imaginative prices for cars and guides. However, it does have some good English-speakers, so if you're desperate, call them at ℂ 0311/8581-5102.

FAST FACTS

Banks, Foreign Exchange & ATMs   There's a handy branch of the **Bank of China** on the north side of the Dōngfāng Dàshà, Zhōngshān Xī Lù 97, close to the railway station. Hours are Monday through Friday from 8:30am to noon and 2:30 to 5:15pm. Forex is available at counters 4 to 7. Another useful branch lies near a KFC just west of the World Trade Plaza on Zhōngshān Dōng Lù (same hours). Both branches have ATMs that accept foreign cards.

Internet Access   Dial-up is ℂ **163** or 169.

Post Office   The post office near the railway station (corner of Gōnglǐ Jiē and Zhōngshān Xī Lù) is open from 8:30am to 6:30pm. There's a more centrally located post office in Jiànshè Nán Dàjiē; its hours are 8:30am to 9pm.

Visa Extensions   The city **PSB** is 1 block north of Zhōngshān Xī Lù, and 2 blocks east of Zhōnghuá Běi Dàjiē, at Límíng Jiē 8. The visa office has a separate entrance on the east side of the building. Walk up Qīngnián Jiē on the west side of the Huáběi Shāngchéng (department store), across the next junction, and the office is on your left (ℂ **0311/8686-3176**). Hours are Monday to Friday from 8:30am to noon and 2:30 to 5:30pm.

WALKING TOUR   THE PAGODAS OF ZHĚNGDÌNG ✿✿

Getting There:	Take minibus no. 201 from the enclosure between Zhàn Qián Jiē and the railway station; it drops you at Zhèngdìng bus station for ¥3 (40¢). Ignore *sānlúnchē* (three-wheeler) drivers and take minibus no. 1 from the same spot to its terminus outside Lóngxīng Sì (¥1/15¢). A *sānlúnchē* will cost you ¥5/65¢. A harder-to-find alternative is a tourist service which runs every 15 minutes from near the no. 50 bus stop farther south on the road running directly in front of the station, just north of the bus station, to outside Kāiyuán Sì; the fare is ¥3 (40¢). It is possible to stay at the (nominally) four-star Golden Star Holiday Hotel (ℂ **0311/825-8888**), just north of Lóngxīng Sì, at Xīngróng Lù 68.
Start:	Lóngxīng Sì
Finish:	Chánglè Mén
Time:	At least half a day
Best Times:	Weekdays between 8am and 4pm

In once-important, long-irrelevant Zhèngdìng, only a little exertion brings a lot of pleasure, including sights like some of the oldest surviving wooden buildings in China, a vast 27m (90-ft.) 10th-century bronze statue of Guānyīn, four very different pagodas, and a fragment of city wall.

Bus no. 1 terminates at the main entrance. We recommend that you purchase an all-inclusive ticket (tàopiào) for ¥60 ($7.50), which covers all the sights described here, except for the Línjì Sì, which is managed by the Religious Affairs Bureau. The ticket includes entrance to a Confucian Temple of minor interest, containing a rather gruesome exhibition on the Japanese occupation.

① Lóngxīng Sì

Open 8am to 5:30pm; ¥30 ($3.75), the Lóngxīng Sì dates its foundation to the Suí dynasty (581–618), and has three particularly unusual and interesting halls. The **Móní Diàn (Manichean Hall)**, built around 1052, rebuilt in 1563, and restored with tact from 1977 to 1980, is almost square in plan, with gabled porches on all four sides. Inside, five gilded figures are approached across a dark uneven floor past vast columns, some of which have a slight lean; the walls carry faint traces of early frescoes, miraculously unretouched. Through a gate beyond, a small altar building houses a two-faced, four-armed and rather delicately executed figure from 1493, hung with scarves of honor. To the right the Pavilion of Kindness contains a 7.4m (24-ft.) Maitreya carved from a single piece of wood. To the left, the two-story **Zhuǎnlún Cáng Diàn (Turning Wheel Storage Hall)** of the Northern Sòng (960–1127) seems to have three stories due to an external gallery with "waist eaves." The ground floor is dominated by a 7m-high (23-ft.) octagonal revolving bookcase, as complex in its design as a miniature temple. The climax is the **Pavilion of Great Benevolence,** also Northern Sòng, a vast hall seven bays wide containing a massive 27m (90-ft.) bronze Guānyīn with a "thousand arms" whose angularity give her a rather crustacean look. The figure was cast upon the instructions of the first Northern Sòng emperor in about 971. You can climb several dusty floors to look her in the eye. The rearmost Míng-era hall was brought

to the site from another temple in 1959, and contains a remarkable three-layered statue of 12 figures seated on lotus thrones. One side hall contains a bizarre exhibition (¥5/60¢) that includes what is claimed to be a 2,100-year-old Hàn dynasty jade burial suit, reconstructed from hundreds of small jade plates and held together with cloth-covered gold wire. If it's the genuine article, it's priceless, but the presence in the exhibition of a pickled turtle, a dilapidated butterfly collection, and other bric-a-brac suggests otherwise. Continue through to **Kūnlú Diàn (Hall of Vairocana),** an exquisitely-carved effigy of four bodhisattvas, dating from the late Míng.

Leaving the temple, note the rough map near the ticket office to the right. Turn right (west) from the temple and walk for 10 minutes.

② Tiānníng Sì

If you are here in the spring, the *wútóng* (Chinese parasol) trees you'll see will have spectacular cascades of pink blossoms. The **Língxiāo Tǎ** (pagoda), all that remains of the temple, is clearly visible to your right. Open 8am to 5:30pm; ¥5 (65¢), the Sòng dynasty nine-story octagonal brick structure, at 41m (134 ft.), is the tallest of the town's remaining pagodas. To climb it, enter from the far (north) side. If you are lucky the attendant will hand you a torch, but if not, the climb to the second, third, and fourth floors is through narrow passages within the brick walls, with short periods of pitch darkness to start with. Keep your head *down.* The remainder of the climb to the ninth floor is by wooden staircases in the interior. A central set of trunks bound with hoops of iron, which radiate support beams, sit on fat brackets.

From the top, looking southwest, you can see the squat, square form of your next destination.

Return to the main road and turn right. After less than 5 minutes, Lìshǐ Wénhuà Jiē "Historical and Cultural Street" is on the left at a bizarre statue-cum-roundabout. Turn left. There's a supermarket with snacks on the corner, and the street has a number of modest restaurants, which are less modest than anything else in the town. Kāiyuán Sì is a short distance down to the right.

❸ Kāiyuán Sì

Two minor buildings stand here, including a heavily renovated late-Táng bell tower, which can be climbed for a closer view of a 2.9m (9½-ft.) bronze bell. Open 8am to 5pm; ¥10 ($1.25).

The nine-story **Xūmí Tǎ** will seem familiar to those who've visited Xī'ān—a tapering, brick, four-sided building, with a projecting ridge between each floor and a plainness that makes the Língxiāo Tǎ look fussy. There are local claims that it dates from 636, but as Xī'ān's Great Goose (p. 255) is supposedly based on information brought back to China by the peripatetic monk, Xuánzàng, and its construction didn't start until 16 years later, one story is wrong (although Xuánzàng is said to have been in the area—see Bǎilín Sì, below). But the stately Xūmí Tǎ certainly looks its age—quite a few of the bricks have fallen out, providing handy niches for nesting sparrows, and it's fenced off. Around the base are eight tubby martial figures, simply carved but full of life. If you do go in, note the carvings of dragons and flowers. The interior floors are missing, and the main floor is slippery with guano, but there's an impressive view up the resulting vertical tunnel.

One area of the temple's ruined remains has been labeled STONE INSCRIPTION GARDEN and contains forlorn rows of chipped statuary and chunks of stelae probably smashed in the Cultural Revolution, along with the cracked remains of the largest *bìxì* you'll ever see, its claws 6 inches long. Often mistakenly described as turtles, *bìxì* are in fact a primitive kind of dragon (not only with claws, but teeth). This one was accidentally discovered in

June 2000 during construction work, as illustrated by photographs in the entrance hall as you leave.

Outside, turn right. You'll see a few street vendors selling birds, flowers, plants, and fish, and almost immediately on the left the entrance to the ancestral hall of the Liáng family.

❹ Liángshì Zōngcí

This hall is a single unit five bays wide in brown wood, containing a small exhibition (pictures, family tree) of the Liáng family. Open 8am to 5pm (closed at lunchtime); ¥3 (40¢).

Outside, turn left. Along the length of this street are antiques and memorabilia shops (with lower prices than most because they are aimed at domestic tourists) selling everything from Buddhist bits and pieces to Máo memorabilia. Still, expect most objects to be fake, and pay only a small fraction of initial asking prices. There are also places to buy ice cream, and assorted restaurants offering *jiǎozi* and Běijīng duck. Keep looking on the left for a large sign with a picture of pagoda, and turn left there.

❺ Línjì Sì

Open 7:30am to 5pm; ¥8 ($1), this temple claims to have been founded by the Eastern Wèi dynasty (534–549). Its **Chénglíng Tǎ** was built to house the remains of the founder of a Zen Buddhist (Chán) sect still popular in Japan, who died late in the Táng dynasty in 867. The slender, octagonal brick pagoda is in a highly ornamental style; an elongated lower floor sits on a brick plinth carved with lotus petals. Eight further tiny stories, each with decorative brick brackets and eave figures, are topped by an umbrella spire. Roughly 30m (98 ft.) high, the pagoda was restored in 2001 and cannot be climbed. A handful of monks are in residence.

Turn right out of the temple and left at the main street. The Guǎnghuì Sì is a well-signposted left turn a few minutes farther along.

❻ Guǎnghuì Sì

This temple's bizarre **Huá Tǎ**, dating from around 1200, is obviously a direct descendant of Indian stupas, consisting of a central brick pavilion topped with a stone spire covered with intricate statuary of elephants, other animals, and figures—some headless, some faceless, and some intact—finished with a brick point on top. The central pavilion is supported by four smaller, rebuilt pavilions. A climb up two floors to a platform (again, watch your head) gives views of the earthen core of the old city wall, the fields still inside it, and a modern mosque. Open 8am to 5:30pm; ¥10 ($1.25).

Again return to the main road and turn left. The south gate of the city wall is straight ahead; the entrance is to the right.

❼ Chánglè Mén

As is usual with city walls, the brick has been taken away to use in domestic construction—all except for those structurally necessary to maintain the gates, unless the wall is breached elsewhere (or removed, earthworks and all). Here the gate and its tower have been rebuilt. Open 8am to 5:30pm; admission is ¥10 ($1.25).

To return to Zhèngdìng, flag down the yellow bus no. 2, which returns in the direction you have walked to the long-distance bus station.

BĂILÍN SÌ & ZHÀOZHŌU QIÁO ☆

Băilín Sì The Cultural Revolution was so thorough here that only the Jīn dynasty (1115–1234) pagoda was left standing. The extensive complex has been reconstructed over the last few years entirely with donations from the faithful, and includes one of the largest "10,000 Buddha" halls in the world.

The temple saw the foundation of a sect of Zen (Chán) Buddhism, and its beginnings date from 220 during the Eastern Hàn dynasty. Xuánzàng is said to have studied here before his trip to India in search of authoritative texts. The temple is entered through a small grove of cypresses (for which it is named), and has a calm bustle of activity from shaven-headed monks in orange and brown robes. One or two English-speakers tend to seek out foreign visitors and are happy to answer queries, show you around, and explain Zen principles and the *Shēnghuó* (life) variant introduced by Venerable Master Jìnghuì, the driving force behind the temple's change from weeds and rubble into an impressive complex. Then-President Jiāng Zémín visited in 2001. Perhaps the rumors are true and he is a closet Buddhist.

Free admission. Open 8am–4pm. In Shíjiāzhuāng, take bus no. 3 to Huáxià Zhàn, the bus station for Zhào Xiàn, to the south of the center on Ān Nán Dàjiē, and catch a bus to Zhào Xiàn (30–45 min.; ¥6/75¢). Jump off at a traffic island with a mini-pagoda in the middle. The road to the left, Shí Tǎ Lù, takes you to Băilín Sì in 10 min. on foot. Alternatively, if you head straight on down Shí Qiáo Dàjiē (Stone Bridge St.), you'll pass the earthen core and one or two watchtowers of the city wall, and get to a major junction straight over which is Zhàozhōu Qiáo, about a 30-min. walk. Or take a *sānlúnchē* (¥3/40¢) or minivan (¥5/60¢).

Zhàozhōu Qiáo ☆ Also known as Ānjì Qiáo (Safe Crossing Bridge) and Dà Shí Qiáo (Big Stone Bridge), this is often labeled the oldest surviving bridge in China. There are probably older bridges, but this one was constructed between 595 and 605, and unlike China's wooden structures it is largely original in its current form. A mecca for architects and civil engineers as well as historians, it was the first bridge in the world to use a segment of an arc rather than a complete semicircle for its arch, giving a far more shallow curve to the road deck and thus making crossings for carts and horses much easier. This was a major design breakthrough, but it would be 800 years before a similar approach would be tried in Europe, and nearly 1,300 years before Europe tried using the spandrel—piercing the buttresses at either end of the bridge so as to reduce pressure on the foundations and allow flood waters to pass without sweeping the bridge away.

The parallel stone ribbons that form the main arch are surprisingly flexible and things of beauty in themselves. Until recently the bridge was still in use, but traffic is now diverted, and some of the damaged carvings on the superstructure, including scowling mythical beasts called *tāotiè,* have been replaced.

Sadly, the bridge's conversion to a tourist sight has brought pedalos (pedal boats) that wallow in the murky, tadpole-filled waters beneath, as well as construction of a hideous parallel concrete pedestrian bridge, mainly to obscure views from the new road bridge and thus increase receipts. But don't let this stop you from viewing China's most significant contribution to architectural method.

See directions for Bǎilín Sì, above. The ticket booth is to the right of the main entrance. Admission ¥25 ($3). 7:30am–7:30pm (to 5:30pm in winter). To find buses to Shíjiāzhuāng, return to the traffic island by foot or taxi, and continue to the next T-junction. (If you turn left and walk for a few minutes, on your right you'll find another, smaller bridge constructed in the same style, with no entrance fee at all.)

CÃNGYÁN SHÃN

This wooded mountain is part of the Tàiháng range, about 80km (50 miles) southwest of Shíjiāzhuāng; its summit is at 1,044m (3,424 ft.). The main point of visiting is a stair-case of more than 300 steps leading up a cleft and beneath two parallel bridges, each topped by a temple, originally Suí dynasty (518–618). The setting is as spectacular as it looks in the closing scene of the feeble *Crouching Tiger, Hidden Dragon* (although the final jump is reportedly from Huáng Shān), and the location, especially from the stairs below and on a misty day, makes for some spectacular photography. The paths which lace the mountainside do not lead to any other equally spectacular sights, and some have crum-bled away. Take a picnic. The 2-hour minibus trip begins rather early in the morning.

Admission ¥40 ($5). Bus: to Cāngyán Shān from the Xīwáng Chángtú Kèyùn Chēzhàn (take bus no. 9 from the rail station to the terminus) in Xīnhuá Lù. It departs at 7am and returns late afternoon. Return fare is ¥26 ($3.25).

WHERE TO STAY
EXPENSIVE

Hébĕi Century Hotel (Hébĕi Shìjì Dàfàndiàn)   This Chinese five-star 29-floor glass cylinder tower opened in 2000 with a cavernous lobby and good-size rooms, if typically tiny bathrooms. The guest rooms have the standard neoclassical cabinetry of international five-stars, but someone involved in the design has been a bit more adventurous with color than is common to Chinese-run hotels, and service is a notch above average, too.

Zhōngshān Xī Lù 145 (just west of the city PSB, corner of Zhōnghuá Bĕi Dàjiē). ☎ 0311/8703-6699. Fax 0311/8703-8866. www.hebei-centuryhotel.com. 439 units. ¥590–¥900 ($74–$113) standard room; ¥1,100–¥6,000 ($138–$750) suite. 30%–50% discounts easily obtained. AE, DC, MC, V. Bus: no. 1 west along Zhōngshān Xī Lù. **Amenities:** 5 restaurants; nightclub; indoor swimming pool; tennis; fitness room; sauna; billiards; children's play area; tour desk; business center. *In room:* A/C, satellite TV, computer (executive floors), broadband Internet access, hair minibar, dryer, safe.

World Trade Plaza Hotel (Shìmào Guǎngchǎng Jiŭdiàn) ✿   This former Crowne Plaza was recently the victim of a buy-out by its Chinese partner. For the moment, this centrally located five-star hotel is the first choice for foreign visitors, but parts of the operation are already veering out of control, particularly the enthusiastic "massage" service, which occasionally solicits from door to door. (A Sofitel, near the railway station, will be open to compete by the time you arrive.) North-facing rooms are quieter, and the larger "executive rooms" *(shāngwù jiān),* which are appealingly arranged with a glass divider between the resting and the work area, are excellent value. The second-floor restaurant offers the finest Western cuisine in town.

Zhōngshān Dōng Lù 303 (opposite Shěng Bówùguǎn/Provincial Museum). ✆ **0311/8667-8888.** Fax 0311/8667-1694. www.wtphotels.com. 238 units. ¥818 ($102) standard room; ¥1,820 ($228) suite; plus 15% service charge. Best rates often 50% less. AE, DC, MC, V. **Amenities:** 3 restaurants; fitness room with access to off-site facilities; Jacuzzi; sauna; limousine service; railway station shuttle; business center with translation services; forex; laundry and dry cleaning. *In room:* A/C, satellite TV, dataport, minibar, safe, iron.

MODERATE

Huìwén Jiǔdiàn　The 26-floor Huìwén, which upgraded from three stars to four stars following renovations in 2003 (though it must have been quite a banquet for the hotel inspectors), is the best choice of a clutch of hotels conveniently opposite the railway station, and less than 10 minutes' walk north of the long-distance bus station. The hotel is adequately clean and well run, but it needs at least one more elevator, and lighting in the bathrooms is poor. Public transport to most out-of-town sites leaves from stops nearby.

Zhàn Qián Jiē 6 (opposite railway station exit—look for Xīnhuá Bookstore sign). ✆ **0311/8787-9988.** Fax 0311/8786-5500. 180 units. ¥268–¥348 ($33–$43) standard room; ¥490 ($61) suite. Discounts around 40%. No credit cards. **Amenities:** 3 restaurants; teahouse; nightclub; fitness room; bowling; pool table; business center. *In room:* A/C, TV, broadband Internet access, hair dryer.

WHERE TO DINE

The usual fast-food culprits are here: KFC is opposite the Yànchūn Garden Hotel, Zhōngshān Dōng Lù 195, and just west of the World Trade Plaza on Zhōngshān Dōng Lù, along with a McDonald's. Extensive Western menus are available at both hotels; you can also find a branch of the excellent Shànghǎi restaurant, **Soup Best Shěn,** at the Yànchūn Garden. There's budget eating opposite the station, including two branches of **California Beef Noodle King (Měiguó Jiāzhōu Niúròu Miàn Dàwáng),** and a branch of the **Mǎlán** noodle chain next to Quánjùdé (see below). At any of these you can fill yourself for ¥5 (65¢). The vast Rénrén Lè Supermarket is located underneath the Máo park, just east of the Yànchūn Garden Hotel. The Great Helmsman transformed into the Great Spruiker. Another supermarket for travel snacks, open from 9am to 7:30pm, is located at Zhōngshān Xī Lù 83, just west of the station. Shíjiāzhuāng is best at offering Běijīng specialties in quieter environments and for lower prices.

Quánjùdé ✦ BĚIJĪNG　The national capital's best-known supplier of its signature roast duck dish provides a better atmosphere, better service, and lower prices at this provincial branch than it does at home. The grand two-story building with a sweeping central staircase bustles pleasantly. The ovens are visible at the rear and use the traditional fruitwood method for baking the duck, which is as moist and succulent as it should be. The downstairs area also offers Shāndōng dishes, which you select from illuminated shelves. Upstairs has full waitress service. If you are by yourself, a half duck *(bàn zhī)* is only ¥49 ($6.10) There's another branch on the south side of Hépíng Xī Lù just west of Píng'ān Jiē.

Jiànshè Nán Dàjiē 7, just south of the Yànchūn Garden Hotel. ✆ **0311/8621-1566.** Meal for 2 ¥150 ($19). No credit cards. 10:30am–2pm and 5–8:30pm.

Shāo'érzǎi CHÁOZHŌU　This branch of the roast goose specialist offers Cháozhōu cuisine's most famous dish, very popular throughout Guǎngdōng and Hong Kong. The large and busy restaurant is set back from the main road in a courtyard, but it's easily spotted by the big roast goose sign.

Zhōngshān Dōng Lù 189, just west of the Yànchūn Garden Hotel. ✆ **0311/8603-3951,** ext. 6666. Meal for 2 ¥60 ($7.50). No credit cards. 10am–1:30am.

The Northeast

by Paul Mooney

Even if the Chinese no longer believe civilization ends at the Great Wall, most tourists still do. The frigid lands to the northeast, once known as Tartary or Manchuria and now referred to simply as Dōngběi (the Northeast), represent one of the least visited and most challenging regions in China and its last great travel frontier.

Dōngběi was the birthplace of China's final dynasty, the Manchu-ruled Qīng (1636–1912). It was declared off-limits to Hàn Chinese from 1644, when the first Qīng emperor took up residence in the Forbidden City, until the dynasty began to lose power in the late 19th century. The ban preserved Dōngběi's image as a mysterious and menacing place separate from China proper.

"The Chinese talk of Tartary as a country half as big as the rest of the world besides," Lord Macartney, George III's emissary to the court of the Qīng Qiánlóng emperor, wrote in the early 18th century. "But their conceptions of its limits are very dark and confused. There is a wide difference between pretension and possession."

Japan and Russia waged a series of battles for control of Dōngběi in the first half of the 20th century, the Chinese finally taking genuine possession of the region after Japan's defeat at the end of World War II. Using Japanese- and Russian-built railroads, China's new Communist leaders made it the center of their efforts to bring the country into the industrial age.

The name "Dōngběi" now conjures images, not of wild invaders on horseback, but of ruddy-faced factory workers famous nationwide for their down-home friendliness.

Despite industrialization, Dōngběi still claims China's largest natural forest, its most pristine grasslands, and one of its most celebrated lakes (Tiān Chí). What makes the region unique, however, are the architectural remnants of the last 350 years—early Qīng palaces and tombs, incongruous Russian cupolas, and eerie structures left over from Japan's wartime occupation.

The region is undergoing a tourism makeover in an attempt to replace income lost with a recent spate of state-owned factory closures. It is still frankly a difficult place to visit, with overpriced hotels, industrial malaise, and a paucity of English speakers. Yet the difficulty offers its own reward: the chance to travel in a place largely free of the exploitation and cultural hyperbole common to tourism in more accommodating parts of China.

Note: Unless noted otherwise, hours listed in this chapter are the same every day.

1 Shěnyáng

Liáoníng Province, 868km (538 miles) NE of Běijīng, 544km (337 miles) SW of Harbin

Shěnyáng is the largest city in Dōngběi and the region's unlovely gateway. A sprawling chaos of dirt and noise where historical buildings stand bathed in the neon of new consumerism, it is the epitome of China's propensity for criminally negligent urban planning. It was the birthplace of the Qīng dynasty in the 15th century and is now the capital of Liáoníng, Dōngběi's southernmost and wealthiest province. Many travelers spend only enough time here to switch trains, but it is worthwhile to linger. The city may be ugly but it is also home to several of Dōngběi's most fascinating historical attractions.

Shěnyáng has existed under various names since the Táng dynasty (618–907) and has been the region's most strategically important city since 1625, when Jürchen founders of the Qīng dynasty (1626–1912) made it their capital (Shénjīng). The Qīng's leaders stayed in the city for 19 years, perfecting a system of government modeled on the Chinese and plotting an attack on the weakened Míng from inside their palace, which still stands in the city center. With the decline of the Qīng at the start of the 20th century, the city (renamed Fēngtiān) fell under the influence of legendary warlord Zhāng Zuòlín. Zhāng ruled Manchuria from his downtown residence courtyard complex just south of the Qīng palace, until his assassination by Japanese soldiers in 1928. The city drifted without obvious leadership until the fall of 1931, when Japan's Kwantung Army (in Japanese: *Kantogun;* in Mandarin: *Guāndōng Jūn*) used the "discovery" of a small hole blasted in their railway line north of the city (known to them as Mukden) as a pretense to invade. The attack, referred to in China as the September 18th (or Mukden) Incident and immortalized in a museum in the north part of the city, eventually led to the establishment of Manchukuo (Mandarin: *Mǎnzhōu Guó*), the puppet state Japan used to mask its territorial ambitions during World War II.

The mayor who transformed Dàlián (p. 169) into the shimmering pride of northern China, now the governor of Liáoníng Province, has vowed to work his magic on the capital. Shěnyáng has never been pretty, but perhaps it doesn't need to be. "[Mukden] is ancient and dusty, with nothing especially attractive," one visiting Catholic missionary wrote in 1919. "I found it very interesting." The same holds true today.

ESSENTIALS

GETTING THERE   Flights connect Shěnyáng's **Táoxiān International Airport (Táoxiān Guójì Jīchǎng)** with every major Chinese city, including Běijīng (16 flights daily), Shànghǎi (nine flights daily), Guǎngzhōu (three flight daily); there are also connections to Seoul (three flights daily) and Tokyo (Tues, Thurs, Sat). Flights can be booked at the **China Northern Airlines** ticket office (**Zhōngguó Běifāng Hángkōng Shòupiào Chù;** ✆ **024/2383-4089**), located at Zhōnghuá Lù 117, north of Shíyī (11) Wěi Lù. The office is open from 8am to 5pm. The airport is 30km (19 miles) south of downtown. An **airport shuttle** runs from the ticket office every half-hour (¥10/$1; 45 min.). **Taxis** at the ticket office offer to take groups for ¥15 to ¥20 ($2–$3) per person; other taxis charge ¥60 ($7.50), including the ¥10 ($1) road toll. Cash and traveler's checks can be exchanged at a kiosk near the international arrivals area.

Shěnyáng has two main **railway stations:** the Russian-built **Shěnyáng Zhàn (Shěnyáng Railway Station)** on the western edge of downtown, and the modern

Shěnyáng Běi Zhàn (Shěnyáng North Station), north of Shìfú Guǎngchǎng. Trains to Běijīng (20 daily; 6–10 hr.; ¥185/$23), Dàlián (18 daily; 4 hr.; ¥55/$7), Chángchūn (24 daily; 3 hr.; ¥47/$6), and Dāndōng (nine daily; 4 hr.; ¥42/$5) stop at both railway stations. Express trains to Shànghǎi (four daily; 25 hr.; ¥405/$51) and Harbin (eight daily; 6½ hr.; ¥76/$10) leave only from Shěnyáng Běi.

Shěnyáng's main **long-distance bus station, Qìchē Kuàisù Kèyùn Zhàn** (ticket office open 7:30am–6pm; ☎ **024/2251-1225**), is on Huìgōng Jiē behind the Times Plaza Hotel. **Luxury coaches,** the best way to travel by bus, go to Harbin (7 hr.; ¥130/$16); Chángchūn (3⅓ hr.; ¥71/$9), Dàlián (5½ hr.; ¥99/$12), and Dāndōng (3 hr.; ¥58/$7).

Shěnyáng

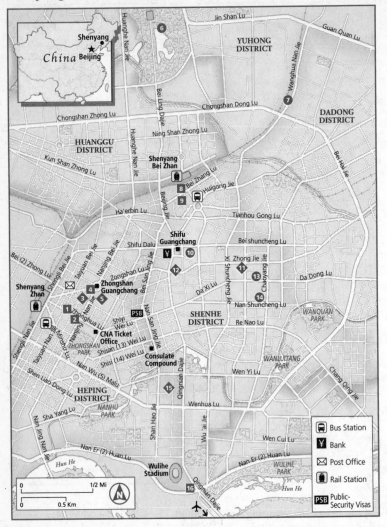

GETTING AROUND   The two areas in Shěnyáng where it is feasible to walk are the old city center, a 5-sq.-km (2-sq.-mile) area surrounding the Imperial Palace (Gù Gōng), and the shopping district east of Shěnyáng Zhàn. Most sights, however, are scattered in the sprawl outside these areas. **Taxis** charge ¥7 ($1) for the first 3km (2 miles), then ¥1 (15¢) for every 600m (⅓ mile). **Buses** charge ¥1 to ¥2 (15¢–25¢) and congregate at the two railway stations. Bus no. 203 travels from Shěnyáng Zhàn via Shífú Guǎngchǎng to Shěnyáng Běi Zhàn; a circle-line *(huán)* bus goes from Shěnyáng Zhàn past Tàiyuán Jiē to Zhōng Jiē (see "Shopping," later in this chapter) and the Gù Gōng. Maps can be bought at Shěnyáng Běi Zhàn.

ACCOMMODATIONS ■

Gloria Plaza Shěnyáng
  (Shěnyáng Kǎilái Dàjiǔdiàn) 9
  沈阳凯莱大酒店
Liáoning Hotel 4
  (Liaoning Fàndiàn)
  辽宁饭店
New World Courtyard
  (Xīnshìjiè Wànyí Jiǔdiàn) 2
  新世界万怡酒店
Shěnyáng Marriott
  (Shěnyáng Huángcháo
  Wànháo Jiǔdiàn) 16
  沈阳皇朝万豪酒店
Shěnyáng Yóuzhèng Dàshà 8
  沈阳邮政大厦
Sheraton Lido
  (Lìdū Xǐláidēng Fàndiàn) 16
  丽都喜来登饭店
Traders Hotel
  (Shāngmào Fàndian) 1
  商贸饭店

DINING ◆

Bar Street
  (Jiǔbā Yītiáo Jiē) 15
  酒吧一条街
Mǎ Family Shāomai
  (Mǎ Jiā Shāomài Guǎn) 11
  玛家烧麦馆
Mulligan's 5
  爱尔兰酒吧
Star Hollywood Café
  (Xīngchén Hǎoláiwù Cāntīng) 3
  星辰好莱坞餐厅
Xīnglóngxuān Jiǎozi Guǎn 12
  兴隆轩饺子馆

ATTRACTIONS ●

9.18 Museum
  (Jiǔyībā Bówùguǎn) 7
  九一八博物馆
Běi Líng 6
  北陵
Gù Gōng
  (Imperial Palace) 13
  故宫
Liáoníng Provincial Museum
  (Liáoníng Shèng Bówùguǎn) 10
  辽宁省博物馆
Zhāng Residence
  (Zhāng Xuéliáng Jiùjū Chénlièguǎn) 14
  张学良旧居陈列馆

FAST FACTS

Banks, Foreign Exchange & ATMs   The main branch of **Bank of China** is at Shìfú Lù 253, west of the Shìfú Guǎngchǎng (open Mon–Fri 8am–noon and 1–4pm; ✆ 024/2285-7569). Traveler's checks and cash can be exchanged at window 28 on the second floor; credit card transactions are handled on the third floor. There are no international ATMs anywhere in town.

Consulates   All consulates are located in a single, heavily fortified compound at the intersection of Shísì (14) Wěi Lù and Běi Sān Jīng Jiē. The **United States Consulate** (open Mon–Fri 8:30am–noon and 1–4:30pm; ✆ 024/2322-1198) is closest to the corner at Shísì Wěi Lù 14. The **Japanese Consulate** (open Mon–Fri 8:45am–noon and 1–5:15pm; ✆ 024/2322-7490) is next door. The surly staff at the **Russian Consulate** (✆ 024/2322-3927), in the rear of the compound, keeps odd hours, doesn't speak English, and will almost never grant you a tourist visa; arrive before 10am if you want to try your luck.

Internet Access   The 24-hour Internet cafe **Tiětōng Xīngànxiàn Wǎngbā** (¥2/25¢ per hour) is 2 blocks east of the railway station on Zhōnghuá Lù. Dial-up is ✆ 165.

Post Office   The main post office is at the corner of Zhōngshān Lù and Tàiyuán Běi Jiē (open May–Sept 8am–5:30pm; Oct–Apr 8am–5pm).

Visa Extensions   Visa extensions are available at the **PSB** Exit/Entry office (© **024/ 2290-0186** or 024/2310-5927) in the old Bank of Communications building (third floor, northeast entrance), at the intersection of Běi Sān Jīng Jiē and Shíyī Wěi Lù (open Mon–Fri 8:30–11am and 1–4pm). Visas take 1 week to process, and require a hotel registration card and proof of at least ¥20,000 ($2,500) in a bank account.

EXPLORING SHĚNYÁNG

The one attraction within walking distance of the downtown hotels is **Zhōngshān Guǎngchǎng (Sun Yat-sen Square),** 4 blocks northeast of Shěnyáng Zhàn on Zhōngshān Lù. It's notable for its striking **statue of Máo,** which stands proudly surrounded by a teeming mass of soldiers, peasants, and workers all bearing weapons of the revolution (guns, sledgehammers, Máo's little red book) and staring grim-faced at the banks and hotels that now surround the square.

Běi Líng 🌟🌟   This august tomb at the center of an Eastern Eden of ponds, pavilions, twisting paths, and 300-year-old pines contains the remains of Qīng dynasty founder Huáng (the Manchurian Tài Zōng emperor, Abahai). The eighth son of Nurhaci, the Jürchen chieftain who unified Manchuria in the early 17th century, Huáng Tàijí rose to power shortly after his father's death, proclaimed the founding of the Qīng dynasty in 1636, then conquered Korea.

Construction of the tomb (also known as Zhāo Líng) began in 1643, the year Huáng Tàijí died, and took 8 years to complete. A central path leads visitors through the front gate, past a stone army of guardian animals and into Lóng'ēn Diàn, a large hall housing the emperor's memorial tablet. Climbing up onto the encircling wall at the northern end will put you at eye level with the tomb itself, a simple dirt hill topped by a lonely tree. Huáng Tàijí's body lies somewhere beneath. The tomb lies at the northern end of Běi Líng Park, former imperial cemetery turned public space. The tomb aside, the park is an excellent respite from the din of the city with its beautiful greenery and myriad kite fliers.

Tàishān Lù 12, at northern end of Běi Líng Dàjiē. Admission ¥30 ($4) 7:30am–6:30pm plus ¥6 (90¢) for Běi Líng Park entrance. Bus: no. 217 from Shěnyáng Běi Zhàn. Taxi: 20 min. from downtown (¥15/$2).

Gù Gōng (Imperial Palace) 🌟   For those who have visited its predecessor in Běijīng, the first and most obvious difference will be size. Shěnyáng's humble imperial abode covers roughly 60,000 sq. m (645,835 sq. ft.), less than a tenth the area of the Forbidden City. This means you don't have to run a tourist marathon to see all the offerings, nor do you need to devote an entire day to exploration.

The palace is largely modeled after Běijīng's Gù Gōng, but architecturally blends intricate Mongolian- and Tibetan-influenced carvings favored by the early Qīng. Unfortunately, many of the exhibitions are poorly cared for, such as Zhōng Zhèng Diàn, where emperor Abahai once attended to political affairs. Viewed from afar, the carved oak throne and emperor-yellow cushion have faded under a thick layer of dust into dull wood and a sickly pale color.

On the northeastern side is the oldest and most impressive structure in the Gù Gōng: **Dà Zhèng Hall (Dà Zhèng Diàn)** and the surrounding **Pavilion of Ten Kings (Shí Wáng Tíng).** The original gate housed to the east of the main entrance is now closed to the public, so visitors will stumble upon this homage to the Manchurian army either from a small door on the west, or from the back. The two pavilions closest to the hall display the offices of the left and right wings, while the

Minorities & the Manchu Myth

Manchurians, one of China's more numerous minorities with a population of 11 million, did not actually exist until a dozen years before they conquered China. Originally a loose alliance of nomadic tribes, they became Manchus (although its exact meaning is unknown, the name was probably taken from a Buddhist term meaning "great good fortune"), after Qīng founder Huáng Tàijí invented the label to unify his people and distance them from their barbarian roots. But it was Nurhaci, Huáng Tàijí's father, who paved the way for the Manchu conquest of Míng China. Nurhaci was bent on instilling loyalty and demanded men who surrendered to him to imitate the Manchu tradition of shaving the front of the forehead and braiding hair in the back into a long "queue," a law that was also enforced during the reign of Huáng Tàijí. By 1645, any man who did not comply faced execution. The Chinese were humiliated by the order at the time, but the queue has recently been reclaimed as Chinese cultural history, and makes frequent appearances on dozens of widely popular Chinese period soap operas.

Manchu culture borrowed heavily from a number of ethnic groups, especially in architecture (see Gù Gōng, below), but many of their customs disappeared after they established the Qīng and adopted Chinese habits—a phenomenon Chinese historians still note with pride. Some aspects of Manchu culture have survived, however. Most notable among these are kàng, heated brick beds still found in some Dōngběi homes, and qípáo (traditional fitted dresses), made famous in 1930s Shànghǎi.

Dōngběi is technically home to more than a dozen other ethnic groups, including Mongolians, Russians, and Koreans. But the majority of them were, at one time or another, considered Manchurian. Victims of successive assimilation, most are now practically indistinguishable from Hàn Chinese. A few distinct minority cultures have managed to survive, if only barely, in the more remote corners of the Northeast. These include a few nomadic **Oroqen** hunters and reindeer-herding **Ewenkis** in the Greater Xīng'ān Mountains (on the border between Inner Mongolia and Hēilóngjiāng Province), and the **Hèzhé,** the majority of whom live in northeastern Hēilóngjiāng Province. Numbering fewer than 5,000, Hèzhé are famous for their fish-skin clothing, a typical suit of which costs between ¥5,000 and ¥6,000 ($625–$750) and uses roughly 250 kilograms (550 lb.) of pike, carp, or salmon.

remaining eight pavilions display various Qīng weaponry and replicas of the armor and the colorful banners (two each of yellow, red, blue, and white) of the eight divisions of the Manchu army. Dà Zhèng Hall is where Dorgon, Huáng Tàijí's younger brother and regent to his successor Shùnzhì (the first Qīng emperor to rule from Běijīng), is said to have given the orders to invade China.

Shěnyáng Lù 771. Admission ¥50 ($6.25) Apr–Oct; ¥40 ($5) Nov–Mar. English guidebook with plenty of grammar mistakes ¥20 ($2.50). 8:30am–5:15pm. Bus: Huán to Gù Gōng stop; walk east along Cháoyáng Lù.

Liáoníng Provincial Museum (Liáoníng Shěng Bówùguǎn) ✿ *Kids* Don't let the giant brontosaurus guarding the entrance wagging its tail and giving a mechanical roar every few seconds deter you; this museum, opened in late 2004, houses an impressive collection of pieces mostly from the Qīng dynasty. The large, circular lay-out gives the museum a comfortable, open feel, while the vaulted ceilings absorb the sounds of chattering tour groups. Notable exhibits include the Zhōngguó Gǔdài Shíbēi Zhì Zhǎn, classical **Chinese stone tablets** tracing calligraphy back to the Han dynasty, and the Gǔdài Huòbì Zhǎn, or the **Chinese Money exhibition,** which dis-plays everything from rudimentary seashell beads to ancient gold ingots from which the auspicious Chinese delicacy *jiǎozi* (steamed dumplings) get their shape. On the third floor, the curators have imported leftover Jurassic Park props. This exhibit appears to be purely for entertainment and does not mean to suggest that dinosaurs ever existed here.

Fǔ Dà Lù 363, at Shìfǔ Guǎngchǎng. Admission ¥20 ($3). Audio tours in English and Chinese (available at coat check) ¥10 ($1) plus ¥100 ($13) and ID deposit. 9am–5pm.

9.18 Museum (Jiǔyībā Bówùguǎn) This revamped museum in northern Shěnyáng offers a decidedly biased view of the Mukden Incident (1931) in which Japan staged an attack on its own South Manchurian railway line at Liǔtiáo Hú as a pretense to invade the Northeast. Four large characters displayed under a clock frozen at 10:20 read *Wù wàng guó chǐ*—**Never forget the national disgrace.** The museum strives to offer a variety of unorthodox presentations. One exhibition, documenting the Rise of the Anti-Japanese Army of Resistance (coincidentally supported by the CPC, and in direct disobedience of Koumintang orders of nonresistance) replicates a guerrilla war-fare conference using full-size wax figures meeting in a large fake forest over the glow of a lamp-infused fire. Nearby are miniature clay figurines behind glass casing, with stunted comical bodies and expressions, celebrating the army's successes. Oil paintings and blown-up photos adorn the walls. The mixing and matching of presentation styles makes for muddled exhibitions. Other displays touch on the Unit 731 biological weapons experiments (see "Harbin," p. 193) and the Nánjīng Massacre (p. 381).

Wánghuā Jiē 46 (at Chóngshān Lù, southeast of Běi Líng). Admission ¥28 ($3.50). 8am–5:30pm. Bus: no. 253 from Dà Xī Mén (west of Gù Gōng).

Zhāng Residence (Zhāng Xuéliáng Jiùjū Chénlièguǎn) This resurrected courtyard house south of the Gù Gōng, originally known as Shuài Fǔ (the Comman-der's Palace), was the home of warlord Zhāng Zuòlín and his celebrated son, Marshal Zhāng Xuéliáng. The residence provides a glimpse into the almost-imperial world inhabited by the powerful warlords who ruled parts of China after the Qīng dynasty collapsed. A study in the Xiǎoqīng Lóu, a small European-styled house next to the main courtyard complex, is where Zhāng Zuòlín died after Japanese assassins exploded a bomb under his private train in 1928.

Corner of Cháoyáng Lù and Nán Shùnchéng Lù. ✆ 024/2484-2454. Admission ¥28 ($3.50). 8:30am–5:10pm. Walk west from Gù Gōng; take a left on Zhèngyáng Jiē.

OUTSIDE SHĚNYÁNG

Qiān Shān ✿ Once a quiet mountain retreat, Qiān Shān, one of Dōngběi's most accessible getaways, is slowly being taken over by hordes of tourists scrambling over the Sòng dynasty temples and zipping through the park on electric shuttle buses that charge ¥10 ($13) a ride. Getting off the main road, which twists through the national park, leads to a more serene and pleasant experience. Climbing is not highly favored by the teems of visitors, so it's quite easy to escape to a pleasant hike off the well-worn paths leading to sites and temples, though you have to climb quite a distance to get away from the karaoke bar speakers blasting homage to the gods on the northeastern slope.

The Běi Bù (Northern Ravine), with signs in English, can be seen in 1 day. Xiānrén Tái (Peak of the Immortals), site of the legendary Dà'ān Temple, requires an overnight trip. There are several affordable hotels in the area. Modest rooms are available in some of the Buddhist temples if you ask nicely.

17km (11 miles) south of Ān Shān. www.qianshan.ln.cn. Admission at main gate ¥50 ($6), temples ¥5–¥20 ($1–$3). Open 24 hr. Bus: Catch large air-conditioned bus to Ān Shān (every 15 min; 2 hr., ¥22/$2.75, plus ¥1/15¢ mandatory insurance) near Wénhuà Gōng, 3 blocks southeast of Shěnyáng Zhàn on Mínzhǔ Lù; then take minibus from Jiàn Guó Nán Lù (40 min.; ¥2/25¢) to Qiān Shān. Last bus back to Shěnyáng leaves Ān Shān at 7pm.

WHERE TO STAY

High season in Shěnyáng runs from March to mid-October. Hotels become especially crowded with a series of industry conventions in early September. Room rates are high, even with the customary 15% discount, but some of the high-end hotels offer good deals in summer.

Budget options are scarce. One affordable choice, the **Peace Hotel (Hépíng Bīnguǎn;** Zhōngshān Lù 97; ✆ **024/2349-8888**), located in a massive brick building painted red and white north of the Shěnyáng Zhàn, has a large variety of clean and simple rooms. A dorm bed costs ¥50 ($6); a standard room costs ¥180 ($23); a nice triple costs ¥260 ($33). The **Měisǎn Bīnguǎn** (Xiǎoxī Lù 48; ✆ **024/2273-5538;** fax 024/2273-5548) is a good value and offers old but tidy rooms with decent bathrooms; a standard room costs ¥160 ($20). It's just a few blocks west of Zhōng Jiē and within walking distance of the Gù Gōng.

VERY EXPENSIVE

Shěnyáng Marriott (Shěnyáng Huángcháo Wànháo Jiǔdiàn) ✦   This ostentatious hotel was the only full-fledged Marriott in China until the chain opened a second branch in Běijīng in 2002. The property is luxurious, but its blinding exterior and the gold-and-crystal garishness of its lobby can leave you craving subtlety. Guest rooms mirror the rest of the hotel, with plush beds and beautiful redwood furniture. Small bathrooms have generous marble fittings. There's an excellent but pricey Japanese restaurant (see Mikado, below) on the premises.

Qīngnián Dàjiē 386. ✆ 024/2388-3456. Fax 024/2388-0677. www.marriott.com. 435 units. ¥968 ($121) standard room. 15% service charge. Rates include breakfast. AE, DC, MC, V. **Amenities:** 3 restaurants; deli; bar; cigar room; small indoor pool; nice exercise room; concierge; business center; forex; salon; 24-hr. room service; same-day dry cleaning/laundry; nonsmoking rooms; executive-level rooms. In room: A/C, satellite TV, dataport, minibar, fridge, hair dryer, safe.

Sheraton Lido (Lìdū Xǐláidēng Fàndiàn) ✦✦✦   This is the best five-star in Shěnyáng. Decorated throughout with fine, original artwork, it offers the city's largest and classiest rooms—a stark contrast in style to the neighboring Marriott's rooms. Standard guest rooms have large bathrooms with separate bathtub and shower. The fourth floor has an indoor climbing wall.

Qīngnián Dàjiē 386 (south of Wǔlǐhé Stadium). ✆ 024/2318-8888. Fax 024/2318-8000. www.sheraton.com/shenyang. 424 units. ¥1,200 ($150) standard room. 15% service charge. Rates include breakfast. AE, DC, MC, V. **Amenities:** 2 restaurants; deli; bar; cigar room; indoor pool; health club and spa; concierge; business center; forex; salon; 24-hr. room service; same-day dry cleaning/laundry; nonsmoking floors; executive-level rooms. In room: A/C, satellite TV, dataport, minibar, fridge, hair dryer, safe.

Traders Hotel (Shāngmào Fàndiàn) ⚝ Its convenient location, in the midst of the Tàiyuán Jiē shopping district and within walking distance of Shěnyáng Zhàn, is the number-one advantage of this Shangri-La managed four-star hotel. Service is stellar, standard rooms are spacious, and the bathrooms virtually spotless. Wireless Internet connection is available on the 21st floor.

Zhōnghuá Lù 68 (at Tàiyuán Jiē). ✆ 024/2341-2288. Fax 024/2341-1988. www.shangri-la.com/shenyang/traders/en/index.aspx. 588 units. ¥1,350 ($169) standard room. 15% service charge. Rates include breakfast for 1. AE, DC, MC, V. **Amenities:** 2 restaurants; deli; bar; small exercise room; Jacuzzi; sauna; concierge; business center; forex; large shopping center; salon; 24-hr. room service; same-day dry cleaning/laundry; nonsmoking rooms; executive-level rooms. *In room:* A/C, satellite TV, broadband Internet access, minibar, fridge, safe.

EXPENSIVE

Gloria Plaza Shěnyáng (Shěnyáng Kǎilái Dàjiǔdiàn) *Value* The Gloria Plaza was the first international hotel to open in the Shěnyáng Běi Zhàn area and is still a reliable luxury standby. Well-maintained guest rooms are unremarkably decorated but comfortable and have small but clean bathrooms.

Yínbīn Jiē 32 (at Běi Zhàn Lù). ✆ 024/2252-8855. Fax 024/2252-8533. www.gphshenyang.com. 289 units. ¥999 ($124) standard room. 15% service charge. Summer discounts exceed 50%. AE, DC, MC, V. **Amenities:** 2 restaurants; bar; health club and spa; concierge; business center; salon; limited room service; dry cleaning/laundry. *In room:* A/C, satellite TV, minibar, fridge.

New World Courtyard (Xīn Shìjiè Wànyí Jiǔdiàn) The New World Courtyard, Shěnyáng's first international joint-venture hotel, is the only real downtown luxury alternative to Traders. Little has been done to update facilities since its opening in 1994, but rooms are spacious and comfortable enough, and service is courteous.

Nánjīng Nán Jiē 2 (at Zhōngshān Lù). ✆ 024/2386-9888. Fax 024/2386-0018. www.courtyard.com. 227 units. ¥1,000 ($125) standard room. 15% service charge. AE, DC, MC, V. **Amenities:** 3 restaurants; rusty exercise room; sauna; concierge; business center; forex; salon; limited room service; in-room massage; dry cleaning/laundry. *In room:* A/C, satellite TV, minibar, fridge.

MODERATE

Liáoníng Hotel (Liáoníng Bīnguǎn) ⚝⚝ *Finds* Originally part of the illustrious Japanese-run Yamato chain, the Liáoníng is one of a very few truly charming hotels in the Northeast. The building (constructed in 1927) underwent an admirable $3.75-million restoration in 2001, giving new life to the original marble staircase with its well-worn brass handrails and intimate green-and-white tile lobby. Guest rooms are high-ceilinged and simply furnished; bathrooms are small but pleasant. The Liáoníng's central location on Zhōngshān Guǎngchǎng adds to the charm.

Zhōngshān Lù 97, south of Zhōngshān Guǎngchǎng. ✆ 024/2383-9166. Fax 024/2383-9103. 79 units. ¥588–¥618 ($74–$77) standard room. No credit cards. **Amenities:** 2 restaurants; outdoor tennis court; exercise room; sauna; beautiful game room (chess and card tables); business center; laundry. *In room:* A/C, TV, dataport, fridge, hair dryer, safe.

INEXPENSIVE

Shěnyáng Yóuzhèng Dàshà *Value* The hallways in this government-run three-star are typically depressing, but its newly renovated rooms are surprisingly comfortable and clean. Prices are far lower than they should be. The hotel is also conveniently located next to Shěnyáng Běi Zhàn.

Běi Zhàn Lù 78. ✆ 024/2259-3333. Fax 024/2252-2369. 214 units. ¥278 ($35) standard room; ¥100 ($12) dorm (not renovated). No credit cards. **Amenities:** Restaurant; business center; laundry. *In room:* A/C, satellite TV, hair dryer.

WHERE TO DINE

Shěnyáng boasts a fair selection of Japanese restaurants. The classiest is **Mikado,** in the Shěnyáng Marriott (see above), with a specialization in teppanyaki and fine sushi served in private tatami-mat rooms. Cheaper and more convenient is the **Qiānyī Lāmiàn Diàn** (Tiānjīn Běi Jiē, north of the Dōngběi Cinema; ✆ **024/2341-9941),** open from 10am to 10pm. The small but lively Japanese noodle shop (with a picture menu) is located just southeast of the Shangri-La. There's a **KFC** on Zhōnghuá Jiē, south of Shěnyáng Zhàn, and a pair of **McDonald's** on Tàiyuán Jiē and Zhōng Jiē; Zhōng Jiē also has a **Pizza Hut.** For groceries, go to one of the city's ubiquitous 24-hour **Civic Moon** convenience stores or the **Carrefour** near Shěnyáng Běi Zhàn.

Mǎ Family Shāomài (Mǎ Jiā Shāomài Guǎn) ⚔ CHINESE/MUSLIM   Great-great-great-grandpa Mǎ is rumored to have first sold these award-winning *shāomài* (steamed open-top dumplings) from a street-side wheelbarrow in 1796. Prices on the menu are for a plate of 10 dumplings, but feel free to mix and match and order less or more accordingly—eight dumplings for one hungry person is more than enough. The most delicious offering here is the *chuántǒng* (traditional) *shāomài,* with beef and ginger. *Yù cuì* (jade green) *shāomài,* with egg and spring onion is excellent vegetarian fare.

Zhèngyáng Jiē, 5-min. walk north of Zhōng Jiē. ✆ 024/2484-5218. Meal for 2 ¥20–¥50 ($3–$6). No credit cards. 10am–9pm.

Xīnglóngxuān Jiǎozi Guǎn ⚔ JIǍOZI   Unmistakable with its bright red facade, this restaurant is cheaper and livelier than the "tourist-approved" Lǎobiān Jiǎozi Guǎn (on Zhōng Jiē), and its *jiǎozi* are just as delicious. Try the *biānxiàn sānxiān* (egg, shrimp, and chives stir-fried before wrapping) or the standard *zhūròu báicài* (pork and cabbage).

Zhōngshān Lù 258, at Yī Jīng Jiē (1 block east of Golden Hotel). ✆ 024/2270-0209. Meal for 2 ¥15–¥40 ($2–$5). No credit cards. 9am–10pm.

SHĚNYÁNG AFTER DARK

Shěnyáng goes to bed at around 10pm on most Saturdays, but late nights can still be had. The places to be seen are **Star Hollywood Café** (Xīngchén Hǎoláiwū Cāntīng on Tóngzé Běi Jiē; ✆ 024/2340-1398) and **Mulligan's,** an Irish pub at Nánjīng Běi Jiē 206 (✆ **024/2334-1888).** Mulligan's, with its wide selection of international beers and a tolerable level of kitsch, is a much better choice. If you order a bottle of whiskey but can't finish it, the bar will hang a name tag on it and throw it in a glass display case near the door, where it will wait until the next night of debauchery. A cheap, adventurous choice for a night out is **Jiǔbā Yī Tiáo Jiē,** or Bar Street. Located on Wényì Lù, Jiǔbā Jiē has an assortment of small joints with lively names like Nothing Is Impossible, The Way to Live Bar, and Yesterday Once More (of which there are two locations within 500m/1,640 ft. of each other). You can take a taxi to Bar Street from downtown for about ¥10 ($1.25). In warm weather, outdoor seating is set up, and with a big group, any of the abashedly neon places would be a fine night out in sleepy Shěnyáng.

2 Dāndōng

280km (173 miles) S of Shěnyáng, 370km (229 miles) NE of Dàlián

Visitors come to **Dāndōng** for one reason: to see North Korea. Situated on a bend in the Yālù Jiāng (Green Duck River) and connected by rail bridge to the North Korean town of

Sinuiju, the city has built a robust economy around the thousands of geographical voyeurs who rush to the border every summer. For all its wealth, Dāndōng remains a Chinese city, with crowded tenement buildings and a new riverside development area already stained by pollution, but it gleams in comparison with its neighbor.

ESSENTIALS

GETTING THERE **Flights** leave the airport (Dāndōng Jīchǎng), 13km (8 miles) west of town, for Shànghǎi (Tues and Sat) and Shēnzhèn (Tues and Sat). Purchase tickets at the **CAAC ticket office** (**Mínháng Shòupiào Chù;** ✆ **0415/221-7999;** open Mon–Sat 8–11:30am and 1–4:30pm) at Jǐnshān Dàjiē 50 (intersection with Sān Wěi Lù). The **airport shuttle** (30 min.; ¥5/65¢) leaves from the CAAC office 2 hours before each flight. By **taxi,** it's a 20-minute ride for ¥30 ($4). Dāndōng's **railway station** is on Shí (10) Wěi Lù, on the western edge of town. Trains go to Běijīng (6:27pm; 14 hr.; ¥263/$32), Shěnyáng (8 daily; 4 hr.; ¥36/$5), Dàlián (6:04pm; 11 hr.; ¥99/$12), Chángchūn (7:13am; 9 hr.; ¥41/$5), and Yánjí (10:05am; 22 hr.; ¥149/$19). **International trains** go to Pyongyang (¥101/$13) and Moscow (¥1,740/ $212); tickets for these are available in the **CITS** foreign office (✆ **0415/214-0145;** open Mon–Fri 8:30–11am and 1:30–5pm). The office is located in the towering, double-spired Shuāngxīng Dàshà across from the railway station (see "Border Crossing: North Korea & Russia," below). The **long-distance bus station** (✆ **0415/213-4571)** is across the street from the railway station, at the corner of Shí Wěi Lù and Gōng'ān Jiē, with coaches to Shěnyáng (¥58/$7), Tōnghuà (¥45/$6), and Běijīng (10am; ¥165/$20). **Dàlián express buses** (**Dàlián Kuài Kè**) (7:35am, 8:30am, 12:30pm, and 1:50pm; 4½ hr.; ¥68/$9) leave from the Bǎoshān Shìchǎng, located 2km (1⅓ miles) east of the railway station, just off Gōng'ān Jiē. **Private cars** at the long-distance bus station will take you to Dàlián in 3½ hours for ¥80 to ¥100 ($10–$12).

VISITOR INFORMATION For tourist complaints call ✆ **0415-3147937.**

GETTING AROUND Most of Dāndōng lies north of a V formed by the Yālù Jiāng and the train tracks. Shí Wěi Lù follows the tracks to the Yālù Jiāng Gōngyuán, facing North Korea. **Taxis** are ¥6 (75¢) in town (negotiate for longer distances).

FAST FACTS

Banks, Foreign Exchange & ATMs Cash and traveler's checks can be exchanged from 8am to 4pm inside the **Bank of China** branch at Jǐnshān Dàjiē 60 (at its intersection with Èr Wěi Lù; open Mon–Fri 7:30–11:30am and 1–5pm). A 24-hour international ATM is located at the bank's entrance.

Internet Access The 24-hour **Wúxiàn Wǎngyuàn** is on Shíyī (11) Jīng Jiē, north of Liù (6) Wěi Lù. It charges ¥2 (25¢) per hour. Dial-up is ✆ **96163.**

Post Office The main post office, open from 8am to 5:30pm, is on the corner of Qī (7) Wěi Lù and Qī Jīng Jiē. Phone cards are sold inside.

Visa Extensions For extensions, go to room 112 of the main **PSB** office at Jiāngchéng Dàjiē 15, behind Shuāngxīng Dàshà (✆ **0415/212-7086;** open Mon–Fri 8am–noon and 1:30–5:30pm). You'll have to show a hotel registration card and proof that you have $100 per day of the extension.

EXPLORING DĀNDŌNG

There isn't much to see at the **North Korean border,** but the contrast between lively Dāndōng and depressed Sinuiju does provide a vivid illustration of the different paths

Bus Station
¥ Bank
✉ Post Office
🚂 Rail Station
PSB Public-Security Visas

Shangshan Jie

Shiyi (11) Jing Jie

To Baoshan
Shichang

Jinshan Dajie   CAAC
Ticket Office

Train
Station

Shí (10) Wei Lù
Jiǔ (9) Wei Lù
Qī (7) Jine Jie
Qī (7) Wei Lù
Liù (6) Wei Lù
Sān (3) Wei Lù
Èr (2) Wei Lù

Liu (6) Jing Jie

CITS

PSB

Jiangcheng Dajie

Bādàjú Seafood Street (Bādàjú Hǎixiān yī tiáo jiē)

Jiangyan Jie

Remains of
Old Bridge

Yalujiang
Gongyuan

Yalu River

ACCOMMODATIONS ■
Guómén Jiǔdiàn 5
国门酒店
Jiāngbīn Hotel
(Jiāngbīn Jiǔdiàn) 2
江滨酒店
Kǎirìdá Hotel
(Kǎirìdá Bīnguǎn) 3
凯日达宾馆
Zhōnglián Dàjiǔdiàn 6
中联大酒店

DINING ◆
Arirang Ālǐláng 7
阿里郎
Dāndōng Cháoxiān Fàndiàn 9
丹东朝鲜饭店
Xiānhǎi Jū Jiǔdiàn 8
鲜海居酒店

ATTRACTIONS ●
Memorial Hall of the War to Resist
U.S. Aggression and Aid Korea
(Kàngměi Yuáncháo Jìniànguǎn) 1
抗美援朝纪念馆
Yālù River Bridge
(Yālù Jiāng Qiáo) 4
鸭绿江桥

OTHER SIGHTS (not on map)
Five Dragon Mountain
(Wǔ Lóng Shān) 五龙山
Tiger Mountain Great Wall
(Hǔ Shān Chángchéng) 虎山长城

to development taken by China and its Communist ally. There are two ways to see the border—by boat and by bridge. Most visitors do both. **Boats** leave from inside the Yālù Jiāng Gōngyuán (6:30am–5:30pm; ¥1/15¢), a 10-minute walk south of the railway station at the end of Shí Wěi Lù. The boats range in size, from large, tacky Chinese-roofed floats to small speedboats. Prices are highly negotiable, but in general, you should not pay more than ¥10 ($1.25) per person, and chartering a small speed boat should cost no more than ¥30 ($3.65). Drivers will hand you a flimsy life jacket, then whip you around to within 3m (10 ft.) of Sinuiju so you can take pictures of the rusting cargo boats, a shipyard, and waving children. A few blocks west, along Jiāngyán Jiē, is the **Yālù Jiāng Qiáo** ✦ (6am–6pm; ¥15/$2), a unique horizontal rotation bridge bombed by the United States in 1950. Korea dismantled its half shortly after the Korean War armistice, rendering the bridge useless. You can wander out to the still-mangled end of the Chinese section, where someone has installed a pair of bomb casings as a reminder.

You might guess what kind of perspective a museum clunkily named the **Memorial Hall of the War to Resist U.S. Aggression and Aid Korea (Kàngměi Yuáncháo Jìniànguǎn; open 8am–5pm; ¥30/$3.65)** might have. Nevertheless, it offers an interesting Communist revisionist's look at the Korean War with black-and-white photos, surprisingly clear English translations, and patriotic music piped in. The museum requires some effort to reach—not just because it's located on a hill on the north side of Shàngshān Jiē, in the northwest part of town, but because the stairs to the memorial are quite a climb. The museum is to the right of the memorial, and behind the museum are some rusty rail cars, tanks, and fighter planes used during the war. Take bus no. 21 from the railway station, get off at the Tǐyùguǎn, and walk northwest.

OUTSIDE DĀNDŌNG

Five Dragon Mountain (Wǔ Lóng Shān) The 20-minute drive from downtown Dāndōng puts you in an idyllic setting with plenty of nice hikes and a temple that houses 20 monks. Ignore the tacky faux-Japanese "villas" at the front of the park, and concentrate on the nature within. It's particularly nice in the autumn when the leaves change colors.

Admission ¥36 ($4.35). Open 24 hr. Round-trip taxi from center of town ¥80 ($9.75). Bus: no. 18.

Tiger Mountain Great Wall (Hǔ Shān Chángchéng) ✿ Tiger Mountain, a short, steep, and impeccably restored section of the Great Wall located 30km (19 miles) northeast of Dāndōng, forms part of China's border with North Korea. A brief hike along the Wall provides beautiful views of surrounding cornfields, and the return path takes you right up against the small stream that separates Chinese and North Korean territory. South Chinese sometimes wander onto stones set in the stream just behind the Wall to trade goods and information with North Korean soldiers and farmers. *Warning:* Cross over on the stones yourself and you risk arrest.

☎ 0415/557-8511. Admission ¥23 ($3). Museum ¥10 ($1). Open 24 hr. Tourist bus (May–Oct; 40 min.; ¥11/$1 round-trip) leaves from left side of long-distance bus station at 8:10am and 1pm, returns from mountain 11:30am and 3pm.

Tips Border Crossing: North Korea & Russia

At press time, United States citizens were not allowed to travel from Dāndōng to North Korea. CITS in Dāndōng can arrange tours for other nationalities, but independent Běijīng-based operations like foreign-run Koryo Tours (www.koryogroup.com) can also pick you up in Dāndōng, charge roughly the same rates, and have more experience with foreigners. The paperwork takes 2 weeks to process.

Crossing the border from Dōngběi into **Russia,** either on the Trans-Siberian train or at one of the border posts in Hēilóng Jiāng and Inner Mongolia, is easier but also requires a visa. Standard tourist visas can usually only be arranged at the Russian Embassy in Běijīng. Keep in mind that you'll have to arrange for a Chinese **double-entry visa** if you plan to come back to China from either country.

WHERE TO STAY

A recent boom in hotels in Dāndōng means that travelers have a lot more choices and bargaining power. The recently renovated **Jiāngbīn Hotel** ✿✿ (Yánjiāng Kāifāqū Fángbà 5 Hào Lóu; ✆ **0415/315-3748;** fax 0415/314-2835; Visa accepted) is the best value in town, with stylish, modern rooms—complete with computer and free Internet access—facing the river (¥300–¥600/$37–$74; 20% discount available). Just down the street is the **Kairida Hotel** (Yánjiāng Kāifāqū Fángbà 1 Hào Lóu; ✆ **0415/345-9995**) a small boutique property that caters to Korean guests. The rooms and bathrooms are small but clean and modern (¥320–¥600/$39–$74; no credit cards). The city's only four-star hotel is the **Zhōnglián Dàjiǔdiàn** ✿ (Shàngmào Lǚyóu Qū A Qū 1; ✆ **0415/317-0666;** fax 0415/317-0888; www.zlhotel.com.cn), located opposite the Yālù Jiāng Qiáo. The hotel offers a nice Western food buffet, a bowling center, a cigar lounge, and surprisingly large rooms with generously sized beds and impeccable bathrooms (¥489–¥658/$60–$80; AE, DC, MC, V accepted). The hotel cafe looks onto North Korea. Across the street is the three-star **Guómén Jiǔdiàn** (Biānjìng Jīngjì Hézuò Qū Huìyǒu Huāyuán 1; ✆ **0415/315-7788;** fax 0415/315-722; (¥498–¥528/$50–$66; no credit cards). Guest rooms lack any character, but at least they come with a pair of binoculars which you can use to gaze at North Korea from rooms overlooking the river. Bathrooms are kept clean and the service is surprisingly good. Management, however, won't offer much of a discount.

WHERE TO DINE

Downtown Dāndōng is full of small, nondescript home-style restaurants and *jiǎozi* houses, and the river promenade has a number of upscale Japanese and Korean eateries. The **Dāndōng Cháoxiǎn Fàndiàn** ✿ (✆ **0415/313-9919;** open 10am–9pm), northeast of the railway station at Qī Jīng Jiē 37, serves the best Korean cold noodles *(lěngmiàn)* in town for a mere ¥3.50 (50¢). Along the strip of Korean eateries that line the river, locals consider **Arirang (Ālǐláng)** ✿ (✆ **0415/212-2333;** 9:00am–9:30pm) the best. The nice Korean setting with comfortable booths and private rooms is a nice place to relax after boating. Try the *shíguō Bànfàn* (stone pot rice), known as bibimbop in Korean, the *huǒguō* (hot pot), the *shēngbàn niúròu* (raw beef). If you're really feeling adventurous, you might consider the *xiānglà gǒuròu* (spicy dog). The best place to try the local seafood, which area residents rave about, is at Xiānhǎ iJū Jiǔdiàn (Bādàjū Hǎixiān Yītiáo jiē; ✆ **0415/216-5763;** open 9am–midnight). It offers a simple, clean interior and a back room full of tanks of live seafood that you can wander through.

3 Dàlián ✿✿✿ & Lùshùn

397km (246 miles) S of Shěnyáng

Dàlián is the supermodel of Chinese cities. Thoroughly modern, sartorially savvy, and unabashedly narcissistic, it is also the largest and busiest port in northern China. Dàlián's straightforward beauty can be refreshing in a region where most towns are of the interesting-but-homely type, and indeed, there are few more enjoyable activities after a week in the Dōngběi gloom than a sunlit stroll along the city's supremely walkable streets. The mere fact that the city has a definable downtown, unlike other cities in China, is to be lauded.

Like Shànghǎi and Hong Kong, the cities to which it is most often compared, Dàlián isn't really Chinese. Located just north of the Lǚshùn naval base at the tip of the Liáodōng Peninsula, it was conceived by Russia's czarist government as an ice-free alternative to Vladivostok. Construction of the port, originally called Dalny, got off to a quick start after Russia secured a lease on the peninsula in 1898; however, it lost the city and Lǚshùn to Japan in the Russo-Japanese War (1904–05). Dàlián (in Japanese: *Dairen*) soon grew into the pleasantly sophisticated port Russia had imagined.

Communist-era industrial development swamped Dàlián in thick clouds of factory smoke, but it was miraculously resurrected in the mid-1990s by Mayor Bó Xīlái, who tried to model the new Dàlián on cities he had seen in Europe. This led him to introduce several revolutionary measures—including a hefty fine for public spitting—that have become a model for urban renewal projects throughout China. Today, Dàlián is considered a vision of China's future both by optimists, who laud its beauty and smoothly functioning modernity, and by more cynical observers, who point wryly to the same silver skyscrapers and note how many are empty. Striking as the modern buildings are, it is the old colonial architecture, remnants of Japanese and Russian rule contrasting pleasantly with the newness around them, that is the city's most interesting attraction.

Fashion designers and consumers from China, Japan, Korea, and Hong Kong descend on Dàlián in mid-September for the 2-week **Dàlián International Fashion Festival (Dàlián Guójì Fúzhuāng Jié).** The festival isn't as important or glamorous as the city claims, but it's worth seeing if you're in the area.

ESSENTIALS

GETTING THERE   Dàlián's **airport (Zhōushuǐzi Guójì Jīchǎng)** is roughly 5km (3 miles) northeast of downtown on Yíngkè Lù (10 min. by taxi; ¥12/$2). Exchange traveler's checks on the second floor, next to the international check-in desk (no credit cards). **China Northern Airlines,** in the Mínháng Dàshà at Zhōngshān Lù 143 (open 6am–6pm; ✆ 0411/8280-2886), sells tickets to Běijīng (11 flights daily), Shànghǎi (seven flights daily), Guǎngzhōu (five flights daily), Hong Kong, and Seoul. **All Nippon Airlines** has a ticket counter on the first floor of the Sēn Mào building (intersection of Zhōngshān Lù and Wǔhuì Lù; ✆ 800/810-5551; fax 0411/369-2508; open Mon–Fri 9am–5pm). The counter sells tickets to Tokyo (daily) and Osaka (Mon–Sat).

Airport shuttles (departing every 2 hr.; 8am–4:40pm; 20 min.; ¥5/$1) from the Furama Hotel (next to the Shangri-La, see below) and Mínháng Dàshà. Or take **bus** no. 701 from the corner of Yùguāng Jiē and Yǒuhǎo Lù (45 min.; ¥1/15¢). By **taxi,** the trip between the airport and downtown takes 10 minutes and costs ¥12 ($2).

Dàlián's **railway station (Dàlián Zhàn)** is in the center of town, opposite Shènglì Guǎngchǎng (Victory Square). Trains go to Běijīng (two daily; 9–12 hr.; ¥269/$34), Shěnyáng (13 daily; 6 hr.; ¥55/$7), Harbin (9:42pm; 9 hr.; ¥231/$29), and Dāndōng (7:37pm; 11 hr.; ¥99/$12). Most **long-distance buses** congregate around Shènglì Guǎngchǎng (✆ 0411/8362-8681). Express air-conditioned coaches to Dāndōng (four daily; 4½ hr.; ¥68/$9) leave from the square's west side; buses to Běijīng (10am and noon; 14 hr.; ¥210/$26) and Chángchūn (four daily; 8 hr.; ¥140/$18) leave from the east side; and buses to Shěnyáng (10 daily; 6 hr.; ¥98/$12) leave from the Bó Hǎi Pearl Hotel next to the railway station.

Ferries leave from the Dàlián Kèyùn Zhàn (✆ 0411/8362-8681), on Gǎngwān Jiē (east end of Rénmín Lù), for Yāntái (8:30am, 12:30pm, and 2pm; 3½ hr.; ¥192/$24), Tiānjīn (even days 5:30pm; odd days 4:30pm; 14 hr.; ¥80–¥1,280/$10–$160), and Incheon (Rénchuǎn) in South Korea (Tues noon and Fri 3:30pm; ¥850–¥1,469/

ACCOMMODATIONS ■
Bó Hǎi Pearl Hotel
  (Bó Hǎi Míngzhū Dàjiǔdiàn) **3**
  渤海明珠大酒店
Dàlián Hotel
  (Dàlián Bīnguǎn) **9**
  大连宾馆
Gloria Plaza Hotel
  (Dàlián Kǎilái Dàjiǔdiàn) **7**
  凯莱大酒店
Jiāshùn Bīnguǎn **15**
  佳顺宾馆
Nikko Hotel Oriental Plaza
  (DōngXù Huángcháo Jiǔdiàn) **17**
  东旭皇朝酒店
Shangri-La Dàlián
  (Dàlián Xiānggélǐlā Dàfàndiàn) **13**
  大连香格里拉大饭店
Swissôtel Dàlián
  (Dàlián Ruìshì Jiǔdiàn) **6**
  大连瑞士酒店

DINING & NIGHTLIFE ◆
Alice Bar No. 2
  (Àilìsī Jiǔbā) **14**
  爱丽丝酒吧
Báixìng Cūn **16**
  百姓村
Dave's Bar **11**
I-55 Coffee Stop
  (Àiwǔwǔ Kāfēizhàn I-55) **5**
  咖啡站
Le Café Igosso
  (Yīgǒusǒu) **8**
  东旭皇朝酒店
Lónghǎi Yúwān
  Měishí Guǎngchǎng **4**
  龙海渔湾美食广场
Powerhouse
  (Bǎohǎo Bā) **10**
  宝宝吧
Russian Street
  (Éluósī Fēngqíng Jiē) **2**
  俄罗斯风情街
Tapas (Dápàsì) **1**
  达帕斯西班牙餐厅
Tiān Tiān Yúgǎng **12**
  天天渔港

$106–$183). The ticket office is open from 4am to 10pm; Yāntái express tickets are also sold at booths near Shènglì Guǎngchǎng. Take bus no. 801 (15 min.; ¥1/15¢) from Yǒuhǎo Guǎngchǎng. The 10-minute taxi ride costs ¥10 ($1).

VISITOR INFORMATION The **Tourism Bureau** has an information line (© 0411/ 8451-9940) and a complaint line (© 0411/8433-9970).

GETTING AROUND Downtown Dàlián is arranged around a series of traffic circles. The two most important are **Yǒuhǎo Guǎngchǎng (Friendship Square)**, dominated by a glass globe in the center, and **Zhōngshān Guǎngchǎng**, the city's transportation center. Ten roads radiate from Zhōngshān Guǎngchǎng, including Rénmín Dàjiē, a major avenue that runs east to the wharf, and Zhōngshān Lù, which runs west past the railway station to the city's far southwestern corner. **Taxis** charge ¥8

($1) for the first 3km (2 miles), then ¥1.80 (25¢) per kilometer. Regular **buses** (without air-conditioning) cost ¥1 (15¢), air-conditioned and mini-buses cost ¥2 (25¢); pay as you get on. Bus no. 801 runs the length of Zhōngshān Lù and Rénmín Dàjiē. A red, trolley-style version of this bus takes tourists on a **sightseeing loop** around the city from Shènglì Guǎngchǎng (every 20 min.; 2½ hr.; ¥20/$3 round-trip). Real Japanese-built trolleys go from Èrqī Guǎngchǎng in the east to Xīnghǎi Gōngyuán in the southwest.

FAST FACTS

Banks, Foreign Exchange & ATMs   The main **Bank of China** branch is in a large tower on the corner of Yán'ān Lù and Báiyù Jiē, behind the Dàlián Hotel on Zhōngshān Guǎngchǎng (open Mon–Fri 8:30am–4:30pm). Traveler's checks and cash can be exchanged at window 32, and credit cards are handled at window 11 (both on the second floor). There are international ATMs next to the old Bank of China on Zhōngshān Guǎngchǎng and inside the Nikko's shopping arcade.

Internet Access   **Búyè Chéng Wǎngyuàn** (24 hr.; ¥3/40¢ per hour) is the most central Internet bar, located underground on the northwest corner of Shènglì Guǎngchǎng. Dial-up is ✆ **165** or 169.

Post Office   The central post office is located several blocks north of Zhōngshān Guǎngchǎng, on the corner of Shànghǎi Lù and Chángjiāng Lù (open May–Sept 8am–7pm; Oct–Apr 8am–6pm).

Visa Extensions   Visa extensions are easy to obtain; you need only a passport and hotel registration to obtain one. Go to the **PSB** Exit/Entry Office on the corner of Yán'ān Lù and Wǔhàn Jiē (second floor; ✆ **0411/8280-2247**; open Mon–Fri 8–11:30am and 1–5pm). Extensions take 5 days to process.

EXPLORING DÀLIÁN

Dàlián's most impressive buildings surround **Zhōngshān Guǎngchǎng.** Highlights are the late Renaissance–style white-brick and green-domed Bank of China (built in 1909) on the north side of the square, and the Dàlián Hotel (see "Where to Stay," below) directly opposite. The city recently made an effort to recapture some of its Russian history with **Éluósī Fēngqíng Jiē (Russian Street),** a collection of mostly new Russian-style structures north of the railway cutout, above Shànghǎi Lù. The large, dilapidated yellow-brick building at the end of the street was the municipal government office when Russia still controlled the city. A stroll around the neighborhood surrounding **Nánshān Rìběn Fēngqíng Jiē** will give you a glimpse of old Japanese housing, though the street itself is full of suspiciously modern homes. For a less pretty but still interesting taste of modern Chinese architecture, head to **Rénmín Guǎngchǎng** (1km/½ mile east of the railway station on Zhōngshān Lù; bus: nos. 801 and 701). This large square, surrounded on three sides by ominous government buildings, is pleasant at night when lights illuminate the fountain; a stone arcade runs along its northern edge.

The Beaches & Bīnhǎi Lù 🅚🅘🅓🅢   Dàlián's seaside location is the major draw for Chinese tourists. Most of its beaches are pebbly and polluted, but the simple presence of the ocean and its attendant sea air provide respite from the rigors of travel. Bīnhǎi Lù meanders next to the coastline and gives breathtaking views of the sea. Start your journey by taking a taxi or bus no. 203 to *Dōnghǎi Gōngyuán* (entrance fee ¥10/$1.25), located about 5km (3 miles) east of downtown. In a nearby plaza at the north gate of

the park, locals enjoy watching the sun rise. Continue on, by taxi, to **Bàngchui Dǎo.** It was once the exclusive playground of Communist Party higher-ups and is now a pristine, hedge-lined country club only accessible by car (15 min.; ¥16/$2). The city's nicest beach is a 30-minute walk past the gate (¥10/$1.25). Just west of Bàngchui Dǎo is **Lǎohǔ Tān (Tiger Beach),** a popular beach that also features Dàlián's best aquatic theme park, **Lǎohǔ Tān Hǎiyáng Gōngyuán** (see below). A few kilometers west is the relatively clean **Fù Jiā Zhuāng Beach** (¥5/65¢). This is where the city's serious swimmers gather for a brisk dip before work. Take bus no. 5 (25 min.) from Qīngnǐwā Qiáo (north of Shènglì Guǎngchǎng). **Xīnghǎi Gōngyuán,** (¥10/$1.25), 5km (3 miles) southwest of downtown, was originally a Japanese resort and is now Dàlián's most accessible but dirtiest beach. Nearby is **Sun Asia Ocean World (Shèngyà Hǎiyáng Shìjiè;** see below).

Jīnshí Tān (Gold Pebble Beach) ★ *(Moments)*

With a little effort you can enjoy a clean beach without loudspeakers, tour groups, or other tackiness that infects the city shores. Hop on the light rail *(qīnggǔ)* at the Dàlián Zhàn railway station and take it to the last stop, Jīnshí Tān; the ride takes about an hour and passes by suburbs and factories along the coast. Taxis are sparse, so once you arrive, take a private car (¥5/65¢) or a horse-drawn carriage (¥10/$1.25) to the area's best strip of beach, **Huángjīn Hǎi'àn.** It's a good swimming spot and the fine-pebble beaches are nearly empty except during the high season (Aug–Sept). About 100m (328 ft.) north of the station is the **Dàlián Wax Museum (Làxiàng Bówùguǎn; ℂ 0411/8790-2006;** open May–Sept 8am–5pm, Oct–Apr 8:30am–4:30pm), where for ¥20 ($2.50) you can stroll past replicas of Jackie Chan, Sun Yat-sen, Adolf Hitler, Zhāng Zǐyí, and Kate Winslet—direct from the set of *Titantic,* with piped-in Celine Dion music.

Lǎohǔ Tān Hǎiyáng Gōngyuán (Tiger Beach Ocean Park)

Tacky cartoonish signboards, dancing clowns, and cheesy shows with dolphins abound, but the locals love it. It's worth a look for its aquarium, its display of polar animals, and a wild bird park, called the niǎoyǔlín. Avoid the "4-dimension pleasure theater" at all costs.

Bīnhǎi Lù No. 9. ℂ 0411/8239-9398. Admission ¥15 ($1.80). 7:30am–5:40pm. Bus: no. 2, 4, 403, 404, 30, 521, or 524.

Lǚshùn

Known to war historians as Port Arthur, Lǚshùn has been the most important, and most sensitive, naval base in northern China for roughly 100 years. Little used during the Qīng dynasty, it became a formidable installation under Russia, was captured and expanded by Japan after the Russo-Japanese War, and was finally returned to Chinese control after World War II. *Warning:* Most of the area is a military zone and officially off-limits to the public; do not cross the railroad tracks which marks off the restricted area. For more information, contact the PSB (ℂ 0411/8661-3411).

Only two historical sights fall north of Lǚshùn Běi Lù, both of which will appeal primarily to World War II buffs. They are only reachable by taxi from Dàlián (3 hr. round-trip; ¥200 – ¥250/$25–$31). Some travel agencies, and even the Dàlián Tourism Bureau, will claim that you can see other sights, but the *only* believable authority here is the PSB (see "Fast Facts," earlier in this chapter).

The **Huìjiàn Suǒ (ℂ 0411/8623-3509;** ¥40/$5; open 7:30am–5pm), in the village of Shuǐshī (Shuǐshī Yíng), is where commanders of the Japanese and Russian armies met to discuss and sign Russia's surrender of Lǚshùn in 1905. The tiny house, chosen because it was the only major structure still standing after both sides bombed the town, contains the original table on which the agreement was signed set beneath a photo of the signatories.

The **203-Meter Mountain (Èrlíngsān Gāodì)** ✿ was Russia's rear defense base during the Russo-Japanese War and the site of one of the war's most pivotal battles. Between 10,000 and 17,000 Japanese soldiers, including the Japanese commander's son, died taking the mountain. A few of the trenches where they fought have been preserved, served by trails near the summit. An exhibition room halfway up the hill contains several Qīng-era photos of the port and a few rusted swords and bullets used in the battle. Most striking is a large, bullet-shaped monument on the summit, erected by the Japanese and defaced by Russian tourists. You can look down into the port itself from here. The site is open 24 hours; admission is ¥30 ($4); for information call ⓒ **0411/8639-8277.**

Shèngyà Hǎiyáng Shìjiè (Sun Asia Ocean World)   Ocean World does not compare with its rival, Tiger Beach Ocean Park, but the recent addition of a polar aquarium and the world's longest underwater aquarium tunnel (116m/380 ft.) may make it a worthwhile stop. Call ahead for free English-speaking guides, who will explain which of the animals in the tanks are edible. Take bus no. 801 from Qīngníwā Qiáo (30 min.).

Just east of Xīnghǎi Park. ⓒ 0411/8468-5136. www.sunasia.com. Admission ¥70 ($9) adults, ¥35 ($4) children. 8am–5pm. Bus: no. 22, 23, 202, 709, 711, 801, K901, 502, 523, or 531.

SHOPPING

Dàlián is a petite female shopper's paradise, with a range of Japanese, Korean, and western fashions. Boutiques scattered around downtown sell knockoff Marc Jacobs and BCBG items for less than ¥150 ($19). **Qīngníwā Jiē,** south of Shènglì Guǎngchǎng (open 9am–9pm), is a materialistic mecca of malls, hotels, fast-food outlets, boutiques, and elaborate window displays unlike anything in China outside Shànghǎi. The prices are very reasonable and the spectacle of so many well-dressed Chinese people in one place is a strange, pleasant shock. If the labyrinth of underground shops, called the **Dìxià Shāngchǎng,** is too overwhelming, try the Japanese department stores Itokin (Yīdūjǐn). **Russian Street (Éluósī Fēngqíng Jiē)** lacks any real Russian people, but is full of stalls with the country's goods, including chocolates, whiskey flasks, vodka, and dolls.

WHERE TO STAY

Dàlián has the Northeast's largest selection of luxury hotels. Rooms are both hard to find and absurdly expensive during the September Fashion Festival, but discounts otherwise typically reach 50%. The city levies a ¥5 (65¢) per-person construction fee on all rooms.

VERY EXPENSIVE

Nikko Hotel Oriental Plaza Dàlián (DōngXù Huángcháo Jiǔdiàn) ✿   Formerly the Hilton, the hotel changed to Japanese management in 2005 but claims to have changed little else. Guest rooms are tastefully modern, decorated in solid colors with lots of glass. Bathrooms are somewhat cramped. Units at the top of the tower sway a bit in the wind, and traffic noise can be problematic, but the views are spectacular. Close to Zhōngshān Guǎngchǎng, the hotel also boasts Dōngběi's only Häagen-Dazs cafe.

Chángjiāng Lù 123 (at Mínshēng Jiē). ⓒ 0411/8252-9999. Fax 0411/8252-9900. www.nikkohotel.com 372 units. ¥935 ($114) standard room; ¥1,008–¥1,168 ($126–$146) suite. 15% service charge. Rates include breakfast. AE, DC, MC, V. **Amenities:** 3 restaurants; bar; indoor pool; outdoor tennis court; luxurious health club and spa; concierge;

business center; forex; small shopping center; salon; 24-hr. room service; same-day dry cleaning/laundry; nonsmoking rooms; executive-level rooms. *In room:* A/C, satellite TV, dataport, minibar, fridge, hair dryer, safe.

Shangri-La Dàlián (Dàlián Xiānggélǐlā Dàfàndiàn) ★★ With the recent turnover in management and ownership of other hotels, Shangri-La's Northeast flagship seems to be the most reliable option. Standard rooms are incredibly spacious, tasteful, and comfortable. Bathrooms, the nicest in town, have separate shower and tub. Service is impeccable. The central courtyard garden is a pleasant place to rest your feet after a walk on Bīnhǎi Lù.

Rénmín Lù 66. ⓒ 0411/8252-5000. Fax 0411/8252-5050. www.shangri-la.com. 562 units. ¥1,577 ($190) standard room. 15% service charge. AE, DC, MC, V. **Amenities:** 3 restaurants; deli; bar; cigar room; indoor 25m (82-ft.) pool; indoor/outdoor tennis courts; health club and spa; concierge; business center; forex; salon; 24-hr. room service; same-day dry cleaning/laundry; nonsmoking rooms; executive-level rooms. *In room:* A/C, satellite TV, minibar, fridge, hair dryer, safe.

Swissôtel Dàlián (Dàlián Ruìshì Jiǔdiàn) Now under Chinese ownership (licensed to use the Swissôtel's name for 2 years), the Swissôtel Dàlián faces a possible downgrade in service, but its unbeatable location, between the Qīngníwā shopping area and the picturesque Láodòng Gōngyuán (Labor Park), makes it a good option for leisure travelers. Guest rooms and bathrooms are a bit small but otherwise classy and very comfortable. The Western buffet offers a great selection of local seafood.

Wǔhuì Lù 21 (back of Qīngníwā shopping area). ⓒ 0411/8230-3388. Fax 0411/8230-2266. www.swissotel-dalian.com. 327 units. ¥1,400 ($175) standard room. 15% service charge. Rates include breakfast. AE, DC, MC, V. **Amenities:** 3 restaurants; outdoor barbecue in summer; deli; bar; indoor pool; large health club; sauna; concierge; business center; forex; salon; 24-hr. room service; same-day dry cleaning/laundry; nonsmoking rooms; executive-level rooms. *In room:* A/C, satellite TV w/pay movies, dataport, minibar, fridge, hair dryer, safe.

EXPENSIVE

Bó Hǎi Pearl Hotel (Bó Hǎi Míngzhū Dàjiǔdiàn) This Chinese-run four-star is typically tacky (note the frightening harpy statues at the door), but the hotel's location directly east of the railway station is as convenient as it gets in Dàlián. Standard rooms are small with lackluster decor and undersize bathrooms. Facilities and staff are slightly above par.

Shènglì Guǎngchǎng 8. ⓒ 0411/8265-0888. Fax 0411/8280-0306. 380 units. ¥730–¥898 ($91–$112) standard room. No credit cards. **Amenities:** 2 restaurants; bar; small indoor pool; sauna; concierge; business center; forex; limited room service; laundry. *In room:* A/C, satellite TV, minibar, fridge, hair dryer.

MODERATE

Dàlián Hotel (Dàlián Bīnguǎn) ★ The Dàlián, built in 1909 on the south side of Zhōngshān Guǎngchǎng, was described in a 1920s guidebook as "one of the finest hotels in the Far East." Originally a part of the Japanese-owned Yamato Hotel chain, it was restored to a semblance of its former appearance in 1997 but still lacks the charm of its counterparts in other northeastern cities. Guest rooms are large with small beds but clean, sizable bathrooms. Furnishings fail to match the grandeur of the building itself, but no other hotel in Dàlián can claim as much history.

Zhōngshān Guǎngchǎng 4. ⓒ 0411/8263-3111, ext. 1101. Fax 0411/8263-4363. www.chinadalianhotel.com. 36 units. ¥598 ($75) standard room. AE MC V. **Amenities:** 3 restaurants; business center; forex; laundry. *In room:* A/C, satellite TV, fridge, hair dryer.

Gloria Plaza Hotel (Dàlián Kǎilái Dàjiǔdiàn) Like the Dàlián Hotel (see above), the Gloria Plaza doesn't quite match its counterparts elsewhere, but discounts make it the most affordable Gloria in the Northeast. Guest rooms are small with tiny bathrooms, but everything is clean and the staff is friendly. Cheaper units on lower floors receive little natural light.

Yīdé Jiē 5 (at Yǒuhǎo Guǎngchǎng). ⓒ 0411/8280-8855. Fax 0411/8280-8533. www.gphdalian.com. 240 units. ¥788–¥988 ($99–$123) standard room. 10% service charge. AE, DC, MC, V. **Amenities:** 2 restaurants; bar; business center; forex; laundry. *In room:* A/C, TV, fridge.

INEXPENSIVE

Jiāshùn Bīnguǎn This amiable guesthouse, sandwiched between a McDonald's and a KFC on Shànghǎi Lù, offers small and simple but clean standard rooms with acceptable bathrooms. Discounts are generous.

Shànghǎi Lù 61 (opposite Paris Shopping Center). ⓒ 0411/8280-7885. Fax 0411/8269-1463. 64 units. ¥260 ($33) standard room. No credit cards. **Amenities:** Restaurant. *In room:* A/C, TV.

WHERE TO DINE

Dàlián's specialty is seafood, but the city is surprisingly cosmopolitan in its international restaurant choices. A branch of the global Japanese chain **Suntory** is on the third floor of the Nikko (ⓒ **0411/8252-9999;** open 11:30am–2pm and 5:30–9:30pm). For excellent **dim sum** head to the Shangri-La Hotel's Shang Palace (Rénmín Lù 66; ⓒ **0411/8252-5000**). A number of **fast-food outlets**—McDonald's, KFC, Pizza Hut—can also be found at Shènglì Guǎngchǎng and on Qīngníwā Jiē. The underground market has a large **food court** with several point-to-choose Chinese stalls. Yǒuhǎo Guǎngchǎng boasts a couple of **burger and pizza restaurants.**

Bǎixìng Cūn ★★ HOME-STYLE This is a delightful, if somewhat stiff, outgrowth of the yuppie countryside trend in Chinese dining. Servers' peasant uniforms are a bit too perfectly pressed, but the glass-topped wood tables and beautiful glazed dishes make for a pleasant setting. The restaurant specializes in clay pot soups, like the light and flavorful *xiānggū guàshì wèi tǔjī* (chicken and mushrooms). Order *yùmǐmiàn bǐng* (corn cakes) to dip in the soup or to sop up sauce left over from one of many well-prepared home-style dishes.

Chángjiāng Lù 128. ⓒ 0411/8258-0228. Meal for 2 ¥60–¥100 ($8–$12). No credit cards. 10am–10pm.

I-55 Coffee Stop (Àiwǔwǔ Kāfēizhàn I-55) ★ AMERICAN Owned by an American expatriate who made sure to include all the details—chalkboard menus and corner couches, world music soundtrack, a Scrabble set propped on a shelf—I-55 is a good place to get an American craving satiated. The cafe roasts its beans on-site and serves a good cup of coffee. The Philly cheesesteak is probably the best you'll get in China, with freshly baked bread, lots of flavorful beef, cheese, and mayo. It also offers good desserts and a weekend breakfast buffet for ¥55 ($6.70). The staff speaks English. Relax with a book on the peaceful outdoor patio.

Gāoěrjī Lù 67 (at Jiniàn Jiē, 2 blocks north of Rénmín Guǎngchǎng). ⓒ 0411/8369-5755. Coffee drinks ¥20–¥30 ($2–$4); breakfast/lunch ¥33 ($4). No credit cards. 9am–midnight. Bus: no. 701, 801, or 401.

Le Café Igosso (Yīgǒusǒu) ITALIAN/FRENCH This Japanese-run bistro, with its dark wood-paneled walls and fine white tablecloths, is as close as you'll get to authentic European dining in the Northeast. Music is subtle, service is silent and attentive, and the wine list is extensive. The English-language menu is mostly Italian, with a few French (foie gras) and Japanese (marinated octopus) selections. The beef carpaccio, drizzled with cream and generously garnished with capers and green onions, is rich but enjoyable. Fresh pasta and risotto dishes are small and simple. Desserts (posted next to the open kitchen) change daily.

Fun Fact Dumplings & Dog Meat

Generally speaking, food is not one of Dōngběi's finer attractions, but there is at least one aspect of Dōngběi cuisine that will appeal to epicures: the delectable meat- and vegetable-filled ravioli-like dumplings known as *jiǎozi.* Cheap and satisfying, *jiǎozi* are popular all over China but are nowhere as divine as in the Northeast. Cooked in one of three ways—boiled *(shuǐjiǎo),* steamed *(zhēngjiǎo),* or pan-fried *(jiānjiǎo)*—they are most commonly filled with a mix of pork and cabbage *(zhūròu báicài)* and served with a soy-and-vinegar dipping sauce, to which you add your own chopped garlic, chili oil, and mustard. Alternatives are endless. Absolutely not to be missed.

Probably more well-known but significantly less appetizing is **dog** *(gǒuròu),* Dōngběi's other signature food. A Korean import shunned by Manchurians but valued among Chinese for its warming properties, it is a winter item most commonly eaten in hot pot. Dog meat turns greenish when boiled; trying it, according to one traveling companion of mine, is "like eating a piece of beef then licking a filing cabinet."

Nánshān Lù 45 (at Kūnmíng Jiē, east of Láodòng Gōngyuán). ⓒ 0411/8265-6453. Main courses ¥40–¥80 ($5–$10). AE, MC, V. 11am–2am.

Lónghǎi Yúwān Měishí Guǎngchǎng ⚔ *(Finds)* SEAFOOD   Yes, it's a gaudy sight, with its faux-marble staircase, but the dishes here will make up for it. Recommended by a local food writer, this recent addition to the Dàlián restaurant scene is located near Xīnghǎi Guǎngchǎng. Try the salt-dried yellow fish *(yánchéng huánghuāyú),* spinach with mussels *(buōcài bàn máoxiàn),* pig stomach cabbage soup *(nòngtáng zhūdǔ wáwácài),* and fish dumplings *(bāyú shuǐjiǎo).* Be prepared for plenty of raw garlic. Each table is set in a private room with a flatscreen television.

Tōngtài Lù 21. ⓒ 0411/8368-5555. Meal for 2 ¥150–¥400 ($18–$50). MC, V. 11am–10pm.

Tapas (Dápàsī) ⚔ SPANISH   On the edge of Russian Street, this two-level restaurant feels more like a hacienda in Galicia than a restaurant in Dàlián. The wine list features wines from Spain, and the menu offers an exhaustive list of tapas good for a snack or a whole meal. Try the gratin mushroom tart, the pancetta with garlic, and the baked peppers on toast. Finish your meal with apple crepes or crème brûlée.

Tuánjié Jiē 19 (near Russian St.). ⓒ 0411/8254-0996. Tapas ¥8–¥30 ($1–$3.60); meal for 2 ¥70–¥100 ($8.50–$12). AE, MC, V. 11:30am–10:30pm.

Tiān Tiān Yúgǎng SEAFOOD   Aquariums inside Dàlián's most prestigious (and expensive) seafood chain contain a truly astounding array of sea life: garoupa, flounder, eel, octopus, crab, clams, mussels, shrimp, lobster, sea snails, sea cucumber, and a host of creatures found only in Chinese waters. Try the *gōngbào yúdīng,* diced shark with peanuts and hot peppers. Also good, and affordable, is the *wénchóng hé tāng,* a delicate soup made with local clams and bok choy. Penny-pinching locals claim they can make the same dishes in their own kitchens. They're lying.

Most convenient branch at Rénmín Lù 10, 1 block east of Zhōngshān Guǎngchǎng. ⓒ 0411/8282-3999. Meal for 2 ¥80–¥400 ($10–$50). MC, V. 9am–9pm.

DÀLIÁN AFTER DARK

The majority of nightspots in Dàlián are neon karaoke dives that cater to naughty Japanese businessmen, but there are a few pleasant exceptions. Resident foreigners favor the subterranean Mǎkèwēi, known to English speakers as **Dave's Bar** (south end of Qīyī Jiē; ✆ **0411/8282-2345;** open 1pm until late), a U.N. of watering holes just northeast of Zhōngshān Guǎngchǎng. Americans, Russians, Europeans, Asians, and Africans mix and flirt at Dave's without prejudice over bottles of Tsingtao beer. **Powerhouse (Bàoháo Bā),** Wǔwǔ Lù 6 in the Zhōngshān District (✆ **0411/8272-7971;** open 5pm–1:30am) has live Chinese rock-'n-roll music and is popular among locals. Just behind the Shangri-La Hotel, **Alice Bar No. 2** (Zhīfú Jiē 8; ✆ **0411/8256-1313;** open 6pm–daylight)—*not* to be confused with Alice's seedier No. 1 bar, just east of the Shangri-La—has a Filipino band nightly and draws the area's expats until the wee hours. **I-55** (see "Where to Dine," above) is open till midnight.

4 Chángchūn

Jílín Province, 302km (187 miles) NE of Shēnyáng, 250km (155 miles) SW of Harbin

Chángchūn is remote enough to feel authentic, is friendly and modern enough to be comfortable, and has just enough pop-history background to make it interesting. Between 1932 and 1945, it was the capital of Japanese-controlled Manchukuo (Mǎnzhōu Guó) and home to puppet ruler Henry Pǔyí, the bespectacled final Qīng emperor best known to Westerners as the subject of Bernardo Bertolucci's lush biopic *The Last Emperor.* The city provided a base for Japan's brutal World War II colonization campaign and was slated to sit at the center of a postwar empire that never materialized.

Chángchūn, now the capital of Jílín Province, has gained fame in the modern era as the Detroit of China, producing first Red Flag cars for Communist Party cadres and later Volkswagens for China's new middle class. Recent economic hardships have sent the city in search of tourism dollars and prompted admirable restorations of several Manchukuo-era buildings. But the city's greatest attraction is still its people, as unpretentious, warm-hearted, and quick-witted as any in the country.

The rest of Jílín Province mirrors Chángchūn in many ways. Less convenient than Liáoníng to the south and lacking the "extreme travel" cachet of Hēilóng Jiāng and Inner Mongolia to the north and west, it quietly offers several of Dōngběi's most enjoyable attractions. **Cháng Bái Shān** (p. 189), a dramatic mountain straddling the China–North Korea border, is the most famous. Just as compelling is the seldom-visited **Yánbiān Korean Autonomous Prefecture** (p. 186) to the north.

ESSENTIALS

GETTING THERE   At press time, a new commercial airport was scheduled to open by the time you read this book. **Flights** at the time of this writing were to/from a civil/military airfield 10km (6 miles) west of town. They included daily flights to Běijīng, Shànghǎi, and Dàlián, and twice-weekly flights to Hong Kong (Tues and Fri). The **China Eastern Airlines** ticket office (**Zhōngguó Běifāng Hángkōng Shòupiào Chù;** ✆ **0431/272-5001** and 0431/272-5026; open 8am–4:40pm) is at Xīnfā Lù 32, through the second door on the building's west side. A taxi from downtown to the airport takes 20 minutes and costs ¥23 ($3). Or take bus no. 364 (40 min.; 6:30am–7pm; ¥1/15¢) from the northwest side of Rénmín Guǎngchǎng.

Express **trains** connect to Běijīng (three daily; 9 hr.; ¥298/$37), Harbin (two daily; 3 hr.; ¥41/$5), Shěnyáng (14 daily; 4 hr.; ¥47/$6), Jílín City (10 daily; 2 hr.; ¥20/$3), Shànghǎi (3:15pm; 27 hr.; ¥437/$55), and Dàlián (8:35pm; 11 hr.; ¥183/$23). The railway station (Chángchūn Zhàn) is north of downtown, at the top of Rénmín Dàjiē.

Air-conditioned **buses** to Harbin (all day; 3 hr.; ¥69/$9) and Shěnyáng (all day; 3½ hr.; ¥72/$9) and the express bus to Jílín City (all day; 1½ hr.; ¥30/$4) leave from a white building at Rénmín Dàjiē 6 (behind the Chūnyí Bīnguǎn). Regular minibuses to Jílín City (3 hr.; ¥15/$2) leave every few minutes from the north side of the building. Private **cars** leave from the railway station parking lot for cities east; prices are negotiable (¥150/$19 to Yánjí is reasonable).

GETTING AROUND   Jetta **taxis** charge ¥5 (65¢) for the first 2.5km (1½ miles), then ¥1.30 (15¢) per kilometer. **Buses** (¥1–¥2/15¢–25¢) are pay-as-you-board. Bus no. 6 runs from the railway station through the middle of town on Rénmín Dàjiē; bus nos. 62 and 362 both wind from the railway station to Rénmín Guǎngchǎng and pass Xīnmín Guǎngchǎng, with stop announcements in English.

FAST FACTS

Banks, Foreign Exchange & ATMs   The most convenient **Bank of China** branch is on Tóngzhì Jiē, south of the Xī'ān Dàlù intersection (open Mon–Fri 8:30am–4:30pm; Sat–Sun 9am–4pm). Traveler's checks and credit card transactions are handled on the second floor (*not* available 11:30am–1pm), and there's an ATM on the first floor. Another ATM across the street from the Shangri-La dispenses up to ¥2,500 ($300).

Internet Access   Xīnhuìyuán Wǎngluò Jùlèbù, on Běijīng Dàjiē midway between Dàqīnghuā Jiǎozi and the Paradise Hotel, and across from the Epoch Hotel, is open from 8am to midnight and charges ¥2 (25¢) per hour. Dial-up is 𝒞 **169.**

Post Office   The most convenient post office (Kuānchéng Yóudiànjú; May–Sept 8:30am–5:30pm; Oct–Apr 8:30am–5pm) is in an old green building south of the long-distance bus station on Rénmín Dàjiē.

Visa Extensions   Visa extensions are easy to obtain (passport and hotel registration only) at the imposing **PSB** Exit/Entry office on Guāngmíng Lù (𝒞 **0431/896-3344,** ext. 4468; open Mon–Fri 8:30–11:30am and 1:30–5pm), behind PSB headquarters on the southwest side of Rénmín Guǎngchǎng.

EXPLORING CHÁNGCHŪN

Chángchūn's chief attraction is the ghost of Japanese occupation, which still lingers in the more than two dozen ministry buildings left scattered throughout the city. The **former Kwantung Army headquarters** is an impeccably preserved Japanese-style castle on Xīnfǎ Lù (now occupied by the Communist Party) near the China Northern Airlines ticket office. Guards might let you roam around the grounds if you promise not to take pictures. There are also a number of buildings lining Xīnmín Lù south of the **Wénhuà Guǎngchǎng (Culture Square),** site of a never-completed imperial Japanese palace and now home to the main building of Jílín University. The grim building southeast of the square, fronted by a statue of infamous Canadian doctor Norman Bethune, is the former site of the **Wěi Mǎnzhōu Guó Guówùyuàn (Manchukuo State Council).** A bizarre English-language tour here (8:30am–6pm; ¥20/$3) includes a ride in a 70-year-old solid brass Otis elevator once used by Henry Pǔyí (see Wěi Huánggōng, below). Bilingual maps are available (¥5/65¢) at the Wěi Huánggōng.

Chángchūn

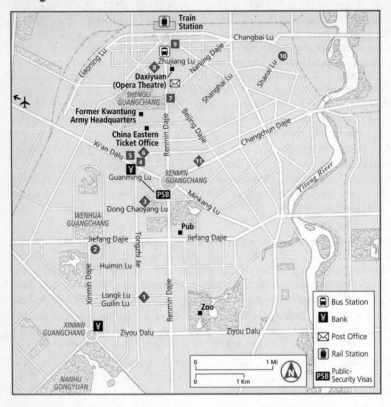

Wěi Huánggōng ✵✵ "The Puppet Emperor's Palace" is where Aisin-Gioro "Henry" Pǔyí, China's last emperor, spent 13 years as an impotent sovereign under Japanese control. This complex of imperial-style buildings, formerly criticized by travelers as shabby and boring, recently underwent a multimillion-dollar makeover and is now among the Northeast's premier historical attractions.

Installed as emperor of China in Běijīng in 1908, at the age of 3, Pǔyí was deposed by Republican forces in 1912 (at a time when he was still breastfeeding) and eventually fell into the hands of the Japanese. In 1932, eager to use Pǔyí's Manchurian face as a screen for its war efforts in the Northeast, Japan convinced him to move to Chángchūn and made him president (later emperor) of Manchukuo. He lived a futile life here, taking orders from the Japanese army and subsisting on a Qīng restoration fantasies, until he was captured by the Soviets in 1945. He spent 14 years in prison, was "rehabilitated," and worked as a gardener until his death in 1967.

The palace was damaged when Soviet troops occupied Chángchūn, so much of the furniture and trappings on display here are replicas. Otherwise, the restoration is meticulous. Most impressive is the Tóngdé Diàn (originally the Jílín Salt Tax Collection Office, and therefore sometimes referred to as the Salt Palace because it was built using money from Japan's salt-mining operations), a building Pǔyí supposedly never

ACCOMMODATIONS ■	DINING ◆

ACCOMMODATIONS ■

Chángchūn Maxcourt Hotel
(Chángchūn
Jílóngpō Dàjiǔdiàn) **5**
长春吉隆坡大酒店

Chūnyí Bīnguǎn **9**
春谊宾馆

Paradise Hotel
(Yuèfǔ Dàjiǔdiàn) **7**
乐府大酒店

Shangri-La Chángchūn
(Chángchūn
Xiānggélǐlā Dàfàndiàn) **4**
长春香格里拉大饭店

DINING ◆

Amigo Bar **11**

Dàqīnghuā Jiǎozi **8**
大清花饺子

French Bakery
(Hóng Mòfáng) **1,6**
红磨坊

Xiàngyáng Tún **3**
向阳屯

ATTRACTIONS ●

Wěi Huánggōng
(Puppet Emperor's Palace) **10**
伪皇宫

Wěi Mǎnzhōu Guó Guówùyuàn
(Manchukuo State Council) **2**
伪满洲国博物馆

used for fear the Japanese had bugged the rooms. The main hall is recognizable as the setting for a dance party scene in *The Last Emperor*, although it was never actually used for that purpose.

Guāngfù Běi Lù 5. ☏ **0431/286-6611.** Admission ¥40 ($5). May–Sept 8:30am–4:20pm; Oct–Apr 8:30am–4pm. Bus: no. 18 (2 stops from the railway station; walk east on Guāngfù Lù), no. 264 (from the Wénhuà Guǎngchǎng).

SHOPPING

Chángchūn is one of China's top producers of ginseng, available in any one of the city's ubiquitous pharmacies. For more conventional shopping, try the upscale **Chóngqìng Lù** or **Guìlín Lù** (east of the Tóngzhì Jiē intersection), a hip and haphazard street lined with Korean clothing shops and stuffed-animal stores. The **underground market** in front of the railway station was once part of an underground bomb shelter connected by tunnels to the Manchukuo ministries.

WHERE TO STAY

Rooms are scarce in late summer, when the city hosts a series of conferences and industry fairs, but discounts of up to 30% are common at other times of the year. Budget hotels generally do not accept foreigners. The city charges a room tax of ¥7 (90¢) per person.

EXPENSIVE

Chángchūn Maxcourt Hotel (Chángchūn Jílóngpō Dàjiǔdiàn) ✿ *Value*   This Malaysian-run four-star claims it will some day surpass the superior Shangri-La, but for now it is content to dominate the city's luxury-hotel price war with generous and flexible package deals (weekend discounts up to 50%)—it's the best deal in town. Bathrooms are small, but guest rooms themselves are some of the most comfortable in the city—especially those on the newly renovated 19th and 20th floors—and service is decent.

Xī'ān Dàlù 823. ☎ **0431/896-2688.** Fax 0431/898-6288. www.maxcourt.com. 228 units. ¥800 ($97) standard room. 15% service charge. Rate includes breakfast. AE, DC, MC, V. **Amenities:** 4 restaurants; bar; small indoor pool; health club; full-service spa; game room w/bowling alley; business center w/Internet access; forex; 24-hr. room service; same-day dry cleaning/laundry. *In room:* A/C, satellite TV w/pay movies, dataport, minibar, fridge, hair dryer, safe.

Shangri-La Chángchūn (Chángchūn Xiānggélǐlā Dàfàndiàn) ★★ The

Shangri-La is Chángchūn's oldest five-star property and still the only hotel in town that provides luxury with class. Standard rooms are spacious, with large beds and generously sized bathrooms, and the hotel's staff is head-and-shoulders above any other in the city. The Shangri-La is centrally located at the edge of the city's most upscale shopping district, a short walk from Rénmín Guǎngchǎng.

Xī'ān Dàlù 569. ☎ **0431/898-1818.** Fax 0431/898-1919. www.shangri-la.com. 458 units. ¥910–¥1,076 ($110–$130) standard room. 15% service charge. Rates include breakfast for 1. AE, DC, MC, V. **Amenities:** 3 restaurants; bakery; outdoor beer garden and evening barbecue; bar; small indoor pool; outdoor tennis court; health center and spa; concierge; business center; forex; salon; 24-hr. room service; same-day dry cleaning/laundry; executive-level rooms. *In room:* A/C, satellite TV, minibar, fridge, hair dryer, safe.

MODERATE

Chūnyí Bīnguǎn The Chūnyí, built in 1909, is the least impressive of the former

Yamato Hotels, and is attractive now only for its convenient location just across the street from the railway station. The original gate is still here, but the exterior is crumbling and the interior retains only a whisper of history. Rooms in the main building, renovated in 2004, are clean and tidy. At press time, rooms in the adjacent tower were undergoing renovations, and already renovated tower rooms were available at a discount.

Rénmín Dàjiē 80 (southeast of railway station). ☎ **0431/209-6888.** Fax 0431/896-0171. 130 units. ¥218–¥260 ($27–$32) standard room. Rates include breakfast. AE, DC, MC, V. **Amenities:** Restaurant; bar currently closed for renovations; laundry. *In room:* A/C, TV.

Paradise Hotel (Yuèfǔ Dàjiǔdiàn) ★ An institution among travelers in

Chángchūn since it opened in 1994, the Paradise is one of a handful of state-run three-stars in China that have a firm grasp on the concepts of service and maintenance. Newly renovated doubles, equipped with a queen-size bed, are cramped. Standard rooms are larger but older. Both are nicely appointed with lacquer furniture, large TVs, and small but very clean bathrooms. Some of the staff speak English. The place fills up in summer, so call ahead.

Rénmín Dàjiē 1078 (south of the Agricultural Bank of China building). ☎ **0431/209-0999** or 0431/209-0999, ext. 1111. Fax 0431/209-0749. yfhotel@hotmail.com. 200 units. ¥288 ($35) standard room. Rates include breakfast for 1. AE, DC, MC, V. **Amenities:** 4 restaurants; bar; business center; laundry. *In room:* A/C, TV, dataport.

WHERE TO DINE

A number of restaurants in Chángchūn serve reasonable regional cuisine. Otherwise, **KFC** and **McDonald's** branches are plentiful throughout the city. There is also a **Pizza Hut** on the right side of the square in front of the railway station.

Dàqīnghuā Jiǎozi ★ *Value* DŌNGBĚI This successful chain, with its nostalgic

Qīng dynasty decor and near-perfect *jiǎozi*, has inspired dozens of imitators but remains unmatched. Don't miss the steamed Manchurian dumplings *(Mǎnzhōu jiǎozi)* filled with pork, shrimp, egg, and Chinese chives. The pan-fried *yuānyang jiǎozi*, filled with shrimp, egg, and squash, are also quite good.

Lóngjiāng Lù 1 (at Běijīng Dàjiē). ☎ **0431/856-3893.** Photo menu. Meal for 2 ¥20–¥50 ($3–$7). No credit cards. 9am–10pm.

French Bakery (Hóng Mòfáng) ✿ WESTERN   Now with two locations, this dark and low-ceilinged cafe with French movie posters pasted to its fake brick walls has long been a haven for Chángchūn's foreign residents. A very clean kitchen produces simple sandwiches, omelets, pizza, and near-authentic pastries. Coffee drinks are genuine. Olive oil, Tabasco sauce, Heinz barbecue sauce, and ground coffee are for sale on a small shelf near the door.

Guìlín Lù 745 (east of Tóngzhì Jiē intersection). ✆ 0431/562-3994. Meal for 2 ¥18–¥25 ($2–$3); coffee ¥10–¥15 ($1.25–$2). No credit cards. 8am–10:30pm. Also at Chóngzhì Hútòng 137 (walk 1 block north of the Shangri-La Hotel on Chóngqìng Lù, then make a left at the Charter Shopping Center); ✆ 0431/898-1958; 9:30am–midnight.

Xiàngyáng Tún ✿✿✿ HOME-STYLE   This delightful countryside eatery, with a statue of Máo out front and calligraphy-covered walls in the main dining room, is the favorite for home-style fare. Try the *jiājī dùn zhēnmó*—tender pieces of chicken stewed with mushrooms in a dark savory sauce—and the *dà páigu* (big ribs), a melt-in-your-mouth house specialty with meat that literally falls off the bone.

Dōng Cháoyáng Lù 3 (east of Tóngzhì Jiē intersection). ✆ 0431/898-2876. Meal for 2 ¥30–¥60 ($4-$7.50). No credit cards. 10:30am–11pm.

CHÁNGCHŪN AFTER DARK

Chángchūn is the birthplace of *èrrénzhuàn,* a mix of stand-up comedy and opera that is thoroughly vulgar and, for those who can understand Mandarin, very entertaining. Real fans head to the raucous, smoke-filled **Hépíng Dàxìyuàn**, a block north of the post office on Rénmín Dàjiē (✆ **0431/893-4304**), where tawdry performances get audiences roaring with laughter and keep them that way most of the night. Nightly shows at 7:40pm cost ¥10 to ¥50 ($1.25–$6). Two popular disco clubs are the **Mayflower (Wǔyuèhuā Jiǔbā;** ✆ **0431/893-322**), tucked underground on the south side of the Wénhuà Huódòng Zhōngxīn on Rénmín Dàjiē, a few blocks south of Rénmín Guǎngchǎng, and **Amigo Bar** (✆ **0431/897-3222**), on Chángchūn Dàjiē, northeast of Rénmín Guǎngchǎng and just east of Qīngmíng Jiē. Both are popular with foreigners and stay open late.

5 Jílín City

Jílín Province, 128km (79 miles) E of Chángchūn

Jílín, one of the oldest settlements in the province and a legendary shipbuilding center during the Qīng dynasty, is famous now for its delicate winter scenery. The city's original name was *Jílín Wūlā* (Manchurian for "along the river"), because it straddles a bend in the Sōnghuā Jiāng (Sungari River). It was hit hard in World War II and, despite one of the country's more impressive urban renewal plans, it will probably never recover its old prestige. Most visitors now use it as a staging point for trips to the Cháng Bái Shān Nature Preserve (p. 189).

ESSENTIALS

GETTING THERE   Trains travel from Jílín to Chángchūn (10 daily; 2 hr.; ¥20/$3), Yánjí (six daily; 7 hr.; ¥52/$7), Shěnyáng (seven daily; 9 hr.; ¥116/$15), and Běijīng (7:02pm; 11 hr.; ¥256/$32). The **railway station (Jílín Zhàn)** is north of the river, at the intersection of Zhōngkàng Lù and Chóngqìng Jiē; the ticket office is open from 5am to 1:30am. The main **long-distance bus station (Gōnglù Kèyùn Zǒng Zhàn or Chàlù Xiāng)** is at Zhōngkàng Lù 13, west of the railway station; buses leave from here for Tōnghuà (all day; ¥42/$5.25), Harbin (all day; ¥43/$5.40), and Yánjí (8am; 6 hr.; ¥44/$5.50). **Express buses** to Chángchūn (every 30 min., 6am–6pm; 1½ hr.; ¥30/$3.75) depart from the Línjiāng Mén Kèyùn Zhàn on Xī'ān Lù, a block west of Línjiāng Guǎngchǎng. **Flights** to Běijīng (Wed and Sat) and Shànghǎi (Wed and Sun) leave from the Gūdiànzi Jīchǎng, 30km (19 miles) west of the city. The **CAAC ticket office** (**Mínháng Shòupiào Chù;** ⓒ **0432/245-4260;** open 8am–5pm) is behind the Dōngguān Hotel at Chóngqìng Lù 1. An **airport shuttle** leaves from here every Wednesday and Sunday at 11:30am and costs ¥10 ($1.25). A **taxi** to the airport costs ¥30 ($3.75).

VISITOR INFORMATION   For tourist complaints, call ⓒ **0432/245-7524.**

GETTING AROUND   Jílín Dàjiē, the main thoroughfare, runs north–south through the middle of town. Most **buses** (¥1/15¢) stop at the railway station; bus no. 103 leaves from the railway station and travels along Jílín Dàjiē. **Taxis** charge ¥5 (65¢) for the first 2km (1¼ miles) and ¥1.80 (25¢) per kilometer after that.

FAST FACTS

Banks, Foreign Exchange & ATMs   The main **Bank of China** branch is inconveniently located on Shēnchún Jiē, at the east end of the Línjiāng Qiáo (Línjiāng Bridge). It's open May through September from 8:30am to 4:30pm and October through April from 8:30am to 4pm. Windows on the left handle traveler's checks and credit card transactions (*not* available 11:30am–1pm). There's an international ATM just inside the door.

Internet Access   There are several **24-hour Internet bars** charging ¥2 (25¢) per hour north of the Tourism Hotel (see below) on Cháoyáng Jiē. Dial-up is ⓒ **16300.**

Post Office   The main post office is on Jílín Dàjiē (open 8:30am–4:30pm), north of the Jílín Bridge.

EXPLORING JÍLÍN

Jílín is host to a scene of unearthly beauty in winter, when steam rises from the Sōnghuā River and condenses on nearby trees. The phenomenon, dubbed *wùsōng* (ice-rimmed trees) 雾凇 in Mandarin, is a by-product of the nearby Fēngmǎn Hydroelectric Dam, which feeds warm water into the Sōnghuā and keeps it from freezing despite air temperatures of −22°F (−30°C). To see this, get up early and walk along any section of the pleasant riverside promenade that follows Sōnghuā Jiāng Lù. Also beautiful is an old **Catholic Church (Tiānzhǔ Jiàotáng),** built in 1917 and restored in 1980, opposite the promenade on the west side of Jiāngchéng Guǎngchǎng; it isn't open to tourists, but you might convince someone in the attached hospice to let you in for a look.

IN TOWN

Wén Miào   This decrepit, charming Confucian temple is notable for its exhibition on the Qīng dynasty imperial examination system, inside the first hall on the right. A mural at the entrance to the exhibit depicts a mountain of men stepping on each other in an effort to climb the Confucian hierarchy. Inside are reproductions of "cheat sheets"—pieces of clothing covered in thousands of near-microscopic characters found on Qīng-era candidates in Běijīng.

Nánchāng Lù. Admission ¥15 ($1.80). 8:30am–4:00pm; closed holidays. Bus: no. 103 to Jiāngchéng Guǎngchǎng, then walk east 2 blocks on Jiāngwān Lù and turn left at the Jiāngchéng Hotel.

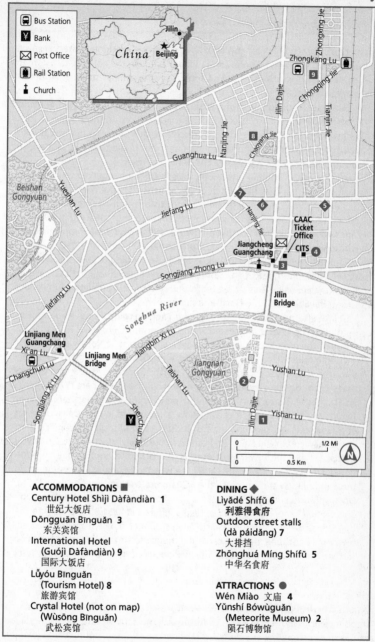

Jílín City

Legend:
- Bus Station
- ¥ Bank
- Post Office
- Rail Station
- Church

China
Jilin
Beijing

Beishan
Gongyuan

Zhongkang Lu

Zhongxing Jie

Chongqing Jie

Tianjin Jie

Jilin Dajie

Guanghua Lu

Nanjing Jie

Chaoyang Jie

Yueshan Lu

Jiefang Lu

Nanjing Jie

CAAC Ticket Office

CITS

Jiangcheng Guangchang

Songjiang Zhong Lu

Jiefang Lu

Jilin Bridge

Songhua River

Linjiang Men Guangchang

Xi'an Lu

Jiangbin Xi Lu

Linjiang Men Bridge

Jiangnan Gongyuan

Yushan Lu

Changchun Lu

Songjiang Xi Lu

Taishan Lu

Shenchun Jie

Jilin Dajie

Yishan Lu

0   1/2 Mi

0   0.5 Km

ACCOMMODATIONS ■
Century Hotel Shìjì Dàfàndiàn 1
　世纪大饭店
Dōngguān Bīnguǎn 3
　东关宾馆
International Hotel
　(Guójì Dàfàndiàn) 9
　国际大饭店
Lǚyóu Bīnguǎn
　(Tourism Hotel) 8
　旅游宾馆
Crystal Hotel (not on map)
　(Wùsōng Bīnguǎn)
　武松宾馆

DINING ◆
Lìyǎdé Shífǔ 6
　利雅得食府
Outdoor street stalls
　(dà páidǎng) 7
　大排挡
Zhōnghuá Míng Shífǔ 5
　中华名食府

ATTRACTIONS ●
Wén Miào 文庙 4
Yǔnshí Bówùguǎn
　(Meteorite Museum) 2
　陨石博物馆

Wild China: Yánbiān

Koreans first fled across the border to Yánbiān, a seldom-visited area of greener-than-green hills and fertile fields nestled in the northeastern corner of Jílín Province, after the first of several severe famines struck the Korean peninsula in 1869.

Subsequent diasporas in the 20th century, the result of continued food shortages and a pair of brutal Japanese occupations, turned the area into what many now call the Third Korea. Now officially called the Yánbiān Cháoxiān (Korean) Autonomous Prefecture, it is home to the largest population of ethnic Koreans outside the peninsula itself.

Many parts of Yánbiān have only recently been opened to tourists, and even those areas that have been open for years see few Westerners. Facilities are minimal and English almost nonexistent. But people adventurous enough to travel here can enjoy one of Dōngběi's most peacefully stunning landscapes—a sublime combination of Scotland and Japan—and interact with one of China's only truly bicultural societies.

The capital of Yánbiān is **Yánjí**, a rapidly developing city where all of the street signs, and most of the residents, are bilingual. Bland and somewhat rigid, its chief value is as a base for journeys to the surrounding countryside, Cháng Bái Shān, and the North Korean border.

A late-afternoon bus ride through the **Yánbiān countryside** ✿✿✿, as sunlight glitters on fields of rice and warms the upturned roofs of Korean huts, is one of the most exquisite experiences available in the Northeast. The best excuse to take such a ride is **Fángchuān,** a tiny town at the end of a needle-thin strip of Chinese territory between North Korea and Russia, and China's preeminent border-viewing spot. A view from the tower here (¥20/$3) provides vistas of Russia, North Korea and, on a clear day, the northern edge of Japan. You have two choices as to how to get there: public transportation or taxi. A **taxi** will save you a lot of hassle; a round-trip ride from Yánjí to Fángchuān costs ¥400 ($50). You can have the driver wait for you while you sightsee. Have the driver wait outside the ticketing area or pay an additional ¥10 ($1.25) to take the car all the way to the tower. Otherwise, from the Yánjí railway station, catch the 6:30am bus to Húnchūn (2½ hr.; ¥21/$3). Once you arrive in Húnchūn, take a (¥2/25¢ pedicab ride to the Húnchūn's Zōnghé Shìchǎng, where you can take a minibus (¥10/$1.25 one-way) to the border's edge. It will drop you off about 3km (2 miles) from the viewing tower in Fángchuān, but you can bribe them a few extra dollars to take you farther. Be certain to ask about the availability of return buses to Húnchūn,

Yǔnshí Bówùguǎn (Meteorite Museum) ⓚⓘⓓⓢ   On March 8, 1976, one of the largest meteorite showers in recorded history fell on a 500-sq.-km (195-sq.-mile) area around Jílín, pelting the city with 4,000 kilograms (4.4 tons) of rock and giving it a reason to open this museum. The facility has recently been renovated but has very few English captions. The main reason to come here is the world's largest stony meteorite as schedules are virtually nonexistent and service is largely determined by whether or not there are enough passengers to fill a bus.

Warning: North Koreans continue to flow into Yánbiān, but without official permission. Though identity checks aren't as strict as they used to be, it is always a good idea to carry your passport with you at all times.

GETTING THERE   Trains connect Yánjí to both Běijīng (10:40am; 24 hr.; ¥322/$40) and Chángchūn (two daily; 9½ hr.; ¥119/$15).The **railway station (Yánjí Zhàn)** is to the south, at the end of Zhàn Qián Jiē; the ticket office is open from 4:30am to 10:30pm. **Buses** to Cháng Bái Shān (p. 189) and towns in the countryside leave from the Dōngběiyà Kèyùn Zhàn (on Cháng Bái Lù, northeast of railway station); the ticket office is open from 5am to 4:30pm. Buses also leave from the railway station parking lot. **Flights** to Běijīng (four daily; ¥970/$121) and Seoul (Mon, Wed, and Fri; ¥2,540/$318) depart from a small airport 6km (3¾ miles) west of the railway station; a taxi ride there costs ¥10 ($1.25). Taxis do not use meters; rides are either ¥5/65¢ or ¥10/$1.25, depending on distance. Negotiate the price before you get in. Purchase flight tickets at the **CAAC ticket office** (⌀ 0433/291-5555; open 8am–9pm) inside the Xiǎngyǔ Dàjiǔdiàn above the Yánxīn Bridge, north of the railway station.

WHERE TO STAY & DINE   Yánjí's most convenient hotel is the **Dōngběiyà Dàjiǔdiàn** (Cháng Bái Lù 109; ⌀ 0433/290-9222; fax 0433/282-0970), next to the long-distance bus station on Cháng Bái Lù. Avoid old rooms in the tower; go instead for clean and spacious units (¥488/$61 standard room) in the new building in back. The joint-venture **Yánbiān Daewoo (Yánbiān Dàyǔ Fàndiàn)** ⌖, Júzi Jiē 272, 3km (2 miles) north of the post office (⌀ 0433/290-5050; fax 0433/265-7701), is Yánjí's largest and most luxurious hotel. The small but tasteful rooms cost ¥800 ($100) and come with breakfast. Yánjí's food specialty is Korean *lěngmiàn* **(cold noodles)**, semitranslucent wheat noodles served in a cold broth with various toppings. Two restaurants compete for the title of best *lěngmiàn* restaurant in town: **Jīndálái Fàndiàn** ⌖ (Hǎilán Lù 42, at Xīnhuá Jiē; ⌀ 0433/252-8590), and **Fúwù Dàlóu** ⌖ (Guāngmíng Jiē 38; ⌀ 0433/251-8668). The latter offers less of a third-grade cafeteria ambience, but both serve a mean *Mín Sú lěngmiàn* (¥10/$1.25 for a large bowl), the classic cold noodle bowl served with pickled cabbage, beef, pine nuts, and Korean chili paste garnished with an apple slice. Both restaurants are open from 8:30am to 10pm.

(1,774kg/3,921 lb.), which hovers dressed in a blue velvet skirt in the middle of the hall. Records show that the meteorite's impact registered 1.7 on the Richter scale. Visitors are allowed to touch a smaller meteorite in the adjacent room.

Jílín Dàjiē 100. ⌀ 0432/466-1214. Admission ¥40 ($5) adults, ¥15 ($1.80) children. 8:30–11:30am and 1:30–4:30pm. Bus: no. 103 to Jiāng Nán Gōngyuán, then walk south past a large statue of Máo.

WHERE TO STAY

Jílín's hotels are busy year-round but only fill up during major Chinese holidays. Discounts range from 15% to 25% in summer.

EXPENSIVE

Century Hotel (Shìjì Dàfàndiàn) An exaggerated statue of Cretheus on Argus at the entrance is the first of many ancient Greek and Roman flourishes installed throughout this odd hotel. Nominally managed by Swiss-Belhotel but dominated by its Chinese owner, the Century feels grossly out of place in Jílín. Still, it is the city's nicest hotel, and close to the sights. Rooms are spacious and opulent, with fluffy beds, pale walls, and dark wood furniture.

Jílín Dàjiē 77 (at Yìshān Lù). (C) **0432/216-8888.** Fax 0432/216-8777. www.centuryhotel.com.cn. 166 units. ¥800 ($100) standard room. 10% service charge. AE, DC, MC, V. **Amenities:** 3 restaurants; bar; nightclub; small indoor pool; health club and spa; business center; forex; limited room service; dry cleaning/laundry. *In room:* A/C, satellite TV, minibar, fridge, hair dryer, safe.

Crystal Hotel (Wùsōng Bīnguǎn) 🌟 Once the only luxury hotel in Jílín, this four-star still offers the city's best combination of comfort and service. Perched several kilometers northeast of the railway station on the east bank of the Sōnghuā Jiāng, it is far from most sights in the city but provides good views of the ice-rimmed trees in winter. Decent-size rooms are nicer than the hotel's worn exterior would suggest. Corner rooms are larger and offer the best river views. Bathrooms in both are clean. Spacious standard rooms on floors 1 through 3 of satellite building C are a good value at about 50% less than comparable rooms in the main building.

Lóngtán Dàjiē 29 (south of Lóngtán Bridge). (C) **0432/398-6200.** Fax 0432/398-6501. ggwusong@mail.jihua-comm. com.cn. 152 units. ¥750 ($93) standard room; ¥1,000 ($125) corner standard room. AE, DC, MC, V. 15% service charge. Rates include breakfast for 2. **Amenities:** 2 restaurants; bar; small exercise room; nice spa w/river view; bowling alley; business center; limited room service; laundry. *In room:* A/C, satellite TV, fridge, hair dryer (upon request).

MODERATE

Dōngguān Bīnguǎn Built in 1957 just north of the Jílín Bridge, the Dōngguān is a relic, but a convenient one, with a great location and two travel agencies (including a CITS branch) on-site. The main building, a white behemoth with a traditional green tile roof, underwent minor renovations in 2002 and offers worn but clean standard rooms with small bathrooms. Similar rooms on the first floor of the rear building are heavily discounted. The nicest standard rooms are in the new building. Rooms on the south side of the main building and west side of the new building offer views of the river.

Jiāngwān Lù 2. (C) **0432/216-0188** or 0432/216-0118. 168 units. ¥210 ($25) standard room in back building; ¥180 ($22) in main building; ¥280 ($34) in new building. No credit cards. Rates include breakfast. **Amenities:** Restaurant; small business center. *In room:* A/C, TV.

International Hotel (Guójì Dàfàndiàn) This three-star no longer gleams the way it used to but is still the most comfortable and best-equipped hotel in the railway-station area. Rooms are tidy and bright with hard beds. The hotel charges the same price for every room and varies the discount: Well-maintained standard rooms are the most expensive, and older rooms on the seventh and eighth floors are the cheapest.

Zhōngxīng Jiē 20 (southwest of railway station). (C) **0432/255-0703.** Fax 0432/255-3788. 191 units. ¥480 ($60) standard room. No credit cards. **Amenities:** 2 restaurants; exercise room; bowling alley; laundry. *In room:* A/C, TV.

INEXPENSIVE

Lǚyóu Bīnguǎn (Tourism Hotel) *Value*   Located just off Rénmín Dàjiē, halfway between the railway station and the river, the Tourism Hotel is the best deal in town. Guest rooms are large, clean, and comfortable, though with thin walls. Bathrooms are in slight disrepair but clean. The carpets are a bit scuffed but nothing to complain about at this price. The hotel is often full, so call ahead.

Cháoyáng Jiē 88 (on Wénhuà Guǎngchǎng). ✆ **0432/508-3222.** 58 units. ¥180 ($22) standard room. No credit cards. No hot water noon–7pm unless requested. **Amenities:** Restaurant. *In room:* A/C, TV.

WHERE TO DINE

There is a **KFC** inside the Fu-Mart at the intersection of Chóngqìng Lù and Bǎodìng Lù; the Fu-Mart also has a **supermarket.** The Century Hotel's Western restaurant serves decent pizza and salads and offers occasional buffet promotions for about ¥60 ($7.50) per person. There are several **Korean cold-noodle** restaurants around the railway station (see box, "Wild China: Yánbiān," p. 186). For a more adventurous and truly local dining experience, try the block of **outdoor street stalls** *(dà páidǎng)* on Cháoyáng Jiē ✆, just north of Jiěfàng Zhōng Lù. You can choose from hot pot, seafood, or *guōtiě*, meat and vegetables you cook yourself at the table in an iron pan. It's open nightly May through October, from 5pm to 5am.

Lìyàdé Shìfù ✆ MUSLIM   By far the most upmarket Muslim restaurant in the city, Lìyàdé lacks the gritty appeal of Jílín's other Huí minority eateries but still manages to serve some fine mutton dishes. Portions are small but well presented. Don't miss the *shǒusī yángròu,* tender bits of torn lamb served with soy-and-garlic dipping sauce.

Jíyuán Shāngchéng on Jiěfàng Zhōng Lù (west of Jílín Dàjiē). ✆ **0432/208-1010.** Meal for 2 ¥70–¥120 ($9–$15). No credit cards. 10am–10pm.

Zhōnghuá Míng Shìfù DŌNGBĚI   This unpretentious local favorite serves up regional cuisine at reasonable prices. The house specialty is zhēn bù tóng tánròu, pieces of fatty pork braised in a homemade beer-based sauce until melt-in-your mouth tender. Also try the dà bàn shuǐlāpí, a huge plate of mung-bean flour noodles served cold with cilantro, peanuts, bits of pork, and julienned cucumbers, all mixed together with a spicy sesame sauce.

Jiěfàng Dàlù just west of Tiānjīn Jiē, on the south side of the street. ✆ **0432/243-8333.** Meal for 2 ¥50–¥70 ($6–$15). No credit cards. 10:30am–9pm.

6 Cháng Bái Shān

Jílín Province, 565km (350 miles) E of Jílín City

Cháng Bái Shān (Long White Mountain) is the mythical source of Manchurian and Korean culture, the center of the 200,000-hectare (494,000-acre) **Cháng Bái Shān Nature Preserve,** the tallest peak in Dōngběi, and the region's most impressive attraction. The main reason to visit is **Tiān Chí (Heavenly Lake)**—a pristine, 2-million-year-old fog-enshrouded lake set deep in the crater at the top of the mountain. Roughly 13km (8 miles) in circumference, it straddles the Chinese–North Korean border and is the source of the Sōnghuā River. Below the lake, the mountain is home to a truly impressive range of flora—over 80 tree and 300 medicinal plant species, including ginseng, Korean pine, and the rare Cháng Bái larch.

The mountain was considered forbidden territory throughout most of the Qīng dynasty, and Hàn Chinese who wandered into the area, usually in search of ginseng, were sometimes beaten to death with sticks. Extreme as it sounds, visitors today might find themselves wishing for a similar policy to protect the mountain from new hordes of trash-shedding Chinese and South Korean tourists. The mountain's UNESCO World Natural Reserve status has done little to this end and, moreover, seems to be the justification for supplementary admission fees, capitalizing on every single scenic spot on the mountain. By the time you get there, it is more than likely there will be additional fees to enter spots that were previously included in the general admission price.

Snow makes routes impassable from early October to late May, and even in summer the weather is maddeningly unpredictable (bring a raincoat). The best time to visit is early September, when the weather clears somewhat and the lake is most likely to be visible. Unfortunately, September is also when an army of South Koreans flood the area, taking up hotel rooms as far west as Jílín City and driving up prices.

THE NORTHERN APPROACH

One of only two routes open to foreigners (the others enter or venture too close to North Korea), this is the most convenient and scenic way to tackle the mountain. It is possible to see Tiān Chí and return to Èrdào Bái Hé (see below) in a single day using this approach, but it's worthwhile to spend at least 2 days here.

ESSENTIALS

GETTING THERE   The route begins at **Èrdào Bái Hé** (Bái Hé for short), a small town 25km (16 miles) north of the mountain, named for a river that flows down from Tiān Chí. The best way to reach Bái Hé from the north or west is through Yánjí (see "Wild China: Yánbiān," above); during peak season, which starts around mid-June, a **tourist express** leaves Yánjí's long-distance bus station at 5:30am and goes directly to the mountain gate. The 3-hour trip costs ¥55 ($7) one-way; ¥101 ($13) same-day round-trip including lunch. Or you can catch one of several Bái Hé–bound buses (191km/118 miles; 4 hr.; ¥28/$4) that leave from the Yánjí railway station. From the south, the easiest approach is by **train** via Tōnghuà (two daily; 6½ hr.; ¥42/$5).

Buses (¥40/$5) and **private cars** (¥80–¥100/$8–$13) gather every morning at the Bái Hé railway station, at the north end of town, for trips to the *dàozhànkǒu* (vehicle switching station), 17km (11 miles) up the mountain from the main gate. **Admission** at the main gate costs ¥60 ($7.50) for adults and ¥30 ($4) for students and children.

TOURS   Jílín's **Yíntōng Travel Service,** on the fifth floor of the Milky Way Hotel, at the intersection of Bánshān Dàjiē and Zhōngxī Jiē (© **0432/202-0726**, ext. 285; open 8:30am–5pm), offers a 3-day Cháng Bái Shān tour for ¥580 ($73). The tour is certainly reasonably priced but it doesn't leave much time to enjoy anything but the lake. In Yánjí, **CITS** (Jíxī Jiē 4 south of the intersection with Xīn Gōngyuán Lù) offers a 1-day tour for ¥290 ($36), which includes lunch and all fees for the mountain. *Note:* It's extremely difficult to beat the CITS price if you are a solo traveler and want to return to Yánjí the same day.

SEEING THE LAKE

SUVs (30 min.; ¥80/$10 per person) travel from the *dàozhànkǒu* to a parking lot in front of the hot springs just below Tiān Chí. Tickets to see Tiān Chí and the hot springs are ¥40 ($5). From the parking lot you will have to climb an incredible number of paved stairs to view the lake. More enjoyable is the 2-hour hike, which follows a smaller road up a narrow valley, crosses a bridge (¥10/$1.25), then climbs past the 68m (223-ft.) **Chángbái Shān waterfall** to the north shore *(běi pō)* of the lake. Rock slides sometimes block the trail, in which case you may be able to seek out a freelance guide (¥100/$13 per person) to show you an alternate route. Go early in the morning to avoid the crowds. Once you arrive, search out Mr. Sòng, an ex-reporter and photographer who lives by the lake and likes to tell tales of the mythical **Tiān Chí monster** *(guàiwu)* over harsh glasses of Chinese moonshine.

OTHER SIGHTS

Cháng Bái Shān is home to a number of volcanic **hot springs,** the largest of which seeps steaming out of the rock south of the waterfall. Water from the springs commonly reaches 180°F (80°C); vendors sell eggs boiled in the springs (¥10/$1.25 for four). The **Wēnquán Yù,** in a small white building that's a 10-minute walk below the waterfall (on the left side as you descend), charges ¥60 ($7.50) for a pleasant soak in its hot-spring baths. Also on the mountain, 4km (2½ miles) below the *dàozhànkǒu,* is the truly magical **Dìxià Sēnlín (Underground Forest)** ✿ (¥15/$2, includes the **Heavenly Pool (Xiǎo Tiān Chí),** a lush forest that becomes progressively more alien as it descends, with the **Èrdào Bái Hé** 60m (200 ft.) below the mountain stratum (bring bug spray). In Bái Hé itself, between the railway station and the rest of town, is **Měirén Sōng Sēnlín (Sylvan Pine Forest;** 6am–6pm; ¥8/$1) which was being logged at the time of writing, but some stunning forestry was (and hopefully will be) left untouched. Sylvan pines *(měirén sōng)* are a rare species that grow only on the northern slope of Cháng Bái Shān between 650 and 1,600m (2,100–5,200 ft.).

WHERE TO STAY & DINE

Rooms in most hotels are outfitted with **kàng**—heated brick platform beds, favored by Koreans and Manchus, either raised or sunk into the floor and covered with quilts. A group of families have set up small guesthouses next to the railway station in Bái Hé, where it is possible to sleep on a *kàng* and enjoy home cooking for as little as ¥15 ($2).

If you prefer a mattress, Bái Hé's largest and nicest hotel is the **Xīndà Bīnguǎn** (© **0433/572-0111;** fax 0433/572-0555; 134 units), on the east side of Báishān Dàjiē just south of the Měirén Sōng Sēnlín. Simple but spacious and clean rooms with slightly dirty bathrooms cost ¥360 ($45). The brand-new **Fúbái Bīnguǎn** (© **0433/ 571-7565;** fax 0433/571-8372; 32 units), inside the Bái Hé Forestry Bureau complex south of the railway station, has clean guest rooms with small but tidy bathrooms for ¥260 ($33), as well as beds for ¥50 ($6).

If you plan to spend more than a day at Cháng Bái Shān, it makes sense to pay the extra money and stay on the mountain. The **Athlete's Village,** at the to dàozhànkǒu (**Yùndòngyúan Cūn;** © **0433/574-6008;** fax 0433/574-6055; 59 units), offers basic but comfortable rooms with TVs and small, clean bathrooms in a ski-lodge setting for ¥560 ($70). A 15-minute walk up the road, in a large, traditional Korean-style building, is the **Cháng Bái Shān International Hotel (Cháng Bái Shān Guójì Bīnguǎn;** © **0433/574-6004;** fax 0433/574-6002; 42 units), which offers relatively luxurious standard rooms with plush beds and clean marble bathrooms (¥700/$88; AE, DC, MC, V accepted). Next door, the impeccable **Cháng Bái Shān Daewoo (Cháng Bái Shān Dàyǔ Fàndiàn)** ✿✿ (© **0433/574-6011;** fax 0433/574-6012; 59 units) offers a choice of bed or water-heated *kàng* (¥960/$120; AE, DC, MC, V accepted).

All of the hotels mentioned above serve overpriced but adequate food. Restaurants in town are mostly dives, but they are significantly cheaper and serve comparable fare. The best meal (also the most expensive) can be found at the Cháng Bái Shān Daewoo.

THE WESTERN APPROACH

Still in the process of being developed, this route lacks the grandeur of the northern approach but compensates with a more subtle beauty. The starting point is the dusty village of Sōngjiāng Hé, 40km (25 miles) west of Cháng Bái Shān, connected by a newly paved road to a saddle of rock overlooking Tiān Chí on the border with North Korea. The chief attraction here is the plant life, which changes gradually from ghostly forests of birch at the lower elevations to vivid fields of wildflowers and grassy tundra just below the lake. The flowers are at their most vibrant in early June.

ESSENTIALS

GETTING THERE   The best way to get to Sōngjiāng Hé is by bus from Chángchūn (5:30am; 9 hr.; ¥42/$5) or Jílín (6am; 10 hr.; ¥41/$5); or by train from Tōnghuà (8:10am, 12:50am; 4 hr.; ¥29/$4). The long-distance bus station, in a blue speckled building with a red-tile roof, is a 20-minute walk south of the railway station on Zhàn Qián Jiē, the city's main thoroughfare.

TOURS   The Sōngjiāng Hé Forestry Company (© 0439/631-8461), with a travel office inside the Sōngjiāng Hé Bīnguǎn (see "Where to Stay & Dine," below), is the only organization officially allowed to run tours of the western slope. The 2-day tour costs ¥440 ($53) and includes admission and lunch, but no English is spoken. If you can speak Mandarin, it's much cheaper to hire a private car; drivers will approach you at the railway station. A reasonable price range is ¥150 to ¥250 ($19–$31).

EXPLORING THE MOUNTAIN

The Xī Pō Shān Mén (West Slope Mountain Gate), located 44km (27 miles) west of Tiān Chí, is open from 6:30am to 4:30pm; admission is ¥80 ($10). The drive from the gate runs past birch forests and fields of wildflowers, ending at a steep set of stairs that leads to Tiān Chí and the No. 5 border stone, which marks the beginning of North Korea. Birds and Chinese tourists cross the border at will, but soldiers stationed by the stone keep foreigners from doing the same. There is a 3-hour round-trip hike from here to Báiyún Fēng, the highest point (2,691m/8,826 ft.); it's the second peak to the left as you face the lake.

None of the other sights in the area are particularly impressive or worth the extra money your driver will demand.

Tips Hiking West to North

Development of the western approach has made it possible to hike around Tiān Chí and see both sides of the lake in 2 days, provided you have a tent, warm clothes, and plenty of food and water. The **hike from the west shore** ⋆⋆ along the ridge past Báiyún Fēng to the waterfall on the north shore takes roughly 6 hours. Once you reach the waterfall, you can hike down to the hot spring, camp, and catch a ride to Bái Hé the next morning. Buses back to Sōngjiāng Hé (3 hr.; ¥13/$2) leave from the long-distance bus station on Báishān Dàjiē at 2pm.

Warning: The path is rocky and the weather unpredictable—for experienced hikers only.

WHERE TO STAY & DINE

The only proper hotel in Sōngjiāng Hé is the dark **Sōngjiāng Hé Bīnguǎn** (© 0439/ 631-3601; fax 0439/631-8820; www.51766.com/img/bssjh; 88 units) on Gōngyì Dàjiē, across from the Sēnlín Huódòng Zhōngxīn. Partially refurbished rooms with acceptable bathrooms cost ¥240 ($30), but this can be bargained below ¥200 ($25) even in the high season. The hotel serves mediocre food, but independent restaurants aren't much better.

7 Harbin

Hēilóng Jiāng Province, 1,421km (881 miles) NE of Běijīng, 553km (342 miles) NE of Shěnyáng

Harbin (Hā'ěrbīn), originally a Russian-built railway outpost carved out of the wilderness on the banks of the Sōnghuā Jiāng (Sungari River), is the northernmost major city in China and capital of Hēilóng Jiāng Province. Named for the Black Dragon River that separates Dōngběi from Siberia, Hēilóng Jiāng represents China's northern limits. It is the country's coldest province, with winter temperatures that frequently plummet below –40°F (–40°C). Like many border regions, it is an amalgamation of clashing extremes, home to one of China's roughest mountain ranges (the Greater Hinggan or Dà Xīng'ān Lǐng), some of its most fertile soil, its largest oil and coal fields, its most pristine wilderness, and most of its few remaining nomad groups.

Harbin itself suffers from a similar internal antagonism, one that ultimately makes it the most compelling destination in Dōngběi. The city was founded in 1897 as a camp for Russian engineers surveying construction of the eastern leg of the Trans-Siberian railroad (called the China Eastern Railroad, or CER). Demand for labor and the city's laissez-faire atmosphere quickly attracted a diverse population of outcasts from Latvia, the Ukraine, and Poland, as well as Manchuria. It was, at its height, one of the most bizarrely cosmopolitan cities in Asia—cold, dirty, rife with speculation and venereal disease, architecturally vibrant, and a model for ethnic and religious tolerance. The town fell under Japanese control during World War II and was finally recaptured in 1946.

Most original foreign residents fled at the end of World War II. The city has begun to recover some of its former face, however, as trainloads of Russian merchants and prostitutes flood back to take advantage of China's new economic momentum. Harbin attracts visitors year-round, especially in winter, when it hosts the famous **Ice and Snow Festival (Bīngxuě Jié)** ✵. The summer's mild temperatures allow for leisurely strolls past the truly stunning clusters of Russian buildings, with their lonely cupolas and embellished pediments, that still brighten older parts of town.

The Ice and Snow Festival has successfully turned the city's worst feature—villainous winter cold—into its greatest asset. The winter, despite the frostbite-inducing weather, is the best time to come as it's the town's most festive time of year. The festival now covers most of the city and features some truly outstanding ice and snow sculptures. Past highlights have included translucent reproductions of the Great Wall and Běijīng's Gate of Heavenly Peace (Tiān'ān Mén), life-size pagodas, structurally sound multilevel houses, and a massive statue of Elvis—all equipped with internal lights.

It's easy to underestimate the cold (temperatures often drop below –22°F/–30°C), so bring more warm clothing than you think you'll need. Wearing five layers of sweaters and a down coat might sound ridiculous until you get there. Admission can be expensive, but there are increasing numbers of free displays on Zhōngyāng Dàjiē and other major streets. Major venues include **Zhàolín Gōnyuán** on Shàngzhí Jiē for ice sculpture (¥30/$4); **Tàiyáng Dǎo Gōngyuán (Sun Island Park),** across the river for snow sculptures (¥60; $7.50); and the **Ice and Snow Palace (Bīngxuě Gōng),** a collection of buildings constructed entirely of ice and snow on the banks of the Sōnghuā Jiāng (¥100/$13).

ESSENTIALS

GETTING THERE **Flights** connect Harbin with Běijīng, Shànghǎi, Dàlián, and Guǎngzhōu; international routes include Hong Kong (one per week), Seoul (daily), and Niigata (Mon, Wed, Fri, and Sun). The **Tàipíng International Airport (Tàipíng Guójì Jīchǎng)** is 30km (19 miles) south of central Harbin. An ICBC booth next to the international departures area on the second floor exchanges traveler's checks and cash. The **CAAC ticket office (Mínháng Shòupiào Chù;** ✆ **0451/8265-1188;** fax 0451/8231-9343; domestic 6am–9pm, international 8am–4pm) is in a large white tiled building with a red roof, 4km (2½ miles) south of the railway station at Zhōngshān Lù 99. An **airport shuttle** (50 min.; ¥20/$2.50) leaves the CAAC office every 30 minutes from 6am to 6pm. **Taxis** to the airport from downtown (¥60/$7.50) take between 40 minutes and an hour, depending on traffic. Leave early either way.

Harbin's **main railway station (Hā'ěrbīn Zhàn)** is on Tiělù Jiē, between Nángǎng and Dàolǐ districts. Trains depart from here for Běijīng (8:37pm; 11 hr.; ¥281/$35), Dàlián (9:09pm; 9½ hr.; ¥224/$28), Shěnyáng (seven daily; 6½ hr.; ¥139/$17), Qiqihar (10 daily; 4 hr.; ¥37/$5), and Mǎnzhōulǐ (6:48pm; 15 hr.; ¥188/$24). The ticket sales office is on the right side of the station (✆ **0451/8690-2828**); tickets can be bought 5 days in advance. For tickets to Khabarovsk and Vladivostok, visit the **Harbin Railway International Travel Service (Hā'ěrbīn Tiědào Guójì Lǚxíngshè;** ✆ **0451/ 5364-3264;** open Mon–Fri 8am–5pm;) on the seventh floor of the Kūnlún Hotel, west of the main station. **CITS** (Xīdàzhí Jiē 13, west of Hóngbō Guǎngchǎng; ✆ **0451/ 5366-7388;** 8:30am–5:30pm) and the **Hēilóng Jiāng Overseas Tourist Company (Hēilóng Jiāng Hǎiwài Lǚyóu Gōngsī;** 11th floor of Hùshì Dàshà, on west side of railway station; ✆ **0451/5363-4000;** fax 0451/5362-1088) sell tickets for the **Trans-Siberian Railroad** (2 weeks to process).

The central **long-distance bus station (Chángtú Kèyùn Zhàn)** is across from the railway station, in a renovated building next to the Běi Běi Hotel. Luxury air-conditioned buses go to Qiqihar (3½ hr; ¥61/$7.50), Wǔ Dà Liánchí (1:30pm; 5½ hr.; ¥69/$9), and Běijīng (5:30pm; 13 hr.; ¥249/$31). Regular buses go to Yánjí (3:30pm; 9 hr.; ¥112/$14) and Dàlián (4:40pm; 13 hr.; ¥178/$22). The ticket sales office is open from 5:30am to 6pm (luxury tickets at windows 7–11).

GETTING AROUND Nearly everything of interest falls into one of two old districts—Dàolǐ and Nángǎng—divided by the train tracks that run past the main station. The Sōnghuā Jiāng (Sungari River) forms the city's northern border and divides it from Tàiyáng Dǎo, a new island development area that seeks to imitate Pǔdōng in Shànghǎi.

Taxis fall into two categories: Increasingly rare Xiàlìs (¥7/90¢ for the first 3km/2 miles, then ¥1.60/20¢ per kilometer); and more expensive Jettas (¥8/$1 for first 3km/2 miles, then ¥1.90/25¢ per kilometer). A number of useful **buses** (¥1–¥2/ 15¢–25¢) stop at the railway station; **bus no. 13** goes from the station through the heart of Dàolǐ.

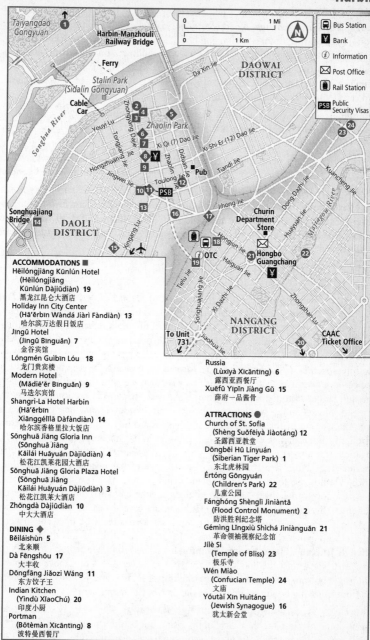

Bus Station
Bank
Information
Post Office
Rail Station
PSB **Public Security Visas**

Taiyangdao Gongyuan

Harbin-Manzhouli Railway Bridge

Ferry

Stalin Park (Sìdàlín Gōngyuán)

Cable Car

DAOWAI DISTRICT

Da Xin Jie

Zhaolin Park

Xi Qi (7) Dao Jie

Xi Shi Er (12) Dao Jie

Zhōngyāng Dàjiē

Tōngjiāng Jie

Youyi Lu

Hongzhuàng Jie

Jingwei Jie

Zhaolin Jie

Diduan Jie

Tiandi Jie

Toulong Jie

Pub

Kuancheng Jie

Măiiagou River

Dong Dazhi Jie

Huáyuán Jie

Songhua River

Songhuajiang Bridge

DAOLI DISTRICT

Xingang Lu

Xingang Lu

Jihong Jie

Churin Department Store

Hongjun Jie

OTC

Haiguan Jie

Hongbo Guangchang

Chang

Xi Dazhi Jie

Tielu Lu

Songhuajiang Lu

NANGANG DISTRICT

To Unit 731

Jiaohua Jie

Jiéfàng Jie

Zhongshan Lu

CAAC Ticket Office

ACCOMMODATIONS ■

Hēilóngjiāng Kūnlún Hotel
(Hēilóngjiāng
Kūnlún Dàjiŭdiàn) **19**
黑龙江昆仑大酒店

Holiday Inn City Center
(Hā'ěrbīn Wàndá Jiàrì Fàndiàn) **13**
哈尔滨万达假日饭店

Jīngŭ Hotel
(Jīngŭ Bīnguăn) **7**
金谷宾馆

Lóngmén Guìbīn Lóu **18**
龙门贵宾楼

Modern Hotel
(Mădíě'ěr Bīnguăn) **9**
马迭尔宾馆

Shangri-La Hotel Harbin
(Hā'ěrbīn
Xiānggélĭlā Dàfàndiàn) **14**
哈尔滨香格里拉大饭店

Sōnghuā Jiāng Gloria Inn
(Sōnghuā Jiāng
Kăilái Huāyuán Dàjiŭdiàn) **4**
松花江凯莱花园大酒店

Sōnghuā Jiāng Gloria Plaza Hotel
(Sōnghuā Jiāng
Kăilái Huāyuán Dàjiŭdiàn) **3**
松花江凯莱大酒店

Zhōngdà Dàjiŭdiàn **10**
中大大酒店

DINING ◆

Běiláishùn **5**
北来顺

Dà Fēngshōu **17**
大丰收

Dōngfāng Jiăozi Wáng **11**
东方饺子王

Indian Kitchen
(Yìndù XiāoChú) **20**
印度小厨

Portman
(Bōtèmàn Xīcāntīng) **8**
波特曼西餐厅

Russia
(Lùxīyà Xīcāntīng) **6**
露西亚西餐厅

Xuěfŭ Yīpĭn Jiàng Gŭ **15**
薛府一品酱骨

ATTRACTIONS ●

Church of St. Sofia
(Shèng Suŏfēiyà Jiàotáng) **12**
圣露西亚教堂

Dōngběi Hŭ Línyuán
(Siberian Tiger Park) **1**
东北虎林园

Értóng Gōngyuán
(Children's Park) **22**
儿童公园

Fánghóng Shènglì Jìniàntă
(Flood Control Monument) **2**
防洪胜利纪念塔

Géming Lĭngxiù Shìchá Jìniànguăn **21**
革命领袖视察纪念馆

Jílè Sì
(Temple of Bliss) **23**
极乐寺

Wén Miào
(Confucian Temple) **24**
文庙

Yóutài Xīn Huìtáng
(Jewish Synagogue) **16**
犹太新会堂

FAST FACTS

Banks, Foreign Exchange & ATMs The main **Bank of China** branch (open Mon–Fri 8:30am–4:30pm) is at Hóngjūn Jiē 20, 1 block north of Hóngbō Guǎngchǎng. Credit cards and traveler's checks are handled at window 2 on the second floor (*not* available 11:30am–1pm). There is an international ATM on the premises. A second branch at Xī Shí (10) Dàojiē 29 (east of Zhōngyāng Dàjiē) exchanges traveler's checks and cash (Mon–Fri 8:30am–4:30pm).

Internet Access Go online at the 24-hour **Yìdù Kōngjiān Wǎngbā** (¥3/40¢ per hour) on the north side of Hóngzhuàn Jiē, a block west of Zhōngyāng Dàjiē. Dial-up is © **16900** or 165.

Post Office The main post office (**Nángǎng Yóuzhèngjú;** open May–Oct 8am–7pm, Nov–Apr 8am–6:30pm) is on the corner of Dōng Dàzhí Jiē and Fèndòu Lù, several blocks east of Hóngbō Guǎngchǎng. Phone cards are sold inside.

Visa Extensions Visa extensions are available inside the **PSB** Exit/Entry Administration Office (© **0451/8466-1435;** Mon–Fri 8–11:40am and 1:30–4:40pm) at Duàn Jiē 26, near the bottom of Zhōngyāng Dàjiē. Passport and hotel registration are required.

EXPLORING HARBIN
ZHŌNGYĀNG DÀJIĒ ✿✿

A cobbled, tree-lined street located in the heart of Dàolǐ District, Zhōngyāng Dàjiē was once the buzzing heart of social and commercial life in Harbin, home to the city's most exclusive hotels and shops. "From 3am until nightfall, it was alive with throngs of people," a Japanese visitor wrote of the avenue, originally known as Kitaiskia (Chinese) Street, in 1926. "The Russian women with their gaudy early summer hats and clothing together with their white shoes formed a spectacle to be seen nowhere else in the Far East save Shànghǎi." The scene today is much the same, but with Russian faces few and far between. Particularly vibrant is the **pedestrian-only section** at the southern end, where Chinese women in absurd fur coats window-shop a new generation of boutiques set up in the old Russian buildings, beautifully restored with explanatory plaques in English. The old-world charm, however, has not stopped the commercial invasion of fast-food restaurants, Wal-Mart, and the Warner Brothers–branded movie theater. The luxury department store Lane Crawford has opened a branch, selling pricey Dunhill, St. John, and Mont Blanc items.

At the top of the street, constructed along a large embankment erected after the Sōnghuā River flooded and buried Harbin under several feet of water in 1932, is **Sīdàlín Gōngyuán (Stalin Park),** a recently repaved stretch of trees and benches where locals gather to exercise and gossip. In the center of the park is the **Fánghóng Shènglì Jìniàntǎ (Flood Control Monument).** The monument commemorates the city's struggle against the floods of 1957, when the river rose 4 feet above street level but was kept from spilling into town by an army of soldiers and volunteers. Water levels from other big floods are marked at the base of the monument.

Church of St. Sophia (Shèng Suǒfēiyà Jiàotáng) ✿✿ The brick spires and green dome of the Church of St. Sophia rising out of the chaos east of Zhōngyāng Dàjiē are the divine reminders of a more inspired age in architecture. Erected in 1907 and rebuilt several times, the church took its current form in 1932. The handiwork is still visible on the vaulted ceilings and painted chambers, despite near-destruction by

Fun Fact Zion That Wasn't

Unlikely as it sounds, Jews fled to Harbin in such numbers in the early 1900s (the population reached 25,000 at its height) that Manchuria ranked just below Morocco and Palestine on early-20th-century lists of potential sites for a Jewish homeland. Fleeing official discrimination and a revival of pogroms in czarist Russia, they were instrumental in Harbin's development but fled en masse for the real Zion shortly after World War II. The only obvious Jewish structures still remaining in the city are the **Modern Hotel** (see "Where to Stay," below); and a **music and Torah school** at Tōngjiāng Jiē 86 (a block west of Zhōngyāng Dàjiē), a ragged structure built in 1919 with Star of David window frames that now houses the No. 2 Korean Middle School (Cháoxiǎn Èr Zhōng).

the Red Guards in the 1960s and a restoration in 1996. The church is now home to the **Harbin Architecture Arts Center.** An exhibition inside contains photos of other churches, old newspaper clippings, and an interesting scale model of Nángǎng District in the 1920s. The rear cloister, used for storage prior to 2002, now contains a small but interesting collection of religious objects. The church's incongruous beauty is enhanced by dozens of white pigeons (kept in place with the promise of free food from feeders in the surrounding square). Pocket-size guides to old Harbin, with color photos and bilingual introductions to several buildings, are sold inside.

Intersection of Tòulóng Jiē and Zhàolín Jiē. Admission ¥25 ($3), child ¥10 ($1.25). 8:30am–5pm. ✆ 0451/8468-6904. Bus: no. 103 from the railway station to Hāyībǎi, then walk 2 blocks east on Tòulóng Jiē.

Dōngběi Hǔ Línyuán (Siberian Tiger Park) *Overrated*   The Siberian Tiger Park is more like an impoverished prison for the tigers—with rusty fences and dilapidated watchtowers—but it may be worth a visit to see the rare felines. Your entrance fee gets you a seat on a typical Chinese minibus that rolls onto the fenced-in .4-sq.-km (.15 square-mile) premises on a dirt road. The bus gets close enough for you to snap good photos and ogle the tigers' paws that are as large as human heads. The park, created in 1986, increased its tiger population from the original 8 to nearly 300, but the facility is more tourist attraction than breeding center. For your sadistic pleasure you may order a meal for the tigers, served via a caged Jeep; on the feeding menu are a live bird (¥40/$5), a live duck (¥100/$13), and a live cow (¥1,500/$188). Sadly, some of the tigers are confined to tiny cages, pacing about in their mini insane asylums; others seems to be in a semipermanent state of slumber.

10km (6 miles) north of the city center. www.dongbeihu.net.cn. Admission (including tour) ¥50 ($6) adults, children ¥25 ($3). May–Sept 8am–6pm; Oct–Apr 8:30am–4pm. Last tour 30 min. before closing. Bus: no. 85 from south end of Gōnglù Dàqiáo (40 min.; ¥2/25¢). Cable car: from Sīdàlín Gōngyuán to Tàiyáng Dǎo Gōngyuán (¥30/$3.75), then minibus to park entrance (20 min.; ¥30/$4).

Értóng Gōngyuán (Children's Park) *Kids*   Built in 1925, this park is famous for its Children's Railroad (Értóng Tiělù), a working pint-size replica of the real thing. The train (¥5/65¢), complete with small hard-seat benches, travels a 2km (1¼-mile) circle from "Běijīng Station" (Běijīng Zhàn) behind the main entrance to "Harbin Station" (Hǎ'ěrbīn Zhàn) at the opposite end of the park and back again.

Fèndòu Lù 295. ✆ 0451/5363-8415. Admission ¥2 (25¢) adults, ¥1 (15¢) children. May–Sept 4:30am–10pm; Oct–Apr 6:30am–6pm. Bus: no. 8 from top of Zhōngyāng Dàjiē. Or walk 4 blocks southeast from the main post office.

Gémìng Lǐngxiù Shìchá Jìniànguǎn   This elegant mansion, built in 1919 by a Polish merchant and opened as a museum in 2002 after a 3-year restoration effort, was where China's top Communist leaders stayed during official inspections of Hēilóng Jiāng. Sumptuously designed rooms on the first floor contain several mementos, including a bathrobe once used by Zhōu Ēnlái. An impressive spiral staircase leads up to the room where Máo slept, still with the original bed.

Yíyuán Jiē (off Hóngjūn Jiē). ✆ 0451/5364-2522. Admission ¥6 (75¢). 9am–4pm. Located behind Sinoway Hotel; it's the 2nd old mansion on the left.

Jílè Sì (Temple of Bliss)   Jílè Sì is the largest active Buddhist temple in Hēilóng Jiāng Province, a beautiful complex welcoming tourists but not made for them. Most impressive are the halls on either side of the main pavilion in the northeastern half, each filled with 500 individually carved arhats *(luóhàn),* or Buddhist saints. The hall on the right is devoted to Manchu namesake Wénshū Púsà (Sanskrit: *Manjusri*), the tiger-riding Boddhisattva of Wisdom (see "Minorities & the Manchu Myth," p. 161). There's a smaller temple next door called Pǔzhào Sì that is open on the 1st and 15th day of each Chinese lunar month.

Dōng Dàzhí Jiē 9. Admission ¥10 ($1.25). May–Sept 8am–4:30pm; Oct–Apr 8am–4pm. Bus: no. 104/14 from Hóngbō Guǎngchǎng to Yóulèyuán; walk northeast on Xuānpǔ Jiē, then take a left on Dōng Dàzhí Jiē.

Unit 731 Museum (Qīnhuá Rìjūn Dìqīsānyāo Bùduì Jiùzhǐ) ✿✿   What happened here is little known in the Western world, which makes this museum a very worthwhile visit despite being located in Harbin's inconvenient suburbs. Between 1939 and 1945, members of Japan's Unit 731 killed roughly 3,000 Chinese, Russian, Mongolian, and North Korean prisoners of war in a series of nauseating experiments designed to perfect their biological weapons program. Japanese soldiers blew up most of the 6-sq.-km (2-sq.-mile) facility at the end of the war, and the unit's existence was kept covered up for decades with the help of the United States government, rumored to have purchased the research with a promise of immunity for participating doctors. A documentary about 731 released in the 1990s prompted Harbin to renovate the facility and add English signs in 2001. Ironically, the museum now stands in an area of town where many of China's pharmaceutical companies are located.

What's best about the museum is that it lets the images and details tell the story, rather than resorting to the heavy-handed propaganda that plagues other Chinese war memorials like the Nánjīng Massacre Site. An exhibition in the main office building contains a series of grim but nicely presented displays on the experiments, in which victims (called *maruta,* Japanese for "log") were frozen, burned, injected with hemorrhagic fever virus, exposed to plague and cholera, and sometimes dissected alive. Most chilling is the medical instruments display (room 9), with its test tubes, needles, saws, and coat rack vivisection hooks (used to "hang human viscera," aka organs). The smokestacks of a large incinerator, where dead *maruta* were burned, still stand on the edge of a weed-strewn field in back.

Once you tour the museum, a guide can take you to the museum's backyard to see where the original germ factory stood (now a pit with overgrown weeds), the remnants of a power-generating facility for the factory, and a series of sheds where the Japanese once bred disease-carrying rats for the experiments.

Xīnjiāng Dàjiē 21 (west of the train tracks), Píngfáng Qū. Admission ¥20 ($2.50). 8–11:30am and 1–4pm. Bus: no. 343 from Kūnlún Hotel (20km/12 miles; 45 min.; ¥2.50/35¢) to museum office; continue in same direction past train tracks. Purchase tickets inside main building.

Wén Miào (Confucian Temple) If you're looking for a brief respite from grimy urban life and a more solemn place than Jílè Sì, visit this wooden temple, one of the largest Confucian temples in China. Built in 1926, Wén Miào, with its 20m-high (66-ft.) ceilings, is now part of Harbin Engineering College campus. At the time of writing, the buildings adjacent to the main palace that make up the temple's main courtyard were being converted into the Nationalities Museum of Hēilóng Jiāng Province. Students painting still lifes in the courtyard and the temple's huge pine trees give it an air of tranquillity.

Wénmiào Jiē 9. Admission ¥15 ($2). 8:30am–4pm. Walk from Jílè Sì across the street to the Harbin Engineering College, then walk inside about 5 min.

Yóutài Xīn Huìtáng (Jewish Synagogue) Once the center of Harbin's vibrant Jewish community that numbered around 20,000 during the early 20th century, this three-story temple underwent an extensive renovation and reopened to the public in 2005. Today, with few Jews remaining in the city, government officials turned the synagogue into a contemporary art museum featuring Jewish and Russian artists.

162 Jīng Wěi Jiē, Dào Lǐ District. ✆ 0451/87630882. Admission ¥10 ($1). 9am–5pm. Bus: no. 2.

WHERE TO STAY

If you want to visit Harbin during the Ice and Snow Festival—December to early March, when thousands flood the city—try to book a room at least 2 weeks to a month in advance. Some hotels offer minor discounts during the festival. Discounts at other times range from 30% to 50%.

EXPENSIVE

Holiday Inn City Center (Hā'ěrbīn Wàndá Jiàrì Fàndiàn) The Holiday Inn, Harbin's finest hotel 5 years ago, now feels more like a midrange Chinese hotel than a respectable joint-venture. But its convenient location at the bottom of Zhōngyāng Dàjiē, solid service, and one of the best Western restaurants in Harbin still make it an attractive option. Rooms are large, clean, and comfortable but somewhat worn and outdated.

Jīng Wěi Jiē 90, Dàolǐ District. ✆ 0451/8422-6666. Fax 0452/8422-1663. holiday@public.hr.hl.cn. 148 units. ¥880 ($110) standard room; ¥1,800 ($200) suite. 15% service charge. Rates include breakfast. AE, DC, MC, V. **Amenities:** 2 restaurants; bar; basic health club; sauna; business center; forex; salon, room service; dry cleaning/laundry; executive-level rooms. In room: A/C, satellite TV, Internet access (¥30/$3 for 3 days), minibar, fridge, hair dryer, safe.

Shangri-La Hotel Harbin (Hā'ěrbīn Xiānggélǐlā Dàfàndiàn) The Shangri-La is the finest hotel in central Harbin, and the only five-star in Dàolǐ District. Rooms, most of which have recently undergone extensive renovations, are comfortable and tasteful. Service is fantastic. The only drawback is that the hotel is not within walking distance of Harbin's fabled architecture, but its location on the river (across from the Ice and Snow Palace) becomes ideal in winter.

Yǒuyì Lù 555 (east of Sōnghuā Jiāng Gōnglù Bridge), Dàolǐ District. ✆ 0451/8485-8888. Fax 0451/8462-1777. www.shangri-la.com. 346 units. ¥1,085 ($136) standard room. 15% service charge. Rate includes breakfast for 1. AE, DC, MC, V. **Amenities:** 2 restaurants; bar; small indoor pool; outdoor tennis courts; health club and spa; concierge; business center; forex; salon; 24-hr. room service; same-day dry cleaning/laundry; nonsmoking rooms; executive-level rooms. In room: A/C, satellite TV, minibar, fridge, hair dryer.

Sōnghuā Jiāng Gloria Plaza Hotel (Sōnghuā Jiāng Kǎilái Huāyuán Dàjiǔdiàn) This new hotel is a welcome addition to Harbin's travel scene, with clean rooms and an unmatched location right next to the Flood Control Monument.

With just 83 rooms few tour groups stay here, making management more attuned to the independent traveler. The suites on the top floor share a common private balcony overlooking the river. (Don't confuse this hotel with the Gloria Plaza, a midprice hotel listed below.)

Èr Dàojiē 259, Dàolǐ District. ⓒ 0451/8677-0000. Fax 0451/8677-0088. 83 units. ¥1,080 ($130) standard room; ¥1,808 ($220) suites. 20%–40% discounts. AE, MC, V. **Amenities:** Restaurant; bar; business center; limited room service. In room: A/C, TV, broadband Internet access.

MODERATE

Lóngmén Guìbīn Lóu ✦✦✦ (Finds)   Built in 1907, this inexplicably ignored yellow-and-white Russian building behind the nondescript Lóngmén Hotel is the most beautifully restored of the old Yamato Hotels. Rooms are spacious and nicely appointed with period furniture. History buffs with money to spare can stay in the suite, outfitted with a beautiful bed from the 1930s, where Zhāng Xuéliáng (see "Shěnyáng," p. 156) held court when in Harbin. Dining rooms on the first floor still display the original Russian woodwork and contain several turn-of-the-20th-century relics, including an old wooden icebox and a still-functioning phonograph.

Hóngjūn Jiē 85 (at Jiànzhù Jiē, opposite the railway station), Nángǎng District. ⓒ 0451/8679-1888. Fax 0451/8363-9700. www.lmhotel.com. 39 units. ¥680 ($85) standard room; ¥1,100 ($133) suite. 40% discount. AE, MC, V. **Amenities:** 4 restaurants; bar; new spa; billiards room; business center; forex; salon; limited room service; dry cleaning/laundry. In room: A/C, TV, minibar, fridge.

Modern Hotel (Mǎdié'ěr Bīnguǎn) ✦   The most glamorous hotel in Harbin during the city's heyday, the three-story Art Nouveau hotel fell on hard times in the early Communist era. While it's improved significantly since, say, the Cultural Revolution, the rooms don't measure up to the history of the place. Still, the location smack in the middle of Zhōngyāng Dàjiē and the fair prices makes it a very good choice. Standard rooms are rather lackluster and devoid of character; bathrooms are small but very clean.

Zhōngyāng Dàjiē 89 (at Xībā Dàojiē, entrance in back), Dàolǐ District. ⓒ 0451/8488-4000. Fax 0451/8461-4997. www.modern.com.cn. 131 units. ¥580 ($73) standard room. Rates include breakfast. AE, DC, MC, V. **Amenities:** 2 restaurants; bar; indoor pool and health club (in neighboring building); business center; forex; laundry. In room: A/C, satellite TV, minibar, fridge.

Sōnghuā Jiāng Gloria Inn (Sōnghuā Jiāng Kǎilái Shāngwù Jiǔdiàn)   The Sōnghuā Jiāng Gloria prospers almost entirely from its location just south of the Flood Control Monument. The hotel, inside a large European-style building, underwent partial renovation in 2001. Rooms are midsize with the green carpets and multilevel ceilings typical of Gloria hotels—worn but still livable. Bathrooms are small and tidy.

Zhōngyāng Dàjiē 257, Dàolǐ District. ⓒ 0451/8463-8855. Fax 0451/8463-8533. www.giharbin.com. 304 units. ¥588 ($74) standard room. AE, DC, MC, V. **Amenities:** 2 restaurants; business center. In room: A/C, satellite TV, minibar, fridge.

INEXPENSIVE

Jīngǔ Hotel (Jīngǔ Bīnguǎn) (Value)   While this hotel might belong in the "moderate" category, the management is so generous with its discount that it is a good choice for the budget traveler. The beds are slightly hard, but the bathrooms sparkling clean. Located on Zhōngyāng Dàjiē, the location puts you in the heart of the pedestrian walk. Some English is spoken by the staff.

Zhōngyāng Dàjiē 185, Dàolǐ District. ⓒ 0451/8469-8700. Fax 0451/8469-8458. 213 units. ¥680 ($85) standard room. 60%–70% discounts. AE, DC, MC, V. **Amenities:** 2 restaurants; business center; ticketing center; bank; forex; bowling; limited room service. In room: A/C, satellite TV, broadband Internet access.

WHERE TO DINE

The basement of the Zhōngyāng Shāngchéng, at Zhōngyāng Dàjiē 100, has a **food court** with point-to-choose Chinese food and a well-stocked **supermarket.** Zhōngyāng Dàjiē is also home to two **McDonald's** and two **KFC** branches. For quick and convenient local food from 9am to 9pm, try the *shāguō shīzitóu* (smoky tofu, carrots, and a large meatball in savory broth) and pancakes *(bǐng)* at **Lǎo Shànghǎi** (© **0451/8262-6335**), located above a bakery at the corner of Zhōngyāng Dàjiē and Dà'ān Jiē.

Běiláishùn MUSLIM   This long-lived Muslim restaurant, named after the legendary Dōngláishùn in Běijīng, is often packed in winter, when believers and atheists alike quiet their shivers over the steam from brass hot pots *(huǒguō)*. Thin-sliced mutton is the main hot pot ingredient, but it's big on the menu, too: Try the *pá yángròu tiáo*—tender, baconlike strips of lamb braised in a simple soy-and-garlic sauce.

Yōuyì Lù 51 (next to Children's Hospital). © **0451/8461-3530**. Meal for 2 ¥40–¥100 ($5–$13). No credit cards. 11am–9pm.

Dà Fēngshōu ★★ *Finds* DŌNGBĚI   Everything about this immensely popular place is authentic Dōngběi: Diners sit on benches and drink beer out of bowls, waitresses unceremoniously dump handfuls of sunflower seeds on the table as appetizers, and the dishes are immense. Avoid the pig-face set dinner and go instead for *jiācháng tǔdòuní*, a Chinese take on garlic mashed potatoes. The entrance is marked by a huge neon sign and a long, lantern-lit pathway.

Yīmiǎn Jiē 283 (north of traffic circle next to railway bridge). © **0451/5364-6824**. Meal for 2 ¥30–¥60 ($4–$7.50). No credit cards. 9am–9pm.

Dōngfāng Jiǎozi Wáng ★★ JIǍOZI   So popular it inspired a region-wide chain, this original branch is classier than other members of the "Eastern Dumpling King" family and serves some of the best *jiǎozi* in China. Order a plate of *sānxiān* (shrimp, pork, and Chinese chive) or *sōngrén yùmǐ* (corn and pine nut) *shuǐjiǎo*, then wander over to the glass-enclosed kitchen to marvel as the restaurant's army of chefs wrap and boil the dumplings with inconceivable speed.

Zhōngyāng Dàjiē 39. © **0451/8465-3920**. Meal for 2 ¥10–¥20 ($1.25–$2.50). No credit cards. 10:30am–9:30pm.

Indian Kitchen (Yìndù Xiǎo Chú) INDIAN   Indian food in northeastern China? It may sounds weird, but this popular Indian-owned chain in China pulls off a decent garlic nan, cashew pilau, and butter paneer. Located on Indian Street (see "Shopping," below), the restaurant is a good choice for vegetarians and meat-eaters alike. The food tends to be more sweet than spicy, but you are free to ask one of the three Indian chefs in the glass-encased kitchen to kick up the heat.

Yìndù Jiē 154, Nángǎng District. © **0451/8263-8888**. English menu. Meal for 2 ¥20–¥60 ($3–$7.50). No credit cards. 10am–2am.

Portman (Bōtèmàn Xīcāntīng) WESTERN   A ritzy place for a meal—you can't miss the white grand piano and giant fireplace surrounded by glass in the center of the four-story restaurant—the Portman serves the most acceptable Western food in Harbin, with decent service and a good atmosphere—without going over the top. The cabbage rolls with cream sauce are juicy and the Russian red soup is hearty with spice. At all costs avoid the mashed potatoes, which have a sweetness to them that should be illegal. If you must have some starchy tubers, go for the potato salad, which is perplexingly like mashed potatoes, but served cold. A wide range of chicken, fish, and steak dishes is also available. Decent live-music performances run every night from 6 to 10pm.

Xīqī Dàojiē 63, just off Zhōngyáng Dàjiē. ✆ 0451/8468-6888. English menu. Meal for 2 ¥20–¥120 ($3–$15). No credit cards. 11am–2am.

Russia (Lùxīyà Xīcāntīng) ✿ RUSSIAN/COFFEE   This small cafe decorated with heirlooms left behind by a Russian family is a rare reminder of China's treaty port days, when expatriates would suffer the chaos of prewar China by day and retreat at night to the softly lit, lace-covered comfort of their homes to drink coffee and write fantastic letters to the people they'd left behind. The cafe, nestled inside the cracked-wall room of an old Russian building near the top of Zhōngyáng Dàjiē, serves a small but satisfying selection of Western dishes. Try the hearty red vegetable soup, or the "pot beef," a steaming stew of beef, carrot, and tomato. Or just spend the day here with a few cups of coffee and a book.

Xītóu Dàojiē 57. ✆ 0451/8456-3207. English menu. Meal for 2 ¥20–¥60 ($3–$7.50). No credit cards. 9am–midnight.

Xuéfǔ Yīpǐn Jiàng Gǔ ✿ DŌNGBĚI   This loud establishment is a favorite among locals. Though there are no English speakers here, the simplicity of ordering is a huge bonus: simply go to the display section in the back and point to what you want. The advertised specialty is the pork ribs (*jiàng gǔ*). If you're adventurous, you can get the *gǔbàng* (pork legs); locals enjoy sucking the marrow out of the bones. Every table setting comes with a pair of plastic gloves that diners don to pick up the giant drumsticks. Also try the tasty four-mushroom soup (Yīpǐn Jūntāng), the pumpkin fries, and the fried crepes with vegetables and egg (Dànhuáng Jūnánguā).

Tōngdá Jiē 329, Dàolǐ District. ✆ 0451/8762-1288. Main courses ¥15–¥50 ($2–$6). No credit cards. 11am–9pm.

SHOPPING

Aside from **Zhōngyáng Dàjiē**, the biggest commercial street is **Guǒgēlǐ Jiē**, where the government has recently organized several streets around themes. There is a street for children (clothing and toys), women (clothing), and, bizarrely, Indians. The Indian street features some saris, but little else from the Indian subcontient is evident here. The **Churin Department Store (Qiūlín Bǎihuò),** located in an immense green baroque-style building on the north side of Dōng Dàzhí Jiē (opposite the main post office), was once one of the largest department stores in East Asia. The first floor is where you'll find Harbin's best *dàlièba*—heavy circular loaves of crusty bread—and Russian-style red sausage (*hóngcháng),* which you can take for a picnic in the nearby Children's Park. A few blocks west, at the intersection of Dōng Dàzhí Jiē and Hóngjūn Jiē, is the **Hóngbō Shìchǎng,** one of the largest underground markets in the Northeast. The market is set up inside an old air-raid shelter, located underneath the former site of the St. Nicholas Church (destroyed by Red Guards in the 1960s), and offers everything from fur hats to black-market video games.

HARBIN AFTER DARK

The Popov distillery left town long ago, but foreign residents still imbibe plenty of vodka at **Blue Kiss (Bùlǔsī Jiǔbā;** ✆ 0451/8468-4277). The drinks-and-dance venue at Dìduàn Jiē 100, near Tòulóng Jiē, is open from 1pm to very late; go late on a weekend night for the must-see variety show, a mix of high-kick quasi-striptease numbers that leaves even regular visitors shaking their heads in slack-jawed wonder. A less raunchy choice, **Portman** (see "Where to Dine," above), is open late and serves passable pitchers of dark draft beer. **St. Petersburg** on Guŏgēlĭ Jiē offers an environment similar to an American chain restaurant (Guāngmáng Jiē 140; © **0451/8260-3737**). Wherever you end up, do try the refreshing and light Harbin Beer, known as Hāpí by the locals, which is China's oldest brew.

8 Wŭ Dà Liánchí

Heīlóng Jiāng Province, 340km (210 miles) NW of Harbin

Wŭ Dà Liánchí (Five Linked Lakes) is an utterly strange health retreat wedged between the Greater and Lesser Hinggan (Xīng'ān) mountains, several hundred miles north of Harbin. The area is named for a series of connected lakes, formed 260 years ago by lava flows from the two youngest of 14 local volcanoes. Wŭ Dà Liánchí is celebrated among Chinese for its pungent natural springs, water from which is rumored to cure everything from gastritis to chronic cardiocerebral angiopathy. The springs are disgusting, but the area's physical oddity is fascinating. Avoid the summer miracle-cure crowd if at all possible.

ESSENTIALS

Air-conditioned Volvo **coaches** (5 hr.; ¥95/$11) leave the **Harbin long-distance bus station** (© **0451/8283-0117**) at 7am, 1:30pm, 4pm and stop at the Worker's Sanatorium (see "Where to Stay," below). Return buses leave from the same spot at 6am, and at 1:30pm during the high season (June–Aug). Brochures with Chinese maps are sold in the Worker's Sanatorium (see below).

EXPLORING WŬ DÀ LIÁNCHÍ

Wŭ Dà Liánchí's most impressive sight is not the lakes but the lava fields, collectively dubbed **Shí Hǎi (Sea of Stone),** which spread out for miles around the area's two largest volcanoes and look vaguely like charred marshmallow. At the center of this is **Lǎohēi Shān** ⚛ (also known as Hēilóng Shān, or Black Dragon Mountain), tallest of the Wŭ Dà Liánchí volcanoes. An hour-long circumnavigation of the crater's edge, with its twisted birch trees and lichen-covered desolation, provides panoramic views. The **Bīng Dòng** (8am–4pm, ¥22/$3), 7km (4⅓ miles) east of the Worker's Sanatorium, is a system of sub-freezing caves that contains an exhibition of colorful but underwhelming ice lanterns.

Private **minivans** are the only way to see most sights in Wŭ Dà Liánchí. Drivers gather near **a large bilingual map** of the area opposite the entrance to Nán Quán (South Spring), a 30-minute walk east of the Worker's Sanatorium. Negotiations for a full tour of the area (25km/16 miles) usually start at around ¥150 ($19) per person (¥100/$13 is fair). Drivers sell **entrance tickets** for ¥55 ($7) that include access to the volcano and lava fields; avoid the ¥2 (25¢) markup by buying them yourself at the volcano entrance.

WHERE TO STAY

Wŭ Dà Liánchí swims with sanatoriums and guesthouses, all offering the same basic accommodations. The most convenient and popular option is the **Wŭ Dà Liánchí Worker's Sanatorium (Gōngrén Liáoyǎngyuàn;** © **0456/722-1569;** fax 0456/722-1814; www.wdgl.com.cn; 350 units), a large complex just east of the central traffic circle. Standard rooms in the main building (¥210/$26) are dark but clean with passable bathrooms. Suites with air-conditioning and 24-hour hot water (¥580–¥880/

$70–$106) are in a separate building. Twenty percent discounts are available. At least one building is kept open all year. Each has its own restaurant, although neither serves particularly great food.

9 Mǎnzhōulǐ

Inner Mongolia, 981km (608 miles) NW of Harbin

A tiny frontier town of 50,000 lost in a sea of grass in the northeast corner of Inner Mongolia, Mǎnzhōulǐ is the East-meets-Wild-West frontier outpost David Carradine should have used as the backdrop to *Kung Fu*. Born almost overnight in the early 1900s, it was once the primary channel for trade between China and Russia. Russians can be seen everywhere in the streets. Most of the signs are written in Chinese, Russian, and Mongolian and many businessmen speak fluent Russian. A new wave of Russian traders has revitalized the city, effecting a return to the rough-and-tumble days of its founding. It is the most convenient base for trips into the gorgeous **Hulun Buir,** home to China's most pristine grasslands.

ESSENTIALS

GETTING THERE   The recently built **Manzhouli Airport** (Mǎnzhōulǐ Xījiāo Jīchǎng) is located 9km (6 miles) southwest of the town. Purchase tickets for flights to Běijīng (daily), Harbin (daily), and Hohhot (Tues, Thurs, and Sat) at the CITS at the International Hotel ticket office (© **0470/622-8319;** 8:30–11:30am and 2–5pm). There is no airport shuttle to Mǎnzhōulǐ airport, but a taxi ride takes 20 minutes and costs ¥30 ($4). **Trains** connect Mǎnzhōulǐ to Běijīng (1:20pm; 30 hr., ¥380/$48), Harbin (6:30pm; 14 hr.; ¥201/$24), Qiqihar (7:10pm; 11 hr.; ¥164/$20), and Hailar (six daily; 3 hr.; ¥22/$3). The Trans-Siberian train comes through once a week, usually Monday morning, with stops in Irkutsk (¥584/$73) and Moscow (¥1,425/$178). The **railway station** (© **0470/225-2261**) is opposite downtown, south of the tracks. Purchase tickets for the Trans-Siberian at the business center inside the International Hotel. (*Note:* you must have arranged a Russian tourist visa in Běijīng if you want to board the train.) The **long-distance bus station** (Guójì Kèyùn Zhàn) is north of the tracks on Yī Dàojiē, a 5-minute walk west of the railway footbridge. Iveco buses depart from here for Hailar (3 hr.; ¥31/$3) every 30 minutes from 7:30am to 5pm.

GETTING AROUND   Most of Mǎnzhōulǐ is located north of the train tracks (behind the railway station) and is easily navigated on foot. **Taxis** charge ¥5 (65¢) anywhere in town; beyond 10km (6¼ miles) add an extra ¥10 ($1.25).

FAST FACTS

Banks, Foreign Exchange & ATMs   The **Bank of China** (open Mon–Fri 8am–noon and 2–6pm) is at Sān Dàojiē 38. Cash and traveler's checks are exchanged in the main hall on the right; credit card transactions (V, MC only) take place inside a separate entrance on the left.

Internet Access   There is a row of 24-hour basement-level **Internet bars** on Èr Dàojiē, near the International Hotel, one of them is called Mèng Gōngchǎng (© **1394/700-8393**); they charge ¥2 (25¢) per hour of access. Dial-up is © **16900** or 16901.

Post Office   The post office (open May–Sept 8am–5:30pm; Oct–Apr 8am–5pm) is located at the corner of Sān Dàojiē and Hǎiguān Lù.

IN & AROUND MĂNZHŌULĬ

A few Russian wood houses still stand in the center of Mănzhōulĭ, and the free flow of cash and vodka lends a certain exhilaration to the place, but most points of interest lie elsewhere. The closest attraction, only 10km (6 miles) west of town, is the old **Sino-Russian border crossing (Guó Mén; 𝄞 0470/629-1562;** 8am–5pm; admission ¥20/$3). If you want your taxi to drive onto the premises, they'll charge you an extra ¥5 (65¢). Nothing much happens here anymore, as most Russians enter China through a new border crossing farther north, but you can still watch trains pass across the border between China and Russia. There is a small exhibition that tells the history of the area inside the building. You'll need your passport to get in. Access is by taxi only (20 min.; ¥20/$2.25 round-trip). A **trade market (Zhōngé Hùshì Màoyì Qū),** is located in a pink Russian-style building beside Guó Mén; it opens in the morning, and all kinds of products, from food to furs can be bought there, including fake ones.

Dálài Hú 𝄞 Also known as Hūlún Hú (*Hulun Nur* in Mongolian), this immense lake emerges seamlessly out of the landscape 36km (22 miles) south of Mănzhōulĭ—a liquid equivalent to the grasslands that surround it. Dálài Hú is China's fifth-largest lake (2,399 sq. km./936 sq. miles) and a popular feeding ground for rare bird species. A small resort on the north shore offers boating, swimming, and fishing. In pleasant weather vendors sell barbecued fish and shrimp skewers fresh from the lake for ¥2 to ¥3 (25¢–40¢). The lake is also open in the winter, but much less interesting without boat access.

The only way to get to the lake from Mănzhōulĭ is by taxi (1 hr.; ¥100–¥150/$13–$18 round-trip). Admission at the main gate, just north of the resort, costs ¥5 (65¢) for each person including driver plus another ¥10 ($1) for taxi entrance. A boat ride on the lake costs ¥20 ($2.50) and motorboat ride costs ¥10 ($1.25) for 10 minutes.

Hulun Buir Grasslands (Hūlúnbèi'ěr Căoyuán) 𝄞𝄞𝄞 No other grasslands in Inner Mongolia can match the Hulun Buir, an emerald expanse shot through with radiant patches of wildflowers that spreads over the hills outside Mănzhōulĭ. The grass here is twice as long as anything found outside Hohhot, and people are scarce. Nothing this beautiful lasts long, though: The season for seeing the grasslands at their most vibrant runs only from late June to mid-August.

The only organization in Mănzhōulĭ officially allowed to arrange tours of the grasslands is **CITS** (inside the International Hotel; 𝄞 **0470/622-2988;** fax 0470/622-4560; open 8:30am–5pm). They offer different types of tours around the grasslands. Three-day tours (¥600/$75 per person) include accommodations in a yurt, horse riding, a mutton banquet, and a visit to Dálài Hú (see above); 2- and 5-day tours are also available. Other attractions around Mănzhōulĭ, such as Golden Shore (Jīn Hǎi'àn) and the Birds' Kingdom (Wūlán Pào), may be added to your tour. If you speak Mandarin and don't mind modest facilities, a better option is to negotiate a stay with one of the local families who approach visitors at the railway station. If you decide to do this, be clear about the details and withhold final payment until your stay is over. Visit www.mzlcits.com for more information.

The Hulun Buir is the backdrop to one of China's most authentic **Naadam** festivals (see also Hohhot, p. 214), held every summer, usually between mid-July and mid-August. Call CITS for details about the date and location.

Zhālàinuò'ěr The turn-of-the-20th-century Russian-built open coal mine (*méikuàng*) is a hideous scar on an otherwise pristine landscape, but few other places in Asia can offer what it does: the chance to see 22 steam trains from the 1920s and

1930s in still-chugging order. CITS (see Hulun Buir Grasslands, above) offers multi-day tours which include a ride on one of the working engines; the price depends on which attractions you choose. It is possible, however, to visit on your own. The mine is 18km (11 miles) south of Mǎnzhōulǐ, and admission is free. The best time to visit is between October and March, when the steam is most dramatic. A bus to Zhālàinuò'ěr (30 min.; ¥3/40¢) leaves from the intersection of Sì Dàojiē and Xīnhuá Lù in Mǎnzhōlǐ and drops you in the center of town. From there, hire a taxi to tour the mine for ¥30 to ¥50 ($4–$6). The easier but pricier option is to simply hire a taxi in Mǎnzhōulǐ for ¥70 to ¥100 ($9–$13).

WHERE TO STAY

All of Mǎnzhōulǐ's hotels are located north of the train tracks. Most offer discounts of 20% or more outside July and August.

Friendship Hotel (Mǎnzhōulǐ Yǒuyì Bīnguǎn) ☆
Fully renovated in 2002, the formerly unremarkable Friendship Hotel now offers the nicest rooms in town, with good service and easy access to the railway station. Standard rooms are spacious, clean, and bright, with large beds and sparkling-clean bathrooms. The hotel isn't as lively as some of its competitors, but this could change as word spreads.

Yī Dàojiē 26 (between Xīnhuá Lù and Hǎiguān Lù). © 0470/624-8888. Fax 0470/622-3828. 80 units. ¥378 ($47) new standard room; ¥428 ($52) older standard room; ¥868 ($105) suite. Rates include breakfast. No credit cards. **Amenities:** 2 restaurants; bar; small indoor pool; business center; forex; laundry. *In room:* A/C, TV, fridge.

Jiāngnán Dàjiǔdiàn
Opened in 2005, this modern hotel is located in the city center and caters to Russian traders, but all are welcome. It's one of the cleanest and newest hotels in town. The rooms are quite spacious but the bathrooms are small with showers only.

Hǎiguān Lù 8. ©0470/6247-888. Fax 0470/6247-990. 72 units. ¥280–¥380 ($34-$46) single room; ¥480 ($58) standard room; ¥880 ($105) suite. No credit cards. **Amenities:** Restaurant. *In room:* TV.

WHERE TO DINE

The local specialty is *shuàn yángròu,* a form of mutton hot pot that uses plain boiling water instead of broth. The best is found at **Jīngdū Huǒguō** (© **0470/622-7370;** open 8:30am–12am; meal for two ¥30–¥50/$4–$6), an unassuming restaurant with a gold sign on Yī Dàojiē. They're famous for their fresh lamb but do offer a vegetarian option (*qīngshuǐ guōdǐ*).

The city's busiest Russian restaurant—and a real find—is **Xīnmǎnyuán Xīcāntīng** (Sān Dàojiē 38; © **0470/622-2008;** open 7am–1am; meal for 2 ¥10–¥30/$1.25–$3.75), a strange and raucous eatery-cum-nightclub located behind the International Hotel (look for the white-and-green awning). Best are the bowls of hearty *sūbā tāng* (beef, potato, and carrot in creamy tomato broth). A branch of **Délifrance** (**Dàmòfáng;** © **0470/629-8765;** open 7am–10pm; ¥12–¥18/$1–$2), directly across from the International Hotel on Sān Dàojiē, serves horrible coffee but has a large variety of satisfying rice plates. The best plates are rice with beef and black pepper and the *sānxiān fàn,* or rice with three flavors.

For a lunch or dinner in the middle of the grasslands, head to **Dōngfāng Hàn** holiday restaurant. Located 20 minutes south of downtown, a taxi ride will cost ¥20 ($2.50). You can order a whole lamb and eat in a yurt, a traditional Mongolian felt tent. Other activities include horseback riding and Mongolian dancing.

6

Along the Yellow River

by Jen Lin-Liu

The six cities and one mountain village featured in this chapter cover an area of northern China that includes parts of Shǎnxī, Shǎnxī, Inner Mongolia, and Níngxià, roughly following the central loop of the Yellow River, north of Xī'ān.

This arid portion of China contains desert, grassland, and, most conspicuously, loess plateau made of the powdery yellow soil that gave the Yellow River and the legendary Yellow Emperor their names. (For an object lesson in what makes the river yellow, wash your T-shirt in the sink after a day of touring the loess cliffs of Yán'ān.) This powder of sand and silt has for millennia been deposited over this part of north and northwest China by winds blowing across the Gobi Desert.

Rich in history, the area lays claim to most of China's oldest surviving timber-frame buildings, its oldest carved Buddhist grottoes, and the mausoleums of nine Xī Xià (1038–1227) emperors. The area around Tàiyuán in Shǎnxī Province is recognized as one of China's "cradles of civilization," and it was here that the mythical sage kings Yáo, Shùn, and Yǔ are said to have performed their miracles.

From Běijīng, Dàtóng is the logical gateway. Going south, a 10-day itinerary might include Dàtóng; the sacred Buddhist mountain, Wǔtái Shān; the Shǎnxī capital of Tàiyuán; and Píngyáo, one of China's best-preserved walled cities. For the grasslands of Inner Mongolia and the relics and monuments of the tribes from beyond the Great Wall, go west from Dàtóng—first to Hohhot, and then to Yínchuān, the provincial capital of Níngxià. There is enough to see for a 3- or 4-day stay in each city. The revolutionary sites and cave dwellings of Yán'ān could be added as the last stop on either itinerary or as the stepping stone between the two.

Piercing winds and icy air currents from the north keep most travelers away from this region from late November to mid-March. Moving south, summer temperatures can be scorching, but evenings are generally comfortable.

Note: Unless noted otherwise, hours listed in this chapter are the same every day.

1 Dàtóng

Shǎnxī Province, 379km (236 miles) W of Běijīng, 284km (176 miles) SE of Hohhot, 350km (217 miles) N of Tàiyuán

In 398, Dàtóng (then Píng Chéng) became the capital of the Xiānběi tribes' first Chinese-style state—as opposed to a tribal confederation—under the Northern Wèi dynasty. Modeled after the Hàn Chinese capital of Cháng'ān (Xī'ān), Dàtóng remained their political center for the next hundred years, and it was during this period that most of the Yúngǎng Buddhist Caves were carved out. Four hundred years after the Wèi moved their capital south to Luòyáng in a step toward Sinicization, the Khitan (or Qìdān) established their Liáo dynasty (907–1125) capital in Dàtóng. Two buildings from that era survive at Huáyán Monastery, which with the Yúngǎng Caves and the spectacular Hanging Temple give ample reasons to visit.

Modern Dàtóng is an industrial center with an abundance of coal that is both a blessing and a curse. Without it, Dàtóng's economy would collapse; with it, skies are rarely clear and lung disease is common. But in 2001, the city began implementing pollution-control measures, and some industries have been closed.

It's possible to visit Dàtóng as a long day trip from Běijīng (see "Tours," below), but to see all the sights, 2 days are needed.

ESSENTIALS

GETTING THERE   Dàtóng's **airport** was scheduled for completion in 2003, but funding problems left the project sitting on the ground. At press time, the airport was expected to open for business at the end of 2005, connecting the city to Běijīng, Shànghǎi, Guǎngzhōu, Chéngdū, and Shěnyáng.

The overnight **train** from Běijīng Xī Zhàn to Dàtóng (N205) is convenient, leaving Běijīng at 11:13pm and arriving in Dàtóng at 6:50am the next morning. Sleepers cost ¥91 to ¥170 ($11–$21). The return train (N214) leaves Dàtóng at 12:27pm, and arrives in Běijīng Xī Zhàn the next day at 6:32pm. Useful trains from Tàiyuán are the express K746 and K748, arriving in Dàtóng at 2:36pm and 8:28pm. Heading west, the Běijīng–Bāotóu line connects Dàtóng with Hohhot (K43/K44; 5 hr.; ¥25/$3); trains on the Běijīng Xī Zhàn and Hohhot line (K89/K90) can be difficult to book in Dàtóng.

Bus trips between Běijīng and Dàtóng take 3 or 4 hours. Large, deluxe buses now travel between the two cities, departing several times a day from the old long-distance bus station, near the railway station, and dropping passengers off at the Liuliqiao Bus Station in the west part of Běijīng. Call ✆ **0352/603-6784** for information; tickets costs about ¥90 ($11). Another "new" station is on Yàntóng Xī Lù near Xīngjiàn Běi Lù. Air-conditioned buses connecting with Hohhot arrive and depart from the old bus station (¥50/$6.10; 3 hr., 40 min.) Departure from Dàtóng is at 8am; the return bus departs Hohhot's long-distance bus station at 2:30pm. Air-conditioned buses also connect with Wǔtái Shān (4 hr.; ¥50/$5.60) and Tàiyuán (3½ hr.; ¥51–¥70/$6.20–$8.50).

GETTING AROUND   Although the city is spread out, it can be toured on foot because the few tourist sights are in a fairly compact area south of Dà Xī and Dà Dōng Jiē. Rates for the two types of **taxis** are ¥5 (65¢) for the first 3km (2 miles), then ¥1.20 (15¢) per kilometer. Beyond 10km (6 miles), the fare is ¥1.80 (20¢) per kilometer. Between 10pm and 7am, the first 3km (2 miles) are ¥5 (65¢), then ¥1.50 (20¢) per kilometer. Most trips within 3km in the city are ¥5 (65¢). Beyond 10km (6¼ miles), the fare is ¥2 (25¢) per kilometer, but the price can be negotiated before you set off.

TOURS   A **CITS** office just inside the main entrance to the railway station (✆ **0352/510-1326;** fax 0352/712-4882) offers useful 1-day tours to the Hanging Monastery and the Yúngǎng Buddhist Caves, or to the Hanging Monastery and the wooden pagoda in Yìng Xiàn. The tour starts at 8:30am from the Yúngǎng Hotel, and departs at 9am from the station; the cost is ¥100 ($13), or ¥210 ($26) including entrance fees and lunch. Some visitors arrive overnight from Běijīng, take this tour, and return overnight. CITS also has offices in the Yúngǎng Hotel (✆ **0352/510-2265**), located in a small building on the right-hand side as soon as you walk through the main gate.

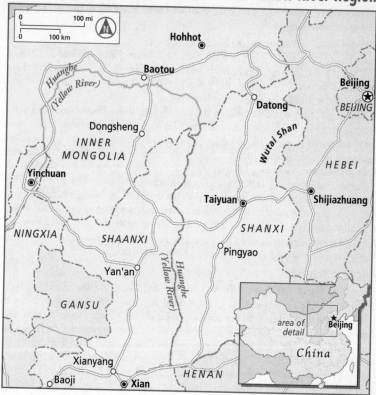

FAST FACTS

Banks, Foreign Exchange & ATMs The main **Bank of China** (Yíngbīn Lù near Hóngqí Nán Jiē; Mon–Fri 8am–noon and 2:30–6:30pm) has full-service foreign exchange. There is no ATM.

Internet Access Internet cafes can be found throughout the city; a convenient *wǎngbā* is directly opposite the railway station. Dial-up is © 169.

Post Office The main post office is on Hóngqí Square (7am–7pm).

Visa Extensions The **PSB** (**Gōngānjú;** open Mon–Fri 8am–noon and 3–6:30pm) is on Xīnjiàn Běi Lù. Visas can be extended while you wait.

AROUND TOWN

If you have time after a visit to Huáyán Sì, Dàtóng's **Jiǔlóng Bì (Nine Dragon Wall;** Dà Dōng Jiē, east of Dà Nán Jiē; ¥10/$1.25; open May–Sept 7:30am–7:30pm, Oct–Apr 8am–6pm; bus: no. 4) is a fine example of a spirit screen, designed to fend off ghosts and evil spirits that can only move in straight lines. The brightly colored glazed wall with nine writhing dragons was built in 1392 in front of a prince's mansion, long ago razed by fire. The much-restored **Shànhuà Sì,** east of Nán Mén Jiē, last rebuilt in 1445, is also a pleasant escape from Dàtóng's dusty streets. Most impressive are the beautiful timber doors of the **Hall of Three Sages (Sān Shèng Diàn; ¥20/ $2.45; open 8am–6pm).**

Huáyán Sì ✦   This monastery has separate upper and lower temples that share a lane. The upper temple's massive main hall, the **Dàxióng Bǎo Diàn** of 1140, is one of China's few surviving 12th-century buildings. Inside are the lined-up Buddhas of the Five Directions (including the center), seated on elaborately decorated lotus thrones and set off by small standing attendants.

Most significant of all the halls in the two temples is the **Bójiā Jiàozàng Diàn** of 1038, a very rare example of a Liáo dynasty building. Inside, Buddhist sutras (scriptures) are stored in one of the finest and best-preserved examples of the miniature timber buildings favored by the period's architects for housing sutras. Named the **Celestial Palace Pavilion (Tiāngōng Lóugé),** the sutra cabinet is an exquisite dollhouse with elaborate bracketing, an arched bridge, curved eaves, and balconies. The 31 elegant stucco statues in the hall also date from the Liáo dynasty. One of the most prized is the female bodhisattva on the right-hand side. Her palms are pressed together as if in prayer, and her lips are parted, revealing her teeth—a rarity in Chinese sculpture.

Both Upper and Lower temples are down a lane off the south side of Dà Xī Jiē. Admission ¥20 ($2.50) each temple. May–Sept 8am–6pm; Oct–Apr 8:30am–5:30pm. Bus: no. 4 from railway station.

OUT OF TOWN

Yúngǎng Shíkū (Yúngǎng Caves) ✦✦✦   Influenced by the Buddhist site of Bamiyan in Afghanistan and the caves of Kizil and Kuqa (in Xīnjiāng, p. 305), the stone carvings of Yúngǎng are the earliest of their kind in China. Hewn in three stages between 460 and 524, they show the movement from a heavy reliance on Indian and central Asian artistic models to an emergence of Chinese traditions. The caves numbered 16 to 20 (the "Five Caves of Tán Yào") were carved between 460 and 465 under the supervision of a Buddhist monk. Caves 1, 2, and 5 to 13 were carved in the second stage, which began in 470 and ended when the Wèi dynasty capital was moved from Dàtóng (at that time Píng Chéng) to Luòyáng in 494. The remaining caves, carved without imperial patronage, are less notable.

For sheer size, **Caves 16 through 20** are the most impressive. Made in part to honor the reigning emperor, Wén Chéng, and his four predecessors, each cave contains one central Buddha figure (representing an emperor) and his attendants. The best of them, **Cave 18,** contains the colossal image of Sakyamuni, the 10 *arhats* (enlightened disciples) associated with him, and two attendant Buddhas. The Buddha to the right of Sakyamuni has a webbed hand—one of the 32 marks of a superior being. His robe was originally red, his face white, and his hair black. Traces of his green mustache and beard can still be seen, and echo the art of Iran.

Largest of the Buddhas in the Tán Yào caves is the sitting figure in **Cave 20,** now exposed by the collapse of the top and sides of the cliff. Holes for beams indicate that a wooden structure was built to protect the Buddha, but that, too, is long gone. The squared figures and static style are typical of this early period of Northern Wèi statuary; they also suggest that the artists may have worked from sketches or drawings brought back by pilgrims from Indian holy sites. Notice in the later carvings the fluidity of line in the postures and draped clothing.

There is much more going on in the second group of caves, many of which depict stories from Buddhist scriptures. **Cave 1** is interesting for its Chinese-style architectural features in the bas-reliefs of buildings, though many of the images have eroded.

Dàtóng

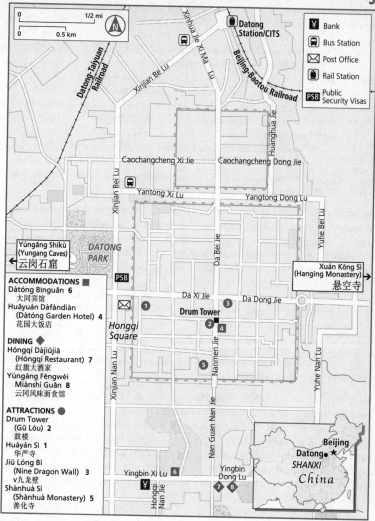

Cave 3 is the largest of the caves. The fuller bodies of the three Buddhist images it contains suggest it was carved as late as the Suí or the Táng dynasties. **Caves 5 and 6** were both carved before 494, but the four-story wooden facade dates to 1651. **Cave 5** houses the largest carving at Yúngǎng—a stunning Sakyamuni in meditation. In **Cave 6** look for the two Buddhas, Sakyamuni and Prabhutaratna, facing each other. This customary pairing alludes to an episode from the Teaching of the Lotus Sutra. In this episode, a stupa (shrine) containing the relics of the Prabhutaratna Buddha appears in the sky. Surrounded by Buddhas and bodhisattvas, Sakyamuni rises to the stupa and unlocks it with his finger. Out comes the extinct Prabhutaratna, who praises and congratulates him. Other episodes from the life of Sakyamuni decorate the walls.

On the entrance arch of **Cave 8** are contented images of Shiva and Vishnu (two of several Hindu divinities who found their way into Buddhism). The discs they hold represent the sun and the moon. Some sources identify the small bird on Vishnu's chest, and the larger one on which his feet rest, as the mythical *garuda*—the vehicle (and disciple) of Vishnu; others, less convincingly, call them phoenixes, a Chinese motif. Traces of ancient Greece appear in the classical bow with inward curve at its center. (As in this relief, the bow is commonly held in the left "wisdom" hand. Presumably the missing right "method" hand held an arrow.) A seated Maitreya Buddha (Future Buddha) dominates **Cave 13.** Most delightful about this statue is the figurine of a four-armed attendant who stands on the Buddha's thigh while supporting its huge raised arm—the artists' solution to a crack in the stone. Allow yourself at least 2 hours to see the main caves.

16km (10 miles) west of Dàtóng. Admission ¥60 ($7.30). 8:30am–5:30pm. Bus: no. 4 (¥1/15¢) from railway station to terminus (Xīnlǐ Kǒu), then bus no. 3 (¥2/25¢) to Yúngāng Caves.

Xuánkōng Sì (Hanging Temple)

This temple, clinging to the side of a cliff, is composed of some 40 connected halls that appear to be supported by toothpicks. Looking more like a wooden model than anything weight-bearing, it is actually supported by sturdy timbers that extend deep into the mountain. Founded in the Northern Wèi dynasty (386–534), the temple contains Buddhist, Daoist, and Confucian chambers, along with a chamber, the Sānjiào Diàn, that combines all three. Sakyamuni is in the center with Confucius to his right and Lǎozǐ to his left. While the temple is marvelous, be prepared for the particularly unattractive surroundings—a huge parking lot and, beyond that, a dam and reservoir.

62km (39 miles) south of Dàtóng. Admission ¥60 ($7.30). Summer 8am–6pm; winter 8am–6:30pm. Minibuses to Húnyuán (near the monastery) leave from the station opposite the railway station when they fill up. Price isn't fixed, so bargain; expect to pay ¥8–¥12 ($1–$1.50). From Húnyuán, it's another 6km (4 miles) to the monastery by minibus (about ¥5/60¢) or taxi (about ¥9/$1.15).

Yìng Xiàn Mù Tǎ (Yìng Xiàn Wooden Pagoda) 🐦

Built in 1056 during the Liáo dynasty, this impressive building is China's oldest surviving wooden pagoda. From the outside, it appears to have only five stories, though it actually has nine; and its complex system of supports includes 54 kinds of brackets. Frescoes on the ground floor and a gilded statue of Sakyamuni date to the Liáo dynasty. During a 1974 renovation, engraved sutras and documents related to the construction of the pagoda were discovered inside one of the statues of Buddha. Unfortunately, visitors are now only allowed to climb to the second level of this delicate structure.

For those on their way from Dàtóng to Wǔtái Shān, it's possible to visit the Hanging Temple and Wooden Pagoda in a day, then spend the night in Yìng Xiàn and leave the next morning for Wǔtái Shān. East of the pagoda, the friendly, affordable **Líhuā Chūn Bīnguǎn,** Yīnghún Lù (eastern extension of Xīnjiàn Dōng Lù; ✆ **0349/502-9593**), is the best hotel in Yìng Xiàn, and its restaurant serves good Cantonese and local dishes. Standard rooms go for ¥88 to ¥108 ($11–$14). The hotel can arrange for north- or southbound hotel pickup. The minibus to Wǔtái Shān charges ¥35 ($4.35) for the 2-hour trip.

76km (47 miles) south of Dàtóng. Admission ¥60 ($7.30). 7:30am–7pm; 8am–6:30pm winter. Minibuses to Yìng Xiàn leave from the station opposite the railway station (¥10–¥15/$1.25–$1.90; 2 hr.) and drop passengers near the Wooden Pagoda. Minibuses also leave from Húnyuán (¥10/$1.25 for the 1½-hr. drive).

Jǐng Xià Yóu (Coal Mine Tour)   One of Dàtóng's latest travel fads is a visit to a local coal mine. You get to suit up in a real coal miner's outfit complete with boots and light-equipped helmet and spend 2 hours underground, albeit at a distance more comfortable than the coal miners are used to. A miner's elevator will take you down into the mine, and then you'll board a small train to reach a point where miners are digging. You may also have lunch with the coal miners in their cafeteria. Tours can be arranged by CITS. To reserve a place call 1 day in advance; a minimum of 10 are required for the tour to run.

30 min. outside Dàtóng. Admission ¥150/$18. Call CITS for reservations ((C) 0352/510-2265).

WHERE TO STAY

CITS agents are likely to meet you coming out of the Dàtóng railway station. They can book a hotel for you on the spot, but you'll get a better discount by shopping around and doing the negotiating yourself. A few years ago, visitors to Dàtóng had limited choices when looking for a hotel; in recent years, however, a number of comfortable and reasonably priced hotels have opened offering a wide variety of choices.

Dàtóng Bīnguǎn   With its manicured gardens, park-size lawn with gazebo, and manor-house facade, this is one of the more pleasant of Dàtóng's hotels. Service is excellent, rooms are clean and comfortable, bathrooms are a decent size, and the price is reasonable. Some of the standard rooms have small balconies, which are worth requesting. Rooms facing the street overlook the front lawn and the adjacent "musical fountain."

Yíngbīn Xī Lù 37. (C) 0352/586-8666. Fax 0352/586-8200. 221 units. ¥380 ($47) single room; ¥350 ($44) standard room. Some rates include breakfast. 30% discount available. 15% service charge. AE, DC, MC, V. Bus: no. 1 or 2. **Amenities:** Restaurant; bar; ticketing; business center; limited forex; limited room service; dry cleaning/laundry. *In room:* A/C, TV, minibar, fridge, hair dryer.

Huāyuán Dàfàndiàn   The Dàtóng Garden Hotel, one of the city's newest hotels, is clean and inexpensive, and the service is friendly—a big improvement over the old state-run hotels that once monopolized the travel business in Dàtóng. The guest rooms in this four-star hotel are well sized and furnished with Míng and Qīng dynasty-style pear-wood furniture. It's also conveniently located in the center of Dàtóng, near the Drum Tower and restaurants and shopping centers.

Dà Nán Jiē 59. (C) 0352/586-5825. Fax 0352/586-5824. 108 units. ¥620 ($75) standard room; ¥680 ($83) deluxe standard. Rates include breakfast. Discount available. 15% service charge. AE, MC, V. **Amenities:** Western and Chinese restaurants; bar; ticketing; business center; forex; limited room service; dry cleaning/laundry. *In room:* A/C, TV, minibar, fridge, hair dryer.

WHERE TO DINE

One of the best restaurants near the hotels is **Yúngǎng Fēngwèi Miànshí Guǎn,** on the south side of Yíngbīn Xī Lù, across from the Yúngǎng Hotel. It's a comfortable little cafe run by a helpful young staff. Some recommended dishes are *shāo qiézi* (stewed eggplant); *sōngrén yùmǐ* (corn cooked with pine nuts); and *chǎo lāmiàn* (fried wheat noodles with ground mutton, spring onion, and garlic). A meal for two costs ¥16 to ¥80 ($2–$10). The three-story **Hóngqí Restaurant** next door is more formal and twice as expensive, but the food is excellent and—with every table celebrating something (often it's a wedding)—the atmosphere is always lively. The restaurant serves Shǎnxī, Sìchuān, and Cantonese dishes. Also on this street is the **Hóngyá Restaurant,** which serves Cantonese food. The Chinese restaurant on the first floor of the Yúngǎng Hotel serves delicious *jiǎozi* (12 per serving) for ¥2.50 (30¢). For vegetarian *jiǎozi,* order a half-hour ahead. They also offer a wide variety of regional dishes.

For a Western breakfast, try the Yúngǎn and the Dàtóng hotels. There's **KFC** at the main square, Hóngqí Guǎngchǎng, and many other branches are scattered around the city.

2 Hohhot (★

Inner Mongolia, 410km (255 miles) W of Běijīng

By Chinese standards, Hohhot, the capital of Inner Mongolia Autonomous Region, has a short history. In 1557, when the Mongolian prince, Altan Khan, ordered the construction of a large Tibetan-Buddhist complex, he had his own agenda. (In a historical twist, his workforce was made up of captured Hàn Chinese artisans and Hàn peasants forced into corvée labor.) Completion of such a complex would legitimize his rule over the southern Mongolian tribes and secure the recognition of the Míng Empire. By 1579, Dà Zhāo Temple, which still survives, was completed, and by 1590 the town of Hohhot (in Mandarin Hūhéhàotè, or simply Hū Shì) had sprung up around it.

From the beginning, the city was both Mongolian and Hàn Chinese, and though the ratio has fluctuated wildly over 4 centuries, the population has always been culturally mixed. In the 19th century, the Huí (Chinese Muslims) became the third-largest ethnic group in the city. Population claims are rarely reliable when they're about China, but it's said that currently for every Mongolian in Hohhot, there are 12 Hàn Chinese.

Hohhot is a pleasant city with some good hotels, excellent restaurants, modern stores, and worthwhile sights.

ESSENTIALS

GETTING THERE   The **airport** is 16km (10 miles) east of town. A taxi into town costs about ¥25 to ¥30 ($3.10–$3.75). Locals negotiate the price in advance and don't use the meter. The CAAC (Zhōngguó Mínháng) shuttle (¥5/60¢) meets flights and is also an option. It leaves from CAAC's main ticket office on Xīlín Guōlè Lù just south of Wūlánqiàtè Xī Jiē 1½ hours before every flight. There are direct flights from many major cities in China, including Běijīng, Shànghǎi, Chéngdū, and Guǎngzhōu. **Mongolian Airlines (MIAT;** © **0471/430-2026)** shares offices with the Mongolian Consulate (Měnggǔ Lǐngshìguǎn) and offers flights to Ulaan Baatar.

The **railway station** is in the north part of town. The fastest trains linking Hohhot with Běijīng are the K89/K90 (10½ hr.), each arriving at 7:20am. Dàtóng is also on this line. Another useful service is the 2003/2004 link with Lánzhōu (7 hr.). Yínchuān and Zhōngwèi are two of the stops on this line. Tickets can be bought in advance at all windows, but sleepers are often in short supply. Try agents in hotels for these.

The **Long-Distance Bus Station** is west of the railway station. There are at least four buses daily to Běijīng (12 hr.; ¥60/$7.50) and daily buses to Dàtóng (5 hr.; ¥40/$5).

GETTING AROUND   Bus fare is ¥1 (15¢); **minibus** fare is ¥1.50 (20¢). The **taxi** rate for the first 2km (1¼ miles) is ¥6 (75¢); after that, it's ¥1 (15¢) per kilometer.

TOURS   The **CITS** office is located on the third floor, Yìshùtíng Nán Jiē 95 (© **0471/ 628-3861**). It can arrange expensive tours to the grasslands with an English-speaking guide. Most hotels have desks offering cheaper, non-English tours. Shop around and bargain.

Hohhot

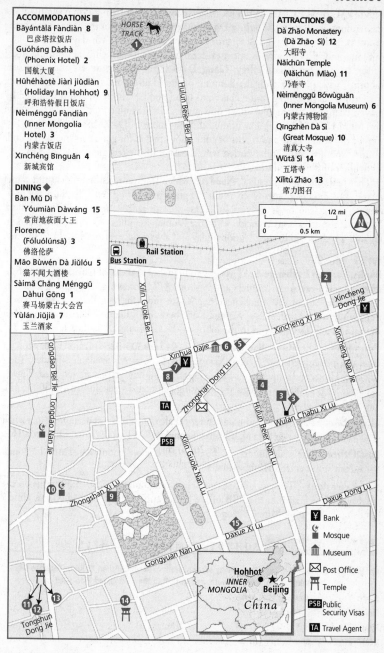

ACCOMMODATIONS ■

Bāyántǎlā Fàndiàn 8
巴彦塔拉饭店

Guóháng Dàshà
(Phoenix Hotel) 2
国航大厦

Hūhéhàotè Jiàrì jiǔdiàn
(Holiday Inn Hohhot) 9
呼和浩特假日饭店

Nèiménggǔ Fàndiàn
(Inner Mongolia
Hotel) 3
内蒙古饭店

Xīnchéng Bīnguǎn 4
新城宾馆

DINING ◆

Bàn Mǔ Dì
Yóumiàn Dàwáng 15
常宙地莜面大王

Florence
(Fóluólúnsà) 3
佛洛伦萨

Māo Bùwén Dà Jiǔlóu 5
猫不闻大酒楼

Sàimǎ Chǎng Ménggǔ
Dàhuì Gōng 1
赛马场蒙古大会宫

Yùlán Jiǔjiā 7
玉兰酒家

ATTRACTIONS ●

Dà Zhāo Monastery
(Dà Zhāo Sì) 12
大昭寺

Nǎichūn Temple
(Nǎichūn Miào) 11
乃春寺

Nèiménggǔ Bówùguǎn
(Inner Mongolia Museum) 6
内蒙古博物馆

Qīngzhēn Dà Sì
(Great Mosque) 10
清真大寺

Wǔtǎ Sì 14
五塔寺

Xílìtú Zhāo 13
席力图召

HORSE TRACK 1

Rail Station
Bus Station

Xinhua Dajie

Xincheng Xi Jie
Xincheng Dong Jie

Wulan Chabu Xi Lu

Zhongshan Dong Lu

Zhongshan Xi Lu

Daxue Dong Lu

Daxue Xi Lu

Gongyuan Nan Lu

Tongshun Dong Jie

Hulun Beier Bei Jie

Xilin Guole Bei Lu

Tongdao Bei Jie

Tongdao Nan Jie

Xilin Guole Nan Lu

Hulun Beier Nan Lu

Xincheng Nan Jie

0   1/2 mi
0   0.5 km

Hohhot
INNER MONGOLIA   Beijing ★
China

¥ Bank
☾ Mosque
🏛 Museum
✉ Post Office
🎋 Temple
PSB Public Security Visas
TA Travel Agent

FESTIVAL & SPECIAL EVENTS Dà Zhào has more than a dozen temple festivals. Among the best are **Sòngjīng Dà Fǎhuì** (8th–15th days of the 1st and 6th lunar months), 8 days of prayer and chanting sutras; **Sòngbālìn** (14th day of the 1st and 6th lunar months), a morning spent exorcising demons—chanting, performing ritual dance, burning of demon effigy; **Liàng Dàfó** (15th day of the 1st and 6th lunar months), which begins with the Sunning of the Maitreya *thangka* (a giant image of the Future Buddha hung in the courtyard to air and be admired), and is followed by prayer, chanting, ceremonial dance and music, circumambulation, and alms-giving; and **Mání Huì** (14th–17th day of the 8th lunar month), Dà Zhào's most solemn festival of the year, 3 days and nights of continuous prayer for good fortune (at the end, visitors who give alms are rewarded with a packet of "sacred medicine," said to cure all manner of illness and disease).

The traditional sports festival, **Naadam,** which features wrestling, horse and camel racing, and archery, occurs when and if the grasslands turn green. That's usually mid-August, but it can be as early as July. Last-minute cancellations aren't uncommon. Note that the dates don't coincide with (the People's Republic of) Mongolia's Naadam festival, which is tied to their National Day and always occurs from July 11 to July 13.

FAST FACTS

Banks, Foreign Exchange & ATMs Two branches of **Bank of China** that have full-service foreign-exchange counters and 24-hour ATM access are at Xīnchéng Dōng Jiē 88 (2 blocks east of the Xīnchéng Dōng/Xī Jiē and Xīnchéng Běi/Nán Jiē intersection); and on the south side of Xīnhuá Dàjiē between Xīlínguōlè Běi Lù and Yíngbīn Běi Lù. There's also an ATM in the lobby of the Guóháng Dàshà hotel.

Consulates The **Mongolian Consulate** (© 0471/4303-3254) issues 30-day tourist visas at Xīnchéng District, Wūlán Xiǎoqū, No. 5. Service is available Monday, Tuesday, and Thursday from 8:30am to 12:30pm. Two photographs are required. The 1-day rush fee is ¥500 ($61); regular processing can take a week and costs ¥300 ($37). Take bus no. 2 or 16.

Internet Access There's a no-name Internet cafe opposite the station, next to a small Bank of China. It's open 8am to 3:30am and charges ¥2 (25¢) per hour. Dial-up is **169.**

Post Office The main branch of the post office is on Zhōngshān Dōng Lù (open 8am–7pm summer, to 6:30pm winter).

Visa Extensions The visa office (Mon–Fri, 8am–noon and 2:30–5:30pm) is on the left beyond the guards at the **PSB office (Gōngānjú)** on Zhōngshān Xī Lù, almost opposite the big pink Mínzú Shāngchǎng.

WALKING TOUR **HOHHOT: TEMPLE TO TEMPLE**

Getting There:	Starting from the railway station, walk west on Chēzhàn Xī Jiē to Tōngdào Jiē. Take bus no. 6 going south, and get off at the stop called Xiǎo Shízì.
Start:	Xiǎo Shízì bus stop
Finish:	Zhōngshān Jiē
Time:	Half a day
Best Times:	8am to 4pm any day

Hohhot's most renowned temples, **Dà Zhào, Xílìtú Zhào,** and **Wǔtǎ Sì,** are in the oldest parts of town—the Yùquán District in the southwest corner of the city. Just to the north is the **Moslem Quarter (Huímín Qū)** with Hohhot's **Qīngzhēn Dà Sì (Great Mosque)**. Before long, every trace of the flat-topped mud and brick houses and storefronts that used to dominate this area will be gone; for a glimpse of the past, go now. By setting out an hour earlier, it's possible to add the Great Mosque to your walk. Better still, devote a full day to the four sites and explore the Moslem Quarter, too.

From the Xiǎo Shízì bus stop, walk about 50m (160 ft.) west on the small street called Tōngshùn Dōng Jiē. The temple is on the right.

❶ Dà Zhào

It's said that at one time this 6th-century temple (Apr–Sept 8am–7:30pm, Oct–Mar 8:30am–5:30pm; ¥15/$1.80) had over 400 lamas in residence. Later, the Qīng government (1644–1911) decreed that no more than 80 could live in Hohhot's earliest Tibetan temple. Today Dà Zhào houses 16 students from all over Inner Mongolia and only about 50 monks, but it is still an active center of Buddhist worship. Unlike Běijīng's famed lamasery, Yōnghé Gōng, Dà Zhào looks and feels much more like the monasteries of Tibet, but with Chinese characteristics. Instead of offerings of *tsampa* (roasted barley), devotees leave mounds of uncooked rice; and the pervading smell is of incense rather than rancid yak butter. But as in Lhasa, worshippers here drape their favorite Buddhas and bodhisattvas with shiny white ceremonial scarves. As you make your way through the complex, look for Dà Zhào's three most prized holdings: the 400-year-old Silver Buddha; in front of it, a pair of vivid golden dragons coiled around two floor-to-ceiling pillars; and exquisite Míng wall murals (in their original paint) depicting stories from Buddhist lore. Go all the way to the back of the complex to find a library full of antique sutras wrapped in orange and yellow cloth. Peek into the less-visited side chambers, too, where you're likely to find a lone lama chanting and playing Tibetan cymbals or a devotee kowtowing in the half-dark.

As you come out of the Dà Zhào temple from the main entrance, turn right, go around the corner, and walk along the west wall for 60m (200 ft.). A lama temple that was once part of the Dà Zhào temple complex is on your left.

❷ Nǎi Chūn Miào

There's no ticket kiosk because this temple, restored in 2004, is rarely visited by anyone outside the neighborhood. A painting of a sinner hanging upside down by his ankles, blood dripping over his face, adorns both panels of the main door. According to a young monk outside the temple, the hall is 300 years old. While the door paintings are considerably more recent, the wall and ceiling paintings inside are darkened with age and are certainly worth a look.

Walk back past Dà Zhào, and continue about 90m (300 ft.) to Dà Nán Jiē. Cross over, turn left, and walk about 30m (100 ft.). This will take only about 10 minutes if you don't stop to take pictures and peer into shops and side alleys along the way.

❸ Xílitú Zhào

The temple (Apr–Sept 8am–7:30pm, Oct–Mar 8:30am–6:00pm; ¥10/$1.25) is visible down the first lane, Dà Nán Jiē, though you wouldn't know it by the plaque above the front gate which uses the name given this temple by the Kāngxī emperor in 1696: Shòu Sì, or Temple of Extended Longevity. Like Dà Zhào, this Buddhist temple was constructed during the Wànlì reign (1572–1620) of the Míng dynasty and remains active, with 16 monks in residence. Razed by fire in the 19th century, it was rebuilt only to be damaged during the Cultural Revolution (1966–76). Its latest humiliation is the transformation of its front buildings into souvenir shops. However, a short distance into the complex, it starts feeling more like a temple than a tourist spot. One highlight is the Buddhist ornaments crowning the central hall. In front is the Wheel of Dharma flanked by two deer, representing the Buddha's first turning of the dharma wheel in the Deer Park. Behind the wheel are two victory banners and a jeweled trident symbolizing the Three Buddhas (past, present, and future) and the Three Jewels (the Buddha, the doctrine, and the monastic community; or body, speech, and mind). Inside the main building is a typical Tibetan prayer hall with cylindrical banners that hang from the ceiling, a white elephant (identified with the Buddha), and sutras lining the walls. On the first day of each lunar month, from 9am to noon, the monks can be heard (and viewed) chanting sutras in the main hall.

The walk from Xílitú Zhào to Wǔtǎ Sì threads through another traditional neighborhood where everyone knows each other and "real Chinese life" abounds. Exiting Xílitú Zhào, turn left (eastward) down Xīngshèng Street and continue walking until you reach a small playground. (En route, you'll pass old brick single-level storefronts on both sides and a toilet on the left.) Pass the playground and turn right, walking along the far side of the playground, which in summer is lined with billiards tables. Continue past a small outdoor market on the right and a narrow lane on your left. At the second narrow lane, Xiǎo Zhào Xiàng, turn left. Ahead, on the right, a new two-story gray building with a traditional Chinese roof takes the place of the mud and brick buildings. You'll see the five spires of Wǔtǎ Sì straight ahead, on Wǔtǎ Sì Hòu Jiē.

❹ Wǔtǎ Sì

This rare Indian-style five-pagoda Buddhist temple (Apr–Sept 8am–6:30pm, Oct–Mar 8am–6pm; ¥10/$1.25) is one of only six *jǐngāng bǎozuò* (diamond throne pagodas) in China. Built between 1727 and 1732, it was quite likely modeled after Běijīng's Wǔtǎ Sì, constructed 300 years earlier. Like that one, Hohhot's Wǔtǎ Sì is the only remaining structure of a much larger temple complex that fell into disrepair. Notable features are the 1,561 stone-carved images of Buddha that cover the middle and top portions of the temple; the graceful bas-relief images of bodhisattvas, bodhi trees, and sacred creatures gracing the base of the temple; and the astronomical map on the back wall purported to be the only one of its vintage written in Mongolian script. Carved in stone, it depicts the 24 seasonal periods of the lunar year, 28 planets, some 270 constellations, over 1,550 stars, and the 12 astrological divisions. Climb to the top of the temple for a view of the changing neighborhood.

To get back to Zhōngshān Jiē from Wǔtǎ Sì, as you leave from the main gate, turn right (eastward) and walk about 100m (330 ft.) to the main street, Gōngyuán Xī Lù. Across the street catch bus no. 26, which will take you to Zhōngshān Road. The bus turns right and follows Zhōngshān a block beyond the Nèiměnggǔ Bówùguǎn (Inner Mongolian Museum), where it turns left (north) onto Hūlúnbèiěr Lù.

IN & AROUND HOHHOT

Nèiměnggǔ Bówùguǎn (Inner Mongolia Museum) ★★ *Kids* Hohhot's museum is home to a rare and magnificent collection of cultural relics left behind by nomadic clans from the north. As befits a collection this important, the displays are adequately lit and include Chinese and English introductions and explanations (though in the case of the minority exhibit their main purpose is to propagandize). The first floor's north wing is devoted to minority costumes, musical instruments, and fishing and hunting implements, but the main attraction is the south wing, which houses skeletal fossils of a broad range of prehistoric behemoths. On the second floor, a fine collection of ruins and relics from the Stone Age forward reflects the artistic refinement and creative abilities of the various northern cultures. Not to be missed are the graceful gold Xiānbēi belt buckles, to which a 4th-century poet compared a maiden's "exquisite neck." Also of note are sets of pottery figures from a nearby Northern Wèi tomb. Among them is a pair of troll-faced pottery tomb-guardians, and eight pottery figurines of a musical troupe and a dancer who look more like a mime troupe, their wooden instruments having long ago disintegrated. After seeing this collection, you may never think of ancient Mongols, Huns, or Tartars in terms of "hordes" again.

Xīnhuá Dàjiē 2. Admission ¥10 ($1.25). Apr–Sept 9am–5pm (last ticket 4pm); Oct–Mar 10am–4:30pm (last ticket 3:30pm). Bus: no. 4 or 15 on Xīnchéng Xī Jiē; no. 19 on Zhōngshān Lù.

Qīngzhēn Dà Sì (Great Mosque)   As beautiful as this 360-year-old mosque is, it has yet to become a standard tourist sight. Typically, a few seniors are chatting and passing time in the courtyard. The buildings include the prayer hall with a beautiful ceiling painted with pink flowers; the teaching hall; and a 15m-tall (49-ft.) wooden pavilion (a Chinese version of the minaret), which, with permission, can sometimes be climbed. (*Note:* A sign in Chinese at the mosque's entrance requests no shorts, short skirts, smoking, or loud talking.) The back exit leads through a small street lined with food stalls on one side and tables and chairs on the other. Here you'll find Muslim snacks such as noodles and kabobs. To get back to Tōngdào Jiē, walk the full length of the lane.

Tōngdào Jiē (near Zhōngshān Xī Lù intersection). Free admission. 10am–4pm. Bus: no. 3, 19, or 21 to Tōngdào Jiē and Zhōngshān Xī Lù intersection.

THREE WAYS TO THE GRASSLANDS

BY BUS   Two buses a day go to Xīlāmùrén Dà Cǎoyuán from the bus station. For a day trip, take the 7:50am bus no. 123 to Zhāo Hé (terminus Chágānhādá) for ¥14 ($1.70), and return on the last bus around 3pm (check on the exact time before leaving). The drive takes about 2½ hours—much of it through the scrub, wild grass, and cultivated forests that carpet the Dà Qīng Mountain range. About 65km (40 miles) out of Hohhot, the bus makes a 10-minute stop in the small town of Wǔchuān. Before leaving Wǔchuān, let the driver know you wish to get off at **Lǚyóu Dùjiàcūn (Traveler's Holiday Village),** which is about 30km (19 miles) from Wǔchuān. A set of tourist *ger* (the Mongolian word for the circular felt tents known in central Asia as yurts) are visible across the street about 300m (1,000 ft.) away. Mr. Bāo, who operates these with his wife, has horses, and though he's not inclined to let you ride off on your own, he and his yellow dog are affable riding companions. (When the mood strikes, he breaks into song—anything from Mongolian folk to "The East Is Red.") With an hour, he can take you to a famous *oboo* (stone memorial) in the area. More time allows you to ride deeper into the grasslands and visit a herdsman's family living in a real *ger* rather than one for tourists. The going rate of ¥15 to ¥25 ($1.80–$3) per hour includes use of one of the guide's horses, though the first asking price will probably be in the ¥50 ($6.10) range. The Bāo family can also prepare a delicious Mongolian lunch (even vegetarian, if requested), which will include Mongolian milk tea and the homemade snacks that go with it. You may get *shǒubā ròu* (handheld meat)—mutton on the bone, eaten with the hands. The return bus passes the spot by the roadside where you were dropped off in the morning.

BY TAXI   If you balk at taking a crowded, smoke-filled rattletrap with no air-conditioning, opt for a private taxi. Drivers are at the ready at the bus and railway stations.

Skulls for Sale

It's not unusual on warm summer evenings to see someone peddling cow or sheep skulls on the city squares. Their buyers are probably opening a new business soon. A traditional belief is that after you eat a cow or sheep, its spirit is still alive. If you display the skull in a prominent place, the living spirit will attract other cows or sheep your way. The skull continues to be a symbol of good luck and a promise that business will thrive. The first asking price for a cow skull is ¥280 ($35), for a sheep skull, ¥160 ($20).

Prices can vary drastically, so ask around and compare. (This will amount to you and the driver pushing a calculator back and forth at each other.) Round-trip fare should be under ¥200 ($24), but you'll want to be certain the driver is taking you to a set of *ger* where you'll be able to ride horses and get a Mongolian meal.

TOURS   One-day tours to Xīlāmùrén Dà Cǎoyuán start at ¥270 ($33) per person for a group of two to five. The tour includes a visit to a herding family, performance of Mongolian song and dance, and a wrestling demonstration. Unless you speak Mandarin, **CITS** is the most reliable way to go, though not the most adventurous. The office is in the Tōngdá Fàndiàn, Suite 530, on Chēzhàn Dōng Jiē (© **0471/628-3861**).

SHOPPING

The **Mínzú Shāngchǎng (Mongolian Minority Department Store)**—one of the biggest stores in Hohhot—is a one-stop shopping opportunity on Zhōngshān Xī Lù at the Gōngyuán Jiē intersection. On the first floor are a **bakery** and a large, well-stocked **supermarket** that's worth a visit if you're shopping for food, travel snacks, or alcohol. The second floor has Mongolian handicrafts, traditional costumes, swords, teapots, jewelry, and more. For travel snacks, you could also visit **Parkson** supermarket, which has just about anything you could want. Be prepared to check your backpack or let it be sealed in shrink-wrap so you can keep it with you. Store hours are from 9am to 8pm. It's located at Zhōngshān Xī Lù 212 at Tōngdào Nán Jiē.

WHERE TO STAY

Bāyàntǎlā Fàndiàn   Renovated in 2002, the VIP Building in this clean, appealing hotel near Xīnhuá Guǎngchǎng offers a cheerful lobby and an atypically attractive elevator. Rooms have the usual twin beds and small bathrooms, but everything is spotless and well maintained. The VIP Building boasts a branch of Běijīng's most famous Peking Duck restaurant, Quánjùdé. Though the "Main Building" is less charming, it, too, is clean, and offers dorm beds for as low as ¥20 ($2.50) in a setting a notch above the usual dorm standard.

Xīlínguōlè Běi Lù 42 (between Xīnhuá Dàjiē and Zhōngshān Xī Lù). © **0471/696-3344**. Fax 0471/696-7390. 173 units with bathroom in VIP Building; 244 economy units (some with shower only, some with common bathroom) in Main Building. ¥380 ($47) standard room in VIP Building (off season as low as ¥200/$25); ¥600 ($73) suite. Rates in VIP Building include breakfast. ¥280 ($34) standard room in Main Building. Off season ¥160–¥220 ($20–$27). No credit cards. Bus: no. 34 or 35 from the railway station. **Amenities:** 2 restaurants; small business center; dry cleaning/laundry. *In room:* A/C, TV.

Guóháng Dàshà (Phoenix Hotel)   Completed in 2001 and owned by Air China, this four-star hotel equals or surpasses a good number of China's so-called five-star hotels. From the moment you step into the lobby, you know you're in an international hotel. Most of the staff have been trained in Shànghǎi and are competent and eager to please. Guest rooms are spacious and bathroom facilities are high in quality. The rooms have blond wood desktops and crisp white down comforters; they are light, airy, and well maintained. Big discounts make this hotel a bargain.

Xīnchéng Běi Jiē (north of Xīnchéng Běi/Nán Jiē and Xīnchéng Xī/Dōng Jiē junction). ✆ 0471/481-6611. Fax 0471/696-1479. www.ni-phoenix.com.cn. 280 units. ¥600–¥760 ($73–$93) standard room; ¥880–¥1,080 ($117–$132) suite. Rates include breakfast or use of sauna/swimming pool. Usual discount 25% with breakfast; 35% without breakfast. Bus: no. 2 from the railway station. AE, DC, MC, V. **Amenities:** 2 restaurants; bar; large indoor pool; outdoor tennis court; health club and sauna; complimentary airport transfer; very helpful business center; ATM; forex; limited room service; laundry/dry cleaning. In room: A/C, satellite TV w/pay movies, dataport, minibar, fridge, hair dryer, safe.

Hūhéhàotè Jiàrì Jiǔdiàn (Holiday Inn Hohhot) 🐕

The city's first four-star hotel, located 16km (10 miles) from the airport and 3km (2 miles) from the railway station, is within walking distance of Hohhot's shopping and commercial areas. As one of the newer hotels in town with international management, this should be the safest bet in town. There is a Western restaurant serving Western and Asian dishes and a Chinese restaurant serving Cantonese, Sìchuān, and Húnán specialties.

Zhōngshān Xī Lù. ✆ 0471/635-1888. Fax 0471/635-0888. 204 units. ¥425 ($52) standard room; ¥600 ($73) deluxe. Rates include breakfast. AE, DC, MC, V. **Amenities:** 2 restaurants; business center; health center w/sauna/whirlpool; dry cleaning/laundry; coin-op washer/dryer; ATM. In room: A/C, satellite TV, high-speed Internet, coffeemaker, hair dryer.

Nèiměnggǔ Fàndiàn (Inner Mongolia Hotel) 🐕

The Nèiměnggǔ was entirely rebuilt to five-star standards in 2001. In addition to having all the trappings of an international hotel (including a sweeping lobby staircase), it has the best non-Chinese cuisine in the province, served in three of Hohhot's handsomest restaurants. Guest rooms and bathrooms are spacious and attractive, service is excellent, and the decor in the hotel's lounges, bars, and tearooms is elegant. Located around the corner from the Xīnchéng Hotel, it hasn't the gorgeous grounds of its competitor, nor the warmth, but there is a public park right across the street. Get the best of both five-star worlds by staying at the Xīnchéng and dining here.

Wūlánchábù Xī Lù (east of Hūlúnbèièr Nán Lù). ✆ **0471/693-8888.** Fax 0471/695-2288. www.nmghotel.com.cn. 345 units. ¥996–¥1,536 ($124–$190) business or deluxe room; ¥788–¥830 ($98–$103) standard room; from ¥1,660 ($207) suite. 20% discount possible. AC, MC, V. Bus: no. 37 from the railway station to Wūlán Chábù Xī Lù; from there, walk east. **Amenities:** 4 restaurants; bar; large indoor pool; health club; Jacuzzi; sauna; business center; forex; 24-hr. room service; dry cleaning/laundry. In room: A/C, satellite TV w/pay movies, dataport, minibar, fridge, hair dryer, safe.

Xīnchéng Bīnguǎn 🐕🐕 *Kids*

The grounds of this hotel and garden complex in the heart of the city cover 119,000 sq. m (1,280,904 sq. ft.) and include a lake, a park, a large sports complex, and a set of *ger* tents. Originally built in 1958, the Xīnchéng underwent a 2001 renovation that produced Hohhot's first five-star hotel. (Some economy rooms are still available, though dorms are gone.) This is the place to take a break from traveling. If you have kids, send them off to swim, bowl, or play video games while you treat yourself to a massage in what the expats say is the best spa in town. If you opt for a deluxe standard, ask for a room with a front view (overlooking gardens, a fountain and, in the distance, a bustling avenue) in the renovated Building A.

Hūlúnbèièr Nán Lù 40. ✆ 0471/666-0322. Fax 0471/657-1141. www.xincheng-hotel.com.cn. 300 units in buildings A and B; 5 villas with luxury rooms. ¥130–¥180 ($16–$22) economy standard (shared bathroom); ¥300–¥600 ($37–$75) deluxe standard; (¥3,000–¥15,000 ($375–$1,875) presidential suite. AE, DC, MC, V. Bus: no. 37 from railway station. For under $1, a taxi saves you the long walk across the immense grounds to the hotel's front door.

Amenities: 12 restaurants; bar; large pool; indoor tennis courts; squash court; health club; sauna; bike rental; bowling alley; billiards; video arcade; business center; forex; limited room service; massage; dry cleaning/laundry. *In room:* A/C, satellite TV, dataport, minibar, fridge, hair dryer, safe.

WHERE TO DINE

There's a **KFC** on the first floor of the Parkson Building and another next to the Mínzú Shāngchǎng. But Hohhot's varied and satisfying Mongolian cuisine, a big change from the mainstream Chinese diet, should get priority.

Bàn Mǔ Dì Yóumiàn Dàwáng ✿✿✿ 〈Value〉 MONGOLIAN

Eating in this lively restaurant specializing in pastas and pancakes made of husked wheat will put you in a good mood. The decor is a mix of Mongolian *ger* and prettified farmhouse. The walls are brightly decorated with floral and folk designs. The waitresses, dressed in equally bright colors and busy patterns, are friendly and efficient. Private rooms have imitation *kàng* (coal-heated brick beds). Best of all, the food is inexpensive and exceptionally tasty. Try house specialties like *wōwo*, husked wheat pasta shaped by curling the dough around the little finger then pressed together in a bamboo steamer, forming what looks like honeycomb made of pasta. *Dùndun*—husked-wheat pancakes filled with carrots, potato, and cabbage—are rolled up and sliced like Mediterranean levant sandwiches. Also try *wō bǐng*, or corncakes, which diners dunk like doughnuts into a soup of vinegar, sesame oil, and soybeans.

Dàxué Xī Lù (across from the pharmaceutical company Táng Yàoyè). ✆ **0471/691-0168**. Reservations recommended. Meal for 2 under ¥40 ($5). No credit cards. 10:30am–10pm.

Florence (Fóluólúnsā) ✿ 〈Value〉 ITALIAN/AMERICAN

This attractive restaurant serves authentic pasta, pizza, and baked lasagna. The chef has worked in several international hotels—most recently in Xī'ān's Sheraton—which may be how poached salmon, lobster Newburg, and T-bone steak ended up on an Italian menu (not to mention the burger, fries, and club sandwich). Though neither the selection nor the dishes themselves demonstrate creativity, this is the best place to satisfy a craving for Western food. You can also drop in for tiramisu and espresso or order takeout. A violin soloist serenades diners nightly, and dinner is by candlelight, but dress is as casual or formal as you like.

In the Nèiměnggǔ Fàndiàn, Wūlánchábù Xī Lù (east of Húlúnbèièr Nán Lù). ✆ **0471/693-8888**. English menu. Pasta, pizza, and sandwiches ¥32–¥48 ($4–$6); steaks, seafood ¥78–¥128 ($9.75–$16). AE, DC, MC, V. 5:30–9:30pm.

Māo Bùwén Dà Jiǔlóu ✿ HOME-STYLE/JIǍOZI

In addition to local specialties and 80 kinds of *jiǎozi* (¥16–¥20/$2–$2.50 for 40), the menu includes Cantonese, Sìchuān, and Shāndōng specialties. The best time to come is between 8pm and 2am, when you'll find the place packed with locals enjoying a late supper of cold dishes and beer topped off by a plate of *lā miàn* (you can watch the chef stretch and swing the dough as it is transformed into noodles before your eyes). Highly recommended dishes are *suāncài ròu chǎo fěn* (wheat noodles mixed with shredded pork, green pepper, cabbage, and spices); *sù hézi* (fried vegetable pie stuffed with chives, crumbled scrambled egg, carrots, and tree ear fungus); the refreshingly light *shénxiān báicài tāng* (immortals' cabbage soup), which includes cabbage, shrimp, mushrooms, and carrots; and *tèsè kǎo rǔniú* (barbecued marinated veal). Before barbecuing, the veal is soaked for a day in a marinade containing over two dozen herbs and spices, the sum of which are said to balance *yīn* and *yáng*.

Húlúnbèièr Běi Kǒu 91 (at Zhōngshān Dōng Lù intersection). ✆ **0471/629-6558**. Meal for 2 ¥20 ($2.50) and up. No credit cards. 10am–2am.

Yùlán Jiǔjiā ★★ *Finds* MONGOLIAN   There's no better place to be introduced to Mongolian cooking than this clean, friendly, family-operated restaurant named after its female proprietor, Chén Yùlán. Though no one speaks English, the staff will bring out ingredients from the kitchen to show you what goes into any particular dish. Their best Mongolian specialties include various types of *guōzǎi*. This stew comes to the table in a pot with flame underneath. Unlike hot pot, the ingredients are already cooked when the dish is set in front of you. Just stir it a bit and remind your waiter to put the flame out when it gets too hot. A Mongolian favorite is *guōzǎi suāncài* (pickled vegetables and sheep organ *[yáng zásuì]* stew) made of mutton, sheep heart, lung, liver, intestines, cilantro, hot pepper, green vegetable, and spices. A Mongolian friend says Yùlán's version of this is exactly right. If you're not inclined to eat internal organs, the dish is also made with the same vegetables and spices combined with mutton *(yángròu)*, beef *(niúròu)*, or chicken *(jīròu)*. *Chǎo miàn* are Mongolian-style fried wheat noodles that can be ordered with or without meat and include cilantro, sesame seeds, and garlic. *Nǎichá*, the milk tea of Hohhot—made with cow's milk—is absent the pungent mutton taste associated with milk tea of the outer steppe. Here, the tea is usually served salted with a dish of sugar on the side. Snacks such as *guǒtiáo* (sticks of crisp fried dough) and pats of *nǎipízi* ("milk skin" which, in taste and texture, falls between cream and fresh butter) are eaten on their own or tossed into the tea along with *chǎo fěn*, processed millet that looks like tiny yellow beads. *Liángfěn* are thick translucent grain noodles served cold in a thin broth made of vinegar, soy sauce, sesame seeds, and hot pepper. If the slimy texture of the noodles isn't an obstacle, you'll find this a delicious dish. In addition to Mongolian specialties, the chef makes a variety of noodle dishes, vegetable and meat dumplings, and delicious *jiācháng cài* (Chinese home-style fare).

Just down the alleyway that runs along the north side of the Bāyàntǎlā Hotel on Xīlínguōlè Běi Lù. It's the 1st restaurant on your right. ☎ **0696/3344-6101**. Meal for 2 ¥20–¥40 ($2.50–$5). No credit cards. 10am–10pm (to 9pm in winter).

HOHHOT AFTER DARK
Sàimǎ Chǎng Měnggǔ Dàhuì Gōng   A performance stage and over 100 *ger* (or yurts) have been erected on the large open field next to Hohhot's horse-racing track. They comprise one big restaurant specializing in Mongolian fare—from noodles to an entire barbecued goat. Even if you're not interested in eating, the time to come is between 6:30 and 9pm, when Mongolian folk musicians and dancers perform on the outdoor stage free of charge. On hot summer nights, Mongolians and Hàn alike bring their families for an inexpensive evening out. The combination of *ger*, outdoor music, and a crowd lends a county-fair atmosphere.

Sàimǎ Chǎng (Hohhot's horse-racing track). No credit cards. Restaurant: 9am–2:30pm and 5–10pm. Performance: 6:30–9pm. Performance canceled in snow or heavy rain. Bus: no. 13 north along Hūlúnbèiěr Lù to the racetrack.

3 Yínchuān ★

Níngxià Province, 1,369km (845 miles) W of Běijīng, 723km (450 miles) NW of Xī'ān

Compared to the other major cities in this chapter—particularly the dirty duo of Dàtóng and Tàiyuán—Yínchuān is a breath of fresh air. Capital of the Níngxià Huí Autonomous Region, it has a population under a million, its tree-lined streets still have relatively few automobiles, and it is rumored (read: reported by the *People's Daily*) to be the quietest city in China. It has also escaped the extreme poverty associated with this province by having the good fortune to be hydrated by the Yellow River and an irrigation system first built during the Hàn dynasty. Over a third of the region's population is Huí (Chinese Muslims), and a significant percentage live in the capital, adding a cultural diversity less apparent in other Chinese capitals. This is an easy town to settle down in for a few days. Hotel rates aren't exorbitant, the food is good, and most of the sights are within walking distance or easy to get to by bus or taxi.

The best time to visit is between May and October. Though summer temperatures can soar, the dry climate makes even the hottest days bearable. **Note:** Yínchuān holds its annual Motorcycle Tourism Festival June 16 to June 22. The emphasis is on tourism, so unless you're prepared for throngs of unregenerate cap-wearing tourists and dancers in go-go boots performing the "songs and dances of the Western Xià," it may be a good time to stay away.

The (Nearly) Lost Dynasty of the Xī Xià

After Genghis Khan died in 1227 near the Xī Xià (Western Xià) capital of Zhōngxīng Fǔ (present-day Yínchuān), his corpse was carried in an ox-drawn chariot—the centerpiece of a grand procession that led back to the Mongolian steppe. En route, any person or beast in the procession's path was slaughtered—in offering to the Khan's spirit and to keep news of his death from spreading. As dour as it must have been, the escorting soldiers might have smiled to themselves in the knowledge they were returning home victorious—having once and for all defeated the Xī Xià (Western Xià) dynasty (1038–1227), which had lasted almost 200 years.

Today the Xī Xià is somewhat of a mystery. It was never recognized as a legitimate dynasty by the Chinese, so there is no official history of the empire or its people, the Tangut; and Xī Xià documents—written in a system fashioned after but different from Chinese—have been difficult to decipher. It's known that the ancient Tangut nomads came from what is now Sìchuān, Qīnghǎi, and Tibet. By the Táng dynasty (618–907), they had a leader and were one of the major players (along with the Khitan and Jurchen) in the ongoing struggle for territory. By the early 11th century they had defeated the Sòng imperial army, declared an independent empire, and extracted an annual tribute of tea, cloth, silk, and silver from the Sòng empire. Almost a century later, the Xià's alliance with the Jīn (the Jurchen state) ignited the wrath of Genghis Khan, who personally led his troops south to destroy the "Great Xià," as they called themselves. At its height, the Xī Xià empire controlled much of what is now Qīnghǎi, Gānsù, Níngxià, and Inner Mongolia. This obscure Buddhist state left behind imperial mausoleums, religious monuments, its own written language, and cultural relics that reveal a passion for Buddhist art, fine pottery, sculpture, and exquisite gold and silver artifacts. Much of what remains can be seen in and around Yínchuān.

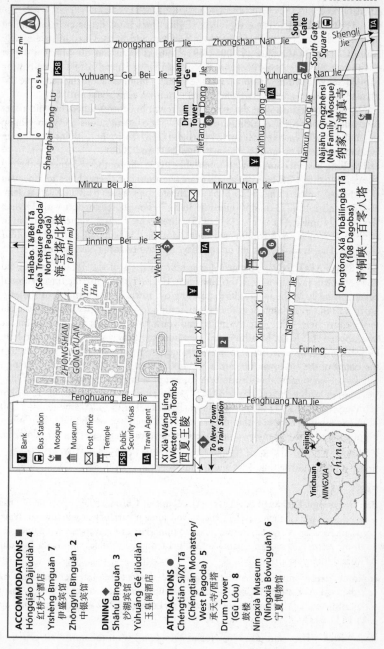

Zhongshan Bei Jie
Zhongshan Nan Jie
South Gate
South Square
Shengli Jie

Yuhuang Ge Bei Jie
Yuhuang Ge
Yuhuang Ge Nan Jie

PSB

Shanghai Dong Lu

Drum Tower
Jiefang Dong Jie
Xinhua Dong Jie
Nanxun Dong Jie

Najiāhù Qìngzhēnsì (Nà Family Mosque) 纳家户清真寺

Minzu Bei Jie
Minzu Nan Jie

Hǎibǎo Tǎ/Běi Tǎ (Sea Treasure Pagoda/ North Pagoda) 海宝塔/北塔 (3 km/1 mi)

Jinning Bei Jie
Wenhua Xi Jie

Qīngtóng Xiá Yībǎilíngbā Tǎ (108 Dagobas) 青铜峡一百零八塔

Yin Hu

ZHONGSHAN GONGYUAN

Jiefang Xi Jie
Xinhua Xi Jie
Nanxun Xi Jie

Funing Jie

Fenghuang Bei Jie
Fenghuang Nan Jie

Xī Xià Wáng Líng (Western Xia Tombs) 西夏王陵

To New Town & Train Station

¥ Bank
🚌 Bus Station
☪ Mosque
🏛 Museum
✉ Post Office
🏛 Temple
PSB Public Security Visas
TA Travel Agent

China
Beijing ★
Yinchuan
NINGXIA

ESSENTIALS

GETTING THERE   There are direct **flights** from most major cities, including Běijīng, Shànghǎi, Chéngdū, Guǎngzhōu, Tàiyuán, and Xī'ān. Discounts are usually available. The **CAAC** office (© **0951/691-3456**) is located in the Mínháng Hotel (Mínháng Dàshà) at the intersection of Nánhuán Dōng Lù and Běi Jiē. A bus costing ¥15 ($1.90) to **Hédōng Airport** leaves the hotel 95 minutes before flights for the 25-minute trip. Buses meet every flight. A taxi into town costs about ¥40 ($5).

The **railway station** is in the new part of town, but there's a booking and ticket office in the old town on Xīnhuá Dōng Jiē. Major connections are with Běijīng (K177/K178; 20 hr.) and Xī'ān (2585/6 and 2587/8; 15 hr.). Trains connecting Hohhot and Lánzhōu stop in Yínchuān (no. 2003 and 2004).

The **long-distance bus station (qìchēzhàn)** is in the southeast corner of the old city on Shènglì Běi Jiē. From Xī'ān, there are five afternoon sleeper buses to Yínchuān (720km/447 miles; 15 hr.; ¥125/$15) and three express buses daily to Xī'ān at 7am, 8:40am, and 9am (723km/450 miles; ¥136/$17). Four buses connect with Tàiyuán (763km/474 miles; ¥115–¥122/$14–$15); three express buses connect with Yán'ān (449km/279 miles; ¥78/$9.50); and with Lánzhōu (514km/320 miles; ¥41–¥89/$5–$11). Tickets can be bought up to 4 days in advance at the bus station.

GETTING AROUND   Yínchuān has a new town (as of the 1960s) and an old town. The railway station is in the new town, but everything else the traveler would need or want is in the much more charming old town 10km (6 miles) to the east. **Taxis** wait in the parking lot at the railway station to transport passengers to the old town. Most prefer not to use the meter, and you'll have to negotiate for a reasonable fare (about ¥15/$1.90). **Minibus** no. 1 goes from the railway station to the Nán Mén Qìchēzhàn (South Gate Bus Station) via Jiěfàng Jiē, which runs east to west through the center of the old town; the fare is ¥3 (40¢). **Bus** no. 11 from the railway station follows the same route, but turns north instead of south at the end of Jiěfàng Dōng Jiē. Bus fare within the old city is ¥1 (15¢). Taxi rates are ¥5 (60¢) for the first 3km (2 miles), then ¥1.20 (15¢) per kilometer. Beyond 8km (5 miles), the rate is ¥1.50 (20¢) per kilometer. Fares within the old town will rarely exceed ¥6 (75¢). *Tip:* When negotiating trips to out-of-town sites, local residents calculate ¥1 (15¢) per kilometer.

TOURS   Níngxià **CITS**, at Běijīng Dōng Lù 375 (© **0951/671-9792**), arranges pricey tours to nearby sites, Zhōngwèi, and Shāpōtóu.

FAST FACTS

Banks, Foreign Exchange & ATMs   The **Bank of China,** at Jiěfàng Xī Jiē 80, has a 24-hour ATM. Change traveler's checks and foreign currency at window 10. Bank hours are Monday to Friday from 8:30am to 6pm. For cash advances on credit cards, go to the second floor of the branch at Xīnhuá Dōng Jiē 5, which also has a 24-hour ATM and foreign exchange.

Internet Access   Just south of the Yùhuáng Gé, there's a true Internet bar *(wǎngbā)* at Yùhuáng Gé Nán Jiē 53. Cocktails are served up front; the computers are in a small room at the back. The bar is open 24 hours and charges ¥2 (25¢) per hour. Dial-up is © **163** or 169.

Post Office   The main post office (open 8am–6pm) is on the northwest corner of the Jiěfàng Xī Jiē and Mínzú Běi Jiē intersection.

Visa Extensions   The Exit-Entry Office of the **PSB** is in the northeast quadrant of the old town at Yùhuáng Gé Běi Jiē 105, entered from Shànghǎi Dōng Lù (© **0951/ 501-5976**). It's open Monday through Friday from 8:30am to noon and 2:30 to 6:30pm. The official processing time is 3 to 5 days, but it's usually done overnight. Take bus no. 4 from Wénhuà Jiē.

IN & AROUND THE TOWN

Chéngtiān Sì and Níngxià Bówùguǎn (Chéngtiān Temple and Níngxià Museum)   The museum, which doesn't keep the most reliable hours, is on the grounds of Chéngtiān Temple, which also goes by the name of its Xī Tǎ (West Pagoda). First erected in 1050, the pagoda did not survive Yínchuān's devastating 1739 earthquake. The existing pagoda dates from 1820, and visitors are allowed to climb the 11-story building.

The museum collection is divided into four parts, distributed among three buildings. The first two sections share a building and are devoted to the history, language, and relics of the Western Xià dynasty. Of all the sites in and around Yínchuān, these two rooms have the most helpful English explanations. The advantage to making this your first stop is a better understanding of the culture that is most connected with the out-of-town tombs and pagodas. The second building houses relics of the Communist revolution and has no English labeling. A third hall focuses on the Huí (Muslim) "nationality," and has only an English introduction.

Jinníng Jiē 6. Admission to museum and pagoda ¥22 ($3). 8:30am–6pm. Bus: no. 2.

Hǎibǎo Tǎ/Běi Tǎ (Sea Treasure Pagoda/North Pagoda)   In a province that has more than its share of stately pagodas, Hǎibǎo Tǎ is one of the loveliest. Originally built in the 5th century, it was toppled by the 1739 earthquake and rebuilt in the original style some 30 years later. Restored since then, it has retained its distinctive cross-shaped ground plan that adds depth and complexity to the four-sided tower. Its rare peach-shaped steeple of glazed green tiles is one of only two—the other crowns Chéngtiān Temple's West Pagoda.

3km (1 mile) north of town along Jinníng Běi Jiē. Admission ¥5 (60¢). Summer 8am–6pm; winter 9am–5pm. No public bus. Taxi from town center ¥5 (60¢).

Nàjiāhù Qīngzhēnsì (Nà Family Mosque)   A good time to visit this 490-year-old wooden mosque is morning, as the town begins to stir. From the three-storied entrance gate, you can look east over the flat-topped brick houses and into small yards and alleys. The population of greater Yǒngníng (which is a half-hour drive south of Yínchuān) is about 80% Huí, while this old village that immediately surrounds the mosque is 100% Huí—that being one of the requisites of residing in this well-preserved section of town. To this day a majority of residents are part of the Nà family after which the mosque was named. According to the septuagenarian caretaker, the mosque escaped the destruction of the Cultural Revolution because the tightly knit community kept constant watch over it and refused entrance to the Red Guards. These days, visitors are invited into the pretty and peaceful courtyard. If you come alone or with only a few people, the caretaker may also let you into the prayer hall.

23km (14 miles) from Yínchuān in the town of Yǒngníng, at Guó Dào 109. Admission ¥10 ($1.20). 6am–noon and 1:30–4pm. Bus: green no. 9 opposite Nán Mén to Yǒngníng; you'll be dropped at the Xīnzhàizi Lùkǒu (Xīnzhàizi intersection). Walk west about 300m (1,000 ft.). You'll cross a small timber bridge. Look for the mosque on your left.

Qīngtóng Xiá Yībǎilíngbā Tǎ (108 Dagobas) Little is known about the 108 dagobas that stand like bowling pins on the side of the Qīngtóng Gorge, near the Yellow River. In the Míng dynasty they were referred to as the "ancient pagodas" (*gǔ tǎ*) and their origin was already a mystery. Today scholars associate them with the Western Xià dynasty because other relics and remains from the Xià culture have been unearthed in the vicinity. Their shape—like a Buddhist alms bowl—is similar to that of the classic Tibetan stupa, supporting the accepted belief that Tibetan Buddhism thrived in this area during the Western Xià and Yuán dynasties. Extensive repairs were made to them in 1987, but the dagobas are unusual and worth the visit. On the way, consider stopping at the Nàjiāhù Qīngzhēnsì (see above).

82km (51 miles) south of Yínchuān, near Qīngtóng Xiá Zhèn. Admission ¥10 ($1.20). 7:30am–7pm. Bus: no. 153 to Qīngtóng Xiá Zhèn (not to be confused with Qīngtóng Xiá Shì, where the bus may stop on the way). Minibuses wait at the drop-off point. The asking price will be higher if the minibus isn't full. Hard bargaining might get it down to ¥20 ($2.50). If the minibus is full, it should be considerably less. To walk from the drop-off junction, take the road to the right. Turn left at the hydroelectric plant; then continue toward the right until you reach the dam. (Signs in English point the way.) Cross the Yellow River by ferry (¥15/$2 round-trip), then hike up and over. Follow the trail to the dagobas. A taxi from Yínchuān and back, including road toll and parking, should be around ¥200 ($24) and take 1 hr., 40 min. one-way.

Xī Xià Wáng Líng (Western Xià Tombs) As the tourism bureau develops this spot, it is fast acquiring a theme-park aura. But if you can forgive the modern "Spirit Way" (fashioned after the path to the Míng tombs), skip the cheesy reenactment scenes of Xià life in the "Art Hall," and ignore promoters' claims that these are "China's Pyramids," you'll be able to appreciate this intriguing site. The tombs of nine Xià kings are spread across a 5×11km (3×7-mile) area at the foot of the Hèlán Mountains. In the fashion of Táng imperial tombs, each of these was originally surrounded by a 1-hectare (2½-acre) mausoleum composed of eight different types of traditional buildings. While only ruins survive, all but one of the nine imperial tombs remain intact. Dotting the landscape, the eerie, mud-encased pyramids resemble giant termite mounds. A two-story museum contains most of the relics, such as compelling stone plinths carved to look like potbellied gnomes on their knees, eyes and foreheads bulging as if from the weight they bear.

38km (24 miles) west of Yínchuān on eastern slopes of Hèlán Mountains. Admission ¥35 ($4.25). For now, no public buses. Taxi round-trip: negotiate for ¥80–¥100 ($10–$13).

SHOPPING

The largest supermarket in town is the **Huálián Supermarket** (9am–10pm) under Nán Mén Square opposite the bus station.

WHERE TO STAY

Hóngqiáo Dàjiǔdiàn This is the closest Yínchuān gets to a four-star hotel. Rooms are well maintained and carpets are clean while midsize bathrooms have combo tub/showers. The hotel isn't in the heart of the tourist area, but it's only a few blocks west of Gǔ Lóu (the Drum Tower), which is the center of town. It's popular, and is especially busy on weekends.

Jiěfàng Xī Jiē. ✆ 0951/691-8888. Fax 0951/691-8788. 192 units. ¥339–¥382 ($42–$47) standard room. 10% discount often available. AE, DC, MC, V. Bus: no. 1 or 11 from railway station. **Amenities:** 3 restaurants; bar; fitness center; ticketing; business center; forex; limited room service; dry cleaning/laundry. *In room:* A/C, satellite TV, minibar, fridge, hair dryer, safe.

Yīshèng Bīnguǎn   This budget hotel north of Nán Guān Mosque is modest, exceptionally clean, and one of the few inexpensive guesthouses in Yínchuān that isn't dismal. Guest rooms are small and bright; each has a private bathroom and shower without a separate cubicle. The hotel's location—within walking distance of Nán Mén, the bus station, and the Nán Guān Mosque—makes it prime for sightseeing.

Nánxūn Dōng Jiē 67 (northeast corner of Nánxūn Dōng and Yùhuáng Gé Nán Jiē intersection). ✆ 0951/604-1888. 12 units. ¥138 ($17) standard room. 20% discount sometimes available. No credit cards. Bus: no. 2 or 17. **Amenities:** Teahouse. *In room:* TV.

Zhōngyín Bīnguǎn   Opened in 1997 and yet to be renovated, this hotel has still been maintained better than most. The rooms are clean and airy, and except for a few spots of peeling wallpaper, they don't show extreme wear. With the discount, the value is good.

Fùníng Jiē 27. ✆ 0951/501-1918. Fax 0951/504-7545. 50 units. ¥200–¥260 ($25–$32) standard room; ¥580–¥880 ($72–$110) suite. Nondiscounted rates include breakfast. 20% discount available. AE, DC, MC, V. Bus: no. 1 or 11 from railway station to Fùníng Jiē, then walk 2 min. south. **Amenities:** 2 restaurants; bowling alley; ticketing; business center; limited room service. *In room:* A/C, TV, minibar, fridge, hair dryer, safe.

WHERE TO DINE

Shāhú Bīnguǎn ✿ *(Value)* CHINESE FAST FOOD   By 7am customers are lined up at this restaurant's outdoor stand to buy *bāozi* (stuffed steamed buns) for takeout. Generous portions of good, inexpensive food have turned this restaurant into the most popular breakfast spot in Yínchuān. According to one taxi driver, a ¥3 (40¢) *bāozi* at Shāhú is one and a half times the size of a ¥3-*bāozi* anywhere else. For very little money you can sample lots of local specialties; choose from among noodle dishes, savory pancakes, eight-treasure soups *(bābǎo zhōu)*—of which there are many kinds—and every sort of *bāozi, jiǎozi,* and *hézi* (steamed buns, Chinese ravioli, fried meat or vegetable pies). A sample breakfast costing just ¥8 ($1) includes a bowl of noodles, three vegetarian *bāozi,* two fried *jiǎozi,* and two crepes stuffed with chives, egg, and cilantro. And there are many more choices for meat eaters and vegetarians alike. Customers pay food servers with coupons purchased in advance from the cashier. Unspent coupons can also be redeemed there.

Wénhuà Xī Jiē 22 (on the ground floor of the Shāhú Hotel). Meal for 2 ¥16 ($2). No credit cards. 6:30am–2pm and 5–10pm. Bus: no. 4 or 18.

Yùhuáng Gé Jiǔdiàn ✿✿ HOME-STYLE   This family-operated restaurant at the west end of town is out of the way but worth the trip. The decor is simple and characteristic of this style of restaurant—fluorescent lights and neat rows of tables for four—but what it lacks in ambience it makes up for in great food. Try the *guàntāng bāozi.* These unleavened *bāozi* served in a bamboo steamer are a Xī'ān specialty. The choice of stuffing includes beef *(niúròu),* mutton *(yángròu),* or vegetable *(sùxiàn).* Their version of *tǔdòu sī* (shredded potatoes with slivers of green and red pepper) is also delicious, as is sweet *bābǎo zhōu* (eight treasure soup), made with sesame seeds, peanuts, rice, lotus seeds, and *gǒuqí* (sometimes translated "wolfberry"), the ubiquitous dried fruit from this area that resembles a red raisin and is considered good for the health by Chinese.

Jiěfàng Xī Jiē 158. ✆ 0951/505-4758. Meal for 2 ¥20–¥50 ($2.50–$6.25). No credit cards. 10am–10pm.

4 Yán'ān

Shǎnxī Province, 371km (230 miles) N of Xī'ān

For 10 years between 1937 and 1947, the dusty, desolate town of Yán'ān in Shǎnxī Province (spelled with two a's to distinguish it from its neighbor, Shānxī) was the site from which the Chinese Communist Party consolidated power and spread revolution. It was here that Máo seized leadership of the party and formulated the theories that came to be known as "Máo Zédōng Thought." As the Japanese took control of the eastern part of the country, intellectuals from all over China moved to impoverished Yán'ān, eager to make their contribution and share in the collective experiment. Among them were the writer Dīng Líng (who was chastised by Máo for her essay on International Women's Day—"Thoughts on March 8"—which pointed out gender inequities in Yán'ān) and the Shànghǎi starlet Jiāng Qīng, who became Máo's third wife and, later, a key player in the Cultural Revolution. This part of northern Shǎnxī was also the location of Chén Kǎigē's affecting 1984 film *Yellow Earth,* about the impact on villagers of a young Communist soldier who goes into the countryside to collect folk songs.

Like Máo's birthplace of Sháo Shān, Yán'ān was a place of pilgrimage during the 1960s, and today is a major point for Chinese making Red Tours, or visiting revolutionary sites. The appeal of this part of Shǎnxī is its very austerity—the cave dwellings, the dry terraced hills, and the yellow loess that covers it all. The "revolutionary sites" that have become such a part of the founding myth of the PRC will also draw anyone with an interest in modern Chinese history. *Note:* Please turn to appendix A for Chinese translations of key locations.

ESSENTIALS

GETTING THERE   **Yán'ān Airport** is 10km (6 miles) northeast of town. A **CAAC shuttle bus** (© 0911/211-1111) costing ¥5 (60¢) runs between the airport and the Mínháng Bīnguǎn (Jīchǎng Lù); it departs from the CAAC office an hour before flights and meets all arrivals. Yán'ān is connected by air with Běijīng and Xī'ān (daily).

The Yán'ān **railway station** is at the south end of town, with services from Xī'ān (4761/4762, 7551/7552; ¥76/$9.20 hard sleeper, or ¥96/$12 for soft sleeper). The best chance of getting a sleeper leaving Yán'ān is through your hotel or CITS. At the station, same-day tickets go on sale at 3:30pm. Arrive by 3:15pm and be prepared to fight your way to the window.

Buses arrive and depart from the railway station parking lot and the **qìchēzzhàn (bus station)** east of town on Dōng Guān Jiē. From Píngyáo or Tàiyuán, it's easiest to go to Xī'ān first, then transfer to bus or train for Yán'ān. Buses connecting Xī'ān and Yán'ān leave throughout the day for the 6- to 7-hour journey costing ¥40 to ¥120 ($4.90–$15). Overnight buses also connect Yán'ān to Luòyáng and Yínchuān.

GETTING AROUND   Shaped like a Y, the city of Yán'ān traces the Yán River as it forks to the east and west. The town is small by Chinese standards and easy to navigate on foot, since its commercial district is concentrated in a few blocks around Zhōngxīn Jiē (Central St.) and Dà Qiáo Jiē (Big Bridge St.). City **bus** rides cost ¥1 (15¢). Rates for the two types of **taxis** are ¥5 (60¢) or ¥6 (75¢) for the first 3km (2 miles), then ¥1.20 (15¢) per kilometer or ¥1.30 (15¢) per kilometer. Between 10pm and 7am, the first 3km (2 miles) are ¥5.90 (75¢) or ¥6.90 (85¢). Most destinations within the city are under ¥10 ($1.25).

TOURS   CITS (© 0911/212-3320) is a short distance down the alley next to the Yán'ān Bīnguǎn. The office is on the second floor of the brick compound to your right. Hours are Monday through Friday from 8am to noon and 2 to 6pm, but the office is occasionally empty even then.

FAST FACTS

Banks, Foreign Exchange & ATMs   The **Bank of China,** at Zhōngxīn Jiē and Běi Guān Jiē, changes cash. It's open Monday through Friday from 8am to noon and 2:30 to 6pm (to 5:30pm in winter).

Internet Access   Huànyǐng Wǎngbā, a small 24-hour Internet room, is in Qǔyì Guǎn, the lane next to the Yán'ān Bīnguǎn, at the top of the outdoor stairway. The access rate is ¥2 (25¢) per hour. Keep your eyes open as you travel around the town and you'll find many other Internet cafes conveniently located around the city. Dial-up is © **163.**

Post Office   The post office is on Zhōngxīn Jiē, south of Yán'ān Bīnguǎn. It also offers 24-hour Internet access.

IN & AROUND TOWN

Between 1936 and 1947 the Communists had four different bases in Yán'ān; each of which comprised cave homes common to the area. Each site is actually very similar, featuring homes cut out of the side of the loess hills, and with a spartan air about them. The rooms are simple, with only basic comforts, such as a desk, chair, and *kàng,* the coal-heated brick platform beds. Shops at each of the sites sell a variety of revolutionary kitsch. You can take public bus nos. 1, 7, 8, and 13 to visit these sites. A taxi can be hired to visit all four for about ¥100 ($13).

Bǎo Tǎ (Bǎo Pagoda)   Built in the Sòng dynasty and renovated in the 1950s, the 44m (144-ft.) Bǎo Pagoda, which can be seen from anywhere in the city, is a national symbol of China. The structure is located on a hill on the southeast side of the Yán River and offers excellent views of the city and nearby countryside.

Bǎo Pagoda, seen from anywhere in the city, can be reached on foot from the downtown area within just a few minutes. Admission ¥20 ($2.45) and another ¥5 (60¢) to climb the pagoda. 8am–6pm (to 5:30pm in winter).

Fènghuáng Shān (Phoenix Hill)   During the months after the Long March when the Communist Party first arrived in Yán'ān, it chose this site for its headquarters. Of greatest interest are the cave dwellings of Máo Zédōng, Zhōu Ēnlái, and Zhū Dé, who lived here between 1937 and 1938. Brick floors, simple wooden furniture, and graceful window lattices give these austere rooms a cozy quality. On display are intriguing photographs from the Yán'ān years, Yán'ān currency, and the raised *kàng.* On sale are attractive black-and-white prints with proletarian themes by a local artist.

Entrance on Zhōngxīn Jiē, a few hundred yards south of the Yán'ān Hotel, before the post office. Admission ¥7 (75¢). 8am–6pm (to 5:30pm in winter).

Gémìng Jìniànguǎn (Revolutionary Memorial Hall/Museum)   While Máo lies under glass in Běijīng, the trusty white steed that transported him through northern Shǎnxī in 1947 stands stuffed behind glass at this museum. According to the sign on the window, the horse, who was then living in the Běijīng Zoo, one day turned in the direction of Zhōng Nán Hǎi (where Máo was living at the time), neighed loudly, and went on to join Marx. Unfortunately, there is no English signage, so without a familiarity with the players, the photographs on display have little meaning. That said, the museum houses an interesting collection of old weapons, many of them handmade and crude, personal effects, and military gear. Unless you have a deep knowledge of Communist Party history, the museum—established in 1950 as "a classroom for advancing patriotism, revolutionary tradition, and the Yán'ān spirit"—shouldn't take more than a half-hour of your time.

Northwest of the city center along Zǎoyuán Lù. Admission ¥15 ($1.85). 8am–6pm (to 5:30pm in winter).

Wángjiāpíng Gémìng Jiùzhǐ (Former Revolutionary Headquarters at Wángjiāpíng)
A 5-minute walk south of Gémìng Jìniànguǎn is the site of the general office of the Eighth Route Army and headquarters of the CCP Central Military Commission from 1937 to 1947. Máo, Zhū Dé, Zhōu Ēnlái, and other top brass also lived here at various times. In March 1947, as the Guómíndǎng (KMT) army moved into northern Shǎnxī, the CCP abandoned Yán'ān, and during the following 13 months of Nationalist government occupation, the Wángjiāpíng buildings were destroyed. Some years later, after the end of the civil war, they were restored according to the original layout and design. The simple mud dwellings and halls, with their low-pitched rooflines and arched doorways and windows that mimic the surrounding hills, are worthy of Frank Lloyd Wright in the way they blend with the natural environment. The site is similar to Fènghuáng Shān (above), but on a much larger scale. If you don't have time for both, this is the one to see.

Situated on Zǎoyuán Lù. Admission ¥12 ($1.50). 8am–6pm (to 5:30pm in winter).

Yángjiālíng Jiùzhǐ (Yángjiālíng Revolutionary Headquarters)
The Communist pantheon of Máo, Zhū Dé, Zhōu Ēnlái, and Liú Shàoqí all lived here at one time or another, but this was also the site of the famous Yán'ān Forum on Literature and Art in May 1942. The forum, in which Máo argued that art and literature should serve the people, was to have a profound impact on the arts in China in the following decades. Visitors to Máo's room toss cigarettes onto the former leader's bed as a sign of respect.

Northwest of the Revolutionary Memorial Hall. Admission ¥15 ($1.85). 8am–6pm (to 5:30pm in winter).

WHERE TO STAY
Many Yán'ān hotels still cannot accept foreigners, so choices are limited.

Yán'ān Bīnguǎn   Dignitaries such as Ho Chi Minh, Lee Kuan Yew, Zhōu Ēnlái, and Jiāng Zémín have stayed at this Soviet-style hotel, but until an upgrade in 2000, it had only three stars. In some ways, nothing's changed. Although guest rooms are clean and comfortable (but absolutely generic), water pressure is poor and there's only cold water from the sink faucet. The hotel is several decades old and still feels like a government hotel, which it is. The staff seems slightly suspicious of guests.

Zhōngxīn Jiē 56. ✆ **0911/288-6666.** Fax 0911/288-6534. 193 units. ¥480–¥580 ($60–$72) standard room; ¥1,160–¥2,880 ($145–$360) suite. Most rates include breakfast. 20% discount available. 10% service charge. No credit cards. Bus: no. 2, 3, or 12 from railway station. **Amenities:** 2 restaurants; bar; indoor pool; ticketing; business center; forex; limited room service; dry cleaning/laundry. *In room:* A/C, TV, Internet access, fridge.

Yàshèng Dàjiǔdiàn   A welcoming, efficient staff and bustling lobby make this three-star hotel instantly more inviting than the Yán'ān Bīnguǎn. And while its hallways are dim and rather cavernous, guest rooms are almost comparable to those at the four-star Yán'ān. Slightly smaller, they are nonetheless clean and well maintained. An advantage to the location is that the area is lively and full of restaurants and food stalls.

Èr Dào Jiē, Zhōng Duàn. ⓒ **0911/213-2778.** Fax 0911/213-2779. 189 units. ¥228–¥380 ($28–$47) standard room. No credit cards. **Amenities:** 2 restaurants; ticketing; business center; forex; limited room service; dry cleaning/laundry. *In room:* A/C, TV.

Yínhǎi Guójì Dàjiǔdiàn (Silver Seas International Hotel)   The city's newest and most fashionable hotel is conveniently located in the center of the city, just 5 minutes from the rail station. The staff is professional, and unlike the other hotels in Yán'ān, the rooms of this four-star property are bright, modern-looking, and spacious.

Dà Qiáo Jiē. ⓒ **0911/213-9999.** Fax 0911/213-9666. 212 units. ¥598–¥688 ($72–$83) superior and deluxe rooms. No credit cards. **Amenities:** 2 restaurants; pool; health club; ticketing; business center; forex; 24-hr. room service; dry cleaning/laundry. In room: A/C, TV, Internet access, fridge.

WHERE TO DINE

One of the best areas to find good, inexpensive dishes is along Èr Dào Jiē in the vicinity and north of Yàshèng Hotel. In warm weather this is a popular stretch for evening strolls. Along nearby Dà Qiáo Jiē, you'll also find outdoor stalls and small restaurants selling *jiǎozi* (Chinese ravioli), meat kabobs, *yángròu pào mó* (mutton soup), and pasta, including *dāoxiāo miàn*—knife-pared noodles—made by paring slices off a block of pasta dough into a large pot of boiling water. Supposedly, in earlier days, the chef placed a clump of dough atop his cotton skullcap and, with a knife in each hand, whittled away above his head—pasta strips flying—until all the dough was in the pot.

Wúqí Dàjiǔdiàn ✿✿ SHĂNXĪ   Despite its simple, somewhat dingy (but clean) appearance, this is probably the best restaurant in the city. Locals crowd the place every evening, chatting noisily as they toast each other between mouthfuls of tasty Shǎnxī specialities. The drink of choice is *mǐjiǔ*, an alcoholic beverage made from millet; this local version, served heated from a small kettle, is a bit cloudy and sweet, and it goes well with the local cuisine. Among the tasty offerings are *huángmómo* (sweet steamed millet cake), *yóumómo* (fried doughnut made of millet), *kǔcài tǔdòu* (mashed potatoes with wild vegetables), *niúròu liángfěn* (bean-starch noodles fried with beef), *qiáomiàn héle* (pressed buckwheat noodles with a vinaigrette dressing), and *yóugāo* (a pan-fried sticky rice cake).

Běiguān Jiē, opposite Yánán Middle School. ⓒ **0911/213-9720.** Fax 0911/213-2779. Meal for 2 ¥25–¥40 ($3–$5). No credit cards. Breakfast 7–9am; lunch 10am–2pm; dinner 4:30–9:30pm.

5 Píngyáo ✿

Shānxī Province, 616km (383 miles) SW of Běijīng, 100km (62 miles) S of Tàiyuán, 540km (335 miles) NE of Xī'ān

The great majority of Chinese cities have histories extending back hundreds and often thousands of years, but few have anything outside of a museum to show for it. The central Shānxī city of Píngyáo is an exception. This 2,700-year-old city had its heyday during the late Míng and Qīng dynasties, and the walled city that survives today was largely built then, though a few Yuán dynasty structures also survive. Chinese and overseas travelers come to this area to see some of the best-preserved traditional architecture in China: gray-brick courtyard homes *(sìhéyuàn)*, extravagant family mansions (one of which was the set for Zhāng Yìmóu's *Raise the Red Lantern*), a Míng city wall, Daoist and Buddhist temples, and China's earliest commercial banks. Visitors also get to stay in restored courtyards, sleep on a *kàng* (heated brick bed), and eat wonderful Shānxī cuisine, which for some reason has yet to catch on in the West.

But Píngyáo isn't all quaintness and old-world charm. Like any place in China dependent on tourism, it has an overabundance of vehicles of every kind, fake antiques, touts, and, well, tourists. As more residents of the old city are moved to modern apartments with modern plumbing, this World Heritage city faces the threat of becoming an over-precious imitation of itself. But for now, Píngyáo still has the vitality of a thriving town behind the veneer of an ancient one. *Note:* Turn to appendix A for Chinese translations of key locations.

ESSENTIALS

GETTING THERE   Overnight **trains** from Běijīng save you a night's hotel stay and arrive in Píngyáo in the morning. The Tàiyuán–Yùnchéng train, the K25/K27, stops in Píngyáo; so does the Xī'ān–Tiānjīn train, the 2562; and the Tàiyuán–Xī'ān train, the 2535. For sleepers, you may have to leave from Tàiyuán. Luxury **buses** from Běijīng's Lìzé Qiáo Long-Distance Bus Station leave every 20 minutes (6 hr.; ¥120/ $15). Transfer to a direct Iveco bus to Píngyáo (2 hr.; ¥25/$3.15). The new expressway from Běijīng to Píngyáo has reduced the total drive to 6 hours. There are three to six buses daily connecting with Xī'ān (8 hr.; ¥115/$14).

GETTING AROUND   Trains and buses arrive at the Píngyáo **railway station** in the "modern" city that is west of the ancient wall. The 7-minute ride by **bicycle rickshaw** to the old city is ¥5 to ¥10 (60¢–$1.20), depending on your negotiating skills. Taxis are only allowed into the narrow streets of old Píngyáo during the very early morning hours, so if you arrive later in the day, walk a short stretch or take a bicycle rickshaw. The better courtyard hotels will arrange free pickup with a taxi for people arriving on the morning train. Most of the courtyard hotels are in the vicinity of the Shì Lóu (Market Building)—the tallest building in sight—at the center of the ancient town, on Nán Dàjiē (also called Míng Qīng Jiē).

The old town has only four main streets and a number of small lanes, so most places are within walking or biking distance. A ride on a motorcycle or bicycle rickshaw to places within the wall costs only a few yuán. A bicycle rickshaw that can accommodate two people can be hired for ¥40 ($5) for a whole day. Several of the courtyard hotels rent bicycles. There's also **bike rental** at Xī Dàjiē 50 (near Běi Dàjiē).

TOURS   Most of the courtyard hotels can arrange cars and buy bus and train tickets for a small fee.

FAST FACTS

Banks, Foreign Exchange & ATMs   None available, but many of the hotels will exchange major foreign currencies, including U.S. dollars, euro, and yen.

Internet Access   Internet cafes can be found throughout the old town, and in the dining and lobby areas of many courtyard hotels. They charge ¥5 (60¢) per hour. Dial-up is ✆ **169.**

Post Office   The old town's post office is at Xī Dàjiē 1.

EXPLORING THE TOWN

The ancient town within the 6km-long (4-mile) city wall is ideal for walking. Take your map, head in any direction, and you're bound to find traditional architectural and cultural gems. On the way, you'll get to see how some of the 30,000 current residents of Píngyáo live. While in the past tickets had to be purchased separately for each site, visitors must now buy a 2-day pass for ¥120 ($15) that allows entrance to the town's 20 most popular sites. These sites are openfrom 8am to 7pm in the summer, to 6pm in the winter. A few lesser-known sites in town still require a separate ticket.

A good first stop is the three-story **Shì Lóu (Market Building)** that marks the city center and affords the best view of the old town. The well-preserved Míng dynasty **ancient city wall** *(gǔ chéngqiáng),* made of rammed earth and bricks, also affords views of the old city and outlying areas. It takes about an hour to walk the circumference of the wall. Near the center of town, **Rì Shēng Chāng** and **Bǎi Chuān Tōng**—headquarters of two of 19th-century China's leading money exchanges—are reminders that this remote town was once the financial center of the Qīng government. Both compounds have been transformed into museums that look much more like elegant courtyard residences than banks. Restored and rebuilt, Rì Shēng Chāng (Xī Dàjiē 38) is an engaging museum consisting of three courtyards and almost two dozen halls and rooms.) Bǎi Chuān Tōng (Nán Dàjiē 109) is now a furniture museum consisting of bedrooms, parlors, a kitchen, and a room for taking snuff (and probably opium)—all furnished and decorated in Míng and Qīng styles.

A few blocks southeast of the Market Building on Chénghuáng Miào Jiē are three Daoist temples in one, the **Chénghuáng Miào, Cáishén Miào,** and **Zàojūn Miào,** honoring the City God, the God of Wealth, and the Kitchen God. The separate but connected buildings are meant to imitate the arrangement of the government seat and its offices. Start at the Temple of the City God. At the back, where scriptures would normally be, the walls have *trompe l'oeil* murals of bookshelves filled with books and scrolls. Turn right (east) to get to the Kitchen God Temple. To get to the less obvious Temple of the God of Wealth, go to the back of the first temple and take the door to the left (west). This Míng dynasty complex burned down twice and was last rebuilt in 1864. Follow Chénghuáng Miào Jiē west (where it becomes Zhèngfǔ Jiē) to visit the **Xiànyá Shǔ** (or Yámen). This was the administrative office that meted out justice, such as it was, during the Míng and Qīng dynasties. On the east side, there was a summoning drum *(dēngwén gǔ).* When someone had a complaint, they beat the drum to call for the Yámen chief, who would then hear the case and make his judgment. You may catch performers in rehearsal for operas and reenactments of trials that are performed here at select times throughout the week. A fine example of a wealthy urban residence, the former home of pioneering banker Léi Lǚtài, **Léi Lǚtài Gùjū,** Shūyuàn Jiē, is also worth a visit for its four rows of connecting courtyards, each in a different style. In the front courtyard, a "certified fortune-teller" reads hands, faces, and astrological charts—alas, only in Chinese.

A Buddhist temple (open 8am–6pm; ¥20/$2.45) within biking or driving distance of Píngyáo is **Zhènguó Sì,** 12km (7½ miles) northeast of the old town. Its **Wànfó Diàn (Palace of Ten Thousand Buddhas),** from the Táng dynasty, is another of China's oldest timber-frame buildings. Inside, its impressive statuary dates to the Five Dynasties (907–960). One of the pleasures of this less-visited temple is its tranquil atmosphere, due in part to an absence of touts and souvenir stalls.

OUT OF TOWN
Qiáo Jiā Dàyuàn 👍👍   This is the best-known of Shānxī's merchant-family mansions *(dàyuàn,* or "grand courtyards"), and where Zhāng Yìmóu's *Raise the Red Lantern* was filmed. Almost midway between Tàiyuán and Píngyáo, it is easily reached from either city. Containing six large courtyards and 313 houses, the compound was constructed in 1755 by Qiáo Guìfā, the first member of the family to strike it rich selling tea and bean curd in Bāotóu, beyond the Great Wall. Returning to his hometown, he built his dream home, to which successive generations added until it reached its present size. Give yourself at least 2 hours.

Admission ¥40 ($5). 8am–7:30pm (to 6pm in winter). Avoid weekends. Buses between Píngyáo and Tàiyuán will drop you off. Follow signs to Qiáo Family Courtyard (10-min. walk). Round-trip taxi 40 min. from Píngyáo, 45 min. from midtown Tàiyuán, is ¥150 ($18).

Shuānglín Sì ✿   This Buddhist temple is 6km (4 miles) southwest of Píngyáo and easily reached by bicycle, motor-rickshaw (¥20–¥30/$2.45–$3.65 round-trip), or taxi ¥50 ($6). Built in the 6th century, the complex underwent large-scale renovations during the Míng dynasty. It is most famous for the 2,000-plus painted statues distributed among 10 halls in three connected courtyards. Highlights include the arhats in **Tiānwáng Diàn.** Princely and dignified, they are a refreshing change from the usual gilded, grotesque variety. Statues of worshippers depict commoners in everyday dress looking humble and devout and nothing like the serene, finely clad bodhisattvas nearby. In the **Púsa Diàn (Bodhisattva Palace),** which contains a thousand-armed Guānyīn, look up at the ceiling where the green, three-clawed, round-bellied figure of a guard keeps watch.

Qiáotóu Cūn. Admission ¥25 ($3). 8am–6pm (8:30am–5pm winter).

Wáng Family Courtyard (Wáng Jiā Dàyuàn) ✿✿   Sixty kilometers (37 miles) south of Píngyáo, this *dàyuàn* dwarfs the Qiáo family's mansion. First constructed in the mid–17th century, its expansion continued for over a century. Walking through the 123 courtyards and 1,118 houses takes around 3 hours, but the time is well spent. The decorative lattice screens and windows, shaped openings between rooms and courtyards, and undulating partition walls are exquisite examples of Míng and Qīng vernacular architecture. Rarely are so many classic styles found all in one place. Also of note and well worth looking for are the cave dwellings at the compound's periphery.

Admission ¥60 ($7.30). 8am–7:30pm (to 6pm in winter). Buses connect Tàiyuán and Píngyáo to the town nearest Wáng Jiā Dàyuàn, Língshí Chéng. Buses between Língshí Chéng and Wáng Jiā Dàyuàn leave every 10 min. and cost ¥1 (15¢). Round-trip taxi from Píngyáo is ¥200 ($24).

Yí Yuán (Grace Vineyard) ✿✿ *Finds*   This Hong Kong–Chinese joint venture winery, which is run by a French wine master, produces probably the best wine in China—but it's exported to Europe. This countryside winery, about 90 minutes from Píngyáo on the road to Tàiyuán, is a pleasant place to visit. You can sample some of the excellent wine, examine the state-of-the-art production facilities, and walk through the vineyard and adjoining fruit orchards.

Free admission. Round-trip private taxi (¥300/$37) can be arranged through the Tiān Yuán Kuí hotel listed below.

WHERE TO STAY

There are now many courtyard hotels within the old town, and more opening every day. Prices vary and bargaining is expected. Standard and deluxe rooms are decorated in Qīng style and have large *kàng* heated brick beds and small modern bathrooms. Budget rooms have conventional beds and less traditional ornamentation. Guesthouses do not accept foreign credit cards, but the better ones exchange major foreign currencies. Most, including the two guesthouses recommended here, have bike rentals for ¥2 to ¥15 (25¢–$1.85) per day.

Déjū Yuán ✿✿   A gracious host, excellent cooking, and attention to decor make this—along with Tiān Yuán Kuí (below)—one of the top two courtyard guesthouses in town. Attractive standard rooms come with large *kàng* beds. A three-room suite has two bedrooms connected by a living room and is ideal for families. Bathrooms are slightly bigger than those elsewhere in town.

Xī Dàjiē 43. ✆ **0354/568-5266.** Fax 0354/568-5366. www.pydjy.com. 19 units. ¥138–¥288 ($17–$36) small to large standard rooms; ¥160–¥488 ($20–$61) suite. 20% discount Nov–Mar. No credit cards. **Amenities:** Restaurant; ticketing; free transport from railway station; laundry. *In room:* A/C, TV.

Tiān Yuán Kuí 🐦🐦 Like Déjū Yuán, this appealing courtyard guesthouse, which opened in 2000, gets a mix of Chinese, European, and North American guests. Aware of growing competition, its savvy proprietors have continually renovated and added services and facilities to keep ahead of the pack. In 2003 the guesthouse added Internet access and a sauna. One of its biggest attractions is its Shǎnxī opera performances *(Jìn jù),* which are likely to occur on hot summer nights when the guesthouse is full and the performers available.

Nán Dàjiē (Míng Qīng Jiē) 73. ✆ **0354/568-0069.** Fax 0354/568-3052. www.pytyk.com. 20 units. ¥120–¥150 ($15–$19) standard room; ¥150 ($19) 2-person room. No credit cards. **Amenities:** Restaurant; ticketing; free transport from railway station; dry cleaning/laundry; Internet access. *In room:* A/C, TV, no phone.

WHERE TO DINE

Most Píngyáo restaurants specialize in Shǎnxī and local cuisine, which emphasize wheat pastas, meat pies, Píngyáo beef (similar to corned beef in color and taste), and fried cakes and breads. Two of the best restaurants in town are in the recommended **Déjū Yuán** and **Tiān Yuán Kuí** guesthouses. Dinner for two costs ¥30 to ¥50 ($3.65–$6.10). Nearly every restaurant in town serves a version of *lǎolao yóumiàn* (sometimes called *wōwo*). These small rings of husked-oat pasta are served pressed together in a bamboo steamer. The sauce that accompanies the dish varies from place to place, but Déjū Yuán serves one of the best. The pasta is so substantial that it almost tastes like cornmeal, while the tomato-based sauce—flavorful and slightly hot—is reminiscent of a light tamale sauce. *Xiāngsū jī* (crispy aromatic chicken) is also highly recommended, as is the lightly sweet *yóuzhá gāo* (crispy puff with date and red bean paste). Try corned beef with potatoes *(tǔdòu shāo niúròu)* at Tiān Yuán Kuí; or try any of their numerous noodle dishes, made from husked oat, yellow bean, or sorghum flour. Most famous is the pasta shaped like little cats' ears *(māo ěrduo).* Both restaurants also serve excellent Western breakfasts, including delicious omelets and fruit crepes. For a drink or dessert, try the Sakura Café, which also has a popular branch in Lìjiāng, Yúnnán province, located on the corner of Xī Dàjiē and Nán Dàjiē.

In the lanes, look for the **mobile stand** selling "beggar's" chicken *(jiàohuā jī).* The chicken is wrapped in two layers of paper, then packed in loess mud ("yellow earth") and cooked over an open fire for 2 hours.

6 Tàiyuán

Shǎnxī Province, 500km (310 miles) SW of Běijīng, 651km (405 miles) NE of Xī'ān

During the 77 years of disunion that followed the collapse of the Táng dynasty, northern China was up for grabs by the various kingdoms that came to be known as the Five Dynasties (907–960). Each laid claim to Tàiyuán (then called Jìnyáng) until the first emperor of the Sòng dynasty (960–1279) stepped in and annihilated the city, going so far as to divert the Fén River so that it would wash away any evidence that Jìnyáng ever existed. Modern Tàiyuán—the capital of Shǎnxī Province—is located on the site of the rebuilt city.

Today things are more tranquil, but not necessarily better for your health. A 1999 report found this sooty industrial city to be the most polluted in the country and city officials, shamed into action, began to take strides toward cleanup. Still, you may want to limit your stay in this environmentally challenged city to a day or two at most.

ESSENTIALS

GETTING THERE   **Wǔsù Airport** is 15km (9 miles) southeast of town. Useful connections include flights from Hong Kong (one flight weekly), Běijīng (several flights daily), Shànghǎi (one or two flights daily), and Xī'ān (four flights daily). **China Eastern Airlines** runs an airport shuttle bus from its office at Yíngzé Dàjiē 158, 2 hours before flights; shuttle fare is ¥10 ($1.20). The main **railway station** is on the east side of town at the start of Yíngzé Dàjiē. An overnight connection with Běijīng leaves either point around 9pm and arrives by 7:30am (K701/K702; ¥230/$28 soft sleeper). The K717 from Běijīng's West Station leaves at 9:50pm and arrives at 7:10am. Other useful connections are Dàtóng (K745/K746, K747/K748; 6½ hr.; ¥156/$19 soft sleeper); Píngyáo on the Tàiyuán–Yùnchéng route (K25/K27; 2 hr.; ¥10–¥28/$1.20–$3.40); Xī'ān on the Tiānjīn route, which also stops in Píngyáo (2562; from Tàiyuán to Xī'ān 2535; 11½ hr.; ¥180/$22 soft sleeper). Most long-distance buses connect with Tàiyuán's **Main Bus Station (Qìchēzhàn)** opposite the railway station, but a few from Wǔtái Shān arrive at a small bus station 7km (4 miles) southwest of the city. From there, bus no. 815 (¥1/15¢) leaves every 5 minutes for the railway station and main hotel area. Luxury buses link Tàiyuán's Main Bus Station with Běijīng's Lìzé Qiáo Bus Station (6 hr.; ¥120/$15), Píngyáo (2 hr.; ¥15–¥25/$1.85–$3), Wǔtái Shān/Táihuái (4 hr.; ¥43/$5.25), and Dàtóng (5 hr.; ¥70/$8.55).

GETTING AROUND   City **bus** fare is ¥1 (12¢); with air-conditioning, the fare is ¥2 (25¢). The most common **taxi** is the Fùkāng. The fare for the first 4km (2½ miles) is ¥7 (85¢); after that it's ¥1 (15¢) per kilometer. Beyond 10km (6¼ miles), it's ¥1.50 (20¢) per kilometer.

TOURS   A helpful branch of **CITS** is at Píngyáng Lù 38 (© 0351/882-2777).

FAST FACTS

Banks, Foreign Exchange & ATMs   The **Bank of China** (open Mon–Fri, 8am–noon and 2:30–6:30pm; to 6pm in winter) at Yíngzé Dàjiē 288 has an ATM and full foreign-exchange facilities.

Internet Access   There's a small 24-hour *wǎngbā* at Shàngmǎ Jiē 54, on the way to Chóngshàn Sì. It charges ¥2 (25¢) per hour. The **Xīnyí Wǎngbā**, with the same hours and rates, is just around the corner at Shàngmǎ Jiē 20. Enter through a courtyard with grapevines. Internet dial-up is © 169.

Post Office   The main post office (Mon–Fri, 8am–noon, 2:30–6:30pm; winter 6pm) is opposite the railway station.

Visa Extensions   The **PSB** is at Hóujiā Xiàng 9 (© 0351/461-2787; open Mon–Fri 8:15–11:45am and 2:45–5:45pm).

EXPLORING TÀIYUÁN

A new provincial museum is rumored to open at the end of 2005, but for the time being the collection is divided between two sites—the Daoist temple Chúnyáng Gōng and the former Confucian temple Wén Miào. **Chúnyáng Gōng** (Qǐfēng Jiē 1, around the block from KFC) is dedicated to Lǚ Dòngbīn, the Táng dynasty poet, calligrapher, and wine connoisseur who, by the time of the Sòng dynasty, was worshipped as one of

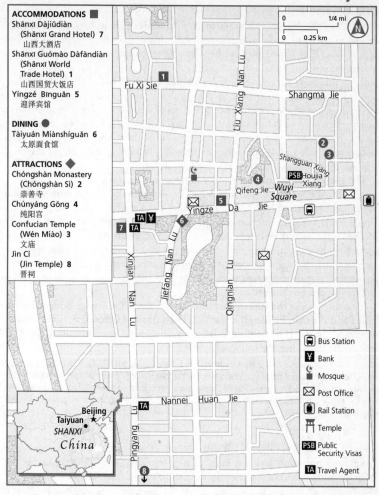

the Eight Immortals of Daoism. He's usually depicted as an impassive scholar with two long wisps of mustache and a thin pointed beard, holding a double-edged sword given to him by a dragon. The main hall is the **Lǚ Zǔ Diàn,** which is dedicated to him. Behind that is a tight group of halls, each containing a portion of the museum's collection. Pieces of pottery are from the Sòng and Jīn dynasties, and the bronze collection has wine vessels that date from the Shāng dynasty (1600–1045 B.C.) The temple is open from 9am to 6pm (to 5pm in winter); admission is ¥5 (60¢). The painting and calligraphy portion of the collection (from the Míng and Qīng dynasties) is in the former **Confucian Temple (Wén Miào)** on Shàngguān Xiàng. The grounds have gardens and covered walkways, making this a pleasant place to amble. Hours are from 9am to noon and 2:30 to 6:30pm in summer; 9am to 5pm in winter. Admission is ¥2 (25¢).

OUT OF TOWN

Jìn Cí (Jìn Temple) ⭐⭐   The site of Jìn Cí is a large park with gardens and a lake, as well as pavilions, halls, and temples from various dynasties, beginning with the Sòng (960–1279). It isn't known when the original temple was built, but the earliest written reference to Jìn Cí is from the 6th century. As you stroll the grounds, the one building that must not be overlooked is **Shèngmǔ Diàn (Hall of the Holy Mother).** Located at the back of the park, it is recognizable by its double-eaved roof and its extraordinary writhing dragons, each carved out of wood and coiled around one of the building's eight front columns. First completed in 1032, the hall was restored several times—most recently in the Míng dynasty—but without ever altering the original architectural style and design. Today, along with a handful of other Shānxī buildings, it is one of the earliest surviving wooden halls in China.

The contents of the hall are equally impressive. Inside is a statue of the honored matriarch—the mother of the founder of Jìn—surrounded by a retinue of life-size handmaidens, actresses, and eunuchs. Dating to the Sòng, these gorgeous painted clay figures reveal much about court customs and dress. Sitting in lotus position, the Holy Mother is the picture of composure. Standing third in attendance on her right is a eunuch with one ear bigger than the other and one eye crossed—from listening intently to his mistress while never daring to look at her directly. Some of the actresses are dressed as male characters, evident from their stances—toes pointed outwards—and flat-topped headdresses.

Directly opposite the Hall of the Holy Mother, across the **Flying Bridge Over the Fish Pond (Yúzhǎo Fēiliáng),** is the **Xiàn Diàn (Hall of Offerings),** where offerings were made to the Holy Mother, believed to have magic powers. Built in 1168 and rebuilt 400 years later, the hall was last restored in 1955.

Admission ¥40 ($5). Summer 8am–6:30pm; winter 8:30am–5:30pm. Bus: no. 804 (¥2/25¢) from railway station or on Xīnjiàn Nán Lù, just south of Yíngzé intersection in front of the Industrial and Commercial Bank. On arrival, motorcycle-taxi drivers may try to convince you that the distance to the temple is too far to walk; in fact, it's a short (10-min.) walk through the park. Cross the parking lot and go through a small film-and-map store to the park entrance on the other side.

WHERE TO STAY

Shānxī Dàjiǔdiàn (Shānxī Grand Hotel)   Plush sofas, high-ceilinged guest rooms, and real plants give this hotel an edge over the Yíngzé Bīnguǎn (see below). Business suites include a computer in the room and free Internet access.

Xīnjiàn Nán Lù 5. ⓒ 0351/404-2899. Fax 0351/404-2891. 166 units. ¥680 ($85) standard room; ¥1,530–¥1,700 ($190–$210) suite. Most rates include breakfast. 30% discount available. 15% service charge. AE, DC, MC, V. Bus: no. 1 from railway station. **Amenities:** 2 restaurants; bar; indoor pool; health club; sauna; bowling lanes; ticketing; airport shuttle; business center; forex; limited room service; dry cleaning/laundry. *In room:* A/C, satellite TV, dataport, minibar, fridge, hair dryer, safe.

Shānxī Guómào Dàfàndiàn (Shānxī World Trade Hotel) ⭐   This is Tàiyuán's first five-star hotel, and while the lobby is grand, and the rooms quite spacious and comfortable, the service is still a bit rough around the edges for an expensive hotel. That said, this is the most comfortable and modern hotel in the city, with facilities and amenities that can be found in most five-star international hotels.

Fùxī Jiē. ⓒ 0351/868-8888. Fax 0351/868-9888. www.sxwtc.com. 398 units. ¥740 ($90) standard room; ¥1,265 ($155) deluxe. Discount available. AE, DC, MC, V. **Amenities:** 2 restaurants; bar; indoor pool; fitness center; sauna; ticketing; business center; forex; limited room service; dry cleaning/laundry. *In room:* A/C, satellite TV, dataport (select floors), minibar, fridge, hair dryer, safe.

Yíngzé Bīnguǎn   Last renovated in 1999, this pleasant hotel has a four-star (west) and a two-star (east) wing, and is conveniently located less than 3km (2 miles) south of the railway station. Management and staff go out of their way to meet guests' needs, and the business center's post office is convenient and reliable. Guest rooms are the standard issue (two beds, two chairs, and coffee table) but are clean and well maintained. For convenience and cordiality, this hotel is number one; for luxury, it is second to the Shānxī Grand Hotel.

Yíngzé Dàjiē 189. ⓒ **0351/882-8888.** Fax 0351/882-6688. book@shanxiyingzehotel.com. 457 units. West wing ¥580 ($72) standard room; ¥880–¥2,600 ($110–$325) suite. East wing ¥230 ($29) standard room. 20% discount available. AE, DC, MC, V. Bus: no. 1 or 6 from railway station. **Amenities:** 3 restaurants; bar; indoor pool; outdoor tennis court; fitness center; sauna; ticketing; business center; forex; limited room service; dry cleaning/laundry. *In room:* A/C, satellite TV, dataport (select floors), minibar, fridge, hair dryer, safe.

WHERE TO DINE

Shānxī cuisine is famous for its buckwheat, sorghum, bean, and potato-flour pastas—all currently enjoying increased popularity in China—as well as for its vinegar *(cù)*. A favorite dish that employs potato-flour noodles, vinegar, soy sauce, and spring onion is *liángfěn*. Served cold, the dish is particularly refreshing on muggy summer evenings. Like Italian pastas, *cuōjiāner* (twisted points), *māo ěrduo* (cats' ears), and a variety of others are named for their shapes. Two winter specialties are Shānxī beef or lamb hot pot *(huǒguō)* and—for breakfast—mutton soup *(tóunǎo)*. Made with fatty mutton, yam, lotus, and herbs (to mask the gamy taste), it goes well with the flatbread called *xiǎobǐng* and fortifies you against the winter cold.

The best place to get these local specialties is at the **night market** Māoér Xiāng, which is lined with some small stands and a number of restaurants serving local specialities and various other Chinese cuisines.

For fast food, **McDonald's** is on Yíngzé Dàjiē catty-corner from Wǔyī Square; it's open from 7am to midnight. **KFC** is on the corner of Liǔxiàng Nán Lù and Yíngzé Dàjiē and elsewhere around the city. The **Tiānlóng Supermarket,** on the northwest corner of Yíngzé Dàjiē and Xīnjiàn Lù, has a decent **bakery** as well as a variety of snacks and a well-stocked supermarket.

Tàiyuán Miànshíguǎn ⚔ *Value* SHĀNXĪ   This excellent restaurant serves typical Shānxī dishes. Try *guòyóu ròu* (pork "passed through oil"), *māo ěrduo* (cats' ears), actually small triangles of dough served in a soup or fried with meat and vegetables, *liángfěn*, a cold potato-flour noodle dressed in vinegar and soy sauce, and other local dishes. The restaurant, which has two large levels, is bright and very clean, and is popular with businesspeople and upper-middle-class Chinese.

Jiěfàng Lù 17. ⓒ **0351/404-1881.** Meal for 2 ¥25–¥40 ($3–$5). No credit cards. 10am–3pm and 5:30–9:30pm.

7 Wǔtái Shān ⚔

Shānxī Province, 327km (203 miles) SW of Běijīng, 210km (130 miles) S of Dàtóng, 238km (148 miles) N of Tàiyuán

The mountain known as Wǔtái or "Five Platforms" is actually a cluster of mountains, which long ago collectively became the northernmost sacred peak of Buddhism. Situated roughly halfway between Dàtóng and Tàiyuán, Wǔtái Shān is, in Buddhist lore, the earthly residence of the great bodhisattva Manjusri. Often depicted astride a lion, he is said to embody the perfection of wisdom. To this day, though tourists far outnumber them, pilgrims come entreating Manjusri to reveal himself again. The peaks of Wǔtái Shān have an average height of 2,000m (6,561 ft.) above sea level, and from northeast to southwest they stretch 120km (75 miles). Cradled at their center is the small town of Táihuái Zhèn, with an elevation of 1,680m (5,500 ft.). Part tourist slum, part sacred site, the town is a combination of souvenir shops, restaurants, temples, and shrines. Summer is the best time to visit—when Wǔtái Shān offers an escape from the heat and humidity of lower climes. In July and August, the average temperature is only about 50°F (10°C), with warm days and cool nights. Even at this most temperate time of year, the mountain itself is rarely overcrowded during the week. Weekends are another story, and national holidays should be avoided at all costs. Winters are severely cold, with temperatures dipping as low as –40°F (–40°C). Even in June, snow is not unheard of.

One of the liveliest of Wǔtái's temple festivals is held on the 14th and 15th days of the 6th lunar month, when demons are exorcised and the Diamond Sutra is honored in a ritual dance. All who join the parade from Púsa Dǐng to Luóhàn Temple are promised blessings. *Note:* Turn to appendix A for Chinese translations of key locations.

ESSENTIALS

GETTING THERE   Most visitors arrive by bus from Tàiyuán to the south or Dàtóng to the north. Wǔtái Shān has no airport. The Wǔtái Shān **railway station** is in Shāhé, 48km (30 miles) and an hour-plus drive from Táihuái. There are daily fast trains to and from Běijīng on the Běijīng–Tàiyuán line (K702/701; 6½ hr.; ¥268/$33 air-conditioned soft sleeper); and to and from Tàiyuán (4 hr.; ¥50/$6.10 air-conditioned car). **Buses** between Shāhé Railway Station and Táihuái Zhōngxīn Tíngchē Station leave regularly throughout the day for ¥20 ($2.45). A **taxi** between Shāhé and Táihuái is at least ¥100 ($12). Allow 2 hours if you're catching a train in Shāhé. There are daily buses from Tàiyuán (3½–4 hr.) and Dàtóng (about 5 hr.). Buses drive into town and will drop you at your hotel if you know where you're staying. Air-conditioned luxury buses to Tàiyuán (¥50/$6) depart throughout the day beginning at 6am from the Wǔtái Shān Bus Station on the main street just south of the Friendship Hotel turnoff. The ticket office opens at 5:30am. Buses to Dàtóng leave from various small hotels on the main street beginning around 6am. The fare for an air-conditioned bus is ¥50 ($6). If you'd rather not have to wave one down, ask your hotel or a CITS branch to arrange hotel pickup (no service fee). In summer only, a direct bus to Hohhot leaves daily around 6am from Yíngfáng Street.

Admission to the Wǔtái Shān area is ¥95 ($12). All vehicles are stopped at the gate while an attendant collects money and passengers grumble about government corruption and the latest price hike.

GETTING AROUND   The town of Táihuái in the center of Wǔtái Shān is small enough to cover on foot in a half-hour. The main street (Táihuái Jiē/Yíngfáng Jiē) runs north–south along the Qīngshuǐ River. Minivans troll the stretch from town to the area in the south where the best hotels are, picking up passengers for a few yuán. The mountains rise to the immediate east, while two small streets running west off the main street lead to Táihuái's temple area. Although the streets have names, nobody uses them; even maps dispense with them. Directions to anyplace begin with the name of the nearest temple, many of which can be reached on foot. A cable car goes up to **Dàilóu Peak,** east of the village.

TOURS   Tour buses and taxis go to the mountain temples from the **Wǔtái Shān Tour Taxi Ticket Office (Wǔtái Shān Lǚyóu Chē Chūzū)** on Yíngfáng Street (across from the White Pagoda and the parking lot/night market). Buses carry 15 passengers and don't set out until they're full. They charge ¥30 to ¥35 ($3.75–$4.40) for tours to any one of the five peaks. A 6-hour tour of 10 temples and lamaseries around the mountains (including Nán Shān Sì and Lóngquán Sì) costs ¥48 ($5.85). Taxis will take groups of four to the same sights for ¥5 to ¥10 (60¢–$1.20) more per person. **CITS** has a number of branch offices in Táihuái. The main office is at Míng Qīng Jiē 18 (© **0352/510-2265;** open 7:30am–8pm). They don't have their own vehicles, but they will arrange a car, driver, and English-speaking guide for a full-day tour to the outlying temples for about ¥400 ($48) for two to four people.

FAST FACTS

Banks, Foreign Exchange & ATMs   The **Bank of China** (open 8am–noon and 2:30pm–6:30pm; winter 8:30am–6pm), Yíngfāng Jiē, only exchanges U.S. dollars; no traveler's checks. Restaurants will sometimes change foreign currency, but it's best to arrive with enough yuán for the duration of your stay.

Internet Access   Fēiyǔ Diànnǎo (8am–midnight; ¥4/50¢ per hour) is on the main street as you head south, just before the turnoff to the Friendship Hotel. Look for the ENGLISH INTERNET sign. There are several other Internet cafes in the area around the main street.

Post Office   The post office (8am–8pm; winter 8am–6pm) is on Yíngfāng Jiē after it rounds the corner from the main street, half hidden by souvenir stalls. The entrance is up a staircase behind the stalls.

AROUND THE MOUNTAINS

One of the delights of Táihuái Village is the variety of people it attracts. Nuns, monks, and lamas from different orders and from all over China, Japan, Nepal, and Thailand come to Wǔtái Shān in the summer—some to climb the five terraces, others to simply take part in the many temple activities. The mountain also has a special religious significance for Tibetan Buddhists and so attracts Tibetan monks, nuns, and laypeople from all over China. Ask around and you will usually learn of some mass gathering in one or another of the temples. Alms meals *(dǎzhāi)* for the nuns and monks (paid for by wealthy patrons to amass good karma) take place frequently all summer. Observers are welcome as long as you're quiet and very discreet with cameras.

TEMPLES IN TÁIHUÁI

There are close to a dozen temples in the small town of Táihuái Zhèn. West of town, next to the bell tower, **Xiǎntōng Sì** is the largest and one of the oldest of the temples at Wǔtái Shān. It was first built in A.D. 68; the surviving halls date to the Míng and Qīng dynasties. Climb the belfry for a commanding view of the town and mountains. Also be sure to visit the **Tóng Diàn (Bronze Hall),** which is lined with thousands of miniature statues said to symbolize the myriad bodhisattvas to whom Manjusri read the Buddhist scriptures while he lived on Wǔtái Shān. The bronze roof and outside structures are remarkable for their flawless imitation of timber construction and wood design.

A 5-minute walk south of Xiǎntōng Sì is **Tǎyuàn Sì,** easily recognized by its tall white pagoda which dominates Táihuái's skyline and has become the symbol of Wǔtái Shān. A smaller pagoda is said to contain strands of Manjusri's hair. Equally famed is the two-story **Sutra Library** in Tǎyuàn Sì. At its center is a revolving wooden bookcase that dates from the Míng dynasty. Now empty and unable to turn, it once held more than 20,000 volumes of Buddhist scriptures, written in Chinese, Mongolian, and Tibetan.

Admission to temples ¥3–¥6 (40¢–75¢). 6am–7pm or later.

MOUNTAIN TEMPLES

The temples on the mountains are generally of less note than those in town, but two of the most famous are **Nán Shān Sì** and **Lóngquán Sì**. The former is 2km (1¼ miles) south of Táihuái Zhèn. Lóngquán Temple is another 2km (1¼ miles) in the same direction, so they are easily visited together and, within a few hours, can be done on foot. Like several of Wǔtái's temples, they claim 108 stairs leading to the entrance gate. Though none of them seem to have exactly that number, the point is that the steps represent the 108 worries (or delusions) of mankind. With each step a worry is cast off, so that by the time visitors reach the gate, you are cleansed with sweat and worry-free. A variation on the theme equates the silent and earnest counting of each stone stair with the meditative chanting of the Buddhist rosary (of 108 beads). With every step, the pilgrim has a chance to reach a pure land, free of temptations and defilements. Founded in the Later Liáng dynasty (907–923) and rebuilt in 1937 on seven terraced levels, Nán Shān Sì is one of Wǔtái Shān's largest temples. Visitors come to see its 18 superb clay arhats (enlightened disciples) in the **Hall of the Great Buddha (Dàfó Diàn)**—the sleeping arhat is considered the best for its lifelike posture and craftsmanship. In the same hall, to the right of the large gilded Sakyamuni, look for the white marble statue of Avalokitesvara (Guānyīn) holding a plump baby boy on her knee. Worshippers bring offerings to her in hopes of male offspring. Located at the foot of Wǔtái Shān's central peak, Lóngquán Sì or Dragon Spring Temple has three courtyards connected to one another by moon-shaped gates. The main halls can be found in the east courtyard. At the front, the **Hall of Celestial Kings (Tiān Wáng Diàn)** houses, among others, the Buddha With a Cloth Sack (Bùdài Fó). This rotund Buddha with an exposed potbelly was a Táng dynasty monk who—with his walking stick and sack of worldly belongings—roamed from place to place carefree and begging. He had in his favor the gift of predicting the future and forecasting the weather, and was believed to be an incarnation of Maitreya, the Future Buddha. A purely Chinese creation, he only appears in temples built after the Míng dynasty (1368–1644). The stupa in the central courtyard contains the remains of Pǔjì, the abbot of Nán Shān Temple who died in 1917 believing he, too, was an incarnation of Maitreya. The four images on the sides of the stupa are of Pǔjì/Maitreya at different ages.

TEMPLES BELOW

Two of only three Táng dynasty (618–907) wooden buildings still standing in China—**Nánchán Sì** and **Fóguāng Sì**—are located between Wǔtái Shān and Tàiyuán. With 120km (75 miles) separating them, visiting both in 1 day is best done en route from one town to the other rather than as a day trip from either point. Since both are also well off the main road, they aren't on the regular bus route. Depending on the day of the week and the time of year, a taxi between Tàiyuán and Táihuái Village that includes stops at both temples costs between ¥200 and ¥500 ($24–$61). A day trip from Táihuái Village to both temples and back costs ¥150 to ¥300 ($18–$37). Allow 6 to 7 hours for the round-trip. Buses to Tàiyuán pass the turnoffs to these temples, and those with light luggage can hop off and negotiate with waiting taxis for each side trip.

Nánchán Sì (Temple of Southern Meditation) ✿
About 177km (110 miles) south of Wǔtái Shān, turning west off the main road to Tàiyuán, a dusty loess road leads to this tranquil ancient temple. It's said that this temple escaped the great Táng persecution of Buddhism in 845 because it was so far from the assemblage of temples

on Wŭtái Shān. Today, its small, perfectly proportioned main hall, **Dàfó Diàn (Hall of the Great Buddha),** is reason enough to make the trip. Built in 782, the wooden-frame building has been much restored, but—unlike the other halls in this complex, which are distinctly of Míng and Qīng design—it has retained its original proportions and graceful Táng design. Features to notice are its gently sloping roof, markedly different from the steep gabled roofs of the previous Northern Wèi and Suí dynasties. Along the main roof ridge, the pre-Míng ornaments that curl toward each other are called *chīwěi,* meaning "owl tails." The word refers to a mythical sea monster—one of the sons of the dragon—believed to protect against fire. Inside the hall are 17 Táng dynasty painted clay statues stationed around the large figure of Sakyamuni. The large statue in the far left corner is Manjusri riding a lion.

Fóguāng Sì (Temple of Buddha's Light) ⚔ The temple is 35km (22 miles) south of Táihuái Village. First built during the Northern Wèi dynasty when Buddhism was the official religion, it had greatly expanded by the time it fell victim to the Táng anti-Buddhist campaign of 845. After its total destruction, it was rebuilt 12 years later with the help of a female benefactor named Níng Gōngyú. The one hall associated with her, **Dōng Dàdiàn (Eastern Great Hall),** survives today. Like the Nánchán's Hall of the Great Buddha, it is the only Táng-style building amidst a cluster of mostly Míng and Qīng dynasty halls.

To get to the Eastern Great Hall, follow the cobblestone path through the first courtyard. This leads through a deep archway similar to a city-wall gate, followed by a steep stone staircase. The statues, calligraphy, and wall paintings within are from the Táng (618–907) and Sòng (960–1279) dynasties, while the 296 arhats (enlightened disciples) on either side—remainder of the original 500—date to the Míng. Note the more elaborate bracketing, double roofs, and ridge ornaments of this hall compared with the simple elegance of Nánchán Sì.

SHOPPING

All manner of Buddhist art, clothing, and accouterments are sold in several small shops on and off the main street. Paintings on fabric *(tiáofú)* and religious scrolls sell for around ¥25 ($3).

WHERE TO STAY

Wŭtái Shān has a number of commendable hotels south of town and some satisfactory budget hotels in town. High season is May through October, but even then, hefty discounts are possible Monday to Thursday. There are a numerous small, very inexpensive hotels in the center of Táihuái Zhèn, but cleanliness is a problem, so they're only for people traveling on a very tight budget. You'll be approached by hotel touts if you get off the long-distance bus in this part of town.

Qīxiángé Bīnguǎn ⚔ Off the main road and next to the mountain, Qīxiángé has the best setting and is especially quiet and relaxing, though slightly far from town. The nicest rooms are in the Yèdòu 3 building, but the best views are in the Jǐnxiù building opposite, which is next to the mountain. Slightly smaller, the rooms are still comfortable, and they face a small mountain road favored by cycling teams for their daily workouts.

Off the main street, about 5km (3 miles) south of town. Look on the left for a small bridge that spans a stream. After crossing the bridge, continue for about 200m (650 ft.). Hotel is on the left. ✆ **0350/654-3475.** Fax 0350/654-2183. 93 units. ¥380 ($46) standard room; ¥898 ($110) suite. Some rates include breakfast. 10%–20% discount available. No credit cards. **Amenities:** Restaurant; bar; gym; ticketing; business center; limited room service; dry cleaning/laundry. *In room:* TV, hair dryer.

Yínhǎi Shānzhuāng Built in the Qīng style, this four-story complex, with its gray buildings, red trim, and bright green and gold roofs with upturned eaves, looks almost like another mountain temple. Mostly catering to tour groups, the hotel is a bit dark, but is probably the best hotel in Wǔtái Shān. For the best view, request a room facing south and the Nánchán Sì, which is just a 20-minute walk away.

Xiǎo Nánpō Cūn, on the main street, 3km (2 miles) south of town, opposite Nánchán Sì. © 0350/654-3676. Fax 0350/654-2949. 80 units. ¥625 ($76) standard room; ¥1,280 ($160) suite. 30% discount sometimes available. No credit cards. **Amenities:** 2 restaurants; bar; ticketing; limited room service. *In room:* TV, fridge (some rooms), hair dryer.

WHERE TO DINE

Fúrén Jū Jiǔlóu ✿ SHĀNXĪ Serving everything from dog, deer, and donkey to delicious sesame paste with transparent green-pea noodles *(májiàng fěnpí)*, this clean, pleasant restaurant specializes in local dishes such as *dà dùn gǔtou* (seared pork ribs), *jiàng mèn xiǎo tǔdòu* (stewed baby potato with sesame paste), and *shāo táimó* (simmered wild mushrooms). A sandwich board with some English and photographs of many of the dishes takes the anxiety out of ordering.

Yíngfāng Jiē (on the main street in the north part of town; just south of Guǎnghuà Temple). © 0350/654-5646. Meal for 2 ¥30–¥50 ($3.75–$6.25). No credit cards. 6am–11pm.

Jìngxīn Zhāi ✿✿ VEGETARIAN This restaurant has a worn look to it, but serves excellent vegetarian food. Try some of the following dishes as you listen to soft Buddhist chants being played over and over again: *xǐqì yángyáng* (spicy mock chicken cubes fried with dried red peppers*)*, *luóhàn zhāi* (traditional mixed vegetables fried with bean-starch noodles), *huākāi xiànfó* (mock ham on a bed of braised tofu), and *sùpái* (deep-fried "meat" smothered with succulent brown sauce).

Just off the main street in the north part of town. © 0350/654-5036. Meal for 2 ¥60–¥200 ($7–$24). No credit cards. 11am–3pm and 5–10pm.

Yīzhǎn Míngdēng Quánsù Zhāi ✿✿ VEGETARIAN This clean and pleasant restaurant serves delicious, reasonably priced vegetarian dishes that make it popular with local and visiting monks, nuns, and laypeople. It's a bright, comfortable spot with a large window overlooking the main street. Some of the excellent dishes here include *báiguǒ nánguā bǎo* (stewed gingko nut with pumpkin), *lǎncài ròumò sìjìdòu* (olive leaf fried with string beans), *huākāi xiànfó* (braised tofu in aromatic broth), *jǐnshàng tiānhuā* ("shredded pork" with yúxiāng flavor), and *tiěbǎn hēijiāo niúpái* (grilled "steak" with black-pepper sauce).

On the main street in the north part of town, opposite the taxi rental office. © 0350/654-5674. Meal for 2 ¥40–¥80 ($5–$10). No credit cards. 7:30am–11pm.

7

The Silk Routes

by Jen Lin-Liu

China was first known in the West as Seres, the land of silk or serica. The Romans were entranced by this strong but delicate thread, and believed it was combed from trees. But it was also viewed as a decadent, effeminate luxury—for the appetite of Rome's better classes for silk was rarely sated, and without a luxury (other than glass) to export in return, silk imports emptied Rome's coffers. As a result, in A.D. 14 the Roman Senate forbade the wearing of silk by men, and Caligula, who was fond of diaphanous silk garments, was disparagingly referred to as Sericatus.

In Táng China, silk was the most important form of legal tender; taxes, fines, and officials' wages were all measured in bales of silk. Silk was used to buy off raiding armies of Uighurs and Tibetans and (it was hoped) make them a bit less barbaric.

The term *Silk Road,* coined in the 19th century by German geographer Ferdinand von Richthofen, is both an evocative and misleading appellation. The trade routes that connected China and the West from the 1st century B.C. until the 10th century A.D. carried a whole inventory of luxuries and necessities beyond silk, from gold and jade to wool and rhubarb. Nor was the road traveled from end to end. Chinese merchants rarely went beyond the edges of the **Taklamakan Desert** before turning the goods over to Sogdian or Parthian caravans, who were left to face the forbidding

mountain passes of the Pamirs. Only devoted missionaries went farther, like the legendary monk Xuánzàng, who spent 15 years traveling across India and central Asia in search of Buddhist sutras.

Silk was just one of many goods transported over these vast distances. Apricots, peaches, and pears reached the West, while China gained the fig tree and the grapevine. China imported spices, woolen fabrics, horses for military campaigns, and foreign novelties such as musical instruments, coral, colored glass, and jewels, which fascinated the courts.

Traders also brought foreign ideas, and were soon followed by missionaries of many faiths. Nestorian Christianity, Zoroastrianism, Manichaeism and, most significantly, Buddhism, were welcomed by a confident and cosmopolitan civilization. Doctrines and art spread eastward, leaving spectacular monuments in the cave temples of **Dūnhuáng, Mài Shān,** and **Kizil.**

The Silk Road wasn't one road at all, but a series of routes emanating from the capital of Cháng'ān. From Cháng'ān, camel trains would follow the Wèi River west before branching into several different routes.

The southern route passed through **Dūnhuáng, Miran,** and **Khotan,** in the shadow of the mighty **Kūnlún Shān,** whose meltwater streams fed thriving Buddhist communities. Intrepid travelers today, tolerant of bare-bones transportation and accommodations, can still traverse the route, which will lead to quiet towns such as Khotan with ancient markets and traditions undisturbed by either tourism or modernization.

The middle route was initially (1st c. B.C.–A.D. 4th c.) popular, allowing merchants to float on barges down the Tarim River from the garrison town of Lóulán to Korla and **Kuqa.** But when the river changed course, and Lop Nor Lake "wandered off," this route was abandoned. Thanks to more recent nuclear testing, which finally ended in 1996, this route will likely remain closed for the half-life of plutonium-239.

The northern routes, skirting the northern and southern foothills of **Tiān Shān (the Heavenly Mountains),** were menaced by Kazakh and Kyrgyz bandits. The bandits are less of a problem these days, and most travelers follow the northern route along the Hé Xī corridor to the mighty fort of **Jiāyù Guān,** the peerless Buddhist caves of Dūnhuáng, and the grape trellises of **Turpan.** Beyond, the road leads to fascinating oasis towns such as Kuqa, and the great market town of **Kashgar,** skirting the northern edge of the Taklamakan Desert. (Taklamakan is commonly translated as "go in and you don't come out," but in ancient Uighur it means "vineyard," evoking a time when the region was more fertile.) The desert dunes have been marching south for many years, threatening the oasis towns of the ancient southern route.

The present character of the Silk Road is Islamic rather than Buddhist. An exodus of the Turkic Uighur peoples from western Mongolia displaced the Indo-European inhabitants, the Táng dynasty fell, and Islam gradually spread east through the Tarim Basin. With the rise of sea trade, land routes fell into disuse. Settlements and temples (which also functioned as

banks) were abandoned to the desert. They remained undisturbed until the turn of the 20th century, when archaeologists from Britain, France, Germany, Russia, Japan, and (later) America came searching for lost Buddhist kingdoms.

The adventurers saw the Hàn Chinese as fellow colonizers, keeping the Turkic Uighurs in their place. British diplomat Eric Teichman believed "the Turkis are a patient, contented and submissive people, made to be ruled by others." Xīnjiāng means "new territories," rather a giveaway in itself, but many Hàn guides will try to persuade you that this region has always belonged to China. Most Uighurs would prefer to rule themselves, and they still practice a form of Islam that is both tolerant and catholic, recalling a time when towns such as Kashgar were centers of Islamic learning.

Turkic Uighurs make up the majority of the population in Xīnjiāng, but they are gradually being displaced by a wave of migrants from the east. After an absence of over a millennium, Hàn Chinese are reasserting control over the Silk Routes with a ruthlessness that the Wǔdì emperor (reigned 141–87 B.C.)—the first ruler to control the Silk Routes—would have envied.

Travel along the Silk Routes has always been arduous, temperatures are extreme, and the distances involved are considerable. Peak season is early May, and mid-July to mid-October. Outside of Xī'ān, Lánzhōu, Dūnhuáng, and Ürümqi, expect little in the way of luxurious lodgings. The more adventurous should seek out the Uighur trading centers of Kashgar, Khotan, and Kuqa, or the Tibetan monastic settlements of **Xià Hé** and **Lángmù Sì.** *Note:* Unless otherwise noted, hours listed for attractions and restaurants are daily.

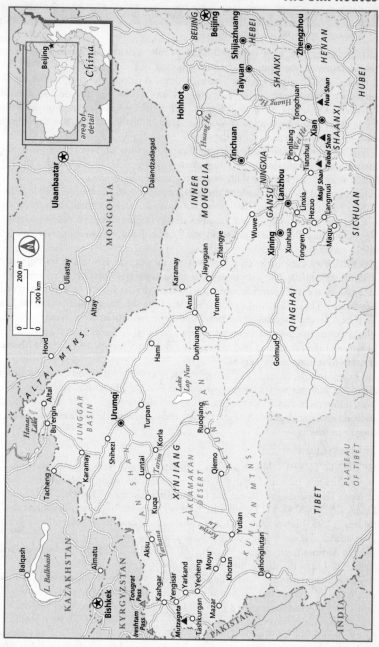

The Silk Routes

1 Xī'ān

Shǎnxī Province, 1,200km (744 miles) SW of Běijīng

Surrounded by rich loess farmland, Xī'ān (Western Peace), the present capital of Shǎnxī Province, was home to the ruling houses of the Qín, Hàn, Suí, and Táng dynasties, when it was known as Cháng'ān (Eternal Peace). The city reached a peak during the Táng dynasty (618–907), when it was the military and trading base for China's shaky control of the Silk Routes. During the Xuánzōng reign of the Táng (712–755), Cháng'ān boasted two million taxable inhabitants and was the largest, most cosmopolitan settlement in the world.

The scale of the metropolis is readily imagined—what are now referred to as the city walls were rebuilt during the Míng dynasty (1644–1911) on the remains of Táng palace walls. The Táng city walls extended 8km (5 miles) north–south and almost 10km (6 miles) east–west, and the south gate opened onto a tree-lined avenue 150m (500 ft.) wide, down which foreign emissaries would once approach the metropolis. The Táng era was a high point for advocates of "foreign religions" as Manicheans, Nestorians, and Buddhists flocked to the capital. Buddhism in particular enjoyed royal patronage.

Surviving monuments open a window onto the imperial power and cosmopolitan style of the old capital. The short-lived totalitarian state of Qín Shǐ Huángdì is reflected in the awe-inspiring massed terra-cotta armies of the **Qín Bīngmǎyǒng Bówùguǎn.** The influence of Buddhism is clear from the majestic spire of the **Dà Yàn Tǎ (Great Goose Pagoda),** constructed under the supervision of Xuánzàng (d. 664), who returned to China in 645 after 15 years of travel across India and central Asia. Evidence of the flourishing trade along the Silk Routes may be found in the **Shǎnxī History Museum** and **Fǎmén Sì.**

There is enough to see in and around Xī'ān to keep even the most energetic visitor busy for a week or two. It's the most-visited town on the Silk Routes, which brings the usual annoyances. Most locals are easygoing and disparaging of their ancient capital, endlessly shaking their heads in regret that their ancestors "fell behind" their richer cousins in Běijīng.

ESSENTIALS

GETTING THERE   Numerous direct **flights** connect Xiányáng Airport with all major cities in China, including Běijīng, Shànghǎi, Chóngqìng, Chéngdū, Kūnmíng, Ürümqi, Lhasa, and Hong Kong. The **CAAC office,** located at Dōngmén Wài, Shìmào Dàshà, (© **029/8248-1111**), will deliver airline tickets free of charge. An **airport shuttle bus** (¥25/$3) leaves from the CAAC office on the hour from 5am to 5pm; aim to leave at least 2 hours before your flight. You can also book tickets through the **Xī'ān Huá'ān Airlines** ticket office at Nán Dàjiē 60 (© **029/8724-1503**). Discounts are possible. A **taxi** from the airport into town costs about ¥150 to ¥180 ($18–$20).

The **railway station** is located outside the northeast side of the city wall, 20 minutes by double-decker bus no. 603 from the main hotel area. The station is open 24 hours, and all windows (except 15, 16, and 18) can be used. There is no longer a foreigners' counter, but window 17 should have an English speaker. Ticket refunds can be obtained from window 2. The fastest trains to Běijīng are the T42 (14 hr.) at 6:02pm, and the T232 at 5:31pm. Other useful trains are the T140 to Shànghǎi (16½ hr.) at 6:44pm; the K84 to Guǎngzhōu (27 hr.) at 9:03am; the K119 to Lánzhōu (9 hr.) at 10:32pm; the K165 at 11:10pm, which passes through Chéngdū (14 hr.) and

Tips Alternate Ways to Book Rail Tickets

The station can get crowded, so either book tickets through your hotel, which will charge between ¥40 and ¥80 ($5–$10) to book a ticket, or visit a branch of the **Industrial and Commercial Bank of China (Gōngshāng Yínháng),** which levies a reasonable ¥5 (65¢) service charge. The closest branch to the railway station is 1.6km (1 mile) south of the station at Wǔlùkǒu Gōngháng, Jiěfàng Lù 288; it's open weekdays from 8am to 6pm, and on weekends from 9am to 5pm. The **city branch** is cater-cornered to the Home Club Department Store at Mùtou Shì 9 (© **029/95588**) and is open weekdays 8am to 8pm; weekends 9am to 3pm.

terminates in Kūnmíng (36 hr.); the K60 to Zhèngzhōu (7 hr.) at 4:24pm; the T69 to Ürümqi (31 hr.) at 8:21am; and the 2334 to Chóngqìng (14 hr.) at 2:16pm.

The **bus station (Xī'ān Qìchē Zhàn;** © **029/8742-7420)** is directly opposite the railway station. Regular buses connect with Zhèngzhōu (573km/355 miles; 9 hr.; ¥111/$13), Luòyáng (425km/264 miles; 7 hr.; ¥65/$8), Tàiyuán (685km/425 miles; 12 hr.; ¥128/$16), and Tiānshuǐ (380km/236 miles; 6 hr.; ¥60/$7.50). Six buses connect with Píngyáo (7am–12:30pm; 8 hr.; ¥ 115/$14) and with Yán'ān (402km/249 miles; 6 hr.; ¥52–¥68/$6.50–$8.50). Five afternoon sleeper buses connect with Yínchuān (720km/446 miles; 15 hr.; ¥110/$14).

CITY LAYOUT   The center of town is generally denoted by the massive Míng **Bell Tower (Zhōng Lóu),** which marks the crossroads between the main north–south and east–west roads—which connect with the four main city gates. The main arteries are **Běi, Nán, Dōng,** and **Xī Dàjiē** (North, South, East, and West aves.). Most of the main hotels, and many of the main sights and restaurants, are along these roads.

GETTING AROUND   There are two ways to travel by **bus.** If there's no conductor, expect to pay a flat fare of ¥1 (15¢); no change is given. If there is a conductor, the fare ranges from ¥.50 to ¥2 (5¢–25¢).

Most **taxis** are green Santana sedans that charge ¥6 (75¢) for the first 3km (2 miles), then ¥1.40 (20¢) per additional kilometer; add ¥1 (15¢) if you're traveling between the hours of 10pm and 5am. Tiny Alto hatchbacks charge slightly less. You'll encounter few problems with drivers overcharging or failing to start the meter, but they will round the fare up or down to whole yuán, so don't sit around waiting for change.

Xī'ān is flat and thus suitable for **biking,** but the streets are congested, and any traffic rules that may exist are ignored by motorists. Only recommended for the experienced urban cyclist.

TOURS   Many travel agencies and hotels offer 1-day tours of the sights around Xī'ān. The most popular tour follows the **Eastern Route (Dōng Xiàn),** which usually includes the **Terra-Cotta Warriors (Qín Bīngmǎyǒng Bówùguǎn), Huáqīng Chí (Huáqīng Pools),** and **Bànpō Bówùguǎn.** The less-traveled **Western Route (Xī Xiàn)** should include Fǎmén Sì, Qián Líng (Táng dynasty tombs), and perhaps Máo Líng (Hàn dynasty tombs) and Xiányáng Bówùguǎn (Xiányáng Museum); in this book, we'll focus on the Eastern Route.

CITS, at Cháng'ān Běi Lù 48 (© **029/8526-2066;** fax 029/8526-7487; www. citsxa.com), offers the most reasonably priced tours in town, charging ¥260 ($30) for the Western Route, and ¥285 ($32) for the Eastern Route daily. They have a competent

Xī'ān

Legend:
- Bus Station
- ¥ Bank
- P Police
- ✕ Post Office
- Rail Station
- TA Travel Agent

Map labels:

Fenghe Lu
Jinhua Bei Lu
Jinhua Nan Lu
Changle Lu
Dong Guang Zhengjie
XINGQINGGONG PARK
Dorgmen Gate (East Gate)
Huancheng Donglu
Dong Xinjie
Dongwu Lu
Jiefang Lu
Xia Lu
Shangde Lu
Xi Xinjie
Xiyi Lu
Xiwu Lu
Heping Lu
Yanta Lu
Juhua Yuan
CITY WALL
Youyi Dong Lu
Jianshe Lu
Tiyuguan Lu
Beimen Gate (North Gate)
Bei Dajie
Dong Dajie
Zhong Lu
Nan Dajie
Nammen Gate (South Gate)
Chang'an Lu
Xia Zhai Dong Lu
Huancheng Beilu
Lianhu Lu
Bei Yuan Men
Zhubashi
Fen Xiang
Nan Dajie Xi Shun Cheng
Huancheng Nanlu
Zhouque Dajie
Nan Er Huan
Youyi Xi Lu
Sajiaqiao Lu
Xi Dajie
Ximen Gate (West Gate)
CITY WALL
Huancheng X
Xiguan Zhengjie
Daqing Lu
Fenghao Dong Lu
Laodong Lu

N
1/2 mi
0.5 km
0

China
Beijing
SHANXI
Xi'an

ACCOMMODATIONS ■

Bell Tower Hotel
(Zhōnglóu Fàndiàn) **6**
钟楼饭店

Howard Johnson Ginwa Plaza Hotel
(Jīnhuā Háoshēng Guójì Dàjiǔdiàn) **13**
金花豪生国际大酒店

Hyatt Regency Xī'ān
(Kǎiyuè Fàndiàn) **11**
凯悦饭店

Jiěfàng Fàndiàn 10
解放饭店

Melody Hotel
(Měilún Jiǔdiàn) **5**
美伦酒店

Shangri-La Golden Flower
(Jīnhuā Fàndiàn) **25**
金花饭店

Shàng Hǎo Bīnguǎn 19
上好宾馆

Sheraton Xī'ān
(Xǐláidēng Dàjiǔdiàn) **1**
喜来登大酒店

Wǔyī Fàndiàn
(May First Hotel) **8**
五一饭店

Xī'ān Shūyuàn Qīngnián Lǚshè
(Xī'ān Shūyuàn Youth Hostel) **9**
西安书院青年旅社

DINING ◆

Dé Fā Chāng 4
德发昌

Fánjì Làzhī Ròudiàn 7
樊记腊汁肉店

Highfly Pizza
(Gāofēi Bǐsà) **15**
高飞比萨

Jiǎsān Guàntāng Bāozi 3
贾三灌汤包子

Lǎ Sūn Jiā 23
老孙家

Shǎnxī Grand Opera House
(Shǎnxī Gēwǔ Dà Xìyuàn) **14**
陕西歌舞大戏院

Táng Dynasty
(Táng Yuè Gōng) **16**
唐乐宫

Wénháo Záliáng Shífǔ Lǎo Diàn 20
文豪杂粮食府老店

ATTRACTIONS ●

Bànpō Bówùguǎn
(Bànpō Neolithic Village) **26**
半坡博物馆

Bā Xiān Ān
(Temple of the Eight Immortals) **24**
八仙庵

Bēilín Bówùguǎn
(Forest of Stelae) **12**
碑林博物馆

Dà Qīngzhēnsì
(Great Mosque) **2**
大清真寺

Dà Yàn Tǎ
(Great Goose Pagoda) **22**
大雁塔

Shǎnxī Lìshǐ Bówùguǎn
(Shǎnxī History Museum) **21**
陕西历史博物馆

Small Goose Pagoda
(Xiǎo Yàn Tǎ) **17**
小雁塔

Zhōng Běi Jiùhuò Shìchǎng 18
中北旧货市场

branch in the lobby of the Shēnyè Dàshà, Jiěfàng Lù (© 029/8740-7066). Another option is the **Golden Bridge Travel Service** at Tǐyùguǎn Lù 111 (© **029/8761-6633;** fax 029/8761-5577; gbtour@pub.xaonline.com), which charges ¥210 ($25) for the Eastern Route and ¥170 ($20) for the Western Route. Some major hotels offer their own tours.

FAST FACTS

Banks, Foreign Exchange & ATMs   The most effective **Bank of China** is the city branch at Jiěfàng Lù 157 (© **029/8745-3386;** open 8am–8pm Mon–Fri, 9am–5pm weekends) It's about 400m (¼ mile) south of the railway station, on the west side of Jiěfàng Lù, next to the Silk Road Hotel. The provincial branch is located in the center of town, on the corner of Júhuā Yuán at Dōng Dàjiē 306 (© 029/8745-1651). Foreign exchange counters are located on the second floor; windows 14 to 16 and ATMs downstairs accept foreign credit cards. There's also a branch, with an ATM, just 180m (590 ft.) south of the Bell Tower at Nán Dàjiē 29 (© 029/8728-1287; open Mon–Fri 8am–6pm, Sat–Sun 9am–5pm). A branch in the west of town, at Liánhú Lù 95 (© 029/8731-6657), changes traveler's checks and cash at counter 4, and is open weekdays from 8:30am to noon and 2 to 6pm.

Internet Access   In the railway area, there are many Internet cafes on Shàngdé Lù. A reasonable choice is **Wǎngshì Rú Fēng Internet Cafe** (on the east side of the road, just south of the intersection with Xī Bā Lù), which charges the standard rate of ¥3 (40¢) per hour. Avoid the Internet bar on the opposite side of the road, which has a "special price" for foreign guests *(wàibīn)* that's interestingly not mentioned in the English translation of its price list. Just north of Nán Mén is **Potman Internet Cafe** at Nán Dàjiē 9 (© **029/8727-0874**). Dial-up is © **169.**

Post Office   The **main branch** is at the northwest corner of the Bell Tower at Běi Dàjiē 1, open 8am to 8pm.

Visa Extensions   Extensions can be obtained from the PSB, located 2 blocks west of the Bell Tower on the south side of the road at Xī Dàjiē 138 (© **029/9727-5934;** open Mon–Fri 8am–noon and 2–6pm); they take 3 days to process.

EXPLORING XĪ'ĀN

Bā Xiān Ān (Temple of the Eight Immortals) ✦ Ⓕ finds   Tucked away in a narrow
alley the tour buses can't reach is the most charming temple in Xī'ān. As with the Great Mosque, the walk into it is half the adventure, with a flea market out front in some of the temple's old buildings. This becomes a huge antiques market on Wednesday and Sunday mornings (see "Shopping," below). Inside the temple, monks, their hair tied up in traditional Daoist fashion, play chess and are always keen for a chat. The folk legend of the **Eight Immortals (Bā Xiān)** is said to have originated here during the late Táng dynasty. As you look at the temple murals, note the influence of Confucianism on its supposed alter-ego, Daoism: The eight Immortals have a strict hierarchy, with Lǚ Dòngbīn in front on his tiger, the rotund Tiěguǎi Lǐ waddling along with his crook to his side, and the one woman, Hé Xiāngū, near the back, carrying a lotus flower.

Wǔ Dào Shízi Dōngjiē (from Ān Rén Fáng, continue east 135m/450 ft. before heading south down the 1st alley on your right; turn right when the road meets a T-junction. Immediately take a left and continue south to the back of the temple, following the incense vendors). Admission ¥3 (40¢). 7:30am–6pm. Bus: no. 13 or 42 from the station, or bus no. 4 or 11 from the Bell Tower to Ān Rén Fáng.

Běilín Bówùguǎn (Forest of Stelae) ✎ Formerly the Shǎnxī Provincial Museum, the Forest of Stelae is situated in a former Confucian temple (ca. 1087) that the literature describes as "unsophisticated and elegant." Originally forming the basis of a Táng university, many of the stelae have traveled a long way to get here; they were floated downriver on rafts to Luòyáng during the Sòng dynasty before returning here in 1087. Stelae are often borne on bìxì, legendary turtle-like creatures descended from the Dragon King *(lóngwáng)* that were renowned for their incredible strength.

In the main courtyard, the first major stele was composed by the Xuánzōng emperor in 745; the exposition on filial piety predated the influential "three character classic" *(sān zì jīng)*. Room 1 houses the Confucian classics, including The Analects, The Spring and Autumn Annals. Candidates for official examinations would pore over rubbings taken from these stelae and would be expected to know the classics by heart—an educational style that unfortunately still holds sway in China. Immediately to your left in room 2 is the Nestorian Stele. Nestorian Christians were drummed out of the Church for maintaining that Jesus was both human and divine and that Mary was the mother of "the man Jesus," and not the mother of God. The stele records the visit of a Nestorian priest to Cháng'ān and the founding of a Nestorian chapel, providing evidence of a Nestorian presence in China as early as A.D. 635. The influence of other faiths is clear—the Maltese cross is set amid Daoist clouds, supported by a Buddhist lotus flower. Rooms 2 and 3 also house the work of master calligraphers, such as Wáng Xīzhī, whose writings are still used as models by calligraphy students. Room 4 has pictorial stelae, including a famous image of Confucius. Here you will encounter a demonstration of "rubbing," whereby moistened paper is hammered onto the inked stones, color is tapped on using a wooden disk wrapped in a cloth, and the impression is dried before being gobbled up by Japanese tour groups. It isn't a gentle process, and it's easy to see why many stelae are almost unreadable. Double back to your left to enter rooms 5 to 7, as well as a gallery of stone sculpture containing an exquisite statue of a bodhisattva that shows Indian and Grecian influences. Before you leave, rest in one of the 1950s cinema seats that line the courtyard.

Wényì Běi Lù 18. ✆ 029/8725-8448. Admission ¥35 ($4.20). 8:30am–6:30pm. Bus: no. 14, 402, or 239.

Dà Qīngzhēnsì (Great Mosque) ✎ Founded during the height of the Táng dynasty in 742, this is one of the most tranquil places in town and the center of a sizable Muslim community, residents in Xī'ān for over 1,200 years. As with Bāxiān Ān, half the adventure is getting there, as you veer left just north of the Drum Tower. The covered alleyway, Huàjué Xiàng, has good-humored vendors selling all manner of weird merchandise (see "Shopping," below) and it may take you a few attempts to find the mosque. The courtyards are spacious and have a gardenlike feel, with a wonderful fusion of Arabian and Chinese architectural styles. To the right of the entrance is a hall filled with exquisite Míng furniture. The central courtyard has a triple-eaved octagonal pagoda from which worshippers are called to prayer. The prayer hall is normally closed to non-Muslims. As this is an active mosque, be circumspect in taking photographs. Avoid visiting on Friday, when access to the mosque is restricted. Be sure to bring mosquito spray in the summer.

Huàjué Xiàng 30. ✆ 029/8727-2541. Admission ¥12 ($1.50). Apr–Oct 8am–7pm; Nov–Mar 8am–5pm. Bus: no. 221, 29, 6, or 618.

Dà Yàn Tǎ (Great Goose Pagoda) & Dà Cí'ēn Sì (Temple of Great Goodwill) ✎
This is the best-known temple in Xī'ān, and worth a visit if, like many in the U.K. and

Australia, you were entranced by the TV version of "Monkey" as a child. The scripture-collecting journey of Xuánzàng (596–664) to India, on which the show was based, lasted 15 years, and was immortalized and lampooned in Wú Chéng'ēn's novel *Journey to the West (Xī Yóu Jì)*. But the journey was not the end of Xuánzàng's travails. Upon his return, he requested the construction of a pagoda to house the scriptures; his request was accommodated inside a temple built from 647 to 652 by Prince Lǐ Zhì in honor of his mother, Empress Wén Dé. Construction of the pagoda commenced in 652, in a style similar to those seen by Xuánzàng in India—hence the simple, tapering structure. Xuánzàng is credited with translating 75 texts into over 1,000 volumes, an amazing feat since the originals contained a host of specialized terms with no Chinese equivalents.

Halls at the back of the temple contain murals depicting Xuánzàng's journey—in many pictures, he is shown holding a fly whisk, intended to send evil spirits into flight. To the left and right of the pagoda's south entrance are prefaces to the texts written by Tàizōng and Gāozōng. Above the east and west doors are barely visible Táng carvings of the Buddha. The temple's perimeter has recently undergone redevelopment and the result is as good as Chinese urban planning gets. To the north of the pagoda is the north plaza *(bei guangcang)*, which boasts a large pool of fountains, benches, and retail shops lining the mall. A water fountain and light show kicks off nightly at 8pm in the winter, 9pm in the summer.

Admission ¥35 ($4). 8:30am–6:30pm. Bus: no. 5 (from the station).

Shǎnxī Lìshǐ Bówùguǎn (Shǎnxī History Museum) ᖇᖇᖇ If you visit one museum in China, make it this one, for its unrivalled collection of treasures. As you enter, start with the hall on the left, pull on a jacket to brave the fierce air-conditioning, and ignore the man who tries to drag you to his display of "original art." Items are displayed chronologically, starting with the Shāng dynasty (ca. 17th c.–11th c. B.C.) and the Zhōu dynasty (ca. 11th c.–221 B.C. on the ground floor, including items that speak to eating, drinking, and merriment in the Western Zhōu (ca. 11th c.–771 B.C.).

Things take a martial turn as you enter the Qín dynasty (221–206 B.C.): Aside from the bronze swords and rusting iron weapons (which gave the Qín a decisive military edge), a striking exhibit is a **tiger-shaped tally** covered in characters *(dùhǔ fú)* which gave its owner, one General Dù, imperial authorization to mobilize over 50 soldiers at will. As you move on to the Táng dynasty (618–907), the influence of Buddhist art from the Silk Routes becomes apparent—carvings are more sophisticated, and bright colors are introduced. Perhaps the most startling exhibits are the frescoes *(bìhuà)* relocated from the Táng tumuli around Xī'ān. A depiction of ladies-in-waiting *(gōngnǔ tú)* ᖇᖇ shows nine women carrying the tools of their trade—candelabras, fans, cloth bundles, powder boxes, even fly swatters. Two of them are dressed in male clothing. Another fresco *(mǎ qiú tú)* shows noblemen enjoying the newly imported game of polo. **Ceramic tomb guardians** point to a lively trade with the outside world—there's a trader from Africa and a fanciful depiction of a man on horseback battling a leopard. You can easily spend 3 or 4 hours here.

Xiǎo Zhài Dōng Lù 91. ✆ 029/8525-4727. Admission ¥35 ($4.40). 8am–5pm. Bus: no. 5 (from the station) or 610 (from just north of the Bell Tower to Lìshǐ Bówùguǎn).

Xī'ān Chéngqiáng (City Wall) ᖇ The largest and best-preserved city wall in China is definitely worth a visit. The pieces of the wall have recently been reconnected so that you can do the 14km (8¾-mile) loop around it by foot, bicycle, or a golf cart. The walls were built during the early Míng dynasty, on the remains of Táng palace

walls. The original city walls were much farther out, well past Dà Yàn Tǎ. The surrounding moat is currently being cleaned up in phases, and should be completed by the Olympics in 2008. The South Gate (Nán Mén) is the best place to start your exploration. Individual (¥10/$1.25) and tandem bicycles (¥20/$2.50) may be hired by the hour from here, or just east of Hépíng Mén. A ride on a golf cart around the wall costs (¥50/$6). To do the entire loop takes 3 to 4 hours by foot, 2 to 3 hours by bicycle, and 1 hour by cart. The wall provides little protection from sun or wind, so dress accordingly.

Admission ¥40 ($4.80). Apr–Oct 8am–10pm; Nov–Mar 8am–6pm.

AROUND XI'ĀN
EASTERN ROUTE (DŌNG XIÀN)

Of the two common tours from Xi'ān, the Eastern Route is shorter, less expensive, and more popular than the Western Route. There is enough to keep you interested for a whole day, but organized tours of the Eastern Route include "shopping" and sights of dubious merit. While tours are convenient if you have the time, you can do without one. If you are short on time, simply visit Bīngmǎyǒng as a half-day trip.

Bīngmǎyǒng (Terra-Cotta Warriors) ✿✿✿   This is the reason most visitors come to Xi'ān, and unlike many big sights in China, it does not disappoint. Amazingly, the warriors are just one piece of Qín Shǐ Huáng's attempt to reconstruct his empire for the afterlife. The tomb to the west is still to be fully excavated, and is said to include a full reconstruction of the ancient capital, complete with rivers and lakes of mercury. According to historian Sīmǎ Qiān, over 700,000 workers were drafted for the project, and those involved in the construction of the tomb were rewarded with graves beside their emperor. Tourism officials pray that the warriors are "just the tip of the iceberg," but it is just as likely that the tomb was plundered during the Táng or Sòng dynasties.

It's hard not to get a shiver down your spine as you survey the unromantically named **Pit 1,** with four columns of warriors in each of the 11 passageways; there are over 6,000 infantry in battle formation, stretching back 182m (600 ft.). Originally painted in bright colors, they were constructed from interchangeable parts luted together by clay. Because the heads were hand-molded, no two appear the same. Qín Shǐ Huáng's army was drawn from all over his vast empire, and this ethnic diversity is reflected in the variety of hairstyles, headdresses, and facial expressions. Even on the mass-produced bodies, the level of detail is striking, down to the layering of armor and the studs on archers' shoes that prevented them from slipping. The average height of the warriors is 1.8m (5 ft. 11 in.); senior officers are taller. **Pit 2** holds 1,400 soldiers and cavalry and a taller (nearly 2m/6½ ft.) general; pit 3 houses the headquarters, with 68 senior officers.

A **small hall** just to the right of pit 1 contains a display of two magnificent bronze chariots, reconstructed from nearly 3,500 pieces excavated from a pit to the west of the tomb.

The tour bus will drop you off in a parking lot; you can either walk the 1km (2/3 mile) to the museum's entrance or take a trolley for ¥5 (65¢) round-trip ticket. An English-speaking guide (¥100/$13) can be arranged on the spot at the tour guide center (*dǎoyóu fúwù zhàn*) located near a red umbrella to the right of the entrance.

Ⓒ 029/8391-1961. Admission: Main exhibits Mar–Nov ¥90 ($11); Dec–Feb ¥65 ($8). 8am–5pm. Bus: no. 306 (leaves from the front of the railway station, on the east side). Take the large A/C bus (¥5/65¢) rather than the minibuses that leave when full. Round-trip taxi from the city costs ¥200 ($25).

Bànpō Bówùguǎn (Bànpō Neolithic Village)   If you're interested in archaeology, this is an essential visit. Otherwise, you can give it a miss. Given the amount of material unearthed here since its discovery in 1953 (tools, pottery, burial jars, etc.), it's amazing that only one-fifth of the site has been excavated (mostly due to the cost of preserving what has been discovered). The village, traced back to the Yǎngsháo culture, was occupied from about 5000 to 4000 B.C.

Bànpō Bówùguǎn (from the Bànpō Bówùguǎn bus stop, walk back toward town and turn left at the 1st cross street). Admission ¥25 ($3). 8:30am–5pm. Bus: no. 11 (from just north of the Bell Tower) or no. 105 (from the station). Continuing on to Huáqīng Pools and Bīngmǎyǒng is tricky, but possible. Take bus no. 105 back toward town as far as Wànshòu Lù. Catch bus no. 512 north far as Wáng Jiā Fén (3 stops) and then catch bus no. 306 east.

SHOPPING

Bā Xiān Ān   The outdoor antiques market on Wednesday and Sunday mornings is the most atmospheric in town. Despite a sign warning that antiques must be declared with Customs before you leave China, there's no guarantee that what you buy is a genuine antique. But there is a buzz to the place, and you can find some wonderful Cultural Revolution kitsch, ceramics, bronze Buddhas, and Qīng coins. See the Bā Xiān Ān review in "Exploring Xī'ān," above, for directions.

Gǔ Wénhuà Jiē   This enjoyable street for browsing is east of Nán Mén, on the way to Bēilín Bówùguǎn. Shops sell huge paint brushes, rubbings, paintings, and musical instruments, and you can watch artists at work in this faithfully restored street.

Huàjué Xiàng   The most enjoyable place to shop for souvenirs is the covered alleyway that leads to **Dà Qīngzhēnsì.** Shopping here is blood sport, and you are the game, but the vendors are friendly. Interesting finds include *fēng shuǐ* compasses, Máo lighters, Tibetan prayer wheels, Little Red Books in French, and gnarled walking sticks.

Zhōng Běi Jiùhuò Shìchǎng   With peasants finding that their fields are full of valuable antiques stored in the graves of their prosperous ancestors, digging is going on at a furious pace in the countryside surrounding Xī'ān. Factories producing excellent copies are also very busy. If you're after a genuine antique, you have some chance of finding one here. There are fakes aplenty, but this market is geared to locals, so asking prices are not as absurd as elsewhere. There are bronzes of all kinds, heroic comic books from the Cultural Revolution, and weird kama sutra–inspired wood carvings. Be wary when purchasing bronzes, which tended to be melted down and reused over the ages (unless they were buried). Your best bets are ceramics and pottery. Open April through October 9:30am to 6pm, and November through March 10am to 6pm. Zhū Què Dàjiē Zhōng Duàn 2. Bus no. 6 from south of Bell Tower to Zhōngtǐ Guǎngchǎng; continue south.

WHERE TO STAY

The locals don't go anywhere near the railway station unless they are catching a train, and if you have any amount of time on your hands, it's best to follow their example. If you must, try the **Jiěfàng Fàndiàn,** Jiěfàng Lù 181 (© **029/8769-8888;** fax 029/8769-8666; www.jiefanghotel.com; ¥280/$35 standard room, ¥480/$60 suite), directly across from the railway station on the left; it has a restaurant and very negotiable rates. Buses for Bīngmǎyǒng, Fǎmén Sì, and Huá Shān leave from outside the Jiěfàng, and there's a CITS office inside.

The major attractions and restaurants are clustered around the southern and central parts of town, which are safer places to find lodgings. Discounts of as much as 50% or more off the rack rates are achieved with little bargaining.

VERY EXPENSIVE

Hyatt Regency Xī'ān (Kǎiyuè Fàndiàn)   If you're used to the luxuries of the Hyatt brand, you might be a little disappointed here. While it still remains the five-star hotel with the best location, the service is inattentive and the rooms are smaller than average. Some of the facilities—particularly the bathrooms—are showing signs of wear, although major renovations are planned. If you stay here, try to upgrade to the executive rooms, which include free entrance to a quiet ninth-floor lounge.

Dōng Dàjiē 156. ☎ 029/8723-1234. Fax 029/8721-6799. www.hyatt.com. 315 units. ¥1,400 ($175) standard room; from ¥2,400 ($300) suite. 15% service charge. 10%–20% discounts. AE, DC, MC, V. Bus: no. 611 from the station to Dàcháshì; continue south for 54m/180 ft. and cross to the street's southeast side. **Amenities:** 2 restaurants; bar; cafe; tennis courts; health club and spa; bike rental; concierge; airport shuttle; 24-hr. business center; 24-hr. forex; salon; 24-hr. room service; in-room massage; same-day dry cleaning/laundry; executive-level rooms; wireless access in atrium (¥10/$1.25 per hour). *In room:* A/C, TV, broadband Internet access (¥30/$3.70 per day), minibar, fridge, iron, safe.

Shangri-La Golden Flower (Jīnhuā Fàndiàn) ✿✿   Of Xī'ān's several five-star hotels, the Shangri-La boasts the best rooms: spacious, with either king- or queen-size beds, and well-appointed with nice bathroom and lighting fixtures. Service is solid here. Located outside the city wall, the hotel is inconvenient for walking around, but a 15-minute taxi ride will get you to the center of town. Stay here if you're in town just to see the Terra-Cotta Warriors, as it is closer to the expressway leading to the treasures than other luxury hotels.

Chánglè Xī Lù 8 (3km/2 miles east of city wall). ☎ 800/942-5050 or 029/8323-2981. Fax 029/8323-5477. www.shangri-la.com. 453 units. ¥1,821 ($227) standard room; from ¥3,446 ($430) suite. 15% service charge. 30% discounts. AE, DC, MC, V. Bus: no. 13 (from the station) or 45 (from east of Bell Tower to Jīnhuā Lù). **Amenities:** 2 restaurants; bar; cafe; large indoor swimming pool; health club and spa; concierge; tour desk; airport shuttle; 24-hr. business center; 24-hr. forex; salon; 24-hr. room service; in-room massage; same-day laundry/dry cleaning; executive-level rooms. *In room:* A/C, satellite TV, broadband Internet access (executive rooms), minibar, fridge, iron, safe.

Sheraton Xī'ān (Xǐláidēng Dàjiǔdiàn) ✿✿   Located over 1.6km (1 mile) west of the city walls, the Sheraton has improved remarkably in recent years, and service is the best in Xī'ān. Renovations are ongoing. Rooms are modern and well appointed, with sturdy beds and plush carpets. After a day braving the grimy air of Xī'ān, you can seek refuge in the immaculate bathrooms. The Gate West Restaurant offers tasty Western fare.

Fēnghào Dōng Lù 262. ☎ 029/8426-1888. Fax 029/426-2188. www.sheraton.com/xian. 338 units. ¥1,370–¥1,743 ($165–$210) standard room; from ¥2,615 ($315) suite. 15% service charge. AE, DC, MC, V. Bus: no. 611 from the station and west of the Bell Tower to Fēnghào Dōng Lù. **Amenities:** 3 restaurants; cafe; bar; large indoor swimming pool; health club; spa; game room; concierge; tour desk; airport shuttle; 24-hr. business center; 24-hr. forex; salon; 24-hr. room service; in-room massage; same-day laundry/dry cleaning; executive-level rooms. *In room:* A/C, satellite TV, broadband Internet access (¥30/$3.70 per day), minibar, fridge, hair dryer, iron, safe.

EXPENSIVE

Bell Tower Hotel (Zhōnglóu Fàndiàn)   This is a solid choice one notch down in price from the international hotels with a fantastic location. Rooms are spacious and bathrooms are modern and clean. The lunch buffet on the second floor is still the best all-you-can-eat value in town. In the hotel are branches of both CITS and Golden Bridge Travel. Service seems to be surprisingly competent for a state-run hotel.

Nán Dàjiē 110 (southwest corner of Bell Tower). ☎ 029/8760-0000. Fax 029/8721-8767. 300 units. ¥850 ($106) standard room; from ¥2,380 ($297) suite. 15% service charge. 40% discount. AE, DC, MC, V. Bus: no. 603 from the station. **Amenities:** 2 restaurants; cafe; health club; game room; concierge; tour desk; business center; 24-hr. forex; shopping arcade; next-day laundry/dry cleaning. *In room:* A/C, TV, minibar, fridge, hair dryer.

Howard Johnson Ginwa Plaza Hotel (Jīnhuā Hǎoshèng Guójì Dàjiǔdiàn) ✦
While the brand name may conjure memories of cheap motels and roadside diners in the U.S., Howard Johnson's has arrived in Xī'ān in style. Located right outside the southern city wall, this is one of the best-run new hotels on the market. The lobby is Miami-style tacky, but the rooms are tastefully done, and bathroom fixtures are modern. Some rooms have great views of the wall—try to book one of these. The hotel is well equipped to deal with English-speaking travelers with at least one overseas employee on staff at all times. Wireless Internet connections are available at all the restaurants, the lobby, club floor lounge, and banquet rooms.

Huángchéng Nán Jiē 18. ☎ **029/8842-1111.** Fax: 029/8206-8888. 324 units. ¥888–¥988 ($111–$125) standard room; ¥1,288–¥1,888 ($161–$256). 15% service charge. AE, DC, MC, V. **Amenities:** 3 restaurants; lobby lounge; concierge; business center; gift shop; 5 nonsmoking floors. *In room:* A/C, satellite TV, minibar, hair dryer, safe.

MODERATE
Melody Hotel (Měilún Jiǔdiàn)   For location and price, this is the best midrange choice in town. Rooms are clean and bright, and it's worth paying a little extra for a view of the Drum Tower, which is directly opposite. The Melody opened in 2001 and is an entirely private venture. If you've ever wanted to try the full-body shower featured in the movie *Shower (Xǐzǎo)*, this is the place.

Xī Dàjiē 86 (opposite the Drum Tower). ☎ **029/8728-8888.** Fax 029/8727-3601. 142 units (shower only). ¥498 ($62) standard room; ¥888 ($111) suite. AE, DC, MC, V. **Amenities:** Restaurant; bar; exercise room; concierge; same-day laundry/dry cleaning. *In room:* A/C, TV, minibar, fridge, hair dryer.

Wǔyī Fàndiàn (May First Hotel)   Stung by exclusion from various travel guides, the first hotel in town to accept foreigners is frantically renovating from the top floor downwards. Some of the wallpaper looks unchanged since the hotel's opening in 1946, so be sure to ask for a room on the refurbished seventh floor. May First requires that their staff take classes in English and politeness, which is more than can be said for some five-star hotels in town. Lugging your bags up the stairs to reception is inconvenient, but with a bustling food court downstairs and elevators that only take four people, a stay here is reminiscent of Hong Kong in the 1970s.

Dōng Dàjiē 351 (225m/750 ft. east of Bell Tower, on north side). ☎ **029/8721-2212.** Fax 029/8721-3824. www.may-first.com. 129 units. ¥230–¥288 ($29–$36) standard room. AE, DC, MC, V. **Amenities:** Restaurant; food court; tour desk; same-day laundry/dry cleaning. *In room:* A/C, TV.

INEXPENSIVE
Shāng Hǎo Bīnguǎn *Value*   This is a small, friendly hotel with prices well below what you would expect to pay for comfortable, clean, and spacious midsize rooms. The staff speaks almost no English so you'll need your phrasebook, but this is a steal. The hotel is situated in one of Xī'ān's liveliest areas, a taste of "real China."

Jiànshè Xī Lù 8. ☎ **029/8553-9111.** 56 units (shower only). ¥120 ($15) twin with shared bathroom; ¥150 ($19) standard room; ¥320 ($39) suite. Rates easily reduced by 40%. No credit cards. Bus: no. 601 from north of Bell Tower, or no. 5 from the railway station to Lǔ Jiā Cūn; walk south for 45m (148 yd.) and turn right onto Jiànshè Lù. The hotel is 90m (300 ft.) ahead, on the north side, directly opposite a hospital. **Amenities:** Restaurant; bar; next-day laundry/dry cleaning. *In room:* A/C, TV.

Xī'ān Shūyuàn Qīngnián Lǚshè (Xī'ān Shūyuàn Youth Hostel) ✦✦ *Finds*
Youth hostels are taking over the budget accommodations niche in China, and this one is the best option in town. A magnificent restored courtyard residence, it formerly housed the Xiányáng County government. Chinese visitors wonder why foreigners put up with rooms that have concrete-and-tile floors and hot water that only runs

from 6pm to 12:30am (although you can ask for it at other times). What you get is a friendly English-speaking staff, an excellent location, impartial and useful information, and that rare commodity in China—ambience.

Nán Dàjiē Xī Shùn Chéng Xiàng 2A (27m/90 ft. west of the South Gate, just inside the city wall). ✆ 029/8728-7720. Fax 029/8728-7720. 45 units (shower only). ¥160 ($20) standard room; from ¥30–¥50 ($4–$6) dorm. No credit cards. Bus: no. 603 from the railway station to Nán Mén. **Amenities:** Cafe; bike rental; concierge; tour desk; railway station courtesy car; laundry and kitchen facilities; Internet access. *In room:* A/C, TV, no phone.

WHERE TO DINE

Dé Fā Chāng ✿ (Kids) DUMPLINGS
Dumplings are raised to a high art form at this lively restaurant located next to the Clock Tower Square. Tasty *xiǎochī*, or little eats, resembling flying saucers, mouse heads, and walnuts will come in steady stream to your table. The 18-course dumpling meal is a steal at ¥60 ($7.50).

Zhōnglóu Guǎngchǎng. ✆ 029/8721-4060. Meal for 2 ¥120 ($15). No credit cards. 7am–9pm.

Fánjì Làzhī Ròudiàn SHĂNXĪ
This is the most famous vendor of Shǎnxī's most widely consumed snack—*ròu jiā mó*, finely chopped pork pressed between two halves of a solid steamed bun. Xī'ān's answer to the hamburger makes a perfect snack on the run, but you can almost feel your arteries clogging up as you wolf it down. Ask for the good-quality (*yōuzhì*) bun (¥4/50¢).

Zhúbāshì Jiē 46 (from Gǔ Lóu, the shop is opposite, 45m/150 ft. south of Xī Dàjiē on the road's east side). Meal for 2 less than ¥20 ($2.50). No credit cards. 7am–9pm. Bus: no. 610 from the station to Gǔ Lóu.

Highfly Pizza (Gāofēi Bǐsà) WESTERN
Outside of the five-star hotels and the inevitable KFCs, Xī'ān offers little in the way of Western food; it's a relief to find pizza (the four-cheese and pepperoni pizzas are superb), real oven-baked penne, tuna sandwiches, chocolate brownies, even Texas stew. There are vegetarian options, the kitchen is spotless, and the entire restaurant is nonsmoking.

Hépíng Mén Wài Shènglì Fàndiàn. ✆ 029/8785-5333. Meal for 2 ¥60–¥100 ($7.50–$13). No credit cards. 9am–10:30pm. Bus: no. 5 (from station) or no. 601 (from north of Bell Tower to Hépíng Mén).

Jiǎsān Guàntāng Bāozi ✿ MUSLIM
Still the most famous of the Jiǎ Brothers' restaurants, you'll know you're there when you see the monstrous blue arch over the entrance and a wall festooned with photographs of Xī'ān notables—TV hosts, writers, and musicians. The specialty dish is *guàntāng bāozi,* with a choice of beef, lamb, or "three flavors"—lamb, mushroom, and prawn. The dumplings have piping-hot soup inside, so let them cool before testing your chopstick skills. This dish is best washed down with *bā bǎo tián xīfàn,* a sweet rice porridge filled with peanuts, sultanas, hawthorn, and medlar berries.

Běi Yuàn Mén 93 (135m/450 ft. north of Drum Tower, on the east side). ✆ 029/8725-7507. Meal for 2 less than ¥20 ($2.50). No credit cards. 8am–midnight.

Lǎo Sūn Jiā ✿ SHĂNXĪ
The original restaurant, opened in 1898, is still the best place to sample Xī'ān's most celebrated dish, *yángròu pàomó*. There are now three branches, two of them on Dōng Dàjiē. The branch with the best reputation at the moment is located inside a large hotel. On the first floor, you can dine with the masses—not recommended unless you want to be the main attraction. The second floor is a point-to-choose *xiǎochī* (snack) restaurant. Recommended dishes include the lamb dumplings (*suān tāng shuǐjiǎo*) and a local favorite, *fěnzhēng yángròu,* two steamed buns perched delicately to the side of a pile of mince and flour. Order *yángròu pàomó* on the third floor. You will face an empty bowl and two steamed buns, as

well as plates of chili, coriander, and cloves of garlic that have been marinated in vinegar and sugar for several months. Tear the buns into tiny pieces and pop them into the empty bowl. When you've finished, your bowl will be taken away and refilled with broth and noodles. Stir in the coriander and chili, and when your palate gets greasy, nibble a clove of garlic and encourage your friends to do likewise. If the star dish doesn't fill you up, the stewed oxtail *(hóngshāo niúwěi)* and bok choy with mushrooms *(bìlù zá shuāng gū)* are recommended. Don't bother with the fourth floor, unless you are entertaining a government official looking for a bribe.

Dōng Guān Zhèng Jiē 78 (from Dōng Mén, cross the road, walk 27m/90 ft. north, turn right, and walk 45m/150 ft. east). ⓒ 029/8221-2935. Reservations recommended on weekends (3rd floor). ¥60 ($7.50) on 2nd floor, ¥200 ($25) on 3rd floor. No credit cards. 11am–9pm. Bus: no. 45 from just east of Bell Tower to Dōng Mén.

Wénháo Záliáng Shífǔ Lǎo Diàn SHĂNXĪ This is one of the more affordable and healthy theater/banquet restaurants in Xī'ān. You won't leave with a grumbling stomach after you polish off up to eight appetizers, eight main courses, and 20 snacks *(xiǎo chī)*. There are three different banquets available, and if you book in advance, you may be able to get a table close to the shadow puppet show (see "Chinese Shadows," below), which is held every night on the third floor. Worth looking out for are a delicious steamed corn bun *(wōtóu)* and a nutty sweet-potato pancake *(shǎn nán xiāngyù bǐng)*.

Jiànshè Lù 2. (From Lǔ Jiā Cūn, walk south 54m/180 ft. and turn right into Jiànshè Lù. The restaurant is 225m/750 ft. ahead, on the north side.) ⓒ 029/8553-5555. Reservations recommended. Meal for 2 ¥120–¥200 ($15–$25). No credit cards. 9:30am–11pm. Bus: no. 606 (from just north of Bell Tower) or no. 5 (from the railway station to Lǔ Jiā Cūn).

XĪ'ĀN AFTER DARK
THE PERFORMING ARTS

Two companies perform Táng-style banquets and musicals to entertain visitors. The competition for the group-tour dollar is fierce.

Shǎnxī Grand Opera House (Shǎnxī Gēwǔ Dà Xìyuàn) While it can't compete with Táng Yuè Gōng (see below) as a spectacle, this opera company has a more authentic feel, with revolutionary credentials tracing its origins to the Northwest Culture Work Group in Yán'ān. If you opt for the dinner, you'll gorge on dumplings with 20 different fillings. Be sure to book in advance; the busy season (May–Oct) may offer two performances nightly (call ahead). Voice-overs are in Chinese and English. If you attend one show, dinner starts at 7pm and the show starts at 8:30pm. If you attend two shows, the first performance is at 6pm, dinner at 7:10pm, and the second show at 8:40pm. Wén Yì Lù 165. ⓒ 029/8785-6012. Reservations essential. Dinner and show ¥198 ($25);

Chinese Shadows

Píyǐng was the staple entertainment of rural Shǎnxī before karaoke. Puppets are carved from leather and dyed dazzling colors—many date from the Qīng dynasty (1644–1911). There are over 600 different plays, ranging from legends to love stories to kung-fu epics. Unlike opera, this is loud, irreverent entertainment for the masses. This art will probably die out in Shǎnxī; its main exponent is a septuagenarian, and his only student is a few years younger. It takes 10 years to learn the craft, and for most, driving a taxi is a more appealing option. For now, the puppet troupe (Shǎnxī Hù Xiàn Píyǐng Yìshùtuán) also performs at Dōngfāng Dàjiǔdiàn.

show only ¥118 ($15). AE, DC, MC, V. Bus: no. 14 from the station, or no. 208 from south of the Bell Tower to Diǎo Jiǎ Cūn.

Táng Dynasty (Táng Yuè Gōng)   Run by a Hong Kong entrepreneur, this show delivers all your fantasies of Asia at once: lavish costumes modeled on the Mògāo cave paintings, a six-course banquet (watch out for the rice wine), hammy acting, and some amazing music and dance. Gāo Míng's performance of the Spring Oriole's Song on a vertical bamboo flute, the *pái xiāo*, is almost worth the money in itself. If you can get past the slickness and the feeling that it's just for foreigners (the voice-overs are all in English), the show makes a spectacular night out. Dinner starts at 7pm; the show begins at 8:30pm. Cháng'ān Lù 75. (② 029/8782-2222. Fax: 029/8526-1619. www.xiantangdynasty. com. Reservations essential. Dinner and show ¥410 ($51); show and cocktail ¥200 ($25). AE, DC, MC, V. Bus: no. 603 from station or north of Bell Tower to Cǎo Cháng Pō.

A SIDE TRIP FROM XĪ'ĀN: THE POTTERS OF CHÉN LÚ ★★

This tiny group of villages in undulating terrain north of Xī'ān has been turning out exquisite pottery since the Táng dynasty, and is free of the hype that surrounds Jǐngdé Zhèn (p. 513). Locals joke that Chén Lú "eats pottery," and while this may be fiction, walls are made of ceramic urns rather than bricks. Elegant cups that would fetch tidy sums in Xī'ān lie by the side of the road. No fewer than 17 small factories turn out different styles of pottery, ranging from the sleek black *hēiyòu* to the rusty shades of *tiěxiù huā* and the blues and whites of *qīng huā*. It's an old-fashioned town: People call each other "comrade" *(tóngzhì)* without the overtone of homosexuality that it now usually bears in urban China, wear Léi Fēng hats with thick tops and earflaps without irony, and offer cigarettes on reflex when they meet a stranger.

If you visit on a day trip, it's doubtful you'll have time to explore all the factories and shops. The best bargains are found in the factory showrooms, where the starting prices will have you offering more money, but you're more likely to come across original works in the houses of individual artisans. The main factory, **Chén Lú Táocí Chǎng** (② 0919/ 748-3343; www.yaozc.com), has an exhibition of antique ceramics, including Táng dynasty moxibustion cups, hat canisters from the Yuán dynasty, and ceramic pillows— still used by villagers today! Visit the exhibition before going on a spending spree, as staff can advise you on which factories make which kinds of pottery. Exquisite bowls in *qīng huā* style cost as little as ¥10 ($1.25), while original works are considerably more expensive. Individual artisans are proud to display their wares and may hail you in the street. Well-known artisans include **Xú Kuàilè** (② 0919/748-2235) and **Wáng Àiguó** (② 0133/0919-9977).

The guesthouse at Chén Lú isn't someplace you'd willingly reside. But in this relaxed town, you won't be short on offers to stay and dine with the villagers, whose houses often have domed roofs in the manner of pottery kilns. Before you agree, check what sort of headrest your host has in mind. Ceramic pillows take some getting used to.

Chén Lú is a 1½-hour drive from Xī'ān, but most tour agencies will look blank when you mention it. A taxi should cost no more than ¥300 ($37) for the round-trip. Air-conditioned buses depart for Tóngchuān (100km/62 miles; 1½ hr.; ¥15/$1.90) from the main bus station every 20 minutes from 6:30am to 9pm. In Tóngchuān, continue north to the first roundabout for 630m (2,066 ft.), or catch bus no. 8 to the roundabout at Yígǔ Liángzhàn. From south of the roundabout, white minivans leave when full for Chén Lú (18km/11 miles; 40 min.; ¥3/40¢).

2 Huá Shān

Shǎnxī Province, 120km (74 miles) E of Xī'ān

The first king of Shāng made a sacrifice on Huá Shān in 1766 B.C., and Hàn Wǔdì (reigned 141–87 B.C.) declared it the Sacred Mountain of the West. The mountain's present popularity with Chinese tourists was aided by Jīn Yōng's martial-arts novel *Huá Shān Lùn Jiàn*, which is filled with heroic swordsmen, mythical beasts, and beautiful maidens. Add a popular soap-opera set against the granite bluffs, precariously perched pine trees, and Daoist temples dangling from precipitous peaks, and Huá Shān's popularity with the locals was guaranteed. Huá Shān sees few foreign visitors, which is a shame, because the climb is a more pleasant experience here than at many other holy mountains in China (where you can be pestered off the mountain by local tourists who see you as part of the entertainment). The scenery is spectacular, the Daoist monks are friendly, and the air is clear enough to make the sunrise worth seeing. The best times to visit are mid-autumn, when the trees are a magical, colorful jumble, or spring, when the wildflowers bloom. Winter is picturesque but bitterly cold.

ESSENTIALS

GETTING THERE   Huá Shān can be visited as a 1- or 2-day trip from Xī'ān. An air-conditioned **bus** leaves from the front of the Jiěfàng Hotel every hour from 7:20am (2 hr.; ¥18/$2.20). Ignore touts who try to drag you away to their minibuses. If you are walking up, ask the conductor to drop you at Huá Shān Kǒu, a village at the base of the mountain, or say that you are walking the *lǎo lù* (old road). To reach the chairlift, stay on the bus to the park entrance and connect with another bus (¥10/$1.25) that takes a further 25 minutes to reach the cable car. Entry to Huá Shān is ¥70 ($9). The last bus returns to Xī'ān from the cable car stop at 4pm, and minibuses run until 7pm.

Connect by **rail** via Huá Shān railway station. There is a minibus every half-hour to Huá Shān Kǒu (20 min.; ¥3/40¢, 1½ hr.); or hail a red minivan that will take you there for the same price. Trains back to Xī'ān (2 hr.) cost between ¥10 ($1.25) and ¥20 ($2.50) and depart every hour or so.

VISITOR INFORMATION   The **Huá Shān Tourist Bureau** (© **0913/436-6650;** fax 0913/436-3578) is inside the Huá Shān Financial Hotel.

EXPLORING THE AREA

Consider the cable car, especially if you only have 1 day in your schedule. The mountain is a tough 2,000m (6,600-ft.) climb, especially if you don't have a head for heights. If you have 2 or more days, walk up and stay at one of the guesthouses on the mountain. You will enjoy a feeling of smugness when you meet the masses piling out of the cable cars at **North Peak (Běi Fēng).** By staying on the mountain, you can see the sunrise and the sunset, and enjoy the mountains when the light is soft. Admission to the mountain is now a whopping ¥100 ($13).

Chinese guidebooks recommend climbing up at night with a flashlight to see the sunrise (presumably skipping the entrance fee). The locals say, "You don't fear what you can't see" *("Bú jiàn bú pà").* This is not sensible. The cable car (¥110/$14 round-trip; ¥60/$7.50 one-way) reaches Běi Fēng in 10 minutes, about 4 hours quicker than you would on foot. If you want to save your knees and leave yourself more time on the mountain, take the cable car down.

On the old road, it's 8km (5 miles) to Běi Fēng, all uphill. You can take a taxi for ¥20 ($2.50). The last mile to North Peak is steep, narrow, and slippery, particularly through **Heaven's Well (Tiān Jǐng).**

Chinese tour groups, bedecked in yellow hats and white gloves, will gape at you, and souvenirs, bottles of water, and cucumbers will be waved in your face, but there is an enjoyable spirit of camaraderie among the hikers. And at least one of the souvenirs is worth purchasing. Every Chinese visitor has his or her name engraved on a brass padlock (¥2/25¢) wishing good health for the family, and attaches it to one of the many chain railings.

WHERE TO STAY & DINE

Outside of early May and mid-October, there is a surplus of accommodations on Huá Shān, so discounts of 30% to 50% are easily obtained. Dining on the mountain is basic and over-priced; take as much food as you can carry.

If you arrive at Huá Shān late at night, there are a couple of passable hotels in **Huá Shān Kǒu,** and unlike the lodgings on Huá Shān itself, they have showers. The dark, midsize rooms of the **Huá Shān Jīnróng Bīnguǎn (Huá Shān Financial Hotel),** Yù Quán Lù Zhōng Duàn (© **0913/436-3119;** fax 0913/436-3124; ¥388/$48 twin, from ¥588/$75 suite), are overpriced, and service can be distant. The best rooms are in building 4, which was renovated in 2001. The Huá Shān Tourist Bureau and a restaurant are located here. The **Xī Yuè Bīnguǎn,** Yù Quán Lù Zhōng Duàn (© **0913/436-8298;** ¥198/$25 twin), easily spotted because of its traditional sloping tiled roof, is friendlier and a better value than the Financial. It was renovated in 2002 but the money ran out, leaving the corridors dark and dank.

On the mountain, facilities are basic, there are no bathrooms or showers, and pit toilets are common. Problems with wastewater treatment may lead to the closure of many hotels, so call ahead to check if your intended lodgings are still there. The **Běi Fēng Fàndiàn,** Huá Shān Fēngjǐng Qū Běi Fēng (© **0913/430-0062;** ¥300 ($37) twin without bathroom), is a 5-minute walk from the cable car—perfect for the lazy and the late. Both the sunset and the sunrise can be enjoyed from the North Peak. The hotel offers a competent staff, clean rooms, a restaurant, and magnificent views.

3 Tiānshuǐ

Gānsù Province, 385km (239 miles) W of Xī'ān, 294km (182 miles) SE of Lánzhōu

Tiānshuǐ is divided into two parts—the main town of **Qín Chéng,** and the smaller township of **Běidào Qū,** 15km (9 miles) down the Wèi river valley to the west. Both townships are unexceptional; the main reason to visit is a clamber around the stunning Buddhist caves of Màijī Shān, a 1-hour bus ride from Běidào Qū. *Note:* Please turn to appendix A for Chinese translations of key locations.

GETTING THERE   The **railway station** is in the north of Běidào Qū, with many trains from Lánzhōu (6 hr.) and farther west, and from Xī'ān (6 hr.) and farther east. Tiānshuǐ's allocation of tickets is limited, so you may need to proceed through CITS in Qín Chéng. Heading west for Lánzhōu are the T75 (11:27am), T113 (9:39am), and T117 (12:20pm). For trains beyond Lánzhōu, try the T53 (29½ hr.; no reserved seats; 4:27pm), or T69 (11:44am). To Xīníng, the speediest choice is the T151 (8 hr.; 7am). To Chóngqìng, the only direct train is the 1084 (20 hr.; 12:12am). Pray for an upgrade. To Xī'ān, take the K120 (1:26am) or T54 (6:32pm) that continues to Shànghǎi. Běijīng trains include the T70 (5:59pm), T152 (7:17pm), and T76 (11:09pm).

Connecting with Xī'ān (370km/229 miles; 6 hr.), the **bus** is your best option. From the **Běidào Qū long-distance bus station** on Jiāotōng Lù (© **0938/273-6388**) there are eight buses a day to Xī'ān (7am–4:30pm; ¥60/$7.50); half-hourly buses to Lánzhōu (8am–5pm; 381km/236 miles; 7 hr.; ¥58/$7); and buses to Yínchuān on alternate days (noon; 610km/378 miles; 17 hr.; ¥75/$9). Buses for Lánzhōu also depart from the railway station between 7:30am and 5pm.

The main bus station in Qín Chéng is 3 blocks east and 2 blocks north of the main square at Shāndōng Lù 31 (© **0938/821-4028**). Eleven buses depart daily for Xī'ān from 7am to 8pm. Buses depart every half-hour for Lánzhōu (¥50/$6); at 6am and 5pm for Yínchuān (¥60/$7.50); and at 6:30am for Línxià (396km/246 miles; 13 hr.; ¥47/$5.90).

GETTING AROUND   Bus no. 6 from the railway station connects Qín Chéng with Běidào Qū (15km/9¼ miles; 30 min.; ¥2.40/30¢). The first bus is at 6:20am; the last bus departs at 11:30pm. Taxis in both areas cost ¥4 (50¢), white minivans ¥3 (40¢).

TOURS & GUIDES   Two hundred meters (656 ft.) east of the Bank of China is **CITS,** on the first floor of Shì Cáizhèng Jú, Mínzhǔ Dōnglù (© **0938/821-3621;** fax 0938/821-3621; www.tianshuitour.com). They are useful if you are looking for an English-speaking guide (¥150/$20 per day), but don't expect obligation-free advice. They are open from 8:30am to 6pm.

FAST FACTS
Banks, Foreign Exchange & ATMs   The main **Bank of China** is located at Jiànshè Lù 8 (© **0938/821-3515**) in Qín Chéng, 800m (2,624 ft.) east of the northeast corner of the main square on the north side of the road. The building has massive bronze lions out front. It's open from 8am to 6pm on weekdays.

Internet Access   An **Internet bar** on the second floor of Gōnghuì Dàshà charges ¥2 (25¢) per hour. Dial-up is © **169.**

Post Office   The main post office is located on the northwest corner of the main square in Qín Chéng.

SEEING THE SIGHTS
Màijī Shān Shíkū 🏵🏵   These are the most remarkable Buddhist caves in China, demonstrating a fine range of statuary styles amid spectacular scenery. Located 30km (19 miles) southeast of Tiānshuǐ, the haystack-shaped mountain is home to 194 extant caves, most on the western side of the mountain. The first caves were carved out during the Later Qín (384–417), a non-Hàn dynasty established during the Sixteen Kingdoms Period. Unlike other Buddhist caves, these saw little construction during the Táng dynasty, due to a series of earthquakes. The most serious occurred in 734, when the middle part of the grottoes collapsed. Significant statuary dates from the Northern Wèi, Northern Zhōu, and Suí dynasties.

Unlike other sites, the statuary here was not carved from the crumbling red rock, but added to it. **Grotto 18** explains the method of construction: A wooden superstructure is hauled up the mountain, bored into the soft cliffs, and coated with clay. Striking grottoes include **no. 191,** which houses a menacing winged figure with bulging eyes as its centerpiece; **no. 13,** with a huge Buddha and two attendant bodhisattvas dating from either the Northern Zhōu dynasty or the Suí dynasty; and **no. 5,** with a sensuous bodhisattva dating from the Táng dynasty. As you scramble up the ladders that connect the caves, the charming scenery complements the statuary.

Many of the most interesting caves are off-limits without payment of between ¥300 ($37) and ¥600 ($75) per group. If you have either the money or many like-minded friends, cave **no. 133** from the Northern Wèi (which is actually a tomb) is recognized as Màijī Shān's best. It contains 18 carved granite stones that depict the life of the Buddha. A sublime statue stands to the right, depicting one of Buddha's disciples, Bhiksu, smiling enigmatically as he listens to the master. When (now ex-) Prime Minister Zhū Róngjī visited in 2001, he was depressed by the poverty he saw on his tour of Gānsù. After staring at this statue, his good humor returned.

Buses for Màijī Shān (1–1½ hr.) leave Běidào Qū railway station from 7am, with the last bus leaving the mountain at 6pm. The bus will stop at a ticket office, where you pay ¥72 ($9) to enter the "scenic area." Collect a map of the area, which is included in the price but is not offered without prompting. The bus stops farther up the mountain; the 10-minute walk to the ticket office takes you through souvenir stalls and excited locals letting off firecrackers. There are no English-speaking guides, so unless you are fluent in Mandarin, there is no need to pay for a guide. Take a picnic, and leave time to explore the surrounding mountains and the botanical gardens.

© **0938/223-1031.** Admission: Scenic area ¥72 ($9) entrance to the caves, ¥50 ($6) for a guide; entrance to "special caves" up to ¥600 ($75). 9am–6pm. Minibus from railway station ¥5 (65¢).

WHERE TO STAY

Unless you have an early bus to catch from the main bus station in Qín Chéng, stay in Běidào Qū, which is handier for both the railway station and Màijī Shān. Discounts of 20% are easily obtained at all establishments. Going against the trend elsewhere, the best hotels in Běidào Qū are near the railway station and the best among them is the two-star **Màijī Dàjiǔdiàn**, Tiānshuǐ Huǒchē Zhàn Guǎngchǎng Xī Cè (© **0938/492-0000;** ¥204/$26 twin, ¥58/$72 suite). The hotel has bright, clean rooms (the best are on the sixth floor, facing away from the railway station), an efficient staff, and a restaurant. If you decide to stay in Qín Qhéng, the recently renovated two-star **Tiānshuǐ Dàjiǔdiàn,** Dàzong Lù Nán Kǒu 1 (© **0938/828-9999;** fax 0938/821-1301; ¥146/$18 twin, ¥217/$27 suite), is the best choice for facilities and location. But if you want to spent the night at Màijī Shān, **Zhíwùyuán Zhāodàisuǒ** (© **0938/223-1029;** ¥100/$13 twin in old wing, ¥280–¥360/$35–$44 cabin) is a real find. The setting is the botanical gardens behind the mountain, amid imposing oak and birch forests and the cabins are good value—you can pay by the bed. By car, take a road to the left 720m (2,362 ft.) past the scenic area ticket office and continue uphill for 3km (2 miles), or walk 15 minutes past the Màijī Shān caves.

WHERE TO DINE

Běidào Qū may not be a culinary paradise, but it sports honest eateries serving generous portions for around ¥10 ($1.25) per person. Elbow past the locals to find a seat in **Niú Dàwǎn,** a halal (Muslim) restaurant north of the bus station on Ér Mǎ Lù. There's one dish to order—*niúròu miàn* (beef noodles), and two choices to make—thick *(kuān)* or thin *(xì)* noodles, and whether to add more beef *(jiā ròu)*.

A friendly establishment just west of the Gōnghuì Dàshà, the **Tiān Xǐ Xiǎochīdiàn** is run by three retired sisters and serves generous portions for around ¥10 ($1.25) per person. Filling *chǎo miàn* (stir-fried noodles) or a stone bowl of bubbling *shāguō jī kuài* (chicken clay pot) are perfect after a hike in the mountains.

4 Lánzhōu

Gānsù Province, 665km (412 miles) W of Xī'ān, 514km (319 miles) SW of Yínchuān

This was once the point where the Silk Routes crossed the Yellow River; however, whatever charms the old town possessed were buried long ago. In 1998, **Lánzhōu** won the title of the planet's most polluted city by a considerable margin (Chinese towns filled 7 of the top 10 places). This dubious distinction led to humorous attempts to rectify the problem—one entrepreneur got backing for a scheme to knock a hole in the surrounding mountains to "open the window" on Lánzhōu's smog. Alas, after 18m (60 ft.) of leveling, and much talk of villas and technology parks, this grand dream of moving the mountain ended when planners discovered that Lánzhōu was hemmed in, not by one mountain, but by 24km (15 miles) of mountains. Plans to convert the city's largest polluter—a coal-fired power station—to natural gas also fell through when the German partner found that the numbers didn't add up.

Lánzhōu offers a glimpse of what lies farther northwest, but there are few reasons to linger. The museum is worth a look, and the town is a comfortable base for trips south to Bǐnglíng Sì, Xiàhé, and Lángmùsì. But your first action should be to book a ticket out of town.

ESSENTIALS

GETTING THERE   The airport is 75km (47 miles) to the north. **China Eastern Airlines** (© 0931/882-1964; fax 0931/882-8174; open 8am–9pm) has its main office opposite the JJ Sun Hotel. They can book tickets on any Chinese airline. Buses for the airport (1 hr.; ¥30/$3.60) leave 3 hours before each flight.

Queues at the new **railway station** (© 0931/492-2222) in the south of town can range from very short to very long. It's worth a shot to go directly here if you hoping to head out of town quickly. Sleeper tickets may also be purchased through your hotel; from various branches of the Industrial and Commercial Bank (Gōng Háng; © 0931/881-8544); or from the largest ticket outlet in the Railway Bureau (Tiělùjú) at Hézhèng Lù 156, on the first floor of the Jīnlún Dàshà. Take bus no. 34 from the station to Tiělùjú.

Trains originating in Lánzhōu connect with Běijīng (T76: 6:56pm, 22 hr.; K44: 4:03pm, 27 hr.), Shànghǎi (T118: 12:05am, 25 hr.), Ürümqi (T295: 4:25pm, 24 hr.,), Xī'ān (K120: 8:40pm, 10 hr.), Guǎngzhōu (K228: 9:25pm, 36 hr.), Chéngdū (K348: 3:46pm, 22 hr.), Píngliáng (N906: 7:32pm, 12 hr.), Jiāyùguān (N907: 8:40pm, 14 hr.), Xīníng (T653: 8:25am, 3 hr.; T655: 3:43pm), and Golmud (N903: 5:49pm, 18 hr.). The speediest connection with Yínchuān is the N902 at 9:48pm (9 hr.).

Bus insurance, which costs ¥30 ($3.70) and is required for travel in Lánzhōu, Xià Hé, and Hézuò, may be purchased from **China Life** (© 0931/840-1757, ext. 8102) at Bīnhé Dōng Lù 573; take bus no. 7 from the station to Qiáo Nán Zhàn, then continue west for about 360m (1,200 ft.). The **West Bus Station** is at Xījīn Dōng Lù 486 (© 0931/266-3285). Bus insurance (plus ¥10/$1.25 commission) may be purchased from counter 2, tickets from counter 3. Buses connect with Hézuò (258km/160 miles; 6 hr.; ¥32/$4 or ¥44/$5.40 Iveco) every half-hour from 7am; with Línxià (149km/92 miles; 4 hr.; ¥27/$3.20) every hour from 8:30am; and with Xīníng every hour from 7:30am. The final bus for these destinations is at 4pm. There are three direct buses to Xià Hé (256km/159 miles; 6 hr.) at 7:30am (¥45/$5.50); 8:30am and 2pm (¥44/$5.40); and three direct buses to Liújiā Xiá (2 hr.; ¥11/$1.30) at 7:30am, 8:30am, and 10am. Every other day there is a bus to Tóngrén (10 hr.; ¥38/$4.70).

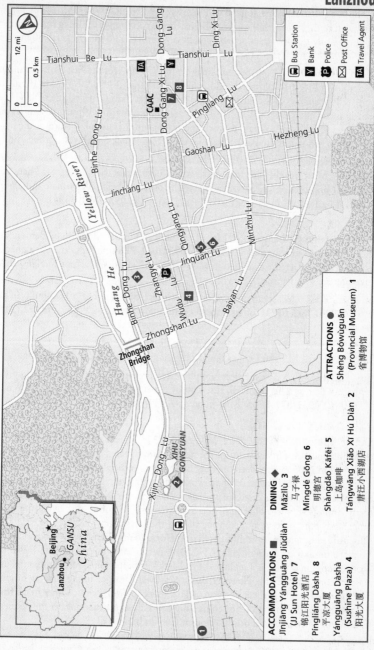

Lánzhōu

Legend:
- Bus Station
- Bank
- Police
- Post Office
- TA Travel Agent

Map labels:

Tianshui Be Lu

Tianshui Lu

Dong Gang Lu

Ding Xi Lu

Dong Gang Xi Lu

CAAC

Pingliang Lu

Hezheng Lu

Gaoshan Lu

Binhe Dong Lu

Jinchang Lu

Qingyang Lu

Minzhu Lu

Jinquan Lu

Zhangye Lu

Binhe Dong Lu

Baiyin Lu

Wumu Lu

Zhongshan Lu

Zhongshan Bridge

Huang He

(Yellow River)

Xijin Dong Lu

XIHU GONGYUAN

Beijing

Lanzhou

GANSU

China

ACCOMMODATIONS ■

Jǐnjiāng Yángguāng Jiǔdiàn
(JJ Sun Hotel) 7
锦江阳光酒店

Pingliáng Dàshà 8
平凉大厦

Yángguāng Dàshà
(Sushine Plaza) 4
阳光大厦

DINING ◆

Mǎzilù 3
马子禄

Míngdé Gōng 6
明德宫

Shàngdǎo Kāfēi 5
上岛咖啡

Tángwāng Xiǎo Xī Hú Diàn 2
唐汪小西湖店

ATTRACTIONS ●

Shěng Bówùguǎn
(Provincial Museum) 1
省博物馆

269

The **long-distance bus station** at Píngliáng Lù 133 (© **0931/456-2222**) is just northwest of the railway station. Half-hourly buses connect with Xīníng from 7am to 7:30pm. Daily sleeper buses depart for Lhasa (5pm; ¥352/$44); Xī'ān (5:30pm; 13 hr.; ¥130/$16); and Yán'ān (5:30pm; 16 hr.; ¥169/$20).

GETTING AROUND   Green Santanas charge ¥7 (90¢) for the first 3km (2 miles), then ¥1.40 (20¢) per kilometer; add a night surcharge (¥1.60/20¢) from 10pm to 5am. Yellow *miàndī* vans charge ¥5 (60¢) for the first 3km (2 miles), then ¥1 (15¢) per kilometer thereafter; and ¥1.20 (15¢) per kilometer from 10pm to 5am. Buses start at ¥1 (15¢), which is paid to a conductor. Bus no. 1 is useful; it starts at the railway station and passes the Bank of China, the JJ Sun Hotel, Northwest Airlines, Sunshine Plaza, and the Lánzhōu Museum.

TOURS   Most **hotels** have tour desks which offer tours to Bǐnglíng Sì. There are numerous branches of **CITS,** each accusing the others of being illegitimate. A helpful branch is located at Lǚyóu Dàshà, Nóngmín Xiàng (© **0931/881-9394**).

FAST FACTS

Banks, Foreign Exchange & ATMs   The **Bank of China** (Mon–Fri 8:30am–noon and 2:30–6pm) at Tiānshuǐ Lù 589 (© **0931/841-7284**) accepts traveler's checks (counter 48) and credit cards (counter 47). The ATM doesn't accept foreign cards. Take bus no. 1 to Pánshí Lù.

Internet Access   Just south of Lánzhōu University, **E Sù Wǎngbā,** at Tiānshuǐ Nán Lù 286 (© **0931/863-6171**), offers a speedy connection and classical music for ¥2 (25¢) per hour.

Post Office   The post office (Mínzhǔ Dōng Lù 104; Mon–Fri 8am–7pm) is located on the corner of Mínzhǔ Dōng Lù and Píngliáng Lù near the East Bus Station.

Visa Extensions   Visa extensions are processed promptly up to 2 weeks before the expiration date at a helpful **PSB,** just west of the city government building at Wǔdū Lù 310 (© **0931/871-8606**; 8am–noon and 2:30–6pm).

EXPLORING LÁNZHŌU

Shěng Bówùguǎn (Provincial Museum)   As of press time, this museum had closed its doors to undergo a huge renovation. It's expected that it will reopen again sometime in 2006 in a modern building but museum officials aren't getting more specific than that. Call ahead to see if the work is done. In the case that it's been reopened, call ahead to arrange an English-speaking guide. The late Neolithic pottery is particularly impressive, most of it from the region around Tiānshuǐ, displaying the rapid progress in both pottery and painting during this period (ca. 3000–1900 B.C.). The museum's most famous exhibit is the **Flying Horse (Tóng Bēn Mǎ)** ⊛, taken in 1969 from the tomb of an Eastern Hàn (25–220) general near Wǔwēi. Staff admit that the bronze horse on display is a replica; the real article is in the vaults of the museum, and another copy is in Běijīng. However, the original was damaged in the copying process, and the mold was either lost or destroyed, so this copy is priceless. Other items from the tomb include bamboo strips containing meticulous instructions on the etiquette of drinking, marriage, and death. Allow at least an hour.

Directly opposite the Friendship Hotel. © 0931/234-6306. From Yǒuyì Bīnguǎn, cross the road and continue west for 135m (450 ft.). Admission ¥15 ($1.90); English-speaking guide about ¥40 ($4.80). 9am–4:30pm. Bus: no. 1 to Yǒuyì Bīnguǎn.

A NEARBY GROTTO

Once a long day trip from Lánzhōu, Bǐnglíng Sì may now be visited on the way to Xià Hé; set out early to avoid being stuck in Línxià (p. 271). The town nearest Bǐnglíng Sì is Liújiā Xiá, which was recently connected with Lánzhōu by an expressway. The trip takes about 90 minutes. Unless you have a passion for cave temples, this one's probably not worth the long haul from Lánzhōu, but if you're heading south to Xià Hé and the weather is fine, it makes for an agreeable outing.

On arrival at Liújiā Xiá, you'll be bundled off to the ticket office, where you purchase an entry ticket for the Sān Xiá Dam (¥15/$1.90)—formerly China's largest and single reason that the Yellow River ends well short of the sea—and a boat ticket. The public ferry costs ¥30 ($3.70), though the staff will deny its existence. It's better to take the fast boats instead, as they get you to the caves 2 hours faster. A round-trip ticket is ¥70 ($8.70); rates are slightly lower for groups. You can rent an entire boat, which will seat 6, for ¥350 ($44). Those continuing to Línxià (25km/16 miles; 40 min.; ¥5/60¢; last minibus 6pm) and then to Xià Hé (107km/66 miles; 2½ hr.; ¥9/$1.10) should ask to be dropped at Liánhuā Tái on the way back. (If you've got your private boat, you can ask that they take you here.) The last bus back to Lánzhōu (¥10/$1.25) leaves at 6:30pm. If you stay in Liújiā Xiá, the best lodgings are the Huáng Hé Bīnguǎn and the cheaper Liú Diàn Bīnguǎn.

There's a mock-fort hotel to the left (west) of the grottoes. Head straight for the caves, as most boats only wait for an hour. Two-thirds of the caves were carved in the Táng dynasty, but examples range from the Northern Wèi (368–534) to the Míng dynasties. Pay ¥35 ($4.20) at the ticket office and turn right; follow a narrow pathway around. A 27m (90-ft.) Maitreya (Buddha of the Future) with prominent nipples—a decidedly non-Hàn Chinese touch—dominates the valley. Higher up the cliff face is **Cave 169** ⚐ (¥300/$37 extra!), one of the most ancient in China, showing Indian influences. Unlike most cave temples, the upper caves are natural. Unfortunately, 200 lower caves were flooded when the dam was completed.

WHERE TO STAY

Lánzhōu may be a dump, but it has new hotels with comfortable beds. Budget options are few, but 30%-to-50% discounts are negotiable at most establishments.

Jǐnjiāng Yángguāng Jiǔdiàn (JJ Sun Hotel)   A quick taxi ride from the railway station, this Hong Kong–managed hotel is not as great as the four stars hanging in the foyer might lead you to believe, but it's an acceptable option anyhow. The beds are a bit hard, and the rooms carry a slightly antiseptic smell. On the plus side, the staff is professional, guest rooms are spotless, and bathrooms are immaculate.

Dōnggǎng Xī Lù 589. ☎ 0931/880-5511. Fax 0931/885-4700. www.jjsunhotel.com. 236 units. ¥800 ($100) twin; ¥768 ($96) standard room; from ¥1,440 ($180) suite. Rates include full breakfast. 15% service charge. AE, DC, MC, V. **Amenities:** 2 restaurants; cafe; concierge; business center; 24-hr. forex; same-day dry cleaning/laundry. *In room:* A/C, TV, broadband Internet access (¥30 ($3.80) per day), minibar, fridge, hair dryer, safe.

Píngliáng Dàshà *(Finds)*   Hidden away down a lane to the east of the JJ Sun, this hotel is such good value that it's often full, so call ahead to check (but not to book . . . you're charged more if you book in advance). Guest rooms are fresh and bright, and bathrooms are less cramped than those at many four-star hotels in town. A 30% discount is standard.

Dōnggǎng Xī Lù 449-1. ☎ 0931/873-3986, ext. 8000. 50 units. ¥200–¥220 ($25–$27) standard room; ¥580 ($72) suite. Rates include full breakfast. No credit cards. **Amenities:** Restaurant; next-day dry cleaning/laundry. *In room:* A/C, TV.

Yángguāng Dàshà (Sunshine Plaza) ✿✿ (Value) (Kids)   Easily the best hotel in town, the Sunshine Plaza has great service and comfortable rooms. It's been successful enough that it will have just finished an expansion by the time you arrive. Three English-speaking Indian staff members make communication easy. The rooms are nicely carpeted, beds are plush, and raised sitting areas are a nice touch. Massage shower heads with six jets are state-of-the-art. The game room is inspired; you can practice your golf swing, grand-prix driving, skiing, dancing, and even shuffleboard, a spectator sport in China. Facilities for travelers with disabilities are available.

Qīnyáng Lù 408. ✆ 0931/460-8888. Fax 0931/460-8889. www.sunshineplaza.com.cn. 233 units (shower only). ¥980 ($123) standard room; ¥1,180 ($148) suite. Rates include 1 breakfast. 15% service charge. AE, DC, MC, V. **Amenities:** 2 restaurants; nightclub; huge game room; concierge; courtesy car; business center; executive business services; 24-hr. forex (no traveler's checks); 24-hr. room service; same-day dry cleaning/laundry. *In room:* A/C, satellite TV, broadband Internet access, minibar, fridge, hair dryer, safe.

WHERE TO DINE

Those craving junk food will find a **KFC** on the northeast corner of Zhōngshān Lù and Zhāngyè Lù. Take bus no. 1 to Xīguān Shízì. **Shàngdǎo Kāfēi,** Nánguān Shízì Shíyóu Dàshà 1 Lóu (✆ **0931/844-8396**), serves eminently drinkable coffee—but be sure to specify hot *(rè),* iced *(bīng),* or by the pot *(hú).* The simple menu offers toast, waffles, and steaks.

Mǎzilù ✿✿ (Value) GĀNSÙ   Be prepared to have one of the best noodle experiences of your life. The drafty, warehouse-style restaurant, open for breakfast and lunch, doesn't have much atmosphere, but no one's here for the decor—it's all about the beef noodles, which is the only thing you can get here. Lánzhōu niúròu lāmiàn has migrated to all parts of the country by way of little street-side noodle shops, but this is the real deal, and known by locals as the best place to sample the dish. Pay your ¥3 (40¢) to the cashier, who will give you a ticket to collect your bowl at the back of the restaurant. The tender, thin noodles are boiled in a huge vat of beef broth, then chili and sesame sauce and bits of beef are tossed in at the last minute.

Dàzhōng Xiàng. No phone. Meal for 2 ¥6 (80¢). No credit cards. 6:30am–2:30pm.

Míngdé Gōng ✿ GĀNSÙ   The Míngdé Gōng, a four-story palace that gets progressively more luxurious as you ascend (culminating in dark wood-paneled rooms, gold-plated cutlery, and some of the biggest karaoke TVs you'll ever see), is the flag-bearer for Gānsù cuisine—"lǒng cài." While the boss is a Huí entrepreneur, the chefs hail from Běijīng and Guǎngzhōu. Signature dishes include *měnggǔ yángpái* (Mongolian lamb), the huge and spicy *kǎo yángtuǐ* (roast leg of lamb with walnuts), a deep-fried lamb and green-pepper pancake *(bóbǐng yángròu),* and the sweet vegetarian dish, *xāshì jǐnjú bǎihé.*

Jiǔquán Lù 191. ✆ 0931/466-8588. Meal for 2 ¥90–¥170 ($11–$21). No credit cards. 10:30am–10pm.

Tángwāng Xiǎo Xī Hú Diàn GĀNSÙ   Regional specialties are scarce, but locals are proud of *shǒuzhuā ròu* (grabbed meat): hunks of beef dunked in salt and pepper and chased by a clove of raw garlic (optional!). Ask for a lean portion *(shòu fěn),* unless you want to guzzle on huge lumps of lard. The *xìliè niúròu miàn* (beef noodles) are also first-rate. Lánzhōu's liveliest night market, Xiǎo Xīhú Yèshì, is directly across the road.

✆ 0931/260-2398. Meal for 2 less than ¥40 ($5). No credit cards. Open 24 hr. Bus: no. 1 to Xiǎo Xī Hú.

5 Línxià

Gānsù Province, 149km (92 miles) SW of Lánzhōu, 107km (66 miles) NE of Xià Hé

"All writers agree on the commercial ability and energy of the T'ung-kan [Huí], as well as on their surliness, ill manners and hostile suspicion of strangers. . . ." This judgment by American journalist Owen Lattimore seems harsh until you visit Línxià, a predominantly Huí town (with a smattering of Bǎo'ān and the Altaic Dōngxiāng minorities). Those wishing to stay in a traditional, non-Uighur Islamic town should visit Xúnhuà in eastern Qīnghǎi. But for those arriving from the north, an overnight stay here in Línxià may be unavoidable.

GETTING AWAY   The **West Bus Station (Xī Zhàn;** ✆ **0930/621-2177)** is less prone to thievery than the **South Bus Station (Nán Zhàn;** ✆ **0930/621-2767).** There are buses every half-hour for Lánzhōu (149km/92 miles; 4 hr.; ¥27/$3.50) from 7am to 3pm; Hézuò (106km/66 miles; 2 hr.; ¥13/$1.60) every half-hour from 6:30am; Xīníng (269km/167 miles; ¥34/$4) at 6am; Xià Hé (107km/66 miles; 2½ hr.; ¥14/$1.50) from 7am to 4:30pm; Xúnhuà (115km/71 miles; 2½ hr.; ¥12/$1.50) and Tóngrén (183km/113 miles; 5 hr.; ¥20/$2.40) at 6:30am; and Yù Mén (973km/ 603 miles; 20 hr.; ¥75/$9.40), just beyond Jiāyù Guān, at noon. Nán Zhàn has more buses to Xià Hé—every half-hour from 6:30am to 4:50pm.

WHERE TO STAY

If you stay overnight, there's the **Línxià Fàndiàn** at Hóngyuán Lù 9 (✆ **0930/ 623-2805;** fax 0930/621-4412), with rooms with twin beds in the old wing from ¥120 ($15), and in the new wing from ¥180 ($23). Head east from Xī Zhàn along Mínzhǔ Xī Lù, then turn down the first street on your right (south).

6 Hézuò

Gānsù Province, 258km (160 miles) SW of Lánzhōu, 72km (45 miles) SE of Xià Hé

Aside from a substantial Tibetan population, the capital of Gān Nán (Southern Gānsù) Prefecture is much like any other Hàn town of recent construction. As a transit point, it is much preferred to Línxià.

ESSENTIALS

GETTING THERE   Hézuò has two bus stations. The new **South Bus Station (Qìchē Nán Zhàn;** ✆ **0941/821-3039)** is inconveniently located in the far south of town; the ticket office is on the right as you enter. Buses connect with Xià Hé (72km/45 miles; 1½ hr.; ¥9/$1.10) every 30 minutes between 6:30am and 5pm. Buses connect with Línxià (106km/66 miles; 2 hr.; ¥13/$1.60) every 20 minutes from 6am to 5:40pm. Six buses depart for Lánzhōu (258km/160 miles; 6 hr.; ¥32/$4 or ¥44/$5.40 for Iveco) between 6:20am and 10am. Buses for Lángmù Sì (173km/107 miles; 5 hr.; ¥20/$2.40) depart at 7am and 9:40am. The **Central Bus Station, Hézuò Qìchēzhàn** (✆ **0941/821-2422),** also has buses for Ruò'ěrgài (7 hr.; ¥37/$4.60) in northern Sìchuān at 7:30am, continuing on to Aba (583km/361 miles; ¥77/$9.60) the following day. Every second day at 6am there are buses to Xīníng (331km/205 miles; 12 hr.; ¥43/$5.30).

Bus insurance may be obtained from **China Life,** about 450m (1,500 ft.) north of Hézuò Qìchēzhàn, just across a bridge on the left (west) side of the road at Téngzhī Zhōng Jiē 46 (✆ **0941/821-2219).** It's open Monday through Friday from 8am to 6pm, weekends from 9am to 4pm.

FAST FACTS

Visa Extensions   The Hézuò PSB office is on Rénmín Lù, near the large square (© 0941/821-3953).

EXPLORING HÉZUÒ

Mǐlārèpà Tower ⚿   Part of the Hézuò Monastery, this nine-story tower was built in 1678, but was burned down during the Cultural Revolution. In the late 1980s, government officials allowed the tower's rebuilding, which was completed in 1994. It's worth a rickety climb up the nine floors not only for the artifacts but also for the decent view of the city from the top. A nice monk named Chinpa who oversees the grounds may invite you in his office for tsampa and tea if you speak a bit of Chinese or Tibetan.

At the north end of Rénmín Lù. Admission ¥20 ($2.50) (though if you look Chinese, they'll let you in for ¥10/$1.25!). Open daylight hours.

WHERE TO STAY

Huáng Hé Fàndiàn   Renovations have brought something startling to this run-of-the mill hotel: large bathrooms! Guest rooms are sizable and airy, beds are new and firm, and the staff actually seems to give a damn. There is a merciful absence of sleaze, so for the moment, the home of the Mǎqū County Government is the best budget choice in town.

Mǎqū Xiàn Zhèngfǔ Zhù Hézuò Bànshìchù on Rénmín Jiē. © 0941/821-0158. 29 units (12 with bathroom). ¥100 ($13) twin; from ¥180 ($22) suite; ¥45 ($5.60) dorm bed. No credit cards. **Amenities:** Restaurant; teahouse. *In room:* TV.

Xiāngbālā Dàjiǔdiàn   One of Hézuò's newer establishments, this is the most comfortable hotel in town. Aside from the annoying instrumental music piped in through speakers in the lobby and the hallways (during working hours), there's nothing offending about this three-star place. Rooms are clean and bathrooms have been well scrubbed. The first floor features a Tibetan-style bar that features a nightly dancing and singing performance.

Rénmín Jiē 53. © 0941/821-3222. Fax: 0941/821-8899. 90 units. ¥ 280 ($35) standard room; from ¥880–¥1,280 ($105–$150) suite. No credit cards. **Amenities:** 3 restaurants; business center. *In room:* TV.

WHERE TO DINE

There's a market with an interesting mix of street stalls and small restaurants selling dumplings, Muslim food, and noodles not far from the bus station on the corner of Rénmín Lù and Dōng Èr Lù. Once you've sated your hunger, you can stroll around the market, which features everything from live birds to athletic shoes.

7 Xià Hé (Labrang) ⚿⚿⚿

Gānsù Province, 256km (159 miles) SW of Lánzhōu, 72km (45 miles) W of Hézuò

The delightful monastery town of **Xià Hé** is nestled north of the banks of the **Dà Xià Hé (Sāng Qǔ)** at an elevation of 2,900m (9,500 ft.). Not surprisingly, it gets very cold in winter, dipping to –4°F (–20°C); even in August, the average temperature is a cool 59°F (15°C). The town is divided into two sections. Primarily Huí and Hàn at its eastern end, it changes abruptly to Tibetan as you approach the monastery in the west. *Note:* Please turn to appendix A for Chinese translations of key locations.

ESSENTIALS

GETTING THERE   Buses (© 0941/712-1462) connect with Hézuò (72km/45 miles; 1½ hr.; ¥9/$1.10) every 30 minutes from 6:10am to 5:10pm; Línxià (107km/66

miles; 2½ hr.; ¥13/$1.60 or ¥18/$2.20 Iveco) every 30 minutes from 6am to 5pm; Lánzhōu (256km/159 miles; 5–6 hr.; ¥45/$5.50) at 6:30am, 7:30am, 8:30am, and 2:30pm; Tóngrén (107km/66 miles; 4 hr.; ¥17/$2.10) at 7:30am; and Amchog (72km/45 miles, 2 hr.; ¥15/$1.80) at 12:30pm and 3:40pm. The Tóngrén service connects with a Xīníng bus. Insurance may be purchased at the bus station; refuse payment for "excess luggage."

Minivans connect with Lángmù Sì (7 hr.; ¥300/$37); service is arranged outside Tara Guesthouse or at the bus station. *Warning:* If you're taking the rough but scenic route southeast via Amchog, hire a Tibetan driver and bring cigarettes; banditry, in the form of determined children with large rocks, is common.

GETTING AROUND **Bicycles** can be rented from Tara's Guesthouse for ¥10 ($1.25) per day.

TOURS & GUIDES Tsewong of Tsewong's Café is a good resource for travel information and can put you in touch with local drivers and tour guides.

FAST FACTS

Banks Forex services are unavailable in Xià Hé.

Internet Access Inexpensive Internet access can be found at the 24-hour **Lèlè Wǎngbā** (© **0941/712-1502**), in a courtyard diagonally opposite the bus station. A cup of tea is provided, and you can watch novice monks transfixed by ultraviolent computer games.

Post Office The post office (open 8am–6pm) is just downhill from Xīnhuá Shūdiàn, opposite the China Life Building.

Visa Extensions You used to be able to previously get them done here, but now it's only possible in at the Hézuò PSB office (see p. 274).

EXPLORING XIÀ HÉ

A 3km (2-mile) clockwise perambulation (kora) of the monastery is an excellent way to begin the day. You may find yourself befriended by delightful elderly pilgrims or by young monks keen to practice their English. If your schedule allows, time your visit to coincide with the **Monlam Festival,** held on the 4th to 16th days of the first lunar month (Feb–Mar). The monastery is open to all during the festival, and on the 13th day you can watch the "sunning of the Buddha." An enormous *thangka* (silk painting) is spread across a **Thangka Wall** on the south bank of the Sangchu. When sanctified, it effectively becomes the Buddha in the minds of believers. The following days feature religious dancing and the offering of *torma* (butter sculptures).

A hike up into the hills gives you a magnificent view of the monastery. Just west of it is a small, friendly nunnery.

Lābǔléng Sì (Labrang Monastery) 🏵🏵 As any monk you come across will tell you, Labrang Monastery, founded in 1709, is one of the six largest monasteries of the Geluk order, and the largest monastery in Amdo. Unlike most large religious institutions, it escaped desecration during the Cultural Revolution, although the number of monks and nuns was reduced from over 4,000 to the present number of just over 1,000. The head lama ranks behind only the Dalai Lama and the Panchen Lama, and with the passing away of the sixth incarnate lama (whose stupa rises in the south of the complex), the monastery is in transition. There are colleges for esoteric and exoteric Buddhism, astronomy, mathematics, geography, and medicine. Amdo monks see

themselves as the true holders of the faith—looking down on the Khampas and central Tibetans as soldiers and politicians respectively—and the monks take pride in the appearance of their monastery. Stunning *thangkhas* adorn the walls, and many beams and finials are inscribed with sacred and protective script.

The most striking building is the **Assembly Hall** ⚔, with its golden roof. This is a recent addition, as the original burned down in 1985. The **museum** and a display of frozen **butter sculptures**—including memorable sculptures of Jiāng Zémín and his cronies—are also worth seeking out. English-speaking tours are the only way to gain admission to the monastery; if you arrive late, you'll find yourself tacked on to a Hàn tour. Once inside, you're free to wander. Just to the right of the main entrance is the School of Buddhist Studies, where monks are often keen to practice their English.

Admission ¥31 ($3.90) for English tour; free otherwise. Tours leave twice a day from the front gate but times vary so it's best to check once you arrive. Closed Nov–Feb.

AROUND XIÀ HÉ

About 13km (8 miles) up the Dà Xià Hé are the grasslands of Sāngkē (entry ¥3/40¢), an ideal place for horse riding (¥20/$2.50 per hour). The grasslands are most spectacular in July and August, when the canola is flowering. Minivans wait outside the Tara Guesthouse and charge about ¥60 ($7.50) round-trip; or you can ride out by bike in an hour or so. (Bikes may be rented from Tara Guesthouse for ¥10–¥20/$1.25–$2.50 per day.) Some of the recent tourist developments—there are 18 "holiday villages" in the grasslands—are so appalling they are attractions in their own right. More spectacular grasslands are reached by turning left onto a seasonal road 12km (7½ miles) beyond town; continue southeast up the Xià Hé valley and over a pass towards the monastery town of **Amchog (Ā'mùqùhū).** Vast grasslands populated by marmots, vultures, and real nomads are your reward.

WHERE TO STAY

Lābǔléng Bīnguǎn (Labrang Hotel)   Once Xià Hé's premier hotel, the Labrang Hotel, situated far west of town, beyond the monastery, is desperately in need of a makeover. The last lick of paint was applied in 1995, and it shows. The Tibetan villas to the north of the complex feature enormous bathrooms, thick rugs, and obscene brown padded walls. The south building *(nán lóu)* is an unimaginative construction, although waking to the sound of a bubbling brook is pleasant.

Láizhōu Cūn 70, 747100. ✆ 0941/712-1849. Fax 0941/712-1328. 98 units (36 with shower only). ¥180–¥220 ($22–$27) standard room; ¥480 ($60) suite. No credit cards. **Amenities:** 3 restaurants; bar; bike rental (¥20/$2.50 per day); concierge; business center; same-day laundry. *In room:* TV.

Overseas Tibetan Hotel (Huáqiáo Fàndiàn) ⚔   The manager, Losang, is a Nepalese Tibetan who earned an MBA in the U.S. and does his best to instill a service ethic into his often lethargic staff. Once a dreary concrete monolith, this hotel has been greatly improved by successive additions to the second and third floors. The hotel offers a range of accommodations. The midsize rooms with twin beds on the third floor were added in 2001 and are the best in town, with tasteful Tibetan decorations and well-appointed bathrooms. The first-floor dormitory rooms are dank.

Rénmín Xī Jiē 77, 747100. ✆ 0941/712-2642. Fax 0941/712-1872. othotel@public.lz.gs.cn. 35 units (20 without bathroom). ¥140–¥200 ($18–$25) standard room; ¥80 ($10) twin without bathroom; ¥20 ($2.50) dorm bed. No credit cards. **Amenities:** Restaurant; bike rental (¥10/$1.25 per day); concierge; next-day laundry; Internet access. *In room:* TV.

Tara Guesthouse (Zhuómǎ Lǚshè) *Overrated*   If any hostel deserves the dreaded "backpacker mecca" title, this establishment does. Tara wrote to complain about the review we gave her establishment in our first edition, but we're sorry to say, Tara, that our second visit here was an even bigger disappointment. While popular with foreign travelers and boasting a prime location, only stay here if other hotels are booked. Don't be fooled by the cozy feel of the rooms; the service borders on hostile and you'll have to wrangle with the staff, who speak poor English, to get toilet paper. The dormitories on the first floor carry a pungent aroma of yak butter and wet socks. The communal showers and toilets, once unspeakably rank, are somewhat improved.

Yǎgē Táng 268, 747100. ⓒ 0941/712-1274. t-dolma@yahoo.com. 19 units (shared bathroom). ¥15–¥30 ($1.80–$3.70) dorm bed; ¥50 ($6.20) single; ¥70 ($9) standard. No credit cards. **Amenities:** Bike rental. *In room:* TV, no phone.

WHERE TO DINE
Everest Cafe WESTERN/CHINESE   Attached to the Overseas Tibetan Guesthouse, the restaurant is conveniently located for you to grab breakfast in the mornings before you start your pilgrimage around the monastery. The also offer a range of sandwiches, milkshakes, and *lassis*. The Chinese food is reminiscent of what you'd find at a Chinese restaurant in America.

Rénmín Xī Jiē 77. ⓒ 0941/712-2642. Meal for 2 ¥30–¥50 ($2.80–$6). No credit cards. 6:30am–11pm.

Tsewong's Cafe   WESTERN/CHINESE   Opened by a former employee of the Overseas Tibetan Guesthouse, this cafe serves better than average Western food in a clean environment. Try the advertised "real pizza by oven"—the crust is nice and cheesy and the sauce consists of fresh tomatoes. The green-pepper topping is deceptively spicy. The Chinese dumplings and the chocolate pancakes with Nutella are also popular. Tsewong is also a great resource for information about day trips around Xià Hé.

Rénmín Xī Jiē, located on the same side of street as the Overseas Tibetan Hotel, about 100m (328 ft.) in the opposite direction of the monastery on the 2nd floor. ⓒ 0941/712-2804 or 1389-397-9763. tsewongt@yahoo.com. Meal for 2 ¥30–¥80 ($2.80–$10). No credit cards. 7am–11pm.

8 Lángmù Sì (Taktsang Lhamo) ★★
Gānsù Province, 431km S of Lánzhōu, 91km NW of Ruò'ěrgài

Perched on the border of Sìchuān and Gānsù, this Tibetan monastic center is slowly becoming known to Chinese tourists, but still lacks the commercial feel of Xià Hé. The tranquil mountain village is reminiscent of Lìjiāng before it was "discovered." It is hoped Lángmù Sì can escape UNESCO listing for a few more years.

ESSENTIALS
GETTING THERE   Daily **buses** connect with Hézuò (173km/107 miles; 5 hr.; ¥20/$2.50) at 7am and 8am and with Línxià (279km/173 miles; 7 hr.; ¥30/$3.70) at 8am. From the south, a bus connects with Ruò'ěrgài (91km/56 miles; 2 hr.; ¥15/$1.90) every second day at noon. There are plans for a daily Sōngpān bus; a minibus to Sōngpān may be arranged through the Renchin Hotel (¥1,000/$125 for an 11-seat bus). The hardy can walk 3km (2 miles) north to the intersection and wait for buses from Hézuò, which pass by after 11am.

EXPLORING LÁNGMÙ SÌ
The town is home to two major Geluk monasteries, **Sertri Gompa** (¥10/$1.25 admission) and **Kirti Gompa** (¥15/$1.80 admission), situated in Gānsù and Sìchuān respectively. Both were razed during the Cultural Revolution and rebuilt during the early 1980s. Together, they house about 1,000 monks. True to the factional traditions

of Tibetan Buddhism, they refer to each other as "that place in the other province." While the buildings are of recent construction, both are lively centers of worship, and the sound of monks chanting the scriptures may be heard throughout the day. A magnificent view of the surrounding countryside may be had from Sertri Gompa.

There are some delightful rambles around Lángmù Sì. If you head southwest beyond the Richen Hotel and Kirti Gompa, a succession of narrow ravines and moraine valleys crowded with wildflowers, birds, and bubbling springs show the way to an abrupt pass. Continuing over the pass, you eventually connect with the Lángmù Sì–Mǎqū road, but this is a strenuous tramp through wild nomad country and should only be attempted by well-equipped parties. Another stiff hike is to the top of the distinctively shaped **Huā Gài Shān (Flower Cap Mountain);** this is best done as a horse trek (¥100/$13 per day), camping overnight on the peak. Traditionally, only men are allowed to sleep on the mountain, but this taboo is relaxed for foreigners. On a clear morning, you can see the holy mountain of Amnye Machen in Qīnghǎi. On the 15th day of the 6th month of the lunar calendar, a magnificent **"sunning of the Buddha" festival** takes place on a broad plateau just below the peak, the consecration of the *thangka* heralded by lamas trumpeting from the summit. A nearby hot spring is also a popular destination for horse treks.

Lángmù Sì is a popular spot to attend a **sky burial** or *chadur* (¥10/$1.25 admission). To reach the spot, head past the gate of Sertri Gompa and veer towards the left, walking about 1km (⅔ mile). A map posted at the gate of Serti Gompa is also helpful to look at. In this arid, treeless land, an alternative to cremation or burial had to be found for the people of the Tibetan plateau. The remains of the deceased (whose soul is thought to have already left the body) are dismembered and offered to huge vultures. Nothing is wasted. Even the bones are ground up by attendants. If attending the funeral of a stranger doesn't put you off, be aware that Lángmù Sì is a small town, so you may have to wait a few days for someone to die. A large breakfast beforehand is not advised.

WHERE TO STAY

Gānsù Dácāng Lángmù Bīnguǎn   This is the most comfortable guesthouse in town, though it's a standard two-star Chinese establishment lacking any character. The rooms come with private bathrooms—hard to come by in Lángmù Sì—but the water is either excruciatingly hot or ice cold and the tubs could use a good scrubbing.

Lángmù Sì. ⓒ 0941/667-1388, 1389/391-5888, or 1323/965-1666. 20 dorm beds, 1 standard room. ¥15 ($1.80) dorm bed; ¥50 ($6.20) standard room. No credit cards. *In room:* No phone.

Nomad's Youth Hostel (Lùpéng Qīngnián Lǚguǎn)   Recently opened by an avid Chinese backpacker from Hénán province, this second-floor guesthouse has great service, charming wood floors, and a row of airy communal rooms with dorm beds. Try to snag the one standard room here by calling in advance. When the hostel is full, Tibetan dance performances are held in the grounds behind the hostel, which inevitably turn into a late-night drinking fest. The owner, Mr. Zhāng, is an encyclopedia of travel information and can help arrange treks around the area. There is usually an English-speaking staff member around.

Lángmù Sì. ⓒ 1351/941-5604 or 1351/941-5602. Fax 0941/667-1460. lphy717@163.com. 20 dorm beds, 1 standard room. ¥15 ($1.80) dorm bed; ¥50 ($6.20) standard room. No credit cards. *In room:* No phone.

Sana Hotel (Sānà Bīnguǎn)   The plentiful standard rooms don't come with private baths but offer a nice view of the temple from their windows and the sound of a running river creek will lull you to sleep. The Muslim owner Yáng Jīncài is a jolly fellow who will encourage you to soak in the hot springs.

Lángmù Sì. ⓒ **0941/667-1062**. 30 units. ¥15 ($1.90) dorm bed; ¥35 ($4.10) standard room. No credit cards. *In room:* No phone.

WHERE TO DINE

Ali's Café 🦋🦋 (ⓒ **0941/667-1090**) was difficult to find, but worth the effort for homey ambience, cheap prices, and the affable owner, Ali—a great place to relax after a hike. At press time, however, the tiny restaurant was about the be torn down to make way for a new road—call Ali to find out where he's moved. Hearty backpacker fare is offered by **Lesha's Cafe** (ⓒ **0941/667-1179**), across the bridge between the Lángmù Sì Bīnguǎn and the Renchin Hotel. Fans of "competitive eating" should inquire about the Yak Burger Challenge. One new entry on the dining scene worthy of note is **Shànghǎi Times (Shànghǎi Shíguāng)** (ⓒ **0941/667-1508** or 1389/398-9290), which offers freshly ground coffee with one refill for ¥10 ($1.25) and a decent spaghetti Bolognese.

9 Jiāyù Guān

765km NW of Lánzhōu, 383km E of Dūnhuáng

At the northwest end of the narrow **Hé Xī corridor** lies a fort that marks the western extremity of the Míng Great Wall. During the Míng dynasty, **Jiāyù Guān** was regarded as the end of the Chinese world, beyond which lay the strange lands and peoples of the western lands. Just as transportation to Australia struck fear into Britons, exile ranked just behind decapitation and death by strangulation in the Qīng penal code. Many common criminals passed through the gates of Jiāyù Guān, but so did victims of court intrigues, such as commissioner Lín Zéxú (1785–1850), who tried to suppress the opium trade in Guǎngzhōu (Canton) but found himself banished to Yīníng. The only people regarded as less fortunate were those who built the Míng Wall. Its construction was estimated to have claimed eight million lives—one life for every yard. Jiāyù Guān today is a quiet and semiprosperous steel town. It's worthwhile to spend a day here to visit the fort.

ESSENTIALS

GETTING THERE   The **airport** is 15km (9 miles) northeast of downtown. A taxi there costs ¥25 ($3), or you can take a shuttle bus for ¥9 ($1.10). **CAAC** is at Xīnhuá Zhōng Lù 4–3 (ⓒ **0937/628-8777;** open 8:30am–5:30pm), about 90m (300 ft.) south of the main roundabout. Because all flights leave at 6pm, the airport shuttle departs from outside the CAAC office at 4:30pm. Jiāyù Guān is connected with Lánzhōu (daily), Dūnhuáng (daily), and Xī'ān (daily).

The **railway station** (ⓒ **0937/597-2512**) is 4km (2½ miles) southeast of the center of town. A taxi from the station should cost ¥10 ($1.25). Heading west, your chances of obtaining a sleeper ticket are slim. Proceed through CITS (¥30/$3.70 commission), or buy a hard-seat ticket and try to upgrade. Heading east, there are two new trains to Lánzhōu, for which tickets can be readily purchased—the N908 (4:53pm; 14½ hr.) and the faster T658 (8:32pm; 9½ hr.).

The **bus station** is on the southeast corner of Shènglì Zhōng Lù and Xīn Xī Lù. Daily buses connect with Dūnhuáng at 9am (383km/237 miles; 6 hr.; ¥46/$5.70); air-conditioned coaches depart at 10:30am, 11:30am, 2:30pm, and 4pm (¥67/$8.30). Sleeper buses for Lánzhōu (765km/474 miles; 13 hr.; ¥135/$16) leave at 3pm, 5pm, and 5:40pm. Bus insurance costing ¥30 ($3.70), which is essential for those traveling east, may be purchased at **Zhōngguó Rénshòu Bǎoxiǎn Gōngsī (China Life)** just south of the Bank of China, at Xīnhuá Zhōng Lù 36 (© **0937/626-1434**). It's open weekdays from 8:30am to 12:30pm and 2:30 to 6:30pm, weekends from 11am to 4pm.

GETTING AROUND   Santana **taxis** cost ¥7 (90¢) for the first 3km (2 miles), ¥1.20 (15¢) per kilometer thereafter, with a night surcharge of ¥1.40 (20¢) from 10pm to 5am. *Xiàlì* taxis charge ¥6 (75¢) for the first 3km (2 miles), with other rates the same as a Santana taxi's. **Bus** nos. 1 and 2 run from the railway station; both cost ¥1 (15¢). With wide, tree-lined bicycle lanes, **bikes** are the best way to get around. The standard rate is ¥2 (25¢) per hour, or ¥10 ($1.25) per day.

TOURS   Jiāyù Guān International Tours is run by the friendly Qín Jiǎn. His office is on the second floor of Shènglì Běi Lù 2 (© **0937/622-2586;** fax 0937/622-6931; www.westtour.cc). Hours are from 8:30am to 12:30pm and 2:30 to 6:30pm. Rates for train tickets and tours are reasonable.

FAST FACTS

Banks, Foreign Exchange & ATMs   You can change traveler's checks at the **Bank of China** (open weekdays 9pm–5pm, weekends 9:30am–4:30pm) at Xīnhuá Zhōng Lù 42, but your credit card will be of no use. Nor are there ATMs for international cards.

Internet Access   The best Internet cafe is **Jīn Chángchéng Wǎngbā,** located on the second floor of the Wénhuà Huódòng Zhōngxīn, just south of the night market. Dial-up is © **169.**

Post Office   The main post office (© **0937/632-4185;** open 8:30am–7pm) is on the southeast corner of the main roundabout at Xīnhuá Zhōng Lù 1.

Visa Extensions   The **PSB** is moving to Yíngbīn Zhōng Lù (© **0937/631-6927,** ext. 3016), but if you ask your hotel, a PSB officer will come to you.

EXPLORING JIĀYÙ GUĀN

Jiāyù Guān Chénglóu (Jiāyù Guān Fort) 🐾🐾
The Míng dynasty's rebuilt section of the Great Wall is still most people's image of China; this final outpost of the Wall is the best-preserved and most spectacular. First built in 1372, then expanded and reinforced in 1539, it was the final project of the Míng rebuilding. Entering from the east, you first come to the **Wénchāng Pavilion,** restored in the late Qīng dynasty, where intellectuals were said to compose poems, lamenting their rotten luck in being sent to live with the barbarians beyond the Wall. Before leaving, they could enjoy performances at the open-air theater opposite. After passing through **Guānghuá Mén,** the first of the three main 17m (56-ft.) towers, they would hurl a stone against the Wall to find out whether they would ever return to civilization. If the stone bounced back, all was well, but if it slithered quietly down the Wall, hope was lost.

Another legend associated with the Wall shows that obsession with quantification started long before 1949. The project's supervisor demanded an exact estimate of the number of bricks to be used in the construction of the fort; if the number was off by one brick, the death penalty awaited one Engineer Yì. When the fort was completed, Yì found that there was one brick left over. Faced with evidence of his failure, Yì declared it "the brick to balance the fort" *(dìng chéng zhuān)* and walked away unscathed. The brick sits on the side of **Huì Jì Mén,** and locals joke about tripping on it. The second main tower, **Róu Yuān Mén,** represents the Míng policy of peaceful coexistence with the minorities beyond the Wall, a policy that ended in the Qīng

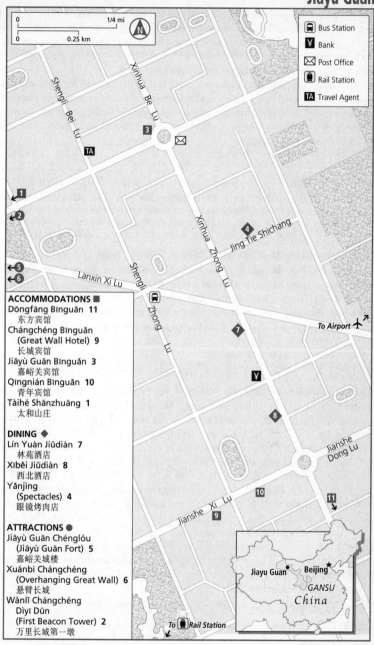

Jiāyù Guān

Bus Station
¥ Bank
Post Office
Rail Station
TA Travel Agent

Shengli Bei Lu

Xinhua Bei Lu

TA

Xinhua Zhong Lu

Jing Tie Shichang

Shengli Zhong Lu

Lanxin Xi Lu

To Airport ✈

¥

Jianshe Dong Lu

Jianshe Xi Lu

ACCOMMODATIONS ■
Dōngfāng Bīnguǎn **11**
　东方宾馆
Chángchéng Bīnguǎn
　(Great Wall Hotel) **9**
　长城宾馆
Jiāyù Guān Bīnguǎn **3**
　嘉峪关宾馆
Qīngnián Bīnguǎn **10**
　青年宾馆
Tàihé Shānzhuāng **1**
　太和山庄

DINING ◆
Lín Yuàn Jiǔdiàn **7**
　林苑酒店
Xīběi Jiǔdiàn **8**
　西北酒店
Yǎnjìng
　(Spectacles) **4**
　眼镜烤肉店

ATTRACTIONS ●
Jiāyù Guān Chénglóu
　(Jiāyù Guān Fort) **5**
　嘉峪关城楼
Xuánbì Chángchéng
　(Overhanging Great Wall) **6**
　悬臂长城
Wànlǐ Chángchéng
　Dìyī Dūn
　(First Beacon Tower) **2**
　万里长城第一墩

To 🚉 Rail Station

Jiayu Guan · Beijing ★
GANSU
China

dynasty, when Xīnjiāng was dragged back into the Chinese empire. Inside the main courtyard is the **Yóujī Yámen,** where the unfortunate generals were stationed with their families. The building is unremarkable but for an **antiques shop** on the east side. Most items are copies, and all are overpriced, but there are genuine pieces left over from the relocation of the museum from Jiāyù Guān to the fort.

Continuing west, you face the massive outer Wall, over 10m (33 ft.) high, and pass through **Jiāyù Guān Gate.** Chinese tour groups joke about forgetting their passport, ride camels, and dress up in funny minority costumes, but in the past it was no joke. Locals called it the Gate of Sighs, and the walls were scrawled with hastily composed poems by unfortunate exiles.

The **Great Wall Museum** (admission included in the price of the ticket; located near the fort's exit; 8:30am–8pm July–Oct, 8:30am–7pm Nov–June) is worth a visit for its well-curated exhibition of photos and models of various spots along the Great Wall.

Admission ¥60 ($7.50), including entry to the Chángchéng Bówùguǎn (Great Wall Museum). July–Oct 8:30am–7:30pm; Nov–June 8:30am–5:30pm. (Times listed are hours of ticket booth; the fort closes a half-hour after the last ticket sold.) Take a taxi (¥12/$1.40), ride a bike, or walk the 5km (3 miles) from town. Turn right about 1km after the railway bridge, follow a line of concrete camels, and eventually turn left at a signposted fork in the road.

Wànlǐ Chángchéng Dìyī Dūn (First Beacon Tower)

Seven kilometers (4⅓ miles) away from the Fort lies this fairly untouched crumbling bit of the Great Wall and watchtower. A visit here is preferable over a visit to the Overhanging Great Wall because it feels less fake, and the river that runs through a steep gorge near the tower makes for a dramatic sunset photo op. You can strap on a body harness and be pitched out over the gorge via a cable ¥35 ($4.30), but remember that, in the event of an accident, you're unlikely to sue and win in China. Make sure your taxi waits for you as it's difficult to arrange a car back to town.

Admission ¥21 ($2.60). July–Oct 8:30am–8:30pm; Nov–June 9am–6:30pm. Take a taxi, round-trip for ¥20 ($2.50).

Xīnchéng Wèi Jìn Mù (Wèi–Jìn Tombs)

Twenty kilometers (12 miles) northeast of Jiāyù Guān, this is sometimes misleadingly called the Dìxià Huàláng (Underground Art Gallery). There are thousands of tombs in this area dating from the Wèi (220–65 B.C.) and Jìn (A.D. 265–420), but only one is open to the public. You will see the tomb of a sixth-rank official, the lowest rank in the imperial pecking order. The valuables were plundered soon after the tomb was sealed, probably by the builder, judging from the accuracy of the thief's tunnel. Compared with Buddhist art, the murals in the tomb are crude cartoons. Detailed instructions on slaughtering pigs, goats, and cows leave no doubt as to what the owner was hoping for in the next world. There is evidence that sericulture had already spread to this part of the empire, that barbecues were enjoyed before Australia was colonized, and that officials were plumper than their servants. Murals detail the official's trip to the capital in Luòyáng, doubtless the highlight of his career. The remaining contents of the tomb are on display in an **exhibition center,** and include black stone pigs found in the hands and the mouth of the official's corpse. He liked his pork.

Admission ¥31 ($3.90); guide fee ¥50–¥100 ($6.50–$13), depending on depth of explanation. 8:30am–8:30pm.

Xuánbì Chángchéng (Overhanging Great Wall) *Overrated*

Built in 1539, this is supposedly as far as northwest as the Wall goes, but that's a myth. (There are sites farther west near Dūnhuáng.) This is part of the government's effort to capitalize on tourism by creating as many useless sites as possible in an effort to boost tourism revenues. Farmers were putting the masonry to better use before this section of the Wall

Gliding Heaven

Gliding above Jiāyù Guān Fort, the Overhanging Great Wall, and the surrounding snowcapped peaks provides an unforgettable experience. Start at the **Jiāyù Guān Gliding Base (Huáxiáng Jīdì; © 0937/638-1070)**, located inside the old airport, 25km (16 miles) northeast of town. The gliding season is from mid-June to September, when the warm ascending air flow of the Jiāyù Guān basin can lift gliders nearly 6km (4 miles) up. If you don't have a gliding license, training courses are available, but you'll need a very good translator. Basic and overpriced accommodations are available at the base. Whatever your arrangements, make them at least a month in advance, and be sure to get them in writing. It may be best to proceed through CITS.

was restored in 1988. It's a sweaty 20-minute climb into the desolate **Hēi Shān (Black Mountains)** as the Wall rises at a 45-degree angle for 500m (1,640 ft.). Chinese tourists arrange stones into the equivalent of "John loves Mary." Farms in the village below are a small finger of green in an immense desert. This section is 8km (5 miles) north of the fort, and can be reached by taxi or bike. Take plenty of water.

Admission ¥21 ($2.60). Apr–Oct 8:30am–8:30pm; Nov–Mar 8:30am–6pm.

SHOPPING

Much of the stock in the **Bǎihuò Dàlóu**, on the northeast side of the main roundabout, looks like it hasn't moved since the Cultural Revolution. This is a chance to pick up Seagull cameras, mahjong tiles, and chess sets at 1960s prices.

WHERE TO STAY

Jiāyù Guān suffers from a glut of mediocre three-star options. Outside the busy season in early May and mid-July to October, occupancy rates run as low as 20%—so discounts of at least 40% can be obtained. During the busy season, a 20% discount should be given.

EXPENSIVE

Chángchéng Bīnguǎn (Great Wall Hotel)   A favorite with tour groups since 1987, this sprawling, comfortable three-star hotel, whose exterior is a tacky replica of the Jiāyùguān Fort outlined in white Christmas lights at night, is probably the most used to dealing with foreign tourists. Service in the hotel is friendly and efficient, but they won't offer much of a discount in the high season.

Jiànshè Lù 6 (from Sīfǎjú walk back 50m/164 ft. and the hotel is on your right). © 0937/622-5213. Fax 0937/ 622-6016. 156 units. ¥280–¥380 ($35–$48) standard room; ¥780–¥2,080 ($98–$260) suite. AE, DC, MC, V. Bus: no. 2 to Sīfǎjú. **Amenities:** Restaurant; swimming pool; exercise room; bike rental; concierge; tour desk; business center; 24-hr. forex; same-day laundry/dry cleaning. *In room:* A/C, TV.

Jiāyù Guān Bīnguǎn ✿   Right in the center of town, this four-star hotel has been giving birth to new wings since 1983, most recently the west wing. The rooms are the cleanest and most comfortable in town, and service is very professional. This is where government officials stay when they come to town.

Xīnhuá Běi Lù 1. © 0937/620-1588. Fax 0937/622-7174. 180 units. ¥398–¥568 ($47–$71) standard room; from ¥1,080–¥1,280 ($135–$160) suite. AE, DC, MC, V. Bus: no. 1 to Yóudiàn Dàlóu. **Amenities:** 2 restaurants; exercise room; game room; concierge; tour desk; business center; 24-hr. forex; same-day laundry and next-day dry cleaning. *In room:* A/C, TV, fridge, hair dryer.

MODERATE/INEXPENSIVE

Dōngfāng Bīnguǎn *Value*   This brand-new hotel in the center of the city offers decent rooms at a good price. Beds can be a bit hard and bathrooms are slightly cramped. Service is friendly, though little English is spoken.

Yíngbīn Lù, Shānchūn Zōnghé Lóu. ✆ 0937/630-1866. Fax 0937/630-1027. 65 units (shower only). ¥280 ($35) standard room; ¥480–¥520 ($60–$65) suite. 20% discount standard. No credit cards. **Amenities:** Restaurant; business center. *In room:* A/C, TV, hair dryer.

Tàihé Shānzhuāng ✿ *Value*   Located within the grounds of the Jiāyù Guān Fort, this replica of a Qīng dynasty courtyard house allows you to spend more time at Jiāyù Guān's main attraction and to view the fort at sunrise and sunset, when the earthen ramparts are highly photogenic. Make sure to get the suite as other rooms do not come with private bathrooms. Beds are hard and bathrooms are slightly grimy but the atmosphere is unbeatable. The restaurant fare is decent. Combined with the magnificent fort, this guesthouse makes for the pretty good "real China" experience.

Jiāyù Guān Guānchéng (150m/492 ft. past the back entrance to the fort). ✆ 0937/639-6616. Fax 0937/639-6914. bjyggch@public.lz.gs.cn. 18 units (shower only). ¥120 ($15) standard room; ¥360 ($45) suite. No credit cards. **Amenities:** Restaurant; same-day laundry. *In room:* A/C, TV.

WHERE TO DINE

Jiāyù Guān is a prosperous steel town, so the restaurants—unlike the hotels—do well year-round. The main outdoor food markets are Fùqiáng Shìchǎng and Jìngtiě Shìchǎng. The night market on the north side of Jìngtiě Shìchǎng is the liveliest in town. Sheep carcasses dangle, beer flows, and vendors make fun of their regular customers. No one knows the name of the night market's greatest showman, who is simply called **Yǎnjìng (Spectacles)**. His shop is easy to spot, under a sign with a caricature of a man with huge glasses and a smock. The caricature is on the mark and Spectacles will serve you tasty Uigher lamb skewers (*yángròu chuàn*) or mini–lamb chops (*yángpái*) by the handful (*bǎ*)—about 20 in each serving, give or take a couple. But make sure you know what you're eating.

Lín Yuàn Jiǔdiàn ✿✿ CANTONESE   With a Cantonese chef poached from one of Xī'ān's top restaurants, this is where the locals go for a treat. The *fùguì niúròu* is akin to roast beef on sesame toast. *Jiāngnán qiánjiāng ròu*, lightly battered chicken in sweet-and-sour sauce, complements the Cantonese favorite, *xīqínbǎihé chǎo xiān yóu* (fresh squid on a bed of celery, field mushrooms, and lotus).

Xīnhuá Zhong Lù 34. ✆ 0937/628-6918. Meal for 2 ¥80–¥120 ($10–$15). No credit cards. 11am–11pm. Bus: no. 1 to Bǎoxiǎn Gōngsī.

Xīběi Jiǔdiàn ✿ *Value* GĀNSÙ/UIGHUR   The specialty here is the *kǎo yángpái* (grilled rack of lamb), which is the best I've tasted. Dipped in a salt-and-pepper concoction, the lamb is grilled so that the meat is tender and the outer layer crisp. One large order of lamb (*yángròu*) and a couple of local beers (*píjiǔ*) makes a fantastic meal for two.

Xīnhuá Nán Jiē, 100m (328 ft.) south of the Xīnhuá Supermarket (Xīnhuá Chāoshì). ✆ 0937/623-3208. Meal for 2 ¥80 ($10). No credit cards. 9am–10pm. Bus: no.1 to Xīnhuá Supermarket.

10 Dūnhuáng

Gānsù Province, 383km (237 miles) W of Jiāyù Guān, 524km (325 miles) NE of Golmud

Dūnhuáng's name (blazing beacon) derives from its function as a Hàn Chinese garrison town, but the Táng name of Shā Zhōu (sand district) describes it better, hemmed

Dūnhuáng

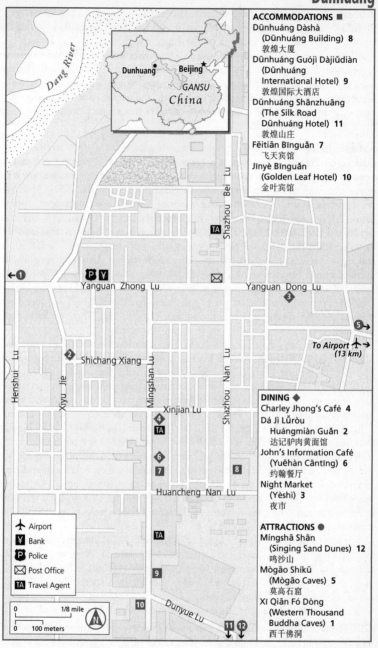

Dang River

Dunhuang   Beijing ★

GANSU
China

Shazhou Bei Lu

TA

Yanguan Zhong Lu   Yanguan Dong Lu

P   ¥   ⊠

3

5 →

To Airport ✈ →
(13 km)

Henshui Lu

2   Shichang Xiang

Xiyu Jie

Mingshan Lu

Shazhou Nan Lu

Xinjian Lu

4
TA

6

7   8

Huancheng Nan Lu

TA

9

10

Dunyue Lu

11 12
↓   ↓

✈ Airport
¥ Bank
P Police
⊠ Post Office
TA Travel Agent

0   1/8 mile
0   100 meters

N

in by sand dunes and bleak, pebbly desert. The middle and southern Silk Routes set off from Dūnhuáng, passing through the remote garrison town of **Lóulán** (abandoned when Lop Nor Lake "wandered off" in the 4th c.) and through the **Lop Desert**.

A large number of the early residents of Dūnhuáng were not Hàn, and the town came under the sway of the Tibetans, the Uighurs, and the Xī Xià, only really becoming a Hàn town after the colonization of the western regions was initiated during the Qīng dynasty. The town is dependent on tourism, and despite efforts to develop other sites, it is the peerless **Mògāo cave-temple complex** that makes Dūnhuáng the essential stop on the Silk Routes.

ESSENTIALS

GETTING THERE   The **airport** is 13km (8 miles) east of Dūnhuáng, just past the turnoff to the Mògāo caves. CAAC once ran a bus to the airport, but you are now at the mercy of taxi drivers without meters, who should charge no more than ¥30 ($3.80) from the center of town. The most useful office of **CAAC** (open 8am–6pm summer, 8am–12:30pm and 2:30–6pm winter) is opposite the Tàiyáng Dàjiǔdiàn at Shā Zhōu Běi Lù 5 (© 0937/882-2389). They will deliver tickets to your hotel, so there is no need to book tickets through hotel travel agencies, who will charge up to ¥70 ($8.40) for making a local call. There is a friendly office of **Northwest Airlines** 150m (492 ft.) north of Fēitiān Bīnguǎn on Míng Shān Lù (© 0937/882-9710; fax 0937/883-9888; open 7:30am–7:30pm). Daily flights connect with Lánzhōu (¥890/$111) and Ürümqi (¥620/$77). Five flights connect with Xī'ān (Mon–Fri; ¥1,340/$167) and four flights connect with Běijīng (Mon, Wed, Fri, and Sun; ¥1,620/$202). There are fewer flights in winter.

Dūnhuáng is 2 to 3 hours or 130km (81 miles) southwest of the **railway station** at Liǔyuán. From the station, you will have no trouble finding minibus drivers, who ask ¥30 ($3.70) for the ¥15 ($1.90) trip. Taxis will make the trip for ¥80 to ¥100 ($10–$13). If you are the last tourist around after a train pulls away, you can bargain hard as the station suffers from a glut of drivers. Buses for the railway station leave the long-distance bus station at 7:30am, 9:30am, 11am, noon, 2pm, 4pm, 6pm, and 7:30pm. Or you can hire a taxi for ¥120 ($15) or a minivan for ¥100 ($13). Heading west, the best choice of trains is the K889 for Ürümqi (12 hr.) at 8:06pm, which originates in Dūnhuáng. It's difficult to get train ticket out of Dūnhuáng during the high season; you can try your luck at the railway station or at a train ticket counter located in front of the grounds of the Dūnhuáng Hotel on Yángguān Dōng Lù. Or you can buy a hard-seat ticket or platform ticket at Liǔyuán and try to upgrade. If you arrive at the station early, there is a rest area on the second floor which charges ¥5 (65¢) for a cup of tea and a bit of peace and quiet.

The **bus station** is on Míng Shān Lù (© 0937/882-2174), diagonally opposite the Fēitiān Bīnguǎn. Daily buses connect with Jiāyù Guān at 11:30am (383km/237 miles; 6 hr.; ¥43/$5.40), 1pm (¥56/$6.90), and 2:30pm (¥66/$8.20); with Lánzhōu at 8:30am (1,148km; 17–20 hr.; ¥133/$17) and 10:30am (sleeper bus; ¥214/$27); with Golmud at 8am (524km/325 miles; 11 hr.; ¥61/$7.60) and 7:30pm (sleeper bus; ¥99/$12); and with Xīníng at 10am (1,067km/662 miles; 22 hr.; ¥183/$23).

GETTING AROUND   Taxis fill Dūnhuáng's narrow streets; most are gypsy cabs. The rate should be ¥5 (65¢) for a short ride; ¥10 ($1.25) for a longer one. Get around on foot, or hire a **bike** for ¥1 (15¢) per hour. There are also three **bus** routes.

TOURS   CITS is inside the compound of the Dūnhuáng Guójì Dàjiǔdiàn at Míng Shān Lù 32 (© **0937/882-2474;** fax 0937/882-2173; www.dhcits.com; open Mon–Fri 8am–12:30pm and 3–6:30pm summer, 8am–12:30pm and 2:30–6pm winter), on the right as you enter.

EXPLORING DŪNHUÁNG

Míngshā Shān & Yuèyá Quán (Singing Sand Mountains & Crescent Moon Spring) ⚛

When Aurel Stein settled down by the spring to churn out his memoirs, he opined, "It lay hidden away amidst high sands beyond the southern edge of the oasis and about three miles from the town. For the desert wanderer there could be no more appropriate place of rest, I thought, than this delightful little pilgrimage place enclosed all around by sand-ridges rising to over 75m (250 ft.) in height. There was a limpid little lake, of crescent shape and about a quarter of a mile long, which has given the locality its name and its sanctity."

Stein's peaceful temple was razed during the Cultural Revolution and is now a souvenir shop. The limpid "lake" is a fenced-off muddy pond reduced to half the original size, a result of the ongoing exploitation of underground water. The pilgrimage is marked by a gauntlet of stalls selling stuffed camels, batik, and glow-in-the-dark cups, culminating in a ticket office charging ¥80 ($10) to see a naturally formed attraction. Inside the entrance there are camels (¥30/$3.70) or carts (¥10/$1.25) to take you to the lake, and toboggans (¥10/$1.25) to take you down the sand dunes, which make for a fun, if sandy experience. If you've never seen desert dunes, it's worth the effort, especially just before sunrise or sunset, when the delicate contours and colors of the dunes are beguiling. The best way to avoid the crowds is to hike up the wooden stairs near the toboggan for ¥10 ($1.25) and then find your own way down, following a ridge.

Admission ¥80 ($10). 7am–10pm. Taxi ¥10 ($1.25) or minibus no. 3.

Mògāo Shíkū (Mògāo Caves) ⚛⚛⚛

Here is the biggest, best-preserved, and most significant site of Buddhist statuary and frescoes in all of China—and the best-curated site, too. A guide is compulsory, as is leaving your bag and camera (no charge) at the gate. Generally the guides, who all have bachelor's degrees, are excellent, sometimes going well beyond the script. Tours, which depart every few minutes and are limited to about 20 people, usually take 2 hours and cover half of the caves that are open to the public. It is worth spending the entire day at Mògāo Shíkū, even though this means that you have to pay for admission twice. Tours in the afternoon are less crowded, and you may get a guide to yourself. Or come right as the caves open in the morning, before the tour groups arrive. You might be able to successfully lobby for your own private tour guide by telling them it's unfair that they charge foreigners ¥20 ($2.50) more than Chinese tourists (which they might counter by saying that English-speaking guides demand more money).

To the left of the ticket office is the **Dūnhuáng Research Institute** ⚛, which includes a copy of the one of the earliest grottoes, **Cave 275,** dating from the short-lived 5th-century Northern Liáng dynasty, and including a *Jataka* (moral story) from one of the historical Buddha's previous lives. He is depicted as a Kushan king, allowing an attendant to cut the flesh from his leg as ransom for a dove that sits in his palm. *Jataka* were popular in the early caves, gradually being displaced by stories from the Mahayanist sutras in later caves as the influence of the "Pure Land Sect" of Chinese Buddhism grew. The subject matter of these *Jataka* was frequently gory. **Cave 285,** for example, tells the tale of 500 rebels who fought against the corrupt King Prasenajit and had their eyes gouged out and were banished to the wilderness before the gods took pity on them and allowed them to be tonsured as monks, their sight restored by the Buddha. Upstairs is a somewhat out-of-place exhibition of Tibetan bronze statues, both complete and beheaded, that were rescued from Red Guards by the canny curator.

All together, there are 492 caves, of which you will see less than a dozen on the 2-hour tour. Your first stop on the tour will be **Cave 17** (the Library Cave). The cave was sealed off sometime after 998 (the year of the last dated manuscript), perhaps out of fear of the spread of Islam—the Buddhist kingdom of Khotan was captured and sacked in 1006. In 1900, the cave was rediscovered by Wáng Dàoshi (Abbot Wáng), the self-appointed guardian of the caves. First among the villains was archaeologist Aurel Stein, a Hungarian who obtained British citizenship (and later a knighthood), who arrived during the winter of 1907. The Chinese commentary is only slightly more damning than the English translation, accusing Stein of "purchasing by deceit" over 7,000 complete manuscripts and silk paintings from the "ignorant" Abbott Wáng for a paltry £130. Next came young French Sinologist Paul Pelliot, whose mastery of Chinese gave him a selectivity his predecessor lacked—Stein returned to London with over 1,000 copies of the Lotus Sutra. Pelliot obtained thousands of documents for even less—only £90! The Chinese save their greatest condemnation for Langdon Warner, who removed 12 murals **(Cave 323)** and a statue **(Cave 328)**. Warner justified his theft as a way of avoiding the "renovations" funded by Abbot Wáng. A map illustrates how the contents are spread around the world.

Curators, fearing that increased tourist activity is damaging the coloration of the frescoes, are closing some caves to the public. The caves depicting acts of love-making, much touted in other guidebooks, are generally off-limits. Remarkable early caves (usually open) include **Cave 257,** commissioned during the Northern Wèi (A.D. 386–535), which contains a *Jataka* of the deer king; and **Cave 428,** where an early incarnation of the historical Buddha sacrifices himself to feed a tigress and her cubs. Later caves, such as **Cave 96,** which houses a 33m (100-ft.) Buddha, and **Cave 148,** which contains a serene 17m (56-ft.) Sleeping Buddha, indicate that artisans from the Táng court found their way to Mògāo. Some lower caves were affected by floodwaters from the Dàquán River, and sunlight has caused lead-based pigments to turn black, but the overall state of preservation is incredible. Caves are grouped roughly by period, and it is intriguing to view the steady transformation of facial features from Greco-Indian to plumper, more feminine Chinese features.

Admission ¥120 ($15), includes English-speaking guide. 8:30am–4:30pm (ticket booth hours; the caves close at 6pm). To reach the caves, minibuses leave from Fēitiān Bīnguǎn and Charley Jhong's Café (both on Míng Shān Lù) at 8am (30 min.; ¥20/$2.50 round-trip). If you plan to see Mògāo Shíkū as a half-day trip, get there as early as possible; buses return to Dūnhuáng at 12:30pm. Taxis, highly recommended, cost ¥50 ($6.20) each way.

Xī Qiān Fó Dòng (Western Thousand Buddha Caves)   The missionary Mildred Cable described the scene: "At the edge of the cliff was a rough opening, and from it a very precipitous path led down to a narrow ledge from which the new caves opened . . . they were comparable to the better known Thousand Buddha Grottoes . . . the figures were free and stately, with flowing lines and elegant draperies, and the frescoes showed the same clear warm tints."

Located 35km (22 miles) southwest of town, the valley is easily accessed as a half-day trip, but it's still a scramble down to the caves. They were largely built by locals from the nearby village of Nán Hú, and have several *Jataka* stories not covered by the Mògāo caves. Most of the statuary (with the exception of caves 5 and 16) was repainted to poor effect during the Qīng dynasty. The most spectacular murals are located in **Cave 15** ✿, which is not open to the casual visitor without payment of an additional fee. The stunning blues and muscular bodhisattvas of the Northern Wèi **(Cave 5)** and Northern Zhōu **(Cave 6)** are in real contrast to the plump, feminine bodhisattvas of the Middle Táng **(Cave 15)**. To reach the site, a taxi may be hired for ¥60 ($7.50); or take any bus heading west from Dūnhuáng for ¥5 (65¢). From the road, it's a 15-minute walk south to the cliff face, with a set of stairs to the left leading down to the ticket office.

Admission ¥30 ($3.70). 8am–6pm. No English tour guide. Taxis make the trip from Dūnhuáng for ¥70 ($9) round-trip.

A SIDE TRIP TO HÀN DYNASTY RUINS ✿

If you're a history buff who is tired of seeing fake renditions of the Great Wall, this 92km (57-mile) journey into the desert to visit these desolate Hàn dynasty ruins is a worthwhile day trip. The ruins comprise three separate locations: **Yùmén Guān (Jade Gate),** an ancient watchtower made of mud, straw, and stone, and the lesser-known **Hé Cāngchéng** and **Hàn Chángchéng.** On the way to these ruins you'll pass another historic site called Yángguān (Sun Gate). Yùmén Guān and Yáng Guān were the traditional border crossings that marked the beginning of the territory ruled by the Hàn dynasty. Today, however, Yáng Guān is a tacky site geared towards Chinese tour groups; it features an unspectacular watchtower surrounded by a fake village, and a terribly curated museum. Skip this and continue to the Yùmén Guān ticket counter, which appears in the middle of the desert, along a long stretch of road. Pay here (¥30/$3.75) and drive for another 30km (19 miles) to reach Yùménguān. The highlight of the three is Hàn Chángchéng ✿✿, which translates at River Warehouse Town. It's 13km (21 miles) east of Yùmén Guān on a dirt road and is a rather crumbling building that was used as a storage unit. Five kilometers (8 miles) to the east of Yùmén Guān is Hàn Chángchéng, which features one watchtower and a several-hundred-meter-long remnant of the Great Wall. Few tour groups, if any, make it out here. Plan for a trip that takes roughly 7 hours. A round-trip taxi ride costs ¥350 ($44).

WHERE TO STAY

Dūnhuáng has a surplus of accommodations. During the peak season, hotels offer 20% discounts; during the low season, discounts of up to 60% are readily negotiated.

VERY EXPENSIVE

Dūnhuáng Shānzhuāng (The Silk Road Dūnhuáng Hotel) ✿✿   This four-star Hong Kong venture is the finest hotel on the Silk Routes, and one of the most unique hotels in the country. It lies 4km (2½ miles) south of town, just before the Míng Shān Dunes, which loom in the background. Designed by a Chinese-American architect, the gigantic, airy lobby gives you a sense of calm that rarely exists in China. The main building mimics the look of the Mògāo Caves, and the high-ceilinged rooms feature finely crafted wooden furnishings and cool stone floors that mesh perfectly with the desert surroundings. Bathrooms, which feature showers lined with black stone, are fantastic. Bill Gates was duly impressed with the villas, which feature a mixture of Táng and Hàn architectural styles. An aptly named "student building" with beds for ¥80 ($10) also houses the staff. Service is top-notch. The rooftop patio ✿ is a must for a sunset and beautiful views of the dunes—it's open to the public in the evenings. If you ask management breakfast can be served on the patio for hotel guests. Dinner at the restaurant adjoining the hotel is decent, featuring spicy Chinese dishes, and there's a nightly dance performance that begins at 9pm. The hotel features a very professional massage center, as opposed to the dodgy kind that are offered at many Chinese hotels.

Dūnyuè Lù. ✆ 0937/888-2088. Fax 0937/888-2086. www.dunhuangresort.com. 233 units, 21 villas. ¥800 ($100) standard room; from ¥1,200 ($150) suite; from ¥2,000 ($250) villa. 13% service charge. AE, DC, MC, V. **Amenities:** 2 restaurants; cafe; bar; sauna; bike rental; concierge; tour desk; evening shuttle bus to town; 24-hr. business center; 24-hr. forex; salon; 24-hr. room service; massage; same-day laundry/dry cleaning. In room: A/C, limited satellite TV, fridge, hair dryer.

EXPENSIVE

Dūnhuáng Guójì Dàjiǔdiàn (Dūnhuáng International Hotel) ✵ ⓥⓐⓛⓤⓔ While its bathroom-tile exterior surely won't win any awards, the rooms here are some of the best in town for the price (though, with a recent upgrade from three to four stars, the rate may increase). Recently renovated, the rooms are decorated in simple tones and feature modern headboards and comfy beds. Service is hit or miss. You can save ¥100 ($13) by choosing a standard room over an executive room; the only difference being that the executive rooms feature slightly more modern bathrooms. The Korean restaurant on the premises serves barbequed beef.

Míngshān Lù 28. ✆ 0937/882-8638. Fax 0937/882-8678. jqdhgj@public.lz.gs.cn. 160 units. ¥ 488–¥588 ($61–$74) standard room; ¥988–¥1,288 ($124–$161) suite. AE, DC, MC, V. Rates include full breakfast. **Amenities:** 3 restaurants; cafe; bar; concierge; tour desk; business center; 24-hr. forex; 24-hr. room service; massage; same-day laundry/dry cleaning; karaoke. In room: A/C, TV, minibar, fridge, safe.

MODERATE

Dūnhuáng Dàshà (Dūnhuáng Building) This unglamorous three-star hotel is owned by the Tax Department, so there is no danger of it running short of money for renovations, which are continuous. Rooms are clean and bright, and the hotel's location—in a quiet area south of the center of town—is a definite advantage.

Shā Zhōu Nán Lù 15. ✆ 0937/882-5007. Fax 0937/882-5006. 101 units. ¥480 ($60) standard room; ¥880 ($110) suite; ¥50 ($6) dorm bed. 20% discount. No credit cards. **Amenities:** Restaurant; bar; concierge; business center; same-day laundry/dry cleaning. In room: A/C, TV, fridge.

Jīnyè Bīnguǎn (Golden Leaf Hotel) Located 1.6km (1 mile) south of the center of town, this is a decent three-star choice. Staff is friendly and rooms are in good condition. An orchard provides grapes, apricots, and peaches for the hotel restaurant. Ask for a room overlooking the orchard, as rooms facing the main road are noisy. "Golden leaf" is a reference to tobacco: The hotel is owned by the Gānsù Tobacco Company.

Míng Shān Lù 37. ✆ 0937/885-3338. Fax 0937/885-1248. 92 units. ¥422 ($53) standard room; ¥888 ($111) suite. Rates include full breakfast. No credit cards. **Amenities:** Restaurant; bar; large exercise room; game room; concierge; tour desk; business center; same-day laundry/dry cleaning. In room: A/C, TV, fridge.

INEXPENSIVE

Fēitiān Bīnguǎn (Fēitiān Hotel) Among the hotels at the bottom of the market, this is probably the safest bet and a well-trodden place for foreign backpackers. Book ahead during the busy season as rooms fill up in advance. The hotel is conveniently located across the street from the long-distance bus station and near the Western-cafe ghetto that seems to be expanding on Míng Shān Lù. Staff is friendly.

Míng Shān Lù 22. ✆ 0937/882-2337. 55 units. ¥30 ($3.80) dorm bed in a triple room; ¥240–¥280 ($30–$35) standard room. Discounts of 20%–40% on standard room. No credit cards. **Amenities:** 2 restaurants; business center; travel agent; same-day laundry. In room: A/C, TV.

WHERE TO DINE

Clustered around the Fēitiān Hotel are small restaurants with English menus, offering "Western" food and overpriced Chinese fare. Favorites are **Shirley's, Charley Jhong's Café,** and **John's Information Café,** all located on Míng Shān Lù. Charley's has the best service. A favorite local drink served at many restaurants, including John's, is the delicious *xìngpíshuǐ* (dried apricot juice), which is generally home-brewed by soaking the apricots in water, then adding sugar for a tart and sweet combination.

Dá Jì Lǘròu Huángmiàn Guǎn *(Finds)* GĀNSÙ   Surprisingly, the specialty dish of Dūnhuáng is *lǘròu huángmiàn* (donkey meat yellow noodles). More surprisingly, it's delicious. It is claimed that the method of making the noodles is revealed in Cave 265, but the cave isn't open to the public and the owners of this noodle shop aren't talking. The noodles are cooked with tomato, tofu, mushrooms, and plenty of garlic—a small plate *(xiǎopán)* is more than sufficient. To accompany the main dish, order some donkey meat *(lǘròu)*. Half a *jīn (bàn jīn)*, which is half a kilo, is enough for two. The meat is lean and tastes a little like roast beef. You'll be served a bowl of finely chopped garlic, to which you should add chili sauce and vinegar to taste, before dipping the meat in it. If you want to meet some locals, this market street is a better choice than the tacky main night market *(yèshì)*. An after-dinner stroll through the charming narrow lanes provides a rewarding glimpse of the old town.

Dà Shìchǎng. ¥10 ($1.25) per person. No credit cards. 10:30am–10:30pm.

11 Turpan (Tŭlŭfān) ⭐⭐

Xīnjiāng Province, 187km (116 miles) SE of Ürümqi

Early European visitors were preoccupied with the overwhelming heat of this delightful oasis town. Set in the **Turpan Depression,** 154m (505 ft.) below sea level at its lowest point at **Lake Ayd Inkol (Àidīng Hú),** the town experiences midday temperatures hovering above 113°F (45°C) during the summer months. The American journalist Lattimore found some relief: "Over the central streets, which are at once passageways and market-places, are trellises, covered with mats, gourd-vines, and the branches of willows and poplars. In the chequered shade the people step softly, loose-robed and barefooted or slipper-shod; as they chatter in Turki, guttural but soft, the eyes of women flash under stenciled eyebrows and the teeth of men flash from black beards . . ."

The green fields that surround Turpan are sustained by the *karez* irrigation system, thought to have been introduced in Persia 2 millennia ago. A web of 1,000 miles of covered water channels brings water from the mountains to the north and west of Turpan. Keeping the *karez* clear requires considerable effort, and locals are proud of this ongoing engineering achievement. Turpan is surrounded by significant ancient sites, all readily accessed by car or minibus. Often an independent kingdom, it has maintained a strong sense of local identity, and observes a relaxed and tolerant version of Islam.

The annual grape festival, which runs in late August for about a week, brings fruit vendors, winemakers, and loads of tourists from around China. It's a fun time to visit—as the city becomes a lively, teeming mass of humanity, you can sample unlimited grapes on the trellis-lined streets or Turpan and witness a fantastic fireworks display on the night before the festival officially kicks off.

ESSENTIALS

GETTING THERE   The nearest **airport** is at Ürümqi, though there is talk of a Turpan airport opening in coming years. Check with CITS in Turpan, listed below.

The **railway station** is located 54km (33 miles) north of Turpan in drab town of Dàhéyàn. Minibuses connect with **Turpan's long-distance bus station** for ¥7.50 (90¢). The Turpan **long-distance bus station** in Dàhéyàn is reached by heading up the hill in front of the station, taking the first right turn, and continuing along the road for about 180m (600 ft.). The bus station is on your left. Some buses wait at the station, along with individual taxis that charge ¥10 ($1.25), as long as they are able to fill a car with three or more passengers. The way back to the railway station is a bit more arduous; bus schedules seem erratic, and you'll have to fight through the crowds to buy your ticket at the counter. It's best to take a taxi to the railway station for ¥60 ($7.50).

To connect with Kashgar, the best choice is the N947 at 6:07pm; the trip takes 20 hours. Except in peak season, sleeper tickets are readily purchased in Dàhéyàn. Those heading to Ürümqi are better served by bus. Heading east, sleeper tickets are tighter; your chances are best on the T198 to Zhèngzhōu (37 hr.) at 7:25pm and the 1068 to Xī'ān (40 hr.) at 9:31pm. Otherwise, proceed through CITS or John's Information Café, which charges a ¥50 ($6) commission.

The **bus station** is at Lǎo Chéng Lù 27 (© **0995/852-2325**), about 90m (300 ft.) west of the central roundabout. Buses for Ürümqi (187km/116 miles; 2½ hr.; ¥25/$3; taxi (Santana) ¥65/$8 per person) leave every half-hour from 7:30am to 8:30pm. There are daily buses for Kuqa (638km/396 miles; 15 hr.; ¥62/$7.70; ¥84/$10 upper berth, ¥97/$12 lower berth) and a sleeper bus for Kashgar (1,385km/859 miles; 26 hr.; ¥171/$21 upper berth, ¥196/$25 lower berth). Both depart at 11am.

GETTING AROUND Turpan is a small town, and nearly everything is within walking distance of the center, marked by the intersection of Lǎo Chéng Lù and Gāochāng Lù. Taxis within the city cost ¥5 (65¢). Most sights are outside town and require a **taxi, minibus,** or **bike,** which can be hired from John's Information Cafe. Your presence is noted by local drivers when you arrive. They will politely but insistently offer tours of the eight sights *(bāge dìfāng)*. Decline.

TOURS   CITS is located to the left of front gate of the Oasis Hotel (before you enter the gate) at Qīngnián Lù 41 (© **0995/852-8962;** turpancits@sina.com; open 8am–9pm).

FAST FACTS
Banks & Foreign Exchange   You can change traveler's checks and draw money on your credit card from counters 3 to 5 at the **Bank of China,** just west of the main roundabout, at Lǎo Chéng Lù 18. It's open 9:30am to 1pm and 4:30 to 7:30pm.

Internet Access   Dial-up is © **165.**

Post Office   The main post office (open 9am–7:30pm summer; 9:30am–7pm winter) is west of the bus station.

Visa Extensions   The **PSB office** (Mon–Fri 9:30am–1pm and 4:30–7:30pm) on Lùzhōu Dōng Lù (© **0995/856-4409**) takes an hour or so to process extensions.

SEEING THE SIGHTS
Tǔlǔfān Bówùguǎn   Although the space-age exterior and lobby belie the sloppily curated interior, this is worth an hour of pottering, especially in the midday heat. Many of the exhibits are from the **Astana graves,** and attest to the preservation qualities of Turpan's arid climate. You'll see dumplings, cakes, and sultanas, all at least 13 centuries past their best. Other grave goods include a rooster-shaped pillow to ensure its owner didn't sleep through the afterlife, and the naturally mummified bodies of some of the inhabitants. The macabre nature of the exhibit attracted experts from the **Běijīng Natural History Museum,** who have added a reproduction of a Gāochāng army general and his wife. The final exhibition hall features the skeleton of a 9m-long (30-ft.) herbivorous dinosaur, *Paraceratherium Tienshanensis,* and various *Jurassic Park*–inspired replicas. Gāochāng Lù 26. Admission ¥20 ($2.50). 9:30am–7:30pm.

DINING ◆

Ātàichì Cāntīng **8**
阿太赤餐厅

John's Information Café
(Yuēhàn Cāntīng) **10**
约翰餐厅

Shìjì Xīng **1**
世纪星

ATTRACTIONS ●

Sūgōng Minaret
(Sūgōng Tǎ) **11**
苏公塔

Turpan Bazaar
(Tǔlǔfān Bāzhā) **5**
吐鲁番巴扎

Tǔlǔfān Bówùguǎn
(Turpan Museum) **2**
吐鲁番博物馆

ACCOMMODATIONS ■

Dōngfāng Jiǔdiàn **9**
东方酒店

Hóngyuǎn Jiǔdiàn **4**
鸿远酒店

Jīnxīn Bīnguǎn **6**
金新宾馆

Lǚzhōu Bīnguǎn
(Oasis Hotel) **7**
绿洲宾馆

Tǔlǔfān Dàfàndiàn
(Grand Turpan Hotel) **3**
吐鲁番大饭店

AROUND TURPAN

The "eight sights" around Turpan can easily be visited in 1 day. These are the ancient city of **Gāochāng,** the **Astana tombs,** the **Bezeklik Caves,** the **Flaming Mountains** (made famous by Ang Lee's travelogue *Crouching Tiger, Hidden Dragon*), **Pútao Gōu (Grape Valley), Sūgōng Minaret (Sūgōng Tǎ),** the *karez* irrigation channels, and the ancient city of **Jiāohé.** Private minibus drivers charge around ¥50 ($6) per person for the tour. The air-conditioned CITS minibus (which runs July–Oct) is worth considering, as it includes an English-speaking guide and costs ¥80 ($10) per person. Hiring a taxi allows you to be selective, and prices can be as low as ¥150 ($19) for a Santana in the off season, rising to a CITS high of ¥350 ($44).

Several of the eight sights are not worthwhile. The ticket seller at Astana tells you to "save your money for the museum." The road to Gāochāng passes the Flaming Mountains, and Bezeklik is in them, so don't stop at the designated photo op unless you enjoy being pestered by small children selling bells or absolutely need a photo next to a giant tacky thermometer that's been built. The *karez* wells are unimpressive, and there are grape vines in Turpan, so there's no need to pay ¥20 ($2.50) for an overpriced meal at Grape Valley. Organize a half-day tour including Gāochāng, Bezeklik, Sūgōng Minaret, and Jiāohé, or take a 1-day tour with a visit to Tuyoq in the morning. Sūgōng Minaret and Jiāohé can also be reached by bike.

Bózīkèlīkè Qiān Fó Dòng (Bezeklik Thousand Buddha Caves)

The setting of Bezeklik Caves, in a ravine deep in the Flaming Mountains, is more spectacular than the contents of the caves. Bezeklik was stripped by several German expeditions—led by Albert Grünwedel and his nominal understudy, Albert von Le Coq—and relocated to the Museum für Indische Kunst in Berlin. Grünwedel was reluctant to remove Buddhist antiquities, but Le Coq deemed it essential for their preservation, sparing them from Muslim iconoclasts and practical-minded farmers who would scrape off paintings for use as fertilizer. Nearly all the large wall paintings were destroyed during Allied bombing raids on Berlin in 1943 and 1945. What little is left, particularly in Cave 39, hints at a distinctly Indo-Persian style. The new *Journey to the West* statue outside is rather special.

Admission ¥20 ($2.50). Summer 9am–8:30pm; winter daylight hours.

Gāochāng (Karakhoja)

Located 45km (28 miles) southeast of Turpan, Gāochāng was founded during the Hàn dynasty as a garrison town to supply troops engaged in the conquest of the "Western Regions." Gāochāng rose to prominence, becoming the capital of the region and maintaining its influence even when it passed from Chinese hands. Xuánzàng visited in A.D. 630, and the king of Gāochāng was so impressed by his preaching that he took the young monk captive. Xuánzàng went on a hunger strike and was released with a promise to return. He wriggled out of his pledge, returning to China by the southern Silk Route. In any event, the king was dead before he returned, as Turpan returned to Chinese control.

During the Táng dynasty, Gāochāng was a thriving artistic and spiritual center for Buddhism and Manichaeism, and most relics recovered by Albert von Le Coq, Stein, and Chinese archaeologists date from this period. There is a **Manichean shrine** northeast of the city walls, but the contents of its library were thrown into a river 5 years before Le Coq arrived. The man feared "the unholy nature of the writings and . . . that the Chinese might use the discovery as a pretext for fresh extortions."

Gāochāng is a significant site, but aside from the city walls and the restored **Buddhist temple,** the weathered mud-brick buildings are hard to discern. A donkey-cart ride to the Buddhist temple costs ¥5 (65¢) each way.

Admission ¥30 ($3.80). 7:30am–dusk.

Jiāohé (Yarkhoto) ✿

Ten kilometers (6¼ miles) west of Turpan, these ruins are better preserved and enjoy a more spectacular location than Gāochāng, though they are historically less significant. If you have time for only one set of ruins, come here—it's closer and more dramatic. Originally a Hàn garrison town, it has no city walls, as the site (which means "meeting of the rivers") is bounded by steep ravines. A clear central avenue runs east–west through the town, with residential, religious, and governmental areas delineated. The reason for the demise of the settlement during the Yuán dynasty is unclear, but the depth of the numerous wells suggests the water supply may have run out. Sunset is the best time to go; not only for photos, but to avoid most of the tour groups. Walk in a clockwise direction to further avoid the remaining tour groups, who always seem to make their pilgrimages in a counterclockwise circle. Jiāohé can be reached by taxi for ¥30–¥40 ($3.80–$5) round-trip; make sure your driver waits for you as there aren't many spare drivers in the parking lot. Or make it a pleasant bike ride.

Admission ¥40 ($5). Summer 8am–8:30pm; winter 10am–6:30pm.

Sūgōng Tǎ or Émǐn Tǎ (Sūgōng Minaret)   The mosque was built in 1778 by Prince Suleiman in honor of his father, Prince Emin, one of the few rulers of Turpan to have made the pilgrimage to Mecca. One of the first Western visitors was Francis Younghusband, who was less than overawed: "Some three miles from Turfan we passed a mosque with a curious tower, which looked as much like a very fat factory chimney as anything else. It was about eighty feet high, circular, and built of mud bricks, and it was ornamented by placing the bricks at different angles, forming patterns."

The most spectacular building is the minaret, actually about 10m (34 ft.) in diameter and 40m (132 ft.) tall. The style is neither Hàn nor Huí, but similar to those found farther west on the Silk Routes. The mosque is not the oldest in Turpan, but it's the best preserved. It's open for worship at 2:30pm on Friday, when entry for non-Muslims is restricted.

Admission ¥30 ($3.80). 9am–7pm. Bus: no. 6 to the terminus; continue east for 10 min.

TUYOQ: A UIGHUR STRONGHOLD *𝘢*

Less than 20km (12 miles) beyond Gāochāng, the idyllic Uighur village of Tuyoq is a fine day trip, and can be included in a tour. A leisurely day trip to Tuyoq, stopping at Gaochang on the way back, can be arranged with individual taxis for ¥200 ($25). Direct buses to Tuyoq (¥6/75¢) leave Turpan at noon, 2pm, and 4pm. Buses to **Lǔkèqìn** (¥9.50/$1.20) pass Tuyoq, and leave from 10am; the last bus back to Turpan leaves Lǔkèqìn at around 5pm, passing Tuyoq about 20 minutes later. Bus station staff, in the pay of taxi drivers, will do everything they can to persuade you that the bus goes nowhere near Tuyoq. If you catch the Lǔkèqìn bus, you will be dropped at the south end of the sprawling settlement, leaving a hot but fascinating 5km (3-mile) walk north to the village proper. Three-wheelers also make the trip for ¥3 (40¢).

Tourist officials hope that the recent opening of some Buddhist caves here will boost revenues; the village now charges a ¥30 ($3.80) fee to walk into the area, regardless of whether or not you'd like to see the caves. The caves have been severely damaged and all that's left of the four open to the public are small patches of cave paintings with the faces of Buddhas scratched out. Bring a flashlight for a closer look. The village itself is nice to wander through, and several courtyard homes will open their doors for you at lunchtime. The cost of a meal should be ¥10 ($1.25)—make sure you agree on the price before you settle in.

WHERE TO STAY

For a town that receives so many tourists, it's a shame there aren't better hotels. You may wonder why some of the below hotels are included; it's for a lack of better options! During the peak season, discounts of 20% are standard. During the off season, discounts of 40% to 60% are possible.

Dōngfāng Jiǔdiàn ⚹ *Value*   This new no-frills two-star hotel is a gem for budget travelers: It offers a great location next to the bazaar and bus station, comfortable beds, and clean bathrooms. Service is kind and efficient and the environment is calmer than the well-trodden backpackers' Jiāotōng Bīnguǎn a few doors down.

Lǎochéng Xī Lù 324. ✆ **0995/626-8228.** Fax 0995/8531-1328. ¥300 ($38) standard room; ¥380 ($48) suite. No credit cards. 40%–50% discount even in high season. *In room:* A/C, TV.

Hóngyuǎn Jiǔdiàn   Popular with tour groups, this place boasts a prime location and decent amenities. Staff is helpful, and rooms are spotless and have nice high ceilings. Some of the rooms are in better shape than others—so look at a few before you pick a room. Beds can be a bit too stiff. A lively night market in front of the hotel appears at 7pm. Avoid the hotel's karaoke-sauna-massage parlor complex.

Gāochāng Lù (Lǚyóu Wénhuà Guǎngchǎng Xī Cè). ✆ 0995/857-8177. Fax 0995/857-8180. 60 units. From ¥380 ($48) standard room; ¥580 ($73) suite. No credit cards. **Amenities:** Restaurant; concierge; tour desk; business center; same-day laundry/dry cleaning. *In room:* A/C, TV.

Jīnxīn Bīnguǎn (Jīnxīn Hotel)   One of the newer establishments in town (and one of the taller buildings around), the rooms feature new furniture and shiny floors. Beds are comfy, and bathrooms are well kept. The hotel is well-managed, and they're used to dealing with foreigners. The one disadvantage is the karaoke parlor on the ninth floor that often reverberates with the bad sounds of government cadres well into the night; stay on the seventh floor or below.

Lúzhōu Zhōng Lù 390. ✆ **0995/856-0222.** Fax 0995/856-0403. 40 units. ¥380 ($48) standard room. 20% discount. No credit cards. **Amenities:** Restaurant; conference room; karaoke. *In room:* A/C, TV.

Lǚzhōu Bīnguǎn (Oasis Hotel)   Managed by the same Hong Kong entrepreneur who created the Silk Road Hotel in Dūnhuáng, this three-star hotel set in rambling grounds is showing signs of age and group-tour syndrome. The only reason to stay here is for the Uighur-style rooms on the first floor, with low beds perched on a raised platform and richly colored rug. Book ahead and specify that you want a *"mínzú tèsè fángjiān"* (minority-flavored room). Service is remarkably helpful.

Qīngnián Lù 41. ✆ **0995/852-2491.** Fax 0995/852-3348. 193 units (28 with shower only). ¥140 ($17) economy room; ¥528 ($66) standard room; ¥1,088 ($136) suite. Room rates readily reduced by 40%. AE, DC, MC, V. **Amenities:** 3 restaurants; bike rental; billiards room; concierge; tour desk (CITS); business center; 24-hr. forex; same-day laundry. *In room:* A/C, TV.

Tǔlǔfān Dàfàndiàn (Grand Turpan Hotel)   The rooms are some of the best in town, but the service could possibly be the worst in town. This hotel recently experienced a change in its management (it was formerly Hong Kong run), and as a result the front desk is terribly managed and has problems dealing with even the smallest request. Spacious rooms in the new wing with clean bathrooms meet four-star standards; dorm beds are clean if not a bit pricey. Don't get this confused with the Turpan Hotel, which is a lesser operation that is popular with backpackers.

Gāochāng Zhong Lù 422. ✆ **0995/855-3868.** Fax 0995/855-3908. xjturpanhotel.com. 149 units (38 with shower only). ¥60 ($7.50) dorm bed; ¥380 ($47) standard room; from ¥880 ($110) suite. AE, DC, MC, V. **Amenities:** 2 restaurants; cafe; exercise room; large game room; concierge; business center; 24-hr. forex; same-day laundry/dry cleaning. *In room:* A/C, TV, minibar, fridge, safe.

WHERE TO DINE

Western breakfasts can be found at the Oasis Hotel for ¥25 ($3), as well as at **John's Information Café.** Hotels offer safe but boring Muslim and Chinese fare and evening performances of singing and dancing. For real food, head for the bazaar just west of the Bank of China, where you can enjoy pastries stuffed with minced lamb *(samsa, kǎo bāozi),* kabobs, and homemade ice cream scraped from gigantic sweet orange mounds. At night, the market in front of the Hóngyuán Bīnguǎn offers fantastic kabobs, Uighur dumplings, and noodles. Just point to what you want. If you want singing and dancing as well . . .

Ātàichì Cāntīng UIGHUR   The original dinner and dance restaurant for the locals is feeling the competition from Shìjì Xīng (below); call ahead to see if it's open. Although its underground location keeps it cool, there is a dungeon-like feel to it, and the print of a whole roast sheep sitting contentedly on a tablecloth in a meadow may be enough to convert you to macrobiotics. Busiest on Friday and Saturday, the banquets (minimum six people) are an excellent way to try a variety of foods without wearing out your phrasebook.

Dà Shízì (on the southeast side of the main intersection, downstairs through a clothing shop). ☎ 0995/852-9775. Banquets ¥39–¥89 ($4.90–$11) per person. No credit cards. 7–10pm (performance starts 9pm).

Shiji Xīng ✿✿ UIGHUR   Set in grape fields north of town, with a meltwater stream flowing by, this is a favorite among locals for carousing late into the night. Bakri, a Uighur entrepreneur, caters to the fantasies of both locals and foreigners, recruiting handsome waiters from Khotan and dancers from all over Xīnjiāng. Grapevines hang above the tables, and discreet fans keep you cool. Waiters shuffle on their knees across elevated platforms and somehow manage to look elegant. *Shìjì xīng yángpái* (lamb chops) is worth the expense, and don't miss the chance to cook your own kabobs. For the long-suffering China traveler, a real treat—dessert! Sweets *(tiánshí)* are not on the menu, but a platter of shortbread and gingerbread biscuits, many with tart apricot fillings, can be arranged. Try mulberry wine *(sāngshèn jiǔ),* less sickly-sweet than most in the region. The wine will help if you get hauled up on stage.

Xīn Zhàn Dīngzì Lùkǒu ☎ 0995/855-1199. Meal for 2 ¥40–¥120 ($5–$15). No credit cards. Open at 1:30pm; performance at 9:30pm. Bus: no. 2 or 201 to Xīnzhàn; walk 135m (450 ft.) to the northwest side of the T-junction.

12 Ürümqi (Wūlŭmùqí)

Xīnjiāng, 1,470km (911 miles) NE of Kashgar, 692km (429 miles) E of Yīníng

Early visitors gave mixed reviews. Missionary Mildred Cable thought the town "has no beauty, no style, no dignity and no architectural interest. The climate is violent, exaggerated and at no season pleasant . . . ." However, acerbic American author Owen Lattimore loved Ürümqi "in the spring, when along the liquescent streets the Chinese began to appear in gay colors and flowered silks and satins, and the Turkis, abandoning the reds and purples of their long winter gowns, to put on the white cotton robes of warm weather; and in the beginning of summer, when the early leafage of trees was not yet dulled with dust, and to walk on the city walls at sunset was the crowning glory of the day."

Opinions on the town are still divided, but everyone agrees that Ürümqi is best avoided in winter. Ringed by factories and relying on coal heating, the town sees its first snow coated by a film of soot within hours. For those who fly in from the east, it provides a tantalizing first taste of a different culture, and there are fascinating markets to explore.

ESSENTIALS

GETTING THERE   **Ürümqi airport,** to the north of town, has a brand-new domestic terminal and a ramshackle international terminal. It's clear which is which. Taxis into town cost around ¥30 ($3.70), or you can lug your bags for 10 minutes to the south and catch the slow but cheap bus no. 2 for ¥2 (25¢). Air tickets may be booked over the phone (© **800-893-9800**), and substantial discounts are available if you book up to 10 days in advance. The main ticket office for **Xīnjiāng Airlines** (© **0991/233-0000**) is opposite the Huádū Dàjiǔdiàn on Yǒuhǎo Nán Lù, just north of the post office. There are also ticket offices at the **airport** (© **0991/380-1652**) and the Bogda Hotel (© **0991/886-3910**). Several daily flights connect with Běijīng, Xī'ān, Kashgar, Yīníng, and Dūnhuáng. There are also daily connections with Shànghǎi, Guǎngzhōu, Chéngdū, and Khotan. There are flights for Lánzhōu (daily) and Xīníng (daily). Xīnjiāng Airlines has international connections with Moscow (5 hr.; Wed and Sun), Almaty in Kazakhstan (1½ hr.; Mon and Fri), Islamabad in Pakistan (2½ hr.; daily), Tashkent (2½ hr.; Wed and Sat), Bishkek in Kyrgyzstan (2 hr.; Tues–Wed and Fri–Sat), Novosibirsk in Russia (2 hr.; Mon–Tues and Thurs–Sat), and Hong Kong (5 hr.; Wed, Fri, and Sun). **Siberian Airlines** (© **0991/286-2326**) has an office in the Túnhé Huáměi Dàjiǔdiàn, on the corner of Qítái Lù and Cháng Jiāng Lù, with flights to Novosibirsk on Tuesday and Saturday.

Ürümqi's **railway station** is located in the southwest corner of town. Nearly all trains from the east and west terminate here. Tickets (for same-day travel only) may be purchased at the station in a building behind and to the right of the main entrance. To purchase sleeper tickets, either proceed through your hotel and pay around ¥30 ($3.70) commission, or queue up with the masses at the **railway ticket office** (© **0991/581-4203**) at Jiànshè Lù 3, in the courtyard of the Láiyuǎn Bīnguǎn, and pay ¥5 (65¢) commission. There are direct express trains to Běijīng (T70; 45 hr.) at 2:19pm, and to Shànghǎi (T54; 49 hr.) at 2:55pm, passing through Lánzhōu and Xī'ān. There are also speedy connections with Lánzhōu (T198; 23 hr.) at 5:28pm, and with Dūnhuáng (N950; 13 hr.) at 7:44pm. Sluggish trains head for Chóngqìng (1084; 56 hr.) at 8:10 pm, and for Chéngdū (1014; 53 hr.) at 11:35pm.

Tickets for Almaty in Kazakhstan may be purchased in the foyer of the **Yà'ōu Bīnguǎn** (© **0991/583-5408;** fax 0991/585-6699). It's open Thursday, Friday, and Sunday from 10am to 1pm and 3:30 to 6pm; Monday and Saturday from 10am to 1pm, 3:30 to 6pm, and 9:30 to 11pm. The Kazakh train runs on Monday (¥394/$49 hard sleeper, ¥625/$78 soft sleeper) and the Chinese one on Saturday (¥409/$51 hard sleeper, ¥589/$74 soft sleeper). Both trains leave at 11pm, arriving on Wednesday and Monday mornings respectively. The Kazakh train is more comfortable.

From the **main bus station** at Hēilóngjiāng Lù 51, buses connect with Yīníng (692km/429 miles; 12 hr.; ¥113/$14)at 11am, 1pm, 4pm, 5pm, 6pm, 7pm, and 8pm; and with the border town of Tǎchéng (633km/392 miles; 11 hr.; upper berth ¥85/$11, lower berth ¥95/$12) at 7pm and 8pm. The **Southern Bus Station** (© **0991/286-6635**) has regular connections with Turpan from 8:40am to 9:20pm (187km/116 miles; 2½ hr.; ¥25/$3); Kuqa (745km/462 miles; 17 hr.; ¥84/$10 upper berth, ¥94/$11 lower berth) every half-hour from 2pm to 7:30pm; Kashgar (1,470km/911 miles; 30 hr.; ¥149/$18 upper berth, ¥168/$20 lower berth) every half-hour from 9:30am to 2:20pm; and Héjìng (376km/233 miles; ¥55/$6.90) at 11am. Bus nos. 1, 7, and 101 all connect with this bus station. Buses across the Taklamakan Desert to Khotan (1,777km/1,101 miles; 25 hr.; ¥360/$45 for a luxury sleeper or ¥233/¥265 [$29/$33] for upper/lower berth) leave from

Ürümqi

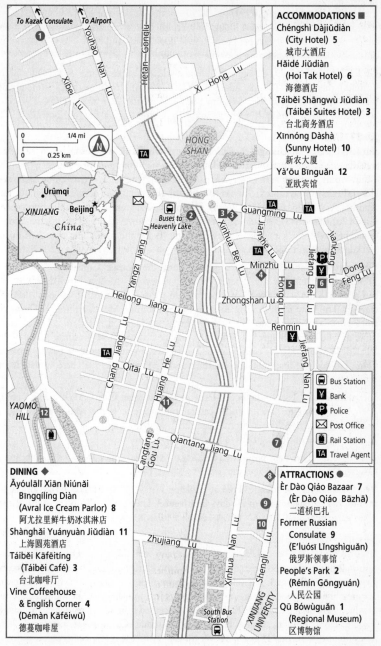

To Kazak Consulate   To Airport

Youhao Nan Lu

Xibei Lu

0   1/4 mi
0   0.25 km

N

Ürümqi

XINJIANG   Beijing ★

China

Hetan Gonglu

Xi Hong Lu

HONG SHAN

Buses to Heavenly Lake

Yangzi Jiang Lu

Guangming Lu

Xinhua Bei Lu

Jianshe Lu

Minzhu Lu

Hongqi Lu

Zhongshan Lu

Renmin Lu

Jierang Bei Lu

Jiankang

Dong Feng Lu

Heilong Jiang Lu

Chang Jiang Lu

Qitai Lu

Huang He Lu

Cangfang Gou Lu

Qiantang Jiang Lu

Zhujiang Lu

Xinhua Nan Lu

Shengli Lu

XINJIANG UNIVERSITY

YAOMO HILL

South Bus Station

ACCOMMODATIONS ■
Chéngshì Dàjiǔdiàn
   (City Hotel) 5
   城市大酒店
Hǎidé Jiǔdiàn
   (Hoi Tak Hotel) 6
   海德酒店
Táiběi Shāngwù Jiǔdiàn
   (Táiběi Suites Hotel) 3
   台北商务酒店
Xīnnóng Dàshà
   (Sunny Hotel) 10
   新农大厦
Yà'ōu Bīnguǎn 12
   亚欧宾馆

DINING ◆
Āyóulālǐ Xiān Niúnǎi
   Bīngqílíng Diàn
   (Avral Ice Cream Parlor) 8
   阿尤拉里鲜牛奶冰淇淋店
Shànghǎi Yuányuàn Jiǔdiàn 11
   上海圆苑酒店
Táiběi Kāfēitíng
   (Táiběi Café) 3
   台北咖啡厅
Vine Coffeehouse
   & English Corner 4
   (Démàn Kāfēiwū)
   德蔓咖啡屋

Bus Station
Bank
Police
Post Office
Rail Station
Travel Agent

ATTRACTIONS ●
Èr Dào Qiáo Bazaar 7
   (Èr Dào Qiáo Bāzhā)
   二道桥巴扎
Former Russian
   Consulate 9
   (E'luósī Lǐngshìguǎn)
   俄罗斯领事馆
People's Park 2
   (Rémín Gōngyuán)
   人民公园
Qū Bówùguǎn 1
   (Regional Museum)
   区博物馆

the **Hétián Bànshìchù** (© **0991/464-1250**) on the west side of Hétán Gōnglù, 180m (600 ft.) south of the Kèlāmǎyī Dōng Lù overpass. Luxury sleeper buses depart at 4pm and 6pm, while ordinary sleeper buses leave at noon, 2pm, and 8pm. The ticket office is on the right, a window beyond a row of pool tables.

GETTING AROUND   A legion of Santana and *Xiàlì* **taxis** charge ¥6 (75¢) for 3km (2 miles), then ¥1.30 (15¢) per kilometer; ¥2.10 (25¢) midnight to 7am. For the useful **bus** nos. 1, 2, and 7, pay ¥1 (15¢) into a box as you enter, or ¥.50 to ¥2 (5¢–25¢) to a conductor. Riding a **bike** through the smog and traffic snarls is not recommended.

FAST FACTS

Banks, Foreign Exchange & ATMs   The main **Bank of China** (open summer weekdays 9:30am–7pm, winter weekdays 10am–6:30pm, and year-round weekends 11am–4pm) is opposite the Hoi Tak Hotel at Dōngfēng Lù 1. Credit cards and traveler's checks are accepted. An ATM (left of the entrance) accepts foreign cards. Another ATM is located at the Jiěfàng Lù branch, just west of the Xīnhuá Bookstore. Credit cards and traveler's checks are accepted at counter 23, and there's the added convenience of black market dealers operating *inside* the bank. The branch is open weekdays 9:30am to 1:30pm and 4 to 7pm.

Consulates   Transit visas are available from the **Kazak Consulate** (© **0991/ 383-2324**) at Kūnmíng Lù 31 for ¥174 ($22). They are issued in 5 to 7 days. Or you can pay ¥348 ($43) to have them issued in 1 to 3 days. The consulate is open Monday through Thursday from 9:30am to 1pm in the summer, Monday through Thursday from 10am to 1pm in the winter. Two photos are required, visas are collected after 1:30pm, and a handling fee of ¥85 ($11) may be charged. The consulate is not easily located, so take a taxi. Or catch bus no. 2 as far as Xiǎo Xīgōu, walk east along Sūzhōu Dōng Lù, take the first right, and continue about 315m (350 yd.). The consulate is on the left (east) side.

Internet Access   East of the Bogda Hotel is **169 Internet Cafe** (© **0991/233-7169**), open from 10am to 2am. A more central Internet cafe is the **Xīnguāng Wǎngbā** (© **0991/283-1848**), open from 10am to midnight, on the second floor of the Liántōng Dàlóu on Jiěfàng Běi Lù. Dial-up is © **16900.**

Post Office   The main post office on Yángzǐ Jiāng Lù is open from 9:30am to 8pm. Overseas mail is handled at counter 3.

Visa Extensions   A friendly **PSB** at Jiànkāng Lù 27 (© **0991/283-4489**) offers 1-month visa extensions up to 20 days in advance. The entrance is to the right of the main gate, marked ALIENS RECEPTION ROOM ÜRÜMQI.

SEEING THE SIGHTS

Qū Bówùguǎn (Regional Museum)   This massive building underwent a full renovation in 2005, and should be shiny and sparkling with new exhibitions when you arrive. Don't miss the 12 remarkably well-preserved **mummies** ✿✿, many with Indo-European features: high cheekbones, long noses, brightly colored woolen kilts. The mummies, some of which have been dated to 2000 B.C., were unearthed from tombs scattered around the Taklamakan in **Lóulán, Astana, Hāmì,** and **Charchan (Qiěmò)**—see map on p. 249. They do little to further Hàn claims over Xīnjiāng. Add the cost of preservation and you might believe, as some suggest, that additional finds are being deliberately left in the ground. Hàn Chinese chauvinists point out that Uighurs, a Turkic people who migrated from western Mongolia, have nothing in common with the indigenous Indo-European Tocharians, who spoke a language that resembles a Celtic tongue. But there are enough blue- or green-eyed folk on the streets of Turpan and Kuqa (former Tocharian strongholds) to suggest that interbreeding was common. As my Uighur companion remarked, "So we killed all of them?"

Hàn Chinese guides make much of the relatively young mummy of General Zhāng (d. A.D. 633), commander of the armies in Gāochāng, whose wife rests in the Turpan Museum. Other interesting items on exhibit are lead and bronze eyeshades used in sandstorms, and a hunting boomerang unearthed in Hāmì.

Xī Běi Lù 132. Admission not determined at press time. 9:30am–5:30pm. Bus: no. 7 to Bówùguǎn; the museum is opposite.

SHOPPING

You'll find a wide range of Uighur handicrafts on sale at **Èr Dào Qiáo Bazaar,** but the environment has recently been turned into a tacky tourist trap. On what used to be on airy outdoor market now stands a Hong Kong developer's interpretation of Uighur architecture, massive beige-brick buildings, complete with a Carrefour and KFC. For more of a local flavor, head to **Rìbīyǎ Dàshà,** a building erected by the Uighur businesswoman Rebiya Kadeer who became famous in the Western press after being jailed by China as a political prisoner. Outside, around the perimeters of the building, bright fabrics, televisions, jewelry, and appliances are sold. Also nearby is **Báihétíyà'ěr Huángjīn Shǒushìdiàn** at Jiěfàng Nán Lù 197, which sells affordable gold, silver, and platinum jewelry. The necklaces are particularly elegant. Watch the Uighur women bargain, and see if you can get a similar price.

For carpets, you should avoid Èr Dào Qiáo Bazaar and its scary assortment of pushy salespeople who don't know the first thing about carpets. Head to the **Carpet Factory of the People's Government (Rénmín Dàhuìtáng Gōngyì Lǐpǐn Xiāoshòu Zhōngxīn)**— where government officials shop for gifts for foreign dignitaries. Here, they sell mostly new carpets, in both silk and wool varieties, fit for export. Goods can be bargained down by 50% at least. If you have trouble getting in (the store is located within the People's Government Compound), give them a call (© 0991/483-6698 or 0/1399-912-2631) and they'll escort you from the gate. Shopping here is generally reserved for the rich and the well-connected Chinese and Uighurs; it's open from 9am to 5pm. Another area to check out carpets in Tiánhǎái Lù, behind Èr Dào Qiáo Bazaar. There are several stores here that will have some antiques, but prices are high.

Dōngfēng Chāoshì, at Xīnmín Lù 5, is an excellent place to stock up on snacks before long train and bus rides. Take bus no. 1 or 101 to Běi Mén, and continue north for about 135m (450 ft.).

Those hunting for books on Buddhist art will find an excellent selection of pictorial and theoretical works at Tiān Zhī Yá Shūshè, in a small lane just east of Xīnhuá Bookstore, at Jiěfàng Nán Lù 348.

WHERE TO STAY
VERY EXPENSIVE/EXPENSIVE
Hǎidé Jiǔdiàn (Hoi Tak Hotel) ⚹   The Hoi Tak benefits from aggressive Hong Kong management, rigorous staff training, and plenty of capital from its parent company for renovations. The 36-story building is the largest in town, and on the rare days when the pollution haze clears, a magnificent view of the Tiān Shān range can be enjoyed.

Dōngfēng Lù 1. (C) **0991/232-2828.** Fax 0991/232-1818. www.hoitak.com. 318 units. ¥1,400–¥1,600 ($175–$200) standard room; from ¥2,080 ($260) suite. 50% discounts are standard. 15% service charge. AE, DC, MC, V. **Amenities:** 4 restaurants; bar; cafe; nightclub; large indoor pool; health club; 8-lane bowling alley; billiards and table tennis rooms; concierge; tour desk; courtesy car; business center; 24-hr. forex; salon; 24-hr. room service; in-room massage; same-day dry cleaning/laundry. *In room:* A/C, satellite TV, broadband Internet access, minibar, fridge, hair dryer, safe.

Táiběi Shāngwù Jiǔdiàn (Táiběi Suites Hotel) ⭐⭐ *(Value)*   Plunked down in the middle of Ürümqi is this extremely stylish new hotel aimed at Taiwan hipsters and business executives. The rooms are the best in Xīnjiāng—plush minimalist sofas and armchairs and comfy large beds give the rooms a professional, modern feel. The bathrooms, with sparkling new fixtures, come with separate shower and tubs. The hallways and lobby buzz with a muted ambience. Rates here are cheaper than at the Hoi Tak and the Xīnjiāng Grand Hotel for now, though they may increase as the hotel gains a loyal following. The **Táiběi Kāfēitíng (Táiběi Café)** on the third floor offers fantastic coffee and desserts (reviewed below).

Xīnhuá Běi Lù 108. (C) **0991/887-8888.** Fax 0991/882-8999. www.taipeihotel.com. 150 units. ¥688 ($66) standard room; ¥888–¥1,288 ($111–$161) suite. 20% discounts. AE, DC, MC, V. **Amenities:** Restaurant. In *room:* AC, TV, broadband Internet access, minibar, fridge.

MODERATE/INEXPENSIVE

Chéngshì Dàjiǔdiàn (City Hotel) ⭐   Right in the center of town, located on a busy, crowded street, the facilities and service at this three-star hotel are better than you would anticipate for the outlay. The beds are firm, the dark wood-paneled floors are a rare treat, and the bathrooms are spotless, if a little cramped. Service has improved to meet the expectations of the primarily foreign clientele. Taking the elevator here feels a bit like stepping into the United Nations—you'll be sharing your space with Russians, Africans, and Americans.

Hóngqí Lù 119. (C) **0991/230-9911.** Fax 0991/230-5321. xjcityhotel@163.com. 226 units. ¥322–¥522 ($40–$65) standard room; from ¥690 ($86) suite. Discounts of 20%. 15% service charge. Rates include breakfast. AE, DC, MC, V. **Amenities:** 2 restaurants; nightclub; teahouse; billiards room; concierge; tour desk; business center; 24-hr. forex; same-day dry cleaning/laundry. *In room:* A/C, TV, minibar, fridge, safe.

Xīnnóng Dàshà (Sunny Hotel)   A favorite with Russian traders, this two-star hotel is handy to the Uighur part of town and the South Bus Station. True to its name, rooms are bright, and recent renovations have delivered well-sprung beds and squeaky-clean bathrooms. Try to get a room on an upper floor, as there is plenty of bustle around the hotel.

Shènglì Lù 175. (C) **0991/285-0033,** ext. 8007. Fax 0991/287-2378. 100 units. ¥260 ($32) twin; ¥480–¥580 ($60–$72) suite. 30% discounts possible for short stays; up to 60% possible for longer stays. No credit cards. **Amenities:** 2 restaurants; concierge; tour desk; business center; next-day dry cleaning/laundry. *In room:* A/C, TV, fridge.

WHERE TO DINE

The streets around Èr Dào Qiáo are full of Uighur restaurants serving tasty dumplings stuffed with lamb and pumpkin, lamb skewers, and *langman,* or noodles. If you get sick of Uighur food, try one of the following:

Āyóulālī Xiān Niúnǎi Bīngqílíng Diàn (Avral Ice Cream Parlor) ⭐⭐ *(Moments)*
DESSERT   Uighurs seem enjoy the Western tradition of loving good ice cream—as evidenced in the soft-serve machines on street corners everywhere in Xīnjiāng. Here, ice cream is elevated to haute cuisine (though still at Uighur prices) at this parlor with wooden walls and glass tables. There are only a few flavors on offer—the trademark

Avral (a butterscotch with local berries), cherry, and chocolate. It's become an institution in Ürümqi.

Shènglì Lù 193. ¥10 ($1.25) per person. No credit cards. Bus: no. 101 to Èr Dào Qiáo; walk south under the overpass, keeping to the west side.

Shànghǎi Yuányuàn Jiǔdiàn ⚜ *Value* SHANGHAI   After the wilds of Xīnjiāng, the subtle flavors and genuinely friendly service of this unlikely restaurant may be just what you need. There is a well-translated menu, which is a relief, as Shànghǎi cuisine has a weakness for euphemistic and flowery names. Those with few cholesterol concerns should try the *Yuányuàn hóngshāo ròu* (Yuányuàn pork). Vegetarian choices are extensive. The one jarring note is the TV blaring in the corner.

Huáng Hé Lù 83. ☎ 0991/583-0777. Reservations recommended. Meal for 2 ¥60–¥140 ($7.50–$17). No credit cards. 12:30pm–12:30am.

Táiběi Kāfēitíng (Táiběi Café) ⚜ TAIWANESE   This new restaurant, part of the Taipei Suites Hotel, is representative of the hip, new edge that's seemed to penetrate Ürümqi in the past few years. The cozy booths with window views of the city, shaded by dark red curtains, are a particularly nice place to escape the hustle and bustle of the city. You can try your luck with the entrees, which range from set Japanese meals to pizza, but it's the rich coffee and mountainous piles of ice and fruit desserts that the Taiwanese call *bàobīng* that stand out.

Xīnhuá Běi Lù 108. ☎ 0991/887-8888. Meal for 2 ¥100 ($13). AE, DC, MC, V. Open 24 hr.

Vine Coffeehouse & English Corner (Démàn Kāfēiwū) WESTERN   A West Indian cafe is not something you expect to find in downtown Ürümqi, but this oasis in a sea of blandness is a delight. The halal menu was established by the head chef of the Plaza Hotel, Curaçao. Try his signature dish, the Jacques Steak, pan-fried with green peppers, tomatoes, and onions, and served with sides of potatoes, coleslaw, and (in a concession to local tastes) rice. Other hits are the soup de jour, chicken a la king, and the cookies under the front counter. "English Corner" is currently held on Thursday and Sunday nights; it's a nice way to meet locals, and possibly find a guide who isn't out to bilk you. The restaurant is down a small alley off Mínzhǔ Lù.

Mínzhǔ Lù 65. ☎ 0991/230-4831. Main courses ¥20–¥35 ($2.50–$4.40). No credit cards. Tues–Sat 1:30–11:30pm.

ÜRÜMQI AFTER DARK

Most Hàn Chinese believe that Uighurs, like all minorities, love to sing and dance *(néng gē shàn wǔ)*. As one Chinese guidebook notes, "although very few Uighurs speak Chinese well, they will often spontaneously break into song and dance to show their friendship." If you're already not exhausted by all the singing and dancing, the best-known song-and-dance troupe is the **Xīnjiāng Gēwǔ Tuán** (☎ 0991/286-6572), which performs at different venues around town. They are housed in the former Russian Consulate, at Shènglì Lù 193, whose elegant, decaying buildings and grounds are a must-see for aficionados of the Great Game, a drawn-out battle of espionage fought out in central Asia between Russian (and later Soviet) diplomats and their counterparts in British India.

AROUND ÜRÜMQI

While Ürümqi has improved, an explosion in domestic tourism means that **Tiān Chí** (**Heavenly Lake;** admission ¥60/$7.50) is on the way to becoming the world's largest public convenience. A "paving-the-lake" operation is underway, but it's still a more pleasant destination than **Hanas Lake** in the north of Xīnjiāng. If you do go, stay the night, as the lake is more tranquil after buses return to Ürümqi around 5pm. Avoid Rashid's Yurt, which is listed in every guidebook—fame is not good for everyone. Buses depart for the lake from the entrance to Ürümqi's **Rénmín Gōngyuán** at 9am (120km/74 miles; 1½ hr.; ¥40/$5 one-way, ¥60/$7.50 round-trip). A similar day trip is to **Báiyáng Gōu (White Poplar Gully),** where you can ride horses, stay in yurts, and enjoy lush countryside. Buses depart at 9:40am (76km/47 miles; 1½ hr.; ¥40/$5) and return midafternoon.

13 Kuqa (Kùchē) (★

Xīnjiāng Province, 748km (464 miles) SW of Ürümqi, 723km (448 miles) E of Kashgar, 591km (366 miles) SE of Yīníng

A maverick Silk Route kingdom, **Kuqa** was the center of the ancient kingdom of **Qiūcí.** The inhabitants were Indo-European Tocharians, who migrated down from Anatolia (Turkey) and the Caucasus. Drawing on inspiration from Gandhara and Persia, Kuqan musicians and artists were very much the fashion in the cosmopolitan capital of Cháng'ān. Monks adhered to Hinayana Buddhism, in contrast to other Tarim basin towns and China proper, which adhered to the more complex Mahayana tradition.

Kuqa's most famous son was **Kumarajiva** (A.D. 343–413), uniquely qualified to be a translator, with a Brahmin father and a Kuqan mother. His father wanted him to be ordained as a Buddhist monk, but his mother sent him to Kashmir and Kashgar to be instructed in Indian literature, astronomy, and Buddhism. He arrived in Cháng'ān in 401 as a prisoner of Chinese raiders, and soon caught the eye of the fervently Buddhist Tibetan ruling house. Kumarajiva oversaw the largest "translation team" in history. Although the Kuqan scholar was skeptical that the scriptures could ever be rendered faithfully from the Sanskrit, the team of around 1,000 scholars translated the *Diamond Sutra,* which became one of the most influential texts in Chinese Buddhism.

Present-day Kuqa is a friendly, ramshackle Uighur town. The fertile soil and relatively temperate climate yield delicious apricots, grapes, peaches, and plums. *Note:* Please turn to appendix A for Chinese translations of key locations.

ESSENTIALS

GETTING THERE There are two flights a day from Ürümqi. For times, check with **CAAC** on Wénhuà Lù (© 0997/713-4250) or with the **airport** (© 0997/712-2051).

The **railway station** is on the southwest side of town. Taxis (¥10/$1.25) and bus no. 6 (¥1.50/20¢) take you into town. Heading west, the N947 train for Kashgar (9 hr.) leaves at 5:40am; the 8873 at 11:28am. Heading east, the N948 for Ürümqi (14 hr.) leaves at 1:51am; the 5808 at 10:48pm (16 hr.) and the 8874 at 7:59pm (20 hr.) leave at more agreeable hours. The railway ticket office, open from 9am to noon, 1 to 8pm, and 9pm to midnight, sells tickets for the day of travel; your best chance of securing a sleeper ticket is CITS, which charges ¥50 ($6) commission.

The **bus station** at Tiān Shān Lù 125 (© 0997/712-2379) refuses to divulge information, and is gratuitously discourteous. There are no direct buses to Kashgar, and no guarantee of a berth on sleeper buses from Korla. However, there are buses to Aksu (275km/171 miles; 7 hr.; ¥23/$2.90), where it is possible to board a sleeper bus to Kashgar. Heading west, regular buses connect with Lúntái (111km/69 miles; 2 hr.; ¥10/$1.25); with Korla (285km/173 miles; 8 hr.; ¥25/$3); and with Ürümqi (748km/464 miles; 17 hr.; ¥70–¥80/$8.70–$10). There are two buses to Yīníng

(591km/366 miles; 20–25 hr.; ¥75/$9.40), through spectacular mountain scenery around Bayan Bulak. Buses to Xīnyuán also pass through Bayan Bulak (245km/152 miles; 10 hr.; ¥40/$5).

GETTING AROUND   **Taxis** have no meters; most trips within town cost ¥5 (65¢). There are **three-wheelers** and **pedicabs,** as well as six **bus** routes. Bus fare is ¥1 (15¢). Donkey-drawn **carts** for ¥1 (15¢) connect the bus station with the old part of town.

TOURS   **Kuqa International Travel Service,** a branch of CITS, is located inside the Qiūcí Bīnguǎn, at Tiān Shān Lù 93 (② **0997/713-6016;** fax 0997/712-2524; open 9:30am–1:30pm and 4–8pm).

FAST FACTS

Banks   The **Bank of China** (open weekdays 9:30am–8pm summer, 10am–7:30pm winter), Tiān Shān Lù 25, can draw money on credit cards, but it doesn't change traveler's checks.

Internet Access   **Liánxiǎng Wǎngbā** at Wǔyī Lù 6–78 charges ¥2 (25¢) per hour for an excellent connection. Dial-up is ② **16300.**

Post Office   The post office is at Wénhuà Lù 8, open from 9:30am to 8:30pm.

EXPLORING KUQA

Friday is the most interesting day to be in town, as humanity pours in from the surrounding countryside for the **Kuqa Bazaar** ⊛⊛, filling the old town with unforgettable sights and smells. Eric Teichman, making the first motorized journey across Xīnjiāng, found himself greatly inconvenienced: "The streets were so packed with Turki peasants that it was difficult to force a passage with the trucks. . . . We lost our way in the maze of narrow streets round the bazaar of Kuchar and it was after 4 p.m. by the time we cleared the town."

There has been no attempt to "modernize" this bazaar, which spills out in front of the mosque, just across the **Kuqa River.** Get there early when the light is ideal for photography. On any day of the week, the old town is worth exploring. Make for the **Kuqa Grand Mosque (Kùchē Dà Sì),** the only mosque in Xīnjiāng that retains a religious court (ca. 17th c.), whose influence is considerably less than when it was founded by Hoja Yisak. Bus no. 1 connects the old town with the bus station, or you can hail a donkey-drawn cart.

Kizil Thousand Buddha Caves (Kèzī'ěr Qiān Fó Dòng)   Those without a special passion for cave temples should save themselves for Dūnhuáng, but for those seeking a complete picture of the transmission of Buddhist art and ideas, this site might offer some more insights. Seventy-eight kilometers (48 miles) from Kuqa, the site can be reached by arranging a tour or hiring a taxi (¥180/$23 for round-trip).

The site, along with several other Xīnjiāng tourist spots, were recently handed over to a private company to be managed, and they've jacked up the prices of admission dramatically. You'll also have less choice over which caves you see—for visits to particular caves, you'll have to fax a letter in advance to ask for permission. Currently, only the Western Section (Xī Qū) is open to the public, and none of the caves actually have much in them except for **Cave 17,** which has several walls worth of Buddhist cave drawings intact. Even so, the blue tones in some of the caves, produced by lapis lazuli from Afghanistan (which was worth twice its weight in gold during the Middle Ages), are stunning.

The site predates Dūnhuáng, and painting continued until the Míng dynasty, when Islam fully displaced Buddhism. The site lies in a spectacular and remote valley beside the Muzart River, where the lack of Hàn influence is striking. Persian, Gandharan, Indian, and Grecian motifs dominate. Black suns, Garuda (a bird god borrowed from Indian mythology), and Apollo riding in a chariot are common decorations on the axis of the roofs. Most caves have a central pillar for perambulation, with a sleeping Buddha at the rear, presided over by mourning disciples. Buddhas and bodhisattvas are lean and muscular, with Indian features.

Unfortunately, little statuary remains, and many of the wall paintings have been removed to Europe and Japan. The eyes and mouths of most remaining images have been defaced by Muslim iconoclasts. There are also some inappropriate recent additions, particularly a ridiculous man-made lake less than 180m (600 ft.) from the caves, which depend on aridity for their preservation. **The Exhibit of Kizil Artifacts** ✦, just inside the entrance, is worthwhile, especially if you've already made the trip out here. It features reproduction drawings from many caves that you won't be allowed to enter, and other artifacts.

Admission ¥35 ($4.30) plus ¥100 ($13) for a mandatory tour guide. The price of a tour guide can be shared among several tourists, but few individual travelers visit the site. ⓒ 0997/893-2235. Fax 0997/893-2247 (fax request if you're seeking permission to visit closed caves). Summer 9am–7:30pm; winter 10am–6pm.

Sūbāshí Gǔchéng   Originally called Jarakol (Headwater) Temple when it was established in the 4th century, this ruined town 24km (15 miles) northeast of Kuqa is evidence of Buddhist parishioners' penchant for spectacular sites. Kumarajiva and Xuánzàng both preached here, the latter recording, "The images of the Buddha in these monasteries were beautiful almost beyond human skill: and the Brethren were punctilious in discipline and devoted enthusiasts." A large fire devastated the town in the 9th century, and it was gradually abandoned from the 11th century as the populace converted to Islam. There were still Buddhist relics (brought by Prince Asoka) housed in the main pagoda when the enigmatic Count Otani visited during the early 19th century.

Admission ¥15 ($1.90). Open daylight hours. Taxi: ¥40 ($5).

WHERE TO STAY

Kùchē Fàndiàn ✦   This is the best place to stay in town. Located about 3km (2 miles) from the railway station, this three-star hotel, popular with foreign tour groups, has plenty of choices of rooms. You can choose from rooms in buildings 8 and 9 and also the villas. Building 9 has larger bathrooms than building 8 but your best option is a standard room in the villas (if not already booked by tour groups), which offer peace within the hotel's large compound. Orchards and a lake on the premises make for relaxing strolls.

Tiān Shān Dōng Lù 8. ⓒ 0997/723-3156. Fax 0997/713-1160. 340 units. ¥388–¥488 ($49–$61) standard room; ¥880–¥1,888 ($110–$236) suite. 20% discount. No credit cards. Bus: no. 6 from the railway or bus station. **Amenities:** 2 restaurants; bar; business center; karaoke; exercise room; sauna; gift shop; same-day laundry. In room: A/C, TV.

Qiūcí Bīnguǎn   Located in a compound set off of the street, the hotel looks vaguely central Asian, vaguely Communist. This is a decent budget option, with bright, airy rooms and bathrooms that are in pretty good shape. Standard rooms can be bargained down to ¥120 ($15) even in the high season. The staff seems friendly and helpful.

Tiān Shān Xī Lù 93. ⓒ 0997/712-2005. Fax 0997/712-4397. 56 units. ¥280 ($35) standard room; ¥360 ($45) suite. No credit cards. **Amenities:** 2 restaurants; tour desk (CITS); same-day laundry. In room: A/C, TV.

WHERE TO DINE

Wúmǎi'ěrhóng Měishí Chéng (Omarjan Muhammed Food City) ✿✿ UIGHUR
Elsewhere, you can polish off 20 kabobs and still not be sated, but three kabobs are sufficient at Kuqa's most famous eatery. Chinese businessmen stroll in before noon and groups of Uighurs soon follow. The *pilao*, or rice pilaf, is excellent, as is the *langman* (spicy cold noodles). Other items worth trying include *lǎohǔ cài*, a spicy salad of cucumber, carrot, and red peppers; and the fruit salad *(shuǐguǒ shālà)*.

Tuánjié Lù. ☎ **0997/766-2428** or 0997/766-1987. Meal for 2 ¥20–¥100 ($2.50–$13). No credit cards. 9am–1:30am.

Wūqià Guǒyuán Cāntīng (Uqa Bhag Resturani) ✿ UIGHUR   At this restaurant, a favorite among Kuqans for special occasions, you risk becoming the guest of honor, especially if you're game to sing, dance (be prepared to make a fool of yourself attempting Uighur-style dancing), and imbibe. The *dàpán jī* is an excellent value, though you'll need a party of four to polish off this tasty meal of whole chicken, peppers, potato, and tomatoes covered in thick noodles. Other dishes include spicy beef strips *(gānzhá niú ròu tiáo)* and a cold platter of sweet cucumber *(tángbàn huángguā)*. The restaurant is in a garden to the right of another Uighur eatery.

Tuánjié Lù 1–13. ☎ **0997/712-4003.** Meal for 2 ¥60–¥150 ($7.50–$19). No credit cards. 1:30–11:30pm. Donkey cart south from the intersection of Tiān Shān Lù and Yǒuyì Lù.

14 Kashgar (Kāshí)

Xīnjiāng Province, 1,470km (911 miles) SW of Ürümqi, 520km (322 miles) NW of Khotan

The northern and southern Silk Routes joined at ancient **Kashgar** and bifurcated again, leading south through the **Pamirs** to Gilgit, and west through **the Ferghana Valley** to Samarkand. At the height of the Hàn and Táng dynasties, Kashgar was in Chinese hands. The Chinese were routed by the Arabs in 751 in the Battle of Talas River (northeast of Tashkent). This allowed Islam to spread east into the Tarim Basin, displacing Buddhism and Manichaeism. Kashgar subsequently became a center of Islamic scholarship and, but for a brief return during the Mongol Yuán dynasty, it lay outside the sphere of Chinese influence. During the Qīng dynasty the Chinese reasserted control, and Kashgar became a key site for players of the **Great Game**—it boasted both a Russian and a British consulate.

Trade is the lifeblood of Kashgar, and with the opening of border crossings at **Khunjerab, Torugart,** and the **Irkeshtam route to Osh,** it is now once again an international trading center. Kashgar's strategic position has unfortunately made it a priority in efforts to "Sinicize" border areas, and with the opening of the railway line in 2000, Hàn settlers are arriving by the trainload, a glimpse of what's in store for Lhasa.

The **old town** maintains its charm. The markets are a riot of color and exotic scents, donkeys pull rickety carts laden with watermelons and cotton bales in and out of town, gray-bearded mullahs call the faithful to prayer on every street corner, and serene old men enjoy long chats over tea.

ESSENTIALS

GETTING THERE   The **airport** is 12km (7½ miles) north of downtown. Take a taxi from the airport for ¥10 ($1.25), or you can take bus no. 2, which terminates to the west of the Peoples' Square. The **CAAC** airline ticket office at Jiěfàng Nán Lù 95 (☎ **0998/282-2113**) does not deliver tickets. Do your best not to resemble a separatist; bring your passport and buy your ticket on the spot. Two daily flights connect with Ürümqi, and onward **flights** can also be booked. Discounts can be obtained by booking up to 15 days in advance.

The **railway station** is southeast of town. Take a 15-minute taxi ride for ¥10 ($1.25), or take bus no. 28 to immediately east of the Peoples' Square. The station only sells tickets from the same day, and is open from 8:30am to 6pm, so if you want sleeper tickets, proceed through a travel agency (**Bīng Shān Lǚxíngshè,** in the foyer of the Peoples' Hotel, charges the lowest commission for train tickets; call ✆ **0998/ 283-7286**), or line up at the Kāshí Huǒchēzhàn Shìnèi Shòupiào Chù (ticket office) at Jiěfàng Běi Lù 226. Despite a sign promising "warm service," you may witness brawls between Uighur queue jumpers and Hàn security guards. Tickets can be purchased 5 days in advance. The ticket office is open from 10am to 7pm in summer, 10:30am to 7:30pm in winter. The N948 for Ürümqi (23 hr.) leaves at 4:49pm, and the 8874 (30 hr.) departs at 9:29am.

Most **buses** connect to the grandly named **International Bus Station (Guójì Qìchēzhàn)** in the north of town at Jīchǎng Lù 29 (✆ **0998/282-2913**). Sleeper buses link with Ürümqi daily between 10am and 9pm; you can opt for fast, comfortable buses (24 hr.; ¥213/$27 lower berth, ¥186/$23 upper berth) or for cheaper, slow buses (30 hr.; ¥167/$21 lower berth, ¥144/$18 upper berth). And there are buses to Aksu (468km/290 miles, ¥41/$5 upper berth, ¥57/$7 lower berth) at 10am and 9pm, Kuqa (723km/448 miles, ¥76/$9.50) at 5pm and 6pm, and Korla (1,003km/622 miles). There are five departures daily for the long and scenic trip over the mountains to Yīníng (1,644km/1,019 miles; 2 days; ¥194/$24 lower berth, ¥173/$22 upper berth, ¥144/$18 seat) at 3pm, 6pm, and 8pm. Buses to Sost in Pakistan (2 days; ¥270/$34) at noon everyday stop overnight in Tashkurgan. Those only traveling to Tashkurgan are still forced to take the "international" (295km/183 miles; ¥62/$5.20 plus ¥1/15¢ insurance), unless it's not running. Do a dry run to check. The ¥26 ($3.20) premium buys you nothing—except the feeling that you have been cheated— because locals on the same bus pay the real price.

Twice a week there is a direct bus to Bishkek for the scenic ride over the Torugart Pass (¥420/$50) at 9am every Monday, but at press time, foreigners were not allowed on it. Until the pass is upgraded to a "first level" border crossing, travelers will need to charter a vehicle through a travel agency in Kashgar. The Caravan Cafe and John's Information Cafe provide the most reliable services.

It is now possible to take a bus to Osh in southern Kyrgyzstan via Irkeshtam for ¥420 ($50). No permit is required, only a valid Kyrgyz visa. At present, the bus departs at 9am on Monday. In winter, you may need to proceed through travel agencies.

The **Dìqū Kèyùn Zǒng Zhàn (Regional Bus Station)** on Tiānnán Lù has buses to Khotan every 90 minutes from 9:30am to 9:30pm (520km/322 miles; ¥50/$6.20 seat, ¥74/$9.30 upper berth, ¥85/$10 lower berth), and daily local buses to Tashkurgan at 9:30am (294km/182 miles; ¥37/$4.60), which you will not be allowed to board if there is a bus leaving from the International Bus Station. There are regular buses to Yèchéng (Karghalik), for those considering the illegal journey to Tibet (see below).

The confusion between Xīnjiāng time and Běijīng time reaches its apogee at Kashgar's bus terminals. The International Bus Station posts its times according to Xīnjiāng time (2 hr. behind Běijīng time), but issues tickets with the Běijīng time printed on them. The Regional Bus Station does the opposite. Confused? You will be.

Kashgar

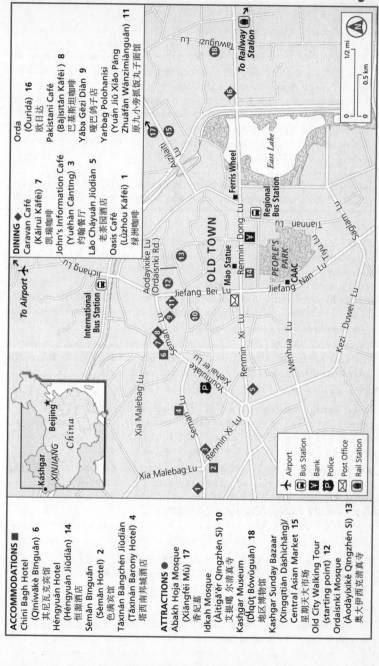

ACCOMMODATIONS ■

Chini Bagh Hotel
(Qìníwǎkè Bīnguǎn) **6**
其尼瓦克宾馆

Héngyuán Hotel
(Héngyuán Jiǔdiàn) **14**
恒源酒店

Sèmǎn Bīnguǎn
(Sèmǎn Hotel) **2**
色满宾馆

Táxínán Bāngchén Jiǔdiàn
(Táxínán Barony Hotel) **4**
塔西南邦城酒店

ATTRACTIONS ●

Abakh Hoja Mosque
(Xiāngfēi Mù) **17**
香妃墓

Idkah Mosque
(Àitígǎ'ěr Qīngzhēn Sì) **10**
艾提尕尔 尔清真寺

Kashgar Museum
(Dìqū Bówùguǎn) **18**
地区博物馆

Kashgar Sunday Bazaar
(Xīngqītiān Dàshìchǎng)/
Central Asian Market **15**
星期天大市场

Old City Walking Tour
(starting point) **12**

Ordaisnki Mosque
(Àodàyìxīkè Qīngzhēn Sì) **13**
奥大伊西克清真寺

DINING ◆

Caravan Café
(Kǎiruì Kāfēi) **7**
凯瑞咖啡

John's Information Café
(Yuēhàn Cāntīng) **3**
约翰餐厅

Lǎo Cháyuán Jiǔdiàn **5**
老茶园酒店

Oasis Café
(Lǜzhōu Kāfēi) **1**
绿洲咖啡

Orda
(Ōurìdá) **16**
欧日达

Pakistani Café
(Bājīsītǎn Kāfēi) **8**
巴基斯坦咖啡

Yāba Gēzi Diàn **9**
哑巴鸽子店

Yarbag Polohanisi
(Yuán Jiǔ Xiǎo Páng
Zhuāfàn Wánzimiànguǎn) **11**
原九小旁抓饭丸子面馆

309

The Back Door to Lhasa

From **Yèchéng**, a short minibus ride for ¥2 (25¢) takes you to **Aba**, the main point for hitching a ride to **Ali (Shíquán Hé)**, the main town in western Tibet. Truck drivers ask in the vicinity of ¥1,000 ($125) and may be bargained down to ¥600 ($75) for the 1,100km (680-mile) trip that takes at least 4 days. It is likely to take several days to arrange a lift. Aside from travelers' tales of Frenchmen freezing to death in the backs of trucks, be aware that you are putting your driver at risk. If you make it to Ali without incident, expect to be fined by the PSB and issued with an Aliens Travel Permit (¥50/$6) to continue on to Lhasa. It is now possible to undertake the journey legally, but for a price. The **Caravan Cafe** (©/fax **0998/284-2196**; www.caravancafe.com) asks ¥18,000 ($2,250), which includes permits, a 4WD, and a driver. Meals and accommodations are not included. The **Kashgar Mountaineering Association** (© **0998/252-3660**; fax 0998/252-2957; www.ksalpine.com) may also be persuaded to arrange this trip.

TOURS & GUIDES   Those interested in adventure travel such as the popular trek out to **Mustagh Ata;** an assault on the world's second-highest mountain, **K2;** or following in the footsteps of Swedish explorer Sven Hedin into the mountains south of Khotan, should connect with either the **Caravan Cafe** (see "Visitor Information," below) or the **Kashgar Mountaineering Association** at Tǐyù Lù 45 (© **0998/252-3660;** fax 0998/252-2957; www.ksalpine.com). They are friendly and experienced mountain guides, and if you want a trekking permit, you must go through them.

VISITOR INFORMATION   Reliable information may be obtained from the **Caravan Cafe** (©/fax **0998/284-2196;** www.caravancafe.com) or **John's Information Cafe** (©/fax **0998/255-1186;** johncafe@hotmail.com).

FAST FACTS

Banks, Foreign Exchange & ATMs   Both traveler's checks and credit cards are accepted at counter 1 of the **Bank of China** (weekdays 9:30am–1pm and 4–7pm) on the west side of the Peoples' Square. There is no ATM, but it is possible to draw money against a personal check with your American Express card.

Internet Access   Access is available at **John's Information Cafe** for ¥6 (75¢) per hour (open 9am–12:30am), or at **Yīmèi'ér Wǎngbā** at Rénmín Dōng Lù 49 (on the second floor of a bathhouse immediately west of the Máo statue) for ¥3 (40¢) per hour (open 10am–2am). Dial-up is © **16900.**

Post Office   The post office (open 9:30am–7pm) at Rénmín Xī Lù 7 has a counter on the second floor for troublesome foreigners.

Visa Extensions   The **PSB** is located about 180m (600 ft.) south of the Chini Bagh Hotel at Yóumùlākè Xiéhǎi'ér Lù 137. They process visa extensions in half a day, but will only extend them up to 5 days before the visa expires.

EXPLORING KASHGAR

Though the wide, main streets brought in by the Hàn have threatened Kashgar's atmosphere, little of **old town** ✦✦✦ has changed. The dusty alleys, colorful residential doorways, and mud-brick walls remain as they have been for decades. Kids with henna-dyed feet and fingernails will approach you speaking a few words of Chinese and English; men with donkey carts trudge down narrow passages; bakers arrange round large slabs of nan in coal ovens built into the ground. At prayer time, a rush of feet shuffle toward the local mosques. A family might invite you in for a cup of tea on their carpet-lined porch within a residential courtyard. Spending time watching how citizens of Kashgar live is one of the most rewarding experiences on the Silk Road. Unfortunately, the experience has been dampened a bit since the government turned out the management of several tourist sites to a Hàn company. Ticket booths now front certain neighborhoods, charging anyone who looks like a tourist ¥30 ($3.80) for a peek. You can avoid this ridiculous fee by entering the neighborhoods from **Sèmǎn Lù,** just east of the Jiěfàng Běi Lù intersection on the south side. Working backward, you'll encounter the money-grubbers once you reach Àodàyīxīkè Lù to the south, but by that point, you'll have already been through the area deemed worthy of tourism. Turning right, or west on **Àodàyīxīkè Lù,** will put you on a busy commercial street where street vendors sell boiled lamb's heads, fresh yellow figs, Hami melon, and rotisserie chicken. You can continue south into a set of residential neighborhoods that have not been savvy enough to charge tourists yet. Proceeding west toward Jiěfàng Běi Lù, old men sitting on rows of old iron benches watch Uighur music videos while drinking a yogurt-and-ice concoction. Just before you reach Jiěfàng Běi Lù, there will be an alley to your left. Proceed south and you'll see hat vendors touting a range of eclectic styles, ranging from fluffy sheepskin caps with earflaps to tall, narrow white-and-black felt ones worn by Kyrgyzs to cowboy hats that seem to be popular with Chinese tourists. Following this road down, you'll continue through a weave of streets that will eventually spit you out on **Rémín Dōng Lù.** Walking west on Rémín Dōng Lù, you'll pass Peoples' Square and the notorious, giant Máo statue that is also one of the largest in China. Note that you'll see some Uighur couples taking pictures in front of it.

Abakh Hoja Mosque (Xiāngfēi Mù) The tomb of one of Kashgar's most renowned kings and spiritual leader of the **Bái Shān sect** is several miles northeast of town. Five generations of his family are housed in a domed mausoleum decorated with green, blue, red, and white tiles. The cool interior houses 58 tombs draped with silks. The admission ticket means that the tomb is not a center of worship, but the adjacent mosque is active; devotees seem oblivious to police, who photograph anyone with a beard. The **Gāodī Mosque** ☞ to the left of the entrance has swastika motifs decorating its columns, trays for washing corpses, and wooden stretchers for transporting them to the graveyard. The cemetery is now cut off from the mausoleum by a high wall, hopefully not impeding the smooth passage of believers to the afterlife.

The tomb is known to the Chinese as **Xiāngfēi Mù,** or **Tomb of the Fragrant Concubine,** a member of the Hoja clan known for her "exceptional body aroma," probably due to the sprig of oleaster she was fond of wearing. A favorite of the Qiánlóng emperor (1711–99), she constantly refused his advances, but all tales have him devastated by her death. She was either murdered by Qiánlóng's mother, committed suicide rather than sleep with the emperor, or died naturally, depending on which account you believe. The sedan just inside the tomb is labeled as the one that brought her back to her beloved Kashgar, although her remains are almost certainly buried in the Eastern Qīng Tombs in Héběi. If the ticket office tries to sell you tickets to other "attractions" involving singing and dancing minorities, hold your ground or simply walk off.

Admission to the tomb ¥15 ($1.90), admission to the Gāodī Mosque ¥5 (65¢). Open daylight hours. Bus: no. 20 from Peoples' Sq. to the terminus. Taxi ¥10 ($1.25).

Idkah Mosque (Àitígǎ'ěr Qīngzhēn Sì)   More of a relief from the bustling market than an attraction in itself, the prayer hall and leafy courtyard of Xīnjiāng's largest mosque (ca. 1442), the heart of Islamic Kashgar, can house up to 20,000 worshippers. Whether that would make a dent in the crowd outside is doubtful.

Admission ¥10 ($1.25). Sat–Thurs 9am–9pm.

Kashgar Sunday Bazaar (Kāshí Xīngqītiān Dà Shìchǎng) *Overrated*   You might expect the world's most famous open-air market to be safe from the meddlings of bureaucracy, if only in the name of financial gain. But you would be wrong. The Bazaar is now *two* bazaars. The original site is marked as KASHGAR INTERNATIONAL TRADE MARKET OF CENTRAL AND WESTERN ASIA. But the animals are gone, and so is the charm. This market is enjoyable on any day *except* Sunday; on those days it is possible to bargain for carpets, hats, and knives at leisure. Bus nos. 7 and 20 have to squeeze through crowds.

The livestock market, squeezed out by the imperatives of modernization and property development, is located several miles southeast of town, next to a four-lane motorway. Known as the **Ivan Bazaar** *📷📷*, it still feels like a bazaar. Efforts to herd all the traders into an enclosure are cheerfully ignored by small traders, who haggle on the road outside, blocking traffic. Ignore demands for payment on entry, unless you have donkeys to trade. Bearded Uighur men in traditional blue and white garb sharpen their knives and trim their sheep; small boys wearing Inter Milan strips gorge themselves on Hami melons; Kyrgyz in dark fur hats pick up and drop dozens of lambs to test their weight and meatiness before settling deals with vigorous and protracted handshakes. No fewer than 10 people act as witnesses.

Arrive early while the market is setting up, and the light is perfect for some unforgettable photography. Shelter under colorful awnings during the midday heat, enjoying tea, buns stuffed with minced lamb *(samsas),* and bagels. Taxis (¥15/$1.90), noisy three-wheelers (¥3/40¢), and donkey carts (¥2/25¢) connect the Kashgar Bazaar with the Ivan Bazaar; or simply hire a bike and follow the crowds.

Ordaisnki Mosque (Àodàyīxīkè Qīngzhēnsì)   Islamic readers looking for a less scrutinized place to worship can visit the oldest mosque in Kashgar (c. 1119), about 270m (900 ft.) east of Idkah Square on Ordaisnki Road. Follow your nose—the city government has so much respect for religion it has placed four huge rubbish bins outside!

SHOPPING

The lanes surrounding the **Idkah Mosque** are ideal for browsing for gifts. Just north of the mosque is a line of carpet shops with nice antique rugs from Khotan, Afghanistan, and Turkmenistan. Prices start around ¥1,000 ($125). Another great place for browsing is the **Middle and Western Asia International Trade Market (Zhōngxīyà Guójì Màoyì Shìchǎng)** on Àizīrè Jiē. Wares include embroidered fabrics, dried fruit, spices, and wooden handicrafts.

Those craving a real supermarket will find one in the underground premises of **Jiāhé Chāoshì** at Kèzīlè Dūwéi Lù, Jīn Shān Míngdiàn Dìxià Dàtīng.

WHERE TO STAY

Kashgar's hotels are overpriced, given the quality. Most foreigners stay at either the Chini Bagh Hotel or the Sèmǎn Hotel, which, despite being located on the grounds of the former British and Russian consulates respectively, are less than fabulous.

Chini Bagh Hotel (Qīníwǎkè Bīnguǎn) Though the hotel is located on the grounds of the former British consulate, the consulate and any remaining character are tucked at the very back of the grounds, past the two main ugly white-tiled buildings. Four room choices fit a range of budgets. The cheapest rooms are located in the Jīngyuán Building, located towards the back of the complex; the building has a nice patio and a bit of Uighur flavor (the best hotel in Kashgar in the 1980s, actually), but rooms and bathrooms are very worn and slightly grimy now. The North Building (Běilóu) offers pleasant rooms with cozy beds but bathrooms in desperate need of renovation. Rooms in the Friendship Building (Yōuyìlóu), the circular building at the front of the complex, are the most popular and meet three-star standards, though bathrooms are still a bit worn. Finally, for ¥1,800 ($225) you can rent out the entire second floor of the former British consulate, which consists of three falling-apart bedrooms with bad Chinese furniture and bathrooms that look like they were last remodeled sometime before the Cultural Revolution. The first floor was recently renovated and now serves Uighur-style lunch and dinners. The hotel's location is spectacularly close to the old Uighur parts of town, which makes it a good choice.

Sèmǎn Lù 144. ⓒ 0998/282-2103. Fax 0998/284-2299. 337 units (shower only). From ¥380 ($47) standard room; ¥680–¥1,800 ($85–$225) suite; ¥120 ($15) triple without bathroom. Discounts of 30% are standard. Rates include breakfast. AE, DC, MC, V. **Amenities:** 3 restaurants; concierge; tour desk; 2 business centers; forex counter (8am–midnight); same-day laundry/dry cleaning. In room: A/C, TV, safe and fridge (Friendship bldg.)

Héngyuán Jiǔdiàn (Héngyuán Hotel) For the budget-conscious that want private rooms with bath, this is probably the best option in town. Rooms are modern, and bathrooms are clean. Though its location on Peoples' Square—just steps away from the notorious Máo Zédōng statue—is solidly in Hàn Chinese territory, the hotel also puts you within a 10-minute walk of Idka Mosque. Rooms can be bargained down dramatically from their rack rates even during the high season, and the management is rather friendly and helpful, though little English is spoken.

Rémín Dōng Lù 42. ⓒ **0998/283-8000.** Fax 0998/284-1988. 80 units. ¥280–¥360 ($37) standard room. No credit cards. **Amenities:** Restaurant; travel agency; salon. In room: A/C, TV.

Sèmǎn Bīnguǎn (Sèmǎn Hotel) You should consider staying at this hotel only if you can get a deal (¥400/$50) on one of the pricier rooms (¥650/$81) in building 1 or 3 ⓕ—they're some of the best in town, with a central Asian feel with intricately carved walls, beaded lampshades, and nice carpets. Bathrooms are decent, but are still a bit worn for three-star hotel. You could also take up residence at the former Russian consulate, though these rooms have a slightly tacky feel with "brick" wallpaper covering the walls and rather uncomfortable beds. (But the rooms at this consulate are better than the ones at the Chini Bagh.) The rest of the rooms here are only for the very budget-minded who won't fret about ugly furniture, very lumpy beds, and dingy bathrooms. If you're in a common room without bath you'll have to share a rather unpleasant shower and toilet with other backpackers. The hotel is ground zero for foreign tourists who frequent the travel agencies and restaurants nearby, but its location is not as good as the Chini Bagh's for those who prefer to spend time in the old quarter of town rather than eating banana pancakes with foreigners.

Sèmǎn Lù 337. ⓒ **0998/255-2861.** Fax 0998/255-2861. 212 units, 120 of which are Uighur-style rooms. ¥160–¥650 ($20–$80) standard room; ¥1,280 ($160) suite. AE, DC, MC, V. **Amenities:** 4 restaurants; concierge; tour desk (CYTS); business center; same-day laundry/dry cleaning. In room: A/C, TV.

Tǎxīnán Bāngchén Jiǔdiàn (Tǎxīnán Barony Hotel) Located on a stretch of road between the Sèmǎn and the Chini Bagh hotels, this new hotel is one of the few in town that meets four-star standards. The hotel, however, has a rather empty feel despite its amenities, and its claim to be "internationally managed" appears to be a hoax. Still, the bathrooms are the most modern in town and rooms are decorated in nonoffending modern tones. Beds are very firm.

Sèmǎn Lù 242. (𝐶) **0998/258-6888.** Fax 0998/258-5888. 108 units. ¥880 ($110) standard; ¥1,280 ($160) suite. 20%–40% discounts. AE, DC, MC, V. Amenities: Restaurant; concierge; conference center; gift shop; gym; billiards; business center; same-day laundry/dry cleaning. In room: A/C, TV, broadband Internet access, minibar, safe.

WHERE TO DINE

If you tire of lamb, try the delicious *chapattis* and *parathas* at the tiny **Pakistani Café** 𝓐𝓐 (no phone), 100m (328 ft.) to the left if you're coming out of the Chini Bagh Hotel on Sèmān Lù. Another good bet is the whole pigeon soup at **Yǎba Gēzi Diàn** 𝓐 ((𝐶) **0998/222-2282),** across the street and about 300m (981 ft.) to the left of the Chini Bagh Hotel.

Caravan Cafe (Kǎiruì Kāfēi) 𝓐𝓐 WESTERN After some time in Xīnjiāng, the caffeine-deprived may dream of the smell of freshly ground coffee or of lattes with perfectly formed froth, perhaps accompanied by a cinnamon roll and a bowl of muesli with yogurt, served by handsome and courteous waitstaff. Fortunately, this is no mirage—the coffee, the food, and the service are 100% real and 100% Western. Managed by Westerners with a passion for central Asia, and staffed by friendly English-speaking Uighurs, the Caravan Cafe can also arrange top-of-the-line adventure travel to the Taklamakan Desert, Shipton's Arch, and Mustagh Ata. If you want to know what's going on in town, make this your first port of call.

Sèmǎn Lù 120. (𝐶) **0998/298-1864.** www.caravancafe.com Main courses ¥19–¥33 ($2.40–$4.10). No credit cards. Thurs–Tues 9am–9:30pm. Closed Jan to mid-Apr.

Lǎo Cháyuán Jiǔdiàn 𝓐 UIGHUR When the locals treat themselves, they make for this eatery, an institution since 1989. Service can be frosty, and the pseudo-Arabian decor is tacky. Let the food take center stage. All dishes are well presented, often with fancy garnishes, something you don't see a lot of in southern Xīnjiāng. For starters, try *bàn sān sī,* a finely sliced salad of capsicum, onion, carrot, cucumber, and noodles; or try the old favorite, roast peanuts. Recommended main courses are a tender beef stir-fry *(chǎokǎo ròu)* and the dry-fried spring chicken *(gānbiān tóngzǐjī).* The local delicacy is field mushrooms steamed with bok choy, ginger, and garlic *(bāchǔ mógu),* although their slippery texture won't be to everyone's taste.

Rénmín Xī Lù 251. (𝐶) **0998/282-4467.** Meal for 2 ¥70–¥150 ($8.70–$19). No credit cards. 10am–1:30am.

Orda (Ōurìdá) 𝓐 UIGHUR This is Uighur dining, made easy; with its kitchen in the center of the restaurant you can just point to what you want. Orders are taken at a register, and the food arrives at your table seconds later. Try the *pilao* (rice pilaf) set meal, which comes with yogurt, which you can dole onto your rice to give it a creamy texture. The atmosphere is pleasant, with walls decorated in colorful tiles and Uighur musicians that play traditional instruments. If you order the fruit plate, remember to eat the watermelon first, before the grapes and the Hami melon—it's an Uighur taboo to do it in reverse!

Rénmín Dōng Lù (Diqu Sifa Duimian). (𝐶) **0998/265-2777.** Meal for 2 less than ¥50 ($6.50). No credit cards. 10:30am–10pm. Bus: no. 10.

Yarbag Polohanisi (Yuán Jiŭ Xiăo Páng Zhuāfàn Wánzimiàn Guăn) ⚁
UIGHUR   Kashgar's best-known restaurant has been packed with locals for the several years, taking shade under a willow tree. Alas, old willow trees are not in the picture for the new Kashgar. City planners have arranged a date with the bulldozer, leaving the new restaurant with the unwieldy name "The pilaf and noodle restaurant that was once next to the no. 9 Primary School." The willow tree remains the logo, and the larger premises will continue to serve savory pilaf and beef ball noodles *(wánzimiàn)*.

Jiěfàng Běi Lù (135m/450 ft. south of Sèmăn Lù). Meal for 2 less than ¥20 ($2.50). No credit cards. 8am–8pm.

AROUND KASHGAR

Shipton's Arch (Tushuk Tash)   The world's largest natural arch stands, largely unheralded, about 50km (31 miles) northwest of Kashgar. Located at an elevation of 3,168m (10,394 ft.), the arch towers 366m (1,200 ft.) above the canyon floor. It is composed of crumbling conglomerate and is exceedingly difficult to reach. Eric Shipton, Britain's final representative in Kashgar and an accomplished mountaineer, failed several times from the southern route via Muk and Mingyol, finally gaining access from the north via Artux and Karakum. His wife described the scene: "We found ourselves looking straight across at the immense curve of the arch. Its upper half soared above us, but the walls continued down into an unfathomable gorge below. It was as if we stood on a platform some few feet away from a giant window. . . ."

The Caravan Cafe runs day tours to the arch for ¥1,200 ($150) for four people. The tour includes a car, driver, and a ladder necessary to scale a steep portion of the canyon.

Tomb of Mohammed Kashgari   The tomb of this eminent 11th-century translator lies 30km (19 miles) southwest of Kashgar, west of the charming Uighur town of **Opal (Wūpà'ěr)**. The scholar spent most of his years in Baghdad and is credited with compiling the first Turkic dictionary in Arabic. Hire a jeep for ¥300 ($37); or take a taxi (¥120/$15) or bus no. 4 (¥2.50/30¢) from Kashgar's Opal bus station (a block south of the Sèmăn Hotel) as far as Shūfù, then share a taxi to Opal for ¥5 (65¢). Donkey carts, charging ¥4 (50¢), leave for the tomb from under a red-and-yellow arch in the center of Opal.

15 Tashkurgan (Tăshíkùèrgān)

Xīnjiāng Province, 295km (183 miles) SW of Kashgar

Tashkurgan marked the end of the Silk Routes for Chinese traders arriving from Kashgar or Yarkand. Their goods would be transferred to Bactrian, Persian, or Sogdian caravans, which continued on to Gilgit and thence either south to the Indian Ocean along the Indus River, or west through Kabul, Herat, and Meshed, ultimately reaching the Mediterranean Sea at Antioch or Tyrus. Described by British consul Eric Teichman as the "storm centre of Asian politics," the town has a strong military presence. Those heading to Pakistan must spend the night here.

ESSENTIALS

GETTING THERE   The road from Tashkurgan to Kashgar was under repair at press time, so what is currently a 12-hour nightmare will someday be a smooth 6-hour journey. Roughly two-thirds of the way to Tashkurgan is **Karakul Lake,** over which towers the magnificent **Mustagh Ata.** Buses leave for Karakul and Tashkurgan starting at 9:30am at Kashgar's Dìqū Bus Station. The cost is ¥44 ($5). Or you could consider renting a Land Cruiser and driver for four people for between ¥800 and ¥1,000 ($100–$125) for 2 days. The icy lake is surrounded by yurts that take in visitors. Room and board can be negotiated for ¥40 ($5) per person, but many of the locals are quite pushy. If you encounter this, just walk on; there are plenty of other yurts. Highly recommended are the yurts that you'll come across before you get to the parking lot and official entrance of the lake, where they'll charge you ¥50 ($6) for a "ticket" to Karakul. You can hop on the back of a motorbike and ride around the lake for ¥20 ($2.50). *Warning:* Do not camp alone—recently, an Italian tourist almost met an untidy end here. Returning to Kashgar from Karakul may be a little trickier—buses are supposed to stop on their way back from Tashkurgan, but they'll often plow ahead without stopping. You can try your luck at noon, when one bus is supposed to come by, and then at 1pm.

Beyond Karakul is the town of **Subash (Sūbāshí),** starting point for hikes to Mustagh Ata. It may be possible to stay here, as a less-touristed alternative to Karakul Lake. Beyond Subash, there is a magnificent moraine valley, a highlight of the trip. Buses return to Kashgar at 9:30am for ¥62 ($7.70). There is a cheaper local bus, but you will not be allowed to buy a ticket for it. You can continue to **Sost** for ¥225 ($28); the 8-hour trip arrives in town in late afternoon after many inspections.

SEEING THE SIGHTS

Tashkurgan Fort   Dating from the 14th century, this substantial fort is accessed by a small lane just east of the Pamir Hotel. Tickets are rarely collected, and an impressive view of the surrounding fields, mountains, and military complexes can be enjoyed. The best view of the fort is from the pastures below in the early morning light.

Admission ¥10 ($1.25). 8:30am–5pm.

WHERE TO STAY

The only thing recommending either of the hotels open to foreigners in Tashkurgan is their existence. Substantial discounts are always obtainable, as Tashkurgan is not a major destination for Chinese tourists.

Jiāotōng Bīnguǎn (Traffic Hotel)   Described by one travel guide as "the worst hotel in the world," the hotel is still stung by this assessment. On those grounds, this establishment is entitled to a "most-improved" award. Rooms facing south are sunnier. The Muslim restaurant is often the site of the Tajik equivalent of a Scottish *ceilidh,* with plenty of drinking and dancing—all arms, wrists, and hips—that will test your sense of rhythm.

Kāshígàlè Lù 50. ⓒ 0998/342-1192. Fax 0998/342-1576. 30 units. ¥100 ($13) twin; ¥300 ($37) suite; from ¥10 ($1.25) dorm bed. No credit cards. **Amenities:** Restaurant; cafe; same-day laundry. *In room:* TV.

Pàmǐ'ěr Bīnguǎn (Pamir Hotel)   This apathetic two-star hotel on the far side of town offers slightly more comfortable rooms with temperamental showers that allegedly run for 16 hours a day. Just which 16 hours is a matter of speculation. Rooms in the newer wing are worth the extra outlay. The only excitement the last time we visited was an exhibition on ETHNIC SEPARATISM AND TERRORISM, enthusiastically attended by brigade after brigade of adolescent Hàn soldiers. The author missed an invitation.

Kāshígàlè Lù 207. ⓒ/fax 0998/342-1085. 70 units (30 with open shower). ¥80–¥180 ($10–$23) twin; ¥200 ($25) suite. No credit cards. **Amenities:** Restaurant; bike rental; same-day laundry. *In room:* TV.

WHERE TO DINE

Fine treats are offered at the **Pamir Restaurant (Pàmǐ'ěr Kuàicān; ⓒ 0998/ 283-3228),** about 27m (90 ft.) north of the main intersection on the right (east) side.

Excellent Sichuanese fare is served up diagonally across from them, at **Chuānfū Dàpáidàng.**

16 Khotan (Hétián) 🕁🕁

Xīnjiāng, 520km (322 miles) SE of Kashgar, 1,509km (936 miles) SW of Ürümqi

Khotan was once a more important trading and religious center than Kashgar. From ancient times, jade was "fished" from the 24 rivers in the Khotan area, and "jade routes" to Mesopotamia and China flourished from the 3rd millennium B.C. onwards. Passing through on his way to India in the 5th century, the Chinese Buddhist monk Fǎxiǎn found a purely Buddhist population in the order of "several myriads." Returning to China after his adventures in India, Xuánzàng found a thriving center: ". . . the country produced rugs, fine felt, and silk of artistic texture, it also yielded black and white jade. The climate was genial, but there were whirlwinds and flying dust. The people were of gentle disposition, and had settled occupations. The nation esteemed music and the people were fond of dance and song; a few clothed themselves in woolens and furs, the majority wearing silk and calico. . . . The system of writing had been taken from that of India."

From 1901, Aurel Stein visited several sites around Khotan, concluding that the ancient capital was at **Yoktan (Yāotègān),** 9.7km (6 miles) to the west. He found Roman coins, and some delightful paintings and sculptures (ca. 2nd c.) showing Grecian influence. Unconnected by rail and thus safe from inundation by Hàn settlers, Khotan is home to the liveliest **bazaar** in Xīnjiāng, and is a must for those hoping to experience traditional Uighur culture and markets. *Note:* Please turn to appendix A for Chinese translations of key locations.

ESSENTIALS

GETTING THERE Khotan's **airport,** 10km (6¼ miles) west of downtown, was undergoing renovations at press time. Daily connections with Ürümqi are expected. The **CAAC** air ticket office, on Wūlǔmùqí Nán Lù (✆ **0903/251-2178**), is open from 10am to 1pm and 4 to 6pm.

The main **bus station** (✆ **0903/251-3533**) is at Hémò Lù 5, north of town, on the south side of Highway 315. Comfortable sleeper buses at 1pm and 5pm cross the Taklamakan Desert Highway to Ürümqi (1,509km/936 miles; 25 hr.; ¥367/$46). Cheaper, less comfortable sleeper buses run every 2 hours between 10am and 8pm. For Kuqa, buy a ticket to Lúntái (874km/542 miles; 14 hr.; ¥147/$19). You are dropped off in the forlorn settlement of Lúnnán, about 30km (19 miles) south of Lúntái. A seat in a taxi to Lúntái should cost ¥10 ($1.25). Ask to be dropped at the bus station (qìchē zhàn), where buses for Kuqa (110km/68 miles; 2 hr.; ¥10/$1.25) leave when full. A daily bus at 9am visits the oasis towns east of Khotan, stopping at Keriya (Yùtián; 177km/110 miles; 3 hr.; ¥15/$1.90), Niya (Mínfēng; 294km/182 miles; 5 hr.; ¥25/$3), and Charchan (Qiěmò; 603km/374 miles; 11 hr.; ¥50/$6). Sleeper buses for Kashgar leave at 5:30pm, 8:30pm, and 9:15pm (509km/316 miles; 13 hr.; ¥87/$11), while hard-seat buses depart at 9am, 10am, and noon (¥57/$7.10). There are daily sleeper buses to Yīníng at 11am and 1pm (2,469km/1,531 miles; 3 days; ¥265/$33).

GETTING AROUND **Taxis** are plentiful and do use their meters. They charge ¥5 (65¢) for 3km (2 miles), then ¥1.30 (20¢) per kilometer. **Bus** fare is usually ¥1 (15¢), paid to the conductor.

TOURS & GUIDES **CITS** is on the third floor of a building 180m (600 ft.) south of the Bank of China, at Tāmùbāgé Lù 23 (© 0903/251-6090; fax 0903/202-2846). It's open from 9:30am to 1:30pm and 4 to 8pm. While rates charged for guides are reasonable, you're better off arranging your own transport.

FAST FACTS

Banks, Foreign Exchange & ATMs   If you are continuing east along the southern Silk Route, change your money in Khotan, as there are no facilities before Golmud or Dūnhuáng. The **Bank of China** at Wūlǔmùqí Nán Lù 14 accepts credit cards and traveler's checks. It's open weekdays in summer from 9:30am to 1:30pm and 4 to 8pm; weekdays in winter from 10am to 2pm and 3:30 to 7pm. No ATMs are available.

Internet Access   The 24-hour **Xīn Shíkōng Dìdài,** just west of the Hétián Yíng Bīnguǎn, charges ¥4 (50¢) per hour for an excellent connection. Dial-up is © 165.

Post Office   On the southwest corner of the main intersection at Běijīng Xī Lù 1 (© 0903/251-1166), the post office is open in summer from 9am to 8:30pm and in winter from 9:30am to 8pm.

Visa Extensions   The **PSB** at Běijīng Xī Lù 22 (© 0903/202-3614) offers one of the speediest visa extensions available—it takes less than half an hour! It's open weekdays from 9:30am to 1:30pm and 4 to 7:30pm.

EXPLORING KHOTAN

Sunday Market, Xīngqītiān Dàshìchǎng ✿✿✿ (Moments)   This is everything the Kashgar Market once was. You'll need an early start and a lot of film stock to make the most of Xīnjiāng's liveliest **bazaar,** set in the heart of the Uighur part of town. The intersection between Gǔjiāng Běi Lù and Jiāmǎi Lù marks the center of the action, and you're unlikely to see a Hàn face as the streets fill with livestock and people throughout the day. Jewelers pore over gemstones, blacksmiths busy themselves shoeing horses and repairing farm tools, blanket makers beat cotton balls, rat-poison sellers proudly demonstrate the efficacy of their products—the sights and smells are overwhelming. Don't miss the **horse riding enclosure** toward the north side of the melee, where buyers test the roadworthiness of both beast and attached cart, with frequent spectacular tumbles. Head southeast from the bus station or simply follow the crowds.

SHOPPING

Ancient Old Wool and Silk Carpet Shop   Across the street from the Hétián Hotel, this little shop has a decent selection of carpets from the surrounding areas. While the shops carries just a few hard-to-find antique carpets, this is probably the best selection you're going to get for old carpets in Khotan, as most stores only sell new ones, in fairly tacky designs, to locals. If the store is closed when you come by, give the owner Abdujilil a call, and he'll come by on his motorbike to open up the shop, which is usually open 9am to 9pm. Wūlǔmùqí Nán Lù 35. © 0903/202-4040 or 0/1307-008-9909.

Jade Factory (Gōngyì Měishù Yǒuxiàn Gōngsī)   Khotan has long been China's source of jade (nephrite). The jade was first noticed by Zhāng Qiān, sent to Khotan on a reconnaissance expedition by Hàn Wǔdì, prior to the first successful Chinese invasion of the Western Regions. He believed women were adept in finding the gem, and they would dive for jade in the rivers around Khotan. Diving in the muddy and much diminished Khotan River now is not recommended, regardless of your gender. Those contemplating jade purchases should do your homework with a reputable jeweler before leaving home. While this shop is reliable, fake jade is one commodity

Khotan never runs short of. Visit the dusty workshop behind the shop, where artisans turn, carve, and polish the jade. The Jade Factory is open from 9:30am to 8pm. Tǎnǎiyī Lù 4. © 0903/202-2370.

WHERE TO STAY

Khotan, surprisingly enough, has plenty of decent, midrange options. Bargain hard— you can get up to 60% off rack rates.

Hétián Yíng Bīnguǎn Set in sprawling grounds with rose gardens, trees, and buildings of varying vintage, rooms in the new four-story three-star main building are decent, with good bathrooms. The dormitories are a good value—but showers could use a little scrubbing. The only hazard is portly men from Sìchuān watching TV in their underwear.

Tǎnǎiyī Běi Lù 4. © 0903/202-2824. Fax 0903/202-3688. 78 units (53 with bathroom). From ¥20 ($2.50) dorm bed; ¥110–¥180 ($14–$22) twin; ¥380–¥480 ($47–$60) suite. No credit cards. **Amenities:** 2 restaurants; business center; same-day laundry. *In room:* A/C, TV.

Wēnzhōu Jiǔdiàn (Wēnzhōu Hotel) Once the nicest hotel in Khotan, this hotel has recently been supplanted by the Zhèjiāng Hotel next door. This hotel is still a good midrange option. Formerly known as the Tiānhǎi Dàjiǔdiàn, the three-star establishment has a good staff, nice rooms, and clean bathrooms. Rooms should be cheaper here than at the Zhèjiāng, since they're a notch down in quality.

Běijīng Xī Lù 5. © 0903/203-7666. Fax 0903/203-7222. 64 units. ¥218 ($27) twin; ¥388 ($48) suite. 30% discounts are standard. No credit cards. **Amenities:** Restaurant; concierge; business center; same-day laundry/dry cleaning. *In room:* A/C, TV, water cooler.

Zhèjiāng Dàjiǔdiàn (Zhèjiāng Hotel) *Value* Brought to you by coastal Chinese investors is this new four-star hotel that seems to have broken out of the mold of the usual Chinese hotel with sleek, modern rooms that are the most comfortable in town. Bathrooms are sparkling clean. The location, right next to the main square in town, puts you at the Sunday market with a quick 10-minute taxi ride. The level of English service is impressive for such a far-flung establishment. When we visited after it first opened, they were offering enormous 60% discounts on their rooms—hopefully, the same will be true when you arrive.

Běijīng Xī Lù 9. © 0903/202-9999. Fax 0903/203-6688. 73 units. ¥468 ($56) standard room; ¥788 ($96) suite. 60% discounts. AE, DC, MC, V. **Amenities:** Restaurant; nightclub; concierge; business center; conference rooms; sauna. *In room:* A/C, TV, minibar, safe.

WHERE TO DINE

Nàwǎkè Lù Gāoyáng Kǎoròu, Kuàicāndiàn *A* UIGHUR The prize for Xīnjiāng's best *samsa*—a package of lamb and spices baked in pastry—is safe with this delightful open-air restaurant, the last in a line of eateries with blue awnings. Customers queue up for some time waiting for them, so be patient. The kabobs and nan are also excellent if you're short on time. The slightly sweet medicinal tea is common to many restaurants, and the tea leaves *(jiànkāng chá)* can be purchased from the **Uighur Hospital,** Jiāmǎi Lù 2.

Nàwǎkè Lù. © 0903/202-5132. Meal for 2 less than ¥50 ($6). No credit cards. 8am–10:30pm.

Toraq Cafe (Húyáng Línghóng Kāfēitīng) UIGHUR This little unpretentious cafe is a great place to unwind and have a cup of coffee. While they only serve instant coffee, at least they have a wide range of international brands to choose from. The Uighur owners also serve a sampling of different Uighur dishes, like *samsa* and lamb

Wild China: Yīníng (Gulja)

Yīníng, 692km (429 miles) west of Ürümqi, has always been a tenuous possession of the Chinese empire, surrounded by the richest farmland in central Asia, and closer to Moscow than Běijīng. During the Qīng dynasty, it was the farthest point of banishment. Surrounded by high peaks and blessed with a mild climate, Yīníng is now a Hàn city with a smattering of Kazaks and Uighurs; it boasts hearty cuisine and access to the fascinating **Qapqal Xībó Autonomous County (Cháb ù Chá'ěr Xiàn)**.

The colonization of Xīnjiāng began with the fierce ancestors of the current residents of **Qapqal**, 25km (16 miles) west of Yīníng. In 1764, 1,000 Xībó soldiers (followed "secretly" by 4,000 family members) were dispatched from Manchuria by the Qiánlóng emperor, with the promise that they would be allowed to return after 50 years. After putting the natives to the sword and hunting the region's animals to near extinction, the Xībó accepted the fact that there was no prospect of a return home, settled down, and took to farming.

While the **Manchu language** died out in northeast China, this outpost maintained their written and spoken language, and traditions such as the **hanging family tree** (*jiāpǔ*). Most houses have one, with coins to represent the family coming into money, clubs and arrows the birth of a boy, and ribbons and boots the birth of a girl. Catch a bus from outside the Yīníng bus station to Chá Xiàn (30 min.; ¥5/65¢) and take a three-wheeler (¥5/65¢) onward to **Jìngyuǎn Sì** (admission ¥10/$1.25). An exhibition of **Xībó** history inside this lamaist temple is fascinating, but alas, the guide speaks fluent Russian and awaits her first Russian visitor. Wander among the fields of sunflowers and wheat, dotted with light blue courtyard houses with earthen roofs.

GETTING THERE   The **airport** is connected to town by taxi (¥10/$1.25). **CAAC** (© 0999/822-1505) is in the foyer of the **Yóudiàn Bīnguǎn**, Jiěfàng Lù 162. Flights connect with Ürümqi, Xī'ān, and Wǔhàn. The **bus terminal** on Jiěfàng Lù in the northwest of town (© 0999/802-3413) has connections with Ürümqi (12 hr.) and Kashgar (52 hr.) via the wild Mongolian minority town of Bayan Bulak. Tickets for Almaty (12 hr.; ¥260/$32; Mon, Wed, Thurs, and

---

skewers. They stay open late and serve a selection of whiskeys and beers. Come here for a drink if you'd like to escape the usual sleaziness of Chinese bars.
Wūlǔmùqì Lù 69. © 0903/688-2424. Meal for 2 less than ¥40 ($5). No credit cards. 8am–midnight.

AROUND KHOTAN

Carpet Factory (Dìtǎn Chǎng)   In the 1980s, factory inspections were an unavoidable part of any trip to China. Fortunately, you can examine the workings of this factory without listening to a cadre reciting statistics concerning output, expected turnover, and the area of the factory down to the last square meter. Workers sit outside the main carpet-making hall, their hands, feet, and hair stained red by henna dye. The gentle rattle of the looms and swoosh of the combs is almost drowned out by the

Sat) are purchased at the hotel reception **immediately** inside the bus termi-nal. There are abundant **taxis,** which charge ¥5 (65¢) for 2km (1¼ mile), then ¥1.30 (20¢) per kilometer thereafter; add ¥.20 (5¢) from midnight to 5am. **Buses** charge ¥1 (15¢), dropped in a box when you board. A **tandem bike** may be rented at **Diāokè Shíguāng** (Jiěfàng Lù 64; ⓒ **0999/838-2369**), which also serves excellent coffee and traditional Tajik ice cream.

WHERE TO STAY & DINE   **Yīlí Bīnguǎn** (Yíngbīn Lù 8; ⓒ **0999/802-2794**; fax 0999/802-4964) is Yīníng's oldest hotel, set in the extensive (30,000 sq. m/322,917 sq. ft.) grounds of the former **Soviet consulate,** which are particu-larly charming in autumn. Midsize twins for ¥160 to ¥488 ($20–$61) in build-ings 2 and 3 to the west of the complex are the best choice. Yīníng's swankiest three-star hotel, the **Yīlìtè Dàjiǔdiàn** (Shènglì Jiē 98; ⓒ **0999/803-5600**; fax 0999/802-1819), is situated on the northeast corner of the Peoples' Square, the scene of anti-government riots in 1997. While this 12-story glass-and-tile monolith is out of place in sleepy Yīníng, standard rooms at ¥298 ($36) are spotless and bright. Discounts of 30% are available.

For dining, **Guǒyuán Cāntīng** (Yīlí Hé Mínzú Wénhuà Cūn Xiàng Nèi 500 Mǐ Chù; ⓒ **0999/832-3580**) charges less than ¥100 ($13) for a meal set in an apple orchard on the north bank of the Yīlí River. (Turn left down the final road before the Yīlí Bridge south of town and continue for 455m/1,500 ft. The entrance is on the right.) Enjoy steamed dumplings (*yóu tǎzi*), a local version of *samsa* with three fingerprints in each bun (*yībǎzhuā*), whole chicken with vegetables and noodles (*dàpán jī*), and the filling *náng bāo ròu,* a huge plate of lamb and vegetable stew on a wheat pancake. Sup honeyed rye beer called *kvass (géwǎsī),* and make friends with the local Uighurs. Try the most renowned Kazakh dish, *nàrén,* at **Nàrén Cāntīng** (Xīnhuá Xī Lù 7; ⓒ **0999/803-2434**). *Nàrén* is roasted horse meat (taken from the waist) served on a pile of thick noodles with a side serving of nan and an appetizing salad of tomato, cucumber, and Spanish onion; it costs less than ¥40 ($5). The genial owner, Tal-gat, will cajole you to try horse's milk or yogurt, but these sour concoctions are an acquired taste. The regular yogurt (*niúnǎi*) is creamy and delicious.

banter of Uighur women—there can be as many as eight of them working on one car-pet. At the back is the inevitable shop, but much of the art of carpet weaving was lost during the Cultural Revolution, so you won't find anything to match the splendor of carpets in your average Uighur home. The factory is open Monday through Saturday from 9:30am to 1:30pm and 3:30 to 7:30pm.

Nàwǎkè Jiē 6. ⓒ 0903/205-4553. Take a cab (about ¥20/$2.50) or bus no. 2 east along Běijīng Lù to the terminus, then bus no. 5 heading south, again to the end of the line.

Silk and Mulberry Research Center (Sī Sāng Yánjiūsuǒ) ⓐ

Khotan is said to have broken the closely guarded Chinese silk monopoly in the 5th century. According to legend, a Chinese princess was instructed by the king to smuggle silk-moth eggs in her hairpiece, as frontier guards, however zealous, would never touch a lady's hair.

The front building houses offices, and possibly someone willing to show you around, but the surest way to see the center is to arrange a tour through CITS, who will also show you "their" traditional silk makers. You can view the entire mysterious process, from sorting and boiling the cocoons, to reeling off the thread—typically 900m (2,950 ft.) long—through to the final weaving into the wavelike ikat patterns characteristic of Khotan silk. While the primitive (and deafening) technology makes for a good tour, business is not good. A sign near the gate opens with a statement of the company's bold production targets, and ends with the modest objective, DON'T LOSE MONEY *(bù kuā)*. You'll find few tasteful products in the shop; buy your silk in a large city. This difference in tastes is nothing new. Chinese silk patterns were never in vogue among the Romans, who usually imported silk thread—Plinius recorded that Chinese cloth would be unraveled and rewoven.

Hémò Lù 107. Bus: no. 1 from north of the main roundabout on Hétián Lù to the terminus, then walk back about 225m (750 ft.).

8

Eastern Central China

by Jen Lin-Liu

If Shǎnxī Province is the cradle of Chinese civilization, then the stretch of eastern central China between the Yellow River (Huáng Hé) and the Yángzǐ River (Cháng Jiāng)—an area covering the provinces of **Hénán, Shāndōng, Jiāngsū,** and **Ānhuī**—can be seen as the crucible in which Chinese culture subsequently developed and flourished. Bounded by the Yellow Sea and the East China Sea on the east, and buffered from ethnic minority influences from the north, west, and south, this swath of China is a region that, except for some Western influence late in China's history, has remained unapologetically and overwhelmingly "Hàn" Chinese in character.

Early Chinese civilization may have developed around the Yellow River in Hénán Province with the Shāng dynasty (1700–1100 B.C.), but Chinese culture as it is widely perceived today really started to take shape only some 600 years later with the birth of the most influential figure in Chinese history, Confucius, in **Qūfù** in Shāndōng Province. By the time of the "golden age" of the Hàn dynasty (206 B.C.–A.D. 220), Confucianism, that quintessentially Chinese philosophical tradition, had become the official state philosophy, and would be put to the test in the subsequent 2,000 years of dynastic changes. Arguably, no region or place in China has seen the rise and fall of more dynasties than this eastern central section of the country, with the ancient capitals of **Luòyáng** (capital of nine dynasties), **Kāifēng** (six dynasties), and **Nánjīng**

(eight dynasties) serving as China's seat of power 23 times. Today, though none of these former capitals has retained much of their previous glory, all contain vestiges of a Chinese imperial past, and are worth visiting. Chinese history buffs may be interested as well in some lesser-known but intriguing finds such as the **miniature terra-cotta army** in Xúzhōu, and the **horse and chariot funeral pits** in Zībó.

The influence of that other indigenous Chinese religious-philosophical tradition, Daoism, is also very strong in this region, which is home to two of Daoism's sacred mountains: **Tài Shān,** the most climbed mountain in China, and **Sōng Shān,** the central Daoist mountain. Though not indigenous to China, Buddhism's influence on Chinese culture has also been profound. Some of China's finest Buddhist art and sculpture can be seen at the magnificent **Lóngmén Grottoes (Lóngmén Shíkū)** in Luòyáng.

Historically, this region has also been the cultural bridge between the political center of gravity mostly in the north, and the economic center in the south, especially around the fertile lower deltas of the Yángzǐ River. The physical link was the great Chinese engineering feat of the **Grand Canal,** built between the Suí dynasty (581–618) and the Yuán dynasty (1206–1368) to link the Yángzǐ and Yellow rivers. Although much of the canal is no longer navigable, it gave rise in its heyday to many flourishing river towns, including Sūzhōu, Zhōu Zhuāng, and the underrated but delightful **Yángzhōu,** the

Eastern Central China

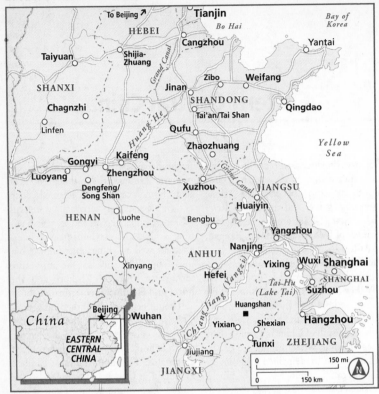

To Beijing ↗
Tianjin
HEBEI
Bo Hai
Cangzhou
Bay of Korea
Yantai
Taiyuan
Shijia-Zhuang
Grand Canal
Zibo
Weifang
SHANXI
Jinan
SHANDONG
Chagnzhi
Tai'an/Tai Shan
Qingdao
Linfen
Huang He
Qufu
Yellow Sea
Zhaozhuang
Kaifeng
Gongyi
Zhengzhou
Grand Canal
JIANGSU
Luoyang
Dengfeng/Song Shan
Xuzhou
Luohe
Huaiyin
HENAN
Bengbu
Yangzhou
Xinyang
ANHUI
Nanjing
Yixing
Wuxi
Shanghai
Hefei
Tai Hu (Lake Tai)
SHANGHAI
Suzhou
China
Beijing ★
Wuhan
Chang Jiang (Yangzi)
Huangshan
Hangzhou
EASTERN CENTRAL CHINA
Yixian
Shexian
Jiujiang
Tunxi
ZHEJIANG
JIANGXI
0   150 mi
0   150 km
N

economic and cultural capital of southern China during the Suí and Táng dynasties. The gardens that were built here by merchants and retired officials, with rocks hauled up from nearby **Tài Hú (Lake Tài)**, have created in many a mind's eye the quintessential Chinese garden. But it is at nearby **Huáng Shān (Yellow Mountain)** that you find the ultimate Chinese landscape, as wispy clouds hover over a lone pine tree on a distant mountaintop.

Today, this eastern central region of China continues to function as a modern crucible of sorts. Traveling in this area,

you will encounter two of China's richest provinces (Shāndōng and Jiāngsū) bordering one of its poorest (Ānhuī). You will see some of China's oldest temples standing next to some of its newest skyscrapers. In the country of Lǎozǐ, this tug between such opposing forces should come as no surprise. It is, after all, quintessentially Chinese. The region sees hot, humid summers, while winters can be bone-chillingly cold; spring and fall are the best times to visit. ***Note:*** Unless otherwise noted, hours listed for attractions and restaurants are daily.

1 Zhèngzhōu

Hénán Province, 689km (413 miles) SW of Běijīng, 998km (599 miles) NW of Shànghǎi

Zhèngzhōu, a sprawling industrial city of six million and a major railway stop on the Běijīng–Guǎngzhōu rail lines, was once a former ancient Shāng dynasty (1700–1100

Zhèngzhōu

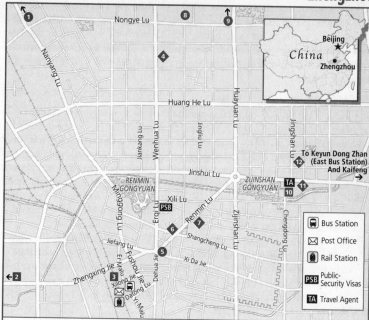

🚌 Bus Station
✉ Post Office
🚉 Rail Station
PSB Public-Security Visas
TA Travel Agent

ACCOMMODATIONS ■

Crowne Plaza/Holiday Inn Zhèngzhōu
(Zhèngzhōu Huángguān Jiàrì Bīnguǎn) 11
郑州皇冠假日宾馆

Express by Holiday Inn Zhèngzhōu 11
(Kuàijié Jiàrì Jiǔdiàn)
快捷假日酒店

Hénán Gōngyè Dàxué Bīnguǎn
(Hénán Industrial University Hotel) 4
河南工业大学宾馆

Sofitel Zhèngzhōu
(Suǒfēitè Dàjiǔdiàn) 10
索菲特大酒店

Tiānquán Dàjiǔdiàn 3
天泉大酒店

Yùdá Guómào Fàndiàn
(Yùdá Palace Hotel) 2
裕达国贸饭店

DINING ◆

Bellagio (Lùgǎng Xiǎozhèn) 12
鹿港小镇

Héjì Huìmiàn 7
合记烩面

Hénán Shífǔ 6
河南食府

Mama Mia Pizzeria (Māma Mīya Bǐsà) 11
妈妈咪呀

ATTRACTIONS ●

Èrqī Tǎ (Monument to the February 7
Worker's Uprising) 5
二七塔

Hénán Bówùguǎn
(Hénán Provincial Museum) 8
河南博物馆

Huáng Hé Huāyuán Kǒu Lǚyóu Qū 9
黄河花园口旅游区

Yellow River Tourist Zone 1
(Huáng Hé Yóulǎn Qū)
黄河游览区

B.C.) capital, though few traces of its 3,000-year history remain. Many travelers simply overnight here en route to Kāifēng and Luòyáng, but there are a few lesser known but intriguing sights in the surrounding area. Zhèngzhōu's proximity to the Yellow River (30km/18 miles to the north) also makes it a convenient base from which to explore the river. *Note:* For Chinese translations of selected establishments listed below, see appendix A.

ESSENTIALS

GETTING THERE Zhèngzhōu is connected by **air** to many major Chinese cities, including Běijīng (1 hr., 20 min.), Guǎngzhōu (2 hr., 20 min.), Hong Kong (2½ hr.), and Shànghǎi (1 hr., 20 min.). Tickets can be purchased at the **CAAC office** at Jīnshuǐ Lù 3 (© 0371/6599-1111). The airport is about 35km (21 miles) southeast of the city. Sofitel and Crowne Plaza have booths at the airport and can arrange transportation into the city if you contact them ahead of time. **Taxis** make the run for around ¥100 ($13). **CAAC airport shuttles** (40 min.; ¥15/$1.90; 6am–6pm) depart every hour for the airport from the Airport Hotel (Mínháng Dàjiǔdiàn) at Jīnshuǐ Lù (© 03716578-1111, ext. 6528) and also meet incoming flights.

Trains run from Zhèngzhōu's **railway station** (© 0371/835-6666) to Luòyáng (2 hr.), Kāifēng (1 hr.), Xī'ān (10 hr.), Běijīng (12 hr.), Shànghǎi (14 hr.), Guǎngzhōu (36 hr.), and a host of other cities in between. Tickets can be purchased at the advance booking office at Èrqī Lù 133 (© 0371/6626-2008; open 8:30am–noon and 2:30–5pm) or at the Crowne Plaza Hotel's booking office (Ān Ān Booking Center; © 0371/6597-6760 or 0371/6595-0055, ext. 1772).

From the **long-distance bus station** (*chángtú qìchēzhàn;* © 0371/6698-3995) opposite the railway station, Iveco buses depart for Luòyáng (every 15 min. 5:30am–8pm, every half-hour 8–10pm; 2–2½ hr.; ¥25/$3), Kāifēng (every 20 min. 5:40am–8pm; 1½ hr.; ¥13/$1.50), Dēngfēng (every 20 min. 6am–8pm; 30 min.; ¥15/$1.80), and Gǒngyì (every half-hour 7am–6pm; 1½ hr.; ¥15/$1.80). If you're heading to Kāifēng (every 20 min. 6:20am–8pm; 1 hr.; ¥12/$1.40) it's highly recommended that you leave from the **East Bus Station (Kèyùn Dōng Zhàn)** on Jīchǎng Lù; it will cut down your travel time significantly. If you're traveling in the summer, make sure to ask if your bus has air-conditioning (*yǒu méi yǒu kōngtiáo?*). For guaranteed air-conditioning, a private bus service, **Hénán Yǔtōng Kuàiyùn** (© 0371/6593-5888), runs air-conditioned buses to Luòyáng (every half-hour 7:30am–7pm; 2 hr., 10 min.; ¥30/$3.75), Běijīng (7:50am, 9:50am, 1:50pm, and 10:20pm; 8 hr.; ¥150–¥210/$18–$26), and Xī'ān (9:30am and 1:30pm; 5½ hr.; ¥98/$13). Buses leave from the bus station as well as from the front of the Crowne Plaza.

GETTING AROUND Taxis charge ¥7 (85¢) for 3km (2 miles), then ¥1 (15¢) per additional kilometer until 10km (6 miles), after which the price rises to ¥1.50 (20¢) per kilometer. From 11pm to 5am, prices rise to ¥9 ($1.10) per 3km (2 miles). City **buses** cost ¥1 (15¢) flat fare. Bus no. 26 runs from the railway station to Jīnshuǐ Lù via Rénmín Lù, while bus no. 16 runs from Èrmǎ Lù to the Yellow River.

FAST FACTS

Banks, Foreign Exchange & ATMs A convenient **Bank of China** branch (open Mar–May and Sept–Nov 8am–6pm; Dec–Feb 8am–5:30pm; June–Aug 8am–6:30pm) is across from the Crowne Plaza Hotel at Jīnshuǐ Lù 8. Counter 7 is for foreign exchange. There is an ATM at this location.

Internet Access   Free wireless laptop access is available in the lobby of the Crowne Plaza Hotel. Dial-up is ✆ **169.**

Post Office   The post office (open 8am–8pm) is just south of the railway station.

Visa Extensions   The **Gōngānjú (PSB)** is located at Èrqī Lù 70 (open Mar–May and Sept–Nov Mon–Fri 8:30am–noon and 2–6pm; Dec–Feb Mon–Fri 8:30am–noon and 2–5:30pm; June–Aug daily 8:30am–noon and 3–6:30pm). Allow 5 business days, though emergency 1-day visas can also be processed.

EXPLORING ZHÈNGZHŌU

The 11-story twin-tower pagoda in the heart of town is the **Èrqī Tǎ (Monument to the February 7 Workers' Uprising),** which commemorates the February 7, 1923, strike on the Běijīng–Hànkǒu rail line against the warlord authorities. The workers were fighting for their rights and freedom to organize, but the uprising was bloodily suppressed.

Hénán Bówùguǎn (Hénán Provincial Museum) ✿✿   Located in the northern part of town, this marvelous museum—the fourth largest in China, it claims—is well worth a couple of hours of your time. Housed in a pyramid-shaped structure, it has a strong collection of prehistoric and early Chinese artifacts such as oracle bones, tools, and pottery from the Yǎngsháo culture, the Lóngshān culture, and the early Xià, Shāng, and Zhōu dynasties, as well as bronzes, jades, and Hàn dynasty funeral objects. Exhibits are well documented in English, and the English-language audio tour—¥30 ($3.75) with a deposit of either ¥400 ($50) or your passport—is quite helpful. English-speaking museum guides are available for ¥100 ($13).

Nóngyè Lù 8. Admission ¥20 ($2.50). 8:30am–6pm. Bus: no. 2, 9, 10, or 29.

Huáng Hé (Yellow River) ✿   Prone to flooding because of silt deposits in its upper reaches, the mighty Yellow River (Huáng Hé) has long been known as "China's Sorrow," having wreaked untold damage and taken countless lives through the ages. Here, the river can be visited from two different locales. The first is at **Huáng Hé Yóulǎn Qū (Yellow River Tourist Zone),** a large artificial park on the southern bank of the river. You can take the official hydrofoil on a 40-minute round-trip tour for ¥65 ($8) per person, which includes a stop at a sandy islet in the middle of the river.

About 15km (9 miles) east of the Yellow River Tourist Zone, the **Huáng Hé Huāyuán Kǒu Lǚyóu Qū** was where Chiang Kai-shek ordered his army to blow up the dikes in order to halt the advance of the Japanese troops in 1938. The tactic worked temporarily, but in the process it flooded 44 counties, killed almost a million people, and left another 12 million homeless and destitute. Today, stone tablets in this tourist park commemorate the event, as does a four-character inscription, ZHÌ LǏ HUÁNG HÉ, on the embankment by Máo Zédōng, meaning "Control the Yellow River."

Yellow River Tourist Zone: Admission ¥25 ($3). 8am–6pm. Bus: no. 16 (¥4/50¢) from corner of Èrmǎ Lù and Zhèngxing Jiē to its terminus. Huāyuán Kǒu Tourist Region of the Yellow River: Admission ¥10 ($1.25). 8am–6pm. Bus: no. 310 from Èrqī Pagoda to the last stop.

WHERE TO STAY
EXPENSIVE
Crowne Plaza/Holiday Inn Zhèngzhōu (Zhèngzhōu Huángguān Jiàrì Bīnguǎn) ✿✿✿   Situated in the northeastern part of town, this hotel chain is in the rather unusual position of having the five-star **Crowne Plaza** and the four-star **Holiday Inn** right next to each other and sharing many of the same facilities and management.

The three-star **Express by Holiday Inn Zhèngzhōu** (see listing below), converted from the former International Hotel, joined the party in 2005 (but does not share in the amenities). Don't let the copious use of marble and gold trim keep you from the Crowne Plaza; this is the best hotel in the province. Rooms are spacious, beds are luminously comfortable, and bathrooms are stocked with accessories. Service is extraordinarily warm and helpful, and the breakfast buffet offers expertly cooked omelets and delicious breads and fruit. There's free broadband access in all rooms and free wireless access in the lobby. The large indoor pool with a sunroof and chirping birds is one of the best in China, and an a new driving range, added behind the Holiday Inn (¥100/$13 for two buckets of balls), adds to the allure. Rooms at the Holiday Inn, geared more toward the business traveler looking for a less flashy, quieter environment, are smaller but were recently renovated and are very comfortable with clean and modern bathrooms.

Jīnshuǐ Lù 115. (© 0371/6595-0055. Fax 0371/6599-0770. www.crowneplaza.com/hotels/cgoch or www.holiday-inn.com/hotels/cgcch. Crowne Plaza 221 units; Holiday Inn 202 units. Crowne Plaza: ¥1,360 ($170) standard room; ¥1,632 ($204) suite. Holiday Inn: ¥1,088 ($136) standard room; ¥1,520 ($190) suite. 35%–40% discounts possible. 15% surcharge. AE, DC, MC, V. **Amenities:** 5 restaurants; bar; lounge; indoor pool; health club and spa; driving range; sauna; concierge; airport shuttle (incoming free; outgoing ¥40/$5); business center; wireless Internet access in lobby; forex; shopping arcade; salon; limited room service; massage; laundry/dry cleaning; nonsmoking rooms; executive rooms. *In room:* A/C, satellite TV, broadband Internet access, minibar, hair dryer, safe.

Sofitel Zhèngzhōu (Suǒfēitè Dàjiǔdiàn)
While the public areas of this hotel are elegant, the rooms here can't compare to those at the Crowne Plaza or the Holiday Inn—though impeccably clean (as are the bathrooms), they are in need of renovation, and the furniture looks cheap and worn. Service is first-rate, and the staff is professional and helpful.

Chéngdōng Lù 289. (© 0371/6595-0088. Fax 0371/6595-0080. www.accorhotels-asia.com. 241 units. ¥990 ($124) standard room; ¥1,328 ($166) suite. 30% discounts possible. 15% surcharge. AE, DC, MC, V. **Amenities:** 2 restaurants; bar; lounge; indoor pool; health club and spa; sauna; concierge; business center; forex; shopping arcade; salon; limited room service; massage; laundry/dry cleaning; nonsmoking rooms; executive rooms. *In room:* A/C, satellite TV, broadband Internet access, minibar, hair dryer, safe.

Yùdá Guómào Fàndiàn (Yùdá Palace Hotel) 🐟🐟
This handsome, modern, 45-story building is Zhèngzhōu's grandest and most opulent hotel, but its location in the western part of town makes it inconvenient for independent travelers. Rooms are enormous—the largest in the city—comfortable, and gorgeously furnished with classic Italian furniture and a high-tech Bose surround-sound audio system. The spacious all-marble bathrooms come with separate tub and shower, except for corner rooms. The hotel, when it opened, lured away staff from the Westin in Shànghǎi, but now appears to be completely local.

Zhōngyuán Xī Lù 220. (© 03716/743-8888. Fax 0371/6742-2539. yudaeo@public2.zz.ha.cn. 356 units. ¥1,494 ($180) standard room; ¥2,490 ($300) suite. 15% surcharge. AE, DC, MC, V. **Amenities:** 5 restaurants; bar; lounge; disco; indoor pool; health club; sauna; concierge; business center; forex; shopping arcade; salon; limited room service; massage; laundry/dry cleaning; nonsmoking rooms; executive rooms. *In room:* A/C, satellite TV, broadband Internet access, minibar, hair dryer, safe, scale.

MODERATE
Express by Holiday Inn Zhèngzhōu (Kuàijié Jiàrì Jiǔdiàn) 🐟
If you'd like to stay at an internationally managed hotel but balk at the prices, this new property is a good option. While it has a slightly institutional feel (note the staff uniforms, for example—employees look like fitness coaches), this hotel will suit any international

traveler fine, if you don't require too many frills. Rooms are bright and modern and come with free broadband Internet access.

Jīnshuǐ Lù 114. © 0371/6595-6600. Fax 0371/6595-1526 www.ichotelsgroup.com/h/d/6c/1/en/hd/cgoex. 269 units. ¥538 ($66) standard room; ¥688 ($85) suite. Rates include breakfast for 2. 20% discounts possible. AE, DC, MC, V. **Amenities:** High-speed Internet access; laundry facilities. *In room:* A/C, TV, hair dryer, iron/ironing board.

Tiānquán Dàjiǔdiàn Conveniently located next to the railway station, this three-star hotel offers relatively clean accommodations at reasonable prices. Guest rooms are a little dark, with forgettable furnishings, but are otherwise quite comfortable. Bathrooms are a bit old, but clean. Be sure to ask for a room in the back, as the honking taxis in the front of the square can be a rude surprise at 3am. The staff tries to be helpful.

Xī Dàtóng Lù 1. © 0371/6698-6888. Fax 0371/6699-1814. 214 units. ¥358–¥388 ($44–$48) standard room; from ¥1,198 ($149) suite. Rates include Chinese breakfast. 30% discounts possible. MC, V. **Amenities:** Restaurant; bar; nightclub; exercise room; salon; business center; gift shop; limited room service; laundry. *In room:* A/C, TV.

INEXPENSIVE

Hénán Gōngyè Dàxué Bīnguǎn (Hénán Industrial University Hotel) *Value*
Located just opposite the university's campus gates in the northeastern part of town, not far from the Hénán Provincial Museum, this basic guesthouse is one of the best budget choices in town. Rooms are a little musty but well kept and the bathrooms are clean and outfitted with new fixtures. Little English is spoken at the front desk, but the receptionist says a staff member is usually on duty to help with translations.

Wénhuà Lù 48. © 0371/6388-7704. 46 units. ¥120 ($15) standard room. No credit cards. *In room:* A/C, TV.

WHERE TO DINE
EXPENSIVE

Mama Mia Pizzeria (Māma Mīya Bǐsā) *ITALIAN/CONTINENTAL* This low-key restaurant offers many of the comfort foods of home. The ambience is casual and unpretentious, with low lighting and checkered tablecloths. Pizzas and pastas are popular here; the spaghetti carbonara is pretty good. Other favorites include the U.S. Angus T-bone steak and the grilled salmon. Service is attentive.

In the Crowne Plaza Hotel, Jīnshuǐ Lù 115. © 0371/6595-0055. Main courses ¥40–¥160 ($5–$20). AE, DC, MC, V. 11:30am–2:30pm and 5:30–10pm.

MODERATE

Bellagio (Lùgǎng Xiǎozhèn) *TAIWANESE* This popular Taiwanese chain with outposts in Běijīng and Shànghǎi has made its first foray into the Chinese hinterlands with this branch, just steps from the Crowne Plaza/Holiday Inn/Sofitel ghetto. Stylishly decorated with red-velvet booths, satin curtains, and bamboo, the interior attracts China's nouveau riche and hipster crowds. But even without the cool interior, this place would do well on the merits of its dishes, which include delectable island specialties such as stewed fatty pork, fried tofu, and stir-fried dragon beans. The specialty drinks, like the blended mango with coconut and sago, are refreshing snacks in themselves. Good for a late-night bite, too.

Jīng Èr Lù 2. © 0371/6598-1533. English menu. Meal for 2 ¥100–¥200 ($12–$24). No credit cards. 11am–2am.

Hénán Shífǔ *HÉNÁN* Located in a recessed courtyard off Rénmín Lù in the center of town, this is one of Zhèngzhōu's more popular and long-standing restaurants. The decor here is traditional Chinese with a loud festive atmosphere during peak dining hours. The food is uniformly excellent and intriguing, especially the *xiāngmá shāobǐng jiā niúròu* (also known as Zhèngzhōu's "hamburger"); it consists of marinated cold beef sandwiched in fried sesame bread—a subtle but sublime mix of cold and hot, savory and sweet. Other noteworthy dishes include *bā sùshíjǐn*, a vegetarian dish of mushrooms, seasonal greens, and bamboo shoots; and *guōtiē dòufu*, a tofu casserole. Service is efficient and friendly but the staff doesn't speak English, nor is there an English-language menu.

Rénmín Lù 22. ✆ 0371/6622-2108. Meal for 2 ¥60–¥160 ($7.50–$20). No credit cards. 11am–2:30pm and 5:30–9:30pm.

INEXPENSIVE

Héjì Huìmiàn MUSLIM/NOODLES   The specialty at this always crowded Muslim restaurant in the center of town is the *tèyōuhuìmiàn* (house specialty noodles), which consists of fresh coarse noodles served with a variety of mushrooms and small chunks of lamb in broth. Chilies, cilantro, and vinegar can be added at the table to taste. The first floor offers no-frills fast-food dining: Order your noodles for at the counter by simply asking for a small bowl *(xiǎo wǎn)* ¥5.50 (70¢) or a large bowl *(dà wǎn)* ¥6 (75 ¢); then grab a table and hand your ticket to the waitress. You'll be served within minutes. The second and third floors offer a la carte dining in a more pleasant, well-lit environment, but menus are in Chinese only.

Rénmín Lù 3. ✆ 0371/6622-8026. Meal for 2 ¥25–¥60 ($3–$7.50). No credit cards. 1st floor: 10:30am–10pm; 2nd and 3rd floors: 11am–3pm and 5–10pm.

ZHÈNGZHŌU AFTER DARK

Target Pub (Mùbiāo Jiǔbā) at the south end of Jīng Liù Lù (✆ 0138/038-57056), is a cool place for those in the know. You can actually have a conversation here or simply sit at the bar and let Lǎo Wáng regale you with tales of off-roading in Lhasa, Mongolia, and the Gobi Desert. Bellagio (see "Where to Dine," above) is open until 2am and offers a great date environment.

2 Dēngfēng & Sōng Shān

Hénán Province, 63km (40 miles) SW of Zhèngzhōu, 87km (53 miles) SE of Luòyáng

Located south of the Yellow River in northwest Hénán Province, Sōng Shān is the central mountain of the five holy Daoist mountains. Today, it's better known as the home of the Shàolín Temple (Shàolín Sì), birthplace of the eponymous brand of kung-fu martial art (Shàolín *gōngfu*) that has long been popular in Asia but has only in recent years become increasingly known to the Western world. The main town serving Sōng Shān is Dēngfēng (meaning "Ascending to Bestow Honor"), named by the Táng dynasty empress Wǔ Zétiān who preferred Sōng Shān to Tài Shān (Mount Tài) in Shāndōng Province, traditionally the favorite mountain of most emperors. Sōng Shān can be visited in conjunction with Luòyáng, or as a day trip from Zhèngzhōu. *Note:* For Chinese translations of selected establishments listed in this section, please turn to appendix A.

ESSENTIALS

GETTING THERE   The nearest **airport and rail connections** are in Zhèngzhōu, but air and rail tickets can be bought at **CITS** at the Guólǚ Dàlóu on Běihuán Lù Xīduàn (✆ 0371/6288-3442). At press time, **buses** make the run to Zhèngzhōu for ¥12 ($1.50) in a half-hour. From Dēngfēng, it's a 20-minute, ¥5 (60¢) **minibus** ride to Shàolín Sì (Shàolín Temple). Minibuses also connect Dēngfēng to Luòyáng (every 20 min. 6am–5pm; 1½ hr.; ¥13/$1.60) and Gǒngyì (8:30am, 9am, 1:30pm, 3pm,

3:30pm; 1 hr.). In Dēngfēng, all minibuses depart from the ramshackle **West Bus Station (Xī Kèchēzhàn)** on Zhōngyuè Dàjiē just west of Sòngyáng Zhōng Jiē. Buy your tickets on the bus. A **taxi** from Zhèngzhōu to Dēngfēng will cost about ¥400 ($50), subject to negotiation.

GETTING AROUND   The town of Dēngfēng is small enough to **walk** or traverse by **bus** (¥.50/5¢). Bus no. 2 runs from the Sòngyáng Academy (Sòngyáng Shūyuàn) through town to the Zhōngyuè Miào (temple). Bus no. 1 connects the Tiānzhōng Hotel with the West Bus Station.

FAST FACTS

Banks, Foreign Exchange & ATMs   The **Bank of China** (open Mon–Fri 8am–noon and 3–6:30pm in summer, 8am–noon and 2:30–5:30pm in winter) is at Shàolín Dàdào 114; there's an ATM on premises.

Post Office   The main post office (open 8am–6:30pm) is at Sōng Shān Lù 86 (corner of Àimín Lù).

EXPLORING THE CENTRAL MOUNTAIN

Sōng Shān is made up of two mountain ranges, each with 36 peaks and dotted throughout with temples and pagodas. The larger range to the east is known as **Tàishì Shān,** and the lesser range to the west is **Shàoshì Shān.**

TREKKING THE MOUNTAIN   Ascending the **eastern** or greater range (**Tàishì Shān**) of Sōng Shān is more challenging as there are no cable cars to bail out the weary. The trail typically starts behind the Sòngyáng Academy (Sòngyáng Shūyuàn). Stone steps lead all the way up to the 1,470m-high (4,900-ft.) **Jùnjí Fēng** where, unlike at China's other sacred mountains, there is no temple or building at the summit, just patches of grass and all of Sōng Shān below you. Allow 4 hours to reach the top. A ¥40 ($5) entrance fee get you into the Tàishì Shān Scenic Area and is required to go up the road to the **Sōngyuè Temple Pagoda.** You can use the same ticket to get into Shàolín Monastery.

Climbing the **western** or lesser range (**Shàoshì Shān**) is made easier by two cable cars. The **Sòngyáng Suǒdào,** a pleasant ¥20 ($2.50), 20-minute ride on a chairlift, is located about 150m (492 ft.) west of Tǎ Lín (Forest of Stupas) and runs less than halfway up the mountain. The ride (or hike) back down affords some marvelous views of the Shàolín Monastery and the Forest of Stupas nestled in the foothills. The **Sōng Shān Shàolín Suǒdào** is another 300m (984 ft.) from the lower terminus of the first gondola, and is a ¥100 ($13), 40-minute cable-car ride that goes past Ladder (Tīzi) Gully to just below the summit. From here, trails lead to the **Sōng Shān Diàoqiáo,** a suspension bridge stretched over a deep ravine of tall bald rocks. You can climb back down either the northern side of Shàoshì Shān underneath the cable cars, or the sheer southern face lined with steep narrow trails. At the parking lot below Sānhuáng Xínggōng (Sānhuáng Palace), you can hire a taxi back to Dēngfēng. For the relatively fit, climbing Shàoshì Shān takes 5 to 6 hours round-trip.

SHÀOSHÌ SHĀN

Shàolín Sì (Shàolín Monastery) ✿   Most visitors these days come to Sōng Shān not for the mountain climbing but for this famous monastery, better known for its martial arts than for its religious affiliations. Today's Shàolín, more loud marketplace than quiet monastery, is overrun with vendors, tourists (up to 10,000 a day in the summer), and martial-arts students.

Located 15km (9 miles) west of Dēngfēng at the northern base of Shàoshì Shān, the monastery was built in A.D. 495 during the Northern Wèi dynasty. Legend has it that the Indian monk Bodhidharma (Dámó in Chinese), founder of the Chán (Zen) school of Mahayana Buddhism, retreated here in 527 after failing to convince the emperor of Liáng in Nánjīng of the "nothingness" of everything. With the Chán emphasis on meditation, Dámó is said to have sat praying in a cave for 9 years. As an aid to, or perhaps relief from, meditation, Dámó's disciples apparently developed a set of exercises based on the movements of certain animals like the praying mantis, monkey, and eagle, which eventually developed into a form of physical and spiritual combat known as Shàolín kung-fu (*gōngfu*). In the Táng dynasty, Prince Lǐ Shìmín (later to be the Táng Tàizōng emperor) was rescued from a battle by 13 Shàolín monks. Thereafter the emperor decreed that the monastery always keep a troop of fighting monks, a practice that reached its apogee during the Míng dynasty (1368–1644), when 3,000 Shàolín monks were engaged in fighting Japanese pirates off the coast of China. The Shàolín monks' exploits, depicted in countless popular Hong Kong and Chinese films, have in recent years caught on with Western audiences. These days, it's not unusual to see Western faces leaping and stomping at the more than 60 martial-arts schools around the monastery.

Pugilism aside, the temple itself has a number of religious relics and frescoes worth viewing. In the **Wénshū Diàn (Wénshū Hall)**, visitors can squint at a piece of cave wall supposedly imprinted with Dámó's shadow from all those months of meditation. In the last hall, **Qiān Fó Diàn (Thousand Buddha Hall)**, is a gorgeous Míng dynasty fresco of 500 *arhats* (Buddhist disciples) worshipping Pílú, a celestial Buddha embodying wisdom and purity. Visitors can also view martial-arts performances for ¥20 ($2.50) throughout the day on the temple grounds.

About 400m (1,312 ft.) west of the temple is the impressive **Tǎ Lín (Forest of Stupas)** ⚔, the monastery's graveyard where 243 brick stupas built between the Táng (618–907) and Qīng (1644–1911) dynasties contain the remains of notable monks. The oldest stupa, honoring Táng dynasty monk Fǎwán Chánshī, was built in 791 and features a simple stupa on a two-tiered brick pedestal. High on the mountain behind the forest is the **cave (Dámó Dòng)** where Dámó was said to have meditated for 9 years.

Shàolín Sì. ¥ 40 ($5) includes admission to the Forest of Stupas. 8am–5pm. To reach Shàolín Temple, see "Getting There," above, for directions.

Martial Arts Training

The **Shàolín Wǔshù Guǎn (Martial Arts Training Center;** ✆ **0371/6274-9016)**, inside the main entrance near the Shàolín Monastery, has a very basic hostel for students and an inexpensive restaurant. Fees for foreigners average ¥125 ($15) per day for classes and lodgings.

The **Shàolín Sì Tǎgōu Wǔshù Xuéxiào (Shàolín Monastery Wǔshù Institute at Tǎgōu;** ✆ **0371/6274-9627;** www.shaolin-kungfu.com), just outside the monastery's main entrance, is one of the largest and oldest schools, with 7,000 students. The fee for foreigners is ¥160 ($20) per day, including lodgings.

It is also possible to study at one of the many private schools in the area. A very unfriendly **CITS** (Běihuán Lù Xīduàn, Guólǚ Dàlóu; ✆ **0371/6288-3442;** fax 0371/6287-3137) can arrange such study trips with students staying from a week to 6 months and longer. The office is open Monday through Friday from 8am to noon and 2:30 to 6pm.

TÀISHÌ SHĀN
Sōngyuè Tǎ (Sōngyuè Pagoda) ✦   Five kilometers (3 miles) northwest of town, nestled at the foot of the Tàishì Shān Scenic Area (Fēngjǐngqū) is the oldest surviving (A.D. 520) brick pagoda in China, originally part of the Sōngyuè Temple built in 509 as an imperial palace for the Xuán Wǔ emperor of the Northern Wèi. The Táng Gāozōng emperor and empress Wǔ Zétiān stayed at this temple every time they visited Sōng Shān. One of the few relics from the temple still stands today: The gracefully curving, 15-story hollow pagoda is 40m (131 ft.) tall. It features arched doorways and windows at its thick base, and increasingly narrow upper stories separated by layers of stepped brickwork. Today, the pagoda is still beautiful but not well kept, and it seems to attract more bats than humans. Motorcycle taxis run here from the nearby Sòngyáng Academy for around ¥10 ($1.25) each way.

Tàishì Shān Scenic Area (Fēngjǐng Qū). Admission: Tàishì Shān Scenic Area ¥10 ($1.25); Sōngyuè Pagoda ¥4 (50¢). 8am–6pm.

Zhōngyuè Miào   Located about 5km (3 miles) east of Dēngfēng on the road to Zhèngzhōu, this is the largest Daoist temple in Hénán Province, and one of the oldest dating to before 110 B.C. Today's complex dates to the Qīng dynasty (1644–1911). In the courtyard after the Chóngshèng gate (Chóngshèng Mén) are four 3m-high (9¾-ft.) Sòng dynasty iron guards originally cast in 1064 with weapons in their hands, but these were supposedly sawed off during the Cultural Revolution (1966–76). Just before the central gate (Língjí Mén) is a rather unusual 1604 **stele with carvings** of the five sacred Daoist mountains: Sōng Shān stands in the middle, Tài Shān in the east, Héng Shān Běi in the north, Héng Shān Nán in the south, and Huá Shān in the west. The temple's central hall, the impressive golden-roofed, double-eaved **Zhōngyuè Dàdiàn**, resembles the Forbidden City's Tàihé Gōng and has a statue of the god of Sōng Shān.

Zhōngyuè Dàjiē. Admission ¥15 ($1.90). 8am–6:30pm. Bus: no. 2.

A UNIQUE OBSERVATORY
Gàochéng Guānxīng Tái ✦   Located about 8km (5 miles) southeast of Dēngfēng, this intriguing observatory is a welcome change for those who've had their fill of temples and pagodas. Built in 1276 by Guō Shǒujìng, a Yuán dynasty astronomer, this 10m-high (33-ft.) pyramidic brick structure is China's earliest surviving observatory. In Guō's time, a long stone beam from a runnel in the back wall was fitted with shadow markers and used to measure time and seasonal solstices.

Gàochéng Zhèn. Admission ¥10 ($1.25). 8am–6pm. From Dēngfēng, catch any Gàochéng-bound minibus or *miàndī* taxi (¥2–¥3/25¢–30¢) from the corner of Yángchéng Lù and Shàolín Dàdào in the southeastern part of town.

WHERE TO STAY
Fēngyuán Dàjiǔdiàn   This three-star hotel is just west of the Tiānzhōng and has several wings with two grades of standard rooms. Opt for the more expensive rooms (¥388/$48), which at least are larger, newer, and brighter—and the best rooms you'll find in town. The staff tries to be helpful.

Zhōngyuè Dàjiē 18. ☏ 0371/6286-5080. Fax 0371/6286-7090. 132 units. ¥238–¥388 ($29–$48) standard room; ¥888 ($111) suite. 20%–30% discounts possible. No credit cards. **Amenities:** Restaurant; bar; lounge; sauna; concierge; business center; forex; shopping arcade; salon; limited room service; massage; laundry. *In room:* A/C, TV.

Shàolín Guójì Dàjiǔdiàn (Shàolín International Hotel)   The first hotel in this area to cater to Western tourists, this three-star property is still popular with independent travelers, but the facilities and service do not match those at the Fēngyuán hotel. The hotel's redemption is that it puts you close to the temple. Rooms are comfortable enough, even though they're unremarkably decorated with standard-issue brown furniture and old carpets. Bathrooms could use a scrubbing.

Shàolín Dàdào 16. ⓒ 0371/6286-6188. Fax 0371/6285-6608. 60 units. ¥258–¥358 ($32–$44) standard room; ¥576 ($72) suite. 20%–30% discounts possible. No credit cards. **Amenities:** Restaurant; bar; lounge; sauna; concierge; business center; shopping arcade; salon; limited room service; massage; laundry. *In room:* A/C, TV.

WHERE TO DINE

For the adventurous, there is a **night food market** in the evenings at the corner of Zhōngyuè Dàjiē and Càishì Jiē, a block east of Sōng Shān Zhōng Lù, where you can eat your fill of spicy kabobs, stir-fries, and the local noodles, *dāoxiāo miàn*. The **Jīnguàn Miànbāo Xīdiǎn Fáng** on the western side of Sōng Shān Zhōng Lù, just north of Shàolín Dàdào, has a wide selection of breads and pastries and is open from 6:30am to 9:30pm. Just up the street from the bakery is the small **Xiāngjī Wáng,** selling fried chicken. A favorite restaurant frequented by foreigners who live at Shàolín is **Sìjì Chūn (Four Seasons)** (ⓒ 01390/381-1423 or 0371/6274-9987; 500m/1,625 ft. to the right after you leave the temple; open 6am–11pm). The proprietor, Mr. Chiu (aka "Uncle Tom," as he's been dubbed by foreigners), makes delicious fresh-cut fries, sweet-and-sour chicken and fish, kung pao chicken, and potatoes and chicken. If you can't find the place, give him a call and he'll pick you up in his trishaw.

3 Luòyáng

Hénán Province, 322km (200 miles) E of Xī'ān, 150km (93 miles) W of Zhèngzhōu

Situated in western Hénán Province at the junction of the Grand Canal and the ancient Silk Road, Luòyáng (literally "north of the river Luò") was the capital of nine dynasties from the Eastern Zhōu (770–221 B.C.) to the Late Táng (923–936). Today, this industrial town with a population of 1.3 million is better known as home to the magnificent UNESCO World Heritage Site **Lóngmén Grottoes (Lóngmén Shíkū)** ✿✿✿, a must-see for anyone interested in Buddhist art and sculpture. A visit in April will allow you to take in Luòyáng's famous **Peony Festival** as well. *Note:* For Chinese translations of selected establishments listed in this section, please turn to appendix A.

ESSENTIALS

GETTING THERE   Luòyáng's small airport is located about 11km (7 miles) north of the city center. There are daily **flights** from Luòyáng to Běijīng (1½ hr.) and Shànghǎi (1 hr., 40 min.), as well as weekly flights to Xī'ān (1 hr.), Chéngdū (1 hr., 15 min.), and Chóngqìng (1½ hr.). Tickets can be purchased at the **CAAC office (Mínháng Shòupiào Chù;** ⓒ 0379/6231-0121) on Jīchǎng Lù just north of the railway station. **CITS** is at Jiǔdū Xī Lù 4, Lǚyóu Dàshà (ⓒ 0379/6432-5061); they can also arrange tickets.

From the **railway station** (ⓒ 0379/395-2673) just north of the city center on Dàonán XīLù, trains run to Běijīng (express train 8 hr.), Shànghǎi (15 hr.), Xī'ān (6 hr.), Zhèngzhōu (2 hr.), and Kāifēng (3 hr.).

From the **long-distance bus station (chángtú qìchēzhàn;** ⓒ 0379/6323-9453), opposite the railway station on Jīngyuàn Lù, buses run to Zhèngzhōu (every 20 min. 5:40am–7pm; 2–2½ hr.; ¥24–¥30/$3–$3.75), Kāifēng (every 30 min. 6:40am–6pm; 3 hr.; ¥3/$4.50), and Dēngfēng (hourly; 1½ hr.; ¥13/$1.60). **Private car** rental from Zhèngzhōu to Luòyáng will run around ¥300 ($38) one-way and ¥400 ($50) round-trip. Your hotel can arrange this.

GETTING AROUND Most **taxis** charge ¥6 (75¢) for 3km (2 miles), then ¥1 (15¢) per kilometer until 10km (6 miles), after which the price rises to ¥1.50 (20¢) per kilometer. From 10pm to 5am, prices rise to ¥5.80 (75¢) for 2km (1¼ miles), then ¥1.75 (20¢) per kilometer thereafter. The bus costs ¥1 (15¢). From the railway station, bus no. 81 runs to the Lóngmén Grottoes, bus no. 83 runs to the airport, and bus no. 11 runs to the western part of town via the Friendship Hotel.

FAST FACTS

Banks, Foreign Exchange & ATMs The **Bank of China** (open Mon–Fri 8am–6pm) is located at Zhōngzhōu Zhōng Lù 439. Foreign exchange is available at counter 17. An ATM is located here.

Post Office The main post office (open 8am–9pm) at Zhōngzhōu Zhōng Lù 216 has a Western Union in addition to the usual services.

Visa Extensions Located at Kǎixuán Xī Lù 1, the **Gōngānjú (PSB; ✆ 0379/ 6393-8397;** open Mon–Fri 8am–noon and 3–6:30pm in summer, 8am–noon and 2–5:30pm in winter) can process visa extensions in 3 business days.

SEEING THE SIGHTS

Lóngmén Shíkū (Dragon Gate Grottoes) ✿✿✿ Located 13km (8 miles) south of
the city center, along the banks of the Yī River (Yī Hé) which divides Xiāng Shān to the east from Lóngmén Shān to the west, these caves are considered one of the three great sculptural treasure troves in China. (The other two are the Mògāo caves in Dūnhuáng, and the Yúngǎng Grottoes in Dàtóng, the precursor to Lóngmén.) In general, the limestone is harder at Lóngmén than at Yúngǎng, and the caves closer to the river, making it easier to discern the details but more difficult to see the caves as a whole.

The first caves were carved in the Northern Wèi dynasty in A.D. 493, when the Xiào Wén emperor moved his capital from Píngchéng (today's Dàtóng) to Luòyáng. Over the next 400 years, cave art and sculpture flourished, reaching their zenith during the Táng dynasty (618–907) and even continuing into the Northern Sòng. Benefactors of the Lóngmén Caves included imperial families, high-ranking officers, Buddhist leaders, and merchants as well as common folk, many of whom could only afford the smaller honeycomb niches. Today, there are 2,300 caves and niches with more than 2,800 inscriptions and over 100,000 Buddhist statues on both East Hill and West Hill. About 30% of the caves are from the Northern Wèi dynasty (386–584); their statues are more elongated, static, and lacking in complexity and detail than the later Táng dynasty sculptures which account for about 60% of the caves, with their fuller figures, gentle features, and characteristic liveliness. The section of Lóngmén Shíkū currently open to visitors is concentrated in a 1km-long (⅔ mile) stretch on the West Hill side of the Yī River. Morning is the best time to visit the Lóngmén Grottoes, which mainly face east and catch the light from the rising sun. Try to arrive before 8am to avoid the tour groups which usually descend on the caves around 9am.

Following are the best caves of the lot, starting at the entrance and running south. Displays have rudimentary English captions, but even for the most independent traveler, this is one of those times when a guided tour is highly recommended. English-speaking guides are available for hire just inside the main entrance for ¥100 ($13).

The entrance to the grottoes has recently been restructured so that you have to take a golf cart about 500m (1,625 ft.) from the parking lot to the main gate. A round-trip in the golf cart costs ¥4 (50¢). Once you've toured the first side of the mountain, you will have to either walk across a long bridge to get to the other side, or take a boat for ¥20 ($2.50) per person.

Bīnyáng Sān Dòng (Three Bīnyáng Caves) Carving of these caves began in the Northern Wèi dynasty from 500 to 523, but the carver died in 523 after completing only the middle cave. The other two were finished later. All three were commissioned by the Xuán Wǔ emperor, who dedicated the middle cave to his father, the Xiào Wén emperor, the southern cave to his mother, and the northern cave to himself. The figures in the middle cave are comparatively longer and thinner than their fleshier, curvier Suí and Táng dynasty counterparts in the other two caves. Missing reliefs are now in the Metropolitan Museum of Art in New York and the Nelson-Atkins Museum of Art in Kansas City.

Wàn Fó Dòng (Ten Thousand Buddha Cave) ⚘ Finished in 680, this exquisite cave actually contains carvings of 15,000 Buddhas, mostly in small niches in the north and south walls, with the smallest Buddha measuring only 4 centimeters (1½ in.) in height. Even more remarkable is the fact that this cave was commissioned by two women, an indication perhaps of the comparatively elevated status of females during empress Wǔ Zétiān's reign. The centerpiece of the cave is the Amitabha Buddha, whose delicate rounded features are said to be modeled on those of one of the cave's patrons.

Liánhuā Dòng (Lotus Flower Cave) Carved during the Northern Wèi dynasty around 527, this cave's highlight is a lotus flower, measuring 3m (10 ft.) in diameter, carved in high relief on the ceiling. Representing serenity and purity, lotus flowers are common motifs in Buddhist art. Surrounding the lotus are some faded but still fine apsarases (Buddhist flying nymphs).

Fèngxiān Sì (Ancestor Worshipping Temple) ⚘⚘⚘ Carved in the Táng dynasty between 672 and 675, this majestic cave is the largest and most beautiful at Lóngmén. Originally started by the Táng Gāozōng emperor, it was expedited by empress Wǔ Zétiān, an ardent Buddhist, who poured money (from her cosmetics budget, it is said) into its completion, no doubt because the central Buddha's face is thought be modeled on hers. This main Buddha, Vairocana, seated on a lotus flower, is a stunning 17m (56 ft.) tall, with a 4m-high (13-ft.) head, 1.9m-long (6-ft.) earlobes, a wide forehead, a full nose, and serene eyes, which were painted black at one time.

Flanking the Buddha are the disciple Kasyapa (the elder) to the left, and Sakyamuni's cousin, the clever disciple Ananda (the younger), to the right. Beside the disciples are two attending bodhisattvas (Buddhas who delay entry into nirvana in order to help others), Manjusri and Samantabhadra, who are decorated with exquisitely fine beads and ornamental drapes. It is said that this tableau of statues is a distilled replica of the Táng imperial court, with the dignified main Buddha representing the emperor (or empress), the obedient disciples representing the ministers, the heavenly kings standing in for the warriors and soldiers, the richly dressed bodhisattvas evoking the imperial concubines, and the flying devas (spirits) recalling palace maids.

Fun Fact **A Brilliant Coincidence?**

Each winter solstice, there is a moment when the sun and the moon are said to shine on the Vairocana Buddha's halo at the same time, illuminating the head in a cosmic union of *yīn* and *yáng*. Coincidence or deliberate planning?

Yàofāng Dòng (Medical Prescription Cave)   This small cave was first carved in the Northern Wèi dynasty but was appended in the subsequent dynasties. The main Buddha here is a Northern Qí (550–577) creation, its fuller figure emblematic of the transition from the thin Wèi figures to the fuller Táng sculptures. At the entrance are stelae carved with Chinese medicine prescriptions for 120 diseases, including diabetes and madness.

Gǔyáng Dòng   First carved during the Northern Wèi sometime between 488 and 528, this is the oldest cave at Lóngmén, though additions were being made well into the Táng dynasty by different benefactors. Nineteen of the famous "Lóngmén Twenty" (20 pieces of calligraphy deemed especially fine and representative of their time) are found here. The central Buddha's head was restored during the Qīng dynasty, and is said to resemble Daoist master Lǎozǐ.

Shíkū Dòng (Stone Room Cave)   This last of the major caves was carved in the Northern Wèi between 516 and 528 and has the best worshipping scenes in Lóngmén. On both sides of the wall are niches with low-relief carvings of officials in high hats, court ladies in flowing robes carrying single lotus flowers, and servants carrying sheltering canopies, all in a procession to honor Buddha.

Luòlóng Lù. Admission ¥80 ($10). Apr–Oct 6:30am–6:30pm; Nov–Mar 7am–6pm. Bus: no. 53, 60 (from the western part of town opposite the Friendship Hotel), or 81 (from the railway station) run to the caves (35–45 min., ¥1.50/20¢). Taxi: about ¥30 ($3.75).

OTHER ATTRACTIONS

Báimǎ Sì (White Horse Temple)   It is more than likely that earlier Buddhist temples were built along the Silk Routes in what is today's Xīnjiāng (the path by which Buddhism entered China), but this is widely held to be the first officially sanctioned Buddhist temple built in China proper. Located 13km (7 miles) to the east of Luòyáng, this temple was built by the Eastern Hàn Míng Dì emperor (reigned A.D. 58–76) to honor and house two Indian monks who, the story goes, came from India bearing Buddhist scriptures on two white horses. Two stone horses (likely from the Sòng dynasty) stand guard outside the gate to today's temple, mostly a Míng construction. Just inside the main entrance in the southeastern and southwestern corners of the complex are the tombs of the two Indian monks. In the impressive Yuán dynasty Dàxióng Diàn (Great Hall), there are 18 arhats (disciples) of ramie cloth.

Báimǎ Sì Lù. Admission ¥35 ($4.50). 7:30am–6pm. Bus: no. 56 (from Xīguā stop on Zhōngzhōu Zhōng Lù).

Gǔmù Bówùguǎn (Ancient Hàn Tombs) ✿   This fascinating museum features 25 reconstructed underground ancient tombs dating from the Western Hàn dynasty (206 B.C.–A.D. 9) to the Northern Sòng dynasty (960–1127). By the Eastern Hàn dynasty (25–220), the use of hollow bricks with painted designs had given way to larger stone vault tombs made of more solid carved brick. Eleven of the tombs also have elaborate wall murals, the most famous of which is the Western Hàn "Expelling the Ghost Mural Tomb" which features a faded but still gorgeous fresco of celebrants holding a feast before the exorcism. The tombs are about 10km (6 miles) north of town on the road to the airport.

Jīchǎng Lù. Admission ¥15 ($1.80). 9am–6pm. Bus: no. 83 (Gǔmù Bówùguǎn stop).

Luòyáng Bówùguǎn (Luòyáng Museum)   Standouts in this museum of local relics include a section dedicated to the Xià (2200–1700 B.C.) and Shāng dynasties (1700–1100 B.C.), with an emphasis on items excavated at Èrlǐtóu (an important

Shāng site 30km/18 miles east of Luòyáng), including jade, bronzes, and pottery arti-facts; Hàn dynasty exhibits of painted pottery and tomb frescoes; and some fine Táng dynasty glazed pottery.

Zhōngzhōu Zhōng Lù 298. Admission ¥10 ($1.25). 8am–6:30pm. Bus: no. 4, 11, or 50.

Wángchéng Gōngyuán Every April during the Luòyáng Peony Festival (Apr 15–25), this park, built on the former site of a Zhōu dynasty city, Wángchéng, is awash in a riot of colors: red, white, black, yellow, purple, pink, blue, green, and every shade in between. Luòyáng produces the best peonies China has to offer, so don't miss paying a visit if you're in town then. For an extra ¥5 (60¢) you can visit the zoo. The zoo and gardens, which open at the crack of dawn, are perfect for early risers.

Zhōngzhōu Zhōng Lù. Admission ¥5 (60¢). 5am–8:30pm. Bus: no. 2, 4, 101, 102, or 103.

WHERE TO STAY

Luòyáng has several low-quality four-star rated hotels with reasonable prices. Most hotels regularly give 20% to 30% discounts unless otherwise noted. There is usually a 5% city tax but no additional service charge. If you're going to be in town for the Peony Festival, book a room in advance.

EXPENSIVE

Huáyáng Guǎngchǎng Guójì Dàjiǔdiàn (Huáyáng Plaza Hotel) ⌾ This white behemoth, which opened in 2005, looks more like a casino than a hotel. Thankfully, the tackiness of the exterior does not come indoors; guest rooms are classy with tasteful headboards, plush and comfy beds, and subtle lighting fixtures. They're the finest you'll find in town. Bathrooms can be a bit cramped but they're sparkling clean and modern. Some guests to the new hotel complain that service is a bit shaky and unprofessional.

Kǎixuán Xī Lù 88. ⌾ 0379/6558-8123. Fax 0379/6488-4777. 530 units. ¥700–¥1,280 ($88–$160) standard room; ¥1,380–¥1,800 ($172–$225) suite. AE, DC, MC, V. **Amenities:** 2 restaurants; bar; lounge; indoor pool; health club; sauna; concierge; tour desk; business center; forex; laundry/dry cleaning. *In room:* A/C, satellite TV, minibar, hair dryer, safe.

MODERATE

Mǔdān Chéng Bīnguǎn (Peony Plaza) ⌾ This four-star hotel offers some of the flashiest and most modern accommodations in town. A wall of smoked blue glass on the outside, the 28-story tower has a massive three-story atrium lobby, a revolving rooftop restaurant, and a wide range of facilities. Guest rooms are cozy enough but the furniture is showing wear. Bathrooms are a good size and come with scales. Service is not quite up to four-star international standards but is adequate. A Western buffet breakfast is served.

Náncāng Lù 2. ⌾ 0379/6468-1111. Fax 0379/6493-0303. 163 units. ¥547 ($68) standard room; ¥782 ($97) suite. AE, DC, MC, V. **Amenities:** 3 restaurants; bar; lounge; indoor pool; health club; sauna; concierge; business center; forex; shopping arcade; salon; limited room service; laundry/dry cleaning. *In room:* A/C, satellite TV, minibar.

Xīn Yǒuyì Bīnguǎn (New Friendship Hotel) Located in the western part of town, this three-star annex to the old Friendship Hotel, renovated in 2000, has pleas-ant, modern rooms. Units come with the usual nondescript brown furniture but beds have clean linens and are comfortable. Bathrooms are small but clean. The hotel also has a Western restaurant, part of its entertainment center that includes a pool table, coffee bar, and shuffleboard.

Xīyuàn Xī Lù 6. ⌾ 0379/6468-6666. Fax 0379/6491-2328. 120 units. ¥358–¥458 ($45–$57) standard room; ¥716 ($89) suite. AE, DC, MC, V. **Amenities:** 2 restaurants; bar; lounge; sauna; concierge; business center; forex; shopping arcade; salon; limited room service; laundry. *In room:* A/C, satellite TV, fridge.

INEXPENSIVE

Míngyuǎn Dàjiǔdiàn (Míngyuǎn Hotel) *Value*   Not far from the railway station, this hotel, which is affiliated with Hostelling International, gets a fare share of greasy-haired foreign backpackers. The rooms, which are characterless but totally adequate, are a better bargain than the dorm beds, which come with an attached bath. Bathrooms, though somewhat worn, are acceptably clean. The karaoke on the lower floors of the building may give the place a slightly dodgy feel.

Jiěfàng Lù 20. © 0379/6319-0378. Fax 0379/6319-1269. 80 units. ¥60 ($7.50) dorm bed; ¥188 ($24) standard room. No credit cards. **Amenities:** Restaurant; sauna; karaoke. *In room:* A/C, TV.

WHERE TO DINE

For Western food, hotel dining offers the most reliable fare. The Luòyáng Peony Hotel (Luòyáng Mǔdān Dàjiǔdiàn) at Zhōngzhōu Xī Lù 15 (© **0379/6485-6699**) has a Western dining room that serves fish and chips, pizzas, and lamb chops for dinner at ¥20 to ¥40 ($2.50–$5) per entree. There's a **KFC** at Zhōngzhōu Zhōng Lù 251 and a **McDonald's** at the Shànghǎi Shìchǎng Bùxíng Jiē (pedestrian street).

MODERATE

Churrascaria Do Brasil BRAZILIAN   This Chinese-style Brazilian barbecue offers all-you-can-eat lunch and dinner buffets. Choose from any number of meats, including beefsteak, lamb, chicken wings, cuttlefish, even spicy vegetarian chicken. Chefs deliver the grilled skewers right to your table, accompanied by a variety of cold Chinese dishes, dim sum, dumplings, and fruit.

Jīnghuá Lù 278 (near north entrance of Workers Cultural Palace). © 0379/6492-2839. Lunch ¥38 ($4.50) per person; dinner ¥45 ($5.80) per person. No credit cards. 11am–2pm and 6–9pm.

Lǎo Luòyáng Miànguǎn (Old Luòyáng Noodle House) *✦* HÉNÁN   Bright, unpretentious, and packed with locals, this a fantastic place for a casual meal. Order the *zhájiàngmiàn* (noodles with bean sauce) and the *tángcù lǐjī* (sweet-and-sour fish). The place is tastefully decorated with simple Míng-dynasty style chairs and appears to be fairly clean.

On Chángchūn Xī Lù, near the corner of Jīnghuá Lù (no number). © 0379/6531-5535 or 0/1393-790-0607. No English menu. Meal for 2 ¥60 ($7.50). No credit cards. 9:30am–2:30pm and 5–10pm.

Zhēn Bù Tóng *✦* LUÒYÁNG   The specialty at this popular restaurant housed in a huge five-story Chinese-style building is the famous *Luòyáng Shuǐxí* (Water Banquet), consisting of 8 cold and 16 hot dishes variously cooked in broth, soup, or juice (examples include *zhēnyāncài*, a soup made of ham, radish, mushrooms, and eggs; and *mìzhī tǔdòu*, sweet-potato fries in syrup). The full complement of dishes, designed for a table of 10 people, costs ¥688 ($86), but happily, the first-floor dining hall offers more reasonably sized four- or five-dish minibanquets. The staff is a little surly, but this is a unique local dining experience that shouldn't be missed.

Zhōngzhōu Dōng Lù 369. © 0379/6395-2338. Reservations recommended. Meal for 2 ¥40–¥80 ($5–$10). No credit cards. 9:30am–2:30pm and 4:30–9pm.

4 Kāifēng *✦*

Hénán Province, 70km (43 miles) E of Zhèngzhōu

Located in central Hénán Province, just 9km (6 miles) south of the Yellow River (Huáng Hé), Kāifēng has a history lasting more than 2,700 years as the capital of seven dynasties. Its heyday was during the Northern Sòng, when it was known as East Capital (Dōngjīng), the most prosperous city in the world, with a population of 1.5 million. Kāifēng is also believed to be the first place the Jews settled when they arrived in China. Having survived fire, earthquake, and flooding from the Yellow River, Kāifēng today is a sleepy but charming town not yet overtaken by massive development, though the government's efforts to capitalize on tourism are kicking into high gear.

ESSENTIALS

GETTING THERE   The nearest major **airport** is at Zhèngzhōu. Frequent **trains** serve Kāifēng from Zhèngzhōu (50 min.), Xī'ān (2 daily; 9 hr.), and Shànghǎi (3 daily; 13 hr.). Kāifēng's railway station is in the south part of town.

Buses run to Zhèngzhōu (every half-hour 7am–7pm; 1 hr., 20 min.; ¥12/$1.40) from the **Kèyùn Xī Zhàn (West Bus Station)** on Yíngbīn Lù; but as this bus station seems to have some unscrupulous and dodgy drivers, go to the **long-distance bus station (Qìchē Zhōngxīn Zhàn)** across from the railway station. Private **taxi** rental between Zhèngzhōu and Kāifēng costs around ¥300 ($37) round-trip.

GETTING AROUND   Taxis cost ¥5 (60¢) for 3km (2 miles), then ¥1 (15¢) per kilometer. Between 11pm and 6am, the rate increases to ¥5.60 (70¢) for 3km (2 miles), then ¥1.20 (15¢) per kilometer. All **buses** cost ¥1 (15¢) per ride. **Tricycle taxis** cost ¥2 (25¢) for most places within the city walls.

Bus no. 1 runs from the railway station through the center of town to the Dragon Pavilion and Iron Pagoda. Bus no. 15 connects Pō Pagoda in the southeast to the Dragon Pavilion in the northwest. Kāifēng is also an easy city to get around by **bike,** which you can rent at a small stand just north of the CITS office on Yíngbīn Lù for ¥10 ($1.25) per day (¥100/$13 deposit).

VISITOR INFORMATION   Kāifēng's **Tourism Bureau (Lǚyóujú;** ✆ **0378/398-4817,** ext. 6507) can answer basic questions about accommodations and sights. For information on Kāifēng's Jewish history or to see the Jewish stelae in the museum, contact **CITS** (Yíngbīn Lù 98; ✆ **0378/393-9032**), actually a subsidiary of the Tourism Bureau. **Tourism Complaints** can be reported by calling ✆ **0378/397-2220.**

FAST FACTS

Banks, Foreign Exchange & ATMs   There's a **Bank of China** (open Mar–May and Sept–Nov 8am–6pm; Dec–Feb 8am–5pm; June–Aug 8am–6:30pm), equipped with ATMs, at Zhōngshān Lù 32.

Post Office   The main post office (open 8am–6:30pm) is at Zìyóu Lù 33.

Visa Extensions   The **PSB** is at Zhōngshān Lù Zhōngduàn 86 (✆ **0378/315-5561;** Mon–Fri 8:30am–noon and 3–6pm, 8:30am–noon and 2:30–5:30pm in winter).

EXPLORING KĀIFĒNG

Dà Xiàngguó Sì   Originally built in A.D. 555, this temple, one of China's more famous Buddhist shrines, had its heyday during the Sòng dynasty (960–1279), when there were 64 Sutra Halls on the premises. Destroyed in the flood of 1642 and rebuilt in 1766, the temple's main attraction is the magnificent four-sided statue of Avalokitesvara (the male Indian bodhisattva who became transfigured over the years into the female Guānyīn), with a thousand hands and a thousand eyes (all-seeing and compassionate), who stands surrounded by 500 arhats. Weighing 2,000 kilograms (2¼

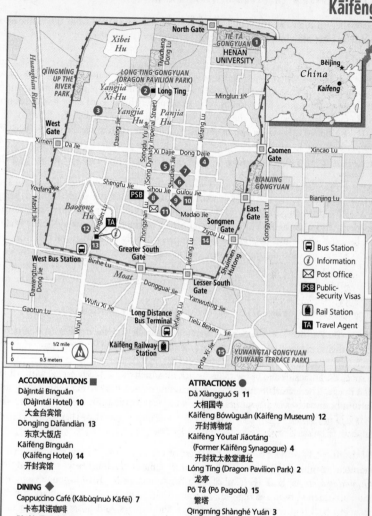

Kāifēng

tons), the 7m-high (23-ft.) statue was said to have been carved from the trunk of a thousand-year-old ginkgo tree and required 58 years to complete.

Zìyóu Lù 54. Admission ¥20 ($2.50). 8am–6:30pm. Bus: no. 5, 9, or 15.

Kāifēng Bówùguǎn (Kāifēng Museum)   Located just south of Lord Bāo Lake (Bāo Gōng Hú), this rather dilapidated and neglected museum is ordinarily not worth visiting, but the fourth floor houses three stone tablets that record early Jewish history in Kāifēng. In order to see the stelae, you should contact CITS (Yíngbīn Lù 98; **℃ 0378/393-9032**) a day or two in advance to get permission to see the tablets (¥40/$5 per person).

Yíngbīn Lù 26. ℃ 0378/396-6049. Admission ¥10 ($1.25). Tues–Sun 8:30–11:30am and 3–6pm. Bus: no. 1, 7, or 12.

Lóng Tíng Gōngyuán (Dragon Pavilion Park)   This park sits on the site of the former imperial palaces of six dynasties from the time of the Later Liáng dynasty (907–923) through part of the Jīn dynasty (1115–1234). The park's entrance is at the northern end of **Sòngdū Yùjiē (Imperial Street of the Sòng Dynasty)**, once exclusively reserved for use by the emperor, imperial family, and aristocrats. Inside the park's main entrance, the imperial way continues past two lakes, Pānjiā Hú to the east and Yángjiā Hú to the west, and ends at the foot of Lóng Tíng (Dragon Pavilion), reconstructed in 1692 for worship of the emperor. Seventy-two steep steps to the top reward you with views of Kāifēng.

Zhōngshān Lù Běiduàn. Admission ¥25 ($3). Nov–Mar 7am–6pm; Apr–Oct 7am–7pm. Bus: no. 1.

Pō Tǎ (Pō Pagoda) ⚔   Tucked away in a maze of alleys in the southeastern corner of town, this hexagonal pagoda, the oldest standing building in Kāifēng, was originally built in 974 with nine floors. The 37m-tall (121-ft.), three-story Míng dynasty pagoda is covered both inside and out with gray brick tiles, each meticulously carved with a Buddha image. There are 108 such images, including those of Sakyamuni, Amitabha, and various bodhisattvas and apsarases. Hiring a taxi is the easiest way to reach the pagoda.

Pō Tǎ Xī Jiē 30. Admission ¥5 (60¢). 8am–5:30pm. Bus: no. 15 (ask to be dropped off at Pō Tǎ Xī Jiē, then follow the red arrows on the walls).

Qīngmíng Shànghé Yuán ⚔   Just west of the Lóng Tíng Gōngyuán, this manufactured theme park is modeled after the famous 12th-century scroll painting *Qīngmíng Shànghé Yuán* (Festival of Pure Brightness on the River)—now hanging in the Forbidden City in Běijīng—that depicts Kāifēng at its height. The park contains reconstructed traditional restaurants, shops, and bridges, and hosts performances by dancers and musicians that re-enact Sòng dynasty rituals. Young women demonstrating traditional embroidery emulate skilled artisans in the imperial workshops who embroidered the emperor's robes using silk threads that were one-fifth the thickness of today's threads, and pulled by needles as thin as human hairs.

The highlight of the park for interested Western visitors is the **Jewish Cultural Exhibit Center (Yóutài Wénhuà Zhǎnlǎnguǎn)**, located in the western part of the park behind the Wáng Yuánwài Jiā building. The history of Jews in the city (see "Kāifēng's Jews," below) is documented in four rooms, with exhibits on early Jewish life in the city, as well as photographs of Jewish graves and synagogues that once stood in Kāifēng. If you're here when the center is closed, check with the Tourist Service Center just before the park's main entrance. The eager-to-please staff will often open up the Jewish Center for inquiring Western guests. For ¥5 (60¢) with a ¥20 ($2.50) deposit, the Tourist Service Center also provides an occasionally clumsy but nevertheless helpful audio tour of the park in English.

Lóng Tíng Xī Lù 5. Admission ¥40 ($5). 9am–10pm; Jewish Cultural Center Fri–Mon 9–11:30am and 2:30–6pm. Bus: no. 1.

Shānshǎngān Huìguǎn ✦ This magnificent guild hall was built during the reign of the Qiánlóng emperor (1736–96) by businessmen from the three provinces of Shānxī, Shǎnxī and, later, Gānsù, who were living in Kāifēng. All the buildings, from the stage, bell tower, and drum tower, to the double-eaved, three-gate archway and the Main Hall, are decorated with overwhelmingly vivid and exquisite wood, brick, and stone carvings.

Xúfǔ Jiē 85. Admission ¥20 ($2.50). 8am–6pm. Bus: no. 1 or 14.

Kāifēng's Jews

The origins of Kāifēng's Jewish community are a mystery. Three stone tablets (dated 1489, 1663, and 1679) from Kāifēng's old synagogue record different dates of arrival. Although inscriptions on the 1663 stele points record the arrival of Jews during the Zhōu dynasty (1100–221 B.C.), it is now more widely accepted that the early Jews likely came from Persia via the Silk Routes sometime in the late 10th century during the Sòng dynasty. According to the 1489 stele, the first arrivals were traders who were invited to stay on in Kāifēng by the Sòng emperor, who also bestowed his surname and those of his six ministers on the Jews who were said to have arrived with 73 surnames, and who subsequently took on the Chinese surnames of Zhào, Lǐ, Ài, Zhāng, Gāo, Jīn, and Shí. A synagogue was established in 1163 but was often rebuilt, usually after natural disasters like the Great Flood of 1642, which damaged much of the town.

By most accounts, the Jews in Kāifēng did not retain any contacts with other Jews outside of China. The first Western report of their existence came from Jesuit priest Matteo Ricci in 1605 when he met Ài Tiān, a Kāifēng Jew who had come to Běijīng seeking office. Ricci later sent one of his Chinese converts to Kāifēng who confirmed Ài Tiān's story that the town had many Israelite families, and a magnificent synagogue containing the five books of Moses.

The Jewish community continued to worship in Kāifēng until the flood of 1852 again destroyed their synagogue, which was never rebuilt after that. Evidence indicates that the remaining Jews became completely assimilated. Today, with renewed interest in the Jews of Kāifēng, there are a few self-identified Chinese Jews making themselves known again, the most notable being Zhāng Xīngwàng, who has been working with the Kāifēng Museum to preserve the history of Kāifēng's Jews. He can be contacted through CITS or the Kāifēng Tourism Bureau (Lǚyóujú; ✆ **0378/398-9388**, ext. 6507). In the United States, information about Kāifēng's Jewish heritage, sometimes including special-interest tours, is available through the Sino-Judaic Institute, 232 Lexington Dr., Menlo Park, CA 94205 (www.sino-judiac.com).

Tiě Tǎ (Iron Pagoda) 🏛️   Kāifēng's most famous landmark is located in the northeast corner of town. This beautiful 11th-century pagoda is actually a brick structure whose facade of glazed brown tiles gives the impression of cast iron. Originally built in 1049, the building has survived earthquakes, fires, and the great flood of 1642, which buried the base under several meters of silt. The 13-story, 55m-tall (180-ft.) octagonal structure has brick panels featuring exquisite designs of apsarases, *qílín* (Chinese unicorns), dragons, and flowers. For another ¥10 ($1.25), you can climb the 168 steps to the top, though the experience can be a bit claustrophobic.

Jiěfàng Lù 175. Admission ¥20 ($2.50). 7am–7pm. Bus: no. 1 or 3.

WHERE TO STAY

Dàjīntái Bīnguǎn (Dàjīntái Hotel) *Value*   This guesthouse's location and price make it a standout. Located next to the night market, the rooms are nothing special, just standard two-star fare, but you'll be saving a few bucks by opting to stay here over competitors. Bathrooms are very clean, and the tile floors in the rooms sparkle. Rooms that face the street might be a tad noisy, especially at night when the market kicks into full gear.

Gǔ Lóu Jiē 23. ✆ 0378/255-2888. Fax 0378/595-9932. 114 units. ¥130–¥160 ($16–$20) standard room. 25% discounts. No credit cards. **Amenities:** Restaurant; tour desk. *In room:* A/C, TV.

Dōngjīng Dàfàndiàn   Located across from the West Bus Station, this sprawling hotel had a portion of its rooms renovated in 2005. The lily pond and pavilions are charming, but the guest rooms are rather characterless, and bathrooms could be a bit cleaner. The staff doesn't speak much English but tries to be helpful. Rooms in the VIP building are gaudily decorated and overpriced—you're better off staying the recently renovated building 4.

Yíngbīn Lù 99. ✆ 0378/398-9388. Fax 0378/393-8861. 221 units. ¥200–¥800 ($25–$100) standard room. MC, V. **Amenities:** 2 restaurants; bar; lounge; indoor pool; health club; sauna; concierge; tour desk; business center; forex; shopping arcade; salon; limited room service; laundry/dry cleaning. *In room:* A/C, TV, fridge.

Kāifēng Bīnguǎn (Kāifēng Hotel) 🏛️   This is hands-down the best choice in town. Situated in a courtyard with a variety of rooms to fit different budgets, this hotel offers a charming environment and friendly service. The building in the center of the courtyard was a Buddhist nunnery in the early 20th century and is now a protected landmark; the rooms in this building are nice, though a bit gaudy in style. The hotel's best rooms are in the slightly less historic building 5, each room recently remodeled and outfitted with sleek white armchairs and modern beds. The bathrooms are sparkling clean and feature massaging shower heads. For a slightly cheaper room, but with cheesy decor, ask for a room in building 4. Note that this building is branded under the name "Jiālǐ Jū," or "Grand Land Hotel," though it is owned and managed by Kāifēng Bīnguǎn.

Zìyóu Lù 66. ✆ 0378/595-5589. Fax 0378/595-3086. 187 plus units. ¥180–¥468 ($23–$56) standard room; ¥1,680–¥2,680 ($210–$325) suite. AE, DC, MC, V. **Amenities:** Restaurant; concierge; business center; bike rental; laundry. *In room:* A/C, TV, broadband Internet access.

WHERE TO DINE

Hotels catering to foreigners all have Chinese restaurants that offer decent if forgettable fare, with a meal for two averaging ¥40 to ¥80 ($5–$10). The **Dìyīlóu Bāozi Guǎn (Number One Dumpling Restaurant)** at Sìhòu Jiē 8 (✆ **0378/565-0780; open 10:30am–11pm)** is a local institution specializing in dumplings and buns. Their *xiǎolóng bāo*, small dumplings filled with pork and a hint of broth, are a must-try. A bit farther to the east at Gǔ Lóu Jiē 66 is another informal diner, the **Xīnshēng Měishíyuán** (ⓒ 0378/596-8918), which offers a wide variety of noodles, kabobs, stir-fries, pastries, and snacks. There is no English menu, but purchase your meal tickets for ¥8 ($1) and up, then go around to the different stalls and order. For decent coffee, Western meals, and an eclectic variety of Asian fare head to **Cappuccino Café (Kǎbùqínuò Xīcāntīng)** ⓖ (Gǔ Lóu Jiē 65; ⓒ 0378/597-3666; 9am–2am; no credit cards), located near Dàjīntái Hotel. The cafe offers an English menu, friendly service, and live music nightly, delivered from a white grand piano in the center of the restaurant. Try the black pepper steak–fried rice, served on a hot iron plate. The Dōngjīng Hotel also has a **fast-food eatery** out front that offers convenient and inexpensive dining for ¥4 to ¥8 (50¢–$1) per person. Just point to choose from the many buffet dishes that are constantly being replenished.

For the more adventurous, the **night market** ⓖ which starts around 7pm on Sìhòu Jiē and closes early in the morning, offers delicious local snacks such as *wǔxiāng shāobǐng* (five-spice roasted bread) and *zhīma duōwèi tāng* (sesame soup). The shish kabobs, especially the *yángròu chuàn* (spicy lamb kabob), are grilled over an open fire and are especially tasty. The market is located on a street filled with charming old architecture in a variety of styles, which makes for a pleasant stroll even if you're aren't hungry.

SHOPPING

Sòngdū Yùjiē (Imperial Street of the Sòng Dynasty) is lined with shops that sell souvenirs, embroidery, silk screen paintings, calligraphy, paintings, seals, and ink stones. A new touristy shopping district called Gǔdài Wénhuà Qū (Gǔdài Culture Area) should be open by the time you get here. For specialty snacks from Hénán, visit the **Kāifēng Tǔtèchǎn Shìchǎng** (open 8:30am–9pm), on Lóng Tíng Xī Lù, near Sòngdū Yùjiē. Goodies include *huāshēng gāo* (peanut cake) and *xìngrén chá* (almond tea), which is more like a gelatin than a tea.

5 Jì'nán

Shāndōng Province, 497km (308 miles) S of Běijīng

With few tourist attractions, the capital of Shāndōng Province is a major rail and air junction that's best used as a base for exploring more worthwhile attractions in nearby towns such as Tài'ān, Qūfù, and Zībó. *Note:* For Chinese translations of selected establishments listed in this section, please turn to appendix A.

ESSENTIALS

GETTING THERE   Jì'nán is connected by **air** to many Chinese cities, including Běijīng (1 hr.), Shànghǎi (1 hr., 40 min.), Xī'ān (1½ hr.), Guǎngzhōu (2½ hr.), Chóngqìng (2 hr.), Zhèngzhōu (1 hr.), and Hong Kong (2½ hr.). CAAC buses (1 hr.; ¥15/$1.90) depart for the Yáo Qiáng Airport 40km (25 miles) to the east from the CAAC office at Luòyuán Dàjiē 198 every hour from 6:10am to 6:10pm. Buses also meet incoming flights but end their run at the long-distance bus station *(chángtú qìchēzhàn)* in the northern part of town at Běiyuán Lù. Plane tickets can be purchased at the **CAAC office** (ⓒ 0531/8602-2338) from 7am to 9:30pm. **China Eastern Airlines** is at Jīngshí Lù 408 (ⓒ 0531/8796-4445; open 8am–8pm).

From Jì'nán's main **railway station** (ⓒ 0531/8242-8862) in the west of town, trains run to Běijīng (16 trains daily, 4½–7 hr.), Shànghǎi (6 trains daily, 9–14 hr.), Tài'ān (1 hr.), Yánzhōu (2 hr.), Qūfù (3 hr.), Zībó (1 hr.), Wéifāng (2½ hr.), Qīngdǎo

(5 hr.), and Xī'ān (19 hr.). Train tickets can be bought 5 days in advance at the railway station.

From the **long-distance bus station** (*chángtú qìchēzhàn;* ✆ **0531/96369**) in the northern part of town, buses depart for Tài'ān (every 30 min. 6:30am–6:30pm; 1–1½ hr.; ¥13–¥20/$1.50–$2, different types of buses), Qūfù (every 20 min. 6:30am–6:30pm; 1½–2 hr.; ¥21/$2.80), Qīngdǎo (every 30 min. 6am–6:30pm; 5 hr.; ¥50–¥95/$6–$12), Zībó (every 30 min. 6:10am–6:40pm; 1 hr., 40 min.; ¥20–¥30/$2.50–$3.75), and Wéifāng (every 30 min. 6:30am–5pm; 3 hr.; ¥32–¥40/$4–$5).

GETTING AROUND   Most **taxis** charge ¥7 (90¢) for 3km (2 miles), then ¥1.20 (15¢) per kilometer until 5.5km (3½ miles), after which the price rises to ¥1.80 (25¢) per kilometer. From 10pm to 5am, the cost after 3km (1¾) is ¥1.40 (15¢) per kilometer, then ¥2 (25¢) per kilometer after 5.5km (3½ miles).

TOURS   The **China Shāndōng Travel Service (Zhōngguó Shāndōng Lǚxíngshè)** at Lìshān Lù 185 (✆ **0531/8260-8108**) can arrange customized tours of other Shāndōng destinations like Tài Shān, Qūfù, Wéifāng, and Zībó.

FAST FACTS

Banks, Foreign Exchange & ATMs   The **Bank of China** at Luòyuán Dàjiē 22 (Mon–Fri 8am–noon and 1:30–6pm) is open for foreign exchange.

Post Office   The main post office (open May–Sept 8am–7:30pm and Oct–Apr 8am–7pm) is in the old part of town at Jīng Èr Lù 162 (corner of Wéièr Lù).

Visa Extensions   The local **PSB** is in the old part of town at Jīng Sān Lù 145 just east of Wěi Wǔ Lù (✆ **0531/8508-2461;** open Mon–Fri 8–11:30am and 2–5:45pm.). The surly staff at counters 2 and 3 can process visa extensions; allow 5 business days.

EXPLORING JÌ'NÁN

Jì'nán is known for its 72 famous **springs** around town, which are really only worth visiting during the rainy season (July–Aug) when water levels are actually high enough to produce any activity. The most famous and also the first of the 72 springs is **Bàotū Quán (Bàotū Spring)**, located in the center of town at Bàotū Quán Nán Lù 1; admission is ¥15 ($1.90) in the evening and ¥20 ($2.50) during the daytime. The Qīng Qiánlóng emperor drank from the spring waters and declared it the "First Spring Under Heaven" *(Tiānxià Dìyī Quán)*. The park is open from 7am to 10pm. The best time to visit it is in the evenings, under a starlit sky. You can enjoy tea in the pavilion by the spring.

More interesting is a walk around the western part of town near the railway station. This area was the **old German Concession,** which came into being when Jì'nán was opened to foreign trade in 1906. There are still a number of German-style buildings around, but you'll have to look for them under webs of telephone poles and wires, and years of grime and soot.

Dà Míng Hú Gōng Yuán (Dà Míng Hú Park)   Located in the heart of town, this lake park, popular with locals, is situated by springs. The park is most famous for its lotus flowers, which are best viewed during the Lotus Festival (July–Aug). There's a memorial for the female poet Lǐ Qīngzhào, who romanticized the park's flowers 800 years ago in her poems. A sightseeing cable car whisks you to the top of hill in 13 minutes and costs ¥10 ($1.25).

Mínghú Lù, Lì Xiá District. Admission ¥15 ($2) or ¥20 ($2.50) (includes visit to skippable stone museum). Winter 6:30am–5:30pm; rest of year 6:30am–6:30pm. Bus: no. 41 or 66.

WHERE TO STAY

Nearly all rooms in Jì'nán come with free broadband access, either in room or in the hotel's business center. Inquire at check-in.

EXPENSIVE

Crowne Plaza Guìhé Jì'nán (Guìhé Huángguān Jiǔdiàn) ✦✦✦   This latest arrival (June 2002) on Jì'nán's luxury hotel scene, a handsome structure with thick Western-style columns and arches, sits atop six floors of the Guìhé Shopping Center and offices. Arranged around a square atrium coffee shop, rooms are large and beautifully appointed, with full amenities. Marble bathrooms are brightly lit and spacious, and come with separate tub and shower. The only flaw seems to be that some of the bathrooms are already showing cracks. Service is efficient.

Tiāndìtán Lù 3. ✆ 0531/8602-9999. Fax 0531/8602-3333. www.sixcontinentshotels.com. 306 units. ¥1,079–¥1,245 ($130–$150) standard room; ¥1,494–¥1,826 ($180–$220) suite. 40%–60% discounts online. AE, DC, MC, V. **Amenities:** 4 restaurants; bar; lounge; indoor pool; health club; sauna; concierge; airport shuttle service; business center; forex; shopping arcade; salon; 24-hr. room service; massage; babysitting; same-day laundry/dry cleaning; nonsmoking rooms; executive rooms; rooms for those w/limited mobility. *In room:* A/C, satellite TV, broadband Internet access, minibar, hair dryer, safe.

Sofitel Silver Plaza Jì'nán (Suǒfēitè Yínzuò Dàfàndiàn) ✦✦✦   Until the arrival of the Crowne Plaza, this was *the* hotel at which to stay, and it continues to attract a large percentage of the foreign market with its good service and luxurious facilities. In the center of town, this modern 49-story edifice incorporates classical European elements in its decor, from chandeliers and thick columns in the lobby to traditional furniture in the rooms. Guest rooms are spacious and offer impeccable luxury and comfort, high above Jì'nán. The marble bathrooms, which come with separate tub and shower, are on the small side. The hotel is a tightly run operation with friendly and obliging staff.

Luóyuán Dàjiē 66. ✆ 0531/8606-8888. Fax 0531/8606-6666. www.accorhotels.com/asia. 326 units. ¥1,241 ($150) standard room; ¥1,718 ($209) suite. Discounts up to 40%–60%. AE, DC, MC, V. **Amenities:** 6 restaurants; bar; lounge; nightclub; indoor pool; health club; sauna; concierge; airport shuttle service; business center; forex; shopping arcade; salon; 24-hr. room service; massage; laundry/dry cleaning; nonsmoking rooms; executive rooms. *In room:* A/C, satellite TV, broadband Internet access, minibar, hair dryer, safe.

MODERATE

Qílǔ Bīnguǎn ✦   Located in the southern part of town, this four-star outfit is rather bland and tired on the outside, but the lobby, decorated in dark woods, is quite elegant. Guest rooms are average, aged with faded pink carpets, but otherwise functional and clean as are the clashing yellow and green marble bathrooms. The hotel has been preparing to open a five-star 42-story wing for some time now, but no one seems to take them seriously.

Qiān Fó Shān Lù 8. ✆ 0531/296-6888. Fax 0531/296-7676. qlhotel@public.jn.sd.cn. 255 units. ¥298–¥398 ($37–$49) standard room; ¥1,680 ($210) suite. 40% discounts possible. AE, DC, MC, V. **Amenities:** 3 restaurants; bar; lounge; health club; sauna; bowling alley; concierge; airport shuttle service; business center; forex; shopping arcade; salon; limited room service; massage; laundry/dry cleaning; clinic. *In room:* A/C, satellite TV, minibar, hair dryer, safe.

Silver Plaza Quan Cheng Hotel (Yínzuò Quánchéng Dàjiǔdiàn) ✦   This four-star hotel in the heart of town offers modest accommodations at reasonable prices. Rooms in the south tower, renovated in 2002, are elegant and have modern furniture and comfortable beds with pristine white comforters. The marble bathrooms are on the small side, but are bright and clean. North tower rooms are larger though the furniture and carpets are worn. Service is adequate and some staff members speak a little English.

Nánmén Dàjiē 2. ✆ **0531/8692-1911.** Fax 0531/8692-3187. Quancheng@jn-public.sd.cninfo.net. 400 units. ¥580–¥680 ($70–$82) standard room; ¥680–¥880 ($82–$106) suite. 20%–30% discounts. 10% service charge. AE, DC, MC, V. **Amenities:** 2 restaurants; bar; lounge; nightclub; exercise room; sauna; concierge; airport shuttle service; business center; forex; shopping arcade; salon; limited room service; massage; laundry/dry cleaning. *In room:* A/C, satellite TV, free Internet access, minibar, hair dryer.

INEXPENSIVE

Guì Dū Dàjiŭdiàn Conveniently located about 1km (⅔ mile) from the railway station, this hotel sits on a quiet street near city government offices. The rooms in the auxiliary building, which lacks an elevator, are cheaper and smaller. Rooms in the main building are a little dark and old but have decent-size bathrooms.

Shēng Píng Jiē 1. ✆ **0531/8690-0888.** Fax 0531/8690-0999. www.guidu.com.cn. 236 units. ¥238–¥298 ($29–$36) auxiliary building; ¥568–¥1,180 ($68–$142) main building. AE, DC, MC, V. **Amenities:** Restaurant; business center; concierge; airport shuttle service; massage. *In room:* A/C, TV, free Internet access in main building.

Ji'nán Tiĕdào Dàjiŭdiàn Well located right next to the railway and bus stations, this three-star hotel offers surprisingly plush accommodations with an elegant marble lobby. Guest rooms are more sedate and come with rather worn, unexciting brown furniture, while bathrooms are small but acceptably clean. Rooms in the front can be a little loud from the noise in the square, so avoid those if you want to sleep.

Chēzhàn Jiē 19. ✆ **0531/8601-2118.** Fax 0531/8601-2188. 260 units. ¥220 ($27) standard room; ¥400 ($48) suite. AE, DC, MC, V. **Amenities:** 2 restaurants; bar; lounge; nightclub; exercise room; sauna; concierge; business center; forex; shopping arcade; salon; limited room service; massage; laundry/dry cleaning. *In room:* A/C, TV, free Internet access on floors 6–8.

WHERE TO DINE

The top hotels offer the most reliable, if expensive, Western food. **Kentucky Fried Chicken** is at Cháoshān Jiē opposite Silver Plaza, and **McDonald's** is at Quánchéng Lù 180. There is a **bakery,** Dàsānyuán, at Cháoshān Jiē Bĕishŏu; it's open from 8am to 9pm.

Inexpensive Chinese food is available 24 hours a day at **Xīn Lán Bái (Blue & White)** at Hēihú Quán Xī Lù 109 (✆ **0531/8691-0628**), a fast-food diner around the corner from the Crowne Plaza. Simply point to choose from the usual array of cold appetizers, eggplant, tofu, vegetables, chicken, noodles, and soups, priced from ¥3 to ¥10 (40¢–$1.25) per dish.

There are restaurants serving traditional Shāndōng cuisine on Cháoshān Jiē near the heart of the town. Try the *mǎ pópo mèn shuāngsŭn* (steamed bamboo and asparagus) the various kinds of *zhōu* (rice porridge) at Lǎo Hángzhōu Jiŭ Wǎn Bàn (Cháoshān Jiē 18; ✆ **0531/8612-7228**), where a meal for two costs ¥30 to ¥50 ($4–$6). The restaurant provides special slender chopsticks that are unique to the coastal town of Hángzhōu.

6 Tài Shān & Tài'ān

Shāndōng Province, 66km (40 miles) S of Ji'nán; 68km (42 miles) N of Qūfù

Inscribed on the UNESCO World Heritage List in 1987, Tài Shān (Great Mountain) is the most famous of the five Daoist sacred mountains in China, located midway between Bĕijīng and Shànghǎi. Its base, in the town of Tài'ān, is 150m (492 ft.) above sea level, and its summit is at 1,545m (5,068 ft.). With annual visitors numbering over four million, Tài Shān is and has always been the most climbed mountain in China. The first emperor of China scaled it. From the summit, Confucius declared

Huáqiáo Dàshà **24**
(Overseas Chinese Hotel)
华侨大厦

Tài Shān Bīnguǎn **21**
泰山宾馆

Tài Shān Dàjiǔdiàn **22**
泰山大酒店

Shénqí Bīnguǎn **6**
神憩宾馆

ATTRACTIONS ●

Bìxiá Cí **5**
(Temple of the Princess
of the Azure Clouds)
碧霞祠

Dài Miào **23**
岱庙

Dàizōng Fāng **4**
岱宗坊

Dàzhòng Qiáo **20**
大众桥

Dǒumǔ Gōng **15**
斗母宫

Duìsōng Tíng **9**
(Opposing Pines Pavilion)
对松亭

Hēilóng Tàn **18**
(Black Dragon Pool)
黑龙潭

Hóng Mén Gōng **17**
(Red Gate Palace)
红门宫

Huímǎ Líng **13**
回马岭

Jīngshí Yù **14**
(Stone Sutra Valley)
经石峪

Nántiān Mén **3**
(South Gate of Heaven)
南天门

Pǔzhào Sī **19**
(Temple of Universal Light)
普照寺

Riguān Fēng **7**
(Sunrise Watching Peak)
日观峰

ATTRACTIONS (cont.)

Shíbā Pán **10**
(Eighteen Bends)
八盘

Wǔsōng Tíng **11**
(Five Pine Pavilion)
五松亭

Wúzì Bēi **2**
无字碑

Yītiān Mén **16**
(First Gate of Heaven)
一天门

Yíngkè Sōng **8**
(Welcoming Guest Pine)
迎客松

Yùhuáng Miào **1**
玉皇庙

Zhōng Tiān Mén **12**
(Middle Gate of Heaven)
中天门

Hou Shi Wu Cable Car

Taohua Yuan Cable Car

Taohua Yuan Entrance

Zhong Tiěn Mén Cable Car

Beijing
SHANDONG
China Tai Shan

CITS

Hongmen Lu

Longtan Lu

Long Distance Bus Station

Buses to Jinan and Qufu

Tai'ěn Train Station

Daizhong Dajie

Qingnian Jie

Xiachang Jie
Shengping

Cai Yuan Dajie

Hushan Lu

PSB

🚌 Bus Station
¥ Bank
ⓘ Information
✉ Post Office
🚉 Rail Station
PSB Public-Security Visas

The Great Mountain

The significance of Tài Shān to the Chinese can be traced to their creation myth in which Pán Gǔ, after creating the sky and earth, died from exhaustion, his head and limbs falling to earth as five sacred mountains. Tài Shān, formed from the head and situated in the east (an auspicious direction signifying birth), became the most revered of the sacred mountains. The other four mountains are Sōng Shān in Hénán (center), Héng Shān Běi in Shānxī (north), Héng Shān Nán in Húnán (south), and Huá Shān in Shǎnxī (west). Although Tài Shān is not particularly high, the ancient Chinese came to regard it as the symbol of heaven. Historically, the Chinese emperor was considered to be the son of heaven, and many emperors, starting from China's first, the Qín Shǐ Huángdì emperor, climbed the mountain to perform sacrificial ceremonies to express their gratitude for being chosen to lead all below them, and to report to heaven on their progress. This also served to legitimize the emperors' power, as only those able to scale the mountain successfully were considered legitimate rulers. Today, hundreds, if not thousands of historical relics, carved inscriptions, temples, and sacrificial altars provide a fascinating record of the imperial presence on the mountain. Countless ordinary Chinese have also made the pilgrimage to this holiest of holy mountains. They believed that the god of Tài Shān ruled the heavens and the earth and governed life and death. Although he has continued to be greatly revered through the years, his daughter Bìxiá (Princess of the Azure Clouds) has for many years now surpassed him in popularity. Today's pilgrims, many of them elderly, female, and peasant, scramble up the mountain paths, stopping at every altar to light incense and pray to the goddess for blessings and protection.

that "the world is small," while Máo Zédōng proclaimed that the "East is Red." Today, tourists and pilgrims, young and old, continue to make the journey, accompanied practically each step of the way by vendors peddling everything from snacks to souvenirs. Neither the highest nor the most impressive mountain in China, Tài Shān attracts visitors because of its cultural and historical significance, much of which, along with the colorful legends surrounding the different sights along the way, is lost on Westerners. However, the mountain still offers scenic vistas, interesting cultural immersion, and a good workout. During the annual International Tài Shān Climbing Festival in early September, hundreds of runners race up the mountain. Check with CITS or Tài'ān Tourism (see below) for the exact dates.

ESSENTIALS

GETTING THERE   The nearest major **airport** to Tài Shān is at Jǐ'nán, 66km (40 miles) south. From the **Tài'ān railway station** (© 0538/219-6222) located just west of the center of town, trains run to Běijīng (7 hr.), Jǐ'nán (1 hr.), Shànghǎi (11 hr.), and Qīngdǎo (6 hr.). There are also frequent **buses** to Jǐ'nán (every 20 min. 6am–6pm; 1 hr., 10 min.; ¥13/$1.50) and Qūfù (every 30 min. 6am–6:30pm; 1 hr., 10 min.; ¥13/$1.50) that depart from the square in front of the railway station. From the **Tài'ān long-distance bus station** (*chángtú qìchēzhàn;* ✆ **0538/833-2656**) in the western part of town on Dōngyuè Dàjiē Xīshǒu, buses run to Běijīng (8:30am and 9:10am; 5 hr.), Shànghǎi (7 and 8pm; 10 hr.), and Jǐ'nán (every 30 min. 6:20am–6:40pm; 1 hr.).

GETTING AROUND   **Taxis** are plentiful in town and charge ¥5 (60¢) for 2km (1¼ miles), then ¥1.50 (20¢) per kilometer. From 10pm to 5am, the price rises to ¥5.80 (75¢) for 2km (1¼ miles), then ¥1.75 (20¢) per kilometer. **Bus** no. 3 (¥1/15¢) runs from the railway station to Dàzhòng Qiáo and also into town and up Hóngmén Lù to the main entrance of Tài Shān.

TOURS & GUIDES   **CITS,** at Hǔshān Lù 158 (✆ **0538/826-2456**), can arrange private guided tours of Tài Shān for around ¥700 ($88), including transportation, English-speaking guide, entrance fees, and lunch. They can also arrange accommodations and book tickets.

VISITOR INFORMATION   The **Tài'ān Tourism Bureau,** located just outside the railway station to the right as you exit (✆ **0538/820-9949**), can answer questions and direct travelers to hotels, sights, and travel agencies.

FAST FACTS

Banks, Foreign Exchange & ATMs   The **Bank of China** is located at Dōngyuè Dàjiē 48. Foreign exchange is available Monday through Friday from 8am to noon and 1:30 to 6pm. There are no ATMs here.

Internet Access   There are **Internet cafes** along Hóngmén Lù north of Dàizōng Dàjiē. Most are open 24 hours and charge ¥2 to ¥3 (25¢–30¢) per hour. Dial-up is ✆ **169.**

Post Office   The main post office (open Nov–Apr 8am–6pm; May–Oct 8am–7pm) is at Dōngyuè Dàjiē 5.

Visa Extensions   The **Gōngānjú (PSB)** is in the eastern part of town at Dōngyuè Dàjiē Dōngshǒu (✆ **0538/827-5264;** open Mar–Oct Mon–Fri 8am–noon and 2:30–6:30pm, Nov–Feb Mon–Fri 8am–noon and 1:30–5:30pm). Allow 2 to 3 business days. Take a taxi or catch bus no. 4.

SEEING THE SIGHTS

Dài Miào ✎   Chinese emperors would come to this awesome temple at the southern foot of Tài Shān to offer sacrifices and pay homage to the god of Mount Tài before tackling the mountain. The present structures date mostly from the Sòng dynasty (A.D. 960–1127). Built in 1009, the awesome nine-bay **Tiānhuáng Diàn (Hall of Heavenly Gifts),** decorated with yellow glazed tiles, red pillars, and colorful brackets, houses a statue of the god of Tài Shān and a gorgeous, if faded, 62m-long (203-ft.) **Sòng wall mural** ✎ depicting, from right to left, the Zhènzōng emperor (998–1023) as the god of Tài Shān embarking on an inspection tour. In the courtyard in front of the Hall of Heavenly Gifts, blindfolded visitors to the **Cypress of Loyalty** literally run circles around a nearby rock (three times clockwise, three times counterclockwise), after which they try to touch the fissure on the south side of the tree. It is said that those who succeed (and very few do) will have luck.

In the back of the complex is a lovely 1615 bronze pavilion, **Tóng Tíng,** which was formerly housed in the Bìxiá Temple on the mountaintop. West of the pavilion is an octagonal iron pagoda, **Tiě Tǎ,** originally built in 1533 with 13 stories, each one cast separately, but only three survive today. The northern gate of the temple marks the beginning of Hóngmén Lù and the imperial way up the mountain.

Shēng Píng Jiē. Admission ¥20 ($2.50). 7:30am–6pm. Bus: no. 1 or 4.

CLIMBING THE MOUNTAIN

Tài Shān is a challenging but manageable climb. There are two trails up to the midway point, Zhōng Tiān Mén (Middle Gate of Heaven): a shorter but less-often hiked **western route** (7.8km/4¾ miles) which starts at Dài Miào but detours west before Hóng Mén; and the much more popular **eastern route** (11km/6½ miles) which runs from Dài Miào up to the main entrance on Hóngmén Lù. As the former imperial way, the eastern route features more cultural and religious sights. The relatively fit should allow a total of about 4 to 5 hours to reach the summit: It's 2 hours to the halfway point, where there are some hotels and a cable car, and another 2 hours minimum to reach Nán Tiān Mén (South Gate of Heaven) near the summit. Water and snacks become increasingly expensive the higher you climb, so think about packing enough beforehand. A walking stick, which can be purchased in stores in town or at the mountain's entrance, can come in handy. Temperatures at the summit can differ considerably from Tài'ān's, so dress in layers. Climbing Tài Shān would not be complete without viewing sunrise from the summit. Some Chinese climb at night, making it to the top just in time to catch the first rays, but this is not advisable for the average foreigner. If you plan to overnight at the top, be sure to pack warm clothing and a flashlight.

BY BUS & CABLE CAR   Those not inclined to climb day *or* night can now take one of three cable cars up to Nán Tiān Mén, though you'll still have to walk another 1.5km (1 mile) to the summit. The first and most popular option involves taking bus no. 3 (or a taxi) from the railway station to Dàzhòng Qiáo (Tiān Wài Cūn also), where you transfer to a minibus (¥20/$2) to Zhōng Tiān Mén. You will have to purchase a ticket for entrance to Tài Shān, which costs ¥100 ($12), here. (There are also direct buses to Zhōng Tiān Mén from the railway station, but these only run in the morning.) From Zhōng Tiān Mén, the 10-minute ride to Nán Tiān Mén on a six-person cable car costs ¥45 ($5.60) one-way. The second cableway runs between the Tiānjiē Suǒdào Zhàn and Táohuā Yuán (Peach Blossom Ravine) on the western flanks of the mountain and costs ¥20 ($2.50) one-way. The third option connects the summit to the more rural Hòu Shí Wù (Rear Rock Basin) and Tiānzhú Fēng (Tiānzhú Peak) on the northeast side of the mountain; the cost is ¥20 ($2.50) one-way.

ENTRANCE FEES   Ticket prices vary depending on your point of entry. Admission at the Hóngmén Lù main entrance, favored by most climbers, and at Wàn Xiān Lóu costs ¥80 ($7.50), or ¥60 ($5.60) November through January. At Táohuā Yuán and Dàzhòng Qiáo (used by buses and hikers of the western route), prices are ¥80 ($10); ¥60 ($7.50) November through January.

EASTERN ROUTE   Heading north from Dài Miào, visitors soon pass through the Míng dynasty **Dàizōng Fāng,** a three-portal gate that leads to **Yī Tiān Mén (First Gate of Heaven),** which marks the beginning of the imperial ascent. Just inside is another arch commemorating the site where Confucius is said to have rested when he visited the mountain. North of the arch is **Hóng Mén Gōng (Red Gate Palace),** which is also the main entrance to the mountain. Purchase your ticket here. One kilometer (⅔ mile) farther is **Dǒumǔ Gōng,** a Daoist nunnery whose origins are obscure, though the temple was completely renovated in 1542; it houses a statue of the goddess Dǒumǔ with 24 heads and 48 hands and eyes in the hollows of her palms. Behind Dǒumǔ Gōng, a

1km (⅔-mile) detour to the east leads to **Jīngshí Yù (Stone Sutra Valley)**, an enormous flat piece of rock carved with the text of the Buddhist *Diamond Sutra*. Another 1.8km (1 mile) farther along the main path, an arch, **Huímǎ Líng,** commemorates the spot where the Táng Xuánzōng emperor had to dismount and continue by sedan chair when his horses could no longer navigate the steep twists and turns.

Less than a kilometer away, **Zhōng Tiān Mén (Middle Gate of Heaven)** marks the halfway point up the mountain (elev. 850m/2,788 ft.), as well as the intersection of the eastern and western routes. There are restaurants, snack shops, and very crude hostels, as well as a cable car that runs to Nán Tiān Mén. A little farther on, those continuing on foot approach **Wǔ Sōng Tíng (Five Pine Pavilion)**, where the Qín emperor Shǐ Huángdì sought shelter from the rain in 219 B.C. He later conferred on the sheltering pine the title of fifth-grade official, hence the name of this spot. Just to the north, **Yíngkè Sōng (Welcoming Guest Pine),** immortalized in countless paintings, extends a drooping branch in welcome. Recharge at **Duì Sōng Tíng (Opposing Pines Pavilion)** before the final assault on the daunting **Shíbā Pán (Eighteen Bends),** the steepest and most perilous 1,633 steps of the mountain. Allegedly built in the Táng dynasty (618–907), the steps lie at a gradient of 80 degrees and rise over 400m (1,312 ft.) in height. Emperors used to be carried up this final stretch in sedan chairs. Today's climbers can only cling to the side railings as you straggle up the steps.

At the top, **Nán Tiān Mén (South Gate of Heaven)** (elev. 1,460m/4,788 ft.) is probably the most welcome and most photographed sight of Tài Shān. Originally built in 1264, this two-story red arched gate tower was completely renovated in 1984. A little farther on, the shop-lined **Tiān Jiē (Heavenly Lane)** brings you to a small Míng dynasty **Wén Miào (Temple to Confucius)** rebuilt in 1995, and above that the hotel Shénqì Bīnguǎn. Below, on the southern slope of the summit, is **Bìxiá Cí (Temple of the Princess of the Azure Clouds),** built in 1009 and renovated and expanded during the Míng and Qīng dynasties. Admission is ¥5 (60¢); hours are from 8am to 6pm. The roof of the main hall is covered with copper tiles, while those on the side chambers are cast with iron to protect the buildings from the fierce elements on the summit. Elderly and female pilgrims flock here to burn incense and pray to Bìxiá and her different incarnations, Yǎnguāng Nǎinai (Goddess of Eyesight), and Sòngshēng Niángniang (Goddess of Fertility).

Northeast of the temple, **Dàguān Fēng** is a gigantic sheer cliff face carved with inscriptions by different emperors, including the Táng Xuánzōng emperor and the later Qīng Kāngxī and Qiánlóng emperors. A little farther north of here is the highest point of Tài Shān, **Yùhuáng Dǐng** (elev. 1,545m/5,067 ft.). A temple, **Yùhuáng Miào,** houses a Míng dynasty bronze statue of the Jade Emperor, considered by many Daoists to be the supreme god of heaven. Outside the temple is the 6m-high (19-ft.) **Wúzì Bēi (Stele without Words).** One version has it that the first Qín emperor had this tablet erected in A.D. 219, but years of exposure to the elements have weathered away the text. Another story tells of the stele being erected by the sixth emperor of the Hàn dynasty, who modestly left it blank to suggest that the virtue of the emperor was beyond words. About 200m (656 ft.) to the southeast is **Rìguān Fēng (Sunrise Watching Peak),** where hundreds of bleary-eyed visitors wrapped in thick jackets congregate every morning around jutting **Tànhǎi Rock** to watch the sunrise. It is on this peak that emperors such as the Táng Gāozōng and Xuánzōng emperors and the Sòng Zhènzōng emperor conducted the Fēng and Shān ceremonies. In 1747, two boxes of jade inscriptions by the third emperor of the Sòng dynasty, once thought to be lost during the Míng dynasty, were unearthed here.

If you choose this route, you should take a minibus to **Zhōng Tiān Mén (Middle Gate of Heaven)** for ¥20 ($2.50) and then climb to **Nán Tiān Mén (South Gate of Heaven)** yourself. You can then ride the cable car (¥45/$5.60) back down to **Zhōng Tiān Mén,** as it is rather steep to climb down.

WESTERN ROUTE This route has fewer cultural attractions than the eastern route and emphasizes more natural sights such as pools and forests. The trail (not always clearly marked) converges at times with the main road running to Zhōng Tiān Mén. A little over 3km (2 miles) down from Zhōng Tiān Mén is **Shànzǐ Yá,** strangely shaped rock formations named for various animals they resemble. About 2km (1¼ miles) farther down past Chángshòu Qiáo (Longevity Bridge) is the main attraction, **Hēilóng Tán (Black Dragon Pool),** a pleasant enough waterfall in the summer and early fall. Another kilometer (½ mile) brings you to Dàzhòng Qiáo and the terminus for the Zhōng Tiān Mén buses. The path continues to **Pǔzhào Sì (Temple of Universal Light),** a Buddhist temple built during the Northern and Southern dynasties (A.D. 420–589) and rebuilt in the Míng. Between 1932 and 1935, Féng Yùxiáng (1882–1948), the "Christian General," stayed in the hall in the back of the temple complex. Born in Ānhuī Province, Féng was a warlord of the north who supported Sun Yat-sen but who later mounted a challenge to Chiang Kai-shek in 1929. He used to baptize his troops with a fire hose, and is buried on the southern slope of Tài Shān. From the temple, it's another 2km (1¼ miles) to the Dài Temple.

WHERE TO STAY

Huáqiáo Dàshà (Overseas Chinese Hotel) This 14-story hotel is supposed to be the most luxurious in town, but it is a rather colorless place even though its rooms and facilities meet the minimum standards for a four-star hotel. Guest rooms are fitted with large twin beds and standard nondescript brown furniture, and are comfortable enough for a night or two. The decent-size bathrooms are a little dark but clean.

Dōngyuè Dàjiē Zhōngduàn. ✆ **0538/822-8112.** Fax 0538/822-8171. www.huaqiaohotel.com. 205 units. ¥400–¥600 ($48–$73) standard room; ¥800–¥1,580 ($97–$191) suite. 30%–60% discounts possible online. 10% service charge. AE, DC, MC, V. **Amenities:** Restaurant; bar; lounge; indoor pool; health club; sauna; bowling alley; concierge; tour desk; business center; free Internet access; forex; shopping arcade; salon; limited room service; massage; laundry/dry cleaning. *In room:* A/C, TV (in-house movies), minibar, safe (select rooms), computers (14th floor only).

Tài Shān Bīnguǎn A trusty old standby, this popular, well-located hotel between the main gate of Tài Shān and the Dài Temple is comfortable and reasonably priced. Last renovated in 1999, guest rooms come with high ceilings and basic but functional furniture. Bathrooms are clean. The whole place has a friendly feel to it and the staff seems to know what they're doing. CITS is conveniently located right next door.

Hóngmén Lù 26. ✆ **0538/822-4678.** Fax 0538/822-1432. www.tsgnestandhotel.com. 110 units. ¥300–¥420 ($38–$52) standard room; ¥680–¥1,080 ($85–$135) suite. 30% discounts possible online. AE, DC, MC, V. **Amenities:** Restaurant; bar; lounge; exercise room; sauna; concierge; tour desk; business center; forex; shopping arcade; salon; limited room service; massage; laundry/dry cleaning. *In room:* A/C, TV, fridge, hair dryer.

Tài Shān Dàjiǔdiàn This modern 19-story hotel located a block east of the Dài Temple has a perfect view of Tài Shān, especially from the higher floors. The rooms are huge, but they are gaudily decorated in floral prints and come with small twin beds and generic brown furniture. Renovations notwithstanding, bathrooms are a little weathered but are spacious and clean.

Dàizōng Dàjiē 210. ✆ **0538/822-7211.** Fax 0538/822-6162. 183 units. ¥200–¥460 ($24–$56) standard room; ¥680–¥880 ($82–$110) suite. 30% discounts possible. AE, DC, MC, V. **Amenities:** 2 restaurants; Internet bar; lounge; nightclub;

health club; sauna; concierge; airport shuttle service; business center; forex (US$, yen, HK$ only); shopping arcade; salon; limited room service; massage; laundry/dry cleaning; nonsmoking rooms; executive rooms. *In room:* A/C, TV w/Internet access (¥8/$1 per hour).

ON THE MOUNTAIN

Shénqì Bīnguǎn   This overpriced, overrated three-star perched atop some steep steps is nevertheless the best place to stay at the summit. It's only 30m (98 ft.) from Yùhuáng Dǐng and 100m (328 ft.) from Rìguān Fēng. Rooms are somewhat dark but are clean enough and come with small twin beds and a small, clean bathroom; TVs are in place, but they receive no stations. The hotel only has hot water between 8:30 and 11pm. Thick jackets are provided for the sunrise viewing and the staff will make sure you're awake in time. A buffet lunch or dinner starts at ¥30 ($4).

1km (½ mile) from Nán Tiān Mén along Tiānjiē. ⓒ **0538/822-3866.** Fax 0538/833-7025. www.shenqihotel.com. 66 units. ¥680 ($85) standard room. Discounts possible up to 20% except on Sat nights Apr–Oct. AE, DC, MC, V. **Amenities:** Restaurant; bar; sauna; forex (US$ only); store; salon. *In room:* A/C, TV.

WHERE TO DINE

In Tài'ān, the **Bǎihuā Cāntīng** restaurant in the Tài Shān Bīnguǎn (ⓒ **0538/822-4678,** ext. 666; 10am–2pm and 5:45–9pm) offers decent Chinese food in a clean environment. Simply point to your choices from the many dishes on display on long counters. A meal for two runs ¥60 to ¥80 ($7.50–$10). **Huánqiú Xīshì Miànbāo Fáng** (Hóngmén Lù 7) sells pastries and snacks for the long hike. There is a **McDonald's** at Shēng Píng Lù 2, and a **KFC** next to the railway station.

On the **mountain,** food is comparatively more expensive along the trail and on the summit than in town. Trailside vendors offer ice cream, bottled drinks, instant noodles, and boiled eggs. At the summit, **Shénqì Bīnguǎn** has a restaurant that serves both basic Chinese fare *(jiācháng cài)* as well as delicacies made from local ingredients such as pheasants, wild vegetables, and local medicinal herbs. A meal for two is ¥80 to ¥120 ($10–$15).

7 Qūfǔ ⓐ

Shāndōng Province, 150km (90 miles) S of Jǐ'nán, 68km (42 miles) S of Tài'ān

Qūfǔ, the home of Confucius, is a small town of 630,000 people, 125,000 of whom are surnamed Kǒng (though few are direct descendents). The town is dominated by the magnificent Temple of Confucius, the Confucian Mansion, and the Confucian Forest, all UNESCO World Heritage Sites. Qūfǔ is often visited as a somewhat hurried day trip from Jǐ'nán. If you would like a more leisurely appreciation of the sights or merely wish to soak up the rarefied air, consider staying overnight and combining this with a visit to nearby Tài Shān. If you like celebrations, the ideal time to visit is on the occasion of Confucius's birthday, September 28. During this time, there are parades and musical and dance performances throughout Qūfǔ. Book well in advance. *Note:* For Chinese translations of selected establishments listed in this section, please turn to appendix A.

ESSENTIALS

GETTING THERE   The nearest major **airport** is in Jǐ'nán, 150km (90 miles) away. The **train** situation is a little confusing, as there are two railway stations: **Qūfǔ Zhàn,** about 5km (3 miles) southeast of the city center, where several trains a day stop between Běijīng and Rìzhào and between Jǐ'nán and Rìzhào. The K51 from Běijīng

Confucius Says . . .

Confucius's tremendous impact on Chinese society was not felt during his lifetime. Born Kǒng Qiū (also Kǒng Zhòngní) to a minor noble family, Confucius (551–479 B.C.) spent most of his life wandering the country as a teacher after the various feudal lords with whom he sought positions all rejected him. Confucius himself never wrote his teachings down. It was only later, over the course of several generations, when his disciples like Zēngzǐ and Mèngzǐ collected and compiled his teachings in *The Analects (Lún Yǔ)*, that Confucianism began to take firm hold.

A philosophical tradition that has come to underpin much of Chinese society, Confucianism is a series of moral and ethical precepts about the role and conduct of an individual in society. Essentially conservative, Confucius was concerned about the breakdown in human, social, and political affairs he observed in the world around him during the Spring and Autumn Period of the Eastern Zhōu dynasty (770–221 B.C.). Expounding on the traditional rites and rituals set forth during the previous Western Zhōu dynasty (1100–771 B.C.), Confucius formulated a code of conduct governing what he saw as the five basic hierarchical relationships in society: between father and son, husband and wife, older and younger brothers, ruler and subject, and friend and friend. At its crux was the supreme virtue of benevolence *(rén)*, and the ideal relationship was one in which the dominant figure (always the male) would rule benevolently over the subordinate, who would in turn practice obedience and piety *(xiào)* toward the authority figure. This concept of *xiào*, which so permeates Chinese familial relations (from parents to in-laws to siblings), is the glue that holds much of Chinese society together.

After an inauspicious beginning when the Qín dynasty Shǐ Huángdì emperor (China's first) rejected all things Confucian and implemented a

(9 hr.) arrives in Qūfù at 7am, while the return K52 departs Qūfù at 9:27pm. Bus no. 5 runs from the railway station into town, though service is infrequent. **Yánzhōu Zhàn** (② 0537/341-5239), 15km (9 miles) west of Qūfù, sits on the Běijīng–Shànghǎi rail line and sees much more traffic. From Yánzhōu, there are daily connections to Tài'ān (1 hr.), Jǐ'nán (2 hr.), Běijīng (5 hr.), and Shànghǎi (10 hr.). There are a limited number of assigned berths on trains serving both stations, so be sure to book your ongoing ticket as soon as you reach town. To avoid the hassle of running back and forth between Yánzhōu and Qūfù, use a ticketing agency like the **Qūfù Shòupiào Chù** in the north Dà Chéng Lù (Huádēng Jiē) (② 0537/335-2276). They have the only computer booking system in Qūfù. The staff here is friendly and helpful.

From the **Qūfù Qìchē Zhàn** (② 0537/441-1241), located one long block south of the Temple of Confucius at the corner of Shéndào Lù and Jìngxuān Dōng Lù, **buses** run to Jǐ'nán (every 20 min. 5:40am–5:30pm; 2½–3 hr.; ¥21/$2.60), Tài'ān (every 30 min. 6:40am–5:30pm; 1 hr., 10 min.; ¥13/$1.60), Wéifāng (7:40am, 10am, 1:40pm; 4 hr.; ¥38/$4.75), and Qīngdǎo (every hour 7–11am and 7–11pm; 7 hr.; ¥61/$7.60). There are several sleeper buses to Běijīng daily, but they are often book-burning campaign in 213 B.C., Confucianism became the official state philosophy from the Hàn dynasty (206 B.C.–A.D. 220) until the fall of the Qīng in 1911, with different rulers seizing on different aspects of Confucius's teachings to justify their rules and methods. Over the years, Confucianism underwent many changes, but Confucian temples *(wén miào)* continued to proliferate and the stature of the Kǒng family continued to rise; by the Qīng dynasty, the Kǒng family had attained a status equal to that of the imperial family. To be sure, there were many detractors throughout the years, too, none more so than during the Cultural Revolution (1966–76) when, encouraged to reject tradition and authority, children openly criticized and humiliated their parents and teachers. The bonds of *xiào* were broken.

Today, Confucianism struggles to remain relevant. Some younger people scoff at it for being rigid and outdated, while a smaller group lays at its feet the onus of over 2,000 years of Chinese patriarchy. Indeed, where once the concept of *zhòngnán qīngnǚ* (the value of males over females), an extension of Confucius's emphasis on the importance of male heirs to continue the family lineage, was held absolute and paramount, today that practice is being very slowly, if not surely, challenged. Yet those fearing the imminent demise of Confucianism need only take a closer look at the family flying a kite in the park, at the crowds who show up to sweep the graves of their ancestors, at the teeming masses who burden the Chinese transportation system in the days leading up to the Spring Festival (Chūn Jié) so they can all rush home to celebrate the Chinese New Year with their family, at the peasant woman who is allowed to have a second child if her first one is a girl. For good or ill, tradition is alive and well, and the family is still the strongest and most important social unit in Chinese society.

booked (7:40am, 3pm; 8 hr.; ¥100/$12). **Minibuses** run to the railway station at Yánzhōu (every 15 min. 6:30am–5:30pm; 25 min.; ¥3/35¢). The taxi to **Yánzhōu Zhàn** from town costs ¥30 ($4) and takes 20 minutes.

GETTING AROUND   It is possible to tour temple, mansion, and cemetery on foot, though hiring a pedicab or horse-drawn taxi to the cemetery is an inexpensive option. Unmetered *miàndī* (minivan) **taxis** cost ¥5 (60¢) per 2km (1¼ miles). Around town, **horse-drawn carriages** cost ¥2 to ¥4 (25¢–50¢) per person, while a **tricycle taxi** costs ¥1 to ¥3 (15¢–35¢) per person. You can hire a tricycle taxi for one day for ¥20 to ¥30 ($2.50–$3.50), but make sure you agree on the price and what attractions you want to see before starting the ride. The infrequent **bus** no. 1 runs from the southwest of town past the bus station all the way up Gǔ Lóu Jiē to the Confucian Forest. Bus no. 2 travels an east–west route along Jìngxuān Jiē.

VISITOR INFORMATION   The **Qūfù Tourist Information Center** at Gǔ Lóu Běi Jiē 4 (© **0537/441-4001;** open 8am–6:30pm) can provide information and direct travelers to sights and accommodations.

FAST FACTS

Banks, Foreign Exchange & ATMs   The **Bank of China** is at Dōngmén Dàjiē 96 just east of Gǔ Lóu Běi Jiē. Foreign-exchange hours are Monday to Friday from 8am to noon and 3 to 6pm.

Internet Access   Dial-up is ⓒ **169.**

Post Office   Located north of the Drum Tower at Gǔ Lóu Běi Jiē 8–1, the post office is open from 8am to 6:30pm.

Visa Extensions   The **PSB (Shì Gōngānjú)** is at Wǔyúntǎn Lù 1 (ⓒ **0537/ 296-0153;** open Mon–Fri 8am–noon and 2:30–6pm). Take a taxi or bus no. 3 from the Kǒngfǔ Fàndiàn (Kǒngfǔ Hotel) at the corner of Dàtóng Lù and Jìngxuān Lù, and ask to be let off at Wǔyúntǎn.

EXPLORING QŪFǓ

Kǒng Miào (Confucius Temple) 𝔯𝔯𝔯   One of the great classical Chinese architectural complexes (along with Běijīng's Forbidden City and Chéngdé's Imperial Summer Resort), the magnificent Confucius Temple was first built in 478 B.C. by the king of Zhōu, Lǔ Àigōng, who converted three rooms from Confucius's residence into a temple to offer sacrifices to the Sage. The temple grew from the Western Hàn dynasty (206 B.C.–A.D. 24) onward due to the increasing number of titles conferred on Confucius. Many of today's structures, done in typical imperial fashion with red pillars and yellow-glazed tiles, and oriented on a north–south axis, date to the Míng and Qīng dynasties.

Over a kilometer long, the temple is first approached from the main south gate in Qūfǔ's city wall. Then, a series of gates and courtyards lead eventually to **Dàzhōng Mén,** a gate and former temple entrance (during the Sòng). In the next courtyard is the marvelous three-story, triple-eaved **Kuíwén Gé (Worship of Literature Pavilion),** first built in 1018 and rebuilt in 1191. This wooden building with stone pillars survived a major earthquake during the reign of the Qīng dynasty Kāngxī emperor (1654–1722) that destroyed much of the rest of Qūfǔ. In the next courtyard are **13 stelae pavilions** all constructed during different periods, from the Jīn (A.D. 265–420) to the Republican period (1914–19), and housing stelae recording the visits of different emperors.

The central gate, **Dàchéng Mén,** leads into the heart of the temple complex and the magnificent **Dàchéng Diàn (Hall of Great Achievements)** 𝔯𝔯𝔯, originally built on this site in 1021 and rebuilt in 1724. Constructed on a two-tiered sculptured marble terrace, the building is supported by 28 carved stone pillars and majestically capped by a double-eaved, yellow-tiled roof. Individually carved from whole blocks of stone, the 10 columns in front each depict two dragons playing with pearls amid a sea of clouds. The remaining 18 octagonal pillars each bear 72 smaller dragons. Inside the temple is a statue of Confucius flanked by four of his students. These statues, destroyed during the Cultural Revolution, were replaced in 1983. Also on display is a set of bronze vessels and musical instruments that were used in ceremonial rites to honor the Great Sage, still occasionally performed here. In front is **Xìng Tán (Apricot Altar),** where it is said Confucius used to deliver lectures to his 72 disciples. Behind the Great Hall is the **Hall of Bedroom** used to honor Confucius's wife, Lady Yuángōng, who married him at the age of 19 and died 7 years before her husband.

The original Confucius's temple stands in the eastern section, only three shanties by legend. Also noteworthy is a 3m-deep (10-ft.) **well** in the eastern section of the complex from which Confucius is said to have drunk. East of the well, a screen wall, **Lǔ Bì,** commemorates the successful attempt by the ninth generation of Confucius's descendant Kǒng Fǔ to hide all the Confucian classics such as *The Analects* and *The Book of Rites* in the walls of Confucius's residence during Qín Shǐ Huángdì's book-burning campaign in 213 B.C. The books were later discovered during the Hàn dynasty (206 B.C.–A.D. 220), when the residence was torn down in order to enlarge the temple.

Admission ¥105 ($13) for entrance to Kǒng Miào, Kǒng Fǔ, and Kǒng Lín. English-speaking guide (at temple entrance) ¥100 ($13). 7:30am–6pm.

Kǒng Fǔ (Confucian Mansion) ✮✮✮

Until 1949 the mansion on the northeast side of the Confucius Temple had been home to 77 generations of Confucius's direct descendants, although the mansion's present location dates only from the end of the 14th century and the complex really grew to its current size (with a total of 463 halls) only in the Míng and Qīng dynasties.

Here lived the Yǎnshèng ("Continuing the Line of the Sage") duke, a title first conferred upon the 46th-generation descendant of Confucius by the Sòng Rénzōng emperor in 1055, and subsequently passed down. During the Míng dynasty, the duke's stature grew, and by the time of the Qīng, he and the Kǒng family had attained a status equivalent to that of the imperial family. He was exempted from taxes, given power over his own court of law and subjects, and was the only one besides the emperor who could ride his horse within the Forbidden City. The Qīng Qiánlóng emperor (reigned 1736–96) even married his daughter to a Yǎnshèng duke in 1772, because only marriage to someone from a family equal in stature could dispel the misfortune that had been predicted for her by fortunetellers on account of the mole on her face. To circumvent the law that prohibited Manchus from marrying the Chinese, Qiánlóng first gave her to a Chinese official, Yú Mínzhōng, for adoption, and her name was changed from Àixīn Juéluó to Lady Yú.

The mansion is divided into three sections. The front part is reserved for formal and public business, the second serves as private family quarters, and the third is a garden. Inside the main gate is a large courtyard with the free-standing **Chóngguāng Mén,** a gate built on eight stone drums that was only opened when emperors or imperial edicts arrived. In the three halls to the north, starting with the main hall, **Dà Táng,** the Yǎnshèng duke proclaimed imperial edicts, received visitors, and tended to business. In the second hall, where the duke received high-ranking officials, are seven tablets inscribed by various emperors, including one with the character *shòu* (longevity) inscribed by the empress dowager Cíxǐ. Northeast of the third hall is a small alley leading to a four-story **Bīnān Lóu (Tower of Refuge),** which was meant to shelter the duke in case of attack. It was never used.

Behind the third hall, the **Nèizhái Mén (Gate to the Inner Apartments)** marks the beginning of the private quarters restricted to family members and a handful of trusted, mostly female servants. Even the water carrier had to pour his well water through a tiny trough in the wall just west of the gate. Behind the Front Reception Hall used for family banquets, weddings, and funeral ceremonies, the two-story **Qiántáng Lóu** was where the 76th duke, Kǒng Lìngyí, lived with his wife, Madame Táo, his two concubines, and his two daughters from Concubine Wáng. After the 76th duke's death, one concubine gave birth to the 77th duke, Kǒng Déchéng. It is widely held that Madame Táo, who produced no surviving heirs herself, poisoned his mother 17 days after she gave birth. The boy was to grow up with his sisters in relative isolation under the tyrannical Madame Táo, Qūfǔ's equivalent of the powerful and manipulative empress dowager Cíxǐ. As depicted in *The House of Confucius* by Déchéng's sister Kǒng Démào and Kē Lán, life in the Confucian Mansion in those days was full of intrigue and betrayal for the adults and loneliness and sadness for the children. Déchéng married and lived here until 1940, when he fled the Japanese invasion and then the Communists, ending up in Táiwān; he was the last of Confucius's descendants to occupy the mansion.

A large garden in the rear occupies the rest of the mansion grounds. A complete tour of the mansion will take 2 hours. Budget another 1 to 2 hours if you want to tour Kǒng Miào. It's best to do both in the morning hours, as there are fewer tourists.

Entrance opposite the back gate of Kǒng Miào. Admission by combination ticket; see Kǒng Miào, above. 7:30am–6pm.

Kǒng Lín (Confucian Forest & Cemetery) ✿✿✿

Slightly over a kilometer (½ mile) north of the Confucian Mansion and Temple, Kǒng Lín is the burial ground for Confucius and his family, and is the largest and oldest cemetery park in China. Covering 2 sq. km (1¼ sq. miles), the forest has thousands of graves and over 20,000 trees, including cypresses, maples, and willows, many collected and planted by Confucius's disciples over the years. It's interesting to note that women, monks, criminals, and aborted fetuses cannot be buried here. Some 4,000 remaining gravestones span the dynasties and of different styles make the cemetery worth visiting. It is a place both large and atmospheric enough to lose yourself in for a few hours. It can be delightfully eerie in the morning before the fog lifts. A pleasant way to tour the forest is by bike ✿, which can be rented at the entrance for ¥10 ($1.25); the price includes a guide who will take you around the main road (7.5km/4¾ miles) of Kǒng Lín. You can take a sightseeing car for ¥10 ($1.25), but you must wait for the car to fill up before it leaves, which can take awhile.

The walkway leading to the forest from the south is lined with 73 trees on the right representing Confucius's age when he died, and 72 trees on the left signaling the number of his disciples. Passing through another two gates, visitors arrive at the forest proper, which is surrounded by a 3m-high (10-ft.) and 5m-thick (16-ft.) wall. To get to Confucius's grave, turn left inside the second entrance, walk along the **Imperial Carriageway** for about 200m (654 ft.), cross the Míng **Zhūshuǐ Bridge,** and continue along the "Spirit Way" *(shén sào),* which is flanked by four pairs of Sòng dynasty stone sculptures. At the end of the Spirit Way is **Confucius's tomb,** a mound of packed earth in front of which are two stelae. The front Míng dynasty tablet is inscribed with the characters DÀCHÉNG ZHÌ SHÈNGWÉN XUĀN WÁNG MÙ or "Tomb of the Ultimate Sage of Great Achievements." Local lore has it that the last two characters, *"wáng mù"* (king's tomb), are partially hidden from view by the stone altar in front to reassure visiting emperors who came to pay their respects that no matter how respected and exalted the Sage was, there was only one emperor. To the right (east) of Confucius's grave is that of his son Kǒng Lǐ, who died before his father. To the south lies the tomb of Confucius's grandson, Zǐsī, who was Mencius's (Mèngzǐ's) teacher and the author of *The Doctrine of the Mean.*

Following the main road to the left of Confucius's grave brings you to a group of Míng Tombs. Continuing to the north eventually leads you to an archway and **tomb for Lady Yú,** the Qiánlóng emperor's daughter. (While Confucian wives were allowed to be buried in the forest, Confucius's female descendants were restricted to burial outside the forest.) Not far to the east is the **Tomb of Kǒng Shàngrèn** (1648–1718), a 64th-generation descendant and author of the famous classical play *Táohuā Shàn (The Peach Blossom Fan).* East of Kǒng Shàngrèn's tomb is the Tomb of the 76th Yǎnshèng duke, Kǒng Língyí, and his wretched wife Madame Táo. Concubine Wáng was also reburied here, despite laws prohibiting concubines from being buried within the forest. Following the road south brings you back to the main entrance.

Líndào Lù. Mar–Nov 8am–6pm; Dec–Feb 8am–5:30pm. Bus: no. 1.

OTHER ATTRACTIONS

Kǒngzǐ Yánjīuyuàn (Confucius Academy) ✦   Designed by the famous Chinese architect Wú Liángyōng, this academy is a combination museum, research center, and exhibition space. Six rooms in the museum are dedicated to Confucius's life and theory, with drawings of the Sage and also some antiques from Kǒng Fǔ (Confucian Mansion) on display. Unfortunately, the place lacks English signage and English-speaking guides, but it's still worthwhile for the fantastic architecture.

Dà Chéng Lù 9. Admission: ¥30 ($4), includes guide (no English-speaking guides available, though). 7:30am–5:30pm.

Shào Hào Líng (Tomb of the emperor Shào Hào) ✦   Located 4km (2½ miles) east of town, this unusually shaped tomb was built in 1111 by the Sòng Huīzōng emperor to honor Shào Hào, one of the legendary five emperors who succeeded the even more legendary first Chinese emperor, Huáng Dì (the Yellow Emperor). This flat-topped pyramid-shaped structure capped by a small brick altar with a yellow-tiled roof was supposedly built from ten thousand pieces of stone. Also here are two 17m-tall (56-ft.) stelae, **Wànrénchóu Jùbēi (Sorrow of Ten Thousand Stelae),** meant to honor the Yellow Emperor, but the Sòng dynasty was driven from power before the stelae could be erected. Lying facedown since then, the tablets were hacked at by zealous Red Guards during the Cultural Revolution but were restored and set upright in 1992.

4km (2½ miles) northeast of Qūfǔ in Jiùxiàn Village. Admission ¥10 ($1.25). 8am–5pm. Shào Hào Líng is best reached by taxi (about ¥10–¥15/$1.25–$2) Bus: no. 2 from outside the bus station heading east on Jīngxuān Dōng Lù. Ask to be dropped of at Shào Hào Líng, then head north for another 400m (1,308 ft.).

WHERE TO STAY
MODERATE

Quèlǐ Bīnshè (Quèlǐ Hotel) ✦   The best place to stay in town, this three-star hotel just east of the Confucius Temple has traditional Chinese buildings in a courtyard setting. Legend has it that Confucius lived nearby. Rooms, while not luxurious, are spacious, comfortable, and decorated in a style that combines traditional Chinese motifs with modern flourishes. Bathrooms have black marble walls and are a bit old but acceptably clean. Service is occasionally spotty but the hotel has a good restaurant that serves Confucian banquets and acceptable Western meals.

Quèlǐ Jiē 1. ☎ 0537/486-6818. Fax 0537/441-2022. www.quelihotel.com. 160 units. ¥298 ($36) single; ¥398 ($49) standard room; ¥988 ($123) suite. MC, V. **Amenities:** Restaurant; bar; bowling alley; sauna; concierge; business center; shopping arcade; salon; limited room service; laundry/dry cleaning. In room: AC, TV w/free Internet access, fridge w/beverages.

INEXPENSIVE

Qūfǔ Yóuzhèng Bīnguǎn (Qūfǔ Post Hotel)   This two-star hotel just east of the Confucius Mansion is an acceptable alternative if the Quèlǐ is full. Rooms are clean and comfortable enough. Bathrooms are tired but otherwise clean. The staff doesn't speak English but tries to be helpful.

Gǔ Lóu Běi Jiē 8. ☎ 0537/448-3888. Fax 0537/442-4340. 66 units. ¥260 ($33) standard room; ¥1,080 ($135) suite. 20%–40% discounts possible. No credit cards. **Amenities:** Restaurant; salon; laundry/dry cleaning. In room: A/C, TV.

Yù Lóng Dàjiǔdiàn (Yù Lóng Hotel)   Located in the north part of the old town, the quiet hotel has a good view of the city wall. It provides huge and acceptably clean

rooms, though the furniture is worn. The staff is friendly, and they can book train tickets for you.

Běi Mén Dà Jiē 1. ✆ 0537/441-3469. Fax 0537/441-3209. ¥ 280 ($34) standard room; ¥1,688 ($204) suite. 30%–50% discounts possible. No credit cards. **Amenities:** Restaurant; laundry/dry cleaning. *In room:* A/C, TV, dial-up Internet access ¥.70 (1¢) per minute.

WHERE TO DINE

The **Confucius Restaurant and Western Dining Room** in the Quèlǐ Hotel offers the best dining in a relatively clean environment, but watch out for shenanigans with prices. Just to the east of the Quèlǐ, the clean and well-lit **Kǒng Fǔ Dàjiǔjiā** (✆ 0537/ 441-1048) has an English menu and serves local Confucian specialties like *yángguān sāndié* (chicken, vegetables, and egg folded together like a fan), *dàizi shàngcháo* (stewed pork, chicken, chestnuts, and ginseng), and *shī lǐ yínxìng* (sweet ginkgo). A meal for two averages ¥80 to ¥160 ($10–$20). No credit cards. An inexpensive choice for lunch or dinner is **Kǒng Fǔ Jiā Yàn Táng** (Kǒng Miào Dōng Jiē; ✆ 0537/448-8959), which provides decent Confucian food. Try *shénxiān yāzi* (fairy duck) and *shī lǐ yínxìng* (sweet "poem" gingko). You can order half portions, which makes it ideal if you're traveling in alone or as a couple. No credit cards. Farther east along Wǔmǎcí Jiē, a lively **night market** proffers a variety of snacks, including delicious grilled kabobs, roasted nuts, and bean curd.

SHOPPING

Popular souvenirs include the "Four Treasures of the Study": seals, ink stones, calligraphy brushes, and rice paper, all of which are available at **Chūnqiū Gé** at Gǔ Lóu Běi Jiē 5 (open 8am–7:30pm). The store also sells ceramics, jewelry, cloisonné, and jade, and accepts international credit cards.

QŪFŪ AFTER DARK

The Quèlǐ Hotel (see above) has nightly **Confucian musical performances.** Tickets range from ¥60 to ¥80 ($6–$10) and are sold in the hotel lobby. From April to October, there are nightly "Confucius Dream" musical performances at 8:30pm at **Xìng Tán Jùchǎng (Apricot Altar Theater;** ✆ 0537/442-4095) where some of the rites mentioned in the *Analects (Lún Yǔ)* are performed. The theater is on Dà Chéng Lù, about 800m (2,624 ft.) south of Kǒng Miào (Confucius Temple).

8 Qīngdǎo ✦✦

Shāndōng Province, 318km (197 miles) E of Jǐ'nán, 890km (551 miles) SE of Běijīng

Qīngdǎo's strategic location at the mouth of a natural inlet on the south coast of the Shāndōng Peninsula has long made it attractive to foreign powers. When two German missionaries were killed in the Boxer Rebellion at the end of the 19th century, that was all the excuse Kaiser Wilhelm II needed to wrest Qīngdǎo, then a small fishing town, from the weak Qīng government, which ceded the port to the Germans on November 14, 1897, for 99 years. The Germans moved in, set up the Tsingtao Brewery, established churches and missions, built a railway to Jǐ'nán, and stationed 2,000 men in the garrison. But they were forced out at the beginning of World War I in 1914, and the Japanese took over, staying on after the 1919 Treaty of Versailles granted them authority over all ex-German territories in China. The Japanese ceded Qīngdǎo back to the Guómíndǎng (Nationalist Government) in 1922 but occupied the town again from 1938 to 1945 during World War II.

Today, Qīngdǎo, which has retained much of its Teutonic architecture, remains one of China's more charming and relaxing cities. With its year-round mild climate, Qīngdǎo also hosts many fairs and festivals throughout the year, the most famous of which is the annual Qīngdǎo International Beer Festival, held the last 2 weeks of August and attracting upwards of a million visitors. Summers see the town packed with Chinese visitors, making spring and fall better times to visit if you hope to avoid the crowds. Tranquillity will be more elusive in the coming years as Qīngdǎo gets ready to host the watersports events of the 2008 Summer Olympics.

ESSENTIALS

GETTING THERE   Qīngdǎo is well connected by **air** to many Chinese cities, including Běijīng (1¼ hr.), Guǎngzhōu (2 hr., 45 min.), and Shànghǎi (70 min.). Tickets can be purchased at the **CAAC office (Mínháng Dàshà)** at Xiānggǎng Zhōng Lù 30 (© **0532/8577-5555**). International destinations served include Hong Kong, Seoul, Fukuoka, Tokyo, Pusan, and Bangkok. **Dragonair** (© **0532/8577-6159**) has an office at the Hotel Equatorial, Xiānggǎng Zhōng Lù 28, as does **Japan Airlines** (Xiānggǎng Zhōng Lù 76; © **0532/571-0088**). Qīngdǎo's **Liú Tíng Airport** (© **0532/8471-5777**) is located 30km (19 miles) north of the city; the 40-minute taxi ride costs ¥80 to ¥100 ($10–$12). Airport shuttles charging ¥15 ($1.90) depart from the Hǎitiān Fàndiàn (Hǎitiān Hotel), and make a stop at the Equatorial Hotel on the hour between 6am and 8pm. The bus also meets incoming flights.

An express overnight **train** from Běijīng (T25) takes 10 hours, and a slow overnight train from Shànghǎi (2106) takes 18½ hours. Several trains a day connect to Wéifāng (2 hr.), Zībó (3–4 hr.), Jì'nán (4–5½ hr.), Tài Shān (6 hr.), and Qūfù/Yánzhōu (7 hr.). Tickets can be bought at the railway station (© **0532/8297-5207**) at Tài'ān Lù 2, 5 days in advance.

The long-distance bus station is in the northern part of town, but the **bus station** (© **0532/8371-8060**) just outside the railway station should serve most travelers' needs. Intra-province buses depart from the lot south of the railway station for Wéifāng (every 40 min. 6:20am–5:30pm; 2 hr., 40 min.; ¥31/$3.80) and Jì'nán (every 30 min. 6am–5:30pm; 5 hr.; ¥50–¥95/$6–$12). Purchase your tickets at the little green kiosks. Long-distance sleeper buses depart from the front of the railway station for destinations farther afield such as Shànghǎi (7pm; 10½ hr.; ¥180/$23) and Hángzhōu (3:50pm; 14 hr.).

Ferries to Incheon, South Korea, run four times a week. Tickets can be bought at the **Qīngdǎo Port Passenger Terminal (Qīngdǎo Gǎng Kèyùn Zhàn)** at Xīnjiāng Lù 6 (© **0532/8282-5001**). **Orient Ferry Ltd.** (Hǎitiān Hotel, Xiānggǎng Xī Lù 48, room 1267/68; © **0532/8389-7636**) also operates regular ferries to Shimonoseki (40 hr.) in Japan; a one-way ticket costs between ¥1,230 and ¥4,785 ($154–$598).

GETTING AROUND   Downtown and the German Quarter can be toured on foot, but taxis and buses are more convenient ways to get to some of the beaches and attractions farther afield. **Taxis** charge ¥7 (85¢) for 3km (2 miles), then ¥1.50 (20¢) per kilometer until 8km (5 miles), when the price rises to ¥2.15 (25¢) per kilometer. **Bus** nos. 26 and 301 run from the railway station along the southern edge of the peninsula towards the commercial district on Xiānggǎng Zhōng Lù; the fare is ¥1 (15¢).

VISITOR INFORMATION   A **Tourism and Information Service Center** (© **0532/8296-2000;** open 9am–5pm) is located 200m (656 ft.) to the left when you

Qīngdăo

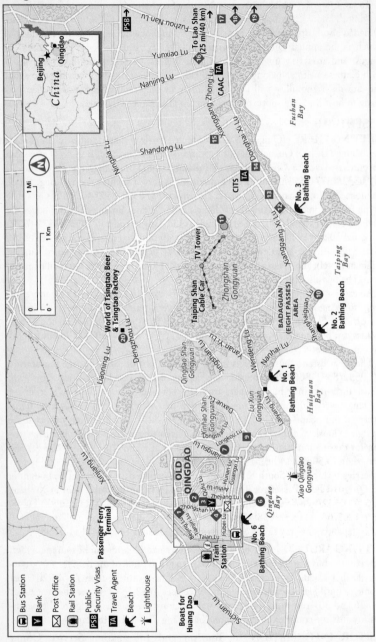

Boats for Huang Dao

Passenger Ferry Terminal

Legend:
- Bus Station
- ¥ Bank
- Post Office
- Rail Station
- PSB Public-Security Visas
- TA Travel Agent
- Beach
- Lighthouse

OLD QINGDAO

Train Station

No. 6 Bathing Beach

Xiao Qingdao Gongyuan

Qingdao Bay

Huiquan Bay

No. 1 Bathing Beach

No. 2 Bathing Beach

No. 3 Bathing Beach

BADAGUAN (EIGHT PASSES) AREA

Taiping Bay

Fushan Bay

TV Tower

Taiping Shan Cable Car

Zhongshan Gongyuan

World of Tsingtao Beer & Tsingtao Factory

To Lao Shan (25 mi/40 km)

CAAC

CITS

PSB

Streets:
Fuzhou Nan Lu, Yunxiao Lu, Nanjing Lu, Shandong Lu, Ningxia Lu, Xanggang Zhong Lu, Donghai Xi Lu, Xanggang Xi Lu, Xanggang Lu, Shanghaiguan Lu, Nanhai Lu, Wendeng Lu, Yanan Yi Lu, Jingshan Lu, Daxue Lu, Longkou Lu, Longshan Lu, Jiangsu Lu, Zhejiang Lu, Guangxi Lu, Hunan Lu, Anhui Lu, Hubei Lu, Taian Lu, Hubei Lu, Zhongshan Lu, Sichuan Lu, Dengzhou Lu, Laoning Lu, Xinjiang Lu, Lu Xun Gongyuan, Huiquan Lu, Qingdao Shan Gongyuan, Xinhao Shan Gongyuan

Scale: 1 Mi / 1 Km

China — Beijing, Qingdao

ACCOMMODATIONS ■

Crowne Plaza Qīngdǎo
(Qīngdǎo Yízhōng
Huángguān Jiàrì Jiǔdiàn) **17**
ê碌阁弥谢诩偃站频

Dōngfāng Fàndiàn **9**
东方饭店

Hǎitiān Fàndiàn **13**
海天饭店

Kǎilái Guójì Jiǔdià (Gloria Inn) **14**
凯莱国际酒店

Qīngdǎo Fàndiàn **3**
青岛饭店

Shangri-La Hotel Qīngdǎo
(Qīngdǎo Xiānggélǐlā Fàndiàn) **15**
青岛香格里拉饭店

DINING ◆

Chūnhé Lóu **1**
春和楼

Eden Café **4**
伊甸休闲餐厅

Gāoshì Jiǔdiàn
(Steven Gao's Restaurant) **16**
高氏酒店

Tǔdàlì **12**
土大力

Yíjǐng Lóu Hǎixiān Dàshìjiè
(Yíjǐng Lóu Seaview
Seafood Restaurant) **18**
怡景楼海鲜酒家

ATTRACTIONS ●

Huāshí Lóu **10**
花石楼

Huílán Gé **6**
回澜阁

Jīdū Jiàotáng
(Protestant Church) **7**
基督教堂

Qīngdǎo Píijiǔ Chéng
(Qīngdǎo Beer Park) **19**
青岛啤酒成
*only open during the
Tsingtao Beer Festival

Qīngdǎo Yíng Bīnguǎn
(Qīngdǎo Welcome
Guesthouse) **8**
青岛迎宾馆

Tiānzhǔ Jiàotáng
(Catholic Church) **2**
天主教堂

World of Tsingtao Beer
(Qīngdǎo Píijiǔ Chǎng) **20**
青岛啤酒厂

Zhàn Qiáo **5**
栈桥

Zhàn Shān Sì **11**
湛山寺

exit the railway station. They can provide information and direct travelers to sights and accommodations.

TOURS & GUIDES   If you haven't become frustrated enough by other **CITS** offices around the country, you can give this one a shot. It's is located at Xiānggǎng Xī Lù 73 (𝄞 **0532/8389-3001;** fax 0532/8389-3013). For the latest information on the city and the rest of the province, look for the monthly English-language *Red Star* magazine, available at most international hotels or on the Internet at www.myredstar.com.cn.

FAST FACTS

Banks, Foreign Exchange & ATMs   The **Bank of China** at Yúnxiāo Lù 1 has an ATM on premises and is open for foreign exchange Monday through Friday from 8am to 5pm. Another branch at Zhōngshān Lù 68 has similar hours. An **HSBC** ATM is also conveniently located inside the Crowne Plaza Hotel (Yízhōng Huángguān Jiàrì Jiǔdiàn).

Internet Access   There is a small **Internet cafe** across from the post office on Ānhuī Lù. It's open from 9am to midnight. Dial-up is 𝄞 **163.**

Post Office   Located at Ānhuī Lù 5 (open 8am–6pm) and another in the commercial district at Xiānggǎng Zhōng Lù 56 (open 8:30am–5:30pm).

Visa Extensions   The **PSB** office for visa extensions ((C) **0532/8579-2555,** ext 2860; open Mon–Fri 8:30–11:30am and 1:30–5:30pm) is inconveniently located in the eastern part of town at Níngxià Lù 272. Bus no. 301 runs there from the railway station.

EXPLORING THE CITY
GERMAN QĪNGDǍO

Many houses and shops in the former German Concession still retain their original European architecture. In addition to the sights that follow, other noteworthy buildings include the **Railway Station** at Tài'ān Lù 2, a classical European structure built in 1901 with a 35m-high (115-ft.) bell tower; the former **Public Security Bureau** at Húběi Lù 29, built in 1904 and 1905 in the style of a medieval village church; and the **Princess House** at Jūyōngguān Lù 10, a villa built in 1903 by the Danish consulate general for a Danish princess.

East of the old town near the Number Two Bathing Beach, the **Bā Dà Guān (Eight Passes)** area, named for the eight famous passes of the Great Wall, was and still is the toniest address in town. Unfortunately for the visitor, most of the well-preserved European mansions and villas here are hidden behind high walls and fences. Still, it's a lovely area to stroll, as the streets are wide and sheltered by a canopy of trees, with each street (or "pass") planted with a different bloom, including crab apples, peaches, pines, magnolias, and ginkgoes.

Huāshí Lóu ✿   This Bavarian medieval castle built in 1903, with a tall round turret, chimneys, balconies, and Greek-style columns, was originally a Russian aristocrat's villa but was later taken over by the German governor general as a fishing retreat. In 1946, Chiang Kai-shek secretly retreated here to plan the Guómíndǎng's next moves. These days, the villa, a big hit with wedding parties, can't exactly be called quiet or relaxing. Climbing to the top affords the visitor a grand view of the surrounding Bā Dà Guān area.

Huánghǎi Lù 18. Admission ¥5 (60¢). 7am–5pm. Bus: no. 26 or 31.

Jīdū Jiàotáng (Protestant Church) ✿✿   One of Qīngdǎo's more attractive sights, this simple but beautiful church was designed by German Curt Rothkegel in the style of a Western medieval castle and completed in 1908. A red tile roof and a pretty green bell tower with a three-sided clock face cap the squat yellow structure. Visitors can climb the tower to see the original bells that still toll here. More popularly known to locals as Zhōngbiǎo Lóu (Clock Tower), the building was spared destruction during the Cultural Revolution, as few knew it was a church.

Jiāngsū Lù 15. Admission ¥3 (35¢). Mon–Sat 8:30–11:30am and 1:30–4:30pm; Sun 1:30–4:30pm. Bus: no. 1 to Jiāngsū Lù.

Qīngdǎo Yíngbīnguǎn (Qīngdǎo Welcome Guest House) ✿✿✿   Built between 1905 and 1908 in the style of an old fortress with Tudor motifs, this magnificent building, the former residence of the German governor general, looks like it leaped from a Grimm Brothers' fairy tale. In 1934, the house became a hotel and is now a museum. Visitors can see the office where Máo Zédōng slept during his month-long summer holiday in July 1957. Much of the stained glass, dark woods, and plush furnishings have survived, including an exquisite green marble fireplace with ornamental tiles in the study and an original 1876 German grand piano.

Lóngshān Lù 26. Admission ¥10 ($1.25). 8:30am–5pm. Bus: no. 25, 26, or 214 to Dàxué Lù.

Tiānzhǔ Jiàotáng (Catholic Church) ✿   The former St. Michael's Cathedral was designed by German architect Pepieruch in a Gothic and Roman style and built between 1932 and 1934 with 60m-high (197-ft.) twin bell towers housing four bronze bells. Much of the church's interior was destroyed during the Cultural Revolution. Today, the inside has been given a bit of a tacky paint job and all the stained glass is new except for the small triangular panels in the round window in the eastern wall of the church. The Sunday morning 8am service is open to the public.

Zhèjiāng Lù 15. Admission ¥5 (60¢). Mon–Sat 8am–5pm; Sun noon–5pm. Bus: no. 26.

World of Tsingtao Beer ✿   The Tsingtao beer factory was closed to the public until recently; now, it's become a must-see attraction for most visitors to Qīngdǎo. The well-curated museum offers a history of the beer, which debuted in China in 1903 as a British-German venture. Displays of print and film advertisements from the 1930s are worth checking out as is the actual bottling assembly line. The tour ends at the Tsingtao Bar, where you'll be treated to a pitcher of beer and given a souvenir—not a bad PR pitch. English signage in the museum is adequate for explaining most of the exhibits but you can call ahead to arrange for an English-speaking guide.

Dēngzhōu Lù 56. ✆ 0532/383-3437. Admission ¥50 ($6). 8:30am–5pm.

BEACHES

Qīngdǎo's beaches are a top attraction for many Chinese, attractive if you're coming from any one of China's many dull, gray, overcrowded cities. Just don't expect a white-sand tropical paradise. From June to September, the beaches are packed. All the main public beaches, seven in the urban area, have changing booths where you can shower for ¥3 (35¢), as well as medical stations and lifeguards on duty. Watersports range from water-skiing to parasailing.

Starting from the western tip of the peninsula, the beach nearest the railway station is the **Number Six Bathing Beach (Dìliù Hǎishuǐ Yùchǎng);** its rocky terrain makes it the least desirable for sunbathing. The big attraction here, however, is Qīngdǎo's former pier, **Zhàn Qiáo** (¥2/25¢; open 7am–8:30pm), originally built in 1892 for the Qīng army. It now juts 440m (1,300 ft.) into the bay and is popularly considered the city's symbol. At the end of the pier is the octagonal Huílán Gé (¥4/50¢), a pavilion which currently houses a small tacky aquarium with a coral exhibit.

Continuing east around the headland into the next bay past the aquarium, the 800m-long (2,624-ft.) **Number One Bathing Beach (Dìyī Hǎishuǐ Yùchǎng)** is Qīngdǎo's longest, but the sand here is somewhat coarse and pebbly. Around the next headland is the **Number Two Bathing Beach (Dì'èr Hǎishuǐ Yùchǎng)** ✿, much nicer and more secluded than either numbers One or Six. Little wonder that this beach used to be popular with political figures like Máo Zédōng and other government officials. You must pay a ¥2 (25¢) entrance fee from 9am to 6pm, but at other times, it's free. In the next bay is the 400m-long (1,312-ft.) **Number Three Bathing Beach (Dìsān Hǎishuǐ Yùchǎng)** ✿, also nice, quiet, and a bit out of the way.

Far out to the west, half an hour by boat and then another half-hour by bus, is the beach of **Huáng Dǎo** ✿, cleaner and quieter than Qīngdǎo's beaches, and until recently known only to locals—a real find. Take the Qīngdǎo Huáng Dǎo Lúndù (ferry) (hourly 6:30am–9pm; 30 min.; ¥10/$1.25) from the local ferry terminal (Lúndù Zhàn) on Sìchuān Lù west of the railway station, then bus no. 1 to its terminus.

PARKS

Qīngdǎo has a multitude of parks, some of them worth exploring. **Zhōngshān Gōngyuán** (Xiānggǎng Xī Lù; ¥5/60¢; 6am–6pm) offers some pleasant strolls and is especially pretty during April and May when the cherry trees are in bloom. Northeast of the park is the **Tàipíng Shān Gōngyuán,** where visitors can take a cable car up to a TV tower at the summit. The cable-car fare is ¥10 ($1.25) one-way, ¥20 ($2.50) round-trip. At the summit you can see lovely views of the city. From there, you can hike down the way you came, take the cable car, or hike down the back of the mountain to **Zhàn Shān Sì** (Zīquán Lù 4), the largest Buddhist temple in Qīngdǎo. Admission to the temple is ¥5 (60¢); hours are from 8:30am to 4:30pm. Note that the cable-car terminus is still a 15-minute walk to Zhàn Shān Sì; the fare to Zhàn Shān Sì is ¥20 ($2.50) one-way, ¥35 ($4.25) round-trip.

Xìnhào Shān Gōngyuán (Signal Hill Park), at Lóngshān Lù, just west of the Qīngdǎo Welcome Guest House, was the location of a German navigating signal tower in 1898. Today the tower has been replaced by someone's bad idea of post-modernist architecture—three carbuncular mushroom-domed pink buildings meant to simulate signaling torches. Kitsch aside, the revolving viewing platform inside the main "mushroom" does afford some lovely views of Qīngdǎo. Admission is ¥2 (25¢) for the park only, ¥12 ($1.50) including tower entrance. Hours are from 7am to 7pm (to 6pm in winter). **Qīngdǎo Shān Gōngyuán,** northwest of Zhōngshān Gōngyuán, has the remains of an old German fort (or rather, the underground command post). Admission is ¥8 ($1); hours are from 8:30 to 11:30am and 2 to 5pm.

OTHER ATTRACTIONS

About 15km (9 miles) east of town, **Qīngdǎo Píjiǔ Chéng** (Xiānggǎng Dōng Lù and Hǎi'ěr Lù) is a European-themed amusement park only open during the 2-week International Beer Festival in September. In this Bavarian bacchanal, there's something for everyone, from amusement park rides for kids, to drinking contests for adults, to go-karting for the kid in the adult. The beer festival also takes place closer to town at the Huìquán Guǎngchǎng, which offers a slightly more sanitized, calmer experience next to the ocean. Both are worth checking out, though you can expect a lot of kitchiness at the first location. Check with CITS for exact dates.

WHERE TO STAY

Qīngdǎo has a glut of upmarket hotels, many of which offer 20% to 30% discounts. All rooms are subject to a 15% surcharge unless otherwise noted.

VERY EXPENSIVE/EXPENSIVE

Crowne Plaza Qīngdǎo (Qīngdǎo Yìzhōng Huángguān Jiàrì Jiǔdiàn) 🌟🌟
Located in the heart of the commercial and shopping district, this latest addition to the five-star hotel scene, recently upgraded from the four-star Holiday Inn, is popular with Western independent and business travelers. Rooms have a slightly claustrophobic, dark feel as windows are small, but they are well furnished and the beds are fairly luxurious. Views of the sea are especially fine. Service here is better than at the pricier Shangri-La. With six restaurants on the premises, the hotel also has some of the most diversified dining choices; the Italian restaurant offers some of the best western food in town.

Xiānggǎng Zhōng Lù 76. ⓒ 0532/8571-8888. Fax 0532/8571-6666. www.sixcontinentshotels.com. 388 units. ¥996 ($124) standard room; ¥1,411 ($176) suite. AE, DC, MC, V. **Amenities:** 6 restaurants; bakery; bar; lounge; indoor pool; health club and spa; sauna; bowling alley; concierge; free airport shuttle service; business center; forex; shopping arcade; salon; 24-hr. room service; massage; babysitting; same-day laundry/dry cleaning; newsstand; nonsmoking rooms; executive rooms. *In room:* A/C, satellite TV, broadband Internet access, minibar, hair dryer, safe.

Hǎitiān Fàndiàn ✿✿

Located just east of the Bā Dà Guān District and overlooking the sea, this five-star, 15-story, two-building Goliath of a hotel claims that all its rooms have sea views except for a few singles in the back. Rooms are comfortable and stylishly decorated with sleek modern furniture. The marble bathrooms are small but are otherwise clean and stylish, and come with dedicated potable water.

Zhàn Shān Dàlù 39. ✆ **0532/8387-1888.** Fax 0532/8387-1777. 606 units. ¥1,400 ($175) standard room. AE, DC, MC, V. **Amenities:** 2 restaurants; bar; lounge; indoor pool; tennis court; health club; sauna; bowling alley; concierge; tour desk; business center; forex; shopping arcade; salon; 24-hr. room service; massage; laundry/dry cleaning; newsstand. *In room:* A/C, satellite TV, minibar, hair dryer, safe.

Shangri-La Hotel Qīngdǎo (Qīngdǎo Xiānggélǐlā Fàndiàn) ✿✿

Located in Qīngdǎo's commercial center, this hotel is a top-notch choice for visitors who don't mind spending the extra cash. The rooms are spacious and have carefully designed lighting fixtures and bathrooms. Offering the full range of facilities and fine dining, the signature Shangri-La luxury is still very much in evidence here, though service is not up to par with the brand's other Chinese locations.

Xiānggǎng Zhōng Lù 9. ✆ **800/942-5050** or 0532/8388-3838. Fax 0532/8388-6868. www.shangri-la.com. 502 units. ¥1,560 ($195) standard room; from ¥2,560 ($320) suite. AE, DC, MC, V. **Amenities:** 2 restaurants; bakery; bar; lounge; indoor pool; outdoor tennis court; health club and spa; Jacuzzi; sauna; concierge; airport shuttle service; business center; forex; shopping arcade; salon; 24-hr. room service; massage; babysitting; same-day laundry/dry cleaning; newsstand; nonsmoking rooms; executive rooms. *In room:* A/C, satellite TV, broadband Internet access, minibar, hair dryer, safe, DVD player (in executive rooms and suites).

MODERATE

Dōngfāng Fàndiàn ✿

For those who don't require a beach location, this four-star hotel, about a 10-minute walk from the Protestant Church, is probably the best deal around. Many Western travelers give it good marks for its comfortable, clean rooms at reasonable prices. It's not luxurious, but there's a full range of facilities and the service is quite good overall. The helpful staff speaks some English.

Dàxué Lù 2. ✆ **0532/8286-5888.** Fax 0532/8286-2741. 146 units. ¥788 ($98) standard room; from ¥980 ($122) suite. AE, DC, MC, V. **Amenities:** 3 restaurants; bar; lounge; tennis court; health club; sauna; concierge; business center; forex; shopping arcade; salon; limited room service; laundry/dry cleaning. *In room:* A/C, satellite TV, minibar, hair dryer, safe.

Kǎilái Guójì Jiǔdiàn (Gloria Inn) ✿

This Hong Kong–managed three-star hotel catering mostly to Japanese, Korean, and domestic guests is the place to stay if you want to be closer to the sea and don't require luxurious amenities. An ugly white-tiled structure on the outside, the hotel has rooms that are comfortable enough. Bathrooms are bright and clean. The rooms facing the sea are bigger and a bit pricier. Views from seaside rooms are somewhat restricted by apartment blocks, but they are pleasant. Service is decent, though getting an extra towel is harder than it should be.

Dōnghǎi Lù 21. ✆ **0532/8387-8855.** Fax 0532/8386-4640. 238 units. ¥680–¥880 ($85–$110) standard room. AE, DC, MC, V. **Amenities:** 2 restaurants; bar; lounge; indoor pool; health club; sauna; salon; concierge; business center; forex; shopping arcade; airport shuttle service; limited room service; massage; babysitting; same-day laundry/dry cleaning; nonsmoking rooms; executive rooms. *In room:* A/C, satellite TV, minibar.

Qīngdǎo Fàndiàn

Within walking distance of the railway station, this three-star hotel offers a wide array of rooms at attractive discounts. The more expensive rooms have been recently renovated and are quite comfortable. Bathrooms run small but are

Wild China: The Funeral Pits of Zībó

Once the capital of the Qí State—during the Spring and Autumn (722–481 B.C.) and Warring States periods (475–221 B.C.)—Zībó today is a dusty industrial town better known for its glass and ceramic production.

The town is located 116km (70 miles) east of Jì'nán in Shāndōng Province, but most of its worthwhile sights are actually in Línzī District about 35km (21 miles) east of Zībó. The **Línzī Zhōngguó Gǔchē Bówùguǎn (Lí Museum of Chinese Ancient Chariots)** 𝔞𝔞 (Qílín Zhèn, Hòulì Guānzhuāng), is about 6km (3½ miles) from the Línzī bus station. Admission is ¥25 ($3) and hours are from 8am to 6pm. Here you'll see two fascinating ancient horse-and-chariot funeral pits which predate Xī'ān's terra-cotta army by more than 280 years. The horses' remains, dating from the Spring and Autumn Period, have been left as they were found. The first pit contains the remains of 10 chariots and 32 horses, all facing west. From the positions of the horses, with bronze bits still intact, archaeologists concluded that the animals were either anesthetized or otherwise rendered unconscious before burial. The second pit features the bones of four horses plus six chariots, which remain buried underneath the horses. Visitors can get a close look, which is a fascinating, if eerie, experience.

Ten minutes to the northwest, **Xūn Mǎ Kēng (Ancient Horse Relics Museum)** 𝔞 (Héyátóu Cūn; ¥10/$1.25; 7:30am–6:30pm) is a series of over 20 tombs believed to have belonged to Qí Jǐng, the 25th monarch of the Qí State. The tombs contain the fossils of 600 horses. Only **tomb 5 (106 horses)** in the southwestern section is open, however. Unearthed in 1982, the horses are arranged in two rows with their heads facing outward. No other funerary objects were found, as the tombs were long ago robbed.

Ceramic production developed around Zībó as early as the period of the Hòulì culture 8,000 years ago. Four exhibit halls at the town's ceramics museum, **Zībó Zhōngguó Táocí Guǎn** 𝔞 (Xīncūn Xī Lù; ¥20/$2.50; May–Oct 9–11:30am and 3–6pm; Nov–Apr 9–11:30am and 2–5pm), trace the evolution of Zībó's ceramics from the Neolithic Lóngshān and Hòulì cultures to its zenith in the Táng and Sòng dynasties with the development of celadon ware and black glaze porcelain. Notable items on display include the dainty eggshell earthenware of the Lóngshān culture and the rare "Blue and

---

clean. Cheaper rooms have no carpets, are very basic but clean, and come with showers only. The staff here is friendly and a few of them speak decent English.

Zhōngshān Lù 53. ☏ 0532/8578-1888. Fax 0532/286-2464. 198 units. ¥230–¥498 ($28–$62) standard room. Discounts possible up to 40%. MC, V. **Amenities:** 3 restaurants; bar; exercise room; sauna; ticket agency; business center; forex; salon; limited room service; laundry. *In room:* A/C, TV.

WHERE TO DINE

Qīngdǎo's seafood and its variations of local Shāndōng cuisine *(lǔ cài)* are all worth trying. Two long blocks east of the Shangri-La Hotel along Xiānggǎng Zhōng Lù is

Yellow Celestial Dragon" patterned porcelain reserved strictly for use by the emperor. The store here (open 8–11:30am and 2:30–6pm, 5pm in winter) sells surprisingly inexpensive locally produced vases, cups, and individual sculptures. Only cash is accepted.

GETTING THERE   From Zībó's **railway station** (© 0533/258-2522) in the southern part of town, daily trains run to Jì'nán (2 hr.), Wéifāng (1 hr.), Qīngdǎo (5 hr.), and beyond. From Zībó's **bus station** (© 0533/288-9261), just west of the railway station, buses run to Jì'nán (every 20–30 min. 5:30am–6:40pm; 1½ hr.; ¥20 –¥30/$2.50–$3.75), Qīngdǎo (every half-hour 6:30am–4:30pm; 3½ hr.), Wéifāng (every half-hour 6:30am–5:30pm; 1½ hr.), and Tài'ān (every half-hour 6:30am–5:20pm).

GETTING AROUND   Take bus no. 6 or minibus no. 20 for ¥3 (35¢) from Dōngyī Lù just east of the railway station to its terminus at Línzī Bus Station; then take tourist bus no. 5, which stops at all the main sights listed here (¥4/50¢ for the entire loop). Alternatively, a **taxi** from Zībó will cost ¥60 to ¥80 ($7.50–$10) one-way. In town, taxis charge ¥5 (60¢) per 3km (2 miles), then ¥1.20 (15¢) per kilometer thereafter.

WHERE TO STAY & DINE   Located in its own garden compound in the center of town, the four-story, four-star **Zībó Bīnguǎn** (Zhōngxīn Lù 189; © 0533/ 228-8688; fax 0533/218-4990) offers rooms that lack charm but are comfortable, with clean bathrooms. Rooms go for ¥380 ($48), and can be discounted 40%. The 31-story **Zībó Fàndiàn** ⌥ (Zhōngxīn Dàdào 177; © 0533/218-0888; fax 0533/218-4800) was the town's first four-star hotel (1999). What it lacks in charm is made up for with a host of modern conveniences. The rack rates are absurd here, but you can bargain them down considerably. Standard rooms, with discount, cost ¥238 ($30) and have large, comfortable beds and standard four-star furnishings, though the carpets are old. The spacious marble bathrooms are dark but clean. Suites can be had for ¥580 ($72). The hotel's revolving restaurant on the 31st floor offers Shāndōng cuisine (also known as "Lǔ") in one of the city's more elegant settings. The Demeanor Bar serves real cappuccino and Colombian coffee, plus cocktails and imported wine. **Western fast food** is available at **McDonald's** (Zībó Shāngshà at Zhōngxīn Lù and Měishí Jiē) and at **KFC** (Měishí Jiē 17).

Yúnxiāo Lù, a lively street of bars and restaurants serving all types of Chinese cuisine into the wee hours.

The most authentic Western fare is still to be found in hotels like the Crowne Plaza and the Shangri-La. The **Eden Café** in Parkson department store on Zhōngshān Lu 44–60 (© 0532/202-1022) serves some credible pizzas, pastas, burgers, and even a New Zealand beef tenderloin; main courses range from ¥28 to ¥88 ($3.50–$11). **McDonald's** and **Kentucky Fried Chicken** have outlets in both the German Concession and the commercial center around Xiānggǎng Zhōng Lù. Coffee aficionados can get a fix at

Starbucks on Xiānggǎng Zhōng Lù in the Sunshine Plaza (Yángguāng Dàshà) or at **SPR Coffee** at the Oceanwide Elite Hotel on Tàipíng Lù, not far from Zhōngshān Lù.

Chūnhé Lóu ✿ SHĀNDŌNG   This long-standing institution for Shāndōng cuisine is located in an old two-story corner building in the German Concession. The first floor serves casual fast food while the second floor has large tables and private rooms. Despite the modest ambience, the food has its devotees. House specialties include *yóubào hǎiluó* (fried sea snails), *sōngshǔ guìyú* (deep-fried sweet-and-sour fish), and *xiāng sū jī* (fragrant chicken).

Zhōngshān Lù 146. ✆ 0532/8282-4346. Meal for 2 ¥80–¥150 ($10–$18). No credit cards. 1st floor 6am–2:30pm and 5–9:30pm; 2nd floor 10:30am–2:30pm and 5–9:30pm.

Gāoshì Jiǔdiàn (Steven Gao's Restaurant) ✿ SEAFOOD/HOME-STYLE   Guitars and posters of Jim Morrison and Axl Rose decorate the walls of this three-story restaurant located on food street Yúnxiāo Lù. Try the *jīngjiàng ròusī* (shredded pork Peking style), *suànxiāng gǔ* (fried pork chop with garlic), or *shāo èrdōng* (sautéed mushrooms with asparagus); or choose from the tanks of fresh seafood out front.

Yúnxiāo Lù 38. ✆ 0532/8573-6676. English menu. Meal for 2 ¥60–¥120 ($7.50–$15). V. Open 24 hr.

Tǔdàlì KOREAN   Located just west of the Shangri-La Hotel, this late-night Korean barbecue diner has a cozy and informal feel, with its exposed wooden beams and plenty of wall graffiti from happy and appreciative patrons. Barbecued meat and vegetable skewers are the main attractions here, along with other tasty Korean staples like kimchi fried rice and *chap chae* (stir-fried yam noodles).

Xiānggǎng Xī Lù 52. ✆ 013583229720. Picture menu. Meal for 2 ¥30–¥60 ($3.75–$7.50). No credit cards. 4pm–4am.

Yíjīng Lóu Hǎixiān Dàshìjiè (Yíjīng Lóu Seaview Seafood Restaurant) ✿✿ SEAFOOD/SHĀNDŌNG   Seafood doesn't get more delicious or fresh than this at this popular chain, especially when you're asked to point and choose it from the tank yourself. Ordering is supereasy here: There's no menu—just a range of aquariums and sample dishes on display. A waiter will follow you around to write down what you want. The highlight of our meal was the fresh *huālóng,* a lobsterlike creature without claws, prepared three ways: served raw (brought to our table with the head still moving), deep-fried with salt and pepper, or made into a rice porridge. Other highlights included *yóuba gǔfǎ zhēng qiézi* (steamed eggplant), *gōngzhǔ yú* (princess fish cooked in oil and steamed), and *tiěbǎn hélí kǎo dàn* (iron plate clams with scrambled eggs). Service is good, though comically formal—they presented our Sprite the way a sommelier would show a bottle of wine before opening it. Make sure to book a private room facing the sea if you're at the Dōnghǎi Lù location, the best of the three.

Three locations: Dōnghǎi Lù in Yínghǎi Dàshìjiè, ✆ 0532/8592-9138; Táiwān Lù, ✆ 0532/8569-1111; and Xiānggǎng Lù, ✆ 0532/8588-3388. Meal for 2 ¥300–¥500 ($36–$60). No credit cards. 10am–2pm and 4:30–9pm.

A NEARBY ATTRACTION

Láo Shān ✿✿   Located 40km (24 miles) east of Qīngdǎo, Láo Shān is a mountain range that is part Daoist sanctuary, part natural wonder, with waterfalls, streams, and walking trails snaking through wooded hills, and jagged cliff faces rising dramatically from the blue sea. Daoism spread to the mountain during the Western Hàn dynasty (206 B.C.–A.D. 9), and emperors throughout the ages have dispatched envoys to scale the mountain in search of the elixir of life. While the water that originates from here didn't perform any miracles, today it is famous and is used in brewing Tsingtao beer.

Admission to Láo Shān is ¥80 ($10), but thanks to greedy tourist officials you must now purchase additional tickets, ranging from ¥4 (50¢) to ¥30 ($3.60), to gain entry to specific attractions on the mountain. The most popular sightseeing route is the **southern route,** which takes in Daoist temples, caves, and ponds, with stupendous sea views along the way. The main Daoist temple here is **Tàiqīng Gōng,** first built in 140 B.C., now with over 140 rooms and an equally mind-boggling number of gods from the Daoist pantheon. Admission is ¥10 ($1.25); hours are from 8am to 6pm. East of the temple, a trail leads up to **Yǎkǒu temple,** where you can either take a cable car or continue on foot up to Yáo Lake and Míngxiá Cave, where admission is ¥4 (50¢). The trail down leads past **Shàngqīng Gōng** (¥4/50¢), another Daoist temple; and the impressive waterfall, **Lóngtán Pù.**

To get to Láo Shān, tourist buses depart from the eastern end of Qīngdǎo's railway station square every half-hour from 6:30am to 6pm. The 1-hour trip costs ¥20 ($2.50). Public bus no. 304 runs from the Ferry Terminal (Lúndù) on Sìchuān Lù all the way to Yǎkǒu. The Tàiqīng Gōng cable car costs ¥50 ($6.25) round-trip (¥40/$5 in low season).

9 Nánjīng ✶✶

Jiāngsū Province, 306km (189 miles) NW of Shànghǎi

First the nation's capital in the early years of the Míng dynasty (A.D. 1368–1644), then the capital of the Republic of China from 1911 to 1937, and now capital of Jiāngsū Province, this bustling city of six million is left off many China itineraries, lacking many visible reminders of what has in fact been a highly tumultuous and storied past. Except for Zhōngshān Lín, the tomb of Sun Yat-sen, the scope of Nánjīng's attractions do not accurately reflect the magnitude and importance of its place in China's history, which is a shame, because the city deserves at least a day or two of your time. In addition to some Míng dynasty attractions, there are reminders that Nánjīng was also the seat of the Tàipíng Rebellion and the site of one of history's most brutal massacres. Spring and fall are the best times to visit, as Nánjīng in the summer is well-known as one of China's three furnaces.

ESSENTIALS

GETTING THERE   From Nánjīng's **airport,** just under 50km (31 miles) southwest of the city, daily flights connect to Běijīng, Guǎngzhōu, Wǔhàn, Chéngdū, Kūnmíng, Guìlín, and Hong Kong. There are also twice-weekly flights to Macau and Bangkok. Tickets can be purchased at hotel tour desks and at the **CAAC** at Hànzhōng Lù 180 (✆ 025/8449-9378). **China Eastern** has a 24-hour office at Zhōngshān Dōng Lù 402 (✆ 025/8445-4325), while **Dragonair** offices are at Hànzhōng Lù 2, nos. 751–753 (✆ 025/8471-0181). CAAC airport shuttles depart from the CAAC office every 30 minutes from 6am to 6:30pm, and also meet arriving flights. The trip takes 50 minutes and costs ¥25 ($3). *Note:* The bus leaves once full; those left behind must take taxis. A metered **taxi** into the Xīnjiēkǒu area should run about ¥140 ($18), including toll.

When construction ends on Nánjīng's **railway station** (Lóngpán Lù 264; ✆ 025/ 8582-2222), it is hoped by the time you read this, it will be linked to Nánjīng's subway, which opened in fall 2005. The city is an important rail junction along the Běijīng–Shànghǎi railway line. Trains heading east to Shànghǎi (2½–3 hr.) connect to Wúxī (1½–2 hr.) and Sūzhōu (2–2½ hr.). There is no direct train to Hángzhōu,

Nánjīng

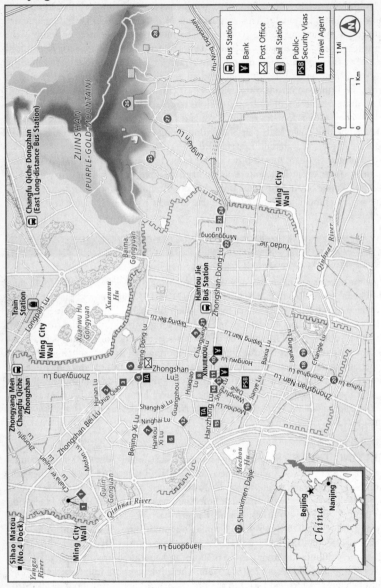

Legend:
- Bus Station
- ¥ Bank
- ✉ Post Office
- Rail Station
- **PSB** Public-Security Visas
- **TA** Travel Agent

1 Mi
1 Km

Changfu Qiche Dongzhan (East Long-distance Bus Station)

ZIJINSHAN (PURPLE-GOLD MOUNTAIN)

Hu-Ning Expressway

Longwang Lu

Ming City Wall

Qinhuai River

Yudao Jie

Minggugong Lu

Zhongshan Dong Lu

Hanfou Jie Bus Station

Baima Gongyuan

Xuanwu Hu

Xuanwu Hu Gongyuan

Train Station

Longpan Lu

Ming City Wall

Zhongyang Lu

Taiping Bei Lu

Beijing Dong Lu

Zhongshan Lu

Changjiang Lu

XINJIEKOU

Hongwu Lu

Taiping Nan Lu

Baixia Lu

Jiankang Lu

Changle Lu

Zhongshan Nan Lu

Zhongyang Men Changfu Qiche Zhongzhan

Zhongshan Bei Lu

Hunan Lu

Shizi Qiao

Beijing Xi Lu

Shanghai Lu

Guangzhou Lu

Ninghai Lu

Hankou Xi Lu

Zhongshan Lu

Wangfu Dajie

Hanzhong Lu

Mochou Lu

Jianye Lu

Jiankang Lu

Yuhua Lu

Yuhua Lu

Chang'er Huaqu Lu

Mofan Lu

Gulin Gongyuan

Qinhuai River

Mochou Hu

Shuiximen Dajie

Ming City Wall

Sihao Matou (No.4 Dock)

Yangzi River

Jiangdong Lu

China

Beijing

Nanjing

374

ACCOMMODATIONS ■

Celebrity City Hotel
(Míngrén Chéngshì Jiǔdiàn) **3**
名人城市酒店

Central Hotel
(Zhōngxīn Dàjiǔdiàn) **8**
中心大酒店

Crowne Plaza Nanjing Hotels and Suites
(Qiáo Hóng Huángguān Jiǔdiàn) **14**
金鹰皇冠酒店

Hilton Nánjīng
(Nánjīng Xīěrdùn Guójì Dàjiǔdiàn) **23**
南京希尔顿国际大酒店

Hotel Sheraton Nánjīng Kingsley
Hotel and Towers
(Nánjīng Jīnsīlì Xǐláidēng Jiǔdiàn) **15**
南京金斯利喜来登酒店

Jīnlíng Fàndiàn **11**
金陵饭店

Nánshān Bīnguǎn **6**
南山宾馆

Shangri-La Dīngshān
(Dīngshān Xiānggélǐlā) **1**
丁山香格里拉大酒店

DINING ◆

Bella Napoli
(Bèilānábōlǐ YìdàlìCāntīng) **10**
贝拉那波意大利餐厅

Jīnhé Tài Cāntōng
(Golden Harvest Thai Opera Café) **2**
金禾泰餐厅

Jīnyīng Dàjiǔlóu **13**
金鹰大酒楼

Lǎo Zhèng Xīng **19**
老正兴菜馆

Míng Yuán **1**
明园

New Magazine Café
(Xīn Zázhì Kāfēi) **7**
新杂志咖啡

1912/Coffee Beanery
(Juéshìdǎo Kāfēi) **9**
爵士岛咖啡

Swede & Kraut **12**

ATTRACTIONS ●

Cháotiān Gōng **16**
朝天宫

Dàzhōng Tíng **5**
大钟亭

Fūzǐ Miào
(Confucian Temple) **19**
夫子庙

Gǔ Lóu **4**
鼓楼

Jiāngnán Gòngyuàn Lìshǐ
Chénlièguǎn **19**
江南贡院历史陈列馆

Línggǔ Sì **27**
灵谷寺

Nánjīng Dàtúshā Jìniànguǎn
(Memorial to the Victims of the
Nánjīng Massacre) **17**
南京大屠杀纪念馆

Míng Xiào Líng
(Ming Filial Tomb) **25**
明孝陵

Míng Gù Gōng **22**
明故宫

Nánjīng Bówùguǎn
(Nánjīng Museum) **24**
南京博物馆

Sòng Měilíng's Villa
(Sòng Měilíng Gōngguǎ) **28**
宋美龄公馆

Tàipíng Tiānguó Lìshǐ Bówùguǎn
(Tàipíng Heavenly Kingdom
Historical Museum) **18**
太平天国历史博物馆

Zhōnghuá Mén Chéngbǎo **20**
中华门城堡

Zhōngshān Líng **26**
中山陵

Zǒngtǒng Fǔ
(Presidential Palace) **21**
总统府

although the 701 goes there via Shànghǎi. Heading west, there are trains to Huáng Shān (6½–10 hr.). You can buy tickets on the second floor of the three-story annex west of the station's exit. A special window selling only Shànghǎi tickets is marked in green; its hours are from 7 to 11am and from 11:30am to 6:30pm. You can also buy tickets at the Gǔ Lóu ticket-booking office at Zhōngshān Lù 293.

Nánjīng has seven **long-distance bus stations,** but the main one, Nánjīng Zhōngyāng Mén Chángtú Qìchē Zǒngzhàn, at Jiànníng Lù 1 (© **025/8553-1288**), just west of the Nánjīng Railway Station, should serve most travelers' needs. From here, large, air-conditioned buses run to Sūzhōu (every 20 min.; 2 hr., 40 min.; ¥46–¥64/$5.75–$8), Shànghǎi (every half-hour; 3½ hr.; ¥82–¥88/$10–$11), and Hángzhōu (hourly; 5 hr.; ¥98/$12). The Hànfú Jiē Bus Station (Chángtú Qìchēzhàn) at Chángjiāng Lù 296 (© **025/8454-1359**) also serves the same destinations. The East Long-Distance Bus Station (Chángtú Qìchē Dōng Zhàn) at Huāyuán Lù 17 services Yángzhōu (every half-hour; 1 hr.; ¥25/$3) and Yíxīng (every 20 min. 6:20am–6:40pm; 2½ hr.; ¥44/$5.50). There are also express "business" buses for ¥88 ($11) that leave for Shànghǎi at 8, 9, and 10am and 2, 3:30, and 4:30pm from the back entrance of the Jīnlíng Hotel.

For those with time to spare, **boats** run to Shànghǎi (daily; 19 hr.), Chóngqìng (daily; 6 days), and all points in between, from the rather forlorn **Sìhào Mǎtóu (No. 4 Dock;** © **025/5858-2345)** at the northwest edge of town. Ticketing hours are from 7 to 11am and from 12:30 to 8:30pm. Few travelers choose this option.

GETTING AROUND Nánjīng is a sprawling city not particularly conducive to walking, with sights scattered in different directions. The rate for **taxis** is ¥7 (90¢) for 3km (2 miles), then ¥2.40 (30¢) per kilometer. From 11pm to 6am, the price rises to ¥2.70 (35¢) per kilometer after 3km. Rickety motorcycle taxis charge ¥3 (40¢) for the first kilometer, after which you're on your own with your powers of negotiation. Be sure to agree on a price beforehand. **Buses** are a convenient and cheap way to get around Nánjīng, although they are almost always full. Pay ¥2 (25¢) for air-conditioned buses and ¥1 (15¢) for all others. No change is given. Some of the main bus routes include: no. 1: Nánjīng Railway Station–Xīnjiēkǒu–Fūzǐ Miào; no. Y1: Nánjīng Railway Station–Xīnjiēkǒu–Zhōngshān Líng; no. Y2: Yǔhuā Tái–Zǒngtǒng Fǔ–Zhōngshān Líng.

TOURS **Jiāngsū Zhōngshān International Travel Service** (Zhōngshān Běi Lù 204; © **025/8342-9700**) works with the major hotels to offer a standard 1-day tour of Nánjīng, including visits to Zhōngshān Líng (Dr. Sun Yat-sen's Mausoleum), Zǒngtǒng Fǔ (the Presidential Palace), and Cháotiān Gōng (Worshipping Heaven Palace), among other places. The cost of ¥150 ($18) includes entry fees and the use of a guide and bus driver.

VISITOR INFORMATION *MAP,* the free local English-language monthly magazine featuring the latest on dining and entertainment in Nánjīng, is available in any of the top hotels or in Western restaurants. Try the government-run **Nánjīng Tourist Information Center (Nánjīng Lǚyóu Zīxún Fúwù Zhōngxīn;** © **025/5226-9008**; 9am–5pm) in Confucius Temple for advice on sightseeing, restaurants, and hotels. The office is staffed by two very helpful employees.

FAST FACTS

Banks, Foreign Exchange & ATMs The main branch of the **Bank of China** is located at Zhōngshān Nán Lù 148. Hours for foreign exchange are Monday through Friday from 8:30am to noon and 2 to 5pm. ATMs accept international cards. Another branch is at Hóngwǔ Lù 29 with the same hours.

Internet Access Bring your passport or ID for Internet access at **China Telecom,** Zhōngyāng Lù 2 on the second floor (open 8:30am–5:30pm, ¥2/25¢ per hour). Dial-up is ✆ **169.** Free wireless laptop access is available the **Coffee Beanery** (in the 1912 entertainment complex at the corner of Chángjiāng Hòu Jiē and Tàipíng Běi Lù) and at all locations of **New Magazine Café** (see "Where to Dine," later in this section).

Post Office The main post office (8am–6:30pm) is at **Gǔ Lóu,** Zhōngshān Lù 366.

Visa Extensions The **PSB** is located at Hónggōng Cí 1 (✆ **025/8442-0004;** Apr–Sept Mon–Fri 8:30–11:30am and 3–5:30pm; Oct–May Mon–Fri 8:30–11:30am and 2:30–5pm). Same-day visas are possible. From Xīnjiēkǒu, walk 5 minutes south on Zhōngshān Nán Lù, then head west onto Sānyuán Xiāng for about 300m (980 ft.).

EXPLORING NÁNJĪNG
HISTORICAL SIGHTS

Sadly, Nánjīng's Míng legacy can be found in only a few buildings and ruins today. In the center of town, the drum tower **Gǔ Lóu** was built in 1382 and contained a series of drums used to mark the night watches, welcome guests, and occasionally warn of approaching enemies (admission to grounds free, ¥ 5/60¢ to enter the second floor of tower and teahouse). Close by is a pavilion, **Dàzhōng Tíng,** which houses a 23,000-kilogram (25-ton) bronze bell from 1388. Toward the eastern part of town are the ruins of the first Míng dynasty imperial palace, **Míng Gù Gōng.** All that remains of the once massive palace, destroyed in the Tàipíng Rebellion, are the Wǔ Mén (Meridian Gate) that once marked the front gate of the palace wall, five small marble bridges, and 12 large plinths that were once the foundation of another large gate. Sections of the Míng **city wall** are still visible.

Zhōnghuá Mén Chéngbǎo ✿
Located in the southern part of town, this is the biggest and best-preserved of the city wall's original 13 gates. Built by the Hóngwǔ emperor between 1366 and 1386, the wall, at 33km (20 miles), was the longest city wall in the world, made of uniform bricks cemented with a mortar of lime, sorghum, and glutinous rice. Zhōnghuá Gate, first built in 1386, actually consists of four rows of gates, the first one 53m (173 ft.) long. Each gate entrance had a vertically sliding stone door lifted with a mechanical winch. Twenty-seven arched vaults inside the first gate could house up to 3,000 soldiers, who were set to ambush the enemy should the latter be so unfortunate as to be trapped within the gates. Climb to the top for some good views of the city, and to gaze at the kitschy fake guards. Along the way, watch for bricks that still bear the carvings of their maker and supervisor. In front of the walls, locals fly kites bought from vendors for ¥8 ($1).

Zhōnghuá Mén. Admission ¥10 ($1.25). 8am–10pm.

Zǒngtǒng Fǔ (Presidential Palace) ✿✿
As the seat of government of the Liǎngjiāng viceroy's office (1671–1911), the Tàipíng Heavenly Kingdom (1853–64), Sun Yat-sen's provisional government (1912), and the Nationalist government (1927–37 and 1946–49), this fascinating but often overlooked site has borne witness to all the important events and personalities in Nánjīng's history. Though this presidential palace dates from the Míng dynasty, today's buildings were all built after 1870. Just inside the main entrance, the Great Hall marked by the words TIĀN XIÀ WÉI GŌNG (The world belongs to all) used to be the first in a series of nine magnificent halls during the Tàipíng Heavenly Kingdom. On January 1, 1912, provisional president of the new Chinese republic Sun Yat-sen held his inauguration here.

The Tàipíng Heavenly Kingdom

During the mid–19th century, natural disasters, catastrophic floods and famines, Western excesses, and Qīng government neglect and corruption had all coalesced to create widespread unrest in China. It was in such a setting that the largest uprising in modern Chinese history occurred. Known as the **Tàipíng Rebellion,** its impact continues to be felt even today.

The Tàipíng Rebellion started in the mind of Hóng Xiùquán (born Hóng Huǒxiù, 1814–64), a teacher and a farmer's son from Guǎngdōng Province. After Hóng failed his civil-service exams for the third time, he had a feverish dream of a bearded man and a younger man, whom he later decided were God the Father and Jesus. Hóng also kept seeing part of his own name, "Huǒ" in the Christian tract, which he interpreted as another divine calling. Convinced that he was God's son and Jesus' younger brother, and his mission from God was to "slash the demons"—the twin demons of the Manchu government and the traditional Chinese folk religion—Hóng formulated his own ideology, a mix of Christian ideals and Confucian utopianism. He soon amassed a large anti-Manchu, anti-establishment following in the south and in 1851 led a group of 20,000 followers to establish the **Tàipíng Heavenly Kingdom,** with Hóng himself as king. Using their army and any number of ragtag peasant militias they could muster along the way, the Tàipíngs swept up through south and central China and established themselves in Nánjīng in 1853, renaming the city Tiānjīng (Heavenly Capital).

The Tàipíngs preached a new order based on the equal distribution of land, equality between the sexes, monotheism, and the existence of small communities ruled by religious leadership, an order that, save for the religious bit,

After the second hall, the next series of rooms were used by Chiang Kai-shek, the leader of the Nationalist Party, to receive foreign guests, among them U.S. Gen. George Marshall, who was attempting to broker a truce between Chiang and Máo Zédōng. In the back, Chiang Kai-shek's former office has an interesting old-fashioned hand-operated Otis elevator, which has now been restored. In Xūyuán, the garden on the western side of the compound, a stone boat is the only remaining original artifact from the days of the Tàipíng Heavenly Kingdom.

Chángjiāng Lù 292. Admission ¥30 ($3.75) Oct 16–Apr 14; ¥40 ($5) Apr 15–Oct 15. English-speaking guides ¥60 ($7.50). Apr–Oct 7:30am–6pm; Nov–Mar 8am–5pm. Bus: no. 1, 2, 29, 44, 65, 95, or 304.

Fūzǐ Miào (Confucian Temple) Kitschy it may be, but this is where you'll get a good idea of the modern interests of Nánjīng's youth. Once a place of intense study and quiet contemplation, Fūzǐ Miào is now the site for everything from tattoo parlors to pirated music stores selling the latest Mandarin hits. To the right (east) was once the Jiāngnán Gòngyuàn, an academy first built in 1169 and which later became the largest imperial civil examination halls during the Míng and Qīng dynasties, with over 20,000 cells for examinees. Today, a handful of rooms have been restored into a museum, the **Jiāngnán Gòngyuàn Lìshǐ Chénlièguǎn.** Tourists can reenact part of the examination process by donning period robes and Míng dynasty hats and sequestering themselves in the was to prefigure some of the tenets of the Chinese Communist movement. Feudalism, slavery, concubinage, arranged marriages, opium smoking, foot binding, prostitution, idolatry, and alcohol were all to be abolished (at least in theory). While women under the Tàipíng were allowed a greater degree of freedom (there was even a Tàipíng army made up entirely of female troops), Tàipíng morals continued to stress obedience and chastity in women. Hóng Xiùquán and other Tàipíng leaders also continued to keep harems, in that way no different from any of China's emperors or even Máo Zédōng, who was known to maintain his own.

In the end, however, the Tàipíngs were doomed by a combination of internecine struggles, corruption, defections, flawed policies, and external forces made up of a reconstituted Qīng army aided by Western powers who had apparently decided they would rather deal with the devil they knew (the Qīng government) than contend with the uncertainties of a strong Tàipíng force, even though they were closer to them in ideals. The counter-attack was brutal and merciless, and by the time the Chinese army suc-ceeded in crushing the revolt 14 years after it began, a reported 30 million lives had been lost. Hóng Xiùquán himself died of illness in 1864 but his suc-cessor, his 14-year old son, was killed by Qīng troops.

It is uncanny how so many facets of the Tàipíng Rebellion would be echoed in later Chinese events. The ability of one man to command such a large fanatical uprising and sustain it for so long would later be paralleled in Máo's Cultural Revolution (1966–76). The effects of such large mass upris-ings also help explain the current Chinese leadership's fear of them.

cells, which have white walls, bare concrete floors, and two boards stretched across the cells as a seat and a table.

Jiànkāng Lù. Confucian Temple ¥15 ($1.90); museum ¥10 ($1.25). 8am–10pm (last ticket sold at 9pm). Bus: no. 1 from Nánjīng Railway Station and Xīnjiēkǒu to Fūzǐ Miào.

Cháotiān Gōng   One of the earliest documented sites in Nánjīng, this former foundry and soldier training ground during the Spring and Autumn Period (722–481 B.C.) was a temple used by the Hóngwǔ emperor (1382–98) as a ceremonial place of worship, hence Cháotiān or "heaven-worshipping." The place was rebuilt in the Qīng dynasty as a Confucian temple and academy. Today, the main hall, Dàchéng Diàn, houses a fascinating **Six Dynasties museum.** Exhibits include a locally unearthed Roman glass, a compass vehicle, and immortality pills, which obviously didn't work. The English explanations are quite good. Outside of the temple, an antiques market sells jade knickknacks and Máo posters.

Cháotiān Gōng 4. Admission ¥30 ($4). 8am–5pm. Bus: no. 4 from Fūzǐ Miào to Cháotiān Gōng.

MEMORIALS & MUSEUMS

For ¥80 ($10) you can buy a combination ticket that will give you access to Zhōngshān Líng, Míng Xiào Líng, and Línggǔ Sì; a shuttle (¥3/45¢) runs between these sights from morning until evening.

ZĪJĪN SHĀN

Zǐjīn Shān (Purple Gold Mountain), located on the eastern edge of town, got its name from the mountain's purple shales, which were said to have lent the place a mysterious purple aura at dawn and dusk. Covered with dense forests and dotted with the occasional lake, the mountain has always been a pleasant retreat for locals seeking relief from Nánjīng's heat. It's also home to some important historical sites. Spend the day if you can, but if you have limited time, then the highlight is surely Zhōngshān Líng.

Zhōngshān Líng ✿✿ This magnificent mausoleum for Dr. Sun Yat-sen (Sūn Zhōngshān), widely revered as the founder of modern China, has become a mecca for Chinese tourists seeking to pay their respects. Sun Yat-sen died in Běijīng in 1925 but wasn't interred here until 1929, when construction of the mausoleum was complete. (In 1912, while hunting with friends in Zǐjīn Shān, Sun had expressed his wish to be buried here.) The tomb itself is at the end of a long, steep set of stairs beginning with a Memorial Archway made of white Fújiàn marble and capped by blue glazed tiles. Symbolizing the white sun on the blue background of the Guómíndǎng flag, the colors also marked a departure from the yellow tiles used to honor all of China's previous emperors. At the top of the 392-step grand tomb passage, a white marble statue of Dr. Sun sits under the pretty mosaic roof of the Memorial Hall. The Republican government's constitution is inscribed on the side walls. Dr. Sun's marble coffin lies in the hushed domed chamber in the back. On the way down, you'll be treated to a nice view of downtown Nánjīng and its surroundings. Make sure to get here early or late in the afternoon, as the place fills up like a zoo.

Admission ¥40 ($5), or by ¥80 ($10) combination ticket (see "Memorials & Museums," above). Apr–Nov 6am–7pm; Dec–Mar 6am–5:30pm. Bus: no. Y1 (from the Nánjīng Railway Station) or 9 (from Xīnjiēkǒu).

Míng Xiào Líng (Míng Filial Tomb) ✿ More peaceful than Sun Yat-sen's mausoleum is the tomb of the founder of the Míng dynasty, Zhū Yuánzhāng (1328–98), also known as the Hóngwǔ emperor. The tomb served as a model for subsequent Míng and Qīng emperors' tombs in Běijīng. The site has recently been polished up with funds from UNESCO after being deemed a World Heritage Site, but the explanations of the tombs are only in Chinese with strange diagrams. Zhū Yuánzhāng was the only Míng emperor to be buried in Nánjīng. The Sacrificial Palace, one of the tomb's main buildings built in 1383, houses memorial tablets. The Míng Tower, a rectangular citadel, served as the command point of the tomb. Nearby, **Shíxiàng Lù** is a pleasant walkway half a kilometer long lined with stone carvings of 12 pairs of animals. The second half of the passageway, flanked by pairs of soldiers and mandarins, leads to Four Square Pavillion, which consists of a tall stone tablet enclosed by four walls. Built in 1413, the pavilion's tablet contains 2,000 characters inscribed with the life story of the emperor Zhū Yuángzhāng, written by his son Zhū Dì.

Admission ¥50 ($6), or by ¥80 ($10) combination ticket (see "Memorials & Museums," above). Apr–Nov 6:30am–6:30pm; Dec–Mar 7am–6pm. Bus: no. Y2 or Y3.

Línggǔ Sì Hidden amid the tall conifers east of Zhōngshān Líng, the fascinating Wúliáng Diàn (Beamless Hall), the only surviving edifice of this original Míng dynasty temple, is notable for having been built entirely from bricks without a single wood beam. From the outside, the building is beautiful, but unfortunately, the inside has been turned into a wax museum of key historical leaders from the early 20th century. China's Republican government erected a cemetery on the grounds of the temple in 1933 to commemorate soldiers.

Admission ¥15 ($1.90), or by ¥80 ($10) combination ticket (see "Memorials & Museums," above). Apr–Nov 6:30am–6:30pm; Dec–Mar 7am–6pm.

Sòng Měilíng's Villa   A beautiful, high-ceiled villa with a traditional Chinese roof, this is where Chiang Kai-shek and his wife, better known as Madame Chiang Kai-shek, often spent weekends when China's capital was located in Nánjīng. The second floor consists of a massive bedroom, parlors, and a dining room decorated with large National government maps.

Admission ¥10 ($1.25). 7:30am–6pm.

OTHER ATTRACTIONS

Nánjīng Bówùguǎn (Nánjīng Museum) ⟨★⟩   Situated in an impressively sleek and clean building, the Nánjīng Museum is worth at least an hour or two of your time. Standouts include the **Lacquerware Hall** with an exquisitely carved Qīng dynasty throne; the **Jadeware Hall** featuring an Eastern Hàn dynasty jade burial suit sewn together with silver from A.D. 200; and the **Fabric Embroidery Hall,** where visitors can view a demonstration of cloud-pattern brocade weaving on an old-fashioned loom. The basement level houses a nice folk-art section and earthenware from the Táng dynasty. The museum shop sells a wide selection of art and crafts.

Zhōngshān Dōng Lù 321. Admission ¥20 ($2.50). 9am–4:30pm. Bus: no. Y1, Y2, or 9 to Zhōnghuá Mén.

Nánjīng Dàtúshā Jìniànguǎn (Memorial to the Victims of the Nánjīng Massacre) ⟨★⟩   While worth a visit, this memorial museum, commemorating the atrocities suffered by the Chinese during the Japanese invasion of Nánjīng in 1937, certainly does

The Nánjīng Massacre

On December 13, 1937, Japanese troops invaded Nánjīng. What followed were the darkest 6 weeks of Nánjīng's history, as over 300,000 Chinese were bayoneted, shot, burned, drowned, beheaded, and buried alive. The city was looted and torched, and corpses were thrown into the Yángzǐ River. Women suffered the most: During the first month of occupation, 20,000 cases of rape were reported in the city. Many of those who survived were often tortured.

During this time, a small number of Western businessmen and American missionaries, who stayed behind when their compatriots fled after the departing Chinese government, used their privileged status as foreign nationals to create a 3.9-sq.-km (1½-sq.-mile) safety zone covering today's Hànzhōng Lù in the south, Zhōngshān Lù in the east, Shǎnxī Lù in the north, and Xīkàng Lù in the west. Around 250,000 Chinese found safe haven in 25 refugee camps inside it. The head of the safety zone was German businessman John Rabe, chosen in part because he was a Nazi. Often described as the Oskar Schindler of China, Rabe's initial determination to save his Siemens Chinese employees eventually took on a larger purpose as he even sheltered hundreds of Chinese women in his own backyard. There were countless individual moments of courage, too, as Chinese clawed their way out of mass graves, crawled to hospitals with bullet wounds, or sheltered their brethren at great risk to themselves.

a heavy-handed job of explaining history, from the funerary-style orchestral music piped on the grounds to the giant statues of human limbs that greet visitors at the museum's entrance. Located at Jiāng Dōng Mén, itself an execution and mass burial site during the invasion, the museum consists of an outdoor exhibit, a coffin-shaped viewing hall containing some excavated victims' bones, and pictures and artifacts documenting the Japanese onslaught, the massacre, and the aftermath. Photographs of tortures and executions, many taken by Japanese army photographers, are quite gruesome, as are reproductions of the blood-soaked clothing of the victims. The final room documents the reconciliation, however tenuous, between the Chinese and Japanese.

Chátíng Dōng Jiē 195, Jiāng Dōng Mén. Free admission. 8am–5pm. Bus: no. Y4 or 7.

Tàipíng Tiānguó Lìshǐ Bówùguǎn (Tàipíng Heavenly Kingdom Historical Museum) The largest uprising in modern Chinese history, the Tàipíng Rebellion is documented here in pictures and artifacts including Tàipíng maps, coins, and weapons. Unfortunately, the descriptions don't explain the rebellion particularly well. The museum itself is located in **Zhàn Yuán,** a garden that was the residence of the Tàipíng "Eastern Prince," Yáng Xiùqīng, and the young "Western Prince," Xiāo Yǒuhé. Visitors can relax in the garden and ponder China's 5,000 years of history while watching goldfish in a pond.

Zhàn Yuán Lù 128. Admission ¥10 ($1.25). Museum 8am–5pm; park 8am–11pm. Bus: no. Y2 to Chánglè Lù.

WHERE TO STAY

The glut of upmarket hotels in Nánjīng has resulted in generous discounts, averaging between 30% and 50% in low season (plus a 15% service charge).

VERY EXPENSIVE

Shangri-La Dīngshān (Dīngshān Xiānggélǐlā) ✿✿✿ Although its location in the northwest part of the city makes it less accessible to sights and restaurants in town, this classy hotel delivers the signature service of the Shangri-La name. Rooms, all tastefully furnished in a mix of contemporary and Asian styles, are the largest and most luxurious in Nánjīng: Each has a private balcony, separate study area, and large bathroom. There is also a four-star annex with smaller and slightly less luxurious rooms, but offering the same friendly and efficient service.

Cháhāěr Lù 90. ✆ 025/5880-2888. Fax 025/5882-1729. www.shangri-la.com. 453 units. ¥1,810 ($220) standard room; from ¥2,900 ($350) suite. AE, DC, MC, V. **Amenities:** 3 restaurants; bar; lounge; nightclub; indoor pool; health club and spa; sauna; concierge; shuttle service to town; business center; forex; shopping arcade; salon; limited room service; massage; laundry/dry cleaning; executive rooms. *In room:* A/C, satellite TV, broadband Internet access, minibar, hair dryer, safe.

EXPENSIVE

Crowne Plaza Nánjīng Hotels and Suites (Qiáo Hóng Huángguān Jiǔdiàn) ✿✿ Suites are this hotel's specialty, which accounts for its popularity with business travelers, but tourists love it, too, for its prime location a block west of Xīnjiēkǒu, right in the thick of the city. Unconventionally located in an office building, the hotel has its entrance and concierge on the first floor, its lobby and other facilities on the seventh and ninth floors, and its guest rooms on the 37th to 58th floors. Guests are treated to a personalized sit-down check-in, then whisked up to their rooms high above the city center. Look down from the city's tallest building and understand why the hotel prides itself on its views, especially at night when the daytime smog gives way to twinkling neon lights. Guest rooms are classically furnished and bathrooms have separate shower and tub.

Hànzhōng Lù 89. ⓒ **025/8471-8888.** Fax 025/8471-9999. www.crowneplaza.com. 300 units. ¥864 ($108) standard room; ¥1,264–¥1,504 ($158–$188) suite. AE, DC, MC, V. **Amenities:** 4 restaurants; bar; lounge; nightclub; indoor pool; health club; sauna; concierge; airport shuttle; business center; forex; shopping arcade; salon; 24-hr. room service; massage; babysitting; laundry/dry cleaning; executive rooms. *In room:* A/C, TV, broadband Internet access, dataport, minibar, hair dryer, safe.

Hilton Nánjīng (Nánjīng Xīěrdùn Guójì Dàjiǔdiàn) ⌗   Inconveniently located at the eastern end of town at Zhōngshān Mén, the Hilton is showing signs of age. Though it has an impressive lobby, the rooms could be better. There's noticeably fewer staff than in competing hotels, but the Hilton folks try to make up for any inconvenience by being extra helpful and offering huge discounts. Rooms are very comfortable but they are not always well fitted for the modern, connected traveler (there's a distinct shortage of electrical outlets in the standard rooms, for example).

Zhōngshān Dōng Lù 319. ⓒ **025/8480-8888.** Fax 025/8480-9999. www.hilton.com. 561 units. ¥1,440 ($200) standard room; ¥2,000 ($250) executive room. Discounts possible up to 60%. AE, DC, MC, V. **Amenities:** 4 restaurants; deli; bar; lounge; disco; indoor pool; tennis courts; health club and spa; sauna; bowling alley; concierge; business center; forex; shopping arcade; salon; limited room service; laundry/dry cleaning; executive rooms. *In room:* A/C, satellite TV, broadband Internet access (executive rooms), minibar, hair dryer, safe.

Hotel Sheraton Nánjīng Kingsley Hotel and Towers (Nánjīng Jīnsīlì Xīláidēng Jiǔdiàn) ⌗⌗   Located about 1km (⅔ mile) west of Xīnjiēkǒu, this sleek and modern glass tower with a state-of-the-art elevator control system (makes a maximum of three stops per run) is a popular choice with foreign business travelers. Travelers fed up with shabby three-star accommodations in China will find the Sheraton a welcome change. The Sheraton also boasts the largest hotel swimming pool and health club in town. Rooms are tastefully decorated and comfortable, and afford good views of the city; those on executive floors come with personal butler service. Bathrooms are large and contain separate shower and tub.

Hànzhōng Lù 169. ⓒ **025/8666-8888.** Fax 025/8666-9999. www.Sheraton.com/Nanjing. 350 units. ¥1,494 ($180) standard room; ¥1,660–¥2,490 ($200–$300) suite. AE, DC, MC, V. **Amenities:** 4 restaurants; bar; lounge; disco; indoor pool; tennis court; health club and spa; sauna; salon; concierge; business center; forex; shopping arcade; limited room service; massage; laundry/dry cleaning; executive rooms. *In room:* A/C, TV, dataport, broadband Internet access, minibar, hair dryer, safe.

Jīnlíng Fàndiàn ⌗   Don't let the fact that this is a state-owned hotel turn you off. The 37-story Jīnlíng has been a local institution since it opened in 1983 and has worked to keep its reputation. Its exalted status has made it arrogant on occasion but its wide range of facilities and shops, not to mention its ideal location right at the city center, make it the place to be for many business travelers and tourists. Standard rooms run small but are functional, and come with large plasma-screen TVs that guests rave about. Rooms are decorated in a smart, minimalist style and bathrooms are sparkling clean.

Xīnjiēkǒu. ⓒ **025/8471-1888.** Fax 025/8471-1666. www.jinlinghotel.com. 600 units. ¥1,410 ($176) standard room; ¥2,490–¥3,485 ($311–$435) suite. AE, DC, MC, V. **Amenities:** 7 restaurants; bar; lounge; karaoke; disco; cigar bar; indoor pool; health club and spa; simulated golf driving range; bowling alley; concierge; business center; forex; shopping arcade; salon; limited room service; laundry/dry cleaning; executive rooms. *In room:* A/C, TV, broadband Internet access, minibar, hair dryer, safe.

MODERATE
Celebrity City Hotel (Míngrén Chéngshì Jiǔdiàn)   This hotel was meant to be a Marriott, but after negotiations fell through, it opened at the end of 2004 as a Chinese-owned four-star establishment. Rooms are tastefully decorated, and deluxe rooms come with desktop computers. One big draw is that the hotel offers free broadband Internet

access in its rooms. Bathrooms have a slight funky smell to them, but on the plus side, they come with a self-cleaning Japanese-style toilet and a massaging shower head.

Zhōngshān Lù 30. ☎ 025/8312-3333. Fax 025/8212-3888. www.yilaicch.com. 368 units. ¥1,080 ($135) standard room; ¥1,380 ($173) deluxe room; ¥1,480 ($185) suite. 50% discounts possible. AE, DC, MC, V. **Amenities:** 2 restaurants; bar; indoor swimming pool; fitness center; sauna; game room; conference center; limited room service; massage; karaoke; nonsmoking rooms; rooms for those w/limited mobility. *In room:* A/C TV, broadband Internet access, desktop computer (deluxe rooms and suites).

Central Hotel (Zhōngxīn Dàjiǔdiàn) ✎ Looking somewhat weathered on the outside, this popular four-star hotel in the round still draws visitors with its spacious, recently renovated rooms, competitive prices, and great location a block north of Xīnjiēkǒu. Amenities, however, do not seem particularly standardized in the rooms, so be sure to request rooms containing whatever specific item you may need. Bathrooms are clean.

Zhōngshān Lù 75. ☎ 025/8473-3888. Fax 0258/473-3999. 320 units. ¥880–¥980 ($110–$123) standard room; ¥2,200 ($275) suite. 40% discounts possible. AE, DC, MC, V. **Amenities:** 5 restaurants; bar; lounge; nightclub; outdoor pool; health club; sauna; bowling alley; game room; concierge; business center; forex; shopping arcade; salon; limited room service; laundry. *In room:* A/C, satellite TV, broadband Internet access (select rooms), minibar, hair dryer, safe.

INEXPENSIVE

Nánshān Bīnguǎn Located in the southwestern corner of the Nánjīng Normal University campus about a 15-minute taxi ride northwest of Xīnjiēkǒu, this hotel is a no-frills budget choice that's nevertheless clean and comfortable. The hotel also houses foreign students studying at the university. Rooms are spartan but the small bathrooms are clean.

Nínghǎi Lù 122. ☎ 025/8371-6440. Fax 025/8373-8174. 200 units. ¥198 ($25) standard room; ¥268–¥588 ($33–$73) suite. No credit cards. **Amenities:** Cafeteria; Internet bar; ticket service; salon. *In room:* A/C, TV.

WHERE TO DINE
EXPENSIVE

Jīnhé Tài Cāntīng (Golden Harvest Thai Opera Café) THAI Located in the Húnán Lù dining area known as Shīzi Qiáo, this restaurant serves decent Thai food and is popular with Nánjīng's expats. A golden Buddha statue outside greets arriving guests, while the decor inside is tasteful and subdued. Besides the typical solid curries and pad Thai, Golden Harvest features several specialties, including a good fried crab with Thai curry sauce and a casserole of baked king prawns with vermicelli noodles.

Húnán Lù Shīzī Qiáo 2. ☎ 025/8324-2525. Reservations recommended. English menus with pictures. Meal for 2 ¥150–¥250 ($19–$31). No credit cards. 10:30am–2:30pm and 5–10:30pm.

Jīnyīng Dàjiǔlóu ✎ HUÁIYÁNG Established in 1998 with only eight tables, this restaurant has since grown into a top restaurant with two locations. The house specialty is *Tiānmùhú yútóu,* a delicious white fish–head soup made with fish from nearby Tiānmù Lake. Other tasty dishes here include *shuǐjīng xiārén* (tender sautéed shrimp) and *pánsī yú* (deep-fried fish-tail filets in sweet-and-sour sauce).

Nánjīng location: Wángfǔ Dàjiē 9. ☎ 025/8452-0088. Reservations recommended. Meal for 2 ¥120–¥250 ($15–$31). No credit cards. 11:30am–2:30pm and 5:30–10pm.

Míng Yuán ✎✎✎ DĪNG SHĀN/HUÁIYÁNG For amazingly good cuisine that's unique to Nánjīng, head out to the Shangri-La Hotel located on a small hill, Dīng Shān, in the northwest part of town. Created here by chefs more than 20 years ago, Dīng Shān cuisine has become an integral part of Nánjīng's culinary lore. Among the restaurant's many specialties, the drunken crab Dīng Shān style (crab steeped in wine, honey, and spices for a week and served raw) is exquisite, as is the sautéed Yúnnán mushroom with crab paste (crab and wild mushrooms served in a spicy sauce). Finish with the signature fish noodle, very fine handmade noodles cooked in a rich fish broth.

Shangri-La Dīng Shān, Cháhǎěr Lù 90. ✆ 025/5880-2888. Reservations recommended. Main courses from ¥160 ($20). AE, DC, MC, V. 11:30am–2pm and 5:30–10pm.

MODERATE

Bella Napoli (Bèilānábōlǐ Yìdàlì Cāntīng) ITALIAN   The fine homemade pasta and wood-fired pizzas at this classic-style Italian eatery should satisfy anyone's craving for home. Naples-born chef Giuseppi Parisi offers up to 98 dishes, including the not-quite-Italian king prawns and T-bone steak, but his signature dish is his own creation, the Mezza-Luna, a half-moon pizza that's part calzone. Bella Napoli is located 1 block east of Xīnjiēkǒu.

Zhōngshān Dōng Lù 75. ✆ 025/8471-8397. Main courses ¥45–¥128 ($5.60–$16). AE, DC, MC, V. Sun–Thurs 11am–2pm and 5–10:30pm; Fri–Sat 11am–midnight.

Swede & Kraut EUROPEAN   The restaurant gets its name from its owners, a Swede and a German. The restaurant, open for dinner only, serves Wiener schnitzel, pizzas, pastas, and salads. Recommended are the decent pastas (with fresh-grated Parmesan), good steaks, and excellent profiteroles for dessert. Located near Nánjīng University, this is a popular place for expats and well-heeled locals.

Xīnjiēkǒu, Huáqiáo Lù 33. ✆ 025/470-1292. Main courses ¥38–¥98 ($4.75–$12). No credit cards. 9:30am–10:30pm. Bus: no. 29 to Huáqiáo Lù.

INEXPENSIVE

Lǎo Zhèng Xīng NÁNJĪNG STREET FOOD   For a fun and authentic experience, head to this cafeteria located in Confucius Temple. In true state-owned fashion, diners go to the cashier to trade money for paper tickets, before heading to individual stalls where the tickets can be redeemed for an array of snacks, including steamed dumplings and glutinous rice wrapped in bamboo leaves. The best part is just being able to point to what you want. The adventurous should try the duck-blood vermicelli (*yaxue fensi*).

Confucius Temple. No phone. ¥4–¥10 (50¢–$1.20) per person. No credit cards. Mon–Fri 9am–9pm; Sat–Sun 9am–9:30pm.

New Magazine Café (Xīn Zázhì Kāfēi) ECLECTIC 🐾   You might come here for the free wireless access but you should stay for the food, which ranges from Western-style pastas to chicken teriyaki to Sichuanese spicy noodles. Teas, in flavors from hazelnut to almond, are brought to the table in porcelain pots resting on a small fire. The cafe also features a rack of Chinese magazines for sale and a range of pastries.

Three locations. Hànkǒu Lù 42, ✆ 025/8324-8932; Chángbái Jiē 488, ✆ 025/8451-2013; and Húnán Lù 18, ✆ 025/5792-3505. Main courses ¥25–¥40 ($3–$5). No credit cards. 9:30am–1:30am.

SHOPPING

Nánjīng's biggest **art gallery,** Jīnyīng Yìshù Zhōngxīn Huàláng (Golden Eagle Art Center), located at Hànzhōng Lù 89, 11th floor, has a large collection of traditional Chinese ink paintings, calligraphy, and modern oil paintings. Nánjīng Yúnjūn Yánjiūsuǒ (Brocade Research Institute) at Chátíng Dōng Lù 240 (open 8:30am–4:30pm) sells **cloud dragon brocade** once reserved exclusively for use by emperors. Prices are high but this is the real deal. The Nánjīng Gōngyì Měishù Dàlóu Gòuwù Zhōngxīn at Běijīng Dōng Lù 31; 9am–5:40pm) has two floors of fairly expensive **handicrafts** from all over China, including jade, silk embroidery, fans, lacquerware, pottery, and jewelry. At the other end of the price and taste spectrum, shops at Fūzǐ Miào sell all kinds of local products, including rain flower pebbles, rain flower tea, hanging ornaments, and Nánjīng salted duck.

The trendy **night market** on Húnán Lù between Zhōngshān Běi Lù and Zhōngyāng Lù sells everything from Tibetan silver jewelry and tattoo patches to rock-bottom priced CDs and DVDs. The smaller but calmer night market at Yúnnán Lù hosts vendors who sell ethnic batik arts, embroidered bags, jewelry, underwear, and household items.

NÁNJĪNG AFTER DARK

To find out what's happening in the arts, pick up a copy of the free English-language monthly *Map*.

Chinese *kūn jù* opera is usually performed at the **Jiāngnán Theater** (Yánlíng Xiāng 5; ⓒ 025/440-4281), while traditional Běijīng Opera is performed at the **People's Theater** (Yánggōngjǐng 25; ⓒ 025/450-1314, ext. 8009). Performances usually begin at 7:30pm.

Around the corner from the Presidential Palace, **1912** is a district of bars, cafes, clubs, and restaurants that debuted in 2005; check with your hotel for more info. **Danny's Irish Pub (Dānnī'ěr Ài'ěrlán Jiǔbā)**, located on the fourth floor of the Sheraton Hotel, Hànzhōng Lù 169 (open 6:30pm–2am) is the most popular bar with Nánjīng's expatriates. For dancing, **Time Tunnel (Shíguāng Suìdào)**, at Tàipíng Nán Lù 354, has the largest dance floor in Nánjīng and a nightly laser show to boot. The wild **Scarlet (Luànshì Jiārén)**, at Gǔ Lóu Chēzhàn Dōngxiāng 29, has been known to give foreigners a discount on entry fees in order to entice the locals.

10 Yángzhōu ⓒ⁄ⓒ

Jiāngsū Province, 240km (149 miles) NW of Shànghǎi, 100km (62 miles) NE of Nánjīng

Located at the junction of the Yángzǐ River and the Grand Canal, Yángzhōu was known during the Suí and Táng dynasties as the economic and cultural center of southern China, home to scholars, painters, poets, literati, and merchants. It was also the playground of the rich and famous, starting with the 6th-century Suí Yángdì emperor, who visited courtesans here. The Qīng Qiánlóng emperor visited six times. Today Yángzhōu is a charming town with broad, tree-lined boulevards and a network of canals and lakes. Known for its handicrafts, cuisine, and landmarks, Yángzhōu certainly has enough to keep you occupied for a couple of days, but it can also be a day trip from Nánjīng.

ESSENTIALS

GETTING THERE   The nearest **airport** is in Nánjīng and the closest **railway** station is in Zhènjiāng. **Buses** serve Zhènjiāng (every 15 min. 6:30am–6:25pm; 1 hr.; ¥13/$1.50) and Nánjīng (every 20 min. 6:30am–6pm; 1½ hr.; ¥25/$3) from the **West Bus Station (Yángzhōu Xī Zhàn;** ⓒ 0514/786-1812) in the southwest of the city. Buses to Shànghǎi (7 daily 6:40am–3pm; 3–3½ hr.; ¥70–¥84/$9–$11) and Sūzhōu (7 daily 7:15am–4:40pm; 2 hr.; ¥57/$7) depart from the **long-distance bus station** (*chángtú qìchēzhàn*) in southeast Yángzhōu on Dùjiāng Nán Lù 27 (ⓒ 0514/781-3658).

GETTING AROUND   Most of Yángzhōu's sights are clustered in the north of town. **Taxis** charge ¥6 (75¢) for 3km (2 miles), then ¥1 (15¢) per kilometer until

Yángzhōu

China
Beijing ★
Yangzhou

Pingshantang Lu
To Han Dynasty Tomb Museum
Changchun Lu
Youyi Lu
Shikefa Lu
Bai Ta
Shou Xi Hu Gongyuan
Da Hongqiao Lu
Shou Xi Hu entrance
Yanfu Lu
Grand Canal
Dongguan Jie
PSB
Siwangting Lu
Huaihai Lu
Dongguan Men
Wenchang Xi Lu
TA
Wenchang Zhong Lu
Daxue Lu
Wenhe Lu
Guoqing Lu
Gangquan Lu
Guangling Lu
Natong Lu
1/2 Mi
.5 Km
To Xizhan (West Bus Station)
Jiangyang Zhong Lu
Jiangyang Dong Lu

Bus Station
¥ Bank
Mosque
Pagoda
Post Office
PSB Public-Security Visas
TA Travel Agent

ACCOMMODATIONS ■

Grand Metropole Hotel
(Yángzhōu Jìnghuá Dàjiǔdiàn) **12**
扬州京华大酒店

Xīyuán Dàjiǔdiàn 5
西园大酒店

Yángzhōu Bīnguǎn 6
扬州宾馆

Yángzhōu State Guesthouse
(Yángzhōu Yíngbīnguǎ) **3**
扬州迎宾馆

DINING ◆

Fùchūn Cháshè 13
富春茶舍

**Gāojiāzhuāng Hǎixiān
Cháoshì Jiǔlóu 8**
高家庄海鲜超市酒楼

ATTRACTIONS ●

Dàmíng Sì 1
大明寺

Gè Yuán 9
个园

Hàn Mù Bówùguǎn
(Hàn Dynasty Tomb Museum) **4**
汉墓博物馆

Hé Yuán 14
何园

Mountain Flattening Hall
(Píng Shān Táng) **1**
平山堂

Pǔhādīng Yuán 11
普哈丁园

Shòu Xī Hú (Slender West Lake) 2
瘦西湖

Wàng Shì Xiǎ Yuàn 10
汪氏小园

Yángzhōu Shì Bówùguǎn (Yángzhōu City Museum) 7
扬州市博物馆

10km (6 miles), after which the price rises to ¥1.50 (20¢) per kilometer. **Bus** no. 5 (¥1/15¢) runs from the long-distance bus station in the southwest of town up Huái-hǎi Lù to Dàmíng Sì.

TOURS & GUIDES **China Travel Service (CTS)** at Wénchāng Zhōng Lù 200 (© 0514/734-0524; Mon–Fri 7:30am–8pm) can arrange accommodations, plane tickets, and city tours. English-speaking guides will cost around ¥200 ($25) a day, transportation not included.

The Grand Canal

At 1,800km (1,116 miles), the Grand Canal (Dà Yùnhé) is the longest canal in the world. Together with the Great Wall of China, this waterway, which runs from Běijīng to Hángzhōu, is one of China's great engineering feats. The first 85km (52 miles) were constructed as early as 495 B.C., but the Herculean task of linking the Yellow River and Yángzǐ River began in earnest in the early 7th century, when the second Suí dynasty Yáng Dì emperor had the waterway dug from his capital at Luòyáng to Běijīng in the north and to the Yángzǐ River basin. Due to the differences in terrain and water levels, locks and dams had to be built along the way.

The original purpose of the canal was to transport the plentiful grains of the affluent south to the poorer north, but over the course of the years, the canal became a major trade conduit as commodities such as tea, silk, porcelain, lacquerware, and salt were all shipped up north. By the time of the Yuán dynasty (1206–1368), the final stretch of the canal was completed, linking Běijīng all the way to Hángzhōu. Many of the bricks and stones used to build Běijīng's temples and palaces arrived via the canal. By the time of the Southern Sòng dynasty (1127–1279), political power had shifted south to Jiāngsū and Zhèjiāng provinces, as the Sòng emperors moved their capital to Hángzhōu and the Míng emperors established themselves in Nánjīng.

The canal only fell into disuse in the early 20th century, thanks to constant flooding from the Yellow River, silting, and the development of rail lines. Today, the navigable sections are primarily south of the Yángzǐ River in the region known as Jiāngnán, which includes the cities of Wúxī, Yángzhōu, Sūzhōu, and Hángzhōu. Even here, some sections are so shallow and narrow that they are accessible only to small, flat-bottomed boats. North of the Yángzǐ, much is silted up and impassable.

Tourists wanting to experience life on the canal can sail between Hángzhōu and Sūzhōu and/or Wúxī. In Sūzhōu, canal boat passage can be booked at travel agencies or directly at the dock, Nán Mén Lúnchuán Kèyùn Mǎtóu, at Rénmín Lù 8 (© 0512/6520-5720). Boats, which are bare-bones basic, depart from the Sūzhōu Boat Terminal daily at 5:30pm, arriving in Hángzhōu at around 7am. The reverse voyage also departs Hángzhōu at 5:30pm and gets into Sūzhōu at around 7am. Tickets either way cost the same and can be purchased in Hángzhōu at the Wǔlín Mén Kèyùn Mǎtóu (© 0571/8515-3185). For information on boats to and from Wúxī, see "Getting There" in the "Wúxī, Tài Hú & Yíxīng" section, below.

FAST FACTS

Banks, Foreign Exchange & ATMs   The **Bank of China** at Wénchāng Zhōng Lù 279 conducts foreign exchange Monday to Friday from 8:30 to 11:45am and 3 to 5:30pm. An ATM is located here.

Internet Access   There's a **24-hour Internet cafe** at Liùhú Lù 34. It charges ¥2 (25¢) per hour. Dial-up is © **163.**

Post Office   Located at Wénchāng Zhōng Lù, it is open from 8am to 6:30pm.

Visa Extensions   The **PSB** is at Huáihǎi Lù 100, © **0514/734-2097** (open Mon–Fri 8am–noon and 3–6pm, 2:30–5:30pm in winter).

EXPLORING YÁNGZHŌU

GARDENS

Shòu Xī Hú (Slender West Lake) ✿✿   Located in the northwest part of town, Yángzhōu's premier attraction got its name during the Qīng dynasty, when Hángzhōu poet Wáng Kāng, on passing through the area, noted that it resembled a slender version of Hángzhōu's West Lake (Xī Hú). The most popular photo spot is the impressive **Wǔ Tíng Qiáo (Five Pavilion Bridge),** built in 1757 by a salt merchant who, in anticipation of the Qiánlóng emperor's arrival, modeled the bridge after one in the imperial resort (Bìshǔ Shānzhuāng) in Chéngdé, Héběi. Many Qīng dynasty salt merchants competed with each other to build gardens in order to impress the emperor.

   Bái Tǎ (White Dagoba), a white Tibetan-style stupa, was built by another ingratiating salt merchant more than 200 years ago. The story goes that during one of his six visits to the lake, the Qiánlóng emperor remarked on the area's resemblance to Běihǎi Park in Běijīng and inquired if there was a similar dagoba here. Eager to please, the salt merchant said yes, then spent the whole night panicking when the emperor insisted on seeing the dagoba. Finally, the merchant hit upon the idea to have a dagoba made out of salt, a tactic that apparently worked the next day when Qiánlóng saw the white structure from afar. Thereafter, the merchant commissioned a real dagoba to be built. The **Diàoyú Tái (Angler's Terrace)** on **Xiǎo Jīn Shān (Small Golden Hill)** is where Qiánlóng came to fish, although he was such a terrible angler that the merchants took to putting fish on his hooks in order to avoid imperial wrath.

Dà Hóngqiáo Lù 28. Admission ¥50 ($6). 6:30am–6:30pm.

Gè Yuán ✿   This garden was built over 160 years ago as part of a salt merchant's residence. It features a ponderous rockery section quite cleverly designed according to the four seasons. "Summer," for example, features Tài Hú rocks designed to resemble clouds in the sky after a storm; magnolia trees provide welcome shade. There's also a variety of exotic bamboo here, including purple, turtle, and yellow bamboo.

Yánfù Dōng Lù 10. Admission ¥30 ($3.75). 8am–6pm.

Hé Yuán ✿✿   Smaller than Gè Yuán, this garden offers some peace and quiet. Located in the southeast part of town, it is more residence than garden but still has its share of rockeries, pavilions, and ponds. Trees, plants, and an elevated walkway are used rather ingeniously to make the garden appear much larger than it really is, a tactic employed in many classical southern Chinese gardens.

Xúníngmén Jiē 77. Admission ¥30 ($3.75). 7:30am–6pm.

Wàng Shì Xiǎo Yuàn ✿   Located in the center of town on Dōng Quān Mén, the street of preserved historic homes (including that of former Chinese president Jiāng

Zémín), this impressive late Qīng dynasty residence of a local salt merchant is simple and understated from the outside but has almost 100 rooms inside, with the main rooms situated on a central axis. The furnishings are fine and reflect the wealth and status of the owner. The main Chūn Huī Shì (Spring Hall), for example, contains a German chandelier, expensive marble wall panels whose patterns resemble Chinese landscapes, and a poem by Táng dynasty poet Bái Jūyì.

Dōngquān Mén Lìshǐ Jiēqū 14. Admission ¥10 ($1.25). 8am–6pm.

OTHER ATTRACTIONS

Dàmíng Sì ⚔ Built more than 1,600 years ago, this major Buddhist temple is today best known for its **Jiàn Zhēn Memorial Hall,** dedicated to a Táng dynasty abbot of the temple, Jiàn Zhēn (688–763), who in 742 was invited to teach in Japan. After five unsuccessful attempts to cross the ocean in a wooden boat, Jiàn Zhēn finally made it to Japan in 753, old and blind. He spent the next 10 years introducing Chinese Buddhism, medicine, language, and architecture to the Japanese. The Jiàn Zhēn Memorial Hall, built in 1974, is modeled after the main hall of the Toshodai Temple in Nara, Japan, which Jiàn Zhēn built. A cedarwood statue of the teacher stands in the hall and there are still religious and cultural exchanges between Nara and Yángzhōu.

South of the temple is **Píng Shān Táng (Mountain Flattening Hall),** where famous Sòng dynasty writer Ōuyáng Xiū (1007–72) came to drink wine and write poetry when he was governor of Yángzhōu. From here, his perspective was on the same level as the nearby hills, hence the hall's name.

Píng Shān Táng 1. Admission ¥20 ($2.50). Apr–Nov 7:30am–5:30pm; Dec–Mar 7:30am–4pm. Bus: no. 5.

Hàn Mù Bówùguǎn (Hàn Dynasty Tomb Museum) ⚔⚔⚔ This fascinating Western Hàn tomb of the king of Guǎnglíng Kingdom, Liú Xū, the fifth son of the Hàn Wǔ Dì emperor (140–86 B.C.), is worth visiting. Sixty years in the making, Liú Xū's tomb is a grand five levels deep. The second airtight layer is made up of 840 nánmù (cedarwood) bricks linked to each other lengthwise by tiny hooks on the inside surfaces. These bricks could only be dissembled, and the wall breached, by locating the first brick. On the third level was the warehouse, while the living quarters occupied the fourth level; the fifth and bottom level contained a coffin on wheels. In the northwest part of the tomb, there is even a bathroom, making this the first Hàn tomb to contain such! Despite the seemingly impenetrable defenses, the tomb was actually robbed about 100 years later. The thieves were able to dig right down to the residential level with relative ease, suggesting that the tomb was robbed by descendants of the very people who built it. East of Liú Xū's tomb is that of his wife, who died 10 years after him. Three levels deep, the queen's tomb, also made from nánmù, is approached from the bottom level.

Yòuyì Lù 16 (3km/2 miles north of town). Admission ¥15 ($1.90). 8:30am–4:30pm. Bus: no. 5.

Pǔhādīng Yuán ⚔ The central tomb at this Sòng dynasty Muslim graveyard belongs to Pǔhādīng, 16th descendant of the prophet Muhammad, who visited Yángzhōu to help spread Islam. He built the Crane Mosque (Xiān É Sì) in town, and was buried in this graveyard in 1275 in a simple, stepped stone grave enclosed in a rectangular structure with a vaulted roof. Also here are the tombs of Muslim traders and other Arabs from the Yuán to the Qīng dynasties.

Jiěfàng Nán Lù 17. Admission ¥12 ($1.50). 8am–5pm.

Yángzhōu Shì Bówùguǎn (Yángzhōu City Museum) Just east of the Yángzhōu Hotel, this museum is housed in a temple complex dedicated to a local hero, a late Míng dynasty official named Shǐ Kěfǎ, who led Yángzhōu's citizenry against the advancing Qīng army. Shǐ was killed when he refused to surrender, his body cut up into five pieces and strewn to the wind. In the 10 days after his death, which came to be known as "Ten Days in Yángzhōu," Qīng troops killed 80,000 Yángzhōu residents. Shǐ's jade belt, clothes, and cap are buried in the tumulus behind the hall. The museum itself features some Hàn coffins, a Táng canoe, and a jade funeral suit with copper threads.

Fēnglè Shàng Jiē 2. Admission ¥10 ($1.25). 8:15–11:30am and 2:30–5:30pm.

WHERE TO STAY
EXPENSIVE
Grand Metropole Hotel (Yángzhōu Jīnghuá Dàjiŭdiàn) ⚛ There's not much individual charm to this modern four-star outfit with joint Hong Kong management, but it does offer all the standard conveniences and comfortable, clean rooms. The staff is used to dealing with foreign business travelers and can usually handle most travelers' needs.

Wénchāng Xī Lù 1. ⓒ 0514/732-3888. Fax 0514/736-8999. 242 units. ¥805 ($100) standard room; ¥1,035 ($129) executive room. AE, DC, MC, V. **Amenities:** 2 restaurants; pastry shop; bar; lounge; health club; concierge; business center; forex; shopping arcade; salon; limited room service; laundry/dry cleaning; executive rooms. In room: A/C, TV, minibar, hair dryer, safe.

MODERATE
Xīyuán Dàjiŭdiàn ⚛ With an ideal location—you can walk to many sights including Shòu Xī Hú or simply stroll along the nearby canals—and an interesting history—supposedly constructed on the site of Qiánlóng's imperial villa—this four-star hotel is the most popular choice with Western tour groups and independent travelers. Units are furnished with comfortable beds, clean bathrooms, and the usual amenities, though some rooms show signs of age. Service is acceptable, but nothing more.

Fēnglè Shàng Jiē 1. ⓒ 0514/734-4888. Fax 0514/723-3870. 253 units. ¥500–¥680 ($62–$85) standard room; ¥1,600 ($200) suite. 30%–40% discounts possible. AE, DC, MC, V. **Amenities:** 2 restaurants; bar; lounge; indoor swimming pool; tennis court; concierge; business center; forex; shopping arcade; salon; limited room service; laundry/dry cleaning; executive rooms. In room: A/C, TV, minibar, hair dryer, safe.

Yángzhōu State Guesthouse (Yángzhōu Yíngbīnguǎn) ⚛ Set on lovely expansive green grounds next to Slender West Lake, this hotel, which used to be closed to the public and used only for visiting high dignitaries, is the best in town. Former Chinese president Jiāng Zémín, who is from Yángzhōu, stays in building 1 when he is in town. Rooms are nicely decorated with colorful pillows and modern furniture. Bathrooms, impeccably clean, have a separate tub and shower.

Yǒuyì Lù 48. ⓒ 0514/732-5288. Fax 0514/733-1674. 100 units. ¥680 ($65) standard room; ¥880 ($110) suite. 20% discounts possible. AE, DC, MC, V. **Amenities:** 2 restaurants; teahouse; bar; lounge; indoor swimming pool; tennis courts; concierge; business center; forex; salon; limited room service; laundry. In room: A/C, TV.

WHERE TO DINE
The Xīyuán and Grand Metropole hotels both have restaurants serving decent Western food. Western fast food is also available at **Kentucky Fried Chicken** (Wénhé Běi Lù 48), **McDonald's** (Wénhé Lù 3), and **Pizza Hut** (Wénhé Nán Lù 120).

MODERATE
Gāojiāzhuāng Hǎixiān Chāoshì Jiŭlóu ⚛ HUÁIYÁNG/NÍNGBŌ   This place is fantastic, partly because there is no hard-to-decipher menu; actually, there's no menu at all, just point to your selection from sample dishes on display at the front of the

Huáiyáng Cuisine

As one of the four major schools in Chinese cooking, Huáiyáng cuisine (referring to the region between the Yángzǐ River and the Huái River in northern Jiāngsū) has its origins in Yángzhōu, even though it has been as much influenced these days by the different regional cooking styles of Jiāngsū and Zhèjiāng provinces. The Míng dynasty Hóngwǔ emperor employed a chef from Yángzhōu, as did the famous 20th-century Chinese opera singer Méi Lánfāng. Unlike Sìchuān cooking with its reliance on peppers, Huáiyáng cuisine aims to preserve the basic flavor of ingredients in order to achieve balance and freshness. River fish, farm animals, birds, and vegetables feature prominently. Some of the more famous dishes include *xièfěn shīzitóu* (lightly braised meatballs with crabmeat, also known as Lion's Head Meatballs), *chāihuì liányútóu* (stewed fish head with tofu, greens, and radish), and *bāshāo zhěng zhūtóu* (stewed pig's head in a red glaze).

restaurant, like a live seafood supermarket with fish, crab, and fresh vegetables. The restaurant features a sleek modern interior with private rooms.

Chángzhēng Lù 2. ☎ 0514/732-4737. Meal for 2 ¥100–¥200 ($13–$25). No credit cards. 9am–8:30pm. Bus: no. 8 or 30.

INEXPENSIVE

Fùchūn Cháshè ✿ TEAHOUSE/DUMPLINGS   Indulge in one of Yángzhōu's favorite pastimes, drinking morning tea, at one of Yángzhōu's oldest teahouses. The ritual starts with a pot of tea and a round of nine different snacks, including Yángzhōu's famous *bāozi* (steamed buns), which come with chicken, bamboo shoots, shrimp, crabmeat, tofu, or a variety of bean pastes. These steamed buns are also available at dinner, as are a variety of *jiǎozi* (dumplings). This restaurant is so popular that it has branches in other Chinese cities and even Tokyo.

Déshēng Qiáo 35 (off Guóqìng Lù). ☎ 0514/723-3326. Meal for 2 ¥20–¥50 ($2.50–$6.25). No credit cards. 6am–9pm.

SHOPPING

Yángzhōu is famous for its **lacquerware,** which has a tradition stretching back to 475 B.C. Red lacquered vases, mother-of-pearl inlaid screens, ink slabs, fans, jewelry, teapots, and lacquered furniture can all be purchased at the **Yángzhōu Qīqì Yǒuxiàn Gōngsī** at Yánhé Jiē 50 (open 8:30–11:45am and 2–6pm). Prices range from the reasonable for small handicrafts to the thousands of dollars (yes, dollars) for the larger pieces of furniture. International credit cards are accepted.

11 Wúxī, Tài Hú & Yíxīng

Jiāngsū Province, 128km (79 miles) NW of Shànghǎi

Located in the southern part of Jiāngsū Province, Wúxī, literally "without tin," was once "yǒu xī" ("has tin"). The town changed its name during the Hàn dynasty when nearby deposits of tin were mined out. A Grand Canal port, Wúxī itself is not an exciting city but it's the best base for a visit to Tài Hú (Lake Tài), one of China's four largest freshwater lakes and its most fabled body of water. On the west shore of Tài Hú is Yíxīng, famous for its purple clay pottery. *Note:* For Chinese translations of selected establishments listed in this section, please turn to appendix A.

ESSENTIALS

GETTING THERE   Wúxī has a small airport which is seldom used. Shànghǎi offers the nearest major **airline** connections. Wúxī is connected by daily **trains** to Shànghǎi (1–1½ hr.), Sūzhōu (25–35 min.), Hángzhōu (4½ hr. via Shànghǎi), and Nánjīng (2 hr.). The **railway station** (© 0510/580-2297) is in the northern part of town (counters 7–9 sell same-day tickets for Shànghǎi, Sūzhōu, and Hángzhōu).

From the **Wúxī Qìchēzhàn (Wúxī Bus Station)** (© 0510/230-0751) just north of the railway station, buses head to Shànghǎi (every 20 min. 6:30am–7pm; 2 hr.; ¥30–¥43/$3.75–$5.40), Sūzhōu (every 15 min. 6:50am–6:15pm; 45 min.; ¥18/$2.25), Hángzhōu (every 40 min. 7am–5:20pm; 4 hr.; ¥64–¥78/$8–$9.75), Yíxīng (every 15 min. 6:10am–6pm; 90 min.; ¥11/$1.40), Nánjīng (every 20 min. 6am–7pm; 2 hr.; ¥40–¥52/$5–$6.50), and Yángzhōu (every 45 min. 7am–5:30pm; 90 min.; ¥42–¥51/$5.50–$6.25).

To get to Hángzhōu along the Grand Canal, a **boat** departs daily from the Húbīn Mǎtóu (Húbīn Dock) on Húbīn Lù at 5:30pm and arrives in Hángzhōu the next morning at 7am. A berth in a standard room costs ¥114 ($14); in a quad ¥82 ($10). Conditions are spartan at best. Tickets can be bought at the **Hángyùn Dàshà (Ferry Building; © 0510/586-8704;** open 7:30am–5:30pm) at the dock.

GETTING AROUND   **Taxis** cost ¥8 ($1) for 3km (2 miles), then ¥2.30 (30¢) per kilometer, then ¥2.80 (35¢) per kilometer after 8km (5 miles). Public **bus** no. 1 (¥1/15¢) and tourist bus no. G1 (same fare) run from the railway station to Yuántóuzhǔ. Bus no. 2 from the railway station stops at Xīhuì Gōngyuán.

TOURS & GUIDES   **China Travel Service (CTS),** located directly across from the railway station at Chēzhàn Lù 88 (© 0510/230-0584; fax 0510/230-4143), can arrange customized tours around the city and to the pottery shops and caves in Yíxīng County. The shamelessly exorbitant rate is about ¥1,500 ($188) in high season for a 2-day tour (for one to three persons) of Wúxī and Yíxīng with private car, English-speaking guide, and lunch, although there's room for bargaining.

FAST FACTS

Banks, Foreign Exchange & ATMs   The **Bank of China** at Zhōngshān Lù 258 conducts foreign exchange Monday through Friday from 8am to 5pm. There is an ATM inside the bank.

Internet Access   Dial-up is © 163.

Post Office   There's a post office (7:30am–6:30pm) on Rénmín Zhōng Lù, west of Zhōngshān Lù.

Visa Extensions   The **Gōngānjú (PSB)** is located on the second floor at Chóngníng Lù 56 (© 0510/270-0123, ext. 22215) and is open Monday through Friday from 8 to 11:30am and 1:30 to 5:30pm (2:30–5:30pm July–Sept). Allow 5 business days.

EXPLORING WÚXĪ

Tài Hú (Lake Tài)   With its northern banks grazing the southwest edge of Wúxī, China's most fabled body of freshwater is the main attraction in town. Covering over

2,400 sq. km (950 sq. miles) with an average depth of only 2m (7 ft.), the lake is dotted with islands, fishing trawlers, low cargo boats, and small sampans. Often shrouded in mist, Tài Hú is also the source of many fantastically shaped limestone rocks that were submerged for years to achieve the desired effect, and that now decorate many a classical Chinese garden. It is said that the Huìzōng emperor of the Sòng dynasty nearly bankrupted the country's treasury in pursuit of increasingly bizarre Tài Hú rocks. For all its fabled status and storied history, however, today's lake, at least the parts accessible to tourists from Wúxī, is a bit of a disappointment, unashamedly geared as it is to the mass tourist trade.

The lake's most popular scenic spot is the peninsula **Yuántóuzhǔ (Turtle Head Isle).** From the park's entrance, most tourists head straight for the ferry docks at the western edge of the peninsula. You can walk, take the tourist train (¥6/75¢ one-way, ¥10/$1.25 round-trip), or ride the elevated tram (¥10/$1.25 one-way, ¥16/$2 round-trip) to the docks. The area south of the docks has some pleasant trails and is worth exploring if you have the time. A lighthouse marks the westernmost tip of the peninsula.

From the docks, ferries shuttle visitors to **Sān Shān Dǎo,** a hilly island connected by causeways to two flanking islets. The 15-minute boat ride, the highlight of a visit to Tài Hú, is usually refreshing, though you're likely to find yourself on a boat with chattering schoolchildren and loud tourists. The island itself is a tacky, commercialized affair complete with pushy vendors and wretched performing monkeys. All the structures here date to the mid-1980s, when the island was first opened to tourists.

Yuántóuzhǔ. Admission ¥70 ($8.75) (includes ferry ride). 6am–5pm. Bus: no. 1 or 212.

Xīhuì Gōngyuán   This park in the northwestern part of town is dominated by two hills that have become symbols of Wúxī: **Xī Shān** after which the city was named, and **Huì Shān** to the west. It's a bit of a climb up to the seven-story octagonal brick-and-wood **Lóngguāng Tǎ (Dragon Light Pagoda)** atop Xī Shān, but there are some good views of the Grand Canal snaking through the city. From 8:30am to 5pm you can also ride a chairlift (¥15/$1.90 one-way, ¥22/$2.75 round-trip) from the bottom of Xī Shān to the peak on Huì Shān. The ride offers even more commanding views of the surrounding area.

At the foot of Huì Shān is the famous Míng dynasty garden, **Jìchàng Yuán,** laid out in classical southern style with walkways, rockeries, ponds, and pavilions. The garden is said to have so captivated the Qiánlóng emperor on one of his visits south that he commissioned a copy of it to be built in the Yíhé Yuán (Summer Palace) in Běijīng. Just southwest of the garden is the **Second Spring Under Heaven (Tiānxià Dì'èr Quán),** three wells containing the putative second-best water source in China for brewing tea, according to Lù Yǔ's Táng dynasty *Chá Jīng (Tea Classic).* From May to October, nightly traditional music performances are held in the garden.

Huìhé Lù. Admission to park ¥10 ($1.25); Jìchàng Garden ¥15 ($1.90) or ¥20 ($2.50) 6–10pm. Park: Apr–Oct 5am–6pm; Nov–Mar 5:30am–5:30pm. Jìchàng Garden: May–Oct 7am–10pm; Nov–Apr 7am–6pm. Bus: no. 2.

WHERE TO STAY

Most hotels regularly offer 20% to 30% discounts, and add a 15% service charge.

EXPENSIVE

Húbīn Fàndiàn ⚑⚑   Set on beautiful grounds along the shores of Lake Tài, this hotel is a good place to escape the bustle of the city. A five-star hotel, this 10-story European-style luxury hotel boasts whitewashed walls, elegant marble floors, and wrought-iron balustrades and balconies. Rooms are not outstanding but they do have thick carpets, redwood furniture, and some gorgeous views of the lake. Bathrooms are small and slightly worn.

Húbīn Lù 388. ✆ 0510/510-1888. Fax 0510/510-2637. 281 units. ¥700–¥1,200 ($88–$150) standard room; ¥1,800 ($225) suite. AE, DC, MC, V. **Amenities:** 3 restaurants; bar; lounge; outdoor pool; tennis court; health club and spa; sauna; bowling alley; concierge; business center; forex; shopping arcade; salon; limited room service; massage; laundry/dry cleaning; executive rooms. *In room:* A/C, TV, minibar, hair dryer.

Sheraton Wúxī Hotel & Towers (Xǐláidēng Dàfàndiàn) ✿✿ This five-star hotel in the center of town offers all the luxuries you'd expect in a top international hotel. Even though it's showing signs of age, it's still the best place to stay for efficient service and first-rate facilities. Rooms are spacious, comfortable, and equipped with a full range of amenities, including robe and slippers. Marble bathrooms are bright and clean. The hotel's four restaurants offer reliable fine dining. Staff is friendly and very helpful.

Zhōngshān 443. ✆ 0510/272-1888. Fax 0510/275-2781. www.sheraton.com. 396 units. ¥1,185 ($143) standard room; from ¥1,869 ($224) suite. AE, DC, MC, V. **Amenities:** 4 restaurants; bar; lounge; cigar bar; indoor pool, health club and spa; Jacuzzi; sauna; concierge; business center; forex; shopping arcade; salon; 24-hr. limited room service; massage; same-day laundry/dry cleaning; executive rooms. *In room:* A/C, satellite TV, dataport, broadband Internet access (select rooms), minibar, hair dryer, safe.

Tài Hú Fàndiàn ✿ Somewhat inconveniently located 10km (6 miles) west of the city center, on the northern banks of Lake Tài across from Yuántóuzhǔ, this five-star resort offers a blissful escape from city bustle, but it's not very practical for the individual traveler. The hotel's sprawling grounds also contain private villas, landscaped gardens, and the resort's private dock, with plans underway for an 18-hole golf course. For such luxury, the standard rooms are surprisingly small and simply decorated, though all the usual amenities are here. Bathrooms are also on the small side but are clean.

Huánhú Lù, Méi Yuán. ✆ 0510/551-7888. Fax 0510/551-7784. www.taihuhotel.com. 257 units. ¥700–¥1,280 ($87–$160) standard room; from ¥1,500 ($187) suite. AE, DC, MC, V. **Amenities:** 4 restaurants; bar; lounge; 2 pools; 18-hole golf course; tennis courts; health club and spa; Jacuzzi; sauna; bowling alley; concierge; tour desk; business center; forex; shopping arcade; salon; massage; limited room service; laundry/dry cleaning. *In room:* A/C, satellite TV, minibar, hair dryer, safe.

MODERATE
New World Courtyard Wúxī (Wúxī Xīnshìjiè Wànyí Jiǔdiàn) ✿✿ This hotel, without official rating, is the equivalent of a top four-star hotel catering mostly to business travelers and a few tour groups. Located in the heart of town, the hotel prides itself on having the largest standard guest rooms around. Rooms are tastefully decorated and fitted with a full range of amenities. Bathrooms are spacious and clean. Service is friendly and efficient.

Zhōngshān Lù 335. ✆ 0510/ 276-2888. Fax 0510/551-7784. www.courtyard.com. 266 units. ¥860 ($107) standard room; ¥2,000 ($250) suite. AE, DC, MC, V. **Amenities:** 3 restaurants; bar; lounge; health club and spa; sauna; concierge; tour desk; business center; forex; shopping arcade; salon; limited room service; massage; laundry/dry cleaning; executive rooms. *In room:* A/C, satellite TV, broadband Internet access, minibar, hair dryer, safe.

WHERE TO DINE
The top hotels all offer reliable dining. Western fast food is readily available in the center of town, with three **KFC outlets** (9:30am–10:30pm) within a block south of Jiěfàng Lù, and a **Pizza Hut** at Rénmín Zhōng Lù 127 (10am–10:30pm). **McDonald's** is at Zhōngshān Nán Lù 217 (8am–11pm). Bābǎibàn (Yaohan Department Store) at Zhōngshān Lù 168 has a **food court** on the sixth floor.

MODERATE

Sān Fēng Jiǔjiā ✿ WÚXĪ   While Wúxī isn't exactly known for its cuisine, this restaurant does a superb job making the best of the regional fare. Order the *páigǔ,* delicious Chinese-style baby-back ribs cooked in sugar and soy sauce, or the local specialty *miànjīn,* which are fried balls of flour that a shredded and stir-fried with meat and vegetables. The restaurant also features fresh seafood and fresh squeezed juices.

Zhōngshān Lù 240. ✆ **0510/272-5132.** Meal for 2 ¥80–¥160 ($10–$20). No credit cards. 11am–1:30pm and 5–8pm.

Wúxī Kǎoyā Guǎn (Wúxī Roast Duck Restaurant) ✿✿ WÚXĪ   This popular four-story restaurant serves its excellent signature Wúxī roast duck in two ways: with steamed bread, chives, cucumbers, and sweet sauce; and as a soup. Other specialties include *Tàihú yínyú* (deep-fried Lake Tài fish) and the mouthwatering *Wúxī xiǎolóng* (Wúxī dumplings). Service is friendly.

Zhōngshān Lù 222. ✆ **0510/272-9623.** Reservations recommended. English menu. Meal for 2 ¥90–¥200 ($11–$25). No credit cards. 11am–2pm and 5–9pm.

INEXPENSIVE

Wángxìng Jì DUMPLINGS   One of Wúxī's most famous and popular places for casual dining, this assembly-line cafeteria has no decor to speak of, but the crabmeat dumplings *(xièfěn xiǎolóng)* and pork wontons *(xiānròu húntun)* are pretty good. A variety of noodles is also available here. Don't expect much from the apathetic service, and try your best to grin and bear the beggars who stumble in here asking for money—or a dumpling.

Zhōngshān Nán Lù 221. ✆ **0510/275-1777.** Meal for 2 ¥20–¥40 ($2.50–$5). No credit cards. 7am–9pm.

SHOPPING

Wúxī's famous folk-art **Huìs Hān clay figurines,** which some consider rather ugly, are available at the **Huì Hhān Clay Figurine Factory** store at Xīhuì Lù 26 (open 8:30am–5pm). Credit cards are accepted.

A SIDE TRIP TO YÍXĪNG

Located 60km (37 miles) southwest of Wúxī on the western shores of Tài Hú, Yíxīng is famous for its "Yíxīng ware" pottery, specifically small teapots and decorative objects made from a distinctive dark red clay (often referred to as "purple sand" due to a high level of iron in the soil). You can see a collection of Yíxīng pots, flasks, and urns from over 6,000 years ago, as well as the latest vases and teapots from contemporary masters, at the ceramics museum **Yíxīng Táocí Bówùguǎn** (Dīngshān Běi Lù 150; ¥20/$2.50; 7:30am–5pm) in Dīngshū Town, 15km (9 miles) southwest of Yíxīng. Recently renovated, the museum offers coherent explanations in English and is pretty well put together for a small-town museum. It's worthwhile for visitors who are really into pottery. You can purchase a certified Yíxīng teapot set (teapot with six cups) for ¥200 to ¥300 ($25–$38) at the museum store. Outside are workshops where visitors can watch ceramics artisans at work. Across the highway is a dusty pottery market, where amazing deals can be struck for a wide range of pottery ranging from ¥5 to ¥200 ($2.50–$25).

Yíxīng also has some karst caves near Dīngshū Town. **Shànjuǎn Dòng** (¥38/$4.75; open 7:30am–5pm) located 25km (15 miles) southwest of Yíxīng, has three main chambers of oddly shaped rocks. Visitors may climb to the upper cave or take the more interesting short ride on a flat-bottomed boat in the lower cave along a 120m-long (393-ft.)

underground stream that leads out to a tacky temple complex commemorating China's Romeo and Juliet, Liáng Shānbó and Zhù Yīngtái. Twenty-two kilometers (13 miles) southwest of town, a Daoist temple fronts the large **Zhānggōng Dòng** (¥30/$3.80; 7:30am–5:30pm) which contains a labyrinthine 72 halls. The Hall of the Dragon King has wide steps that run all the way to the top of the hill, where there's a view of the dusty countryside.

Wild China: The Water Village of Tónglǐ

Now that Sūzhōu, once the "Venice of the East," has grown into a modern city; visitors searching for a more traditional Yángzǐ River delta water town should visit the Sòng dynasty town of **Tónglǐ**, 20km (12 miles) southeast of Sūzhōu and 80km (49 miles) west of Shànghǎi. The entrance fee for all sights is ¥50 ($6.25); hours are from 8am to 5pm. (Zhōu Zhuāng, another delta town, has unfortunately evolved into a massive tourist trap.)

The main attraction in Tónglǐ is **Tuìsī Yuán (Retreat and Reflection Garden)** ⋇, in the center of the old town. Built in 1886 by a dismissed court official, the garden contains the family's residences in the west, meeting and entertaining rooms in the center, and a small but cleverly designed landscaped garden in the east. The use of winding walkways with different-shaped windows, jutting pavilions, and a reflecting pond make the garden appear larger than it is.

West of the garden are two of the town's better-preserved traditional residences. **Jiāyīn Táng,** built in the 1910s as the residence of a famous local scholar, Liǔ Yàzǐ, has high white walls and doorways fronted by upturned eaves. The highlight at **Chóngběn Táng,** also with four courtyards and three doorways, is the refined brick, stone, and wood carvings of propitious symbols such as cranes and vases. Connecting the two residences are three bridges: **Tàipíng Qiáo (Peace Bridge), Jílì (Luck) Qiáo,** and **Chángqìng (Glory) Qiáo.** It was the custom in the old days to carry a bride in her sedan chair over all three. Today, tourists can don proper wedding finery and also be carried across the bridges in an old-fashioned sedan chair.

GETTING THERE   From the bus station *(qìchē zhàn)* in the new part of town on Sōngběi Gōng lù, **buses** run to Sūzhōu (hourly 7am–5pm; 1 hr.; ¥12/$1.50). In Shànghǎi, the Jǐnjiāng Optional Tours Center at Chánglè Lù 191 (© 021/6466-2828) can organize a private tour with an English-speaking guide, air-conditioned car, and lunch for about ¥1,200 ($150) for one person and ¥650 ($81) each for two. Alternatively, a Tónglǐ tourist bus (2 hr.; ¥110/$13 round-trip) leaves from the Shànghǎi Stadium at 9am (returns at 4pm) and 10am (returns at 4:30pm).

WHERE TO DINE   Several small restaurants along **Míngqīng Jiē** serve basic *jiācháng cài* (Chinese home-style cooking) at reasonable prices; a meal for two averages about ¥30 to ¥50 ($3.50–$6). **Nányuán Cháshè,** located in a restored Qīng dynasty building, serves tea and local snacks. Local specialties include *zhuàngyuán tí* (the Tónglǐ version of braised pigs' trotters), *xiǎo xūnyú* (small smoked fish), and *mín bǐng* (a sweet glutinous rice pastry).

From the **Yíxīng Bus Station (Shěng Qìchēzhàn; ℡ 0510/794-5031)**, buses depart regularly for Wúxī (90 min.; ¥11/$1.40) and Nánjīng (2½ hr.; ¥44/$5.50). Once in Yíxīng, tourist bus no. Y1 (¥5/60¢) will take you from the bus station to the ceramics museum and Zhānggōng Dòng (Zhānggōng Cave), while tourist bus no. Y2 heads to Shànjuǎn Dòng (Shànjuǎn Cave).

Yíxīng is usually a day trip from Wúxī or Nánjīng, but for those who wish to stay over, the renovated three-star **Yíxīng Guójì Fàndiàn (Yíxīng International Hotel)** ✵, Tōngzhèngguān Lù 52 (℡ **0510/791-6888;** fax 0510/790-0767) has clean and comfortable rooms for ¥420 to ¥580 ($52–$72). The rooms are fitted with all new furniture, fridge, and satellite TV. The hotel has three restaurants serving decent fare.

12 Héféi

Ānhuī Province, 615km (381 miles) NW of Shànghǎi, 321km (199 miles) NW of Huáng Shān

As the provincial capital of Ānhuī, this industrial city of 1.3 million has few attractions for the tourist but sees a constant flow of business travelers. Héféi is also home to the University of Science and Technology, where Chinese dissident Fāng Lìzhī was vice-president until he sought asylum in the West after the 1989 Tiān'ān Mén Square massacre. *Note:* For Chinese translations of selected establishments listed in this section, please turn to appendix A.

ESSENTIALS

GETTING THERE   Héféi has daily **flights** to Běijīng (2 hr.), Guǎngzhōu (3 hr.), Xī'ān (1½ hr.), Hángzhōu (50 min.), Shànghǎi (1 hr.), and Qīngdǎo (1 hr.), and several flights a week to Guìlín (90 min.), Huángshān (50 min.), Hong Kong (2 hr.), Jǐ'nán (1 hr.), and Zhèngzhōu (1 hr.). Tickets may be purchased at the 24-hour **CAAC Booking Center (Mínháng Shòupiào Zhōngxīn)** at Měilíng Dàdào 458 (℡ **0551/ 467-9999).** Taxis (20 min.; ¥20/$2.50) are your best option for getting to Héféi's airport, which is about 10km (6 miles) south of town. There are no airport buses, but public **bus** no. 11 runs there from the railway station.

From Héféi's railway station (℡ **0551/267-6822)** in the northeast part of town, **trains** run to Běijīng (12 hr.), Zhèngzhōu (9 hr.), Shànghǎi (7–10 hr.), Huáng Shān (8 hr.), Xī'ān (18 hr.), and Hángzhōu (8 hr.). Tickets can be purchased at the railway station or, more conveniently, at ticket outlets in town at Chángjiāng Zhōng Lù 376 (℡ **0551/264-0000).**

Héféi has several bus stations, but the **long-distance bus station** (*chángtú qìchēzhàn;* ℡ 0551/429-7013) at the corner of Shènglì Lù and Míngguāng Lù should serve most travelers' needs. Buses run to Shànghǎi (every 40 min. 6:20am–5:40pm; 6½ hr.; ¥120/$15), Zhèngzhōu (9:30am and 3:50pm; 10 hr.; ¥87/$11), Huáng Shān (7:40am; 6 hr.; ¥63/$8), and Nánjīng (7:10, 9, and 11:40am and 12:40 and 3:30pm; 2½ hr.; ¥52/$6.50).

GETTING AROUND   Taxis charge ¥5 (60¢) for 3km (2 miles), then ¥1.20 (15¢) per kilometer. From 11pm to 5am, prices rise to ¥6 (75¢) for 3km, then to ¥1.45 (20¢) per kilometer.

Most public **buses** (¥1/15¢ flat fee) require exact change. Bus no. 1 runs from the railway station down Shènglì Lù onto Chángjiāng Zhōng Lù before heading south on Jīnzhāi Lù. Bus no. 11 runs from the railway station to the airport along Chángjiāng Zhōng Lù.

FAST FACTS

Banks, Foreign Exchange & ATMs   The **Bank of China** is at Chángjiāng Zhōng Lù 313. Foreign exchange is available at all counters Monday through Friday from 8am to noon and 2:30 to 6pm (2–5:30pm Nov–Apr). An ATM is located here.

Internet Access   Dial-up is ⓒ **163.**

Post Office   The post office (8am–8pm) is at Chángjiāng Zhōng Lù 146.

Visa Extensions   The **Héféi Municipal Administration Service Center (Shì Xíngzhèng Fúwù Zhōngxīn)** is at Jiǔ Shíqiáo Jiē 45 (ⓒ **0551/262-7613**). Open year-round Monday to Friday from 8am to noon; May to October, 3 to 6pm and November to April 2:30 to 5:30pm.

EXPLORING HÉFÉI

Héféi's nicest park, **Bāo Hé Gōngyuán** in the center of town, has an arched bridge over a placid lake, whispering willows on the shores, and schools of fish in lily ponds, all making for some pleasant strolls. Entrance is free and the park is open 24 hours The park is also home to **Bāo Gōng Mùyuán (Lord Bāo's Tomb)** at Wú Hú Lù 58. It commemorates one of China's most respected iconic figures, local son Bāo Zhěng (999–1062), a conscientious and impartial Northern Sòng dynasty judge who fought for the common folk. Admission to the tomb is ¥15 ($1.90).

For an eclectic range of activities, head to **Xiāoyáojīn Gōngyuán.** It features a peaceful lake where the elderly practice tai-chi, but also offers a range of tacky roller-coaster-type rides for kids, a petting zoo, a circus, paintball, and, best of all, crocodile wrestling. Admission is ¥20 ($2.50) and the cost of individual activities ranges from ¥3 to ¥20 (40¢–$2.50); the park is open from 6am to 6pm.

North of the Xiāoyáojīn Gōngyuán along the pedestrian street **Shāngyè Bùxíng Jiē** is **Lǐ Hóngzhāng Gùjū** (Huáihé Lù 208; ¥15/$1.90; 8:30am–5:30pm), the former residence of Lǐ Hóngzhāng (1823–1901), a highly successful Qīng dynasty military commander who is perhaps best known as one of the chief architects of the destruction of the Tàipíngs (p. 378). His residence has been well preserved, complete with beautiful lattice windows and Qīng dynasty furniture.

The **Ānhuī Shěng Bówùguǎn (Ānhuī Provincial Museum),** at Ānqīng Lù 268 (¥10/$1.25; Tues–Sun 8:30–11:30am and 2:30–5pm), is a rather forlorn place. It has a modest bronze collection, some Hàn tomb engravings, and a fairly comprehensive display on the Huīzhōu-style architecture of southern Ānhuī. The museum closes early if there are no visitors, which is often. There's a decent flower and bird market outside of the museum.

WHERE TO STAY

EXPENSIVE

Holiday Inn Héféi (Héféi Gǔjǐng Jiàrì Jiǔdiàn) ⋇⋇   Just east of the commercial heart of town, this luxurious five-star 29-story hotel has rooms that are large, well appointed, and decorated with classical furniture. The marble bathrooms are a bit small but very clean. Rooms on the higher floors provide panoramas of the city. Service is professional and efficient.

Chángjiāng Dōng Lù 1104. ⓒ 0551/220-6666. Fax 0551/220-1166. hihfe@mail.hf.ah.cn. 338 units. ¥678–¥768 ($84–$96) standard room; from ¥828 ($103) suite. AE, DC, MC, V. **Amenities:** 4 restaurants; bar; lounge; disco; cigar bar; indoor pool; health club; concierge; business center; forex; shopping arcade; salon; limited room service; massage; laundry/dry cleaning; executive rooms. In room: A/C, satellite TV, broadband Internet access, minibar, hair dryer, safe.

Novotel Héféi (Héféi Nuòfùtè Qíyún Shānzhuāng) *&&* Renovated in 2002, the trendy four-star Novotel has standard rooms that are a little small but perfectly comfortable. They are fitted with modern light-wood furniture and all the expected amenities. Bathrooms are sparkling clean. Consider upgrading to a superior room, which is spacious and refreshingly decorated with hip blue and orange futon sofas. Service is excellent and the staff is professional and exceedingly friendly.

Wú Hú Lù 199. ✆ 0551/228-6688. Fax 0551/228-6677. www.accorhotels.com/asia. 245 units. ¥598 ($72) standard room; ¥888 ($108) superior; ¥1,150 ($143) suite. Discounts possible up to 50%. AE, DC, MC, V. **Amenities:** 3 restaurants; pastry shop; bar; lounge; health club; concierge; tour desk; airport shuttle; business center; forex; shopping arcade; salon; 24-hr. room service; massage; laundry/dry cleaning; executive rooms. *In room:* A/C, satellite TV, broadband Internet access, minibar, hair dryer, safe.

MODERATE

Huáqiáo Fàndiàn (Overseas Chinese Hotel) This midrange three-star hotel has a great location right in the heart of town and is a good choice if you're on a budget. Rooms in building B are fairly large are nicely decorated. Building A is a notch down, but staying here will save you a bit of cash. In general, bathrooms are clean enough, save for the occasional stained bathtub.

Chángjiāng Zhōng Lù 98. ✆ 0551/265-2221. Fax 0551/264-2861. 268 units. ¥300–¥550 ($38–$68) standard room. 30%–50% discounts possible. V. **Amenities:** 2 restaurants; bar; lounge; concierge; business center; shopping arcade; salon; limited room service; laundry. *In room:* A/C, TV, hair dryer.

WHERE TO DINE

All the top hotels catering to foreigners serve very credible Western and Chinese food. For Western fast food, there's a **Pizza Hut** at Huáihé Lù 77 and a **McDonald's** at the intersection of Sūzhōu Lù and Chángjiāng Lù.

Jīn Mǎn Lóu Huāyuán Jiǔdū *&* CHÁOZHŌU/CANTONESE This popular, clean restaurant offers reliable and tasty fare at very reasonable prices, though service is uneven. Start with a cold dish of spicy mushrooms with broad beans or the house specialty, *tàijí sùcài gēng,* a puréed vegetable soup. Graduate to the *huāshì xiǎochǎo,* a light stir-fry mix of pork, leeks, and bean curd strips. Also try *suàn zhēng shànbèi,* garlic steamed scallops with glass noodles.

Tóngchéng Lù 96. ✆ 0551/287-7777. Meal for 2 ¥40–¥120 ($5–$15). No credit cards. 11am–2pm and 4–9pm.

Lǎo Xiè Lóngxiā *&&* SEAFOOD Located on a street that's been dubbed "*lóngxiā yī tiáo lù*" or "a street filled with lobsters," this restaurant packs them in every night of the week. *Lóngxiā* really means Chinese-style crayfish here, which is steamed in spices and served with beer. In the warmer months, locals cram themselves on outdoor tables and enjoy grilled corn on the cob, fish, and meat and vegetable skewers along with the crayfish. The mustachioed Mr. Xiè has been at it for more than a decade, and while there are other restaurants on the street that serve the same thing, he keeps drawing the crowds that come until the wee hours of the morning.

Lóngxiā yī tiáo Lù. No phone. Meal for 2 ¥20–¥50 ($2.50–$6). No credit cards. 10am–4am.

Noodles in Chopsticks (24 Xiǎoshí Miàn) *&* NOODLES Located in the Holiday Inn, this noodle house will satisfy your hunger pangs 24 hours a day. There's a noodle for practically every taste, from the simple Sìchuān-style *dāndān miàn* (spicy noodles with meat sauce) to Japanese udon; egg and spinach noodles may substitute regular noodles in any of the dishes.

Holiday Inn, 2nd floor. ✆ 0551/288-7777. Meal for 2 ¥20–¥60 ($2.50–$7.50). AE, DC, MC, V. Open 24 hr.

13 Huáng Shān ⭐⭐⭐

Ānhuī Province, 501km (315 miles) SW of Shànghǎi, 65km (40 miles) NW of Túnxī

If you climb one mountain in China, let it be Huáng Shān (Yellow Mountain). Located in southern Ānhuī Province, and inscribed on the UNESCO World Heritage List in 1990, Huáng Shān, with its 72 peaks, is China's most famous mountain for scenic beauty. Having no religious significance, the mountain is known instead for its sea of clouds, strangely shaped rocks, unusual pine trees, and bubbling hot springs—four features that have mesmerized and inspired countless painters and poets for over 1,500 years.

Huáng Shān is enshrouded in mist and fog 256 days a year, while snow covers the mountain peaks 158 days a year. Trails are usually packed with hikers from May to October, so April is often cited as the best time to visit. Local tourism authorities, however, like to boast that each season highlights a uniquely different aspect of Huáng Shān, and have taken to pushing Huáng Shān winter tours, when hotel, restaurant, and ticket prices are at least lower. Whenever you visit, allow at least 2 days for the mountain, and another day or two for the attractions around **Túnxī.**

ESSENTIALS

GETTING THERE   The nearest **airports** and **railway stations** are at Túnxī, 65km (40 miles) and a 1½-hour bus ride away. In Tāngkǒu, the nearest town serving the mountain, buses leave for Túnxī from the **long-distance bus station** (*chángtú qìchēzhàn;* ✆ 0559/556-2590) just before the main gate to Huáng Shān and from the main bridge area in town. Tickets may be purchased at the bus station or at the **Lìdū Hotel (Lìdū Jiǔdiàn;** ✆ 0559/235-3952). Slow long-distance buses also run to Héféi (6:50–7:10am, 3–3:40pm; 6 hr.; ¥63/$7.50), Shànghǎi (6:20am; 8 hr.; ¥101/$12), and Hángzhōu (6–8am, 2pm, and 5:20pm; 6 hr.; ¥55/$6.80).

GETTING AROUND   *Miàndì* (van) taxis charge ¥3 to ¥5 (35¢–60¢) for trips in town. The start of the Eastern Mountain Trail (Eastern Steps) or the cable car at Yúngǔ is another hour away by minibus (¥5/60¢) or taxi (approximately ¥30/$3.75 per trip or ¥10/$1.25 per person depending on the number of people). The Peach Blossom Hot Springs area and the start of the Western Mountain Trail (Western Steps) will require a 30-minute walk or a taxi ride from the Tāngkǒu bus station (¥10–¥15/$1.25–$2). If you want to take the cable car up the western slopes, take a minibus for ¥5 to ¥10 (60¢–$1.25) or a taxi for around ¥40 ($5), subject to bargaining, from Tāngkǒu to the Mercy Light Temple (Cíguāng Gé).

EXPLORING THE MOUNTAIN
ORIENTATION & INFORMATION

Buses from Túnxī usually drop off passengers in Tāngkǒu by the bridge or at the bus station in upper Tāngkǒu near the Huáng Shān Front Gate.

There are two main trails up the mountain. The 7.5km-long (4½-mile) **Eastern Steps** (3–4 hr. hike) are compact and steep and are generally considered less strenuous than the 15km-long (9¼-mile) **Western Steps** (4–6 hr. hike), which are longer and steeper but which have some of Huáng Shān's most spectacular vistas. For the fit, it's entirely possible to climb the mountain in the morning and descend in the afternoon in about 10 hours. But an overnight stay at the summit would allow a more leisurely appreciation of the sights and views along the way.

Sedan chairs can be hired on both routes and can cost up to ¥500 ($62) for a one-way trip, though there is plenty of room for bargaining. Just be very clear beforehand on all the terms of the deal, including exact starting and ending points, and the price per passenger. If you hire a porter to tote your bags, be clear as to whether you're being charged by the piece or by weight. If the latter, insist, if you can, that the items be weighed *before* you embark so you have an idea of the total cost, and not when you're at the end point, for the load at the end has an uncanny way of weighing three times more than you'd imagined.

For those preferring the path of least resistance, there are three **cable cars** going up the mountain: the Eastern Trail's **Yúngǔ Sì cable car** (Mar 15–Nov 15 6:30am–4:30pm; otherwise 8am–4pm) has a waiting line for the 6-minute ascent that can take up to 1 to 2 hours. The Western Trail's **Yùpíng cable car** (Mar 15–Nov 15 6:30am–5pm; otherwise 8am–4pm) runs from Cíguāng Gé (Mercy Light Temple) to Yùpíng Lóu, which is just over halfway up the western slope; the third, with a length of 3,709m (12,166 ft.) and less frequently used because it spits you west of the summit, is **Tàipíng cable car** (same times as above). The trip back to Tāngkǒu takes 1 hour by taxi or infrequent minibus. The one-way cost of each cable car is ¥66 ($8.25); or ¥56 ($7) from November 16 to March 14. When climbing the mountain, always carry layers of clothing: sweaters and raincoats as well as T-shirts. Hats and umbrellas are useful, too, as temperatures, even in summer, are subject to sudden changes due to the altitude and winds. You might also consider packing your own food and drink, as these become considerably more expensive the higher you climb.

From March 10 to November 15, the park entrance fee is ¥131 ($16); from November 16 to March 9 it's ¥86 ($11).

EASTERN STEPS At 7.5km (4½ miles) long, these paved, cut-stone stairways are considerably easier to negotiate than the Western Steps, though this is definitely not a walk in the park. Shortly after the start of the trail, considered the Yúngǔ Sì cable car terminus, see if you can spot Eyebrow Peak (Méimao Fēng) to the south, said to resemble what else but a pair of eyebrows. When you're not huffing and puffing, the climb, which takes you past bubbling streams and pretty pine and bamboo forests, is quite pleasant.

WESTERN STEPS Most hikers begin their assault on the 15km (9-mile) Western Steps at **Cíguāng Gé,** where you can burn incense and offer prayers for safe trails, not a bad idea considering that the serpentine Western Steps, hewn out of the sheer rock face, can be precipitously steep and narrow at places. There are rest stops along the way at the **Yuèyá Tíng (Crescent Moon Pavilion)** and the **Bànshān Sì (Mid-Level Temple,** a misnomer—it should be the Quarter-Way Temple, for that's about where you are).

The real midpoint of the trail is **Yùpíng Fēng (Jade Screen Peak),** with the Yùpíng Lóu Bīnguǎn nestled like a jewel among the pointed vertical peaks. About 20 minutes by foot to the west is the upper terminus for the Yùpíng *suǒdào* (cable car). Before you reach Jade Screen Peak, however, a narrow path hewn between two large rocks named **Yī Xiàn Tiān** (literally "A Thread of Sky" because only a sliver of sky is visible through this passage) leads to the distinctive **Yíngkè Sōng (Welcoming Guests Pine),** which extends a long tree branch as if in greeting.

South of Jade Screen Peak, an incredibly steep and exposed stairway (often called the Áoyú Bèi—Carp's Backbone) snakes its way to the magnificent **Tiāndū Fēng** ✦✦✦, the third-highest peak at 1,810m (5,937 ft.). Young lovers often bring padlocks inscribed

ACCOMMODATIONS ■
Běihǎi Bīnguǎn 5
北海宾馆

Shīlín Dàjiǔdiàn 3
狮林大酒店

Táoyuán Bīnguǎn 12
桃源宾馆

Xīhǎi Fàndiàn 2
西海饭店

Yúngǔ Shānzhuāng 9
(Cloud Valley Villa Hotel)
云谷山庄

Yùpíng Lóu Bīnguǎn 7
(Jade Screen Hotel)
玉屏峰

ATTRACTIONS ●
Bànshān Sì 10
(Mid-Level Temple)
半山寺

Cíguāng Gé 11
慈光阁

Fēilái Shí 6
(Rock that Flew from Afar)
飞来石

Páiyún Tíng 1
(Cloud Dispelling Pavilion)
排云亭

Qīngliáng Tái 4
(Refreshing Terrace)
清凉台

Yíngkè Sōng 8
(Welcoming Guests Pine)
迎客松

China ANHUI
Huang Shan
Beijing ★

Taiping Cable Car

BEIHAI (NORTHERN SEA OF CLOUD)

Shǐxìn Fēng
▲ (Beginning to Believe Peak)
始信峰

DONGHAI (EAST SEA OF CLOUD)

Guāngmíng Dǐng
光明顶

Yúngǔsī cable car
云谷索道

Liánhuā Ūēng
(Lotus Flower Peak)
莲花峰

▲ Tiāndū Fēng
(Heavenly Capital Peak)
天都峰

Yùpíng Suǒdào
(cable car)
玉屏索道

▲ Mountain
⛩ Temple

Huang Shan Gate

Wuhui Hwy.

0 ___ 1 mi
0 ___ 1 km

Huang Shan

Tāngkǒu

with their names to affix to the railings at the peak in proof and hope of being "locked" together in eternal love. The **views** from this "heavenly capital" are simply extraordinary. If you suffer from vertigo or agoraphobia, give this peak a pass. At press time, Tiāndū Fēng was closed for maintenance, and no date was set for reopening.

Past the Jade Screen Hotel is Huáng Shān's highest summit, **Liánhuā Fēng (Lotus Flower Peak;** elev. 1,873m/6,143 ft.), so named because it resembles a lotus shoot among fronds. From here it's another 20 to 30 minutes or so to the second-highest peak, **Guāngmíng Dǐng** (elev. 1,860m/6,100 ft.), where there's a weather station and a hotel. A little farther along is the famous **Fēilái Shí (Rock that Flew from Afar),** a large vertical rock standing on a tapered end. Another half-hour brings you to the Běihǎi Bīnguǎn.

ON THE SUMMIT The highlight at the summit is the **Běihǎi Sunrise** ✿✿, the only reason for overnighting on the summit. Weather permitting, the moment when the first golden ray hits and spills onto the sea of clouds is truly breathtaking. Be fore-warned, however, that you'll be sharing this special moment with hundreds of other chattering tourists bundled up in the thick jackets provided by the summit hotels. The **Qīngliáng Tái (Refreshing Terrace),** less than 10 minutes from the Běihǎi Bīnguǎn, is the best place to view the sunrise. Alternatively, the **Páiyún Tíng (Cloud Dis-pelling Pavilion)** between the Fēilái Shí and the Xīhǎi Fàndiàn is the place to catch the equally pretty sunsets. Another popular photo op is the **Shǐxìn Fēng (Beginning to Believe Peak)** between the Běihǎi Bīnguǎn and the Yúngǔ cable car terminus.

WHERE TO STAY & DINE

Tāngkǒu's hotels are not quite up to international standards but are adequate in a pinch. Hotels at the hot springs are generally overpriced, and staying there only makes sense if you plan to indulge in the waters or if you plan an early-morning assault on the Western Trail. The Yúngǔ Sì area is more remote, and hotels there generally cater to large tour groups. Although prices are significantly higher on the summit, spend-ing a night at the top in order to catch the famed Běihǎi sunrise is highly recom-mended. Phone ahead for reservations, particularly if you plan to visit May through October when rooms are difficult to come by.

TĀNGKŎU

There's a **bakery,** Wèitèjiā Miànbāofáng, on Yín Shí Jiē, the main street under the bridge. Next door is a mini-**supermarket** where you can stock up on snacks, groceries, and drinks for the climb.

Hóngdàshī Jiŭdiàn This two-star hotel just down the street from the Zhōunán Hotel has unremarkable rooms with firm beds and forgettable furniture, but at least the rooms are very clean and the furniture is still new. Bathrooms are basic but clean and there's 24-hour hot water. The staff can't muster much English, but they put on a nice game face.

Yánxī Jiē. ✆ **0559/556-2577.** Fax 0559/556-1888. 35 units. ¥320–¥380 ($40–$48) standard room. 20% discounts possible, up to 40% in low season. No credit cards. **Amenities:** 2 restaurants; lounge; concierge; store; salon; limited room service; laundry. *In room:* A/C, TV.

Mr. Chéng's Restaurant HOME-STYLE CHINESE Currently located at Yánxī Jiē, this restaurant (which will likely have moved by the time you read this) dishes up big por-tions of familiar favorites like *gōngbào jǐdīng* and fried spare ribs in soy sauce. For some-thing local, try *Huáng Shān èrdōng,* a stir-fry of winter mushrooms and bamboo shoots picked from the surrounding hills. The very friendly, English-speaking Mr. Chéng can also help with tour information and with booking accommodations and train tickets.

Yánxī Jiē. ✆ **0/13085592603.** English menu. Meal for 2 ¥40–¥80 ($5–$10). No credit cards. 7am–10pm (to mid-night Mar 10–Nov 15).

Zhōunán Dàjiŭdiàn This two-star hotel east of the bridge has basic but clean rooms with comfortable beds and the standard no-frills amenities. But there's a hair dryer in every room! The staff speaks minimal English but tries to be helpful.

Yánxī Jiē. ✆ **0559/556-3518.** Fax 0559/556-3519. 77 units. ¥340–¥380 ($42–$47) standard room. 35% discounts possible. No credit cards. **Amenities:** Restaurant; tour desk; store; salon; limited room service; laundry. *In room:* A/C, TV, hair dryer.

WĒNQUÁN (HOT SPRINGS)

Táoyuán Bīnguǎn This large three-star hotel is the inn of choice and is where the Western Trail begins. Rooms were renovated in 2002; bathrooms, however, are still small and dark. The staff can handle the basics, but little more.

Huáng Shān Fēngjǐngqū Wēnquán. © 0559/558-5666. Fax 0559/558-5288. 108 units. ¥600 ($75) standard room; ¥1,880 ($235) suite. AE, DC, MC, V. **Amenities:** Restaurant; bar; lounge; concierge; business center; forex; shopping arcade; salon; limited room service; laundry. *In room:* A/C, TV.

YÚNGǓ SÌ (CLOUD VALLEY TEMPLE) CABLE CAR STATION

Yúngǔ Shānzhuāng (Cloud Valley Villa Hotel)   Down the road from the Yúngǔ Sì cable car, this remote three-star hotel popular with Taiwanese tour groups is nicely designed in the traditional Huīzhōu architectural style, with stark white walls and gray tiled roofs. Rooms are a little dark and damp, but are otherwise furnished with the basic amenities.

Yúngǔ Sì. © 0559/558-6444. Fax 0559/558-6018. 100 units. ¥580 ($72) standard room; ¥1,280 ($155) suite. 20%–40% discounts possible. No credit cards. **Amenities:** Restaurant; bar; lounge; sauna; concierge; business center; forex (US$ only); salon; limited room service; laundry/dry cleaning. *In room:* A/C, TV.

SUMMIT AREA

Běihǎi Bīnguǎn   As the oldest hotel (1958) on the mountain, this three-star outfit has at least staked out the best position and is closest to the sunrise-viewing spot. Front rooms, which have good views of Starting To Believe Peak, are otherwise quite drab. Rooms in the back wing are newer and nicer and fitted with Chinese furniture, comfortable beds, and jackets for the sunrise-viewing. Service is uneven.

Běihǎi Fēngjǐngqū. © 0559/558-2555. Fax 0559/558-1996. 230 units. ¥700–¥850 ($87–$106) standard room. 10% discounts possible. AE, DC, MC, V. **Amenities:** Restaurant; bar; lounge; concierge; salon; limited room service. *In room:* TV, heater.

Shílín Dàjiǔdiàn ✦   This four-star hotel has rooms that are small but cozy and furnished with the usual amenities. Bathrooms are small but clean and come with showers only. The hotel's restaurant can serve Western breakfasts upon request. Service is adequate if not particularly memorable.

Běihǎi Fēngjǐngqū. © 0559/558-4040. Fax 0559/558-1888. www.shilin.com. 142 units. ¥960 ($120) standard room. AE, DC, MC, V. **Amenities:** 2 restaurants; bar; lounge; concierge; business center; forex; shopping arcade; salon; limited room service; laundry; nonsmoking rooms. *In room:* A/C, TV, minibar.

Xīhǎi Fàndiàn ✦   A nicer but pricier option is this four-star Swiss-designed hotel, popular with American, European, and Japanese tour groups. Rooms, resembling ship cabins, are fitted with comfortable beds and rattan furniture. Some bathrooms are a little run-down. Staff is friendly and helpful. It's as comfortable as staying on the summit can be. The restaurant offers a decent breakfast buffet for ¥40 ($5) per person.

Xīhǎi Fēngjǐngqū. © 0559/558-8888. Fax 0559/558-8988. 125 units. ¥1,080 ($130) standard room; ¥1,730 ($216) suite. 30% discount possible. AE, DC, MC, V. **Amenities:** 2 restaurants; bar; concierge; business center; forex (US$ and yen only); store; salon; limited room service. *In room:* Satellite TV, minibar, heater.

14 Túnxī

Ānhuī Province, 67km (41 miles) SE of Huáng Shān, 27km (17 miles) W of Shè Xiàn

After arriving in Túnxī, the gateway to Huáng Shān, it used to be that visitors would bypass this small town and head directly for the mountain. Nowadays, however, the beautiful countryside around Túnxī, with its paddy fields and gorgeous traditional architecture, provides a draw in its own right, and a visit here is well worth combining with your trip to Huáng Shān. *Note:* For Chinese translations of selected establishments listed in this section, please see appendix A.

ESSENTIALS

GETTING THERE Located about 8km (5 miles) northwest of town, **Túnxī airport** has daily flights to Shànghǎi (1 hr.), Běijīng (2 hr.), Guǎngzhōu (1½ hr.), and Hángzhōu (1 hr.); and less frequent flights to Hong Kong (2 hr.), Héféi (a half-hour), Guìlín (1½ hr.), and Xī'ān (3 hr.). Tickets can be bought at the **CAAC office (Míngháng Shòupiào Chù)** at Huáshān Lù 23 (② 0559/293-4111). Taxis to the airport cost ¥20 ($2.50).

There are two **trains** a day connecting Túnxī to Shànghǎi (12 hr.; ¥171/$21 soft sleeper, ¥103/$13 hard sleeper). Tickets can be bought at the **railway station** (② 0559/211-6222), at CITS, or at hotel tour desks.

Tāngkǒu-bound **buses** (1½ hr.; ¥13/$1.60) regularly leave from Túnxī's bus station *(qìchēzhàn)* and the square in front of the railway station. They start as early as 6:30am to catch arriving train passengers and run until around 6pm. Buses become less frequent in the afternoon and only depart when full.

GETTING AROUND Taxis charge ¥5 (60¢) for 2km (1¼ miles), then ¥1.80 (25¢) per kilometer thereafter until 10km (6 miles), then ¥2.70 (35¢) per kilometer. Smaller *miàndī* (van) taxis charge ¥3 (40¢) per 2km (1¼ miles) or ¥5 (60¢) for destinations in town. Private taxi rental out to Yī Xiàn will run around ¥300 ($38), subject to negotiation.

TOURS & GUIDES CITS at Bīnjiāng Xī Lù 1 (② 0559/251-5303; fax 0559/251-5255) can arrange private day trips to surrounding areas like Yī Xiàn and Shè Xiàn. Car hire for a day (guide not included) will run ¥300 to ¥400 ($38–$50) depending on your itinerary; an English-speaking guide will cost another ¥100 to ¥200 ($15–$25). Unless you look Chinese or have some *guānxi* (connections) with the local PSB, it's easier to have CITS get your permit for ¥60 ($7.50) to visit Yī Xiàn, even if you use none of their other services.

FAST FACTS

Banks, Foreign Exchange & ATMs The **Bank of China** at Xīn'ān Běi Lù 9 is open for foreign exchange Monday through Friday from 8am to noon and 2:30 to 5:30pm. There is an ATM outside the bank.

Internet Access There is a **24-hour Internet cafe** at the southern end of Xiānréndòng Lù; it charges ¥2 (25¢) per hour. Dial-up is ② 163.

Post Office The post office (open 8am–8pm) is in the southern part of town at Qiányuán Nán Lù 39.

Visa Extensions The **PSB** is at Chánggān Lù 108 (② 0559/231-8768; Mon–Fri 8–11:30am and 3–5:30pm).

WHERE TO STAY

EXPENSIVE

Huáng Shān Guójì Dàjiǔdiàn (Huáng Shān International Hotel) ⚔ This four-star hotel in the northwestern part of town is the choice for visiting Chinese dignitaries and the most popular choice with Western visitors, although it's starting to show signs of age. Rooms are spacious, comfortable, and equipped with extra amenities like robes, bathroom scale, and in-house movies. Bathrooms are bright and clean, and the service is quite friendly and efficient. The hotel's restaurant, featuring Ānhuī cuisine, is known by locals as one of the better establishments in town.

Huáshān Lù 31. ⓒ **0559/256-5678.** Fax 0559/251-2087. 215 units. ¥680 ($80) standard room; from ¥1,480 ($175) suite. 20% discounts possible; 40% discounts possible Nov–Mar. AE, DC, MC, V. **Amenities:** 2 restaurants; bar; lounge; outdoor tennis court; health club; concierge; tour desk; business center; forex; shopping arcade; salon; limited room service; laundry/dry cleaning. *In room:* A/C, TV, minibar, hair dryer (4th floor and up), safe (select rooms).

Huáng Shān Guómài Dàjiǔdiàn) ⚞

Five minutes south of the railway station, this modern 11-story hotel has the most convenient in-town location of the four-star establishments. Business travelers seem to favor this hotel, which has classy rooms equipped with comfortable beds and the standard amenities. The staff speaks some English and can be helpful when they're not harried.

Qiányuán Nán Lù 25. ⓒ **0559/235-1188.** Fax 0559/235-1199. 153 units. ¥680 ($85) standard room; ¥1,280–¥3,800 ($160–$475) suite. 10% discounts possible. AE, DC, MC, V. **Amenities:** 3 restaurants; bar; lounge; health club; concierge; business center; forex; shopping arcade; salon; limited room service; laundry/dry cleaning; executive rooms. *In room:* A/C, satellite TV, minibar, hair dryer, safe.

Jiànguó Shāngwù Jiǔdiàn (Jiànguó Garden Hotel) ⚞

Located near the International Hotel on the road to the airport, this four-star hotel catering mostly to Asian tour groups is a modern (built in 2000) but charmless white-tiled affair on the outside. Happily, rooms are more tastefully decorated with comfortable beds and inoffensive furnishings. The clean bathrooms have weighing scales and the basic amenities. The friendly staff speaks a little English.

Jīchǎng Dàdào 6. ⓒ **0559/256-6688.** Fax 0559/235-4580. www.hs.jg.com. 130 units. ¥680–¥780 ($85–$97) standard room; ¥1,380–¥4,800 ($172–$600) suite. 20% discounts possible. AE, DC, MC, V. **Amenities:** 2 restaurants; bar; lounge; outdoor pool; outdoor tennis court; health club; concierge; business center; forex; shopping arcade; salon; limited room service; laundry/dry cleaning. *In room:* A/C, TV, hair dryer.

MODERATE

Huáng Shān Huāxī Fàndiàn   Located in the southwest part of town near Túnxī's Old Street, this three-star hotel used to be one of the main outfits catering to foreigners before all the new four-star hotels set up shop. Today, it still has its appeal and is often fully booked. Rooms in the main building were renovated in 2002 and are simply furnished but comfortable. Bathrooms are basic but clean.

Xīzhèn Jiē 1. ⓒ **0559/232-8000.** Fax 0559/251-4990. 282 units. ¥480–¥680 ($60–$85) standard room; ¥1,280 ($160) suite. 20% discounts possible. AE, DC, MC, V. **Amenities:** Restaurant; bar; lounge; concierge; business center; shopping arcade; salon; limited room service; laundry. *In room:* A/C, TV.

WHERE TO DINE

Bǎo Húlu DUMPLINGS/NOODLES   This no-frills but clean eatery in the western part of town is very popular with locals for breakfast and lunch. Popular menu items include *zhēngjiǎo* (steamed dumplings), *niúròu miàn* (beef noodles), and *Yángzhōu chǎofàn* (Yángzhōu fried rice).

Yán'ān Lù 81. Meal for 2 ¥15–¥25 ($2–$3). No credit cards. 7am–10pm.

Lǎo Jiē Dìyī Lóu ⚞ HUĪZHŌU   Housed in a traditional three-story Huīzhōu-style building at the eastern end of Old Street, this is a clean and therefore excellent place to try Huīzhōu cuisine, which is typically strong and pungent, emphasizing spicy and salty flavors. Specialties include *Huáng Shān sùwèiyuán* (stir-fried mountain vegetables, tofu, pumpkin, bamboo shoots, mushrooms, and medicinal herbs), *wǔcài shànsī* (eel stir-fried with peppers, mushrooms, and bamboo shoots) and *chòu dòufu* (smelly tofu). The food is tasty but service is a bit uneven.

Lǎo Jiē 247. ⓒ **0559/253-9797.** Meal for 2 ¥50–¥100 ($6–$12). No credit cards. 9am–2pm and 4:30–9pm.

SHOPPING

In the southwestern part of town 1 block north of the river is **Lǎo Jiē (Old Street),** a 1.3km (¾-mile) street lined with restored Sòng dynasty wooden houses and shops. The usual souvenirs are here, from ethnic batik and Máo buttons to Chinese paintings and dried foodstuffs. Shops are open from 8am to 10pm. This is a fun place to stroll even if you're not in the buying mood.

AROUND TÚNXĪ

Formerly known as Huīzhōu (from which Ānhuī derived part of its name), this region was home to many wealthy salt merchants who in the Míng and Qīng dynasties built many memorial arches and residences in such a unique style as to create a distinct regional *Huāzhōu* style of architecture. The district of Huīzhōu and the counties of Shè Xiàn and Yī Xiàn are famous for their well-preserved memorial arches *(páifang),* memorial halls *(cítáng),* and traditional villages lined with narrow streets and flowing streams.

Yī Xiàn is approximately 50km (30 miles) northwest of Túnxī, while the **Huīzhōu District** and **Shè Xiàn** are to the north and northeast. All three can easily be visited as separate day trips, but a combination of the three will be trickier. It is possible to visit both Shè Xiàn and Yī Xiàn in a long day, but you'll most likely only be able to visit one

Huīzhōu Architecture

The main courtyard in Huīzhōu houses is flanked on three sides by buildings with downward-sloping roofs, meant to aid the collection of rainwater, which symbolized wealth. This open-air courtyard provides the only illumination as there are few, if any, outside windows. Buildings typically have two or three overhanging stories; these upper floors were the havens (or prisons) of the women of the house, who had to rely on peepholes and small windows in the closed-off verandas to survey the goings-on in the courtyard below.

The average family home had a single courtyard, but those of higher status were allowed two or even three courtyards. Because building courtyards beyond one's rank was a punishable offense, many owners attempted to enhance their prestige by building more side rooms and by improving the ornamental and decorative fixtures in the house. As a result, many of Huīzhōu's houses have some of the best stone, brick, and wood carvings in China.

Huīzhōu houses are also separated from each other by high, crenellated walls called **horse-head walls *(mǎtóu bì),*** so named because the wall is said to look like a horse's head with its convex-shaped, black-tiled gable roof over stark white or gray stones. These walls were used both to prevent fires and to deter burglars and bandits, especially when the merchants were away on business.

Stone **memorial archways *(páifang)*** built to honor ancestors typically have calligraphic inscriptions detailing the reason for the arch, have two or four supporting posts, and have anywhere from two to five tiered roofs.

or two sights in each place and you won't have time to linger. You'll also have to rent a private taxi or car for the day (see "Tours & Guides," above), since public transportation to and between sights is slow and infrequent. If you have some command of Chinese or would simply like to brave it on your own, you can hire a taxi in Túnxī for the day to **Xīdì, Hóng Cūn,** and **Nánpíng** in Yī Xiàn for ¥250 to ¥300 ($30–$38), and to **Shè Xiàn, Qiānkǒu,** and **Chéngkǎn** for around ¥280 ($35). Minibuses also leave for Shè Xiàn (30 min.; ¥4/50¢) and Yī Xiàn (1 hr.; ¥8/$1) from the bus station and the roundabout in front of the railway station. Note that you will have to get a **permit** for ¥60 ($7.50) to visit Yī Xiàn (deemed a "sensitive" area because of some nearby military bases), which you can do either at the PSB (Gōngānjú) or through CITS. The PSB requires that individuals applying for a permit have a sponsoring agency, which can sometimes, though not always, be the taxi driver you hire for the day.

YĪ XIÀN

The first village you encounter on the way to Yī Xiàn (7km/4 miles away) is **Xīdì** ✦ (¥50/$6.25; open 8am–6pm), a UNESCO World Heritage Site famous for its over 300 well-preserved ancient residences. The houses, with their amazingly ornate stone, brick, and wood carvings, are really the highlight here at this boat-shaped village which dates to the Northern Sòng dynasty (960–1127) but which developed into its present size during the Míng and Qīng dynasties. The memorial archway (built in 1578) which greets visitors when you first arrive is the sole remaining archway in the village and is said to have survived the Cultural Revolution because it was covered with Máo slogans.

Another UNESCO World Heritage Site, **Hóng Cūn** ✦✦ (¥55/$6.50; open 8am–5:30pm), located 11km (7 miles) northeast of Yī Xiàn town, is probably the most picturesque of the towns, with two spots in the village vying for top honors: the exterior view with an arched bridge across a large lily pond; and the crescent-shaped pond Yuèzhǎo Táng, whose reflection of the surrounding traditional houses on a clear day is truly magnificent. If these vistas appear familiar, it is probably because the two locations were used in the movie *Crouching Tiger, Hidden Dragon*. Water is the main feature at this village, with the two large ponds connected to a series of flowing streams and canals which pass by every house, providing water for washing, cooking, and bathing, and which taken altogether are said to outline the shape of a bull.

Just over 5km (3 miles) west of Yī Xiàn, **Nánpíng** ✦ (¥20/$2.50; open 8am–5:30pm) is a late Táng, early Sòng dynasty town that served as the location for Zhāng Yìmóu's 1990 film *Jú Dòu*. All the houses in the village have concave corners that bow inward, the absence of rigid sharp edges symbolizing the avoidance of quarrels in the community. With 72 lanes that seem to double back on each other like an Escher maze, the village is best visited with a local guide (included in the price of admission), even though he or she speaks practically no English.

SHÈ XIÀN

Although Shè Xiàn has 94 memorial arches scattered throughout the county, **Tángyuè Páifang Qún (Tángyuè Memorial Arches)** ✦, with its collection of seven four-pillared arches, is the best place to view these impressive structures. Located about 6km (3¾ miles) west of Shè Xiàn, the arches may be viewed from 6:30am to 6:30pm for a fee of ¥35 ($4.30). The arches were built by a salt merchant family named Bāo over the course of 400 years in the Míng and Qīng dynasties. If you're coming by minibus (¥4/50¢) from Túnxī, ask to be dropped off at the archways. From there, it's another 1.5km (1 mile) to the arches. Walk or take a tricycle taxi for ¥5 to ¥10 (60¢–$1.20).

Shè Xiàn claims the only eight-pillared memorial archway in China, the **Xǔguó Shífáng (Xǔguó Stone Archway)** ⚘⚘. Built in 1584 to honor a local scholar named Xú Guó, this magnificent structure has eight pillars decorated with carved lions, phoenixes, and *qílín* (Chinese unicorns). Up the hill from the archway and down a left side street is **Dòushān Jiē** (¥10/$1.25), a narrow alley lined with traditional houses and shops.

HUĪZHŌU QŪ (HUĪZHŌU DISTRICT)

The highlight at **Chéngkǎn** village ⚘⚘ (¥35/$4.30 Mar 16–Nov 15; ¥25/$3 otherwise; 7am–5:30pm; 8am–4:30pm Nov 16–Mar 15), 34km (20 miles) north of Túnxī is **Bǎolún Gé (Bǎolún Hall)** ⚘⚘, an impressive building alone worth the trip. Located in the back of the **Luó Dōngshū Cí (Luó Dōngshū Ancestral Hall),** the bottom half of the structure, with stone square pillars supporting exquisitely painted (though now faded) wooden beams and brackets, was built in the Míng dynasty to honor the Luó family ancestors. The top half, with wooden windows and tiled roof, was built 70 years later to honor the emperor. At Zhōngyīng Jiē 12 is a Qīng dynasty house worth visiting for its intricately carved wooden doors and panels.

Qiánkǒu village has a Museum of Ancient Residences (¥10/$1.25; open 7:30am–6pm), a collection of 12 Míng dynasty Huīzhōu-style residences formerly scattered throughout Shè Xiàn county but relocated here and restored to their original state. This museum provides a comprehensive overview of the local architecture if you don't have time to tour individual towns.

Shànghǎi

by Sharon Owyang

As China's largest city, and its economic, commercial, and financial capital, Shànghǎi is the heart of and key to China's future. No other super city in China, including Hong Kong and Běijīng, is more vibrant or fascinating, or has such a unique colonial past.

As Chinese cities go, Shànghǎi is comparatively young, gaining its identity only after the First Opium War in 1842 opened up this heretofore small fishing village at the mouth of the Yángzǐ River to foreign powers. The British, French, Americans, Germans, and Russians moved in, erecting their distinct Western-style banks, trading houses, and mansions, leaving an indelible architectural legacy to this day.

During its heyday in the 1920s and 1930s when it grew to be Asia's leading city, Shànghǎi, dubbed the "Paris of the East" (and more ignominiously, the "Whore of Asia"), was a cosmopolitan and thriving commercial and financial center that attracted legions to its shores: explorers and exploiters, gangsters and businessmen alike. In 1990, after 40 years of commercial slumber imposed by the Communist victory in 1949, Shànghǎi was picked to spearhead China's economic reform, and the city has not looked back or paused for breath since.

Shànghǎi was not always fun to tour, but it is now. After the building boom of the 1990s tore the city apart, new roads, highways, tunnels, and bridges, not to mention new hotels, restaurants, and sights, now make Shànghǎi a city that a visitor can once again comfortably enjoy and explore.

Today, there are neighborhoods of foreign architecture that have been preserved and restored, and are wonderful for a stroll. Shànghǎi's great river of commerce, the Huángpǔ, a tributary of the Yángzǐ River, is lined with a gallery of colonial architecture, known as the Bund, grander than any other in the East, much of it recently refurbished, and beckoning to the curious visitor and savvy locals alike. The mansions, garden estates, country clubs, and cathedrals of the Westerners who made their fortunes here a century ago are scattered throughout the city, and there is even a synagogue, dating from the days of an unparalleled Jewish immigration to China.

At the same time the creations of a strictly Chinese culture have not been erased. A walk through the chaotic old Chinese city turns up traditional treasures: a teahouse that epitomizes Old China; a quintessential southern-Chinese classical garden; active temples, and ancient pagodas.

But the city is not only a museum of East meeting West on Chinese soil. Overnight Shànghǎi has become one of the world's great modern capitals, the one city that best shows where China is headed at the dawn of the 21st century. Across the Huángpǔ River, Pǔdōng, serving as the face of new Shànghǎi, now boasts the tallest hotel in the world, Asia's largest shopping mall, China's largest stock exchange, and one of the highest observation decks in Asia, the Oriental Pearl TV Tower.

More than just in the facades of its buildings, Shànghăi is also once again establishing itself as a leading trendsetter when it comes to fashion, design, culture, and the arts. And in matters culinary and commercial, Shànghăi is arguably also the best city in China for dining and shopping.

Bearing the burden of all these superlatives, the Shanghainese—frank, efficient, chauvinistic, and progressive—are using their previous international exposure to create China's most outward-looking, modern, and brash metropolis, one due to host the World Expo in 2010.

Visitors dizzy from the frenzy can find, within an easy day trip of Shànghăi, two famous, more pastoral destinations that should not be missed. To the northwest, Sūzhōu, with its classical gardens and canals, is known as the "Venice of China." To the southwest is Hángzhōu, renowned for beautiful West Lake and the surrounding tea plantations. Winter in Shànghăi is windy and chilly; summer is oppressively hot and humid, making late March or late October/early November the ideal time to visit. **Note:** Unless otherwise noted, hours listed for attractions and restaurants are daily.

1 Orientation

ARRIVING

BY PLANE Shànghăi has an older airport to the west, **Hóngqiáo International Airport,** and a newer airport to the east, **Pŭdōng International Airport,** which began operations late in 1999. Virtually all of the international carriers use the Pŭdōng airport, which serves all major international destinations from Amsterdam to Vancouver. Every major city in China is also served with multiple daily flights, mostly to and from Hóngqiáo, but the most important, such as Bĕijīng, also have services to Pŭdōng.

The **Pŭdōng International Airport** (© 021/3848-4500), your likely point of arrival, is located about 45km (28 miles) east of downtown Shànghăi. Transfers into the city take 45 minutes to 1 hour. The international arrivals hall (ground level) has hotel counters, bank counters for money exchange (directly across from the baggage-area exits), and several ATMs. There is a Tourist Information Center (TIC) counter, as well as a branch of China International Travel Service (CITS) here.

The older **Hóngqiáo Airport** (© 021/6268-8899), now largely reserved for flights within China, is located 19km (12 miles) west of the city center. There are two arrival halls, A and B, each with hotel counters, though the majority of the hotels are represented in Arrival Hall B. Also here is a **Tourist Service Center** open 10am to 9:30pm (© 021/6268-8899) that provides maps and information and can also help with hotel reservations. There is no money exchange here, but an ATM that accepts foreign cards can be found in Arrival Hall A.

GETTING INTO TOWN
FROM THE AIRPORT
Hotel Shuttles Many of Shànghăi's hotels maintain service counters along the walls in the main arrivals halls in both airports, with free or inexpensive shuttle buses offered at Hóngqiáo Airport. In Pŭdōng, the hotel's airport staff will help you find a taxi or arrange for an expensive private car to take you to the hotel in the city.

Airport Taxis The legitimate taxis are lined up just outside the arrivals halls of both airports. Taxis into town from Hóngqiáo Airport take anywhere from 20 to 40 minutes depending on traffic and should cost between ¥40 and ¥80 ($5–$10). Taxi transfers on the new highway to hotels in Pǔdōng and downtown Shànghǎi run between 45 minutes and 1½ hours for ¥150 ($19) and up. Insist on seeing the meter started.

Metro   The world's first commercially operating maglev (magnetic levitation) line uses German technology to whisk you the 30km (19 miles) between Pǔdōng Airport and the Lóngyáng Lù metro station in Pǔdōng in 8 minutes (¥50/$6 one-way; ¥80/$10 round-trip). Maglev trains run every 15 minutes between 8:30am and 5:30pm daily. For information, dial © 021/6255-6987. From the Lóngyáng Lù station, travelers can connect to the rest of Shànghǎi using metro line 2. The latter is supposed to connect directly with the old Hóngqiáo Airport sometime in the near (but uncertain) future, too.

Airport Buses   There are many buses (© 021/6834-6912) making transfers from **Pǔdōng** airport into town: Airport Bus Line no. 1 goes to Hóngqiáo Airport; airport Bus Line no. 2 (Jīchǎng Èr Xiàn) goes from Pǔdōng to the City Air-Terminal Building (Chéngshì Hángzhàn Lóu) at Nánjīng Xì Lù 1600 every 15 to 20 minutes, from 7:20am to the last flight arrival, with taxis providing the final link to hotels. Bus no. 5 goes to the Shànghǎi Railway Station. Fares range from ¥17 to ¥25 ($2–$3). There are also shuttle buses that serve some hotels directly: Bus A serves the City, and the Jǐnjiāng and Garden hotels; Bus B, the Hilton, Equatorial, and Shànghǎi hotels; Bus C, the Peace and the Sofitel Hyland; and Bus "Pǔdōng A" makes a loop of the Pǔdōng hotels including the Shangri-La, Grand Hyatt, and Intercontinental hotels. Hotel bus tickets are ¥30 ($3.60). Check at the airport bus counter in the arrivals hall for the number and schedule of the bus that stops at your hotel or at the one nearest it.

From **Hóngqiáo,** several buses also make the run into town. A CAAC shuttle, Mínháng Zhuānxiàn (Airport Special Line), goes to the Chéngshì Hángzhàn Lóu (City Air-Terminal Building) at Nánjīng Xī Lù 1600, every 20 minutes from 6am to 8:30pm. Tickets cost ¥4 (50¢). Airport Bus Line no. 1 (Jīchǎng Yī Xiàn) goes to Pǔdōng Airport (buses depart every 20 min. from 6am–9pm). Bus no. 941 goes to the railway station and bus no. 925 runs to People's Square (Rénmín Guǎngchǎng).

BY TRAIN
Shànghǎi Railway Station (Shànghǎi Huǒchēzhàn; © 021/6354-3193 or 021/6317-9090) is massive but modern. You will have to walk a block to the metro Line 1 station (follow the signs) or hail a taxi (¥2/25¢ surcharge) on the lower level of the terminal., unless you are staying at the Holiday Inn Downtown, which is just a block south, across the shopping plaza. Five dedicated soft-sleeper express trains (Z1, Z5, Z7, Z13, and Z21) run every evening overnight from Běijīng Zhàn, arriving between 7 and 7:30am. (12 hr.; ¥478–¥499/$60–$63) while the return trips depart every evening between 7 and 7:30pm. Round-trip Běijīng–Shànghǎi tickets (return trip within 3–20 days) can now be purchased up to 20 days in advance. The K100 arrives on alternate days from Hong Kong's Hung Hom Station at 4:38pm (25 hr.; HK$530/US$69 hard sleeper, HK$825/US$108 soft sleeper, HK$1,039/US$135 deluxe soft sleeper—two beds but no private bathroom). There are trains to and from every other major city in China, as far away as Ürümqi. There is an English-language ticket counter at the station (usually counter 41).

BY SHIP
International arrivals from Japan are at the **International Passenger Terminal (Guójì Kèyùn Mǎtóu)** at Yángshùpǔ Lù 100 (© 021/6595-9529), not far north of the Bund. Ships of the **Japan-China International Ferry Company (Chinajif)** line leave

either Osaka or Kobe every Saturday, arriving in Shànghăi about 48 hours later; they leave Shànghăi for alternately Kobe or Osaka every Tuesday. See **www.fune.co.jp/chinjif/jikoku.html** for the schedule. The **Shànghăi Ferry Co. Ltd.** has a weekly sailing from Osaka on Friday, and to Osaka on Tuesday; see **www.Shanghai-ferry.co.jp** (in English). Tickets are available at the terminal or at travel agencies such as CITS. Domestic ships arriving from Dàlián, the Yángzĭ River, and Pŭtuó Shān now arrive at the **Wúsōng Passenger Terminal** (Shànghăi Găng Wúsōng Kèyùn Zhōngxīn, Sōngbăo Lù 251; ℂ **021/5657-5500**), at the intersection of the Huángpŭ and Yángzĭ rivers. If you arrive here as an independent traveler, you will have to hail a taxi at the passenger terminal to reach your hotel, which is likely another 30 to 45 minutes away.

VISITOR INFORMATION

The official **Tourism Hotline** (ℂ **021/6439-0630** or 021/6439-8947) can be helpful, but even better is the 24-hour **Tourist Information Line** maintained by Spring Travel Service (ℂ **021/6252-0000**). There are about a dozen **Travel Information Service Centers (TIC)** in the city, and they appear to only sell tours and book hotels but, depending on who's behind the desk, you may get some guidance. The main office is at Zhōngshān Xī Lù 2525, room 410 (ℂ **021/6439-9806**), with smaller branch offices scattered throughout the city.

The best sources of **current information** about Shànghăi events, shopping, restaurants, and nightlife are the free English-language newspapers and magazines distributed to hotels, shops, and cafes around town, such as *that's Shanghai* (www.thats shanghai.com), and *City Weekend* (www.cityweekend.com.cn). The newspaper *Shanghai Daily* (www.shanghaidaily.com) provides the sanitized official view.

CITY LAYOUT

Shànghăi, with one of the largest urban populations on Earth (13.5 million registered permanent residents, plus three million registered migrants), is divided by the Huángpŭ River into Pŭdōng (east of the river) and Pŭxī (west of the river).

For the traveler, the majority of Shànghăi's sights are still concentrated **downtown** in Pŭxī, whose layout bears a distinct Western imprint. After the First Opium War in 1842 opened Shànghăi up to foreign powers, the British, French, Germans, Americans, and others moved in, carving for themselves their own "concessions" where they were subject not to the laws of the Chinese government but to those established by their own governing councils. Colonial Shànghăi is especially visible downtown, along the western shore of the Huángpŭ River up and down the **Bund (Wàitān),** which has always been and still is the symbolic center of the city; from here, **downtown Shànghăi** opens to the west like a fan. Today's practical and logistical center, however, is **People's Square (Rénmín Guăngchăng),** about a mile west of the Bund. This is the meeting point of Shànghăi's two main subway lines, as well as the location of the Shànghăi Museum, Shànghăi Art Museum, and Shànghăi Grand Theatre. The Bund and People's Square are linked by several streets, none more famous than **Nánjīng Lù,** historically China's number-one shopping street.

Southwest of the Bund is the historic **Nánshì District,** Shànghăi's Old Chinese city. As its name suggests, here are located some typically Chinese sights, such as the quintessential Southern-Chinese Garden, Yù Yuán, the famous Húxīn Tíng teahouse, and several temples.

A mile or so west of the Bund and south of Nánjīng Lù, Shànghăi's former **French Concession** is still one of Shànghăi's trendiest neighborhoods, chock-full of colonial architecture and attractions. It is also home to some of the city's most glamorous shops and restaurants, as seen in the mega-development **Xīn Tiāndì.** Farther west still is the **Hóngqiáo Development Zone,** where modern commercial and industrial development was concentrated beginning in the 1980s.

North Shànghǎi has a scattering of interesting sights, including the Jade Buddha Temple, the Lǔ Xùn Museum, and the Ohel Moshe Synagogue. **South Shànghǎi** has the Lónghuá Pagoda, the Shànghǎi Botanical Garden, and the cafes and shops of Héngshān Lù.

East of the Huángpǔ River, the new district of **Pǔdōng** is today all about Shànghǎi's future, as epitomized by its ultramodern skyscrapers such as the Oriental Pearl TV Tower and the 88-story Jīn Mào Building, which houses the highest hotel in the world.

NEIGHBORHOODS IN BRIEF

The Shànghǎi municipality consists of 15 districts, 4 counties, and the Pǔdōng New Area, and covers an area of 6,341 sq. km (2,448 sq. miles), with its urban area measuring 2,643 sq. km (1,020 sq. miles). The eight main urban districts, running from east to west, are identified here.

Pǔdōng The Pǔdōng New Area was formerly a backwater beginning on the east bank of the Huángpǔ River directly across from the Bund and downtown Shànghǎi. Rapid urbanization began in 1990.

Huángpǔ (Downtown Shànghǎi) The city center of old Shànghǎi lies in a compact sector west of the Huángpǔ River and south of Sūzhōu Creek. It extends west to Chéngdū Běi Lù (the North–South Elevated Highway) along Nánjīng Road and encompasses the Bund, People's Square, and the Shànghǎi Museum.

Nánshì (Old Town) Immediately south of downtown and the Bund, between the Huángpǔ River and Xīzàng Nán Lù, this area includes the old Chinese city, the Yù Garden, and the Confucian Temple.

Hóngkǒu (Northeast Shànghǎi) Immediately north of downtown Shànghǎi, across Sūzhōu Creek, this residential sector along the upper Huángpǔ River was part of the International Concession in colonial days.

Lúwān (French Concession) Beginning at People's Square (Xīzàng Lù) and continuing west to Shǎnxī (Shaanxi) Nán Lù, this was the domain of the French colonial community (up until 1949).

Jìng Ān (Northwest Shànghǎi) North of the French Concession, this district has its share of colonial architecture, Chinese temples, and the modern Shànghǎi Centre.

Xúhuì (Southwest Shànghǎi) West of the French Concession and south along Héngshān Lù, this is one of the city's top addresses for cafes, bars, and shops.

Chángníng (Hóngqiáo Development Zone) Starting at Huáihǎi Xī Lù, directly west of the Xúhuì and Jìng'ān districts, this corridor of new international economic ventures extends far west of downtown, past the Shànghǎi Zoo, to the Hóngqiáo Airport.

2 Getting Around

BY METRO

The Shànghǎi metro *(dìtiě)* is the fastest and cheapest way to cover longer distances: just ¥3, ¥4, or ¥5 (35¢, 50¢, or 65¢) per ride, depending on the number of stops. Operating from 5:30am to 11pm, the metro now has two main lines and a light rail line, though there are plans to extend the number to eleven lines in the next decade. Currently, **metro line 1,** the red line, which has been extended, winds in a roughly north–south direction connecting the Shànghăi Railway Station in the north to points southwest past Shànghăi Stadium. Its central downtown stop is People's Square (Rénmín Guăngchăng) near Nánjīng Xī Lù, which is where it connects with **metro line 2,** the green line, which runs east–west from Pŭdōng across downtown Shànghăi. At press time, **metro line 4,** tracing a southern ring around the downtown area and extending into Pŭdōng was expected to be operational in early 2006. See the map on the inside back cover for all stops.

NAVIGATING THE METRO Subway platform signs in Chinese and *pīnyīn* indicate the station name and the name of the next station in each direction, and maps of the metro system are posted in each station and inside the subway cars. English announcements of upcoming stops are also made on trains. To determine your fare, consult the fare map posted near the ticket counters and on ticket vending kiosks. Fares range from ¥2 (25¢) for the first few stops to ¥4 (50¢) for the most distant ones. **Hang onto your electronic ticket, which you have to insert into the exit barrier when you leave.**

Note: Light Rail line 3, which currently circles the western outskirts of the city, is seldom useful for sightseeing, although it does stop near Lŭ Xùn Park, where the metro lines do not extend.

BY TAXI

With over 40,000 taxis in the streets, this is the visitor's most common means of getting around Shànghăi. Taxis congregate at leading hotels, but are better hailed from street corners. Your best bets for service and comfort are the turquoise-blue taxis of **Dà Zhōng Taxi** (© 021/6258-1688), the yellow taxis of **Qiáng Shēng Taxi** (© 021/6258-0000), and the blue taxis of **Jǐnjiāng Taxi** (© 021/6275-8800). Regardless of the company, the fare is ¥10 ($1.25) for the first 3km (1¾ miles), and ¥2 (25¢) for each additional kilometer. There's a 30% surcharge for trips after 11pm, and for bridge and tunnel tolls. Expect to pay about ¥20 to ¥35 ($2.40–$4.20) for most excursions in the city and up to ¥60 ($7.20) for longer cross-town jaunts.

BY BUS

Public buses *(gōnggòng qìchē)* charge ¥1 (15¢) per ride (¥2–¥3/25¢–30¢ if air-conditioned), but they are more difficult to use and less comfortable than taxis or the metro. Tickets are sold on board by a roving conductor, though some buses have no conductors and require exact change. Be prepared to stand and be cramped during your expedition, and take care with backpacks and purses, as these are inviting targets for thieves.

BY BRIDGE, BOAT & TUNNEL

To shift the thousands of daily visitors between east and west Shànghăi, there are seven basic routes. Three are by bridge, each handling around 45,000 vehicles a day: the 3.7km-long (2⅓-mile), harp-string-shaped **Nánpŭ Dàqiáo,** and the **Lúpŭ Dàqiáo,** both in the southern part of town; and the 7.6km-long (4¾-mile) **Yángpŭ Dàqiáo** northeast of the Bund. A fourth route (and the cheapest) is by water, via the **passenger ferry** that ordinary workers favor. The ferry terminal is at the southern end of the Bund on the west shore (ticket price: ¥2/25¢), and at the southern end of Riverside Avenue at Dōngchāng Lù on the east shore. Three more routes across the river make use of tunnels. The Yán'ān Dōng Lù Tunnel is plied by motor vehicles (though taxis are barred

8–9:30am and 5–6:30pm); metro line 2 is filled with German-made subway cars; and the **Bund Sight-Seeing Tunnel (Wàitān Guānguāng Suìdào)** is equipped with glassy tram cars that glide through a tacky subterranean 3-minute light show with music and narrative (8am–10:30pm; ¥30/$3.75 one-way, ¥40/$5 round-trip).

FAST FACTS: Shànghăi

If you don't find what you're looking for in these listings, try the **Tourism Hotline** ((C) 021/6439-0630 or 021/6439-8947) or inquire at your hotel desk.

American Express Holders of an American Express card can make inquiries about currency exchange, emergency card replacement, and personal check cashing at Nánjīng Xī Lù 1376, Shànghăi Centre, room 455 ((C) **021/6279-8082;** fax 021/6279-7183; Mon–Fri 9am–noon and 1–5:30pm). Tickets, bookings, and tours are not handled directly by American Express in their Shànghăi office.

Banks, Currency Exchange & ATMs The most convenient place to exchange currency is your hotel, where the rates are similar to those at the Bank of China and exchange desks are often open 24 hours. Convenient **Bank of China** locations for currency exchange and credit card cash withdrawals are located on the Bund at the Bank of China building, Zhōngshān Dōng Yī Lù 23 ((C) **021/6329-1979);** at Nánjīng Xī Lù 1221 ((C) **021/6247-1700);** at Yán'ān Xī Lù 2168 ((C) **021/6278-5060);** and at Huáihăi Zhōng Lù 1207 ((C) **021/6437-8753).**Bank hours are Monday to Friday from 9am to noon and 1:30 to 4:30pm, and Saturday from 9am to noon.

There are also branches of **Hongkong and Shanghai Bank (HSBC)** at the Shànghăi Centre (Nánjīng Xī Lù 1376) and at G/F, HSBC Tower, Yīn Chéng Dōng Lù 101, Pǔdōng. **Citibank** has a branch at the Peace Hotel on the Bund (Zhōngshān Dōng Yī Lù 19; (C) **021/6329-8383;** Mon–Fri 9am–4:30pm, Sat 10am–3pm) that can change U.S. traveler's checks and cash. All have 24-hour **ATMs,** which accept many international cards. *Note:* You must retain your foreign exchange receipts if you wish to reconvert Chinese currency back to your home currency before you depart China.

Doctors & Dentists Shànghăi has the most advanced medical treatment and facilities in China. The higher-end hotels usually have in-house or on-call doctors, but almost all hotels can refer foreign guests to dentists and doctors versed in Western medicine. The following medical clinics and hospitals specialize in treating foreigners and provide international-standard services: **World Link Medical and Dental Centers,** Nánjīng Xī Lù 1376, Shànghăi Centre, Suite 203 ((C) **021/ 6279-7688);** and Unit 30, Mandarine City, Hóngxǔ Lù 788, Hóngqiáo District ((C) **021/6405-5788),** have 24-hour emergency services, offer Western dental care, OB-GYN services, and maintain a website (www.worldlink-shanghai.com); walk-in hours at both branches are from 9am to 7pm Monday through Friday, from 9am to 4pm Saturday, and from 9am to 3pm Sunday. In addition, World Link has a Specialty and Inpatient Center at Dànshuǐ Lù 170, third floor ((C) **021/6385-9889).** The **Huá Shān Hospital,** Wūlǔmùqí Zhōng Lù 12, Jìng'ān District ((C) **021/ 6248-9999,** ext. 1921), has a special Foreigner's Clinic on the 19th floor, and a 24-hour hot line ((C) **021/6248-3986).** A representative office of **AEA International (SOS Alarm Centre),** Zūnyì Nán Lù 88, Shartex Plaza 2606 ((C) **021/6295-8277),** provides medical evacuation and repatriation throughout China on a 24-hour basis; for emergency medical evacuation, call © **021/6295-0099.**

Dental care to foreign visitors and expatriates is provided by World Link Monday to Saturday (see above); by **Dr. Harriet Jin's Dental Surgery,** Huáihăi Xī Lù 55, Sun Tong Infoport Plaza, room 17C (© **021/5298-9799**), open from 9am to 6pm Monday through Friday, from 9am to 1pm Saturday; by the Canadian-managed **Sino-Canadian Shànghăi Dental Center** on the seventh floor of the Ninth People's Hospital, Zhìzàojú Lù 639 (© **021/6313-3174**), which is closed Sunday; and by **DDS Dental Care,** Táojiāng Lù 1, second floor (© **021/6466-0928;** www. ddsdentalcare.com). DDS Dental Care has multilingual Western-trained dentists, a lab, and a 24-hour emergency number (© **1301-288-1288**).

Embassies & Consulates The consulates of many countries are located in the French Concession and Jìng'ān districts several miles west of the city center. The consulates are open Monday through Friday only, and often close for lunch from noon to 1pm. The Consulate General of the **United States** is at Huáihăi Zhōng Lù 1469 (© **021/6433-6880;** fax 021/6433-4122; www.usembassy-china.org.cn/ shanghai). The **Canadian** Consulate General is in the Shànghăi Centre at Nánjīng Xī Lù 1376, West Tower, Suites 604 and 668 (visa section, © **021/6279-8400;** fax 021/6279-8401; www.shanghai.gc.ca). The **New Zealand** Consulate General is at Huáihăi Zhōng Lù 1375, Suite 15A (© **021/6471-1108;** fax 021/6431-0226; www. nzembassy.com). The Consulate General of **Australia** is in CITIC Square at Nánjīng Xī Lù 1168, 22nd floor (© **021/5292-5500;** fax 021/5292-5511; www. aus-in-shanghai.com). The **British** Consulate General is in the Shànghăi Centre, Nánjīng Xī Lù 1376, Suite 301 (© **021/6279-8400;** fax 021/6279-7651; www. britishconsulate.sh.cn).

Hospitals See "Doctors & Dentists," above.

Internet Access Business centers at most three-star and up Shànghăi hotels now provide online access and e-mail services. Dial-up Internet access (© **16300,** with the same user name and password) is available in any hotel room with a phone, but broadband Internet access is now commonplace in Shànghăi's top hotels, many of which also offer wireless access in their lobbies and executive lounges. The most reliable and the cheapest Internet access can be found at the **Shànghăi Library (Shànghăi Túshūguăn),** Huáihăi Zhōng Lù 1557 (© **021/6445-2001**), in a small office on the ground floor underneath the main entrance staircase. It's open from 9am to 8:30pm (¥4/50¢ per hour).

Maps & Books The biggest and best selection of English-language books in Shànghăi, as well as the bilingual *Shànghăi Tourist Map,* can be found at the **Shànghăi Foreign Language Bookstore (Shànghăi Wàiwén Shūdiàn),** Fúzhōu Lù 390 (© **021/6322-3200;** 9:30am–6pm). The **Shànghăi Museum,** Rénmín Dà Dào 201 (© **021/6372-3500**), has selections of books on Shànghăi and Chinese art and culture, as do the gift shops and kiosks in major hotels, such as the Hilton and the Jīnjiāng (which carry foreign newspapers as well). Most hotel concierges should also be able to provide bilingual maps of the city.

Pharmacies The best outlet for Westerners is **Watson's Drug Store** which has branches throughout town, including at Huáihăi Zhōng Lù 787–789 (© **021/ 6474-4775;** 9:30am–10pm). Prescriptions can be filled at the **World Link Medical**

Center, Nánjīng Xī Lù 1376, Shànghǎi Centre, Suite 203 (© **021/6279-7688**).

Post Office Most hotels sell postage stamps and will mail your letters and parcels, the latter at a hefty fee. The main post office (*yóuzhèngjú;* open 7am–10pm) is located at Běi Sūzhōu Lù 276 (© **021/6324-0069**), at Sìchuān Běi Lù, in downtown Shànghǎi just north of Sūzhōu Creek; international parcels are sent from a desk in the same building, but its entrance is actually around the corner at Tiāntóng Lù 395. Another post office where employees can speak some English is at Shànghǎi Centre, Nánjīng Xī Lù 1376, lower level (© **021/6279-8044**).

Taxes Most four- and five-star hotels levy a 10% to 15% tax on rooms (including a city tax), while a few restaurants and bars have taken to placing a similar service charge on bills. There is no sales tax.

Taxis See "Getting Around," above.

Visa Extensions The **PSB** office for visa extensions is at Wúsōng Lù 333, north of the Bund (© **021/6321-1997**).

Weather The *China Daily* newspaper, CCTV 9 (CCTV Central Television's English language channel), and some hotel bulletin boards furnish the next day's forecast. You can also dial Shànghǎi's weather number, © **121**.

3 Where to Stay

With so many international chains and new luxury hotels, Shànghǎi offers excellent accommodations, but few bargains. The room rates listed are rack rates, but you'll be able to negotiate much better rates in person. The top hotels all levy a service charge of 10% to 15%, though this is usually waived or included in the final negotiated price at smaller hotels. All rooms have TVs with foreign channels unless otherwise noted.

HUÁNGPǓ (DOWNTOWN)
VERY EXPENSIVE
JW Marriott (Wànháo Jiǔdiàn) ✿✿✿   Opened in October 2003, China's first JW Marriott, ideally located a short walk from both subway lines and attractions such as the Shànghǎi Museum, Grand Theatre, Nánjīng Lù Pedestrian Mall, and Xīn Tiāndì, is a handsome five-star hotel lodged primarily on the 38th to 60th floors of Tomorrow Square. Boasting a penthouse library billed as the tallest library in the world by the Guinness Book of World Records, and China's first Mandara Spa, the hotel offers luxurious rooms furnished with three telephones, CD radio, laptop safe, thick bathrobes, and brilliant city views. Marble bathrooms have separate showers with power massage jets and antifog mirrors.

Nánjīng Xī Lù 399 (at Huángpí Běi Lù, west side of Rénmín Gōngyuán). © **800/228-9290** or 021/5359-4969. Fax 021/6375-5988. www.marriott.com. 342 units. ¥3,154 ($380) standard room; ¥3,652 ($440) executive level; from ¥3,984 ($480) suite. Discounts 40%–60%. AE, DC, MC, V. Metro: Rénmín Guǎngchǎng. **Amenities:** 3 restaurants; 2 lounges; indoor/outdoor pool; health club w/Jacuzzi and sauna; Mandara Spa; concierge; business center; salon; 24-hr. room service; babysitting; same-day dry cleaning/laundry; nonsmoking rooms; executive-level rooms. *In room:* A/C, satellite TV, broadband Internet access, minibar, coffeemaker, hair dryer, iron, safe.

The Westin Shànghǎi (Shànghǎi Wēisītīng Dàfàndiàn) ✿✿✿ *Kids*   Located a 5-minute walk from the Bund, the award-winning 26-story Westin offers large guest rooms headlined by Westin's patented Heavenly Bed, and plushly furnished with large

Shànghǎi Accommodations & Dining

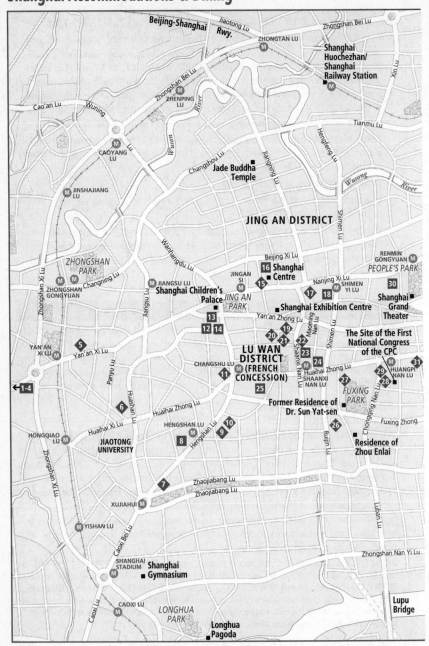

Beijing-Shanghai Rwy.

Jiaotong Lu

ZHONGTAN LU

Zhongshan Bei Lu

Shanghai Huochezhan/ Shanghai Railway Station

Cao'an Lu

Wuning

Zhongshan Bei Lu

ZHENPING LU

Tianmu Lu

CAOYANG LU

Changzhou Lu

Jianping Lu

Wusong River

Jade Buddha Temple

JINSHAJIANG LU

Hengfeng Lu

JING AN DISTRICT

RENMIN GONGYUAN

PEOPLE'S PARK

ZHONGSHAN PARK

Changning Lu

Beijing Xi Lu

Shimen Lu

ZHONGSHAN GONGYUAN

Wanhangdu Lu

JIANGSU LU

JINGAN SI

16 Shanghai Centre

15

Nanjing Xi Lu

SHIMEN YI LU

30

Shanghai Grand Theater

Shanghai Children's Palace

JING AN PARK

17 **18**

13

Shanghai Exhibition Centre

Yan'an Zhong Lu

12 **14**

Maoming Nan Lu

The Site of the First National Congress of the CPC

YAN'AN XI LU

5

Yan'an Xi Lu

Panyu Lu

20 **19**

21

22

Shaanxi Nan Lu

23

31

LU WAN DISTRICT (FRENCH CONCESSION)

CHANGSHU LU

11

24

HUANGPI NAN LU

29

←1-4

Huashan Lu

Huaihai Zhong Lu

SHAANXI NAN LU

25

FUXING PARK

27

28

Chongqing Nan Lu

6

Huaihai Xi Lu

Huaihai Zhong Lu

HENGSHAN LU

Former Residence of Dr. Sun Yat-sen

Fuxing Zhong

HONGQIAO LU

Zhongshan Xi Lu

JIAOTONG UNIVERSITY

8

Hengshan Lu

9

10

26

Ruijin Lu

Residence of Zhou Enlai

YISHAN LU

7

Zhaojiabang Lu

Zhaojiabang Lu

XUJIAHUI

Luban Lu

Zhongshan Nan Yi Lu

Caoxi Bei Lu

SHANGHAI STADIUM

Shanghai Gymnasium

CAOXI LU

Caoxi Lu

LONGHUA PARK

Lupu Bridge

Longhua Pagoda

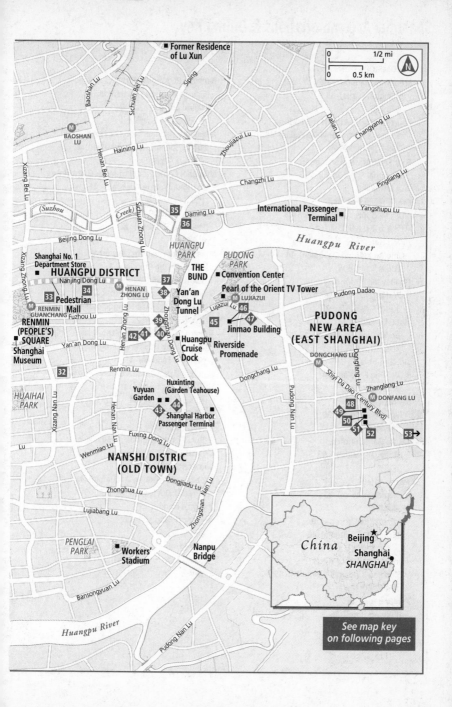

Former Residence of Lu Xun

Baoshan Lu

Sichuan Bei Lu

Siping

Zhoujiazui Lu

Dalian Lu

Changyang Lu

BAOSHAN LU

Haining Lu

Henan Bei Lu

Changzhi Lu

Pingliang Lu

Xizang Bei Lu

(Suzhou)

Creek

Sichuan Zhong Lu

35

Daming Lu

International Passenger Terminal

Yangshupu Lu

Huangpu River

36

Beijing Dong Lu

HUANGPU PARK

PUDONG PARK

Shanghai No. 1 Department Store

HUANGPU DISTRICT

THE BUND

Convention Center

Pudong Dadao

Nanjing Dong Lu

HENAN ZHONG LU

37

Yan'an Dong Lu Tunnel

Pearl of the Orient TV Tower

LUJIAZUI

33 Pedestrian Mall

34

38

LUJIAZUI

M

Lujiazui Lu

46

PUDONG NEW AREA (EAST SHANGHAI)

Xizang Zhong Lu

RENMIN GUANGCHANG

Fuzhou Lu

39

45

47

RENMIN (PEOPLE'S) SQUARE

Yan'an Dong Lu

42 41

40

Jinmao Building

DONGCHANG LU

Shanghai Museum

Renmin Lu

Huangpu Cruise Dock

Riverside Promenade

Dongchang Lu

Shiyi Da Dao (Century Blvd)

Danglang Lu

32

Huxinting (Garden Teahouse)

Zhanglang Lu

HUAIHAI PARK

Yuyuan Garden

44

48

DONFANG LU

M

49

Henan Nan Lu

43

Shanghai Harbor Passenger Terminal

Pudong Nan Lu

50

Lu

Fuxing Dong Lu

51

52

53

Wenmiao Lu

NANSHI DISTRIC (OLD TOWN)

Dongjiadu Lu

Zhongshan Nan Lu

Zhonghua Lu

Lujiabang Lu

China

Beijing

PENGLAI PARK

Workers' Stadium

Nanpu Bridge

Shanghai
SHANGHAI

Bansongyuan Lu

Huangpu River

Pudong Nan Lu

See map key on following pages

421

Shànghǎi Accommodations & Dining Key

ACCOMMODATIONS ■

Broadway Mansions Hotel
(Shànghǎi Dàshà) **35**
上海大厦

Courtyard by Marriott Hotel Pǔdōng
(Shànghǎi Qílǔ Wànyí Dàjiǔdiàn) **48**
上海齐鲁万怡大酒店

Four Seasons Hotel Shànghǎi
(Shànghǎi Sì Jì Jiǔdiàn) **18**
上海四季酒店

Grand Hyatt Shanghai
(Jīn Mào Jūn Yuè Dàjiǔdiàn) **46**
上海金茂君悦大酒店

Hilton Hotel
(Jìng'ān Xīěrdùn Dàjiǔdiàn) **14**
静安希尔顿大酒店

Holiday Inn Pǔdōng
(Pǔdōng Jiàrì Jiǔdiàn) **52**
上海浦东假日酒店

Hotel Equatorial
(Guójì Guìdū Dàjiǔdiàn) **13**
国际贵都大酒店

Jǐnjiāng Hotel
(Jǐnjiāng Fàndiàn) **24**
锦江饭店

JW Marriott
(Wànháo Jiǔdiàn) **30**
万豪酒店

Okura Garden Hotel
(Huāyuán Fàndiàn) **23**
花园饭店

Peace Hotel
(Hépíng Fàndiàn) **37**
和平饭店

Portman Ritz-Carlton Hotel
(Bōtèmàn Dàjiǔdiàn) **16**
上海波特曼丽嘉酒店

Pǔdōng Shangri-La Hotel
(Pǔdōng Xiānggélǐlā Fàndiàn) **45**
浦东香格里拉大酒店

Pǔjiāng Fàndiàn
(Pǔjiāng Hotel) **36**
浦江饭店

Ramada Pǔdōng Airport
(Shànghǎi Jīchǎng Huáměidá
Dàjiǔdiàn) **53**
上海机场华美达酒店

Regal International East Asia Hotel
(Fùháo Huánqiú Dōngyà Jiǔdiàn) **8**
富豪环球东亚酒店

Shànghǎi Conservatory of Music Guest House
(Shànghǎi Yīnyuè Xuéyuàn) **25**
上海音乐学院

Shànghǎi Hotel
(Shànghǎi Bīnguǎn) **12**
上海宾馆

Shànghǎi International Airport Hotel
(Guójì Jīchǎng Bīnguǎn) **1**
上海国际机场宾馆

Shànghǎi Marriott Hotel Hóngqiáo
(Shànghǎi Wànháo Hóngqiáo Dàjiǔdiàn) **2**
上海万豪虹桥大酒店

Sheraton Grand Tài Píng Yáng
(Xǐ Lái Dēng Háo Dá Tài Píng
Yáng Dà Fàndiàn) **4**
喜来登豪达太平洋大饭店

Sofitel Hyland Hotel
(Hǎilún Bīnguǎn) **34**
海伦宾馆

St. Regis Shànghǎi
(Ruìjì Hóngtǎ Dàjiǔdiàn) **50**
上海瑞吉红塔大酒店

The Westin Shànghǎi
(Shànghǎi Wēisītīng Dàfàndiàn) **42**
上海威斯汀大饭店

Yangtze Hotel
(Yángzǐ Fàndiàn) **33**
扬子饭店

YMCA Hotel
(Qīng Nián Huì Bīnguǎn) **32**
青年会宾馆

DINING ◆

work desk, fax machine, high-speed Internet access, and deluxe bathroom that includes a separate stall with a "rainforest" shower. The Westin Kids Club consists of a separate area with adjoining outdoor terrace and paddle pool. Adults meanwhile can avail themselves of the sybaritic experience at the hotel's Banyan Tree Spa. Service throughout is impeccable.

Hénán Zhōng Lù 88, Wàitān Zhōngxīn (3 blocks west of the Huángpǔ River). *(?)* **888/WESTIN-1** or 021/6335-1888. Fax 021/6335-2888. www.westin.com. 301 units. ¥2,988 ($360) standard room; ¥3,735 ($450) executive level; from ¥4,067 ($490) suite. Discounts 40%–50%. AE, DC, MC, V. Metro: Hénán Zhōng Lù. **Amenities:** 3 restaurants; deli; 2 lounges; juice bar; 20m (66-ft.) indoor/outdoor pool; state-of-the-art health club and spa w/Jacuzzi and sauna; children's programs; concierge; 24-hr. business center; salon; 24-hr. room service; babysitting; same-day dry cleaning/laundry; executive-level rooms; 3 rooms for those w/limited mobility. *In room:* A/C, satellite TV, broadband Internet access, minibar, coffeemaker, hair dryer, safe.

EXPENSIVE

Peace Hotel (Hépíng Fàndiàn) *(?)* *(Overrated)*   Built in 1929, the Peace—known in its heyday as the Cathay Hotel—is Shànghăi's best known historic hotel. The lobby is an Art Deco masterpiece and the view from the rooftop is magnificent. Rooms, renovated in 2003, are spacious, with large closets and high ceilings, though some retain their old furnishings. For all the Peace's fame and ideal location on Nánjīng Lù and the Bund, the amenities and service—inefficient and uninspired—barely rise to the four-star level (even though the hotel is rated five stars). The former Palace Hotel across the street has now been turned into the south wing of the Peace.

Nánjīng Dōng Lù 20 (on the Bund). *(?)* **021/6321-6888.** Fax 021/6329-0300. www.shanghaipeacehotel.com. 380 units. ¥1,320–¥1,820 ($160–$220) standard room; ¥2,077 ($250) executive level; from ¥2,460 ($320) suite. Discount up to 40%. AE, DC, MC, V. Metro: Hénán Zhōng Lù. **Amenities:** 3 restaurants; 2 lounges (jazz bar, rooftop bar); tiny health club w/sauna; concierge; tour desk; small business center; salon; 24-hr. room service; babysitting; same-day dry cleaning/laundry; nonsmoking rooms; executive-level rooms. *In room:* A/C, satellite TV, dataport, minibar, coffeemaker, hair dryer, safe.

Sofitel Hyland Hotel (Hăilún Bīnguăn) *(?)*   This Accor-managed four-star, 30-story tower in the heart of the pedestrian sector of Nánjīng Lù has a superb downtown location. Rooms, equipped with two phones, robes, slippers, and standard amenities, are quite small but are comfortable enough. Sofitel Club rooms are slightly larger and include a Western buffet breakfast. There's a European, even French feel to the hotel. Service is mostly efficient, if brusque at times.

Nánjīng Dōng Lù 505 (on Nánjīng Lù Pedestrian Mall). *(?)* **800/221-4542** or 021/6351-5888. Fax 021/6351-4088. www.accorhotels.com. 389 units. ¥1,722 ($210) standard room; ¥1,927 ($235) executive level; from ¥2,624 ($320) suite. AE, DC, MC, V. Metro: Hénán Zhōng Lù. **Amenities:** 4 restaurants; deli; 2 lounges; health club w/Jacuzzi and sauna; concierge; tour desk; business center; salon; 24-hr. room service; same-day dry cleaning/laundry. *In room:* A/C, satellite TV, dataport, minibar, coffeemaker, hair dryer, safe.

MODERATE

Yangtze Hotel (Yángzǐ Fàndiàn) *(?)*   Located a block south of the Nánjīng Lù pedestrian mall and a block east of People's Square, this striking 1934 Art Deco hotel has undergone a complete refurbishment and is today a very popular midrange choice amongst Chinese business travelers. Rated only three stars, the hotel offers in-room amenities that rival those at four-star outfits farther down Nánjīng Lù. Rooms, a portion of which were renovated in 2002, are spacious and come with thick drapes, comfortable beds, and broadband access. The majority of the staff tries to be helpful.

Hànkǒu Lù 740 (east of Xīzàng Zhōng Lù, 1 block south of Nánjīng Dōng Lù). *(?)* **021/6351-7880.** Fax 021/6351-6974. www.e-yangtze.com. 183 units. ¥980 ($120) standard room; ¥1,280 ($160) executive rooms; ¥1,980 ($240) suite. Discounts 30%–40%; 10% service charge. AE, DC, MC, V. Metro: Rénmín Guăngchǎng. **Amenities:** 2 restaurants; lounge;

bar; business center; salon; limited room service; laundry service. *In room:* A/C, TV, broadband Internet access, dataport, minibar, hair dryer, safe.

INEXPENSIVE

YMCA Hotel (Qīngnián Huì Bīnguǎn)   Built in 1929, this historic 11-story brick building is today one of the more popular budget hotels in town, with a slightly dilapidated air but a great location right in the heart of old Shànghǎi. Rooms are drab and not well maintained, and the beds occasionally lumpy, but bathrooms are at least fairly clean. Dorm rooms with shared bathroom facilities are available but are spartan at best. A cafe that serves Western food is a big draw for international backpackers. Front-desk staff speaks a little English and can be helpful when pressed.

Xīzàng Nán Lú 123 (southeast of Rénmín Guǎngchǎng, north of Huáihǎi Zhōng Lù). ✆ **021/6326-1040.** Fax 021/6320-1957. www.ymcahotel.com. 150 units. ¥580 ($70) standard room; ¥680 ($82) executive; ¥100 ($13) dorm bed. 10% service charge. AE, DC, MC, V. Metro: Rénmín Guǎngchǎng. **Amenities:** Restaurant; cafe; health club; small business center; salon; room service; next-day dry cleaning/laundry. *In room:* A/C, TV, minibar.

LÚWĀN DISTRICT (FRENCH CONCESSION)
VERY EXPENSIVE

Okura Garden Hotel Shànghǎi (Huāyuán Fàndiàn) ⚘⚘   The top hotel in the French Concession, the five-star Japanese-managed Okura was built in 1990 on the site of the 1920s French Club and Cercle Sportif. The fine Art Deco features of the original structure have been preserved in its east lobby and grand ballroom. Rooms, undergoing renovations for the next few years, are of average size, with marble bathrooms that contain automated bidets. With extensive and first-rate facilities and highly efficient service, there's little to complain about here.

Màomíng Nán Lù 58 (1 block north of Huáihǎi Zhōng Lù). ✆ **021/6415-1111.** Fax 021/6415-8866. www.garden hotelshanghai.com. 500 units. ¥2,240–¥2,740 ($270–$330) standard room; ¥2,820–¥3,860 ($340–$465) executive level; from ¥3,735 ($450) suite. Discount 40%. AE, DC, MC, V. Metro: Shǎnxī Nán Lù. **Amenities:** 4 restaurants; cafe; 3 bars; 25m (82-ft.) indoor swimming pool; 2 lighted outdoor tennis courts; health club w/Jacuzzi and sauna; concierge; tour desk; business center; salon; 24-hr. room service; same-day dry cleaning/laundry; nonsmoking rooms; executive-level rooms. *In room:* A/C, satellite TV, broadband Internet access, minibar, hot-water maker, hair dryer, safe.

EXPENSIVE

Jǐnjiāng Fàndiàn   The most famous hotel in the French Concession, the Jǐnjiāng opened its doors in 1929 as the Cathay Mansions but is best remembered as the location for the signing of the Shànghǎi Communique by President Nixon and Zhōu Ēnlái in 1972, reestablishing U.S.-China relations. Today's complex includes: the 1929 North Building (Běi Lóu), remodeled as a five-star hotel; the central Grosvenor House (1931), with its facade an imitation of the Barclay-Vessey Building in New York City, recently redone as a five-star all-suite deluxe hotel; and the old South Building (Nán Lóu), at press time set to reopen as another five-star aspirant. However, everything's just a bit worn here for a "luxury" hotel, and the service, still lagging behind the international chains, is adequate though hardly exemplary.

Màomíng Nán Lù 59 (1 block north of Huáihǎi Zhōng Lù). ✆ **021/6258-2582.** Fax 021/6472-5588. www.jinjianghotel shanghai.com. 515 units. ¥1,640–¥1,960 ($205–$245) standard room (North Building); from ¥2,400 ($300) suite. Discount 30%. AE, DC, MC, V. Metro: Shǎnxī Nán Lù. **Amenities:** 3 restaurants; food street on hotel grounds; 20m (66-ft.) indoor swimming pool; health club w/Jacuzzi and sauna; 6-lane bowling alley; concierge; tour desk; business center; shopping street; salon; 24-hr. room service; same-day dry cleaning/laundry; nonsmoking rooms; executive-level rooms. *In room:* A/C, satellite TV, dataport, minibar, coffeemaker, hair dryer, safe.

JÌNGĀN DISTRICT (NORTHWEST SHÀNGHĂI)
VERY EXPENSIVE

Four Seasons Hotel Shànghăi (Shànghăi Sìjì Jiŭdiàn) 🏵🏵🏵   A 2002 arrival on Shànghăi's luxury hotel scene, the 37-story Four Seasons offers top-quality pampering. Each guest room is lavishly furnished with three telephones, thick robes, and laptop safes. The patented Four Seasons bed alone is worth the stay. Marble bathrooms have separate shower and tub. Best of all, this hotel delivers impeccable service, from its 24-hour butler service for each guest to the highly efficient and friendly multilingual staff throughout the hotel. Nánjīng Lù is a 5-minute walk away, the Shànghăi Museum a 10-minute stroll.

Wēihăi Lù 500 (at Shímén Yī Lù, between Nánjīng Xī Lù and Yán'ān Zhōng Lù). ✆ 800/819-5053 or 021/6256-8888. Fax 021/6256-5678. www.fourseasons.com. 439 units. ¥3,100–¥3,300 ($375–$400) standard room; from ¥4,100 ($495) suite; ¥400–¥600 ($50–$75) extra for executive lounge benefits. AE, DC, MC, V. Metro: Shímén Yī Lù. **Amenities:** 4 restaurants; lounge; jazz bar; 20m (66-ft.) indoor pool; state-of-the-art health club and spa w/Jacuzzi and sauna; concierge; 24-hr. business center; salon; 24-hr. room service; babysitting; same-day dry cleaning/laundry; nonsmoking floors; rooms for those w/limited mobility. *In room:* A/C, satellite TV, broadband Internet access, minibar, coffeemaker, hair dryer, safe, butler service.

Hilton Hotel (Jìngān Xīěrdùn Dàjiŭdiàn) 🏵🏵 *Value*   Shànghăi's first foreign-owned hotel (1987), the Hilton still rates among the very best of the city's hotels, and it's a favorite of Western business travelers. The services are top-notch, the staff competent. Guest rooms, undergoing renovations at press time, are spacious and bright and will include flatscreen TVs and broadband connection once renovated.

Huáshān Lù 250 (1 block south of Yán'ān Zhōng Lù). ✆ 800/445-8667 or 021/6248-0000. Fax 021/6248-3848. www.hilton.com. 720 units. ¥2,722 ($328) standard room; ¥3,220 ($388) executive level; from ¥5,926 ($714) suite (up to 60% discount pending occupancy). AE, DC, MC, V. Metro: Jìng Ān Sì. **Amenities:** 6 restaurants; deli; 2 lounges; indoor swimming pool; outdoor tennis court; squash court; state-of-the-art health club and spa w/Jacuzzi and sauna; concierge; business center; 24-hr. room service; babysitting; same-day dry cleaning/laundry; nonsmoking rooms; executive-level rooms. *In room:* A/C, satellite TV, broadband Internet access, minibar, coffeemaker, hair dryer, safe.

Portman Ritz-Carlton Hotel (Bōtèmàn Dàjiŭdiàn) 🏵🏵🏵   Despite some heavy competition, the 50-story Portman is tenaciously guarding its position as Shànghăi's top choice hotel for many business travelers and world leaders. Rooms are plush, elegant, and fitted with all the amenities you could want. As expected, service is professional and excellent. The adjacent Shànghăi Centre has airline offices, a medical clinic, a supermarket, a post office, automatic teller machines, a performing arts theater, upscale boutiques, and a little-known cafe called Starbucks.

Nánjīng Xī Lù 1376 (Shànghăi Centre). ✆ 800/241-3333 or 021/6279-8888. Fax 021/6279-8800. www.ritzcarlton.com. 578 units. ¥3,075 ($370) standard room; ¥3,985 ($480) executive level; from ¥4,400 ($530) suite. AE, DC, MC, V. Metro: Jìng'ān Sì. **Amenities:** 4 restaurants; 2 lounges; indoor/outdoor 20m (66-ft.) swimming pool; indoor tennis court; 2 indoor squash courts; indoor racquetball court; 3-story health club; Jacuzzi; sauna; concierge; 24-hr. business center; shopping arcade; grocery; salon; 24-hr. room service; babysitting; same-day dry cleaning/laundry; nonsmoking rooms; executive-level rooms; World Link Medical Center; rooms for those w/limited mobility. *In room:* A/C, satellite TV, broadband Internet access, minibar, coffeemaker, hair dryer, safe.

EXPENSIVE

Hotel Equatorial (Guójì Guìdū Dàjiŭdiàn) 🏵   This four-star hotel, located just north of the Hilton, and managed by a Singapore group, offers bright, fully equipped, comfortable rooms. Fitness facilities, refurbished in 2002 at a cost of $1.5 million, are extensive, as are the dining options. Staff is generally helpful and speak decent English.

Yán'ān Xī Lù 65 (south of Jìng'ān Gōngyuán). ✆ 021/6248-1688. Fax 021/6248-1773. www.equatorial.com. 509 units. ¥1,886 ($230) standard room; ¥2,132 ($260) executive floor. Discount up to 60%. AE, DC, MC, V. Metro: Jìng

Ān Sì. **Amenities:** 5 restaurants; deli; 2 lounges; 20m (66-ft.) indoor swimming pool; lighted outdoor tennis court; squash court; health club w/Jacuzzi and sauna; 6-lane bowling alley; concierge; tour desk; business center; shopping arcade; salon; 24-hr. room service; babysitting; same-day dry cleaning/laundry; nonsmoking rooms; executive-level rooms. *In room:* A/C, satellite TV, broadband Internet access, minibar, coffeemaker, hair dryer, safe.

MODERATE

Shànghǎi Hotel (Shànghǎi Bīnguǎn)   If you want to be near the French Conces-sion with access to the shops and restaurants of Héngshān Lù, but the prices at the adjacent Hilton and Equatorial hotels are too steep, the 30-story, locally managed Shànghǎi will work. Most guests are Chinese, but the staff can handle non-Chinese guests as well. Partially renovated in early 2004, guest rooms are fully modernized.

Wūlǔmùqí Běi Lù 505 (west of the Hilton, south of Yán'ān Zhōng Lù). (021/6248-0088. Fax 021/6248-1056. 543 units. ¥988 ($123) standard room; ¥1,888 ($236) executive level; from ¥2,588 ($323) suite. Discount 20%–30%; 10% service charge. AE, DC, MC, V. Metro: Jing'ān Sì. **Amenities:** 3 restaurants; small health club w/Jacuzzi and sauna; tour desk; business center; shopping arcade; 24-hr. room service; next-day dry cleaning/laundry. *In room:* A/C, TV, mini-bar, hot water maker, hair dryer.

CHÁNGNÍNG (HÓNGQIÁO DEVELOPMENT ZONE)
VERY EXPENSIVE

Shànghǎi Marriott Hotel Hóngqiáo (Shànghǎi Wànháo Hóngqiáo Dàjiǔdiàn) 🎇 This grand five-star, eight-story Marriott is the top hotel address in the Hóngqiáo Airport neighborhood. Guest rooms are large, with comfortable beds, DVD players, and Internet broadband access. The zoo is a short walk away, but other attractions require a taxi ride to town. The hotel is often sold out during weekdays but offers substantial discounts on weekends.

Hóngqiáo Lù 2270 (6.4km/4 miles east of Hóngqiáo Airport). (800/228-9290 or 021/6237-6000. Fax 021/6237-6222. www.marriott.com. 315 units. ¥1,900 ($237) standard room; ¥2,500 ($312) executive level; from ¥3,300 ($412) suite. Discount up to 50%. AE, DC, MC, V. **Amenities:** 3 restaurants; deli; lounge; sports bar; indoor pool; outdoor tennis court; health club w/Jacuzzi and sauna; concierge; business center; salon; 24-hr. room service; same-day dry cleaning/laundry; executive-level rooms. *In room:* A/C, satellite TV, dataport, minibar, coffeemaker, hair dryer, safe.

Sheraton Grand Tàipíngyáng (Xǐláidēng Háo Dá Tàipíngyáng Dà Fàndiàn) 🎇🎇 Business travelers love this 27-story five-star Sheraton, not just for the location (halfway between the old Hóngqiáo Airport and downtown), but for the highly efficient service and the lush yet homey atmosphere. Rooms, renovated in 2002, are a tad on the small side but are lushly decorated with rich carpeting, overstuffed chairs, and a classical rolltop desk right under Chinese artwork. Bathrooms are sleek and modern with glass sinks. The hotel can also arrange tee times and transportation to the Shànghǎi International Golf and Country Club.

Zūnyì Nán Lù 5 (1 block north of Yán'ān Xī Lù). (800/325-3535 or 021/6275-8888. Fax 021/6275-5420. www. sheratongrand-shanghai.com. 496 units. ¥2,656–¥2,988 ($320–$360) standard room; ¥3,154 ($380) executive-level standard room; from ¥3,884 ($468) suite. AE, DC, MC, V. **Amenities:** 5 restaurants; deli; 3 lounges; indoor swimming pool; health club w/Jacuzzi and sauna; concierge; business center; salon; 24-hr. room service; babysitting; same-day dry cleaning/laundry; nonsmoking rooms; executive-level rooms; rooms for those w/limited mobility. *In room:* A/C, satellite TV, broadband Internet access, dataport, minibar, coffeemaker, hair dryer, iron, safe.

XÚHUÌ (SOUTHWEST SHÀNGHǍI)
EXPENSIVE

Regal International East Asia Hotel (Fùháo Huánqiú Dōngyà Jiǔdiàn) 🎇 The best luxury hotel in the district, the 22-story, internationally managed Regal has bright, modern guest rooms with bedside electronic controls, robes, slippers, and all the amenities of a five-star establishment. Its Shànghǎi International Tennis Center offers Shànghăi's best facilities, including a center court that seats 1,200 spectators. It's located along trendy Héngshān Lù, and the metro is just a block away. Service is efficient enough, but drops off when it gets busy.

Héngshān Lù 516 (west of Wúxīng Lù). ⓒ **800/222-8888** or 021/6415-5588. Fax 021/6445-8899. www.regal-eastasia. com. 300 units. ¥2,740 ($335) standard room; ¥3,740 ($455) executive level. Discounts 30%–40% low season, otherwise 10%–20%. AE, DC, MC, V. Metro: Héngshān Lù. **Amenities:** 3 restaurants; lounge; 25m (82-ft.) indoor pool; 10 championship tennis courts; indoor squash court; extensive health club and spa w/Jacuzzi and sauna; game room; 12-lane bowling alley; concierge; tour desk; business center; salon; 24-hr. room service; babysitting; same-day dry cleaning/laundry; nonsmoking rooms; 4 executive-level floors. *In room:* A/C, satellite TV, broadband Internet access, minibar, coffeemaker, hair dryer, safe.

INEXPENSIVE
Shànghăi Conservatory of Music Guest House (Shànghăi Yīnyuè Xuéyuàn)
It doesn't get any cheaper than this for French Concession accommodations. The conservatory has spartan standard rooms in ugly concrete bunkers, but considerably nicer are the three standard rooms (¥300/$38) with wooden floors, original fireplaces, en-suite bathroom, and spacious balconies on the second floor of the colonial-style Zhuānjiā Lóu (Experts' Building), once the Brazilian consulate. The conservatory's restaurant serves decent and inexpensive *jiācháng cài* (home-style cooking).

Fēnyáng Lù 20 (east of Chángshú Lù, south of Huáihăi Zhōng Lù). ⓒ **021/6437-2577.** Fax 021/6437-2577. 60 units. ¥100–¥300 ($13–$38) standard room. No credit cards. Metro: Chángshú Lù. **Amenities:** Restaurant; laundry.

HÓNGKŎU DISTRICT (NORTHEAST SHÀNGHĂI)
MODERATE
Broadway Mansions Hotel (Shànghăi Dàshà)   Reverting to its original name, the 19-story Broadway Mansions, originally built in 1934, and once housing the Foreign Correspondents' Club, is now a four-star hotel offering spacious rooms (renovated in 2003) with high ceilings, firm beds, and central air. The rooms facing the Sūzhōu Creek are absolutely worth splurging on, as there are few other places where you can wake up to the creek, the Bund, *and* Pŭdōng outside your window.

Běi Sūzhōu Lù 20 (north of the Bund across the Sūzhōu River, just west of the Wàibáidù Bridge). ⓒ **021/6324-6260.** Fax 021/6306-5147. www.broadwaymansions.com. 233 units. ¥1,082–¥1,378 ($132–$168) standard room; ¥1,680 ($205) executive level; from ¥2,870 ($350) suite. Discount up to 50% in low season. AE, DC, MC, V. **Amenities:** 3 restaurants; bakery; lounge, bar; health club; sauna; concierge; business center; salon; 24-hr. room service; same-day dry cleaning/laundry; executive-level rooms. *In room:* A/C, satellite TV, broadband Internet access (executive rooms only), minibar, hair dryer, safe.

INEXPENSIVE
Pŭjiāng Hotel (Pŭjiāng Fàndiàn)   An inexpensive, somewhat grotty backpackers' favorite in the last decade, this just-north-of-the-Bund hotel, once Shànghăi's oldest hotel, the Astor House, has upgraded into a three-star outfit. Though dorms (unrenovated) are still a bit dank, refurbished standard rooms have firm and comfortable beds and bathrooms are large and clean. Visitors can also choose from four restored "celebrity rooms," including one occupied by Albert Einstein in 1922 (room 304).

Huángpŭ Lù 15 (northeast side of Sūzhōu Creek, north of the Bund). ⓒ **021/6324-6388.** Fax 021/6324-3179. www.pujianghotel.com. 116 units. ¥580–¥980 ($72–$122) standard room; ¥1,280 ($160) celebrity room; ¥1,280–¥1,680 ($160–$210) executive room; ¥150 ($19) dorm. 20%–40% discount on standard rooms, 10% service charge. AE, DC, MC, V. Metro: Hénán Zhōng Lù (about a mile away). **Amenities:** Restaurant; Internet cafe; spa; bike rental; tour desk; self-service laundry. *In room:* A/C, TV, fridge (select rooms).

PŬDŌNG (EAST OF RIVER)
VERY EXPENSIVE
Grand Hyatt Shànghǎi (Shànghǎi Jīn Mào Jūnyuè Dàjiǔdiàn) ✷✷   Currently the world's tallest hotel, running from the 54th to the 88th floors of the Jīn Mào Tower, the ultraluxurious Grand Hyatt is more of a novelty hotel than a practical one. The views of the Bund and Pŭdōng are astonishing, as are the lush guest rooms, which combine Art Deco and traditional Chinese motifs with high-tech designs, but the burden of renown has made the staff a bit standoffish. The hotel's highflying address means you should allow extra time to get to your destination.

Shíjì Dà Dào 88, 54th floor, Jīn Mào Tower (southeast of the Oriental Pearl TV Tower). ✆ 800/233-1234 or 021/5049-1234. Fax 021/5049-1111. www.hyatt.com. 555 units. ¥3,500 ($425) standard room; ¥3,700 ($450) executive-level room; from ¥4,600 ($560) suite. AE, DC, MC, V. Metro: Lùjiāzuǐ. **Amenities:** 6 restaurants; food pavilion; 2 lounges; nightclub; indoor "skypool" (world's highest swimming pool); health club w/Jacuzzi and sauna; concierge; tour desk; 24-hr. business center; salon; 24-hr. room service; same-day dry cleaning/laundry; executive-level rooms. *In room:* A/C, satellite TV, dataport, minibar, coffeemaker, hair dryer, safe.

Pŭdōng Shangri-La Hotel (Pŭdōng Xiānggélǐlā Fàndiàn) ✷✷✷   In the never-ending quest to be the biggest and boldest in Shànghǎi, the Shangri-La has added a sleek new tower annex, a world-class "Chi" spa, and new convention facilities, making it now the largest hotel in town. Already, it boasts the best location in Pŭdōng with a gorgeous view of the Bund across the river. Guest rooms are spacious and comfortable, with Bund-view rooms worth the extra $20. Staff is exceedingly friendly and the service is of a high international caliber.

Fùchéng Lù 33 (southwest of the Oriental Pearl TV Tower/Dōngfāng Míngzhū, adjacent to Riverside Ave/Bīnjiāng Dà Dào). ✆ 800/942-5050 or 021/6882-8888. Fax 021/6882-6688. www.shangri-la.com. 981 units. ¥1,992 – ¥2,158 ($240–$260) standard room; ¥2,324 – ¥3,320 ($280–$400) executive level; from ¥4,000 ($500) suite. Discount 40%. AE, DC, MC, V. Metro: Lùjiāzuǐ. **Amenities:** 7 restaurants; deli; lounge; nightclub; indoor lap pool; tennis court; health club and full-service spa w/Jacuzzi and sauna; concierge; tour desk; large business center; 24-hr. room service; babysitting; same-day dry cleaning/laundry; executive-level rooms. *In room:* A/C, satellite TV, broadband Internet access, minibar, fridge, coffeemaker, hair dryer, safe.

St. Regis Shànghǎi (Shànghǎi Ruìjí Hóngtǎ Dàjiǔdiàn) ✷✷✷   This handsome robust hotel may well be *the* luxury hotel to stay at in town were it not for its less convenient location in Pŭdōng. Standard rooms, the largest in the city (48 sq. m/157 sq. ft.), are gorgeously furnished with comfortable sofas, ergonomic Herman Miller "Aeron" chairs, Bose CD radios, and "rainforest" showers in the spacious marble bathrooms. St. Regis butlers, on call 24 hours a day, can press clothing, serve free in-room coffee and tea, make dinner reservations, and help with any Internet hookup problems. Two ladies'-only floors feature women butlers and a host of special in-room amenities including toiletries by Bulgari.

Dōngfāng Lù 889 (south central Pŭdōng). ✆ 800/325-3589 or 021/5050-4567. Fax 021/6875-6789. www.stregis.com. 318 units. ¥3,070 – ¥3,237 ($370–$390) standard room; from ¥3,570 ($430) suite. Discount up to 60%. AE, DC, MC, V. Metro: Dōngfāng Lù. **Amenities:** 3 restaurants; 2 lounges; indoor pool; tennis court; state-of-the-art health club and full-service spa w/Jacuzzi and sauna; concierge; tour desk; business center; salon; 24-hr. room service; babysitting; same-day dry cleaning/laundry; 24-hr. butler service; 1 room for those w/limited mobility. *In room:* A/C, satellite TV, broadband Internet access, minibar, coffeemaker, hair dryer, safe.

EXPENSIVE
Holiday Inn Pŭdōng (Shànghǎi Pŭdōng Jiàrì Jiǔdiàn) ✷ 𝘝𝘢𝘭𝘶𝘦   Though appealing mostly to businesspeople, this thoroughly Western 32-story Holiday Inn offers excellent value for tourists, especially after discounts. Guest rooms are spacious and

Airport Hotels

There are plenty of hotels with free shuttle service near Hóngqiáo Airport. The closest five-star hotel is the **Marriott Hotel Hóngqiáo** (p. 427), which is still about 6.4km (4 miles) to the east. The highly efficient, Japanese-managed, 308-unit **Shànghăi International Airport Hotel (Shànghăi Guójì Jīchăng Bīnguăn,** Hóngqiáo Lù 2550; ⓒ 021/6268-8866; fax 021/6268-8393), is the nearest major hotel within a 10-minute walk from the airport. Rooms (¥880/$110 standard room, 10% service charge) are cozy, modern, and clean, and flight schedule monitors are mounted in the cheery lobby. A free shuttle is available to Hóngqiáo and Pŭdōng airports.

The only hotel currently serving Pŭdōng Airport is the newly opened (2003) **Ramada Pŭdōng Airport** (Shànghăi Jīchăng Huáměidá Dàjiŭdiàn, Qíháng Lù 1100; ⓒ 021/3849-4949; fax 021/6885-2889; www.ramada airportpd.com), a 2- to 3-minute free shuttle ride or a 10-minute walk from the airport. The hotel has 370 units. Rooms (¥880/$100 standard room; 15% service charge, 40% discount) are clean and comfortable with the usual amenities. Both Western and Chinese dining are available.

bright, with bird's-eye maple furniture, comfortable beds, and all the amenities you're likely to need. The white tile bathrooms are spotless, and service is efficient and professional. The nearby metro 2 subway station, which is within walking distance, allows easier access to the rest of Shànghăi.

Dōngfāng Lù 899 (south central Pŭdōng). ⓒ 800/465-4329 or 021/5830-6666. Fax 021/5830-5555. www.holiday-inn.com. 318 units. ¥1,500 ($187) standard room; ¥2,000 ($250) executive level; from ¥2,000 ($250) suite. Discounts up to 50% low season. AE, DC, MC, V. Metro: Dōngfāng Lù. **Amenities:** 4 restaurants; deli; pub; bar; indoor pool; large health club w/Jacuzzi and sauna; game room; concierge; tour desk; business center; salon; 24-hr. room service; babysitting; same-day dry cleaning/laundry; nonsmoking rooms; executive-level rooms; rooms for those w/limited mobility. *In room:* A/C, satellite TV, dataport, minibar, coffeemaker, hair dryer, safe.

MODERATE
Courtyard by Marriott Hotel Pŭdōng (Shànghăi Qílŭ Wànyí Dàjiŭdiàn) ⓐ
Opened in 2002, the Courtyard is a thoroughly modern and busy four-star hotel catering to business travelers. The comfortable rooms are of average size, with modern furniture and the Courtyard's signature floral bedspreads. The subway is just 2 blocks away, meaning a nonbusiness traveler could stay here comfortably, especially if a bargain room rate can be secured.

Dōngfāng Lù 838 (at intersection with Wéifáng Lù). ⓒ 021/6886-7886. Fax 021/6886-7889. www.courtyard.com. 218 units. ¥1,495 ($180) standard room; ¥1,985 ($240) executive level; from ¥2,315 ($280) suite. Discount up to 50%. AE, DC, MC, V. Metro: Dōngfāng Lù. **Amenities:** 2 restaurants; lounge; fitness center w/sauna; concierge; business center; salon; 24-hr. room service; babysitting; same-day dry cleaning/laundry; executive-level rooms. *In room:* A/C, satellite TV, dataport, minibar, coffeemaker, hair dryer, safe.

4 Where to Dine

Dozens of promising, mostly upscale, international restaurants and cafes open every month, too many to keep up with. The emphasis is on Shànghăi's own renowned cuisine, commonly referred to as *běnbāng cài*. The most celebrated Shànghăi dish is hairy

Three on the Bund (Wài Tān Sān Hào)

One of the splashiest and most luxurious developments to hit Shànghǎi, **Three on the Bund** is a "lifestyle destination" that has brought some world-class swank to the Bund. Built in 1922, this former Union Insurance Company Building now houses an art gallery, exclusive fashion outlets (including a Giorgio Armani store), and a luxurious Evian spa, but it's the fine-dining restaurants, all offering stunning vistas of the Bund and Pǔdōng, that are drawing the crowds. For even more exclusive and intimate dining, the domed **Cupola** atop the building offers private dining for two, service by a private butler, and a menu from any of the following outlets. *Note:* Reservations required at Jean Georges, Laris, Whampoa Club, and the Cupola; reservations recommended at New Heights.

Jean Georges ✿✿ (fourth floor; ✆ 021/6321-7733; 11:30am–2:30pm and 5:30–10pm). From *amuse-bouche* to dessert, it's the finest contemporary and light French fare from world-renowned chef Jean-Georges Vongerichten. There are over 5,000 bottles of wine to choose from, and a 30-seater wine cellar private dining room, all cloaked in dark blue and deep wine hues. Expect a dinner for two to hover immodestly around ¥2,000 ($250).

Whampoa Club ✿✿ (fifth floor; ✆ 021/6321-3737; 11:30am–2:30pm and 5:30–10pm). Putting a creative spin on classics learned from a passel of old-time Shànghǎi master chefs, Chef Jerome Leung focuses on bringing out the flavors of classic Shànghǎi dishes. Indulge in the tasting menu, which was delicious when I was there, though there have been occasional reviews of inconsistency. A professional tea sommelier can help with selecting from over 50 teas from all over China.

Laris ✿✿✿ (sixth floor; ✆ 021/6321-9922; 11:30am–2:30pm and 5–10:30pm). In a light breezy setting, larger-than-life Australian chef David Laris creates some wonderful "New World" cuisine inspired by his previous culinary stints in Hong Kong, Vietnam, Macau, and London (as executive chef of Mezzo). Seafood gets top billing here (seared scallops on parsnip mash with oyster lemon foam, anyone?), with a crustacean-stocked seafood bar and a special Chocolate room (which churns out the Laris signature chocolate) getting raves from guests. Save room for the Pandan Leaf Panna Cotta.

New Heights ✿ (seventh floor; ✆ 021/6321-0909; 11:30am–3:30pm and 6–11:30pm) is the option for casual, more affordable bistro-type fare, with rooftop views of the Bund and Pǔdōng rivaling that of M on the Bund next door. Dinner for two should be in the ¥400 ($50) range. In the back of New Heights is a music lounge, **Third Degree** (7pm–2am), which serves live music with its cocktails.

Three on the Bund is located at Zhōngshān Dōng Yī Lù 3 (entrance on side street at Guǎngdōng Lù 23; ✆ 021/6323-3355; www.threeonthebund.com). Take the metro to Hénán Zhōng Lù.

crab, a freshwater delicacy that reaches its prime every fall. Also popular are any number of "drunken" dishes (crab, chicken) marinated in local Shàoxīng wine, and braised meat dishes such as lion's head meatballs and braised pork knuckle. Shànghăi dim sum and snacks include a variety of dumplings, headlined by the local favorite *xiǎolóng bāo*, as well as onion pancakes and leek pies, all of which deserve to be tried.

The boom in Shànghăi restaurants has brought with it a dramatic increase in Japanese, Thai, European, and American restaurants, too, with the international fast-food chains, from Starbucks to McDonald's, seemingly on every corner. For restaurant locations, see the map on p. 420.

HUÁNGPŬ (DOWNTOWN)
VERY EXPENSIVE
Bund 18 INTERNATIONAL   The latest redevelopment on the Bund—in the lavishly restored Chartered Bank of India, Australia, and China building—features **Sens & Bund** (sixth floor) ✿✿✿, the first China foray of Jacques and Laurent Pourcel, fresh from their three-star Michelin restaurants in France. At press time, their haute French cuisine, with equally haute prices, was already attracting repeat customers. Garnering more complaints, especially of rude service and only mediocre food is the Cantonese restaurant **Tán Wài Lóu** (fifth floor). **Bar Rouge** on the rooftop is currently the place for the jet set to see and be seen with their cocktails.

Zhōngshān Dōng Yī Lù 18. www.bund18.com. Reservations required. AE, DC, MC, V. Sens & Bund, 6th floor, ✆ 021/6323-9898. Main courses ¥150–¥280 ($18–$35). 11:30am–2:30pm and 6:30–10:30pm. Tán Wài Lóu, 5th floor, ✆ 021/6339-1188. Meal for 2 ¥800 ($100) and up. 11am–2:30pm and 6–10:30pm. **Bar Rouge**, 7th floor, ✆ 021/6339-1199. 11:30am–2am. Metro: Hénán Zhōng Lù.

M on the Bund (Mǐshì Xīcāntīng) ✿✿✿ CONTINENTAL   Lodged atop a handsome seven-story colonial building on the Bund, this is the restaurant that 7 years ago put Shànghăi dining on the world map. All Art Deco elegance, M boasts a terrace that affords unsurpassed views of the Bund, the Huángpŭ River, and Pǔdōng's skyscrapers, as well as a "Glamour Room" for nightly dinner and drinks. The very fine menu changes frequently to take advantage of fresh local ingredients, but signature dishes include the slow-baked leg of lamb and the exquisitely sublime Pavlova dessert.

Zhōngshān Dōng Yī Lù 5, 7th floor (entrance on side street at Guǎngdōng Lù 20). ✆ 021/6350-9988. Reservations required. Main courses ¥150–¥280 ($18–$35). AE, DC, MC, V. 6–10:30pm; Tues–Fri 11:30am–2:30pm; Sat–Sun brunch 11:30am–3pm; Sun tea 3:30–5:30pm. Metro: Hénán Zhōng Lù.

EXPENSIVE
Shànghăi Uncle (Hǎishàng Āshū) ✿✿✿ SHÀNGHĂI   If you only get to try one Shanghainese meal, let it be at this cavernous and brash red-themed restaurant in the basement of the Bund Center where old Shànghăi favorites are given a modern makeover. Menu favorites include the unbelievably tender pine seed pork rip, Shànghăi traditional smoked fish, and the fusion-influenced cheese baked lobster with homemade noodles. Mezzanine booths offer the best viewing spots.

Yán'ān Dōng Lù 222, Wàitān Zhōngxīn (Bund Center), Basement (between Hénán Zhōng Lù and Jiāngxī Zhōng lù). ✆ 021/6339-1977. Xúhuì branch: Tiānyáoqiáo Lù 211, 2nd floor (north of Nándān Dōng Lù), ✆ 021/6464-6430. Reservations highly recommended. Meal for 2 ¥160–¥250 ($20–$31). AE, DC, MC, V. 11am–11pm. Metro: Hénán Zhōng Lù.

NÁNSHÌ DISTRICT (OLD TOWN)
EXPENSIVE
Lǚ Bō Láng *Overrated* SHÀNGHǍI   Housed in a three-story traditional Chinese pavilion just south of Yù Yuán in the old Chinese city, this restaurant has become a de rigueur stop on the average tourist itinerary strictly on the basis of its celebrity guest list (Fidel Castro, President Bill Clinton). Specialties such as the seasonal *Yángchéng Hú* crab, shark's fin, and President Clinton's favorite *sānsī méimao sū* (eyebrow-shaped pasty stuffed with pork, bamboo, and mushrooms) sell well, though prices are generally inflated. The automatic 10% service charge is a guarantee that you won't get much in the way of service.

Yù Yuán Lù 115 (south shore of teahouse lake). ✆ 021/6328-0602. Reservations recommended. Meal for 2 ¥120–¥250 ($14–$30). AE, DC, MC, V. 7am–12:30am. Metro: Hénán Zhōng Lù.

INEXPENSIVE
Nánxiáng Mántou Diàn DUMPLINGS   Tourists flock to this dumpling restaurant just west of the Bridge of Nine Turnings in old town for its award-winning *Nánxiáng xiáolóng* (¥8/$1 for a steamer of 16 dumplings), steamed pork dumplings with delicious broth that squirts all over the moment you bite into the wrapper. The take-out counter is on the first floor, three dining rooms are on the second, and the crowds are everywhere.

Yù Yuán Lù 85 (west shore of teahouse lake). ✆ 021/6355-4206. Meal for 2 ¥16–¥80 ($2–$10). No credit cards. 7am–8pm. Metro: Hénán Zhōng Lù (1.6km/1 mile away).

LÚWĀN DISTRICT (FRENCH CONCESSION)
VERY EXPENSIVE
Lan Kwai Fong at Park 97 ⚜⚜ INTERNATIONAL   Located in Fùxīng Gōngyuán, the oh-so-chic Hong Kong import Park 97, one of Shànghǎi's trendiest restaurant complexes since 1997, now comprises four outlets. **Baci Italian Cuisine** is justifiably known for its fresh pasta dishes and very thin-crusted pizzas, but its most popular offering is its weekend brunch. A children's menu is also available for brunch. **Tokio Joe** has sushi creations and delicious rolls, with three-course moderately priced set meals. **California Club** is a very hip and loud disco (aesthetically and acoustically) that opens onto Baci; while **Upstairs at 97** is a lounge bar with a slightly mellower live band (usually jazz or Latin).

Gāolán Lù 2 (inside west gate of Fùxīng Gōngyuán). ✆ 021/5383-2328 (Baci/Tokio Joe/California Club). Reservations recommended on weekends. Main courses ¥50–¥250 ($6–$30). AE, DC, MC, V. Baci 11:30am–11pm. Tokio Joe Mon–Fri 11:30am–2:30pm and 6–11pm; Sat–Sun 11:30am–11pm (lunch served until 6pm). California Club and Upstairs at 97 9pm–2am (till 4am Fri–Sat). Metro: Huángpí Nán Lù.

Xīn Tiāndì Restaurant Mall ⚜⚜⚜ INTERNATIONAL   A Starbucks stands at its entrance, the First National Congress of the Communist Party at its flanks, and in its midst, brilliant restorations of Shànghǎi's colonial Shíkù Mén ("stone gate") architecture. The place is Xīn Tiāndì (literally "New Heaven and Earth"), an upscale cultural mall where the moneyed East meets the moneyed West. Here you'll find the city's hottest dining spots. Located downtown a block south of the Huángpí Nán Lù Metro station, Xīn Tiāndì is a 2-block pedestrian mall with enough good eating to require weeks to experience it all. The best and the priciest are listed below.

　　Crystal Jade Restaurant (Fěicuì Jiǔjiā) ⚜⚜⚜ (South Block/Nánlǐ 6–7, second floor–12A and B; ✆ 021/6385-8752; Mon–Fri 11am–3pm and 5–11:30pm,

Sat–Sun 10:30am–3pm and 5–11:30pm) serves arguably the best *xiǎolóng bāo* (steamed dumplings with broth) and *lāmiàn* (hand-pulled noodles) south of the Yángzǐ. Reserve in advance or risk a long wait.

KABB (Kǎibó Xīcāntīng) ✿ (North Block, House 5, Unit 1; ✆ **021/3307-0798;** Mon–Fri 9:30am–midnight, Sat–Sun 9:30am–2am), a spiffy American bar and comfort food cafe.

La Maison (Lèměisōng Fǎguó Cāntīng) (North Block, House 23, Unit 1; ✆ **021/ 3307-1010;** 11:30am–12:30am), a strictly French cafe, with French prices and its own bakery.

Luna ✿ (North Block, House 15, Unit 1; ✆ **021/6336-1717;** 11:30am–1:30am), a Continental cafe with heavenly surroundings.

Paulaner Brauhaus (Bǎoláinà) (North Block, House 19–20; ✆ **021/6320-3935;** 11am–2am), the Shànghǎi standby praised for its excellent German food, with authentic brews to match.

Star East (Shànghǎi Dōngmèi) (North Block, House 17, Unit 1; ✆ **021/ 6311-4991;** 11:30am–2am), international film star Jackie Chan's slick five-story Cantonese restaurant and bar, where Western set meals are available as well.

T8 ✿✿✿ (North Block, House 8; ✆ **021/6355-8999;** lunch Wed–Mon 11:30am–2pm, dinner daily 6:30–11pm) is the restaurant whose service and chefs have quickly rivaled those at M on the Bund, only with less attitude. Service and management are superb and unobtrusive, the decor is super chic and the food is irresistible, especially the Sìchuān seared king prawns, the slow-cooked lamb, the Sìchuān pie, and the to-die-for chocolate addiction plate.

Va Bene (Huá Wàn Yì) ✿✿ (North Block, House 7; ✆ **021/6311-2211;** 11:30am–2:30pm and 5–11:30pm), an upscale Italian diner (from the owners of Hong Kong's Gaia) with warm Tuscan decor, patio dining, and a wide range of antipasti, pasta, and gourmet pizzas, all made from the freshest ingredients.

Yè Shànghǎi ✿ (South Block, House 6; ✆ **021/6311-2323;** 11:30am–2:30pm and 5:30–11pm), an elegant touch of old Shànghǎi, which Hong Kong visitors claim is better than the original back home.

Zen (Xiānggǎng Cǎidié Xuān) ✿ (South Block, House 2; ✆ **021/6385-6395;** 11:30am–11:30pm), a modern Cantonese restaurant by way of Hong Kong, with excellent dim sum for lunch.

EXPENSIVE

Lan Na Thai (Lán Nà Tài) ✿✿ *(finds)* THAI This popular Thai restaurant is located on the second floor of a beautiful colonial mansion (the "Face" building) on the north end of the Ruìjīn Hotel estate. The prawn cake, satays, and papaya salad are superb and authentic, as are the soft-shell crabs. Service is discreet and gracious, making this an ideal spot for a relaxing lunch or fine candlelit dinner.

Ruìjīn Èr Lù 118 (building 4, Ruìjīn Guest House; south of Fùxīng Zhōng Lù). ✆ 021/6466-4328. Reservations recommended on weekends. Meal for 2 ¥200–¥320 ($25–$40). AE, DC, MC, V. 11:30am–2:30pm and 5:30–11pm. Metro: Shǎnxī Nán Lù.

MODERATE

Dī Shuǐ Dòng ✿✿ *(finds)* HÚNÁN Rivaling Sìchuān cuisine in spiciness, the lesser-known cooking of Húnán Province can be tried at this delightful restaurant atop a flight of rickety wooden stairs inside a small French concession storefront. Highly recommended are the *làzi jǐdīng* (spicy chicken nuggets), *suān dòujiǎo ròuní* (diced sour beans with minced pork), *duòjiāo yútóu* (fish head steamed with red chili), and *xiāngwèi hóngshǔ bō* (fragrant sweet potato in monk's pot). Service is no-nonsense, even occasionally impatient, but the food is superb and shouldn't be missed.

Màomíng Nán Lù 56 (north of Chánglè Lù). ✆ 021/6253-2689. Meal for 2 ¥80–¥140 ($10–$18). No credit cards. 11am–12:30am. Metro: Shǎnxī Nán Lù.

Zǎozi Shù ✿ VEGETARIAN Serving some of Shànghǎi's best vegetarian food, this popular, health-conscious restaurant eschews alcohol, dairy, MSG, and smoking, while serving organic tea and fruit as an appetizer. The bean curd skin roll is a delicious starter and you can't go wrong with most of the pure vegetable dishes, though the fake meat dishes don't always hold up as well.

Sōngshān Lù 77, 1st floor (inside the Shànghǎi Huánggōng complex, south of Huáihǎi Lù, 1 block east of Huángpí Nán Lù). ✆ 021/6384-8000. Reservations recommended. Meal for 2 ¥60–¥100 ($7.50–$13). AE, DC, MC, V. 10:30am–9pm. Metro: Huángpí Nán Lù.

JÌNGĀN DISTRICT (NORTHWEST SHÀNGHǍI)
VERY EXPENSIVE
Shintori Null II (Xīndūlǐ Wúèr Diàn) ✿✿ JAPANESE The crowd at this nouvelle Japanese restaurant set inside an industrial bunker is well heeled, black-clad, and a bit precious, but the sushi and sashimi are fine and fresh. A fun way to go may be to make a meal from a selection of appetizers such as cuttlefish in butter sauce, grilled codfish with *monomiso*, foie gras on radish, and vermicelli noodles served in an ice bowl. Service is efficient and friendly, which lends some much-needed warmth to the place.

Jùlù Lù 803 (west of Fùmín Lù). ✆ 021/5404-5252. Reservations required. Meals for 2 ¥250–¥600 ($31–$75). AE, DC, MC, V. Mon–Fri 5:30–10:30pm; Sat–Sun 11:30am–2pm and 5:30–10:30pm. Metro: Chángshú Lù.

EXPENSIVE
Méilóngzhèn ✿ SHÀNGHǍI Established in 1938, this Shànghǎi institution still draws the crowds after all these years. Its cuisine has evolved over time from strictly regional fare to one incorporating the spices and chilies of Sìchuān cooking. Popular favorites include deep-fried eel, Mandarin fish with noodles in chili sauce, Sìchuān duck, and Méilóngzhèn special chicken, served in small ceramic pots. The atmosphere is a bit stodgy with Qīng dynasty furniture and carved wooden paneling. Staff alternates between attentive and harried.

Nánjīng Xī Lù 1081, building 22 (east of Shànghǎi Centre at Jiāngníng Lù). ✆ 021/6253-5353. Reservations recommended. Meal for 2 ¥120–¥240 ($14–$29). AE, DC, MC, V. 11am–2pm and 5–10pm. Metro: Shímén Yī Lù.

Mesa (Méisà) ✿✿ CONTINENTAL This modern minimalist restaurant with stark walls, floor-to-ceiling windows, and an open kitchen serves the comfort foods of home while making good use of fresh local ingredients. The menu changes frequently but established favorites include the soy and ginger salmon with green tea soba, the T-bone steak, and the beef pie. Wines, chosen from an impressive list, are served in specially imported glasses. Save room for the homemade desserts.

Jùlù Lù 748 (east of Fùmín Lù). ✆ 021/6289-9108. Reservations required. Main courses ¥90–¥200 ($11–$25). AE, DC, MC, V. Mon–Fri 6–11pm; Sat–Sun 9:30am–5pm and 6–11pm. Metro: Chángshú Lù.

MODERATE
Bǎoluó *Value* SHÀNGHǍI A strictly local experience, Bǎoluó buzzes every night with barely controlled chaos. The extensive Chinese-only menu features many local favorites given a slight twist, including *huíguō ròu jiābǐng* (twice-cooked lamb

wrapped in pancakes), *sōngshŭ lúyú* (sweet-and-sour fried fish), *xièfĕn huì zhēnjūn* (braised mushroom with crabmeat), and the more unusual *qīngzhēn dòuní* (creamy mashed beans).

Fùmín Lù 271 (north of Chánglè Lù, 1 block east of Chángshú Lù). ☎ 021/6279-2827. Reservations highly recommended. Meal for 2 ¥80–¥140 ($10–$18). No credit cards. 11am–6am. Metro: Chángshú Lù.

INEXPENSIVE
Element Fresh (Yuán Sù) ⊛ AMERICAN   This hip eatery in the Shànghăi Centre serves a range of soups, sandwiches, and salads that are fresh, healthy, and an instant cure for any homesickness. Also on the menu is a slew of smoothies, fresh fruit and vegetable juices, pastas, and a handful of Asian set meals, as well as some very popular breakfast sets. The place is jam-packed at lunchtime as is the patio during the warmer months.

Nánjīng Xī Lù 1376, no. 112 (ground floor, Shànghăi Centre). ☎ 021/6279-8682. Reservations recommended. Main courses ¥35–¥85 ($4.50–$11). AE, DC, MC, V. 7am–11pm. Metro: Jìng'ān Sì.

XÚHUÌ DISTRICT (SOUTHWEST SHÀNGHĂI)
VERY EXPENSIVE
La Villa Rouge (Xiăo Hóng Lóu) ⊛⊛ CONTINENTAL/FUSION   The 1921 red-brick mansion housing this fine dining outlet was once the original EMI Recording Studios. Amidst the grand staircases, large glass windows, and traditional recording instruments, fusion-influenced degustation menus are the way to go if you're blessed with an expense account; typical a la carte items such as beluga caviar, foie gras, lobster, and beef tenderloin can add up as well. An after-dinner drink in the bar or on the patio during warmer months is a classy way to spend an evening.

Héngshān Lù 811 (in Xújiāhuì Gōngyuán). ☎ 021/6431-9811. Reservations required. Main courses ¥190–¥420 ($24–$52). AE, DC, MC, V. 11:30am–10pm (bar is open until 1 or 2am Fri–Sat). Metro: Héngshān Lù or Xújiāhuì.

EXPENSIVE
Simply Thai (Tiāntài Cāntīng) ⊛⊛ THAI   Located in a cozy two-story cottage, Simply Thai is the top choice with many Shànghăi expatriates (Thais included) for unpretentious, authentic, and reasonably priced Thai food. Especially pleasing are the refreshing pomelo (grapefruit) salad with pineapple appetizer, *tom yam* shrimp soup, panaeng pork curry, and seafood with glass noodle salad. Patio dining in the warmer months provides a lovely respite from the city bustle.

Dōngpíng Lù 5, Unit C (between Héngshān Lù and Yuèyáng Lù). ☎ 021/6445-9551. Reservations recommended. Meal for 2 ¥150–¥300 ($18–$36). AE, DC, MC, V. 10am–1am. Metro: Héngshān Lù or Chángshú Lù.

MODERATE
Indian Kitchen (Yìndù Xiăochú) ⊛ INDIAN   This small, intimate restaurant in the heart of the French Concession is a favorite with locals and expatriates for authentic Indian food that's also easy on the wallet. Besides the signature chicken tandoori, the mutton curry and the flaky spring onion *parotas* are especially fine. Staff seems a little hesitant at times, but the line that forms nightly outside the door should be plenty reassuring.

Yǒngjiā Lù 572 (between Yuèyáng Lù and Wūlǔmùqí Nán Lù). ☎ 021/6473-1517. Reservations recommended. Meal for 2 ¥130–¥200 ($16–$25). AE, DC, MC, V. 11am–2:30pm and 5–11pm. Metro: Héngshān Lù.

Lái Fú Lóu ⊛ HOT POT   The sleek Lái Fú Lóu offers some of the most elegant and private hot pot dining in town. There's a wide variety of soup bases to choose from. Many folks opt for the *yuānyāng* version, which contains both a potent spicy stock and a more benign pork-based broth. Besides all the usual meat and vegetable ingredients, the restaurant also specializes in hand-made *yúwán* (fish balls) and *dànjiǎo* (egg-wrapped dumplings).

Huáihǎi Zhōng Lù 1416, 2nd floor (at intersection of Fùxīng Xī Lù). ✆ 021/6473-6380. Reservations recommended. Meal for 2 ¥80–¥120 ($10–$15). AE, DC, MC, V. 11am–4am. Metro: Chángshú Lù.

CHÁNGNÍNG DISTRICT (HÓNGQIÁO DEVELOPMENT ZONE)
MODERATE

Bā Guó Bù Yī 🎗🎗 SÌCHUĀN   Those seeking authentic Sìchuān fare can find it at this popular batik-themed eatery where chili alerts in the Chinese-only menu will let you know what you're in for. Try *làzi jīdǐng* (chicken nuggets in a sea of red chili peppers), *huíguō ròu* (twice-cooked pork with chili and scallions), *shuǐzhǔ yú* (fish slices and vegetables in a flaming spicy broth), and *dāndān miàn* (noodles in spicy peanut sauce), but order lots of cold beer to put out the three-alarm fire in your mouth.

Hóngqiáo Lù 1676 (east of Shuǐchéng Lù). ✆ 021/6270-6668. Reservations required. Meal for 2 ¥80–¥160 ($10–$20). No credit cards. 11:30am–2pm and 5–9pm.

1221 🎗🎗 SHÀNGHǍI   Very chic, this is a very popular place among resident foreigners and business travelers for reasonably priced fine Shànghǎi dining that's neither too greasy nor too sweet. Standouts include drunken chicken, Shànghǎi smoked fish, lion's head meatballs, braised pork with preserved vegetables, and stir-fried shredded beef with *yóutiáo* (a fried salty doughnut).

Yán'ān Xī Lù 1221 (between Pānyú Lù and Dīngxī Lù). ✆ 021/6213-6585. Reservations recommended. Meal for 2 ¥120–¥250 ($15–$30). AE, DC, MC, V. 11am–2pm and 5:30–11pm.

INEXPENSIVE

Lǎo Tán 🎗 *(Finds)* GUÌZHŌU   Miáo minority cuisine from Southwestern China's Guìzhōu Province can now be found in Shànghǎi in this boisterous second-floor restaurant tucked away just east of the Crowne Plaza hotel. Worth trying are *suān jiāngdòu làròu* (sour diced long beans with chilies and smoked bacon), *huǒyàn niúròu* (beef with red and green peppers on a bed of leeks cooked over a slow flame), *gānguōjī guōzi* (spicy chicken with peppers), and *gānbiān tǔdòu* (fried potato pancake)—a perfect accompaniment to just about any dish.

Xīngfú Lù 42, 2nd floor (north of Fǎhuázhèn Lù, 1 block east of Fānyú Lù). ✆ 021/6283-7843. Reservations highly recommended. Meal for 2 ¥60–¥100 ($7.50–$13). No credit cards. 11am–2pm and 5–11pm.

PǓDŌNG NEW AREA
VERY EXPENSIVE

Canton (Yuè Zhēn Xuān) 🎗🎗🎗 CANTONESE/DIM SUM   With a 360-degree view from this grand height, elegant decor, impeccable service, and master chefs from Hong Kong, the Grand Hyatt's Canton is the most luxurious restaurant for haute Cantonese cuisine in Shànghǎi. The shark's fin and bird's nest soups are superb; the abalone and other seafood dishes are surprisingly delicate; and the dim sum dumplings are wonderful.

Shìjì Dà Dào 88 (55th floor, Jīn Mào Tower, Grand Hyatt Hotel). ✆ 021/5049-1234, ext. 8898. Reservations required. Meal for 2 ¥200–¥400 ($25–$50). AE, DC, MC, V. 11:30am–2:30pm and 5:30–10pm. Metro: Lùjiāzuǐ.

Danieli's (Dānní'àilì) 🎗🎗🎗 ITALIAN   Worth a special trip out to Pǔdōng, this fine Italian restaurant atop the St. Regis Hotel features all manner of excellent *pesci* and *carni,* but it's the pastas that fans love (giving this restaurant "the best pasta" award in a local expatriate dining magazine competition). To top it off, the views are exquisite, the wine list extensive, and the service highly attentive.

Dōngfāng Lù 877 (29th floor, St. Regis Hotel). © 021/5050-4567. Reservations required. Main courses ¥90–¥250 ($11–$31). AE, DC, MC, V. 11:30am–2:30pm and 5:30–10pm. Metro: Lùjiāzuǐ.

MODERATE

Sū Zhè Huì (Jade Garden) ✿ SHÀNGHĂI This branch of one of the more highly regarded and popular Shànghăi chain restaurants offers diners its signature local dishes as well as Hong Kong–style dim sum in a classy and refined setting. Menu items of note include tea-smoked duck, wine-preserved green crab, *mìzhī huǒfǎng* (pork and taro in candied sauce), and *qícài dōngsǔn* (fresh winter shoots with local greens)—something you're unlikely to get back home.

Dōngfāng Lù 877 (just north of the St. Regis hotel). © 021/5058-6088. Meal for 2 ¥77–¥120 ($9.60–$14). AE, DC, MC, V. 11am–11pm. Metro: Dōngfāng Lù.

5 Exploring Shànghăi

THE BUND (WÀITĀN)

The Bund (Embankment) refers to Shànghăi's famous waterfront running along the west shore of the Huángpǔ River, forming the eastern boundary of old downtown Shànghăi. Once a muddy towpath for boats along the river, the Bund was where the foreign powers that entered Shànghăi after the Opium War of 1842 erected their distinct Western-style banks and trading houses. Today, a wide avenue (Zhōngshān Dōng Yī Lù) fronts the old buildings, which date mostly from the prosperous 1920s and 1930s. On the east side of the road, a raised pedestrian promenade affords visitors pleasant strolls along the river and marvelous views of both the Bund and Pǔdōng—its modern skyscrapers constituting Shànghăi's "21st Century Bund"—across the river.

The Bund, stretching for 1.6km (1 mile) from Sūzhōu Creek in the north to Jīnlíng Lù in the south is well worth strolling by day or at night. The chief colonial buildings, running north to south, include: the **former British Consulate** (No. 33–53), its two remaining faded but still stately buildings part of a compound slated for redevelopment; **Banque de L'Indo-Chine** (No. 29), built in 1911; **Glen Line Building** (No. 28), built in 1922 and briefly the American Consulate after World War II; **Jardine Matheson** (No. 27), 1922, one of the first and most powerful foreign trading offices in Shànghăi; **Yangtze Insurance Building** (No. 26), 1916, with a fine restored lobby; **Bank of China** (No. 23), dating from 1937; **Peace Hotel** (No. 20), the former Cathay Hotel (1929), worth a tour in its own right for its spectacular Art Deco interiors; the former **Palace Hotel** (No. 19), 1906, built by the Sassoon family and now part of the Peace Hotel; **Chartered Bank of India, Australia, and China** (No. 18), 1923, newly restored into a stunning high-end restaurant and retail complex; **North China Daily News Building** (No. 17), built in 1921; **Bank of Táiwān Building** (No. 16), built in 1924 as a Japanese bank; **Russo-Chinese Bank Building** (No. 15), dating from 1901; **Bank of Communications Building** (No. 14), a 1940 edifice with an entrance framed in copper sheets; **Shànghăi Customs House** (No. 13), dating from 1927 and still housing some dank offices and apartments; **Hongkong and Shanghai Bank** (No. 12), dedicated in 1923, with its not-to-be-missed restored lobby dome just inside; **Hospital of the Shànghăi Navigation Co.** (No. 7), built in 1906 and the site of China's first switchboard; **China Merchants Bank** (No. 6), built in 1906; the former **Nishin Navigation Company** (No. 5), 1925, its seventh floor now housing the restaurant M on the Bund; **Union Insurance Company Building** (No. 3), 1922, also known as Three on the Bund, one of Shànghăi's hippest "lifestyle destinations" complete with international caliber restaurants and luxury shops (see box on p. 431); and **Shànghăi Club** (No. 2), 1910, former home of the legendary Long Bar.

YÙ GARDEN (YÙ YUÁN)

Yù Yuán is a pleasant enough, well-contained classical Chinese garden, if not quite the loveliest of its kind, as local boosters would have you believe. Bearing the burden of being the most complete classical garden in urban Shànghăi and therefore a must-see for every tourist, this overexposed garden overflows daily with hordes of visitors, and is no longer the pastoral haven it once was. Built between 1559 and 1577 by local official Pān Yǔnduān as the private estate for his father, Yù Yuán (meaning Garden of Peace and Comfort) is a maze of Míng dynasty pavilions, elaborate rockeries, arched bridges, and goldfish ponds, all encircled by an undulating dragon wall. Occupying just 2 hectares (5 acres), it nevertheless appears quite expansive, with room for 30 pavilions.

Located in the heart of old town (Nánshì), a few blocks southwest of the Bund in downtown Shànghăi (nearest metro: Hénán Zhōng Lù, which is still 1.6km/1 mile away), Yù Yuán has a ticket window on the north shore of the Húxīn Tíng Teahouse pond (© **021/6326-0830**). The garden is open from 8:30am to 5pm; admission is ¥30 ($3.75).

The layout of Yù Yuán, which contains several gardens-within-gardens, can make strolling here a bit confusing, but if you stick to a general clockwise path from the main entrance, you should get around most of the estate and arrive eventually at the Inner Garden (Nèi Yuán) and final exit.

Halls and pavilions of note (in clockwise order from the north entrance) include the **Hall for Viewing the Grand Rockery (Yáng Shān Táng),** a graceful two-story tower serving as the entrance to the marvelous rock garden behind, which consists of 2,000 tons of rare yellow stones pasted together with rice glue and designed by a famous garden artist of the Míng dynasty, Zhāng Nányáng; the **Hall of Heralding Spring (Diăn Chūn Táng),** the most famous historical building in the garden, where in 1853 the secret Small Sword Society (Xiăodāo Huì) plotted to join the peasant-led Tàipíng Rebellion and help overthrow the Qīng dynasty; and the **Hall of Jade Magnificence (Yù Huá Táng),** opening to the most celebrated stone sculpture in the garden, the **Exquisite Jade (Yù Líng Lóng),** which was originally procured by the Huìzōng emperor of the Northern Sòng (reigned 1100–26) from the waters of Tài Hú (Lake Tài) where many of the bizarre rocks and rockeries found in classical Chinese gardens were submerged to be naturally carved by the currents. Such rocks represent mountain peaks in classical Chinese garden design. Just before the **Inner Garden (Nèi Yuán),** where local artists and calligraphers often display and sell their works, is the garden's main exit.

SHÀNGHĂI BÓWÙGUĂN ✿✿✿

Frequently cited as the best museum in China, the Shànghăi Museum has 11 state-of-the-art galleries and three special exhibition halls arranged on four floors, all encircling a spacious cylindrical atrium. The exhibits are tastefully displayed and well lit, and explanatory signs are in English as well as Chinese. For size, the museum's 120,000 historic artifacts cannot match the world-renowned Chinese collections in Běijīng, Taipei, and Xī'ān, but are more than enough to fill the galleries on any given day with outstanding treasures.

Shànghǎi Attractions

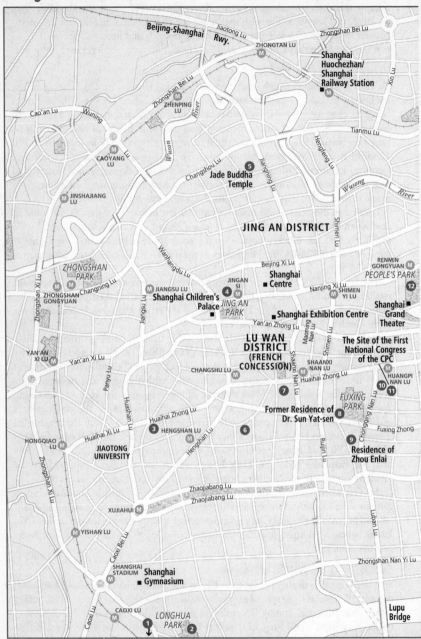

Beijing-Shanghai Rwy.

Jiaotong Lu

ZHONGTAN LU Ⓜ

Zhongshan Bei Lu

线 号 二

Shanghai Huochezhan/ Shanghai Railway Station

Ⓜ

Zhongshan Bei Lu

Zhongshan Bei Lu

ZHENPING LU Ⓜ

Cao'an Lu

Wuning

Wusong River

Tianmu Lu

Hengfeng Lu

CAOYANG LU Ⓜ

Changshou Lu

Jiangning Lu

Ⓜ JINSHAJIANG LU

Wusong River

⑤ Jade Buddha Temple

JING AN DISTRICT

Shimen Lu

ZHONGSHAN PARK

Wanhangdu Lu

Beijing Xi Lu

RENMIN GONGYUAN *PEOPLE'S PARK*

Zhongshan Xi Lu

Changning Lu

Ⓜ ZHONGSHAN GONGYUAN

Ⓜ JIANGSU LU

JINGAN SI ④

■ Shanghai Centre

Nanjing Xi Lu

SHIMEN YI LU Ⓜ

⑫

JING AN PARK

Shanghai Children's Palace ■

■ **Shanghai Exhibition Centre**

Shanghai Grand Theater

YAN'AN XI LU

Yan'an Xi Lu

Ⓜ YAN'AN XI LU

Panyu Lu

Huashan Lu

Jiangsu Lu

Yan'an Zhong Lu

LU WAN DISTRICT (FRENCH CONCESSION)

Shaanxi Nan Lu

Maoming Nan Lu

Shimen Lu

The Site of the First National Congress of the CPC

⑩

HUANGPI NAN LU ⑪

CHANGSHU LU Ⓜ

⑦

SHAANXI NAN LU

Huaihai Zhong Lu

FUXING PARK

Former Residence of Dr. Sun Yat-sen ⑧

Chongqing Nan Lu

Fuxing Zhong

HONGQIAO LU Ⓜ

Huaihai Xi Lu

Huaihai Zhong Lu

③ HENGSHAN LU Ⓜ

⑥

Hengshan Lu

Rujin Lu

⑨ **Residence of Zhou Enlai**

Luban Lu

JIAOTONG UNIVERSITY

Zhaojiabang Lu

Zhaojiabang Lu

Zhongshan Xi Lu

XUJIAHUI Ⓜ

Ⓜ YISHAN LU

Caoxi Bei Lu

Zhongshan Nan Yi Lu

SHANGHAI STADIUM

Shanghai Gymnasium ■

Caoxi Lu

Ⓜ CAOXI LU

LONGHUA PARK

① ↓

②

Lupu Bridge

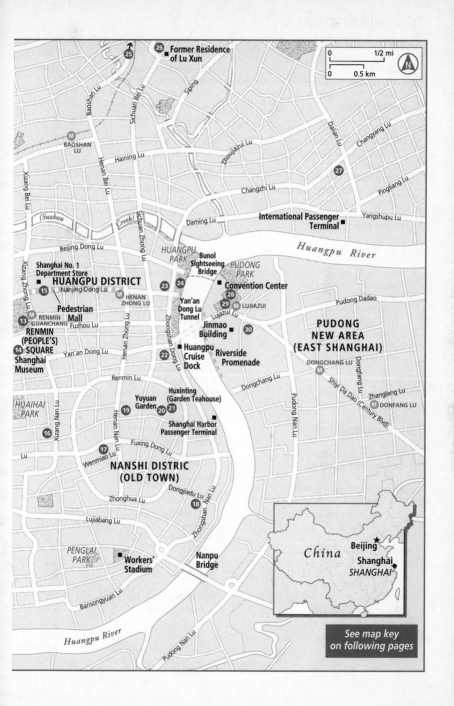

25

26 Former Residence
of Lu Xun

1/2 mi

0.5 km

N

BAOSHAN
LU

Baoshan Lu

Sichuan Bei Lu

Siping

Zhoujiazui Lu

Dalian Lu

Changyang Lu

Haining Lu

Henan Bei Lu

27

Pingliang Lu

Changzhi Lu

Yangshupu Lu

(Suzhou

Creek)

Sichuan Zhong Lu

Daming Lu

International Passenger
Terminal

Huangpu River

Beijing Dong Lu

HUANGPU
PARK

Bunol
Sightseeing
Bridge

PUDONG
PARK

Xizang Bei Lu

Shanghai No. 1
Department Store

HUANGPU DISTRICT

15 Nanjing Dong Lu

23

24

Convention Center

28

Pudong Dadao

Xizang Zhong Lu

Pedestrian
Mall

13

HENAN
ZHONG LU

RENMIN
GUANGCHANG

Fuzhou Lu

Henan Zhong Lu

Zhongshan Dong Lu

Yan'an
Dong Lu
Tunnel

29

LUJIAZUI

Lujiazui Lu

30

PUDONG
NEW AREA
(EAST SHANGHAI)

RENMIN
(PEOPLE'S)
SQUARE

14

Shanghai
Museum

Yan'an Dong Lu

Jinmao
Building

22

Huangpu
Cruise
Dock

Riverside
Promenade

DONGCHANG LU

Pudong Nan Lu

Shiyi Da Dao (Century Blvd)

Dongfang Lu

Renmin Lu

Dongchang Lu

DONGCHANG LU

Zhangliang Lu

Xizang Nan Lu

HUAIHAI
PARK

16

19

Yuyuan
Garden

20 21

Huxinting
(Garden Teahouse)

DONFANG LU

Henan Nan Lu

Shanghai Harbor
Passenger Terminal

Lu

17

Wenmiao Lu

Fuxing Dong Lu

NANSHI DISTRIC
(OLD TOWN)

Dongjiadu Lu

Zhongshan Nan Lu

Zhonghua Lu

18

Lujiabang Lu

PENGLAI
PARK

Workers'
Stadium

Nanpu
Bridge

China

Beijing ★

Shanghai
SHANGHAI

Bansongyuan Lu

Huangpu River

Pudong Nan Lu

See map key
on following pages

441

Shànghǎi Attractions Key

The Bund
   (Wài Tān) 24
   外滩
Confucius Temple
   (Wén Miào) 17
   文庙
Dǒngjiādù Fabric Market
   (Dǒngjiādù Lù Zhīpǐn Shìchǎng) 18
   董家渡路织品市场
Dōngtái Lù Antiques Market
   (Dōngtái Lù Gǔwán Shìchǎng) 16
   东台路古玩市场
Friendship Store
   (Yǒuyì Shāngdiàn) 22
   友谊商店
Fúyòu Market 19
   福佑市场
Húxīn Tíng Teahouse
   (Húxīn Tíng Cháshè) 21
   湖心亭茶社
Jade Buddha Temple
   (Yùfó Sì) 5
   玉佛寺
Jīn Mào Tower
   (Jīn Mào Dàshà) 30
   金茂大厦
Jìng'ān Sì
   (Jìng'ān Temple) 4
   静安寺
Lónghuá Sì
   (Lónghuá Temple) 2
   龙华寺
Lǔ Xùn Park and Memorial Hall
   (Lǔ Xùn Jìniànguǎn) 26
   鲁迅纪念馆
Nánjīng Road Pedestrian Mall 15
   南京路步行街
Ohel Moshe Synagogue
   (Móxī Huìtáng) 27
   摩西会堂
Oriental Pearl TV Tower
   (Dōngfāng Míngzhū
   Guǎngbō Diànshì Tǎ) 28
   东方明珠广播电视塔
Peace Hotel
   (Hépíng Fàndiàn) 23
   和平饭店

Shànghǎi Art Museum
   (Shànghǎi Měishùguǎn) 12
   上海美术馆
Shànghǎi Botanical Gardens
   (Shànghǎi Zhíwùyuán) 1
   上海植物园
Shànghǎi Circus World
   (Shànghǎi Mǎxì Chéng) 25
   上海马戏城
Shànghǎi Municipal History Museum
   (Shànghǎi Shì Lìshǐ Bówùguǎn) 29
   上海市历史博物馆
Shànghǎi Museum of Arts and Crafts
   (Shànghǎi Gōngyì Měishù
   Bówùguǎn) 6
   上海工艺美术博物馆
Shànghǎi Museum
   (Shanghai Bówùguǎn) 14
   上海博物馆
Shànghǎi Urban Planning Centre
   (Shànghǎi Chéngshì Guīhuà
   Zhǎnshìguǎn) 13
   上海城市规划展示馆
Site of the First National
   Congress of the Communist Party
   (Zhōnggòng Yīdà Huìzhǐ) 11
   中共一大会址
Soong Ching-ling's Former Residence
   (Sòng Qìnglíng Gùjū) 3
   宋庆龄故居
Sun Yat-sen's Former Residence
   (Sūn Zhōngshān Gùjū
   Jìniànguǎn) 8
   孙中山故居纪念馆
Xiāngyáng Clothing Market
   (Xiāngyáng Shì
   Lǐpǐn Shìchǎng) 7
   襄阳饰礼品市场
Xīntiāndì
   (New Heaven and Earth) 10
   新天地
Yù Yuán
   (Yù Garden) 20
   豫园
Zhōu Enlái's Former Residence
   (Zhōu Gōng Guǎn) 9
   周公馆

Located downtown on the south side of People's Square (Rénmín Guăngchăng) at Rénmín Dà Dào 201 (© **021/6372-3500**), the museum has its main entrance on the north side of the building, facing the three monumental structures that now occupy the north half of the square (Grand Theatre to the west, City Hall in the middle, Shànghăi Urban Planning Exhibition Center to the east). Metro lines 1 and 2 both have their main stations on the northeast corner of People's Square. The museum is open 9am to 5pm (no tickets sold after 4pm). Admission is ¥20 ($2.50). Audio phones providing narratives of the major exhibits in English, French, Japanese, Spanish, German, and Italian are available for rent (¥40/$5 plus a deposit of ¥400/$50 or your passport) at the counter to your left as you enter the lobby.

The first floor contains major galleries displaying bronzes and stone sculptures. The second floor has wonderful displays of ceramic ware. The third floor has separate galleries for paintings, calligraphy, and personal seals. The fourth floor has exhibits of jade, coins, furniture, and minority cultures. Though visitors all have their individual favorites, the Bronze Gallery and the Stone Sculpture Gallery on the first floor, the Painting Gallery on the third floor, and the Jade Gallery on the fourth are generally considered the most impressive.

HUÁNGPŬ RIVER CRUISE

The Huángpŭ River (Huángpŭ Jiāng) is the city's shipping artery both to the East China Sea and to the mouth of the Yángzǐ River, which the Huángpŭ joins 29km (18 miles) north of downtown Shànghăi. It has also become a demarcating line between two Shànghăis, east and west, past and future. On its western shore, the colonial landmarks of the Bund serve as a reminder of Shànghăi's 19th-century struggle to reclaim a waterfront from the bogs of this river (which originates in nearby Diānshān Hú or Lake Diānshān); on the eastern shore, the steel-and-glass skyscrapers of the Pŭdōng New Area point to a burgeoning financial empire of the future.

The Huángpŭ's wharves are the most fascinating in China. The port handles the cargo coming out of the interior from Nánjīng, Wŭhàn, and other Yángzǐ River ports, including Chóngqìng, 2,415km (1,500 miles) deep into Sìchuān Province. From Shànghăi, which produces plenty of industrial and commercial products in its own right, as much as a third of China's trade with the rest of the world is conducted each year.

Several boat companies offer cruises, but the main one is the **Shànghăi Huángpŭ River Cruise Company (Shànghăi Pŭjiāng Yóulǎn),** at Zhōngshān Dōng Èr Lù 219 (© **021/6374-4461**), located on the southern end of the Bund Promenade; there's another office farther north at Zhōngshān Dōng Èr Lù 153. They have a daily full 3½-hour afternoon cruise (2–5:30pm) with the possibility of a full morning cruise during the summer. Prices for this cruise start at ¥70 ($9) and top out at ¥120 ($15). This company also offers nightly hour-long cruises as well as hour-long cruises (¥25–¥35/$3–$4.50) on weekdays running every 2 to 3 hours between 9:30am and 10pm.

The granite offices, banks, consulates, and hotels of Shànghăi's past colonial masters form a stately panorama along the Bund, while the Oriental Pearl TV Tower, the Jīn Mào Tower, and other new skyscrapers soar on the Pŭdōng side. As the ship heads north of the Bund, hugging the west shore are the old "go-downs" or warehouses of the many foreign trading firms. This area, known as Hóngkŏu District, and the district to the east, Yángpŭ District, have been marked for rapid development after Pŭdōng, though new modern towers (all no more than 4 years old) have already started to stake out the skyline. Eventually, all of this waterfront will be developed into a series of marinas and a combination of industrial and recreational areas.

As the Huángpŭ slowly curves northward again, you'll pass the **Yángpŭ Cable Bridge,** which, like the **Nánpŭ Cable Bridge** to the south, is one of the largest such structures in the world. Boasting the longest span in the world, some 602m (1,975 ft.), the Yángpŭ Bridge is considered the world's first "slant-stretched" bridge. Its total length is about 7.6km (4¾ miles), and 50,000 vehicles pass over its six lanes daily.

What overwhelms river passengers even more than the long industrial shoreline is the traffic slinking up and down the waterway from the flotilla of river barges to the large rusting hulls of cargo ships. The Huángpŭ is, on the average, just 183m (600 ft.) wide, but more than 2,000 oceangoing ships compete with the 20,000 barges, fishing junks, and rowboats that ply the Huángpŭ every year.

The Huángpŭ eventually empties into the mighty Yángzĭ River at **Wúsōng Kŏu,** where the water during high tide turns three distinct colors, marking the confluence of the Yángzĭ (yellow), the Huángpŭ (gray), and the South China Sea (green). Before this, there's an ancient **Wúsōng Fort,** from which the Chinese fought the British in 1842. The passenger terminal for Yángzĭ River cruises is also here. This marks the end of Shànghăi's little river and the beginning of China's largest one. As your tour boat pivots slowly back into the narrowing passageway of the Huángpŭ, you can look forward to a return trip that should be more relaxed.

TEMPLES

Confucius Temple (Wén Miào)
Built in 1855 on the site of an earlier temple, and restored in 1999 to celebrate the 2,550th birthday of Confucius, this temple honoring China's Great Sage offers quiet refuge from the crowded streets of the old Chinese city. Inside are statues of Confucius flanked by his two disciples, Mencius (Mèngzĭ) and Yànhuī; the Zūnjīng Gé, a former library now containing a display of unusually shaped rocks; and, near the entrance, Kuíxīng Gé, a three-story, 20m-high (66-ft.) pagoda dedicated to the god of liberal arts, the only original structure left. A lively book market is held here Sunday mornings.

Wénmiào Lù 215, Nánshì (north side of Wénmiào Lù, 1 block east of Zhōnghuá Lù). ✆ 021/6377-9101. Admission ¥10 ($1.25). 9am–4:30pm.

Jade Buddha Temple (Yùfó Sì) ⚡ *Overrated*
Though an active Buddhist monastery today, the real emphasis at Shànghăi's most popular temple is squarely on tourism. The chief attractions are two gorgeous white jade Buddhas, each carved from an individual slab of Burmese jade and brought to Shànghăi in 1881 by the monk Huìgēn. The first—a lustrous seated Buddha weighing 205 kilograms (455 lb.), measuring 1.9m (6 ft. 5 in.), and adorned with jewels and stones—can be found in the Cángjīng Lóu in the northeast of the compound, while a smaller 1m-long (3 ft. 4 in.) sleeping Buddha is in the Wòfó Sì, northwest of the main hall.

Ānyuán Lù 170, Pŭtuó (northwest Shànghăi, west of Jiāngníng Lù, 6 long blocks north of Bĕijīng Xī Lù). ✆ 021/6266-3668. Admission ¥10 ($1.25). 8am–4:30pm.

Jìng'ān Sì (Jìng'ān Temple)
Always lively and crowded, this garishly decorated and recently renovated temple has the longest history of any shrine in Shànghăi: about 17 centuries. Its chief antiquities are a Míng dynasty copper bell (the Hóngwŭ Bell) that weighs in at 3,175 kilograms (3.5 tons), and stone Buddhas from the Northern and Southern States Period (A.D. 420–589).

Nánjīng Xī Lù 1686, Jìng Ān (corner of Huáshān Lù). ✆ 021/6248-6366. Admission ¥10 ($1.25); ¥30 ($3.75) 1st and 15th day of Spring Festival (usually late Jan and early Feb). 7:30am–5pm. Metro: Jìng Ān Sì.

Lónghuá Sì (Lónghuá Temple) 🞭🞭   Shànghăi's largest temple features the city's premier pagoda (Lónghuá Tă). The seven-story, eight-sided, 1,000-year-old wood-and-brick pagoda is pretty, but it is not open for visits. The temple is active, its main halls impressive, its courtyards crowded with incense-bearing supplicants. Lónghuá is also famous for its midnight bell-ringing every New Year's Eve (Dec 31–Jan 1). The Bell Tower's 3,000-kilogram (3.3-ton) bronze bell, cast in 1894, is struck 108 times to dispel all the worries said to be afflicting mankind. For a small fee, you, too, can strike the bell, but for three times only.

Lónghuá Lù 2853, Xúhuì. 🕿 021/6456-6085. Admission ¥10 ($1.25). 7am–4:30pm. Metro: Shànghăi Tǐyùguăn (a long, unpleasant walk; easier to reach by taxi).

PARKS & GARDENS
Shànghăi Botanical Gardens (Shànghăi Zhíwùyuán) 🞭 *Kids*   Located in the far southwest of town, the city's premier garden, covering 81 hectares (200 acres), is divided into different sections featuring peonies, roses, bamboo, azaleas, maples, osmanthus, magnolias, and orchids (considered the best in China). The hallmark section is the Pénjǐng Yuán (Bonsai Garden), which requires a separate admission (¥7/90¢), with hundreds of bonsai displayed in a large complex of corridors, courtyards, pools, and rockeries.

Lóngwú Lù 1111, Xúhuì. 🕿 021/5436-3369. Admission ¥15 ($1.80). 7am–5:30pm (to 4:30pm in winter).

MUSEUMS & MANSIONS
Lǔ Xùn Park and Memorial Hall/Former Residence of Lǔ Xùn (Lǔ Xùn Gōngyuán/Lǔ Xùn Gùjū)   Named for China's best-known 20th-century writer, Lǔ Xùn (1881–1936), who lived in this neighborhood from 1927 until his death, this park contains Lǔ Xùn's mausoleum and a museum devoted to his life, the Lǔ Xùn Memorial Hall. A 10-minute walk east of the park, **Lǔ Xùn's Former Residence** is a three-story brick house where he lived from 1933 to his death, and largely decorated as it was then.

Jiāngwān Dōng Lù 146, Hóngkǒu. 🕿 021/5696-2894. Park free admission; includes Lǔ Xùn's tomb. 6am–6pm. Lǔ Xùn Memorial Hall (inside park on east side; 🕿 021/6587-6682); admission ¥8 ($1); 9am–4pm. **The Former Residence of Lǔ Xùn**, Shānyīn Lù 9 Lane 132, Hóngkǒu (from park, take a left out the main entrance, follow Tián'ài Lù south until it curves left onto Shānyīn Lù); admission ¥8 ($1); 9am–4pm. Light Rail: Hóngkǒu Zúqiú Chăng.

Ohel Moshe Synagogue (Móxī Huìtáng)   Shànghăi experienced several waves of Jewish immigration, beginning with the arrival of Sephardic Jews in the late 1840s, and lasting into the 1930s with a wave of European Jews fleeing Hitler. This synagogue, built in 1927 by the Ashkenazi Jewish community of Shànghăi, no longer serves as a synagogue, but as a museum devoted to the Jews in Shànghăi (whose number topped 30,000 just before World War II). The best way to visit this, as well as other sites in the Hóngkǒu District that formed Shànghăi's "Little Vienna," is on the **"Tour of Jewish Shànghăi"** 🞭 conducted by appointment with Dvir Bar-Gal (🕿 **0130/0214-6702;** www.shanghai-jews.com).

Chángyáng Lù 62, Hóngkǒu District. 🕿 021/6512-0229. Admission: ¥50 ($6.25) donation. Mon–Fri 9am–4pm.

Shànghăi Art Museum (Shànghăi Měishùguăn) 🞭   Relocated in 2000 to the historic clock tower building on the northwest end of People's Park, the museum is more to be seen for its monumental interior architecture than for its art. The fastidiously restored interiors of this 1933 five-story landmark recall colonial times when People's Park was a racecourse and the grandstand (1863) stood where this museum is now. Today, in addition to the artwork, there is a classy American restaurant, Kathleen's 5, on the fifth floor.

Nánjīng Xī Lù 325, Huángpǔ (northwest edge of People's Park at Huángpí Lù). ⓒ 021/6327-2829. www.sh-art museum.org.cn. Admission ¥20 ($2.50). 9am–5pm (last tickets sold 4pm). Metro: Rénmín Gōngyuán.

Shànghăi Municipal History Museum (Shànghăi Shì Lìshǐ Bówùguǎn) ★★

This excellent museum tells the history of Shànghăi with special emphasis on the colonial period from 1860 to 1949. Exhibits include dioramas of the Huángpǔ River, the Bund, and foreign concessions, evoking the street life and lost trades of the period; dozens of models of Shànghăi's classic avenues and famous buildings; and intriguing artifacts such as an ornate wedding palanquin, and visiting chits used in brothels. Signs are in English and Chinese.

Lùjiāzuǐ Lù 2, Oriental Pearl TV Tower basement, Pǔdōng. ⓒ 021/5879-3003. Admission ¥35 ($4.25). 9am–9:30pm. Metro: Lùjiāzuǐ.

Shànghăi Museum of Arts and Crafts (Shànghăi Gōngyì Měishù Yánjiūsuǒ Jiùgōngyìpǐn Xiūfù Bù)

With its expansive lawns, stained-glass windows, and dark wooden paneling, this 1905 French Concession mansion gives a fine picture of how the colonials lived in old Shànghăi. After 1960, this became the Shànghăi Arts and Crafts Research Center, and its many rooms were converted to studios where visitors could watch artisans work at traditional handicrafts. Today, a few artists' studios remain, along with a formal museum of the crafts produced in Shànghăi over the past 100 years. A salesroom is attached, of course.

Fēnyáng Lù 79, Lúwān District (at intersection of Yuèyáng Lù and Táojiāng Lù). ⓒ 021/6437-3454. Free admission. 8:30am–4:30pm. Metro: Chángshú Lù.

Shànghăi Urban Planning Centre ★★ (Finds)

One of the world's largest museums showcasing urban development, this exhibit is much more interesting than its dry name suggests. On the third floor is a showstopper: an awesome vast scale model of urban Shànghăi as it will look in 2020, a master plan of endless skyscrapers punctuated by patches of green. See this and understand how and why Shànghăi is going to be *the* city of the future.

Rénmín Dà Dào 100, Huángpǔ (northeast of the Shànghăi Museum; entrance on east side). ⓒ 021/6372-2077. Admission ¥25 ($3.10). 9am–4pm (to 5pm Fri–Sun). Metro: Rénmín Guǎngchǎng.

Site of the First National Congress of the Communist Party (Zhōnggòng Yīdà Huìzhǐ)

This historic building of brick and marble—a quintessential example of the traditional Shànghăi style of *shíkù mén* (stone-framed) houses built in the 1920s and 1930s—contains the room where on July 23, 1921, Máo Zédōng and 12 other Chinese revolutionaries founded the Chinese Communist Party. Supposedly the original teacups and ashtrays remain on the organizing table.

Xīngyè Lù 76, Lúwān (south end of Xīn Tiāndì). ⓒ 021/5383-2171. Admission ¥3 (35¢). 9am–4pm. Metro: Huángpí Nán Lù.

Soong Ching-ling's Former Residence (Sòng Qìnglíng Gùjū)

Soong Ching-ling (1893–1981) is revered throughout China as a loyalist to the Communist cause. Born in Shànghăi to a wealthy family, she married the founder of the Chinese Republic, Dr. Sun Yat-sen, in 1915. This house served as her residence from 1948 to 1963. The 1920s villa is little changed; the rooms are much as Soong left them. There is also a collection of her personal letters, photos, and books from her college days at Wesleyan College.

Huáihǎi Zhōng Lù 1843, Xújiāhuì (east of Tiānpíng Lù). ⓒ 021/6437-6268. Admission ¥8 ($1). 9am–4:30pm.

Sun Yat-sen's Former Residence (Sūn Zhōngshān Gùjū)   Sun Yat-sen (1866–1925), beloved founder of the Chinese Republic (1911), lived here with his wife, Soong Ching-ling from 1918 to 1924, when the address would have been 29 Rue de Molière. Here Sun's wife later met with such literary stars as Lǔ Xùn and George Bernard Shaw, and political leaders including Vietnam's Ho Chi Minh. An English-speaking guide leads visitors through the house. The backyard has a charming garden.

Xiāngshān Lù 7, Lúwān (west of Fùxīng Park at Sīnán Lù). ✆ 021/6437-2954 or 021/6385-0217. www.sh-sunyat-sen. com. Admission ¥8 ($1). 9am–4:30pm. Metro: Shǎnxī Nán Lù.

Zhōu Ēnlái's Former Residence (Zhōu Gōng Guǎn)   China's most revered leader during the Máo years, Premier Zhōu Ēnlái (1898–1976), used to stay at this ivy-covered house when he visited Shànghǎi in 1946. Used more as office than residence, the house served before 1949 as the Communist Party's Shànghǎi office. Zhōu's old black Buick is still parked in the garage.

Sīnán Lù 73, Lúwān (2 blocks south of Fùxīng Zhōng Lù). ✆ **021/6473-0420.** Admission ¥2 (25¢). 9am–4pm. Metro: Shǎnxī Nán Lù.

SPECIAL ATTRACTIONS

Húxīn Tíng Teahouse (Húxīn Tíng Cháshì)   Shànghǎi's quintessential teahouse has floated atop the lake at the heart of old town, in front of Yù Yuán, since 1784. Believed to be the original model for Blue Willow tableware, the two-story pavilion with uplifted black-tiled eaves is a relaxing place to idle over a cup of tea and escape the old town crowds.

Yùyuán Lù 257, Nánshì (at pond in the center of the Old Town Bazaar). ✆ **021/6373-6950.** Free admission. 8:30am–10pm. Metro: Hénán Zhōng Lù.

Jīn Mào Tower (Jīn Mào Dàshà) 🏵🏵   Built in 1998 as a Sino-American joint venture, this tallest building in China, and currently the third-tallest building in the world at 421m (1,379 ft.), is sublime, blending traditional Chinese and modern Western tower designs. Offices occupy the first 50 floors, the Grand Hyatt hotel the 51st to the 88th floors, while a public observation deck on the 88th floor ("The Skywalk") offers views to rival those of the nearby Oriental Pearl TV Tower (its admission charge is also lower). Enter the building through entrance 4.

Shìjì Dà Dào 2, Pǔdōng (3 blocks southeast of Oriental Pearl TV Tower). ✆ 021/5047-5101. Admission ¥50 ($6). 8:30am–10pm. Metro: Lùjiāzuǐ.

Oriental Pearl TV Tower (Dōngfāng Míngzhū Diànshì Tǎ) 🏵   Built in 1994 at a height of 468m (1,550 ft.), this hideous gray tower with three tapering levels of pink spheres (meant to resemble pearls) is hailed as Asia's tallest TV tower and the third-tallest in the world. For most visitors, the observation deck in the middle sphere (263m/870 ft. elevation), reached by high-speed elevators, is just the right height to take in panoramas of Shànghǎi (when the clouds and smog decide to cooperate, that is).

Lùjiāzuǐ Lù 2, Pǔdōng. ✆ 021/5879-1888. Admission ¥50–¥100 ($6–$12), depending on sections visited. 9am–9:30pm. Metro: Lùjiāzuǐ (Exit 1).

Peace Hotel (Hépíng Fàndiàn) 🏵🏵🏵   As the ultimate symbol of romantic colonial Shànghǎi, this Art Deco palace was built in 1929 by Victor Sassoon as part office and residence (Sassoon House) and part hotel (the Cathay Hotel), the latter becoming one of the world's finest international hotels in the 1930s. Stroll the wings of the finely restored lobby, then take the elevator to the gorgeous eighth-floor ballroom. You

Formula One Fever

Formula One racing officially roared into China with the **Shànghǎi Grand Prix** in September 2004. Located in the northwestern suburb of Āntíng in Jiādìng County, about 40 minutes from People's Square, the Shànghǎi International Circuit (Shànghǎi Guójì Sàichēchǎng), which will host F1 races in China until 2010, features a stunning track in the contours of a Chinese character, and a 10-story glass-and-steel grandstand. Tickets range from ¥160 ($19) for practice sessions to ¥3,700 ($340) for top seats overlooking the finish line on the last day. Tourist bus line no. 6B (¥4/50¢) makes the run to Āntíng from the Shànghǎi Stadium. For more information, call ✆ 021/9682-6999 or 021/6330-5555 or visit www.icsh.sh.cn.

can walk up to the roof and garden bar (cover charge of ¥50/$6.25; one soft drink included) for a superb view of the Bund, Pǔdōng, and the Huángpǔ River.

Nánjīng Dōng Lù 20, Huángpǔ (on the Bund); ✆ 021/6321-6888. Free admission. 24 hr. Metro: Hénán Zhōng Lù.

TOURS

Most Shànghǎi hotels have tour desks that can arrange a variety of day tours for guests. These tour desks are often extensions of **China International Travel Service (CITS),** with its head offices near the Shànghǎi Centre at Běijīng Xī Lù 1277, Guólǚ Dàshà (✆ **021/6289-4510** or 021/6289-8899, ext. 263; www.scits.com). The FIT (Family and Independent Travelers) department can be reached at fax 021/6289-7838. There's another branch at the Bund at Jīnlíng Dōng Lù 2 (✆ **021/6323-8770**) where you can purchase airline and train tickets.

If you have little time, **group tours** are convenient, efficiently organized, and considerably less expensive than private tours. These tours cost about ¥250 to ¥400 ($30–$48) per person. The **Jǐnjiāng Optional Tours Center,** which has its head office in the CITS building (Běijīng Xī Lù 1277, room 611; ✆ **021/6445-9525;** fax 021/6472-0184; www.jjtravel.com) and a desk in the Jǐnjiāng Tower Hotel at Chánglè Lù 161 (✆ **021/6415-1188,** ext. 80160) offers a typical group tour of Shànghǎi by bus, with English-speaking guide and lunch, for ¥250 ($31); sites include Yù Yuán, the Bund, Jade Buddha Temple, Xīn Tiāndì, People's Square, the Shànghǎi Museum, and a quick drive-by of Pǔdōng. Hotel desks have a wider range of group tour itineraries to select from, but at higher prices than those offered by the Jǐnjiāng Optional Tours Center. Another option is **Gray Line Shànghǎi,** located at Běijīng Xī Lù 1399, fifth floor (✆ **021/6289-4655;** www.grayline.cn), part of the international chain.

6 Shopping

Shànghǎi's top street to shop has always been **Nánjīng Lù,** enhanced recently by the creation of the **Nánjīng Lù Pedestrian Mall** downtown, where the most modern and the most traditional modes of retailing commingle. More popular with locals, however, is **Huáihǎi Zhōng Lù,** the wide avenue south of Nánjīng Road and parallel to it. The modern shopping malls here have better prices than you'll find on Nánjīng Road.

Some of the most interesting shopping in the French Concession is concentrated in the **Màomíng Lù/Chánglè Lù** area, while the **Old Town Bazaar** in Nánshì is the best place to shop for local arts and crafts, and antiques.

To preview what's available and for last-minute purchases, try the **Friendship Store (Yǒuyì Shāngdiàn)** at Jīnlíng Dōng Lù 68 (© **021/6337-3555;** metro: Hénán Zhōng Lù). It's open from 9:30am to 9:30pm.

There are 250 **antiques** stalls located in the basement of the **Huá Bǎo Lóu** on "Shànghǎi Old Street" near the Temple of the Town God at Fāngbāng Zhōng Lù 265, Nánshì (© **021/6355-2272;** metro: Hénán Zhōng Lù), but the chances of buying something authentic are as slim as anywhere else in China. Still, it's worth a browse.

For **ceramics,** the largest shop, complete with its own museum, is the **Jǐngdé Zhèn Ceramics Shànghǎi Art Centre,** open from 9am to 5pm at Dàdùhé Lù 1253, Chángníng, on the west side of Chángfēng Gōngyuán (© **021/6385-6238**). A more convenient outlet is **Shànghǎi Jǐngdé Zhèn Porcelain Artware,** open from 10am to 10pm at Nánjīng Xī Lù 1185 (© **021/6253-3178;** metro: Jìng Ān Temple). Or try the **Shànghǎi Arts and Crafts Museum (Shànghǎi Gōngyì Měishùguǎn)**, open from 8:30am to 4:30pm, at Fēnyáng Lù 79, Xújiāhuì (© **021/6437-0509;** metro: Chángshú Lù).

Pearls, jade, gold, and silver jewelry can be found at **Amy's Pearls** in Gǔběi New Town, open from 9am to 7pm at Gǔběi Lù 1445 (© **021/6275-3954**) or at Xiāngyáng Nán Lù 77, Xúhuì (metro: Chángshú Lù; www.amy-pearl.com); and at **Lǎo Fèng Xiáng Jewelers** on the north side of the Nánjīng Lù Pedestrian Mall, open from 9am to 9pm at Nánjīng Dōng Lù 432 (© **021/6322-0033;** metro: Hénán Zhōng Lù). **Pearl Village (Zhēnzhū Cūn),** located in the Old Town Bazaar at Fúyòu Lù 288, Yàyì Jīndiàn, third floor, Nánshì (© **021/6355-3418;** metro: Hénán Zhōng Lù) has over 50 vendors representing pearl dealers, farms, and factories from throughout China.

Silk and wool yardage, along with a wide selection of shirts, blouses, skirts, dresses, ties, and other finished silk goods, have make **Silk King (Zhēnsī Dà Wáng)** the top silk retailer in Shànghǎi. Silk or wool suits can be custom tailored in as little as 24 hours. Branches are at Nánjīng Dōng Lù 66 (© **021/6321-2193;** metro: Hénán Zhōng Lù); at Nánjīng Xī Lù 819 (© **021/6215-3114;** metro: Shímén Yī Lù); and Huáihǎi Zhōng Lù 550 (© **021/5383-0561;** metro: Huángpí Nán Lù).

MARKETS & BAZAARS

DŌNGJIĀDÙ FABRIC MARKET (DǑNGJIĀDÙ LÙ ZHĪPǏN SHÌCHǍNG) ✿

Located at Dǒngjiādù Lù and Zhōngshān Nán Lù in the southeastern corner of the old Chinese city, this gem of a market features hundreds of stalls selling bales of fabric (silk, cotton, linen, wool, and cashmere) at ridiculously low prices. Many stalls have their own in-house tailors who can stitch you a suit, or anything else you want, at rates that are less than half what you'd pay at retail outlets like Silk King. Turnaround is usually a week or more. Open 9am to 5pm.

DŌNGTÁI ANTIQUES MARKET ✿

Located on Dōngtái Lù and Liùhé Lù, 1 block west of Xīzàng Nán Lù, Lúwān, this market features dealers specializing in antiques, curios, porcelain, furniture, jewelry, baskets, bamboo- and wood carvings, birds, flowers, goldfish, and colonial-era bric-a-brac. Open from 9am to 5pm.

FÚYÒU MARKET

Still the best place to rummage through lots of junk for the chance to find the rare real nugget, this favorite for weekend antique and curio hunting, is located in the Cángbǎo Lóu (building) at Fāngbāng Zhōng Lù 457 and Hénán Nán Lù (in the Old Town Bazaar, Nánshì). Come as near to dawn as possible on Saturday or Sunday morning, preferably the latter, when vendors come in from the surrounding countryside and display goods ranging from porcelains, old jade pendants, and used furniture, to old Russian cameras, Buddhist statues, and carved wooden screens. Open 9am to 5pm; the weekend market (on the third and fourth floors) runs from 5am to 6pm, but tapers off by noon.

XIĀNGYÁNG CLOTHING MARKET ⚐   At the intersection of Huáihăi Zhōng Lù and Xiāngyáng Lù, Xúhuì (between the Shănxī [Shaanxi] Nán Lù and Chángshú Lù metro stations), is Shànghăi's version of Běijīng's famous Silk Alley—and a paradise for those looking for runoff (or knockoff) "Prada" bags, "Rolex" watches, and "North Face" jackets at a fraction of retail prices. Haggling is expected, but *do not* go with itinerant vendors who approach with laminated photos of their wares, no matter how enticing the price. Open from 8am to 9pm.

7 Shànghăi After Dark

Well into the 1990s, visitors retired to their hotels after dark, unless they were part of a group tour that had arranged an evening's outing to see the Shànghăi acrobats. In the last few years, however, the possibilities for an evening on the town have multiplied exponentially, and Shànghăi, once dubbed the "Whore of Asia" for its debauchery, is fast becoming again a city that never sleeps.

THE PERFORMING ARTS

Shànghăi acrobatics are world-renowned, and a performance by one of the local troupes makes for a diverting evening. These days the juggling, contortionism, unicycling, chair-stacking, and plate-spinning have entered the age of modern staging; performances are beginning to resemble the high-tech shows of a Las Vegas–style variety act. That's exactly what you'll see at the **Shànghăi Circus World (Shànghăi Măxìtuán),** Gònghé Xīn Lù 2266 (© 021/6652-1196), a circus of many acts, headlined by acrobats. The Shànghăi Acrobatic Troupe, one of the world's best, tours the world, but can often be found performing at the **Shànghăi Centre Theatre (Shànghăi Shāngchéng Jùyuàn),** at Nánjīng Xī Lù 1376 (© 021/6279-8663), in a 2-hour variety show with about 30 acts. Check with the box office as performance schedules vary seasonally.

Shànghăi has its own **Chinese opera** troupe that performs Běijīng opera *(Jīng Jù)* regularly at the Yìfú Theatre at Fúzhōu Lù 701, Huángpŭ (© 021/6351-4668). Most opera performances these days consist of abridgements lasting 2 hours or less (as opposed to 5 hr. or more in the old days), and with their martial arts choreography, spirited acrobatics, and brilliant costumes, these performances can be a delight even to the unaccustomed, untrained eye. Regional operas, including the Kūn Jù form, are also performed in Shànghăi. Check with your hotel desk for schedules.

JAZZ BARS

Shànghăi was China's Jazz city in the pre-revolutionary days (before 1949), and the place to meet for drinks to music was the Peace Hotel bar—a tradition that continues, though mostly for tourists these days, in the **Peace Hotel Old Jazz Bar** at 8pm nightly (Nánjīng Dōng Lù 20; © 021/6321-6888). Most of the top-end hotel lounges and bars also offer jazz performances, albeit of the easy-listening variety, by international artists. For more modern and improvisational sounds, check out the following spots: the long-running **Cotton Club,** Fùxīng Xī Lù 8 (© 021/6437-7110); the stylish **House of Blues and Jazz,** Màomíng Nán Lù 158 (© 021/6437-5280); and the jamming and jam-packed **Club JZ,** Fùxīng Xī Lù 46 (© 021/6415-5255).

The **Shànghǎi International Jazz Concert Series** has been held the second week of November each year since 1996; ask your hotel concierge for details.

DANCE CLUBS, DISCOS & BARS

Some of the top spots to dance the night away are the Hong Kong–style **California Club** (Gāolán Lù 2, Lan Kwai Fong at Park 97); **Babyface** (Màomíng Nán Lù 180, Lúwān), an ultrapretentious but popular club; **Guandii** (Gáolán Lù 2, inside Fùxīng Gōngyuán, Lúwān), attracting a Taiwan, Hong Kong and hip local crowd in a garden setting; the always jam-packed **Pegasus** (Huáihǎi Zhōng Lù 98, second floor, Lúwān); **Judy's Too** (Màomíng Nán Lù 176), popular with Western expatriates; the hot Mexican-themed **Zapata's** (Héngshān Lù 5, by Dōngpíng Lù); and the spectacular nightspot complex in the Grand Hyatt Hotel on the Pǔdōng side, **Pu-J's** (Podium 3, Jīn Mào Tower).

Among the best bars are the romantic **Face** (building 4, Ruìjīn Èr Lù 118) in the heart of the French Concession; **Glamour Room** (in M on the Bund, Guǎngdōng Lù 20, seventh floor), with great views; **Bar Rouge** (Zhōngshān Dōng Yī Lù 18, seventh floor), with its Bund views and creative drinks; **Malone's** (Tóngrén Lù 255 near Shànghǎi Centre), Shànghǎi's best American-style pub; and **O'Malley's** (Táojiāng Lù 42, off Héngshān Lù), China's best Irish-style pub, with good food, too. In Pǔdōng, **Cloud Nine** and **the Sky Lounge** (Shìjì Dà Dào 88, Grand Hyatt Hotel, 87th floor), atop the Grand Hyatt Hotel, offer the headiest views, but the drinks are overpriced and the service lackadaisical.

Gay-friendly nightspots (subject to change, as the scene shifts but never disappears) include **Eddy's,** Huáihǎi Zhōng Lù 1877, by Tiānpíng Lù (© **021/6282-0521**); **Home,** Gāolán Lù 18, west of Sīnán Lù (© **021/5382-0373**); and the recently refurbished **Vogue in Kevin's,** Chánglè Lù 946, no. 4, at Wūlǔmùqí Běi Lù (© **021/6248-8985**).

8 Sūzhōu

81km (50 miles) NW of Shànghǎi

Sūzhōu's interlocking canals, which have led it to be called the "Venice of the East," its classic gardens, and its embroidery and silk factories, are the chief surviving elements of a cultural center that dominated China's artistic scene for long periods during the Míng and Qīng dynasties. Rapid modernization in the last decade has robbed the city of much of its mystique, but enough beauty remains to merit at least a day of your time. *Note:* For Chinese translations of selected establishments listed in this section, please turn to appendix A.

GETTING THERE

At press time, the most popular **trains** for day-trippers from Shànghǎi include the T702 which leaves Shànghǎi at 7:55am and arrives at 8:42am; and the T706, which departs at 8:37am and arrives at 9:15am. Return trains to Shànghǎi in the afternoon include the 5073, which departs at 5:10pm and arrives at 6:13pm; and the T711, which departs at 6:01pm and arrives at 6:52pm. There is also a new express direct train between Sūzhōu and Běijīng (11½ hr.), Z85/Z86, leaving each city nightly around 7:30pm. The **railway station, Sūzhōu Huǒchē Zhàn** (© **0512/6753-2831**), is in the northern part of town on Chēzhàn Lù, just west of the Rénmín Lù intersection.

Sūzhōu is also well connected by **bus** to Shànghǎi, Wúxí, and Hángzhōu. There are two main bus stations: the **Qìchē Běi Zhàn** (© **0512/6753-0686**) in the north; and the **Qìchē Nán Zhàn** (© 0512/6520-4867) in the south. From the North Bus Station, buses depart for Shànghǎi (every 20 min. 7am–6:20pm; 90 min.; ¥30/$3.75), Wúxī (every 30 min. 7:15am–5:50pm; 1 hr.; ¥19.50/$2.45), and Hángzhōu (every hour 5:30am–6:50pm; 3–4 hr.; ¥52/$6.50).

Sūzhōu is also linked to Hángzhōu to the south by overnight passenger **boats** (13 hr.) on the Grand Canal. Tickets (¥78–¥788/$9.75–$98 per berth depending on class of service) can be bought at hotel tour desks and at the dock itself, Nánmén Lúnchuán Kèyùn Mǎtóu at Rénmín Lù 8 (© 0512/6520-5720; 6:30am–5:30pm) in the southern part of town.

Check with your hotel tour desk to book a bus tour of Sūzhōu. The **Jǐnjiāng Optional Tours Center,** Chánglè Lù 161, in the lobby of the Jǐn Jiāng Tower Hotel (© 021/6445-9525 or 021/6415-1188, ext. 80160), offers a convenient 1-day group bus tour with an English-speaking guide and lunch, departing daily between 8:20am and 9am (from three pick-up points in town) and returning in the late afternoon. The price is ¥350 ($42) for adults, ¥175 ($21) for children 2 to 11, and free for children under 2. The same tour operator can also arrange a private tour with a guide, air-conditioned car, lunch, and door-to-door service (¥1,400/$168 for one person, ¥650/$81 each for two to five people).

EXPLORING SŪZHŌU

Central Sūzhōu, surrounded by remnants of a moat and canals linked to the Grand Canal, has become a protected historical district, 3×5km (2×3 miles) across, in which little tampering and no skyscrapers are allowed. More than 170 bridges arch over the 32km (20 miles) of slim waterways within the moated city. The poetic private gardens number about 70, with a dozen of the finest open to public view. No other Chinese city contains such a concentration of canals and gardens.

CLASSIC GARDENS

Sūzhōu's magnificent formerly private gardens are small, exquisite jewels of landscaping art, often choked with visitors, making a slow, meditative tour difficult. Designed on principles different from those of the West, these gardens aimed to create the illusion of the universe in a limited setting by borrowing from nature and integrating such elements as water, plants, rocks, and buildings. Poetry and calligraphy were added as the final touches. Listed below are some classic gardens worth visiting.

FOREST OF LIONS GARDEN (SHĪZI LÍN YUÁN) ✿✿   Built in 1342 by a Buddhist monk and reportedly last owned (privately) by relatives of renowned American architect I. M. Pei, this large garden consists of four small lakes, a multitude of buildings, and Sūzhōu's largest and most elaborate collection of tortured rockeries, here said to resemble lions. Many of these oddly shaped rocks come from nearby Tài Hú (Lake Tài), where they've been submerged for a very long time to achieve the desired shapes and effects. The garden is located at Yuánlín Lù 23 (© 0512/6727-2428). It's open 7:30am to 5:30pm; admission is ¥20 ($2.50).

HUMBLE ADMINISTRATOR'S GARDEN (ZHUŌ ZHÈNG YUÁN) ✿✿
Usually translated as "Humble Administrator's Garden," but also translatable tongue-in-cheek as "Garden of the Stupid Officials," this largest of Sūzhōu's gardens, which dates from 1513, makes complex use of the element of water. Linked by zigzag bridges, the maze of connected pools and islands seems endless. The creation of multiple vistas and the dividing of spaces into distinct segments are the garden artist's means of expanding the compressed spaces of the estate. As visitors stroll through the

garden, new spaces and vistas open up at every turn. The garden is located at Dōng Běi Jiē 178 (© **0512/6751-0286**). It's open 7:30am to 5:30pm; admission is ¥50 ($6.25).

LINGERING GARDEN (LIÚ YUÁN) ✿✿   This garden in the northwest part of town is the setting for the finest Tài Hú rock in China, a 6m-high (20-ft.), 5-ton castle of stone called Crown of Clouds Peak (Jùyún Fēng). Liú Yuán is also notable for its viewing pavilions, particularly its **Mandarin Duck Hall,** which is divided into two sides: an ornate southern chamber for men, and a plain northern chamber for women. Lingering Garden is located at Liúyuán Lù 338 (© **0512/6533-7903**). It's open 7:30am to 5:30pm; admission is ¥30 ($3.75).

MASTER OF THE NETS GARDEN (WǍNG SHĪ YUÁN) ✿✿✿   Considered to be the most perfect, and also smallest, of Sūzhōu's gardens, this a masterpiece of landscape compression. Hidden at the end of a blind alley, its tiny grounds have been cleverly expanded by the placement of walls, screens, and pavilion halls, producing a maze that seems endless. In the northwest of the garden, don't miss the lavish **Diànchūn Yí (Hall for Keeping the Spring),** the former owner's study furnished with lanterns and hanging scrolls. This was the model for Míng Xuān, the Astor Chinese Garden Court and Ming Furniture Room in the Metropolitan Museum of Art in New York City. Master of the Nets Garden is located at Kuòjiē Tóu Xiàng, off Shíquán Jiē (© **0512/ 6529-3190**). It's open 8am to 5:30pm; admission is ¥20 ($2.50). In the summer, daily performances of traditional music and dance are staged in the garden (7:30pm; ¥80/$10).

TIGER HILL (HǓ QĪU SHĀN) ✿   This multipurpose theme park can be garishly tacky in parts, but it's also home to some local historic sights, chief among them the remarkable leaning **Yúnyán Tǎ (Cloud Rock Pagoda)** at the top of the hill. Now safely shored up by modern engineering (although it still leans), this seven-story octagonal pagoda dating from A.D. 961 is thought to be sitting on top of the legendary grave of Hé Lǔ, the 6th-century B.C. king of Wú, and also Sūzhōu's founder. His tomb, thought to include his arsenal of 3,000 swords, is said to be guarded by a white tiger (hence the name of the hill). Partway up Tiger Hill is a natural ledge of rocks, the **Ten Thousand People Rock (Wànrén Shí),** where according to legend a rebel delivered an oratory so fiery that the rocks lined up to listen. Tiger Hill is located 3km (2 miles) northwest of the city at Hǔqiū Shān 8 (© **0512/6532-3488**). It's open 8am to 5:30pm; admission is ¥60 ($7.50) March to May and September to November; ¥40 ($5) otherwise.

WATER GATES & CANALS

Sūzhōu is not only the city of gardens, but of canals. In the southern part of town in the scenic area just south of the Sheraton Hotel known as **Gūsū Yuán (Gūsū Garden),** you'll find in the southwestern corner **Pán Mén (Pán Gate),** built in A.D. 1351, and the only major piece of the Sūzhōu city wall to survive. **Pán Mén** once operated as a water gate and fortress when the Grand Canal was the most important route linking Sūzhōu to the rest of China. To the south is a large arched bridge, **Wúmén Qiáo,** a fine place to view the ever-changing canal traffic. Near the main garden entrance in the east is **Ruìguāng Tǎ,** a seven-story, 37m-high (122-ft.) pagoda built in A.D. 1119 (admission ¥6/70¢ to climb) that affords some excellent views of the old city from its top floors. The rest of the grounds is not very interesting. Gūsū Yuán is located at Dōng Dà Jiē 1. It's open 8am to 5:30pm; admission is ¥20 ($2.50).

SILK FACTORIES

Sūzhōu is synonymous not only with gardens and canals, but also with silk. Its silk fabrics have been among the most prized in China for centuries, and the art of silk embroidery is still practiced at the highest levels. The **Sūzhōu Silk Museum (Sūzhōu Sīchóu Bówùguǎn)**, Rénmín Lù 2001 (© **0512/6753-6506**), just south of the railway station, takes visitors through the history of silk in China, with an interesting section on sericulture complete with silkworms, cocoons, and mulberry leaves. Weavers demonstrate on traditional looms. The museum is open 9am to 5pm; admission is ¥7 (90¢).

The **Sūzhōu Cìxiù Yánjiūsuǒ (Sūzhōu Embroidery Research Institute),** Jǐngdé Lù 262 (© **0512/6522-4723**), is both a factory and sales outlet that has become a de rigueur stop on group tour itineraries. The silk embroideries here are exquisite and not surprisingly, expensive. The institute is open 9am to 4:30pm; admission is free.

WHERE TO STAY & DINE

If you plan to spend the night in Sūzhōu, the top hotel is the five-star **Sheraton Sūzhōu Hotel & Tower (Sūzhōu Wúgōng Xǐláidēng Dàjiǔdiàn),** Xīn Shì Lù 259, near Pán Mén in southwest Sūzhōu (© **800/325-3535** or 0512/6510-3388; fax 0512/6510-0888; www.sheraton.com/suzhou). With 407 rooms starting at ¥1,660 ($200; usually no more than 10%–20% discount) for a standard room, this luxury hotel receives rave reviews for its quality service and its Chinese-style buildings. Another good choice is the 296-unit **Gloria Plaza Hotel Sūzhōu (Kǎilái Dàjiǔdiàn),** east of city center at Gānjiāng Dōng Lù 535 (© **0512/6521-8855;** fax 0512/6521-8533; www.gphSuzhou.com). Rooms (¥980–¥1,180/$118–$142 standard; 30% discounts) were renovated in the last 3 years and have all the expected amenities. For those on a budget, the lovely 37-unit **Scholars Inn (Shūxiāng Méndì Shāngwù Jiǔdiàn),** opened in 2003 in the center of town at Jǐngdé Lù 277 (© **0512/6521-7388;** fax 0512/6521-7326; www.sscholarsin@163.com) offers simple but clean standard rooms with air-conditioning, phone, TV, and showers for ¥300 to ¥520 ($38–$65).

Although hotel restaurants offer the most reliable fare and accept credit cards, Sūzhōu has a number of good restaurants that deserve to be tried, many of which are located on Tàijiān Nòng (Tàijiān Lane), also known as Gourmet Street, around the Guānqián Jiē area. One of the most famous local restaurants is the over 200-year-old **Sōng Hè Lóu (Pine and Crane Restaurant)** at Guānqián Jiē 141 (© **0512/6727-7006;** 8am–9pm), which serves Sūzhōu specialties such as *Sōngshǔ Guìyú* (squirrel-shaped Mandarin fish), *Gūsū Lǚyā* (Gūsū marinated duck), and *Huángmèn Hémàn* (braised river eel). Dinner for two ranges from ¥100 to ¥200 ($13–$25).

9 Hángzhōu

185km (115 miles) SW of Shànghǎi

Seven centuries ago, Marco Polo pronounced Hángzhōu "the finest, most splendid city in the world . . . where so many pleasures may be found that one fancies oneself to be in Paradise." Hángzhōu's claim to paradise has always been centered on its famous **West Lake (Xī Hú),** surrounded on three sides by verdant hills. The islets and temples, pavilions and gardens, causeways, and arched bridges of this small lake (about 5km/3 miles across and 14km/9 miles around) have constituted the supreme example of lakeside beauty in China ever since the Táng dynasty when Hángzhōu came into its own with the completion of the Grand Canal (Dà Yùnhé) in 609. Hángzhōu reached its zenith during the Southern Sòng dynasty (A.D. 1127–1279), when it served as China's capital. In 2003, much to the horror of purists, Xī Hú was enlarged in the western section with an additional causeway along its new western shoreline. New sights, shops, and restaurants were added to the eastern and southern shores. *Note:* For Chinese translations of selected establishments listed in this section, please turn to appendix A.

GETTING THERE

Hángzhōu has an **airport** (© **0571/8666-1234** or 0571/8666-2999) about a 30-minute drive from downtown, with international connections to Hong Kong, Macau, Bangkok, Tokyo, and Singapore; and domestic connections to Běijīng and other major Chinese cities. A taxi into town costs around ¥130 ($16) while an air-conditioned bus (© **0571/8666-2539;** ¥15/$1.90) runs to the railway station and the Marco Polo Hotel (nearest stop to the Shangri-La Hotel).

By **train,** the N509 leaves Shànghǎi at 7:38am, arriving in Hángzhōu at 10:19am. The return N510 departs Hángzhōu at 6:25pm and arrives at 9:20pm. Soft-seat train tickets cost about ¥50 ($6) plus a typical ¥20 ($2.50) service charge if purchased from hotel tour desks. There is also a new express direct train between Hángzhōu and Běijīng (13½ hr.), with the Z10 leaving Hángzhōu nightly at 6:03pm and Z9 leaving Běijīng at 6:53pm. The no. 7 bus connects the railway station to downtown and to the Shangri-La Hotel for ¥1 (15¢), and its air-conditioned version, the K7, connects them for ¥2 (25¢). For train information, call © **0571/5672-0222;** ticket booking is from 8am to 5pm (© **0571/8782-9983**). **Bus** services are quicker and more frequent. There are regular departures from the East Bus Station to Shànghǎi until 7pm. There are also connections with Sūzhōu, Shàoxīng Níngbō, and Wēnzhōu.

There are also overnight **boats** sailing the Grand Canal between Hángzhōu and Sūzhōu, with departures leaving from the Hángzhōu Wǔlín Mén Mǎtóu at 5:30pm and arriving in Sūzhōu around 7am. For information and bookings, call © **0571/ 8515-3185.**

Check with your hotel tour desk to book a **bus tour** of Hángzhōu. The **Jǐn Jiāng Optional Tours Center,** Chánglè Lù 161, in the lobby of the Jǐn Jiāng Tower Hotel (© **021/6445-9525** or 021/6415-1188, ext. 80160), offers a convenient if expensive 1-day group bus tour with an English-speaking guide and lunch, departing at 8am every Tuesday, Thursday, Friday and Saturday, and returning in the late afternoon. The price is ¥500 ($60) for adults, ¥250 ($30) for children 2 to 11, and free for children under 2. The same tour operator can also arrange a private 1- or 2-day tour (on any day) with a guide, air-conditioned car, lunch, and door-to-door service for significantly more. If you're staying at the Shangri-La Hotel (see below) in Hángzhōu, their business center can also organize half- or full-day city tours.

EXPLORING HÁNGZHŌU

The city surrounds the shores of West Lake, with modern Hángzhōu spread to the north and east. The lake is best explored on foot and by boat, while sights farther afield will require a taxi or bus. Taxis cost ¥10 ($1.25) for 4km (2½ miles), then ¥2 (25¢) per kilometer. Add 20% after 8km (5 miles). Buses cost ¥1 to ¥2 (15¢–25¢) depending on whether they have air-conditioning. Bus no. K7 runs from the railway station to Língyǐn Sì via the northern shore of the lake (Běishān Lù) and the Shangri-La Hotel, while bus no. 27 runs along Běishān Lù to Lóngjǐng Cūn (Dragon Well Village), and bus no. Y1 makes a loop of the lake starting from Língyǐn Sì.

XĪ HÚ (WEST LAKE)

Strolling the shores and causeways of West Lake and visiting the tiny islands by tour boat should not be missed. A **Lakeshore Promenade** ⚲—a combination walkway and roadway—encircles the lake, with the busiest parts along the eastern edge of the lake. The once-busy thoroughfare Húbīn Lù has now become a pedestrian walkway home to such outlets as Starbucks and Häagen-Dazs, while the area immediately to the south around Nánshān Lù and Xīhú Dà Dào is now known as Xī Hú Tiāndì (West Lake Heaven and Earth), a miniature version of Shànghăi's Xīn Tiāndì, right down to the *shíkù mén* (stone-frame) style housing and with some of the exact same restaurants. Following are the top attractions around the lake:

SOLITARY ISLAND (GŪSHĀN DĂO) ⚲   Situated just off the lake's northwest shore, this big island is accessible via the **Xīlíng Bridge** in the west. A roadway sweeps across the island, which is home to a number of minor sights including Hángzhōu's famous restaurant, Lóu Wài Lóu, and the large **Zhèjiāng Provincial Museum (Zhèjiāng Shěng Bówùguăn;** ✆ **0571/8798-0281),** which contains the oldest grains of cultivated rice in the world (developed 7,000 years ago in a nearby Hémǔdù village). The museum is open from 9am to 4pm; admission is free.

BAI CAUSEWAY (BÁI DĪ) ⚲⚲   Solitary Island is connected in the east to downtown Hángzhōu by Bái Dī, a man-made causeway providing some of the finest walking around West Lake. It runs east for half a mile, rejoining the north shore road (Běishān Lù) at **Duàn Qiáo (Broken Bridge),** so named because when winter snows first melt, the bridge appears from a distance to be broken.

CRUISING WEST LAKE ⚲⚲   All along the lakeshore, but particularly on Húbīn Lù and near Gūshān Dăo (northwest corner of the lake), there are boats for hire, from 3m (10-ft.), heavy wooden rowboats (where you take the oars) to small junks propelled by the owner's single oar to full-fledged ferries—flat-bottomed launches seating 20 under an awning. To tour the lake in a small junk, you have to bargain for the fare (usually about ¥60–¥80]/$7.50–$10 for an hour on the water). Passenger ferries sell tickets for ¥35 to ¥45 ($4.40–$5.60), which includes entrance to the Island of Small Seas (below). There are ticket booths across the street from the Shangri-La Hotel and along the east side of the lake.

ISLAND OF SMALL SEAS (XIĂO YÍNG ZHŌU) ⚲⚲⚲   Make sure your boat docks on this island at the center of West Lake. The **Island of Small Seas** was formed during a silt-dredging operation in 1607. As a Chinese saying goes, this is "an island within a lake, a lake within an island." Its form is that of a wheel with four spokes, its bridges and dikes creating four enclosed lotus-laden ponds. The main route into the hub of this wheel is the **Bridge of Nine-Turnings,** built in 1727. Occupying the center is the magnificent **Flower and Bird Pavilion,** an exceedingly graceful structure that is notable for its intricate wooden railings, lattices, and moon gates, though it only dates from 1959. It's open 8am to 5pm; admission is ¥20 ($2.50).

THREE POOLS MIRRORING THE MOON (SĀN TÁN YÌN YUÈ) ⚲⚲   Located just off the southern shore of the Island of Small Seas are three little water pagodas, each about 2m (6 ft.) tall that have "floated" like buoys on the surface of West Lake since 1621. On evenings when the full moon shines on the lake, candles are placed inside. The effect is of four moons shimmering on the waters. Even by daylight, the three floating pagodas are quite striking.

SŪ CAUSEWAY (SŪ DĪ) 🎔🎔   The best land view of the Three Pools Mirroring the Moon is from the Sū Causeway, the great dike that connects the north and south shores along the western side of West Lake. (A third causeway added in 2003, the Yánggōng Dī running parallel to Sū Dī in the west, is primarily for vehicles and is not as scenic.) Running nearly 3km (2 miles), Sū Dī is lined with weeping willows, peach trees, and shady nooks and crosses six arched stone bridges.

LÉI FĒNG TǍ (LÉI FĒNG PAGODA) 🎔 *Finds*   Completely rebuilt in 2003 on the south bank of West Lake, this modern steel-and-copper pagoda affords some of the best panoramic views of the lake. Beneath the modern construction are the brick foundations of the original Léifēng Pagoda built in 977. The bricks you see were part of an underground vault used to store precious Buddhist relics, including a rare wood-cut sutra, which was found among the ruins. The pagoda and surrounding gardens are open 8am to 5:30pm (to 10pm July–Aug, and to 9pm in Sept for sunset and night-time views); admission is ¥40 ($5).

OTHER ATTRACTIONS

LÍNGYǏN SÌ (LÍNGYǏN TEMPLE) 🎔   Located in the lush hills just west of West Lake, Língyǐn Sì (Temple of the Soul's Retreat) has been rebuilt a dozen times since its creation in A.D. 326. More of an amusement park than quiet temple, the whole complex is open from 7am to 6pm; admission is ¥25 ($3.10), while entrance to the temple itself is a separate ¥20 ($2.50).

The main attraction on the way to the temple is a limestone cliff, called **Fēilái Fēng (Peak That Flew from Afar)**, so named because it resembles a holy mountain in India seemingly transported to China. The peak, nearly 150m high (500 ft.), contains four caves and about 380 Buddhist rock carvings. The most famous carving is of a Laughing Buddha from the year A.D. 1000. Scholars have deemed these stone carvings the most important of their kind in southern China.

The present temple buildings go back decades rather than centuries. The main Dàxióng Bǎodiàn (Great Hall) contains a gigantic statue of Buddha carved in 1956 from 24 sections of camphor and gilded with nearly 3,000 grams (104 oz.) of gold—not a bad modern re-creation.

LÓNGJǏNG WÈNCHÁ (DRAGON WELL TEA VILLAGE)   West of West Lake is the village of **Lóngjǐng (Dragon Well)**, the source of Hángzhōu's famous **Lóngjǐng tea,** grown only on these hillsides and revered throughout China as a supreme vintage for its fine fragrance and smoothness. The best tea here is still picked and processed by hand. A popular stop near the village is the **Zhōngguó Cháyè Bówùguǎn (Chinese Tea Museum),** open 8am to 5pm. Here you can comb through the extensive displays of Chinese teas, pots, cups, and ceremonial tea implements. Admission is free.

ZHŌNGGUÓ SĪCHÓU BÓWÙGUǍN (CHINA SILK MUSEUM)   Though Sūzhōu may be better known as a silk capital, Hángzhōu, too, produced its share of this much sought-after commodity. This large museum south of West Lake boasts a surprisingly comprehensive exhibit with displays ranging from mulberry bushes and silkworms to traditional looms and exquisite pieces of damask brocades, all well annotated in English. The museum is located at Yùhuáng Shān Lù 73–1 and is open 8:30am to 4pm; admission is free.

WHERE TO STAY & DINE

If you're spending the night, the best hotel is the very fine five-star, 383-unit **Shangri-La Hotel Hángzhōu (Hángzhōu Xiānggélǐlā Fàndiàn),** Běishān Lù 78, on the north shore of West Lake (© **800/942-5050** or 0571/8797-7951; fax 0571/8799-6637). Standard rooms with hillside or garden views cost ¥1,400 to ¥1,900 ($175–$238), while a room with a view of West Lake costs between ¥1,880 and ¥2,350 ($235–$294). You can expect a 35% discount off the rack rate. Another good option is the newly opened (2003) 200-unit **Sofitel Westlake Hángzhōu (Hángzhōu Suǒfēitè Xīhú Dàjiǔdiàn),** Xīhú Dà Dào 333, on the eastern shore of West Lake (© **800/221-4542** or 0571-8707-5858; fax 0571/8707-8383). Standard rooms start at ¥1,500 ($188) before the average 40% discount.

For dining, try the Hángzhōu institution **Lóu Wài Lóu,** Gūshān Lù 30 (© **0571/8796-9023**), on Solitary Hill Island, between the Xīlíng Seal Engraving Society and the Zhèjiāng Library. Hours are 11:30am to 2pm and from 5 to 8pm; specialties, such as Beggar's Chicken *(jiàohuà jī),* cost about ¥100 ($12) here, but a main course of local *dōngpō* pork costs half that. In the summer, this restaurant offers dinner cruises on West Lake. The Shangri-La Hotel's signature restaurant, **Shang Palace** (© **0571/8797-7951**), is more elegant and also more expensive, with a meal for two costing ¥200 ($25) and up. The international restaurants at the new development **Xī Hú Tiāndì (West Lake Heaven and Earth)** on the southeastern shore of the lake should provide plenty of comfort food.

The Southeast

by Christopher D. Winnan

A quick glance at the topography of this area speaks volumes. Apart from a few, scattered river deltas, this is harsh and unforgiving mountain country, with just a narrow ribbon of land next to the sea, into which most of China's modern coastal cities are all tightly squeezed.

Although the indigenous peoples of this area were assimilated Borg-style by Hàn colonists long ago, the isolated terrain has fostered a strong feeling of independence in the coastal dwellers, forever aware that "the mountains are high and the emperor far away." In fact, it was probably their relative isolation and the establishment of small cell network economies that led to their early successes.

Few people realize that it was this part of the world that Columbus sought when he first set sail for the East Indies. While Europe had been blindly staggering through the dark ages, some of the foremost trading ports of their time had developed in this region. From then on it was only a matter of time before the industrialization that swept across 18th-century Europe was to have similar disastrous effects in China. The institutionalized xenophobia, currently aimed at Japan, was earlier focused on England. China's rewritten history lay the blame for the subsequent "Opium Wars" firmly at the feet of the British, rather than the emerging global economy and its mercenaries such as the East India Company. Endless statues, museums, and memorials maximize the "humiliations" of the Opium Wars for propaganda purposes, and yet nobody even dreams of a cigarette war in retaliation for the 10,000 Chinese that now die from smoking-related illnesses every week. Still, beyond the misguided nationalism, this region is a treasure trove of history for those willing to dig just a little bit further than the official media mouthpieces.

The relentless pressure and pace of the modern economy in business cities like Guǎngzhōu and Wēnzhōu can make them appear harsh and unfriendly. Tourists are relatively few compared to the unending stream of businessmen, here to put yet more Chinese to work in factories. It is hardly surprising that foreigners are often treated with such mistrust and suspicion. Mass migration from the hinterland has put even more pressure on rapidly expanding urban areas until they now suffer the same problems that plague oversized cities all over the world: pollution, rising crime, and social misery. The region now resembles a huge cargo ship in which the load is concentrated on only one side and it is listing dangerously.

Traveling throughout the region provides an excellent opportunity to see the process in action. Industrialization in the cities destroys the traditional economies of the hinterlands, which then takes its revenge by mass migration to the cities, poisoning them further and making them even more unmanageable. The flat delta areas have become toxic rat's nests of industrialization, as more and more rice paddies are concreted over to build ever more factories and express highways. Only the old and infirm remain in the

The Southeast

rural areas, and with less and less land to cultivate every year, it is difficult to imagine how China can continue to feed itself.

Indeed, rapid development had laid to waste some former treaty ports, but others have taken care to preserve their Western heritage, and some of those laced by canals have preserved areas of ancient waterfront housing of considerable charm. An hour or two inland, you'll see that farming remains as primitive as ever, but it's quite picturesque.

Summers are hot and extremely humid around the coast; the mild months of October to March are the best times to visit, although some offshore islands are appreciated year-round for their breezes. Inland Jiāngxī suffers from drier but furnacelike summers and chilly dank winters, making spring and autumn the best times to travel. *Note:* Unless otherwise noted, hours listed for attractions and restaurants are daily.

1 Shàoxīng

Zhèjiāng Province, 58km (36 miles) SE of Hángzhōu, 128km (80 miles) W of Níngbō

Chairman Máo said, "Shàoxīng is the home of celebrities," by which he meant a lineup of officially sanctified educators, writers, protorevolutionaries, and Communist cadres, some of whom had fame thrust upon them for propaganda reasons, but whose houses and mansions have as a result been preserved and opened to the public. A quiet, relaxed, waterside town, Shàoxīng is the alternative to Zhèjiāng's capital, Hángzhōu (p. 454), with less reputation but with more to see. It's yet another "Venice of China," and one which you can actually explore by boat. It doesn't receive the volume of visitors it deserves.

Redevelopment has been far kinder here than in most towns, and the main north–south shopping street has been rebuilt with five-story buildings that retain traditional black-and-white tones and other hints of local style, while housing several Hong Kong–clothing names and a lot more besides. But behind all this, many of the older streets survive in areas of ramshackle (and occasionally restored) ancient housing that unexpectedly crop up squeezed between waterways and newer construction.

The gondolas of this "Venice" are the black-awning boats *(hēi péng chuán),* narrow craft with arched, woven bamboo awnings (painted black), propelled by wiry boatmen acrobatically using hands and feet to work the oars.

ESSENTIALS

GETTING THERE The nearest **airport** is at Hángzhōu, and there's a bus from there to Shàoxīng's Wángcháo Jiǔdiàn; the trip takes 1½ hours. To get to the Hángzhōu airport from Shàoxīng, there are seven services a day between 8:30am and 5:10pm. Shàoxīng is on the **railway line** from Shànghǎi via Hángzhōu to the terminus at Níngbō but the railway carries little traffic, and buses are more frequent. There are five train services from Hángzhōu between the K869 at 7:30am and the K867 at 7:18pm. The trip takes about 2¼ hours; soft seat costs ¥19 ($2.40). Taxis are lined up to the left as you leave the railway station; buses into town leave from the right (bus nos. 1, 2, and 4 take you into the center). Leaving Shàoxīng, rail travel for longer distances involves changing at Hángzhōu; and in the case of coastal destinations to the south, it also involves long, slow loops through the interior. For train information, call © **0575/802-2584,** or 0575/514-4422 for ticket booking. Agents ask a ¥10 ($1.25) commission for tickets from Shàoxīng to Hángzhōu and Shànghǎi, but ¥30 ($3.75) for hard sleepers and ¥50 ($6.25) for soft sleepers for departures from Hángzhōu—book at least 3 days in advance. Try the **Zhèjiāng Kuàijī Mountain Tour Co Ltd.,** Rénmín Zhōng Lù 45 (© 0575/513-9886), which is also the main **air ticket** agency, just east of the Bank of China. Or try CTS at Shàoxīng Rénmín Zhōng Lù 367 (© 0575/511-6282). CTS also offers English-speaking guides for a ridiculous ¥300 ($37) per day.

The main **Long-Distance Bus Station (Kèyùn Zhōngxīn)** to the northeast of the city center offers highly comfortable *háohuá gāosù kōngtiáo chē,* the luxury high-speed air-conditioned buses that are a better choice than trains down the coast. Departures are announced in astonishingly clear English. Tickets are on sale at the bus station from 5:30am to 7:30pm (© 0575/801-8852). Buses arrive here directly from Shànghǎi, Hángzhōu, Sūzhōu, and Wēnzhōu. There are plentiful taxis, or bus no. 3 will take you along Shènglì Dōng Lù to Jiěfàng Běi Lù at the main town square (Chéngshì Guǎngchǎng). The bus trip to Hángzhōu's **Qìchē Dōng Zhàn (East Bus Station)** is 60km (28 miles) and costs ¥19 ($2.30). There are departures every 40 minutes for Níngbō between 6:40am and 6pm, for ¥38 ($4.75); the fare for a regular bus is ¥18 ($2.20). The 239km (149-mile) bus trip to Sūzhōu costs between ¥20 and ¥51 ($2.50–$6.30), depending on the quality of bus and route taken. Shànghǎi is 230km (144 miles) by the expressway and costs ¥60 to ¥70 ($7.50–$8.75), but as little as ¥18 ($2.20) by regular bus on regular roads. The trip to Wēnzhōu is 350km (219 miles) and costs ¥108 ($13).

GETTING AROUND   Santana and Fùkāng **taxis** have a flagfall of ¥5 (65¢) which includes 4km (2½ miles); after that, it's ¥2.20 (30¢) per kilometer. There are no "one-way" extras or night surcharges, and as a result, *sānlúnchē* (cycle rickshaws) tend to take over at night. They also provide all-day access to narrower streets at typically ¥3 (40¢) minimum per trip. **Buses** charge a flat fee of ¥1 (15¢) upon boarding, or up to ¥3 (40¢) on longer journeys with a conductor. Shàoxīng's center is small enough to tackle on foot, Jiěfàng Běi Lù and Jiěfàng Nán Lù being the main north–south arteries, but buses are useful for access to the Long-Distance Bus Station (bus no. 9) and the railway station (bus no. 1 or 7), and for reaching sights just out of town.

VISITOR INFORMATION   The official Shàoxīng website is at **www.sx.gov.cn/english/index.asp**; or call © 0575/860-6879 or 0575/512-0742.

FAST FACTS

Banks, Foreign Exchange & ATMs   The main **Bank of China** (open 8am–5pm) is at Rénmín Zhōng Lù 201, west of the junction with Zhōng Xīng Zhōng Lù.

Internet Access   Apart from the typically large *wǎngbā* that are springing up everywhere, China Telecom (Zhōngguó Diànxìn) has a small Internet cafe in its Dōng Jiē office, which is open 24 hours and charges ¥2 (25¢) per hour. Dial-up is © **163.**

Post Office   The post office (open 7:30am–9:30pm) is at Dōng Jiē 27, just east of Jiěfàng Nán Lù.

FLOATING AROUND SHÀOXĪNG

According to local theory, the rivers run north–south through the town, and the streams east–west, and it's still possible to travel between certain points by boat. However, only tourists do this, and mostly at the East Lake (Dōng Hú) just outside town. But being propelled through the town itself beneath some of its ancient bridges is rather more enjoyable.

Lǔ Xùn Jìniànguǎn   Lǔ Xùn is often considered China's greatest 20th-century writer, but this museum doesn't do him justice. The main point in visiting here is to

Shàoxīng

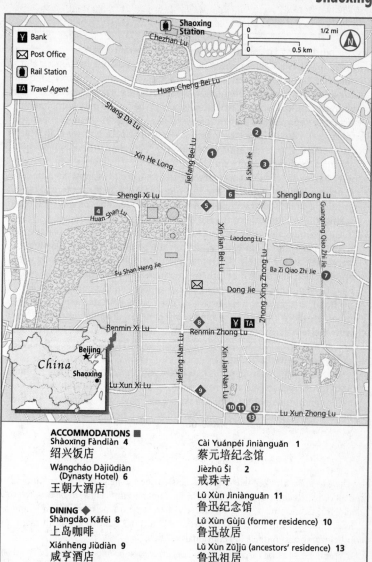

ACCOMMODATIONS ■

Shàoxīng Fàndiàn **4**
绍兴饭店

Wángcháo Dàjiǔdiàn
(Dynasty Hotel) **6**
王朝大酒店

DINING ◆

Shàngdǎo Kāfēi **8**
上岛咖啡

Xiánhēng Jiǔdiàn **9**
咸亨酒店

Yuánlín Dàjiǔdiàn **5**
园林大酒店

ATTRACTIONS ●

Bā Zì Qiáo **7**
八字桥

Cài Yuánpéi Jìniànguǎn **1**
蔡元培纪念馆

Jièzhū Sì **2**
戒珠寺

Lǔ Xùn Jìniànguǎn **11**
鲁迅纪念馆

Lǔ Xùn Gùjū (former residence) **10**
鲁迅故居

Lǔ Xùn Zǔjū (ancestors' residence) **13**
鲁迅祖居

Sān Wèi Shūwū **12**
三味书屋

Shūshèng Gùlǐ
(The Master Calligrapher's
Native Place) **3**
书圣故里

The Straight Story

The big bust of Lǔ Xùn (1881–1936) in the entrance hall of the Lǔ Xùn Jìniànguǎn has a Stalinesque air, but the writer wasn't one to follow Stalin's line that art should represent class struggle (even though other Chinese writers sympathetic to communism were doing so). Often labeled China's greatest 20th-century writer, Lǔ Xùn is one of the few to gain both Communist Party approval and admiration even from the Party's greatest critics. His short stories are unforgettable, bite-size pieces of pure bitterness, in which his characters' good intentions are always followed by backsliding, their attempts to change society are always thwarted by its inertia, and they are swept away by circumstances beyond their control. His most famous creation, the hapless subject of *The True Story of Ah Q,* manages to end up in front of a firing squad without having the first idea how or why, and represents the witless state of the nation as a whole.

Lǔ Xùn flays the weaknesses of Chinese character, which he blames for both China's miseries in general and for the result of the 1911 revolution, which he saw as merely the replacement of one set of scoundrels with another. Had he not died before the Communist triumph of 1949, he would have been making the same point all over again (and this museum wouldn't be here). He remains popular today even with educated young people otherwise more interested in China's emerging sex, drugs, and hanging-out-with-Westerners genre (mostly banned in China), or in books which more accurately depict the lawless underbelly of modern Chinese society than the officially approved accounts.

Lǔ Xùn's works can be picked up in English translation at many Xīnhuá Bookstores, and some can be read online at www.chineseliterature.com.cn/modernliterature/ml.htm. The infrastructure may have changed, but the mind-set hasn't, and though Lǔ Xùn may have been dead for nearly 70 years, he tells it like it is.

buy the *tào piào,* a ticket that allows access to several neighboring Lǔ Xùn–related sites, all of which are much more interesting. The museum claims to be devoted to his "ideological development," but fortunately there are no labels in English to put you to sleep. Still, you can see it all here, from the author's desk to his death mask, plus period clothing and models of traditional festivals.

Lǔ Xùn Zhōng Lù 393. Admission ¥30 ($3.75), which includes 2 neighboring buildings owned by his family, and where he went to school (see below). 8am–4:45pm. The museum is a 5-min. walk east of the Xiánhēng Jiǔdiàn; you'll pass the Gùjū (former residence) on the way. Bus: no. 1 from station or anywhere in Jiěfàng Lù.

Lǔ Xùn Gùjū ✿   Turn right as you leave the Lǔ Xùn museum and walk back to Lǔ Xùn's former residence, almost next door. This is one of the most pleasant old buildings open to the public in Shàoxīng, dating from the early 1800s. Lǔ Xùn was born here in 1881 and lived here until his family sold the building in 1918. Alterations were made, but the layout has been "reconstructed according to the description of Lǔ's relatives and friends." The long, slender building has a series of black-pillared, white-walled courtyards on two axes, and is brightened by red-painted window screens and plants. That's the original pearwood bed in his bedroom, and it was here that he wrote his first story, *Memories of the Past*.

Admission by ticket purchase at Lǔ Xùn Museum or Lǔ Xùn Zǔjū—see museum entry above for times and prices.

Sān Wèi Shūwū Cross the road from the Lǔ Xùn Gùjū and turn left (east). The Sān Wèi Study, where Lǔ Xùn was a student from age 12 to 17, is a short way along just across a bridge to the right, beneath which several *hēi péng chuán* wallow waiting for business.

This was a private school in a late-Qīng building, of which you can see three brick-floored white-walled rooms filled with old furniture; one piece is helpfully labeled THIS IS LǓ XÙN'S DESK. There's a brick board used for teaching calligraphy, and it's not difficult to imagine a dozen or so little pigtailed heads bowed over trying to copy it. At the exit there's the inevitable shop, but appropriately with a calligrapher who will write whatever you like on fans. Watch how he holds the brush, hand bent upright at the wrist and rigidly gripping it partway down, his whole arm moving to make each stroke.

Admission by ticket purchase at museum or across the road at the Lǔ Xùn Zǔjū—see museum entry for times and prices.

Lǔ Xùn Zǔjū Lǔ's real family name was Zhōu, and for generations this was the family residence, now converted into a small but moderately interesting museum of folk customs. Some of the rooms here are labeled in English, such as the main family hall for ancestor worship, and the room where the children were given their primary education. There's a series of seven interlocking courtyards with dark, black pillars and white walls; they are quiet and cool—you could sit for hours. Intricate miniature waxworks are used to illustrate marriage customs, teahouse life, and other traditions.

Lǔ Xùn Zhōng Lù. Admission ¥30 ($3.75), which includes the 3 preceding sights. 8am–4:45pm. Bus: no. 1 from station or anywhere in Jiěfàng Lù.

Bā Zì Qiáo 🐟 It is claimed that Shàoxīng has 229 bridges, but the one "in the shape of the character for 'eight'" is perhaps the most famous, and can be reached by boat

---

Tips Winning the Boat Race

Puttering about the narrow backwaters of the town in one of Shàoxīng's black-awning boats is more entertaining than boating at the overrated East Lake. Pricing for the black-awning boats is regulated, so don't let any boatman persuade you otherwise. The boat takes up to three people, at a fixed rate, to each destination. Once you've finished with the Sān Wèi Shūwū and the Lǔ Xùn Zǔjū opposite, consider a trip from there to the Bā Zì Qiáo (Bridge in the Shape of the Character for "Eight") for ¥65 ($8). Compare the characters on the map key (p. 463) with those on the signboard to check current rates, but for now the prices from here are: East Lake (Dōng Hú) ¥68 ($8.50), Lǔ Xùn Wénhuà Guǎngchǎng (the square at the junction of Lǔ Xùn Zhōng Lù and Jiěfàng Lù, not far west of here) ¥26 ($3.25); or putter round wherever you like for ¥65 ($8) per hour. Other destinations include the less romantic Long-Distance Bus Station (Kèyùn Zhōngxīn) for ¥80 ($10). Even the price of having your picture taken on a boat is regulated: ¥2 (25¢).

or on foot from several directions, perhaps best from the south. From Rénmín Zhōng Lù, head north up the right bank of the canal. The bridge ahead at Dōng Jiē is attractive, and once you've climbed up to road level and gone down the other side on ramps, there's ancient housing to the left and right. The Bā Zì Qiáo, rebuilt during the Southern Sòng era in 1256, is straight ahead and attractively bearded with creeper, its eightness the result of long ramps with a gentle gradient to either side.

Honk If You Like Calligraphy

Wáng Xīzhī (ca. 303–61), known as the Sage of Calligraphy, was an official of the Eastern Jin dynasty, whose family moved to Shàoxīng in his youth. Tradition provides him with the usual perfect childhood, in which he spent so much time studying calligraphy that he would absent-mindedly dip food instead of brush into the ink when eating.

Accounts of his adult life are both more believable and more entertaining. Wáng had a penchant for geese—which seems obvious until you remember that the Chinese didn't use quills. The birds were allowed to roam his house, where they would sometimes swallow valuables, including on one occasion a string of pearls. Once he offered a monk a copy of a key Daoist text executed in his own hand and priceless even then, in order to acquire an entire flock of pedigree geese. Another story tells how he traveled to see a bird rumored to have a particularly beautiful call, only to find that its owner had prepared her VIP guest a goose dinner. He was miserable for days afterward.

Although he was also skilled in formal characters and in *cǎo* (grass) style (in which characters are often scribbled with a single continuous stroke of the brush), his fame rests principally on his *xíng* (walking) style of calligraphy—a semi-cursive, free-flowing, very personal style which was to become a model for generations of student scribes.

What particularly ties him to the Shàoxīng area is what is said to be the finest calligraphy ever, the *Lán Tíng Jí Xù (Preface to the Orchid Pavilion Collection)*. In 353 he invited 41 guests to a literary drinking session at the Lán Tíng (just outside town—see below), where they sat on either side of a stream down which small cups of wine were floated. Guests had to compose a poem in the time it took for the cup to float past them, and if they failed they had to drink up. One river of wine later, 26 participants had produced a volume of 35 poems, for which a warmed-up Wáng dashed off an elegant 28-line, 324-character masterpiece about what a good time they'd had. Subsequently, when sober, he was unable to reproduce the same form.

Three hundred years later, the Táng Tàizōng emperor was so taken by this document that he had copies made, and then was buried with the original. This dog-in-the-manger approach ensured immortality for Wáng and his *Preface*, although the poems it introduced are now rarely read.

After you recross the bridge and turn left, the canal-side path runs between one- and two-story white houses up to and over the seven-sided arch of the **Guǎngníng Qiáo** of 1574, then abandons the canal (which swings left), narrows, and squeezes between houses. Through open doors people can be seen playing cards or mahjong, and vendors on tricycles sing out their wares (little cakes, *dòufu* skin). This alley, Guǎngníng Qiáo Zhí Jiē, ends at Shènglì Dōng Lù. A taxi, bus no. 6, or your feet can take you west to the main square.

Bā Zǐ Qiáo Zhí Jiē runs east from Zhōng Xīng Zhōng Lù. To follow the route above, take bus no. 22 from Jiěfàng Běi Lù to Értóng Gōngyuán stop. Continue east on the north side of the road, and take the 1st left turn after Mǎ Nòng.

Shūshèng Gùlǐ (The Master Calligrapher's Native Place) 🐟 Among several
areas of ancient housing left standing in Shàoxīng, this is perhaps the most pleasant, although it's been tidied up for tourists. The best entry point is from Zhōng Xīng Zhōng Lù along Qiáo Zhí Jiē, just north of the junction with Shènglì Dōng Lù, at the memorial arch (*páifāng*).

The two-story houses are constructed of stone and wood, painted white, often with their fronts to the stone-flagged street, and their backs to the waterways. At the first main junction, across the bridge, turn right into Fǔ Shān Jiē, at the top of which lies the **Jièzhū Sì** (¥5/65¢; open 8am–5:30pm), a single hall five bays wide with circular stone screens at either end carved with images of playful deer. Once the residence of Wáng Xīzhī, the Master Calligrapher himself, the hall contains a small exhibition on his life, and copies of his work.

As you return down Fǔ Shān Jiē, make your first left into a narrow street and you'll come immediately to a bridge giving views of people washing their clothes, and traditional housing hung with washing and lanterns. Across the bridge, the path at water level to the right offers plenty of photo ops and brings you back to Qiáo Zhí Jiē again. Turn back onto Fǔ Shān Jiē and left onto Bǐjià Qiáo (Pen Rack Bridge) at the end of which, you will find a carpenter who still makes paddles and boats.

AROUND SHÀOXĪNG

Lán Tíng (Orchid Pavilion) This well-kept and fragrant garden, a short bus ride
southwest of the city, is named for a 5th-century B.C. orchid plantation. It is full of stands of feathery bamboo and banana palms which surround temples and pavilions of fairly recent construction. Some house imperial stelae that eulogize the Master Calligrapher, others have rubbings of stelae showing the poets sitting on streamside rugs, and the walls of one structure are lined with copies of the Orchid Pavilion poems. The literary event itself has been re-created annually in March since 1984.

Down a zigzag path and across a bridge is a museum of calligraphy, where there are claims that calligraphy has a 6,000- to 7,000-year history. Samples on display begin with early rune-like characters.

The stream used for the drinking game (see the "Honk If You Like Calligraphy" box, above) meanders through the site, and there's a goose pond that would have pleased Wáng Xīzhī. Just at the start of the path to the museum are stone tablets on which you can use the brushes provided to practice your characters in water—the ultimate palimpsest.

About 14km (9 miles) and 30 min. southwest of town. Admission ¥25 ($3). 7:30am–5pm. Bus: no. 3 from Jiěfàng Lù (¥1.50/20¢). 1st bus out at 6am; last bus back at 6:58pm.

SHOPPING

Shàoxīng souvenirs include *chòu dòufu* ("stinky" tofu), invented here, and Shàoxīng "yellow wine" (made from rice, and some of it distinctly red rather than yellow), both available in ornate jars. Shàoxīng makes 250,000 tons of wine a year, but as with the tofu, you may prefer the jar to the contents. The rear of the ground floor of the **Huáyì Gōngsī,** just south of the central square on the east side of Jiěfàng Běi Lù, has a useful market with many types of wine in ordinary bottles at supermarket prices (as well as travel snacks). Hours are from 8:30am to 9pm.

The lively **Fúhé Jiē Shìchǎng** street market runs parallel to Jiěfàng Nán Lù on the east side, south from Lǔ Xùn Zhōng Lù. It's worth visiting more for local color than for actual shopping, although you can look out for the black felt hats (*wǔ zhān mào*) favored by the boatmen.

WHERE TO STAY

Low season, from November to March, brings significant discounts.

Shàoxīng Fàndiàn   This is an attractive hilltop collection of low-rise buildings of brick and wood in local style, all white walls and curling eaves, arranged around pools stocked with fish and the odd black-awning boat for local color. Once the big official place to stay (for big officials), it has managed to keep up with the times. Buildings 1 and 3 have smaller rooms, building 5 is more upmarket with larger rooms with wooden floors, and building 6 is more luxurious still. Bathrooms stay a standard small size, but grow in amenities. The hotel has three stars but its VIP building has an upper-four-star ambience, and much of the complex was refurbished in 2000.

Huán Shān Lù 9. ⓒ **0575/515-5858.** Fax 0575/515-5565. 210 units. ¥350 ($44) single; ¥400–¥550 ($50–$69) standard room; ¥900–¥2,600 ($113–$325) suite. Rates include breakfast. Discounts 30% or 40% (no breakfast). AE, DC, MC, V. **Amenities:** 3 restaurants; fitness room; sauna; bowling alley; business center (Internet ¥10/$1.25 per hour). *In room:* A/C, TV, fridge.

Wángcháo Dàjiǔdiàn (Dynasty Hotel)   This 26-floor circular glass tower wants to be the International Hotel but it isn't, although it is the town's best three-star. Haggle to make sure breakfast is included. "Junior" rooms have no windows but can be bargained down to ¥150 ($19). Some superior twins have interesting triangular shapes, larger-than-average bathrooms and, on one side of the hotel, views over an area of preserved old houses. Refurbished in 2002, guest rooms and bathrooms, while standard, are fresh. There's a battered rooftop "English pub" with views, and an "English corner" where students practice their English (with beer) on Thursday.

Shènglì Dōng Lù. ⓒ **0575/512-5888.** Fax 0575/512-5798. dynastyh@mail.sxptt.zj.cn. 149 units. ¥260 ($33) junior room; ¥345–¥400 ($43–$50) standard room; ¥648 ($81) suite. 10% tax (usually not charged). Discounts 30%–40%. AE, DC, MC, V. **Amenities:** 3 restaurants; bar; pool; exercise room; tour desk; airport shuttle; business center. *In room:* A/C, TV, fridge, hair dryer, safe.

Xiánhēng Jiǔdiàn (Old Xiánhēng Hotel)   Opened in 1998, this three-star is in battered but acceptable condition for the price (after bargaining). It's a five-story concrete building with hints of local style, handy for a lively street market and the Lǔ Xùn–related sights. Rooms are functional. The restaurant in the hotel is poor, although the one just outside (see Xiánhēng Jiǔdiàn below) is of more interest.

Lǔ Xùn Zhōng Lù 179. ⓒ **0575/511-6666.** Fax 0575/512-6179. 64 units. ¥280 ($35) single; ¥350–¥420 ($44–$53) standard room; ¥480 ($60) triple. Rates include breakfast. Discount 40%. AE, DC, MC, V. Bus: no. 1 from the station. **Amenities:** Restaurant; business center. *In room:* A/C, TV.

WHERE TO DINE

Most kitchens close at 8pm so be sure to eat before 7:30pm. The Shàoxīng Guójì Dàjiǔdiàn offers a decent Western breakfast in its ground-floor coffee shop for ¥65 ($8), along with assorted Italian and Asian dishes.

Shàngdǎo Kāfēi WESTERN   Branches of this Taiwanese joint-venture are far better choices for something familiar than the usual American fast-food chains. Green sofas and decent coffee at Western prices (in fact, the coffee costs as much as a meal) are the signature, together with an assortment of one-plate dishes, Western and Chinese, which include hefty portions of very buttery spaghetti and adequate sandwiches. **Omar Coffee,** just west of the Dynasty Hotel, is a detailed copy of the formula, with the same gauche charm.

Rénmín Zhōng Lù 239. ✆ 0575/514-0890. Main courses ¥20–¥60 ($2.50–$7.50), mostly at the lower end. No credit cards. 8am–2am.

Xiánhēng Jiǔdiàn SHÀOXĪNG   To the right as you face the hotel of the same name, this simple, concrete-floored restaurant with moon gates between rooms is of more literary than epicurean fame, but it attempts to re-create a 19th-century wine-shop atmosphere. Originally set up in 1894 by some distant relatives of Lǔ Xùn, it became famous through his mournful short story about the eponymous intellectual bum, Kǒng Yǐjǐ. Buy tickets from a desk in the center, then point to dishes at a counter to the left, such as local specialty *chòu dòufu* ("stinky" tofu). Order a measure of rather dark, sweet, sherrylike "wine" *(tài diāo jiǔ)* from a front counter.

The restaurant actually inside the hotel has indifferent service. The dishes are cooked with Shàoxīng wine, but the prices are high for what you get. Try "stinky" tofu steamed with mincemeat (called "rotten thousand sheet steamed meat cake" or *méi qiān zhāng zhēng ròubǐng*), and "drunken" bamboo shoots *(jiǔ niàng zāo sǔn).*

Lǔ Xùn Zhōng Lù 179. ✆ 0575/511-6666. Meal for 2 ¥40 ($5). No credit cards. 7:30am–8pm.

Yuánlín Dàjiǔdiàn SHÀOXĪNG   This large, high-ceilinged hall with modern rippled ceilings and upmarket decor is belied by inept service and tiled floors. But the local dishes are good. Try *qīng zhēng chòu dòufu* (steamed "stinky" tofu), *ròu tiáo mèn cài* (pork strips with vegetables), *Xiāo Shān luóbo gān* (shredded radish), *Yuèzhōu zāo jī* ("drunken" chicken), and *yóu zhá chòu dòufu* (fried "stinky" tofu).

Shènglì Dōng Lù 58. ✆ 0575/522-0788. Meal for 2 ¥60 ($7.50); more for seafood. No credit cards. 10:50am–1:30pm and 4:50–8:30pm.

2 Níngbō

Zhèjiāng Province, on the coast, 186km (116 miles) E of Hángzhōu

Thanks to the international attention that Shànghǎi has received in recent years, Níngbō has been inspired to transform itself from container port and manufacturing base to a burgeoning new tourist destination. The city center has almost completely reinvented itself, with a spanking new shopping plaza that showcases a 95m (312-ft.) musical fountain and probably the largest Starbucks in Asia. Best of all, authorities recently invested in a brand-new tourist office, complete with colorful brochures and English-speaking (to a degree) staff. No longer solely a stop-off point on the way to Pǔtuó Shān, Níngbō is now a gateway to dozens of new and interesting destinations that probably will not make it into most guidebooks for another 5 or 10 years. Choose the right time of year to come and Níngbō makes an excellent base for exploring original destinations that few others have even heard of, let alone visited.

Although Níngbō seems proud of its long history of foreign trade, the last remnants of its treaty-port-era architecture around the port were coming down as this book went to press, except for a few token buildings at the city's central Y-shaped river confluence, Sān Jiāng Kǒu.

The city is bustling and prosperous, and looks best at night with bridges and the old Catholic church colorfully illuminated. The center is being rebuilt in part with a brisk modernism that resembles a Silicon Valley high-tech campus more than a standard Chinese town. *Note:* For Chinese translations of selected establishments listed in this section, please turn to appendix A.

ESSENTIALS

GETTING THERE   Níngbō is connected with Běijīng (four flights daily), Hong Kong (four flights daily with China Eastern and occasionally with Dragonair), Guǎngzhōu (eight flights daily), and Shànghǎi (five flights daily). There are also daily flights to major cities across the southeast. Airport buses meet arrivals and bring them to the CAAC office southeast of the center at Xīngníng Lù 91 for ¥8 ($1); the ride takes 25 minutes. Outbound buses leave from 6am to 6pm on the hour, except 1pm. Take a bus 2 hours before your flight. CAAC has telephone numbers for booking tickets with free delivery; call ✆ **0574/8783-6750** or 0574/8783-4202. For **airport inquiries,** call ✆ **0574/8783-4202.** The stylish modern **railway station** sits at the end of the line from Hángzhōu via Shàoxīng. Destinations farther afield usually involve changing at Hángzhōu, so trains to Hángzhōu are comfortable all-seat daytime services: Hángzhōu ¥29 ($3.50) hard seat, ¥44 ($5.50) soft seat; Shàoxīng ¥17 ($2.10) hard seat, ¥28 ($3.50) soft seat. The ticket office (open 5:50am–7:55pm) is to the right of the railway station's main entrance. There's a left-luggage office (open 6:30am–8pm) inside the main hall. For **train inquiries,** call ✆ **0574/8731-2084.** Ticket windows are open from 5:50am to 7pm. The main **South Bus Station (Qìchē Nán Zhàn;** ✆ **0574/8713-1834)** has several competing companies offering rapid luxury services to points south and west, including Hángzhōu (¥42/$5.35) every 10 minutes from 6am to 7:30pm; Shànghǎi (¥96/$12; both Héngfēng Lù and Xújiāhuì stations are served) every 15 to 20 minutes from 6:20am to 7pm; and Wēnzhōu (11 daily; ¥116/$14). The main ticket office of the South Bus Station is open from 5:20am to 7pm, but there's a separate side entrance for some departures, to the right as you face the building. Bus services in Zhèjiāng Province are punctual, comfortable, and very well run. The **Zhèjiāng Quik (Zhèjiāng Kuàikè)** company is particularly good, serving Hángzhōu and Wēnzhōu (✆ **0574/8714-2846**). The **East Station (Qìchē Dōng Zhàn),** ✆ 0574/8792-4570 in Yáo'ài Lù, reached by bus no. 514 from the railway station, has minibuses to out-of-town sights. Níngbō also has a variety of **sea connections** to and from Pǔtuó Shān, the easiest of which is the ¥58 ($7.25) bus-and-speedboat combination, which leaves from the **Lúnchuán Mǎtóu (Ferry Dock),** reached by bus no. 1 from the railway station. See "Pǔtuó Shān," below, for more information. For **ferry inquiries** call ✆ 0574/8735-6332.

GETTING AROUND   Taxis cost ¥8 ($1) for 4km (2½ miles), then ¥1.80 (25¢) per kilometer, and 50% more after 6km (3¾ miles). Add 20% more from 10pm to 5am. Most **buses** charge a flat fare of ¥1 (15¢).

VISITOR INFORMATION   The smart new tourist office is conveniently located at Qìzhǎ Lù 169, Tiān Yī Square. It's open 9am to 9pm (© **0574/8727-9988;** nbtic@163.com).

FAST FACTS

Banks, Foreign Exchange & ATMs   A **Bank of China** (open 8am–5:15pm; 8:40am–5:05pm weekends and holidays) is in Zhōngshān Dōng Lù, opposite a KFC. At Yàoháng Jiē 139, another Bank of China (open 8:30–11:20am and 2–5:30pm), windows 10–12, offers foreign exchange. There are no ATMs accepting foreign cards.

Internet Access   The **Piàojǐng Wǎngbā** (open 8am–9pm) on Huálóu Jiē, just off Kāimíng Jiē, charges ¥3 (40¢) per hour, as do most other Internet cafes in town. Dial-up is © **163.**

Post Office   The main post office (open 7:30am–8pm) is at Sān Jiāng Kǒu, at Zhōngshān Dōng Lù and at Líng Qiáo Lù.

Visa Extensions   Extensions are available from the office to the left of the **PSB**'s main tower at Zhōng Xīng Lù 658 (© **0574/8706-2000;** open Mon–Sat 8:30–11am and 2–5pm).

SEEING THE SIGHTS

Sights at **Sān Jiāng Kǒu** include the **Tiān Hòu Gōng** devoted to the protector of sailors (¥10/$1.25; open 8am–5pm) and the French-built **Catholic church** of 1872, near opposite ends of the Jiāng Xià Qiáo (bridge).

Tiān Yī Gé Bówùguǎn ⚑   This 16th-century library is the most famous of a collection of ancient buildings housing a fine museum of local culture and various oddities, unusually well-lit and displayed. It's not exactly crowded—if you enter from the west through the Xī Dà Mén, you may have to wake the attendant in order to buy a ticket.

The Tiān Yī Gé (1561–66), the oldest surviving library building in China, is past some beautifully carved screens, old residences containing an unexciting literary exhibition (mainly genealogies in Chinese only), and a gelatinous pond. In the Níngbō style, it's six bays wide, which makes the entrance off-center.

Surrounding pavilions, in various degrees of modernization, contain exhibitions of painting and calligraphy of modest interest, but the **Bǎi É Tíng,** a pavilion made entirely of stone in imitation of wood, from bracket sets to carvings of writhing dragons, is remarkable.

The **main exhibitions** ⚑ are in Qīng-era (1644–1911) ancestral halls on the south side of the site (there's a map on the back of the ticket), through a passage beneath a rockery, and they concentrate on local culture and history. There's a second entrance here (the Xīnán Mén), and the displays are ordered accordingly, so walk through and start on the south side. The exhibitions include an entertaining account of the history of mahjong, labeled in English, with a series of courtyards set out with giant mahjong tiles and explanations of the origins of their symbols. A substantial bronze has three life-size characters playing the game, and you can sit to be photographed as the missing fourth. The empty chair has a promising hand, but there's no way the Chinese would miss this opportunity to triumph over foreigners, and their own man (there's also a Westerner and a Japanese in the game) is just in the process of winning with a particularly high score. The rear hall has an excellent display of sets of bone, bamboo, bronze, and plastic mahjong tiles as well as an impressive collection of Sichuan long cards.

The neighboring **theater stage** *(xìtái)* ✦ suggests great wealth. Its canopy has vast upturned pointed eaves. Superb water dragons, fish, and other figures on the roof are supported by fabulously complicated bracket sets beautifully gilded and carved. Little potted plants add a further splash of color to the already fabulous red-and-gold detailing. The historical relics exhibition in surrounding halls has some fine objects, including bizarre urns carved with lively figures, delicate Sòng celadon ware, and an ornately detailed bridal sedan chair, all in a nicely air-conditioned if English-free interior.

Tiān Yī Jiē. Admission ¥20 ($2.50). Apr 21–Oct 21 8am–5.30pm; Oct 22–Apr 20 8am–4:30pm.

AROUND NÍNGBŌ

Bǎoguó Sì ✦   Set in a leafy hillside site, this temple, founded in 845, has a Táng dynasty stele and a main hall (dated 1013), which is claimed to be the oldest surviving wooden structure south of the Cháng Jiāng (Yángzǐ). Surrounding structures dating from the Míng and Qīng dynasties house 17 small but interesting exhibitions. In the main hall, three caissons sit on seven layers of gradually angled bracket sets in one of the most intricate roofing structures you'll see in China. Supporting *guāléng* ("melonlike division") pillars are ribbed with eight segments, and lean alarmingly. Higher halls hold displays that include 108 statues of Guānyīn, and a 724-volume limited-edition sutra collection. The rearmost hall has a small exhibition devoted to Mínzhōu marriage customs, including a magnificent bridal sedan chair.

② 0574/8758-6317. Admission ¥12 ($1.50). 8.30am–6.30pm. Bus: no. 332 from Xīn Mǎlù north of the ferry port to terminus (¥1/15¢; every 30 min. 5:50am–5pm).

WHERE TO STAY

Several hotels here, even modest two-stars, have notices at their entrances that emphasize the dual economies separating the rich from the poor: DRESSED IN RAGS, PLEASE DON'T ENTER. But they are just the same as shabby hotels elsewhere in China—though a new Hyatt is on the way.

Jīngǎng Dàjiǔdiàn (Golden Port Hotel)   Popular with Japanese tours, and well positioned close to the port for those moving on to Pǔtuó Shān, this four-star tower has superb views over the confluence of the rivers at Sān Jiāng Kǒu. The standard rooms are very plain, and the pricier rooms have bizarre pseudo-European furnishings. Still, the guest rooms are well maintained and of a good size, the bathrooms standard, and the building within walking distance of the last remnants of the old foreign quarter.

Yángshàn Lù 51. ② 0574/8766-8888. Fax 0574/8767-8888. www.jingang-hotel.com. 260 units. ¥580–¥960 ($73–$120) standard room; ¥1,800–¥6,800 ($225–$850) suite. 50% discounts typical. AE, DC, MC, V. **Amenities:** 3 restaurants; bar; 2 lounges; outdoor tennis court; fitness room; sauna; bowling alley; game room; concierge; business center (Internet ¥12/$1.50 for 10 min.); forex; salon; 24-hr. room service; executive-level rooms. *In room:* A/C, satellite TV, broadband Internet access (¥20/$2.50 per day), fridge, hair dryer, safe.

Wénchāng Dàjiǔdiàn (Mandarin Prosperous Hotel)   Well located for city-center sightseeing and shopping, this four-star tower has great views over the city. The standard rooms are spacious and clean, the service enthusiastic and helpful.

Wénchāng Lù 2, off Zhōngshān Xī Lù. ② 0574/8726-8668. Fax 0574/8726-8188. www.mandarin-nb.com. 199 units. ¥688–¥988 ($86–$125) standard room; ¥1,800–¥6,800 ($225–$850) suite. 50% discounts typical. AE, DC, MC, V. **Amenities:** 3 restaurants; lobby bar; teahouse; fitness room; sauna; bowling alley; concierge; business center; forex; salon; 24-hr. room service; executive-level rooms. *In room:* A/C, video on demand and satellite TV, fridge, hair dryer, safe.

WHERE TO DINE

There's plenty of seafood flopping about in buckets or tanks at the entrances to restaurants, but nothing spectacular, so you might as well eat in your hotel.

Several all-day or 24-hour **fast-food outlets** dot the South Bus Station/Railway Station/Níngbō Hotel area, offering noodles from ¥3 (40¢). In the evenings, Uighurs produce kabobs on Huálóu Jiē. The usual Western fast-food outlets are highly visible, including **McDonald's** on Zhōngshān Dōng Lù just east of the river. There's a branch of the Taiwanese **Shàngdǎo Kāfēi,** with its green sofas and usual mix of sandwiches and pastas, just south of the Níngbō Fàndiàn. Even so, now that Tiān Yī Square has been completed, it boasts the largest assortment of restaurants, cafes, and fast-food joints in town including a **Pizza Hut,** a **Starbucks,** and more than a dozen Chinese venues to try.

3 Pŭtuó Shān

Zhèjiāng Province, a small island offshore from Níngbō

Pŭtuó Shān is regarded as the earthly address of Guānyīn, the goddess of mercy (originally Avalokitesvara, and male, turned female in China en route to Japan, where she is the equally female Kannon).

There are multiple legends to explain the connection between the bodhisattva and this undistinguished outcrop, all dating from the 9th century, and all involving the rescue or assistance of monks, Indian, Chinese, and Japanese. In one tale, a monk taking a Guānyīn statue from Wǔtái Shān (p. 241) to Japan was caught in a storm, and promised to build a monastery to Guānyīn if he was rescued. An invisible hand guided his boat to Pŭtuó Shān, and he built Pǔjì Sì.

Pŭtuó Shān is a small island about 4 miles long and 3 miles wide, one of more than 100 in the Chusan archipelago, usually reached by a combination of bus and fast ferry from the mainland port of Níngbō. It's a summertime weekend holiday resort for urbanites from Shànghǎi trying to escape the heat, who fly into Zhōu Shān airport on the neighboring island of Zhūjiājiān and take boats from there. Summer periods, as well as weekends for most of the year, should be avoided because hotel prices are extortionate then, as are prices in restaurants.

There's an entrance fee of ¥110 ($14), payable as you alight from the boat. Individual temples and other sights slap on additional admission charges of ¥2 and ¥16 (25¢–$2), turning this holy island into little more than a tacky Buddhist Disneyland.

ESSENTIALS

GETTING THERE   There are **flights** to the nearest airport (on Zhōu Shān, a neighboring island) from major cities that include Běijīng (four weekly), Shànghǎi (two or three daily), Xī'ān (four weekly), and Xiàmén (once daily). Returning, departure tax for the short hop to Shànghǎi is only ¥10 ($1.25). Buses take passengers to a ferry to Pŭtuó Shān. For tickets out, try the **Pŭtuó Shān Jīchǎng Shòupiào Chù** in the main square, across from Pǔjì Sì, near the exit to the bus station. The ferry/bus link to the airport costs ¥12 ($1.50); call ✆ **0580/609-3101** for bookings. **China Eastern** airlines has an office in the Xī Lěi Xiǎo Zhuāng hotel (✆ **0580/609-1931**). Peak season is July through September.

There are regular **sailings** to Pŭtuó Shān from Níngbō, although the first half of the 2-hour, 20-minute journey is done by bus (11 departures, 6am–4:30pm), the rest by passenger speedboats called *kuàitǐng* (¥58/$7.25). The Lúndù Mǎtóu is in Wài

Mǎlù, just north of Níngbō's Yǒng Jiāng and Xīn Jiāng bridges. The port *(kèyùn zhàn)* at Pǔtuó Shān has a left-luggage office in the ticket office to the left as you leave. The road up to the left is the quickest one to town, or take the bus for ¥3 (40¢) to Pǔjì Sì and neighboring hotels. A cheaper but longer sea route is via **Shěnjiāmén;** luxury buses depart from Níngbō's North bus station (Běi Zhàn) 26 times a day from around 7:10am to 4:30pm and arrive at a bus station opposite the port at Shěnjiāmén, for about ¥30 ($3.75). Boats leave every 30 minutes from Pǔtuó Shān between 7am and 8pm for a fare of ¥15 ($1.90). Shěnjiāmén also has 11 daily buses directly to and from Shànghǎi (6 hr.; ¥120/$15) and one to Hángzhōu (5 hr.; ¥77/$9.80) at 12:40pm.

There are daily direct **boats** to and from **Shànghǎi** taking 12 hours for ¥79 to ¥720 ($9.90–$90), and a twice-daily combination of 2½ hours by speedboat and 2 hours by bus for ¥180 to ¥220 ($23–$28). Tickets for all sailings can be bought at the pier on Pǔtuó Shān, in Shànghǎi at the main ferry ticket office on the Bund, or through agents.

GETTING AROUND   Taxis and **pedicabs** are tiresome and unreliable, but the **minibus** service is well regulated. Each major stop has its own line, with signs in English and clearly written prices of ¥2 to ¥6 (25¢–75¢). For those who don't want to make the penitential trudge up Fódǐng Shān (not a serious climb in holy mountain terms—under an hour), Huìjì Sì is now accessible in 10 minutes by a smart European **cable car** system. The station at the bottom is currently a mass of new construction with a host of new temples being built on the opposite mountain.

FAST FACTS

Banks, Foreign Exchange & ATMs   The **Bank of China** (open 8–11am and 1–4:30pm) is on Méi Cén Lù opposite the Bǎotuó Hotel.

Internet Access   Dial-up ℂ **163** works, but other Internet access is limited.

Post Office   The post office is located on Méi Cén Lù (open 7:30am–4:40pm).

A QUICK TRIP AROUND A SMALL ISLAND

Attractions on the overrated Pǔtuó Shān consist of several Buddhist temples of ancient foundation but modern restoration, modern attractions designed to extract a few more *kuài* from visitors, and some scenic pleasures.

The center of activity is an area of stone-edged lotus ponds, crossed by bridges and surrounded by a number of hotels, reached by bus or by a 1km-to-2km (½-mile–1¼-mile) walk from the dock. **Pǔjì Sì** (open 5:30am–6pm; ¥5/65¢) stands on the west side. Yellow roofs indicate past imperial approval, and the sound of recorded chanting reveals the temple's active and commercial bent. Inside there's a mixture of the devout, those going through the motions (just in case), and those merely having fun. But the four heavenly kings in the first hall are good and gaudy, and the large main hall is filled with kneelers and lit-up gilded statues, all modern.

From the northeast corner of the square, walk past the battered finger of the 14th-century **Duōbǎo Tǎ** and a hotel belonging to a tobacco company, and you'll find a collection of bus stands with English signs. You can take a bus to the **Fǎyǔ Sì** and start a climb to the top of **Fódǐng Shān,** or stay on the bus a little farther to the cable car *(suǒdào)* station. The cable car makes the 10-minute trip to the summit from 6:30am to 5pm for a fare of ¥25 ($3) up, ¥15 ($1.90) down, ¥40 ($5) round-trip. Walk uphill and turn right to reach **Huìjì Sì;** try to avoid tripping over those who've done it the hard way—a procession of muddy figures who throw themselves prostrate, stand up at the point their heads have reached, and throw themselves prostrate again, effectively

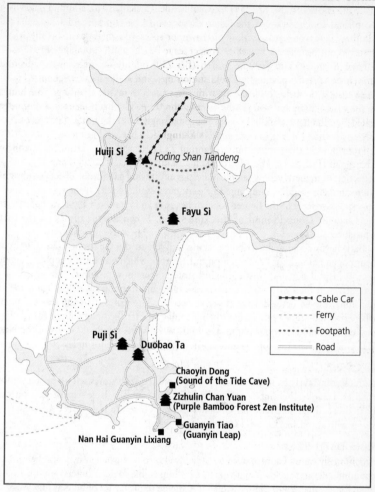

Huiji Si

Foding Shan Tiandeng

Fayu Sì

Cable Car

Ferry

Footpath

Road

Puji Sì

Duobao Ta

Chaoyin Dong
(Sound of the Tide Cave)

Zizhulin Chan Yuan
(Purple Bamboo Forest Zen Institute)

Guanyin Tiao
(Guanyin Leap)

Nan Hai Guanyin Lixiang

measuring the entire length of the route with their bodies in a combined test of spiritual and physical fitness.

The temple (open 5am–6:30pm; ¥5/65¢) contains four particularly enormous and gaudy heavenly kings, the two white-faced ones looking rather jolly, and the same mix of piety, devotion, and sightseeing as down below. But surprisingly authentic full-scale ceremonies are also held here, with persistent percussion and chanting from less-than-authentic staff posing as monks.

The route out of the temple is lined with souvenir sellers whose principal sales pitch is *"Lái!"* (Come!). At the junction, before taking the pilgrimage route down to **Fǎyǔ Sì,** walk 5 minutes up to **Fódǐng Shān Tiāndēng** (beacon), which is little more than a stone plinth next to a military installation bristling with aerials and a rather vicious-looking German Shepherd that may make you have second thoughts. But the views make the effort and the ¥2 (25¢) fee worthwhile. Particularly on a humid day, when the mist is caught between the other islands, you'll be reminded of Chinese scroll paintings, and you can see most of the other spots you might visit on the island stretched out below you, as well as "1,000 Steps Beach" and "100 Steps Beach."

Fǎyǔ Sì (open 5am–6:30pm; ¥5/65¢) is a 30-minute descent down paths and uneven stone stairs, past many a cold-drink seller, and audio speakers cunningly disguised as plastic rocks to fill the air with the sounds of mystic chanting. This brings you to a side door, and you do the temple in reverse. The main hall has a very large seated Buddha figure, and very lively dragons dangle from the beams. Statues of particularly lifelike *luóhàn (Chinese saints)* shout, preach, beg, and grimace.

From outside the temple, buses charging ¥3 (40¢) will take you to the **Zǐzhúlín Chányuàn (Purple Bamboo Forest Zen Institute)** (open 4:30am–6pm; ¥5/65¢), a collection of modern yellow temple buildings of dizzying gaudiness. There's a substantial recumbent Buddha, and some fine perforated stone screens at the rear exit—note the expressive faces of the figures—which heads to an imitation Táng-style hall, above the **Cháoyīn Dòng (Sound of the Tide Cave).** When the sea rushes in, the cave reproduces the sound of chanting (if you have a highly active imagination).

Back beyond the main entrance, paths lead left to the **Guānyīn Tiào (Guānyīn Leap;** open 6am–6pm; ¥2/25¢), a prominent rock which was once a popular suicide spot. A helpful sign and twisting flights of stone stairs now prohibits this. The deities themselves in their dirty cases are expressionless and unimpressive although some of the stone, carved bases deserve closer inspection. The real treat is the rear chamber, where it is the murals rather than the idols that capture the imagination. A little farther on is a brand-new but impressive 33m-tall (109-ft.) statue of Guānyīn, the **Nán Hǎi Guānyīn Lìxiàng** (open 6am–6:30pm; ¥6/70¢), visible for miles.

SHOPPING

Lanes leading away from the main square are packed with stores selling plaster saints, rosaries, karaoke-chanting VCDs (which you may already have experienced on the boat over), dried starfish, and gewgaws galore. There are also several convenience stores with travel snacks, drinks, and mineral water.

WHERE TO STAY

Traditionally canny Chinese seem remarkably easy to fool when away from their home environment, and they will tell you that it's impossible to get a hotel room on Pǔtuó Shān for less than ¥400 ($50)—which in Chinese terms is a lot of money. July, August, and September; the first weeks of May and October; and weekends for much of the rest of the year are indeed very busy, and the hotels charge what they like. But off peak, and avoiding weekends, demand discounts of 50%, which may rise to 70% if you negotiate amiably. Even at peak times, discounts of 20% to 50% may be available.

Many hotels on Pǔtuó Shān are not open to foreign visitors. The general quality of those that are open to foreigners is above average for Chinese-run hotels, but prices are still disproportionate to the quality of service provided. The three-star, 159-room **Xī Lěi Xiǎo Zhuāng,** Xiānghuá Jiē 1 (© 0580/609-1505; fax 0580/609-1812), is one of the better hotels, not least because it is less greedy than some others at the more comfortable end of the scale. Built in 1991 and refurbished in 2001, the hotel is a collection of buildings, with block no. 1 the best and approaching a Chinese four-star in quality. Staff speak some English, foreign credit cards are accepted, and rooms are in general small but well-appointed. Standard rooms cost ¥493 to ¥792 ($62–$99), and suites cost ¥2,080 to ¥3,800 ($260–$475). The two-star **Bǎotuó Bīnguǎn,** Méi Cén Lù 118 (© **0580/609-2090;** fax 0580/609-1148), has rooms renovated in 2001 that were still fresh and comfortable at press time and were worthy of three stars elsewhere. Standard and triple rooms cost from ¥400 to ¥560 ($50–$70), and suites cost ¥1,080 ($135); off season, prices are 50% less.

If budget matters to you, talk to the people who will approach you at the dock, offering **private rooms** with common bathroom facilities for a bargainable ¥40 ($5) a bed. The legality is in doubt but a brisk business is done, and photo albums are ready with photos of the accommodations, so there seem to be no problems.

WHERE TO DINE

Fresh seafood is plentiful on menus on Pǔtuó Shān. It's at its cheapest at small, open-fronted restaurants on the two roads leading up from the docks, and in the cluster of store-filled alleys north of Pǔjì Sì. Your meal will be squirming, flopping, or slithering in tubs and bowls at the entrance until you order it.

Hotel restaurants tend to take advantage of tourists by offering both high prices and small portions, but the restaurant in the **Xǐlěi Xiǎo Zhuāng** (© **0580/609-1505,** ext. 502; open 6:30–9am, 12:50–2pm, and 5–9pm) has a wide variety of standard Chinese dishes and a respectable vegetarian menu. A meal for two will cost around ¥100 ($13).

In the square outside Pǔjì Sì, the **Báihuà Cháyì Sùzhāi Guǎn** (© **0580/609-1208**) has a pleasant interior. It offers a broad vegetarian menu as well as standards, for about ¥80 ($10) for two. Farther up the street, past the shops that sell the monk's out-fits (only ¥80/$10 for an arresting saffron number) and the beauty salons (!) there are a number of little holes-in-the-wall that provide tasty local fare at reasonable prices.

4 Wēnzhōu

Zhèjiāng Province, 470km (294 miles) S of Hángzhōu, 436km (272 miles) N of Fúzhōu

Hemmed in by mountains and looking to the sea, Wēnzhōu, with its own peculiar local dialect, is an unlovely modern trading creation based on an early treaty port. It sits on a small seaside plain laced with canals, but it is no Shàoxīng. Opened by an Anglo-Chinese convention of 1876, it never amounted to much.

Apart from being a useful starting point to visit the bridges of Tàishùn County (see below), Wēnzhōu is also a fascinating place to see what deplorable damage the modern economy can do to an ancient agrarian culture. From the designer boutiques and European car dealers downtown, through the poverty of the surrounding shanty towns to the utter hopelessness of those left behind in the villages, visitors can see very clearly how dual economies are tearing the nation apart. Nowhere else is the wealth gap more pronounced than in a city that the propagandists have made famous for its concentration of millionaires. The official media constantly lauds "the Wēnzhōu model" which, like "socialism with Chinese characteristics," is a way of talking about raw capitalism without having to admit to the Communist Party's U-turn, when in reality it is simply innumerable sweatshops churning out cheap plastic tack that ranges from disposable lighters at best to sordid, ugly sex toys at worst. It's also famous as a source of fake everything—it's said that within a week of the latest *prêt-à-porter* fashions appearing in Paris, there are knockoff versions on sale here. There's even a fake McDonald's (Màidāngláo) and KFC (Kěndéjī) combination called Màikěnjī. *Note:* For Chinese translations of selected establishments listed in this section, please turn to appendix A.

ESSENTIALS

GETTING THERE Wēnzhōu is connected by **air** to 38 Chinese cities as far-flung as Ürümqi, including Běijīng (two to three flights daily), Guǎngzhōu (four or five flights), Hángzhōu (four or five flights), Shànghǎi (both airports six or seven flights), and Shēnzhèn (three to five flights). There are also five flights a week from Hong Kong. The main **CAAC ticket office (Wēnzhōu Mínháng Shòupiào Chù)** is at the junction of Mínháng Lù and Jǐnxiù Lù (☎ **0577/96555** domestic, or 0577/883-24311 international—only Hong Kong from Wēnzhōu). Prices include ticket delivery. The airport is 25km (16 miles) east of town, served by an airport bus that makes 13 trips from 5:40am to 8pm for a fare of ¥10 ($1.25). Wēnzhōu has a **railway station** but not many useful connections; these are all to the interior, notably to Wǔchāng. The ticket office (open 8am–7pm) is at the far left side as you face the station. Left luggage is to the right; it's open from 6am to 11:40pm and charges ¥5 (65¢) per piece. The fastest way along the coast north or south is by luxury **bus** on the new coastal highways. Buses from Níngbō and Shàoxīng (4 hr.) mostly arrive at the **Xīnchéng Kèyùn Zhōngxīn Zhàn** (☎ **0577/8891-1927**), well to the southeast of the center and northeast of the railway station. This is the main station for the excellent Zhèjiāng Quik company's connections with Níngbō (13 departures 7:30am–5:10pm; ¥116/$14), Shàoxīng (9:30am and 2:40pm; ¥108/$13), and Hángzhōu (25 departures 6:40am–6:20pm; ¥120/$15). The **Wēnzhōu Kèyùn Zhōngxīn Zhàn,** south of the center, has buses to Tàishùn, a winding 191km (119 miles) away (5 hr.; ¥54/$6.50), with departures at 7am, 9am, 1:30pm, and 3:30pm. Call the operator direct at ☎ **0137/678-8822.** Despite the rural destination, the bus is large and comfortable, but tickets can only be bought on the day of travel. There are also minibuses that arrive every 30 minutes from 8am to 2pm. The ticket windows are to the left of the entrance. The **Xīn Nán Zhàn,** just west of the railway station, has buses to Fújiàn Province, but as elsewhere in China, cross-border services are more limited. The best bus to Fúzhōu is a luxury daytime sleeper bus at 8:30am (8 hr.; ¥154/$19). The bus station automatically adds ¥2 (25¢) in insurance. There's also an overnight sleeper service. The bus is a surprise: Shoes must be taken off and placed in a bag provided. Berth allocation is random, so come early. There are also services from here to Nánjīng, Shànghǎi, Guǎngzhōu, and beyond.

GETTING AROUND **Taxis** have a flagfall of ¥10 ($1.25) which includes 4km (2½ miles); after that, it's ¥1.50 (20¢) per kilometer, and 50% more after 6km (3¾ miles). Add another 20% from midnight to 5am. Public **buses** have a minimum fare of ¥1.50 (20¢); most charge that as their flat fare. Buses serve all parts of the city and while the signs at stops do not have any English, route maps give very useful visual representations. There are **ferries** to Jiāngxīn Island (see below) from the Jiāngxīn Mǎtóu (dock), well-marked in English on Wàng Jiāng Dōng Lù. From the dock there are also **tourist river trips** for ¥50 ($6.25) at 6:30pm (☎ **0577/8819-9073**).

FAST FACTS

Banks, Foreign Exchange & ATMs The main branch of the **Bank of China** (open 8am–6pm) is at the east end of Rénmín Xī Lù at Xīnhé Jiē. Go to counter 4/5 *opposite* the foreign-exchange sign.

Internet Access *Wǎngbā* are almost everywhere but the library on Gōng Yuán Lù (☎ **0577/8882-4163**) offer cleaner, quieter facilities. Dial-up is ☎ **163.**

Post Office The main post office branch (open 7:30am–5:30pm) is at Xǔ Shān Lù 73. There's also a branch just east of the railway station, beyond the Wànháo Grand Hotel.

Visa Extensions   The city **PSB** Aliens Entry-Exit Bureau (© **0577/8808-9888;** open Mon–Fri, 8:30am–noon and 2–5:30pm) is at the end of an alley on the west side of Rénmín Guǎngchǎng at Guǎngchǎng Lù Xī Gōngxié 86.

AROUND CENTRAL WĒNZHŌU

The warren of streets north of **Wǔ Mǎ Jiē,** particularly between (and along) Jiěfàng Běi Lù and Fǔqián Jiē, has a number of ancient facades and a labyrinth of girly shopping with a faint air of London's Carnaby Street in the 1960s. Wǔ Mǎ Jiē itself has been pedestrianized and received a heavy-handed restoration, although several faintly Art Deco buildings sport slightly unlikely mid-19th-century dates.

Jiāngxīn Gū Yǔ ("solitary island in the heart of the river" in a very literal translation) makes for a pleasant stroll despite the piped music from speakers in the trees and, in the evenings, the howls of the damned from the opposite shore. Or it may just be karaoke.

Small as the island is, it has a central lake and is dotted with pavilions outlined in gaudy lights, a Sòng dynasty well, a temple or two, Soviet-style heroic monuments to the People's Liberation Army, and two pagodas. The **Dōng Tǎ,** at the eastern end, built in 869 and restored in the Míng and Qīng dynasties, reportedly owes its topless state to a consular complaint about the noise of roosting birds. The local mandarin simply removed the roof. The lighthouse here, established by foreign residents, was included by the International Association of Lighthouse Authorities in 1997 on a world list of 100 historical lighthouses, and is still in service. In roughly the middle of the island's southern side, the **Xī Tǎ** was built in 969 and its most recent restoration was in 1982. Its seven six-sided stories look like freshly poured concrete. Ferries leave for the island every 30 minutes from the Jiāngxīn Mǎtóu in Wēnzhōu, from 8am to 11:30pm for ¥10 ($1.25) round-trip.

WHERE TO STAY

There are plain and simple budget accommodations around the railway station for about ¥200 ($25).

Fán Dōng Bīnguǎn   An unappealing, nominally three-star hotel in a white-tile building, but in an excellent location directly opposite the Xīnnán Bus Station, just west of the railway station, this is among the better budget accommodations in this neighborhood, and will do for those merely passing through. Modest functional guest rooms have decent bathrooms with shower cubicles. Cheap point-to-order fast food on one side of the hotel and a convenience store on the other help those facing the 4-hour trip to Fúzhōu prepare for the journey.

Wēnzhōu Dà Dào, Huǒchēzhàn Xī Shǒu. © **0577/8678-5588.** Fax 0577/8678-3732. 60 units. ¥228–¥318 ($28–$40) standard room; ¥358 ($45) triple. Discounts up to ¥110 ($14). No credit cards. **Amenities:** Restaurant. In room: A/C, TV.

Jiāngxīn Liáoyǎngyuàn ★ (Finds)   A rare opportunity (see also "Xiàmén," p. 502) to stay in an old colonial consulate building, this one is British and dates from 1894 (the manager says 1886); it was once a workers' sanatorium. This is far from the highest class of hotel you'll see in China, but it has the merit of relative peace and quiet on Jiāngxīn Island, with views across to the city. There are only six very oddly shaped rooms, the best of which is vast and high-ceilinged with a modern bathroom and shower cubicle, and a balcony with a view across the water. Others are small with simple (or sometimes common) bathrooms. A former consular residence building to one side has dorm beds for ¥80 ($10), which includes three meals of unknown quality.

Jiāngxīn Yǔ. ⓒ 0577/8820-1269. Fax 0577/8820-1213. 6 units. Various rooms ¥200–¥500 ($25–$63). 50% discounts weekdays off peak. No credit cards. Above on the right as you exit the ferry. **Amenities:** Restaurant. *In room:* A/C, TV.

WHERE TO DINE

Despite all their wealth, Wēnzhōunese are still decidedly provincial when it comes to eating. A couple of the flashier hotels recently imported celebrity chefs from Hong Kong, but the locals simply turned their noses up at Cantonese and sent the disappointed chefs back to Central with their tails between their legs. The Taiwanese coffee shop and snack chain **Shàngdǎo Kāfēi** has six branches across Wēnzhōu, including the one at Wēndí Lù, Chéngkāi Huāyuàn 10 (ⓒ 0577/8865-3063). **KFC** and **McDonald's** outlets are dotted around town, and there's a **Pizza Hut** on Wǔ Mǎ Lù.

Fruit Restaurant (Chún Sōng Láng Shuǐguǒ Fáng) ✦ *Finds* FUSION Tucked away on a little side street next to the Chocolate Club, this initially appears to be a simple juice bar but is much more than that. Sure you can try all kinds of exotic juices (star fruit, papaya, even the dreaded, foul-smelling durian), but there is a great selection of food on the English menu, too. My favorite was the stir-fried rice with mango and frogs' legs, but the steak set with papaya sauce ran a close second—all washed down with a refreshing kiwi and lemon juice. Not only one of the best places in Wēnzhōu, but surely one of my personal faves on the entire east coast.

Chún Sōng Láng Shuǐguǒ Fáng, Cái Qiáo Xiàng, off Shènglì Lù. No phone. Meal for 2 ¥80 ($10). No credit cards. 11am–11pm.

THE BRIDGES OF TÀISHÙN COUNTY ✦✦

Yes, corridor bridges *(láng qiáo)*—a few are the simple roofed horizontal spans as seen in *The Bridges of Madison County* (which was a big hit in China), but with Chinese characteristics. Other bridges are the longer, writhing affairs the Chinese call *wúgōng qiáo*—"centipede bridges"—which rear up over rivers, sometimes incorporating two-story shrines in their off-center humps. Some stand incongruously beautiful in the middle of hideous small towns, some are at rural dead ends reached by unpaved roads and surrounded by Míng-era housing, and still others are deep in the countryside, reachable by walking down steep stone staircases—until last century the regions' highways, and still the routes by which farmers get their goods to market. The area gains no stars for its accommodations (it's often hard to pay more than ¥20/$2.50 for a bed) or its transport. But its rickety buses wind on flagstoned routes past water buffaloes pulling plows, guided by peasants in *suōyī*—rainwear made from tree bark. Only 5 years ago, these bridges were almost unheard of, and now thanks to numerous websites, articles, and CCTV documentaries, these rural backwaters are becoming more and popular for domestic tourists. We made the mistake of traveling during National Week and were almost run off the road numerous times by private cars.

Although Tàishùn (also known as Luóyáng Zhèn) can be reached by sleeper bus from other points in Zhèjiāng, it's best to start from Wēnzhōu and travel light. Use your Wēnzhōu hotel or the railway station left-luggage office, and bring just a day pack. You can do the trip in 3 to 4 days, covering about four towns and eight bridges; the best times to travel are in March and from August to October.

Catching a morning bus to **Tàishùn** will get you there in the early afternoon. Try not to get a seat at the front of the bus as this is probably one of the most hair-raising, purgatorial bus rides that you will take during your entire stay. Few other routes have sick buckets along the center aisle—and they seemed to get used most every trip.

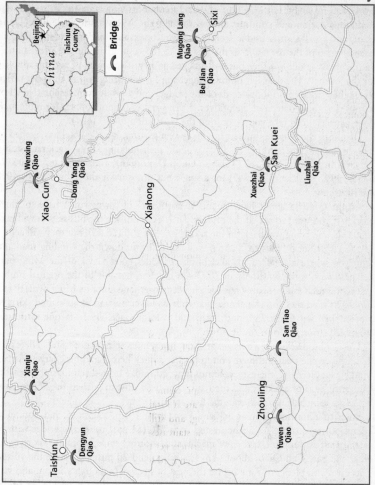

Roads cling precariously to the sides of heavily forested mountains, and precipitous drops can be seen just inches away beyond the concrete barriers, an alarmingly high number of which seemed to be missing. Clouds can come in quickly, bringing visibility down to a few meters, but even this barely slows the drivers.

Tàishùn is a noisy, dirty place but it does make a useful base. There's a chance to move straight on to peaceful **Zhōulǐng** if you wish, but a night here is worthwhile in order to see the **Xiānjū Qiáo,** and to make other preparations. You may well be accosted by accommodations touts as you leave the bus station (which closes at 4pm), but turn left to find for yourself a number of small **hotels** with clean simple rooms, private bathrooms, and usually fans or air-conditioning (for which you may have to pay extra). Rooms with two or three beds cost ¥50 to ¥70 ($6.25–$8.75) after bargaining. Selecting one a little farther from the bus station will make for a more slightly more peaceful night, but only until the tractors start arriving at dawn. Turn right out of the bus station and continue around to the right at the traffic circle onto Dōng Dàjiē, and you'll shortly find a Xīnhuá Shūdiàn (bookshop) on your right, selling an essential map of the town and of the area for ¥5 (65¢). Just back up the street a little, on the opposite side is a tiny, but well-stocked bakery, if you need to pick up supplies for the journey. The next left onto Guǎngchǎng Lù will bring you to the **post office** where they stock colorful postcards of the bridges and a lovely commemorative set of stamps that show sixteen of the bridges. A *bèngbèngchē* (onomatopoeia for motorized three-wheelers) can take you there from the bus station for ¥3 (40¢).

Thanks to the growing interest in *láng qiáo,* a smarter, upscale hotel has opened to cater to digital-camera-toting, rich city types in their hulking SUVs. Rack rates at the **Tàishùn International Hotel (Tàishùn Guójì Dàjiǔdiàn),** Yóuzhèng Lù 2 (© 0577/ 6756-9999), start at ¥378 ($47) for a single but this quickly drops by 30% or 40% just by asking.

Xiānjū Qiáo ia about 8km (5 miles) northeast of town; you'll have to move quickly if you want to see all the bridges. Surly taxis outside the bus station will take you, wait, and bring you back for the asking price of ¥50 ($6.25), but they will accept ¥30 ($3.75). Local buses to Xiānrén will also take you down the winding road and drop you where a modern, parallel bridge provides good views of the Míng one. Repaired with some sensitivity in 2002—as much as possible of the original timber was kept, much as it probably has been in many overhauls since its Míng dynasty creation—its tiled roof forms a gentle arc, while its lower portion wears slatted skirts to protect the long timbers supporting it, and it leaps gracefully from one intricately assembled stone platform to the other.

The last bus back to town passes at about 4pm, but you may not mind. There's little traffic on the road, although you may meet a duck herder and his charges. As you wind back up the hill, there are columns of wood smoke from distant farmhouses, the loudest noise is of crickets, and the road turns from dust to ancient flagstones, passing large "armchair" tombs set in the lush hillside.

Buses to **Zhōulíng** leave at 6:30am, 7am, 8am, 10am, 12:30pm, and 3pm. The 48km (30-mile) trip takes 2¼ hours and costs ¥10 ($1.25). To see the bridge with by far the prettiest location, take the 8am bus and, shortly before Zhōulíng, ask to be let off at the **Sān Tiáo Qiáo,** about 6km (3¾ miles) and 20 minutes before the village. This gives you plenty of time before the next bus passes (although you can also visit it as an excursion from the village or, with an early start, on the way back). The bridge is a 30-minute walk through the countryside. Steps lead up the embankment to meet a cart track which winds around steep-sided hills laced with thread-like waterfalls. After a few minutes, take some shallow stone steps to the left and follow the edges of paddy fields (look lost, and farmers will direct you). The path drops away steeply, becoming a long stone staircase past rice terrace after rice terrace and the occasional mournful tethered goat bleating a greeting. Wildflowers are sprinkled at the edges of the paddies, whose waters reflect the sky, and frogs scatter at your footsteps. Finally, the bridge comes into view, looking like a small house that woke up, yawned, and stretched across the river, linking three of the beautifully stone-stepped paths that would have been the highways of their time (which is why the bridge is called "three roads bridge"). Inside, as with all the bridges, there are benches where peasants put down their bamboo shoulder poles for a rest in the shade before attempting the climb. Although plain, the bridge is perhaps Tàishùn County's oldest, first erected in the Táng dynasty (618–906). If you are lucky, the rushing of the river, bird song, and the chirping of crickets provide the only sounds. Alas, thanks to the growth in popularity of these bridges, you may now also notice the litter and the graffiti. Fújiàn Province is nearby, and you might want to wait for the afternoon bus (which should pass at about 3pm) or take one of those winding staircases and see just how far you can go.

From where you began at the entrance of the bridge, try following the path that leads up in the opposite direction but on the same side of the valley. This is actually a peasants' shortcut up over the mountain and down through to **Zhōulǐng.** As you begin descending again, simply look over to the houses beyond the paddy fields, and if you are lucky, a passing tractor will give you the bearings of the main road. Make sure that you bear left when you hit this road; otherwise, you will end up back where you started. Walking to **Zhōulǐng** only takes a couple of hours and allows you examine the countryside up close, and in much more detail than you could if you were whizzing by in a minibus. You'll pass irrigation systems that have been there for centuries and strange ancestral temples that have probably been there even longer. (The truly inquisitive may discover, as I did, the foulest toilet this side of the Yángzǐ.) Up this close, though, it is easy to see the trauma that the Chinese countryside is undergoing. Stark, boxy houses (most of them empty) and new roads are pushing agriculture farther and farther away from the fertile valley floors. The few farmers that still work these areas are forced to work ever steeper inclines to make way for the dubious benefits of modern transportation. Most of the remaining population that has not fled for the cities falls into two categories, those so old that all they can do is sit and smoke all day and an alarmingly large number archetypal village idiots, the disturbing results of 5,000 years of inbreeding. Streams are choked with garbage and the mountains themselves are battered and scarred as dynamite and bulldozers hurry to connect tiny communities that have previously been isolated for millennia.

The road, already surfaced, ends at the hamlet of **Zhōulǐng,** and the bus stops outside the only accommodations, the **Zhōulǐng Xiāng Lǚshè (© 0577/6768-2368).** There's a simple restaurant and shop at the front with ridiculously cheap home cooking. Rooms on two floors above are reached through the kitchen and entered from balconies overlooking a square mainly populated by ducks and chickens. The best beds cost ¥20 ($2.50). There are two or three beds to a room, with fan, TV, and common bathroom. Everything's clean, but the shower head on the bathroom wall is not particularly practical. The friendly owner is also a schoolteacher and wannabe travel agent. His parents do the cooking and may volunteer to show you ancient Míng dynasty mansions, some of which are vast affairs home to dozens, all with the same family name. The odd slogan on the walls shows that the Cultural Revolution did reach here (*Zédōng sīixiǎng wàn suì!*—Long live [Máo] Zédōng thought!), but unlike in urban China, where the whole period is an embarrassment, no one could be bothered to erase them. The post office is in someone's front room. Chickens wander through the bank. It's desperately quiet—at least until dawn rouses a large population of cockerels, and the 6am, 7am, and 8am buses (one of which you'll want to catch) give blasts of the horn before departure.

The town's own *láng qiáo,* the **Yùwén Qiáo,** is a squarish, two-story houselike bridge, with a wooden superstructure built over a conventional stone semicircular arch. It's only 5 minutes from the hostel along a stone-flagged path, which quickly becomes no more than the lip of rice paddies. There's a rapidly rushing brown-and-white river a few feet below. The fields maintain the orderliness of the countryside, which is always in such contrast to the disorder of the cities; the iridescent green of the freshly sprouted rice and salad vegetables are arranged in neat rows. Peasants bent over paddies wear the stiff clothing woven from tree bark that gives them a slightly batlike appearance, topped with a pointed straw hat. Much of the hillside here is covered with a local fern that manages to look like a vast flock of green birds just taking flight. A wooden staircase partway across the bridge leads to the upper story, but this is locked. Beyond the stairs, behind panes of glass, are plaster gods with bowls of incense in front of them. An enticing stairway leads up the hillside from one end of the bridge, but at the other an unpaved road passes through the end of it. A concrete lip directs traffic, but there are huge dents and scratches in the ancient pillars, some of which are knocked off-center.

Sān Kuí, on the way to Zhōulǐng, is only 1¼ hours back. It's an unlovely small town ruined by hideous new construction. But it contains a *láng qiáo* larger than others yet seen. Beds go for ¥15 ($1.90) in hostels around the bus station, but it's best to move on after seeing the two bridges here. The first bridge, the **Xuēzhái Qiáo,** is a 5-minute *bèngbèngchē* ride (¥3/40¢) from the bus station. It is bizarrely located in surroundings of ramshackle modern drabness, which would make the bridge itself drab were it not for its flamboyant roof, deep skirts, and colorful ceramic fishes on the roof, tails up, spouting water to repel fire. The bridge launches itself off steep stone buttresses to either side, and is still in use.

The **Liúzhái Qiáo** is a ¥4 (50¢) ride (fee includes waiting time and return to the bus station) back past the bus station and onward about the same distance again (it would take a maximum of 30 min. to do all this on foot). When you can't go any farther due to the narrowness of the way, the driver directs you down a path past ancient houses where toothless old ladies are ankle-deep in chickens. Around past the edges of paddies, dragonflies dart at you and ducklings paddle amid the rice plants. The bridge, hidden behind a substantial three-story mud building, is only seen at the last moment. The most colorful yet, it has curly upturned eaves and resembles two gabled mansions with a horizontal two-story connecting section. The bridge is topped with yellow-bodied, blue-headed dragons with large pointed teeth and tails thrashing the air.

Dating from 1405, the bridge is a little ramshackle and hardly looks as if it's been restored at all, except for new stonework in a buttress at one end. Benches inside give you views across trickling waters to banana palms and rice paddies, sheds of mud brick, and elegantly precise dry-stone walls retaining the rice paddies. Only a 10-minute walk from the drop-off point, the bridge is completely beyond the range of the town's rather negative atmosphere.

To reach the **Běi Jiàn Qiáo** (also known as the Xià Qiáo, or lower bridge), return to the crossroads and turn left onto Sìshuǐ Zhōng Lù, following the canyonlike street around to the right. Just outside of town, a path down to the left leads along the edge of the river to the bridge, which stands at a confluence. Two vast old trees grow from the stone base on which some ancient housing sits; the trees almost seem to be holding up the bridge and houses. The red-skirted bridge has a separate central roof with sharply pointed upturned eaves, and on its ridge there's a face-off between two lively lime-green dragons. The complexity of the interior bracketing gives this away as a Qīng rather than Míng construction. Triple niches midway house a small Buddha figure. A petition in angry red characters (making them hostile to the Chinese eye) but in respectful language is addressed to every agency conceivable, asking them to halt construction of a dam that would damage this bridge. At press time, the petition had been up for more than a year—astonishing in a country where the ruling elite brooks no dissent, and where local officials mainly run things for their own benefit.

The **Mùgǒng Láng Qiáo (Wooden Arch Corridor Bridge),** also known as the Dōng Xī Qiáo (Bridge Over the East Stream) and Shàng Qiáo (Upper Bridge), is back in town and a short walk past the central crossroads within the built-up area. The broad spread of the eaves at its entrances still draws pedestrians to make the climb over the arch despite the horizontal road bridge directly alongside. The separate central roof is even more pronounced, each sharply upturned corner and each end of the ridge decorated with thrashing fish. Three interior niches are painted with dragons and *Chiling* (a Chinese version of the Chimera).

From the central crossroads there are two buses a day to **Xiǎo Cūn,** which pass by at around 6am and 11:30am. The 25km (15-mile) trip takes 1 hour and costs ¥8 ($1). Again, the bus will drop you at a crossroads. On Yuè Shān Xī Lù to the left is the **Ā Guó Fàndiàn** (© 0577/6763-5118), with a few clean beds with common bathroom, tiled floors, and fans. The rate is ¥20 ($2.50) per bed. Below is a popular restaurant with good food at low prices. The friendly owners are keen to promote knowledge of their local *láng qiáo,* one of which, the **Wénxīng Qiáo,** is indeed the most spectacular to be seen on this trip.

The bridge is reached by turning right out of the hotel, and left at the crossroads down Wángfèng Nán Lù. There's a lively market here on the 7th, 17th, and 27th of every lunar month, full of modern misses in see-through blouses, tight jeans, and gold high heels, with mobile phones, who seem to spring out of nowhere. Busy at 8am, it's all over by 11am.

Walk out of town for 2km (1¼ miles), until at the 5.5km marker stone you see a path down to the left which winds around the paddies' edges. The Wénxīng Qiáo is not a centipede, but a stretching cat. From steep stone steps the bridge makes a gradual rise, levels out, swoops to the top, and then drops steeply to the stone steps on the other side. As a result, the two-story center section with its turned-up eaves has a drunken tilt.

The central shrine seems to be fully active, and incense is lit to its three gods (responsible, from left to right, for land, the world, and domestic affairs) on the 1st and 15th of the each lunar month. You'll find a bamboo canister of sticks (*shén gōng pàn jí,* roughly "God impartially judges your luck" written on the outside) with which to tell your fortune. Shake the canister, pick a stick at random, read the number carved on the flattened end, and find the matching numbered couplet on the wall. Five signboards from different dates recount the shrine's repairs and who paid for them, which inadvertently tells you something about China's modern history: One is dated by the year of the then-reigning emperor, another suggests they don't know who's in charge, another dates from the 19th year of the republic, and finally, in 1987, the date is from the Gregorian calendar. Currencies change, and the characters go from traditional full form to the post-reform modern simplified form.

The bridge is busy on market day, with everyone from little old ladies going shopping, to wiry farmers carrying goods to sell on shoulder poles (ducks hanging upside down by their webbed feet), to young women in spangled shoes carrying umbrellas to shade themselves from the sun. (In New China no young woman wants to be mistaken for a peasant—not even a peasant woman.) Across the bridge is a small guardhouse; above it, a path to the right leads to a charming meadow above the bridge perfect for photography.

The **Dōng Yáng Qiáo** is down Yuè Shān Dōng Lù—turn right out of the hotel and proceed straight at the crossroad. The bridge is less than 3km (less than 2 miles) out of town—a three-wheeler out here will cost ¥3 (40¢), or with waiting time and a return trip, it will cost a maximum of ¥9 ($1.10). At the .9km stone after the 41km stone, there's a small turn to the left, from which a path alongside a stream leads left to the bridge. It's buzzed by fast-moving violet butterflies and lumbering orange ones, the 747s of the butterfly world.

Dating only from the 10th year of the republic (1921–22), the bridge is in complete contrast to its flamboyant neighbor but is of considerable charm. A narrow staircase rises parallel to the stream; turn right from it onto the short, level bridge, which has a higher central roof section and is supported by a stone pier midstream. No shrine or boards with names of donors here—the red characters stenciled on one wall mean, "It is prohibited to fish using electricity."

You can walk back to, or be dropped at, an area of ancient housing at the edge of town called **Xú Ào**. Its mid-Qīng wooden courtyard houses have remained almost completely undisturbed except by the occasional telephone and electricity pole and, in the past, by two fires—one 6 years ago, one 60 years ago. The dark wooden mansions sit on carefully assembled dry-stone bases and seem deserted except for the odd filament of wood smoke, washing hung out to dry, and recently bundled brushwood leaning against the walls of the courtyards, where ducklings wander. In neighboring fields, peasants have pulled the rice and now they're churning the fields with water-buffalo-drawn plows driven by rhythmic shouts and calls to turn the beast left and right.

Buses for **Tàishùn** pass through the crossroads every few minutes. The 36km (23-mile) trip takes 1 hour and costs ¥7.50 (90¢). The luxury buses to **Wēnzhōu** leave from **Tàishùn** at 8am, 9:10am, 1:30pm, and 2:20pm (© **0137/678-8822**). There are also sleeper services to **Hángzhōu**, **Shànghǎi**, **Níngbō**, and **Xiàmén**, all several hundred kilometers and a few centuries away.

5 Fúzhōu

Fújiàn Province, 436km (272 miles) S of Wēnzhōu, 310km (194 miles) N of Xiàmén

Fúzhōu is a more attractive city than Wēnzhōu to the north, but only just and there is not of a great deal of interest. It's a useful starting point for reaching Wǔyí Shān; otherwise, proceed south to Quánzhōu or north to Zhèjiāng Province.

One of the first five treaty ports, Fúzhōu had brief success trading principally tea. Foreign tea-tasters worked long, frantic days for 6 to 9 weeks during the tea-tasting season, and idled away much of their time for the rest of the year with alcohol and billiards. Even still, they had half of their salaries left, some of which they invested in the firms for which they worked and turned into small fortunes.

At the height of the tea trade, fortunes were quickly won and lost, and tea traders lived in substantial mansions, but by 1885 all was in decline. Still, the words *tea* in English, *thé* in French, *tè* in Italian, *té* in Spanish, and *tee* in German, all indicate that tea first reached them from Fújiàn, where the local language says *te*. The old-fashioned U.K. English slang *char*, Portuguese *chá*, and so on originated in Cantonese and ports farther south. *Note:* For Chinese translations of selected establishments listed in this section, please turn to appendix A.

ESSENTIALS

GETTING THERE Shuttle buses from the **airport** run 55km (34 miles) to a turning opposite the CAAC ticketing office, which is south of the city center on Wǔyī Zhōng Lù. The shuttles depart from 6am to 7pm and cost ¥20 ($2.50). Fúzhōu has connections to 43 mainland cities, plus Hong Kong, Macau, and Bangkok (twice weekly). Mainland destinations include Běijīng (seven to eight daily) Shànghǎi (one or two daily), Guǎngzhōu (four daily), and Xiàmén (two to five daily). The **CAAC** office (© **0591/8334-5988** domestic, or 0591/331-4957 international), open from 8am to 8pm, gives decent discounts when they're available and delivers tickets free of charge, but check prices with other agents. Bus nos. 36 and 37 from the city center stop outside.

There's nowhere in Fújiàn Province you can't reach more quickly by bus than by **train,** since the line goes several hundred kilometers inland before turning north or south, then has to travel back out to the coast again. Wǔyí Shān is an option, with four trains daily in each direction. There's a daily train to Shànghǎi, the K164 at 2:48pm (19 hr.; ¥379/$48 soft sleeper, but the number of tiresome peddlers suggests there may often be a premium to pay); and a daily train to Nánjīng West, the 2002 at 11:26am (24 hr.; ¥438/$55). There's a sleeper ticket office straight ahead as you enter the ticket hall (to the left of the station as you face it). It sells tickets up to 5 days in advance from 8am to noon and 3 to 5pm. Main ticket windows are open from 8am to 7pm. Ticket agencies in town typically want a ¥10 ($1.25) commission for local destinations (Wǔyí Shān, Xiàmén) and ¥30 ($3.75) for longer distances. Left luggage is on the left of the station forecourt as you leave.

Buses from Wēnzhōu in Zhèjiāng Province arrive at the **Chángtú Qìchē Běi Zhàn** on the north side of town (© **0591/8758-0118**) from 5:30am to 10:40pm. Connections to the north include Wēnzhōu (436km/272 miles; ¥115/$14 at 8:30am, ¥163/$20 sleeper bus at 6:15pm) and Hángzhōu (906km/565 miles; ¥260/$33 at 4pm). To the south, buses depart for Quánzhōu (13 departures 7am–7:20pm, ¥69/$8.60; and 11 departures on smaller buses 7:30am–5:40pm, ¥52/$15) and Xiàmén (310km/194 miles; every 20–30 min. 7am–7:20pm; ¥70–¥80/$8.75–$10). You can get a Mandarin speaker to call the Wēnzhōu bus operator directly at © **130/5775-8315.** The **South Bus Station** on Wǔyī Zhōng Lù, open from 5:30am to 5:30pm, has tickets to all the same destinations, plus to Wǔyí Shān (369km/231 miles; ¥81–¥103/$10–$13). But the most useful services are from an efficient private operation outside the Mǐn Jiāng Fàndiàn, the (wait for it) **Fújiàn Zhōngyǒu Mǐn Jiāng Gāosù Gōnglù Kèyùn Shǐfá Zhàn** at the junction of Wǔsì Lù and Hú Dōng Lù. Inside the ticket office, open from 6am to 11pm, are photographs of all the different buses, complete with destinations and prices: Xiàmén (57 departures 6:15am–11pm, which will also drop you at Quánzho]li]u) and beyond, to Guǎngzhōu and Shēnzhèn. There's one sleeper service to Hong Kong (5:30pm; ¥388/$49). For bookings call © **0591/8760-8848** (up to 7 days in advance). There's also a useful **air ticket agency** here (© **0591/8753-6250** domestic, or 0591/754-6815 international).

GETTING AROUND   Xiàlì and some Fùkāng **taxis** charge ¥7 (90¢) for 3km (1¾ miles), then ¥1.40 (20¢) per kilometer up to 5km (3 miles), and ¥2.10 (25¢) per kilometer thereafter. Santanas charge ¥8 ($1), ¥1.80 (25¢), and ¥2.70 (35¢) respectively. All taxis add 20% from 11pm to 5am. **Buses** charge a flat fare on entry (¥1/15¢, or ¥2/25¢ if air-conditioned).

VISITOR INFORMATION   For tourist complaints call © **0591/8760-1364.**

FAST FACTS

Banks, Foreign Exchange & ATMs   The main **Bank of China** (open 8am–5:45pm Mon–Fri; 8:30am–5pm weekends and holidays) is at Wǔsì Lù 136. There's an ATM outside the bank. Most other Bank of China ATMs in the city accept foreign cards, too. (If you are heading north to Zhèjiāng, note that there are almost no useful ATMs there whatsoever.)

Internet Access   There are plenty of Internet cafes, usually open 24 hours and charging ¥3 (40¢) per hour, which is a relief as the provincial library (227 Huadong Lù) does not have a computer in sight. The **Jīntài Wǎngbā** is centrally located on Jīntài Lù just east of Bāyīqī Běi Lù. Dial-up is © **8163.**

Post Office   The main post office (open 7:30am–7:30pm) is on the corner of Dōng Jiē and Bāyīqī Běi Lù.

Visa Extensions   Extensions are available at the **Provincial PSB** at Huálín Lù (© **0591/8709-3486**). Go to the office to the left of the gate to sign in, then cross to the right for the visa office (open Mon–Fri, 8am–noon and 3–6pm).

EXPLORING FÚZHŌU

Fúzhōu's attitude toward its **treaty port** history is ambivalent. The drive south down Bāyīqī Lù toward the Jiěfàng Bridge over the Mǐn River demonstrates this well, while it also indicates the threadbare nature of China's supposedly vast economic growth. South of the junction with Gōngyè Lù, the street narrows and there are ramshackle shophouses in wood, with the odd 100-year-old European-influenced building. On the east side, after a stretch of particularly fine higgledy-piggledy three-story wooden buildings, there's a sudden broadening of the street with halted construction to either side, then vast mansions with neoclassical porticoes and domes from mixed periods and out of scale with each other. There's shiny shopping at ground level, but it's deserted.

Just before the bridge there are even larger and more grotesque examples of petty theft from a Western architectural pattern book, including something that looks like it was supposed to turn into a large church before construction was once again halted.

"Méi yǒu qián!" says the taxi driver. "No money!" It's always like this in China, he complains. *"Kāi kāi tíng tíng, kāi kāi tíng tíng"*—stop and start, stop and start.

Beyond the bridge, old mansions, consulates, and other buildings of the former European residents still stand, including several churches and religious institutes. Some of the old buildings have been adapted for modern purposes, their spires, turrets, crenellations, porticoes, and pillars the models for the hideousness on the north side of the river. After crossing the bridge, take any climbing path that suits you into the labyrinth around **Yāntái Shān Gōngyuán (Beacon Hill Park).** Keep your eyes open for Home Counties chimneys behind high walls topped with barbed wire or bougainvillea.

WHERE TO STAY & DINE

As provincial capital, Fúzhōu has several Chinese five-star hotels, but you'd be better off staying at the new **Ramada Plaza.** The **Ramada (Měilún Huáměidá Guǎngchǎng Dàjiǔdiàn),** on the North Ring Road at Běi Huán Xī Lù 108 (© **0591/8788-3999;** fax 0591/8786-9613; www.ramadainternationalhotel.com), has 323 units with every modern convenience and a number of foreigners working where it matters, particularly in the restaurants. The Ramada's Plaza Café serves good Western and Asian buffets, and a Hong Kong chef in the hotel's Fortune Hall Cantonese restaurant ensures high standards there. Standard rooms cost from ¥500 ($63) and suites from ¥1,600 ($200), plus a 15% service charge, but they can be bargained well down.

The new 414-room **Fúzhōu Shangri-La (Fúzhōu Xiānggélǐlā Dàjiǔdiàn),** Xīn Quán Nán Lù 9 (© **0591/8798-8888;** fax 0591/8798-8798; slfz@shangri-la.com),

Early Morning Snacks

Be sure to get out in the early morning to taste a local specialty for breakfast called "guō biān hǔ," a soup made with rice powder with a mild oyster flavoring. Of course "yóu bǐng" or the flat bing (doughy cake) with vegetables and peanuts is great with the soup.

has all the luxuries that we have come to expect from this international chain and then some. This is perhaps the only place that you will be able to find nonsmoking rooms, a real luxury in a region dominated by chain-smoking neocapitalists.

Among the Chinese five-stars, the **Golden Resources International Hotel (Jīnyuán Guójì Dàjiǔdiàn),** Wēnquán Gōngyuán Lù 59 (© **0591/8708-8888;** fax 0591/8708-8999), opened in 2001, has vast and glitzy public areas and attentive staff with English speakers. Comfortably furnished guest rooms come with movie channels, piped drinking water in the bathrooms, and piped geothermally heated water in the bathtubs. The hotel is popular with businesspeople visiting the neighboring exhibition center. Standard rooms cost from ¥800 ($100), and suites cost from ¥1,380 ($172), plus a 15% service charge, with 30% discounts available.

The **Apollo Hotel (Ā Bō Luó Dàjiǔdiàn),** WǔyíZhōng Lù 132, (© **0591/ 8305-6789**), is the first drop-off point for the bus heading downtown from the airport making it perhaps the most useful hotel to visitors. Rack rates are posted at ¥500 to ¥600 ($62–$75) but this quickly drops to the ¥200-to-¥300 range ($25–$38) if you ask for a lower floor such as the 10th, even though the facilities are almost identical. Rooms are spacious and the beds comfortable. The staff in general is quite helpful, though those stationed at lobby travel agency are not. There is a huge Wal-Mart located just opposite the hotel, good for provisions for that next bus, train, or plane ride.

For those in a hurry for something familiar, there's a **McDonald's** and a **Pizza Hut** near the Jùchūn Yuán. A row of wannabe-Western bars on Wēnquán Gōngyuán Lù, opposite the Golden Resources Hotel, have Scottish, Wild West, and Harley Davidson themes.

6 Wǔyí Shān

Fújiàn Province, 369km (231 miles) NW of Fúzhōu, 364km (228 miles) SE of Nánchāng

The mountains of Wǔyí Shān are just as beautiful as anywhere in Yúnnán or Guǎngxī; in fact, choose the right time of year, get away from the domestic tourists, and you'll find one of the best places in China for hiking, climbing, and exploring. The resort area has a well-deserved reputation for rip-offs, but there are ways to avoid the scams and enjoy one of the most spectacular parts of China.

It's the resort area you'll want, rather than the town, and the airport and the railway station are between the two. The resort itself is an ugly sprawl of restaurants and guesthouses clustered alongside a highway that stretches back to the main town. Most of the hotels are on the east bank of the Chóngyáng Xī, with a little spillover onto the west bank, where the Fēngjǐngqū (scenic area) can be found. This is prime Chinese tourist territory, especially the "gànbù" variety—middle-aged office types that do not mind being herded around in Day-Glo baseball caps. Avoid summers, the weeklong public holidays at the beginning of May and October, and weekends between those two holidays. But in November, daytime temperatures are a pleasant 59°F (15°C), just right for walking, and the trees change color prettily. *Note:* For Chinese translations of selected establishments listed in this section, please turn to appendix A.

ESSENTIALS

GETTING THERE   The **airport** is served by flights from Běijīng (at least one daily), Fúzhōu (once daily), Guǎngzhōu (at least one daily), Shànghǎi (two daily), and Xiàmén (once daily). There are occasional flights from other cities. Bus no. 6 passes the airport entrance and runs the 8km (5 miles) to the resort for ¥1 (15¢). The **railway station** is a little farther from the resort, also passed by bus no. 6, and three-wheelers run a shuttle the few hundred meters to the main road. There are useful train services from Hángzhōu (509km/318 miles; ¥205/$25 soft sleeper), Nánchāng (364km/221 miles; ¥159/$20), Jiǔjiāng (499km/312 miles; ¥205/$25), Shànghǎi (710km/444 miles; ¥276/$34), Xiàmén (590km/369 miles; ¥232/$29), Quánzhōu (593km/371 miles; ¥232/$29), and other cities. Ticket offices are open from 3:30 to 5:30am, 8:30am to noon, 1:30 to 5:30pm, and 8:30 to 11:30pm. Agents in Wǔyí Shān want a ¥35 ($4.40) commission for rail tickets.

GETTING AROUND   Within the resort, everything is walkable. **Bus** no. 6 is the most useful of all; coming from Wǔyí Shān town, it passes both the railway station and the airport, runs through the middle of the resort down Chóngyáng Dào, turns west along Wàngfēng Dào, crosses the Chóngyáng Xī (river), and continues to Xīng Cūn. Minibuses in fairly good condition with air-conditioning cost a little more, but rides are typically ¥1 (15¢). *Miàndī* (minivans) to most destinations are ¥2 (25¢) if you use them like buses, with others hopping on and off; you can use them to get to Xīngcūn for the *zhúfá* (bamboo rafts), to get to the airport, or to get to the railway station. Bus no. 5 runs to the railway station when trains are scheduled, but not frequently. *Sānlúnchē* three-wheelers that charge ¥1 (15¢) are everywhere but they do not understand that visitors might want to walk anywhere. If you try to take one any distance, they will be straight onto one of their taxi friends to take over. It is generally assumed that you want to get wherever you are going as quickly as possible, when really the three-wheelers offer the chance to see and hear nature up close, something that most domestic tourists miss as they zip from sight to sight in their air-conditioned coaches.

FAST FACTS

Banks, Foreign Exchange & ATMs   The **Bank of China** (open 8am–5:30pm), with an ATM outside, is at Sān Gū Jiē.

Internet Access   There are *wǎngbā* (open 8am–midnight; ¥2–¥4/25¢–50¢ per hour) in back streets south of Wàngfēng Dào. As you walk east from the river, look for the *wǎngbā* characters on your left.

Post Office   The post office (open 7:50am–9pm summer; 8am–5:30pm winter) is on Wàng Fēng Lù.

WǓYÍ SHĀN FĒNGJǏNGQŪ

The scenic area spreads across the river west of the resort, and is best appreciated either from the top of one of the peaks or from a bamboo raft *(zhúfá or zhúpái)* on **Jiǔ Qǔ Xī (Nine Bend Stream)**.

There's a constant stream of buses (¥1/15¢) and minivans (¥2/25¢) from Chóngyáng Dào or Wàngfēng Lù to the village of **Xīng Cūn**; they drop you off either in the village center or at the dock itself. If you are dropped off in the center, fork right, follow the road to the left, and take the first major right turn down toward the river. The ticket office is down on the right, about 5 minutes' walk altogether. The overpriced *zhúfá* depart in groups intermittently between 7:30am and 4pm. Tickets are on sale about 20 minutes before each departure; they cost ¥100 ($13) plus an optional ¥1 (15¢) for insurance.

The river ride of about 9.5km (6 miles) takes an hour and 40 minutes, a lot of it right next to the main highway. The river is only a meter deep in some parts, and is clear enough to let you see the bottom. It's at its highest in July, and if it rises to a 2m (5½-ft.) height, trips are suspended.

The scenery is a slightly scaled-down version of that around Guìlín, but more interesting due to the tilted strata which give the cliffs the look of a sandwich with everything on it. Various rocks are said to resemble an elephant trunk, a turtle, a frog, and two lions playing with a ball, but you'd never be able to say which was which without assistance. In common with the Yángzǐ trip, there are cliff-side burial places. Two large caves high up, which are supposed to contain 3,800-year-old tombs along with some wooden remains, can be seen protruding from the cliffs, more easily visible than those elsewhere. The river winds sinuously around its nine bends, bird song echoes between the cliffs, the metal tips of the bamboo poles rattle against the river bottom, flights of widgeon whir past, and there's the occasional brilliant flash of a kingfisher. Some stiller water is supposed to run deep indeed—down to 28m (92 ft.).

The disembarkation point is just before the river's confluence with the Chóngyáng Xī, in manicured gardens a short walk from the base of **Dà Wáng Fēng.** You have the option of returning to the road to flag down a passing bus back to the resort, or you can walk towards the peak past various tawdry shopping opportunities and purchase one of two *tào piào.* One of the tickets is for the immediate area, which includes the two most commonly climbed peaks; it's valid for 2 days and costs ¥62 ($7.75). The other ticket offers wider access around the scenic area from 6am to 8pm.

Climbing **Dà Wáng Fēng** officially takes 1½ hours, but it can be scaled by the moderately fit in an hour. At the top, the views are principally over the confluence of the rivers and the not particularly attractive sprawl of the resort. As you climb, you have several choices of route, which all lead eventually to the top; the routes include two horizontal galleries cut into the rock, the higher of which involves slightly less bending. It can be slippery when wet. The lower stairways wind wonderfully, but in some cases they are only wide enough for one—awkward when you encounter tour groups. At some points, the only thing that will catch you if you fall is a stand of bamboo.

You'll probably want to climb **Tiānyóu Shān,** farther east and included in your ticket, on another day. The turnoff is about halfway to Xīng Cūn, and the entrance to the mountain about 5km (3 miles) from the resort. A *miàndī* will bring you here for ¥10 ($1.25), dropping you a 10- to 15-minute walk from the gate. If you're fit, the climb will not take more than about 30 minutes.

The slogan "If you haven't climbed Tiānyóu Shān, you haven't seen Wǔyí Shān" is much bandied about, and this is the one peak all the tour groups climb, mostly in the morning—so leave it until the afternoon. The paths are more solid, are broader, and have more handholds than the paths of Wǔyí Shān. Views are pretty, and you look down to the loop of the river's fifth and sixth bends, around which might drift some rafts. Halfway up, a pretty waterfall, multithreaded and glued to the cliff face, moves in slow motion. Near the top are a house built for Chiang Kai-shek's wife, Soong Mei-ling, and a flat open space with teahouses. As you jostle your way to the top, the views show you why you should consider extending your stay—the peak opposite also has a staircase snaking up it, but no sign of modern concrete additions, and no people.

WHERE TO STAY

Hotels are legion (more than 60 in the resort area alone), most of them the elevator-free four-story kind. Most date from a building boom in 1995, but others are just 2 or 3 years old, and more are going up all the time. The resort is very busy at Spring Festival (Chinese New Year) and during the first weeks of May and October. But on weekdays for the remainder of the May-to-October period, supply still outstrips demand, and you can pay half price. Outside those times you need not pay more than a third of the first asking price. Almost all the hotels have two or three stars; in addition to the choices below, glance into a few others. Avoid those with "beauty parlors" too full of beauties and those with karaoke. Although temperatures are well above freezing even in December, make sure that your hotel has the heat turned on and has hot water 24 hours during low season.

Bǎodǎo Dàjiǔdiàn   Centrally located next to the bank, this property has recently been upgraded to four-star standing, with an odd circular central atrium that allows the wail of karaoke to drift up from the basement. The lobby is full of furniture carved from tree trunks, but the guest rooms are less imaginative. The hotel has expanded along the main street and now has even more rooms and facilities than before.

Wàngfēng Lù. ✆ **0599/523-4567**. Fax 0599/525-5555. 220 units. ¥780 ($48) single; ¥880 ($110) standard room; from ¥1,800 ($225) suite. 60% discount off season. AE, DC, MC, V. **Amenities:** 2 restaurants; business center; game rooms; conference facilities; forex. *In room:* A/C, TV, fridge.

Jīn Gǔ Yuán Da Jiǔdiàn   One of the newest hotels in town (opened May 2005), this three-star property has been decorated in a sophisticated, modern style—modern for Wǔyí Shān at least. The staff is a friendly bunch, but do not expect any English to be spoken. The location is close to the center of the resort and currently offers the best value around.

Dà Wàngfēng Lù. ✆ **0599/523-9888**. Fax 0599/523-5866. 52 units. ¥480–¥690 ($60–$86) standard room; ¥1,698 ($213) suite. 70% discount off season; 40% otherwise. No credit cards. **Amenities:** Restaurant. *In room:* A/C, TV, fridge.

Wǔyí Shānzhuāng (Wǔyí Mountain Villa) ✿   The resort's most prestigious hotel is just across the Chóngyáng Xī, in a peaceful location at the foot of the Dà Wáng Fēng. It's a collection of chalet-style buildings set around well-maintained gardens, the newest of which is rated four stars. One restaurant overlooks a pool, which is seen through a waterfall that runs off the roof. The first choice for visiting party officials, with photos of various Communist Party leaders all over the walls, this kind of hotel tends to rest on its laurels. This is certainly true here, where service is poor unless you arrive in a cavalcade of red flag limousines.

Wǔyí Gōng. ✆ **0599/525-1888**. Fax 0599/525-2567. 167 units. www.wysvilla.com ¥888 ($111) standard room; ¥988 ($125) standard room in new wing; ¥1,388–¥2,888 ($174–$360) suite. 30% discount in off season. AE, DC, MC, V. **Amenities:** 3 restaurants; teahouse; small outdoor pool; sauna; tour and ticket desk; forex; limited room service; massage. *In room:* A/C, TV, fridge, hair dryer, safe.

WHERE TO DINE

Restaurants in tourist areas like this typically offer low-quality cuisine at extortionate prices; Wǔyí Shān is no exception. All the restaurants have the same exotic displays of mushrooms, snakes, and bee larvae as well as standard meat and vegetables. Proprietors are especially keen to take advantage of rich but scarce foreigners. We only met one other non-Chinese during our entire stay, a Chicagoan who was beating himself up for letting this resort of conmen and tricksters turn him into an angry, "ugly American,"

Tips Cheap Eats on the Street

The cheapest and probably the best food can be found at a handful of *yóu zhá* stalls outside the Bǎodǎo Hotel. These nocturnal street eateries, frequented mainly by local foot-massage girls, offer a wide range of pan-fried meat and vegetables on kabob sticks. The small pumpkin cakes are delicious and fried banana with ketchup seems to be a popular if strange local specialty.

hardly surprising when he had just been charged ¥450 ($56) for a simple meal that would have been overpriced at $45.

Wǔyí Shān resort is not yet ready for overseas visitors. There are no English menus and Westerners are seen as money trees to be shaken endlessly, rather than guests to be looked after. This is a shame because the mountains are definitely some of the most spectacular in the country, but returning to the resort area in the evenings is a tribulation that most travelers could do without. The most comfortable dining is inside hotels, overpriced and of modest, if acceptable, quality. (Most three-star hotels charge under ¥100/$13 for a meal for two.)

SIDE TRIPS FROM WŪYÍ SHĀN

The Wǔyí mountains deserve a lot more time than most people give them, usually because they tire quickly of the mercenary resort, or the endless streams of tourists at the main attractions. Independent travelers are so unusual that incredulous locals will constantly ask, "Ň shì yí gè rén ma?" ("Are you traveling alone?"). Following are two memorable day trips.

DÀ HÓNG PÀO

For ¥5 (65¢) you can hire a three-wheeler to take you to the small parking lot just below the stone Buddha; then walk the last 5 minutes up to the ticket office. For ¥22 ($2.75), you can follow the official route to visit three small tea bushes, known as Dà Hóng Pào, which purportedly yield the rarest and most expensive tea in China. When you actually arrive at the trees you may walk past them, as I did, without even noticing—rather disappointing after treks up seemingly endless flights of steps and back down deep terraced gorges. At the bottom of the stairs that lead back up to the tea trees, look for a sign that points out an alternative route to the water curtain cave (Shuǐ Lián Dòng), as well as the intriguing words NON TOUR ROUTE. *This* is where the real adventure begins. The path is far from virgin as the plastic bags and empty bottles quickly attest, but after a 15-minute stroll you will be rewarded with a hidden valley, draped at one end by a splashing ribbon of water cascading down 30m (98 ft.) into an icy cold rock pool. The path has just about disappeared by this point, but old campfires show that you are not the first one; you'll probably have to try a few routes across the bare rocks to get to the flowing water, but I recommend that you persevere and jump in. I was exhilarated when I finally made it to the base of what I quickly christened Frommer's Falls.

A number of paths continue up through the small tea plantations, each one almost begging to be explored. Along the way are caves, waterfalls, and the occasional tea farmer to greet. The paths are sturdy rock steps and are sometimes carved into the very cliff faces themselves. All the time new vistas and views appear, each one seemingly more spectacular than the last.

Backtrack to the NON TOUR ROUTE sign and head for the water curtain cave. The path forks, one way heading to the cave the other passing China's greediest cold drinks vendor, selling bottles of water at 10 kuài ($1.25) each. Continue toward the cave and the path will deposit you at the rear of the newly constructed Ever Happy Temple (Tiān Xīng Yǒng Lè), populated with even more grabby vendors, this time posing as monks. Follow the stairs that lead down to the parking lot and ticket office, and you have inadvertently discovered a sneaky back entrance where you can avoid the exorbitant ticket prices.

WŬYÍ SHĀN VIRGIN FOREST

About 48km (30 miles) east of Wǔyí Shān, past the village of Xīngcūn, is the so called Virgin Forest. A moto (motorbike) will take you out through the uninspiring farmland, past hastily constructed water wheels and a mini hydroelectric station for ¥10 or ¥20 ($1.25 or $2.50). There are signs for Lóng Chuán, but bear right and follow signs for the Virgin Forest (Yuánshǐ Sēnlín Gōngyuán); adventurous travelers will be rewarded with an unpaved road that follows a boulder-strewn river through deep, wooded gorges. Despite the name, you'll pass a few construction crews, making this area ready for package tourists some time in the future. Most of the trees are still relatively young and it is easy to imagine how areas like this were devastated during the Great Leap Forward. Now, 1,000 shades of green surround bubbling rapids, punctuated by rocks of every size from small pebbles to boulders the size of small houses. Trickling waterfalls line the road every 90m (300 ft.) and wildlife abounds, with more species of bird than a Cantonese restaurant. Walk for about 90 minutes until you come across a quarry that scars this otherwise magnificent landscape and scramble across the rocks to one of the miniature beaches for a bit of lunch and a paddle. The clear mountain water is bracing to say the least. Or perch yourself up on one of the 20-ton boulders (as I did while writing this!), forget that this is China, and simply enjoy nature at her very best. The road continues upstream, but that pleasure I shall leave for you to discover by yourself and perhaps the next edition. For more information, call ✆ **0599/510-8155** or 0599/511-3055; or write slgy@yahoo.com.cn.

SHOPPING

Various gift shops around town sell mountain produce such as dried roots, berries, and mushrooms, and specialist shops sell supposedly medicinal products (yes, including snake oil), but everything is priced ridiculously. When I inquired about a painting I picked up in Guǎngzhōu for ¥50, the guy took one look at me and asked for ¥5,000.

7 Quánzhōu ✪

Fújiàn Province, 593km (371 miles) SE of Wǔyí Shān, 109km (68 miles) N of Xiàmén

Quánzhōu was once Zaytun, "one of the two greatest havens in the world for commerce," according to Marco Polo. "Twice as great as Bologna," said Franciscan friar Odoric da Pordenone, who was in China from 1323 to 1327. "The harbour of Cìtóng is one of the greatest in the world—I am wrong; it is *the* greatest. I have seen there about an hundred first-class junks together; as for small craft, they were past counting," said Moroccan Ibn Battuta, who visited the area in 1345 to 1346. The Franciscan bishop of Zaytun wrote of Genoese merchants in 1326, and the city had other foreigners, including many Arabs.

Quánzhōu

Bus Station
Bank
Police
Post Office

ACCOMMODATIONS ■
Jiàn Fú Shāng Wù Jiǔdiàn (Jian Fu Business Hotel) **12**
建福商务酒店

Quánzhōu Hángkōng Jiǔdiàn (Xiàmén Airlines Quánzhōu Hotel) **10**
泉州航空酒店

Quánzhōu Jiǔdiàn **11**
泉州酒店

DINING ◆
Háokèlái Niúpái (Houcaller Beefsteak) **7**
豪客来牛排

Měicān Yì Tiáo Jiē **13**
美餐一条街

Number 2 Bodhi Food (Pútí Zhāi) **3**
菩提斋

Qīng Qí Shén **9**
清其神

Shàngdǎo Kāfēi **11**
上岛咖啡

ATTRACTIONS ●
Guāndì Miào **10**
关帝庙

Kāiyuán Sì **2**
开元寺

Luòyáng Qiáo **5**
洛阳桥

Maritime Museum (Hǎiwài Jiāotōng Shǐ Bówùguǎn) **4**
海外交通史博物馆

Mùou Bówùguǎn (Puppet Museum) **8**
木偶博物馆

Quánzhōu Museum (Quánzhōu Bówùguǎn) **1**
泉州博物馆

Statue of Zhèng Chénggōng **6**
郑成功

Tiānhòu Gōng **12**
天后宫

But after the Míng expulsion of the Mongol Yuán dynasty in 1368, China gradually closed itself up, and by the time of Europe's next contact, via the Portuguese in the 16th century, Zaytun had withered. In the 19th and 20th centuries, while almost all its neighbors became treaty ports with resident foreigners and trading, Quánzhōu was overlooked.

Today Quánzhōu's center has been overtaken by a different kind of commerce, mainly cheap sneakers and plastic sandals that smell like mustard gas. The suburbs are filled with factories and white-tiled blocks of apartments. The downtown area is even more depressing, with Wēnlíng Nán Lù, the main drag, consisting primarily of karaoke clubs interspersed with sleazy short-time hotels, along with a few large brothels thinly disguised as hotels. That said, Quánzhōu's interesting history is now receiving more of the attention it deserves, with two new excellent museums and a host of attractions to see outside the town.

ESSENTIALS

GETTING THERE   The nearest **airport** is at Xiàmén, 40km (25 miles) away, and many bus services there pick up and drop off at its entrance. The railway line down to Quánzhōu is new, and the **railway station** is in the northeast suburbs. Bus nos. 19 and 23 run from the railway station to the center of town. Train tickets are on sale from 6:30 to 11:30am, 1:30 to 5pm, and 6:30 to 8:30pm. Trains to Zhèjiāng and elsewhere in coastal Fújiàn have to perform long loops. There are no longer any sleeper trains for Wǔyí Shān, for that you have to travel to Xiàmén, but the early riser can enjoy the winding mountain line by taking the K955 at 6:32am and arriving at 4:53pm (K9856 and K955: 594km/368 miles; ¥149/$19 hard sleeper, ¥232/$29 soft sleeper).

The main bus station, the **Kèyùn Xīn Zhàn,** is full of yelling louts and has buses to Wǔyí Shān (but train is better); to Xiàmén (20 departures 6:35am–5:40pm; ¥19–¥20/$2.30–$2.40; luxury bus ¥32/$4); and to Fúzhōu (12 departures 8:05am–5:25pm; ¥34–¥41/$4.20–$5). There are also sleeper buses to Jiāngxī destinations, Tàishùn, Wēnzhōu, Shàoxīng, and Hángzhōu. Some express buses to Xiàmén drop off passengers at the airport entrance. Some luxury services from and to Fúzhōu terminate next to the **Huáqiáo Dàshà,** as do luxury buses to Shēnzhèn (© 0595/2228-7158) and a daily bus to Guǎngzhōu and Zhūhǎi for Macau (© 0139/6022-9688). The same Huáqiáo Dàshà office has tickets for **flights** from Xiàmén (© 0595/2218-2573).

GETTING AROUND   While most youngsters seem to have bicycles with strange plastic spokes, older motorcyclists will beep at you and wave spare helmets until you want to hit them. Jetta **taxis** are ¥6 (75¢) for 2km (1¼ miles), then ¥1.60 (20¢) per kilometer up to 4km (2½ miles), then ¥1.80 (25¢) per kilometer up to 30km (19 miles), then ¥2 (25¢) per kilometer up to 50km (31 miles), and after that, ¥2.20 (30¢) per kilometer. At night, from 11pm to 5am, rates begin at ¥1.80 (25¢) per kilometer. To get to the suburbs, **buses** charge a flat fare of ¥1 (15¢) on entry; buses without air-conditioning but with conductors charge ¥2 (25¢).

VISITOR INFORMATION   For complaints, call © 0595/2227-4888.

FAST FACTS

Banks, Foreign Exchange & ATMs   The main branch of the **Bank of China** (8–11am and 2:30–6pm) is in Fēngzé Jiē just west of the Xiàmén Airlines Hotel. Counter 14 handles checks and credit card withdrawals; it also handles cash exchanges during the same hours. ATMs at branches around town all accept foreign cards.

Internet Access   The **Dàdì Wǎngbā** (open 8am–3am; ¥2–¥3/25¢–40¢ per hour) is just east of the PSB on Dōng Lù. The **Huánqiú Wǎngbā** is at Zhuàngyuán Jiē 127, and another *wǎngbā* is opposite it at no. 138. Both are full of chain-smoking youngsters hurling obscenities at each other. A quieter alternative, with two dozen or so PCs, is the public library at Dōnghú Lù 752 (open 8–11:30am and 2:30–10pm; ¥2/25¢ per hour). Dial-up is © 8163.

Post Office   The main post office (open 8am–8pm) is at Wēnlíng Běi Lù 209, at the junction of Jiǔyī Lù.

Visa Extensions   Extensions are harder to obtain here than in most places. The **PSB** on Dōng Hú Lù (© **0591/2218-0323;** open Mon–Fri 8–11am and 3–6pm) requires evidence of the possession of $100 per day, for a single extension of up to 30 days.

EXPLORING THE CITY

Quánzhōu has its fair share of the hideous white-tiled buildings that infest most cities; in fact, the tallest building in the city is already derelict, and new chunks of concrete masonry litter the sidewalk below every day—well worth avoiding. Other tour books drone on about saintly tombs and Arab mosques but the really interesting spots are to be found elsewhere.

Kāiyuán Sì   This large and once-celebrated temple suffered terrible destruction in the 20th century, but its large main courtyard dotted with stelae is pleasant and shady. Gaudy apsaras (female spirts of nature) support the beams of its main hall, which holds five Buddhas, behind which the 18 *luóhàn* stand on either side of a Guānyīn. In a hall farther back, deeper than it is wide, a three-tiered terrace supports a seated figure on a "thousand Buddha"–studded lotus; a canopy overhead is carved with clouds and gilded birds. To either side of stairs on four sides are large bug-eyed figures with raised fists. The ceiling is fantastically ornate, with layers of brackets in ever-diminishing sizes to a central circle.

Farther west, a 1,300-year-old mulberry is locked away for its own protection. The registers of a plump squat stone pagoda of five stories is carved with figures out of a solid chunk of granite; its solid stone brackets imitating wood are home to generations of swallows. There's another, similar pagoda on the east side.

176 Xī Jiē. Admission ¥4 (50¢). 8am–6pm.

Maritime Museum (Hǎiwài Jiāotōng Shǐ Bówùguǎn) ★★★   The newly constructed Maritime Museum, east of the library on Dōng Hú Lù is one of the most interesting museums in China, especially for anybody that already has a penchant for the sea. The first floor displays the sort of ranting xenophobia that is par for the course in most Chinese museums, with exhibits that explain how Táiwān was "recovered from the greedy grasp of Dutch invaders" and how Quánzhōu was infested with Japanese pirates, spitefully described as "pygmy bandits." The real gems are on the second floor: a priceless collection of hundreds of intricate scale models representing the whole of China's seafaring history. Each ship was handmade by master craftsman Chén Yánhóng, and the level of detail is extraordinary. Highlights include imperial warships, caterpillar-like articulated vessels, and battleships that conceal secret launches. The English labels are better than you might expect although as always the Chinese claim to have invented anything worth inventing long before the West. In this particular field, this includes anchors, rudders, watertight compartments, paddlewheels, and even catamarans. Despite this pomposity, the models are of excellent quality and nobody leaves unimpressed.

Back on the first floor directly below the seafaring exhibit visitors will find a collection of carved stonework, dating from the peak of Quánzhōu's heyday. The displays are a lot less accessible for the casual visitor than the model ships but their significance is attested to by the fact that UNESCO funds are being used to help save these historical artifacts. Some of the inscriptions are carved in Syriac script, the written form of Aramaic, the language that was supposedly spoken by Jesus. During my visit, the stones were being examined in detail by academics from Cambridge in England and

Macquarie in Australia. Five-hundred years ago, this place was already a magnet for travelers of the world. Even though he ended up on the other side of the world, Columbus risked everything to find this already mythical city that had been made famous long before in the seven voyages of Sinbad, the tales of Marco Polo, and the mystical Christendom of Prester John.

Dōnghú Lù. © 0595/2210-0561. Admission ¥10 ($1.25). Tues–Sun 8:30am–5:30pm.

Quánzhōu Museum (Quánzhōu Bówùguǎn) The brand-new Minnan-style Quánzhōu Museum is so new that you may be the only visitor in the place. The museum provides the usual political propaganda, but this is made up for by a very interesting *National Geographic*–style documentary, describing the *Tàixīng* wreck and how treasure hunters salvaged more than 350,000 pieces of porcelain from the ocean floor.

During my visit, not all exhibits were open and the shops were just in the process of stocking their shelves, but one item caught my eye, the *Guide to Quánzhōu Tourism*, a strangely translated book that talks about "interflow between Quánzhōu and the alien countries." Although the descriptions are very brief and overly official, at just ¥15 ($1.90) it is a useful book to have if you plan to explore this area further.

Note: At press time, the exit on to the ring road had not yet been completed, so you may find yourself forced to walk a good 10 minutes back into town before you can hail a cab.

North section of Xīhú Lù. © 0595/2228-3914. Admission ¥10 ($1.25). 9am–5:30pm.

Luòyáng Qiáo At the edge of the northeastern suburbs, this 11th-century bridge is reached by a short walk from the terminus of bus no. 19, up winding Fèngguān Jiē, through a village of mixed modern and ancient housing, down to where the bridge runs for 1.1km (¾ mile) across stinking mud flats.

Built between 1053 and 1059, this is no technological marvel. It consists of 46 spans of 11m (36-ft.) beams between large, boat-shaped piers. But its length of 1,200m (3,936 ft.) is impressive, and it weaves slightly on its way from bank to bank as if strong tides have succeeded in dragging some of its massive piers out of place. There are guardian figures at the entrance and ancient stelae on an island a short way across, where there's also a memorial to the bridge's architects. The mud flats are alive with fiddler crabs, and farmers sink thigh-deep in the foul-smelling ooze checking nets and slabs of stone that attract the mollusks; the crabs are said to act as a living glue within the crevices of the piers, holding them together.

Admission ¥2 (25¢). Bus: no. 19 from center (passes new bus station, Tombs of the Islamic Saints, and railway station) to terminus at Qiáo Nán (about 40 min.).

Statue of Zhèng Chénggōng At 38m (125-ft.) high, 42m (138-ft.) long, and weighing in at 500 tons, this huge monument to Chinese propaganda is visible from just about any part of the city. Standing atop a mountain beyond the northern suburbs, this Míng pirate routed the Dutch from Táiwān and unlike pirates of other nationalities, has been a national hero ever since. The best way to get to this massive monolith is as a side trip on the way back from Luòyáng Bridge. Once the general comes into view, jump off the bus and hail a moto to take you the rest of the way for ¥5 or ¥10 (65¢ or $1.25). Up close, however, the monster statue of the great patriot on horseback is rather disappointing, being of a hollow metal-plate construction rather than local stone as one might have expected. The views of Quánzhōu are unbeatable, but standing below the giant stallion, try not to look up unless you want an eyeful of enormous equine testicles.

Qīng Yuán Shān   This hilly spot boasts nine Buddhist and Daoist statues, more Islamic tombs, and inscriptions (as befits a seaport) praying for wind. The Lǎo Jūn Yán, a Sòng dynasty statue of Daoism's semimythical founder, Lǎozǐ, at the base of the hill near the ticket office, is almost a symbol of the town—a benevolent, balding, bewhiskered, and big-eared seated figure, broader (8m/26 ft.) than he is high, and of considerable charm.

Admission ¥15 ($1.90) Lǎozǐ statue only, ¥30 ($3.75) for all but the statue, ¥40 ($5) whole park. 5am–6pm. Bus: no. 3, 15 min. from center to terminus (¥2/25¢).

Mùǒu Bówùguǎn (Puppet Museum)   While the idea of a puppet museum may sound a little dull, Quánzhōu is full of surprises. I was initially inspired to visit this place after seeing a short puppetry documentary, known locally as "jiā lǐ opera" at the Quánzhōu Museum. The marionettes here have up to 30 strings and can be manipulated in the most fascinating ways. Have you ever seen a puppet disrobe or pour itself a drink? There are some useful captions in English and Chinese. Quánzhōu now hosts an annual puppetry festival that attracts practitioners from all over the world. Check locally for more details.

24 Tóngzhēng Xiàng, behind the Ashab Mosque. Free admission. 9am–6pm.

A WALK AROUND THE WALLS OF CHÓNGWǓ 🏯🏯

A little over 50km (30 miles) from Quánzhōu, Chóngwǔ has one of the best-preserved city walls in China. Measuring 2.5km (1½ miles) long and dating from 1387, it is not yet the victim of much official recognition, and consequently is more natural than walls at Píngyáo (p. 235).

The bus ride there departs from the main bus station every 30 minutes from 7am, with the last one heading back at 6pm; the fare is ¥9 ($1). The often crowded minibus takes an indirect 90-minute route through towns and villages almost entirely devoted to stonemasonry. Stone is the traditional building material in this area and is still used in preference to concrete; stacked beams everywhere look like a rough-hewn giant's Jenga tower. Houses are blockish, plain, and flat-roofed, the occasional external stairway giving them a decidedly Middle Eastern look, reinforced by the tendency of local women to wear headscarves.

Before you even arrive at the old town, it is worth getting off the bus and walking the last part of the way to see the amazing output of all the local **stone factories.** Alight at the roundabout with the three laughing Buddhas (known in Chinese as Mí Lè Fó) and the huge triangular billboard. From there on in, not only do statues of every description line the road, but the front lots of the factories have thousands more. Apart from a complete pantheon of Asian deities, there are local celebrities of every age, right up to modern times with Mickey Mouse, Pokemon, and Hello Kitty. Many of the designs are semi-abstract and some even down right erotic. Unfortunately, this wonderland of stonework may make the statue park a little drab when you finally arrive at Chóngwǔ.

Modern Chóngwǔ, reached after 1½ hours, is typically unlovely, but walk straight from the bus terminus, and where the road swings right, go straight on up the narrower street of small shops. Continue uphill until you arrive in less than 10 minutes at the modest east gate of the old walls, its enceinte still intact. Through that gate, turn immediately right into an alley called Cuì Shí Xiàng that is barely wider than your shoulders, and find steps up. Turn right and walk clockwise.

The wall is very solid, with varied construction styles much less regular than walls elsewhere. It's sometimes overgrown, but accessible. At each gate in the wall the enceinte is entered from one side with a turn forcing you to pass through the wall itself. You can look down on the passage of beeping motorbikes, and on meat sold from open trestles in the shade. Elsewhere, geese, ducks, and hens in backyards look up startled at your passage.

This makes an interesting contrast to other old towns such as Lìjiāng and Dàlí, where the whole layout has been expanded to make it more accessible for tourists. Inside Chóngwǔ, conditions are cramped and claustrophobic. The stench of open sewers pervades the narrow alleys and yet motorbikes scream though the dark confines pinning pedestrians up against the walls, assuming that they manage to sidestep the sewers. Here is an authentic view of what really happens when an ancient Chinese town meets the 21st century head on.

After the north gate the wall has been cleared a little and rises to views of the sea across the roofscape. There's a modern statue of a heroic defender looking out to sea, and a little temple on the wall topped with marvelous dragons with green bodies and red tails and faces. Firecracker residue and incense ash indicate the temple's popularity. Another temple below is worth descending to see, its walls papered with lists of contributors to its restoration, and its hall again topped with rampant polychromic dragons.

Below the east gate, a group of bad modern statuary looks out over broad sand beaches, and there's a modern lighthouse at the southeast corner. Actually the **statue park** (¥25/$3) is worth a visit as it contains a truly bizarre sight, the 24 virtues of filial piety. Taken from a collection of popular Chinese folk tales available in every bookstore, the statues are great examples of Asian weirdness. Madam Táng breastfeeds her grandmother for she has no teeth, Guō Jù buries his own son alive because he is too poor to feed him. I'll leave you to check out the tiger strangling and dung eating for yourself.

On the south side there's more beach, neat topiary-lined pathways, and sun shades. At the south gate, the **Nán Mén Guāndì Miào** is a new but remarkably elaborate temple, its stone pillars carved fantastically into dragons. The ceiling inside is finely carved and gilded, and interior pillars are fabulously carved with birds and figures giving great liveliness to dead stone.

A ticket office at the base of the gate is unmanned but would attempt to charge ¥2 (25¢) to visitors entering from the beach side if anyone could be bothered. The exterior of the wall here is bearded with creeper, and beyond it are cold-drink and ice-cream sellers, sly seafood restaurants, horse rides, lookout points labeled as suitable for photography, and more bad statuary.

The final section is more overgrown but there's a clear path, where you scatter crickets underfoot while ducking under branches.

WHERE TO STAY

Hotels in Quánzhōu are unexceptional, and many at the three- and four-star levels are overpriced considering their dowdiness. Much renovation and new construction are going on, and there may be more choices by the time you arrive.

Jiàn Fǔ Shāngwù jiǔdiàn (Jiàn Fǔ Business Hotel)   Renamed and redecorated since the first edition, the combination of the unbeatable location and "favorable" prices, make this excellent value for money. On the downside, like most Quánzhōu hotels, Jiàn Fǔ has a very active "massage" service. The boss here must have some kind of automatic war-dialer software as the phone rings in your room almost every 10 minutes. Simply unplug the phone when you arrive.

Wēnlíng Lù Nán Duàn. ✆ **0595/2298-7999.** Fax 0595/2298-0889. 80 units. ¥168 ($21) standard room; ¥288–¥5,888 ($36–$736) suite. 10% service fee not charged. AE, DC, MC, V. **Amenities:** Restaurant; karaoke bar; massage (including in-room). *In room:* A/C, TV, fridge.

Quánzhōu Hángkōng Jiǔdiàn (Xiàmén Airlines Quánzhōu Hotel)   An upper-end three-star hotel, with a free shuttle bus to Xiàmén Airport, this fresh, modern, 16-story tower with well-maintained rooms has above-average service, except the first-floor coffee shop, with its awful coffee, understandably always empty. Larger and with more facilities than the Jiàn Fǔ, it has higher prices to match.

Fēngzé Jiē 339. ✆ **0595/2216-4888.** Fax 0595/2216-4777. 177 units. ¥560 ($70) standard room; ¥998 ($125) suite. Rates include breakfast. 10% service fee not charged. 40%–50% discounts available. AE, DC, MC, V. **Amenities:** 2 restaurants; fitness room; business center (Internet ¥30/$3.75 per hour). *In room:* A/C, TV, video on demand, broadband Internet access (on floors 12 and 16; ¥30/$3.75 per day), minibar, fridge, hair dryer, safe.

Quánzhōu Jiǔdiàn   This is one of those rare long-standing state-owned hotels that has actually made some attempts to stay refreshed and train its staff, but even with a discount it's way overpriced. Business from its government connections means that it does not have to work as hard as other hotels as long as it maintains its impressive appearance. Choose a room with a view of the twin pagodas of Kāiyuán Sì. Conference facilities make the hotel popular with both businesspeople and unbusinesslike officials. There is a clothing store just next door, called Binge, which should give you an idea of the type of guest that patronizes this hotel.

Zhuāngfǔ Xiàng 22. ✆ **0595/2228-9958.** Fax 0595/2218-2128. www.quanzhouhotel.com. 295 units. ¥515–¥915 ($65–$115) standard room; ¥1,245–¥5,893 ($155–$737) suite. 15% service charge in 4-star wing, and 10% in 3-star wing. 30% discounts available. AE, DC, MC, V. **Amenities:** 4 restaurants; bakery; indoor pool; outdoor tennis court; fitness room; sauna; bowling alley; game room; concierge; tour desk; business center; forex; salon; limited room service; massage. *In room:* A/C, TV, video on demand, broadband Internet access, fridge, hair dryer, safe.

Quánzhōu Mandarin Hotel (Yù Huāu Jiǔdiàn)   Scheduled to open at press time, this will be Quánzhōu's first five-star hotel. The controlling group already owns five successful hotels in Xiàmén, so it will be interesting to see if they can shake up the market a little here.

Chì Tóng Xī Lù. ✆ **0595/2801-9218.** Fax 0595/2801-9818. 381 units. ¥488–¥988 ($61–$123) standard room; ¥788–¥9,888 ($99–$1,236) suite. AE, DC, MC, V. **Amenities:** 3 restaurants; coffee shop; karaoke; pool; fitness room; sauna; game room; concierge; tour desk; business center; forex; salon; room service; massage. *In room:* A/C, TV, video on demand, broadband Internet access, fridge, hair dryer, safe.

WHERE TO DINE

Food in Quánzhōu is surprisingly lackluster, even in the better hotels (and there's a nasty tendency to add a service charge there, even if one isn't added to the room rate). The staff in the otherwise decent restaurant in the Xiàmén Airlines Quánzhōu Hotel look puzzled at a request for local dishes and can only offer *Xiàmén hǎilì jiān* (Xiàmén-style baby oysters), which means with eggs as a kind of oyster pancake, but that's rather good. The excellent local wheat beer, Huìquán, will please anyone fond of Hoegaarden.

The liveliest eating is in the **Měicān Yì Tiáo Jiē (The Beautiful Food Street)** running north from the arch on Jīnhuái Jiē, 1 block east and parallel to Wēnlíng Běi Lù. Here rows of food stalls with tables and chairs in the open air or in air-conditioned interiors compete for your business until the small hours. There's seafood in buckets, *niúpái* (beefsteak—a local favorite), dumplings, kabobs, hot pot, Sìchuān food, and even Lánzhōu "pulled" noodles. Especially interesting are the Army-themed restaurants with pictures of aircraft carriers and stealth bombers on the walls.

Close by on Wēnlíng Nán Lù is another nighttime food street where hot pot is more popular. Rows of baskets contain kabobs with all manner of food—animal, vegetable, and probably even some kind of mineral, too. Look for the large Chinese gateway next to the Construction Bank building, opposite the strangely named 8.1 Hotel.

Those craving Western food will find **McDonald's, KFC,** and **Pizza Hut** around the center, along with a branch of the ubiquitous **Shàngdǎo Kāfēi,** Túmén Jiē (© **0595/2219-2070**), with its nearly English menu, near spaghetti, sandwiches, and excellent if pricey coffee. An unusual alternative is **Háokèlái Niúpái (Houcaller Beefsteak)** on Wēnlíng Běi Lù north of the post office (© **0595/2219-5779**), which has a brightly lit fast-food interior but offers intelligent service and an English menu. Set meals such as pork chop, salad, bread, soup, tea, and a small glass of a pinkish spirit called *kāiwèijiǔ*—which would literally translate as "start the stomach alcohol"—for a *digestif* are ¥25 to ¥50 ($3–$6.25).

Qīng Qí Shén, behind the Guāndì Miào in Túmén Jiē, is a very pleasant teahouse in a traditional multicourtyard setting, where people sit playing board games beneath caged songbirds or watch the performance of a storyteller, and order snacks and tea from a bamboo slat menu: Oolong (Wūlóng) is ¥70 ($8.75) per pot; ordinary tea from ¥8 ($1).

Near the library, off Dōng Jiē Lù, at Gōng Jiē Xiàng 123, is **Bodhi Food (Pútí Zhāi;** © **0595/2222-6705)**, a vegetarian restaurant popular with local monks. Apart from the usual vegetarian fare, they serve a number of very convincing meat facsimiles including fried ham *(huǒtuǐ)* and mock turtle *(jiǎ yù gū)*. Other delicious options include faux chicken in lemon sauce *(nín méng jīpiàn)* and the deep-fried salad surprise *(shuǐguǒ shālà)*. Most dishes range in price from ¥10 to ¥25 ($1.25–$3.25).

8 Xiàmén ✦✦

Fújiàn Province, 109km (68 miles) S of Quánzhōu, 770km (481 miles) E of Guǎngzhōu

The island of Xiàmén, then better known to foreigners by its Fújiàn name of Amoy, became a foreign concession in 1903, with most of the foreigners living on the tiny islet of Gǔlàng Yǔ just off Xiàmén itself. By the 1930s there were about 500 resident foreigners and nine consulates, several of which still stand, as do the vast, Europeanized mansions of Chinese who returned wealthy from overseas.

Here, more than at any other former treaty port including Shànghǎi, there seems to be something left of the foreign presence and the colonial era, in the largest and best-preserved warren of colonial-era shop-houses in mainland China, and on Gǔlàng Yǔ, the largest and best-preserved collection of colonial mansions. People also seem remarkably relaxed and law-abiding—there's little spitting, little shouting at foreigners, and an unusual tendency to obey road signs.

Much of the island is a hideous white-tiled wasteland to match anything else in China, but even so, the odd turret and spire reflect the city's pride in its stock of

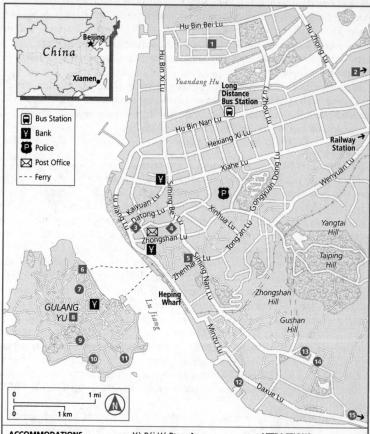

ACCOMMODATIONS

Holiday Inn Crowne Plaza Harbourview (Jiàrì Hǎijǐng Dàjiǔdiàn) 5
假日海景大酒店

Marco Polo Xiàmén 1
马可波罗酒店

Xiàmén Dàxué Guó Jì Xué Sù Jiāo Liǔ Zhōng Xīn (Xiàmén University International Academic Exchange Centre Hotel) 14
厦门大学国际学术交流中心

Xiàmén Xǐ Lài Dēn Jiǔdiàn (Sheraton Hotel) 2
喜来登大酒店

Yè Bái Hé Bīnguǎn (Night Lily Guest House) 8
夜百合宾馆

Yong Shun Bīnguǎn 6
永顺宾馆

DINING

Huā Shēng Tāngdiǎn 3
花生糖点

Miào Xiāng Biǎn Shí 12
妙香扁食

Nán Pǔtuó Sì 13
南普陀寺

Shǔxiāng Yuán Chuān Cài 4
蜀香园川菜

ATTRACTIONS

Húlǐ Shān Pàotái 15
胡里山炮台

Jīnquán Qiánbì Bówùguǎn 11
金泉钱币博物馆

Rìguāng Yán (Sunlight Rock) 9
日光岩

Shūzhuāng Gōng yuán 10
菽庄公园

Xiàmén Shì Bówùguǎn (City Museum) 7
厦门市博物馆

original European architecture. The rest of the island is a refreshing change and full of character—narrow alleys connecting sinuous streets are laced together with power and telephone cables, and house DVD shops, noodle restaurants, and hair salons where no hair is ever cut. Vehicle-free Gǔlàng Yǔ, a few minutes away by ferry, is all pleasant strolls and quiet back streets full of mansions overgrown with brilliant bougainvillea.

In short, Xiàmén is the largely overlooked gateway to China that provides the softest landing of all. The comfortable cruise around the coast from Hong Kong provides the ideal overture to a mainland visit, with Xiàmén a halfway house between orderly former colony and the bedlam that is most mainland cities.

ESSENTIALS

GETTING THERE   Xiàmén's **Gāoqí International Airport** (© 0592/602-8940) is on the north side of the island only 20 minutes from the downtown area. Airport taxis cost little more than ¥30 ($3.50) to downtown, and there's a shuttle to the railway station from the right of the terminal as you leave that charges ¥6 (75¢). The Crowne Plaza and Marco Polo have free shuttles for guests. There are international connections to Bangkok, Hong Kong, Kuala Lumpur, Manila, Osaka, Singapore, and Tokyo, with an assortment of domestic and foreign airlines including JAL, Philippine, ANA, and Dragonair; and regular flights to all major Chinese cities, including Běijīng (five or six flights daily), Guǎngzhōu (five or six daily), and Shànghǎi (nine flights daily). While most airlines maintain offices in the Crowne Plaza or Marco Polo hotels, or in the Yínháng Zhōngxīn at the corner of Húbīn Xī Lù and Xiàhé Lù, you are better off purchasing your tickets from independent agencies, preferably away from your hotel. **Xiàmén Airlines** (© 0592/222-6666) has a 24-hour ticketing and check-in desk for its own passengers and those of China Southern in the Jīnyàn Jiǔdiàn. It also sells tickets for other airlines with reasonable discounts. Its shuttle service is free for guests and for Xiàmén/China Southern passengers; there are eight departures from 5:20am to 7:20pm. Reserve a seat on the shuttle in advance at © 0592/221-8888, ext. 34 or 6110.

At the airport, an **ATM** that accepts foreign cards is upstairs at international departures, as is a **Bank of China** forex counter open from 8:30am to 4:30pm.

On routes to neighboring coastal cities and to Hong Kong, luxury long-distance bus services are quickest, but there are useful **train** connections from Nánchāng (three daily; 837km/523 miles; ¥302/$37 soft sleeper), Wǔyí Shān (K985/988; 587km/367 miles; ¥232/$29), and Shànghǎi (K175; 1,395km/872 miles; ¥472/$59). The mostly single-track route through mountainous Fújiàn Province is pretty and winding, passing sugar-cane plantations and banana palms with bags tied over the fruit to help it ripen. There are also direct services from Běijīng, Nánjīng, and Xī'ān. For **train inquiries,** call © 0592/581-4340; for **bookings,** © 0592/398-8662, up to 12 days in advance. The railway station is a 10-minute cab ride east of the ferry dock, which can also be reached on bus no. 1. Ticket windows are open from 8am to 8:30pm, with tickets available up to 5 days in advance including day of travel. As you face the railway station, booking and left luggage are to the right of the entrance. The **Nánfāng Lǚxíngshè** inside the Hépíng Wharf has computer access to the railway system, and charges a ¥10 ($1.25) service fee per ticket. There is also a useful sleeper service to Wǔyí Shān leaving at 6:55pm arriving in Wǔyí Shān at 7am the next morning.

Southern China's new highway system is now cruised by air-conditioned **buses** with frequent services, many of them luxury foreign makes with attendants and lavatories. For all coastal destinations north in Fújiàn and into Zhèjiāng, as well as south into neighboring Guǎngdōng Province, these buses are far quicker than trains. The main **long-distance bus station (chángtú qìchēzhàn; ⓒ 0572/221-5238)** is on Húbīn Nán Lù, just north of downtown. It sells tickets from 5:30 to 10pm. However, many of the best services also have agencies located conveniently opposite the main ferry terminal to Gǔlàng Yǔ. Try **Lúndù Shòupiào Chù (ⓒ 0592/213-5051)**, next to the Spring Sunlight Hotel, where several services pick up passengers and which has a small waiting room. Sample bus routes: Guǎngzhōu (770km/481 miles; ¥180/$22), Shēnzhèn (680km/425 miles; ¥180/$22). There's even a direct bus route to Hong Kong (830km/519 miles; ¥350/$44). You can also board most bus lines at the **Wúcūn Qìchēzhàn (ⓒ 0592/581-5525)**, opposite the railway station and a little north. Most services starting here go on to the main bus station, but buses from Fúzhōu and Quánzhōu generally terminate here. Services include Wēnzhōu (¥163/$20); Tàishùn (¥150/$19); Wǔyí Shān (¥124/$15) at 8:10am and 1:50pm; Guǎngzhōu (17 departures; ¥110–¥180/$14–$23) from 7:50am to 10:10pm; Shēnzhèn (14 departures; ¥100–¥200/$13–$25) from 8am to 10:30pm; and Quánzhōu (more than 50 departures; ¥32/$3.75) from 6:20am to 9:10pm. The **Fúzhōu Express (ⓒ 0592/221-8591)** takes only 3 hours and 40 minutes to reach Fúzhōu (13 departures 6:30am–6:30pm; ¥80/$10). One Hong Kong service, the **Eternal East Cross-Border Coach Mgt. Ltd. (ⓒ 0592/202-3333,** or 852/2723 2923 in Hong Kong; www.eebus.com), can be booked and boarded at the Crowne Plaza, with daily departures at 7:30am. Although most coastal **ferry** routes are long gone, the service from Hong Kong survives, and makes for a soft landing in mainland China. Service is now provided by the 250-cabin *Wasa Queen* of the **Hong Kong Cruise Ferries** company (www.cruise-ferries.com.hk). Services leave Xiàmén at 6pm on Thursday and arrive in Hong Kong at 3pm the next day. From Hong Kong they leave at noon on Wednesday and arrive in Xiàmén at 10am. One-way fares for cabin berths range from HK$320 to HK$1,120 (US$41–US$143) per person for individual travelers and couples, and about 20% of those fares for each of the third and fourth persons in any group. Prices payable in Xiàmén are local currency equivalents. Prices rise 50% around Chinese New Year. Check the website for up-to-date schedule details, or call Hong Kong (24 hr.) at ⓒ 852/2957 8188, Xiàmén at 0592/202-2517. Xiàmén departures are from the Hépíng Wharf, just south of the Gǔlàng Yǔ ferry terminal.

GETTING AROUND   Both the old town and Gǔlàng Yǔ are easily explored **on foot,** and the other main sights are short **taxi** rides away. Flagfall for taxis is ¥8 ($1) including 3km (2 miles), then ¥2 (25¢) per kilometer up to 8km (5 miles), then ¥3 (40¢) per kilometer. Add 20% from 11pm to 5am. **Buses** are frequent and reliable, with fare boxes into which you deposit ¥2 (25¢) for air-conditioned service, ¥1 (15¢) without. A few non-air-conditioned buses have conductors. There are several **ferry** routes between the **Ferry Dock (Lúndù Mǎtóu)** and Gǔlàng Yǔ. The 5-minute main route is free outbound, but ¥3 (40¢) to return. There's an optional ¥1 (15¢) charge to sit on the top deck in either direction. Ferries run roughly every 10 to 15 minutes from 5:30am, every 20 to 30 minutes after 9pm; the last sailing is at 12:20am. To the right of the ferry boarding point are windows for a **daytime cruise** around Gǔlàng Yǔ and to see Taiwanese Jīnmén Dǎo. The 35-minute cruise departs roughly every 30 minutes from 7:40am to 5pm; call ⓒ 0592/202-3493. The next windows offer a

night cruise (② **0592/210-4896;** 1 hr., 50 min.; ¥118/$15 including snacks). There are also night trips to see the Hǎicāng Dà Qiáo, a large, illuminated suspension bridge just to the north; the 40-minute trip is offered May through October from 8 to 8:45pm for ¥10 to ¥20 ($1.25–$2.50). At the end farthest to the right is a second ferry service to Gǔlàng Yǔ, running to Sān Qiū Tián, a little east of Gǔlàng Yǔ's main dock, beneath the former U.S. consulate. Ferries depart every 30 minutes from 7:15am to 9:40pm; throughout the night, they depart roughly every hour.

VISITOR INFORMATION   For travel complaints, call ② **0592/206-3715.** American Express has an office in the Crowne Plaza, room 212 (② **0592/212-0268;** Mon–Fri 9am–5pm). The staff isn't terribly helpful, but with some prodding they can at least tell you where to find the check-cashing service. For more details about new developments in the area, check the *What's On Xiàmén* website: www.whatsonxiamen. com. There is also a book called *Amoy Magic* that cannot be recommended due to the inane humor, amateurish style, and constant party brown-nosing of the author. Even so, it covers a lot more locations than most Western guidebooks, but you may end up chucking it out of a train window in disgust after reading some of the writer's ridiculous comments.

FAST FACTS

Banks, Foreign Exchange & ATMs   All **Bank of China** ATMs take foreign cards, from the airport, via Gǔlàng Yǔ (at Hǎitān Lù 2), to the convenient Zhōngshān Lù branch (open 8:30am–noon and 2:30–5:30pm) close to the Gǔlàng Yǔ ferry dock in the center of town, which also has forex at counters 2 to 6. There's another Bank of China with forex and ATM in the Yínháng Zhōngxīn on the corner of Húbīn Xī Lù and Xiàhé Lù. Just next door is a branch of the **Hongkong and Shanghai Bank (HSBC),** whose ATMs take almost any card invented.

Internet Access   There are Internet cafes located around the old town, including one on Kāiyuán Lù. A much quieter option is the third floor of Xiàmén Library at Gōng Yuán Nán Lù 2; it's open 8 to 11:30am and 2:30 to 5:30pm. Dial-up is ② **8163.**

Post Office   The main post office (open 7:30am–7:30pm) is in Zhōngshān Lù opposite the Bank of China. There's also a useful branch in Lóngtóu Lù on Gǔlàng Yǔ.

Visa Extensions   The **PSB** (Gōng'ānjú; open Mon–Sat 8–11:45am and 3–5:45pm) is in Chū Mí Yán (② **0592/2262-2207**).

EXPLORING XIÀMÉN

The narrow streets of the **old quarter,** which has the mainland's largest and best-preserved area of treaty port–era shop-houses in a labyrinth of curling streets and narrow lanes, is bounded to the north by Xiàhé Lù and to the south by Zhōngshān Lù, which leads to the ferry docks.

GǓLÀNG YǓ

Amoy, as Xiàmén was then known, was one of the first five treaty ports to be opened to foreign residence and trade after the First Opium War, and a British consulate was opened in 1843. The first foreign settlements were on Amoy proper, but the town was then famously noisome, its alleys, some too narrow to allow the opening of an umbrella, funneling an extravagant palette of aromas from sewers inadequately concealed beneath the pavements. Surprisingly clean now, Xiàmén was then reputed to be the filthiest city in China.

The foreign community therefore moved to the 2-sq.-km (¾-mile) Gǔlàng Yǔ but grew slowly (37 residents in 1836), although in 1852 the site became the first of the "concessions"—areas of land formally set aside for foreign residence, then parceled out to British citizens. By 1880, the now multinational foreign population was around 300 and sustained a daily English newspaper, an ice factory, a club, and tiger shooting (25 were bagged at the beginning of the 1890s alone). Amoy's main export was coolies, the British having forced the Qīng to permit Chinese emigration, and between 1883 and 1897 an estimated 167,000 left for labor overseas, founding Chinatowns around Asia and North America.

In treaty port days all transport was on foot, and no wheeled vehicles were allowed—a rule still enforced with the exception of some quiet electric carts used sometimes to take tourists on a circuit round the island but mostly to quietly sneak up and scare the bejeesus out of them.

First impressions of the island are not very favorable. The ferry disembarkation area consists of huge sliding steel gates that would be more at home on Alcatraz rather than a tourist hot spot. Once through the maximum security–type entrance, the first thing that visitors see is a huge ad for McDonald's.

As you alight from the ferry, an office to the right (© **0130/5551-9326**) offers ferry trips to Jīnmén Island for ¥96 ($12). There are 12 departures between 8:20am and 3:10pm. An office straight ahead as you dock offers a ¥80 ($10) ticket giving entrance to a variety of tawdry modern entertainments such as a fun fair and a laser show, so turn left instead to where the electric cars are parked. Proceed uphill straight to the area of finest mansions, on serpentine Fújiàn Lù and Lùjiāo Lù. The best examples are signposted, yet marked with unhelpful plaques giving construction dates and little more information; the former Japanese consulate is marked, however. Look out for the Catholic church of 1917 at Lùjiāo Lù 34. Some sources claim that 30% of the island's 20,000 residents are still practicing Christians. It's also a tradition that there are more pianos here than anywhere else in China, and tourism promoters claim that Gǔlàng Yǔ is known as "Piano Island," although no one seems to have told the locals this. Bach and Clementi can often be heard being hammered out rhythmically if unimaginatively, but that is only because the local high school uses concerto snippets instead of the usual school bells.

Fújiàn Lù 32 is particularly impressive—a vast porticoed mansion built in 1928 by a Vietnamese-Chinese real estate tycoon; the mansion later served as a hospital during the Japanese occupation of World War II, and today is the Art Vocation University of Xiàmén. Dozens of families now occupy a range of such mansions and have bricked up entrances, walled in balconies to add floor space, and left gardens to turn wild. Pretty winding paths between mansions are now overgrown with hawthorn, but despite the sometimes dismaying crush on the ferry, the island has generous amounts of what China generally lacks—peace and quiet.

Farther on, clockwise around the island, is the **Jīnquán Qiánbì Bówùguǎn,** a museum of ancient coins housed in the handsome British consulate, originally built in 1843 and the earliest foreign building on the island. Recently opened, its hours and entrance fee seem not yet set, but beyond the building is one of the best lookout points back to Xiàmén.

Follow signs down to the beach below. Chinese now paddle where foreigners once held bathing parties that inexplicably involved eating ginger biscuits and drinking cherry brandy.

Just past the beach are shady benches beneath the trees, beyond which a short tunnel takes you through to the next beach. Immediately after that on the left, steps lead up the hillside through gardens to **Rìguāng Yán (Sunlight Rock),** a lookout point perhaps used by pirate and Míng loyalist Zhèng Chénggōng (1624–62), also known as Kongxia, a Dutch corruption of a title awarded him by the expiring Míng. He's an official state hero for being the first Hàn to invade Táiwān, which he did mainly for its silk and sugar, but is idolized for having kicked the Dutch off Táiwān in 1624. A dull museum to his memory is laced with the usual propaganda about how Táiwān has always been "an inseparable part of the motherland." It's a stiff climb (although there's a cable car alternative) and the entrance fee is a hefty ¥60 ($7.50). The view is very overrated, just a busy shipping lane and some ugly container-handling facilities over on the opposite island.

Past the beach, a right turn before a farther tunnel leads you into a maze of old mansions, but signs will direct you to the **Xiàmén Shì Bówùguǎn (City Museum)** at Gǔxīn Lù 43 (open 8:30am–5pm; ¥10/$1.25). The museum is located in possibly the grandest of all the mansions, the swaggering, three-story, cupola-topped Bāguà Lóu or Eight Trigrams Building of 1907, designed by an American for a Taiwanese businessman. The ground floor has early examples of the Mǐn Nán region (Quánzhōu/Zhèngzhōu/Xiàmén) specialty ware, *blanc de chine,* mostly Qīng. There's other material on the Opium War and the Japanese occupation, as well as on the Communist forces' drive to Xiàmén, which forced the Nationalists to Táiwān. The small matter of Jīnmén Island, which sits uncaptured less than 2km (1¼ miles) from the mainland (despite being the subject of two major offensives and the fact that the Chinese shelled the island nonstop for 44 days back in '58), receives no comment. The museum is dusty, echoing, forgotten, and rarely visited, but there are good views from upper balconies (hung with the attendants' washing) for a fraction of the cost of views from Sunlight Rock. A new building to one side has well-presented displays on fishing, local customs, and tea.

AROUND XIÀMÉN

Southeast of the center, a series of sites make a pleasant excursion when seen together. Start by taking a taxi or bus no. 2 or 22 from Sīmíng Lù to the **Húlǐ Shān Pàotái,** a platform (open 8:30am–5pm; ¥25/$3) with a vast Krupp 280-millimeter cannon overlooking the island-dotted ocean and offering a different kind of seashell. The huge gun, one of two originally sited here in 1893, sits on a vast rotating chain-driven mechanism and is credited with sinking a Japanese warship in 1937. When it was first fired, several nearby houses collapsed, too. The other gun emplacement now houses a tacky souvenir shop. There are plenty descriptions in English but they include the usual nationalist claptrap about "British aggressors" and "brave Chinese soldiers." The surrounding sunken barracks area has been turned over to the exhibition of peculiar stones and ancient weaponry that includes a rusty pistol said to have belonged to Opium warrior Lín Zéxú. A boat at the pier below offers 1-hour trips to see Jīnmén and Little Jīnmén islands for ¥96 ($12); call ✆ **0592/208-3759** for information.

Cross the road opposite the cannon and turn left until you find the gate to the university, **Xiàmén Dàxué.** Even the footbridge here is worth a closer look as this innovative tension structure is millennia ahead of almost any other construction in China. This is one of China's older and most pleasant campuses, founded around 90 years ago and heavily funded by donations from Chinese overseas. Wander straight on past substantial brick buildings to a major left turn to the main gate—students will point you in the right direction if you look lost. Just outside the campus, on the right, is **Nán Pǔtuó Sì** (open 3am–6:30pm; ¥3/40¢). It's a temple of little antiquity but fully functional as a place of worship, with the devout on their knees reading scriptures and surely nearly asphyxiated by all the incense smoke. Monks bustle about, and wooden blocks are tossed to obtain the answers to important questions. There's also rock-cut calligraphy, modern stupas containing the remains of recently interred monks, 18 particularly animated *luóhàn* statues, a "thousand-armed" Guānyīn, and an excellent vegetarian restaurant.

WHERE TO STAY

Xiàmén has a variety of shiny business hotels scattered around the island, but at four-star level the two to choose are the Marco Polo and the Crowne Plaza. Upmarket hotels add a 10%-to-15% service charge and there is now an additional 4% local government tax. You'll find abundant budget accommodations on the waterfront north of the Lùjiāng Bīnguǎn and some (much quieter) on Gǔlàng Yǔ, including a former American consulate. Xiàmén holds its annual marathon on the last Saturday of March when almost 20,000 athletes compete for a first prize of $25,000, so don't expect any hotel discounts that particular weekend. Xiàmén tourism is busy March through May, after which Chinese tourism drops to almost nothing, and only the odd foreigner is seen mid-summer; it picks up again September through early October for a trade fair. Typically, 40% discounts are available in nonpeak periods, more in lower-level accommodations.

EXPENSIVE

Holiday Inn Crowne Plaza Harbourview (Jiàrì Hǎijǐng Dàjiǔdiàn)   Rooms on the upper floors of this tapering 22-story tower, visible across the city, are bright and sunny and have good views. The building dates from 1992 but a continuous refurbishment program has kept it fresh. All facilities are of a conventional four-star standard, and service is both attentive and efficient. The hotel is a conveniently short walk from the Hépíng Wharf (for Hong Kong ferries), 5 minutes from the warren of the old town, and a 15-minute stroll along the harbor front from the main ferry to Gǔlàng Yǔ.

Zhènhǎi Lù 12–8. ✆ **0592/202-3333.** Fax 0592/203-6666. www.crowneplaza.com. 349 units. ¥1,280–¥2,080 ($160–$260) standard room; ¥2,800–¥6,560 ($350–$820) suite. 15% service charge. AE, DC, MC, V. **Amenities:** 4 restaurants; 24-hr. coffee shop; cocktail bar; Golf Bar; outdoor swimming pool; fitness room; sauna; concierge; tour desk (and American Express office); free airport shuttle; business center; Internet access; forex; salon; 24-hr. room service; babysitting; same-day dry cleaning/laundry; executive floor. *In room:* A/C, satellite TV, dataport, broadband Internet access (¥10/$1.25 per hour), minibar, fridge, hair dryer, safe.

Marco Polo Xiàmén ✧   Many of the rooms are arranged on eight floors around a central atrium, but a wing off to one side is a better choice for peace and quiet. The guest rooms are well appointed and meet four-star standards, with broadband Internet access and larger-than-average bathrooms. The concierge desk is particularly well staffed with good English speakers, both eager to help and capable of doing so. The center of town is only a few minutes away by taxi.

Jiànyè Lù 8 (off Húbīn Běi Lù on the north shore of Yuàndàng Lake). ✆ **0592/509-1888.** Fax 0592/509-2888. www.marcopolohotels.com. 350 units. ¥1,280–¥2,000 ($160–$250) standard room; ¥1,600–¥7,840 ($250–$980) suite. 15% service charge. AE, DC, MC, V. **Amenities:** 3 restaurants; lobby lounge; poolside bar with views across the lake to the city skyline; outdoor swimming pool; fitness room; sauna; concierge; tour desk; free airport shuttle; business center; forex; shopping arcade; salon; 24-hr. room service; babysitting; same-day dry cleaning/laundry; executive-level rooms. *In room:* A/C, satellite TV, minibar, fridge, hair dryer, safe.

Wild China: The Earth Houses of Yǒngdìng

About 205km (128 miles) inland from Xiàmén, Yǒngdìng is a heartland of the **Hakka** people—Hàn who migrated south from near Kāifēng in five waves beginning more than 1,000 years ago, and who were kept moving around southern China by civil war, famine, and discrimination by earlier Hàn arrivals. They often ended up with the worst farming land on the highest ground. Unlike other Hàn, their women did not bind their feet and worked alongside men in the fields, and so tended to marry only other Hakka. They also maintained what they claim is something close to early Chinese but is unintelligible to speakers of Mandarin, Cantonese, and Mǐn Nán Huà.

Now an officially recognized minority, known as the **Kèjiā** or "guest people," their long exile and continued sense of being outsiders has produced both tangible and intangible benefits for visitors. The Hakka claim to be more hospitable to outsiders than other Chinese, but the need to protect themselves against others has produced the magnificent multistory fortresses called *tǔlóu* or "earth buildings," some home to hundreds, all sharing a single family name.

The *tǔlóu* are spread around nearly 50 counties on the Guǎngdōng-Fújiàn-Jiāngxī border. The concentration easiest to reach, and the one most prepared for visitors, is that at **Húkēng,** where a bus will drop you right outside the ticket office. A fee of ¥40 ($5), valid for 2 or 3 days, includes access to four officially open major *tǔlóu* and another containing a museum, although no one seems to mind if you wander in anywhere else. Helpful English signs are quite common, and there's a primitive hotel in the middle of the village (summer only), but you would be better off having the full experience by staying in an actual *tǔlóu*. Residents with rooms to let (typically for ¥20/$2.50 or so) will persistently approach you, as will motorbike and *sānlúnchē* owners wanting to take you to other villages.

The vast fortresses nestle together on either side of a river in a narrow green valley, and in autumn their khaki tones have splashes of color as crops of plums and persimmons are spread out to dry on flat surfaces. The "earth" is in fact a tamped mixture of sand, lime, and dirt, giving the walls a textured surface. The best-known building is the marvelous circular **Zhènchéng Lóu** of 1912, consisting of an outer four-story ring with each floor divided into 44 rooms and two halls; an inner, two-story ring divided into eight sections; and two tobacco workshops outside, bringing the total number of rooms to 222. As with other *tǔlóu*, windows to the outside world begin two stories up. Balconies run around the interiors, providing access and light. The inner ring joins at a hall for worshipping ancestors, marriage ceremonies, greeting distinguished guests, and other events.

The battered **Huánxīng Lóu** is not an official sight, but it dates from around 1550 and is the oldest in this village. Though battered by flooding, an earthquake, and even an attack during the Tàipíng rebellion (p. 378), some 200 residents remain, all called Lǐ.

Tǔlóu also come in half-moon, pentangle, "five phoenix," and other shapes. The square, fortresslike **Kuíjù Lóu,** dating from 1834, is, at 6,000 sq. m (64,583 sq. ft.) even bigger than the circular buildings. It has an interior of brick and wood more like that of a conventional mansion. The 7,000-sq.-m (75,347-sq.-ft.) **Fúyù Lóu** of 1880, whose residents are all called Lín, has multiple axes, and a five-story earthen tower at the rear. Its beams and pillars are beautifully carved, and it also has some fine inlaid screens, as well as a teahouse and rooms to let.

The last official *tǔlóu* (although residents don't mind if you wander into several others) is the charming **Rúshēng Lóu,** built sometime between 1875 and 1908. It's a single 23m (63-ft.) diameter ring-shaped dollhouse in comparison to the others, which have three stories each of 16 rooms. Finally, the **museum** occupies a rectangular *tǔlóu,* where the music of traditional instruments echoes around the two floors of one courtyard, given over to displays of tobacco knives, tools used in building, and photographs of festivals and other *tǔlóu* that may have you planning trips to other villages. You may see dried persimmons being roasted and pressed into cakes—a local specialty called *shìbǐng.*

GETTING THERE   The best route is by **bus** from Xiàmén, first to **Lóngyán** (4 hr.; ¥55/$6.90) every 45 minutes from 7am to 6:30pm, and then by Iveco minibus to **Húkēng** (13 departures; 2 hr.; ¥15/$1.90) from 7am to 4:50pm. There's also a daily service to Lóngyán from Nánchāng. There are limited **train** services to **Yǒngdìng,** 37km (23 miles) and ¥7 (90¢) by minibus from modern Húkēng, and then a short taxi ride to the old town. But timings are highly inconvenient. The roundhouses are particularly popular with Japanese tourists, and so for those seeking a more comfortable alternative we recommend one of the companies used regularly by the Marco Polo. The example schedule includes 2 days and 1 night.

TOURS   Guided tours are available. For two to three travelers, the **Xiàmén Overseas Tourist Co China** (© 0592/212-7638, 0592/212-7738, or 0592/213-4038; LJW@xmotc.com) charges flat fees for transportation from Xiàmén (¥1,600/ $200), a guide (¥300/$38), and guesthouse accommodations (¥250/$31 per room). Meals cost ¥50 ($6.25) per person per meal, and entry to the *tǔlóu* costs about ¥100 ($13) per person. Rates do not apply for Spring Festival, National Day, or the Labor Day holiday. The **Xiàmén C&D Travel Agency** (© 0592/211-0294) offers a similar package that costs ¥1,400 ($175) per person and includes transportation, guest house accommodations, guide, and meals for individuals or groups smaller than 10.

WHERE TO STAY & DINE   Owners of lodgings will find you, and you get what you pay for. Insist on clean bedding, but expect a single lightbulb, a thermos of boiling water, and a chamber pot to be the sum total of facilities. Make careful note of the locations of the pit toilet and a tap with running water, both down at ground level, before it gets dark. Simple food will be offered, to be eaten in the ground-floor room. Three plain dishes, cooked over wood fires, will cost around ¥20 ($2.50). Take supplementary snacks from Xiàmén. After dark it's eerily quiet, especially in the now sparsely inhabited **Zhènchéng Lóu.** Lín Hóngyuán (© 0130/6245-7844) is among those with rooms there; Lín Qínmíng also has rooms at the **Fúyù Lóu** (© 0130/6245-7844). Slightly less basic accommodations can be found in the new town 5km (3 miles) away.

Xiàmén Xǐláidēng Jiǔdiàn (Sheraton Hotel) As the first five-star hotel in town, the Sheraton has a lot to live up to. The location seems to be more geared toward convention attendees rather than tourists, but as it only opened in August 2005 (*after* my visit to Xiàmén), it will still be setting the standard for all other accommodations. Many of the rooms have superb views over Jiāngtóu Park.

Jiāhé Lù 386-1. ⓒ **0592/552-5888.** Fax 0592/553-9088. 360 units. ¥800–¥1,440 ($100–$180) deluxe room; ¥1,600–¥7,840 ($200–$980) suite. Rates include breakfast. 15% service charge. AE, DC, MC, V. **Amenities:** 2 restaurants; 3 bars including a pool bar and cigar bar; spa; concierge; tour desk with 24-hr. airline ticketing; airport shuttle; business center; forex; salon; 24-hr. room service; executive floor. *In room:* A/C, TV, video on demand, free broadband Internet access, minibar, fridge, hair dryer, safe.

MODERATE TO INEXPENSIVE

Xiàmén Dàxué Guójì Xuéshù Jiāoliú Zhōngxīn (Xiàmén University International Academic Exchange Centre Hotel) This campus hotel offers plain and simple rooms favored by parties of visiting academics but it is well situated for tourists, too. It's located just inside the relaxing confines of the Xiàmén University campus, with the bus station just outside along with plenty of colorful restaurants, aimed at the large student population. Far better than the anonymous business hotels if you actually want to get out and meet the locals.

North Gate, Xiàmén University. ⓒ **0592/208-7988.** Fax 0592/208-6116. 77 units. ¥250 ($32) single; ¥400 ($50) standard room. No credit cards. 10% service charge. **Amenities:** Restaurant. *In room:* A/C, TV.

Yè Bǎihé Bīnguǎn (Night Lily Guest House) ✿✿ *Finds* This is just the kind of accommodations that China needs. Two forward-thinking foreigners have converted this 1930s colonial mansion on Gǔlàng Yǔ into what can only be described as a boutique hotel. There are five guest suites done in wonderfully eclectic styles that mix and match antique Chinese furniture with modern designer bathrooms. The view across to the city is breathtaking but actually finding the place in the maze of higgledy-piggledy streets is a nightmare. Better to call one of the owners in advance who will arrange your collection from the docks.

Bǐshān Lù 11, Gǔlàng Yǔ. ⓒ **0592/206-0920.** Mobile 13599924474. yyzpec@soho.com. 53 units. ¥450 ($57) standard room; ¥500 ($63) triple room. Rates include breakfast. No credit cards.

Yong Shun Bīnguǎn *Overrated* Here's a chance to sleep in a former U.S. consulate, built in 1928 with bricks imported from the States at a cost of $200,000 (the first consulate burned down). The neoclassical portico (with an oddly Egyptian touch to the tops of its pillars) has been glassed in and the upper floor extended into the space. The building was refitted and opened as a hotel in 1999. Unfortunately, nobody speaks a word of English and the only decent views are from the much more expensive suites. The standard rooms I saw were cramped and stuffy, outfitted in way too much beige. The gardens and tennis courts are perfectly manicured so it is perhaps better to come here for a little sun in the afternoon but sleep somewhere else.

Sānmíng Lù 26 (on Gǔlàng Yǔ, a short walk to the right from the main ferry dock, and served less frequently by ferries to a dock immediately beneath it). ⓒ **0592/206-5621.** Fax 0592/206-9762. 29 units. ¥460 ($57) standard room; ¥660 ($82) suite. 30% discounts typical. ¥280 ($35) simple standard rooms in separate newer building. No credit cards. **Amenities:** Restaurant (open intermittently); 2 outdoor tennis courts. *In room:* A/C, TV, fridge.

WHERE TO DINE

Unsurprisingly for a port city, Xiàmén is known for its fresh fish, and seafood can be found for next to nothing in the back streets of the old quarter or at small, hole-in-the-wall restaurants just up from the dock on Gǔlàng Yǔ. Lunch will still be swimming or crawling in plastic tubs set out in the street, and is priced by weight. Júkǒu Jiē has very cheap Sìchuān and Taiwanese restaurants. Try the basic **Shǔxiāng Yuán Chuān Cài** for authentic Sìchuān, upstairs at no. 63, on the west side near the junction with Sīmíng Xī Lù. It stays open as long as there are shoppers; a meal for two costs about ¥40 ($5). Good Western food is still only available in the bigger hotels (the Pan-Asia expat favorites at both the Marco Polo and Crowne Plaza are excellent), but there are two **McDonald's** and a **KFC** in Zhōngshān Lù alone. A waterfront **Pizza Hut** on the 24th floor of a tower in Lùjiāng Dào, visible for miles, has correspondingly excellent views once you get up there.

Vegetarians are well served at the **Nán Pǔtuó Sì.** Tickets must first be purchased from the "Vegetable Dishes Booking Office," signposted in English; it's open from noon to 4pm and 5 to 7pm. Individual dishes cost from ¥8 ($1), but three-dish set meals from ¥30 ($3.75) per person make life easier. The surroundings are undistinguished and practical, but the food is prepared with sensitivity to each ingredient's strengths, and is an excellent value. Try *xiāng ní cáng zhēn* (vegetables mashed into a paste—much more attractive than it sounds), *luóhàn zhāi* (a stew of pine nuts, cabbage, cucumber, corn, mushrooms, and fresh coriander), *dāngguā miànjīn tāng* (Chinese angelica and gluten soup), and *lúsǔn dòufu tāng* (asparagus and tofu soup).

Huáng Zé Hé, or peanut soup, from the Huāshēng Tāng Diàn (peanut snack bar) on Zhōngshān Lù seems to be the local dish that most tourists seek out, but you will have to battle through crowds of red and white baseball caps to get any. A more relaxing option is to head down to the old harbor where a small eatery turns out equally delicious peanut-based dishes. My favorite was the local-style wonton soup *(biǎ nshí)* and the tasty noodles *(bàn miàn)* at Miào Xiāng Biǎn Shí located on Dàxué Lù 102 (☎ **0592/899-1820**), open from 6am to 10:30pm.

9 Jǐngdé Zhèn

Jiāngxī Province, 280km (174 miles) NE of Nánchāng, 430km (267 miles) E of Wǔhàn

Jǐngdé Zhèn is a smallish town in the throes of growing up but without quite the economic clout to do so. For now, areas of ramshackle housing still survive behind the typical white-tile shopping streets but are clearly not due to be around much longer. The main attraction is the pottery industry, but the town doesn't present itself too well and its museum collections are weak, although the Táocí Lìshǐ Bówùguǎn (Ceramic Historical Exhibition Area) is excellent. Local authorities are starting to recognize the importance of tourism and, in 2004, celebrated the area's 1,000th anniversary as an imperial kiln-production center.

During the Sòng dynasty, Jǐngdé Zhèn came to dominate porcelain production and gained its name from a decision by the Sòng Jǐngdé emperor (reigned 1004–07) to upgrade it to a town. It dominated world porcelain production for nearly 1,000 years, not least because Jiāngxī Province has Asia's purest deposits of kaolin clay suitable for firing, and Jǐngdé Zhèn was surrounded by wooded hills providing plentiful quantities of the right kind of firewood (coal causes yellowing in the glaze). Although 17th-century Manchu riots destroyed much of the town, the Yángzǐ to the north, and river systems leading south to Guǎngzhōu, enabled the town to get its wares around China for sale, and later, via the treaty ports, to an increasingly enthusiastic European market. Imperial support also helped—some kilns were employed solely for the making of wares for the emperors and their officials. The first kiln site to produce white china and to use certain underglaze painting techniques, Jǐngdé Zhèn reached its peak of technical brilliance during the mid–17th to late 18th century with the gaudy full-colored enamel overglaze illustrations of *famille vert* and *famille rose* china.

Statues at the end of Zhū Shān Jiē show the process of working the clay, blowing on glazes, carrying items to kilns, and more.

ESSENTIALS

GETTING THERE The **airport** is only 8km (5 miles) out of town, but it has a very limited number of flights only to Shànghǎi, Běijīng, Xiàmén, Chóngqìng, and Shēnzhèn. A **shuttle bus** runs to the Jīchǎng Shòupiào Zhōngxīn (© **0798/822-3907;** ticket office, 8am–5:30pm), in the center of town at Zhū Shān Lù 127. The shuttle fare is ¥5 (65¢) and it leaves for the airport 1½ hours before each flight. A taxi ride costs about ¥20 ($2.50). For more choices, head to Nánchāng's Chāngběi Airport, 6 hours north of Jǐngdé Zhèn.

Rail services are also fairly limited, although there are three trains daily from Běijīng Xī (West), one from Běijīng, two from Shànghǎi, two from Xiàmén, and two from Fúzhōu. However, none start at Jǐngdé Zhèn, so ticket availability is limited. Nánchāng and Jiǔjiāng, both best reached by express bus from Jǐngdé Zhèn, have far more trains. Ticket windows at the station are open from 7:45am to 8pm, with brief breaks.

The **Main Bus Station** (**Kèyùn Zhōngxīn;** © **0798/858-0990**) is on the northwest side of town and is open from 6am to 7pm. Buses to Bōyáng for ferries (see below), and express buses using the highway to Jiǔjiāng and beyond, arrive and depart from here. Destinations include Jiǔjiāng (134km/84 miles; 12 departures 7:30am–6:30pm; ¥30/$3.75), Nánchāng (280km/175 miles; 14 departures 6:30am–7:10pm; ¥60/$7.50 for the best bus), and Wǔhàn (430km/269 miles; 4 departures 7:30am–4:30pm; ¥100/$13), as well as Wēnzhōu, Hángzhōu, Shàoxīng, and Nánjīng. Another bus station (© **0798/820-8156**) opposite the railway station, open from 6:20am to 5:30pm, also serves Jiǔjiāng and Nánchāng.

GETTING AROUND **Taxis** are locally made boxlike Suzukis. Flagfall of ¥5 (65¢) includes 2km (1¼ miles), after which the fare is ¥1 (15¢) per kilometer up to 6km (3¾ miles), then ¥1.50 (20¢) per kilometer thereafter. From 11pm to 5am the fare is ¥1.80 (25¢). **Buses** charge a ¥1 (15¢) flat fare deposited in the slot. Bus no. K35 starts at the Kèyùn Zhōngxīn and goes south past the Jīnyè Dàjiǔdiàn and then east along Zhū Shān Zhōng Lù.

FAST FACTS

Banks, Foreign Exchange & ATMs There's a useful **Bank of China** (open 8am–6pm, to 5:30pm winter) opposite city hall on Zhū Shān Lù. There are no useful ATMs.

Internet Access *Wǎngbā,* such as the one on the south side of Zhū Shān Lù near the junction of Cídū Dà Dào , usually charge ¥2 (25¢) per hour. Dial-up is © **8163.**

Post Office The main post office (open 8am–7pm summer, to 6:30pm winter) is on Zhū Shān Lù.

Visa Extensions The **PSB** (open Mon–Fri 8:30–11:30am and 2:50–5:30pm) is on the west side of Cídū Dà Dào well south of the Zhū Shān Lù junction, in a tall white building with pink steps.

PUTTERING AROUND TOWN

Táocí Lìshǐ Bówùguǎn (Ceramic Historical Exhibition Area) ✿

This is easily the best of several exhibitions devoted to ceramics, and includes several old kilns, areas demonstrating the production process, and ancient houses and temples. The site is down a winding country lane off an urban main street, providing an abrupt transition from town to countryside. The entrance to the left of the ticket office leads to rebuilt ancient kiln types in reddish brick, and a fine old mansion in local style, with black pillars, white walls, and richly carved and gilded interior beams. Glass cases in its three courtyards hold modest displays of ceramics. English signs guide you around the site and visitors can even have a try at the ceramics process themselves.

The **Tiānhóu Gōng** behind the mansion has been heavily reconstructed and is now just a souvenir shop, but beyond that it is a curious temple dedicated to the three deified founders of porcelain making, venerated as the source of Jǐngdé Zhèn's past wealth—the discoverer of china clay, the inventor of forming techniques, and the inventor of firing—worship of whom is unique to Jǐngdé Zhèn. The temple is about 300 years old and seems not to have been renovated since, giving it a rather distressed charm. Blue-and-white porcelain panels give an account of traditional production techniques, and there are statues of the founders at the rear. The one with a red face has not been drinking *báijiǔ*, but has spent too much time close to the kiln. Offerings of plastic fruit and fake ingots suggest the founders are not yet entirely forgotten.

A second entrance to the right of the ticket office leads to an area where, in theory, you can watch the production process in a series of sheds, which begins with pools of clay and continues with racks of pieces in various stages of preparation. But the kiln is no longer fired, there are weeds growing from the clay pits, and this is all for show and shopping.

Behind this area, what looks at first like a dry-stone wall is a large pile of firewood built into the shape of a cottage. Pine wood was carefully cut and stacked this way to guard against rain and spontaneous combustion, and to save the cost of building storage sheds, but the result is a work of art. The duck's-egg-shaped kiln to the right, one of Jǐngdé Zhèn's oldest, occupies only about a quarter of the area of a large barnlike building. The ground floor is a small forest of curved pillars that seem to be largely unfashioned tree trunks, between which are stacked piles of saggars, the rough ceramic outer cases into which pieces were placed for firing. A series of wall-mounted illustrations shows the process.

At the end of the low-ceilinged hall there's a ramp up through a narrow entrance into the arched brickwork of the kiln space itself, where the firewood would have been stacked in patterns depending on the effect required, and saggars containing porcelain requiring different temperatures would have been placed in different positions.

Cídū Dà Dào. Exhibition area (just off Cídū Dà Dào) admission ¥15 ($1.90); Temple admission ¥38 ($4.75). 8am–5pm. Bus: no. 19 to the end of the route. Taxi: about ¥6 (75¢).

Sān Bǎo Shuǐduì (Water-powered Hammers) ✿

A short way into the countryside, some fascinating primitive technology can be seen. Take bus no. K35 for ¥1 (15¢) to the east and alight at the Hútián stop shortly before the terminus where the bus swings right; walk on for 2.5km (1½ miles), or take a taxi. The route leads past shuttered factories and smokeless chimneys peeping from among the green hills. Those few premises still in operation seem to be making saggars rather than finer material, but large trucks still pass, brimful of white clay. The *shuǐduì* can be heard before they are seen, an irregular solid clunking from beneath a thatched hut to the left. Just past it, follow a path that crosses a stream and then swings around to the left to the hut. Inside, four giant wooden mallets with long heads and pointed noses, ingeniously driven by a small water wheel and among the last of their kind, pound soggy masses of clay.

Bus: no. K35 to Hútián; follow directions above.

Táocí Bówùguǎn (Museum of Porcelain) "China is one of China people's contrivance," says an introductory sign helpfully. This old-style (dusty, ill-lit) museum sets out 1,000 years of Jǐngdé Zhèn production, beginning with early shards, proceeding through modest examples of blue-and-white, five-color, and other wares, and ending with the gaudiest although technically impressive modern productions (a vase of flowers in which every single petal, including those of a wilted chrysanthemum, is ceramic, for example).

Liánshè Lù (east side, north of Zhū Shān Lù). Admission ¥15 ($1.90). 9am–5pm.

Xiángjí Lòng Mínzhái Also called the **Pǐntáo Zhái,** this is one of what should eventually be a series of restored Míng-era merchants' houses demonstrating the wealth generated by imperial and private kilns. This sturdy mansion, with its brown pillars and black beams with gold trim, was originally constructed sometime between 1435 and 1449, and contains a small exhibition of photographs of the local area.

Just off the east side of Zhōngshān Běi Lù, immediately north of Zhū Shān. Admission ¥10 ($1.25). 8:30am–5pm.

SHOPPING

Long-distance sleeper buses of the cheaper, more primitive kind leave groaning with vast quantities of rope-bound packages of china. A vast, modern complex opposite the Porcelain Museum has dozens of shops selling nothing but porcelain. Most hotels and museums sell it, too. Even the KFC has it on display. In the various museums, look out for an interesting CD of music performed by the porcelain orchestra.

WHERE TO STAY

The **Jīnyè Dàjiǔdiàn,** in Cídū Dà Dào (© **0798/858-8888;** fax 0798/8566-2233; jd668899@public1.jd.jx.cn), is the best choice (opened in 2002). A three-star hotel in nice condition, it has 21 stories and 228 rooms, but it could do with a few more elevators to reach them. The guest rooms are comfortable and the bathrooms clean. Standard rooms are ¥358 to ¥458 ($45–$57), and suites ¥788 to ¥1,588 ($99–$199), usually with a 30% discount. The usual credit cards are accepted, but there's no foreign exchange. Some "overseas Chinese" tour groups stay here. The restaurant is good value. Of the many budget options along the main street, Zhū Shān Lù, the two-star **Jīnshèng Bīnguǎn** at no. 29 (© **0798/827-1818;** fax 0798/820-7818) is the best choice, refurbished in 2002. Carpetless standard rooms with common bathroom are ¥80 ($10); standard rooms, modest but not too battered, are ¥138 to ¥288 ($17–$36); and triple rooms are ¥180 ($23). Discounts of 15% are easily negotiated. There's a restaurant but no forex service, and credit cards are not accepted. The cheaper standard rooms have bathrooms which double as shower cubicles, but the more expensive rooms have proper bathrooms. April through November is the busy season.

WHERE TO DINE

The restaurant at the **Jīnyè Dàjiǔdiàn** (© **0798/858-7777;** open 6:30–9:30am, 5–9pm, and 9:30pm–2am) offers *Gàn cài* (Jiāngxī dishes) and Chinese standards. The hot dishes (Jiāngxī food is spicy) are labeled *huǒ là*—fiery hot. Try *sāngná niúròu*, "sauna" beef—tender slices in a garlicky, peppery oil, served in a clay pot and cooked by putting small heated stones in the liquid (some Yúnnán dishes are made like this, too). Also try *jǐnggāng lǎobiǎo sǔn*, a peppery dish of solid, chewy, bamboo shoots, with dried tofu. All are good value at around ¥60 ($7.50) for two. **KFC** is now on Zhū Shān Lù, as is the copycat **CFC** or China's Fried Chicken, with identical typeface on the logo. The **Dìyī Lú Miànbāo** (**No. 1 bakery;** open 7am–10:30pm) at the corner of Zhōngshān Lù, has fresh bread and cakes to take on your journey.

10 Guǎngzhōu

Guǎngdōng Province, 163km (102 miles) NW of Hong Kong, 165km (103 miles) NE of Macau

Guǎngzhōu has recently become the workshop of the world. In and around its satellite cities, there are more assembly lines, factories, and mass production than anywhere else on the planet. Visitors seeking nature, history, or even culture are going to be sorely disappointed as Guǎngzhōu is all about one thing—profit. Even so, this massive concentration of commerce provides plenty of interesting color for those who know where to look. Ignore all those remarkably dull sights glorifying the revolutionary credentials of the city and seek out instead what the Cantonese currently have passions for: business and food.

ESSENTIALS

GETTING THERE Guǎngzhōu's new and nearly finished **airport** is barely in Guǎngzhōu anymore. It's way out in the sticks, in a white-tiled cluster called **Huā Dū.** Don't be surprised if your taxi driver asks for the ridiculous sum of ¥150 ($19) just to get out of town.

Fortunately, there are plenty of regular **buses** to dozens of locations within the city at the princely sum of ¥16 ($2). Seven main bus routes traverse Guǎngzhōu but nos. 1 and 2 will probably satisfy the short-term visitor. No. 1 goes to the old station and no. 2 goes through Tiān Hé and past the big hotels on Huǎnshì Lù. For more information contact the **Báiyún Port Bus Service** (© 020/3129-8077). The no. 3 metro line connecting the airport with the city might be open in late 2006 but, then again, this is China. *Tip:* For those heading to Hong Kong from elsewhere in China, it's often considerably cheaper to fly here or (even better) to Shēnzhèn instead, and then take a bus, train, or boat. Guǎngzhōu is also connected internationally to Amsterdam, Bangkok, Fukuoka, Jakarta, Kuala Lumpur, Los Angeles, Melbourne, Osaka, Phnom Penh, Seoul, Singapore, Sydney, and Tokyo. As elsewhere, tickets are best bought from agents rather than directly from airlines. **CITS** (© 020/8669-0179 air tickets; or 020/8666-4661 train tickets; Mon–Fri 8:30am–6:30pm, Sat–Sun 9am–5pm) to the right of the main railway station as you face it is unusually helpful, with some English spoken. Air ticket prices can be bargained down. Buses run to and from CITS to the airport every 30 minutes for ¥3 (40¢).

Most **trains** arrive at the main railway station **Guǎngzhōu Huǒchēzhàn** (known locally as **Lǎo Zhàn**, the old station), which has services from Běijīng Xī, Chéngdū, Xī'ān, Shíjiāzhuāng, Zhèngzhōu, Chóngqìng, Níngbō, Lánzhōu, Wēnzhōu, and many more cities. There are a few services to Shēnzhèn. For information, call © 020/6135-7412 or 020/6135-8952. There's an information counter toward the right-hand end of the railway station as you face it, open from 5am to midnight. The 24-hour

Guǎngzhōu

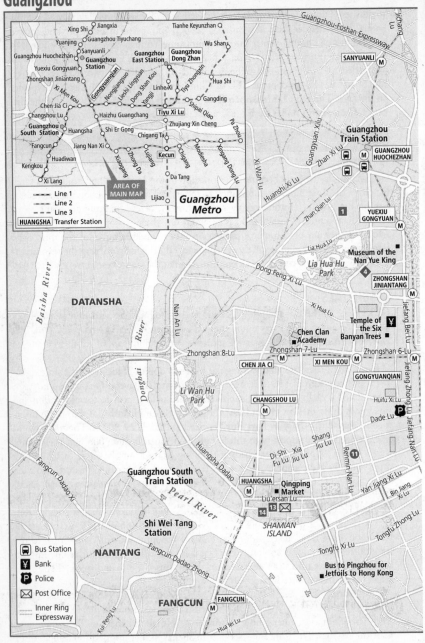

Guangzhou Metro

- —•— Line 1
- —•— Line 2
- —•— Line 3
- **HUANGSHA** Transfer Station

AREA OF MAIN MAP

Xing Shi
Jiangxia
Tianhe Keyunzhan
Wu Shan
Yuanjing
Guangzhou Tiyuchang
Guangzhou Huochezhan
Sanyuanli
Guangzhou East Station
Guangzhou Dong Zhan
Guangzhou Station
Yuexiu Gongyuan
Zhongshan Jiniantang
Gongyuanqian
Nongjiangsuo
Lieshi Lingyuan
Dong Shan Kou
Yangji
Linhe Xi
Tiyu Zhongxin
Hua Shi
Xi Men Kou
Chen Jia Ci
Haizhu Guangchang
Tiyu Xi Lu
Shipai Qiao
Gangding
Changshou Lu
Zhujiang Xin Cheng
Guangzhou South Station
Huangsha
Shi Er Gong
Chigang Ta
Pa Zhou
Fangcun
Jiang Nan Xi
Xiaogang
Zhong Da
Lujiang
Kecun
Chigang
Modiesha
Xingang Dong Lu
Huadiwan
Kengkou
Xi Lang
Da Tang
Lijiao

Guangzhou-Foshan Expressway
Jichang Lu

SANYUANLI Ⓜ

Guangzhou Train Station
🚌🚌 Ⓜ **GUANGZHOU HUOCHEZHAN**

Guangyuan Xilu
Zhan Xi Lu
Huanshi Xi Lu

1

YUEXIU GONGYUAN Ⓜ

Lia Hua Lu
Museum of the Nan Yue King ■

Zhan Qian Lu

Dong Feng Xi Lu
Lia Hua Hu Park

4
ZHONGSHAN JINIANTANG Ⓜ

Xi Hua Lu

Temple of the Six Banyan Trees ¥ ■

DATANSHA

Baisha River
Donghai River

Nan An Lu

Chen Clan Academy ■

Zhongshan 7-Lu
Zhongshan 8-Lu
CHEN JIA CI Ⓜ
XI MEN KOU Ⓜ
Zhongshan 6-Lu

Jiefang Bei Lu
Jiefang Zhong Lu
Jiefang Nan Lu

GONGYUANQIAN Ⓜ

Huifu Xi Lu
Ⓟ
Dade Lu

Li Wan Hu Park

CHANGSHOU LU Ⓜ

Di Shi Fu Lu
Xia Jiu Lu
Shang Jiu Lu

Renmin Nan Lu

11

Guangzhou South Train Station

Huangsha Dadao

HUANGSHA Ⓜ

Qingping Market ■
Liu'ersan Lu

Yan Jiang Xi Lu
Bin Jiang Xi Lu

Fangcun Dadao Xi

Shi Wei Tang Station

Pearl River

14 **13** ✉

SHAMIAN ISLAND

Tongfu Xi Lu
Tongfu Zhong Lu

NANTANG

Fangcun Dadao Zhong

Bus to Pingzhou for Jetfoils to Hong Kong ■

FANGCUN

Kui Peng Lu

FANGCUN Ⓜ

Hua lei Lu

Legend
- 🚌 Bus Station
- ¥ Bank
- Ⓟ Police
- ✉ Post Office
- Inner Ring
- Expressway

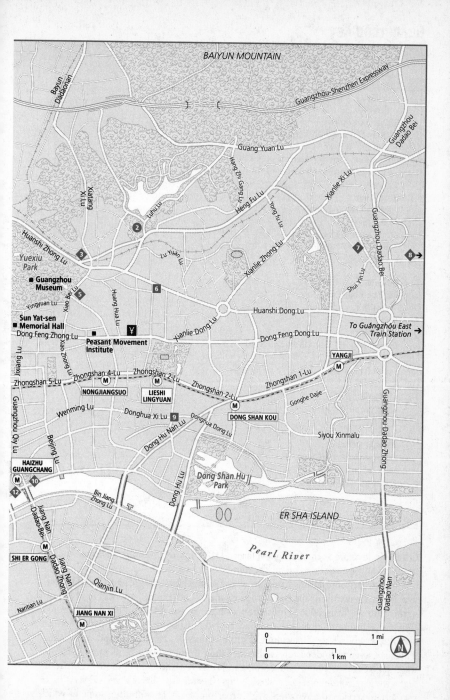

BAIYUN MOUNTAIN

Guangzhou-Shenzhen Expressway

Guang Yuan Lu

Guangzhou Dadao Bei

Bayun Dadaonan

Xiatang Xi Lu

Luhu Lu

Hang Zhi Gang Lu

Heng Fu Lu

Yong Fu Lu

Xianlie Xi Lu

②

Huanshi Zhong Lu

③

Lu Yuan Lu

Xianlie Zhong Lu

⑦

Guangzhou Dadao Bei

⑧ →

Yuexiu Park

■ **Guangzhou Museum**

Yingyuan Lu

Xiao Bei Lu

⑤

⑥

Huanshi Dong Lu

Shui Yin Lu

■ **Sun Yat-sen Memorial Hall**

Dong Feng Zhong Lu

Huang Hua Lu

Xianlie Dong Lu

Dong Feng Dong Lu

To Guǎngzhōu East Train Station →

Guangzhou Qiy Lu

Xiao Zhong Lu

¥

■ **Peasant Movement Institute**

Zhongshan 4-Lu

Zhongshan 2-Lu

Zhongshan 2-Lu

Zhongshan 1-Lu

YANGJI Ⓜ

Guangzhou Dadao Zhong

Zhongshan 5-Lu

NONGJIANGSUO

Ⓜ **LIESHI LINGYUAN**

Wenming Lu

Beijing Lu

Donghua Xi Lu **⑨**

Donghua Dong Lu

Gonghe Dajie

Ⓜ **DONG SHAN KOU**

Siyou Xinmalu

Dong Hu Nan Lu

Dong Hu Nan Lu

Dong Shan Hu Park

HAIZHU GUANGCHANG

Ⓜ **⑩**

⑫

Bin Jiang Zhong Lu

Dong Shan Hu Park

ER SHA ISLAND

Jiang Nan Dadao Bei

Ⓜ

SHI ER GONG

Jiang Nan Dadao Zhong

Pearl River

Guangzhou Dadao Nan

Qianjin Lu

Nantian Lu

JIANG NAN XI

Ⓜ

0		1 mi

0		1 km

N

Guǎngzhōu Key

ticket windows are at the far right-hand end. Buy up to 12 days in advance. The 24-hour left-luggage windows are in the middle.

Direct trains from **Hong Kong** arrive at **Guǎngzhōu Dōng Zhàn (East Station),** which is conveniently at the end of the first metro line (exit D), and will be at the end of the third line from 2006. This station is on the express line from Běijīng Xī through Jiǔjiāng with direct trains that continue to Hong Kong on alternate days There are also direct services to Chángchūn, Tiānjīn, Qīngdǎo, Nánchāng, and other cities. There are seven train departures a day for **Hong Kong** between 9:50am and 5:20pm; the trip takes 1½ to 2 hours and costs from HK$190 (US$23). For more information, see www.kcrc.com/eng/services/services/itts_shedule.asp. There's also a very high-speed train service to **Shēnzhèn,** with departures every few minutes, some of which cover the 139km (87 miles) in under an hour and drop you right next to the border crossing to Hong Kong at Luó Hú/Lo Wu. (A few slower services run to and from the main railway station.) The railway station has a customer service center (open 5:30am–11:40pm), a number of air ticket agents (some surprisingly competitive), and a counter selling tickets for Shànghăi, Tàiyuán, Jiŭjiāng, and Běijīng Xī (West). The main ticket windows, open from 5:50am to 9:40pm with short breaks, are set back on the right, while the left-luggage office (open 8:30am–6:30pm) has moved to the central concourse. The Hong Kong ticket office (open 7:30am–6pm) is at the far end of the concourse, upstairs on the right. The entrance to Hong Kong trains, via Customs, is just beyond that.

Guăngzhōu has multiple **long-distance bus stations.** Luxury buses provide more frequent and rapid connections than trains to all parts of Guăngdōng Province, southern Fújiàn, and eastern Guăngxī. The three most useful stations are all near the main railway station. The **Liúhuā Chēzhàn** (open 5am–10:30pm) is reached by an underpass across the station forecourt and to the right. It has buses to Shēnzhèn (15 departures 6am–10:30pm; ¥60/$7.50; and a few more expensive services); and to Zhūhăi (60 departures 5:45am–10pm; ¥35–¥45/$4.40–$5.60). From the far right-hand corner of the station forecourt as you leave it, turn right along Huánshì Xī Lù, and the 24-hour **Shěng Qìchē Kèyùn Zhàn** is a couple of minutes farther on the right. It has services to Shēnzhèn (¥60/$7.50) every 12 minutes from 6:15am to 11pm; to Zhūhăi Gŏng Běi for Macau (¥55/$6.90) every 20 minutes from 6:30am to 8:30pm; and to Kāipíng (¥35/$4.40) every 40 minutes from 6:30am to 7pm. There are also services to Guìlín, Nánníng, and Běihăi. The **Shì Qìchē Kèyùn Zhàn** opposite, over the footbridge, has more departures to the same destinations.

There are also direct bus services to **Hong Kong airport,** picking up at the China Hotel, White Swan, Garden Hotel, International Hotel, Holiday Inn, and other hotels (eight services 5:45am–4:25pm, HK$250/US$32; buses to Guăngzhōu depart 10:05am–5:15pm from the CTS counter at Hong Kong Airport; call ✆ 020/8333-6888, ext. 5384, or 852/2764 9803 in Hong Kong). Buses also run from The Garden Hotel to Hung Hom Station or Prince Edward MTR in Hong Kong; there are 16 departures from 8am to 7:15pm, and the cost is HK$120 (US$16). There are also services to Macau two to three times daily for HK$53 (US$7).

Unfortunately, nearly all of the ferry services to and from Hong Kong have been discontinued, even though the roads become more and more congested everyday. Boats no longer depart from Guăngzhōu, only some of the satellite towns such as Pānyú and Shùndé. The Garden Hotel still has shuttles to Nánhăi where there is still a boat to Hong Kong that takes about 2½ hours. Shuttle buses leave The Garden Hotel at 9am and 4pm and the cost of the service is ¥170 ($20), ¥180 ($23) for first class. Call the Garden Hotel for more info: ✆ 020/8333-8989.

GETTING AROUND   Taxi fares are among China's most expensive, but taxis are still your best choice for getting around. Flagfall is ¥7 (90¢) including 2km (1¼ miles), then ¥2.60 (30¢) per kilometer up to 15km (9 miles), then 50% more. There are no extra nighttime charges, but beware the 5-to-7pm rush hour, which will add significantly to your costs. The **metro** is the most convenient way to get through Guăngzhōu's heavy traffic but due to pathetic political wranglings, it completely misses many key areas of the city, notably the mainly Hong Kong–invested downtown area around The Garden Hotel. The useful line no. 1 (red on maps) passes Shāmiàn Island (Huángshā Station) and two or three other major sights, ending up at Guăngzhōu East railway station. Line no. 2 (green) opened in 2003 and will eventually reach the current airport; it passes the main railway station and one or two useful hotels. A third line is scheduled to open in 2006 bringing the total distance covered to 37km (23 miles), but the mayor recently announced that he planned to have a whopping 255km (158 miles) of lines by 2010. Tickets cost ¥2 to ¥5 (25¢–65¢) according to the distance to be traveled, as shown on a color-coded sign above ticket machines. Stored-value cards allowing multiple journeys are also available from the metro station ticket desks. The system runs from around 6am to 11pm. Oddly, the metro stations are fairly well signposted, but the entrances are overly discreet. There are English on-board announcements. Ordinary buses charge a flat fare of ¥1 (15¢); newer air-conditioned versions charge a flat fare of ¥2 (25¢).

VISITOR INFORMATION   Guǎngzhōu supports several free magazines that tend to be more advertorial than useful information, obtainable from hotel lobbies and expat hangouts. They contain reviews of new restaurants, clubs, and bars (usually paid for), and intermittently accurate listings. *That's Guangzhou* is marginally better than *South China City Talk,* but not much since the English owner was pushed out in a very hostile takeover by his greedy Chinese bean-counters. *Guangzhou Today* is advertorials from cover to cover.

American Express (© 020/8331-1311; fax 020/8331-1616) has a branch in the office building of the Guǎngdōng International Hotel. It's open Monday through Friday from 9am to 5pm. For official tourist information, call © 020/8668-7051; for complaints call © 020/8667-8043; and for emergency rescue (!) call © 020/8666-6330.

FAST FACTS

Banks, Foreign Exchange & ATMs   Most of the many branches of the **Bank of China** (open 9am–noon and 2–5pm) have forex services and ATMs accepting foreign cards, including the branch inside The Garden Hotel and the nearby Friendship Store. But be prepared to wait. Nearly all banks now have a ticket system like you find at a cheese counter. Just take a number and wait your turn. There's a newly opened branch of the **Hongkong and Shanghai Bank** at the front of The Garden Hotel on Huánshì Lù.

Consulates   The consulate of **Australia** is in room 1509 in the main building of the Guǎngdōng International Hotel (© 020/8335-0909). The consulate of **Canada** is in Suite 801, Wing C in the China Hotel (© 020/8666-0569, ext. 0). The **U.K.** consulate is on the second floor of the Guǎngdōng International Hotel (© 020/8335-1354). The **U.S.** consulate is at Shāmiàn Nán Lù 1 (© 020/8121-8000). Onward visas for **Vietnam** are available on the second floor of B Building North at the Landmark Hotel, Qiáoguāng Lù 8 (© 020/8330-5911); hours are Monday through Friday from 9am to noon and 2 to 5pm. Cambodia, Denmark, France, Italy, Japan, Korea, Malaysia, The Philippines, Poland, Thailand, and The Netherlands also have consulates in Guǎngzhōu.

Internet Access   There are Internet cafes everywhere but most of them are dark, dingy places populated by sad locals. A far cleaner alternative is on the second floor of the Guǎngzhōu library, just outside the Lièshì Língyuán subway stop. No smoking is allowed and the keyboards are still legible—all for just ¥2 (25¢) per hour. Deposit is (¥50/$6.30); have your passport with you in case its requested. It's open Thursday to Tuesday (9am–5pm); on Wednesdays, you can head to the nearby Zhōngshān library (Zhōngshān Lù 4) instead. Dial-up is © 163, or the faster © 96169.

Post Office   There's a useful post office (open Mon–Sat 9am–5pm) in Sān Jiē on Shāmiàn if you happen to be staying in that part of town, but for sending anything bulky, try the branch outside the old railway station, where both of the packing guys are extremely helpful and speak excellent English.

Visa Extensions   The **PSB** is at Jiěfàng Nán Lù 155 (© **020/8311-5808;** open Mon–Fri 8:50–11:30am and 2:30–5pm) at the corner of Dàdé Lù. Pick up an application form upstairs on floor M1 (open 8–11:15am and 2:20–4:45pm) then continue past various travel agencies mostly selling overseas travel to Chinese (air tickets from Guǎngzhōu and Hong Kong airports) to the fourth floor, where there can be long queues. Extensions take five working days to obtain.

EXPLORING GUĂNGZHŌU

History buffs and culture vultures may well be disappointed in Guǎngzhōu as this city moves to a very different beat, the vibrant pulse of international trade. The art museum is one of the best in the country and is definitely worth a visit, but apart from that the real highlights are the markets, the vast bazaars, and the huge numbers of people crammed into this small river delta. Those making a brief trip to Guǎngzhōu from Hong Kong should concentrate on the commerce rather than the culture. The Provincial Museum, the Sun Yat-sen Memorial Hall, the Peasant Movement Institute, and other revolutionary sites are all dull and avoidable.

SHĀMIÀN ISLAND ♠

Forced to relinquish a permanent trading base to the hated barbarians (us) at the end of the First Opium War in 1841, the Guǎngzhōu authorities probably snickered as they palmed off a sandbar to the British and French. Perhaps they snickered less when it was promptly bunded (made secure with artificial embankments); was provided with proper streets, drainage, and imposing buildings; and became home to a prosperous foreign enclave with everything from tennis courts to a yacht club. The rest of Guǎngzhōu lacked even properly surfaced roads well into the 20th century. Resentment from the local authorities manifested itself in dictatorial regulations, restricting traders solely to the island (barely half the size it is today and resulting in the word "cantonment") and forbidding wives or families. There was a death penalty for anybody attempting to learn Chinese, and the only time that the foreigners were allowed to leave the island was by rowboat to visit the notorious flower boats upriver, lucrative sidelines for the same Cantonese merchants that monopolized the vast opium networks that quickly brought China to its knees.

Shāmiàn still retains some of its former grandeur in the mansions which were the foreign residences, business premises, banks, and consulates. The mansions were taken over by dozens of families after 1949, but they were recently restored in many cases to former splendor, with each major building labeled as to its former purpose. Now partly pedestrianized, its broader boulevards are like long thin gardens with a lot of topiary. A line of bars and cafes on the southwest side with views over the Pearl River serves modern expats. Dozens of small businesses close to the modern White Swan Hotel aim to entrap those on organized tours who wander out of the hotel by themselves and think they are being brave. Souvenir stalls, tailoring stores, and teahouses all have inflated prices, and all offer "special discounts" to those with children—the U.S. consulate on the island is the one specializing in adoption matters, and adoptive parents fan out from here to collect their new daughters (almost always daughters) and return to do the paperwork. One or two of the old mansions are roofless and boarded up, but others are open as restaurants, shops, or hotels.

Metro: Huángshā on line no. 1.

Hǎizhū Square Wholesale Market   What was once a stronghold of revolutionary fervor (as can be seen from the rifle-thrusting monument in the center of the round-about) has succumbed entirely to the forces of the free market and is now one of the most colorful markets in Asia, a vast area that stretches from Hǎizhū Square almost as far down as Shāmiàn Island. Apart from the usual toys, furnishings, and electronics, this is a great place to find many of those souvenirs found in tourist shops around the rest of the country, but here at wholesale prices. A short walk to west along Yìdé Lù brings you to even more markets, with vast areas specializing in stationery, toys, and even dried foods. It is a shame that most people stop off in Guǎngzhōu at the begin-ning of their trip into China as this is the ultimate shopping stop and would be much more suitable on the return journey.

Metro: Hǎizhū Square on line no. 1.

Zhuàng Yuán Fāng   Many visitors come to China and focus solely on relics and artifacts from the purported 5,000 years of history. Here instead is a chance to see China's youth, the so called Q generation, up close and personal. Originally a street devoted to costumes, instruments, and props for Cantonese opera, only one or two of this kind of emporium remains, while the rest has been taken over by innumerable fashion stores, and is now the place where many trends and fads are started. Unfortu-nately the current fashions seem to be West Coast hip meets East Coast bag lady. Spiky-haired teenagers puff on orange and strawberry cigarettes while others chomp on stinky fried tofu or even stinkier durian ice cream. Don't be ashamed by the fact that you are probably the oldest person in a 5km radius.

Look for the large new gateway on the left as you head south from Huifú Lù on Rénmín Nán Lù.

Guǎngzhōu Railway Station   Here is a rare chance to see what China is undoubt-edly most famous for: its enormous population. While other tourist highlights such as Tiān'ān Mén Square are usually devoid of life, here is a large public square that per-petually teems with humanity. Certainly one of the best opportunities to visualize what a population of 1.6 billion really looks like. At Chinese New Year, this square is awash with more than 100,000 people a day, and ticket queues stretch kilometers away into the suburbs. Even at the nonpeak times, being in this area is like being out-side the stadium doors as a rock concert finishes and the audience pours out. The area has a bad reputation for crime but this is rather undeserved, especially compared to the new East Station and the central business district of Tiān Hé, where gangs of pick-pockets roam openly and arrogant motorists make the simple act of crossing the road one of the most high-risk events of your entire holiday. Here at the old station, there are at least 18 kinds of uniformed security as well as patrol cars ranging from con-verted golf carts to oversize SUVs. Business people from all over the province and much of the rest of the country converge here at the vast wholesale clothing markets nearby. Simply find a vantage point and look on in awe, as immense flows of human traffic surge endlessly by.

Huādìwān   Few tourists venture south of the river, but those who do are always impressed with Huādìwān in the Fāngcūn District. As you emerge from the subway, head for the furniture stores that feature carving and carpentry from all over the country. This soon transforms into specialist aquaria stores, then more conventional pet stores and across the road into the bird market. This merges towards the main road with a horticultural section that includes exquisite bonsai trees (known locally as *pénjĭng,* the original Chinese name), and a large number of stores featuring "viewing stones," oddly shaped rocks and stones that often resemble dragons, deities, and wild animals.

Huādiwān Subway Station on line no. 1.

Guăngzhōu Art Museum   Guăngzhōu has a number of thinly disguised propaganda venues posing as museums, but this is not one of them. In fact this is a thoroughly new generation of attraction that is a world away from the Peasant Movement Institute and the Mausoleum of the Revolutionary Martyrs. Among the nine permanent galleries, four are dedicated to local artists from the Cantonese school of painting called Lìng-nán that first emerged in the late 1800s. Look for exquisite scrolls featuring rural scenes and pastel blossoms. Another gallery contains a first-class collection of Tibetan *thangkas* (religious icon tapestries) donated by a Hong Kong collector. Take a break by the relaxing fish ponds where huge schools of brightly colored koi carp vie for your attention.

13 Lùhú Lù. Admission ¥30 ($3.75). 9am–5pm.

THE LEANING TOWERS OF KĀIPÍNG ☆☆

Much of southern Guăngdōng is a sprawl of untidy and often grim manufacturing, where sweated labor produces the world's toys. But Kāipíng, 136km (85 miles) southwest of Guăngzhōu, 164km (102 miles) from the Macau border, and also reachable by sea directly from Hong Kong, is China at its most bucolic. Peasants in conical straw hats bend over their plants, and position hand-powered threshing machines on shoulder poles, much as in other provinces. But here they often toil beneath the gaze of extraordinary towers called *diāolóu,* which are partly Portuguese Gothic, like *Citizen Kane's* Xanadu broken into nearly 2,000 fragments and sprinkled across the county. Some squat brick fortresses dating from the 17th century were intended as places of refuge for whole villages. But more alien watchtowers were mostly built by Chinese who traveled out through the treaty ports and returned wealthy in the late 19th and early 20th centuries to buy land, build a house, and marry. Simple concrete towers were merely lookout points intended to provide warning of approaching bandits, but by the 1920s these had evolved into massive fortified residences up to nine stories high, sprouting turrets and loopholes, balconies and cupolas, borrowed from half-understood European styles encountered everywhere from Macau to Manila. Of around 3,000 originals, 1,833 still stand, towering over almost every village. A representative sample can be visited in a day by taxi, or Kāipíng town can used as a base for exploring by public transport and on foot.

There are around 50 buses daily to Kāipíng from Guăngzhōu (about 2 hr.; last bus back at 6pm; ¥30/$3.75), and eight from the Macau border at Zhūhăi Gŏng Bĕi (2½ hr.; last bus back at 6:30pm; ¥45/$5.60). A representative sample of towers can be seen in a day by chartering a taxi in Kāipíng or, with an early start, en route between Macau and Guăngzhōu. There are also nine bus services from Shēnzhèn (299km/187 miles; ¥65/$8). Kāipíng makes a far more pleasant entry point to the mainland from Hong Kong than Shēnzhèn does, and there's a daily high-speed **catamaran** service

from Hong Kong's China (HK) Ferry Terminal at 8:30pm (4 hr.; from HK$180/
US$23) to Kāipíng's Sānbù port, just east of the center (taxi around ¥12/$1.50), with
the return to Hong Kong at 1:30pm costing from ¥160 ($20). See **www.cksp.com.hk**
for more information.

The oldest surviving *diāolóu* is the **Yínglóng Lóu** at **Sān Mén Lǐ**, 15 minutes west
on the main road and passed by many local buses. A narrow pine-lined path leads to
the village, and the tower is through a narrow passage between ancient houses. It's a
three-story solid brick place of refuge, the lower two reddish stories built sometime
between 1436 and 1449, and the upper gray one added in 1919. The villagers suffered
serious flooding in 1884 and 1908, took refuge in the upper stories, and survived.
Their descendants are pleased by your interest and very proud that they kept their
diāolóu when everyone else knocked theirs down (brick can be recycled for other
uses—concrete cannot, so most survivors are of later date); they may unlock the tower
so you can climb the bare interior.

The largest single collection of *diāolóu* is at **Zìlì Cūn**. Almost any bus passing Sān
Mén Lǐ will drop you at the right-hand turn toward **Tángkǒu,** where there's a convenience store and some small restaurants. Motorbikes here will take you to Zìlì Cūn, turning right again where there's a gas station after 4km (2½ miles), and then going through
Tángkǒu. Most buses from Kāipíng drop you at the gas station (every 20 min.;
¥4/50¢), from where it's a 5-minute walk into Tángkǒu and a 45-minute walk beyond
that on a country lane that swings left into Zìlì Cūn at the last moment. Or you can
stay on the bus until a closer stop, when you'll be pointed vaguely across the paddies
and duck ponds to a visible cluster of towers. Taxis from Kāipíng charge about ¥70
($8.75) per hour. They can also take you to Zìlì Cūn and wait for 1 hour for ¥80 ($10).

The 15 towers close together here, like a miniature city, are scheduled to be the first
developed for tourism—a new road big enough to take tour buses is being built. This
is a very impressive group of towers, with little stone paths weaving through the
marshy ground on which they stand; the marsh no doubt contributes to the slight lean
some of them display. Wooden signs indicate a viewing route, but you won't exactly
be elbowing your way through hordes of other visitors, although there's sometimes a
pause as a gaggle of ducks crosses from one damp patch to another. Villagers chop
sugar cane, geese seek shade beneath banana palms, and crabs cluster beneath bridges.
Most of the towers are three or four stories high, made of concrete, their top stories
decked with arches and balustrades, ornamental urns, and turreted corners. Perhaps
the most elegant is the taller **Míngshí Lóu**, on the right toward the rear of the village.
There are plans to open this as a museum, as it retains late-Qīng furnishings and a
top-floor ancestral shrine. The last bus back from the Tángkǒu turning is at 6pm.

Farther southwest, about 35 minutes from Kāipíng on buses heading to **Chìkǎn**
(¥4/50¢), **Xiàbiān Cūn** has a rather different tower, the five-story **Shì Lú** of 1924, to
the left as you enter the village. Cement, unknown in mainland China, had to be
imported from Hong Kong at considerable expense, and the ingenious alternative was
to make a tower of rammed earth, sugar, lime, and sticky rice. The clayey red soil has
left its warm color in the pink-ocher walls, and the pits left by its extraction are now
fishponds beside a row of ancient housing. Limited supplies of cement were reserved
for the tower's top, with its balcony, pepper-potted corners, and domed pavilion.

Farther southwest at **Xiǎngǎng**, 50 minutes and ¥4 (50¢) from Kāipíng, are perhaps
the oddest tower and the most impressive tower of all. Motorbikes meet buses, but it's
much more enjoyable to do this on foot. The first tower is about a 2.5km (1½-mile)

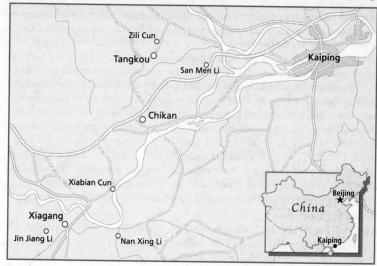

walk. Cross the river bridge with views of river-going vessels, homes to their owners, with firewood stacked on their decks, and turn left onto Dōng Lóng Lù (East Dragon St.). After a short distance, the path passes a gate and shrinks to a track before reaching the unspoiled and friendly little village of Dōng Xī Cūn. The third narrow alley between the traditional houses leads to a vast European-influenced mansion, whose owners went back overseas again and are now said by the villagers to be in San Francisco. Carry straight on and descend to a decent, paved road. Turn left, making a note of where to turn off on your return. Passing the occasional armchair grave, water buffalo wallowing in the paddies, rice and buffalo dung laid out to dry on the road, you reach the first major village on the left; the village of **Nán Xìng Lǐ** is beyond this one on the right. Here's China's answer to Italy's *Torre di Pisa,* a slender six-story concrete finger called the **Nán Xìng Xié Lóu (Leaning Tower of Nán Xìng),** 2m (5½ ft.) in height and inclined severely but very photogenically to one side. It is reflected attractively in the village pond. The tower's top is out of alignment, with an annual lean increase of 2 centimeters (⅘ in.)—so though it has survived since 1902, you'd better see it while you can. Even when just completed, it was already leaning so far the watchman had to put bricks under one side of his bed.

Returning to Xiàngāng, turn right and recross the bridge, then turn left and walk straight out the other side of town; the narrow road wriggles between other *diāolóu* en route. Once you're in the fields, fork left. There are optional diversions into other villages, but swing left at a junction with a modern pavilion, and the **Ruìshí Lóu** in **Jǐn Jiāng Lǐ** will shortly appear on the right across the waterlogged fields. The road leads past it to the village entrance and across the open area at the entrance, where people shoo pigeons away from drying rice. Any narrow alley between the ancient houses where shoeless children scurry among the chickens will take you to the tower's base. This is perhaps the most magnificent *diāolóu* of all, built by a man who ran a bank and herbal medicine store in Hong Kong. Completed in 1925, it took 3 years to construct using local labor but imported materials. The nine-story tower dominates the village, with its corners and windows decorated from top to bottom, a gallery with domed corners running around all four sides, and a two-story octagonal folly at the top. Nearly as elaborate, the neighboring **Shēngfēng Lóu,** completed in 1925 by a returnee from the U.S., has bizarre columns running up two stories of elevated galleries. A motorbike ride out to this village and back will cost around ¥4 (50¢), and to the two sites about ¥10 ($1.25).

There's much pleasure to be had just by rambling at will through the countryside, heading towards any toothy towers visible on the skyline. Few are still occupied, but many are used for storage, and sometimes the remarkably friendly local people, seeing your curiosity, will invite you to inspect the tower and climb to the roof for a panoramic view of the countryside. A small local government team is working to obtain UNESCO World Heritage listing for the towers, and they have already placed plaques with good English at these sites. But they are proceeding cautiously with tourism development, and for now, roads cannot accommodate tour buses. Schemes to control entry to the narrow spaces in the towers are being considered before any are opened as museums.

GETTING AROUND   **Taxis** in Kāipíng are mostly Jettas or Santanas with a ¥5 (65¢) flagfall which includes 2km (1¼ miles), then a fare of ¥2 (25¢) per kilometer. From 11pm to 5am, flagfall is ¥6 (75¢). Rentals for trips out of town should not involve the meter, however. Bargain down from the first asking price of ¥70 ($8.75) per hour, especially if you plan to be out for a few hours. The first price for Tángkǒu, a 1-hour wait, and return is ¥80 ($10). **Buses** to Tángkǒu, Xiǎngǎng, and Chìkǎn leave from two green-arched parking bays at the rear of the bus station. The left is for Tángkǒu and the right for the other towns; there are about one to three buses an hour between about 6:30am and 5:30pm.

For those who want to stay overnight, Kāipíng is a pleasant small town at the confluence of two rivers. There are still sizable communities of émigré Kāipíngrén who return regularly, and many who retire here (buying specially built apartments rather than constructing towers). The five-star **Ever Joint Hotel (Tán Jiāng Bàndǎo Jiǔdiàn)** at Zhōngyín Lù 2 (© **0750/233-3333;** fax 0750/233-8333; www.jmtour.org/tanjiang) doesn't quite deserve its grade but, run by the White Swan people from Guǎngzhōu, it is surprisingly glitzy for such a small town, and is full of "overseas Chinese." Its tower, positioned at the tip of an island dividing the Tán River, has excellent views; standard rooms cost from ¥800 to ¥1,250 ($100–$156), suites from ¥1,200 to ¥8,000 ($150–$1,000). A 10% service charge is not usually added. Discounts of 20% are available year-round, and you can usually bargain from there. A short walk along Xī Jiāo Lù (opposite the bus station entrance) past a KFC, the **Guǎngshì Jiǔdiàn** (© **0750/221-2213;** fax 0750/229-8409) is a modest two-star hotel whose best guest rooms and bathrooms have had a recent refit. "Luxury" rooms can be bargained from ¥173 ($22) to ¥138 ($17), and surprisingly contain a VCD player, for which the hotel will loan free disks. This is the best of the budget hotels. The **Shìjì Zhī Zhōu Cāntīng (Ship of the Century),** Yán Jiāng Xī Lù 18 (© **0750/222-2988;** open 9am–2am) is a two-story boat-shaped restaurant/cafe/bar on the river itself whose "sails" form an awning over a platform with pleasant views. There's an English menu, local and Western dishes (including breakfast), very cold beer, and decent coffee. Main dishes are around ¥20 ($2.50).

WHERE TO STAY

Guăngzhōu is quite expensive. Don't visit in April or October when the main trade fairs are on, as you may have to pay even above rack rates. Sweltering July and August are popular with tour groups. However, from November to March, rates drop, with a further dip in December and after Chinese New Year.

This is one of the last cities where the cavernous hotels with innumerable rooms and endless facilities have survived in any numbers. These are designed to serve the vast numbers of businesspeople attending the main trade fairs in the last 2 weeks of October and April. These have an effect on room rates as far away as Hong Kong, and the major hotels, despite their cavernous size, are likely to be full in that period and offering no discounts. Otherwise, expect to cut 20% to 50% from the prices quoted, although major hotels also add a 10% service charge and a 5% city tax. Lesser hotels conform to normal Chinese standards by not adding service and including city tax in the quoted price.

The larger hotels, with the exception of the White Swan, are in the busiest sections of a busy city, and even if you're used to staying at five-star and four-star accommodations, you should consider smaller, quieter hotels on Shāmiàn Island, which is largely pedestrianized, and where a little peace and quiet can be found. Some of those are conversions of old colonial buildings, of considerably more character than the average hotel, and on a smaller and more human scale.

EXPENSIVE

The Garden Hotel (Huāyuán Jiǔdiàn)
The 30-story Y-shaped Garden Hotel is a Chinese five-star colossus with every imaginable facility, and easily the grandest lobby in Guăngzhōu (reputedly the largest in Asia). Its level of service is among Guăngzhōu's best, and its rooms are slightly more imaginative than the China Hotel's. *Tip:* The road outside, Jiàn Shè Liù Mălù, is infinitely more interesting to shop than the hotel's shopping arcade, with a number of popular coffee shops ranging from Starbucks all the way down to the tiny but reliable Peoples' Cafe tucked away on a side street.

Huánshì Dōng Lù 368. ☎ 020/8333-8989. Fax 020/8335-0467. www.thegardenhotel.comcn. 1,038 units. ¥1,160–¥2,080 ($145–$260) standard room; ¥2,740–¥4,980 ($343–$623) suite. AE, DC, MC, V. **Amenities:** 11 restaurants and bars; swimming pool; tennis and squash courts; fitness room; sauna; children's playground; tour and ticket desk; limousine service; forex; shopping arcade; salon; babysitting; dry cleaning; valet. *In room:* A/C, satellite TV, minibar, fridge.

Globelink Hotel (Quánqiú Tōng Dàjiǔdiàn) ✵
It is surprising that so few Western tourists stay at the Globelink, as it has by far the largest rooms in the city. Its location is very central, with easy access to the subway as well as large shopping areas such

---

⸢Tips⸥ Affordable Accommodating Newcomers

The larger five-star hotels are quickly becoming uncompetitive dinosaurs, thanks to appearance of lean new competitors such as Unotel, which now has eight smart business hotels in Guăngzhōu and two more in Shēnzhèn. Rooms are light, clean, and much more modern that many larger, more expensive places, and with prices starting at just (¥220/$28), they make very sensible options for travelers seeking good value rather than endless facilities. Go to www.unotel.com.cn for full details and locations.

as Běijīng Road, China Plaza, and Hǎiyīn Electronics Market. The staff is friendly and helpful; a few even speak English. Best of all, the discounted prices for this four-star hotel are unbeatable.

Yuèxiù Nán Lù 208. ⓒ 020/8389-8138. Fax 020/8389-8899. globalh@public.guangzhou.gd.cn. 406 units. ¥480 ($60) standard room; ¥580–¥680 ($72–$85) suite. AE, DC, MC, V. **Amenities:** 3 restaurants; lobby lounge bar; nightclub; health club; sauna; business center; forex; salon; health clinic; valet. *In room:* A/C, cable TV, broadband Internet access, minibar.

White Swan Hotel (Bái Tiān'é Bīnguǎn) *(Kids)* This was one of China's first luxury hotels (1982)—an ugly, labyrinthine monster whose dominating location on Shāmiàn Island and views over the Pearl River have all but destroyed the island's colonial atmosphere. The more you pay, the higher your room. Refurbishment is a continuous process, and the hotel is unusual among long-standing hotels in keeping up standards and adding facilities. Some slightly larger rooms come with dataport, some with broadband Internet access, high ceilings, and new furniture. The tacky lobby features a waterfall and fish-stocked pools crossed by bridges. Former guests include Queen Elizabeth II and former U.S. president George Bush. Many agencies organizing adoptions use the White Swan: Every floor is fully stocked with diaper service, parents get a free toy, and the hotel goes quiet at nap time—no wonder it has been nicknamed the White Stork.

Shāmiàn Nán Jiē 1 (on Shāmiàn Island). ⓒ 020/8188-6968. Fax 020/8186-1188. www.whiteswanhotel.com. 843 units. ¥2,320–¥2,800 ($290–$350) standard room; ¥2,960–¥3,440 ($370–$430) suite. Rack rates are halved outside trade fair periods, and can often be bargained down by a further 30%. AE, DC, MC, V. **Amenities:** Multiple restaurants; nightclub; 2 swimming pools; golf driving range; 10 tennis courts; squash court; fitness room; sauna; extensive children's facilities; tour desk; business center; forex; extensive shopping arcade with bakery, florist, bookshop, and pharmacy; salon. *In room:* A/C, satellite TV, dataport, broadband Internet access (select rooms: ¥150/$19 per 24 hr.), minibar, fridge.

MODERATE TO INEXPENSIVE

Guǎngdōng Victory Hotel (Guǎngdōng Shènglì Bīnguǎn) This hotel has two premises within 2 minutes' walk of each other, both in old colonial buildings with some character. The "four-star" version renovated most floors to a good standard in 2002 (the eighth floor was omitted). The rooms have all the standard amenities, plus free TV-based Internet access. Suites have good bathrooms with proper shower cubicles. There are Western and Chinese restaurants and, bizarrely in such an old building, there's a rooftop swimming pool. The three-star building is the original Victory, with an excellent dim sum restaurant in one corner. The rooms are plainer but in better decorative repair than the average three-star hotel. The cheapest have no windows, but the slightly more expensive ones are larger than average and come with small sitting rooms.

Shāmiàn Běi Jiē 53 (4 stars). ⓒ 020/8121-6802. Fax 020/8121-9889. www.gd-victory-hotel.com. 92 units. ¥360–¥530 ($45–$66) standard room; ¥780 ($98) suite. Also at Shāmiàn Dàjiē 54 (3 stars). ⓒ 020/8186-2622. Fax 020/8186-2413. 118 units. ¥360–¥530 ($45–$66) standard room; ¥600 ($75) triple; ¥650 ($81) suite. Rates include service charge and tax. 40% discounts typically available. AE, DC, MC, V. **Amenities:** More than 20 restaurants; swimming pool; business center; forex. *In room:* A/C, TV, fridge.

Hotel Elan (Mǐlánhuā Jiǔdiàn) *(Finds)* Recently opened, and designed by an Australian architect, the Hotel Elan features minimalist yet comfortable rooms in a refreshing break from typically bland Chinese accommodations. It is especially popular with value-seeking business travelers and is a definite step above other previous

favorites in the area such as the Guóxiăng Mansion around the corner or the China Southern Airlines Hotel right by the station. The lobby is stylishly designed and, although small, has become a popular meeting place. There is even a Manchurian restaurant on the ground floor.

Zhàn Qián Héng Lù 32. (©) 020/8622-1788. Fax 020/8666-9420. 70 units. ¥288 ($36) standard room; ¥588 ($74) suite. Rates include service charge and tax. No credit cards. **Amenities:** Restaurant. *In room:* A/C, TV, fridge.

WHERE TO DINE

According to a national survey, the average Cantonese spends ¥4,413 ($554) on dining out annually, which is three times as much as the average Shanghainese, and a whopping seven times more than the national average. While it is Cantonese cuisine that captures the headlines, the local passion for eating has ensured that an eclectic mix of international flavors has established a presence here. Not only does Guăngzhōu provide the chance to sample many provincial cuisines, an abundance of Asian, Middle Eastern, and even European creativity can now to be tasted here.

Guăngzhōu's expat community has changed rapidly in the last few years and this can be seen in the number of international cuisines available. Overpriced generic brands such as the Hard Rock Cafe were not able to survive here but have been replaced with a wide variety of flavors, from Caribbean to Syrian.

Běi Yuán Jiŭjiā CANTONESE   The Cantonese seem to be the most raucous of all Chinese, and the main restaurant choices for classic Cantonese food, or for dim sum, are bedlam. The Běi Yuán dates from the 1920s, although the current two-story building with courtyards is newer, built around a garden and pond. There's dim sum here all day (about ¥4/50¢ per steamer) and a generous menu of Cantonese classics, with some English translations. Try *huādiāo zhù jĭ* (chicken cooked in yellow wine—although some might argue this is really a Zhèjiāng dish), *táng cù sū ròu* (sweet-and-sour pork), and *jiŭhuáng ròu sī* (sliced pork with yellow chives). The typically garish carpets, screens, and chandeliers are in odd contrast to a central green space. There are twin entrances—the left is for the traditional Cantonese dishes; the right is for a Cháozhōu (Chiu Chow) restaurant, with the roast goose dishes typical of that area of northeast Guăngdōng.

Xiăo Běi Lù 202. (©) 020/8356-3365. Meal for 2 about ¥80 ($10). No credit cards. 6:50am–4:30pm and 5:30pm–12:10am.

Dōng Běi Rén MANCHURIAN   One of the most successful chains in the region, Dōng Běi Rén offers the opportunity to try northern cuisine in a southern city. Sample as many different kinds of *jiăozi* (resembling miniature ravioli) as possible. So many trolleys will come wheeling past your table that you may not even need to consult a menu; rest assured that you will not be disappointed by the selection (or the English that's spoken here). Wash it all down with great-value fresh fruit juices or even a sweet red wine that might surprise with its potency. The bright flowery uniforms and decor should make branches easy to spot, but watch out for the copycats that are springing up.

Branches all over the city including Tiān Hé Nán Èr Lù 36 ((©) 020/8750-1711), Táojīn] Běi Lù 2/F ((©) 020/8357-1576), and Lánbăoshí Building of Rénmín Běi Lù ((©) 020/8135-1711). Main courses ¥30–¥50 ($3.75–$6.25). No credit cards. 11am–10pm.

Dōng Jiāng Hăixiān Dà Jiŭlóu CANTONESE SEAFOOD   While Cantonese food can now be found all over the world, the enormous, multistory, football field–size restaurants remain something than can only be seen in Guǎngzhōu. Many places compete to be the largest (the title is currently held by Fishermans' City, more the size of a theme park than a restaurant, in the suburb of Pānyú) but most branches of the Dōng Jiāng chain are vast enough to impress. This particular location stretches over five floors and even spills out on to the sidewalk later in the evening. Huge tanks of seafood fill the first floor with many obscure, strange-looking varieties available at higher prices. Beginners may want to start with a plate full of steamed shrimp and another of steamed crab, and practice eating with their fingers before they proceed onto local exotica such as water beetles and horseshoe crabs. Restaurant rush hour is early Sunday evening, when it seems like every family in the city is heading out to eat. If you can even find a seat, the noise will be deafening, but it will be an experience that you will be unable to replicate elsewhere on the planet.

Yánjiāng Lù 2, beside Hǎizhū Square. (C) 020/8318-4901. Also at Huánshì Zhōng Lù 276, opposite the children's activity center, (C) 020/8322-9188. Meal for 2 about ¥80–¥200 ($10–$24). AE, DC, MC, V. 7am–4am.

Japan Fusion JAPANESE/CANTONESE   Reputedly the largest Japanese restaurant in Asia, but the equally huge menu reveals a strong inclination towards Cantonese flavors. At lunchtime, the vast expanse of tables, teppanyaki plates, and sashimi bars is flooded to capacity, hardly a surprise considering the choice of excellent value set lunches available. Great for lunch on the way to or from the station, but watch out in the evening when prices rise sharply.

2/F Metro Plaza, Tiān Hé Běi Lù 358–378. (C) 020/83884-5109. Set lunches ¥20–¥100 ($2.50–$13); specialty dishes can be much, much higher. AE, DC, MC, V. 11am–11pm.

1920 EUROPEAN   Conveniently located next to the Pearl River, 1920 is ideal for lunch after a morning browsing the markets or before an afternoon stroll around Shāmiàn. This small cafe-style eatery has an outdoor seating area and an upstairs section with live jazz in the evening and a Sunday jazz brunch (10:30am–4pm). Although now under Filipino management, there is still a strong German influence to the menu and the place is popular with tourists and expats alike. On the way out, make sure to check just around the corner to see what Oliver Twist is eating at the bizarrely named Village of Gruel.

Yánjiāng Zhōng Lù 183. (C) 020/8333-6156. www.1920cn.com. Main courses ¥30–¥100 ($3.75–$12). AE, DC, MC, V. 11am–2am.

Qīng Wǎ Jū KOREAN   The large expat Korean community in Guǎngzhōu supports a number of Korean restaurants, but this one is the friendliest and most certainly the best value. A short but succinct picture menu shows all the national favorites without drowning the reader with too much variety. Every dish is accompanied with delicious barley tea and a selection of small dishes including fresh kimchi and delicious pumpkin puree.

Shǔiyìn Lù 117-14, opposite the west gate of Dōng Fēng Park. (C) 020/8725-1929. Main courses ¥30–¥80 ($2.50–$10). No credit cards. 11am–10pm.

11 Shēnzhèn

Guǎngdōng Province on the border with Hong Kong, 163km (102 miles) SE of Guǎngzhōu

Shēnzhèn grew overnight from nothing to metropolis in the 1980s at the instigation of then-supreme leader Dèng Xiǎopíng, and remains the symbol of the reform and opening policy he initiated. It's equally a symbol of everything that's wrong with what China has become—a jostle of shanty-towers with a rootless, money-grubbing, temporary atmosphere. No one's a native, and many Chinese are here illegally. Far from finding the get-rich-quick scheme of their dreams, many often end up in sweat shops or prostitution.

If you're in Hong Kong and are considering Shēnzhèn as a side trip, then be aware that shopping is the main activity. The main point of visiting here is to use its airport to get somewhere else. *Warning:* Although Hong Kong has "returned to the motherland," this is a full-scale **international border crossing** from 6:30am to midnight and is prohibited even to Chinese without the right documentation. Lines can be long, especially at holiday periods. In either direction, allow *at least* an hour, and be sure to collect immigration cards and fill them in while waiting in the queue in either direction. There are lines for Hong Kong residents, mainland Chinese, and foreigners—you'll be sent to the back again if you join the wrong one. Full Chinese tourist **visas** cannot be obtained here. A 5-day permit allowing access *only* to Shēnzhèn can be purchased at the border by citizens of most developed nations for ¥100 ($13), but the list of favored nations changes as high-level diplomatic spats eventually filter down to the ordinary traveler. Last year it was the British who were out of favor, this year it is the Americans who are in the doghouse. *Note:* For Chinese translations of selected establishments listed in this section, please turn to appendix A.

ESSENTIALS

GETTING THERE   It is usually much cheaper to **fly** into Shēnzhèn from other mainland cities than it is to fly directly to Hong Kong, and there are around 60 Chinese cities to choose from, including Běijīng (18 flights daily), Chéngdū (seven flights), Guìlín (four flights), Hángzhōu (six flights), Kūnmíng (five flights), Shànghǎi (17 flights), Xiàmén (12 flights), and Xī'ān (four flights). **Hong Kong** can be reached directly from the airport using TurboCAT (jetfoil/catamaran) services to Kowloon (six sailings, 9am–5:15pm) and the Macau Ferry Terminal on Hong Kong Island (4:30, 6:30, and 7:45pm; HK$189–HK$289/US$25–US$38, can be paid in yuán on the Chinese side). Shuttle buses take passengers the short distance to the pier, and the total journey time is around 55 minutes. There are also services to **Macau** at 9:30am and 1:30pm (HK$171–HK$271/US$22–US$34; can be paid in yuán or Macanese patacas). For current times and services in each direction, see **www.turbocat.com/turbojet_sailing_rev.htm**.

Airport bus no. 330 (© **0755/99788**) runs from the airport to the Huálián Dàshà (a hotel and department store), just west of the center on Shēn Nán Zhōng Lù. The ride takes 40 minutes and costs ¥20 ($2.50); the buses run every 30 minutes from 6:30am to 8pm. When work on an extension to the KCR East Rail line is complete, buses will run to the railway station. For now it's a ¥20 ($2.50) taxi ride farther. (Coming from Hong Kong, ignore touts at Luó Hú, and make for the signposted taxi rank.)

The **railway station** is 2 minutes' walk north of the Luó Hú/Lo Wu border and connected by elevated walkway. Tickets for Guǎngzhōu are on sale at this level, and for elsewhere on the floor below, from 7am to 8pm. The express trains directly from Kowloon to Běijīng and Shànghǎi pass through but do not stop here. Shēnzhèn has its own services from Běijīng Xī, of which the best is the T107 at 8:30pm, passing through Jiǔjiāng and Nánchāng, and arriving at 9:10pm the next day—not bad for 2,373km (1,483 miles). The cost is ¥467 ($58) hard sleeper, ¥720 ($90) soft sleeper.

To Běijīng, the T108 leaves at 1:08pm. Tickets for this and many other **trains** from Shēnzhèn can be bought at CTS in Hong Kong, but there's a much greater choice of services and destinations from Guǎngzhōu. Departures by 200kmph express trains to Guǎngzhōu Dōng (East) leave 45 times a day from 7:18am to 8:45pm. They occasionally continue to the main station.

From **Hong Kong,** the easiest train route is via the KCR East Rail line from Hung Hom or Kowloon Tong to Lo Wu. The first train from Hung Hom is at 5:30am and the last at 11:07pm. *Only stay on for Lo Wu if you plan to cross the border, or you may be fined.* The long-distance bus station, **Luó Hú Qìchēzhàn,** is beneath Luó Hú Commercial City, to your right as you leave Customs. There are rapid bus connections with Guǎngzhōu, Zhūhǎi Gǒng Běi (the Macau border crossing, every 15 min. 7am–8:30pm), Kāipíng, and most other corners of Guǎngdōng Province. A cross-border coach service runs to the Shangri-La hotel directly from Hong Kong Airport's arrivals hall counter 4B; 16 services make the 2-hour trip from 10:30am to 8:30pm for HK$100 (US$13). In the other direction, 10 services operate from 7:30am to 5:50pm. *Warning:* Access to Shēnzhèn is subject to extra controls. Have your passport ready if you're arriving or leaving by bus.

GETTING AROUND   Few people get farther than Luó Hú, with its border station, railway station, bus station, shopping, restaurants, and hotels, all close together. **Taxis** have high rates similar to those in Guǎngzhōu. *Never* deal with touts who approach you at the border. The taxi stand is signposted beyond Luó Hú Commercial City to your right. At the north end of the plaza, with the border on the south side and the station on the west, stands the Shangri-La hotel. The street leading north on the left side is Jiànshè Lù, and the street on the right side is Rénmín Nán Lù; between the two of them, they lead to everything you might want.

FAST FACTS

Banks, Foreign Exchange & ATMs   There's a branch of the **Hongkong and Shanghai Bank** on the Rénmín Nán Lù side of the Century Plaza Hotel—you can't change money here but you can use its ATM outside. A branch of the **Bank of China** (open Mon–Fri 8:30am–5:30pm; Sat–Sun and holidays 9am–4pm), which has foreign-exchange service and an outside ATM, is nearby to the right and beyond the Shangri-La hotel.

Internet Access   The 24-hour **PC-War E-Cafe** even has a nonsmoking area. It's on the fourth floor of the Cybermart at Rénmín Nán Lù 3005 and charges ¥2 (25¢) per hour. Use the side entrance from 7pm to 9am. Dial-up is ⓒ **169.**

Post Office   There's a useful post office (open 9am–noon and 12:30–5pm) at ground-floor level of the north end of Luó Hú Commercial City.

Visa Extensions   Cross into Hong Kong and obtain a brand-new 3-month visa within 24 hours if need be (see chapter 11).

EXPLORING SHĒNZHÈN

Newly minted Shēnzhèn only has the face of modern China to show you, including tawdry and occasionally offensive theme parks. The *Minsk,* certainly out of the ordinary, can be seen as a day trip from Hong Kong.

Minsk **World (Míngsīkè Hángmǔ Shìjiè)** ⓖ ⓚⓘⓓⓢ   Throughout mainland China there's a slightly chilling admiration for military power and for weaponry both high- and low-tech. Much of the admiration for the West (when admitted) is for its ownership of the kinds of munitions that, if our own generals are to be believed, double-check the address, knock politely, and ask for ID before deciding whether or not to explode. The Russian aircraft carrier *Minsk,* launched in 1978 and once the flagship of the Pacific Fleet, is of a more clockwork era, with not a microchip in sight, but its sheer scale and power are still impressive, as is the relentless marketing to which visitors are subjected from the moment they pass the monument to peace at the entrance, a-flutter with doves, to enter what is a large-scale celebration of the weapons of war.

The ticket office is in a vaguely St. Petersburgian fake palace, behind which are a shooting range where you can fire tennis balls at assorted objects, stalls selling animated military dolls, a row of MIG fighter planes, a tank or two, an inflatable Russian bear presiding over a number of centrifugal rides, and a Soyuz space capsule (the genuine article).

The carrier itself has been substantially refitted, with stirring Russian military music playing through a PA system. Your visit commences with a compulsory 10-minute cinema show on the history of aircraft carriers, into which you are ushered by pretty young women in naval uniforms, before you follow a clearly marked route through torpedo hall, bridge, deck, anchor room, missile elevators, and just about every other corner, with informative signage in good English. At every turn there's a souvenir stall (¥15/$1.90 for a postcard!), or a stall selling obsolete military equipment, or another stall selling radio-controlled toys. The deck has occasional reenactments of Russian military parades; the officers' mess is a restaurant serving black bread and imitations of Russian food; and the main aircraft hanger is a disco with neon signs shaped like weaponry, flight-simulator rides, and a stall selling popcorn. If you survive all this, then for ¥30 ($3.75) you can be whizzed around the ship at water level in a small motorboat.

Shātóujiǎo. ¥110 ($14). 9:15am–6pm. Minibus: no. 430, from a local bus terminal just north of Luó Hú Commercial City on the east side of Rénmín Nán Lù; it drops you at the gate of *Minsk* World in 30 min. for ¥4 (50¢). Walk a short distance back up to main road to catch returning buses, however.

SHOPPING

It's an increasingly popular view among residents of Hong Kong that Shēnzhèn is a cheap place to shop. Compared to Hong Kong, it *is* cheap, of course, at least for domestic items, but many proclaiming this view have never been anywhere else in China (and many Hong Kong people have never been to the mainland at all). Those who do go to shop often get no farther than the overrated **Luó Hú Shāngyè Chéng (Luó Hú Commercial City),** five stories of shopping (open 8:30am–11pm) above the bus station to the right as you leave the border is where you find luggage, shoes, bags, CDs, clothes, toys, Chinese medicine, tea, tailoring services, portrait photography,

---

⌢Tips Expert Shopping

Nobody should spend any time in Shēnzhèn without consulting Ellen McNally's excellent insider's guide, *Shop in Shēnzhèn.* Widely available in Hong Kong yet strangely absent on the mainland, this handy little guide goes much further than detailed floor plans for Lo Wu, right out to Hǔmén garment wholesale city. Check the Web at www.shopinshenzhen.com.

bed linens, quilts, electrical goods, leather goods, pearls, jewelry, wigs, massages, pedicures, and even a Cantonese opera house. Of course, as elsewhere in the mainland, nearly everything is fake. "Where else can you get a cotton tailored shirt for around $9?" enthuses one shopping guide. To which the answer might be, "Name a mainland city where you can't—and usually cheaper." This mall's very proximity to rich Hong Kong, almost inside the border post, ought to warn you off in the first place.

WHERE TO STAY

Business-oriented Shēnzhèn tends to be expensive. But if you must spend a night, the best place to stay is the five-star **Shangri-La (Xiānggélǐlā Dàjiǔdiàn)** at Jiànshè Lù 1002 (© **0755/8233-0888;** fax 0755/8233-9878; www.shangri-la.com), visible straight ahead as you leave the border crossing, and 2 minutes from the railway station. This is a luxurious and fully outfitted business hotel with excellent service, four restaurants, and cozy, recently refurbished rooms fitted with everything that you could possibly want in order to shut out the bedlam of Shēnzhèn, including broadband Internet access, satellite TV channels, and in-house movies. Rack rates are from ¥1,865 to ¥4,420 ($233–$553), but special offers and on-the-spot bargaining can produce rates under US$100 (all plus 15%).

Of the budget hotels up Rénmín Nán Lù, the best is probably the **Guǎngxìn Jiǔdiàn,** on the west side, north of Chūnfēng Lù (© **0755/8223-8945**). The lobby is modern and stylish, which makes the grubby corridors beyond a bit of a shock, but refurbishment may have reached that far by the time you visit. Battered guest rooms and bathrooms are clean enough and larger than average, although they have few amenities. Standard rooms are ¥308 ($38), usually reduced to ¥228 ($28); triple rooms are ¥400 ($50), usually reduced to ¥350 ($44).

WHERE TO DINE

Street-level dim sum from 6 to 10:30am, outside the **Yáng Xī Jiǔdiàn** and just around the corner from the Shangri-La in Jiànshè Lù, makes a good and very cheap start to the day. There's Kèjiā food, *jiǎozi,* and familiar Hong Kong fast-food names such as Fairwood in the Luó Hú Commercial City. Keep clear of the restaurants in the railway station building, however, where the food and portions are both miserable, and where there's a 10% charge for nonexistent service. Venture farther up Jiànshè Lù or Rénmín Lù to find an assortment of standard Chinese restaurants and Western fast-food chains. The rotating **Tiara** restaurant on the top (31st) floor of the Shangri-La has an excellent international buffet for around ¥150 ($19) per person, as well as constantly changing views that include the one across the barbed wire to the green New Territories of Hong Kong. The hotel's signature **Shāng Palace** restaurant has top-of-the-line Cantonese food at fair prices for the quality; a meal for two costs around ¥400 ($50). For burger and steak enthusiasts, the hotel also has a branch of the American chain **Henry J. Bean's,** with main courses for ¥100 ($13).

Hong Kong

by Beth Reiber

Viewed from Victoria Peak, Hong Kong surely rates as one of the most stunning cities in Asia, if not the world. In the foreground rise the skyscrapers of Hong Kong Island, while beyond them is the incredible bustle of Victoria Harbour, where all manner of watercraft—from the historic Star Ferries to cruise liners, cargo ships, and wooden fishing vessels—compete for space. On the other side is the Kowloon Peninsula, growing by the minute with ambitious land-reclamation projects, housing estates, and ever-higher buildings, all set against a dramatic backdrop of gently rounded mountains.

Today's Hong Kong is a blend of the exotic and the familiar forged during its 156 years as a British colony—from 1842, when Britain acquired Hong Kong Island as a spoil of the first Opium War, to its 1997 handover to the Chinese. The Chinese government has given Hong Kong status as a Special Administrative Region (SAR), guaranteeing its capitalist lifestyle and social system for 50 years, so to the casual observer little seems changed. English is still an official language, the Hong Kong dollar remains legal tender, and entry formalities are largely the same. Although it's pricier than most other Asian destinations, many travelers find Hong Kong a welcome respite, with all the creature comforts of home.

Hong Kong boasts what is arguably the greatest concentration of Chinese restaurants in the world, along with top-notch restaurants serving dishes from around the globe. The city has also revved up its sightseeing attractions, offering museums, parks, temples, and other amusements. And Macau, with its fascinating blend of Portuguese and Chinese cultures, is just an hour's boat ride away.

1 Orientation

ARRIVING
BY PLANE

Hong Kong International Airport (© **852/2181 0000;** www.hongkongairport.com) is located about 32km (20 miles) from Hong Kong's central business district. In the arrivals hall, just past Customs, visitors can pick up English-language maps and sightseeing brochures and get directions to their hotel at the **Hong Kong Tourist Board (HKTB),** open daily 7am to 11pm. Also in the arrivals hall are the **Hong Kong Hotel Association** (www.hkha.com.hk), open daily from 6am to midnight, with a free booking service to some 60 member hotels; and the **Macau Government Tourist Office,** open daily from 9am to 1pm, 1:30 to 6pm, and 6:30 to 10:30pm. You can also exchange money in the arrivals hall, although because of the unfavorable rates, it's best to change only what's needed to get into town—about US$50 should do it. Otherwise,

Hong Kong

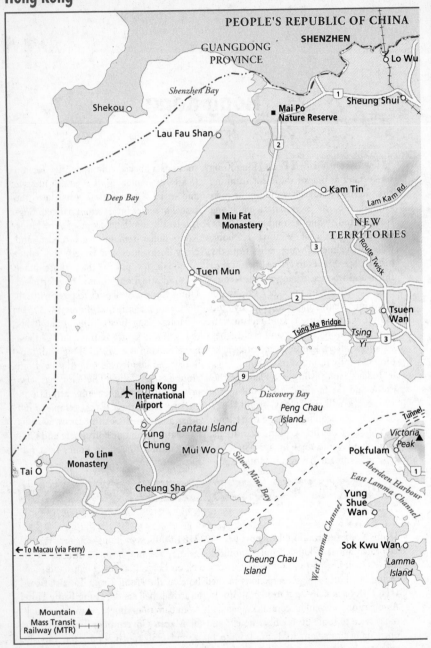

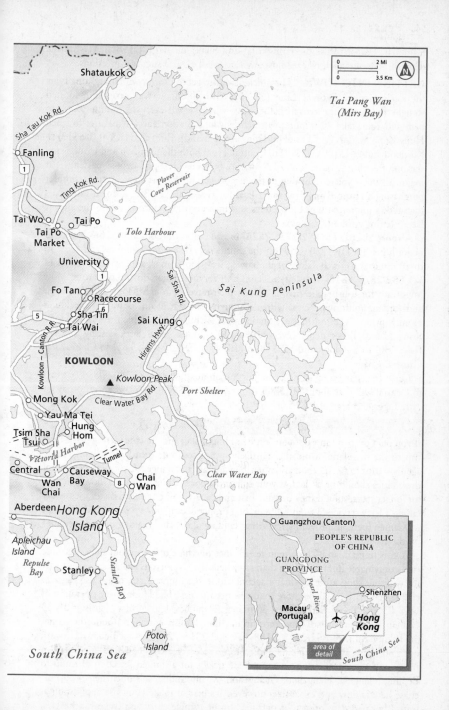

Shataukok

*Tai Pang Wan
(Mirs Bay)*

Sha Tau Kok Rd.

Fanling
1

Ting Kok Rd.

*Plover
Cove Reservoir*

Tai Wo
Tai Po
Tai Po
Market

Tolo Harbour

University
1

Sai Sha Rd.

Sai Kung Peninsula

Fo Tan
Racecourse
6
Sha Tin
Tai Wai

Sai Kung

Hirams Hwy.

5

Kowloon – Canton R.R.

KOWLOON

▲ *Kowloon Peak*

Port Shelter

Mong Kok
Yau Ma Tei
Hung
Hom

Clear Water Bay Rd.

Tsim Sha
Tsui

Victoria Harbor

Tunnel

Central
Causeway
Bay

Wan
Chai

Chai
Wan

Clear Water Bay

8

Aberdeen *Hong Kong
Island*

*Apleichau
Island*

*Repulse
Bay*
Stanley

Stanley Bay

South China Sea

*Potoi
Island*

0   2 Mi
0   3.5 Km

Guangzhou (Canton)

**PEOPLE'S REPUBLIC
OF CHINA**

**GUANGDONG
PROVINCE**

Pearl River

Shenzhen

**Macau
(Portugal)**

✈
**Hong
Kong**

area of
detail

South China Sea

it's much cheaper to use the **Hongkong and Shanghai Bank (HSBC)** ATM at the departures level, which takes almost any card—ask HKTB staff for directions.

GETTING INTO TOWN   The quickest way to get to downtown Hong Kong is via the sleek **Airport Express Line** (✆ **852/2881 8888;** www.mtr.com.hk), located straight ahead past the arrivals hall. Trains, which depart every 12 minutes between 6am and 1am, take 20 minutes to reach Kowloon Station and 24 minutes to reach Hong Kong Station (in Central on Hong Kong Island). Fares are HK$90 (US$12) to Kowloon and HK$100 (US$13) to Central. From both the Kowloon and Hong Kong stations, free shuttle buses (every 12–24 min. 6:18am–11:10pm) deposit passengers at major hotels. If you're returning to the airport via the Airport Express Line, consider purchasing a **Hong Kong Transport Pass** for HK$300 (US$39), a stored-value pass that allows unlimited travel for 3 days and includes the trip from and to the airport (see "Getting Around," below).

Airport Shuttle (✆ **852/2735 7823**) provides door-to-door airport bus service to major hotels for HK$120 (US$16); the shuttle departs every 30 minutes and takes 30 to 40 minutes to reach Tsimshatsui. Slower, with more stops, are **Cityflyer Airbuses** (✆ **852/2873 0818;** www.citybus.com.hk), serving major downtown areas. Most important for tourists are **Airbus A21,** which travels through Mongkok, Yaumatei, and Jordan, and down Nathan Road through Tsimshatsui on its way to the Hung Hom Kowloon–Canton Railway Station; and **Airbuses A11,** which travels to Hong Kong Island. Buses depart every 10 to 30 minutes, with fares costing HK$33 (US$4.30) to Kowloon and HK$40 to HK$45 (US$5.20–US$5.85) to Central and Causeway Bay.

On average, a **taxi** to Tsimshatsui will cost approximately HK$300 (US$39); a taxi to Central will cost about HK$365 to HK$400 (US$47–US$52). Expect to pay an extra luggage charge of HK$5 (US65¢) per piece.

TRAVELING TO & FROM THE MAINLAND

If you plan to spend most of your time in Hong Kong and are considering just a brief trip to the mainland, avoid the massively overpriced tours peddled by Hong Kong agents—trips to Guǎngzhōu and Shēnzhèn are easy to arrange for yourself. Neither of these cities should be picked as your sole experience of the mainland, however; nor, for longer stays, should they be your first choice as a point of entry. Instead, consider taking a ferry service to rural Kāipíng, or a proper oceangoing vessel around the coast to Xiàmén (perhaps providing the softest landing of all), and making easy connections up the coast.

A visit to mainland China requires advance purchase of a **visa,** but these are more easily obtainable in Hong Kong than anywhere else. Numerous agents are eager to act for you, but shop around—many agents within the tourist districts are also eager to charge you 50% to 100% more than you need to pay. The Hong Kong operation of **CTS (China Travel Service)** has 36 branches, the best known of which is at 27–33 Nathan Rd., Tsimshatsui (one floor up in Alpha House, entrance around the corner on Peking Rd.; ✆ **852/2315 7188;** fax 852/2315 7292; www.chinatravel1.com), open 365 days a year. Come here for commission-free ferry, train, and bus tickets to the mainland, as well as advance-purchase tickets for a limited selection of trains to Běijīng, Shànghǎi, Hángzhōu, Guǎngzhōu, Xī'ān, Guìlín, and Shēnzhèn. Visa purchase here is slow and expensive, however. It's best to make your visa application at least 3 business days prior to departure; cost of a single-entry visa (valid for 30 days) is HK$210 (US$27). However, if you're in a hurry, you can obtain a visa more quickly by paying more: For HK$360 (US$47), your visa will be processed and available for pickup by 2pm the next day; for HK$480 (US$62), visa applications made before noon will be available by 5:30pm the same day. Note, however, that at press time, Americans applying for visas were required to pay HK$250 (US$32) in excess of the fees above. Double-entry and multiple-entry 6-month visas are also easily available.

For air tickets, shop around the many budget-travel agents in the area, such as **Shoestring Travel,** also in the Alpha House, fourth floor (© **852/2723 2306;** fax 852/2721 2085; www.shoestringtravel.com.hk). Entry visas are cheaper here, too, but agents farther away from the main shopping streets are even cheaper.

It is possible to visit **Shēnzhèn** for up to 5 days (but go no farther) without purchasing a visa in advance, if you take the option of walking across the border at Lo Wu.

BY PLANE

Various Chinese airlines fly to and from Běihǎi, Běijīng, Chángchūn, Chángshā, Chéngdū, Chóngqìng, Dàlián, Fúzhōu, Guǎngzhōu, Guìlín, Guìyáng, Hǎikǒu, Hángzhōu, Harbin, Héféi, Huáng Shān, Jǐ'nán, Kūnmíng, Nánchāng, Nánjīng, Nánníng, Níngbō, Qīngdǎo, Sānyà, Shànghǎi, Shěnyáng, Shíjiāzhuāng, Tiānjīn, Wēnzhōu, Wǔhàn, Xiàmén, Xī'ān, Zhèngzhōu, and other minor destinations. Hong Kong's more expensive **Dragonair** flies to Běijīng, Chángshā, Chéngdū, Chóngqìng, Dàlián, Fúzhōu, Guìlín, Hángzhōu, Kūnmíng, Nánjīng, Níngbō, Qīngdǎo, Sānyà, Shànghǎi, Wǔhàn, Xiàmén, and Xī'ān. Shop around with travel agencies and bargain for discount fares. Do *not* book with Hong Kong agents in advance online—prices are outrageous. With the exception of rare special offers, it is almost always cheaper to fly from **Shēnzhèn** or Guǎngzhōu to domestic destinations. Be sure to factor in transportation costs to Hong Kong International Airport and to Shēnzhèn or Guǎngzhōu, as well as the mainland domestic departure tax of ¥50 ($6.50), when making comparisons.

Shēnzhèn Airport has service to 57 Chinese cities and can be reached from Hong Kong International Airport via **TurboJET Sea Express** (six sailings, 12:15–7:45pm) to Shēnzhèn's Fú Yǒng Ferry Terminal, followed by a 5-minute shuttle bus to Shēnzhèn Airport. Fares range from HK$210 to HK$330 (US$27–US$43). Transfers to the Sea Express are made *before* Hong Kong Customs, thereby eliminating Hong Kong immigration formalities. In Hong Kong, there are also TurboJET services from Kowloon's China HK Ferry Terminal (eight sailings, 7:30am–5:30pm) and the Macau Ferry Terminal on Hong Kong Island (one sailing, 8am), for HK$189 to HK$289 (US$25–US$38). Passengers should plan on about 1 hour for the total journey time. For full up-to-date times and services in each direction, see www.turbocat.com/turbo jet_sailing_rev.htm.

BY TRAIN

The T98 leaves for Běijīng at 3pm on alternate days, stopping at Dōngguǎn (Chángpíng), Guǎngzhōu East, Sháoguān, Chángshā, Wǔchāng, Hànkǒu, Zhèngzhōu, and Shíjiāzhuāng before arriving in Běijīng West at 3:18pm the next day. The K100 leaves for Shànghǎi at 3pm on alternate days, calling at Dōngguǎn (Chángpíng), Guǎngzhōu East, Sháoguān, and Hángzhōu East before arriving in Shànghǎi at 4:38pm the next day. Tickets can be bought at Hung Hom or any KCR East Rail station, or through travel agents (with no commission payable). Online agents overcharge by as much as 70%. To find out whether your train is departing on odd or even days of the month, go to www.kcrc.com/eng/services/services/itts_intro.asp, or call the **Intercity Passenger Services Hotline** at ⓒ **852/2947 7888,** which also has details on Guǎngzhōu services.

From Běijīng, fares are HK$1,191 (US$155) for *gāojí ruǎnwò*—a bed in a two-bed cabin—HK$934 (US$121) for a soft sleeper, and HK$601 (US$78) for a hard sleeper. From Shànghǎi, fares are HK$530 to HK$1,039 (US$69–US$135).

There are 12 daily services to and from **Guǎngzhōu Dōng Zhàn (East Station)** for HK$190 to HK$230 (US$25–US$30); the trip takes a little less than 2 hours.

From Běijīng and Shànghǎi, passengers are required to alight with all baggage and go through Customs and Immigration procedures about an hour out from Kowloon's Hung Hom Station, at Chángpíng (Dōngguǎn). Leaving Hong Kong, don't bother to stow heavy baggage until after you reboard the train. To and from Guǎngzhōu, formalities are conducted at Guǎngzhōu Dōng station and on the train. Hong Kong Customs and Immigration procedures (including yet another X-ray of baggage) take place at Hung Hom station. Expect to spend about HK$30 (US$3.90) for a taxi to a hotel in Tsimshatsui or Tsimshatsui East.

There are also services every few minutes to and from Lo Wu, Hong Kong's border crossing to Shēnzhèn, the last stop on the KCR East Rail. See "Getting Around," below, and "Shēnzhèn" (p. 532) for details. You should only proceed as far as Lo Wu if you intend to cross the border, which is open from 6:30am to midnight. Lines can be long—allow an hour.

BY FERRY

Up-to-date schedules of TurboJET jetfoil sailings from Hong Kong can be found at www.turbojet.com.hk/turbojet_sailing_rev.htm, or by calling ⓒ **852/2859 3333** in Hong Kong or ⓒ **853/790 7039** in Macau. In addition to the round-the-clock services to Macau from the Macau Ferry Terminal on Hong Kong Island and nine daily sailings from the China (HK) Ferry Terminal in Tsimshatsui in Kowloon (see "Macau," later in this chapter), there are eight daily sailings to Shēnzhèn (six on weekends) from Kowloon and one from Hong Kong, complete with free bus link to the Shēnzhèn airport (about 55 min. altogether). Tickets to Shēnzhèn cost HK$189 to HK$289 (US$25–US$38). There are also direct sailings from Hong Kong International Airport to Shēnzhèn and Macau, as well as three daily sailings from Macau to Shēnzhèn (four on weekends) for HK$171 to HK$271 (US$22–US$35). Tickets are sold at ferry terminals and at the Shun Tak Centre 3/F (200 Connaught Rd. Central, Hong Kong), the TurboJET Service Counter (Sheung Wan MTR Station, exit D), Hong Kong and Macau airports, and China Travel Service branches. Telephone reservations via credit card can be made up to 28 days in advance at ⓒ **852/2921 6688.**

The **Chu Kong Passenger Transport Co.** operates a catamaran service to **Guǎngzhōu** at 8:05am and 2:30pm, taking 2¾ hours to reach Píngzhōu Wharf at Nánhǎi, with a free shuttle bus to Zhōutóuzuǐ, just south of Shāmiàn Island. The catamaran leaves from the China HK Ferry Terminal in Kowloon, and tickets are HK$151 to HK$247 (US$20–US$32). See www.cksp.com.hk or call ⓒ **852/2858 3876** for details. The company also has service to various lesser ports around Guǎngdōng Province, notably **Kāipíng's** Sānbù at 8:30am for HK$185 to HK$205 (US$24–US$27), taking 4 hours. Prices on all routes may rise during public holidays.

BY BUS

CTS sells tickets for a variety of cross-border bus services to destinations around Guǎngdōng Province and beyond, including Guǎngxī's Yángshuò and Guìlín (many more than appear on their website). There are services from Causeway Bay (Metro Park Hotel), Wanchai ferry pier, and Prince Edward MTR station to the China Hotel in Guǎngzhōu (© **852/2789 5401**) for HK$100 (US$13); and direct services from Hong Kong airport to Shēnzhèn (Shangri-La Hotel) and to Guǎngzhōu (White Swan, Garden Hotel, and several others; © **852/2764 9803**). There are also bus services from Hong Kong Airport to the Dōngguǎn area, Huìzhōu, and Shēnzhèn run by **Eternal East Cross-Border Coach Mgt. Ltd.** (© **852/2723 2923;** www.eebus.com).

VISITOR INFORMATION

In addition to its tourist counter in the arrivals hall of Hong Kong International Airport and at Lo Wu Arrival Hall (daily 8am–6pm), the **Hong Kong Tourist Board (HKTB)** maintains two offices in town, on both sides of the harbor. On the Kowloon side, there's a convenient office in Tsimshatsui right in the Star Ferry concourse, and another on Hong Kong Island in the Causeway Bay MTR subway station near exit F. Both offices are open daily from 8am to 8pm. Otherwise, if you have a question about Hong Kong, you can call the **HKTB Visitor Hotline** (© **852/2508 1234**) from 8am to 6pm.

The HKTB publishes a wealth of excellent free literature, maps, and the weekly *What's On—Hong Kong. Where Hong Kong* and *bc* are other free monthly giveaways with event listings.

THE LAY OF THE LAND

The Hong Kong Special Administrative Region (SAR) is located at the southeastern tip of the People's Republic of China, some 2,000km (1,240 miles) south of Běijīng. Hong Kong can be divided into four distinct parts: **Hong Kong Island;** the **Kowloon Peninsula;** the **New Territories,** which stretch north from Kowloon all the way to the mainland border; and 260 **outlying islands,** most of which are barren and uninhabited.

NEIGHBORHOODS IN BRIEF

Hong Kong Island

CENTRAL DISTRICT Central serves as Hong Kong's nerve center for banking, business, and administration. It also boasts some of Hong Kong's most innovative architecture, a couple of the city's poshest hotels, high-end shopping centers, and restaurants and bars catering to Hong Kong's white-collar workers.

LAN KWAI FONG Named after an L-shaped street in Central, this is Hong Kong's premier nightlife and entertainment district, occupying not only Lan Kwai Fong but overflowing into neighboring streets like D'Aguilar and Wyndham.

MID-LEVELS Located above Central on the slope of Victoria Peak, the Mid-Levels is a popular residential area with swank apartment buildings, sweeping views of Central, lush vegetation, and slightly cooler temperatures. Serving white-collar workers who commute to Central is the Hillside Escalator Link, the world's longest people mover.

SOHO This up-and-coming dining and nightlife district, flanking the Hillside Escalator, is named for being

"South of Hollywood Road." It has blossomed into an ever-growing neighborhood of cafe-bars and intimate restaurants specializing in ethnic and innovative cuisine, centered mostly on Elgin, Shelley, and Staunton streets.

WESTERN DISTRICT The Western District is a fascinating neighborhood of shops selling medicinal herbs, ginseng, medicines, dried seafood, and other Chinese products. It's also famous for Hollywood Road (long popular for its many antiques and curio shops) and for Man Mo Temple, one of Hong Kong's oldest.

WANCHAI Notorious for its sleazy bars and easy women, Wanchai has become a little more respectable with new, mostly business-style hotels, the huge Hong Kong Convention and Exhibition Centre, and a small but revitalized nightlife scene.

CAUSEWAY BAY Just east of Wanchai, Causeway Bay is popular as a shopping destination, with Japanese department stores; clothing, shoe, and accessory boutiques; and restaurants. On its eastern perimeter is the large Victoria Park.

ABERDEEN On the south side of Hong Kong Island, Aberdeen was once a fishing village but is now studded with high-rises and housing projects. It remains famous for its hundreds of sampans and junks, and for a huge floating restaurant.

STANLEY Located on the quiet south side of Hong Kong Island, this former fishing village is home to Hong Kong's most famous market, selling everything from silk suits to name-brand shoes, casual wear, and souvenirs.

Kowloon Peninsula

KOWLOON North of Hong Kong Island, across Victoria Harbour, is Kowloon, 7.7 sq. km (4¾ sq. miles) that were ceded to Britain in 1860. Kowloon includes the districts of Tsimshatsui, Tsimshatsui East, Yaumatei, Hung Hom, and Mongkok. Boundary Street in the north separates it from the New Territories.

TSIMSHATSUI Tsimshatsui boasts an excellent art museum, a cultural center for the performing arts, Kowloon Park, one of the world's largest shopping malls, a broad selection of international restaurants, a jumping nightlife, and Nathan Road, nicknamed the "golden mile of shopping."

TSIMSHATSUI EAST This area was built entirely on reclaimed land and is home to several hotels, shopping and restaurant complexes, museums and the new KCR East Tsimshatsui Station, with train service to the New Territories and China and connections to the Mass Transit Railway (MTR) subway system.

YAUMATEI Just north of Tsimshatsui, Yaumatei has an interesting produce market, a jade market, and the fascinating Temple Street Night Market. It also has several moderately priced hotels.

MONGKOK This district north of Yaumatei is a residential and industrial area, home of the Bird Market and the Ladies' Market on Tung Choi Street.

2 Getting Around

Hong Kong is compact and easy to navigate, with street, bus, and subway signs clearly marked in English. Each mode of transportation—bus, ferry, tram, and train/subway—has its own fare system and requires a new ticket each time you transfer from one to another. However, if you're going to be in Hong Kong for a few days, consider purchasing the **Octopus** smart card, which allows users to hop on and off trains, trams, subways, and most buses and ferries without worrying about purchasing tickets each time. Sold at all MTR subway stations and at some ferry piers, it costs a minimum of HK$150 (US$20), including a HK$50 (US$6.50) refundable deposit, and can be reloaded as necessary. For information, call the Octopus Hotline at (©) 852/2266 2266 or check its website at www.octopuscards.com.

Otherwise, transportation on buses and trams requires the exact fare, making it imperative to carry lots of loose change wherever you go.

BY SUBWAY   Hong Kong's **Mass Transit Railway (MTR)** is modern, easy to use, and very fast, consisting of four color-coded lines. Single-ticket, one-way fares range from HK$4 to HK$26 (US50¢–US$3.40), depending on the distance. Credit card–size plastic tickets are inserted into slots at entry turnstiles, retrieved, and inserted again at exits. The MTR operates daily from 6am to 1am, and there are no public toilets at any of the stations or on the trains. For general inquiries, call the **MTR Hotline** at (©) 852/2881 8888 or check www.mtr.com.hk.

BY TRAIN   The **Kowloon-Canton Railway (KCR) Corporation** ((©) 852/2602 7799; www.kcrc.com.hk) operates three rail lines in the New Territories as well as trains to China. Most useful for visitors is the **East Rail,** which offers local commuter travel from the KCR East Tsimshatsui Station in Kowloon up to Sheung Shui in the New Territories. That is, Sheung Shui is where you get off if you don't plan on traveling onward to China. Departing every 3 to 8 minutes daily from 5:30am to midnight, the commuter train from Kowloon to Sheung Shui takes only a half-hour, with a one-way ticket costing HK$9 (US$1.15) for ordinary (second) class and HK$18 (US$2.35) for first class. If you plan on visiting Shēnzhèn, you can continue to the border station of Lo Wu and cross the border on foot. Or, if you have a visa, you can travel onward to Guǎngzhōu, Shànghǎi, and Běijīng.

BY BUS   HKTB has individual leaflets showing bus routes. Depending on the route, buses run from about 6am to midnight, with fares ranging from HK$1.20 to HK$45 (US15¢–US$5.85)—exact fare required. Few drivers speak English, so you may want to have someone at your hotel write your destination in Chinese. In rural areas, you must flag down a bus to make it stop.

BY TRAM   Tramlines, found only along the north side of Hong Kong Island, are a nostalgic way to travel through the Western District, Central, Wanchai, and Causeway Bay. Established in 1904, these old, narrow, double-decker affairs clank their way from Kennedy Town in the west to Shaukeiwan in the east, with one branch making a detour to Happy Valley. Regardless of how far you go, you pay the exact fare of HK$2 (US25¢) or use an Octopus card as you exit. Trams run daily from 6am to 1am.

BY FERRY   A 5-minute trip across Victoria Harbour on one of the white-and-green ferries of the **Star Ferry Company**, in operation since 1898, is one of Hong Kong's top attractions. It costs only HK$1.70 (US20¢) for ordinary (second) class or HK$2.20 (US30¢) in first class on the upper deck. Ferries ply the waters between Central and Tsimshatsui daily from 6:30am to 11:30pm, with departures every 4 to 10 minutes. Besides the Central-to-Tsimshatsui route, Star Ferries also run between Central and Hung Hom and between Tsimshatsui and Wanchai; hover ferries run between Central and Tsimshatsui East.

A large fleet also serves the many outlying islands and the northern part of the mainland, with most ferries departing from the Central Ferry Pier just west of the Star

Ferry terminus in Central. The HKTB has ferry schedules, or call **First Ferry** at *©* **852/ 2131 8181** or check its website at www.nwff.com.hk.

BY TAXI   Taxi drivers in Hong Kong are strictly controlled and as a rule are fairly honest. Fares start at HK$15 (US$1.95) for the first 2km (1¼ miles), then HK$1.40 (US20¢) for each 200m (656 ft.). Luggage costs an extra HK$5 (US65¢) per piece, and taxis ordered by phone add a HK$5 (US65¢) surcharge. Trips through tunnels cost extra: HK$20 (US$2.60) for the Cross-Harbour Tunnel, HK$30 (US$3.90) for the Eastern Harbour Crossing and Lantau Link, HK$45 (US$5.85) for the Western Harbour Tunnel, and HK$5 (US65¢) for Aberdeen. Passengers taking taxis through harbor tunnels must pay *double* the tunnel toll, unless you're traveling in a Hong Kong– or Kowloon-based cab returning to its usual place of operation, in which case just one toll is payable. At major taxi stands, there are separate lines for Kowloon and Island-side taxis. A 24-hour hot line handles complaints about taxis (*©* **852/2527 7177**).

BY MINIBUS   These small, 16-passenger buses are the poor person's taxis. There are two types of vehicles: The green-and-yellow public "light buses," which follow fixed routes, charge fixed rates ranging from HK$2 to HK$20 (US25¢–US$2.60) depending on the distance, and require the exact fare as you enter (many also accept Octopus cards); the red-and-yellow **minibuses** will stop wherever you hail them and do not follow fixed routes. Fares for these range from HK$2 to HK$23 (US25¢–US$3), and you pay as you exit. Just yell when you want to get off.

FAST FACTS: Hong Kong

American Express   American Express offices (Mon–Fri 9am–5pm and Sat 9am–12:30pm) are located up on the first floor of the Henley Building, 5 Queen's Rd. Central, in the Central District (*©* **852/2110 2008**); and at 48 Cameron Rd. (*©* **852/ 2926 1606**) in Tsimshatsui.

Banks, Foreign Exchange & ATMs   Although opening hours can vary among banks, banking hours are generally Monday through Friday from 9am to 4:30pm and Saturday from 9am to 12:30pm. Some banks stop their transactions an hour before closing time. ATMs are everywhere, and almost all accept foreign cards.

Doctors & Dentists   Most first-class hotels have medical clinics with registered nurses, as well as doctors on duty at specified hours or on call 24 hours (see individual hotel listings below). Otherwise, your concierge or the U.S. consulate can refer you to a doctor or dentist. In an emergency, dial *©* **999** or call one of the recommendations under "Hospitals," below.

Embassies & Consulates   The consulate of the **United States** is at 26 Garden Rd., Central District (*©* **852/2523 9011**; 852/2841 2211 for the American Citizens Service; www.hongkong.usconsulate.gov). The consulate of **Canada** is on the 11th to 14th floors of Tower One, Exchange Square, 8 Connaught Place, Central District (*©* **852/2810 4321**; www.dfait-maeci.gc.ca/hongkong). The consulate of the **U.K.** is at 1 Supreme Court Rd., Central District (*©* **852/2901 3000**; 852/2901 3222 for passport inquiries; www.britishconsulate.org.hk). The consulate of **Australia** is on the 23rd and 24th floors of Harbour Centre, 25 Harbour Rd., Wanchai, on Hong Kong Island (*©* **852/2827 8881**; www.Australia.org.hk). The consulate of **New Zealand** is on the 65th floor of Central Plaza, 18 Harbour Rd., Wanchai (© **852/2525 5044**; www.nzembassy.com/hongkong). Most other nations also have representation in Hong Kong, including all of China's neighbors, even hermit kingdoms like North Korea and Bhutan. Collect onward visas here.

Hospitals Try **Queen Mary Hospital,** 102 Pokfulam Rd., Hong Kong Island (© **852/2855 3111**); and **Queen Elizabeth Hospital,** 30 Gascoigne Rd., Kowloon (© **852/2958 8888**).

Internet Access **Itfans,** open daily 8am to 5am at 12–13 Jubilee St., Central, has 100 computers. It charges HK$20 (US$2.60) per hour Monday through Thursday and HK$22 (US$2.85) per hour Friday to Sunday and holidays, plus a HK$10 (US$1.30) membership fee. **Pacific Coffee** is a chain of coffee shops, several with computers offering free Internet access. Its shop no. 1022 in the International Finance Center (IFC), above Hong Kong Station in Central (© **852/2868 5100**), is open Monday through Saturday from 7am to 10pm, Sunday from 8:30am to 9pm. The Peak Tower branch on Victoria Peak (© **852/2849 6608**) is open Monday through Thursday from 8am to 10:30pm and Friday through Sunday from 8am to 11pm.

Newspapers The *South China Morning Post* and *The Standard* are the two local English-language daily newspapers. The *Asian Wall Street Journal, Financial Times, International Herald Tribune,* and *USA Today International* are also available.

Pharmacies There are no 24-hour drugstores in Hong Kong. One of the best-known pharmacies in Hong Kong is **Watson's,** with more than 90 branches, most of them open from 9am to 10pm.

Police You can reach the police for an emergency by dialing © **999,** the same number as for a fire or an ambulance.

Post Offices Air-mail letters up to 20 grams and postcards cost HK$3 (US40¢) to the United States or Europe. Most hotels have stamps and can mail your letters for you. Otherwise, most post offices are open Monday through Friday from 9:30am to 5pm and Saturday from 9:30am to 1pm. The main post office is at 2 Connaught Place, Central District, Hong Kong Island, next to the Star Ferry concourse (© **852/2921 2222**). You can have your mail sent here "Poste Restante," where it will be held for 2 months; be sure to bring along your passport for identification. On the Kowloon side, the main post office is at 10 Middle Rd., which is 1 block north of Salisbury Road (© **852/2366 4111**). Both are open Monday through Saturday from 8am to 6pm and Sunday from 8am to 2pm.

Weather If you want to check the day's temperature and humidity level or the 2-day forecast, dial © **18501** or 187 8066.

3 Where to Stay

Hotel rates listed below are the hotels' official or "rack" rates, which you might end up paying if you come during peak season (Chinese New Year, Mar–Apr, Oct–Nov, major trade fairs). Otherwise, you should be able to get a room for much less by calling the hotel directly to ask whether any promotional rates are available, or by checking the hotel's website.

Hong Kong's top hotels are among the best in the world, many with sweeping views of Victoria Harbour (for which you'll pay extra) and superb service and amenities. Although the greatest concentration of hotels is on the Kowloon side, Hong Kong is so compact and easily traversed by public transportation that location is not the issue it is in larger, more sprawling metropolises. Moderate hotels comprise the majority of hotels in Hong Kong, with smaller rooms compared to their American counterparts and catering largely to tour groups (mostly from mainland China). Inexpensive hotels offer just the basics. A 10% service charge and 3% government tax will usually be added to prices quoted below.

KOWLOON
EXPENSIVE
Hotel Inter-Continental Hong Kong (formerly The Regent Hong Kong) ✿✿✿

The Inter-Continental has the best views of Victoria Harbour from Tsimshatsui. Built in 1981 and rising 17 stories, the hotel is located at the water's edge on reclaimed land. About 70% of its rooms command sweeping views of the harbor with floor-to-ceiling and wall-to-wall windows. Notable hotel features are its high-rated restaurants; spacious bathrooms with sunken bathtub, separate shower unit, and adjoining walk-in closet; an air purification system in all guest rooms; a spa renowned for its healing treatments; and wireless broadband that enables guests to access the Internet even from poolside.

18 Salisbury Rd., Tsimshatsui, Kowloon, Hong Kong. ✆ 800/327-0200 in the U.S. and Canada, or 852/2721 1211. Fax 852/2739 4546. www.hongkong-ic.intercontinental.com. 514 units. HK$3,100–HK$3,700 (US$403–US$481) single or double; HK$500 (US$65) extra for Club Floors; from HK$5,500 (US$714) junior suite. Children under 18 stay free in parent's room. AE, DC, MC, V. MTR: Tsimshatsui. **Amenities:** 5 restaurants; bar; lounge; outdoor pool and whirlpools overlooking Victoria Harbour; fitness room (open 24 hr.); spa; concierge; limousine service; business center; upscale shopping arcade; 24-hr. room service; massage; babysitting; same-day laundry/dry-cleaning service; nonsmoking rooms; executive-level rooms; house doctor. *In room:* A/C, satellite TV w/Internet access and pay movies, broadband Internet access, minibar, coffeemaker, hair dryer, safe.

The Peninsula Hotel ✿✿✿ *Finds*   This is Hong Kong's most famous hotel and *the* place to stay. Built in 1928, it exudes elegance, from its white-gloved doormen to one of the largest limousine fleets of Rolls-Royces in the world. Its lobby, with high gilded ceilings, pillars, and palms, has long been Hong Kong's foremost spot for afternoon tea and people-watching. Its restaurants are among the city's best. After land reclamation lost The Peninsula its harbor view, it remedied the problem in 1993 with the completion of a magnificent 32-story tower, offering fantastic views from guest rooms and its top-floor restaurant, Felix, designed by Philippe Starck. Spacious rooms are so wonderfully equipped that even jaded travelers are likely to be impressed.

Salisbury Rd., Tsimshatsui, Kowloon, Hong Kong. ✆ 800/462-7899 in the U.S. and Canada, or 852/2920 2888. Fax 852/2722 4170. www.peninsula.com. 300 units. HK$3,000–HK$4,900 (US$390–US$637) single or double; from HK$5,600 (US$727) suite. AE, DC, MC, V. MTR: Tsimshatsui. **Amenities:** 6 restaurants; 2 bars; lounge; gorgeous indoor pool w/sun terrace overlooking the harbor; health club; spa; concierge; limousine service; business center; designer-brand shopping arcade; salon; 24-hr. room service; massage; babysitting; same-day laundry/dry-cleaning service; nonsmoking rooms; in-house nurse. *In room:* A/C, cable/satellite TV w/CD/DVD player (free CDs and DVDs), fax, dataport, minibar, hair dryer, safe.

Kowloon

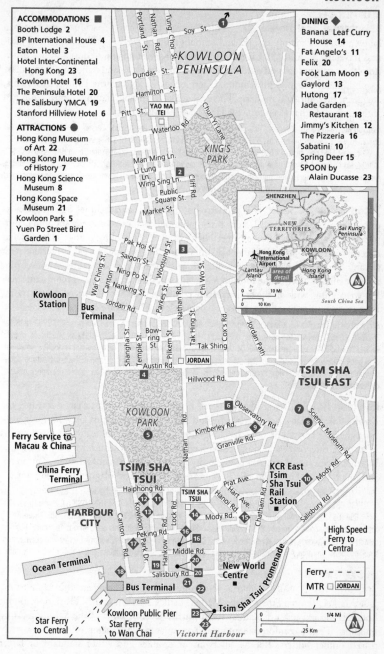

ACCOMMODATIONS ■
Booth Lodge **2**
BP International House **4**
Eaton Hotel **3**
Hotel Inter-Continental
  Hong Kong **23**
Kowloon Hotel **16**
The Peninsula Hotel **20**
The Salisbury YMCA **19**
Stanford Hillview Hotel **6**

ATTRACTIONS ●
Hong Kong Museum
  of Art **22**
Hong Kong Museum
  of History **7**
Hong Kong Science
  Museum **8**
Hong Kong Space
  Museum **21**
Kowloon Park **5**
Yuen Po Street Bird
  Garden **1**

DINING ◆
Banana Leaf Curry
  House **14**
Fat Angelo's **11**
Felix **20**
Fook Lam Moon **9**
Gaylord **13**
Hutong **17**
Jade Garden
  Restaurant **18**
Jimmy's Kitchen **12**
The Pizzeria **16**
Sabatini **10**
Spring Deer **15**
SPOON by
  Alain Ducasse **23**

KOWLOON PENINSULA

Soy St.
Portland St.
Tung Choi St.
Nathan Rd.

Dundas St.

Hamilton St.

Pitt St.
YAO MA TEI
Waterloo Rd.

Chun Yi Lane

Man Ming Ln.
Li Lung Ln.
Wing Sing Ln.
Public Square St.
Market St.

Cliff Rd.

KING'S PARK

SHENZHEN

NEW TERRITORIES

Sai Kung Peninsula

Hong Kong International Airport

Lantau Island

KOWLOON

Hong Kong Island

area of detail

South China Sea

0   10 Mi
0   10 Km

Pak Hoi St.
Saigon St.
Ning Po St.
Nanking St.

Wai Ching St.
Canton
Woosung St.
Parkes St.
Nathan Rd.
Chi Wo St.

Kowloon Station

Bus Terminal

Jordan Rd.

Shanghai St.
Temple St.
Bow-ring St.
Pilkem St.
Tak Hing St.
Cox's Rd.

JORDAN
Austin Rd.
Hillwood Rd.

Jordan Path

TSIM SHA TSUI EAST

Observatory Rd.

Kimberley Rd.
Granville Rd.

Science Museum Rd.

KOWLOON PARK

Ferry Service to Macau & China

China Ferry Terminal

TSIM SHA TSUI

Haiphong Rd.

HARBOUR CITY

Kowloon Park Dr.
Lock Rd.

TSIM SHA TSUI

Prat Ave.
Hart Ave.
Hanoi Rd.
Mody Rd.

Chatham Rd. S.
Mody Rd.

KCR East Tsim Sha Tsui Rail Station

Salisbury Rd.

High Speed Ferry to Central

Peking Rd.
Hankow Rd.
Middle Rd.

Ocean Terminal

Salisbury Rd.

New World Centre

Tsim Sha Tsui Promenade

Ferry - - - -
MTR □ JORDAN

Bus Terminal

Star Ferry to Central

Kowloon Public Pier
Star Ferry to Wan Chai

Victoria Harbour

Tsim Sha Tsui

0   1/4 Mi
0   .25 Km

MODERATE

BP International House *(Kids)*   This 25-story hotel has a spacious but utilitarian lobby and caters mainly to tour and school groups as well as budget-conscious business travelers. Built in 1993 at the north end of Kowloon Park, it's just a stone's throw from the park's indoor and outdoor public swimming pools and a short walk to a playground, making it good for families. Guest rooms, located on the 14th to 25th floors, are clean, pleasant, and modern. There are also very simple "family rooms" equipped with bunk beds that sleep four for HK$1,540 (US$200).

8 Austin Rd., Tsimshatsui, Kowloon, Hong Kong. ℂ **800/223-5652** in the U.S. and Canada, or 852/2376 1111. Fax 852/2376 1333. www.bpih.com.hk. 535 units. HK$990–HK$1,450 (US$129–US$188) single; HK$1,100–HK$1,500 (US$143–US$195) double; HK$1,600–HK$1,800 (US$208–US$234) corporate double room; from HK$3,100 (US$403) suite. Children under 13 stay free in parent's room. Rates include buffet breakfast. AE, DC, MC, V. MTR: Jordan. **Amenities:** Coffee shop; lounge; babysitting; coin-op laundry; laundry/dry-cleaning service; nonsmoking rooms; executive-level rooms. *In room:* A/C, satellite TV w/pay movies.

Eaton Hotel *(Finds)*   This property has more class and facilities than most in its price range. A handsome, 21-story brick building, it's located above a shopping complex not far from the Temple Street Night Market. The lobby lounge is bright and cheerful, with a four-story glass-enclosed atrium that overlooks a garden terrace with a water cascade, where you can sit outside with drinks in nice weather. Another plus is the small but nicely done rooftop pool with sunning terrace. Guest rooms are small but welcoming, with all the basic creature comforts. The highest-priced deluxe rooms have curved, floor-to-ceiling windows giving views of a distant harbor.

380 Nathan Rd., Yau Ma Tei, Kowloon, Hong Kong. ℂ **800/223-5652** in the U.S. and Canada, or 852/2782 1818. Fax 852/2782 5563. www.eaton-hotel.com. 460 units. HK$1,730–HK$2,230 (US$225–US$290) single or double; HK$2,530 (US$329) executive room. AE, DC, MC, V. MTR: Jordan. **Amenities:** 3 restaurants; bar; lounge; small outdoor pool; exercise room; concierge; business center; shopping arcade; room service 7am–2:30am; babysitting; same-day laundry/dry-cleaning service; nonsmoking rooms. *In room:* A/C, satellite TV w/pay movies, dataport, minibar, coffeemaker, hair dryer, safe.

Kowloon Hotel   If you like high-tech hotels but don't want to pay a fortune, the Kowloon is the place for you, right behind The Peninsula and just a few minutes' walk from the Star Ferry. The hotel has long offered the most technically advanced rooms in its price category, each equipped with an interactive telecenter, which provides free Internet access, word-processing capability (in-room fax machines double as printers), and much more. The downside: Rooms are minuscule and plagued by traffic noise.

19–21 Nathan Rd., Tsimshatsui, Kowloon, Hong Kong. ℂ **800/262-9467** in the U.S., or 852/2929 2888. Fax 852/2739 9811. www.thekowloonhotel.com. 736 units. HK$1,300–HK$2,550 (US$169–US$331) single; HK$1,400–HK$2,650 (US$182–US$344) double; from HK$3,700 (US$480) suite. AE, DC, MC, V. MTR: Tsimshatsui. **Amenities:** 3 restaurants; bar; access to nearby YMCA pool and health club (fee charged); tour desk; limousine service; business center; shopping arcade; salon; room service 6am–2am; babysitting; same-day laundry/dry-cleaning service, nonsmoking rooms. *In room:* A/C, satellite TV w/access to Internet, fax, dataport, minibar, coffeemaker, hair dryer, safe.

INEXPENSIVE

Booth Lodge *(Finds)*   About a 30-minute walk to the Star Ferry but close to the Jade Market, Temple Street Night Market, Ladies' Market, and MTR station, Booth Lodge is located just off Nathan Road on the seventh floor of the Salvation Army building. It has a comfortable lobby and an adjacent coffee shop offering reasonably priced dinner buffets. Rooms, all twins or doubles and either standard or larger deluxe, are spotlessly clean. Some face the madness of Nathan Road; those facing the hillside are quieter.

11 Wing Sing Lane, Yau Ma Tei, Kowloon, Hong Kong. © 852/2771 9266. Fax 852/2385 1140. www.boothlodge. salvation.org.hk. 53 units. HK$620–HK$1,500 (US$81–US$195) single or double. Rates include buffet breakfast. AE, MC, V. MTR: Yau Ma Tei. **Amenities:** Coffee shop; tour desk; laundry/dry-cleaning service. *In room:* A/C, satellite TV, free local phone calls, fridge, hair dryer.

The Salisbury YMCA ★★★ (Kids)   For decades the number-one choice among low-cost accommodations, this YMCA offers 19 single rooms (none with harbor view) and more than 250 doubles and twins (the most expensive provide great harbor views), as well as suites with and without harbor views that are perfect for families. Although simple in decor, these rooms are on a par with those at more expensively priced hotels in terms of in-room amenities. For budget travelers, there are also seven dormitory-style rooms, available only to visitors who have been in Hong Kong fewer than 10 days. Great for families is its sports facility boasting two indoor swimming pools (one a lap pool, the other a children's pool), a fitness gym, squash courts, and indoor climbing wall (fees charged). Make reservations in advance, especially for April or October.

Salisbury Rd., Tsimshatsui, Kowloon, Hong Kong. © 800/537-8483 in the U.S. and Canada, or 852/2268 7000 (852/2268 7888 for reservations). Fax 852/2739 9315. www.ymcahk.org.hk. 368 units. HK$700 (US$91) single; HK$800–HK$1,000 (US$104–US$130) double; from HK$1,300 (US$169) suite. Dormitory bed HK$210 (US$27). AE, DC, MC, V. MTR: Tsimshatsui. **Amenities:** 2 restaurants; 2 indoor pools; exercise room; Jacuzzi; sauna; squash courts; climbing wall; tour desk; salon; room service 7am–11pm; massage; babysitting; coin-op laundry; laundry/dry-cleaning service; nonsmoking rooms; bookstore. *In room:* A/C, satellite/cable TV, wireless Internet access, minibar, coffeemaker, hair dryer, safe.

Stanford Hillview Hotel ★ (Finds)   This small, intimate hotel is near the heart of Tsimshatsui and yet a world away, located on top of a hill in the shade of some huge banyan trees, next to the Royal Observatory with its colonial building and greenery. Knutsford Terrace, an alley with trendy bars and restaurants, is just a minute's walk away. Its lobby is quiet and subdued (quite a contrast to those in most Hong Kong hotels) and its staff friendly and accommodating. Rooms are basic and small.

13–17 Observatory Rd., Tsimshatsui, Kowloon, Hong Kong. © 800/858-8471 in the U.S. and Canada, or 852/2722 7822. Fax 852/2723 3718. www.stanfordhillview.com. 163 units. HK$880–HK$1,580 (US$114–US$205) single or double. AE, DC, MC, V. MTR: Tsimshatsui. **Amenities:** Restaurant; lounge; outdoor golf driving nets; exercise room; business center; 24-hr. room service; babysitting; same-day laundry/dry cleaning; nonsmoking rooms. *In room:* A/C, cable TV w/pay movies, Wireless Internet access, minibar, coffeemaker, hair dryer.

CENTRAL
EXPENSIVE
Island Shangri-La Hong Kong ★★★ (Finds)   With Hong Kong Park on one side and the upscale Pacific Place shopping mall on the other, Hong Kong Island's tallest hotel offers the ultimate in extravagance and luxury, rivaling the grand hotels of Europe with its Viennese chandeliers, lush Tai Ping carpets, and artwork throughout. The 17-story atrium, which stretches from the 39th to the 56th floors, features a marvelous 16-story-high Chinese painting, drawn by 40 artists from Běijīng and believed to be the largest landscape painting in the world. Also in the atrium are a private lounge open only to hotel guests, and a two-story old-world-style library. Elegant rooms, among the largest in Hong Kong, face either Victoria Peak or spectacular Victoria Harbour.

Pacific Place, Supreme Court Rd., Central, Hong Kong. © 800/942-5050 in the U.S. and Canada, or 852/2877 3838. Fax 852/2521 8742. www.shangri-la.com. 565 units. HK$2,400–HK$3,700 (US$312–US$481) single; HK$2,600–HK$3,900 (US$338–US$506) double; from HK$5,800 (US$753) suite. Children under 18 stay free in parent's room. AE, DC, MC, V. MTR: Admiralty. **Amenities:** 5 restaurants; lounge; large outdoor heated pool; 24-hr. health club; spa;

Jacuzzi; sauna; steam bath; concierge; tour desk; limousine service; free shuttle to Queen's Pier in Central and Convention Centre; 24-hr. business center; adjoining shopping mall; salon; 24-hr. room service; massage; babysitting; same-day laundry/dry-cleaning service; nonsmoking rooms; executive-level rooms; medical clinic. *In room:* A/C, satellite TV w/movies, fax/printer/scanner, dataport, minibar, coffeemaker, hair dryer, safe.

MID-LEVELS
MODERATE

Bishop Lei International House ★★ *Finds*   Located about halfway up Victoria Peak in a residential area favored by ex-pats, this hotel makes up for its out-of-the-way location with free shuttle service to Central. A half-dozen city buses stop outside its door, and the Hillside Escalator is nearby. It offers tiny standard rooms (with even tinier bathrooms, most with showers instead of tubs) that have large windows letting in lots of sunshine but that face inland. If you can, spring for a more expensive room with fantastic harbor views.

4 Robinson Rd., Mid-Levels, Hong Kong. ⓒ 852/2868 0828. Fax 852/2868 1551. www.bishopleihtl.com.hk. 203 units. HK$1,080 (US$140) single; HK$1,280–HK$1,680 (US$166–US$218) double; from HK$1,880 (US$244) suite. 1 child under 12 can stay free in parent's room. AE, DC, MC, V. Bus: no. 3B, 12, 12M, 23, 23A, and 40 to Robinson Rd. **Amenities:** Coffee shop; small outdoor pool; exercise room; business center; 24-hr. room service; babysitting; same-day laundry/dry-cleaning service; nonsmoking rooms; free shuttle bus to Central. *In room:* A/C, cable TV, dataport, minibar, coffeemaker, hair dryer, safe.

CAUSEWAY BAY/WANCHAI
EXPENSIVE

Grand Hyatt Hong Kong ★★★ *Kids*   Walking into the lobby of the Hyatt International's Asian flagship hotel is like walking into the salon of a 1930s Art Deco luxury ocean liner, with huge black-granite columns, massive flower arrangements, bubbling fountains, and furniture and statuettes reminiscent of that era. Located near the waterfront beside the Convention Centre and only a 5-minute walk from the Wanchai Star Ferry pier where passengers embark for Tsimshatsui, it offers smart-looking, contemporary rooms, and marble bathrooms with separate bathtub and shower areas. Some 75% of the rooms provide a harbor view, while the rest have views of Hong Kong's largest outdoor hotel pool and garden with partial glimpses of the harbor.

1 Harbour Rd., Wanchai, Hong Kong. ⓒ 800/233-1234 in the U.S. and Canada, or 852/2588 1234. Fax 852/2802 0677. www.hongkong.grand.hyatt.com. 572 units. HK$3,600–HK$4,400 (US$467–US$571) single; HK$3,850–HK$4,650 (US$500–US$604) double; HK$4,350–HK$4,750 (US$566–US$617) Regency Club executive-floor double; from HK$5,800 (US$753) suite. Children under 12 stay free in parent's room (maximum 3 persons per room). AE, DC, MC, V. MTR: Wanchai. **Amenities:** 4 restaurants; lounge; champagne bar; huge outdoor heated pool (shared w/adjacent Renaissance Harbour View Hotel and open year-round); children's splash pool and playground; driving range (golf); 2 outdoor tennis courts; health club; jogging track; concierge; tour desk; limousine service; free shuttle to Central, Causeway Bay, and Admiralty; business center; salon; 24-hr. room service; babysitting; same-day laundry/dry-cleaning service; nonsmoking rooms; executive-level rooms. *In room:* A/C, satellite TV w/Internet access and pay movies, fax, dataport, minibar, coffeemaker, hair dryer.

Jia ★★ *Finds*   Hong Kong's hippest boutique hotel, designed by Philippe Starck and opened in 2004, goes out of its way to prove it's no ordinary place of abode, with a staff decked out in chic Shanghai Tang–designed uniforms and stylish rooms bathed in white. Studios and one- and two-bedroom suites are available, complete with kitchens and home entertainment centers. Add a bunch of freebies—like local complimentary telephone calls, Internet access, breakfast, cocktail hour, and access to a local gym—and it seems well positioned for both business and tourist markets.

1–5 Irving St., Causeway Bay, Hong Kong. ⓒ 852/3196 9000. Fax 852/3196 9001. www.jiahongkong.com. 57 units. HK$2,000 (US$260) single or double; from HK$3,000 (US$390) suite. Rates include continental breakfast. AE, DC, MC,

Central Hong Kong

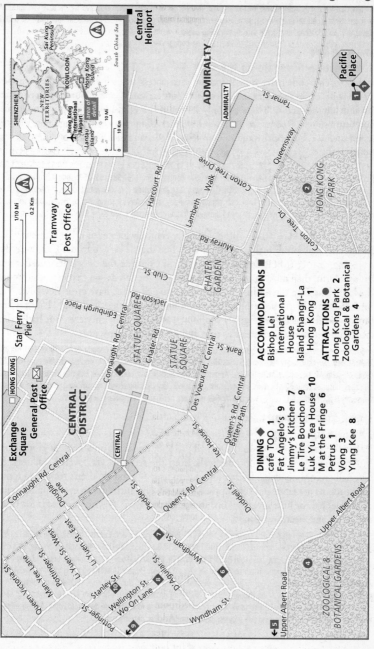

Central Heliport

Pacific Place 1

ADMIRALTY

Tamar St.

Queensway

HONG KONG PARK 2

Cotton Tree Drive

Cotton Tree Dr.

ADMIRALTY

Lambeth Walk

Murray Rd

Harcourt Rd.

CHATER GARDEN

Club St.

Jackson Rd.

STATUE SQUARE

Chater Rd.

Edinburgh Place

Connaught Rd. Central

Bank St. Central

Des Voeux Rd. Central

STATUE SQUARE

Star Ferry Pier

Ice House St.

Queen's Rd. Central

Battery Path

CENTRAL

Exchange Square

HONG KONG

General Post Office

CENTRAL DISTRICT

Connaught Rd. Central

Douglas Lane

Pedder St.

Duddell St.

Queen's Rd. Central

Man Yee Lane

Queen Victoria St.

Pottinger St.

Li Yuen St. West

Li Yuen St. East

Wyndham St. 7

D'Aguilar St.

Stanley St. 10

Wellington St. 8

Wo On Lane

Pottinger St. 9

Wyndham St.

Upper Albert Road 5

Upper Albert Road

ZOOLOGICAL & BOTANICAL GARDENS 4

Upper Albert Road

6

Map inset

South China Sea

Sai Kung Peninsula

KOWLOON

Hong Kong Island

SHENZHEN

NEW TERRITORIES

Hong Kong International Airport

Lantau Island

area of detail

0   10 Mi
0   10 Km

Legend

Tramway

Post Office ⊠

0   1/10 Mi
0   0.2 Km

ACCOMMODATIONS ■
Bishop Lei International House 5
Island Shangri-La Hong Kong 1

ATTRACTIONS ●
Hong Kong Park 2
Zoological & Botanical Gardens 4

DINING ◆
cafe TOO 1
Fat Angelo's 9
Jimmy's Kitchen 7
Le Tire Bouchon 9
Luk Yu Tea House 10
M at the Fringe 6
Petrus 1
Vong 3
Yung Kee 8

V. MTR: Causeway Bay. **Amenities:** Restaurant; bar; free access to nearby health club; rooftop Jacuzzi; sun deck; 24-hr. room service; self-service laundry; same-day laundry/dry-cleaning service. *In room:* A/C, satellite/cable TV w/DVD player, dataport, kitchen, hair dryer, safe, iron/ironing board.

MODERATE

Best Western Rosedale on the Park ★★ *Finds*   This hotel has lots going for it, including complimentary broadband Internet access in each room, cordless phones, fridge (with complimentary soda, beer, and bottled water), and a lounge with computers and Internet access. There are only 13 rooms on each floor, giving it a boutique-hotel atmosphere. Rooms are small but have everything you need, though note that the least expensive "superior" rooms are on lower floors and face another building.

8 Shelter St., Causeway Bay, Hong Kong. © **800/528-1234** in the U.S. and Canada, or 852/2127 8888. Fax 852/2127 3333. www.rosedale.com.hk. 274 units. HK$1,180–HK$1,280 (US$153–US$166) single; HK$1,280–HK$1,380 (US$166–US$179) double; HK$1,580 (US$205) executive double; from HK$1,980 (US$257) suite. Children under 18 stay free in parent's room. AE, DC, MC, V. MTR: Causeway Bay. **Amenities:** 3 restaurants; lounge; small fitness room; business center; room service 7am–1am; babysitting; same-day laundry/dry-cleaning service; nonsmoking rooms. *In room:* A/C, cable TV w/pay movies, high-speed dataport, fridge, coffeemaker, hair dryer, iron/ironing board, safe.

Metropark Hotel ★ *Value*   Although not as centrally located as other Causeway Bay hotels, this newcomer makes up for it with free shuttle service to the Causeway Bay shopping district (MTR and tram lines are just outside the door). It's cheerier and more colorful than most hotels, with a contemporary, fun design that extends through the lobby and into the rooms, the most expensive of which have great views over Victoria Park to the harbor (the cheapest rooms face another building). It offers free broadband Internet service and a rooftop pool complete with views, but bathrooms are small, with showers instead of tubs and limited counter space.

148 Tung Lo Wan Rd., Causeway Bay, Hong Kong. © **800/223-5652** in the U.S. and Canada, or 852/2600 1000. Fax 852/2600 1111. www.metroparkhotel.com. 266 units. HK$1,500–HK$1,800 (US$195–US$234) single or double; from HK$2,600 (US$338) suite. AE, DC, MC, V. MTR: Tin Hau. **Amenities:** Coffee shop; bar; outdoor pool; exercise room; Jacuzzi; sauna; tour desk; business center; 24-hr. room service; same-day laundry/dry-cleaning service; nonsmoking rooms; free shuttle to Causeway Bay. *In room:* A/C, cable TV w/pay movies, dataport, minibar, coffeemaker, hair dryer, safe.

NEAR THE AIRPORT
EXPENSIVE

Regal Airport Hotel ★ *Kids*   Opened in 1998, this is the only hotel at Hong Kong International Airport, a 5-minute walk from the terminal via covered walkway. It's especially recommendable for families due to its very good children's recreation room. Guest rooms are large and soundproof, with modern furniture in eye-popping colors of purple, red, or lime green; all but the cheapest have TVs with keyboards for Internet access and electronic games.

9 Cheong Tat Rd., Chek Lap Kok, Hong Kong. © **800/222-8888** in the U.S. and Canada, or 852/2286 8888. Fax 852/2286 8686. www.regalhotel.com. 1,100 units. HK$2,000–HK$2,800 (US$260–US$364) single or double; HK$2,950 (US$383) Regal Class; HK$3,500 (US$455) Regal Club; from HK$5,000 (US$649) suite. Children under 12 stay free in parent's room (maximum 3 persons per room). AE, DC, MC, V. Airport Express Liner: Hong Kong International Airport. **Amenities:** 5 restaurants; lounge; indoor and outdoor pools; health club and spa; children's recreation room; concierge; limousine service; 24-hr. business center; shopping arcade; salon; 24-hr. room service; babysitting; same-day laundry/dry-cleaning service; executive-level rooms; nonsmoking rooms; house doctor. *In room:* A/C, satellite TV w/Internet connection, games, and pay movies, minibar, coffeemaker, hair dryer, safe.

4 Where to Dine

With more than 10,000 restaurants from which to choose, in a few short days you can take a culinary tour of China, dining on Cantonese, Sìchuān, Shanghainese, Běijīng, Chiu Chow, and other Chinese specialties. Other national cuisines are also popular, including French, Italian, American, Thai, Indian, and Japanese. A welcome trend has seen talented chefs opening neighborhood establishments in ever greater numbers. Avoid dining from 1 to 2pm on weekdays, the traditional lunch hour for office workers.

KOWLOON

For Kowloon restaurant locations, see the map on page 549.

EXPENSIVE

Felix ✸✸✸ *(Value* PACIFIC RIM FUSION   Designer Philippe Starck has made sure that Felix is not your ordinary dining experience, beginning with the elevator's wavy walls and continuing inside the restaurant, where a huge aluminum wall and two glass facades reveal stunning views of Kowloon and Hong Kong Island. The food, featuring Pacific Rim ingredients brought together in East-meets-West combinations, rarely disappoints. You might start with California rolls, followed by the Mongolian-style barbecued rack of lamb. Bargain hunters can dine before 7pm and opt for a three-course fixed-price dinner for HK$340 (US$44). Or just come by for a drink.

In The Peninsula Hotel, Salisbury Rd., Tsimshatsui. ✆ 852/2315 3188. www.peninsula.com. Reservations required. Main courses HK$220–HK$310 (US$29–US$40). AE, DC, MC, V. Daily 6pm–2am (last order 10:30pm). MTR: Tsimshatsui.

Fook Lam Moon ✸✸✸ CANTONESE   Upon entering this restaurant you immediately feel as if you've stepped back a couple of decades. The decor is outdated, and, unless you're a regular, the waiters are indifferent. Yet this remains *the* place to go for exotic dishes, including shark's fin, bird's nest, and abalone. Shark's fin is the obvious number-one choice, with 12 different renditions listed on the menu. If you feel like splurging, prices for half a bowl of shark's fin with crabmeat or shredded chicken begin at HK$300 (US$39). If you're not careful, you could end up spending a small fortune (if you go for the exotic dishes, count on at least HK$1,000/US$130 per person). Some Hong Kong old-timers swear this restaurant serves the best Cantonese food in the world.

There's another branch in Wanchai at 35–45 Johnston Rd. (✆ **852/2866 0663;** MTR: Wanchai), with the same hours.

53–59 Kimberley Rd., Tsimshatsui. ✆ 852/2366 0286. www.fooklammoon-grp.com. Reservations recommended for dinner. Main courses HK$100–HK$190 (US$13–US$24). AE, DC, MC, V. Daily 11:30am–2:30pm and 6–11:30pm. MTR: Tsimshatsui.

Sabatini ✸✸ *(Finds* ITALIAN   The dining hall here is rustic and cozy yet refined, with live guitar music in the evenings. An offshoot of the original restaurant opened by the Sabatini brothers in Rome in 1954, its menu is a faithful replica of the fare served there, with liberal doses of olive oil, garlic, and peppers and including handmade pasta. Popular dishes include Dover sole with Prosecco, green and black olives, and herbed lemon butter; and veal with morel sauce. The list of mostly Italian wines is seemingly endless.

In the Royal Garden, 69 Mody Rd., Tsimshatsui East. ✆ 852/2733 2000. www.rghk.com.hk. Reservations required. Main courses HK$250–HK$385 (US$32–US$50); fixed-price lunch Mon–Sat HK$125–HK$250 (US$16–US$32); Sun and holiday buffet HK$280 (US$36). AE, DC, MC, V. Daily noon–2:30pm and 6–11pm. MTR: Tsimshatsui.

SPOON by Alain Ducasse ✿✿✿ FRENCH Dinner at this sophisticated venue is more than just a meal—it's an experience. The focal point of the dining room is the ceiling, where 550 hand-blown Murano glass spoons are lined up like a landing strip, directing one's attention to the open kitchen and to the stunning harbor view just beyond the massive windows. The menu, featuring the contemporary cuisine inspired by chef and restaurateur Alain Ducasse, gives diners the freedom to mix and match food and cooking styles by selecting an entrée (the steak is to die for), its sauce, and accompanying vegetables. You might, therefore, pair roasted warm salmon with a béarnaise reduction, served with spinach and Swiss chard. Or, your entire group may opt for the Sexy Spoon, a menu created for your table for HK$750 (US$97) per person.

In the Hotel Inter-Continental Hong Kong, Salisbury Rd., Tsimshatsui. ⓒ 852/2313 2256. www.hongkong-ic.inter continental.com. Reservations necessary. Main courses HK$240–HK$375 (US$31–US$49). AE, DC, MC, V. Daily 6pm–midnight. MTR: Tsimshatsui.

MODERATE

Gaylord ✿ INDIAN This long-established, first-floor restaurant in the heart of Tsimshatsui is popular for its authentic North Indian classics, including tandoori, lamb curry cooked in North Indian spices and herbs, chicken cooked in fiery-hot vindaloo curry, prawns cooked with green pepper and spices, and fish with potatoes and tomatoes. There are also a dozen vegetarian dishes. The lunchtime buffet, served every day except Sunday and public holidays until 2:30pm, is a winner. There are also fixedprice dinners, along with a dinner buffet available until 9:30pm.

23–25 Ashley Rd., Tsimshatsui. ⓒ 852/2376 1001. Main dishes HK$78–HK$198 (US$10–US$26); lunch buffet HK$88 (US$11); dinner buffet HK$128 (US$17); fixed-price dinner HK$150–HK$210 (US$19–US$27). AE, DC, MC, V. Daily noon–2:30pm and 6:30–11pm. MTR: Tsimshatsui.

Hutong ✿✿✿ (Finds) NORTHERN CHINESE This stunning restaurant is about as far from a real *hútòng* (ancient Běijīng alleyway) as one can get, since it's located on the 28th floor of a strikingly modern high-rise. Still, the restaurant is to be commended for its down-to-earth yet dramatic setting, with red lanterns providing the only splash of color against a dark, muted interior with fantastic views of Hong Kong. The cuisine uses new ingredients and combinations to create its own trademark dishes, along with classic North Chinese fare, including drunken raw crab (an appetizer marinated 3 days in Chinese wine), the crispy deboned lamb ribs, crispy softshelled crab with Sìchuān red chili, and the lotus root with wild mushroom. Dim sum is available for lunch.

1 Peking Rd. (28th floor), Tsimshatsui. ⓒ 852/3428 8342. www.aqua.com.hk. Reservations required for dinner. Main dishes HK$118–HK$288 (US$15–US$37); fixed-price lunch HK$388–HK$468 (US$50–US$61). AE, DC, MC, V. Daily noon–3pm and 6–11:30pm. MTR: Tsimshatsui.

Jade Garden Restaurant CANTONESE Jade Garden is popular with Chinese families and is the place to go if you don't know much about Chinese food but want to try it. A plus is the view of the harbor afforded by some of the window-side tables. As in most Cantonese restaurants, lunch is dim sum served from trolleys pushed through the aisles. If you'd rather order from the menu or come for dinner, you might consider drunken shrimp boiled in rice wine, deep-fried boneless chicken with lemon sauce, or stir-fried minced pigeon served with lemon leaves.

Star House (4th floor), 3 Salisbury Rd., Tsimshatsui. ⓒ 852/2730 6888. Main dishes HK$60–HK$140 (US$7.80–US$18). DC, MC, V. Mon–Sat 11am–5pm and 5:30–midnight; Sun and holidays 10am–midnight. MTR: Tsimshatsui. Also at 1 Hysan Ave., Causeway Bay (ⓒ 852/2577 9332). Daily 7:30am–midnight.

The Pizzeria *Value* ITALIAN   Located on the second floor of the Kowloon Hotel (just behind the Peninsula), this casual and bustling dining hall offers relaxed meals at good prices. Despite its name, the restaurant specializes in pasta, with an a la carte menu that changes often but has included homemade fettuccine with lobster and spinach in tomato cream sauce, and penne pasta with smoked chicken and porcini mushrooms in creamy herb sauce. There are also five different kinds of pizza and main courses that always include fish.

In the Kowloon Hotel, 19–21 Nathan Rd., Tsimshatsui. © 852/2929 2888, ext. 3322. www.thekowloonhotel.com. Pasta and pizza HK$135–HK$160 (US$18–US$21); main courses HK$190–HK$215 (US$25–US$28); lunch buffet HK$190 (US$23) Mon–Fri, HK$210 (US$26) Sat–Sun. AE, DC, MC, V. Daily noon–3pm and 6–11pm. MTR: Tsimshatsui.

INEXPENSIVE

Banana Leaf Curry House MALAYSIAN/INDIAN/THAI   This fast-growing local chain has more than 100 choices, including chicken, mutton, beef, seafood, and vegetables, cooked in several varieties of curry and presented on banana leaves. The service is brisk and efficient, the prices are reasonable, the tables are crowded, and the atmosphere is that of a school cafeteria. You might want to start with chicken satay and peanut sauce, or samosas with a mint chutney. Main dishes run the gamut from Hăinán chicken and Malaysian curry crab to vegetarian selections.

Golden Crown Court (3rd floor), 68 Nathan Rd., Tsimshatsui. © 852/2721 4821. Main dishes HK$54–HK$128 (US$7–US$17). AE, V. Daily 11am–3pm and 6–11:30pm. MTR: Tsimshatsui. Also at 440 Jaffe Rd., Causeway Bay (© 852/2573 8187). Daily 11am–3pm and 6–11:30pm. MTR: Causeway Bay.

Fat Angelo's *Value* ITALIAN   This local chain offers good value with its hearty, American renditions of Italian food, including pastas ranging from traditional spaghetti marinara to fettuccine with salmon and main courses that include rosemary roasted chicken, grilled salmon with pesto, and eggplant Parmesan, all of which come with salad and homemade bread. The emphasis is on quantity, not quality, though the food isn't bad. And they really pack 'em in; this place is bustling and loud.

33 Ashley Rd., Tsimshatsui. © 852/2730 4788. www.fatangelos.com. Reservations recommended. Pastas HK$88–HK$165 (US$11–US$21); main courses HK$125–HK$188 (US$16–US$24); fixed-price lunch (Mon–Fri only) HK$38–HK$68 (US$4.95–US$8.85). AE, DC, MC, V. Daily noon–midnight. MTR: Tsimshatsui. Also at the Elizabeth House, 250 Gloucester Rd. in Causeway Bay (© 852/2574 6263; MTR: Causeway Bay), and 49A-C Elgin St., Central (© 852/2973 6808; MTR: Central), both open noon–midnight.

Spring Deer Restaurant *Finds* BĚIJĪNG   This long-established restaurant offers excellent Běijīng food at reasonable prices. Your tablecloth may have holes in it, but it will be clean—and the place is usually packed. Best on the menu is its specialty—honey-glazed Peking duck, which costs HK$280 (US$36). You'll probably have to wait 40 minutes for the duck if you order it during peak time (7:30–9:30pm). Chicken dishes are also excellent, as are the handmade noodles. Most dishes come in small, medium, and large sizes; the small dishes are suitable for two people.

42 Mody Rd., Tsimshatsui. © 852/2366 4012. Reservations recommended. Small dishes HK$50–HK$90 (US$6.50–US$12). AE, MC, V. Daily 11:30am–3pm and 6–11pm. MTR: Tsimshatsui.

CENTRAL

For Central Hong Kong restaurant locations, see the map on p. 553.

EXPENSIVE

M at the Fringe ★★★ *Finds* CONTINENTAL   A meal here is a treat in more ways than one—the artsy furnishings are a feast for the eyes, while the food, influenced by cuisines along the Mediterranean, is consistently superb. The handwritten menu changes every 3 months but is always creative and always includes lamb and vegetarian selections. An example of the former is a salt-encased, slowly baked leg of lamb with celery root and potato gratin, French beans, and baby carrots. For dessert, don't pass up the Pavlova.

2 Lower Albert Rd., Central. © 852/2877 4000. www.m-atthefringe.com. Reservations strongly recommended. Main courses HK$208–HK$228 (US$27–US$30). AE, MC, V. Mon–Fri noon–2:30pm; Mon–Sat 7–10:30pm; Sun 7–10pm. MTR: Central.

Petrus ✷✷✷ (Finds) FRENCH   Simply put, the views from this 56th-floor restaurant are breathtaking, probably the best of any hotel restaurant on the Hong Kong side. The restaurant is decorated like a French castle, with the obligatory crystal chandeliers, statues, thick draperies, and murals gracing dome-shaped ceilings. The cuisine emphasizes contemporary Mediterranean/French seasonal ingredients, and the menu changes often but has included such intriguing choices as black truffle soup with duck liver confit ravioli and roast Boston lobster served with vegetables, fennel, morels, and anise star cream sauce.

In the Island Shangri-La (56th floor), Pacific Place, Supreme Court Rd., Central. © 852/2820 8590. www.shangri-la. com. Reservations recommended. Jacket required for men. Main courses HK$320–HK$530 (US$42–US$69); fixed-price lunch HK$310–HK$350 (US$40–US$45); fixed-price dinner HK$800–HK$950 (US$104–US$123). AE, DC, MC, V. Mon–Sat noon–3pm; daily 6:30–10:30pm. MTR: Admiralty.

Vong ✷✷✷ FRANCO-ASIAN FUSION   Chef Jean-Georges Vongerichten set Hong Kong abuzz when he opened on the 25th floor of the Mandarin Oriental Hotel in 1997. With great views, it still serves what may be the best pairing of French-Asian cuisine this side of the hemisphere. All main courses are tempting—perhaps you'll choose the spiny lobster with Thai herbs or the chicken marinated in lemon grass with sweet rice steamed in banana leaf. At lunchtime, you can save money by ordering the Black Plate or White Plate menu, which comes with six exquisitely prepared items for HK$268 (US$35).

In the Mandarin Oriental Hotel (25th floor), 5 Connaught Rd., Central. © 852/2825 4028. www.mandarinoriental.com. Reservations required. Main courses HK$228–HK$338 (US$30–US$44); fixed-price lunch HK$268–HK$288 (US$35–US$37). AE, DC, MC, V. Mon–Fri noon–3pm; daily 6pm–midnight. MTR: Central.

MODERATE

cafe TOO ✷✷✷ (Finds) INTERNATIONAL   The most interesting buffet in Hong Kong, cafe TOO features open kitchens and seven "stations" of food presentations spread throughout the restaurant, thereby giving it a theatrical touch. Browse the appetizer and salad table; a cold seafood counter with sushi, fresh oysters, crab, and other delights; and a Chinese section with dim sum and main courses. Other stations serve Western hot entrees, pastas that are prepared to order (and run the gamut from Chinese to Italian), and Asian dishes from Thai curries to Indian tandoori. The dessert table is the crowning glory.

In the Island Shangri-La Hotel, Pacific Place, Supreme Court Rd., Central. © 852/2820 8571. Reservations recommended. Lunch buffet HK$235 (US$31) Mon–Sat, HK$275 (US$36) Sun and holidays; dinner buffet HK$325 (US$42) Mon–Thurs, HK$355 (US$44) Fri–Sun and holidays. AE, DC, MC, V. Mon–Fri noon–2:30pm and 6:30–9:30pm; Sat–Sun noon–3pm and 7–10pm. MTR: Admiralty.

Jimmy's Kitchen ✷ CONTINENTAL   This restaurant opened in 1928, a replica of a similar, American-owned restaurant in Shànghǎi, and has an atmosphere reminiscent of an American steakhouse, with white tablecloths, dark-wood paneling, and elevator music. The daily specials are written on a blackboard, and an extensive a la carte menu offers salads and soups, steaks, chicken, Indian curries, and a seafood selection that includes sole, scallops, and the local garoupa. It's a good place also for corned beef and cabbage, beef Stroganoff, and hearty German fare.

1 Wyndham St., Central. ✆ **852/2526 5293.** www.jimmys.com. Main courses HK$116–HK$268 (US$15–US$35); fixed-price lunch HK$88–HK$158 (US$11–US$21). AE, DC, MC, V. Daily 11:30am–3pm and 6–11pm. MTR: Central. Also at 29 Ashley Rd., Tsimshatsui (✆ **852/2376 0327**). Daily noon–11pm.

Le Tire Bouchon ✿✿ *Finds* FRENCH   This dark, cozy restaurant near the Hillside Escalator was established in 1986 and claims to be Hong Kong's oldest independent restaurant with a French chef. It serves classic French food heavy on the sauces, like beef filet in port wine and shallot sauce with fresh duck liver, or steak with black-peppercorn sauce. Fatten up even more on one of the sumptuous desserts.

48 Graham St., Central. ✆ **852/2523 5459.** www.hkdining.com. Reservations recommended. Main courses HK$155–HK$210 (US$20–US$27); fixed-price lunch HK$178–HK$198 (US$23–US$26). AE, DC, MC, V. Mon–Sat noon–2:30pm and 6:30–10:30pm. MTR: Central.

Luk Yu Tea House ✿✿ CANTONESE   Luk Yu, first opened in 1933, is the most famous teahouse remaining in Hong Kong, a wonderful Art Deco–era Cantonese restaurant with ceiling fans, spittoons, individual wooden booths for couples, marble tabletops, and stained-glass windows. It's one of the best places to try Chinese teas like *lung ching* (a green tea) or *sui sin* (narcissus or daffodil), but Luk Yu is most famous for its dim sum, served from 7am to 5:30pm. The problem for foreigners, however, is that the place is always packed with regulars who have their own special places to sit, and the staff is sometimes surly to newcomers. In addition, if you come after 11am, dim sum is no longer served by cart but from an English menu with pictures but no prices, which could end up being quite expensive unless you ask before ordering. Bring along a Chinese friend, or consider coming for dinner, when it's not nearly so hectic and there's an English menu listing more than 200 items, including all the Cantonese favorites.

24–26 Stanley St., Central. ✆ **852/2523 5464.** Main dishes HK$100–HK$220 (US$13–US$29); dim sum HK$25–HK$55 (US$3.25–US$7.15). MC, V. Daily 7am–10pm. MTR: Central.

Yung Kee ✿ CANTONESE   Popular for decades, Yung Kee started out in 1942 as a street stall selling roast goose. Its specialty is still roast goose with plum sauce, cooked to perfection with tender meat on the inside and crispy skin on the outside and available only for dinner (a half bird, enough for five or six people, costs HK$160/US$21). Other specialties include roast suckling pig or duck, cold steamed chicken, barbecued pork, bean curd combined with prawns, sautéed filet of garoupa, and thousand-year-old eggs. Dining is on one of the upper three floors, but if all you want is a bowl of congee or takeout, join the office workers who pour in for a quick meal on the informal ground floor.

32–40 Wellington St., Central. ✆ **852/2522 1624.** www.lankwaifong.com. Main dishes HK$68–HK$180 (US$8.85–US$23). AE, DC, MC, V. Daily 11am–11:30pm. MTR: Central.

CAUSEWAY BAY
MODERATE
Red Pepper ✿ SÌCHUĀN   Open since 1970, the Red Pepper has a large following among the city's expats. Specialties include fried prawns with chili sauce on a sizzling platter, fried garoupa with sweet-and-sour sauce, smoked duck marinated with

oranges, and shredded chicken with hot garlic sauce and dry-fried string beans. Most dishes are available in two sizes, with the small dishes suitable for two people.

7 Lan Fong Rd., Causeway Bay. ⓒ 852/2577 3811. Reservations recommended for dinner. Small dishes HK$85–HK$130 (US$11–US$17). AE, DC, MC, V. Daily 11:30am–11:15pm (last order). MTR: Causeway Bay.

Wasabisabi ★★ JAPANESE   This contemporary restaurant looks like it was airlifted straight out of Tokyo, and like that huge metropolis, it's easy to get lost here. Luckily, staff is on hand to lead diners past the mirrors and corridors to the dark and cozy dining room, where diners are faced with all the usual choices like sashimi, sushi, temaki (hand-rolled sushi), grilled dishes (like grilled salmon), and tempura, as well as the Japanese chef's own creations. Top off your meal with a drink at the restaurant's popular bar.

Times Sq. (13th floor), 1 Matheson St., Causeway Bay. ⓒ 852/2506 0009. www.aqua.com.hk. Sushi (2 pieces) HK$40–HK$140 (US$5.20–US$18); main courses HK$75–HK$188 (US$9.75–US$24). DC, MC, V. Daily noon–3pm and 6pm–midnight. MTR: Causeway Bay.

INEXPENSIVE

Open Kitchen ★ *Finds* INTERNATIONAL   This self-serve cafeteria near the convention center is the best place in Wanchai for a quick, inexpensive meal with a view of the harbor. As its name suggests, chefs working in an open kitchen prepare everything from lamb chops and tandoori chicken to grilled salmon and curries. Lighter fare includes a salad bar, soups, and sandwiches.

Hong Kong Arts Centre (6th floor), 2 Harbour Rd., Wanchai. ⓒ 852/2827 2923. Main courses HK$70–HK$110 (US$9.10–US$14). AE, MC, V. Daily 11am–9pm. MTR: Wanchai.

VICTORIA PEAK
MODERATE

Cafe Deco ★ *Overrated* INTERNATIONAL   This chic, airy restaurant boasts the best views in town. To assure a ringside window seat, be sure to make reservations for the second floor at least 2 weeks in advance, emphasizing that you don't want your view obstructed by the Peak Tower, or opt for one of the 16 outdoor tables, which are often easier to get. The food is as trendy as the restaurant, with an eclectic mix of international dishes and ingredients, including tandoori kabobs and dishes, Asian noodles, sushi, grilled steaks and chops, pizzas, create-your-own pastas, soups, sandwiches, salads, and burgers. Unfortunately, main dishes occasionally fall short of expectations. What you're really paying for here is the view.

Peak Galleria, Victoria Peak. ⓒ 852/2849 5111. Reservations recommended for dinner (request window seat with view). Pizzas and pastas HK$98–HK$168 (US$13–US$22); main courses HK$108–HK$248 (US$14–US$32); fixed-price lunch (Mon–Fri only) HK$128 (US$17); Sun brunch HK$250 (US$33). AE, DC, MC, V. Mon–Fri 11:30am–11pm; Sat–Sun 9:30am–11pm (last order). Peak Tram.

The Peak Lookout ★★ INTERNATIONAL   Although it's on the Peak, across the street from the Peak Tram terminus, there are only limited views of the South China Sea from The Peak Lookout's terrace. A former tram station, it's a delightful place for a meal, with exposed granite walls, a tall timber-trussed ceiling, an open fireplace, wooden floors, and a greenhouselike room that extends into the garden. You can also sit outdoors amid the lush growth where you can actually hear birds singing—one of the best outdoor dining opportunities in Hong Kong on a glorious day. The menu is eclectic, offering a combination of American, Chinese, Indian, and Southeast Asian dishes, including tandoori chicken tikka, Thai noodles, penne with prawns, grilled steaks and salmon, and curries like Thai green chicken curry with coconut milk.

121 Peak Rd., Victoria Peak. (℗ 852/2849 1000. Reservations required for dinner and weekends. Main courses HK$125–HK$238 (US$16–US$31). AE, DC, MC, V. Mon–Thurs 10:30am–11:30pm; Fri 10:30am–1am; Sat 8:30am–1am; Sun 8:30am–11:30pm. Peak Tram.

ABERDEEN
MODERATE
Jumbo Kingdom *(Overrated* CANTONESE   There are many other restaurants that are more authentic, are more affordable, and have better food than what you find here—but this floating restaurant has been in operation for more than a quarter of a century and claims to be the largest in the world. Simply take the bus to Aberdeen and then board one of the restaurant's own free shuttle boats, which depart every few minutes. The dining hall, recently renovated, specializes in fresh seafood and changing seasonal dishes. Dim sum is available from an English menu (from carts on Sun and holidays) until 4pm. The floating complex contains shops and an exhibit on the history of Chinese fishing communities.

Aberdeen Harbour, Hong Kong Island. (℗ 852/2553 9111. www.jumbo.com.hk. Main dishes HK$80–HK$400 (US$10–US$52). Table charge HK$8 (US$1.05) per person. AE, MC, V. Mon–Sat 10:30am–10:30pm; Sun 7:30am–10:30pm. Bus: no. 7 or 70 from Central to Aberdeen, then the restaurant's private boat.

5 Exploring Hong Kong

Every visitor to Hong Kong should eat dim sum in a typical Cantonese restaurant, ride the Star Ferry across Victoria Harbour, and, if the weather is clear, take the Peak Tram for the glorious views from Victoria Peak.

VICTORIA PEAK
At 392m (1,308 ft.), Victoria Peak is Hong Kong Island's tallest mountain and offers spectacular views. Since the Peak is typically cooler than the sweltering city below, it has always been one of Hong Kong's most exclusive places to live. More than a century ago, the rich reached the Peak via a 3-hour trip in sedan chairs, transported to the top by coolies. In 1888 the **Peak Tram** began operating, cutting the journey to a mere 8 minutes.

The easiest way to reach the Peak Tram Station, located in Central on Garden Road, is to take the no. 15C open-top shuttle bus that operates between the tram terminal and the Star Ferry in Central (turn left from the ferry pier). Otherwise, the tram terminal is about a 10-minute walk from the Star Ferry. Trams depart from Peak Tram Station every 15 minutes between 7am and midnight. Round-trip tickets cost HK$30 (US$3.90) for adults, HK$14 (US$1.80) for seniors, and HK$9 (US$1.15) for children.

Upon reaching the Peak, you'll find yourself at the very modern **Peak Tower.** Head straight for the viewing terrace on Level 5, where you have one of the world's most breathtaking views: the skyscrapers of Central, the boats plying Victoria Harbour, Kowloon, and the many hills of the New Territories undulating in the background.

The best thing to do atop Victoria Peak, however, is to take an hour-long **circular hike** on Lugard Road and Harlech Road, located just a stone's throw from the Peak Tower. Mainly a footpath overhung with banyan trees and passing through lush vegetation (with glimpses of secluded mansions), the road snakes along the cliff side, offering views of Central District below, the harbor, Kowloon, and then Aberdeen and the outlying islands on the other side. This is one of the best walks in Hong Kong.

> *Tips* **A Money-Saving Museum Pass**
>
> The Museum Pass, available at HKTB for HK$30 (US$3.90), is valid for 1 week and allows entry to the Hong Kong Museum of Art, Hong Kong Museum of History, Hong Kong Space Museum, Hong Kong Science Museum, Hong Kong Museum of Coastal Defence, and Hong Kong Heritage Museum. Museum admission is free to all on Wednesday.

MUSEUMS

Municipal museums are closed December 25 and 26, January 1, and the first 3 days of Chinese New Year.

Hong Kong Heritage Museum ✶✶ *Kids*   Presenting both the history and culture of the New Territories, this museum is probably the best reason to take the KCR to Sha Tin in the New Territories. Come here to learn about the customs, religions, and lifestyles of the early fishermen and settlers and how they have changed over the centuries. See a barge loaded for market, traditional clothing, models of Sha Tin showing its mind-numbing growth since the 1930s, musical instruments, elaborate costumes used in Chinese opera, porcelains, bronzes, jade, and other works of Chinese art dating from the Neolithic period to the 20th century. At the Children's Discovery Gallery, youngsters can practice being archaeologists, wear traditional costumes, and learn about marshes. Plan on spending 2 hours here.

1 Man Lam Rd., Sha Tin. ✆ 852/2180 8188. http://hk.heritage.museum. Admission HK$10 (US$1.30) adults, HK$5 (US65¢) children, students, and seniors. Free admission Wed. Mon and Wed–Sat 10am–6pm; Sun/holidays 10am–7pm. KCR: Tai Wai or Sha Tin, about a 10-min. walk from either.

Hong Kong Museum of Art ✶✶✶   Because of its location on the Tsimshatsui waterfront just a 2-minute walk from the Star Ferry terminus, this museum is the most convenient and worthwhile if your time is limited. Feast your eyes on ceramics, bronzes, jade, cloisonné, lacquerware, bamboo carvings, and textiles, as well as paintings, wall hangings, scrolls, and calligraphy dating from the 16th century to the present. The Historical Pictures Gallery provides a visual account of life in Hong Kong, Macau, and Guǎngzhōu in the late 18th and 19th centuries. Another gallery displays contemporary Hong Kong works by local artists. You'll want to spend at least an hour here, though art aficionados can devote more time by renting audioguides for HK$10 (US$1.30).

Hong Kong Cultural Centre Complex, 10 Salisbury Rd., Tsimshatsui. ✆ 852/2721 0116. www.lcsd.gov.hk/hkma. Admission HK$10 (US$1.30) adults, HK$5 (US65¢) children, students, and seniors. Free admission Wed. Fri–Wed 10am–6pm. MTR: Tsimshatsui.

Hong Kong Museum of History ✶✶✶   If you visit only one museum in Hong Kong, this should be it. Opened in 2001, it's Hong Kong's ambitious attempt to chronicle 6,000 years of history. Through displays that include life-size dioramas, replica fishing boats, reconstructed traditional housing, furniture, clothing, and items from daily life, the museum introduces Hong Kong's ethnic groups, traditional means of livelihood, customs, and beliefs. You can peer inside a fishing junk, see what Kowloon Walled City looked like before it became a park, view the backstage of a Chinese opera, read about the arrival of European traders and the Opium Wars, and study a map showing land reclamation since the 1840s. One of my favorite parts of the museum is a re-created street of old Hong Kong, complete with an original Chinese herbal medicine shop located in Central until 1980 and reconstructed here. There are also 19th- and early-20th-century photographs, poignantly showing how much Hong Kong has changed through the decades. You can easily spend 2 hours here.

100 Chatham Rd. S., Tsimshatsui East. **852/2724 9042.** http://hk.history.museum. Admission HK$10 (US$1.30) adults, HK$5 (US65¢) children and seniors. Free admission Wed. Mon and Wed–Sat 10am–6pm; Sun/holidays 10am–7pm. MTR: Tsimshatsui (a 20-min. walk from exit B2). Bus: no. 5 or 5C from Star Ferry bus terminus.

Sam Tung Uk Museum 🖈🖈 Located in the New Territories but easily accessible from either Central or Tsimshatsui in about 25 minutes via MTR, this is actually a restored Hakka walled village, built in the 18th century by members of the farming Chan clan. It consists of tiny lanes lined with tiny tile-roofed homes, four houses that have been restored to their original condition, an ancestral hall, two rows of side houses, an exhibition hall depicting Tsuen Wan's history, and an adjacent landscaped garden. The four windowless restored houses are furnished much as they would have been when occupied, with traditional Chinese furniture (including elegant blackwood furniture). Although as many as 300 clan members once lived here, the village was abandoned in 1980. Today the museum is a tiny oasis in the midst of high-rise housing projects.

2 Kwu Uk Lane, Tsuen Wan. 🕐 **852/2411 2001.** Free admission. Wed–Mon 9am–5pm. MTR: Tsuen Wan (a few minutes' walk from exit E).

TEMPLES

Man Mo Temple 🖈 Hong Kong Island's oldest and most important temple was built in the 1840s and is named after its two principal deities: Man, the god of literature, and Mo, the god of war. Two ornately carved sedan chairs in the temple were once used during festivals to carry the statues of the gods around the neighborhood. But what makes the temple particularly memorable are the giant incense coils hanging from the ceiling, imparting a fragrant, smoky haze—these are purchased by patrons seeking good health or a successful business deal, and may burn as long as 3 weeks.

Hollywood Rd. and Ladder St., Western District. 🕐 **852/2803 2916.** Free admission. Daily 8am–6pm. Bus: no. 26 from Des Voeux Rd. Central (in front of the Hongkong Bank headquarters) to the 2nd stop on Hollywood Rd., across from the temple. Or, take the Hillside Escalator to Hollywood Rd.

Wong Tai Sin 🖈🖈 Located six subway stops northeast of Yaumatei in the far north end of Kowloon Peninsula, Wong Tai Sin is Hong Kong's most popular Daoist temple. Although the temple dates only from 1973, it adheres to traditional Chinese architectural principles with its red pillars, two-tiered golden roof, blue friezes, yellow latticework, and multicolored carvings. On the temple grounds are halls dedicated to the Buddhist Goddess of Mercy and to Confucius; the Nine Dragon Garden, a Chinese garden with a pond, a waterfall, and a Nine Dragons mural; the Good Wish Garden, with circular, square, octagonal, and fan-shaped pavilions, ponds, an artificial waterfall, and rocks and concrete fashioned to resemble animals; and a clinic with both Western medical services and traditional Chinese herbal treatments.

Wong Tai Sin Estate. 🕐 **852/2327 8141.** www.siksikyuen.org.hk. Free admission to temple, though donations of about HK$1 (US15¢) are expected at the temple's entrance and for Nine Dragon Wall Garden; admission to Good Wish Garden HK$2 (US25¢) extra. Temple daily 7am–5:30pm; gardens Tues–Sun 9am–4pm. MTR: Wong Tai Sin (exit B2) and then a 3-min. walk (follow the signs).

ORGANIZED TOURS & CULTURAL ACTIVITIES

For information and pamphlets on the following tours, stop by HKTB; most hotels also have tour desks.

CITY TOURS   For general sightseeing, the **Gray Line** (© 852/2368 7111; www.grayline.com.hk) offers a variety of tours to such locations as Man Mo Temple, Victoria Peak, Aberdeen, Stanley, Po Lin Monastery on Lantau island, and the New Territories, as well as sunset cruises and visits to the horse races. **Splendid Tours & Travel** (© 852/2316 2151; www.splendidtours.com) also offers a general city tour, excursions to Lantau and the New Territories, night tours, cruises, and organized visits to the horse races.

"MEET THE PEOPLE" *Finds*   Through this unique program of free, 1-hour tours, lectures, classes, and seminars, visitors can meet local specialists and gain in-depth knowledge of Hong Kong's traditions. Programs are updated and revised annually; past offerings have covered Chinese antiques, Cantonese opera, traditional Chinese medicine, feng shui (geomancy), and *tàijíquán* (shadow boxing), with something going on virtually every day of the week. For details on what, when, and where, pick up a *Cultural Kaleidoscope* brochure at HKTB.

OUTDOOR PURSUITS
PARKS & GARDENS

Hong Kong Park *Kids*   Opened in 1991, Hong Kong Park, Supreme Court Road and Cotton Tree Drive, Central, features a dancing fountain at its entrance, Southeast Asia's largest greenhouse with more than 2,000 rare plant species, an aviary housing 800 exotic birds in a tropical rainforest setting, various gardens, a children's playground, and a viewing platform reached by climbing 105 stairs. The most famous building on the park grounds is the **Flagstaff House Museum of Tea Ware** (© 852/ 2869 0690; www.lcsd.gov.hk/hkma), the oldest colonial building in Hong Kong. Completed in 1846 in Greek Revival style for the commander of the British forces, it now displays some 150 items of tea ware on a rotating basis from its 600-piece collection, primarily of Chinese origin and dating from the 7th century to the present day. The park is open daily from 6am to 11pm, the greenhouse and aviary are open daily from 9am to 5pm, and the museum of tea ware is open Wednesday through Monday from 10am to 5pm. Admission is free to everything. Take the MTR to Admiralty Station (exit C1), then follow the signs through Pacific Place and up the escalators.

Yuen Po Street Bird Garden *Kids*   Birds are favorite pets in Chinese households; perhaps you've noticed wooden bird cages hanging outside shops or from apartment balconies, or perhaps you've even seen someone taking his bird for an outing in its cage. To see more of these prized songbirds, visit the fascinating Yuen Po Street Bird Garden, Prince Edward Road West, Mongkok, which consists of a series of Chinese-style moon gates and courtyards lined with stalls selling songbirds, beautifully crafted wood and bamboo cages, live crickets and mealy worms, and tiny porcelain food bowls. Young children love it here. Take the MTR to Prince Edward Road station (exit B1 or B2) and walk 10 minutes east on Prince Edward Road West, turning left at the overhead railway onto Yuen Po Street. Admission to the garden is free and it's open daily from 7am to 8pm.

Zoological & Botanical Gardens *Kids*   Established in 1864, the Zoological and Botanical Gardens, Upper Albert Road, Central, are spread on the slope of Victoria

Peak, making them a popular respite for Hong Kong residents. Arrive early around 7am to see Chinese residents going through the slow motions of *tàijíquán*. The gardens retain some of their Victorian charm, and of the 1,000 species of plants, something is almost always in bloom, from azaleas in the spring to wisteria and bauhinea in the summer and fall. The small zoo houses 600 birds, 90 mammals, and 20 reptiles from around Asia. There's also a children's playground. Admission is free. The eastern part of the park, containing most of the botanical gardens and the aviaries, is open daily from 6am to 10pm, while the western half, with its reptiles and mammals, is open daily from 6am to 7pm. Take the MTR to Central and then walk 15 minutes up Garden Road to the corner of Upper Albert Road. Or take bus no. 3B or 12 from the Jardine House on Connaught Road Central.

TAI CHI

Tàijíquán (shadow boxing), called "tai chi" in the West, is an ancient Chinese regimen designed to balance body and soul and thereby release energy from within. Visitors can join free, 1-hour **lessons** in English, offered by HKTB's "Meet the People" cultural program, every Monday, Wednesday, and Thursday at 8am outside the Hong Kong Cultural Centre on Tsimshatsui near the Star Ferry. For more information, stop by or call HKTB (② **852/2508 1234**).

HIKING

With 23 country parks—amounting to more than 40% of Hong Kong's space—there are many trails of varying levels of difficulty throughout Hong Kong, including hiking trails, nature trails, and family trails. Serious hikers may want to consider the famous **MacLehose Trail** in the New Territories, which stretches about 100km (62 miles) through eight country parks, while the **Lantau Trail** is a 70km (43-mile) circular trail on **Lantau island** that begins and ends at Mui Wo (also called Silvermine Bay). Easier to reach is the 50km (31-mile) Hong Kong Trail, which spans Hong Kong Island's five country parks. The HKTB has trail maps and a hiking and wildlife guidebook called *Exploring Hong Kong Countryside: A Visitor's Companion*. Its website, www.discoverhongkong.com, also lists recommended hikes.

HORSE RACING

If you're here anytime from September to mid-June, join the rest of Hong Kong at the horse races. Introduced by the British more than 150 years ago, horse racing is by far the most popular sporting event in Hong Kong, due to the fact that, aside from the local lottery, racing is the only legal form of gambling in Hong Kong. Winnings are tax-free.

There are two tracks—**Happy Valley** on Hong Kong Island, which you can reach by taking the tram to Happy Valley or the MTR to Causeway Bay; and **Sha Tin** in the New Territories, reached by taking the KCR railway to Racecourse Station. Races are held Wednesday evenings and some Saturday and Sunday afternoons. The lowest admission price is HK$10 (US$1.30), which is for the general public and is standing room only. If you want to watch from the more exclusive Hong Kong Jockey Club members' enclosure, are at least 18 years old, and are a bona-fide tourist, you can purchase a temporary member's badge for HK$50 (US$6.50). It's available on a first-come, first-served basis by showing your passport at either the Badge Enquiry Office at the main entrance to the members' private enclosure (at either track), or at the off-course betting center near the Star Ferry concourse in Central.

You can also see the races by joining an organized tour offered by Gray Line or Splendid Tours (see "Organized Tours & Cultural Activities," above).

SWIMMING

There are numerous public swimming pools, including those at **Kowloon Park,** with admission costing around HK$19 (US$2.45) for adults and HK$9 (US$1.15) for children and seniors. About 40 **beaches** are free for public use, most with lifeguards on duty April through October, changing rooms, and snack stands or restaurants. On Hong Kong Island, beaches include Big Wave Bay and Shek O on the east coast, and Stanley, Deep Water Bay, South Beach (popular with the gay crowd), and Repulse Bay on the southern coast. There are prettier beaches on the outlying islands, including Hung Shing Ye and Lo So Shing on Lamma, Tung Wan on Cheung Chau, and Cheung Sha on Lantau.

OUTLYING ISLANDS

An excursion to an outlying island provides not only an opportunity to experience rural Hong Kong but also the chance to view Hong Kong's skyline and harbor by ferry, and very cheaply at that. I recommend either Lantau, famous for its giant outdoor Buddha and monastery serving vegetarian meals, or Cheung Chau, popular with families for its unhurried, small-village atmosphere and beach. Both islands are reached in about an hour via ferries that depart approximately every hour or so from the Central Ferry Pier, located less than a 5-minute walk west of the Star Ferry in Central (pick up a free timetable at HKTB). Tickets range from HK$10 to HK$31 (US$1.30–US$4), depending on the day (weekdays are cheaper) and class (ordinary and deluxe). Upper-deck deluxe class entitles you to sit on an open deck out back.

In addition to the ferries above, there is also a faster hover ferry service used mostly by commuters, as well as infrequent ferry service from Tsimshatsui's Star Ferry concourse on Saturday afternoon and Sunday. You can also reach Lantau via the Tung Chung MTR Line, with a connecting cable car opening in early 2006 that will deliver visitors directly to the Giant Buddha in just 17 minutes.

LANTAU

Hong Kong's largest island and twice the size of Hong Kong Island, Lantau has a population of 84,000 and is home to Hong Kong's international airport. Luckily, more than half of the mountainous and lush island remains preserved in country parks. After taking the ferry from Central to Silvermine Bay (called *Mui Wo* in Cantonese), then bus no. 2 (or the MTR to Tung Chung, followed by take bus no. 23 or, from 2006, cable car), you'll arrive at Lantau's biggest attraction, the **Giant Tian Tan Buddha,** the largest, seated outdoor bronze Buddha in the world. The nearby **Po Lin Monastery** (© 852/2985 5248) is famous for its vegetarian meals. Both are situated on the plateau of Ngong Ping at an elevation of 750m (2,460 ft.). The Giant Buddha is more than 30m (100 ft.) tall and weighs 220 tonnes (243 U.S. tons); it's reached via 268 steps and offers great views of the surrounding countryside. Admission to the viewing platform is free and it's open daily from 10am to 6pm.

Be sure to explore the grounds of the colorful monastery, established near the turn of the 20th century by reclusive Buddhist monks. Because of the ferry and bus rides required to get there and back, you should allow at least 5 hours for a visit to Lantau.

The biggest thing to hit Lantau since its new airport is **Hong Kong Disneyland** (© **852/1830 830;** www.hongkongdisneyland.com), a 125-hectare (310-acre) theme park reached via the Tung Chung MTR line. Open hours vary with the season, with admission priced at HK$295 (US$38) for adults, HK$210 (US$27) for children, and HK$170 (US$22) for seniors. During peak times (weekends, holidays, and school vacation), admission costs HK$350 (US$45), HK$250 (US$32), and HK$200 (US$26), respectively.

CHEUNG CHAU

If you have only a few hours to spare and don't want to worry about catching buses and finding your way around, Cheung Chau is your best bet. It's a tiny island (only 1 sq. mile), with more than 25,000 people in its thriving fishing village. There are no cars on the island, making it a delightful place for walking around and exploring. The island is especially popular with Chinese families for its rental bicycles and beach, but my favorite thing to do here is to walk the tiny, narrow lanes of Cheung Chau village.

Inhabited for at least 2,500 years by fisherfolk, Cheung Chau still supports a sizable population of fishing families, and fishing remains the island's main industry. Inhabited junks are moored in the harbor, and the waterfront where the ferry lands, known as the **Praya,** buzzes with activity as vendors sell live fish and vegetables. The village is a fascinating warren of narrow alleyways, food stalls, open markets, and shops selling everything from medicinal herbs to toys.

About a 3-minute walk from the ferry pier is **Pak Tai Temple,** near a playground on Pak She Fourth Street. Built in 1783, it's dedicated to the "Supreme Emperor of the Dark Heaven," long worshipped as a Daoist god of the sea. As you roam the village, you'll pass open-fronted shops selling incense, paper funeral objects such as cars (cremated with the deceased to accompany him or her to the next life), medicinal herbs, jade, rattan, vegetables, rice, sun hats, sunglasses, and beach toys. On the other side of the island (directly opposite from the ferry pier and less than a 10-min. walk away) is **Tung Wan Beach.**

6 Shopping

Shopping is one of the main reasons people come to Hong Kong, and at first glance the city does seem to be one huge department store. Good buys include Chinese antiques, clothing, shoes, jewelry, furniture, carpets, leather goods, luggage, handbags, briefcases, Chinese herbs, watches, toys, and eyeglasses. Electronic goods and cameras are not the bargains they once were, though good deals can be found in recently discontinued models. Hong Kong is a duty-free port, so there is no sales tax.

BEST SHOPPING AREAS

Tsimshatsui boasts the greatest concentration of shops in Hong Kong, particularly along Nathan Road, with its many electronics stores (which should be avoided in favor of the reliable chain Fortress). Be sure to explore its side streets for shops specializing in washable silk, casual clothing, and luggage. Harbour City, one of the largest malls in the world, stretches along Canton Road.

For upscale shopping, **Central** is where you'll find international designer labels, in boutiques located in the Landmark and Prince's Building. For one-stop shopping, there's the upscale Pacific Place at Admiralty and the ifc mall beside Hong Kong Station. **Causeway Bay** caters more to the local market, with lower prices, small shops selling everything from shoes and clothing to Chinese herbs, several Japanese department stores, and a large shopping complex called Times Square.

Antiques and curio lovers usually head for **Hollywood Road** and **Cat Street** on Hong Kong Island, where everything from snuff bottles to jade carvings is for sale. Finally, one of my favorite places to shop is **Stanley Market,** on the southern end of Hong Kong Island, where vendors sell business and casual wear, as well as Chinese crafts and products. Another good place to shop for Chinese imports and souvenirs is one of several Chinese **craft emporiums.**

Because shopping is such big business in Hong Kong, most stores are open 7 days a week, closing only for 2 or 3 days during the Chinese New Year. Most stores open at 10am, closing at 7pm in Central, 9 or 10pm in Tsimshatsui, and 9:30pm in Causeway Bay. Street markets are open every day.

SHOPPING A TO Z
ANTIQUES & COLLECTIBLES

The most famous area for antiques and chinoiserie is around **Hollywood Road** and **Cat Street,** both above the Central District on Hong Kong Island. Hollywood Road twists along for a little more than half a mile, with shops selling original and reproduction Qīng and Míng dynasty Chinese furniture, original prints, scrolls, porcelain, clay figurines, silver, and rosewood and blackwood furniture, as well as fakes and curios. Near the western end is Upper Lascar Row, popularly known as Cat Street, where sidewalk vendors sell snuff bottles, reproductions, and other curios.

Arch Angel Antiques   Established in 1988, this is one of Hollywood Road's largest shops for Asian antiques and art, including museum-quality ceramics, furniture, Míng dynasty figurines, terra-cotta animals, boxes, and collectibles. In addition to this three-story main shop, nearby galleries showcase ancient ceramics, bronze Buddhas, terra-cotta figures, and contemporary Vietnamese art. Every antique item for sale is accompanied by a detailed certificate of authenticity. Open daily from 9:30am to 6:30pm. 53–55 Hollywood Rd., Central. ✆ **852/2851 6848.** MTR: Central.

Cat Street Galleries   Cat Street Galleries, on Cat Street, houses several individually owned booths of arts and crafts and expensive antiques from the various dynasties, making it a good place to begin an antiques shopping odyssey. It's open Monday to Friday from 11am to 6pm and Saturday from 10am to 6pm. 38 Lok Ku Rd., Central. ✆ **852/2543 1609.** MTR: Shueng Wan. Bus: no. 26 (from Des Voeux Rd. Central in front of the Hongkong Bank) to the 2nd stop on Hollywood Rd., at Man Mo Temple.

Tips **Buyer Beware**

Hong Kong is a buyer-beware market. To be on the safe side, try to make your major purchases at HKTB member stores, which display the HKTB logo (a gold circle with black Chinese calligraphy in the middle and the words "Quality Tourism Services"). Member stores are listed in a directory called "A Guide to Quality Merchants," free at HKTB, and at www.qtshk.com. Still, it's always a good idea to obtain a receipt from the shopkeeper with a description of your purchase, including the brand name, model number, serial number, and price for electronic and photographic equipment. For jewelry and gold watches, there should be a description of the precious stones and the metal content. If you're making a purchase using a credit card, ask for the customer's copy of the credit card slip, and make sure "HK$" appears before the monetary total.

China Art   The mixed displays of furniture and art give this family-owned shop the elegance of an art gallery. It's one of Hong Kong's best for antique Chinese furniture, including chairs, folding screens, chests, and more, mostly from the Míng dynasty (1368–1644). Located across from the Central Police Station, it's open Monday through Saturday from 10:30am to 6pm and Sunday and holidays from 1 to 6pm. 15 Hollywood Rd., Central. (©) 852/2542 0982. www.chinaart.com.hk. MTR: Central. Bus: no. 26 (from Des Voeux Rd. Central in front of the Hongkong Bank) to Hollywood Rd.

Dragon Culture *(Finds*   All serious fans of Chinese antiques eventually end up here. One of the largest and most knowledgeable purveyors of antiques in Hong Kong, Victor Choi began collecting Chinese antiques in the 1970s, traveling throughout China. He shares his expertise in three books, which you can purchase in his shop. With another gallery at 184 Hollywood Rd. ((©) 852/2815 5227) and one in New York, Choi carries Neolithic pottery, three-color glazed pottery horses from the Táng dynasty, Míng porcelains, bronzes, jade, woodcarvings, snuff bottles, calligraphy, paintings, brush pots, stone carvings, and more, and also provides a certificate of authenticity. Both his Hong Kong shops are open Monday through Saturday from 10am to 6pm. 231 Hollywood Rd., Sheung Wan. (©) 852/2545 8098. www.dragonculture.com.hk. MTR: Shueng Wan. Bus: no. 26 (from Des Voeux Rd. Central in front of the Hongkong Bank) to the 2nd stop on Hollywood Rd., at Man Mo Temple.

True Arts & Curios *(Finds*   This tiny shop is so packed with antiques and curios that there's barely room for customers. Although everything, from snuff bottles, porcelain, antique silver, earrings, and hairpins, to children's shoes (impractical but darling, with curled toes), is stocked, the true finds here are some 2,000 intricate woodcarvings, pried from the doors and windows of dismantled temples and homes. The shop is open Monday through Saturday from 10:30am to 6:30pm and Sunday from 2:30 to 6:30pm. 89–91 Hollywood Rd., Central. (©) 852/2559 1485. MTR: Sheung Wan.

CHINESE CRAFT EMPORIUMS

In addition to the shops listed here, which specialize in traditional and contemporary arts, crafts, souvenirs, and gift items from China, there are souvenir shops at Stanley Market, located in Stanley on the southern end of Hong Kong Island, that carry lacquered boxes, china, embroidered tablecloths, figurines, and other mainland imports. All these items will be much cheaper across the border, of course.

Chinese Arts and Crafts Ltd   In business for more than 30 years, this is the best upscale chain for Chinese arts and crafts and is one of the safest places to purchase jade. You can also buy silk clothing, arts and crafts, antiques, jewelry, watches, carpets, cloisonné, furs, Chinese herbs and medicine, rosewood furniture, chinaware, Chinese teas, and embroidered tablecloths or pillowcases—in short, virtually all the upmarket items produced by China. It's a great place for gifts, though prices are high. Open from 10am to 9:30pm. The shop is located in Star House near the Star Ferry at 3 Salisbury Rd., Tsimshatsui ((©) 852/2735 4061; www.crcretail.com; MTR: Tsimshatsui). Other branches are at Pacific Place, 88 Queensway, Central ((©) 852/2523 3933; MTR: Admiralty); and in the China Resources Building, 26 Harbour Rd., Wanchai ((©) 852/2827 6667; MTR: Wanchai).

Shànghǎi Tang *(Finds*   Step back into 1930s Shànghǎi at this upscale, two-level store with its gleaming wooden and tiled floors, raised cashier cubicles, and ceiling fans. This is Chinese chic at its best, with neatly stacked rows of updated versions of traditional

Chinese clothing ranging from cheongsams and silk pajamas to padded jackets, caps, and shoes—all in bright, contemporary colors and styles. If you're looking for a lime-green or shocking-pink padded jacket, this is the place for you. It's open Monday to Saturday from 10am to 8pm and Sunday from 11am to 7pm. There's a small branch in the Peninsula Hotel, Salisbury Road, Tsimshatsui (© 852/2537 2888; MTR: Tsimshatsui). Pedder Building, 12 Pedder St., Central. © 852/2525 7333. www.shanghaitang.com. MTR: Central.

FASHION

Hong Kong has been a center for the fashion industry ever since the influx of Shang-hainese tailors fleeing the 1949 Communist revolution in China. If you're looking for international designer brands and money is no object, the **Landmark,** located on Des Voeux Road Central, Central, is an ultra-chic shopping complex boasting the highest concentration of international brand names in Hong Kong, including Gucci, Tiffany & Co., Polo/Ralph Lauren, Manolo Blahnik, Marc Jacobs, Versace, Missoni, Kenzo, Sonia Rykiel, Louis Vuitton, Lanvin, and Christian Dior. Other shopping arcades with well-known international designer boutiques include the **Prince's Building,** next to the Mandarin Hotel, and the **Peninsula Hotel,** on Salisbury Road in Tsimshatsui.

For trendier designs catering to an upwardly mobile younger crowd, check out the **Joyce Boutique** chain, established in the 1970s by Joyce Ma to satisfy Hong Kong women's cravings for European designs. Today her stores carry clothing by Issey Miyake, John Galliano, Stella McCartney, Yohji Yamamoto, Rei Kawakubo (Comme des Garçons), and others on the cutting edge of fashion. You'll find Joyce shops at 18 Queen's Rd. Central, Central District (© 852/2810 1120; MTR: Central); 334 Pacific Place, 88 Queensway, Central (© 852/2523 5944; MTR: Admiralty); and Shop G106 in The Gateway, Canton Rd., Tsimshatsui (© 852/2367 8128; MTR: Tsimshatsui).

FACTORY OUTLETS   Hong Kong's factory outlets offer excess stock, overruns, and quality-control rejects. Because these items have been made for the export mar-ket, the sizes are Western. Bargains include clothes made of silk, cashmere, cotton, linen, knitwear, and wool. Most outlets are located in **Hung Hom,** clustered in a large group of warehouse buildings called **Kaiser Estates** on Man Yue Street (take bus no. 5C from the Tsimshatsui Star Ferry bus terminal to Ma Tau Wai Rd., the third stop after the KCR Kowloon Railway Station). On Hong Kong Island, the best-known building housing factory-outlet showrooms is the **Pedder Building,** 12 Pedder St., Central. For a list of factory outlets, along with their addresses, telephone numbers, and types of clothing, pick up the free pamphlet "Clothing & Accessories" at HKTB offices. Most outlets are open from 10 or 11am to 7pm Monday through Friday, with shorter hours on Saturday. Some are open Sunday as well.

MARKETS

Jade Market   Jade is available in all sizes, colors, and prices at this market at the junction of Kansu Street and Battery Street, in two temporary structures in the Yau-matei District. Unless you really know your jade and pearls, you won't want to make any expensive purchases here. It's open daily from 10am to about 4pm (mornings are best), though some vendors stay until 6pm on busy days like Sunday. The market is located near the Jordan MTR station or less than a 30-minute walk from the Star Ferry.

Ladies' Market   Stretching along Tung Choi Street (between Argyle and Dundas sts.) in Mongkok, Kowloon, Ladies' Market specializes in inexpensive women's and children's fashions, shoes, jewelry, sunglasses, watches, handbags (including fake designer bags), and other accessories. Some men's clothing is also sold. Although many of the products are geared more to local tastes and sizes, an increase in tourism has brought more fashionable clothing and T-shirts in larger sizes and you may find a few bargains. In any case, the atmosphere is fun and festive, especially at night. The nearest MTR station is Mongkok. Vendors' hours are daily from 12:30 to 10:30pm.

Li Yuen Street East & West   These two streets are parallel pedestrian lanes in the heart of Central, very narrow and often congested with human traffic. Stalls are packed with Chinese jackets, handbags, clothes, scarves, sweaters, toys, baby clothes, watches, make-up, umbrellas, needles and thread, knickknacks, and even brassieres. Don't neglect the open-fronted shops behind the stalls. These two streets are located just a couple minutes' walk from the Central MTR station or the Star Ferry, between Des Voeux Road Central and Queen's Road Central. Vendors' hours are from 10am to 7pm, daily.

Stanley   Stanley Market is probably the most popular and best-known market in Hong Kong. Located on the southern coast of Hong Kong Island, it's a great place to buy inexpensive clothing, especially sportswear, cashmere sweaters, silk blouses and dresses, and women's suits. Men's, women's, and children's clothing are available. The inventory changes continuously—one year it seems everyone is selling washable silk; the next year it's Chinese traditional jackets or Gore-Tex coats. The market also has souvenir shops selling paintings, embroidered linen, beaded purses, handicrafts, and other products from mainland China.

To reach Stanley, take bus no. 6, 6A, 6X, or 260 from Central's Exchange Square bus terminal near the Star Ferry (bus no. 260 also makes stops in front of the Star Ferry terminal and Pacific Place). The bus ride to Stanley takes approximately 30 minutes. From Kowloon, take bus no. 973 from Mody Road in Tsimshatsui East or from Canton Road in Tsimshatsui. Shops are open daily from 9:30 or 10am to about 6:30pm.

Temple Street Night Market   Temple Street in the Yaumatei District of Kowloon is a night market that comes to life when the sun goes down. It offers T-shirts, jeans, menswear, watches, jewelry, CDs, mobile phones, electronic gadgets, alarm clocks, luggage, and imitation designer watches and handbags. Bargain fiercely, and check the products carefully to make sure they're not faulty or poorly made. The night market is great entertainment, a must during your visit to Hong Kong. North of Temple Street, near Tin Hau Temple, are fortune-tellers and sometimes street performers singing Chinese opera. Although some vendors begin setting up shop at 4pm, the night market is busiest from about 7 until the 10pm closing; it's located near the Jordan MTR station.

7 Hong Kong After Dark

Hong Kong's nightlife is concentrated in Tsimshatsui, in Central's entertainment areas of Lan Kwai Fong and SoHo, and in Wanchai. If you're watching your Hong Kong dollars, take advantage of happy hour, when many bars offer two drinks for the price of one or drinks at reduced prices. Furthermore, many pubs, bars, and lounges offer live entertainment, from jazz to Filipino combos, which you can enjoy simply for the price of a beer. Remember, however, that a 10% service charge will be added to your bill.

In addition to the recommendations below, be sure to watch the nightly "Symphony of Lights" show from 8 to 8:18pm, when an impressive laser and light show is projected from approximately 30 buildings on Hong Kong Island. The best place to watch? From Tsimshatsui's waterfront.

To obtain tickets for the Hong Kong Chinese Orchestra, Chinese opera, rock and pop concerts, and other major events, call the **Urban Council Ticketing Office (URBTIX)** at ✆ 852/2734 9009, or drop by outlets located in City Hall, Low Block, 7 Edinburgh Place in Central, or in the Hong Kong Cultural Centre, 10 Salisbury Rd. in Tsimshatsui. Both are open daily from 10am to 9:30pm. You can also reserve tickets before arriving in Hong Kong, either by calling the Credit Card Hotline at ✆ 852/2111 5999 or through the website www.urbtix.gov.hk.

PERFORMING ARTS
CHINESE OPERA
The most popular regional styles of Chinese opera in Hong Kong are Peking-style opera, with its spectacular costumes, elaborate makeup, and feats of acrobatics and swordsmanship; and the less flamboyant but more readily understood Cantonese-style opera. For visitors, the easiest way to see a Chinese opera is during a festival, such as the Hong Kong Arts Festival, held from about mid-February through early March. Otherwise, Cantonese opera is performed fairly regularly at town halls in the New Territories, as well as in City Hall in Central and at the Hong Kong Cultural Centre in Tsimshatsui. Tickets, ranging from HK$100 to HK$300 (US$13–US$39), usually sell out well in advance, so book before arriving in Hong Kong. Contact HKTB for an updated schedule.

HONG KONG CHINESE ORCHESTRA
Established in 1977, the Hong Kong Chinese Orchestra (www.hkco.org) is the world's largest professional Chinese-instrument orchestra, with 80-some musicians performing both new and traditional works using traditional and modern Chinese instruments and combining them with Western and Chinese orchestrations. Performances are held at the Hong Kong Cultural Centre, 10 Salisbury Rd., Tsimshatsui (✆ 852/2734 2009), and at City Hall, Edinburgh Place, Central District (✆ 852/2921 2840). Tickets range from HK$90 to HK$150 (US$12–US$19).

DANCE CLUBS/DISCOS
C Club   With a seductive interior of velvet sofas and a curved bar, all bathed in red lighting, this basement club packs them in with underground house music and techno. If you come on a weekend, be prepared to wait in the queue of beautiful people lined up outside. It's open Monday to Thursday from 6pm to 2am, Friday from 6pm to 5am, and Saturday from 9pm to 5am. California Tower, 30–32 D'Aguilar, Lan Kwai Fong, Central. ✆ 852/2526 1139. www.lankwaifong.com. No cover Mon–Thurs; cover HK$200 (US$27) Fri–Sat, including 2 drinks. MTR: Central.

Propaganda   Hong Kong's longest-standing and most popular gay disco, Propaganda moved into upgraded quarters a few years back in the new SoHo nightlife district, with a discreet entrance in a back alley (off Pottinger St.). The crowd is 95% gay, but everyone is welcome. Come late on a weekend if you want to see this alternative hot spot at its most crowded. It's open Tuesday through Thursday from 9pm to 3:30am, Friday and Saturday from 9pm to 5am. 1 Hollywood Rd., Central. ✆ 852/2868 1316. No cover Tues–Thurs; cover HK$100 (US$13) Fri; HK$120 (US$16) Sat before 10:30pm; HK$160 (US$21) Sat 10:30pm–3:30am; HK$100 (US$13) Sat after 3:30am. MTR: Central.

THE BAR SCENE

KOWLOON

Aqua Spirit This glam newcomer is one of Hong Kong's hottest bars, due in no small part to its unbeatable location on the 30th floor of a Tsimshatsui high-rise, where slanted, soaring windows give an incredible bird's-eye-view of the city. Circular booths shrouded behind strung beads, designer drinks, and a voyeur's dream location on an open mezzanine overlooking a restaurant on the 29th floor make this one of Kowloon's trendiest venues. There's a HK$120 (US$16) drink minimum, and it's open Sunday to Thursday from 6pm to 1am and Friday and Saturday from 6pm to 3am. 1 Peking Rd., Tsimshatsui. © 852/3427 2288. MTR: Tsimshatsui.

Chasers One of several bars lining the narrow, alleylike Knutsford Terrace, which parallels Kimberley Road to the north, this is one of the most popular, filled with a mixed clientele that includes both the young and the not-so-young, expat and Chinese. It features a house Filipino band nightly from 10:30pm, playing rock, jazz, rhythm-and-blues, and everything in between, free of charge. Happy hour is from 3 to 10pm Monday to Friday and from noon to 9pm Saturday and Sunday. The bar is open Monday to Friday from 3pm to 6am and Saturday and Sunday from noon to 6am. 2–3 Knutsford Terrace, Tsimshatsui. © 852/2367 9487. MTR: Tsimshatsui.

Delaney's This upmarket Irish pub with a convivial atmosphere gets an extra boost from a Tuesday quiz night with prizes for winners and a DJ Friday nights, both free of charge, as well as big soccer and rugby events shown on a big screen. An a la carte menu features Irish stew and other national favorites. Happy hour is from 5 to 9pm daily; regular hours are daily from 9am to 2:30am. There's another Delaney's in Wanchai at 18 Luard Rd. (© **852/2804 2880**). 71–77 Peking Rd., Tsimshatsui. © **852/2301 3980.** MTR: Tsimshatsui.

Lobby Lounge This comfortable cocktail lounge boasts gorgeous, water-level views of Victoria Harbour and Hong Kong Island. You'll fall in love all over again (with Hong Kong, your companion, or both) as you take in one of the world's most famous views (this is a very civilized place for watching the nightly Symphony of Lights laser show) and listen to a live jazz band (from 6–11pm). It's open daily from 8am to 2am. In Hotel Inter-Continental Hong Kong, 18 Salisbury Rd., Tsimshatsui. © 852/2721 1211. MTR: Tsimshatsui.

Ned Kelly's Last Stand This lively Aussie saloon attracts a largely middle-aged crowd with free live Dixieland jazz daily from 9:30pm to 1am. It serves Australian chow and pub grub, and is open daily from 11:30am to 2am (happy hour daily until 9pm). 11A Ashley Rd., Tsimshatsui. © 852/2376 0562. MTR: Tsimshatsui.

CENTRAL DISTRICT

California This was once *the* place to see and be seen—the haunt of young nouveaux riches in search of definition—and it remains a respected and sophisticated restaurant/bar. Consider starting your night on the town here with dinner and drinks; the menu exalts Californian cuisine, though hamburgers (the house specialty) remain hugely popular. Happy hour is from 5 to 10pm. On Friday and Saturday night from 11pm to 4am, the California becomes a happening disco. It's open Monday to Thursday from noon to midnight, Friday and Saturday from noon to 4am, and Sunday from 6pm to midnight. 24–26 Lan Kwai Fong St., Central. © 852/2521 1345. MTR: Central.

Club 97 Opened more than 20 years ago as a disco, this well-known club is now a sophisticated lounge, a reflection of an aging clientele more prone to drinking and conversation than to dancing. Weekly events to watch for are the Friday gay happy hour, complete with drag shows, and the Sunday reggae night. The club is open Monday to Thursday from 6pm to 2am (happy hour 6–9pm), Friday from 6pm to 4am (happy hour 7–9pm), Saturday from 7pm to 4am (happy hour 6–9pm), and Sunday from 8pm to 3am (happy hour 8–10pm). 9 Lan Kwai Fong, Central. (C) **852/2810 933**. MTR: Central.

Insomnia   One of Lan Kwai Fong's most popular bars, this one is aptly named, since live music by a Filipino band doesn't get under way until 10:30pm and it's at its most packed in the wee hours of the morning, when there's no room to spare on the crowded dance floor. Happy hour is from 5 to 9pm. The bar is open daily from 8am to 6am, leaving insomniacs 2 hours with nowhere to go. 38–44 D'Aguilar St., Central. (C) **852/2525 0957**. MTR: Central.

CAUSEWAY BAY/WANCHAI

Dusk til Dawn   This laid-back bar attracts a mostly expat and Southeast Asian clientele, who take advantage of its 5-to-11pm daily happy hour, food and snack menu served until 5am, and nightly free live music starting at 10pm. Open Monday through Saturday from noon to 6am and Sunday from 3pm to 6am. 76–84 Jaffe Rd., Wanchai. (C) **852/2528 4689**. MTR: Wanchai.

Klong Bar & Grill   Wishing to evoke steamy, sensual Bangkok, this new establishment takes its name from the many canals that lace Thailand's capital. Its open-fronted ground-floor bar and grill, with an open kitchen turning out delectable Thai barbecue, looks like any Asian bar, dark and slightly rough around the edges, but go upstairs and it's a whole different place, very posh and with well-dressed urbanites crowded around a huge U-shaped bar and lounging in the corner "opium den." Things do get crazy however, especially when a DJ hits the scene on Friday and Saturday nights and both professionals and amateurs are encouraged to hop on the bar and perform an exotic pole dance, which probably happens most on Wednesday nights when ladies are served free vodka. Still, it's a long cry from Bangkok's nightlife scene. It's open daily from 6pm until 3am or later, with happy hour until 10pm. The Broadway, 54–62 Lockhart Rd., Wanchai. (C) **852/2217 8330**. MTR: Wanchai.

8 A Side Trip to Macau

Macau was established as a Portuguese colony in 1557, centuries before the British acquired Hong Kong. Just 64km (40 miles) west of Hong Kong, across the Pearl River Estuary, Macau is a rather small and unpretentious provincial town, only 27 sq. km (11 sq. miles) in area. Once a sleepy backwater, it has experienced something of a revival in the past few years, with spanking-new boutiques and restaurants, a huge shopping, dining, and entertainment complex called Fisherman's Wharf, and an explosion of world-class casinos that have transformed it into Asia's hottest gambling mecca.

   While much has been lost in the flurry of development, Macau is still a unique destination in the world, an intriguing mix of Chinese and Portuguese traditions and culture. On December 20, 1999, Portugal's 400 years of rule came to an end when Macau was handed back to China. Like Hong Kong, Macau is a Special Administrative Region of China, permitted its own internal government and economic system for another 50 years after the Chinese assumed control. As with Hong Kong, no advance visa is required.

Macau

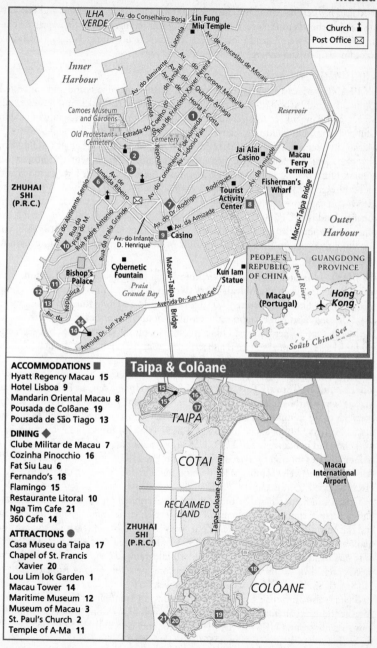

Church ✝
Post Office ✉

ILHA VERDE
Av. do Conselheiro Borja
Lin Fung Miu Temple
Av. de Venceslau de Morais
Lacerda
Av. do Coronel Mesquita
Inner Harbour
Av. do Almirante
Av. Amaral
do Amaral
Av. de Francisco Xavier Pereira
Estrada do Coelho do
Rua de Francisco Xavier Ouvidor Arriaga
Rua da Horta E Costa
Av. Sidonio Pais
Camoes Museum and Gardens
Old Protestant Cemetery
Estrada do Coelho do
Cemetery
Reservoir
Reposuo
Av. do Conselheiro F. de Almeida
Av. de Almeida Ribeiro
❶
Jai Alai Casino
Av. da Amizade
Macau Ferry Terminal
ZHUHAI SHI (P.R.C.)
Rua do Almirante Sergio
Rua da Praia do M.
Rua Padre Antonio
Rua da Praia Grande
❷
❸
Rodrigues
Tourist Activity Center
Fisherman's Wharf
Av. da Amizade
Macau-Taipa Bridge
❼
Av. do Dr. Rodrigo
Av. da Amizade
❽
❾ **Casino**
Outer Harbour
Av. do Infante D. Henrique
❿
Cybernetic Fountain
Praia Grande Bay
Macau-Taipa
Kun Iam Statue
Bishop's Palace
⑫
⑪
Republica
Av. da
⑬
Praia Grande Bay
Avenida Dr. Sun Yat-Sen
Bridge
Avenida Dr. Sun Yat-Sen
⑭
⑭
Avenida Dr. Sun Yat-Sen

PEOPLE'S REPUBLIC OF CHINA
GUANGDONG PROVINCE
Pearl River
Macau (Portugal)
Hong Kong
South China Sea

ACCOMMODATIONS ■
Hyatt Regency Macau **15**
Hotel Lisboa **9**
Mandarin Oriental Macau **8**
Pousada de Colôane **19**
Pousada de São Tiago **13**

DINING ◆
Clube Militar de Macau **7**
Cozinha Pinocchio **16**
Fat Siu Lau **6**
Fernando's **18**
Flamingo **15**
Restaurante Litoral **10**
Nga Tim Cafe **21**
360 Cafe **14**

ATTRACTIONS ●
Casa Museu da Taipa **17**
Chapel of St. Francis Xavier **20**
Lou Lim Iok Garden **1**
Macau Tower **14**
Maritime Museum **12**
Museum of Macau **3**
St. Paul's Church **2**
Temple of A-Ma **11**

Taipa & Colôane

⑮
⑮
⑯
⑰
TAIPA
COTAI
Taipa-Coloane Causeway
Macau International Airport
RECLAIMED LAND
ZHUHAI SHI (P.R.C.)
⑱
COLÔANE
㉑ **⑳**
⑲

Macau has beaches, churches, fortresses, temples, gardens, museums, and fascinating neighborhoods to explore, as well as restaurants serving wonderful Macanese cuisine. What's more, Macau's prices are cheaper than Hong Kong's, including accommodations and dining.

ARRIVING

BY PLANE   Macau International Airport, located on Taipa Island and connected to the mainland by bridge, has international connections to Taipei, Singapore, Seoul, Mania, and Bangkok. It also has flights with Chinese airlines to Chóngqìng, Fúzhōu, Guìlín, Hángzhōu, Kūnmíng, Sānyà, Shànghǎi, Xiàmén, Xī'ān; and flights with Air Macau to Běijīng, Guìlín, Hǎikǒu, Kūnmíng, Nánjīng, Chéngdū, Qīngdǎo, Shànghǎi, and Xiàmén. Several first-class hotels offer complimentary transfers on request. Otherwise, airport bus AP1 travels from the airport to the ferry terminal and Hotel Lisboa; the fare, in Macau pataca currency, is MOP$6 (US80¢). A taxi to the Lisboa costs approximately MOP$40 (US$5.20). Airport-departure tax for flights to the mainland is MOP$80 (US$10) adults, MOP$50 (US$6.50) children 2 to 12; for other destinations, the tax is MOP$130 (US$17) adults, MOP$80 (US$10) children. For those flying on to the mainland within 24 hours of arrival in Macau, departure taxes are waived.

BY BOAT   Macau is easily accessible from Hong Kong by **high-speed jetfoil,** with most departures from the **Macau Ferry Terminal,** located just west of the Central District in the Shun Tak Centre, 200 Connaught Rd., on Hong Kong Island. Situated above Sheung Wan MTR station, the terminal houses jetfoil ticket offices, as well as the Macau Government Tourist Office (room 336, on the same floor as boats departing for Macau). Limited service is also available from Kowloon, from the newer China Hong Kong Terminal on Canton Road, Tsimshatsui.

The fastest, most convenient way to travel to Macau is via a 55-minute ride on jetfoils operated by **TurboJET** (© 852/2859 3333 in Hong Kong, or 853/790 7039 in Macau; www.turbojetc.com.hk), with departures from the Macau Ferry Terminal every 15 to 30 minutes, 24 hours a day. One-way fares Monday through Friday are HK$243 (US$320) for super class and HK$141 (US$18) for economy class; fares on weekends and holidays are HK$259 (US$34) in super class and HK$153 (US$20) in economy. Fares for night service (5:45pm–6am) are HK$274 (US$36) and HK$175 (US$23) respectively. Seniors older than 60 and children younger than 12 receive a HK$15 (US$1.95) discount.

Tickets can be purchased at the Macau Ferry Terminal on Hong Kong Island, the China Ferry Terminal in Kowloon, all China Travel Service branches in Hong Kong, and the TurboJET Service Counter at Sheung Wan MTR Station, exit D. You can also book by credit card by calling © **852/2921 6688.** Note that passengers are allowed only one hand-carried bag, not to exceed 10 kilograms (22 lb.), with one additional piece checked in 20 minutes prior to departure for a fee ranging from HK$20 to HK$40 (US$2.60–US$5.20), depending on weight.

There is also TurboJET Sea Express service directly from Hong Kong International Airport (transfers are made without passing through Hong Kong customs), with four sailings daily costing HK$180 (US$14) for economy class and HK$280 (US$36) for super class.

In Macau, you'll arrive at the **Macau Ferry Terminal,** on the main peninsula. After going through Customs, stop by the Macau Government Tourist Office for a map and brochures. In the arrivals hall is also a counter for free shuttle buses to major hotels. Otherwise, city bus nos. 3, 3A, and 10 travel from the terminal to Avenida Almeida Ribeiro, the main downtown street, for MOP$2.50 (US30¢).

TO THE MAINLAND

Travel to the mainland (on foot across the border to Zhūhǎi, by jetfoil to Shēnzhèn, or by plane) requires a Chinese visa. For all but land crossings, buy visas in Hong Kong (see "Traveling to & from the Mainland" in the Hong Kong section, earlier in this chapter). The **border crossing** is open from 7:30am to 11:30pm, but arrive by 11pm.

Guǎngzhōu can be reached by bus from Zhūhǎi Gǒng Běi bus station, ahead and slightly to the right as you emerge from the Macau/Zhūhǎi border crossing. There are departures every 15 minutes or so between 6am and 8:30pm to Guǎngzhōu Station, from where there's a choice of taxi, bus, or metro to take you the 8km (5 miles) to the airport. There are also frequent services to **Shēnzhèn** and **Kāipíng** between 8:30am and 7:30pm.

VISITOR INFORMATION

There are two **Macau Government Tourist Offices (MGTO)** in Hong Kong—at counter A06 in the arrivals lobby of the International Airport (© **852/2769 7970;** www.macautourism.gov.mo), open daily from 9am to 10pm (closed for lunch 1–1:30pm and dinner 6–6:30pm); and in room 336 on the third floor of the Macau Ferry Terminal, Shun Tak Centre, in Central (© **852/2857 2287**), open daily 9am to 1pm and 2:15 to 5:30pm.

In Macau, you'll find an MGTO at the Macau Ferry Terminal, open daily from 9am to 10pm; there is also an MGTO at Macau International Airport, open for all incoming flights. For complete information, stop by the main Macau Government Tourist Office, Largo do Senado 9, located in the center of town on the main plaza just off Avenida Almeida Ribeiro and open daily from 9am to 6pm. Other tourist information offices are located at **St. Paul's Church,** open daily from 9am to 1pm and 2:15 to 6pm; **Guia Fort and Lighthouse,** open daily from 9am to 1pm and 2:15 to 5:30pm; and the **Border Gate** (also called Barrier Gate and serving visitors from the mainland), open daily from 9am to 1pm and 2:30 to 6pm. Be sure to pick up a free city map, brochures on everything from churches to fortresses, and the tourist tabloid *Macau Travel Talk.* For information by telephone, call the **Tourist Hotline** at © **853/333000.**

GETTING AROUND

Macau comprises a small peninsula and Taipa and Colôane, two islands that have merged due to land reclamation and are linked to the mainland by bridges. The peninsula—referred to simply as Macau and surrounded by an Inner and an Outer Harbour—is where you'll find the city of Macau, as well as the ferry terminal and most of its hotels, shops, and attractions. Macau's main road is **Avenida Almeida Ribeiro;** about halfway down its length is the attractive **Largo do Senado (Senate Square),** Macau's main plaza.

Because the peninsula is less than 4.8km (3 miles) in length and 1.5km (1 mile) at its greatest width, you can walk most everywhere. If you get tired, jump into a metered **taxi,** which charges MOP$10 (US$1.30) at flagfall for the first 1.5km (1 mile), then MOP$1 (US15¢) for each subsequent 200m (656 ft.). **Public buses** run daily from 7am to midnight, with fares costing MOP$2.50 (US30¢) for travel within the Macau

Peninsula, MOP$3.30 (US45¢) for travel to Taipa, and MOP$4 to MOP$5 (US60¢–US65¢) to Colôane. Buses heading for Taipa and Colôane make a stop in front of Hotel Lisboa, located on the peninsula near the Macau-Taipa Bridge. MGTO has a free map with bus routes.

WHERE TO STAY

In addition to the rack rates given below (quoted in Hong Kong dollars; be sure to bargain for a better rate, especially in the off season), there's a 10% hotel service charge and a 5% government tax. If you plan on coming during Chinese New Year, Easter, July, August, or late November when the Grand Prix is held, book well in advance.

EXPENSIVE

Mandarin Oriental Macau ✦✦✦ *(Kids)*   This is a companion hotel of the Mandarin Oriental in Hong Kong, but with room rates much lower than you'd pay in Hong Kong. Located about a 7-minute walk from the ferry terminal in the direction of downtown, a huge land-reclamation project has robbed the hotel of much of its water-front view, but on the plus side the hotel claimed a small portion of the new land for its state-of-the-art resort facility, which includes an outdoor swimming pool; waterfall; water slide, pool, playground, and children's center; and a gorgeous spa. Although the hotel's exterior is rather nondescript, if not downright ugly, its interior is beautifully designed and elegantly decorated throughout with imports from Portugal.

Av. da Amizade 956–1110, Macau. © 800/526-6566 in the U.S. and Canada, or 853/567888 or 852/2881 1288 for reservations in Hong Kong. Fax 853/594589. www.mandarinoriental.com. 435 units. HK$1,900–HK$2,300 (US$247–US$299) single or double; HK$2,600–HK$3,000 (US$338–US$390) Mandarin floors; from HK$5,100 (US$662) suite. AE, DC, MC, V. Free shuttle bus or bus no. 3A from ferry terminal. **Amenities:** 4 restaurants; bar; 24-hr. casino; outdoor heated pool open year-round; kids' pool; 4 outdoor floodlit tennis courts; 2 indoor squash courts; health club and spa; outdoor Jacuzzi; children's day-care center for ages 3–12; playground; game room; concierge; business center; shopping arcade; salon; 24-hr. room service; massage; babysitting; same-day laundry/dry cleaning; nonsmoking rooms; executive-level rooms; doctor on call. *In room:* A/C, satellite TV w/pay movies, dataport, minibar, coffeemaker, hair dryer, safe.

Pousada de São Tiago ✦✦✦ *(Finds)*   Built around the ruins of the Portuguese Fortress da Barra, which dates from 1629, this delightful small inn on the tip of the peninsula is guaranteed to charm even the most jaded of travelers. The entrance is dramatic—a flight of stone stairs leading through a cavelike tunnel that was once part of the fort, with water trickling in small rivulets on one side of the stairs. Once inside, guests are treated to the hospitality of a Portuguese inn, with its ornately carved wooden bedroom furniture imported from Portugal and the use of stone, brick, and Portuguese blue tile throughout. A terrace restaurant is shaded by banyan trees, and most of the rooms, all of which face the sea, have balconies.

Avenida da República, Fortaleza de São Tiago da Barra, Macau. © 853/378111, or 852/2739 1216 for reservations in Hong Kong. Fax 853/552170. www.saotiago.com.mo. 24 units. HK$1,620–HK$1,960 (US$210–US$254) single or double; from HK$2,300 (US$299) suite. AE, DC, MC, V. Free shuttle bus (on request) or bus no. 28B from ferry terminal. **Amenities:** Restaurant; lounge; outdoor pool; room service (8am–10:30pm); babysitting; same-day laundry/dry cleaning. *In room:* A/C, cable TV, dataport, minibar, hair dryer.

MODERATE

Hotel Lisboa *(Finds)*   The Lisboa is in a class by itself. Built in 1969, it's a Chinese version of Las Vegas—huge, flashy, and with a bewildering array of facilities that make it almost a city within a city, and its 24-hour casino has long been one of the most popular in Macau. It has countless restaurants, shops, and nighttime diversions, including the Crazy Paris Show with a revue of scantily clad European women. The rooms are located in an older wing, a newer wing, and a tower that was completed in 1993. The tower, which added 14 floors, offers the best—and most expensive—harbor views, including rooms with traditional Chinese architecture and furniture. Otherwise, rooms seem rather small and old-fashioned. In short, this is the place to be if you want to be in the thick of it. Buses traveling to the outlying islands and other parts of Macau stop right outside the front door, and downtown Macau is only a 5-minute walk away.

Av. de Lisboa 2–4, Macau. ☏ 853/577666, or 852/2546 6944 for reservations in Hong Kong. Fax 853/567193. www.hotelisboa.com. 927 units. HK$1,480–HK$2,800 (US$192–US$364) single or double; from HK$3,800 (US$494) suite. Children under 13 stay free in parent's room. AE, DC, MC, V. Free shuttle bus or bus no. 3, 3A, 10A, or 28B from the ferry terminal. **Amenities:** 18 restaurants (some 24 hr.); 2 bars; lounge; nightclub, 24-hr. casino; outdoor heated pool; health club; shopping arcade; salon; 24-hr. room service; same-day laundry/dry cleaning; nonsmoking rooms. *In room:* A/C, satellite TV w/free movies, minibar, hair dryer, safe.

Hyatt Regency Macau ★★★ (Value) (Kids)
The atmosphere at the Hyatt is both tropical and Mediterranean, with extensive recreational facilities for the entire family, restaurants that are among the best in Macau, and comfortable rooms. Located on Taipa Island with free shuttle service to the mainland (just a 5-min. drive away), the hotel boasts a 1.3-hectare (3-acre) complex set amid lush greenery with an outdoor heated pool open year-round, tennis and squash courts, a fitness center, and more. For families, there's the children's wading pool, playground, game room, a child-care center, and Camp Hyatt (weekends and holidays) for kids ages 5 to 12. If you feel like exploring or dining on local cuisine, the quaint Taipa Village is only a 15-minute walk away.

Estrada Almirante Marquês Esparteiro 2, Taipa Island, Macau. ☏ 800/223-1234 in the U.S. and Canada, 853/831234, or 852/2546 3791 for reservations in Hong Kong. Fax 853/830195. www.macauhyatt.com. 326 units. HK$800–HK$1,750 (US$104–US$227) single or double; HK$1,100–HK$2,050 (US$143–US$266) Regency Club; from HK$5,300 (US$688) suite. Children under 12 stay free in parent's room (maximum 3 persons per room). AE, DC, MC, V. Free shuttle bus or bus no. 28A from the ferry terminal. **Amenities:** 3 restaurants; lounge; 24-hr. casino; outdoor heated pool open year-round; outdoor children's pool; 4 floodlit outdoor tennis courts; 2 indoor squash courts; multi-purpose court for volleyball, basketball, badminton, and soccer; glayground; rental bicycles; health club and spa; wonderful child-care center for children 2–8; Camp Hyatt for children 5–12; game room w/video games, table tennis and pool tables; concierge; free shuttle to ferry and Hotel Lisboa; business center; 24-hr. room service; massage; babysitting; same-day laundry/dry cleaning; nonsmoking rooms; executive-level rooms; in-house nurse and doctor. *In room:* A/C, satellite TV w/pay movies, minibar, coffeemaker, hair dryer, safe.

INEXPENSIVE
Pousada de Colôane ★ (Finds)
This small, family-owned property, perched on a hill above Cheoc Van Beach with views of the sea, is ideal for couples and families in search of a reasonably priced isolated retreat. More than 30 years old but recently renovated, it's a relaxing, rather rustic place, with modestly furnished rooms, all of which have balconies facing the sea and a popular public beach. There's an outdoor terrace where you can relax over drinks, and the inn's Portuguese restaurant is especially popular for the Sunday lunch buffet offered during peak season. The main drawback is one of access, but buses to Macau pass by frequently; when you arrive at the Macau ferry terminal, you're best off traveling to the hotel by taxi.

Praia de Cheoc Van, Colôane Island, Macau. ☏ 853/882144. Fax 853/882251. www.hotelpcoloane.com.mo. 22 units. HK$680–HK$750 (US$88–US$98) single or double. Weekday discounts available. AE, MC, V. Bus: no. 21A, 25, or 26A from Lisboa Hotel (tell the bus driver you want to get off at the hotel). **Amenities:** Restaurant; bar; outdoor pool; children's pool; playground. *In room:* A/C, TV, minibar.

WHERE TO DINE
EXPENSIVE
Clube Militar de Macau ★★ *Finds* MACANESE/PORTUGUESE With its tall ceilings, whirring ceiling fans, arched windows, wooden floor, and displays of antique Chinese dishware, this is one of Macau's most atmospheric dining halls. It's located in a striking pink colonial building, built in 1870 for military officers and opened to the public in 1995. It's best to stick to the classics, such as Portuguese green vegetable soup, roasted codfish with hot olive oil and garlic, seafood stew in a white-wine sauce, sirloin steak Portuguese style, or African chicken. The lunch buffet is a downtown favorite, and the list of Portuguese wines is among the best in town.

da Praia Grande 795. ⓒ 853/714009. Reservations recommended for lunch. Main courses HK$90–HK$168 (US$12–US$22); fixed-price lunch or dinner HK$90 (US$12); lunch buffet HK$130 (US$17). AE, MC, V. Daily noon–3pm and 7–11pm. Bus: no. 3, 3A, 8, 10A, or 10.

Flamingo ★★★ *Value* MACANESE Decorated in hot pink, the Flamingo has a great Mediterranean ambience, with ceiling fans, swaying palms, and a terrace overlooking lush landscaping and a duck pond. An air-conditioned enclosure was recently added for those unaccustomed to alfresco dining, but the real pleasure of dining here is the terrace. The bread is homemade, and the specialties are a unique blend of Portuguese, Chinese, African, Indian, and Malay spices, resulting in delicious, authentic Macanese fare. For an appetizer, try the stuffed crab, followed by a main course like pan-fried Macau sole; spicy king prawns with chili sauce; curried crab; or African chicken.

In the Hyatt Regency Hotel, Taipa Island. ⓒ 853/831234. Reservations recommended Sat–Sun. Main courses HK$70–HK$100 (US$8.85–US$13); fixed-price lunch HK$88 (US$11). AE, DC, MC, V. Daily noon–3pm and 7–11pm. Bus: no. 11, 21, 21A, 22, 25, 26, 26A, 28A, 30, 33, 34, 35, or AP1.

360 Cafe ★ INTERNATIONAL This is Macau's most conspicuous restaurant, more than 219m (730 ft.) above reclaimed ground in the soaring Macau Tower. Opened in 2001, the tower contains an observation deck and lounge, with an admission of HK$70 (US$9.10). Head instead to the tower's revolving restaurant, where for the price of a buffet you have an equally good view. It takes 1½ hours for a complete spin, giving you ample time to sample the various Southeast Asian, Chinese, Macanese, and Continental dishes available as you soak in the view.

In the Macau Tower, Lago Sai Van. ⓒ 853/9888660. www.macautower.com.mo. Reservations recommended weekends. Buffet lunch HK$148 (US$19); buffet dinner HK$238 (US$31). HK$10 (US$1.30) extra weekends and holidays. AE, DC, MC, V. Daily 11:30am–3pm and 7–11pm. Bus: no. 23 or 32.

MODERATE
Cozinha Pinocchio PORTUGUESE/MACANESE Opened in 1977, Taipa Island's first Portuguese restaurant is still going strong, though some who have known it since its early days claim that the atmosphere became more staid when a roof was added to the original roofless two-story brick warehouse. Nevertheless, things are still hopping—people crowd its doors for specialties like curried crab, king prawns, charcoal-grilled sardines, fried codfish cakes, grilled spareribs, roast veal, roast quail, and Portuguese-style cooked fish.

Rua do Sol, Taipa Village, Taipa Island. ⓒ 853/827128. Main courses HK$48–HK$128 (US$6.25–US$17). DC, MC, V. Daily 11:45am–11:45pm. Bus: no. 11, 22, 28A, 30, 33, 34, or 35.

Fat Siu Lau MACANESE This is Macau's oldest restaurant (dating from 1903). Its three floors of dining have been updated, but its exterior matches all the other storefronts on this revamped street—whitewashed walls and red shutters and doors. Dishes include roast pigeon marinated according to a 90-year-old secret recipe; spicy African chicken; curried crab; garoupa stewed with tomatoes, bell pepper, onion, and potatoes; and grilled king prawns.

Rua da Felicidade, 64. ℭ **853/573580.** Main courses HK$45–HK$135 (US$5.85–US$18). DC, MC, V. Daily 11:30am–11:30pm. Bus: no. 3, 3A, 5, 6, 7, 8, 10, 11, 18, 19, 21, or 21A.

Fernando's *Finds* PORTUGUESE For years Fernando's was just another shack on Hac Sa Beach, hardly distinguishable from the others (it's the brick one closest to the beach, below the vines). But then a brick pavilion was added out back, complete with ceiling fans and an adjacent open-air bar with outdoor seating (a good place to wait for a table; reservations are not accepted), and now everyone knows the place. The strictly Portuguese menu includes prawns, crabs, mussels, codfish, *feijoada* (a Brazilian stew), veal, chicken, pork ribs, suckling pig, beef, and salads. Only Portuguese wine is served, stocked on a shelf for customer perusal (there is no wine list). The place is very informal and not for those who demand pristine conditions—there is no air-conditioning, not even in the kitchen.

Praia de Hac Sa, 9, Colôane. ℭ **853/882264** or 853/882531. Reservations not accepted. Main courses HK$60–HK$148 (US$7.80–US$19). No credit cards. Daily noon–9:30pm. Bus: no. 15, 21A, 25, or 26A.

Restaurante Litoral *Finds* MACANESE Exactly which restaurant serves the most "authentic" Macanese food in town is a hotly contested subject, but this attractive restaurant, with its dark-gleaming woods, whitewashed walls, and stone floor, can certainly lay claim to the title. All the traditional favorites are here, including curry crab, curry prawns, African chicken, feijoada, and *minchi,* a Macanese dish prepared with pork cubes, potatoes, onion, and garlic—but Portuguese specialties like codfish baked with potato and garlic, roast Portuguese sausage, and Portuguese green soup are not to be overlooked. Wash it all down with Portuguese wine or beer. The restaurant is located along the covered sidewalk not far from the Maritime Museum and A-Ma Temple.

Rua do Almirante Sergio, 261A. ℭ **853/967878.** Main courses HK$78–HK$148 (US$10–US$19). AE, MC, V. Daily noon–3pm and 6–11pm. Bus: no. 1, 1A, 2, 5, 6, 7, 9, 10, 10A, 11, 18, 21, 21A, 28B, or 34.

INEXPENSIVE

Nga Tim Cafe *Finds* CHINESE/MACANESE This lively, open-air pavilion restaurant is a good place to rub elbows with the natives. It's situated on the tiny main square of Colôane Village, dominated by the charming Chapel of St. Francis Xavier. Its popularity with the locals lends it a festive atmosphere. The food, which combines Chinese and Macanese styles of cooking and ingredients, is in a category all its own, with many dishes not available elsewhere. Try the salt-and-pepper shrimp, chicken in an earthen pot, grilled duck with lemon sauce, steamed chicken with garlic, scallops with broccoli, or crab curry.

Rua Caetano, No. 8, Colôane Village, Colôane Island. ℭ **853/882086.** Main courses HK$32–HK$88 (US$4.15–US$11). MC, V. Daily 11:30am–1am. Bus: no. 15, 21, 21A, 25, 26, or 26A.

SEEING THE SIGHTS

St. Paul's Church ✷✷ The church crowns a hill in the center of the city and is approached by a grand sweep of stairs. However, only its ornate facade and some excavated sites remain. Designed by an Italian Jesuit, it was built in 1602 with the help of

Japanese Christians who had fled persecution in Nagasaki. In 1835, the church caught fire during a typhoon and burned to the ground, leaving its now-famous facade, adorned with carvings and statues depicting Christianity in Asia—a rather intriguing mix of images that includes a Virgin Mary flanked by a peony (representing China) and a chrysanthemum (representing Japan). Beyond the facade is the excavated crypt, where glass-fronted cases hold the bones of 17th-century Christian martyrs from Japan and Vietnam. Here, too, is the tomb of Father Allesandro Valignano, founder of the Church of St. Paul and instrumental in establishing Christianity in Japan. Next to the crypt is the underground Museum of Sacred Art, with religious works of art produced in Macau from the 17th to 20th centuries, including 17th-century oil paintings by exiled Japanese Christian artists, crucifixes of filigree silver, and wooden saints.

Rua de São Paulo. ☏ 853/358444. Free admission. Grounds open daily 24 hr.; museum Wed–Mon 9am–6pm. Bus: no. 2, 3, 3A, 5, 9, 9A, 12, 16, 22, or 25 to Largo do Senado Sq. (off Almeida Ribeiro); then follow the wavy, tiled sidewalk leading uphill to the northeast about 10 min.

Museum of Macau ✿✿✿ A must-see, this very ambitious project beside St. Paul's Church in the bowels of ancient Monte Fortress provides an excellent overview of Macau's history, local traditions, and arts and crafts. Displays, arranged chronologically, start with the beginnings of Macau and the arrival of Portuguese traders and Jesuit missionaries. Particularly interesting is the room comparing Chinese and European civilizations at the time of their encounter in the 16th century, including descriptions of their different writing systems, philosophies, and religions. Other displays deal with the daily life and traditions of old Macau, such as festivals, wedding ceremonies, and industries ranging from fishing to fireworks factories. Displays include paintings and photographs of Macau through the centuries, traditional games and toys, an explanation of Macanese cuisine and architecture, and a re-created Macau street.

Citadel of São Paulo do Monte (St. Paul Monte Fortress). ☏ 853/357911. www.macaumuseum.gov.mo. Admission MOP$15 (US$1.95) adults, MOP$8 (US$1.05) seniors and children. Tues–Sun 10am–6pm. Located next to St. Paul's Church.

Maritime Museum ✿ *Kids* Macau's oldest museum, ideally situated on the waterfront of the Inner Harbour where visitors can observe barges and other boats passing by, traces the history of Macau's lifelong relationship with the sea. It's located at the tip of the peninsula, across from the Temple of A-Ma, in approximately the same spot where the Portuguese first landed. The museum begins with dioramas depicting the legend of A-Ma, protectress of seafarers and Macau's namesake, and continues with models of various boats, including trawlers, Chinese junks, Portuguese sailing boats, and even modern jetfoils. There are also life-size original boats on display, ranging from the sampan to an ornate festival boat, and a small aquarium.

Largo do Pagode da Barra, 1. ☏ 853/595481. www.museumaritimo.gov.mo. Admission MOP$10 (US$1.30) adults, MOP$5 (US65¢) children, free for seniors and children under 10. Sun and holidays, half price. Wed–Mon 10am–5:30pm. Bus: no. 1, 1A, 2, 5, 6, 7, 9, 10, 10A, 11, 18, 21, 21A, 28B, or 34.

Temple of A-Ma ✿✿ Macau's oldest temple is situated at the bottom of Barra Hill at the entrance to the Inner Harbour, across from the Maritime Museum. With parts of it dating back more than 600 years, it's dedicated to A-Ma, goddess of seafarers. The temple was already here when the Portuguese arrived, and they named their city A-Ma-Gao (Bay of A-Ma) after it. The temple contains images of A-Ma and stone carvings of the boat that carried her to Macau, as well as several shrines set on a rocky hillside linked by winding paths through moon gates and affording good views of the Inner Harbour.

Rua de S. Tiago da Barra. Free admission. Daily 6am–6pm. Bus: no. 1, 1A, 2, 5, 6, 7, 9, 10, 10A, 11, 18, 21, 21A, 28B, or 34.

Macau Tower *Overrated*   Does the world really need another tower? Since admission to the observation deck is rather exorbitant by Macau standards, I personally think you are best off coming for a meal in the revolving **360 Cafe** (p. 580). However, thrill seekers take note: Daredevils can tour the observation deck's *outside* ramparts with the safety of harnesses and ropes, which costs MOP$220 (US$29) on weekdays and MOP$250 (US$32) weekends and holidays; half price for children and seniors. Other ways to have fun with Macau Tower: climbing the mast (a 2-hr. ordeal); climbing 32m (106 ft.) up the tower's concrete shaft on what may be the world's highest artificial climbing wall; bungee jumping 233m (769 ft.); and more.

Lago Sai Van. (② **853/933339**. www.macautower.com.mo. Admission to observatory MOP$70 (US$9) adults, MOP$35 (US$4.55) children and seniors. Daily 10am–9pm. Bus: 23 or 32.

MACAU AFTER DARK

Several hotels have casinos, including the **Mandarin Oriental** and **Hotel Lisboa,** open 24 hours. In the past couple years, several themed, Las Vegas–style casinos have opened their doors, including **Pharaoh's Palace,** in the Landmark on Avenida da Amizade (② **853/788111**) and the **Sands Macau,** near the ferry terminal and Fisherman's Wharf (② **853/883388;** www.sands.com.mo). In 2006, Macau's reputation as a gambling destination will skyrocket with the opening of the **Venetian Macau,** a resort on Cotai (the strip of reclaimed land between Taipa and Colôane) complete with casino, hotel, canals, gondolas, shopping mall, and more. For a glimpse of gambling Chinese style, none is more interesting than the ornately decorated **Floating Macau Palace Casino,** moored in the Outer Harbour not far from the Mandarin Oriental Hotel.

One of the few benefits to have arisen from reclaimed-land development on the Outer Harbour is the Docks, a string of sidewalk cafes and bars lining Avenida Dr. Sun Yat-Sen near the Kun Iam Statue; they are busiest from 10pm to 1am.

TAIPA & COLÔANE ISLANDS

Closest to the mainland, **Taipa** has exploded with new construction in recent years, but it's still worth coming to for **Taipa Village,** a small, traditional community with narrow lanes; two-story colonial buildings painted in yellows, blues, and greens; and hanging baskets of flowers. There are a number of fine, inexpensive restaurants here, making dining reason enough to come. For sightseeing, don't miss the **Casa Museu da Taipa (Taipa House Museum),** on Avenida da Praia (② **853/827088**). It's one of five colonial-style homes lining the banyan-shaded street that once belonged to Macanese families in the early 1900s. Combining both European and Chinese designs and furnishings as a reflection of the families' Eurasian heritage, the Casa Museu displays a dining and living room, kitchen, and upstairs bedrooms filled with period furniture. A couple of the other former homes contain displays relating to the history of Taipa and traditional regional costumes of Portugal. Hours are Tuesday through Sunday from 10am to 6pm, and admission is MOP$5 (US65¢). Bus nos. 11, 15, 22, 28A, 30, 33, 34 and 35 all go to Taipa Village.

Farther away and connected to Taipa via causeway and a huge strip of reclaimed land, **Colôane** is less developed than Taipa and is known for its **beaches,** particularly Cheoc Van and Hac Sa, both with lifeguards. To reach them, take bus no. 21A or 26A. Farther along the coast is the quaint, laid-back community of **Colôane Village,** with its sweet **Chapel of St. Francis Xavier,** built in 1928 and dedicated to the Catholic missionary.

For more information on Taipa and Colôane, pick up a free pamphlet from the Macau tourist office called *Macau, Outlying Islands.*

12

The Southwest: Mountains & Minorities

by Christopher D. Winnan

"The most interesting part of China, from a geographical and ethnological point of view, is the West—geographically, because its recesses have not yet been thoroughly explored, and ethnologically, because a great part of it is peopled by races which are non-Chinese." In describing the attraction of southwest China for a few iconoclastic foreigners in 1889, British consul Alexander Hosie may as well be describing the region's appeal today for hundreds of thousands of travelers, both foreign and Chinese. Considerably more explored than in Hosie's day but still retaining large swaths of undiscovered territory, today's splendid southwest is beginning to attract its deserved share of attention, and will be in the years to come one of China's major tourist destinations.

For starters, this region, encompassing the provinces of **Yúnnán, Guìzhōu, and Guǎngxī,** is home to some of China's most spectacular mountain scenery. As the Himalayan mountain range in northwest Yúnnán gives way to the Yúnnán-Guìzhōu plateau to the southeast, the scenery changes from the awesome 5,000m-high (16,400-ft.) glacier peaks of the **Jade Dragon Snow Mountain range** to the lower but no less beautiful famous limestone hills of eastern Guǎngxī. Three of Asia's mighty rivers—the Salween, the Mekong, and the Yángzǐ—cut parallel paths all within 150km (90 miles) of each

other in the northwest mountains before they flow their separate ways, creating in their passage some of the most breathtaking gorges and lush river valleys in the country.

Even more appealing is the fact that this region is easily the most ethnically diverse in China. Twenty-six of China's fifty-six ethnic groups can be found in the southwest, which claims about 45 million of China's 100-million-strong minority population. If geography is destiny, then this inhospitable mountainous terrain, to which many ethnic minorities were historically displaced by earlier expanding Chinese empires, has not only helped create a vibrant kaleidoscope of peoples, languages, and cultures, but it has helped some of these cultures maintain their unique traditional ways in the face of encroaching modernization. At the same time, shared borders with Sìchuān, Tibet, Myanmar (Burma), Laos, and Vietnam have allowed the region to absorb and integrate the colorful and diverse influences of its neighbors. From the Mosu at **Lúgū Lake** to the Dǎi in **Xīshuāngbǎnnà,** and the Miáo around **Kǎilǐ Sān Jiāng,** you will have multiple opportunities to encounter different minorities.

Historically, this area has undertones of the Wild West, with the Miáo and other minorities replacing the American Indians. Although the massacres and genocide have been going on for hundreds of years,

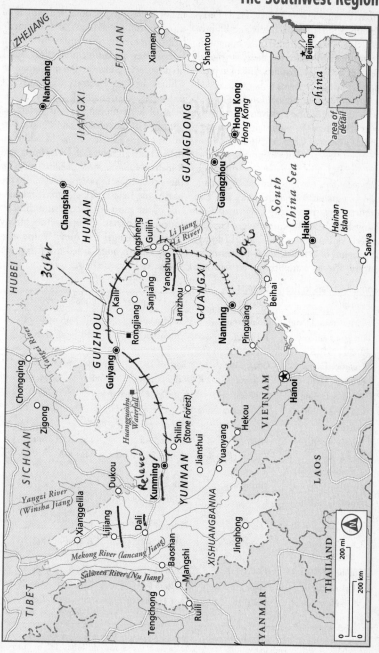

The Southwest Region

ZHEJIANG

Nanchang

JIANGXI

FUJIAN

Xiamen

Shantou

Changsha

HUNAN

GUANGDONG

Hong Kong
Hong Kong

Guangzhou

HUBEI

Yangzi River

Longsheng

Guilin

Li Jiang
(Li River)

Yangshuo

Kaili

Sanjiang

Lanzhou

GUANGXI

Rongjiang

Nanning

Pingxiang

Beihai

GUIZHOU

Guiyang

Chongqing

Zigong

Huangguoshu Waterfall

Shilin
(Stone Forest)

Jianshui

Yuanyang

Hekou

VIETNAM

Hanoi

LAOS

SICHUAN

Dukou

Xianggelila

Lijiang

Dali

Yangzi River (Winsha Jiang)

Kunming

YUNNAN

Mekong River (lancang Jiang)

Baoshan

Mangshi

XISHUANGBANNA

Jinghong

Salween River (Nu Jiang)

TIBET

Tengchong

Ruili

MYANMAR

THAILAND

South China Sea

Haikou

Hainan Island

Sanya

Beijing

China

area of detail

200 mi

200 km

French missionary Father Paul Perry described the situation coldly and bluntly in 1871. "The Chinese government is determined to obliterate these aboriginal peoples by a systematic policy of repression." The policy seems to have succeeded as the indigenous populations are indeed now the minorities, driven relentlessly into these remote mountains by never-ending waves of Chinese colonists.

A traveler can easily spend years in this region and not exhaust its offerings. Between the obvious draws of Guìlín, which ranks as one of China's top five destinations, the backpacker mecca of Yángshuò, and the increasingly popular trifecta of Kūnmíng, Dàlǐ, and Lì Jiāng, is a legion of other delights awaiting discovery. To be sure, travel outside the major tourist destinations and provincial capitals can be arduous and distinctly lacking in luxury, but for those willing to forego a few creature comforts for heaps of discovery, Guìzhōu Province, one of China's best-kept secrets, contains not only spectacular natural scenery in the form of karst mountains and waterfalls, but some of the most dynamic and colorful minority life in China. In addition, the still-quaint towns of Téngchōng and Bǎoshān promise new delights even for the seasoned southwest traveler. In the north, the road to Tibet, which remains one of the most spectacular and difficult journeys, passes through the newly crowned Shangri-La. *Note:* Unless otherwise noted, hours listed for attractions and restaurants are daily.

Some Festivals in the Southwest

Festival	Location	Lunar Calendar	2006	2007
Tàiguǎnrén (Dòng)	Dòng areas	3rd–4th of 1st	late Jan	late Feb
Dragon Lantern (Miáo)	Tái Jiāng	15th of 1st	Feb 5	Feb 23
Huāpào (Dòng)	Cóng Jiāng	28th of 1st	Feb 18	Mar 8
Sānduō (Nàxī)	Lì Jiāng	8th of 2nd	Feb 27	Mar 17
Water Splashing Festival (Dǎi)	Jínghóng Xīshuāngbǎnnà	(Apr 13–15 fixed in Western calendar)		
Sānyuèsān	Dòng areas	3rd of 3rd	Apr 21	Apr 11
Sānyuè Jié (Bái)	Dàlǐ	15th of 3rd	May 3	Apr 23
Sisters' Meal Festival (Miáo)	Tái Jiāng/Shídòng	15th–17th of 3rd	May 3–5	Apr 23–25
Sìyuèbā (Miáo)	Huángpíng	8th of 4th	May 26	May 15
Ràosānlíng (Bái)	Dàlǐ	23rd–25th of 4th	June 10–12	May 30–June 1
Dragon Boat (Miáo)	Shídòng	25th of 5th	July 12	July 1
Chábái Singing (Bùyī)	Xīngyì	21st of 6th	Aug 6	July 26
Huǒbǎ Jié (Bái)	Dàlǐ	24th of 6th	Aug 9	July 29
Zhuàn Shān Jié	Lúgū Hú	25th of 7th	Sept 9	Aug 29
Miáo New Year	Léi Shān	last 10 days of 10th	1st week Nov	Dec 4th week

**Dates are based on information provided by local tourism sources. However, there are many date fluctuations, especially with festivals like the Miáo New Year. Check with the local CITS or other local sources before setting off.

1 Guìlín ★

Guǎngxī Province, 500km (310 miles) NW of Hong Kong, 1,675km (1,039 miles) SW of Běijīng

One of the most-visited Chinese cities, Guìlín (pop. 630,000), located in the north-eastern part of the Guǎngxī Zhuàng Autonomous Region, has long been famous for its limestone karst hills. Formed more than 200 million years ago when the oceans receded from this area, the towers sprout from a patchwork of paddy fields and flowing streams, creating a dreamy, seductive landscape that leaves few souls unstirred. Time and space meet here to produce a masterpiece of nature's handiwork. Though there are a few hills in the city that can be explored, and the Lí River cruise from Guìlín to Yángshuò remains one of top river journeys in the world, Guìlín is also being used as a base to visit the Yáo, Miáo, and Dòng minority villages to the north-west. Unfortunately, the cost of Guìlín's overwhelming popularity is a degree of unrelenting exploitation and extortion audacious even by Chinese standards; foreigners are overcharged for everything.

With summer's heat and humidity and winter's low rainfall affecting water levels in the Lí River, April, May, September, and October are the best months for cruising. April to August also marks the rainy season, however, so be prepared with rain gear. Avoid the first weeks of May and October, when China celebrates national holidays, the Lí River becomes even more congested with tourist boats than usual, and the price of everything doubles at the very least. July can become unbearably hot, and this is the last place on earth that you want to be holed up in your hotel room, clinging to the air conditioner.

ESSENTIALS

GETTING THERE   From Guìlín's airport 30km (19 miles) west of town, **flights** connect to Guǎngzhōu (1 hr.), Běijīng (2½ hr.), Shànghǎi (2 hr.), Kūnmíng (1½ hr.), and Chéngdū (70 min.). There are also international flights to Seoul (4 hr.) and Hong Kong (1½ hr.). Tickets can be purchased at the **Mínháng Dàshà** on Shànghǎi Lù (© **0773/384-3922**), and also at travel agencies or hotel tour desks. **Dragonair** has an office at the Guìlín Bravo Hotel, Rónghú Nán Lù 15 (© **0773/282-3950**, ext. 1150). Airport shuttles depart from the CAAC office every half-hour from 6:30am to 8pm for ¥20 ($2.50); they also meet incoming flights. Taxis to the airport cost around ¥100 ($13). Many expats simply skip Guìlín altogether in preference for a weekend in Yángshuò as the taxi fare is only ¥180 ($23).

Train travel to and from Guìlín is very convenient, although the surrounding mountainous topography means that destinations farther afield often require several days' travel; also, sleeper tickets for those destinations are often difficult to come by. The city has two railway stations, though the main one used by most travelers is the **Guìlín Huǒchēzhàn** (© **0773/383-3124**) in the southern part of town. The T6 to Běijīng (24 hr.) departs at 5:23pm, the K38/35 to Guǎngzhōu (13 hr.) at 6:15pm, the K150 to Shànghǎi (26 hr.) at 4:28pm, and the K155 to Kūnmíng (via Guìyáng, 30 hr.) at 2:08pm. The train to Guǎngzhōu is extremely popular and boasts some of the best staff and rolling stock that a visitor will see. For Chéngdū and Chóngqìng, change trains at Guìyáng (18 hr.). There are trains throughout the day to Nánníng (7–8 hr.). The T5/905 from Běijīng to **Hanoi** stops in Guìlín (only four sleeper berths are available from Guìlín). It's best to have a travel agent or your hotel tour desk arrange tickets because they are extremely difficult to come by.

From the **Guìlín Bus Station (Guìlín Qìchēzhàn; ⓒ 0773/382-2153)** just north of the railway station, large, air-conditioned direct *(zhídá)* buses go to Běihǎi (7 hr.; ¥150/$19) at 8:30am, 9:20am, and 10:20am; to Lóngshèng (3 hr.; ¥15/$1.90) every 40 minutes from 7am to 7pm; to Nánníng (5 hr.; ¥80/$10) every half-hour from 7am to 7pm; and to Guǎngzhōu (9 hr.; ¥150/$19) at 9am, 11am, 9pm, 10pm, and 11pm. Regular minibuses run to Yángshuò (1 hr.; ¥7.50/95¢) from the bus station and outside the railway station. A new private luxury air-conditioned bus to Hong Kong (ⓒ 0773/585-7088) now runs every Friday evening, charging ¥350 ($44) one-way, ¥600 ($75) round-trip. It departs from the Guìlín Guìshān Hotel on Chuānshān Lù at 7pm, stops at the Yángshuò Paradise Hotel at 8pm, and arrives at Huánggǎng in Shēnzhèn at 7am. After passengers go through Customs and Immigration, the bus continues onto Sha Tin, Kowloon Tong, and Tsimshatsui in Hong Kong. For the return, the bus simply retraces the route, departing from Hong Kong's Tsimshatsui at 4pm and arriving in Guìlín the next morning around 7am. There are plans to increase the frequency of this service, but beware this is an arduous night's travel, with road conditions and driving skills that you may not be used to.

GETTING AROUND   Guìlín is a compact area and is easy to get around by foot or bicycle. **Bikes** can be rented at most hotels, including the Bravo Hotel and the Sheraton, for ¥25 to ¥50 ($3–$6) per day plus a deposit of ¥300 to ¥400 ($38–$50).

Taxis cost ¥7 (90¢) for 2km (1¼ miles), then ¥1.60 (20¢) per kilometer. After 4km (2½ miles), the price jumps to ¥2 (25¢) per kilometer. From 11pm to 7am, the fare is ¥7.80 (95¢) for 2km (1¼ miles), then ¥2.40 (30¢) per kilometer until 4km (2½ miles), and ¥3 (40¢) per kilometer after that.

There are also several **buses** geared toward tourists: The free bus no. 58 from 8:30am to 4:30pm runs from Nánxī Park in the south to Reed Flute Cave, stopping along the way at Elephant Hill, Seven Star Park, Fúbō Hill, and Diécǎi Hill. Another free sightseeing minibus travels a similar loop from Seven Star Park to Reed Flute Cave between 8:40am and 4pm, but passengers are required to show their entrance tickets to at least one of the sights.

TOURS   CITS at Bīnjiāng Lù 41 (ⓒ **0773/286-1623;** fax 0773/282-7424) has full-day city tours with English-speaking guides for ¥200 ($25) per person. The CITS Panda Bus picks up daily from the Fǔbó, Sheraton, Bravo, and Royal Garden hotels. CITS can also organize Lí River cruises for ¥460 ($57), day trips to Yángshuò by bus for ¥193 ($24) per person, and overnight trips to Lóngshèng Minority Village and Terrace Fields for ¥450 to ¥550 ($56–$68) per person. The concierge at the Sheraton Hotel, Bīnjiāng Nán Lù (ⓒ **0773/282-5588**), can arrange all of the above, as well as nighttime cormorant fishing trips for ¥65 ($8) and evening cultural performances for around ¥100 ($13).

VISITOR INFORMATION   For information on hotels and sights, there are **Guìlín Tourism Information Service** centers around town, most noticeably outside the railway station (ⓒ 0773/382-7391) and in the Central Square (Zhōngxīn Guǎngchǎng; ⓒ 0773/285-4318).

FAST FACTS

Banks, Foreign Exchange & ATMs   Bank of China (open Mon–Fri 8am–noon and 3–6pm) is at Shànhú Běi Lù 5. It offers forex and an ATM.

Internet Access   Visit the third floor of **Lèqún Shǒujī Chéng** at Zhōngshān Zhōng Lù 49, corner of Lèqún Lù. Internet access is 24 hours, at ¥2 (25¢) per hour. Dial-up is ⓒ **96163.**

Guìlín

ACCOMMODATIONS ■

Guìlín Bravo Hotel
(Guìlín Bīnguǎn) **4**
桂林宾馆

Guìlín Diànxìn Bīnguǎn
(Guìlín Telecom
Hotel) **7**
桂林电信宾馆

Lì Jiāng Waterfall Hotel
(Lì Jiāng Dà Pùbù
Fàndiàn) **3**
漓江大瀑布饭店

Sheraton Guìlín
(Guìlín Dàyǔ
Dàfàndiàn) **2**
桂林大宇大饭店

0 — 1/2 mi
0 — 0.5 km

Shèngli Lu

(Peach Blossom) River

Táohua

Lúdí Yán
(Reed Flute Cave)
芦笛岩

Ludi Lu

Guìlín North
Station

Zhōngshan Bĕilù

China

Beijing ★

GUANGXI

Guìlín ●

Diécǎi Shān
(Folding Brocade Hill)
叠彩山

FULONG
ISLE

Fúbō Shān
(Wave-Subduing Hill)
伏波山

Dúxiù Fēng
(Solitary Beauty Peak)
独秀峰

Xinyi Lu

Yiwu Lu

Jiefang Lu

Binjiang Lu

Zhèngyáng Pedestrian Street
(Zhèngyáng Bùxíng Jiē)
正阳步行街

Lìjun Lu

Táohua

Rong Hu (Banyan Lake)

Ronghu Nan Lu

Shanhu Bei Lu

Zhongshan Lu

¥

1
2
3

Qixia Lu   Liuhe Lu

Qīxīng Gōngyuán
(Seven Star Park)
七星公园

Chuanshan Lu

(Peach Blossom) River

4

Cedar Lake
(Shan Hu)

5 **6**

Nanhuan Lu

ZIZHOU ISLE

TA

Longyin Lu

Camel Hill

Qixing Lu

Dong'an Lu

7

Xiàngbí Shān
(Elephant Trunk Hill)
象鼻山

Minzhu Lu

PSB

← To Airport

Guìlín-Qinglongjie Hwy.

Guìlín Railway
Station

i

Cuizhu Lu   Shanghai Lu

TA

LUOBO
ISLE

Xiadong River

Li River

Zhongshan Nan Lu

CHUAN
SHAN
PARK

DINING ◆

Mi Dié Xiāng
   (Rosemary Café) **1**
   迷迭香

Yíyuán Fàndiàn **6**
   怡园饭店

Zàowángyé Xiāngwèi Jū
   (Vesta Restaurant) **5**
   灶王爷乡味居

Chongxin Lu

WUJIAREN
ISLE

🚌 Bus Station
¥ Bank
ⓘ Information
✉ Post Office
🚉 Rail Station
PSB Public-
   Security Visas
TA Travel Agent

Post Office   The main post office (open 8am–8pm) is at Zhōngshān Zhōng Lù 249.

Visa Extensions   The **Gōngānjú** (PSB; © **0773/582-9930;** open Mon–Fri 8:30am–noon and 3–6pm) is on the east side of the Lí River south off Lóngyǐn Lù.

EXPLORING GUÌLÍN

In the center of town are two of Guìlín's main lakes left over from the moat that ringed the city in the Táng dynasty. To the western side of Zhōngshān Lù is **Róng Hú (Banyan Lake),** named after an 800-year-old banyan tree on its shore. On the eastern side is **Shàn Hú (Cedar Lake),** with its newly erected twin pagodas. A **Liǎng Jiāng Sì Hú (Two Rivers and Four Lakes) boat tour** offers visitors a chance to tour these lakes together with Guì Hú (Osmanthus Lake), Mùlóng Hú (Wooden Dragon Lake), and parts of the Lí Jiāng and Táohuā Jiāng (Peach Blossom) rivers, all of which are now connected by newly dredged waterways. Day sailings for ¥90 ($11) from 9:30am to 4pm, and evening sailings for ¥120 ($15) from 7:30 to 9:30pm, depart from the Jiěfàng Qiáo Mǎtóu (pier) on Bīnjiāng Lù near Jiěfàng Qiáo, and from the Zhīyǐn Tái Mǎtóu on the eastern side of Cedar Lake. Buy tickets at hotel tour desks and at Shízì Jiē next to the Dàshìjiè Bridge (© **0773/282-2666**).

MOUNTAINS & CAVES

Diécǎi Shān (Folding Brocade Hill)   Named for its striated layers of rock that resemble folded brocade, this hill was most popular with poets and painters in the Míng and Qīng dynasties, whose visits were commemorated by scores of inscriptions carved in the rock face. Halfway up the hill is the Wind Cave, a tunnel of cool breezes that extends right through the mountain. The city's highest peak (elev. 223m/731 ft.) has some unobstructed views of the Lí River.

Diécǎi Lù. Admission ¥13 ($1.50). 6:30am–6:30pm (cave 7am–4pm). Bus: no. 2 or 58.

Dúxiù Fēng (Solitary Beauty Peak) ⚐   Tapering to a pavilion-capped peak, this 152m-high (498-ft.) limestone beauty in the middle of town is the most dramatic of Guìlín's hills. A set of steep stairs winds to the top, where awaiting you is a spectacular panorama of Folding Brocade Hill to the north, Wave Subduing Hill to the east, and Seven Star Crag to the southeast. The hill is actually located on the grounds of the 14th-century former palace *(wángchéng)* of a Míng dynasty prince, occupied today by the Guǎngxī Normal University. A gallery sells works by local artists at exorbitant prices.

Wángchéng 1. Admission ¥15 ($2). Apr–Oct 7am–7pm; Nov–Mar 7:30am–6:30pm. Bus: no. 1 (Lèqún Lù stop); from Zhōngshān Lù, take a right onto Xīhuá Lù for about 150m (490 ft.). The park entrance is on your left.

Lúdí Yán (Reed Flute Cave) ⚐⚐   Located a pleasant 45-minute bike ride northwest of town, Reed Flute Cave, whose name derives from the reeds that used to cover the entrance and were used to make flutes, is the most impressive and most popular of Guìlín's caves. Going first thing in the morning or late in the afternoon helps you avoid the overwhelming crowds. At any time, however, individual visitors may have to wait for a group of 20 or more tourists to amass before you can take the 40-minute tour of the cave—and then only with a Chinese-speaking guide. The highlight is the cavernous Crystal Palace of the Dragon King (Shuǐjīng Gōng) with a dense collection of limestone mounds reflected in pools of water, all lit by hundreds of colored lights. Despite the blatantly tacky artifice of it all, most visitors can't help but gasp at the scene before them. This grotto is said to have been an air-raid shelter during World War II.

Lúdí Lù. (If you're biking from the Guìlín Bravo Hotel, go north on Xīnyì Lù, take a left on Lìjūn Lù, and continue as it becomes Xīshān Lù; bear right as the road changes to Táohuā Jiāng Lù, and continue all the way to Lúdí Lù; take a right onto the bridge crossing the Peach Blossom River (Táohuā Jiāng) until you reach the park entrance.) Admission ¥45 ($5.50); in the slow season, ¥40 ($5). Apr–Nov 7:30am–5:20pm; Dec–Mar 8am–4:50pm. Bus: no. 3.

Qīxīng Gōngyuán (Seven Star Park) ✿

Named for its seven hills whose configuration is said to resemble the Big Dipper, this extremely popular park's most famous attraction is the gargantuan **Qīxīng Yán (Seven Star Cave),** which requires about 40 minutes to tour and is full of brightly lit, bizarrely shaped rock outcroppings. Exiting the cave puts you in the vicinity of the aptly named **Luòtuo Shān (Camel Hill).** In the south of the park is the Crescent Moon Peak with its **Lóngyīn Dòng (Dragon Darkness Cave)** and **Guìhǎi Bēilín (Forest of Stelae),** which has thousands of stone tablet inscriptions from the last 1,600 years. There's plenty of room for some pleasant strolls away from the crowds.

Zìyóu Lù. Admission ¥20 ($2.50) park, ¥30 ($2.75) cave. Park 6am–10pm; cave 8am–5:30pm. Bus: no. 10, 11, 14, 28, 52, or 58.

WHERE TO STAY

Hotels are often heavily booked in May, June, September, and October, so plan ahead if want to visit then. Many Guìlín hotels tack on a 15% service charge and a ¥8 ($1) per-person, per-night government tax, which rises to ¥25 ($3.10) during the second to sixth days of the Lunar New Year and also during the May and October national holidays.

EXPENSIVE

Guìlín Bravo Hotel (Guìlín Bīnguǎn) ✿   Catering to foreigners since 1988, this former Holiday Inn, located on the northwestern bank of Banyan Lake, is still the best four-star hotel in town. Rooms are comfortably furnished with large twin beds and soft chairs. Ninth-floor rooms have high ceilings and marvelous views of the lake. Bathrooms are bright and clean.

Rónghú Nán Lù 14. ✆ 0773/282-3950. Fax 0773/282-2101. www.glbravohtl.com. 274 units. ¥960 ($120) standard room; from ¥1,360 ($170) suite. 20%–30% discounts. AE, DC, MC, V. **Amenities:** 3 restaurants; bar; lounge; outdoor swimming pool; rooftop tennis courts; health club; Jacuzzi; sauna; bike rental; concierge; tour desk; business center; forex; shopping arcade; salon; room service; dry cleaning/laundry; nonsmoking rooms. *In room:* A/C, TV, minibar, hair dryer, safe.

Lí Jiāng Waterfall Hotel (Lí Jiāng Dà Pùbù Fàndiàn) ✿   This extravagantly over-the-top five-star—note the enormous man-made waterfall (72m/236 ft. wide×45m/148 ft. high)—aims to be Guìlín's first choice in accommodations. Rooms are large and luxurious enough, but the service is not yet up to the standard of its Western-managed competitors. For now it caters more to northeast Asian tour groups, but special deals are often good enough to entice independent Westerners away from the Bravo and the Sheraton.

North Sānhú Lù 1. ✆ 0773/282-2881. Fax 0773/282-2891. www.waterfallguilin.com. 646 units. ¥1,480–¥2,480 ($185–$310) standard room; from ¥3,150 ($395) suite. 10%–20% discounts. AE, DC, MC, V. **Amenities:** 4 restaurants; bar; lounge; teahouse; nightly minority cultural show; indoor swimming pool; sauna; concierge; business center; forex; shopping arcade; salon; 24-hr. room service; dry cleaning/laundry; 24-hr. medical clinic. *In room:* A/C, TV, broadband Internet access, minibar, hair dryer, safe.

Sheraton Guìlín (Guìlín Dàyǔ Dàfàndiàn)   Though showing signs of age, the Sheraton still offers the best and most efficient service in town. The hotel has an unparalleled location, flanked by the Lí River on one side and the new Zhèngyáng Pedestrian Street with its myriad shops and restaurants on the other. Guest rooms, arrayed around the modern if somewhat dark atrium lobby, are well appointed, with comfortable beds and clean marble bathrooms. The hotel offers very reliable Western dining, and also boasts a 20m-long (65-ft.) swimming pool. Staff is professional, friendly, and very helpful.

Bīnjiāng Nán Lù (west bank of Lí River). ✆ 0773/282-5588. Fax 0773/282-5598. www.sheraton.com/guilin. 430 units. ¥1,245 ($150) standard room. AE, DC, MC, V. **Amenities:** 3 restaurants; bar; lounge; indoor swimming pool; health club; sauna; bike rental; concierge; tour desk; airline-ticketing service; airport shuttle; 24-hr. business center; forex; shopping arcade; salon; 24-hr. room service; babysitting; same-day dry cleaning/laundry. *In room:* A/C, satellite TV, minibar, safe, hair dryer.

MODERATE
Guìlín Diànxìn Bīnguǎn (Guìlín Telecom Hotel) This is a slightly cheaper alternative to the dreary Osmanthus Hotel just up the road, which while having benefited from a number of interior refurbishments, still looks like an asylum from the outside. The Telecom is simpler, but much closer to the station and is a good choice, if you are stuck in Guìlín for the evening but do not want to blow your budget on a five-star. The rooms are spartan but clean, sufficient for an overnight if heading elsewhere.

Zhōngshān Nán Lù 57. ✆ 0773/383-9898. Fax 0773/383-5558. www.gldx.com. 64 units. ¥220–¥380 ($28–$48) standard room; ¥680 ($84) suite. Up to 40% discount. AE, DC, MC, V. **Amenities:** 2 restaurants; karaoke and dance hall; forex; room service; dry-cleaning/laundry. *In room:* A/C, TV, broadband Internet access, fridge.

WHERE TO DINE
Guìlín's most famous local dish is *Guìlín mǐfěn* (Guìlín rice noodles), served at practically every street-corner eatery. Order it dry or in broth, with chicken, beef, even horse meat *(mǎròu),* or plain, then add chives, chili, and pickled sour green beans. Other local favorites, including snake, dog, seafood, and a variety of wild animals sometimes too exotic for foreign tastes, are available in many local restaurants, which usually don't have English menus. For Western food, stick to the international hotel restaurants such as the Sheraton's **Studio Café** and the Guìlín Bravo's **Patio Café.** **McDonald's** and **KFC** are both on Yīrén Lù off the Zhèngyáng pedestrian street.

Mídiéxiāng (Rosemary Café) ✦ WESTERN While the usual traveler's fare such as banana pancakes are ubiquitous in Yángshuò, this is one of the few places in Guilin to have a reliable Western menu. Conveniently located near the Sheraton and just off the pedestrian walking street, Rosemary's is a hit with the overseas tourists that stumble across it. The only downside is that that there are only half a dozen tables and it soon fills up with European package tourists enjoying extended breakfasts or sipping ice-cold watermelon juice to escape the summer heat outside.

Yīrén Lù 1–1. ✆ 0773/281-0063. Meal for 2 ¥80 ($10). No credit cards. 11am–midnight.

Yíyuán Fàndiàn ✦✦ SÌCHUĀN Garnering consistently high marks from travelers, this restaurant serves some excellent spicy dishes, including the tear-inducing diced chicken stir-fried with loads of chilies and garlic; and the *shuǐzhǔ niúròu* (tender beef slices and vegetables in a chili sauce). Calm the palate with *tángcù cuìpí yú* (crispy sweet-and-sour fish), then rev back up to a spicy finish with the *dāndān miàn* (noodles in spicy peanut sauce). The decor is pleasant, and the service is friendly and efficient.

Nánhuán Lù 106. ✆ 0773/282-0470. English menu. Meal for 2 ¥80–¥100 ($10–$13). No credit cards. 11:20am–2pm and 5:20–9pm.

Guìlín's Darker Days

Although the basement-level CD store of the Xīnhuá Bookstore on Zhōngshān Běi Lù is not particularly well stocked, it does offer an insight into Guìlín's past. Check out the heavy steel bomb doors at the entrance, remnants from a paranoid time when every building had such an installation for fear of Soviet attack.

Zàowángyé Xiāngwèi Jū (Vesta Restaurant) ⚔ YÁO/ZHUÀNG   The emphasis at this pleasant restaurant serving authentic Yáo and Zhuàng minority cuisines is on spices and fresh ingredients gathered from the countryside. Specialties include *shāncūn tǔjī* (free-range chicken soup), *záliáng zhútǒng fàn* (bamboo cooked rice), and *shāncūn làròu zhēng yúpiàn* (steamed taro with smoked meat).

Nánhuán Lù 96. ⓒ 0773/282-7769. Meal for 2 ¥80 ($10). No credit cards. 11am–2:30pm and 4:30–9:30pm.

SHOPPING

With generally overinflated prices, Guìlín is no place for bargains. Snacks and candies that make nice gifts include *guìhuā sū* (a crisp, sweet osmanthus cracker) and *guìhuā wángchá* (osmanthus flower tea). The newest attraction, the **Zhèngyáng Pedestrian Street,** has a plethora of shops and stalls selling everything from teapots and jade to clothing and overpriced minority handicrafts and embroidery. The **Guìlín Wēixiào Táng Shàngshà (Guìlín Niko Niko Do Co, Ltd.)** at Zhōngshān Zhōng Lù 187, open from 9am to 10:30pm, is the largest **department store** in town.

GUÌLÍN AFTER DARK

Minority song and dance performances are held nightly at the **Lí Jiāng Theatre (Lí Jiāng Jùyuàn),** Bīnjiāng Lù (ⓒ 0773/286-0288). Performances cost ¥60 to ¥100 ($7.50–$13) and run from 8 to 9:15pm. The **Guìlín Folk Customs Centre (Guìlín Mínsú Fēngqíng Yuán)** at Línjiāng Lù (ⓒ 0773/581-5678) charges ¥60 ($7.50) for shows from 7 to 9:30pm. **The Guìlín Spring Theatre (Chūntiān Jùchǎng)** at Xìnyì Lù 31 (ⓒ 0773/285-6290) offers 7:30pm performances for ¥80 ($10) that are only fractionally better than the other two.

A DAY TRIP FOR ART LOVERS: XIĀNG BĀ DǍO (GRASSROOTS ISLAND)

To alleviate the pressure of so many tourists descending upon the towns of Yángshuò and Guìlín, local authorities opened a sculpture park in 2000, partway between the two. There is a mediocre minorities display, but far more interesting is the Rénwén Shānshuǐ exhibition (humanity and landscape). The park showcases many of China's most well-known, contemporary artists, with an interesting selection of abstract and avant-garde works. Visitors can stay the night on the island where there are tents for hire for ¥180 ($23) per night. A more comfortable alternative might the **Yúnwù Shānzhuāng (Foggy Resort;** ⓒ 0773/384-8899) which has standard rooms starting at ¥280 ($35). This has even inspired some local competition in the form of a second gallery back in town at the Old South Gate (Gǔ Nán Mén), where artists from Guìlín Teachers' College have begun displaying their work.

Buses leave the railway station every 40 min. for ¥5 (65¢). Admission ¥30 ($4).

A POPULAR BOAT TRIP: LÍ JIĀNG (LÍ RIVER)

A boat cruise from Guìlín to Yángshuò along the 432km (270-mile) Lí River is usually sold as the highlight of a Guìlín visit, and indeed, the 83km (52-mile) stretch between the two towns affords some of the country's most breathtaking scenery as the river snakes gracefully through tall karst mountains, gigantic bamboo sprays, and picturesque villages—sights that have inspired countless poets and painters for generations. Unfortunately, such inspiration these days costs a lot more than it used to and, inevitably, monopoly and price-gouging have become the trademarks of this cruise. Foreigners, segregated onto "foreigner boats," pay ¥460 to ¥480 ($57–$60), which is especially egregious considering that Chinese tourists pay less than half that amount. Unfortunately, there is no other way to travel this stretch of the Lí River except on these official tourist authority–sanctioned boats. If time and convenience are your priorities, then take the cruise by all means. Otherwise, if you plan to spend some time in Yángshuò, consider bypassing the cruise; more beautiful karst scenery can be better toured on foot, by bike, or by boat from Yángshuò.

Currently, river trips for foreigners depart from Zhú Jiāng Mǎtóu (Zhú Jiāng Pier) 24km (15 miles) and a half-hour bus ride south of Guìlín at around 8:30am. The first 1½ hours of the cruise to the town of Yángdì is serene and comparatively unexciting but for names of hills along the way, such as a woman yearning for her husband's return, the Eight Immortals, even a calligraphy brush. Visual highlights are clustered between **Yángdì** and the picturesque town of **Xīngpíng**. **Jiǔmǎ Huà Shān (Nine Horses Fresco Hill)** is a steep cliff face with shadings and markings said to resemble a fresco of nine horses. A little farther on, **Huángbù Dàoyíng,** a series of karst peaks and their reflections, is the tableau burnished on the back of a Chinese ¥20 note.

Boats arrive in Yángshuò in the early afternoon after 4 or 5 hours of sailing. There's a stop for shopping, after which tour buses transport passengers back to Guìlín (1 hr.). Tickets for the cruise can be bought at hotel tour desks or at CITS, and include round-trip transportation to Zhú Jiāng Pier, an English-speaking guide, and a Chinese lunch.

Note: See appendix A for Chinese translations of key locations listed above.

2 Yángshuò ✶✶✶

Guǎngxī Province, 65km (40 miles) S of Guìlín

Located at the terminus of the Lí River cruise from Guìlín, the small town of Yángshuò has long been a mecca for backpackers, but long before that, it was a geomancer's delight too. Here the vast landscape is reduced to a garden scale, nature in microcosm, where hills, mountains, oceans, and rivers are reduced to rocks, karsts, streams, and pools. Set amid an awesome cluster of limestone pinnacles—a zigzag, serrated skyline superior even to that of Manhattan—Yángshuò is more beautiful, less expensive, and significantly less crowded than Guìlín. Some of the most impressive karst scenery in Guǎngxī can be found just a short bike ride outside town. With its inexpensive hostels and Western-style cafes, some foreigners have been known to stay for months, sometimes even years. Once a sleepy little town, today's Yángshuò is being overtaken by upscale hotels, new shops and bazaars, and hordes of eager tourists. Perhaps it is no longer the unknown, quiet idyll of years past, but it remains a lovely and relaxing place to break a journey and to soak up some of China's most beautiful scenery.

Yángshuò

ACCOMMODATIONS ■

Hóngfù Fàndiàn
(Hóngfù Palace Hotel) **7**
鸿福饭店

Magnolia Hotel
(Baí Yù Lǎn Dàjiǔdiàn) **12**
白玉兰酒店

New West Street Hotel
(Xīn Xī Jiē Dàjiǔdiàn) **3**
新西街大酒店

Paradise Yángshuò Resort
(Yángshuò Bǎilèlái Dùjià Fàndiàn) **2**
阳朔百乐来度假酒店

Qìng Yuán Hotel
(Qìng Yuán Bīnguǎn) **9**
沁园宾馆

White Lion Hotel
(Wèi Laī Ēn Fàndiàn) **4**
未来恩饭店

DINING ◆

The Balcony **11**
小马的天

Café China **10**
原始人餐厅

Le Vôtre **8**
东得法式餐厅

ATTRACTIONS ●

Bìlián Fēng
(Green Lotus Peak) **6**
碧莲峰

Shānshuǐ Yuán **5**
山水园

Yángshuò Gōngyuán
(Yángshuò Park) **1**
阳朔公园

¥ Bank
🚌 Bus Station
ⓘ Information
✉ Post Office

ESSENTIALS

GETTING THERE   The nearest **rail and air** connections are in Guìlín, but tickets can be purchased here from CITS. From the bus station on Pāntáo Lù, **buses** depart for Guìlín (70 min.; ¥7.50/95¢) every 10 to 15 minutes from 7:30am to 8pm; for Xīngpíng (1 hr.; ¥3.50/45¢) every 15 minutes from 6am to 7:30pm; for Fúlì (20 min.; ¥5/60¢) every 15 minutes from 6am to 7:30pm; and for Gāotián (a half-hour; ¥2/25¢) every 15 minutes from 6:30am to 7pm. Direct buses also run to Guǎngzhōu (8 hr.; ¥150/$19) at 10am, noon, 4pm, and 10pm; and to Shēnzhèn (10 hr.; ¥180/$22) at 5:30pm and 9pm.

Taxis from Guìlín (your hotel in Guìlín can arrange this) will make the trip in an hour at a cost of around ¥250 to ¥300 ($31–$38). If heading straight to Yángshuò, call ahead and your hotel can arrange a taxi for between ¥160 to ¥180 ($20–$23).

GETTING AROUND Yángshuò's main thoroughfare is the cobblestone pedestrian street **Xī Jiē (West Street),** also known as Yángrén Jiē (Foreigner's Street). It runs from Pāntáo Lù to the Lí River boat docks and is where the bulk of travelers' cafes, shops, and basic guesthouses are clustered. The town itself is small enough to be traversed by foot in less than an hour. **Bikes** are the best means of getting to outlying sights, and are available for rent for ¥10 ($1.25) at many Xī Jiē cafes and hotels, as well as at the southern end of Xī Jiē towards Pāntáo Lù. **Motorcycle taxis,** normally ¥3 (40¢) for 3km (2 miles), will offer to take tourists out to Moon Mountain and nearby caves for ¥30 ($3.75), but be sure to agree on all the desired destinations and cost beforehand.

TOURS & GUIDES **CITS** at Xī Jiē 110 (© **0773/882-7102;** fax 0773/882-7102; citsys@sina.com.cn) has three outlets on Xī Jiē and offers many local tours. A 1- or 2-day Lóngshèng Minority Village tour costs ¥150 ($19); the bus leaves Yángshuò at 7:30am and returns at 7pm. There are also Lí River cruises between Yángshuò and Xīngpíng and between Xīngpíng and Yángdī. Day tours can be booked at several travelers' cafes, including **Planet Yángshuò** at Pāntáo Lù 47 (© **1350/7839231**). Be aware that all agents in Yángshuò are now charging a ridiculous booking fee of ¥50 ($6.25) for train and plane tickets, so it would pay to book ahead.

VISITOR INFORMATION The friendly **Yángshuò Lǚyóu Zīxún Fúwù Zhōngxīn (Yángshuò Tourism Information Service Center)** just south of the bus station on Pāntáo Lù (© **0773/882-7922**) can answer basic questions on accommodations, local sights, and tours.

FAST FACTS

Banks, Foreign Exchange & ATMs The **Bank of China** is located at Bīnjiāng Lù 11. Forex hours are Monday to Friday from 9am to 5pm.

Internet Access Internet access is available at a number of cafes and also at **CITS** (Xī Jiē 110) for ¥6 to ¥10 (75¢–$1.25) per hour. Dial-up is © **96163.**

Post Office The post office (open 9am–9:30pm) is at Pāntáo Lù 28.

Visa Extensions The Yángshuò **PSB** office at Chéngběi Lù 39 now tells foreigners that they have to go to Guìlín to renew their visas.

EXPLORING YÁNGSHUÒ

The majority of Yángshuò's treasures are located a bike ride out of town. **Xī Jiē (West Street),** with its souvenir shops and travelers' cafes, has become a bona-fide tourist attraction for Chinese visitors, who completely take over the street starting in the early afternoon when boats from Guìlín pull in. The former Míng dynasty **Jiāngxī Huìguǎn,** once the guild hall for merchants from Jiāngxī Province, has now become part of the Hóngfú Hotel on Xī Jiē, but it's worth a quick pop-in for its finely carved lattice doors and windows.

In the southeastern part of town along the western banks of the Lí River, the **Shānshuǐ Yuán** park (¥21/$3; open 8:30am–6pm) is home to the impressive karst mountain **Bìlián Fēng (Green Lotus Peak),** which towers over the town and the harbor. In the western part of town next to the bus station, **Yángshuò Gōngyuán (Yángshuò Park)** (Diécuì Lù 22; ¥9/$1.10; open 6:30am–7pm) sees few foreign visitors but is full of loafing locals who pay nothing to enter. You can hike to the top of Xīláng Shān for some arresting views of the countryside.

OUTDOOR ACTIVITIES

With so many karst hills and caves around the area, Yángshuò has become a little mecca for **rock climbing,** boasting some 70 climbing circuits. English-speaking Echo at the **Karst Café,** Xiànqián Jiē 42 (© **0773/882-8482**), helps organize and lead both half-day trips for ¥150 ($20) and 1- to 3-day trips for ¥300 ($38) per person per day. During the summer months, some cafes on Xī Jiē will organize **rafting** or **kayaking** trips on the Lí River and on smaller rivers like the Yùlóng Hé (Jade Dragon River). Those preferring something more sedate can take courses on tai chi, Chinese cooking, Chinese calligraphy, Chinese medicine, or Mandarin at various outfits in town, including the **Chinese Culture and Art Promotion Workshop,** Diécuì Jiē 2 (© **0773/881-1121**).

WHERE TO STAY

Xī Jiē, once a backpacker's dream with its cheap hostels and guesthouses, has of late been playing host to some newer, smaller hotels that provide perfectly comfortable and unpretentious accommodations. Larger hotels are along Pāntáo Lù—such as the monstrous, overpriced **New West Street Hotel** (Xīn Xī Jiē Dàjiŭdiàn; © **0773/881-8888**), geared largely to big tour groups—but these lack the charm and personal touches of the guesthouses. Some seriously offensive price gouging occurs during holidays (first week in May and Oct) and peak periods (summer), when rooms can cost up to four times the usual price.

Yángshuò has been in a constant state of flux for some 10 years, and some complain that the town has become crass and overcommercialized. While few tourists would gripe about the availability of air-conditioning in most places, the party atmosphere of West Street, with nightclubs like Babyface raucous until the wee hours, can be a bit unnerving. See Mountain Retreat in the Yùlóng Hé section below if you are looking to escape the scene.

EXPENSIVE

Paradise Yángshuò Resort (Yángshuò Bǎilèlái Dùjià Fàndiàn)   Located in its own compound at the western end of Xī Jiē, this three-star Chinese courtyard–style resort dating from the 1950s once prided itself on offering the only classy accommodations in town for foreign tour groups. Guest rooms are furnished with comfortable beds, and bathrooms are duly clean, but it's really overpriced for its age. Service is efficient, if not exactly warm.

Xī Jiē 116. © **0773/882-2109.** Fax 0773/882-2106. www.paradiseyangshuo.com. 145 units. ¥664 ($80) standard room; from ¥996 ($120) suite. 20% discount. 18% service charge. AE, DC, MC, V. **Amenities:** 2 restaurants; bar; lounge; outdoor swimming pool; health club; bowling alley; sauna; concierge; business center; forex; shopping arcade; salon; room service; next-day dry cleaning/laundry. *In room:* A/C, TV, minibar.

MODERATE

Hóngfù Fàndiàn (Hóngfù Palace Hotel)   Housed in the former Jiāngxī Guild Hall (300 years old), this new treat of a hotel is the brainchild of two French brothers who also run the French restaurant, Le Vôtre, next door. The spacious guest rooms, though a little dark, are simply decorated with traditional Chinese furniture and comfortable beds. Bathrooms are large and clean. The owners have recently opened their own microbrewery; too bad, I was hoping for Yángshuò's first patisserie.

Xī Jiē 79. © **0773/882-9489.** Fax 0773/882-9499. hongfuhotelyangshuo@yahoo.fr. 28 units (shower only). ¥200 ($25) (¥600/$75 in high season) standard room; ¥400 ($62) suite year-round. No credit cards. **Amenities:** Restaurant; bar; concierge; room service; laundry. *In room:* A/C, TV, no phone.

Magnolia Hotel (Báiyùlán Dàjiǔdiàn) ★★★ (Value) One of the newest and definitely the best choice of accommodations in Yángshuò at the moment. Formerly a run-down student dormitory, the Magnolia has been transformed into a great-value boutique hotel by an Australian entrepreneur with an eye for detail and a knack for getting the best out of local staff. A number of tour companies are already using the Magnolia as their number-one choice, and it is easy to see why. Four floors are built around a bright, spacious atrium, with rooms that are equally bright, and outfitted with supercomfortable king-size beds. *Tip:* Ask for room 307; it's much larger than the rest and boasts it own private patio garden.

Diécuì Lù 7. © 0773/881-9288. Fax 0773/881-9218. www.yangshuoren.com. 30 units. ¥200–¥300 ($25–$38) standard room. AE, DC, MC, V. **Amenities:** Laundry/dry cleaning. *In room:* A/C, TV, hair dryer.

Qìng Yuán Hotel (Qìng Yuán Bīnguǎn) (Finds) Here is that great-value, Chinese-style guest house, replete with lots of traditional architectural details, that everybody else is traipsing around looking for. Located far off West Street, the Qìng Yuán is just outside the quiet little square that has developed around Guìhuā Brook, a pleasant area with lots of new bars and restaurants (check out **FlyTime** and the very popular **Bar 98**), that often charge less that half the price of eateries along West Street.

Guì Huā Lù 29. © 0773/881-9999. Fax 0773/881-33333. www.qinyuanhotel.net. 28 units. ¥200 ($25) standard room; ¥400 ($50) suite. 20%–50% discounts. AE, DC, MC, V. **Amenities:** Teahouse; bike rental; limited room service; next-day laundry. *In room:* A/C, TV.

White Lion Hotel (Wèi Lái Ēn Fàndiàn) (Value) This is the hotel that I always choose when I am bringing friends to Yángshuò for the first time. It is right in the heart of West Street, with rooms that actually overlook the bars and shops. Perhaps it's a bit noisy, but it provides a great introduction to Yángshuò. The rooms have a somewhat rustic feel to them with wooden floors and pine furniture, a refreshing change from the anonymous beige of most Chinese hotels. The staff is helpful and can arrange a variety of tours, and even cookery courses at the owner's new restaurant around the corner, Seventh Heaven.

Xī Jiē 103. © 0773/881-2321. Fax 0773/882-7778. www.whitelionchina.com. 27 units. ¥100–¥200 ($13–$25) standard room overlooking West St.; ¥200–¥300 ($25–$38) small suite. No cards accepted. **Amenities:** Coffee shop; free Internet access; self-service laundry. *In room:* A/C, TV.

WHERE TO DINE

There are plenty of cafes on Xī Jiē offering Western, Chinese, and local dishes at very reasonable prices. Although such alfresco dining is extremely pleasant and allows for good people-watching, some tourists have recently complained about being harassed mid-bite by over-eager vendors or would-be English practitioners offering their services as tour guides.

Yángshuò abounds with great cafe food. The **Karst Café** (Xiànqián Jiē 42; © 0773/882-8482) still hangs on the title of best pizza in town, but its enormous "Full Monty" breakfast is worth investigating. At the corner of West Street and Xiànqián Jiē is the internationally owned and operated **Café China** (© 0773/882-7744). The ground floor offers typical West Street fare from rich, creamy cheesecake to thick banana pancakes. Its second and third floors are much more elegant: spacious tables, Asian art, and an atmosphere more inclined toward traveling gourmands than backpackers. The rooftop is one of the best locations in town, with excellent mountain views. Local specialties such as delicious *píjiǔ yú* (fish cooked in beer and spices) and *bàochǎo tiánluó* (Lí River snails stuffed with pork) are extremely reliable here but it might be wise to book a table in advance as this is the number-one choice for Western tour groups.

The Italian gelato stalls around town are worth avoiding as both the cones and the gelato taste unpleasantly chemical. While many places do pancakes, only **The Balcony,** at the bottom of Xiānqián Jiē (© **0773/881-2331**), does exquisite crepes. Sit outside on the balcony terrace for breakfast, or in evening join the French owner Nico, for a drink.

For more elegant dining, charming **Le Vôtre** at Xī Jiē 79 (© **0773/882-8040**), occupying half of the former Míng dynasty Jiāngxī Guild Hall, offers everything from T-bone steaks to Chinese dishes, but signature specialties include escargots, *moules chaude* (steamed mussels), and *filet du canard grillé* (grilled duck filet). Finish off with a crème brûlée or the crêpes suzette. A full bevy of Italian and French wines is available. Main courses range from ¥30 to ¥80 ($3.75–$10).

In answer to requests from visitors for more fine Chinese dining, the owner at Café China opened a new restaurant in May 2005, just outside of town in the small village of Liú Gōng. Ask at Café China or the Magnolia Hotel and staff will organize a boat (¥100–¥150/$13–$19) to take you to this converted village watch tower, less than an hour downstream from Yángshuò. Tourist boats rarely come down this far, so you may have the entire Lí River to yourself as you pass the disused sugar refinery that still sits nestled between riverside peaks. **Liú Gōng Pavilion (Zhī Huán Xuān;** www.yang shuoren.com) overlooks the river with a backdrop of mountains so spectacular that it almost answers the question of divine existence. Recommended are the stir-fried sweet-potato shoots and the Yáo minority-style braised pork wrapped in rice stalks. Two people can eat here very well for less than ¥100 ($13) and even a pot of fresh coffee is only ¥22 ($3). You might like to take your bikes with you on the boat and then ride home via Fúlì. Don't leave too late, though: only a few houses in Liú Gōng village have electricity, and one of the Pavilion staffers might have to guide you over the cobbles by flashlight.

To eat where the locals eat, head 1 block north of Xī Jiē to **Diécuì Lù.** Walk down past the Magnolia and turn left where the buildings end, where the old market was knocked down to make room for new development. The third shop along is a scary-looking noodle store that's popular with local waitresses. Few locals eat banana pancakes, but with these *spicy snail noodles (luó sī fěn)* this is an opportunity to see what people really eat in Yángshuò, and for just ¥2.50 (30¢).

AROUND YÁNGSHUÒ

See appendix A for Chinese translations of key locations.

RIVER TRIPS

There are plenty of opportunities to take shorter and significantly less expensive river trips from the Yángshuò area—check with the travel agencies and backpackers' cafes on Xī Jiē for your options. The fascist Lí River patrol authorities have a stranglehold on all river traffic and there are strict laws about the kinds of boats foreigners can ride on (boat licenses can cost up to a million *yuán*), so stick with the legitimate outfits rather than with the random touts who approach you, no matter how friendly they are.

One of the more popular trips is downriver to the umbrella and fan town of **Fúlì** (see below), but boats only ply this route during the summer and early fall. Another trip is to the town of **Xīngpíng,** about 3 hours upstream from Yángshuò. Official boats make the run in summer for about ¥60 to ¥80 ($7.50–$10) per person. Rather than sail upstream, some tourists prefer to cycle or take a bus to Xīngpíng and catch a boat downstream back to Yángshuò. Some tour operators come up with creative combinations of hiking/river-trip tours, which involve traveling to Xīngpíng by bus or bike, then hiking along the river for part of the way before hopping onto a boat for the rest of the journey.

MOON MOUNTAIN (YUÈLIANG SHĀN) AREA

A pleasant bike trip involves riding 8km (5 miles) out to **Moon Mountain (Yuèliang Shān)** in the direction of Gāotián. Follow Pántáo Lù in the opposite direction from Guìlín until the traffic circle, and bear right onto Kàngzhàn Lù. Once you leave town, you'll be greeted around each bend with unbelievably scenic vistas of karst pinnacles stretching as far as your eyes can see. (It's just a shame that the authorities have not spent any of their profits on road maintenance!)

Along the road to Moon Mountain are several recently built attractions geared strictly towards Chinese tour groups that can be safely missed. About 6km (4 miles) from Yángshuò, the **Gǔróng Gōngyuán** (¥18/$2.25; open 6am–sunset) has an intriguing 17m-tall (56-ft.), over 1,500-year-old banyan tree that looks like a collection of entwined snakes up close and like a giant umbrella from afar. Unlike most alleged antiquities that tourists see, this is the real deal, easily as old as any American redwood. Visit if you have time, but you can see the tree just as easily from atop **Moon Mountain,** 1km (⅔ mile) away (¥8/$1; open 7am–6pm), so named because of the large moon-shaped arch under its peak. A series of steep steps winds through thick bamboo brush all the way to the top, where there are some marvelous views.

If there's an adventurous spelunker in you waiting to break free, there are several interesting caves around here worth exploring. However, some of these are suitable only for the fit, as none have paved paths and all will require you to get down and dirty by crawling through holes and climbing rickety ladders. **Buddha Cave** (¥60/$7.50; open 8am–6pm summer, 9am–5pm winter), along with **Water Cave (Shuǐyán),** have underground pools and rivers on which you can paddle and get that mud bath you've always wanted.

A more civilized alternative is 90 minutes south at the magnificent **Silver Cave (Yínzi Yán;** www.glyinzicave.com) situated in spectacular parkland about 20km (13 miles) south of Yángshuò. Any local agency will arrange tickets and transportation for around ¥80 ($10) per person, which is perhaps a safer option than public transport. We missed the last bus back to town and had to flag down an archaic vehicle (half-tractor, half-tricycle), whose maximum speed turned out to be about half my normal walking pace. After a painfully slow half-hour, we asked how long it would take to get back to Yángshuò. The young peasant girl at the wheel simply shrugged her shoulders; she had never been that far from her village before!

FÚLÌ

Located along the Lí River downstream from Yángshuò, the village of Fúlì, first established over 1,300 years ago during the Táng dynasty, is a popular excursion either by boat or bike. Most travelers seem to prefer the latter for the gorgeous scenery along the 6km (4-mile) ride, especially now that the Pavilion has opened at Liú Gōng. Fúlì holds a **market** every 3 days and while there's not much to buy for tourists (but potentially a lot to lose to pickpockets—be careful!), there's enough local color here to take an hour or so of your time. Just before the market is a lane that winds past traditional stone houses down to the river. To cycle to Fúlì, head east on Pāntáo Lù past the traffic circle and follow the road across the bridge. You can also take a bus from the station on Pāntáo Lù.

XĪNGPÍNG ★★

Surrounded by a jungle of karst pinnacles, the charming, as yet unspoiled village of Xīngpíng about 25km (15 miles) upstream of Yángshuò is being touted by some as the next Yángshuò, meaning the next backpackers' haven, now that Yángshuò has become more of a commercialized circus. Cobblestone streets wend their ways through this quaint village of stone houses that's refreshingly free of souvenir stores, and residents go about their daily business with nary a glance spared for the visitor. The most scenic area is the riverfront; on market days you'll see villagers from the surrounding areas boarding boats laden with everything from live chickens to new aluminum woks. A few cafes and backpackers' hostels have sprung up here, but accommodations and dining are still fairly basic. There are regular buses to Xīngpíng from the Yángshuò bus station, or you can ride your bike here in 3 to 4 hours.

An interesting side trip from Xīngpíng is to **Yúcūn** (literally "Fishing Village"), a tiny, picturesque Míng dynasty village (1506–21) 20 minutes downstream along the Lí River, whose more famous visitors have included Sun Yat-sen in 1921 and Bill Clinton in 1998. Full of traditional Míng and Qīng dynasty houses with white walls and gray-tiled roofs with upturned eaves, as well as the occasional ancestral hall, the village requires a ¥5 (60¢) entrance fee which includes a tour by a Chinese-speaking local. Daily boats make the 20-minute trip to Yúcūn for ¥25 ($3) round-trip. They depart Xīngpíng's waterfront between 8am and 5:30pm (the ticket booth is to the right at the end of the main street), but boats only depart with a quorum of 10, which sometimes can mean a wait of hours in low season. The gorgeous boat ride between Xīngpíng and Yúcūn, however, is generally worth the bit of hassle in getting there.

YÙLÓNG HÉ (JADE DRAGON RIVER) ★★★

One of the loveliest trips outside Yángshuò, this river, sometimes dubbed **Xiǎo Lí Jiāng (Lesser Lí River),** is, if anything, even more beautiful and certainly quieter than the Lí. The river's more famous landmarks may be its bridges, in particular the 59m-long (194-ft.) Míng dynasty **Yùlóng Qiáo (Jade Dragon Bridge)** found in the town of **Báishā,** but it's the scenery of small villages nestled at the foot of karst hills surrounded by rice paddies and a lazy winding river that most visitors remember long after they've left. Many of the travelers' cafes offer full-day tours of the river and surrounding sights, but it's entirely possible to visit on your own. Just pack a picnic, plenty of film, and rain gear, check your bike's tire pressure, and you're off.

There are several routes by which to explore the river. From Yángshuò, head out towards Moon Hill. Before the bridge crossing the Yùlóng Hé, head right on the dirt trail which can, with several deviations, take you all the way up to Báishā and the Jade Dragon Bridge. You can return along these back paths, or head back from Báishā on the main Guìlín–Yángshuò highway. Or reverse the order and take the highway to Báishā (9km/6 miles from Yángshuò), then cycle back down through the villages. Chances are you'll get lost on some of these paths, that can narrow to the width of your bicycle (so get off and walk carefully or you may end up in the mud!), but that's half the fun. Not to worry, the villagers around here are more than happy to set you right, and there are enough paths between the river and the highway that you won't be lost for long.

Alternatively, some travelers have sailed back down the Yùlóng Hé on narrow bamboo rafts for ¥100 to ¥200 ($12–$25), though I don't advise it. Several years ago, there was a boating fatality involving a foreigner in the lower reaches of the river. Because new rules requiring passengers to wear safety jackets seem to be honored more in the breach, this is a risky undertaking at best. Some travelers have settled for sailing down a very short, relatively smooth stretch of the river from Báishā, but even this involves having to get off the raft occasionally so it can be poled down the bigger bumps.

The full journey to Yùlóng Qiáo may be a bit much for some, especially in the summer when heat stroke and sun burn are serious threats on a journey as long as this. A less exhausting alternative is to stop off at **Yángshuò Shèngdì (Mountain Retreat)** ✦✦✦ on the way. Built by a successful American businessman just 5 years ago, this is one of China's true gems and has possibly the best location in the province. Rooms are a good size with massive picture windows and balconies to take advantage of views that are some of the best in the world. The retreat itself has a Confucian academy–type feel to it and is especially popular with corporate groups. Located on Wáng Gōng Shān Jiǎo in Gāotián, Yángshuò, you can contact the hotel by phone (© 0773/877-7091), fax 0773/877-709, or online at www.yangshuomountainretreat.com. Standard rooms go for ¥200 ($25), while a deluxe room costs ¥500 ($62).

Lí Jiāng After Dark

Every night from July through September, 2,000 spectators fill the purpose-built riverside amphitheater for acclaimed director Zhāng Yìmóu's waterborne spectacular, **"Impression, Sanjie Liu."** This innovative new show is on a grand scale with over 200 bamboo rafts in the water at once and a total production crew of some 600. It is a strange but beautiful mix of floodlights, singing, and minority processions against a magical backdrop. Tickets start at ¥180 ($23) and can be arranged through most hotels. The show starts at 8pm but best to get there half-hour early, leaving time to wander Liú Sān Jiě Park. Bring binoculars or rent them for ¥5 (65¢); insect repellent is also a good idea. At the bottom of West Street in Yángshuò, there is an endless succession of boat owners who will happily take you to an alternative viewing point on the river for just ¥20 to ¥30 ($2.50–$3.75); but at this price you will be paying mostly for the mosquitoes. For more info, visit **www.yxlsj.com.**

⌐Moments Taking a Dip in the Yùlóng

For those who'd prefer not to float down the entire length of the Yùlóng, here is an alternative. Mountain Retreat's public relations manager led me down to the river bank where boatmen where playing some kind of noisy brag. For ¥10 ($1.25), one of them agreed to pole us the hundred meters or so up to the next weir, where we promptly jumped off the raft, and spent the rest of the afternoon swimming. Even the boatman stripped down to his skivvies and jumped in with us. So many tourists float down this stretch of water, two rafts even feature an onboard PC and printer, with locals taking digital pictures for a small fee. The Retreat's manager told me that swimming like this was her summertime morning routine, a half-hour dip before returning for breakfast and fresh orange juice. Certainly one of my China highlights!

---

3 Guìyáng

Guìzhōu Province, 450km (270 miles) NE of Kūnmíng

Guìyáng, the capital of Guìzhōu Province, is a natural fortress. The capricious weather and the hostile topography, giving Guìyáng the resemblance of a castle in the mist, seem more at home in Transylvania. Few Hàn Chinese even knew these strange lands existed before the famed geographer Xú Xiákè traveled here in 1636 as part of his 30-year trek exploring China's sacred mountains (on foot and unescorted!) Again and again he was confronted by "massive, labyrinthine heaps of rock towering wavelike into crests or busting out like petals, dizzying in their effect as they jostle and surge toward the sky!"

"Imagine a series of quaintly shaped hillocks littering a landscape that is also pock-marked with deep depressions," explained 17th-century explorer Francis Garnier. "No valleys or mountain ranges. No general sense of direction. The streams flow to all points on the compass. Every step would have led us up against some impossible piece of terrain."

By that time the empire had relocated so many eastern Chinese colonists to this unforgiving land that the province's population had soared from 65 to 150 million. A series of rebellions was dealt with mercilessly by succeeding generations of Tunpuren, or Hàn military colonists. Eighteen-thousand Miáo were killed in 1732, with almost the same number executed and a similar amount enslaved. More than 100 years later the scenario was repeated. The governor of Guìzhōu wrote that the province had lost nine-tenths of its entire population in just 2 decades, either massacred or exiled to the hills of northern Laos, Burma, and Thailand.

Guìyáng remains an important strategic possession in a land where even the locals claim that there is "never three days of sun in a row, never three acres of flat land and never three people with any money." Despite some development, Guìzhōu has remained an impoverished backwater compared to its neighbors. Incomes and literacy rates are well below the national averages, and many villages still lack basic infrastructures such as roads and electricity.

A closer look at the map reveals how these proud, defiant peoples have been dominated and humiliated by Chinese colonists. Name after name stands out like marker flags on a campaign plan: Ānshùn (Peace and Submission); Líping (Pacification of the Lí); Zhènyuán (Pacification of the Distant Tribes); Guiding (Pacification of Guìzhōu); Luódiàn (Extension of Imperial Power); and Kǎilǐ (Village of the Victory Song).

As for the Hàn Chinese contribution, Guìyáng itself is a place many travelers can't wait to get out of, if they make it here at all. Today, gray, dreary buildings still dominate the disarray of so-called development, staggering to cope with its growing population of over a million people. Happily for visitors interested in exploring Guìzhōu's ethnic minority cultures, having to stay over is not as dreaded as it once was. The city is now an essential jumping-off point to see autochthonous cultures, as different to the Hàn Chinese as the Native Americans are to the 21st-century descendants of their European conquerors. With the building of new highways, this transportation hub is an ideal base from which to visit surrounding attractions like the Huángguǒshù Falls and Bouyi minority villages.

ESSENTIALS

GETTING THERE   Daily **flights** connect Guìyáng to Běijīng, Shànghǎi, Guǎngzhōu, Chéngdū, Xī'ān, Kūnmíng, Guìlín, Nánníng, Chóngqìng, and Hong

Kong. Tickets can be purchased at the **CAAC** office at Zūnyì Lù 264 (© **0855/597-7777**) from 8:30am to 8pm. A **China Southwest Airlines** office, located in the Táiwān Dàshà at Zhōnghuá Nán Lù (© **0851/581-1222**), is open from 8am to 10pm. The 12km (8-mile) **taxi** ride to the airport should cost ¥50 ($6.25). **Airport buses** depart from the CAAC office every half-hour for a fare of ¥10 ($1.25); the CAAC office is open from 8:30am to 6:30pm. Getting to the airport is more of a problem. Most drivers demand ¥50 ($6.25) for what is actually a ¥25 ($3) journey, but it is an unavoidable rip-off that is almost worth it if you get to go on the notorious short cut.

Guìyáng's **railway station** (© **0851/818-1222**) in the southern part of town is a modern building with computerized ticketing and all your usual touts. From here, several **trains** a day run to Kǎilǐ (3–4 hr.; ¥25/$3), though it's much faster now to take the 2-hour bus. The K946 train originates in Guìyáng at 7:40am, so it's easier to get an assigned seat on it. The 2079 departs for Kūnmíng (12½ hr.; ¥234/$29 soft sleeper) at 6:50pm; the K922 leaves for Chéngdū (17 hr.; ¥226/$28 soft sleeper) at 4pm; and the 5608 departs for Chóngqìng (10 hr.; ¥150/$19 soft sleeper) at 7:40pm. The T88 departing at 10:36pm is the quickest option for getting to Běijīng (32 hr.; ¥754/$94 soft sleeper). The K112 runs to Shànghǎi (33 hr.; ¥556/$69) at 9:30pm; and the 1688 heads for Guǎngzhōu (33 hr.; ¥337/$42) at 9am, stopping at Guìlín (17 hr.) along the way.

Guìyáng has several bus stations, but the main one that should serve most travelers' needs is the **Sports Stadium Bus Station (Tǐyùguǎn Kèyùn Zhàn)** near the railway station at Zūnyì Lù and Jiěfàng Lù (© **0851/579-3381**). **Buses** run to Kǎilǐ (2 hr.; ¥30–¥35/$3.75–$4.25) every half-hour from 7:30am to 7:30pm; to Ānshùn (1½ hr.; ¥15/$2) every 20 minutes from 7:05am to 7:30pm; and to Róng Jiāng (7 hr.; ¥70/$9) at 1:50pm. Tour buses to Huángguǒshù Falls and Dragon Palace Cave depart from the bus stand just outside the railway station (see "Tours & Guides," below).

GETTING AROUND **Taxis** cost ¥10 ($1.25) for 3km (2 miles), then ¥1.60 (20¢) per kilometer, and ¥1.90 (25¢) per kilometer after 10km (6 miles). From 10pm to 7am, prices rise to ¥12 ($1.50) for 3km (2 miles), then ¥1.90 (25¢) per kilometer, and then ¥2.40 (30¢) per kilometer after 10km (6 miles).

TOURS & GUIDES Companies outside the Tōngdá Fàndiàn near the railway station offer various tours of the Huángguǒshù Falls. For about ¥200 ($25), you get transportation, meals, and a guided tour (in Chinese) of the falls, as well as a Miáo village. You also get either **Tiānxīng Qiáo (Heavenly Star Bridge)** or **Lónggōng Dòng (Dragon Palace Caves)**. Another option is a round-trip bus ride to the falls for ¥60 ($7.50). **CITS,** at Héqún Lù 1, Lóngquán Dàshà, seventh floor (© **0851/690-1660**), can arrange private tours of the same with English-speaking guides, but rates are much higher (starting at around ¥800/$100 a day for car and guide).

FAST FACTS

Banks, Foreign Exchange & ATMs The main branch of the **Bank of China** (© **0851/586-9790;** open Mon–Fri 8:30–11:30am and 2:30–6pm/2–5:30pm in winter) is located at Dūsī Lù 30. The branch has an ATM.

Internet Access A 24-hour Internet cafe at Yán'ān Dōng Lù 20, just east of the Trade Point Hotel, charges ¥2 (25¢) an hour.

Post Office The main post office (open 8:30am–7pm) is at Zhōnghuá Nán Lù 68.

Guìyáng

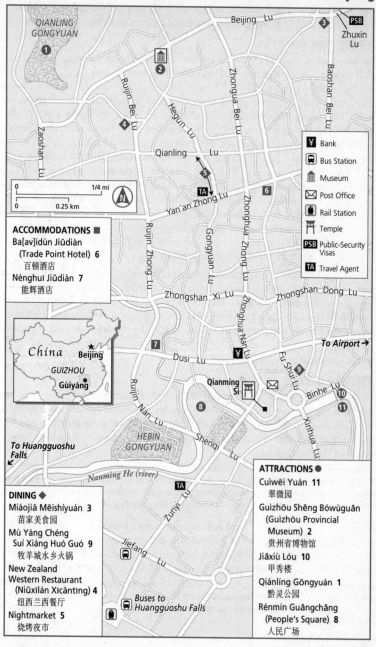

QIANLING GONGYUAN

Beijing Lu

PSB
Zhuxin Lu

Rujin Bei Lu

Zhonghua Bei Lu

Baoshan Bei Lu

Hegun Lu

Qianling Lu

Zaoshan Lu

¥	Bank
🚌	Bus Station
🏛	Museum
✉	Post Office
🚉	Rail Station
⛩	Temple
PSB	Public-Security Visas
TA	Travel Agent

TA

Yan'an Zhong Lu

Rujin Zhong Lu

Gongyuan Lu

Zhonghua Zhong Lu

0   1/4 mi
0   0.25 km

ACCOMMODATIONS ■
Ba[av]idùn Jiǔdiàn
   (Trade Point Hotel) 6
   百顿酒店
Nénghuī Jiǔdiàn 7
   能辉酒店

China
★ Beijing
GUIZHOU
● Gùiyáng

Zhongshan Xi Lu

Zhonghua Nan Lu

Zhongshan Dong Lu

To Airport →

Rujin Nan Lu

Dusi Lu

¥

Fu Shui Lu

Qianming Sī

✉

Binhe Lu

Xinhua Lu

Shenqi Lu

To Huangguoshu Falls ←

HEBIN GONGYUAN

Nanming He (river)

TA

Zunyi Lu

DINING ◆
Miáojiā Měishíyuán 3
   苗家美食园
Mù Yáng Chéng
   Suí Xiáng Huǒ Guó 9
   牧羊城水乡火锅
New Zealand
   Western Restaurant
   (Niǔxīlán Xīcāntīng) 4
   纽西兰西餐厅
Nightmarket 5
   烧烤夜市

Jiefang Lu

Buses to
Huangguoshu Falls

ATTRACTIONS ●
Cuìwēi Yuán 11
   翠微园
Guìzhōu Shěng Bówùguǎn
   (Guìzhōu Provincial
   Museum) 2
   贵州省博物馆
Jiǎxiù Lóu 10
   甲秀楼
Qiánlíng Gōngyuán 1
   黔灵公园
Rénmín Guǎngchǎng
   (People's Square) 8
   人民广场

Visa Extensions   The **PSB** is at Zhúxīn Lù 5 (© **0851/676-5230;** open Mon–Fri 8:30am–noon and 2–5pm). Allow 5 business days for a month-long extension.

SEEING THE SIGHTS

The stretch of the Nánmíng River southeast of the city center is worth a couple hours' stroll at most. From **Rénmín Guǎngchǎng (People's Square)** on Zūnyì Lù (now housing an underground Wal-Mart beneath Louvre glass pyramids), a giant gleaming white statue of Máo Zédōng presides over tai-chi practitioners, kite flyers, and young lovers. Walk along the river to the Fúyù Bridge on which sits **Jiǎxiù Lóu** (¥2/25¢; open 8:30am–5:30pm). Built in 1598 as a meeting place for scholars attending the provincial Confucian examinations, this three-story pavilion has three tiers of soaring eaves supported by 12 stone pillars. The pavilion currently houses a teahouse and a small exhibit of the building's history as it is one of the few remaining traditional wooden buildings in the city. The real find is the open-air **secondhand bookstore** on the ground level which sells rare, hard-to-find travel and nature guides, great for exploring local caves, flora, or minorities, at well below the usual tourist prices. At the other end of the bridge is **Cuìwēi Yuán** (¥3/40¢; open 8:30am–midnight), a series of traditional buildings once part of a Míng dynasty Buddhist temple. Today, it is home to a teahouse favored by mahjong players; pricey shops sell minority goods.

Qiánlíng Gōngyuán   Located on the slopes of 1,395m-high (4,576-ft.) Qiánlíng Shān in the northwest part of town, this lushly forested park offers a pleasant reprieve from the urban jungle. A hike up the steep winding path to the 17th-century temple **Hóngfú Sì** (¥1/15¢; open 8am–6pm) will give you a good workout and a bird's-eye view of the city. A cable car (¥12/$1.50 up; ¥8/$1 down) also makes the trip. Avoid the zoo at all costs.

Zǎo Shān Lù. Admission ¥5 (65¢). 6:30am–10pm.

WHERE TO STAY

Bǎidùn Jiǔdiàn (Trade Point Hotel) ✦✦   This elegant, centrally located four-star hotel is the top choice in town. Guest rooms are a bit small but are well appointed with large beds, soft linens, and comfortable chairs. Bathrooms are clean and well stocked. The hotel provides all you need for a restful night save for the jarring karaoke rooms on the fourth floor.

Yán'ān Dōng Lù 18. © 0851/582-7888. Fax 0851/582-3118. www.trade-pointhotel.com. 254 units. ¥800–¥900 ($100–$112) standard room; ¥1,360 ($170) suite. Discounts up to 50%. AE, DC, MC, V. **Amenities:** 2 restaurants; bar; lounge; health club; sauna; concierge; business center; forex; shopping arcade; room service; laundry/dry cleaning; nonsmoking floor; executive rooms. *In room:* A/C, satellite TV, minibar, hair dryer, safe.

Nénghuī Jiǔdiàn ✦ (Value)   This handsome and modern hotel delivers accommodations and facilities well beyond what its three-star status might suggest. Guest rooms are large and bright with high ceilings, big firm beds, modern furniture, and sparkling bathrooms. Although the hotel originally opened in spring 2002, it is surprisingly well maintained.

Ruìjīn Nán Lù 38. © 0851/589-8888. Fax 0851/589-8622. 125 units. ¥520 ($65) standard room; ¥1,080 ($135) suite. 40% discount. AE, DC, MC, V. **Amenities:** Restaurant; bar; lounge; health club; sauna; concierge; business center; forex; shopping arcade; salon; room service; laundry/dry cleaning; executive rooms. *In room:* A/C, satellite TV, minibar, hair dryer, safe.

WHERE TO DINE

The best Western dining is offered in high-end hotels like the **Trade Point Hotel,** which has a Western buffet. Less exalted fare like **KFC** (open 9am–11pm) is available at Zhōnghuá Nán Lù 246. For local dining, an extremely lively **night market** ✿ on Héqún Lù just north of Yán'ān Zhōng Lù proffers kabobs, grilled meats and vegetables, noodles, dumplings, stir-fries, and hot pot and is, for adventurous patrons, one of the more interesting dining experiences in town. Dog meat is very popular here.

Miáojiā Měishí Yuán ✿ MIÁO   Located down a set of dark steps in a traditional courtyard setting, this casual Miáo restaurant serves some incredibly spicy food. Try, if you dare, the fiery *yáng làjiāo* (hot peppers and chilies that have been blanched, sundried, and fried), *Miáojiā ānyú* (Miáo sour fish), or the delicious *Miáowèi páigǔ* (spicy Miáo spareribs). For something more benign, the *Miáojiā tǔdòu piàn* (deep-fried potato coins) and *ròusī chǎomiàn* (stir-fry noodles with pork) should be comfortingly familiar.

Bǎoshān Běi Lù 433 (opposite Holiday Inn). ✆ 0855/675-1451. ¥25–¥70 ($3–$9). No credit cards. 11am–2:30pm and 5–9:30pm.

Mù Yáng Chéng Shuǐxiāng Huǒguō ✿✿ *Value* HOT POT   While many have seen the latest craze in sushi bars where dishes are pulled around on toy trains with narrow-gauge tracks, here is an improvement on even that idea. All tables (each equipped with their own gas stove) are located alongside a small stream. A succession of small boats floats along and you choose the ingredients that you would like to parboil in your table-top soup dish. There are plenty of safe choices such as lotus root, potato, duck, and quail eggs; for the more adventurous there is stomach (which strangely resembles bathroom carpet both in texture and taste) and fresh pigs' brains. Best of all it costs ¥38 ($6) for all you can eat including soft drinks. Definitely one of the best deals in town. See the special hot pot glossary in appendix B (p. 805) for more ingredients.

Fù Shuǐ Nán Lù 198. ✆ 0851/580-9118. ¥38 ($6). No credit cards. 11am–4am.

New Zealand Western Restaurant (Niǔxīlán Xīcāntīng) WESTERN/ASIAN If you don't want to pay hotel prices for your Western food, this pleasant restaurant delivers the goods at reasonable prices.

Ruìjīn Běi Lù (opposite Guìyáng Dàshà). ✆ 0851/651-2086. Main courses ¥20–¥45 ($2.50–$5.60). No credit cards. 10:30am–midnight.

SHOPPING

You're better off buying minority handicrafts in the outlying villages, but in a pinch, **Cuìwēi Yuán** on the south side of the Nánmíng River has shops selling beautiful but pricey batiks and Miáo and Dòng embroidery. Guìzhōu is home to China's most famous alcohol, Maotai, an appallingly awful 106-proof liquor that most foreigners can take only in extremely small or extremely large quantities.

SIDE TRIPS FROM GUÌYÁNG

A new highway between Guìyáng and the Huángguǒshù Falls enables visitors to make the trip in a day. Those short on time would do well to hire a private car, which your hotel or, in a pinch, CITS, can help arrange. *Note:* Please turn to appendix A for Chinese translations of key locations below.

HUÁNGGUǑSHÙ PÙBÙ (HUÁNGGUǑSHÙ FALLS) ✿

Guìzhōu's premier attraction, and Asia's largest waterfall, is located 150km (90 miles) and just over 2 hours on the highway southwest of Guìyáng. Many foreigners have reported being underwhelmed by the falls (named for the indigenous *huángguǒshù* or yellow fruit tree), possibly because they visited during the dry season (Nov–Apr), when the usual torrents are reduced to a mere trickle. Current rumors suggest that authorities plan to recycle the water in order to make this a year-round attraction. From May to October, the thundering falls can be heard for miles "like a thousand horses galloping," or so it says in the local guide book.

Fed by the Báishuǐ River (Báishuǐ Hé), the main waterfall spans 81m (266 ft.) and plunges down a precipitous 74m (243 ft.) into **Rhinoceros Pool.** The **Water Curtain Cave,** with a separate admission fee of ¥10 ($1.25), is a 100m-long (328-ft.) walkway behind the falls. It promises a wet backstage view of the cascades, especially in the rainy season. There are three entrances to the falls: just south of Huángguǒshù town, next to the Huángguǒshù Bīnguǎn, and next to the cable car. Admission to the falls is ¥40 ($5) February to October and ¥35 ($4.30) at other times.

During the rainy season, other falls to visit include **Dǒubōtáng Pùbù** (about 1km/⅔ mile upstream from the main falls) and **Luósītān Pùbù** (about 1km/⅔ mile downstream). The latest attraction for Chinese tourists is **Tiānxīng Qiáo Jǐngqū (Heavenly Star Bridge Scenic Area;** ¥30/$3.75; ¥25/$3 Nov–Jan) about 8km (5 miles) below the main falls. Highlights include a large cave full of the usual karst formations, a wonderful tableau of stepping stones rising from the water, and a waterfall. It's nice, if you can explore away from the crowds.

The falls are very well lit in the evenings, which makes an overnight stay worthwhile to go with the rainbows that you saw during the day. If you want to spend the night, the three-star **Xīn Huángguǒshù Bīnguǎn** (© **0853/359-2110**) offers the nicest accommodations and a Chinese restaurant. Up a driveway off the main road south of the village, the hotel has large, bright, and comfortable standard rooms with sparkling new bathrooms (shower only) for ¥480 ($60).

LÓNGGŌNG DÒNG (DRAGON PALACE CAVES)

About 132km (79 miles) west of Guìyáng is a string of 90 karst caves that stretch for over 15km (9 miles) through some 20 hills. At present, only 840m (2,755 ft.) of the main **Dragon Palace Cave** (¥50/$6.25; open 8am–6:30pm/5:30pm in winter) is open to the public. Rowboats take visitors through five chambers of colorfully lit, wonderfully weird karst formations, as tacky Muzak plays in the background. When the water levels are low, you'll have to return by boat, but during the rainy season, visitors can climb stone ladders in the last chamber to Tiger's Den, then slowly meander back to the entrance through a stone forest park. Private car hire or an organized tour from Guìyáng are the most convenient ways to visit.

MINORITY VILLAGES

The area southwest of Guìyáng around Ānshùn is home to the **Bouyi,** one of the original peoples of southwest China, who number around 2.5 million today. Related to the Zhuàng, the poorer Bouyi are skilled stonemasons, forced by the rocky karst terrain to build entire hillside villages out of stone. One such village worth visiting is **Shítou Zhài (Stone Village)** ⊛ where, not surprisingly, all the walls, bridges, roads, and houses are made of stone. Home to about 200 households, the village sits along the river Báishuǐ Hé and is surrounded by pretty green paddies. You can pick up some of the Bouyi's famous batik here, since everyone seems to have a batik workshop in their house. Discerning buyers should look for hyperrealistic and even erotic motifs. Shítou Zhài is off the main highway about 15km (9 miles) beyond the Lónggōng turnoff and

5km (3 miles) before Huángguǒshù. Watch for the turnoff and travel another kilometer or so along the dirt road to the village.

About 60km (40 miles) west of Guìyáng, off the main highway between Guìyáng and Ānshùn, the intriguing Míng dynasty village of **Tiānlóng Túnbǎo** ✿✿ (¥20/ $2.50; open 8:30am–7pm) makes for an interesting visit despite it being a tour-group magnet. Tiānlóng Túnbǎo's almost 6,500 inhabitants are descendants of the Hàn Chinese soldiers who were sent to the southwest in 1381 by the first Míng Hóngwǔ emperor. Calling themselves *Lǎo Hàn* (Old Hàn), the villagers regard themselves as a quasi-minority for having retained many of the Míng dynasty Hàn Chinese ways for the last 6 centuries, in particular the women's dress and hairstyles and the dialect they speak. Villagers also perform their own unique brand of opera known as *dì xì* (ground or open-air opera), so named because it's performed not on a stage but on the ground, with the audience standing on surrounding elevated spots to get better views. As with most buildings in the area, the houses in Tiānlóng are also made of stone and have low entrances. The village entrance fee includes a Chinese-language tour of the various ancestral halls and residences in this labyrinthine village.

4 Kǎilǐ & the Miáo & Dòng Autonomous Prefecture

Guìzhōu Province, 184km (110 miles) E of Guìyáng

As the capital of the Qián Dōngnán Autonomous Prefecture of the Miáo and Dòng nationalities in eastern Guìzhōu, Kǎilǐ is the gateway to some of the most fascinating minority villages you're likely to encounter in China. About 65% of the prefecture's population is Miáo, clustered to the east and northeast of Kǎilǐ. The Dòng are to the southeast. This entire region hosts more than 100 festivals (see chart on p. 586) each year, with the greatest concentration around February/March and October/November, making these excellent months to visit. Be warned that travel around the Miáo areas can be difficult due to its narrow, winding roads, but this is often light-years ahead of traveling through some of the Dòng region's backwaters, where a farmer's truck or your own feet might be the only means of navigating pothole-ridden mud paths. In truth, half the fun of traveling in this part of the country is getting there in the first place, so bring your sense of adventure and don't forget the seat cushion. *Note:* Please turn to appendix A for Chinese translations of key locations in this section.

ESSENTIALS

GETTING THERE   Traveling by **train** to Guìyáng (3½ hr.) has become less popular now that buses can whisk travelers there in 2 hours. The faster trains leave Kǎilǐ in the middle of the night, though there's a 10am train (K192) that gets in at 1:51pm and a 4:10pm train (K79) that gets in at 7:47pm. Tickets (hard seats only) can be bought at a counter inside the **Bank of China** at Běijīng Dōng Lù 9–11 (© 0855/ 822-1065; open 8:30am–noon and 2–5:30pm). A taxi ride to town from the **railway station** (© 0855/381-2222) costs ¥10 ($1.25). For destinations farther afield like Kūnmíng (the T61 train departs at 11:59pm and arrives in Kūnmíng at 3:17pm), purchase your tickets in Guìyáng if you want anything more than a hard seat.

From the **bus station** at Wénhuá Běi Lù (© 0855/823-8035), **buses** run to Guìyáng (2 hr.; ¥30–¥35/$3.75–$4.50) every half-hour from 6am to 7:15pm; to Róng Jiāng (6 hr.; ¥28–¥35/$3.50–$4.50) from 6:40am to 3pm; to Cóng Jiāng (9 hr.; ¥45–¥55/$5.50–$6.80) at 6:50am, 8am, and 9am; to Léishān (1 hr.; ¥8/$1) every

The Miáo

The Miáo, also called Hmong, trace their history back 4,000 years to what is now the Yellow River area in central China. As the first Chinese dynasty (221–207 B.C.) came into being and the Chinese empire expanded, the Miáo were driven into the outlying mountain regions. The subsequent southwesterly migration splintered the Miáo into different subgroups with their own dialects, dress, and customs, making them one of the most diversified ethnic groups in China. Black, Red, White, Long-Horned, Flowery, Mountain, and Long-Skirt Miáo are just some names that the Hàn Chinese gave to the Miáo, based on their appearance or locale. Those who continued their southerly migration into Laos, Myanmar, Thailand, and Vietnam are generally known as Hmong. Today there are about eight million Hmong worldwide.

Miáo festivals such as the Miáo New Year, the Sisters' Meal Festival (Zǐmèifàn Jié), and the Lúshēng Festival (dates vary by village) are occasions for young men and women to socialize and find marriage partners. Traditional Hàn Chinese consider attracting attention invites misfortune The events are marked by dancing, the playing of *lúshēng* (a musical instrument made of pipes), buffalo fighting (not as bad as you might imagine), and horse racing. If at all possible, time your visit during one of these occasions. The Miáo are generally very hospitable and will greet visitors with cups of locally brewed rice wine, the ultimate sign of respect from some of the hardiest drinkers around.

half-hour from 7am to 5:30pm; to Tái Jiāng (1 hr.; ¥8/$1) every 40 minutes from 8:30am to 6pm; and to Shídòng (2½ hr.; ¥15/$2) from 8am to 2:50pm.

GETTING AROUND   **Taxis** charge ¥4 (50¢) for in-town destinations, but ¥5 (65¢) if you catch one inside the bus station. Add an additional ¥1 (15¢) to all fares from midnight to 7am. **Bus** no. 2 makes a loop from the railway station in the north down past the long-distance bus station on Wénhuà Běi Lù to the main traffic circle on Běijīng Lù and then down Zhàoshān Nán Lù to the museum, before it returns to the railway station. The bus fare is ¥.50 (5¢).

TOURS & GUIDES   **CITS,** at Yíngpán Dōng Lù 53 (© **0855/822-2506;** www. qdncits.com; open Mon–Fri 9am–6pm) can customize private trips to the Miáo and Dòng regions, especially if you're looking to explore remote villages, but none of it comes cheap. Rates start at around ¥800 ($100) a day for a guide and driver. Bargain hard. The office's top English-speaking guide, the friendly Mr. Lǐ Màoqīng, can answer questions regarding nearby sights.

FAST FACTS
Banks, Foreign Exchange & ATMs   The main branch of the **Bank of China** is at Zhàoshān Nán Lù 6 (open Mon–Fri, 8am–noon and 2:30–6:30pm/2–6pm in winter).

Internet Access   The **Téngxùn Wǎngbā** at the intersection of Běijīng Dōng Lù and Wénhuà Lù (look for the green sign) charges ¥2 (25¢) an hour. Dial-up is © **163.**

Post Office The post office (open 8am–6:30pm/6pm Oct–Apr) is at Běijīng Dōng Lù 1.

Visa Extension The **PSB** is at Yǒnglè Lù 26 (© **0855/853-6113;** open Mon–Fri, 8.30–11:30am and 2–5:30pm). Allow 5 working days.

SEEING THE SIGHTS

Kǎilǐ's highlights are undoubtedly in the villages outside of town. One exception is its **Sunday Market,** where minorities from nearby villages sell all manner of goods around Xīmén Jiē and surrounding side streets. Water buffalo can often go for under ¥500 ($63) but a smarter and more portable might be an item of traditional costume. Minority girls learn to embroider at the same time that they learn to read and write and a festival costume may take up to 5 years' continuous work. The **Minorities Museum (Zhōu Mínzú Bówùguǎn),** at Guǎngchǎng Lù 5; ¥10/$1.25; open 9am–5pm) in the southern part of town, is mildly interesting, with fairly comprehensive if musty displays on the costumes, artifacts, musical instruments, and traditional houses of the Miáo and the Dòng. More curious is the fact that the museum is on the third floor of a forlorn furniture store.

WHERE TO STAY

Guótài Dàjiŭdiàn This three-star hotel right in the center of town is the nicest place to stay in Kǎilǐ and currently gets all the foreign tour groups. Guest rooms are nothing special but are spacious and clean and come with large, comfortable beds and reasonably well-kept furniture. Bathrooms are clean. The staff is efficient and even smiles occasionally.

Běijīng Dōng Lù 6. © **0855/826-9888.** Fax 0855/826-9818. 73 units. ¥258–¥288 ($32–$36) standard room; ¥380–¥880 ($47–$110) suite. 20% discounts. No credit cards. **Amenities:** Restaurant; bar; concierge; shopping arcade; salon; room service; laundry. In room: A/C, TV.

Kǎilǐ Lántiān Dàjiŭdiàn Depressingly old and decrepit on the outside, this hotel in the center of town has surprisingly spacious and comfortable rooms. The ¥218 ($27) rooms are so large they come with a whole living-room set. Beds are a little small but firm. Some of the bathrooms could use a new grout job but are otherwise acceptably clean. Get a room as far away from the sleazy nightclub on the fourth floor as possible.

Běijīng Xī Lù 1. © **0855/827-5980.** Fax 0855/823-4699. 56 units. ¥168–¥218 ($21–$27) standard room; ¥380 ($47) suite. No credit cards. **Amenities:** Restaurant; bar; concierge; room service; laundry. In room: A/C, TV.

WHERE TO DINE

Hotels still offer the best dining options, but restaurants serving a variety of Chinese cuisine are popping up along **Shāngmào Jiē** in the newly developing southern part of town. These spots are geared toward locals, so don't expect English menus. But do venture here if you're tired of hotel food . . . just make sure you recognize the characters for dog meat (*gǒuròu*) if that's not something you're game for.

A lively **night market** in the alley right next to the Guótài Hotel offers barbecue, noodles, dumplings (*jiǎozi*), meat buns (*bāozi*), and fresh fruit. One of the best **bakeries** in town is a 5-minute walk south of the bus station on Wénhuà Běi Lù. It sells pastries, cakes, hot coffee (albeit of the instant variety), teas, juices, and also dumplings (*shuǐjiǎo*).

The closest approximation to Western food can be found at **Màidéshì,** located at Zhāoshān Běi Lù 2, second floor, just north of the post office. It serves fried chicken, chicken burgers, and fries.

AROUND KĂILĬ

If you're short on time, several Miáo villages around Kǎilǐ can comfortably be visited, alone or in combination, as day trips. One of the most popular is **Lángdé** ✿, a lovely traditional Miáo village of about 600 people (all surnamed Chén), located 31km (19 miles) and a 45-minute ride south of Kǎilǐ. Dating from the late Yuán/early Míng dynasty, the village is divided into two sections. If your visit coincides with a tour group's, you may be greeted with songs and rice wine and treated to a bronze-drum dance performance in the upper village square. With its water wheels and wooden stilt houses made from local cedar, the village is a lovely stroll, and the women vendors at the village entrance actually carry some beautiful embroidery amid the rest of their junk. To get there, take the Léishān-bound bus for ¥6 (75¢) and ask to be let off at Lángdé. From the main road, it's still around a 2km (1¼ miles) walk along the Bālā River, through a number of smaller hamlets into the upper village.

Fifteen kilometers (9 miles) southwest of Kǎilǐ, the small village of **Zhōuxī** is host to a grand *lúshēng* festival every year around the 20th day of the first lunar month, when melodious pipes resound through a sea of silver headdresses. To reach Zhōuxī, take a minivan taxi for ¥3 to ¥4 (40¢–50¢) from the corner of Huánchéng Xī Lù and Běijīng Xī Lù.

About 19km (11 miles) northwest of Kǎilǐ and surrounded by tree-covered hills, the village of **Mátáng** ✿✿ is home to about 400 members of the **Géjiā** people (the other Géjiā stronghold is in **Huángpíng Village**). Once lumped in with the Miáo, the Géjiā were formally recognized only in 1993. Unlike the Miáo, who are known to have strong constitutions, the Géjiā toast with rice, not wine. Another distinguishing custom is the Cáiqíng dance (Cáiqíng Wǔ), with its characteristic stomping. The harder the stomp, the deeper the love between the man and the woman. Known for their batik and embroidery, the Mátáng Géjiā are friendly and hospitable. To get here, take a minivan taxi for ¥3 (40¢) or a Yúdòng-bound minibus for ¥2 (25¢) from the corner of Huánchéng Xī Lù and Běijīng Xī Lù. Ask to be dropped off at Mátáng; it's a 15-minute walk to the village. An excellent day trip would take in Lángdé in the morning, and Mátáng in the afternoon.

XĪ JIĀNG ✿✿

Located about 75km (45 miles) southeast of Kǎilǐ in Léishān County, Xī Jiāng is the largest Miáo village in China, with about 1,000 households. Nestled in a valley surrounded by lush bamboo forests, the village has hundreds of dark brown wooden stilt houses built into the side of a hill and, unfortunately for purists, a white concrete building (Xī Jiāng's new school) smack in the middle of it all. Xī Jiāng hosts a massive celebration during the **Miáo New Year Festival** in the 10th lunar month with dances,

---

Tips Local Recipes Best Avoided

Curses, evil eyes, and other forms of witchcraft are still common in these primitive surroundings. One popular concoction to look out for is "gu," a slow-acting poison. To create it, a selection of scorpions, lizards, and snakes are dropped into a jar without any food so that they devour each other. Next, the body of the lone survivor, supposedly gorged with poison, is then crushed to make a mysterious toxin that will kill only the unrepentant.

bullfights, *lúshēng* competitions, and other festivities, most clustered around the basketball court. On the sixth day of the sixth lunar month (usually July or Aug), the **New Rice Tasting Festival** is another raucous celebration. **Market** days in Xī Jiāng (every 7 days for the large market, every 5 days for a smaller market) are also very colorful, as villagers hawk everything from fish to fake hair.

Xī Jiāng can be visited as a day trip with private car hire or overnight if you travel by bus. From Kăilĭ, there are very infrequent direct buses. More reliable is the bus to Léishān (1 hr.; ¥8/$1); from there, transfer to a bus for Xī Jiāng (1 hr.; ¥7/90¢).

The best option among the town's very basic accommodations is the relatively new, relatively clean **Cángzhēn Lóu** (© 0855/334-8068), located down the main street from the old and decrepit Zhèngfǔ Zhāodàisuǒ (Government Guesthouse). It has 30 beds at ¥10 ($1.25) each, in different room combinations with bare concrete floors and communal showers and toilets.

TÁI JIĀNG & FĂNPÁI ⚐

This ordinarily uninspiring town of Tái Jiāng, dotted with more nondescript white-tiled buildings than with the traditional black-and-brown Miáo houses, comes alive during two big Miáo festivals: the Dragon Lantern Festival halfway through the first lunar month, and the Sisters' Meal Festival in the middle of the third lunar month. The town also has a **Wénchāng Gōng** (¥10/$1.25), a former school and Confucian hall built by the most famous Miáo resistance leader, Zhāng Xiùméi, who fought Qīng dynasty troops for 18 years in the mid–19th century. Today, there's a Miáo **embroidery museum** on the premises, which is usually closed unless a visitor shows up and pounds on the door. The town hosts a large and fairly interesting **market** every 6 days.

Tái Jiāng can also be used as a gateway to **Fănpái,** a traditional Miáo village hidden high in the hills above Tái Jiāng, seemingly forgotten by time. The ride to Fănpái can be wonderfully atmospheric, especially on any of Guìzhōu's misty, moody days. In the village, wander around the traditional wooden dwellings or go for a hike in the surrounding hills and watch the villagers work their terrace fields. Minibuses leave every hour for Fănpái (1 hr.; ¥4/50¢) from the main street just before the T-junction.

The best place to stay in Tái Jiāng is **Miáojiāng Bīnguǎn** (© 0855/532-6028) on the road into town. Rooms for ¥70 ($8.75) are basic but clean and have air-conditioning, TV, and 24-hour hot water, but no phone.

The ride from Tái Jiāng to Shídòng (below) takes in some beautiful mountain scenery. Notoriously unreliable buses for Shídòng (2–2½ hr.; ¥7/90¢) depart from the street left of the T-junction hourly from 6 to 11am.

SHĬDÒNG ⚐

About 94km (56 miles) northeast of Kăilĭ, this little Miáo village along the banks of the Qīngshuǐ River hosts two big festivals. The 3-day **Lóngzhōu Jié (Dragon Boat Festival),** in the middle of the fifth lunar month, features dragon boats made from hollowed-out tree trunks that are decorated with a dragon's head and hold up to 30 rowers. Each of the nearby villages enters a boat in the race. This is certainly the place to see **Zǐmèifàn Jié (Sisters' Meal Festival),** during the fourth lunar month, which celebrated with *lúshēng* dances, antiphonal singing, and plenty of opportunities for young Miáo women, gorgeously bedecked with elaborate silver headdresses, to socialize with erstwhile suitors. Several months before the festival, many Shídòng households will be engaged in making silver ornaments for the festival. Silver aficionados may wish to visit here at any time, as Shídòng (in particular the neighboring hamlet

---

Fun Fact **Sisters' Rice Speaks to Suitors**

Sisters' Meal rice is stained bright colors using wild berries and is then wrapped in an indigo cloth, together with a small item that conveys a message. A pair of chopsticks signifies acceptance for a marriage proposal, while a single stick denotes refusal. Garlic shoots or pepper mean "Please look elsewhere," while pine needles remind a suitor that a girl's heart can sometimes be won with satin or silk.

---

of Tánglóng) is renowned for excellent-quality silver. Traditional Chinese consider that attracting attention invites misfortune, but not the Miáo, some of these girls will wear more than 20 kilograms (44 lb.) of silver, engraved, embossed, stippled, and assembled into set pieces. While these ornaments are mostly for private use, it's possible to purchase pieces from enterprising villagers. Ask around.

For now, visit Shídòng as a day trip from Kǎilǐ; local accommodations would make sleeping in one of those dragon boats seem like a night at the Ritz. Return buses to Kǎilǐ stop running around 2pm.

DÒNG REGION

The southeastern part of Guìzhōu is squarely Dòng territory, with over 400 Dòng roofed bridges in Lípíng, Róng Jiāng, and Cóng Jiāng counties. On the southeastern border across from Guǎngxī Province, Zhàoxìng is the largest Dòng village, while the area around Róng Jiāng and Cóng Jiāng is dotted with smaller villages awaiting discovery.

RÓNG JIĀNG & CÓNG JIĀNG

The only reason to stay in Róng Jiāng is its famous and incredibly colorful **Sunday Market,** which spills onto several streets east of the main road. Unless you want to explore the Dòng villages around here, many travelers heading south from Kǎilǐ end up overnighting or changing buses in Cóng Jiāng, which serves as more of a gateway to both Zhàoxìng in the east and Guǎngxī Province in the south.

Róng Jiāng
173km (104 miles) SE of Kǎilǐ

GETTING THERE From the **Main Bus Station (Qìchēzhàn)** in the north of town, **buses,** including minibuses, large air-conditioned buses, and sleepers, run to Kǎilǐ (6–7 hr.; ¥28–¥35/$3.50–$4.50) from 6:30am to 4pm; and to Cóng Jiāng (3 hr.; ¥15/$1.90) from 6:40am to 4:30pm.

WHERE TO STAY & DINE The best place to stay is the **Róng Jiāng Bīnguǎn** at Gǔzhōu Zhōng Lù 47 (© **0855/662-4188;** fax 0855/662-4223), which has basic but comfortable enough standard rooms for ¥160 ($20) with private bathrooms. There's also a restaurant.

Cóng Jiāng
79km (47 miles) SE of Róng Jiāng, 252km (151 miles) SE of Kǎilǐ

Like Róng Jiāng, there's little to recommend Cóng Jiāng itself, but about 7km (4 miles) before the town, on the road from Róng Jiāng, the unusual village of **Bāshā** ★★ makes for a fascinating visit. Although recognized as members of the Miáo, the Bāshā Miáo are practically a tribe unto themselves. They cling to unique traditions such as the men's *hugun* hairstyle, which is created by shaving off all the hair except for what grows on the crown, and coiling what's left into a topknot never to be cut, as hair is considered the lifeline given by ancestors. Wandering through the village, you can hear the pounding of indigo grass and dyed cloth and see swags of glutinous rice hanging on giant racks to dry. Barefoot boys play hide-and-seek, and dogs bark at approaching visitors while pigs snort and wallow deeper in the mud. Living a simple and extremely poor existence, the Bāshā are understandably wary of cadres of tourists tramping through their village. You can only hope that the entrance fees of ¥10 ($1.25) for foreigners and ¥6 (75¢) for Chinese are actually going to the village and not padding some tourist official's pockets. If you're visiting on your own, tread softly and sensitively.

As you leave Cóng Jiāng in the direction of Zhàoxìng, cutting a dashing sight on the left are the three drum towers of **Gāozēng** village. Two of the drum towers are the tallest in the region, at 17 stories and almost 30m (98 ft.) high. The road between Cóng Jiāng and Zhàoxìng offers some of the most picturesque pastoral scenes of terrace fields cut into gently rolling hills.

GETTING THERE   From the **Cóng Jiāng Bus Station (Qìchēzhàn; ⓒ 0855/ 641-3957)** on the eastern side of the river, **buses** run to Róng Jiāng (3 hr.; ¥15/$2) every hour from 7am to 5:20pm; to Kāilĭ (10 hr.; ¥53/$6.60) at 6am, 8am, and 9:20am; and to Sān Jiāng in Guǎngxī Province (3½–4 hr.; ¥15/$2), with nine departures from 6:30am to 3:30pm via Bāluó and Fùlù. To get to Zhàoxìng, take a Lípíng-bound bus for ¥20 ($2.50) from 6:30am to 1:40pm and change at Pílín. You can also

The Dòng

Accounts differ as to the origins of the Dòng people—some say they came from the Yángzǐ River (Cháng Jiāng) region, and others argue that they migrated north from Thailand—but now they are firmly planted in southeast Guìzhōu (2.5 million Dòng residents) and in northeast Guǎngxī Province, where they gravitate toward lush river valleys.

Famed for their (fir) wooden architecture, Dòng villages typically have a Wind and Rain Bridge *(fēngyǔ qiáo)*, which serves not only as a meeting place for villagers but to ward off inauspicious energies from the village. Each village also has one or several drum towers *(gǔlóu)*, each built for a clan with the same surname.

In addition to the many Hàn festivals such as Spring Festival and Festival of the Ghosts, the primarily animist Dòng celebrate many of their own, including one of the biggest, Sānyuèsān, held on the third day of the third lunar month and celebrated with fireworks, dances, sporting competitions, bullfights, and abundant feasting. The Tàiguānrén Festival, which coincides with the Hàn Spring Festival, has visitors from neighboring villages dressed up as bandits, goblins, and strange animals, while a man dressed as a government official *(guānrén)* parades through town dispensing money as a gift to the village. The Firecracker Festival (Huāpào), celebrated in Guǎngxī's Sān Jiāng on the third day of the second month, has participants competing to catch an iron ring that's been blasted out of a small cannon.

change at Luóxiáng, but connecting buses are infrequent; at press time, the dirt road (if it can be called that) between Luóxiáng and Zhàoxìng consisted a series of never-ending potholes.

WHERE TO STAY & DINE The newest place to stay is the **Yuèliang Shān Bīnguǎn** on Jiāng Dōngnán Lù (© **0855/641-4888**), on the eastern side of the river just next to the bus station. Standard rooms with air-conditioning, TV, phone, and 24-hour hot water cost ¥120 ($15). The hotel also has a Chinese restaurant. No English is spoken. Across from the bus station are food stalls that serve basic stir-fries (point to the vegetables you want and say *"chǎo ròu"* if you want them with pork) and noodles to get you through the night. Off the main street west of the river is a small **night market** of barbecue stalls, north of the post office.

ZHÀOXÌNG ✰✰✰

Zhàoxìng, the biggest Dòng village in China with a population of 3,500 people (all surnamed Lù!), is one of those places where the rewards that await you are in direct proportion to the difficulty in getting there. And it is very difficult to get to Zhàoxìng. With a history of over 700 years, this picturesque village of fishponds and rice paddies is extremely welcoming (but largely free of tourists) and boasts the single greatest collection of drum towers (five) in China, ranging from seven to thirteen stories high. With many settlements around the area ripe for exploration, there's enough to occupy you for at least a couple of days; allow an equal amount of time to get here and away. Though Zhàoxìng can be approached from both Kǎilǐ and Sān Jiāng in Guǎngxī Province, the latter has more direct buses.

GETTING THERE The most hassle-free way to get to Zhàoxìng is by private car/taxi hire. From Sān Jiāng in Guǎngxī Province, the 3-hour-plus ride will run between ¥200 and ¥300 ($25–$38) depending on your bargaining powers. The most reliable public bus leaves at 6:50am, costs ¥14 ($1.60), and takes about 4 hours. Unfortunately much of the road is currently under construction so it is probably better to allow 6 hours and perhaps bring a face mask to filter out the incredible amounts of dust. From Zhàoxìng to Sān Jiāng by bus (4–4½ hr.), an early-morning bus departs at 7:30am and another less reliable bus around 9:30am. The quickest way to Kǎilǐ (10 hr.) is to take the 7am bus to Lìpíng and transfer to the 11:40am bus to Kǎilǐ. At press time, there were no direct buses to Cóng Jiāng. The best option is to take a bus to Pílín (2½ hr.), then transfer to a Cóng Jiāng bus that's coming from Lípíng (3 hr.). Alternatively, some folks have hiked an hour to Luóxiáng; or they have taken a local farmer's truck for ¥30 ($3.75) along a wretched pothole-riddled dirt road and transferred to a Cóng Jiāng-bound (¥11/$1.40) bus, which runs every half-hour to hour from 7:30am to around 4pm.

Exploring the Village & Beyond

The main attraction is the village itself, which is divided into five sections organized by clan, each with its own all-wooden **drum tower, wind and rain bridge,** and **theater stage.** Ranging from 7 to 13 stories (the tallest is 25m/82 ft. high), the drum towers have all been rebuilt since they were destroyed by Red Guards during the Cultural Revolution (1966–76). Desperately in need of a fresh coat of paint, the structures are still impressive and continue to play host to large events like weddings, festivals, and funerals, and to less-momentous occasions like a villager's afternoon nap. The rest of the place is filled with photo ops of villagers dyeing cloth, sifting rice, weaving baskets, and building houses.

There are also several villages around Zhàoxìng worth visiting. Three kilometers (2 miles) or an hour's invigorating climb to the south, the village of **Jìtáng** ⚔ has three well-preserved original drum towers that escaped destruction during the Cultural Revolution. The largest, in the middle of the village square, has 11 tiers of eaves and is held up by 16 original stone pedestals. Wander this lovely village, where bales of indigo cloth hang from beautiful traditional wooden houses and friendly children try their Chinese (usually limited to *"nǐhǎo"* meaning "hello") on you. To get there, follow the main street in the direction of Luóxiáng and bear left as the road winds uphill. The village of **Táng'ān** about 4km (2½ miles) to the southeast has some stone terraces worth hiking out to see if you have time.

Where to Stay & Dine

The nicest and most popular place to stay is the all-wooden **Wénhuàzhàn Zhāodàisuǒ** right in the center of town off the main road, just under 50m (164 ft.) from the informal bus stop. The spartan rooms come with nothing more than beds and fans but are otherwise clean, as are the communal showers and toilets. A bed costs ¥20 ($2.50) and a standard room ¥50 ($6.25). The owners don't speak much English but are very friendly and can cook Chinese and Dòng meals as well as pancakes for breakfast. Deeper inside the village, **Lulu's Homestay (Fēngqíng Lǚyóu Shèwài Mínjū Lǚguǎn; ☎ 0855/613-0112)** offers six rooms on the second level of the owner's (Lù Xīnfēng) house, but a new wooden guesthouse was being constructed next door at press time. The new rooms should be basic but clean, with beds averaging ¥20 to ¥25 ($2.50–$3) each. Mr. Lù's wife cooks delicious Dòng meals for ¥10 to ¥20 ($1.25–$2.50) per person, and instant coffee is available. Mr. Lù, with his smattering of English, often leads hikes in the surrounding hills.

Around Zhàoxìng

If you're traveling the road between Zhàoxìng and Sān Jiāng in Guǎngxī Province, you'll notice about 1½ hours south of Zhàoxìng at the hamlet of **Dìpíng** a three-tower **wind and rain bridge** stretching 56m (184 ft.) across the river. Guìzhōu's most impressive bridge of its kind, the structure was built as early as 1883. Keep your eyes peeled for a lovely set of four stamps issued in 1997, featuring the Dìpíng Bridge and three other splendid examples of Dòng architecture.

5 Kūnmíng ⚔

Yúnnán Province, 1,200km (744 miles) NW of Hong Kong, 450km (270 miles) SW of Guìyáng

As the capital of Yúnnán Province, Kūnmíng, also known as the "city of eternal spring," is one of the most pleasant and relaxed cities in China. Though it was founded over 2,000 years ago, the city did not gain prominence until it became the eastern capital of the Nánzhào Kingdom in the 8th century. By the time the Mongols swept through in 1274, Kūnmíng, or Yachi as it was then known, was enough of a flourishing town to have attracted the attention of Marco Polo, who described it as a "very great and noble" capital city. The city's bloodiest period occurred during the Qīng dynasty, with a series of Muslim rebellions. In the late 19th century, foreign influence appeared in the form of the French, who built a narrow-gauge rail line to Vietnam still in use today. During World War II, Kūnmíng played an important role as the terminus of a major supply line (the famous Burma Road) in the Allies' Asian theater of operations.

Kūnmíng

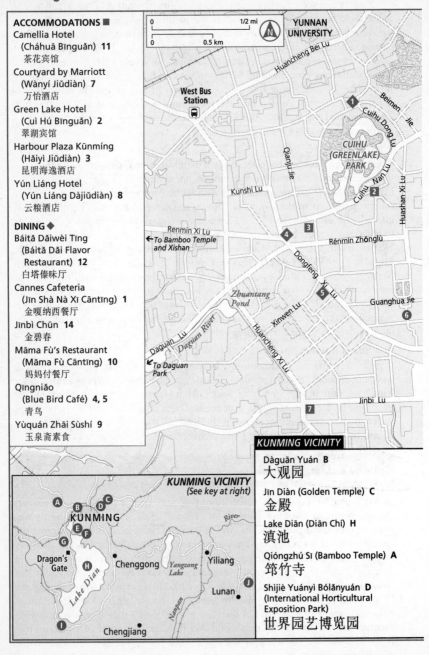

ACCOMMODATIONS ■

Camellia Hotel
(Cháhuā Bīnguǎn) **11**
茶花宾馆

Courtyard by Marriott
(Wànyí Jiǔdiàn) **7**
万怡酒店

Green Lake Hotel
(Cuì Hú Bīnguǎn) **2**
翠湖宾馆

Harbour Plaza Kūnmíng
(Hǎiyì Jiǔdiàn) **3**
昆明海逸酒店

Yún Liáng Hotel
(Yún Liáng Dàjiǔdiàn) **8**
云粮酒店

DINING ◆

Báitǎ Dǎiwèi Tīng
(Báitǎ Dǎi Flavor
Restaurant) **12**
白塔傣味厅

Cannes Cafeteria
(Jīn Shà Nà Xī Cāntīng) **1**
金嘎纳西餐厅

Jīnbì Chūn **14**
金碧春

Māma Fù's Restaurant
(Māma Fù Cāntīng) **10**
妈妈付餐厅

Qīngniǎo
(Blue Bird Café) **4, 5**
青鸟

Yùquán Zhāi Sùshí **9**
玉泉斋素食

KUNMING VICINITY

Dàguān Yuán **B**
大观园

Jīn Diàn (Golden Temple) **C**
金殿

Lake Diān (Diān Chí) **H**
滇池

Qióngzhú Sì (Bamboo Temple) **A**
筇竹寺

Shìjiè Yuányì Bólǎnyuán **D**
(International Horticultural
Exposition Park)
世界园艺博览园

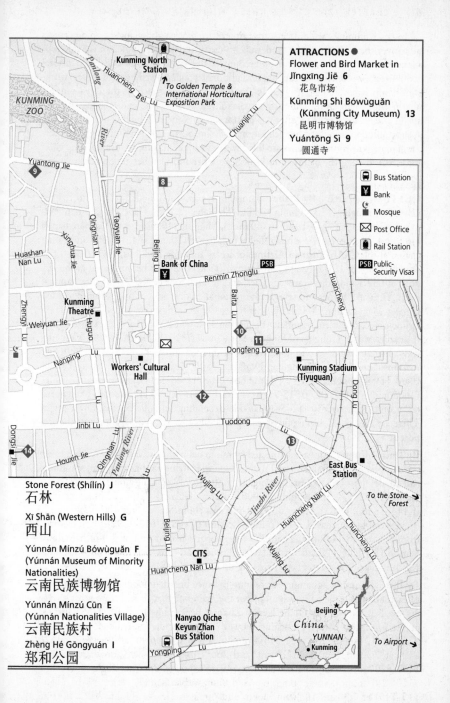

ATTRACTIONS ●

Flower and Bird Market in
Jīngxīng Jiē **6**
花鸟市场

Kūnmíng Shì Bówùguǎn
(Kūnmíng City Museum) **13**
昆明市博物馆

Yuántōng Sì **9**
圆通寺

🚌 Bus Station

¥ Bank

★ Mosque

✉ Post Office

🚉 Rail Station

PSB Public-
Security Visas

KUNMING ZOO

Kunming North Station

To Golden Temple &
International Horticultural
Exposition Park

Yuantong Jie ⑨

⑧

Huancheng Bei Lu

Panlong River

Chuanjin Lu

Qingnian Lu

Taoyuan Jie

Xinghua Jie

Huashan Nan Lu

Beijing Lu

Bank of China ¥

Renmin Zhonglu

PSB

Baita Lu

Huancheng

Zhengyi Lu

Weiyuan Jie

Kunming Theatre

Huguo Lu

Nanping Lu

⑩

⑪

Dongfeng Dong Lu

Kunming Stadium
(Tiyuguan)

Workers' Cultural Hall

⑫

Jinbi Lu

Qingnian Lu

Panlong River

Tuodong

⑬

Dong Lu

East Bus Station

To the Stone Forest

Dongsi Jie ⑭

Houxin Jie

Beijing Lu

Wujing Lu

Jinzhi River

Huancheng Nan Lu

Chuncheng Lù

Stone Forest (Shílín) J
石林

Xī Shān (Western Hills) G
西山

Yúnnán Mínzú Bówùguǎn F
(Yúnnán Museum of Minority
Nationalities)
云南民族博物馆

Yúnnán Mínzú Cūn E
(Yúnnán Nationalities Village)
云南民族村

Zhèng Hé Gōngyuán I
郑和公园

CITS

Huancheng Nan Lu

Wujing Lu

Nanyao Qiche
Keyun Zhàn
Bus Station

Yongping Lu

Beijing
★

China

YUNNAN

Kunming

To Airport

619

Today, Kūnmíng's wide streets, towering office blocks, and giant shopping centers all convey the impression of a modern, 21st-century city. Sadly, much of the development of recent years, most of it on account of the 1999 International Horticultural Exhibition, has come at the expense of traditional wooden dwellings and artisan workshops, which have all been razed in the process, taking much of the city's original charm with them. Still, Kūnmíng remains a highly enjoyable and relaxing place to spend a few days even if its offerings do not match some of Yúnnán's other treasures. A subtropical location and high elevation (1,864m/6,213 ft.) give Kūnmíng a temperate climate year-round. Its days are filled with sunshine, making almost any time good for a visit, though the balmy months of September and October are especially fine.

ESSENTIALS

GETTING THERE   By Plane   Kūnmíng is connected by daily flights to Běijīng (2½ hr.), Chéngdū (1 hr.), Guìlín (1½ hr.), Shànghǎi (2½ hr.), Dàlǐ (½ hr.), Lì Jiāng (40 min.), Xiānggélǐlā (1 hr.), Bǎoshān (40 min.), Mángshì (40 min.), and Xīshuāngbǎnnà (40 min.). There are twice-weekly flights to Lhasa via Xiānggélǐlā. Tickets can be purchased at the **CAAC/Yúnnán Airlines** office at Tuòdōng Lù 28 (© **0871/316-4270** domestic, or 0871/312-1220 international). Tickets can also be purchased at the airport, at CITS and other travel agencies, and at hotel tour desks. On the international front, Yúnnán Airlines and several international carriers serve Hong Kong, Bangkok, Chiang Mai, Yangon, Mandalay, Vientiane, Osaka, Singapore, and Hanoi. Foreign airline offices include: Dragonair (Běijīng Lù 157; © 0871/356-2828); Lao Aviation (Camellia Hotel, Dōngfēng Dōng Lù 96; © 0871/316-3000, ext. 5166); Thai Airways (Běijīng Lù 98, second floor, King World Hotel annex; © 0871/351-2269); Silk Air/Singapore Airlines (Dōngfēng Dōng Lù 25; © 0871/315-7125), Japan Airlines (Bank Hotel, Qīngnián Lù 399; third floor © 0871/315-8111); and Vietnam Airlines (Tuòdōng Lù 80; © 0871/315-7175). The airport is 5km (3 miles) south of city center, a quick ¥15 to ¥30 ($2–$4) taxi ride depending on your destination in town. There are no CAAC airport buses, but public bus nos. 67 and 52 also serve the airport at ¥1 (15¢).

By Train   Kūnmíng is well connected by rail to many major Chinese cities, but these trips require several days and nights. Consider flying for longer distances. Trains run to Běijīng (T62, 42 hr.), Shànghǎi (K80, 46 hr.), Guǎngzhōu (1166, 31 hr.), Guìlín (K182, 17½ hr.), Nánníng (2006, 14½ hr.), Guìyáng (K156, 12 hr.), Chéngdū (K114, 18 hr.), Dàlǐ (K446 or K732, 8 hr.), and Shílín/Stone Forest (K440, 90 min.). Tickets can be purchased at the **railway station** (© **0871/612-2492**) south of town from 6:30am to 11:30pm. The 5933 train departs from Kūnmíng's North Railway Station (Běi Huǒchēzhàn) on Friday and Sunday at 4pm for Hékǒu (17 hr.), after which it continues on to Hanoi, arriving there at 8:10pm local time.

By Bus   Kūnmíng has a number of long-distance bus stations, all within 5 minutes of each other and the railway station, but the main one that should serve most travelers' needs is the **Nányáo Qìchē Kèyùn Zhàn** at Běijīng Lù 60 (© **0871/351-0617**), at the northwest corner of Běijīng Lù and Yǒngpíng Lù. From here, buses go to Xiàguān (17 buses; 5 hr.; ¥104/$13) from 7:30am to 7:30pm; to Lì Jiāng (9 hr.; ¥152/$19) at 7:30am, 9:30am, 11:30am, and 2pm); to Xiānggélǐlā/Zhōngdiàn (12 hr.; ¥162/$20) at 8:20am; to Ruìlì (16 hr.; ¥191/$24) at 3:30pm; to Jǐnghóng (16 hr.; ¥150/$19) at 2pm, 4pm, 6pm, 7pm, and 8pm; to Bǎoshān (7½–8 hr.; ¥116–¥150/$15–$19) at 7:30am, 10:30am, noon, and 6pm; to Hékǒu (11 hr.; ¥112/$14) at

9:45am; and to Jiànshuǐ (4½ hr.; ¥30–¥35/$3.75–$4.35) every half-hour from 7:20am to 9pm. A private bus company, **YNTAC** (© 0871/718-7225), also operates luxury, air-conditioned, nonsmoking buses from Kūnmíng to Xiàguān (5 hr.; ¥103/$13) at 8:30am, 9:30am, 10:30am, 1pm, 2:30pm, and 7pm; and to Lì Jiāng (8 hr.; ¥151/$19) at 8:30am, 9:30am, and 1pm. Buses leave from the Kūnmíng Tǐyùguǎn at Dōngfēng Dōng Lù 99. The **West Bus Station (Xiǎo Xī Zhàn)** at Rénmín Zhōng Lù just west of Dōngfēng Xī Lù, has buses that go to Kūnshān (1 hr.; ¥10/$1.25) every half-hour to hour from 7:30am to 6pm.

GETTING AROUND   Downtown sights can be toured on foot or by bike. If your hotel does not offer bike rental, the Camellia Hotel (see "Where to Stay," below) rents them for ¥2 (25¢) an hour or ¥15 ($1.90) for the day. For a choice of mountain bikes for rent visit **Fat Tyres Bike Shop** at Qiānjū Lù 61, off Cuì Hú Nán Lù (© 0871/530-1755).

Flagfall for Xiàlì and smaller **taxis** is ¥7 (85¢) for 3km (2 miles), then ¥1.60 (20¢) per kilometer until 10km (6 miles), when it goes up to ¥2.40 (30¢) per kilometer. From 10pm to 6am, the cost is ¥8.40 ($1.05) for 3km (2 miles), then ¥1.90 (25¢) per kilometer until 10km (6 miles), then ¥2.70 (35¢) per kilometer. Santana taxis cost ¥8 ($1) for 3km (2 miles) and ¥1.80 (25¢) per kilometer after that; from 10pm to 6am, flagfall is ¥9.60 ($1.20) for 3km (2 miles).

While many of the outlying sights such as the Bamboo Temple and Dragon's Gate can be reached most conveniently by taxi, public **buses** also travel most of these routes. Bus no. 52 runs from the airport to Dà Guān Yuán via the railway station. Bus no. 47 runs from the railway station to the International Horticultural Exposition Park, from where you can either take the cable car or bus no. 10 to the Golden Temple. Bus no. 44 goes from a block north of the railway station to the Yúnnán Nationalities Village. The fare for each bus is ¥1 (15¢).

CONSULATES   Laos   The **Laos consulate** (© 0871/317-6624) is in room 120 of the Camellia Hotel at Dōngfēng Dōng Lù 96 (open Mon–Fri 8:30am–11:30am and 1:30–4:30pm). Transit visas (5–7 days) and standard 15-day tourist visas (valid within 2 months of issue) can be issued in 3 working days (ordinary service) or by the next working day (express service). Fees vary from ¥270 to ¥378 ($33–$47) for ordinary service and from ¥400 to ¥505 ($50–$63) for express service. You cannot currently get a Laos visa at the border. Bring two photos and complete two application forms.

Myanmar   The **Myanmar consulate** (© 0871/316-3000, ext. 6225; fax 0871/317-6309) is located in room 225 of the Camellia Hotel (open Mon–Fri, 8:30am–noon and 1–2pm). Standard 28-day travel visas costing ¥285 ($35) and valid within 3 months of issue can be issued in 3 working days; for same-day service, expect to pay an extra ¥150 ($19). This visa is only good for flying into Yangon or Mandalay. For overland crossing at the Ruìlì border, see "Tours," below.

Thailand   The **Thai consulate** (© 0871/316-2033, ext. 62105; fax 0871/316-6891) is located on the grounds of the Kūnmíng Hotel at Dōngfēng Dōng Lù 50–52 (open Mon–Fri 9am–1:30pm). Note that travelers from most countries won't need Thai visas.

Vietnam   There is no Vietnamese consulate here, but you can apply for 30-day Vietnamese visas for ¥400 ($50) at the **Vietnam Airlines** office, Tuòdōng Lù 80 (© 0871/315-7175). Bring your passport and photo.

OUTDOOR ACTIVITIES Golfers can head to the **Spring City Golf and Lake Resort** located 48km (29 miles) southeast of Kūnmíng; it has a championship 18-hole golf course designed by Jack Nicklaus and another by Robert Trent Jones, Jr. Standard rooms at the five-star resort (© **0871/767-1188;** www.springcitygolf.com) cost ¥1,328 to ¥1,504 ($166–$188), while a round of golf will set you back ¥1,410 to ¥1,760 ($176–$220).

TOURS CITS at Huánchéng Nán Lù 285 (© **0871/353-5448;** fax 0871/316-9240; www.kmcits.com.cn; open Mon–Fri 8:30am–noon and 2–6pm) is often busy juggling international tour groups but can be very helpful with arranging accommodations, ongoing transportation, or customized tours throughout Yúnnán for individual travelers. The **Camellia Travel Service** on the ground floor of the Camellia Hotel at Dōngfēng Dōng Lù 96 is less helpful (© **0871/316-6388;** fax 0871/318-8949, Camellia@ynmail.com; open 8am–10pm). They can arrange travel to **Tibet** by plane (the price per person is inclusive of one-way plane ticket, Tibet Travel Permit, an English-speaking guide, insurance, and accommodations in Tibet for 3 days; call or write for fee) or overland by Land Cruiser from Zhōngdiàn (¥5,000/$625 per person inclusive of transportation, travel permit, and guide, subject to a minimum of four people). Note that travelers to Tibet are still required to join an "organized tour," but the group can consist of just one person (see p. 754 for more details).

For overland travel to **Myanmar** at the Ruìlì border, you will have to be accompanied all the way to Mandalay by an official travel agency–sponsored guide. Jenny in the travel agency (© **0871/316-0003**) in room 208 of the Camellia Hotel just before the Myanmar consulate can handle all the arrangements for you, including the visa. Expect to pay about ¥1,500 ($187) per person for a day trip as far as Lasio, more if you want to travel farther.

FAST FACTS

Banks, Foreign Exchange & ATMs The main branch of the **Bank of China** (open Mon–Fri 8:30am–noon and 2–5pm) is at Rénmín Dōng Lù 448. ATMs here accept international cards.

Internet Access Internet access is available at **China Telecom,** Dōngfēng Dōng Lù 12; open Mon–Fri 8:30am–5:30pm, Sat–Sun 9am–5:30pm; ¥5/60¢ per hour before 10am, ¥6/75¢ per hour otherwise). A ¥20 ($2.50) deposit is required. Dial-up is © **163.** Unfortunately there are no PCs at the library on Zhīchūn Jiē 37, but they do have an extensive section in English about Thailand if you plan on traveling there.

Post Office The main post office (open 8am–8pm) is at Dōngfēng Dōng Lù 14, and another (open 9am–8pm) is west of the railway station.

Visa Extensions The visa office is located at counter 57 of the **People's Service Center** of Kūnmíng Municipality (Kūnmíng Shìzhèngfǔ Biànmín Zhōngxīn), Rénmín Dōng Lù 196 (© **0871/319-6540;** open Mon–Fri 8:30–11:30am and 1–5:30pm).

EXPLORING KŪNMÍNG

Cuì Hú (Green Lake) ✦ Kūnmíng's nicest park is a pleasant retreat from the bustling city even though it can get quite crowded on weekends. Bridges and pavilions connect the various islands on the lake, and sipping tea at a lakeside teahouse is one of the more pleasant activities here. The park is home to the Siberian black-headed gulls, which migrate here during the winter. There are also some great restaurants and accommodations.

Cuì Hú Nán Lù. Free admission. 6am–midnight. Bus: no. 4, 59, 22, 74, 78, 85, or 101.

Kūnmíng Shì Bówùguǎn (Kūnmíng City Museum)   Only worth a visit if you've exhausted the city's other offerings, this museum focuses on the bronzes, drums, jewelry, swords, and other artifacts of the Diān nation unearthed around the Lake Diān area, including a seven-story octagonal Sutra Stone Incantation Pillar built during the Dàlǐ Kingdom (938–1254) to release the soul from suffering. Just opposite is the Museum of Urban Planning, which has some great scale models that give you a bird's-eye view of the city but not a word of English in sight. Still, at least entrance is free.

Tuòdōng Lù 120. Admission ¥5 (60¢). Tues–Sun 10am–4:30pm.

Yuántōng Sì   This unusual temple, the largest Buddhist shrine in Kūnmíng, combines elements from Mahayana, Hinayana (or Theravada), and Tibetan Buddhism (Lamaism). Originally built between 780 and 807, and rebuilt during the Qīng dynasty, the temple is dedicated to the worship of Avalokitesvara (the original male Buddha who was later transfigured into the female Guānyīn in Chinese Mahayana Buddhism). In the back of the complex is a Hinayana-style hall with a bronze statue of Sakyamuni donated by the Buddhist Association of Thailand. To the east is an altar hall of the Lama sect.

Yuántōng Jiē. Admission ¥4 (50¢). 8am–5pm.

WHERE TO STAY

Less conveniently located for the independent traveler in the southwestern part of town is the four-star **Courtyard by Marriott (Wànyí Jiǔdiàn)** 🏵🏵, Huánchéng Xī Lù 300 (© **0871/415-8888;** fax 0871/415-3282; cyhotel@public.km.yn.cn). While not as luxurious as some five-star hotels, it still delivers first-rate facilities and quality service.

Camellia Hotel (Cháhuā Bīnguǎn)   Still the favorite of independent budget travelers but only because of apathy. This two-star is old and run-down but thrives on its longstanding reputation. There are older budget standard rooms that are smaller and more run-down, and basic dorms with shared showers that are in high demand among backpackers. The hotel offers an budget ¥10 ($1.25) Western buffet breakfast. The staff speaks some English and can be helpful when pressed although the travel agency receives varying reports. Look out for the huge solar farm planted on top of the front building.

Dōngfēng Dōng Lù 96. © **0871/316-3000.** Fax 0871/314-7033. 180 units. ¥30 ($3.75) dorm bed; ¥200–¥220 ($25–$28) standard room. AE, DC, MC, V. **Amenities:** 2 restaurants; bar; lounge; bike rental; concierge; tour desk; business center; forex; shopping arcade; salon; room service; laundry/dry cleaning. *In room:* A/C, TV.

Green Lake Hotel (Cuì Hú Bīnguǎn) 🏵🏵🏵   Originally opened by the Hongta tobacco group in 1956, and later by Hilton, this was Kūnmíng's very first hotel to be opened to foreigners. The location easily surpasses any of the downtown five-stars and its two new wings make is a tempting new choice. The rooms are very well maintained and luxuriously appointed with huge king-size beds, making this one of the few locally run five-stars that can give the multinationals a run for their money. The lake is wonderful area to stroll, as is the university, although the military academy can safely be ignored.

South Cuì Hú Nán Lù 6. © **0871/515-888.** Fax 0871/515-3286. 302 units. ¥1,180 ($148) standard room; from ¥1,380 ($173) suite. 35% discounts. AE, DC, MC, V. **Amenities:** 2 restaurants; teahouse; nightclub; indoor pool; health club; driving range; sauna; concierge; tour desk; free shuttle to city center; business center; forex; shopping arcade; salon; 24-hr. butler service; same-day dry cleaning/laundry; *In room:* A/C, satellite TV, broadband Internet access, DVD player, minibar, hair dryer, safe.

Harbour Plaza Kūnmíng (Hǎiyì Jiǔdiàn) ★★★ This luxurious five-star Hong Kong–managed hotel is minutes from Green Lake Park and currently *the* place to stay for high-end tour groups from Europe and America. Guest rooms are simply but tastefully decorated and have comfortable beds. Bathrooms run small but are clean and bright. Staff is poised and efficient.

Hóng Huá Qiáo 20. ⓒ **0871/538-6688.** Fax 0871/538-1189. www.harbour-plaza.com. 300 units. ¥1,038 ($139) standard room. Discounts up to 40%. AE, DC, MC, V. **Amenities:** 3 restaurants; bar; lounge; outdoor pool; health club; sauna; children's playroom; concierge; tour desk; free airport shuttle; business center; forex; shopping arcade; salon; 24-hr. room service; same-day dry cleaning and laundry; executive rooms. *In room:* A/C, satellite TV, minibar, hair dryer, safe.

Yún Liáng Hotel (Yún Liáng Dàjiǔdiàn) ★ *Value* Near the Yuántōng Temple and Green Lake, this is a very well-located business hotel that's a much better choice than the Camellia for budget-minded travelers. Rooms are clean and simple (although the beds are a little hard), while staffers are friendly, but not linguists.

Běijīng Lù 623. ⓒ **0871/617-7188.** Fax 0871/515-5730. 65 units. ¥288 ($38) standard room; from ¥688 ($85) suite. 35% discount. AE, DC, MC, V. **Amenities:** Tour center; salon; in-room massage; karaoke. *In room:* A/C, TV.

WHERE TO DINE

The most famous Yúnnán dish is **"crossing the bridge noodles"** *(guòqiáo mǐxiàn)*, a hot pot consisting of steaming chicken broth to which you add thinly sliced chicken, pork, fish, other meats, vegetables, mushrooms, and rice noodles, all seasoned with peppers and chilies to taste. The oil on top keeps the simmering food hot enough to scald tongues, so be careful with your first bites! According to legend, the dish was invented over a century ago by the wife of a scholar who discovered that a layer of oil on top of her husband's food could keep it warm all the way from her kitchen across the bridge to a pavilion where he was studying for his imperial examinations, hence the dish's name. Another popular local dish is *qìguō jī* (chicken stewed with medicinal herbs). Along with a pharmacopoeia of allegedly healthful herbs and spices that are often used in many local dishes, Yúnnán mushrooms are also valued for their medicinal qualities. Fried goat cheese, Yúnnán sweet ham, and Yúnnán coffee are some other local favorites.

MODERATE

Jīnbì Chūn ★★ DIĀN CUISINE/SÌCHUĀN One of the best dining experiences in town, this restaurant combines the wonderful ambience of a 130-year-old Chinese mansion with delectable local Diān cuisine. This two-story gray-brick building just south of Jīnbì Square has private dining rooms arrayed around a once-open courtyard. Red Chinese lanterns and beautifully carved wooden doors and lattice windows set the right mood. Specialties include *zhēng lǎo nánguā* (steamed pumpkin), *jīnbì yān huóxiā* (spicy prawn sashimi), and *sūpí guànguàn jī* (chicken soup with puff pastry). The restaurant should have an English menu by the time you read this.

Dōngsì Jiē, Dà Huājiāo Xiāng 5. ⓒ **0871/364-1663.** Reservations recommended. Main courses ¥80–¥100 ($10–$12). No credit cards. 11am–10pm.

Yùquán Zhāi Sùshí ★ VEGETARIAN The largest vegetarian restaurant in town, located diagonally across from the Yuántōng Sì, is a clean, low-key, and foreigner-friendly place where Buddhist chants play softly in the background. All the dishes here are made from vegetables, tofu, or soy products but have been known to fool even the most discerning of meat eaters. Try *hóngshāo shīziqiú* (a mushroom ball in soy sauce),

> **Tips Local Flavors**
>
> Just on the other side of the Yuántōng Bridge are a number of holes-in-the-wall serving excellent roast duck. The dish is so popular among locals that whole racks of birds are lined up for the oven every single day. Combined with a couple of fresh fruit juices (¥4–¥6/50¢–75¢) from Fresh, just around the corner opposite the river, this makes an excellent choice for lunch.

cuìpí yā (crispy fried mock duck), and *cuìpí rúyì yú* (crispy mock fish in sweet-and-sour sauce). The staff is attentive and helpful.

Píngzhèng Jiē 88, 2nd floor. © **0871/511-16572.** English menu. Main courses ¥80–¥120 ($10–$15). No credit cards. 9am–9pm.

INEXPENSIVE

Báitǎ Dǎiwèi Tīng (Báitǎ Dǎi Flavor Restaurant) 🍴 DǍI   For a refreshing change of palate, this ethnic Dǎi restaurant, decorated comfortably with rattan furniture and batik prints, serves delicious favorites that include *yēzi qìguō jī* (coconut chicken), *huǒshāo gānbā* (barbecue dried beef), *zhútǒng ròu* (pork cooked in bamboo), and *hùnhé chǎo* (fried mixed vegetables). A variety of local beers and wines are available to complement your meal.

Shāngyì Jiē 143. © **0871/317-2932.** Main courses ¥50–¥70 ($6.25–$8.75). No credit cards. 11:30am–2:30pm and 5:30–9:30pm.

Cannes Cafeteria (Jīn Gā Nà Xīcāntīng) 🍴🍴🍴 MEDITERRANEAN   While this may not be Las Ramblas, Green Lake Park does have a relaxing Latin feel to it at times, especially with all the pavement cafes. The owner of Cannes lived in Spain for more than 20 years and his extensive knowledge of the country's cuisine is reflected in the menu. The second floor is a great place to spend a lazy afternoon; the staff is friendly and the prices reasonable.

Cuì Hú Běi Lù 78, Green Lake. © **0871/519-9696.** Main courses ¥18–¥50 ($2.25–$6.25). No credit cards. 11am–midnight.

Māma Fù's Restaurant (Māma Fù Cāntīng) 🍴 WESTERN/CHINESE   All the Chinese and Western staples are here: fried noodles, fried rice, pancakes, apple pie, sandwiches, pizzas, and spaghetti. The restaurant bakes its own breads. Several doors down, the **Fù Māma Miànguǎn** offers a wide variety of noodle dishes, including *hóngshāo niúròu miàn* (beef noodles), *shànyú miàn* (noodles with eel), and *yìndù gāli jī miàn* (curry chicken noodles). Thanks to its proximity to the Camellia Hotel, the restaurant is very popular with foreigners.

Báitǎ Lù 219 (across from the Kūnmíng Hotel). © **0871/311-1015.** Main courses ¥15–¥40 ($2–$5). No credit cards. 8:30am–11pm. Also at Māma Fù Miànguǎn, Dōngfēng Dōng Lù 58. © **0871/316-7340.** Main courses ¥8–¥20 ($1–$2.50). No credit cards. 8:30am–midnight.

Qīngniǎo (Blue Bird Café) WESTERN/CHINESE   This popular restaurant has two outlets. The one at Dōngfēng Xī Lù is squirreled away in its own alley with alfresco dining on the lovely patio. Unfortunately, it suffers from usually overenthusiastic, not always melodious karaoke aficionados, who can put a damper on a quiet candlelight dinner. The cafe, Xiǎo Xīmén Qīngniǎo on Cuì Hú Nán Lù, is quieter and cozier. Food at both is consistently decent. The menus offer pizza, steaks, and basic Chinese fare familiar to foreigners (kung pao chicken, garlic eggplant).

Qīngniǎo Lǎowū, Dōngfēng Xī Lù 127, buildings 1 and 2. ⓒ 0871/361-0478. Xiǎo Xīmén Qīngniǎo, Cuì Hú Nán Lù 150. ⓒ 0871/531-4071. Main courses ¥18–¥30 ($2.25–$3.75). No credit cards. 9am–2am.

SHOPPING

The area around Zhèngyì Lù and Nánpíng Lù has turned into Kūnmíng's main shopping district. The huge **department store** Kūnmíng Bǎihuò Dàlóu at Dōnfēng Dōng Lù 99 (open 9:10am–10pm) has a supermarket in the basement. The Gǔwán Chéng (open 8:30am–7:30pm) at the southwest corner of Hùguó Lù and Nánpíng Lù has a collection of stores selling **antiques,** curios, and ceramics. Yúnnán's famous **Pǔ'ěr tea** can be purchased at Ten Fu's Tea (Tiān Fú Míngchá), Shāngyì Jiē 41, next to the PSB. Minority women will sometimes gather outside the Camellia Hotel with their **handicrafts** and **batiks.** The Flower and Bird Market in Jǐngxīng Jiē is worth a browse for **souvenirs** and minor, mostly fake, antiques. For something more original, head down Běijīng road past the Jǐndá Hotel and the PLA Headquarters. There are plenty of army surplus shops here that sell everything from fur caps ¥20 ($2.50) to military police ID wallets ¥25 ($3), all of which make very unusual gifts.

KŪNMÍNG AFTER DARK

The 24-hour **Àomā Měilì Restaurant** at Dōngfēng Lù 60 (ⓒ **0871/312-6036**) is a laid-back bar with a good selection of liqueurs, beers, wines, sake, and the usual coffees and teas. The popular **Camel Bar (Luòtuo Jiǔbā)** at Báitǎ Lù 274 (ⓒ **0871/337-6255**) serves inexpensive beer and has live music on weekends. The local bar scene thrives at dark but trendy **The Hump** (ⓒ **0871/364-4197;** open noon–2am or till last customer) has a full bar and posters of American pop and movie stars but attracts highly budget-conscious backpackers rather than regular independent travelers. For more sophisticated venues, try some of the bars around Green Lake.

AROUND KŪNMÍNG

Jīn Diàn (Golden Temple) ✿✿ The centerpiece of this gorgeous Daoist temple complex, located 10km (6 miles) northeast of town, is the small but exquisite Golden Temple, built in 1671 on a two-tiered marble platform ringed by beautifully carved balustrades. The weathered 6.7m-high (22-ft.), 7.8m-wide (25-ft.), 250-ton hall has a double-eaved roof with gables, beams, columns, lattice doors, and lattice windows, all cast in bronze. Inside is a 1.5m-tall (5-ft.) bronze statue of Zhèn Wǔ, the legendary God of the North, flanked by a girl and a boy servant. Beyond the Golden Temple at the summit of the hill is the **Bell Tower (Zhōng Lóu),** a 36m-high (118-ft.), three-story square structure with a total of 36 flying eaves evoking flying phoenixes that was built only in 1983. Inside hangs a 14-ton bronze bell, used to signal time as well as to sound the alarm at the city's southern gate. A ¥15 ($1.90) cable car now runs from the temple to the World Horticultural Expo Garden.

Jīn Diàn Gōngyuán. Admission ¥15 ($1.90). 7am–8pm. Bus: no. 10 or 71 (from Jìnrì Gōngyuán).

Qióngzhú Sì (Bamboo Temple) ✿✿ Built in 639 and rebuilt in 1422 to 1428, this temple houses an incredibly vivid tableau of 500 arhats carved between 1883 and 1890 by Sichuanese sculptor Lǐ Guǎngxiū and his six apprentices, who gave to each arhat a different and incredibly naturalistic facial expression and pose. It is thought that some of these arhats, who range from the emaciated to the pot-bellied, the angry to the contemplative, were carved in the images of the sculptor's contemporaries, friends, and foes. A wildly fantastical element dominates the main hall, where an arhat surfs a wave on the back of a unicorn, while another stretches a 3m (10-ft.) arm upward to pierce the ceiling.

12km (7 miles) northwest of town. Admission ¥4 (50¢). 7:30am–5pm. Bus: no. 1 from Nánpíng Jiē and Zhèngyì Lù to Huángtǔ Pō; transfer to *miàndī* (van) taxis (¥3/35¢) for Qióngzhú Sì.

LAKE DIĀN (DIĀN CHÍ)

China's sixth-largest freshwater lake, located southwest of Kūnmíng, is 40km (25 miles) from north to south and covers an area of 300 sq. km (186 sq. miles). Fishing boats still trawl the lake, but serious pollution has made it difficult for many families to continue to make their living this way. Bordered by hills to the west and industrial settlements to the south and east, the lake has a number of attractions.

Dà Guān Yuán   This pleasant park on the northern shore of Lake Diān boasts nurseries, gardens, and walkways, but it is most famous for its triple-eaved **Grand View Tower (Dà Guān Lóu),** first built in 1682 and rebuilt in 1883. The tower offers unobstructed views of the lake.

Dàguān Lù (3km/2 miles south of Kūnmíng). Admission ¥5 (60¢), dawn to dusk. Bus: no. 4 or 52 (from airport).

Xī Shān (Western Hills)   Sometimes called the Sleeping Beauty Hills—their contours are said to resemble the outline of a sleeping maiden when viewed from afar—this densely forested range of hills on the western banks of Lake Diān is home to a number of Buddhist and Daoist temples and pavilions carved into the sheer rock face.

From the park's entrance, it's a 5km (3-mile) hike uphill to the parking lot and cable-car station, though most visitors prefer to take the bus from Gāoyáo directly to the parking lot. Along the way, the first major temple is the large and impressive Míng dynasty **Huátíng Sì** (¥4/50¢; open 7:20am–6:30pm) which has statues of 500 arhats. About 2km (1¼ miles) later is another Míng temple, **Tàihuá Sì** (¥3/40¢; open 8am–6pm), which was built in 1306 and boasts large gardens that contain camellia, plum, and osmanthus trees.

At the minibus and cable-car terminus is **Niè Ěr Zhī Mù** (¥1/15¢; open 8am–6:30pm), the tomb of the famous Yúnnán musician Niè Ěr, who composed China's national anthem before he drowned prematurely at sea in Japan in 1935. From here, you can take a chairlift for ¥15 ($1.90) to the summit at Dragon Gate (Lóng Mén), or you can take a tram for ¥3 (40¢) to **Sānqīng Gé,** a Daoist temple dedicated to the three main Daoist Gods which marks the beginning of the climb to the Dragon Gate Grottoes (¥20/$2.50). This series of grottoes containing various deities was carved by a local Daoist monk, Wú Láiqīng, and his band of monks between 1781 and 1795, all of whom must have been hanging by their fingertips as they painstakingly hacked away at the sheer rock face. The path on the cliff edge leading to **Dragon Gate** is so narrow that only one person can pass at a time. Below is a precipitous drop of about 600m (2,000 ft.) to the shores of Lake Diān. Those with vertigo should avoid this path. But the views from here of the lake and Kūnmíng in the distance are quite stunning and worth the trip.

To get to Xī Shān, take a taxi for ¥80 to ¥100 ($10–$12), or take local bus no. 5 from the Kūnmíng Hotel to its terminus at the Liù Lù Chēchǎng. Change to bus no. 6, which will take you to the village of Gāoyáo, where minibuses and van taxis will run you up to the tomb of Niè Ěr for ¥5 to ¥15 (60¢–$2). Minibuses also make the run to the tomb from the Liù Lù Chēchǎng, but these are unreliable. You can also leave Dragon Gate by cable car for ¥30 ($3.75) one-way, ¥50 ($6.25) round-trip. It crosses Lake Diān down to Hǎigēng Park and the Yúnnán Nationalities Village. The cable-car terminus is at the tomb of Niè Ěr.

15km (9 miles) west of Kūnmíng.

Zhèng Hé Gōngyuán   Sadly, there's not much to see at this park honoring the Míng dynasty admiral Zhèng Hé, whose amazing explorations in his day have largely been forgotten. Other than the de rigueur statue of the admiral and Zhèng Hé's father's tomb, a museum display in his old residence chronicles his seven sea voyages.

60km (40 miles) southwest of Kūnmíng in Kūnyáng. Admission ¥2.50 (30¢). 8am–5pm. Bus: no. 14 from Xiǎo Xīmén Bus Station to Kūnyáng Bus Station. Exit the station and turn right onto Zhèng Hé Lù for 300m (980 ft.) until the second intersection. The park is to the left.

STONE FOREST (SHÍ LÍN) 🏵🏵

Located 90km (55 miles) southeast of Kūnmíng in the Lǔnán Yí Autonomous County, Shí Lín is Kūnmíng's most famous attraction—a giant forest of limestone rocks formed 270 million years ago when the ocean receded from this area. Millions of years of tectonic shifts and erosion from wind and rain have resulted in today's maze

China's Columbus

China's most famous sailor, Zhèng Hé, was born in 1371 in the town of Kūnyáng. Originally a Huí Muslim named Mǎ Hé, he was captured by the conquering Míng army at age 10, castrated, and forced into service. Rising through the military ranks, he was eventually promoted to serve as a eunuch in the inner court of the Forbidden City, where it is said the emperor gave him the name Zhèng Hé because Mǎ means "horse" in Chinese and horses could not enter the inner court. In 1405, he was appointed admiral of a naval expedition to explore new trade routes and to collect tribute for the Chinese emperor.

Zhèng Hé made seven voyages between 1492 and 1504 compared to Christopher Columbus's four and Vasco da Gama's single sailing in 1497 to 1499. With an armada of 62 ships and a crew of 27,800 men—compared to Columbus's three ships and 87 crew members, and da Gama's four ships and 160 men—the admiral explored territory from Java to the mouth of the Persian Gulf and even down the coast of Africa, sailing to a total of 39 countries, including modern-day Vietnam, Thailand, Yemen, Iran, and Somalia. That Zhèng Hé's feats have remained largely forgotten may have something to do with the fact that his expeditions were less about conquering new lands or disseminating religion than about proclaiming the glory of the Chinese empire to foreigners, who would, the Chinese assumed, recognize China as the Middle Kingdom and render tribute accordingly. It has become an interesting exercise for historians to speculate on what might have happened had the Chinese acted on these explorations of "barbarian" lands. Perhaps we would all be speaking Chinese right now.

Tips **Another, Quieter Stone Forest**

About 8km (5 miles) northeast of the Stone Forest is the 300-hectare (741-acre)
Nǎigǔ Shílín Black Pine Stone Forest (¥25/$3), which predates the Stone Forest
by about 2 million years. The park is a much quieter option; in fact, I only saw
two other French tourists, the entire day that I was there. There are some interesting geological signs in English and the terrain varies from underground karst
caves to magnificent black volcanic lookout points. On your own, catch a horse
and cart for ¥15 ($1.90) from the main road outside the Stone Forest.

---

of sharp-edged fissures and sky-piercing pinnacles, which are punctuated by walkways,
ponds, and pavilion lookouts. Fed by subterranean rivers, **Jiànfēng Chí** is the only
natural body of water in the forest. The reflection of the blue sky, white clouds, and
swordlike stone peaks in the pond makes this one of the most photographed locales
in the forest. **Shīzi Tíng (Lion Pavilion),** the highest point in the Stone Forest, and
Wàngfēng Tíng (Peak Viewing Pavilion) offer the best panoramas.

This geological wonder is quite a sight if you've never before seen a petrified forest,
but some visitors are more amazed at the immense parking lots and long lines at the
ticket offices. It could be the hordes of tourists that tramp through here during the
day, for the forest takes on a much more ethereal and mysterious quality only in the
evening after the tour groups have left. The Stone Forest can be comfortably navigated
in a 2½- to 3-hour loop with plenty of opportunities to get off the trodden path. An
English-speaking tour guide can be hired for ¥80 ($10) but is not really necessary.

This area is also home to the Sāní branch of the Yí minority group. Young Sāní men
and women (allegedly) in colorful costumes greet all arriving visitors and act as tour
guides through the forest, while Sāní vendors sell a variety of handicrafts and some very
nice batiks. There are also Sāní song and dance performances during the day and on
most nights at the Minor Stone Forest (Xiǎo Shí Lín) right next to the Stone Forest.

Another side trip worth considering is the 96m-high (315-ft.), 54m-wide (177-ft.)
Dàdiéshuǐ Fēilóng Pù (¥18/$2.25), Yúnnán's largest waterfall. Hiring a taxi for ¥50 to
¥70 ($6–$8.50) directly from the Stone Forest is the most convenient way to get here.

GETTING THERE   The best way to reach the Stone Forest is via the direct K440
train (90 min.; ¥20/$2.50 one-way, ¥30/$3.75 round-trip), which departs Kūnmíng
at 8:10am and returns from the Stone Forest at 4:30pm. Train tickets for the forest are
sold from 7:30am to 8:10am at a special booth at the southeast corner of the railway
station next to the gate for the Stone Forest train. During other times, purchase Stone
Forest train tickets at counter 3 in the main station or from travel agencies or hotel
desks. Entrance tickets for the Stone Forest can be purchased for ¥80 ($10) on the
train, where attendants may also try to sell you organized tours taking in nearby sights.
Nǎigǔ Stone Forest costs an additional ¥40 ($5) including lunch, and the Dàdiéshuǐ
Waterfall costs an additional ¥50 ($6.25) including lunch. If you decide to join one
of these tours, usually conducted only in Chinese, they will send you to the railway
station in time for the return train to Kūnmíng at 4:30pm. If you do not wish to wait
for the 4:30pm return train, you can catch other, earlier Kūnmíng-bound trains for
¥17 ($2.10) that stop at the Stone Forest on the way (the 1165 leaves Shí Lín at
1:47pm and arrives in Kūnmíng at 3:30pm), although there are no reserved seats.

Avoid anyone who tries to sell you bus rides for ¥30 ($3.75) round-trip, unless you want to spend all your time shopping along the way and only reach the forest in the afternoon. Trips from the Camellia are especially overrated; your ¥90 ($11) includes nothing but a ride in a cramped microbus with a surly driver, who pretends to speak no English. Rather than drive through ghastly industrial towns like "Developing Yíliǎng," the train is a much more scenic option.

WHERE TO STAY & DINE   The sprawling three-star **Stone Forest Xīngyà Fēngqíng Garden** (© 0871/771-0599; fax 0871/771-1599) offers guest rooms that are spacious and comfortable, if a little worn. Rates can easily be discounted to ¥250 to ¥300 ($30–$38); no credit cards accepted.

6 Dàlǐ

Yúnnán Province, 392km (243 miles) NW of Kūnmíng, 15km (9 miles) N of Xiàguān, 150km (90 miles) S of Lì Jiāng

The charming town of Dàlǐ, traditionally one of the best places in China to tune in, turn on, and drop out for a while, remains a wonderful place to visit despite the increasing commercialization brought by tour groups. Its small size belies its important place in Yúnnán's history: During the Táng dynasty (609–960), Dàlǐ was the capital of the Nánzhào Kingdom, and during the Sòng dynasty (960–1079), it was the capital of the Dàlǐ Kingdom. Deserted after Kublai Khan overran Dàlǐ in 1252, it was reconstructed during the Míng dynasty (1382). Today's Dàlǐ is the capital of the Bái Autonomous Prefecture (although it's run from Xiàguān). Located in a mountain valley at an elevation of 1,948m (6,496 ft.), Dàlǐ is sunny year-round, though winter nights can be chilly. The best times to visit are between February and October, when the majority of festivals take place.

ESSENTIALS

GETTING THERE   Dàlǐ's transportation hub is **Xiàguān,** 15km (9 miles) to the south. From the Dàlǐ Airport another 15km (9 miles) northeast of Xiàguān, there are daily **flights** to Kūnmíng (40 min.) and Xīshuāngbǎnnà (50 min.). From the airport to Dàlǐ is about a 1-hour taxi ride, which will cost up to ¥100 ($13). If you need to purchase additional plane tickets, take a taxi into Xiàguān for about ¥40 to ¥50 ($5–$6) (or see the buses below) and go to the **Yúnnán Airlines** ticket office (© **0872/ 231-5339**), located next to the railway station across from the China Telecom building. There is another outlet in the Cāng Shān Fàndiàn at Cāng Shān Lù 118. Travel agencies or your hotel concierge in Dàlǐ may be able to help you purchase airline tickets, but give them as much advance notice as possible and expect to pay a fee for the service.

A popular **train** route is the overnight sleeper from Kūnmíng (8 hr.; ¥161/$20 soft sleeper), which leaves Kūnmíng at 10:34pm and arrives in Xiàguān at 6:22am. A later train departs at 11:16pm and arrives at 7:30am. From the railway station, bus no. 8 (45 min.; ¥3/40¢) runs to the West Gate of the old city in Dàlǐ, while bus no. 10 runs into Xiàguān. Returning to Kūnmíng, trains depart Xiàguān at 9pm and 10:02pm.

Travelers can still take the 9-hour bus trip on the old Burma Road (see box, below) between Kūnmíng and Xiàguān, but most folks these days prefer the far quicker (4–5 hr.) and more comfortable **buses** that travel the new expressway. Coaches have free gifts for passengers, but this is little consolation for travelers leaving Kūnmíng on the most appalling route out of town. Apart from the major construction, once past the

Dàlǐ

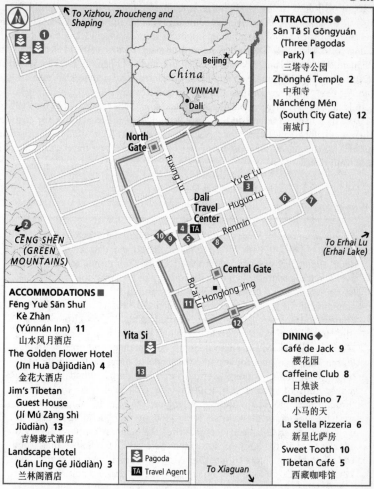

ATTRACTIONS ●

Sān Tǎ Sì Gōngyuán
(Three Pagodas
Park) **1**
三塔寺公园

Zhōnghé Temple **2**
中和寺

Nánchéng Mén
(South City Gate) **12**
南城门

To Xizhou, Zhoucheng and
Shaping

China
Beijing ★
YUNNAN
● Dali

North
Gate

Fuxing Lu

Yu'er Lu **3**

Dali
Travel
Center

Huguo Lu **6** **7**

Renmin

10 **9** **4** **TA**
5 **8**

CĒNG SHĒN
(GREEN
MOUNTAINS)

2

To Erhai Lu
(Erhai Lake)

Central Gate

Bǒ'ai Lu

11 Honglong Jing

12

Yita Si

13

ACCOMMODATIONS ■

Fēng Yuè Sān Shuǐ
Kè Zhàn
(Yúnnán Inn) **11**
山水风月酒店

The Golden Flower Hotel
(Jīn Huā Dàjiǔdiàn) **4**
金花大酒店

Jim's Tibetan
Guest House
(Jí Mú Zàng Shì
Jiǔdiàn) **13**
吉姆藏式酒店

Landscape Hotel
(Lán Líng Gé Jiǔdiàn) **3**
兰林阁酒店

Pagoda
TA Travel Agent

To Xiaguan

DINING ◆

Café de Jack **9**
樱花园

Caffeine Club **8**
日烛谈

Clandestino **7**
小马的天

La Stella Pizzeria **6**
新星比萨房

Sweet Tooth **10**

Tibetan Café **5**
西藏咖啡馆

No. 2 Sewage Treatment Plant, both sides of the roads are filled with parking lots containing bulldozers, dump trucks, and just about every other piece of earth-moving equipment imaginable. Be thankful that you are seeing Yúnnán while it is still there. Most Dàlǐ-bound buses actually stop in Xiàguān, which has several bus stations, but the main one that travelers will likely use the most is the confusingly named **Dàlǐ Qìchē Kèyùn Zhàn** (© **0872/218-9330**) opposite Mínshēng Plaza, on Jiànshè Lù east of Rénmín Lù. From here, luxury air-conditioned buses depart for Kūnmíng (5 hr.; ¥104/$13) every half-hour from 7:30am to 8:30pm; for Lì Jiāng (3 hr.; ¥51/$6.30) at 8:30am, 2pm, 7pm, and 7:30pm; and for Xiānggélǐlā/Zhōngdiàn (6 hr.; ¥86/$11) at 9am and 3pm. There are also regular buses to Lì Jiāng (3 hr.; ¥35–¥50/$4.40–$6.30) every half-hour from 7:20am to 7:30pm; to Téngchōng (5–6 hr.; ¥71–¥81/$8.80–$10) at 10am and 7:30pm; to Bǎoshān (2–6 hr.) hourly from 8:30am to

3:30pm; to Ruìlì (10 hr.; ¥91/$11) at 8:30am and 8pm; and to Jǐnghóng (22 hr.; ¥141/$18) at 7:30pm. A private bus company, **YNTAC** (© 0872/212-5221), operates luxury, air-conditioned, nonsmoking buses from Xiàguān's Cāng Shān Fàndiàn (Cāng Shān Lù 118). The buses go to Kūnmíng (5 hr.; ¥103/$13) at 8:30am, 10:30am, 12:30pm, 1pm, 2:30pm, and 7:30pm; and to Lì Jiāng (3 hr.; ¥55/$6.90) at 8:20am, 1:40pm, 2:40pm, and 7pm. From the center of Xiàguān to Dàlǐ, take bus no. 4 for ¥2 (25¢) from the corner of Jiànshè Lù and Rénmín Lù.

In Dàlǐ, it's best to have a tourist cafe arrange your Dàlǐ–Kūnmíng bus for ¥105 to ¥110 ($13–$14), as they will take care of sending you to Xiàguān for the transfer. There is usually a ¥5 (60¢) fee for this service. Buses to Lì Jiāng also mostly originate out of Xiàguān. Again, the most hassle-free option is to have a travel agency or cafe book your ticket.

The Burma Road

As the Japanese took control of northern and coastal China in 1937, the Kuomintang government, forced to flee to Chóngqìng, decided that a "back door" supply line was needed into the country. They turned to the ancient overland trade routes with India and Burma, also known as the southern Silk Route, which over 2,000 years ago had connected the markets of the Hàn empire with the bazaars of Rome. Between 1937 and 1939, about 200,000 Chinese and Burmese laborers were drafted to build a road from Xiàguān (the stretch from Kūnmíng to Xiàguān had been built in 1935) across the Mekong and Salween rivers to Bǎoshān, to Wǎndīng, and on to Lashio in Burma, where rail lines connected it to Mandalay. Armed with only the most primitive of tools, laborers wrestled large boulders, crushed stone, and moved tons of mud into a 1,100km-long (700-mile) road that wound through thick mountains and dense jungles. The road turned out to be a strategic lifeline for the Chinese. From 1940, up to 18,000 tons of supplies were carried into China each month. When the Japanese captured Burma in 1942 and cut off the Burmese side of the route, another road was built from Ledo in northeast India to meet up with the Burma Road at Bhamo and Muse. This 1,736km-long (1,079-mile) Ledo supply route came to be known as the Stilwell Road after Gen. Joseph B. Stilwell, who ran the Allied operation in the China-Burma-India theater from his base in Kūnmíng. At the same time, a temporary air supply line came over the Himalayan Hump from India, but the treacherous terrain took the lives of over 1,000 airmen, some of whose bodies have never been recovered. Finished in 1944, the Stilwell road was abandoned the following year with the end of the war.

Today, this 940km (564-mile) stretch between Kūnmíng and the border crossing at Wǎndīng (though not currently open for tourist crossings) has once again become the darling of Chinese entrepreneurs eager for Burmese business, with traded items ranging from jade and rubies to heroin and antiaircraft artillery.

The Bái

With a history dating back some 3,000 to 4,000 years around the Ěr Hǎi Lake region, the Bái nationality is one of the oldest and the second largest minority group in Yúnnán. Over 80% of the Bái, now numbering close to 1.4 million, live in Dàlĭ and the surrounding villages and countryside in what is known as the Bái Autonomous Prefecture. More than most minority groups, the Bái, who've had a long illustrious history throughout the Nánzhào and Dàlĭ kingdoms, are one of the best adapted to the Hàn majority. The Bái— the "white"—revere the color, which is regarded as noble and is the main color of their traditional dress.

The Bái celebrate many festivals, the largest of which is Sānyuè Jié (Third Month Festival), which had its origins over a thousand years ago when Buddhist monks and adherents gathered to celebrate Guānyīn's (the Goddess of Mercy) appearance to the Bái. Today's festival, which starts on the 15th day of the third lunar month (usually Apr or early May), has become more secular as the Bái and other minorities from around the area gather in the foothills of Cāng Shān (Green Mountains) for 5 days and nights of singing, dancing, wrestling, horse racing, and large-scale trading of everything from Tibetan-made felt hats and silk floss to horses and medicinal herbs. Ràosānlíng, which involves a procession to three nearby temples, is held between the 23rd and the 25th days of the fourth lunar month (usually May). Huǒbǎ Jié (the Torch Festival) is held on the 24th day of the sixth lunar month (usually July) and involves the parading of flaming torches through homes and fields. There are also fireworks and dragon boat races.

Note: If you get stuck in Xiàguān en route to Dàlĭ, the modern four-star **Mànwān Dàjiǔdiàn** ✦ at Cānglàng Lù (© **0872/218-8188;** fax 0872/218-1742) is the nicest place to stay in town, with large comfortable rooms and bright, clean bathrooms. Standard rooms cost ¥500 ($62); suites are ¥780 to ¥988 ($97–$123).

GETTING AROUND   Old town Dàlĭ is currently undergoing something of a construction boom. The major new Lì Jiāng Highway (whose existence will soon cut the 20-hr. trip from Kūnmíng down to 5 hr.) will bypass the West Gate, taking a lot of congestion away from the north–south running Bó'ài Lù. Still, the old town is so small that it's possible to walk from the North Gate (Běi Mén) to the South Gate (Nán Mén) in half an hour or less if you don't stop at the many shops along the main thoroughfare, Fùxīng Lù. To explore farther afield, **bikes** are the best way to get around and can be rented all along Bó'ài Lù for around ¥10 ($1.25) a day. A **taxi** to nearby sights such as the Three Pagoda Park or the Cāng Shān chairlift will run between ¥5 and ¥10 (60¢–$1.25). Bus no. 2 runs from the Yàxīng (Asia Star) Hotel to the dock at Cǎi Cūn.

TOURS & GUIDES   Many of the Dàlĭ cafes provide a variety of tours, including a **boat trip** on Ěr Hǎi Lake which costs ¥20 to ¥40 ($2.50–$5) per person, depending on group size; or **horseback riding** to a mountain monastery or local Bái village for about ¥40 to ¥60 ($5–$7.50) per person. Local English-speaking guides can be hired through cafes for about ¥30 to ¥50 ($3.75–$6) per hour, or around ¥200 ($25) per day. The **Dàlǐ Travel Center,** next to the Golden Flower Hotel (Hùguó Lù 76; ✆ **0872/267-1282**), offers the above services and also sells bus tickets to local destinations.

FAST FACTS

Banks, Foreign Exchange & ATMs   The **Bank of China** (open Mon–Fri 8am–6pm) is at Fùxīng Lù 333. It has an outside ATM.

Internet Access   Many cafes offer Internet access, mostly with free ADSL, such as the six machines in the **Tibetan Café** at 58 Rénmín Lù. Dial-up is ✆ **163.**

Post Office   The post office (open 8am–6pm) is at the corner of Fùxīng Lù and Hùguó Lù.

Visa Extension   These are available in Xiàguān at the **Gōngānjú (PSB),** located at Tiānbǎo Jiē 21 (✆ **0872/216-6090;** open Mon–Fri 8:30–11am and 2:30–5pm).

EXPLORING DÀLǏ

Old town Dàlǐ, with its 9m-high (30-ft.) battlements, dates from the Míng dynasty (1368–1644), but the current wall was restored and extended only in 1998 as part of a project to gentrify Dàlǐ and attract tourists. From the top of the freshly painted Nán Chéng Mén (South City Gate; ¥2/25¢; open 8am–9pm), there are some lovely views of the town and the Cāng Shān Mountains to the west. You can also walk along the restored city wall to Xī Mén (Western Gate). Of course, if you climb the wall at the southwestern corner, there is no ticket fee.

Unlike Lì Jiāng, Dàlǐ's charm is that visitors still can look beyond the other tourists and see the original residents slowly going about their daily business, as if looking through some kind of time machine. Old people especially move slowly through the main thoroughfares like ghosts, seeing things very differently from the way we do, but always responding positively to any attempt we might make to cross the divide.

Several new construction projects promise more walking streets filled with souvenir stores. There is already one **Foreigner Street**—a photo-op must for domestic tourists (a second one is being rapidly constructed). If you prefer not to be on display, **Rénmín Lù** is a little more laid-back, but the secret quiet spot is up on **Hóng Lóngjǐng,** toward the west wall, where local students practice their tai chi.

Sān Tǎ Sì Gōngyuán (Three Pagodas Park) ⚔   About 2km (1¼ miles) northwest of town at the foot of the Cāng Shān Mountains, Dàlǐ's most famous landmark has unfortunately become a massive tourist trap. Apart from the pagodas, a new temple and a museum have been added to the rear of the park but there is very little of interest inside them; nonetheless, in 2 years, ticket prices have increased fivefold, from ¥10 ($1.25) to ¥52 ($6.50). This once open and informal garden is now sequestered

---

Horse Trekking Takes Its Toll

The horse trek up the mountain to **Zhōnghé Temple** has gone downhill. It is easy to feel sorry for these worn-out horses, but perhaps worse is the damage that is being done to the paths by constant erosion. Look closely as you pass overhead on the chairlift; notice how the paths have been worn over a meter deep in many places.

behind thick red walls. The three pagodas were originally part of Chóngwén Sì monastery and have withstood several earthquakes through the years. The monastery itself was destroyed in the Qīng dynasty, and what you see today dates only from 1999. The central pagoda, the statuesque 16-story, 69m-high (226-ft.) **Qiānxún Tǎ,** resembling Xī'ān's Small Goose Pagoda, was built first between 824 and 859 and is a hollow square brick structure with graceful eaves. Each floor has windows and niches containing Buddhist statues, many of them now defaced if not completely destroyed. The two smaller flanking octagonal pagodas were built later during the 12th century, and have 10 tiers each for a total height of 42m (138 ft.). The pagoda's doors and windows have been filled with concrete to prevent visitors from climbing inside. A popular photo op is from a small lake in the northeast corner of the park that captures the reflections of all three pagodas in a stunning tableau. Apart from that one particular vista, the rest of the site is overrated.

Sān Tǎ Gōngyuán. Admission ¥52 ($6.50). 8am–7pm.

MARKETS
A market visit is highly recommended for a sense of local color. Many of the markets around Dàlĭ are scheduled according to the lunar calendar, so check with the local cafes before you set out. Dàlĭ itself has a market every 7 days (usually on the 2nd, 9th, 16th, and 23rd days of the lunar month). Once the most popular, the Shāpíng market, held every Monday, has become a bit of a commercialized circus (see below). The town of Wāsè on the eastern shores of Ěr Hǎi Lake also has a popular market held every 5 days from 9:30am to 4pm. Foodstuffs and agricultural produce are the main goods here, as the market still caters to locals instead of tourists. The easiest way to visit is to sign up with a local cafe that will arrange round-trip transportation for around ¥28 ($3.50) per person.

WHERE TO STAY
Accommodations can be scarce during festivals and also in June and July, so be sure to book your hotel ahead of time if you plan to visit then. Many guidebooks only list a handful of hideous backpacker haunts such as the MCA Guesthouse and the notorious numbered guesthouses. Fortunately, Dàlĭ is teeming with interesting accommodations that you may well have all to yourself if you time your visit right.

Fēng Yuè Sān Shuǐ Kèzhàn (Yúnnán Inn) *(Finds*   Part guesthouse, part experimental art; but even with the proximity of the stream just outside, this hotel is still no Fallingwater. Opened in 2003, the owner is a successful Běijīng-based artist, and this is where he keeps his lovable mongrel, Big Diamond (Dà Bǎo). Apt really, because this is a lovable mongrel of a hotel, possessing the character that is rarely found in Chinese hotels. A series of interesting rooms cling to the surrounds of a converted studio by means of steel walkways and metal girders. And while most Chinese hotel rooms are arranged neatly off central corridors, rooms here go off in all different directions.

There are few government-approved amenities, but this is more than made up for by eccentric touches, such as being able to watch the fish under your feet as you check your e-mail, or being treated to the unparalleled views from the enormous rooftop. Be sure to request a room with a separate bathroom; the alternative is just too odd.

Hóng Lóngjǐng 3, next to the Yù Yuán Hotel. ✆ 0872/266-3741. 10 units. ¥80–¥120 ($10–$15) standard room. No credit cards. *In room:* TV.

The Golden Flower Hotel (Jīn Huā Dàjiǔdiàn) ✿✿ Certainly the best location in town, this is also the first choice for foreign study groups, which often stop here after long field expeditions in the wilds of Yúnnán. The lobby is a marvelous display of marble and bonsai, while the staff in traditional Bái dress, is friendly and helpful. Some rooms are a bit small but ask for room 2023 or 3023 and you'll be able to invite some friends over for a soccer match. Beds are soft and comfortable, enhanced by the sound of Chinese nightingales and other songbirds in the atrium. Often overlooked by independent travelers, The Golden Flower is worth checking into.

Fùxīng Lù 349. ✆ 0872/267-3343. Fax 0872/267-0573. www.goldenflowerhotel.com. 150 units. ¥288–¥388 ($35–$48) standard room. Up to 50% discounts (low season). No credit cards. **Amenities:** Ticket service; laundry. *In room:* A/C, TV.

Jim's Tibetan Guest House (Jí Mǔ Zàng Shì Jiǔdiàn) ✿✿✿ At the time of writing, this was one of the best hotel choices in town. The location, a bit off the beaten track, is more than made up for by the levels of service, interior decoration, and imagination on the part of the owners, one Kampa Tibetan, and the other Dutch. Rooms are bright and colorful as well as comfortable, but often booked solid with Western tour groups. This is also a great place to eat. For four people or more, go for the Tibetan smorgasbord at ¥30 ($3.80) per person. We counted at least 16 dishes as well as a delicious dessert. You may want to keep away from Jim's No. 1 Whiskey, a local moonshine whose harshness is disguised by a few local herbs, but would probably be better in a tractor carburetor than some unwary tourist's stomach.

Yù Xiù Lù Zhōng Duàn 13, Lù Yù Xiǎoqū. ✆ 0872/267-7824. Fax 0872/266-1822. www.china-travel.nl. 30 units. ¥180 ($23) standard room. No credit cards.

Landscape Hotel (Lán Líng Gé Jiǔdiàn) A slightly more expensive option than The Golden Flower, the beautiful Landscape is an agglomeration of old city houses that have been joined together to form a 163-room hotel incorporating a number of traditional Bái construction styles. With some of the most ornately decorated screen walls in the town, the Landscape offers designs surprises at every turn, from a bubbling stream to a functioning well. This a very popular option with the more upmarket tour groups.

Yù' ér Lù 96. ✆ 0872/266-6188. Fax 0872/266-6189. 163 units. ¥600 ($75) standard room; ¥1,080 ($136) suite. Up to 45% discount (low season). All rates subject to 15% service charge. AE, DC, MC, V. **Amenities:** Laundry. *In room:* A/C, TV, minibar (select rooms), hair dryer.

WHERE TO DINE

Bāba is sold all around northwest Yúnnán, where it mostly consists of a piece of flat rice dough that's grilled or fried and flavored with salty and spicy seasonings. In Dàlǐ, the dough is stuffed with salted vegetables, sweet sauce, chili sauce, crushed peanuts, and *yóutiáo* (fried, salty doughnut) and grilled to tender perfection. This "Dàlǐ calzone" is one of the most popular breakfast items, often sold on street corners like Hùguó Lù and Fùxīng Lù. Other typical local dishes include *shāguō yú* (stewed fish

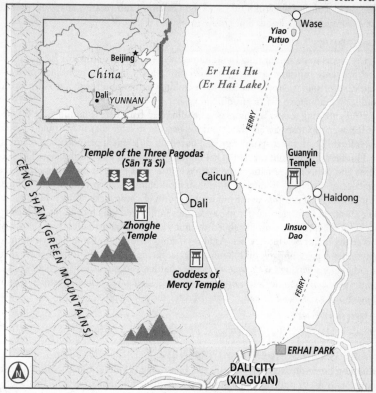

casserole) and the Bái specialty, *rǔshàn* (milk fan), a delicious local goat's cheese sliced in thin layers and fried until "rubbery."

The foreigners' cafes clustered along Hùguó Lù and Bó'ài Lù serve inexpensive and generally tasty Western, Chinese, Bái, and Tibetan meals. **Café de Jack** at Bó'ài Lù 82 (© **0872/267-1572**) has recently been refurbished but as yet the reliability of the menu does not match the new decor. Jack is also the owner of **La Stella Pizzeria** at Hùguó Lù 58 (© **0872/266-2881**), which serves an excellent pizza focaccia and does a very generous goat's cheese and tomato salad. Also popular is the **Tibetan Café** on Rénmín Lù (© **0872/266-4177**), which used to be a lot cozier until they recently invested in a row of PCs to supply free Internet. Even so, this is still the best place to start the day; the unbeatable Dalai Lama's Breakfast Slam consists of Tibetan oats, fresh fruit, yogurt, and jasmine tea. New to the scene, **Sweet Tooth,** at the corner of Rénmín Lù and Bó'ài Lù (open Mon–Sat 10am–10pm), is wildly popular with foreigners but sees very few domestic customers. Set up by an American entrepreneur to provide jobs for Dàlǐ's deaf community, Sweet Tooth's traditional chocolate chip cookies are just what a stressed traveler needs; their Ugly Brownies and huge slabs of Oreo cheesecake will make you wonder if you are still in China.

Finally, down amongst the dopers and the dreadlocks on Rénmín Lù, are a number of small bars and cafes that attract independent travelers. Recommended are **Clandestino** (at #283), a small French-run cafe, and the **Caffeine Club** (nearby, at #370), with its casual attitude and delicious lime crushes.

SHOPPING

There seems to be an alarming trend in tourist towns like Dàlǐ towards fashion shops that sell only **military clothing,** usually with AK47s or M16s as display pieces— hardly surprising when you see that most children here start off with a wooden sword and soon graduate to plastic pistols and rifles.

Dàlǐ's growing season is almost never ending and **fruit** here is nothing like you see in the average supermarket. Watch out for peaches so large that they would frighten even Roald Dahl, sweet syrupy figs, and dozens of different apple-pear combinations.

Hundreds of shops in town sell Dàlǐ **marble,** famous for its beautiful cloudlike patterns and anticorrosive nature; the marble is now even more in demand because the practice of quarrying from the Cāng Shān mountains has been officially prohibited. For now most of it comes in the unfortunate form of cheap tacky ashtrays but a growing number of sculptors are setting up studios in the area, which could be promising. Other local specialties include **sliced walnut vases and lampshades,** but a block of **pu'er tea** might be a little wiser. As always, comparison-shop before you commit to anything: A piece of batik on Hùguó Lù can sometimes cost 10% to 20% more than another along Fùxīng Lù (or vice versa). For **batiks,** you can usually get better prices in the wholesale factories and workshops in Zhōu Chéng (see below). In stores, it's not uncommon to bargain to half or two-thirds of the asking price.

AROUND DÀLǏ

Please turn to appendix A for Chinese translations of key locations.

CĀNG SHĀN (GREEN MOUNTAINS)

Running down the west side of Dàlǐ, the 42km-long (25-mile) Cāng Shān mountain range with its 19 peaks (a number of them permanently snow-covered), 18 streams, and acres of verdant forests, is well worth exploring. The easiest way to ascend the mountain is by chairlift, a lovely ride ¥28 ($3.50) up, ¥20 ($2.50) down, that offers some of the loveliest vistas of the old town and the shimmering blue Ěr Hǎi Lake in the distance. (From the western gate of the old town, head north until you see the sign for the chairlift; or take a taxi for ¥5 to ¥8 (60¢–$1). At the chairlift's upper terminus is **Zhōnghé Sì,** a not particularly memorable temple. The sign for the **Highlander Guest House** (© 0872/266-1599; www.higherland.com/index2.htm) says 100m (328 ft.), what it doesn't say is that it's 100m straight up. At the moment the place has superb potential and will one day be a star attraction, but not yet. Several trails branch out from Zhōnghé Sì. One option if you don't have time to make a day of it is the trek through pretty terrain to **Fèngyǎn Dòng (Phoenix Cave),** which takes you through the back of Lóngquán Mountain (about an hour each way). There's also a vigorous 11km (7-mile), 4½- to 5-hour hike to **Gǎntōng Sì,** a temple first built in 900 on the southern slope of Yīngshèng Peak. The road down the mountain from Gǎntōng Temple will take you back to the main road, from where you can take a taxi or bus no. 4 back to Dàlǐ. Another trail leads to the lovely **Qīngbì Xī** in the valley between Mǎlóng and Shèngyīng peaks. Flowing through three large ponds, this stream eventually empties into Ěr Hǎi.

ĚR HǍI HÚ (ĚR HǍI LAKE)

East of Dàlǐ and north of Xiàguān, Ěr Hǎi Hú, literally named after its resemblance to a human ear (ěr), is one of the seven largest freshwater lakes in China and the second largest in Yúnnán after Diān Chí in Kūnmíng. Originating in the Hēigǔ Shān mountains to the northwest and fed partially by the 18 streams of Cāng Shān, the lake spans 42km (25 miles) from north to south, and 7km (4 miles) from east to west, and has an average depth of 10m (33 ft.). There are many settlements and towns scattered around the lake, along with some tourist traps on the eastern side. **Warning:** Some recent travelers have reported that the lake was unsafe for swimming as it contained the schistosomiasis (bilharzia) parasite; unfortunately, accurate up-to-date information on the situation is hard to come by.

However, a **boat ride** ⟨⟩ on the beautiful lake is one of the highlights of a visit to Dàlǐ. Several ferries cross the lake, from Lóngkǎn to Hǎidōng, Cái Cūn to Wāsè, and Xiàguān to Jīnsuō Dǎo. Giant tourist boats charge ¥90 ($11) to make a 3½- to 4-hour run of the lake from the Táoyuán Mǎtóu (dock) in Zhōu Chéng to Xiàguān, stopping along the way at **Pǔtuó Dǎo, Guānyīn Gé (Guānyīn Pavilion),** and **Jīnsuō Dǎo,** an island full of caves and caverns and inhabited by Bái fishermen. You can also negotiate with smaller private boats, which charge an average of ¥100 to ¥200 ($13–$25) for the round-trip; or get a travelers' cafe in town to help you with any special arrangements.

About 7km (4 miles) north of Xīzhōu, the village of **Zhōu Chéng** is famous for its **tie-dyed batiks** ⟨⟩. The minute you step off the bus, you'll be approached by Bái women who will invite you to visit their batik workshops. This is worth considering, as you can often pick up batik tablecloths or shirts for considerably less than you would pay in the shops in Dàlǐ—subject to bargaining, of course. There is also a local **market** in the center of town; uphill from there, part of the old town is worth exploring. Catch an Ěryuán-bound bus from either Dàlǐ or Xīzhōu.

7 Lì Jiāng ⟨★⟩⟨★⟩⟨★⟩

Yúnnán Province, 527km (316 miles) NW of Kūnmíng, 150km (90 miles) NW of Dàlǐ

Lì Jiāng is as lovely, and as fake, as it gets in China. Located in the northwest part of Yúnnán Province, this capital of the Lì Jiāng Nàxī Autonomous County (pop. 302,000) is home to the Nàxī people (who constitute almost 60% of its population) and to a smaller number of Bái, Tibetan, Yí, Mosu, and Hàn peoples. Though its history dates to the Warring States (475–221 B.C.), its most influential period was when it was governed by Nàxī chieftains during the Míng dynasty (1368–1644).

In February 1996, an earthquake hit Lì Jiāng, killing over 300 people, injuring 17,000 more and destroying 186,000 homes, much of the city. Amazingly, many of the traditional Nàxī houses held up quite well, leading the government in its reconstruction process to pour millions of *yuán* into replacing concrete buildings with traditional wooden Nàxī architecture. The World Bank came up with rebuilding funds, and Lì Jiāng was conferred with the ultimate imprimatur (some would say the kiss of death) as a UNESCO World Heritage town in 1999. All this attention plus the construction of a new airport and hotels has turned it into a major tourist destination with outrageous prices at every turn. Lì Jiāng's old town, with its cobblestone streets, gurgling streams, and Nàxī architecture, thankfully preserves a modicum of traditional ways, but as Hàn merchants move in to cater to hordes of stampeding tourists, many of the Nàxī who still live there (about 6,000 households) are finding their old way of life being challenged.

Located on the road to Tibet in a region widely regarded as being one of the most beautiful in the world, Lì Jiāng also offers a plethora of fascinating side trips that can easily take up to a week or more of your time. Lì Jiāng (elev. 2,340m/7,800 ft.) has a pleasant climate year-round with average temperatures in the spring, summer, and fall ranging between 60°F and 80°F (16°C–27°C). Spring and fall are the best times to visit, as the summer months are unbelievably crowded with Chinese tourists, busier even than the big-city shopping areas.

ESSENTIALS

GETTING THERE   From Lì Jiāng's airport, 24km (15 miles) and a 30-minute taxi ride (around ¥80/$10) southwest of town, there are daily **flights** to Kūnmíng (50 min.) as well as weekly flights to Guǎngzhōu (3 hr.), Shànghǎi (4½ hr.), and Xīshuāngbǎnnà (30 min.). Tickets can be bought at the **CAAC/Yúnnán Airlines** ticket office at Fúhuì Lù, Mínháng Zhàn (© **0888/516-1289**). CAAC airport buses (¥10/$1.25) depart from the office 90 minutes before scheduled departures. There is another CAAC office on the first floor of the Lì Jiāng Dàjiǔdiàn at Xīn Dàjiē (© **0888/518-0280;** open 8:30am–6:30pm).

Though the flight from Kūnmíng to Lì Jiāng only takes a half-hour or so, road transportation in last decade has improved exponentially, reducing a 20-hour journey to just 5 hours once the new Dàlǐ bypass opens in spring 2006. From the main **long-distance bus station** at the southern end of Mínzú Lù (© **0888/512-1106**), **buses** run to Xiàguān (3 hr.; ¥32–¥51/$4–$6.30) every half-hour from 7:10am to 6:30pm; express buses to Xiàguān depart at 8:20am, 11:30am, and 2:30pm. Express buses run to Kūnmíng (7 hr.; ¥152/$19) at 8:20am, 9:20am, 11:20am, and 3:20pm; a sleeper bus to Kūnmíng (9 hr.; ¥105–¥115/$13–$14) runs every half-hour from 5:30 to 8:30pm. Buses also run to Zhōngdiàn/Xiānggélǐlā, passing Qiáotóu (5 hr.; ¥27/$3.40) every hour from 7:30am to 4pm; to Jīnjiāng/Sìchuān (9 hr.; ¥52–¥66/$6.40–$8) at 7:10am, 8:30am, 12:30pm, 2pm, and 6pm; and to Nínglǎng (4 hr.; ¥23/$3) every hour from 7:50am to 3:30pm. A private bus company, **YNTAC** (© **0888/512-5492**), operates luxury air-conditioned buses to Xiàguān (3 hr.; ¥50/$6.25) at 8:30am, 9am, 10:30am, and 5pm; and to Kūnmíng (8 hr.; ¥151/$19) at 8:30am, 9am, and 10:30am. YNTAC buses depart from the Nàxī Dàjiǔdiàn, at Nán Guòjìng Lù about 1km (⅔ mile) west of the bus station.

GETTING AROUND   The old town, off limits to motor traffic, can be comfortably toured on foot. **Taxis** cost ¥6 (75¢) for 3km (2 miles), then ¥1.60 (20¢) per kilometer. From midnight to 7am, in-town taxis charge ¥10 ($1.25) per trip. **Bikes** can be rented from several cafes in the old town and also in Máo Square at Ālǐ Bābā (© **013987047896**) for around ¥15 ($2) a day.

TOURS & GUIDES   Many of the cafes and hostels in old Lì Jiāng have travel agencies that provide day tours and air and bus tickets. The **Dōngbā House,** Xīnyì Jiē, Jīshàn Xiàng 16 (© **0888/517-5431**), can help with backpackers' routes. **Gallery Travel,** diagonally across the way at Jīshàn Xiàng 39 (© **0888/666-0994**), frequently organizes hikes to Tiger Leaping Gorge, skiing trips to nearby Hābā Mountain and Jade Dragon Snow Mountain, and overland trips by Land Cruiser into Tibet (approximately ¥4,500/$562 per person for transportation and Tibet permit, based on four-person minimum). For the less adventurous, Old Lì Jiāng has a **Tourist Consultation Service** just inside the northern entrance on Xīnyì Jiē (© **0888/511-6666**) which offers more sedate day tours of the surrounding areas (in Chinese only).

Lì Jiāng

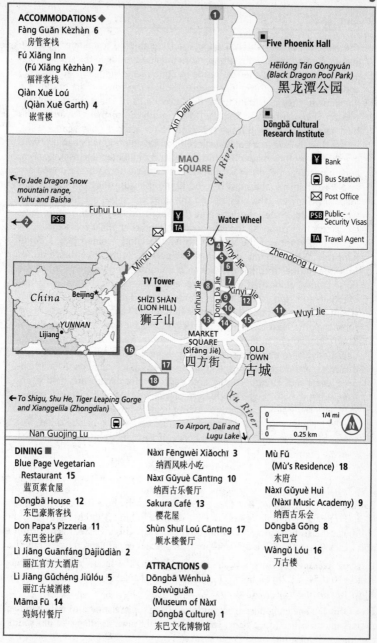

ACCOMMODATIONS ◆
Fàng Guǎn Kèzhàn **6**
房管客栈
Fú Xiǎng Inn
(Fú Xiǎng Kèzhàn) **7**
福祥客栈
Qiàn Xuě Lóu
(Qiàn Xuě Garth) **4**
嵌雪楼

To Jade Dragon Snow
mountain range,
Yuhu and Baisha

Xin Dàjiē

Fuhui Lu

PSB

**MAO
SQUARE**

Yu River

Five Phoenix Hall

Hēilóng Tán Gōngyuán
(Black Dragon Pool Park)
黑龙潭公园

Dōngbā Cultural
Research Institute

¥ Bank

Bus Station

Post Office

PSB Public-
Security Visas

TA Travel Agent

China

Beijing ★

YUNNAN

Lijiang

Minzu Lu

¥
TA

Water Wheel

Xinyi Jiē

Zhendong Lu

TV Tower
**SHĪZI SHĀN
(LION HILL)**
狮子山

Xinhua Jiē

Dong Da Jiē

Xinyi Jiē

Wuyì Jiē

**MARKET
SQUARE
(Sìfāng Jiē)**
四方街

**OLD
TOWN**
古城

To Shigu, Shu He, Tiger Leaping Gorge
and Xianggelila (Zhongdian)

Nan Guojing Lu

Yu River

To Airport, Dali and
Lugu Lake ↓

0   1/4 mi
0   0.25 km

DINING ■
**Blue Page Vegetarian
Restaurant 15**
蓝页素食屋
Dōngbā House 12
东巴豪斯客栈
Don Papa's Pizzeria 11
东巴爸比萨
Lì Jiāng Guānfáng Dàjiǔdiàn 2
丽江官方大酒店
Lì Jiāng Gǔchéng Jiǔlóu 5
丽江古城酒楼
Māma Fù 14
妈妈付餐厅

Nàxī Fēngwèi Xiǎochī 3
纳西风味小吃
Nàxī Gǔyuè Cāntīng 10
纳西古乐餐厅
Sakura Café 13
樱花屋
Shùn Shuǐ Lóu Cāntīng 17
顺水楼餐厅

ATTRACTIONS ●
**Dōngbā Wénhuà
Bówùguǎn
(Museum of Nàxī
Dōngbā Culture) 1**
东巴文化博物馆

**Mù Fǔ
(Mù's Residence) 18**
木府
**Nàxī Gǔyuè Huì
(Nàxī Music Academy) 9**
纳西古乐会
Dōngbā Gōng 8
东巴宫
Wàngǔ Lóu 16
万古楼

The Nàxī

The majority of China's Nàxī population, numbering just under 290,000, lives in Yúnnán, and of this group, more than half reside in the Lì Jiāng Nàxī Autonomous County; the rest reside in Zhōngdiàn, Nínglàng, Yōngshèng, and Déqìn counties to the northwest. Though the Nàxī's exact origins are not known, they are thought to be descendants of the ancient nomadic Tibetan Qiāng tribes of Qīnghǎi. Driven south by northern invaders, the Nàxī have been resident in the Lì Jiāng area for around 1,400 years.

The Nàxī believe in a polytheistic religion called dōngbā (meaning "wise man" or "scripture reader"), which is a blend of Tibetan lamaism, Daoism, and shamanistic beliefs in various gods and spirits in nature. Dōngbā are also Nàxī shamans, the most revered figures because they not only act as mediators between the present and the spirit world but are the only ones who can read, write, and interpret the approximately 1,400 pictographic characters that comprise the Nàxī script created over 1,000 years ago.

The importance of the shaman notwithstanding, women play a dominant role in Nàxī society, which is matrilineal in nature. Inheritance passes from the mother through the youngest daughter, and women control the purse strings, work the fields, and trade at markets. It is the men who traditionally function as child-raisers, gardeners, and musicians. The revival in recent years of traditional Nàxī music has helped keep alive an ancient art form that the Nàxī have been practicing since before the days of Kublai Khan's invasion of Lì Jiāng in the 13th century. Many of the songs, rarely heard anywhere else and some dating as far back as the Sòng and Táng dynasties, are played on rare and unusual musical instruments several hundred years old. Dōngbā music and dance performances are held every evening in the old town, and feature prominently as well in Nàxī festivals, including the traditional Sānduō Festival held on the eighth day of the second lunar month to honor the god Sānduō, believed to be the great protector of the Nàxī against a whole horde of pestilence and disasters.

FAST FACTS

Banks, Foreign Exchange & ATMs   The main branch of the **Bank of China** (open Mon–Fri 8:30am–5:30pm) is on Xīn Dàjiē south of Fúhuì Lù and has an ATM. In the old town, the **Industrial and Commercial Bank of China (ICBC)** across from the post office (open Mon–Fri, 8:30am–5pm) can exchange cash and travelers' checks.

Internet Access   A number of cafes in the old town offer Internet service for around ¥5 to ¥10 (65¢–$1.25) an hour. One of the most reliable is the **Dōngbā House Inn,** Xīnyì Jiē Jīshàn Xiàng 16. Dial-up is © 163.

Post Office   The main post office in new Lì Jiāng (open 8am–8pm) is on Xīn Dàjiē. A smaller post office (open 8am–8pm) is in the old town at Sìfāng Jiē just south of the Xīnhuá Bookstore.

Visa Extensions   The **Gōngānjú (PSB)** is located at Fúhuì Lù (© **0888/518-8437;** open Mon–Fri 8am–noon and 2:30–5:30pm in summer, 8:30am–noon and 2–5:30pm otherwise).

EXPLORING LÌ JIĀNG
OLD TOWN ✷✷

When visitors and travel guide writers gush about Lì Jiāng, they're really referring to its raison d'être, the **old town** *(gǔchéng)*, built over 800 years ago during the Southern Sòng dynasty. A delightful maze of twisting cobblestone streets and Nàxī-style homes but more and more shops, usually of the souvenir variety, the old town still affords glimpses of traditional Nàxī life as residents go about their daily lives despite the staggering crowds and the increasingly commercial tenor of the whole place.

Unlike many ancient towns in China, Lì Jiāng does not have a city wall. It is said that the first ruling family of Lì Jiāng, surnamed Mù, prohibited the building of a wall around the old town because drawing a box around the character of *mù* turned it into the character *kùn*, meaning "difficulty," and was therefore not auspicious. What the old town does have, however, is a web of flowing canals fed by the Yùquán springs in today's Black Dragon Pool to the north. These streams often flow into several three-pit **wells** scattered around the old town with designated pits for drinking, washing vegetables, and washing clothes. You can see such a well at the **Báimǎ Lóng Tán** in the south of town. The **Yīcàn Quán,** for drinking water only, can be found on Mìshì Xiāng next to the Blue Page Vegetarian Restaurant. The old town used to have several water mills as well, but the only one standing today is a reconstructed **water wheel** at the old town entrance. In the center of town is **Market Square (Sìfāng Jiē),** ringed with shops and restaurants. During the day, Nàxī women come here to trade, and on certain evenings, residents will gather here and break into spontaneous circle dances.

From Market Square, a cobblestone path leads uphill along the eastern flanks of **Shīzi Shān (Lion Hill),** which separates the old town from the new. This area, known as Huáng Shān, is one of the region's oldest neighborhoods and is a lovely place to wander, as it's a relatively tourist-free zone. At the top of the hill is the 33m-tall (108-ft.) **Wàngǔ Lóu;** admission is ¥15 ($1.90) and it's open from dawn to dusk. Each meter represents 10,000 of Lì Jiāng's 330,000 people; it is said to be the tallest wooden pagoda in China. Supported by 16 massive 22m-high (72-ft.) pillars made from old local wood, the square pagoda has 13 soaring eaves (representing the 13 peaks of the Jade Dragon Snow Mountain range) and over 2,300 Dōngbā designs carved into the structure. There are some stunning **views** ✷✷ of the old town, new town, and majestic Jade Dragon Snow Mountain range from the top.

Anchoring the southern part of the old town is **Mù Fǔ (Mù's Residence;** ¥35/ $4.30; open 9am–6pm). The former home of the Nàxī ruling family, which ruled Lì Jiāng for 22 generations until 1723, the residence was actually completely destroyed in the Qīng dynasty (1644–1911) and, until the earthquake of 1996, the houses of ordinary Nàxī stood in the palace's stead. Postearthquake authorities apparently determined

---

Tips Lost in Lì Jiāng

If you ever get lost in the old town, just find a stream and walk against the current, as it will invariably lead you back to an entrance of the town.

that World Bank rebuilding funds would be better justified by an imperial residence that could attract legions of tourists rather than by banal domestic housing; the result is the sprawling residence you see today. Stepped into the side of Lion Hill are six main halls separated by courtyards said to resemble those of the Forbidden City, including a meeting hall where the clan chiefs met and a library of Dōngbā writings. From the back of the residence, steps lead up the hill to Wàngǔ Lóu.

Dōngbā Wénhuà Bówùguǎn (Museum of Nàxī Dōngbā Culture) ๙ This museum features exhibits of Nàxī clothing and jewelry, Dōngbā pictographic script, unearthed artifacts from old Lì Jiāng, and a display claiming the region is the real Shangri-La. Explanations are in English. At the museum shop you can have a piece of Dōngbā calligraphy drawn for you by an 85-year-old Dōngbā shaman for about ¥100 ($13).

Hēilóng Tán. Admission ¥5 (60¢). 8:30am–6pm.

Hēilóng Tán Gōngyuán (Black Dragon Pool Park) ๙ About 1.5km (1 mile) north of the old town, this park, which contains the source of much of the old town's water, also offers Lì Jiāng's most famous photo op: the distant snowcapped Jade Dragon Snow Mountain fronted by the park's Déyuè Lóu (Moon Embracing Pavilion), and Wǔkǒng Qiáo (Five Arch Bridge). In the eastern section is the three-story Míng dynasty Wǔfèng Lóu (Five Phoenix Hall), with soaring eaves meant to resemble flying phoenixes. Also here is the Dōngbā Cultural Research Institute (Dōngbā Wénhuà Yánjiūsuǒ), where you can see experts translating Dōngbā pictographs.

Xīn Dàjē. Admission ¥20 ($2.50). 6:30am–8:30pm.

WHERE TO STAY

While new Lì Jiāng has more upscale hotels with modern facilities, none of them can match the charming ambience and coziness of the old town's traditional Nàxī guest-houses and hotels. There are plenty of inns offering basic dormitory-style accommodations, but a notch above these guesthouses are several hotels also housed in traditional Nàxī buildings. The **Fú Xiǎng Inn (Fú Xiǎng Kèzhàn)** ๙ at Jīshàn Xiàng 24, Xīnyì Jiē (② **0888/515-2525;** fax 0888/515-2526), is one such property. Situated just beyond a small stream that seems to be the center of activity for the whole neighborhood, this courtyard inn has 25 passable rooms (¥180/$23), but with big, wide internal balconies. Some rooms even have Jacuzzis, but even this luxury does not match the pleasure of sipping tea under the crimson glow of traditional *dēnglong* lanterns. Operated by the same owners is the **Fáng Guǎn Kèzhàn** at Jīshàn Xiàng 58, Xīnyì Jiē (② **0888/510-2118**); its 19 comfortable rooms have air-conditioning (and central heating during the winter) and private bathrooms for ¥280 ($35).

Lì Jiāng Guānfáng Dàjiǔdiàn The only five-star hotel in town, this modern glass building with the revolving restaurant towers above all others as the symbol of new Lì Jiāng. Distinctly lacking in personal charm, the hotel attracts mostly domestic tour groups. Rooms are not as luxurious as you would expect. The carpets are a little worn and the upholstery clashes with the decor, but the units are otherwise spacious and come with the full amenities. Bathrooms are done in a rather garish tile but are clean.

Xiānggélǐlā Dà Dào. ② **0888/518-8888.** Fax 0888/518-1999. www.gfhotel-lijiang.com. 289 units. ¥960 –¥1,120 ($120–$140) standard room; ¥2,000 ($250) suite. AE, DC, MC, V. **Amenities:** 3 restaurants; bar; lounge; indoor swimming pool; health club and spa; bowling alley; concierge; tour desk; air ticket counter; free airport shuttle; business center; forex; shopping arcade; salon; 24-hr. room service; same-day dry cleaning/laundry. *In room:* A/C, satellite TV, minibar, hair dryer, safe.

Qiàn Xuě Lóu (Qiàn Xuě Garth) 🏵 With its imposing location, the Garth seems to dominate the entire main square and it is difficult to find any courtyards more pleasant than these. Rooms are clean and comfortable but it is the courtyards where you can sit outside, that are more important in Lì Jiāng. Staff can be somewhat elusive, spread out among all the courtyards, private dining rooms, and small gardens. The best part is the viewing terrace that looks directly out over the water wheels and the main square.

Shuāng Shí Duàn, Xīn Huá Jiē (north entrance of old town Lì Jiāng). ℂ 0888/515-1816. Fax 0888/515-1789. 123 units. ¥480 ($60) standard room; ¥640 ($80) deluxe room; from ¥960 ($120) suite. 20%–30% discounts. AE, DC, MC, V. **Amenities:** 2 restaurants; bar; lounge; concierge; business center; forex; shopping arcade; salon; 24-hr. room service; dry cleaning/laundry. In room: A/C, satellite TV, minibar, hair dryer, safe.

WHERE TO DINE

Old town Lì Jiāng offers plenty of friendly cafes and family-operated restaurants catering to foreign travelers with Western, Chinese, and Nàxī food at prices that have recently increased so much they almost match those of the big cities. The classic **Māma Fù** (ℂ 0888/512-2285), located on Xīnyì Jiē just north of the Market Square, serves some of the best pizza around and is also famous for its homemade breads and apple pie. Sit outside by the running stream and watch old Lì Jiāng go by. The **Blue Page Vegetarian Restaurant** at Xīnyì Jiē, Mìshì Xiàng 69 (ℂ 0888/518-5206), is a quiet, cozy place with fresh flowers that serves excellent vegetarian fare such as a mushroom and vegetable pie, vegetarian burgers, and apple crumble. The **Dōngbā House** at Xīnyì Jiē, Jìshàn Xiàng 16 (ℂ 0888/517-5431), offers Tibetan cuisine along with Nàxī, Chinese, and Western food, and some of the best people-watching in the old town. On the west side of the old town, the always-crowded **Sakura Café** at Xīnhuá Jiē, Cuìwén Duàn 123 (ℂ 0888/518-7619), has everything from delicious Korean *bibimbap* (rice with vegetables and meat) to an Israeli chicken-cutlet dinner.

Don Papa's Pizzeria 🏵🏵🏵 *Finds* WESTERN An oasis of sweetness for those who have overloaded themselves on goat cheese, yak butter, and that local specialty, deep-fried insects. Run by a French expat with excellent culinary skills, this somewhat hidden corner store has a great balcony upon which to enjoy a reliable Western breakfast. For the rest of the day, customers can choose from strawberry tartlets, chocolate croissants, and fresh fruit Danish. At dinnertime, among the excellent Italian entrees is a delicious four-cheese pizza, featuring goat cheese, Lì Jiāng cheese, mozzarella, and Parmesan.

Xīnyì Jiē, Jìshàn Xiàng 3 (ℂ 0888/518-3967. Meal for 2 ¥50–¥150 ($6.25–$19). No credit cards. 8:30am–11:30pm.

Lì Jiāng Gǔchéng Jiǔlóu 🏵 YÚNNÁN/NÀXĪ This pleasant, upscale restaurant with alfresco stream-side dining specializes in the *Nàxī sāndiéshuǐ*, a 36-course meal divided into cold, steamed, and sweet dishes. Although this banquet, at ¥488 ($61), is designed for six to eight people, smaller groups can order the half portion for about ¥300 ($38). The restaurant also has a more traditional Chinese menu, and serves hot pot and grilled kabobs as well.

Dōng Dàjiē (entrance to the old town). ℂ 0888/518-1818. Meal for 2 ¥80–¥150 ($10–$19). No credit cards. 9am–midnight.

Nàxī Fēngwèi Xiǎochī 🏵 NÀXĪ This no-frills restaurant serves some of the best local fare in all of Lì Jiāng; witness the crowds that throng here every night. You can dine outdoors by a running stream or on the second floor. Nàxī favorites include *jīdòu chǎo mǐfàn* (fried rice with soya bean), *Lì Jiāng bāba* (a local baked pastry which can be ordered sweet or salty), and *zhá rŭbĭng* (fried goat cheese). If you're with a group of five or more, ask for the *fēngwèi cān,* which consists of 10 to 16 special Nàxī dishes. Service is brusque during peak meal times from 6 to 8pm. The restaurant has a second outlet two doors down.

Xīnhuá Jiē, Shuāng Shí Duàn 22. ⓒ **0888/518-9591.** Meal for 2 ¥20–¥40 ($2.50–$5). No credit cards. 7:30am–11pm.

Nàxī Gŭyuè Cāntīng YÚNNÁN/NÀXĪ   This modest restaurant located down an alley has little atmosphere but serves hearty *guòqiáo mĭxiàn* (crossing-the-bridge noodles) and *qìguō jī* (stewed chicken), as well as Nàxī specialties like *kăo yú* (barbecued fish) and *Lì Jiāng dàguōcài* (vegetables in broth). There are no menus in English, but the staff tries to be helpful.

Dōng Dàjiē (south of Nàxī Gŭyuè Huì/Nàxī Music Academy). ⓒ **0888/666-7577.** Meal for 2 ¥20–¥60 ($2.50–$7.50). No credit cards. 7:30am–11:30pm.

Shùn Shuĭ Lóu Cāntīng NÀXĪ   This is one of the best locations that we found in town, right beside one of the numerous streams, and yet another good choice for experimenting with the more bizarre tastes of Nàxī food such as *shù wā* (frog-skin fungus) or the numerous types of deep-fried insects that are available here. The English menu is a starting point, but as this place is popular among Cantonese diners, see what everybody else is trying before making your own choices.

Băi Suì Fáng, 80, Xīnyì Jiē. ⓒ **0888/5129029.** Meal for 2 ¥40–¥80 ($5–$10). No credit cards. 7:30am–11:30pm.

LÌ JIĀNG AFTER DARK

Attending a Nàxī concert is one of the more popular evening activities in Lì Jiāng. The original Nàxī Orchestra at the **Nàxī Gŭyuè Huì (Nàxī Music Academy)** is led by esteemed Nàxī ethnomusicologist Xuán Kè, who delivers introductions and explanations to the music and instruments in both English and Chinese. Nightly performances are held at the Nàxī Concert Hall (Dōng Dàjiē) from 8 to 9:30pm. Purchase tickets for ¥30 to ¥50 ($3.75–$6.25) ahead of time; performances are frequently sold out. Directly across the street, the **Dōngbā Gōng** offers a second option for Nàxī song and dance performances at 8pm. Tickets are ¥35 ($4.50) or ¥50 ($6.25).

AROUND LÌ JIĀNG

Please turn to appendix A for Chinese translations of key locations.

YÙFĒNG SÌ

Located about 13km (8 miles) northwest of Lì Jiāng at the foot of Jade Dragon Snow Mountain, this small lamasery belonging to the Scarlet Sect of Tibetan Buddhism was first built in 1660. Today it is best known for its *wànduŏ shānchá* (10,000-flower camellia tree). Formed from the merger of two trees planted by monks between 1465 and 1487, the camellia tree is said to bloom 20 times between March and June, bearing a total of 20,000 blossoms! If you're cycling here (2 hr.), follow Xiānggélĭlā Dà Dào out of town. About 5km (3 miles) past the town of Báishā, take a left at **Yùshuĭ Zhài (Jade Water Village),** go past the **Dōngbā Village,** and continue on to Yùfēng Temple.

YÙ HÚ (NGULUKO) 🌸🌸

Just before the Dōngbā Village is the turnoff for the lovely, quiet, tour group–free village that was Joseph Rock's home in the 1920s and 1930s. The Austrian-born botanist and anthropologist, whose *Ancient Nakhi Kingdom of Southwest China* is the definitive account of Nàxī culture and language, is a local legend who lived in Lì Jiāng for 27 years. Following the turnoff—which you can't miss, as large letters proclaim FOLLOW ROCKER'S TRAIL TO SHANGRI-LA (the misspelled name turns out to be an English transliteration of the literal Chinese pronunciation of "Rock," or "Luòkè")—take a right at the first fork for about 3km (2 miles), then follow signs directing you to the village where all the houses are built entirely from large stones and rocks. **Joseph Rock's former residence (Luòkè Gùjū Chénlièguǎn;** ¥10/$1.25; open 8am–6pm) is a two-story wooden house where Rock lived with his Nàxī assistant Lǐ Sīyù. Rock's quarters on the second floor contain his original twin bed, his suitcase, a folding table, two chairs, and kerosene lamps. A newly built exhibition hall next to the residence has displays of Rock's gun, clothing, pictographic cards used to help Rock learn the Dōngbā language, and Rock's own photographs of Nàxī funeral ceremonies and festivals.

BÁISHĀ 🅐

Ten kilometers (6 miles) northwest of Lì Jiāng, 1km (½ mile) off the main road to Jade Dragon Snow Mountain, this dusty historic town is most famous these days for its Míng- and Qīng-dynasty **temple frescoes,** which were painted by Nàxī, Tibetan, Bái, and Hàn artists and hence incorporate elements of Buddhism, Lamaism, and Daoism. The largest fresco, found on the front wall of the **Dàbǎojī Palace** (¥8/$1; open 7:30am–6pm), is a gorgeous Míng dynasty mural of Buddha preaching to his disciples.

In the street behind the Dàbǎojī Palace, visitors can also find Báishā's most famous personality, Dr. Ho (Hé), at his Chinese herbal clinic. Immortalized by travel writer Bruce Chatwin as the "Taoist physician in the Jade-Dragon Mountains of Lì Jiāng," and visited by countless journalists and curious travelers ever since, Dr. Ho can dispense herbs for any ailment and will happily sell you some of his special tea made from home-grown herbs, which has many fans if you believe all the scrapbooks of letters from grateful patients.

For those more interested in local history than local celebrity, the plain that the bus crosses to get to the village conceals the remains of the airstrip used by the Flying Tigers. Unfortunately, there is not much left to look at, but a nose around might inspire the amateur archaeologist in you.

SHÙ HÉ 🅐🅐

Until recently, this village, actually the prototype for Lì Jiāng, was almost unknown to travelers. For a ¥15 ($2) 15-minute taxi ride, you can escape the thronging hordes of Lì Jiāng and visit this little village, Lì Jiāng in microcosm, with two gurgling streams running past every house. There is an old town and a new development with accommodations, restaurants, and even a few bars. At the other end of town is an interesting museum that follows the history of the Horse and Tea Road and features plenty of pictures of Joseph Rock. Look for the very attractive guidebooks of the area, printed on traditional Nàxī paper. Entry into the village costs ¥30 ($4) but the ticket office usually closes around 7pm.

YÙLÓNG XUĚSHĀN (JADE DRAGON SNOW MOUNTAIN) 🅐🅐🅐

This magnificent 35km-long (21-mile) mountain range framing Lì Jiāng is a must-visit. The tallest of the mountain's 13 peaks is the daunting **Shànzifēng (Fan Peak;** elev. 5,596m/18,355 ft.), perennially snowcapped and climbed for the first time only in 1963 by a research team from Běijīng. Today's visitors have a number of options for exploring the mountain. All require you to pay a ¥60 ($7.50) entrance fee to the Jade

Dragon Snow Mountain Scenic Area, about 30km (20 miles) north of town. Many tourists visit as part of an organized tour. To get out here on your own, it's best to hire a private car or taxi for ¥100 to ¥150 ($13–$19), or take a bus for Bǎoshān or Dàjù.

The most popular visit is a round-trip cable-car ride for ¥180 ($22) from the village just inside the main gate to **Bīngchuān Gōngyuán (Glacier Park).** If possible, purchase your ticket in town the day before at the Jade Dragon Snow Mountain ticket office at Xiānggélǐlā Dà Dào and Xiàngshān Dōng Lù, as ornery ticket attendants at the reception center will sometimes insist you cannot purchase a ticket on the spot. Buses for ¥10 ($1.25) round-trip will transport you the 4km (2½ miles) from the reception center to the cable car terminus. From here it's a two-section ride on a chairlift to the foot of Fan Peak. You can climb a wooden walkway all the way up to 4,480m (14,700 ft.), where visitors are greeted with a stunning view of glaciers and with ice caverns. If you feel any altitude sickness, Chinese vendors will happily sell you an oxygen bag for around ¥30 ($3.75).

About 20 minutes north of the reception center past the Báishuǐ Hé River, a 10-minute ride on a chairlift for ¥40 ($5 round-trip) and a 30-minute ramble through groves of spruce and pine trees leads you to **Yúnshān Píng (Spruce Meadow,** elev. 3,206m/10,515 ft.). During the annual Torch Festival, young Nàxī men and women come here to pray for eternal love.

The third cable car, which costs ¥60 ($7.50) round-trip and takes you another 20km (12 miles) north, arrives at **Máoniú Píng (Yak Meadow,** elev. 3,500m/11,480 ft.), the least visited of the three spots. The meadow has grazing yaks, blooming flowers (in spring and summer), and a number of hiking possibilities. One of the more popular routes leads to Xuěhuā Hú (Snow Flake Lake), which brilliantly captures the crystalline reflection of the surrounding mountains.

TIGER LEAPING GORGE (HǓTIÀO XIÁ) 🌾

Often billed as one of the most spectacular sights in Lì Jiāng and a must-hike for trekkers, the 30km-long (18-mile) Tiger Leaping Gorge, which sits between the Jade Dragon Snow Mountain of Lì Jiāng and the Hābā Snow Mountain of Zhōngdiàn to the north, is a tad overrated. To be sure, this canyon, reaching a depth of over 3,000m (9,842 ft.), is pretty enough, and occasionally breathtaking; as treks go, it is a moderately interesting, occasionally strenuous, and infrequently dangerous trek taking 2 to 3 days, but by no stretch of the imagination is it the ultimate of sights, as its renown may have led some to expect.

The gorge is divided into upper *(shàng hǔtiào),* middle *(zhōng hǔtiào),* and lower *(xià hǔtiào)* sections, with two main entrances, one at the town of Qiáotóu at the upper gorge and the other at the town of Dàjù at the end of the lower gorge (¥30/$3.75; open 8am–7pm). Most hikers now start from Qiáotóu, as all foreigners traveling on buses from Lì Jiāng to Dàjù are required to pay the ¥48 ($6) entrance fee to the Jade Dragon Snow Mountain Scenic Area between Lì Jiāng and Dàjù. For most visitors short on time, the gorge can be visited as a day trip from Lì Jiāng or on the way to Shangri-La. Recently, instead of going all the way to Qiáotóu, many private-hire taxis and tour buses like to drop off visitors at a newly constructed parking lot on the south side of the gorge across from the town of Qiáotóu. After paying the entrance fee, it's a 2.6km (1½-mile) walk along a wide paved path to the gorge's most famous sight, the **Tiger Leaping Stone (Hǔtiào Shí),** a large rock in the middle of the raging river which gave the gorge its name. The legend goes that a tiger being chased by a hunter escaped capture by leaping over the river with the help of this rock.

On the north side of the gorge, a new road for buses and cars has been built all the way from Qiáotóu to Tiger Leaping Stone, allowing for even more busloads of tourists to disembark on the northern side of the stone; by the time you read this, the road from Tiger Leaping Stone to Walnut Grove which marks the end of the middle section of the gorge should be paved, which means more exhaust-spewing cars reaching ever deeper into the gorge.

For trekkers approaching from Qiáotóu, there are two paths: the lower path used by buses and cars as described above, which is a relatively easy and flat, if exhaust-filled, hike; and the higher path, which is longer, more strenuous, and more dangerous because of falling rocks and narrower paths. Check with the travelers' cafes in Lì Jiāng beforehand for the latest hiking conditions. It is possible but not advisable to do the hike in a day. Basic but charming guesthouses along the way, all with hot water and restaurants, make overnighting at the gorge a relatively painless affair. In general, hikers on the high path can overnight at **Nuòyǔ** village, 6.3km (4 miles) and 2 hours from Qiáotóu, where the Nàxī Family Guesthouse charges ¥10 ($1.25) per bed. Or you can stay at **Běndìwān** village, 17km (10 miles) and 4 to 8 hours from Qiáotóu, which has several guesthouses; the Halfway Guesthouse (Zhōngtú Kèzhàn) has beds for ¥10 to ¥15 ($1.25–$2), and some of the best views. Some hikers even manage to get to **Walnut Grove (Hétao Yuán)**, 23km (14 miles) from Qiáotóu and 2 to 4 hours from Běndìwān, in one day. However, the middle rapids between Tina's Guesthouse on the lower path and Walnut Grove is one of the prettiest sections of the gorge, so you may want to take your time through there. Guesthouses at Walnut Grove include the very social Sean's Spring Guesthouse (Shānquán Kèzhàn) with beds for ¥15 to ¥20 ($2–$2.50); and the quieter Château Woody (Shānbáiliǎn Lǚguǎn), with beds for ¥10 to ¥15 ($1.25–$2), clean toilets, and great views. From Walnut Grove, you can either hike back to Qiáotóu via the 4- to 5-hour lower path, or you can take a taxi back to Qiáotóu for ¥10 to ¥15 ($1.25–$2). Another option is to continue on to Dàjù, a section considerably less scenic which requires crossing the river; the old ferry costs ¥10 ($1.25), the new ferry ¥12 ($1.50).

To get to Qiáotóu from Lì Jiāng, take a Zhōngdiàn-bound bus (2½ hr.; ¥14/$1.60), which runs every half-hour to hour from 7:30am to 3pm, and ask to be let off at Qiáotóu. From Qiáotóu, the last bus to Lì Jiāng passes at around 6:30pm, while the last bus to Zhōngdiàn passes at around 5pm. The last bus (3 hr.; ¥24/$3) from Dàjù to Lì Jiāng leaves at 1:30pm. Frequent minibuses, running until 5pm, take 2½ hours and cost ¥15 ($2) to get from Dàjù to Zhōngdiàn.

A FASCINATING SIDE TRIP
LÚGŪ HÚ (LÚGŪ LAKE) ★★

Located about 210km (126 miles) northeast of Lì Jiāng in the Nínglàng Autonomous County (Nínglàng Xiàn) at the juncture of Yúnnán and Sìchuān provinces, the pristine and breathtaking **Lúgū Hu (Lúgū Lake)** is the home of the Mosu ("Mósuō" in Mandarin)—the only practicing matriarchal society in the world, with a population of 36,000—and a smaller number of Tibetans and Yí. The relatively remote lake is at least a 5-hour trip by car (up to 8 hr. by minibus with a change in Nínglàng) from Lì Jiāng, and it used to be that only anthropologists and a handful of curious travelers would make the trip. However, as word got out about the unusual Mosu, new roads were built and Chinese visitors have been arriving by the busloads, usually as part of a 2-day tour from Lì Jiāng. It's an interesting world, where women do *all* of the work,

Little-Known History

While many books and brochures talk about the Mosu, this area is also home to the Yí tribe, especially the infamous Norzu clan, slavers who made regular raids into the surrounding lowlands. A fascinating account of life is presented in Alan Winnington's book *Slaves of the Cool Mountains.* The practice was only abolished in 1956.

from child raising to cooking, from planting to governing, and the men are defined by their roles not as fathers but as uncles to the children in their mother's household. On the 25th day of the seventh lunar month (Aug or Sept), the Mosu celebrate their biggest festival, Zhuàn Shān Jié (Mountain-Circling Festival) at the Gému Nushén Shān (Goddess Gému Mountain) on the shores of Lúgū Lake.

Despite the increasingly crass commercialization and crowds, Lúgū Lake is still worth visiting, though an overnight stay is required. Most of the Chinese tour groups arrive in the afternoon and depart after breakfast the next morning, leaving you a good part of the day to explore, take a boat ride on the lake, or engage a Mosu in conversation, all in relative peace before the next batch of tourists arrives in the afternoon.

The 70-sq.-km (27-sq.-mile) freshwater lake (admission ¥35/$4.40) is dotted with many Mosu log cabins, though these have been replaced by three- and four-story hotels in the main village of **Luòshuǐ Cūn** on the western shore. The lake is surrounded by mountains, with the **Gému Nushén Shān** in the north and the hills of Sìchuān's Yányuán County across the lake in the east. Colorfully clothed Mosu women can row visitors in "pig-trough" (*zhūcáo*) boats, for approximately ¥35 ($4.25) per person, out to the two major islands in the lake: **Lǐwùbǐ Dǎo** and **Hēiwǎé Dǎo.** A small **museum** next to the bus station on the main strip has displays (in Chinese only) of Mosu artifacts and hosts evening Mosu song and dance performances. The owners of the **Húsī Teahouse,** transplants from Chóngqìng themselves, are a great source of information on local activities and often lead hikes around the lake. Farther on, **Yóngníng** is home to several more Mosu villages worth exploring.

GETTING THERE Short of joining an organized tour (which travel agencies in Lì Jiāng can arrange), the easiest way to get out to the lake on your own is by private car or taxi hire (5½ hr.; ¥500–¥600/$62–$75 round-trip); you'll have to pay for the driver's food and accommodations separately. Otherwise, take a Nínglàng-bound bus from Lì Jiāng's main bus station, then transfer to a Luòshuǐ-bound minibus (2–2½ hr.; ¥20/$2.50). Leaving Luòshuǐ, a Lì Jiāng-bound bus (¥43/$5) leaves the bus station (*kèyùn zhàn*) along the lakeshore at 7:30am. Alternatively, take a minivan taxi to Nínglàng for ¥20 ($2.50), and then catch a connecting bus back to Lì Jiāng (every hour 7am–3pm).

WHERE TO STAY & DINE A decent option close to the lake is the relatively new **Āxiá Nóngjiā Yuàn** (Āxiá Farmer's House; ✆ **0888/588-6066**), located behind the museum between the lake and the main road. It has 12 clean standard rooms with attached bathrooms for ¥200 ($25), with a 50% discount in low season. Staying along the waterfront is the most pleasant option, but the log cabin guesthouses for ¥10 to ¥15 ($1.25–$2) per bed are very basic, with communal showers and toilets. The **Mósuō Yuàn** (✆ **0888/588-1188**) along the lakeshore is one of the larger guesthouses and is relatively clean. Guesthouse owners can cook you dinner for about ¥10 to ¥20 ($1.25–$2.50). In the evenings, barbecue stalls set up along the waterfront, where you can get any variety of grilled meats and vegetables. The **Húsī Teahouse** along the waterfront offers coffees, teas, juices, and basic but tasty Chinese fare.

8 Xiānggélĭlā (Zhōngdiàn)

Yúnnán Province, 651km (390 miles) NW of Kūnmíng, 198km (119 miles) NW of Lì Jiāng

To its majority Tibetan residents, the capital of the Díqìng Tibetan Autonomous Prefecture, a small town on the road between Lì Jiāng and Tibet, is known as Gyalthang. To the town's smaller Hàn population, it's still called Zhōngdiàn. To tourist authorities, hotel owners, and tour operators around the country, the town is now the earthly paradise of Xiānggélĭlā (that's Shangri-La to you). A rose never had it so difficult, and we'll continue to refer to the destination as "Zhōngdiàn" in practical information. Though Zhōngdiàn was officially renamed Xiānggélĭlā in May 2002 (see sidebar below), you'll be sorely disappointed if you arrive here expecting paradise. Tourist authorities are working hard to build new hotels and roads, but for now this is still a small, dusty town (elev. 3,380m/11,092 ft.) to be visited mostly for its Tibetan monastery if you aren't going to make it to Tibet. The surrounding area, however, does offer some spectacular scenery. *Note:* Please turn to appendix A for Chinese translations of key locations.

Paradise Found?

In 1933, the word *Shangri-La* was introduced into the world's lexicon by novelist James Hilton, who wrote in *Lost Horizon* of four Westerners stranded by a plane crash in an idyllic mountain paradise in the Himalayas called Shangri-La. In this earthly Eden, peace and harmony prevailed. Hilton, who never set foot in China, later hinted that the inspiration for his mythical paradise may well have derived from Joseph Rock's many *National Geographic* articles about northwest China in the 1920s and 1930s. By then, this "magical place" with the lush valley, a monastery, a village, and Mount Karakal, "an almost perfect cone of snow," had stirred the soul of many an explorer, Chinese and Western alike, and the search for the "real" Shangri-La was on.

For the last 70 years, countries like Nepal and Bhutan have laid claim to the title. Within China, some have posited that Lì Jiāng, after all Rock's hometown for 27 years, was the real Shangri-La, while Sìchuān Province claimed that its Yàdīng Nature Reserve in the Konkaling Mountains was the true site. Then, in 1997, the Yúnnán government declared that they had, with "certainty," found Shangri-La—the Díqìng Plateau, 100km (60 miles) north of Lì Jiāng. Citing many similarities to Hilton's description, Zhōngdiàn County, the capital of the Díqìng Tibetan Autonomous Prefecture, officially changed it name to Xiānggélĭlā (Shangri-La) in 2002. Was paradise found after all? Zhōngdiàn may have the official imprimatur, but several rebel experts believe that the real inspiration for Shangri-La can actually be found some 320km (200 miles) to the southeast in the ancient kingdom of Mùlĭ, an area the size of Wales between Dàochéng, Zhōngdiàn, and Jiŭlóng.

ESSENTIALS

GETTING THERE Zhōngdiàn is connected by **flights** to Kūnmíng (50 min.; daily), Chéngdū (1 hr., 10 min.; 3–4 flights a week), and Lhasa (1 hr., 45 min.; 1–2 flights a week depending on season). To fly to Lhasa, you must have your Tibet travel permit in order. Tickets can be purchased at the **Yúnnán Airlines/CAAC** office at Wénmíng Jiē next to the Guāngguāng Hotel (② **0887/822-9901**); it's open from 8:30am to noon and 3 to 8pm (2–5:30pm in winter). Taxi fare to the airport about 6km (4 miles) south of town will cost ¥15 to ¥20 ($1.90–$2.50).

From the **Bus Station (Kèyùn Zhàn)** on Chángzhèng Lù (② **0887/822-2972**), **buses** run to Kūnmíng (9–10 hr.; ¥142–¥175/$17–$21) at 9am, and then hourly from 11am to 8pm; to Xiàguān (8 hr.; ¥42–¥65/$5–$8) every hour from 7am to 8pm; to Lì Jiāng (3½–5 hr.; ¥27/$3.25) every half-hour to hour from 7:10am to 5pm; to Déqīn (7 hr.; ¥30/$3.75) at 7:20am, 8:20am, and 9:20am; to Xiāngchéng (9 hr.) at 7:30am; to Jīnjiāng (10 hr.) at 3:30pm and 5pm; and to Sānbā (5–6 hr; ¥20/$2.50) at 8:30am. The 3:30pm bus to Jīnjiāng will get you there in time to connect with the train to Chéngdū. There has been talk of moving the bus station to the northern part of town along Zhōngxiāng Lù, so check beforehand.

To Tibet You can only travel overland to Tibet by Land Cruiser as part of an official travel agency group with all the requisite Tibet travel permits. If you haven't made prior reservations by the time you arrive in Zhōngdiàn, check first at the travelers' cafes. During the summer, there may be enough interest to pull together a group, but it'll likely cost around ¥5,000 ($625) per person just for transportation and the permit. From Zhōngdiàn, the overland route passes through Déqīn, the last border town in Yúnnán, another 6 to 8 hours away by car. Any questions about Tibet travel permits can be referred to Mr. Lin at the Tibet Tourism Office (see below).

To Sìchuān The back roads into Sìchuān from Zhōngdiàn are no less scenic or any more comfortable than the road to Tibet, but at least you won't have to worry about permits. Busing it to Chéngdū will take at least 6 to 7 days over some very high altitudes (above 4000m/13,120 ft.) and incredibly gorgeous terrain. Hiring a private car will cost around ¥800 to ¥1,200 ($100–$150). From Zhōngdiàn, a 7:30am bus departs every 2 to 3 days for Xiāngchéng in Sìchuān; the trip takes 10 hours. From Xiāngchéng, the route continues to Dàochéng or Lǐtáng, depending on weather and road conditions, then to Kāndìng (11 hr. from Lǐtáng), and finally to Chéngdū (a further 8 hr.).

Return to Dàlǐ ✿ The alternative route back to Dàlǐ that does not stop at Lì Jiāng, is an interesting option for those heading back south. Leaving at 12:30pm and costing ¥42 ($5) , the 6-hour journey starts on the Tibetan plateau and passes a surprising number of breeding centers for the shaggy Tibetan Mastiff, perhaps the only dog in the world with a hardier constitution than a St. Bernard. The road then drops away and descends through endless forest switchbacks, past numerous new hydro plants. After some breathtaking precipices, the surroundings turn agricultural once more and the roads turn to yellow as local farmers spread their rice husks across the road, to be conveniently winnowed by passing minibuses such as yours. Most travelers are very surprised by the huge amounts of one particular crop that grows in this province— opium's natural successor, tobacco.

GETTING AROUND Around town, **taxis** (unmetered) cost ¥5 (60¢) per trip. Bus no. 3 (¥1)/15¢) runs from the Tibet Hotel up the main thoroughfare, Chángzhēng Lù, all the way to Sōngzànlín Sì.

TOURS   CITS at Chángzhēng Lù (© **0887/823-0152**) just north of the bus station offers day tours (in Chinese only) to the surrounding areas. A group package to Sōngzànlín Sì, Bìtǎ Hǎi, and Nàpà Hǎi will run ¥110 to ¥150 ($14–$19). Information on local sights and travel to Tibet and Sìchuān can be picked up at the **Tibet Café** at Chángzhēng Lù (© **0887/823-0282**). Mr. Lin at the **Tibet Tourism Office** (© **0887/688-3996;** mobile 013988717676688) in the Xiāngbālā Hotel can arrange Tibet travel permits.

FAST FACTS

Banks, Foreign Exchange & ATMs   The **People's Bank of China** (Zhōu Rénmín Yínháng; open Mon–Tues and Thurs–Fri, 8:30am–noon and 2:30–5:30pm) is on Chángzhēng Lù. It offers forex, but it won't give cash advances on credit cards.

Internet Access   China Telecom on Chángzhēng Lù 9 has Internet service from 9am to 9pm, at ¥3 (40¢) per hour. Dial-up is © **163.**

Post Office   The post office (open 8:30am–8:30pm, 9am–8pm in the winter) is at the corner of Chéngzhēng Lù and Xiàngyáng Lù and has a nice collection of stamps and cards at very low prices.

Visa Extensions   The visa section of the **Gōngānjú** (**PSB;** Mon–Fri: 8:30–11:30am and 2:30–6pm summer; 9am–noon and 2–5:30pm winter) is located at Chángzhēng Lù 72 just south of the Díqìng Bīnguǎn.

EXPLORING THE TOWN

The largest Tibetan Buddhist temple in southwest China, **Ganden Sumtseling Gompa (Sōngzànlín Sì)** ✿✿✿ (¥10/$1.25; open 7:30am–6:30pm), is located 3km (2 miles) north of town. The Gelukpa (Yellow Hat) monastery was built in 1679 by the fifth Dalai Lama. Modeled on the Potala Palace in Lhasa, the temple was shelled by the Chinese army in 1959 and officially reopened in 1981. About 700 monks currently reside here. The main temple at the top of the hill, a four-story structure with a gold-plated roof reached by climbing a series of steps (or you can have your taxi drive you up to the north entrance *[běimén]*), has a solemn main hall with 108 red pillars and scores of colorful *thangka* hanging from the ceiling. Ascend to the roof, where a simply glorious panorama of Zhōngdiàn awaits you. In the living quarters of the Living Buddha, check out the smooth marks along the floor, where thousands have prostrated themselves in front of the Lama. You may even be able to find a monk who can point out the nearby mountain to the south used for Tibetan sky burials.

Returning to town on Chángzhēng Lù, you'll see a large white **chörten** (Tibetan stupa) on a hill to the west. There is typically a stupa at the entrance to every Tibetan town which, as a symbol of protection, is usually decorated with prayer flags and jewels, and ringed with stones laid by pilgrims as expressions of particular wishes or prayers. Pilgrims entering town are required to circumambulate the stupa three times.

To the south, Zhōngdiàn's **old town** is worth a ramble. From the Tibet Hotel, head east on Tuánjié Lù until it curves south onto Cāngfáng Jiē. You'll soon come to the **Old Town Scripture Chamber (Gǔchéng Zàngjīng Táng).** Admission is ¥5 (60¢) and hours are from 7am to 8pm. The 300-year-old temple housed part of the Red Army on their Long March in 1936. The triple-eaved main hall contains a statue of an all-seeing and omnipotent Buddha with a thousand heads and hands *(qiānshǒu qiānyǎn).*

WHERE TO STAY

The **Tibet Café** has reasonable rooms at perhaps the best prices in town, although the main road can be a little noisy. The Tibet Hotel on the other hand has an impressive reception area but awful rooms and some brainless staff whose entire knowledge of local history could be written on a postage stamp. The rooms are even worse and to be avoided at all costs.

Lóngfèng Xiáng Dàjiŭdiàn (Holy Palace Hotel) ⚝ This imposing Tibetan-style four-star hotel is still popular with upmarket American and European tour groups. Guest rooms are large and fitted with comfortable firm beds and classical European furniture. Bathrooms are clean but somewhat dark.

Hépíng Lù. ☎ 0887/822-9788. 220 units. ¥528 ($66) standard room; ¥1,680–¥1,880 ($210–$235) suite. 20% discount. AE, DC, MC, V. **Amenities:** Restaurant; bar; lounge; concierge; travel agency; business center; forex; shopping arcade; salon; room service; laundry/dry cleaning. *In room:* A/C, TV, hair dryer.

Tiān Jiè Shén Chuān Dàjiŭdiàn (Paradise Hotel) At last, Zhōngdiàn has its first five-star hotel. Arranged around a huge tropical, indoor pool, featuring rock cascades and stepping stones, this must be one of the most out of place hotels in China. Rooms are suitably luxurious, especially the designer bathrooms, but do you really want to experience Guǎngdōng accommodations when you are so close to the kingdom on the roof of the world?

Chángzhēng Lù, Zhōng Duàn. ☎ 0887/822-8008. Fax 0887/822-3776. 300 units. ¥880–¥1,380 ($110–$173) standard room; ¥1,980 ($250) suite. 20%–30% discounts possible. AE, DC, MC, V. **Amenities:** 3 restaurants; bar; lounge; teahouse; indoor swimming pool; sauna; KTV; concierge; business center; forex; shopping arcade; salon; 24-hr. room service; laundry/dry cleaning. *In room:* A/C, satellite TV, broadband Internet access.

WHERE TO DINE

For decent and inexpensive local and Western fare, head to the travelers' cafes in the southern part of town. The most popular of the lot is the cozy **Tibet Café** ⚝ at Chángzhēng Lù near the Martyr's Cemetery (☎ 0887/823-0282). It serves Western staples like pancakes, pasta, and pizza, along with Nàxī and Tibetan specialties (try the yak steak or the hearty fried bread stuffed with yak meat). Main courses cost ¥10 to ¥20 ($1.25–$2.50). **The Snowland Restaurant (Xuě Yù Kāfēitīng),** near the Tibet Hotel, does very reliable breakfasts and the owners are a mine of information for places to visit both in and outside the town. Around Hépíng Lù and Jiàntáng Lù are a number of food stalls and small restaurants that serve Huí Muslim, Sìchuān, and home-style (*jiācháng cài*) Chinese food; none, however, have English menus.

AROUND XIĀNGGÉLĬLĀ

The most popular day trip is to **Báishuǐ Tái (White Water Terraces)** ⚝ (¥30/$3.75; open 8am–6pm), a limestone-deposit plateau at the town of Sānbā about 108km (67 miles) southeast of Xiānggélǐlā. These seemingly sculpted terraces, actually formed from calcium carbonate deposits over hundreds of years, are quite beautiful. It has become de rigueur for visitors to walk barefoot on the terraces, which appear slippery but are actually not. Nearby is the village of Báidì, the cradle of Nàxī Dōngbā culture. To get there, it's best to hire a private car for ¥350 to ¥600 ($45–$75); or join a day tour organized by the travelers' cafes or your hotel concierge desk.

Many tourists combine their Báishuǐ Tái visit with a stop at **Bìtǎ Hǎi (Bìtǎ Lake;** ¥30/$3.75; open 8am–5pm/6pm summer) a nature reserve some 25km (15 miles) east of town whose centerpiece freshwater lake is awash in azalea blooms in June and a riot of autumn colors in September. There are two entrances to the lake: one in the west which is still several kilometers (a half-hour by pony) from the lake; and another in the south, on the road to Báishuǐ Tái. From the southern entrance, it's a 2km (1¼-mile) walk down a log-lined path or a 20-minute pony ride for ¥20 ($2.50) to the lake. Many visitors tend to walk down and ride up, because the walk uphill at this altitude can be quite taxing. The main paths are full of tourists but there are plenty of opportunities to get away for more private hikes.

9 Băoshān & Téngchōng

The Băoshān region located to the west of Dàlǐ has a history that dates from the 4th and 5th centuries B.C., when trade routes extending from Sìchuān to India via Yúnnán and Burma passed right through the towns of Băoshān and Téngchōng. The area came under Chinese control during the Hàn dynasty, and cities along this route flourished well into the Táng dynasty. Overlooked by most travelers today, the region, which is home to several minorities, including the Hàn, Yí, Bái, Dǎi, and Huí, boasts the delightful town of Téngchōng, which has enough volcanoes, hot springs, and traditional Chinese villages nearby to warrant a detour of a few days. Băoshān is Téngchōng's air link to the outside world, but there's not a lot to see here. Worth avoiding in fact, is the Graveyard of National Heroes, which is full of needlessly graphic depictions, and some outrageously anti-Japanese propaganda material that goes a long way to explain much of the xenophobic fervor of the moment.

BĂOSHĀN
Yúnnán Province, 592km (355 miles) W of Kūnmíng, 168km (101 miles) E of Téngchōng

ESSENTIALS
GETTING THERE   Daily **flights** connect to Kūnmíng (40 min.) from Băoshān's airport 10km (6 miles) south of town. The **Yúnnán Airlines** office (✆ 0875/216-1747) is located at the corner of Mínháng Lù and Lóngquán Lù. A taxi from the airport costs about ¥20 ($2.50).

From the **Băoshān Bus Station (Qìchēzhàn;** ✆ 0875/212-2311), **buses** run to Kūnmíng (7½–8 hr.; ¥116–¥150/$15–$19) from 8 to 10am, at 1 and 3:30pm, and from 5:20 to 8:20pm. Buses also run to Xiàguān (3 hr.; ¥31–¥41/$4–$5) every 40 minutes from 7am to 4:20pm; to Téngchōng (3½–4½ hr.; ¥31 ($4.50) every half-hour to hour from 6:40am to 5:30pm; to Ruìlì (5 hr.; ¥43/$5.25) every half-hour from 6:30am to 2:35pm; and to Jǐnghóng (20 hr.; ¥158/$19) at 6pm.

FAST FACTS
Banks, Foreign Exchange & ATMs   The **Bank of China** (open Mon–Fri 8–11:30am and 2:30–6pm) is at Băoxiù Dōng Lù and Zhèngyáng Běi Lù. There is an ATM inside the bank.

Post Office   There is a post office (open 8am–8pm) at Xiàgǎng Jiē and Jiǔlóng Lù.

WHERE TO STAY
For budget options near the station, try the **Huáchéng Hotel** (✆ 0875/220-3999), which is right outside the bus station's rear entrance and offers rooms for ¥150 ($19), or the **Hǎilóng Hotel** (✆ 0875/310-0888), located in the Customs House Building, which cannot possibly be missed as the bus arrives in town. Rooms at the Hǎilóng go for ¥120 ($15).

Lándū Hotel (Lándū Fàndiàn) This three-star hotel located five long blocks west of the bus station is the nicest place to stay in town. Rooms are large and, unlike the hotel's unrepentantly ugly white-tile, smoked-glass exterior, are decorated in a surprisingly understated and tasteful manner. Beds are firm and comfortable; bathrooms are clean and bright.

Bǎoxiù Xī Lù Zhōng Duàn. ⓒ 0875/212-1888. Fax 0875/212-1990. 150 units. ¥400 ($50) standard room; ¥800 ($100) suite. AE, DC, MC, V. **Amenities:** 2 restaurants; bar; lounge; indoor pool; exercise room; bowling alley; concierge; business center; shopping arcade; salon; room service; laundry/dry cleaning. *In room:* A/C, TV, minibar.

TÉNGCHŌNG

Yúnnán Province, 750km (450 miles) W of Kūnmíng, 168km (101 miles) W of Bǎoshān

Téngchōng, a predominantly Hàn town which shares a 148km (89-mile) border with Myanmar (Burma) to the northwest, flourished as an ancient southwestern Silk Route town. However, from the Míng dynasty on, large numbers of its natives went abroad to Burma and Southeast Asia to trade and seek a livelihood, thus creating for Téngchōng a reputation as the "homeplace of the overseas Chinese." The money sent home by the émigrés helped build schools, residences, and memorial halls, and today you can see some charming, well-preserved traditional villages in the area. Téngchōng also sits on the southwestern end of the Héngduàn (transversely faulted) Mountains, in a region where volcanoes abound and earthquakes are frequent. Bubbling over with geothermal energy, the county has over 80 hot springs and fountains.

ESSENTIALS

GETTING THERE The closest airport is at Bǎoshān. From the **Téngchōng Bus Station (Kèyùn Zhàn;** ⓒ **0875/518-1450)** and the **long-distance bus station (Chángtú Qìchēzhàn),** both on Huánchéng Dōng Lù directly opposite each other, **buses** run to Kūnmíng (15 hr.; ¥156/$19) from 1:30 to 7:50pm; to Xiàguān (10 hr.; ¥80/$10) at 8:30am and 7pm; to Bǎoshān (4 hr.; ¥26–¥32/$3.25–$4) every half-hour from 7am to 4:30pm; to Ruìlì (7 hr.; ¥36/$4.40) at 6:20am, 7am, 8:30am, and 11:20am; and to Mángshì (4 hr.; ¥20/$2.50) every half-hour to hour from 7:30am to 3pm.

GETTING AROUND Téngchōng is small enough to explore on foot. **Bikes** are difficult to find, with only the repair shop at Fèngshān Lù 22 having a few old clankers at a ridiculous ¥20 ($2.50) a day. **Taxi** fare costs ¥5 (65¢) for in-town destinations and this price doubles after 11pm. The rest is subject to negotiation.

FAST FACTS

Banks, Foreign Exchange & ATMs The **Bank of China** (open Mon–Fri 8–11:30am and 2:30–6pm) is at Yíngjiāng Dōng Lù 161. There is an ATM outside the bank.

Internet Access **China Telecom** (open 8am–midnight) on Láifèng Dà Dào has Internet service for ¥2 (25¢) an hour.

Post Office The post office (open 8am–5:30pm) is at the corner of Fēngshān Nán Lù and Yíngjiāng Dōng Lù.

Visa Extensions The visa section of the **Gōngānjú (PSB)** is located at Xià Xī Jiē 20, room 107 (ⓒ **0875/513-1046;** open Mon–Fri 8–11:30am and 2:30–5:30pm).

EXPLORING TÉNGCHŌNG

In the southern part of town, the **Láifèng Shān Guójiā Sēnlín Gōngyuán (Láifèng Shān National Forest Park;** open 24 hr.; ¥10/$1.25 admission charged 8am–6pm) is a large and quiet pine forest that offers vigorous hikes, especially up to the summit

Téngchōng

Bank
Bus Station
Post Office
PSB Public-Security Visas

To Yunfeng Shan and Huoshan Gongyuan

9

Guanghua Xi Lu
Lao Huancheng Xi Lu
Huancheng Xi Lu

8

To Heshun (4 km)

Feicui Lu

PSB

2

1

Fengshan Bei Lu
Guanghua Dong Lu

To Baoshan, Dali and Kunming

Fengshan Nan Lu

Yingjiang Dong Lu

Buses to Heshun

Huancheng Dong Lu

4

3

Láifēng Shān Guójiā Sēnlín Gōngyuán (Láifēng Shān National Forest Park)

Laifeng Dadao

6

5

Feicui Lu

7

Minibuses to Rehai

Beijing

China
YUNNAN
Téngchōng

Rehai Lu

To Rehai and Qiluo

ACCOMMODATIONS ■

Róng Hé Dàjiǔdiàn **7**
融和大酒店

Téngchōng Guǎn
Fán Dàjiǔdiàn **9**
腾冲官房大酒店

DINING ◆

Fèngyuán Cāntīng **6**
凤园餐厅

Lào Yìn Xī Cāntīng **5**
烙印西餐厅

Night food market
(shāokǎo yèshì) **8**
烧烤夜市

ATTRACTIONS ●

Diéshuǐ Hé Pùbù **1**
叠水河瀑布

Láifēng Shān Guójiā Sēnlín
Gōngyuán (Láifèng Shān
National Forest Park) **3**
来凤山国家森林公园

Láifēng Sì **4**
来凤寺

Nationalities Cultural
Performance Center **2**
民族文化表演中心

(notice how the path follows a very meandering circuit to avoid all the many graves here), where a pagoda promises to offer spectacular views of the area, but is unfortunately closed all the time. **Láifēng Sì,** an active temple first built during the Táng dynasty and rebuilt in the Míng and Qīng, is also located here.

In the western part of town, the **Diéshuǐ Hé Pùbù** (¥10/$1.25; open 8am–8pm) is a small but pretty waterfall good for a quick ramble or a long picnic. Before you reach the falls, a new **Nationalities Cultural Performance Center** hosts the usual minority performances in summer.

Travel farther afield into the **Gāolí Gòng Shān Nature Reserve,** where one might possibly encounter rare and exotic species such as the red panda, the slow loris, and the takin.

WHERE TO STAY

Róng Hé Dàjiǔdiàn   Under the same management as the three-star Léi Huá down around the corner, the staff here has a much better attitude as well as better prices. This two-star has only been open since May 2005 and as yet, there are no karaoke or massage operations in the hotel, which makes it possibly the quietest option in town.

Rè Hǎi Lù. ☎ **0875/515-2588.** Fax 0875/515-1999. 48 units. ¥80 ($10) standard room; ¥168 ($21) suite. No credit cards. **Amenities:** Laundry. *In room:* A/C, TV.

Téngchōng Guān Fáng Dàjiǔdiàn   Téngchōng's first five-star hotel is impressive but empty, which is a shame because the rooms are beautifully appointed with stylish bathrooms and desks complete with Internet-ready PCs. Little English is spoken, but the location is great, with the low-rise accommodations that are a pleasant change from the glass-and-steel high-rises.

Téng Yuè Lù. ☎ **0875/519-9812.** Fax 0875/513-2999. www.guanfang.com.cn. 288 units. ¥380 ($48) standard room; ¥880–¥1,280 ($110–$160) suite. No credit cards. **Amenities:** 3 restaurants; bar; 5 outdoor swimming pools; indoor swimming pool; outdoor tennis courts; business center; forex; room service; laundry. *In room:* A/C, TV, PC w/broadband Internet access, hair dryer.

WHERE TO DINE

The lively **night food market** *(shāokǎo yèshì)* ✿ has been temporarily relocated to vacant lot on Huángchéng Xī Lù but still has the same delicious array of barbecue skewers, local casseroles, and stir-fries.

Fēngyuán Cāntīng ✿ HOME-STYLE/TÉNGCHŌNG   Extremely popular with locals, this restaurant serves creative cuisine in a traditional two-story Chinese courtyard–style building complete with lattice windows and upturned eaves. Menu items include the delicious *fēngyuán dòufu* (tofu deep-fried in a batter of milk, eggs, and coconut), *dàjiùjià* (a rice-flour pastry stir-fried with ham, mushrooms, and vegetables), and *gōngbào tiánjī* (kung pao frogs' legs). There are no menus in English, but the staff tries to be helpful.

Láifèng Dà Dào. ☎ **0875/518-9898.** Meal for 2 ¥30–¥80 ($3.50–$10). No credit cards. 11am–1pm and 4–9pm.

Lǎoyīng Xīcāntīng TÉNGCHŌNG/WESTERN   Possibly the only place left in town with an English menu, this surprisingly large, two-story restaurant is easy to find, just halfway up Láifèng Xiāng, the road that leads up to the Forest Park in the south of the city. Start with a refreshing lemon juice for just ¥3 (40¢) and browse a very respectable selection of both Chinese and Western dishes. The staff is friendly, but English is greeted with nervous smiles.

Láifèng Xiāng. ☎ **0875/302-8315.** Meal for 2 ¥20–¥40 ($2.50–$5). No credit cards. 11am–9pm.

AROUND TÉNGCHŌNG

Sights around Téngchōng can easily take up to a few days depending on your interests. Ornithologists may be interested in visiting the **Běihǎi National Marshland (Běihǎi Shīdì; ✆ 0785 514-0428; ¥20/$2.50)** 12km (7 miles) northeast of town, a lake where it's possible to tread on large beds of floating grass. The marshland is an hour away by bike; or take a minibus for ¥5 (60¢) from the traffic circle at the intersection of Huǒshān Lù and Huánchéng Xī Lù.

Traditional Villages

Héshùn Qiáoxiāng ✿✿   Located 4km (2½ miles) southwest of Téngchōng, this charming, well-preserved ancient town (¥20/$2.50 8am–6pm, free otherwise) whose name means "peace and harmony" is a must-visit. First established when the militia sent by the Míng dynasty Hóngwǔ emperor to Yúnnán in the early 1400s decided to stay on, Héshùn today has over 1,300 households and over 6,000 people, with another 12,000 former residents living abroad (70% of whom are in neighboring Burma, while others are in Japan, Thailand, India, Canada, and the United States). One of Héshùn's highlights is its **library** ✿, which boasts a collection of 70,000 books (but only 56K Internet access). Built in 1928, this quaint building, complete with creaky wooden floorboards and glass windows, is fronted by a Chinese-style double-eave gate with an inner stone gate with Western-style arches and columns. Next door is the former **Confucian Temple (Wén Miào),** which is now part of the library. Many of Héshùn's pathways are studded with volcanic cobblestones, with a smoother paved stone path down the center for the convenience of elderly and female villagers. The village's many traditional courtyard-style residences are also well maintained. Architectural highlights include the **Liú Family Memorial Hall (Liúshì Zōngcí)** and the **former residence of Ài Sīqí (Ài Sīqí Gùjū;** admission ¥10/$1.25), a Marxist philosopher whose writings are said to have influenced Máo Zédōng.

Visitors wandering around may notice that each section *(xiàng)* of the village, once home to residents with the same last name, has a curved terrace in front of its gate. This "moon terrace" *(yuètái),* which forces the river surrounding Héshùn to curve around it, is meant to prevent wealth from flowing out of the village. In the past, each section used to have a main gate *(lǚ mén)* as well, the keys to which were kept by the eldest resident in that section. The idea was to prevent theft, but it also served to keep young married women at home when their husbands went abroad for business. Tourism has started to have an impact on the area as can be seen from the boating lake complete with water cannon boats and floating mines as targets. On the other side of the water is a far more interesting collection of water wheels and water hammers.

To get there, take bus no. 3 for ¥1.50 (20¢) from the corner of Fěicuì Lù and Fēngshān Lù or from the traffic circle in front of what was the TCC Café.

Volcanoes

The Téngchōng area has 97 volcanoes, all dormant since 1609 when the largest, Dàyīng Shān, just 10km (6 miles) outside the county line, last erupted. About 25km (15 miles) north of town, **Huǒshān Gōngyuán (Volcano Park)** ✿ (¥20/$2.50; open 8am–7pm), is the most accessible cluster. It includes **Dà Kōng Shān (Big Empty Hill),** the largest volcano here, with a height of 150m (492 ft.). You can climb to the top, where there are some commanding views of the surrounding mountains, but the big empty crater now covered with grass is underwhelming. More interesting is the

Crossing into Myanmar

In years past, the town of Ruìlì (827km/496 miles west of Kūnmíng), which currently has China's only overland crossing into Myanmar (Burma), used to have a famous reputation as a Wild West frontier town, but regular crackdowns on the drugs, gambling, and prostitution that made the town so prosperous are now making it a desperate and dangerous location. All the casinos have relocated to jungle areas outside of town, leaving heroin (locally known as *Number 4*) as the current addiction. Watch out for overdosed addicts lying dead on the streets late at night and try not to eat at pavement-side restaurants, unless you want to be stared into submission by entire families of beggars. Not that there is much to see in Ruìlì other than a handful of temples, and unless you simply have to cross into Myanmar via this overland route at the Jiégāo border checkpoint, your time is much better spent elsewhere in Yúnnán. The only other attraction is the gem market and the Burmese trader market next door where you can pick up Mandalay Rum at ¥5 (75¢) a bottle. If you cross, you must be accompanied directly to Mandalay by an official travel agency–sponsored guide (see "Tours," in the "Kūnmíng" section, earlier in this chapter). No day crossings are allowed for foreigners, and all the proper transportation and visa arrangements can take at least 2 weeks.

To get to Ruìlì, the closest airport is at Mángshì, 115km (69 miles) east of Ruìlì, where there are twice-daily **flights** to Kūnmíng (40 min.). Minibuses meet incoming flights and head directly to Ruìlì (2 hr.). In Ruìlì, you can buy plane tickets at the **Yúnnán Airlines** office (© 0692/414-8275) next to the Yǒngchāng Hotel. There is also a daily morning bus that leaves from here directly for the Mángshì airport 3 hours before the first flight. From Ruìlì's **long-distance bus station** (© 0692/414-1423), **buses** run to Kūnmíng (12–15 hr.; ¥179/$22) every 1 to 2 hours from 7am to 7:30pm; to Téngchōng (6 hr.; ¥35/$4.40) from 5:50 to 11:10am; to Jǐnghóng (36 hr.; ¥243/$30) at 8:30am; and to Xiàguān (10 hr.; ¥98/$12) every hour from 4 to 8pm.

In Ruìlì, the nicest and most modern hotel, the four-star **Jǐnchéng Dàjiǔdiàn** at Máohàn Lù Zhōngduàn (© 0692/415-9999; fax 0692/415-9888) lacks personal charm, but it offers comfortable and clean rooms for ¥418 ($52) with up to 50% discounts, but only very grudgingly. The hotel has a full range of facilities and two restaurants serving Chinese and Dǎi food.

bed of black Vesuvianite columns, **Zhùzhuàng Jiélǐ** ✿, formed from the erosion of lava-encrusted rocks, about 12km (7 miles) northeast of the volcano clusters.

To get to the Volcano Park, take a bus to Mǎzhàn for ¥5 (60¢) from the West Bus Station (Xī Zhàn), then walk to the entrance of the park; or hire a taxi for ¥40 ($5) round-trip to take you to the volcanic columns, whose entrance fee is included in park admission. Hiring a private taxi from Téngchōng will run around ¥100 to ¥150 ($13–$19).

Yúnfēng Shān

Located 55km (34 miles) northwest of Téngchōng, this Daoist mountain (¥10/$1.25; open 8am–7pm) with its cluster of monasteries perched atop its peak offers some challenging hikes. However, most visitors prefer the 20-minute cable-car ride to the top for ¥30 ($3.75) one-way, ¥50 ($6.25) round-trip. From the cable car terminus, it's still a steep and lung-straining 20-minute climb to the main temple, **Dàxióng Băodiàn,** first built in the Míng dynasty but seriously damaged during the Cultural Revolution and most recently rebuilt in 1987. On a clear day, the **views** ✦ from the top are spectacular: To the east is the Gāolìgòng Shān mountain range, while just over the hills to the northwest lies Myanmar. Take a Gŭdōng minibus for ¥9 ($1.10) from Téngchōng's west station, and transfer in Gŭdōng to Yúnfēng Shān–bound minivans charging ¥5 (60¢) per person for three or more.

The Final Stretch of the Burma Road

Although the bus ride from Téngchōng to Ruìlì may only cost ¥31 ($3.80), and last a good 10 hours, it offers a spectacular transition from mountain passes to jungle lowland. Descending from the Téngchōng plateau, the bus passes hundreds of small, independent stone cutters, who provide the hundreds of thousands of basalt flagstones that line the streets of the local towns. Dotted among the razorlike teeth of the cutting wheels are sprinkled dozens of decidedly low-tech tunnel entrances and drop shafts, demonstrating clearly why China still maintains the highest mining fatality rates in the world. As the descent continues, the landscape first changes to one of endless rice paddies, often matching the magnificent vistas of Lóngshèng and Yuányáng. Unshod peasants goad stubborn-looking water buffalo, all of which seem to have the same basic steering malfunction.

There is a short lunch stop about two-thirds of the way in a small town that has two restaurants but about a dozen sword and knife shops containing everything from butterflies and stilettos to machetes and sword-sticks.

10 Jǐnghóng & Xīshuāngbǎnnà

Yúnnán Province, 730km SW of Kūnmíng

The Xīshuāngbǎnnà Dǎi Autonomous Prefecture is situated at the subtropical southwestern tip of Yúnnán and shares a border with Burma and Laos. About a third of its 800,000-strong population is Dǎi, another third is Hàn, and the rest comprises minorities such as the Hāní, Lāhù, Bùlǎng, Jīnuò, Yáo, and Yí. With its tropical forests, perennial sunshine, and laid-back lifestyle, the place has always felt more like Southeast Asia than China. Today, with domestic tourists able to travel more easily to the real Thailand and Burma, Xīshuāngbǎnnà, a Chinese approximation of the original Thai *Sip Sawng Panna* ("Twelve Rice-Growing Districts"), is no longer the much-ballyhooed destination it once was, and much of the main town of Jǐnghóng has fallen into a kind of romantic decay. Still, for plant lovers and those with an interest in minority cultures, especially Dǎi culture, Xīshuāngbǎnnà is worth visiting for a refreshing change of pace. The wildly popular Dǎi Water Splashing Festival (Apr 13–15) can be an interesting time to visit, but book well in advance, as flights and accommodations are notoriously scarce at this time. Otherwise, the most pleasant times to visit are between October and February. *Note:* Please turn to appendix A for Chinese translations of key locations in this section.

ESSENTIALS

GETTING THERE   Jǐnghóng is connected by **flights** to Kūnmíng (40 min.), Dàlǐ (45 min.), Lì Jiāng (50 min.), and Bangkok (30 min.). Tickets can be purchased at the **Yúnnán Airlines/CAAC** office located at Jǐngdé Xī Lù 8 (© **0691/212-7040**). Minibuses charge ¥2 (25¢), or ¥3 (40¢) after 10pm; they make runs to the airport every 10 minutes from 7am to 11:30pm. The airport is located about 5km (3 miles) southwest of town, and the minibuses depart from the corner of Jǐngdé Xī Lù and Mínzú Nán Lù. A taxi ride between the airport and town will cost around ¥20 ($2.50).

For destinations such as Kūnmíng or Dàlǐ, it's much more convenient to take the plane, as bus trips are interminably long and smoke-filled, and you may find yourself caught in floods, mudslides, or bus breakdowns. Still, for the intrepid (or the foolish), there's the **bus station** (**Qìchē Kèyùn Zhàn**) on Mínzú Běi Lù (© **0691/212-3570**). Express buses run to Kūnmíng (15 hr.; ¥157/$19) at 10:30am, 2pm, 4pm, 6pm, and

The Dǎi

Historically, the Dǎi (also known as the "Tai") are said to have appeared in the Yángzǐ River valley around the 1st century A.D. but were driven south by the expansion of the Chinese empire. The majority of the Dǎi moved into the northern parts of Southeast Asia and are found today in Thailand, Laos, northeast Myanmar (Burma), and northern Vietnam. The majority of China's Dǎi population of over one million live in the Xīshuāngbǎnnà region and in Déhóng Prefecture. "Dǎi" means "peace and freedom loving," and it is no coincidence that the Dǎi/Thai are often regarded as being some of the most gracious people in the world.

The Dǎi mostly inhabit the plains areas around rivers and lakes. To keep away from the damp earth, they live in bamboo stilt houses, with the second floor given over to the living quarters and the first floor reserved for livestock.

The Dǎi practice Theravada Buddhism, and there are Buddhist temples and pagodas in every village, though individual villages are not beyond their own animistic beliefs and spirit worship. The Water Splashing Festival (Pōshuǐ Jié), a huge tourist attraction, also marks the Dǎi New Year. According to legend, the Dǎi were once terrorized by a sadistic demon who took for himself seven consorts. In an *in vino veritas* moment, the youngest of the consorts, who was plying the demon with strong libations, discovered that he would die if hung by his own hair. As soon as the demon fell into a drunken stupor, she grabbed a strand of his hair and strangled him. The demon's head fell off but burst into unquenchable flames as it rolled through the land wreaking havoc. The seven consorts took turns dousing the ball of fire with water. To this day, water is splashed on everyone in gratitude for deliverance from the demon, and to wash away your own sins as well as any disasters or diseases. The wetter you are, the more luck you're likely to receive in the coming year. The lively festival is also marked by dragon boat races, group dances, temple visits, and rocket launching.

> **Tips Dăi Etiquette**
>
> Always take off your shoes before entering a Dăi temple or household, as a sign of respect. Dress appropriately in temples, don't take photos of the monks or the interiors without permission, don't raise yourself higher than a Buddha figure, and never sit with your feet pointing at the Buddha or at anyone else.

7:30pm; ordinary sleeper buses also make the run (19 hr.; ¥146–¥170/$18–$21) every 40 minutes from 8:20am to 7pm. In addition, buses run to Xiàguān (28–33 hr.; ¥150/$19). Buses also leave for Xiàguān from the new and somewhat forlorn **South Bus Station (Nán Zhàn; ✆ 0691/212-3586)** on Nónglín Lù. Additional buses leave from the **City Bus Station (Shì Kèyùn Zhàn; ✆ 0691/212-8741)** for Hékŏu (¥148/$19) at 7:30am; for Gănlănbà (a half-hour; ¥6.50/80¢) every 20 minutes from 6:30am to 7pm; for Mĕnglún (2 hr.) every 20 minutes from 6:30am to 7pm; for Mĕnghăi (¥8/$1) every 20 minutes from 7am to 6:40pm; for Mĕngyáng every half-hour from 8am to 6:30pm; and for Mĕnglà (5–7 hr.; 4–5 buses a day).

There is no official **boat** service running between Jĭnghóng and Laos and Thailand. Only private small boats currently make the run to Gănlănbà.

GETTING AROUND   **Taxis** cost ¥7 (85¢) for 2km (1¼ miles), then ¥1.50 (20¢) per kilometer until 20km (12 miles), when the cost rises to ¥2.30 (30¢) per kilometer. From 10pm to 6am, the cost is ¥8.40 ($1.05) for 2km (1¼ miles).

TOURS & GUIDES   **CITS** at Lǚyóu Dùjiàqū, Sānhào Lù (✆ 0691/214-8520; Mon–Fri 8:30–11:30am and 3–6pm), can arrange day tours to the surrounding areas, with car hire for a day costing around ¥300 ($38), and an English-speaking guide for another ¥200 ($25) or so, though there's room for bargaining. Travelers' cafes such as the Mĕi Mĕi Café and the Mekong Café can also organize treks to nearby villages.

FAST FACTS

Banks, Foreign Exchange & ATMs   The **Bank of China** (open Mon–Fri 8–11:30am and 3–6pm) is at Mínzú Nán Lù and Jĭngdé Xī Lù.

Internet Access   **Màntīng Lù** has several Internet cafes, including one below the Mekong Café (¥2/25¢ per hour) at Màntīng Lù 111. Dial-up is ✆ **163.**

Post Office   The post office (open 8am–8:30pm) is at Jĭnghóng Xī Lù 2.

Visa Extensions   The **Gōngānjú (PSB)** is at Jĭnghóng Dōng Lù 5 (✆ **0691/213-0366;** open Mon–Fri, 8–11:30am and 3–5:30pm).

EXPLORING JĬNGHÓNG

There is not much to see in Jĭnghóng itself. **Màntīng Gōngyuán** (admission 7:30am–7pm ¥15/$1.90; 7–10:30pm ¥80/$10) in the southeastern part of town, once an imperial garden for the Dăi kings, hosts the annual Dăi Water Splashing Festival. Those who can't make it to the real festival can now be splashed in a faux daily ceremony as meaningless as your clothes are wet. In the rear of the park is the **Zŏngfó Sì,** a Theravada-style temple complex that is the center of Dăi Buddhism, but the stupas and the temples complete with gilded statues of Sakyamuni all date only from the late 1980s. Many of the monks here have studied in Thailand.

The **Tropical Flower and Plants Garden (Rèdài Huāhuìyuán)** ⚝ (¥10/$1.25; open 8am–6pm), in the western part of town, has garnered good reviews from green thumbs impressed with the collection of over 1,000 plants from Yúnnán's tropical forests. Descriptions are mostly in Chinese.

WHERE TO STAY

Dàiyuán Dàjiǔdiàn (Tai Garden Hotel) ⚝   Located in its own compound with a full range of facilities, this is the most luxurious hotel in town, but it's somewhat inconveniently situated in the southwest part of town. Guest rooms are fairly plush, comfortable, and well appointed, with large beds; bathrooms run a little small but are otherwise clean. The staff here is friendly and efficient.

Nónglín Nán Lù 8. ⓒ 0691/212-3888. Fax 0691/212-6060. 172 units. ¥670 ($80) standard room; from ¥1,200 ($150) suite. 20%–40% discounts. AE, DC, MC, V. **Amenities:** 2 restaurants; bar; lounge; outdoor swimming pool; tennis court; health club; sauna; concierge; business center; forex; shopping arcade; room service; laundry. *In room:* A/C, TV (Thailand and Hong Kong satellite channels only), minibar, hair dryer.

Xīshuāngbǎnnà Guānguāng Jiǔdiàn   This newly designated four-star hotel in the tourist development zone is owned by Yúnnán Airlines and has all the modern conveniences. The hotel's aqua-blue smoked glass exterior is a terminal eyesore, but the interior is considerably cheerier than that of most Chinese hotels. Guest rooms are large, comfortable, and fitted with unobtrusive light brown furniture. Bathrooms are clean and come with full amenities.

Lǚyóu Dùjiàqū. ⓒ 0691/214-4888. Fax 0691/214-9666. 154 units. ¥638 ($80) standard room; from ¥1,380 ($170) suite. 20%–40% discounts. AE, DC, MC, V. **Amenities:** 2 restaurants (Western dining available); bar; lounge; health club; concierge; business center; forex; shopping arcade; room service; laundry/dry cleaning; executive rooms. *In room:* A/C, TV, hair dryer.

WHERE TO DINE

Though all five tastes are represented in Dǎi cuisine, the emphasis is on the sour, the pungent, and the fragrant. Famous Dǎi dishes include *kǎo yú* (grilled fish) and *kǎo sǔnzi* (grilled bamboo shoots), often wrapped in banana leaves or lemon grass; *xiāngzhú fàn* (fragrant bamboo rice, or glutinous rice stuffed inside a hollowed bamboo that is then cooked over an open fire), and *suānsǔn zhǔ yú* (fish boiled with sour bamboo shoots).

Informal Dǎi and Western food can be had at the travelers' cafes concentrated around Màntīng Lù, with prices about ¥10 to ¥30 ($1.25–$4) per dish. The pleasant **Mekong Café (Méigōng Cānguǎn)**, at Màntīng Lù 111 (ⓒ **0691/212-8895;** open 8am–1am) is housed in a bamboo building nicely decorated with ethnic art. Menu items range from banana pancakes and pizzas to Dǎi dishes like steamed pineapple sticky rice to a Hāní set meal. There's a book exchange and an eclectic collection of Western music on the second floor. The **Měi Měi Café** (ⓒ **0691/212-7324**) at the Màntīng Lù traffic circle is also popular among travelers for its pizzas and pastas, juices, and coffees. The cafe has a laundry service and organizes treks to the surrounding villages. The **Dōngguǎn Jiǎozi Guǎn** (ⓒ **0691/214-9346**) on Jǐngdé Dōng Lù (open 7am–10pm) serves your basic northern staples like dumplings, noodles, and steamed buns.

Cái Chūn Qīng ⚝ THAI   This clean and informal restaurant along lively Màntīng Lù serves authentic and flavorful food, courtesy of the restaurant's Thai chef. Menu highlights include green papaya salad, *tom yum kung* (spicy shrimp) soup, and steamed fish with chili and lemon. The staff is friendly.

Màntīng Lù 193. ⓒ 0691/216-1758. English menu. Meal for 2 ¥40–¥80 ($5–$10). No credit cards. 9am–9:30pm.

Dăi Jiā Měishí Cūn ✦ DĂI   Located in traditional bamboo buildings on the grounds of the Banna Bīnguǎn, this restaurant offers excellent Dǎi specialties like *kǎo yú* and *kǎo sǔnzi*. The *zhútǒng fàn* (glutinous rice cooked in bamboo) and the *suānsǔn zhǔ jī* (chicken cooked with pickled bamboo) are also worth trying. The costumed staff is friendly and there is a nightly Dǎi song and dance performance.

Gǎnlǎn Zhōng Lù 11. ⓒ 0691/212-3679. Main courses ¥20–¥40 ($2.50–$5). No credit cards. 6:30–9pm.

SHOPPING

Jǐnghóng Nán Lù between Nónglín Lù and Jǐngdé Lù is lined with shops selling **Burmese jade,** jewelry, and gems. You can pick up some of Yúnnán's famous **Pǔ'ěr tea** at the Tiānchéng Dàmàichǎng on Jǐnghóng Běi Lù; it's open from 8am to 11:30pm. **Dǎi minority souvenirs** such as tie-dyed T-shirts and woven bamboo items can be found in shops along Màntīng Lù.

JĪNGHÓNG AFTER DARK

The **Mínzú Fēngqíng Yuán** in the southwestern part of town hosts Dǎi and Jīnuò song and dance performances at ¥80 ($10) per person. The performance starts at 8:30pm and is followed by a barbecue, drinking, and audience participation in group dances and games, which may just make you want to run away. **Màntīng Gōngyuán** features a similar program from 7 to 10pm.

AROUND JĪNGHÓNG
GĂNLĂNBÀ (MĚNGHĂN)

Gǎnlǎnbà (Olive Plain) lies on the Mekong River about 27km (16 miles) southeast of Jǐnghóng. It used to be that you could sail down the Mekong (known in Yúnnán as the Láncāng Jiāng) to Gǎnlǎnbà, but few boats make the trip anymore and it's more convenient to take the minibus from Jǐnghóng's city bus station. The main attraction here is the **Dǎi Minority Folk Customs Park** (Dǎizú Yuán; ¥35/$4.25; open 7:30am–6:30pm). The collection of five pleasant Dǎi villages has now been "preserved" for tourists. The first village of **Mànchūnmàn** has the Mànchūnmàn Fó Sì, a regal temple first built in 1126. There is a gorgeous golden Burmese stupa here surrounded by four smaller golden stupas. Farther in, **Màntīng** village has another impressive temple and white pagoda worth exploring, the **Màntīng Fó Sì Dà Dú Tǎ,** built in 669, which now houses Buddha statues donated by a Thai philanthropist.

MĚNGLÚN

About 42km (25 miles) east of Gǎnlǎnbà, the town of Měnglún is home to China's largest botanical garden, the 900-hectare (2,223-acre) **Xīshuāngbǎnnà Rèdài Zhíwùyuán** (¥35/$4.25; open 24 hours), which boasts around 7,000 species of tropical and subtropical plants from China and abroad. The sprawling grounds are divided into many sections, including a rubber and tea plantation, a stretch of natural tropical rainforest, and a bamboo forest. To get there, take a minibus from the city bus station. From the Měnglún bus station, turn left and walk to the corner of the second block. Turn left and walk down the road flanked by hawkers; follow this road until you come to a ticket booth in front of a footbridge across the Luósuō River. This is the western entrance to the garden. If you're coming by taxi, the entrance is way over in the east, but taxis should be able to let you off close to the Tourist Information Center (Yóukè Fúwù Zhōngxīn) in the middle of the park.

About 8km (5 miles) west of Měnglún (at the 63km marker on the Jǐnghóng–Měnglún road) is the **Bǎnnà Rainforest Valley (Bǎnnà Yǔlín Gǔ; ¥20/$2.50; open 8am–6:30pm)**, a pleasant enough primary rainforest park. It has several aerial walkways and a number of ancient trees that include a giant strangling fig with long, gnarled roots.

MĚNGYǍNG

One of the highlights at this town 20km (12 miles) northeast of Jǐnghóng is an elephant-shaped banyan tree, **Xiàngxíng Róngshù,** that is a magnet for Chinese tourists. Considerably more interesting is the **Jīnuò Folk Custom Village (Jīnuò Mínsú Shānzhài),** about 6km (4 miles) east of Měngyǎng near Jīnuò Shān, home of the Jīnuò people. Though the main village of Bāpō Zhài has been spruced up to become your usual tour group–friendly folk-custom village, it at least affords visitors a friendly introduction to the Jīnuò, who have not always been so welcoming toward individual travelers in the past.

Officially recognized as a minority group only in 1979, the Jīnuò have a population of just over 20,000, all living in 46 villages east of Jǐnghóng. Jīnuò men are famous hunters, while the women are known for their elaborately decorated ear lobes and black teeth, caused by a local medicinal plant used to prevent tooth decay. The Jīnuò's biggest festival is celebrated every February 6 to February 8 with their characteristic solar drum dance, which visitors can now view upon entering the village. You can also visit a typical Jīnuò house, which is built 1m (3 ft.) aboveground and often houses four generations of a family. Admission to the village is ¥35 ($4.40) and includes entry to the Bǎnnà Wild Elephant Valley, as both are managed by the same company.

About 28km (17 miles) north of Měngyǎng, the **Bǎnnà Wild Elephant Valley (Bǎnnà Yěxiàng Gǔ)** (¥25/$3; open 8am–5:30pm) is part of the 1.5-million-hectare (3.7-million-acre) **Sānchàhé Nature Reserve (Sānchàhé Zìrán Bǎohùqū).** There are hiking trails and a 2,063m (6,766-ft.) chairlift ride (¥40/$5) over the forest canopy, all designed to help visitors spot the roughly 40 wild elephants that live here. If you don't manage a sighting, there are wretched performances by more domesticated elephants near the eastern exit. By the southern entrance are some tacky hotels.

To get to the nature reserve, take any Sīmáo-bound bus (1 hr.; ¥10/$1.25) from Jǐnghóng that passes the reserve. A daily tour that takes in the Elephant Valley and Jīnuò village costs ¥120 ($15), and includes admission, transportation, and lunch. The tour bus departs daily at 8:40am from the entrance to Peacock Lake (Jǐnghóng Dōng Lù) and returns around 5pm.

Tips Getting to Laos

The border crossing is at Móhān, a 2-hour bus ride from Měnglà. Make sure your visa is in order—you cannot get one at the border. A morning crossing is best; things seem to wrap up on the Laos side by early afternoon.

Yángzǐ & Beyond

by Dinny McMahon

In addition to shared borders, the land-locked provinces of Sìchuān, Húběi, and Húnán and the municipality of Chóngqìng have in common the world's third-longest river, the Cháng Jiāng ("Long River," aka Yángzǐ), whose navigable reaches start in Sìchuān, thread through Chóngqìng, and roughly define the border between Húběi and Húnán. Now China's heartland, this region—home to the Chǔ, Bā, and Shǔ cultures—was for centuries a land of exile and colonization for the ruling kingdoms of the North China Plain. The Qín (221–206 B.C.) banished thousands to faraway, inhospitable Shǔ (present-day Sìchuān), and China's most famous martyr, Qū Yuán, was exiled to the southern edges of his own Chǔ kingdom where he drowned himself in the Mìluó River (in present-day northern Húnán).

Five hundred years later, this same swath of central China was the battlefield on which the rulers of Wèi, Shǔ, and Wú contended for complete dominion over China. Many sights along the Yángzǐ commemorate the heroes of those 60 years of turmoil known simply as the Three Kingdoms Period (220–280). By the 3rd century, Buddhism and Daoism were spreading rapidly through the region, and many of the hundreds of temples that dot

the sacred mountains of Sìchuān, Húběi, and Húnán were first constructed at this time.

In addition to being the home of five holy Buddhist and/or Daoist mountains, this area contains some of China's most beautiful scenery—in northern Sìchuān and northern Húnán—and lays claim to seven World Heritage Sites.

Until recently, most foreign travelers came to this part of central China to see the Three Gorges—the spectacular 242km (150-mile) channel comprising Qūtáng, Wū, and Xīlíng gorges—but with China's equivalent of the New Deal underway, new airports, rail lines, and expressways are opening all the time, making travel to remote areas much less painful.

If the Three Gorges are on your itinerary, try to leave yourself a few days on either end to explore Chóngqìng and Wǔhàn. And a day trip from Chóngqìng to the Buddhist grottoes at Dàzú is well worth the time. Sìchuān is best explored over 2 or 3 weeks. Use Chéngdū as a place to leave extra luggage and to return to for a break and some urban sightseeing before going out again. In Húnán, do the same with Chángshā. *Note:* Unless otherwise noted, hours listed for attractions and restaurants are daily.

1 Chéngdū 🕊

Sìchuān Province, 504km (313 miles) NW of Chóngqìng, 842km (523 miles) SW of Xī'ān

Ask a resident of Běijīng or Shànghǎi what to do in Sìchuān's capital of Chéngdū, and 9 times out of 10 they'll tell you to drink tea and eat hot pot, such is the city's reputation

The Yángzǐ Region

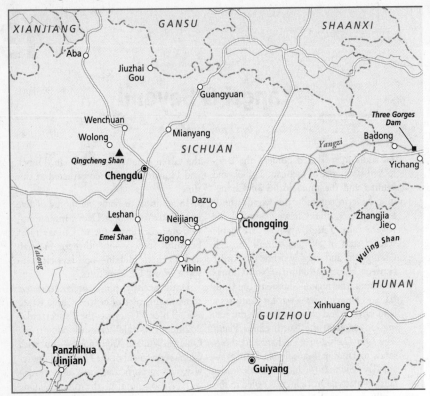

as a culinary capital that knows how to take it easy. Indeed, Chéngdū's cuisine is irresistible and tea drinking is a custom that took hold here 1,300 years ago and never let go. With few genuine ancient sights within the city proper (Dù Fǔ's cottage is only a replica; Wǔhòu Temple is ho-hum), drinking tea may be Chéngdū's most durable link to the past. But what Chéngdū lacks in ancient sites, it makes up for in charm and atmosphere. Like so many cities in central China, Chéngdū has a pretty little river running through it. The narrow Fǔ Hé and its southern tributary form a sort of moat around the city, sections of which are lined with attractive restaurants and teahouses. The city is also in the midst of a building boom, but a few old ramshackle warrens and outdoor markets still survive just west of the city square.

Chéngdū is the gateway to scenic Jiǔzhài Gōu, the Buddhist mountains of Éméi Shān and Lè Shān, and one of the most important panda breeding centers. It's also a traveler's haven and a place to gather information between trips. People are friendly and the pace unrushed. And because Chéngdū is one of the few cities with daily flights to Lhasa, many travelers come here to arrange transportation to Tibet.

ESSENTIALS

GETTING THERE **Shuāngliú Airport** is 17km (11 miles) south of Chéngdū. Destinations include Běijīng (eight or nine flights daily); Guǎngzhōu (eight or nine

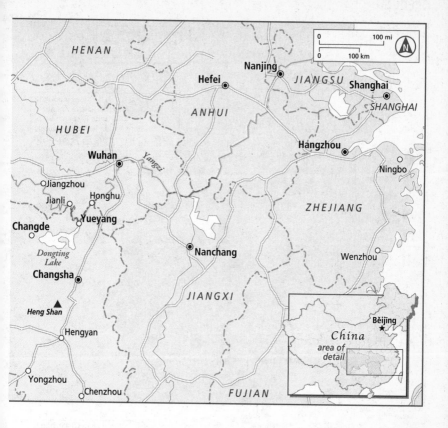

flights daily); Hong Kong (one or two flights daily); and Kūnmíng (8–10 flights daily). To Lhasa, there are one to four flights daily, but it's always best to book the 6am flight; later flights are often canceled or delayed. As of January 2003, travelers were no longer required to enter Tibet with a group of five or more, but Tibet Tourism Bureau (TTB) permits are, for the time being, still required. The price of a one-way flight to Tibet, TTB permit, and airport transfer in Chéngdū is around ¥2,000 ($250). All flights can be booked with any of the several English-speaking travel agents at and near the Traffic Hotel. **Dragonair** has an office in the Sheraton Lido (© **028/8676-8828**) at Rénmín Zhōng Lù 15, 1 Duàn. An **airport shuttle** from the China Southwest office on Rénmín Nán Lù (next to Mín Shān Fàndiàn) takes 45 minutes and costs ¥10 ($1.25); it departs every half-hour. A less direct CAAC shuttle (Mínháng Bānchē), no. 303, leaves every half-hour from 7am to 7pm from the CAAC office at the North Railway Station. The 22km (14-mile) ride takes 70 minutes and costs ¥6 (75¢). A **taxi** from the city center to the airport costs ¥50 to ¥75 ($6.25–$9), including a ¥10 ($1.25) toll.

The main **railway station** is at the northern end of Rénmín Běi Lù, 8km (5 miles) north of the Máo statue in the city center. The ticket office, open 24 hours, is to the right of the main building. Try to purchase tickets at least 2 days in advance. Major

Chéngdū

Sānxīng Duī Bówùguǎn
(Sānxīng Duī Museum)
三星堆博物馆

Xióngmāo Jīdì/
Dàxióngmáo Fánzhí Zhōngxīn
(Panda Research Base/
Giant Panda Breeding Center)
熊猫基地/大熊猫繁殖中心

Er Huan Lu Bei

Er Huan Lu Xi

Yi Huan Lu Bei

Beida Jie

Yi Huan Lu Bei

Sha He (Sha River)

Yi Huan Lu Dong

Ұ Bank

🚉 Rail Station

🏮 Temple

PSB Public-Security Visas

TA Travel Agent

Babao Jie

Wenshu Yuan Jie

Wenwu Lu

PSB

Shuncheng Da Jie

Renmin Zhong Lu

Kuan Xiangzi

Wufu Jie

Er Qiao Lu

Qingyang Zheng Jie

Nan He (Nan River)

Yi Huan Lu Xi

Renmin Xi Lu · Tianfu Square · Renmin Dong Lu

Mao Statue

Bin Long Jie

Da Ci Si Lu

Yi Huan Lu Dong

Wǔguì Qiáo Qìchēzhàn
(Wǔguì Qiáo Bus Station)
五桂桥汽车站

Binjiang Xi Lu

Linjiang Xi Lu

Renmin Nan Lu

Binjiang Zhong Lu · Binjiang Dong Lu

Linjiang Zhong Lu · Linjiang Dong Lu

Wuhou Ci Da Jie

Wuhou Ci Dong Jie

Xin Nan Lu

Yi Huan Lu Nan

Wangjiang Lu

SICHUAN UNIVERSITY

Yi Huan Lu Nan

Renmin Nan Lu

Keihua Bei Lu

Er Huan Lu Nan

Nijia Qiao Lu

Lingshi Guan Lu · Jinxiu Lu

U.S. Consulate

Er Huan Lu Nan

0   1/2 mi

0   0.5 km

N

Tongzi Lin Bei Lu

670

destinations include Běijīng (fast trains 26 hr.; hard sleeper ¥418/$52), Kūnmíng (fast trains 18½ hr.; ¥222/$27), and Shànghǎi (15½ hr.; hard sleeper ¥400–¥500/$50–$62).

Xīn Nán Mén Bus Station (Xīn Nán Mén Qìchēzhàn), at the corner of Xīn Nán Lù and Línjiāng Zhōng Lù and next to the Traffic Hotel, is clean, efficient, and tourist-friendly (has signs in English). Air-conditioned buses leave from here for Lè Shān (2½ hr.; ¥32/$3.90) and for Éméi Shān (2 hr., 15 min.; ¥32/$3.90). Air-conditioned buses to Chóngqìng leave throughout the day from the equally clean, efficient **Wǔ Guī Qiáo Bus Station (Wǔ Guī Qiáo Qìchēzhàn)** southeast of the city center on Yínghuī Lù (4¼ hr.; ¥121/$15). Buses to Jiǔzhài Gōu, Wòlóng, Dūjiāng Yàn, and Qīngchéng Shān now leave from the **Chádiànzi Kèyùn Zhàn** in Chéngdū's western suburbs near the new Third Ring Road (Sān Huán Lù).

VISITOR INFORMATION Pick up the free monthly English-language *Go West Magazine* in hotels and Western-style restaurants for its listings of entertainment and shopping in Chéngdū and Chóngqìng.

GETTING AROUND Chéngdū's flat terrain and many bike lanes make walking and biking easy, but blocks are long, and crossing the river can require a trek before reaching a bridge. Rénmín Lù bisects the city on the north–south axis. Its east–west counterpart is less straightforward: At the heart of the city (Tiānfǔ Sq.), Rénmín Xī Lù runs west from the square and Rénmín Dōng Lù runs east; after a block in either direction, the names change every block or so. Unfortunately, most of Chéngdū's avenues have a multitude of names, making a street map essential. Traffic Hotel (Jiāotōng Bīnguǎn) at Línjiāng Zhōng Lù 77 rents **bicycles** for ¥15 ($1.85) per day with a ¥300 ($25) deposit. Take bus no. 6, 49, 50, or 55 and get off at the Xīn Nán Mén stop. City **buses** (¥1/15¢; air-conditioned ¥2/25¢) serve all parts of the city. Some buses charge ¥1 (15¢) extra at night. Routes are on city maps. Both bus no. 16 and minibus no. 5 (not the full-size no. 5) running the length of Rénmín Lù from the North Railway Station to the South Railway Station are useful lines. The most common **taxi** is the midrange Jetta. Taxi rates are ¥5 (65¢) for the first kilometer, then ¥1.40 (20¢) per kilometer thereafter; the rate increases to ¥2.10 (20¢) per kilometer above 7km (4⅓ miles). From 10pm to 7am the first kilometer costs ¥6 (75¢); after that the fare is ¥1.70 (20¢) per kilometer for the first 7km and ¥2.40 after that.

TOURS Chéngdū has enough good, English-speaking **independent travel agents** that you needn't bother with CITS and its generally higher rates. The best deals can be found inside and in the vicinity of the Jiāotōng Bīnguǎn (Traffic Hotel). The **Traffic Travel Service** (inside the hotel) and **Tiānfǔ International Travel Service** at the entrance to the hotel both book air and train tickets and offer a variety of tour packages. For a **private guide,** Mr. Tray Lee is a highly recommended freelance guide. His prices are competitive, his English excellent, and he's always reachable by mobile phone (© **0139/8160-5307;** message only 028/8555-4250; fax 028/8556-4952; lee_tray@ hotmail.com). His "Sìchuān Opera" tour (see "Chéngdū After Dark," later in this chapter) costs ¥80 ($10) for admission, a backstage visit, one-way transportation, and an English-speaking guide. Die-hards stay for the whole 4 hours, but that's not required. **BikeChina Adventures** (www.bikechina.com/index.htm), an American company based in Chéngdū, arranges adventure bicycle tours through any part of China.

FAST FACTS

Banks, Foreign Exchange & ATMs The **Bank of China** (open Mon–Fri 8:30am–noon and 2–6pm), Zhìmín Lù 36 near the Traffic Hotel and Xīn Nán Mén Bus Station, has full foreign-exchange facilities and an ATM. The branch at Rénmín Nán Lù opposite the Mín Shān Fàndiàn also has an ATM, and is open the same hours.

Consulates   The U.S. Consulate is at Lǐngshìguǎn Lù 4 (© **028/8558-3992;** open Mon–Thurs 8:30am–5:30pm, Fri 9am–4pm; consular.chengdu@state.gov). Take bus no. 16, 61, 49, or 50 to Lǐngshìguǎn Lù.

Internet Access   Try the **Qílín Wǎngbā** and **Jīn Shǒu Wǎngbā,** which both charge ¥2 (25¢) per hour. Both are halfway down the alley off Lǐngshìguǎn Lù near the U.S. Consulate. There is also an Internet cafe on the second floor above **Xīn Nán Mén Bus Station** that is surrounded by computer game machines. It also charges ¥2 (25¢) per hour. Otherwise, you can find Internet cafes around the university, the U.S. Consulate, and the Jiāotōng Bīnguǎn, most of them open 24 hours. Dial-up is © **163.**

Post Office   The Jǐnjiāng Hotel post office (open 8am–noon and 2:30–5:30pm) at Rénmín Nán Lù 80, 2 Duàn, opposite the Mín Shān Fàndiàn, is reliable and conveniently located.

Visa Extensions   The Exit-Entry Office of the **PSB (Jìngwài Rényuán Bànzhèng Qiānzhèng Tīng)** is at Wénwǔ Lù 144 (© **028/8640-7067;** open Mon–Fri 9am–noon and 1–5pm). The entrance is at 391 Shùnchéng Dàjiē. Processing time is officially 5 days, but 3 days seems to be the average, and it's even speedier if you show an ongoing ticket. Take bus no. 55, 62, or 73 from railway stations 16 or 64; get off at the junction of Rénmín Zhōng Lù and Wénwǔ Lù and walk east.

EXPLORING CHÉNGDŪ

The best way to enjoy Chéngdū is to take long walks through the city, relax in a few teahouses and hot pot restaurants, and spread your visits to the best sights over a few days—or longer if you're using Chéngdū as a base from which to visit out-of-town attractions. Here are some of my favorite strolls:

- Much of Chéngdū's Tibetan community lives southeast of the Wǔhóu Temple, and the area around the Southwest Minority Nationalities College and the Tibetan Hospital is interesting for its bookstores, Tibetan shops, and people. **Wǔhóu Cí Héng Jiē,** in particular, has lots of shops selling Tibetan and minority goods. Have lunch at **Xīzàng Fēngqíng Wū** (see "Where to Dine," later in this chapter).

- Directly to the east of Wǔhóu Temple is the most recent addition to Chéngdū's entertainment landscape, **Jǐnlǐ Gǔ Jiē (Jǐnlǐ Ancient Street).** Completed in early 2005, this narrow strip of restaurants, bars, and souvenir stores is built in the style of traditional Eastern Sìchuān architecture and is surprisingly tastefully done. Catering more to locals than tourists, the walk is as interesting for the architecture as it is for the opportunity to just mingle with middle-class Chinese. The strip is also well worth visiting for its alley of traditional Sìchuān street food—an infinitely more hygienic environment than where you'll usually find it.

- Chéngdū's art students used to sell their work on the roads leading into their campus, but the art trade has since been institutionalized and moved into the government building **Sòngxiān Qiáo Yìshù Chéng (Songshan Bridge Art City)** on Huànhuà Běi Lù. While all this might make the complex seem tragically bereft of bohemian spirit, it is worth taking an afternoon to wander through the stalls of "antiques" (both new and old), old party propaganda, Chinese handicrafts, and art. While much of what is on offer is indistinguishable from the pap passed off as Chinese culture in every city you are likely to visit, there are enough gems to warrant some of your time. Of particular interest is the **Zhōngchuān Shōucáng (Zhōngchuān Collection)** (A Qu, second floor no. 53), run by Yáng Xīguāng, a former cadre selling off his extensive personal collection of Cultural Revolution propaganda. Mr. Yáng does not speak English, but the collection more than speaks for itself.

Qīngyáng Gōng (Green Ram Monastery) ⚔ Directly west of the city center, this Daoist monastery is culturally and historically the most important sight in the city. It's said that at Qīngyáng Fair (its first incarnation), Lǎozǐ attained immortality. And it was here that he revealed the *Dàodé Jīng (Classic of the Dào)* to Yǐn Xǐ, frontier guardian at the Hángǔ Pass and last man to see Lǎozǐ before he left the world of men for Mount Kūnlún, gateway to the Western Paradise. Today Qīngyáng Gōng is one of the most active and important Daoist monasteries in China. Among its treasures, of greatest historical significance is a set of rare and elegant pear-wood printing plates of abstracts of scriptures in the Daoist canon. The grounds contain six halls on a central axis, a room for printing Daoist texts that stands to the east, and a room for worshipping Daoist sages that stands to the west. The **Hall of Three Purities (Sānqīng Diàn)** is the monastery's main building, but the most emblematic has to be the **Bāguà Tíng (Pavilion of the Eight Trigrams).** This octagonal building sitting on a square pedestal (symbolic of the Earth) rises 20m (65 ft.) and has two flounces of upturned roofs covered in yellow, green, and purple ceramic tiles. Between the roofs, each facet of the octagon has at its center a plaque of the eight trigrams set off by a pattern of swastikas, symbolic of the sun or the movement of fire. The 81 carved dragons are said to symbolize the 81 incarnations of Lǎozǐ, but the number has closer associations with Chinese numerology and the belief in nine as the most "accomplished" of numbers. A bookstore in the **Hǔnyuán Diàn (Hall of Chaotic Origin)** sells souvenirs alongside Máo bookmarks, Daoist study guides, and a fortune-telling manual called "Unlocking the Secrets of the *Book of Changes.*" If you buy one of the likenesses of Lǎozǐ that comes in a cloth envelope and hand it to the Daoist priest behind the counter, he'll burn incense over it to *kāiguāng* or "open its light."

Escape the din of the city at the partially covered outdoor **teahouse,** where you can sit in a bamboo chair and watch other customers play mahjong and chat with friends (albeit sometimes on cellphones.) Next door is a **vegetarian restaurant,** open 11am to 2pm.

Yī Huán Lù Xī, 2 Duàn (at Yī Huán Lù and Qīngyáng Zhèng Jiē intersection, on the grounds of Wénhuà Gōngyuán/Cultural Park). Admission ¥5 (75¢). 8am–5:30pm. Bus: no. 11, 42, 47, or 59.

Sānxīng Duī Bówùguǎn ⚔ This modern, spiral-shaped museum, opened in 1997, houses one of the most remarkable collections of ancient sculpture, masks, and ritual bronzes in China—don't miss it. Discovered in 1986, these otherworldly, artistically sophisticated tomb relics have sparked debate about the origins of the culture that produced them (as far back as the 14th c. B.C.) and its connection, if any, to the later Shǔ culture. The museum brochure equates the Sānxīng Duī civilization with the Shǔ, but some scholars doubt this, and there are many unanswered questions. For example, why is there no mention of this culture in historical records? When and why did the civilization disappear? Why do many of the masks and human busts seem to have been burned and deliberately shattered—quite possibly by the very people who created them? Still, it's a marvelous collection. Highlights include a delightful ornament-bearing bronze holy tree supported by three kneeling guards and crowned with hawk-beaked birds. The piece most emblematic of the Sānxīng Duī is a 2.4m (8-ft.) standing bronze figure thought to be a sorcerer. Barefoot and standing on a pedestal of zoomorphic design, the creature has a long forehead, oversize eyes, and ears shaped like butterfly wings. Many of the bronze heads wear masks of pure gold. There is also an impressive gold-covered stick believed to be the ritual wand of a shaman. There are photos of the excavation process, English labels and, supposedly, an English-speaking guide on duty for ¥100 ($13). Give yourself about 2 hours to explore the museum.

Guǎnghàn, 40km (25 miles) north of Chéngdū. www.sanxingdui.com/musuem.htm. Admission ¥50 ($6.25). May–Sept 9am–6pm; Oct–Apr 9am–5:30pm. No direct buses to the museum. Go from Zhāojué Sì Qìchēzhàn (Zhāojué Temple bus station) near the zoo to Guǎnghàn. Frequent departures throughout the day. Deluxe A/C bus ¥10 ($1.25), 30-min. ride. Minivans leave Guǎnghàn for Sānxīng Duī every 20 min. for ¥2 (25¢). Return buses depart from same spot.

Sìchuān Dàxué Bówùguǎn (Sìchuān University Museum) 🕸

Construction of a new provincial museum is underway, but it will be hard to match Sìchuān University's fascinating, well-presented collection, which includes Hàn and Táng dynasty Buddhist carvings; important Daoist documents, ritual instruments, talisman blocks, and clothing worn by shamans from the Eastern Hàn dynasty (25–220) to the Qīng dynasty (1644–1912); bronzes from Bā and Shǔ cultures; a shadow puppet theater; and an ethnology collection featuring artifacts from a dozen central China minorities. Rarely are costumes displayed in such a dignified manner and without mannequins.

On the first floor, in the **Hall of Stone Carvings,** look for the exquisite 2m (7-ft.) carved Táng dynasty figure of a **bodhisattva** draped in cloth and jewels. On the second floor, there are several standouts. In the small room of ancient pottery from the Eastern Hàn dynasty, look for the life-size **clay dog** with hanging jowls and bulbous nose. The **Tibetan trumpet** made of a human femur can be found in the Exhibition Hall of Tibetan Artifacts. In the Daoist room, don't miss the **stone certificate of purchase** for a piece of subterranean real estate. In the bureaucratic netherworld, these funerary land deeds were taken to the grave as the deceased's proof of ownership of the land in which he or she was buried. Lastly, located in the same room is a circular **jade disk** *(bì)* from the Shāng dynasty, symbol of Heaven (thought to be round), which was used in worship and burial (when it was probably placed beneath the corpse's back).

Enter through east gate from Wàngjiāng Lù; walk to end, turn right; look for the lotus pond; the museum is adjacent. ✆ 028/8541-2451. Admission ¥10 ($1.25). Mon-Fri 8:30am–5:30pm, closed weekends. Bus: no. 3, 35, 19, or 27.

Wáng Āntíng Xiǎoxiǎo Zhǎnlǎnguǎn 🕸 *Finds*

Informally known as the **Máo Museum,** this very small exhibition hall/apartment is the most eccentric museum you're likely to find in China. The 57,000 badges and Máo pins, along with two more tons of Máo memorabilia still boxed in the attic, were all collected by the museum's owner, Wáng Āntíng—who said that Máo came to him in a dream instructing him to share his collection with the world. In addition to badges, there are busts, buttons, posters, magazines from the 1960s, and photographs from the same era. At the apartment's center, where a dining room table should be, is a large framed sepia-toned portrait of a beatific Máo. In front of it are burning incense and offerings of packages of instant noodles, and usually a plate of pears or a dish of candies. Other photos include one of a decrepit-looking Máo as he shakes the hand of Julie Nixon Eisenhower.

The best day to visit is December 26, when the museum and its small lane are packed with people who've come to celebrate Máo's birthday.

Wǔfú Jiē 23, northwest of the Máo statue; facing Máo, walk left (west). Turn right at the big street with a traffic light; pass Jīnjiābà (lane with a market); turn at the 2nd left down Píngān Xiàng; the entrance to Wǔfú is on the right. Admission is free, however the proprietor will encourage donations to support the museum. 9am–5pm.

Wénshū Yuàn The best things about this active, Táng-founded Buddhist monastery are neither its gilded statues nor its relatively youthful buildings, but its tea-house filled with people reading, knitting, and just relaxing, and its excellent vegetarian restaurant with tables for two and windows overlooking the gardens. Outside, the street is lined with shops selling incense, paper money, and other Buddhist paraphernalia. Inside, locals come to worship and burn incense. The 1st and 15th days of the lunar month are the most active. Another day that draws large crowds is the 19th day of the second lunar month, when the monastery celebrates the birthday of China's favorite bodhisattva, Guānyīn, Goddess of Mercy. The Huáyán Scripture, written in human blood, and the cranial bones of the monk Xuánzàng (p. 255) are among the treasures housed at Wénshū. A pleasing and unusual Sòng fresco of a child worshipping Guānyīn can be found near the gold-plated bronze Guānyīn.

Wénshū Yuàn Jiē, just off Rénmín Zhōng Lù. Admission ¥1 (15¢). 8am–5:40pm; restaurant 10:30am–10:30pm. Enter to the right of main entrance. Bus: no. 16 or 55.

Xióngmāo Jīdì/Dàxióngmāo Fánzhí Zhōngxīn (Panda Research Base/Giant Panda Breeding Center) ✦ This research base, which has elements of a veterinary lab, a park, a panda habitat, and a zoo, is one of the best places to see giant pandas. The much more wild and natural Wòlóng Nature Reserve (p. 689) would be better, but—except in its panda enclosures—panda sightings are few and far between. The stated purpose of the breeding center is to increase the captive population of pandas in order to reintroduce some to the wild. The grounds of the research base, covered with trees, flowers, and 14 species of bamboo, are lovely and, at the very least, provide a pleasant escape from the noise and congestion of Chéngdū proper. As you follow pathways through the reserve you may see not only giant pandas but red pandas (closer to a raccoon than a panda), black-necked cranes, and white storks. You might also run into visiting field researchers. Your best chance of seeing pandas is at feeding time, 8:30 to 10am, although a few, mostly those for breeding, are in cages. Ask if there are cubs around—a mother panda with babe in arms is a sight not to be missed. Allow an hour to get to the base, two to stroll the grounds. Alternately you can take a tour cart for ¥10 ($1.25) and reduce the visit to about 50 minutes; the tour is conducted in Chinese, but at least you go straight to the pandas.

Xióngmāo Dà Dào, northern suburb, northeast of the zoo. ⓒ 028/8351-6748. Admission ¥30 ($3.75). 8am–6pm. Bus: no. 9, 19, 201, or 302 to zoo; from there, ¥8 ($1) taxi or ¥5 (65¢) trishaw.

SHOPPING

Chéngdū abounds in supermarkets, including three **Carrefour (Jiālèfú)** stores (open 9am–10pm). Thanks to discounts and a broad selection of Chinese and imported products, shopping here always feels like the day before Christmas—festive, but impossibly crowded. If you abhor body contact with perfect strangers, go elsewhere. If you don't mind it, the most accessible location is at Bābǎo Jiē 1 (ⓒ **028/8626-6789**). Take bus no. 4, 56, or 76 to Bābǎo Jiē. **Trust-mart (Hǎoyòuduō Chāoshì)**, located at Jǐnxiù Lù 2 near the corner of Kēhuá Běi Lù on the south side of town, is a block long, next to McDonald's and almost opposite KFC. Open from 9am to 10pm, it's a grocery store, drug store, and department store in one, and one of the few stores in China to carry tampons. Take bus no. 6, 76, or 77. The best, most conven-ient supermarket at which to buy snacks for a long train journey is the huge **Rénmín Shāngchǎng (People's Market)** opposite the main railway station. It also has a bak-ery and a fast-food restaurant that serves a Chinese breakfast for ¥1 to ¥4 (15¢–50¢). Open 7:30am to 9:30pm.

WHERE TO STAY
EXPENSIVE
Holiday Inn Crowne Plaza (Zǒngfǔ Huángguān Jiàrì Jiǔdiàn)   Located a few blocks from the city center and next door to Parkson, this five-star international hotel used to be the best in Chéngdū. It still is quite good, with clean bathrooms and pleas-ant staff, but the Sheraton (see below) is a notch above and no more expensive. If you stay here, rooms with a single king-size bed rather than twins are slightly bigger.

Zǒngfǔ Jiē 31, 610016 (4 blocks east of the Máo statue). ✆ **028/8678-6666.** Fax 028/8678-9789. www.ichotels group.com. 434 units. ¥800 ($100) standard room. Most rates include breakfast. 40% discount standard; add 15% service charge. AE, DC, MC, V. Bus: no. 3, 4, 7, 45, 58, or 98. **Amenities:** 4 restaurants; 2 bars; indoor pool; tennis court; health club; sauna; airline, train, and bus ticketing; business center; forex; 24-hr. room service; dry cleaning/laundry. *In room:* A/C, satellite TV, dataport, broadband Internet access, minibar, fridge, hair dryer, safe.

Sheraton Chéngdū Lido (Tiānfǔ Lìdū Xǐláidēng Fàndiàn) ✿   Opened in 2000 1km (½ mile) north of the city center, the Sheraton may be the most attractive of Chéngdū's luxury hotels. The lobby's fountain and large floral arrangement give this spot a warmer ambience than the standard hotel, and the front desk staff is amiable and efficient. Although the standard rooms aren't as spacious as those at the Holiday Inn, the cozy decor is more inviting. Many of the rooms have separate bathroom and shower.

Rénmín Zhōng Lù, 1 Duàn 15. ✆ **028/8676-8999.** Fax 028/8676-8888. www.sheraton.com/chengdu. 402 units. ¥1,440 ($180) standard room. Most rates include breakfast. 40%–50% seasonal discounts; 15% service charge. AE, DC, MC, V. Bus: no. 16. Minibus: no. 5 from railway station. **Amenities:** 2 restaurants; 2 bars; indoor heated pool; health club, Jacuzzi; sauna; airline, train, and bus ticketing; business center; forex; 24-hr. room service; massage; dry cleaning/laundry. *In room:* A/C, satellite TV, dataport, minibar, fridge, hair dryer, safe.

MODERATE
Xīnzú Bīnguǎn (Sunjoy Inn)   Located just a short walk from the U.S. Consulate, this three-star hotel was renovated in 2004. Management and staff pride themselves on continued maintenance of the building and guest rooms; clean hallway carpets and unstained sinks—rarities in all but the priciest hotels—attest to their sincerity. Guest rooms and bathrooms are medium in size. Furnishing is run-of-the-mill but better maintained than most in this range. The hotel is connected to one of the best non-Chi-nese restaurants in Chéngdū, **Tandoor Indian Cuisine** (see "Where to Dine," below).

Rénmín Nán Lù, 4 Duàn 34. ✆ **028/8552-0808.** Fax 028/8554-6598. www.sunjoy-inn.com. 189 units. ¥400–¥460 ($50–$57) standard room. Rates include breakfast. 20% discount is standard. AE, DC, MC, V. Bus: no. 16, 19, or 72. Minibus: no. 5. **Amenities:** 3 restaurants; bar; exercise room; airline, train, and bus ticketing; small business center; forex; 24-hr. room service; dry cleaning/laundry. *In room:* A/C, TV, minibar, fridge.

INEXPENSIVE
Guānhuá Qīngnián Yóushè (Sim's Cozy Guesthouse)   The cheapest of Chéngdū's budget offerings, Sim's is spartan but clean and well-situated—a good starting point for exploring the city. Staying here is also a great way to mingle with Chéngdū locals: It is located on a side street that is not only close to Wénshū Temple,

one of the more lively temples in town, but is also filled with seniors playing mahjong on the side of the road. The hotel has communal bathrooms, a common room with a TV and an extensive DVD collection, and a leafy outdoor area with tables and chairs—ideal in summer to meet fellow travelers. To account for the vagaries of the seasons, ¥10 ($1.25) extra will buy you air-conditioning and ¥5 (65¢) will get you an electric blanket. The hotel staff and the in-house travel agent all speak English.

Xī Zhūshì Jiē 42 (just down from Wénshū Yuàn, on the east side). ℂ **028/8691-4422**. www.gogosc.com. 24 units. ¥70 ($8.50) standard room. No credit cards. Bus: no. 1, 18, 302, or 80. **Amenities:** Restaurant; airline and train ticketing; dry-cleaning/laundry service; Internet access; bike rental.

Jiāotōng Bīnguǎn (Traffic Hotel) ⚓ Catering to independent travelers and back-packers, this one-star hotel puts Internet access, Tibet travel news, rental bikes, and bag storage at your fingertips. Equally important, room rates range from inexpensive to moderate. The staff is friendly and helpful (most speak some English), and the **Anchor Bar** (see below) in front is *the* place to meet other like-minded travelers. Although the elevator has a disturbing rattle, rooms are clean and sort of cozy. At the time of writing the second and third floors were being renovated to the quality of the fourth and the restaurant was undergoing an upgrade.

Línjiāng Zhōng Lù 6 (next to the Xīn Nán Mén Bus Station). ℂ **028/8545-1017**. Fax 028/8544-0977. www.traffic Hotel.com. 151 units. ¥200 ($25) standard room; ¥210 ($26) triple with bathroom; ¥40 ($5) bed in 3-person room with A/C and communal shower/toilet. 10% seasonal discount. No credit cards. Bus: no. 15, 16, 28, or 99. Minibus: no. 5. **Amenities:** 2 restaurants; bar; airline, train, and bus ticketing; business center; forex; limited room service; dry cleaning/laundry. *In room:* A/C, TV.

Yǒuyì Bīnguǎn (Friendship Hotel) ⓥ𝘢𝘭𝘶𝘦 This six-story hotel is popular with young Chinese visitors, but few foreign travelers have discovered it, despite its proximity to the U.S. Consulate. Small, simple, and built around a pleasant garden and pond, it's basic but handy for access to many Chinese and Western restaurants, a coffee shop (Coffee Beanery), and the Trust-mart Supermarket. Although there's no elevator or Internet access, the rooms are clean with a decor that is slightly better than standard. The hotel fills up during the busy season (Mar–Oct), especially on weekends. Without reservations you're unlikely to get a room here during national holidays.

Língshìguǎn Lù 1 (opposite U.S. Consulate). ℂ **028/8522-3442**. Fax 028/8522-1508. 83 units. ¥160–¥200 ($20–$25) standard room; ¥120 ($15) triple. No credit cards. Bus: no. 16. Minibus: no. 5. **Amenities:** Restaurant; airline, train, and bus ticketing; business center; limited room service. *In room:* A/C, TV.

WHERE TO DINE

Anchor Bar (Àn Bā) ⓥ𝘢𝘭𝘶𝘦 HOME-STYLE WESTERN/CHINESE Situated in front of the Traffic Hotel, this cozy little bar is a great place to relax over a cold beer; plus, Internet access is free if you buy a meal there. For the most part, the menu lacks imagination—both in the Chinese and Western offerings—with the exception of an excellent hot Western breakfast. But all is forgiven when you sink into one of the soft, welcoming couches that are a godsend after a day spent pounding city streets. The rest of the decor is Tibetan inspired with warm, earthy colors. The staff speaks limited English but is a friendly lot and will burn your pictures onto a CD, and let you use the TV to watch a DVD after 8pm.

Línjiāng Zhōng Lù 6. ℂ **028/8545-4520**. Main courses ¥15–¥30 ($2–$3.50). No credit cards. 9am until the last customer goes home. Book exchange. Bus: no. 15, 16, 28, or 99. Minibus: no. 5.

Bāguó Bùyì ⚑⚑ ⓥ𝘢𝘭𝘶𝘦 SÌCHUĀN Delicious local fare made with fresh, natural ingredients is served here in artfully rustic surroundings—dried corn stalks and red peppers hang between photographs of farmhouses and peasant life. A spiral wooden staircase wrapped around a large artificial tree leads to second-floor tables with views of the open kitchen. There's enough space for privacy, and service is excellent. House specialties include the gelatinous green turtle stewed with taro *(yùer shāo jiǎyú)*—a regional delicacy, but not to everyone's taste. More reliable would be *huíguō hòupí cài* (twice-cooked thick-skinned greens), a leafy green vegetable boiled and stir-fried in a delicious broad bean sauce, and more inspired than its name suggests. Also try *yěcài bā* (steamed glutinous rice bread with wild vegetable wrapped in corn husks), and *dòufu jìyú* (tofu and golden carp). The tasty sauce, made of tomato, spring onion, chilies, and beans, makes this a particular favorite with locals.

Rénmín Nán Lù 20, 4 Duàn (near Língshìguǎn Lù). ✆ **028/8553-1688.** English menu. Meal for 2 ¥50–¥100 ($6–$12). No credit cards. 11:30am–2:30pm and 5–10pm. Bus: no. 16 or 99.

Càigēn Xiāng ✿ SÌCHUĀN

With four outlets and a cooking school, this is one of Chéngdū's most popular restaurants. Specializing in dishes made with traditional pickled vegetables *(pào cài),* the restaurant has won awards for its *pàojiāo mòyú zǎi* (pickled pepper with baby squid). Two other distinctive dishes are Càigēn Xiāng spareribs *(Càigēn Xiāng páigǔ)* which fall off the bone and are cooked in a delicious sauce that renders them juicy and tender, and fish with pickled vegetables *(pàocài jiāyú).* This is a whole fish served in a red sauce with a variety of fresh and pickled vegetables. Bones have to be dealt with, but the fish is delicate and tasty.

Rénmín Nán Lù (near corner of Tóngzǐ Lín Běi Lù). ✆ **028/8518-5967.** Photo menu. Meal for 2 ¥40–¥200 ($5–$25). No credit cards. 9:30am–9:30pm. Bus: no. 16 or 99 to Jǐnxiù Huāyuán.

Fiesta Thai (Fēicháng Tài Tàiguó Fēngwèi Cāntīng) ✿ THAI

Nestled in next to the Anchor Bar, the food at Fiesta isn't exactly authentic—suffering from the Sìchuān tendency to make everything a little hotter than necessary—but the service and environment more than compensate. The polished wooden floor boards and elegantly dressed serving staff add a touch of class, and the high ceilings add a breezy feeling that makes the restaurant a pleasant escape from the summer heat.

Línjiāng Zhōng Lù 6 (just in front of the Traffic Hotel). ✆ **028/8545-4530.** English menu. Meal for 2 ¥65–¥80 ($8–$10). No credit cards. 5–10:30pm. Bus: no. 15, 16, 28, or 99.

Gingko (Yínxìng) ✿ SÌCHUĀN

As much thought and energy went into the design of this upscale restaurant as into the menu; and in both cases, the results are elegant and sophisticated. Plush chairs and couches in the bar area, and dining tables overlooking the river, invite guests to relax and linger over drinks and dinner. The food is excellent, but expensive. This is one of the few restaurants in Sìchuān where you'll feel out of place unless you dress up to dine. Two of the best house specialties are king crab steamed with peppercorns *(jiāozǐ zhēng guìyú)* for ¥128 ($16) and crispy beef tenderloin *(sūpí niúliǔ)* for ¥48 ($6).

Línjiāng Zhōng Lù 12, about 150m (492 ft.) beyond the Xīn Nán Mén Bus Station. ✆ **028/8555-5588.** www.yxjl.com. English menu. Meal for 2 ¥200–¥400 ($25–$50). No credit cards. 11am–10pm. Bus: no. 16, 78, or 99 along Rénmín Lù to Línjiāng Lù; walk east from there.

Grandma's Kitchen (Zǔmǔ de Chúfáng) AMERICAN HOME COOKING

Farm-style chandeliers and wall lamps, straight-back wooden chairs with gingham cushions, and framed photos on the wall give this split-level restaurant an appropriately homey atmosphere—and goes a long way toward explaining how Grandma's is turning itself into a booming franchise with two locations in Chéngdū and two in Běijīng. The menu might not be entirely familiar—tuna-fish pizza is undoubtedly the result of a recipe confused in the translation—but the rest of the menu, which includes fried chicken, a variety of steaks, and much more, is a prayer answered for any U.S. resident craving a taste of home. The pies and desserts are made at **Grandma's Deli,** next door to the Kēhuá Běi Lù premises, which specializes in sandwiches and homemade desserts. A comfortable atmosphere with small libraries containing donated English-language paperbacks make either Grandma's location a perfect place to hole up on a rainy day and write postcards.

Grandma's Kitchen and Grandma's Deli at Kēhuá Běi Lù 75. ✆ **028/8524-2835.** Bus: no. 55, 110, 49, or 6. Also at Rénmín Nán Duàn Lù 22. ✆ **028/8555-3856.** Main courses ¥35–¥50 ($4.35–$6.25). No credit cards. English spoken. Mon–Fri 8:30am–midnight; Sat–Sun 8am–midnight.

Highfly Pizza (Gāofēi Bǐsà) PIZZA

If you're lonely for friendly faces or other travelers, you'll find both in this cheerful restaurant serving pizzas, salads, and pastas. In general, the dishes are tasty; but the chocolate brownies topped with hot fudge are scrumptious. There's also takeout pizza, and eggs Benedict for breakfast (¥15/$1.80). The waitstaff speaks English.

Línjiāng Zhōng Lù 19. ✆ **028/8665-2656.** Pizza ¥15–¥32 ($2–$4). No credit cards. 9am–10.30pm. Bus: no. 15, 16, 28, or 99. Minibus: no. 5.

Kuàilè Lǎojiā HOT POT

You'll appreciate this hot pot restaurant as much for its good food as for its warmly lit, inviting dining room. The space is large and airy and affords privacy at every table. Ambience aside, the keys to great hot pot are the broth—here it is rich and flavorful—and the dipping sauce. Ingredients vary, but are likely to include bean sprouts, leeks, a variety of mushrooms, sausages, seafood, organ meats, and/or duck tongues. Photographs of dishes and ingredients remove the difficulty of ordering without an English menu. Prices depend on the ingredients you choose—the more exotic, the pricier. I recommend any of the *má là* (hot and numbing) hot pots, but plain mild broth is also available *(báitāng lǔ).*

Língshìguǎn Lù 5 (south side of street, opposite Friendship Hotel; look for blue sign with big yellow dots). ✆ **028/8522-4999.** Meal for 2 ¥100–¥200 ($12–$24). No credit cards. 10:30am–11pm. Bus: no. 16, 50, 72, or 76 to Língshì Guǎn Lù.

Rome Restaurant (Luómǎ Yìdàlì Xīcāntīng) ITALIAN

Formerly a French restaurant, it has made the transition to Italian seamlessly. Service in this small restaurant is friendly and efficient, design is modern and comfortably minimalist, and prices are affordable. The menu is mammoth with something for everyone, but the pork medallions in white wine and lemon sauce are highly recommended. Desserts include chocolate mousse and tiramisu. A small selection of Western wines and liqueurs is available, but more important the restaurant shares the same coffee supplier as the top hotels in town. Not far from Grandma's (see above).

Kēhuá Běi Lù 115 (just north of the west gate of Sìchuān University). ✆ **028/8524-4968.** Meal for 2 ¥50–¥100 ($6.25–$13). No credit cards. 10:30am–10:30pm. Bus: no. 55, 110, 49, or 6.

Tandoor Indian Cuisine (Téngdūěr Yìndù Cāntīng) 🐟🐟 NORTHERN INDIAN

Tandoor's Indian chef clearly takes care in buying and preparing ingredients to make authentic dishes from chiefly the north, but also from southern India. The food and service are equally superb. A delicious specialty from Goa is the Portuguese-influenced pork vindaloo. This very hot dish is made with Indian spices, vinegar, and chilies. One

The Ways of Tea

In the 8th-century *Classic of Tea,* author and tea sage Lù Yǔ says that there are "nine ways by which man must tax himself when he deals with tea."

1. He must manufacture it.
2. He must develop a sense of selectivity and discrimination about it.
3. He must provide the proper implements.
4. He must prepare the right kind of fire.
5. He must select a suitable water.
6. He must roast the tea to a turn.
7. He must grind it well.
8. He must brew it to its ultimate perfection.
9. He must, finally, drink it.

In modern China, there are still many ways to drink tea, from the highly ritualized, heavy-on-equipage style prescribed by Lù Yǔ, to the style favored on long-distance trains (toss a pinch of tea leaves into a glass jar with a screw-top and keep adding water and drinking until you reach your destination). The Chéngdū way doesn't use a teapot or a glass jar: The typical setting is the riverside, a park, or temple grounds—in an outdoor teahouse with bamboo tables and chairs. Here, patrons sip tea from 3-ounce cups that sit on saucers small enough to rest in the palm of the hand while protecting it from the heat of the cup. A lid keeps the tea hot and can be used to sweep aside tea leaves that rise to the top as you drink. Melon seeds, boiled peanuts, or dried squid are typical snack accompaniments.

of the best northern specialties is *murgh malai* kabob, chunks of chicken marinated in ginger-garlic paste, then mixed with cheese, cream, coriander, chili, cinnamon, and anisette, and cooked in a tandoori oven. Connected to the Xīnzú Bīnguǎn (Sunjoy Inn), Tandoor, designed by an Indian architect, is airy and handsome; elegant wooden rafters give it flair, and soft Indian music enhances an already pleasing ambience. Traditional Indian dance performances run nightly from 7 to 8pm.

Rénmín Nán Lù 34, 4 Duàn (directly behind the Xīnzú Bīnguǎn). ⓒ 028/8555-1958. Reservations recommended. Set meals ¥48–¥110 ($6–$14). AE, DC, MC, V. 11:30am–2pm and 5:30–10:30pm. Bus: no. 99 or 16.

Xīzàng Fēngqíng Wū *Value* TIBETAN   Situated in a Tibetan neighborhood and frequented by Tibetans (many Khampas from western Sìchuān), this intimate three-room restaurant (with four to six tables in each room) serves top-quality dishes in a warm, cheerful environment. Tibetan music usually plays in the background, and almost any time of day you'll find monks at several of the tables, eating snacks and drinking milk tea. Three great dishes are *jiāróng suāncài kǎobǐng* (jiāróng Tibetan bread stuffed with pickled cabbage and barbecued pork) for ¥10 ($1.25); *máoniú ròubāo* (yak meat *bāozi*), ¥8 ($1) for 10 *bāozi;* and *suān luóbo chǎo máoniúròu* (pickled cabbage with fried yak meat) for ¥15 ($1.90). For a snack, try Tibetan bread with milk tea. A large pot of tea costs ¥10 ($1.25).

Wǔhóu Cí Dōng Jiē 3, Fù 2 (look for painting of yak on an ocher-yellow building with Tibetan script in blue, red, orange, and yellow). ✆ 028/8551-0112. Menu has some English. Meal for 2 ¥30 ($3.80). No credit cards. 8am–10:30pm. Bus: no. 82 from Traffic Hotel.

TEAHOUSES

For the typical Chéngdū experience, go to Qīngyáng Gōng or Wénshū Yuàn monasteries (see "Exploring Chéngdū," earlier in this chapter). For something trendier, Chéngdū has upmarket teahouses for the connoisseur or connoisseur-in-training. The best of the bunch is **Guǎnghé Chálóu**, on the river at Línjiāng Zhōng Lù 16 (✆ 028/8550-1688). Rattan chairs, palm trees, lots of large potted plants, and blonde wood lend a clean, spalike atmosphere to this teahouse. The Chinese/English menu has pages of teas, some medicinal or therapeutic, others special for the locale in which they're grown. Under "Teas for Women" are "Aloe Beauty Face Tea," "Heart Tea," and "Chinese Yew Tea for Lady." A small pot of "Rose Love Things" is ¥48 ($6), but my favorite is always Wūlóng, of which there are many kinds. The best come from the high mountains of Táiwān and Fújiàn Province. A pot of tea costs ¥38 to ¥68 ($4.75–$8.50). The teahouse is open from 9am to midnight.

CHÉNGDŪ AFTER DARK

Unlike many Chinese cities, Chéngdū offers a variety of ways to pass the evening. **Sìchuān opera** is a favorite for foreign and Chinese tourists alike. Known for its humor and dynamism, an integral part of every performance is *biànliǎn* or "changing faces." The character is often a villain who changes his face to escape recognition. The reputed record is 14 changes in 24 seconds. Over its 300-year tradition, the trick has changed, but it has always been a closely guarded secret within the operatic community. Traditional stick puppets and flame balancing are also incorporated into the drama. Performances are at the teahouse next to the Jǐn Jiāng Theater on Huáxīng Zhèng Lù on Saturday for ¥15 ($2.75). Performances are also held at the strictly-for-tourists **Shǔfēng Yǎyùn** in Wénhuà Gōngyuán, from 8 to 9:30pm; the fee is ¥80 ($10) and performances are held nightly. Take bus no. 25, 46, or 103 to Wénhuà Gōngyuán.

The highlight of Chéngdū's nightlife is unquestionably the **Lotus Palace Bar and Restaurant** (**Liánhuā fǔdǐ;** ✆ 028/8553-7676; 3pm–3am). Nestled halfway down Jǐnlì Ancient Street, you'll first notice the red-and-black lacquered traditional style tables and chairs in a small courtyard to your left. The entrance to the bar itself is hidden behind two heavy black doors and walled in by a granite facade in the traditional Sìchuān style. But once inside the designers have tweaked the traditional design with some modern license: red decor throughout the bar, a Perspex ceiling above the dance floor to see the night sky, silver faux bamboo hanging from the ceiling. Drink prices are reasonable (¥30/$3.75 for a beer or mixed drink) and, if you go early in the evening, the music is sufficiently loungey and good for enjoying a quiet drink; go later and the music gives way to heavier dance mix enjoyed by Chéngdū's young, bright things. Even if the bar is not busy, it is worth a visit to see how China is trying to reclaim its cultural heritage—without giving into kitsch.

2 Éméi Shān ⚹

Sìchuān Province, 143km (89 miles) SW of Chéngdū, 36km (22 miles) E of Lè Shān

Éméi means "lofty eyebrows," but it's also a pun on a poetic expression referring to the delicate brows of a beautiful woman. The mountain was named for two of its high adjacent peaks, whose outlines, according to 6th-century commentary on the "Book of Waterways," did indeed conjure the image of two long, thin, graceful eyebrows. Once richly endowed with both flora and fauna, this sacred Buddhist mountain is still home to 10% of China's plant species; fauna have fared less well. Threatened species include Asiatic black bear, giant salamander (the famous "crying fish," or *wáwa yú* in Chinese), gray-hooded parrotbill, and Asiatic golden cat. You'll also bump into monkeys that want a handout, but try to resist—they already suffer from obesity and hypertension. As of 2002, park wardens have put them on a diet. ***Note:*** For Chinese translations of selected establishments listed in this section, please turn to appendix A.

Come here for scenic hiking and active Buddhist shrines and monasteries (where the monk and nun population was once as threatened as the golden cat but has now returned, albeit in smaller numbers). Nature enthusiasts will delight in the exotic insects and butterflies along the way.

Altitudes on the mountain range from 500 to 3,099m (1,640–10,167 ft.) at the Wànfó Dǐng summit. Not surprisingly, average yearly temperatures vary significantly from one part of the mountain to another. In the subtropical zone at the bottom, the average is 63°F (17°C); at the summit, 37°F (3°C). Bring layers of clothes, and adjust them as you climb and descend. The best months to visit are late August through early October. The busiest months are July and August. Avoid national holidays.

Émei Shān admission ¥120 ($15), student discount ¥60 ($7.50). Entrance to monasteries ¥6–¥20 (75¢–$2.50).

A Proper Visit to Émei Shān

The Chinese say a proper visit to Émei Shān involves at least one of the following:

- Watching the **sunrise** from the summit (which requires staying the night on or near it—the earliest shuttle arrives after sunup).

- Standing in the **Cloud Sea.** Like many a Chinese mountain, Émei is famous for its clouds and mists. The classic experience happens when layers of clouds gather between Jiǔlǎo Dòng and Xǐ Xiàng Chí (Elephant Bathing Pool). You see the clouds above, climb through them, then look down to see clouds billowing and surging at your feet like the sea. Of course, conditions aren't always right.

- Witnessing **Buddha's Halo.** When the sun shines through misty clouds, and you're standing between the clouds and the sun, you can see your shadow outlined by a halo-shaped rainbow. Optimal time: 2 to 5pm. Optimal place: Shèshēn Yán.

- Seeing the **"Strange Lamps" (Guài Dēng).** Photos and witnesses are both scarce, but supposedly in the evening when the moon is waning, especially after it has rained and the sky has cleared, those looking down from Shèshēn Yán at the layers of mountains in the distance can see thousands of floating orbs of light.

ESSENTIALS

GETTING THERE   There are several **trains** from Chéngdū to Éméi Shān on the Chéngdū–Kūnmíng line. The trip takes 2 to 3 hours and costs ¥22 ($3). Minibuses and taxis connect the **Éméi Railway Station** (3.2km/2 miles east of town) with the mountain entrance at Bàoguó. The fare is ¥16 ($2) and it's a 20-minute drive. The bus is faster and more direct than the train.

In Chéngdū, most **buses** to Éméi Shān depart from Xīn Nán Mén; the first leaves at 7am. Buses terminate at the Éméi Shān Bus Station or Bàoguó Town. Bàoguó is preferred, since this is where the mountain trails begin, but fewer buses go there. The Éméi Bus Station is connected to Bàoguó Sì, the monastery at Éméi's entrance, by **minibuses** that make the 20-minute, 6.4km (4-mile) drive for ¥10 ($1.25). You can also take one of the public buses leaving every 5 minutes; the fare is ¥2 (25¢). The bus from Chéngdū costs ¥32 ($3.90) each way and takes 2½ hours. Buses also run between Éméi Shān and Lè Shān bus stations every few minutes. Buy your ticket for the 1-hour trip inside the terminal for ¥8 ($1). Buses unload at Lè Shān's north gate. You can also hop on one of the many Lè Shān–bound minibuses that wait outside the Éméi gate. They don't depart until every seat is taken; the fare is ¥4 (50¢).

VISITOR INFORMATION   The very modern and helpful **Éméi Shān Tourist Center (Lǚrén Zhōngxīn),** near Bàoguó Temple (☏ **0833/559-0111**), provides free information and materials about Mount Éméi. Guides can be hired here, although you're sure to pay less if you hire one of the many freelance guides (whose English may not be as good) outside Bàoguó Temple. For quiet and tranquillity, you may opt to go it alone.

Bilingual maps are sold at the tourist center and at any of the many postcard and book stands near the entrance and along the trail. The map costs ¥3.50 (40¢); one side of the map shows Éméi Shān, the other Lè Shān (see below).

EXPLORING ÉMÉI

There are two main **hiking routes** up Éméi Shān to the Jīn Dǐng summit, and two involving bus and/or cable car. Both hiking routes follow the same path from **Bàoguó Sì** (at the entrance) to **Niúxīn Tíng.** At Niúxīn Tíng, they split into a higher and a lower trail, which meet up again at **Xǐ Xiàng Chí,** where they merge into a single path that leads to **Jīn Dǐng Peak.** Since there are 80km (50 miles) of trails to the peak, a combination of hiking, buses, and cable car is recommended.

You can take a **bus** from Bàoguó Sì to Léidòng Píng; from there, take a **cable car** to the top. Buses travel between Bàoguó Sì and Léidòng Píng all day (5am–5pm holidays and July–Aug; 7am–4pm Nov–Apr; and 6am–4 or 5pm May–June and Sept–Oct). The trip each way takes 2 hours and costs ¥30 ($3.75). The cable car runs the 500m (1,666-ft.) leg between the last parking lot, at Jiēyǐn Diàn (next to Léidòng Píng), and Jīn Dǐng (Golden Peak); round-trip fare is ¥70 ($8.65).

An option is to take the bus as far as **Wànnián Cable Car Station (Wànnián Chēchǎng).** Begin your trek there or take the 8-minute cable car ride to Wànnián Sì and start climbing from there. The cable car ride costs ¥30 ($3.75) for the ascent, ¥20 ($2.50) for the descent, and ¥55 ($6.70) round-trip.

All roads lead to Jīn Dǐng, but the highest peaks are **Qiānfó Dǐng** and **Wànfó Dǐng.** These can be reached by a **monorail** that runs between Jīn Dǐng and Wànfó Dǐng. The round-trip takes 20 minutes and costs ¥45 ($5.60).

Note: If you get caught without enough warm clothing, rent a Chinese army jacket for ¥10 ($1.25) at several spots on the mountain, including the Léidòng Píng (Léidòng parking lot).

WHERE TO STAY

For the most comfort, stay in one of the several full-service hotels near the entrance to Ém“ Shān. At the summit, the **Jīn Dǐng Dàjiǔdiàn** is quite comfortable (see below). Other than that, if you want to overnight on the mountain, be prepared for relatively spartan accommodations. Beginning at Bàoguó Sì—the first temple you encounter upon entering the Ém“ Shān scenic area—and continuing to the summit, all the monasteries have guesthouses with rates ranging from ¥15 to ¥160 ($2–$20) per night. Accommodations are as basic as the rates suggest: The least expensive have dorm-style rooms for four to six people, limited or no hot water, and a hallway bathroom. In the $10-and-higher range, expect air-conditioning and limited hot water. Meals can consist of vegetarian, mock-meat dishes or a simple bowl of noodles for around ¥6 (75¢). Two popular monasteries are **Xiānfēng Sì** and **Xǐ Xiàng Chí.** Guesthouses at the peak and in the vicinity of the cable-car terminus at Jìng Shuǐ offer more comfortable lodging (with TV, air-conditioning, and hot showers) for a bit more—but not all of them accept foreigners. They charge ¥150 to ¥250 ($20–$30).

Ém“ Shān Fàndiàn (Ém“ Shān Hotel)   Completed in 2002, this is the only hotel in Ém“ with an Internet bar—although a couple of bars have also appeared on the main street—and, as of this writing, continues to be fresh and sparkling. Each deluxe standard room is spacious and comfortably furnished with a sofa, chair, and coffee table. Some rooms have picture windows with a garden view. Located next to the bus station, the hotel is convenient for late arrivals or early departures, but it's about 8km (5 miles) from Ém“ Shān. To get to the mountain, catch a bus in front of the station for ¥2 (25¢) or take a taxi for ¥12 ($1.50) or less.

Bàoguó Sì 614201 (by the Ém“ Shān Bus Station, 8km/5 miles from Bàoguó Sì). ✆ **0833/559-0518.** Fax 0833/559-1399. 210 units. ¥300–¥580 ($37–$72) standard room. 20%–30% discounts. Rates include Chinese breakfast. AE, DC, MC, V. **Amenities:** Restaurant; bar; business center; limited room service; Internet access. *In room:* A/C, TV, fridge/minibar in some rooms.

Hóngzhū Shān Bīnguǎn   Located on park grounds with a lake and surrounded by dense forest, this is the most beautiful place to stay at Ém“ Shān, and the choice of visiting dignitaries. Several buildings comprise the hotel, but no matter where you stay, you're guaranteed a gorgeous, wooded view. Wing no. 5, renovated and upgraded in 2002, is the best choice, with four-star accommodations; the guest rooms and bathrooms are large, with tastefully appointed furnishings. Wing nos. 7 and 8 are three-star standard; they're clean and comfortable and recently renovated, but the rooms are a little on the small side.

Ém“ Shān Bàoguó Sì Zuǒcè (approaching Ém“ Shān from town, after passing Ém“ Museum on the right, and just before reaching Bàoguó Sì, turn left and follow road to end). ✆ **0833/552-5888.** Fax 0833/552-5666. www.hzs hotel.com. 283 units. ¥350–¥500 ($44–$62) 3-star standard room; ¥880–¥1,800 ($110–$225) 4-star standard room. Most rates include breakfast. 20%–40% discounts. AE, DC, MC, V. **Amenities:** 2 restaurants; 2 bars; airline, train, and bus ticketing; business center; forex; limited room service; dry cleaning/laundry. *In room:* (4-star): A/C, TV, dataport, minibar/fridge, hair dryer; (3-star): A/C, TV.

Jīn Dǐng Dàjiǔdiàn (Golden Summit Hotel)   If you'd like to see the sunrise, this two-star hotel close to the summit is the place to stay. The rooms may be standard issue, but the views are incredible.

Jīn Dǐng (at the Jīn Dǐng summit). ⓒ **0833/509-8077.** ¥600–¥800 ($75–$100) standard room. 20%–30% discounts. No credit cards. **Amenities:** Restaurant; limited room service. *In room:* TV, heater.

WHERE TO DINE

The two restaurants at **Hóngzhū Shān Bīnguǎn** serve excellent food. The prices are higher than usual, but basic meat and vegetable dishes are still quite reasonable. There are a number of restaurants along the road leading to Bàoguó Sì. The biggest draw for Western tourists is **Teddy Bear Café** (ⓒ **0833/559-0135**), which serves Chinese and Western dishes and has an English menu. Next door is the Teddy Bear Hotel, whose English-speaking staff is extremely useful in organizing tours and booking tickets.

3 Lè Shān

Sìchuān Province, 154km (96 miles) SW of Chéngdū, 36km (22 miles) W of Éméi Shān

The carved stone statue of the Great Buddha (Dà Fó) at Lè Shān is one of Sìchuān's top tourist destinations, but whether it's worth a day in a tight travel schedule is debatable. The thrill of Lè Shān is in your first sighting of the Great Buddha. Whether that's from the top looking down, from a boat looking straight up, or from the path of nine switchbacks (Língyún Zhàndào) looking somewhere in between, the moment it dawns on you that the large, gracefully curved, stone wall (for example) that you're looking at is actually the lobe of a colossal ear, and that the ear is only a small slice of a well-proportioned giant—that moment is thrilling. But after you've marveled at the Great Buddha from all the various angles, what's left to explore is not much more than an overcrowded theme park.

The town of Lè Shān is not without charm, but with a 2,300-year history and situated as it is at a confluence of rivers, it should offer much more than it does. Mass demolition and reconstruction have rendered it indistinguishable (except for its pretty waterways) from a thousand others undergoing the same process. I suggest you skip the town and go directly to the mountain. Lè Shān is best done as a day trip from Chéngdū or as a stopover on the way back to Chéngdū from Éméi Shān. Two to 3 hours is plenty of time to enjoy it. Admission to the mountain is ¥70 ($5) and includes all the sights. It's open from 7:30am to 7:30pm, May through September; and from 8am to 6pm, October through April. *Note:* For Chinese translations of selected establishments listed in this section, please turn to appendix A.

ESSENTIALS

GETTING THERE   Air-conditioned **buses** depart for Lè Shān from Chéngdū's Xīn Nán Mén Bus Station every half-hour from 7am to 7pm for ¥36 ($4.50); the ride takes 2½ hours. They arrive at the Lè Shān Long-Distance Bus Station or a bus stop on the main road into town. Return buses for Chéngdū leave from the Lè Shān entrance every half-hour or so. The last bus returning to Chéngdū from the entrance leaves between 5:30 and 6pm (whenever it fills up). Buses also leave for Chéngdū from Lè Shān's Long-Distance Bus Station every 15 minutes, and from the Central Passenger Station every half-hour. Buses run between Éméi Shān and Lè Shān bus stations every few minutes for ¥7 (90¢). On the return leg to Chéngdū, be aware of which bus station you are being taken to. **Taxi** fare between Éméi and Lè Shān is about ¥60 ($7.50).

GETTING AROUND   Buses arrive in one of three places in Lè Shān: the Long-Distance Bus Station, the Passenger Central Bus Station, or a bus stop on the main road into town. The Long-Distance Bus Station is farthest from the Great Buddha site—a ¥15 ($2) taxi ride. From the Lè Shān bus stop, take bus no. 3 to the Great Buddha for ¥5 (65¢). What should be a 10-minute drive stretches to a half-hour as the driver trawls for passengers along a circuitous route. The bus unloads at Lè Shān's north gate. It's a 7-minute walk to the park entrance, or you can hitch a motorcycle lift for a few *yuán*. Pedicabs are an option that will shave time off the journey between the bus stop and Lè Shān scenic area; they charge ¥8 to ¥10 ($1–$1.25). By taxi from the bus stop to the Lè Shān scenic area, expect to pay ¥12 to ¥15 ($1.50–$1.90). A round-trip **tour boat** or **motorboat** from the north gate to Wūyóu Temple costs ¥50 ($6) and allows time for photos of the Great Buddha. **Ferries** run between the Lè Shān City dock and both Língyún Shān and Wūyóu Sì for ¥5 (65¢); the last boat leaves Lè Shān at 6pm.

At the entrance to Lè Shān scenic area, vendors sell **maps** of the mountain for ¥3.50 (40¢). Maps are also sold at the small stands near the head of the Great Buddha. One side of this bilingual map shows Lè Shān; the other shows Éméi Shān.

EXPLORING LÈ SHĀN

On foot from the entrance, it's a 10-minute walk along a stone path to the Great Buddha. When the road forks into two staircases, take the staircase to the right. This leads around the side of the mountain looking back at the town. It also affords a panoramic view of the three converging rivers, the Mín Jiāng, the Dàdù Hé (Cháng Jiāng), and the Qīngyī Jiāng. The path leads to a terrace and souvenir area beside and around the back of the Buddha's head. From here you can look into his ear and over his shoulder. For a variety of views of Dà Fó, descend the zigzag staircase called **Jiǔqǔ Zhàndao (Path of Nine Switchbacks)** by the statue's right side. This leads to a large viewing platform that puts visitors at toe level.

Dà Fó (The Great Buddha) ✿   At 71m (233 ft.) tall, Lè Shān's Dà Fó—hewn out of a mountain—is similar in size, subject, and artistic medium to the recently demolished Bamiyan Buddhas in the Hindu Kush. Carved some 500 years later, between 713 and 803, Dà Fó is one of the world's largest stone sculptures of Buddha. It was the inspiration of the Buddhist monk Hǎi Tōng, abbot of Língyún Monastery, who hoped that a giant Maitreya Buddha (Future Buddha) overlooking the water might subdue floods and violent currents. In 1996 it was added to UNESCO's World Heritage List, and in 2001 large-scale repairs were started: The Buddha's head, shoulders, and torso were cleaned up and repaired and a cement coating (added in modern times) was removed. The next stage took 10 months and was completed in 2002. Repairs were made to the statue's ingenious, hidden drainage system that slowed, but could not stop, erosion; and cracks as deep as 4m (13 ft.) in the base of the Buddha were filled in. For an idea of how massive this statue is: Each eye is 3m (11 ft.) long; each ear 7m (23 ft.); and his middle finger is 8m (27 ft.) long. His head is covered with 1,021 buns of coiled hair, carved out of tapered stone blocks that fit into his head like pegs in a cribbage board.

Wūyóu Shān   After viewing the Great Buddha, there isn't a lot more to do, except stroll the park grounds and enjoy the views. To reach the adjacent southern hill, Wūyóu Shān, cross the **Háoshàng Dà Qiáo** footbridge on the south side of the Great Buddha. The plain, six-hall monastery by the same name, built in the Táng dynasty and rebuilt many times since, sits atop the hill. The Luóhàn Táng contains an army of terra-cotta arhats, each in a different pose. Most impressive is the view of the rivers from the top of the complex.

WHERE TO STAY & DINE

The best stays in Lè Shān were once within the park itself, but they have all since closed down. A nice alternative is the **Xiāndǎo Dàjǐudiàn (Xiāndǎo Hotel)** which is only a 2-minute walk to the back entrance of the park. Out of the city on Dǎo Lóng Island, it is surrounded by waterways and greenery. Although the rooms can be a little damp, it makes for a pleasant escape from the dust and general blandness of Lè Shān itself. Standard rooms cost ¥268 to ¥388 ($33–$46), but management is open to negotiation. The most comfortable place to stay in downtown Lè Shān is the **Jiā Zhōu Bīngguǎn,** Báitǎ Jiē 19 (© **0833/213-9888;** fax 0833/213-3233). It's as three-star hotel with basic modern rooms for ¥360 ($45) and a restaurant. A number of good small restaurants are also in the vicinity of this hotel. **Yáng's** is inexpensive, with Chinese and Western food and an English menu; it's located at Báitǎ Jiē 49 (© **0833/ 211-2046**). Richard Yang, the proprietor, is a wealth of local knowledge and personal anecdotes. A vegetarian restaurant specializing in faux meat dishes is on Wūyóu Shān behind Dàxióng Temple.

4 Qīngchéng Shān ★

Sìchuān Province, 55km (34 miles) NW of Chéngdū, 16km (10 miles) SW of Dūjiāng Yàn

As a convenient subalpine getaway, Qīngchéng Shān is better than all the other mountains in this chapter. It offers solitary climbing on stone steps and wooden paths through dense forests of pine, fir, and cypress. Along the way are caves, ponds, a pedestrian bridge, ancient ginkgoes, and 16 Daoist and Buddhist monasteries housing statues dating as far back as the 6th century.

More important (though it may have slim bearing on the travel plans of most Westerners), Mount Qīngchéng is considered the birthplace of China's only indigenous religion, Daoism—that is, "organized" Daoism, which gelled a half century after Lǎozǐ. It was to this mountainous part of western Sìchuān (the Shǔ Kingdom) that the pilgrim Zhāng Dàolíng came to cultivate the *Dào*. Some years later, in A.D. 142, the deified Lǎozǐ appeared at Hèmíng Shān (just south of Qīngchéng) and made Zhāng the first Celestial Master. Zhāng went on to establish 24 peasant communities throughout Shǔ, whose customs included confession and the regular payment of 5 pecks of rice to a communal grain reserve.

Less awe-inspiring than other World Heritage mountains, Qīngchéng Shān nevertheless makes an invigorating day trip from Chéngdū. If you wish to stay longer, there is lodging in monasteries and inns on the mountain. Escape crowds and high guesthouse rates by coming midweek. Summer is considered the best time to visit, but it's also the busiest, as Chéngdū residents flee the city heat.

ESSENTIALS

GETTING THERE Buses depart Chéngdū's Xīn Nán Mén Bus Station every 30 minutes from 8 to 10am (1 hr.; ¥28/$3.50); they run in the afternoon as well but are more sporadic. Buses also run more frequently during July and August. Return buses leave every 30 minutes from 3pm to 5pm, from Qīngchéng's main entrance. An option is to take a bus to Dūjiāng Yàn and transfer to a Qīngchéng Qián Shān bus. Buses make the 16km (10-mile) trip between Dūjiāng Yàn and Qīngchéng every half-hour from 6:20am to 5:30pm for ¥4.50 (60¢).

GETTING AROUND The hike to the 1,260m (4,133-ft.) summit is less strenuous than the Éméi trail, but it includes a few short, steep sections. At a leisurely pace,

Shàngqīng Gōng can be reached in about 2 hours. It's possible to cut that time in half by taking the ferry across Yuèchéng Hú and from there a cable car to just below Shàngqīng Gōng. Passage is ¥30 ($3.75) one-way; ¥50 ($6.25) round-trip. The cable shuts at 5:30pm. It's a fun way to go, but you sacrifice seeing the sights. Admission is ¥60 ($7.50).

EXPLORING QĪNGCHÉNG SHĀN
SUGGESTED ROUTE (3–4 HR.)

From the entrance, follow the main trail, keeping to the left. Pass **Yílè Wō (Nest of Pleasures)**; continue to **Tiānshī Dòng (Celestial Master Cave)**. This is the core site of Qīngchéng Shān. The six surrounding peaks were to act as natural inner and outer walls that would protect the area from the world of men. A temple first built in 730 now stands in the spot where Zhāng Dàolíng is supposed to have built a hut for himself. It's said that he planted the **ancient ginkgo tree** that grows here—which would make it about 1,700 years old. Continue on to **Zǔshī Diàn (Hall of the Celestial Master Founder)** and **Cháoyáng Dòng (Facing the Dawn Cave)**. The narrow section of path between these two sights passes through beautiful dark forest and thick undergrowth. Continue on the path; after veering right and passing a couple of viewing pavilions, it leads to **Shàngqīng Gōng (Temple of Highest Clarity)**. First built in the 4th century, the present building is considerably newer. The tearoom here also sells snacks. From here to the summit at **Lǎojūn Gé (Lord Lǎo Pavilion)** is a short but steep climb.

Return Hike: Coming back down the mountain, the road forks at Shàngqīng Gōng. The left trail leads to the cable car. The ride down takes you to the small **Yuèchéng Hú (Moon Wall Lake)**. From here, boats ferry people across for ¥3 to ¥4 (35¢–50¢). If you don't take the cable car, it's only about a half-hour walk through pine forest to the lake.

WHERE TO STAY & DINE

If you've come to watch the sunrise, you'll need to spend the night on the mountain. Tiānshī Dòng, and Shàngqīng Gōng both have basic but clean lodgings for ¥40 to ¥100 ($5–$13), depending on the season. These monasteries also serve vegetarian meals. The **Língyún Shānzhuāng (Língyún Mountain Inn)** near the top cable-car station has lodgings and a restaurant.

5 Wòlóng Nature Reserve (Wòlóng Zìrán Bǎohù Qū)

Sìchuān Province, 135km (84 miles) NW of Chéngdū, 50km (31 miles) NW of Dūjiāng Yàn

Established in 1963, Wòlóng isn't the only place to see giant pandas, nor is it the most convenient. (And erase any notion of observing pandas in the wild.) But scientists here have made more advances in artificial breeding and raising pandas in captivity than anywhere in the world. The Wòlóng Breeding Center currently has about 30 giant pandas ranging in age from newborn to adult, and it is almost always possible to see panda cubs here.

Another aspect of Wòlóng's appeal is location. Situated in the high, densely forested mountains between the Sìchuān Basin and the Qīnghǎi–Tibetan Plateau, the area has a diverse topography that supports a broad range of vegetation and animal life—not that you're likely to see any of the panthers, macaques, white-lipped deer, or takins purported to live on the reserve. Nonetheless, the area is unspoiled and the flora is magnificent (and much more apparent than the fauna). You also have the chance to climb a mountain sans stairs—good news to some. The population is mostly Tibetan and Qiāng farmers who work the fields and make and sell handicrafts.

The best months to visit are May, August, and September. Allow 2 days to see the sights; add another day or two if you want to hike the several marked trails. *Note:* For Chinese translations of selected establishments listed in this section, please turn to appendix A.

ESSENTIALS

GETTING THERE   At least one bus leaves Chéngdū's Chádiànzi Bus Station daily at 11:40am (3¾ hr.; ¥21/$2.60). The return bus passes through Shāwān (also called Wòlóng Zhèn) between 8 and 9am daily; the fare is ¥21 ($2.60). Catch it on the main street or at the Panda Museum parking lot.

GETTING AROUND   Getting around the three main sights must usually be done either on foot or by hiring a private taxi (without a meter). The exception is if you hit it just right and for a few *yuán* can hop on a passing bus from Chéngdū. Hétao Píng— where the breeding center is—and Shāwān (Wòlóng Town), where the museum and most of the hotels are, are on the same road some 6.5km (4 miles) apart.

Tourist and administrative offices share the **Panda Museum** building in Shāwān, on the road from Chéngdū. The museum's parking lot is the terminus for buses from Chéngdū. The **tourist office** can answer questions in English and provide an English-speaking guide to the mountain.

Be sure to carry *yuán*. There are no foreign exchange services, and credit cards are not accepted.

Buy **maps** of the reserve at the Panda Museum in Shāwān or at the Panda Breeding Station in Hétao Píng for ¥5 (65¢).

EXPLORING WÒLÓNG

Most tourists to Wòlóng come for the Panda Breeding Station in Hétáo Píng, which is good enough reason, but there are so few chances in China to enjoy nature, free of crowds, that you may want to do some hiking while you're here. If so, be prepared for temperature fluctuations and rain, especially in summer. Also consider hiring a guide at the Panda Museum if you plan to hike very far. Trails can be faint and muddy, and descents at times slippery (the downside of not having stairs).

A viable **2-day plan** is to arrive in Shāwān in the afternoon. After checking into your hotel, visit the museum for an hour or so and roam around the very small town before dinner. The next morning, get up early and visit the breeding center in Hétao Píng. Spend the late morning and afternoon hiking. Depart the next morning.

Dàxióngmāo Sìyǎng Chǎng (Giant Panda Breeding Station) ✿ *Kids*   The pandas are housed either in enclosures or in semi-natural habitats—if they're being prepared to return to the open reserve. Unfortunately, Wòlóng has had less success with reintroducing pandas to the wild than with captive breeding, so the majority of pandas are in large enclosures that include an indoor room and an outdoor courtyard. For bird's-eye views of the pandas in open-air pens, an elevated trail runs along an adjacent cliff face above the enclosures.

Opposite are the **Lesser Panda Enclosures (Xiǎoxióngmāo Shēngtài Guǎn).** Although the smaller red pandas—related to the raccoon—don't get nearly as much press, they are undeniably appealing and usually more playful.

The best time to visit is between 8:30 and 10:30am, while the pandas feed.

In the town of Hétáo Píng, 5km (3 miles) before Shāwān on the road from Chéngdū. Buses go to Shāwān. If you want to get off here, notify the driver in advance. Admission ¥30 ($3.75). 8:30am–noon and 1–5pm.

Wǔyīpéng Shēngtài Guāncè Zhàn (Wǔyīpéng Field Observation Station)

This used to be an active station for researching and monitoring the giant panda, but it is no longer in use. A visit here makes a nice 1- to 2-hour hike on a steep trail that flattens out the last mile or so. The habitat behind the station is prime forest, and Darjeeling woodpeckers and various species of pheasants have been sighted here.

The cost of a guide from the Panda Museum's Tourist Desk is ¥60 ($7.50) for the round-trip trek (¥100/$13 with lunch) and ¥40 ($5) for the taxi to and from the beginning of the trail, which is about 9km (5½ miles) southwest of the museum. Hire your own taxi round-trip for ¥15 to ¥20 ($2–$2.50), but you'll have to agree on a pickup time. Allow about 3 hours. Pay at the end.

To go on your own from Shāwān, walk south on the main road until you reach a small village. Look for a large sign by the road with two big Chinese characters (for "Distillery"). Cross the wooden bridge on your left and follow it to the mountain. If at that point you regret not hiring a guide, you may be able to persuade one of the farmers on this patch of land to lead you. Unless you speak Chinese, you'll need the Chinese characters to indicate your destination and a calculator to settle on a fee. Expect to pay around ¥20 ($2.50)—more if weather conditions are poor or if the farmer has something else to do.

WHERE TO STAY

Before China's push to join the WTO, Chinese and foreigners were commonly charged different prices for the same service or merchandise. Now, the two-tiered pricing approach has virtually disappeared in large cities. Not so in Wòlóng. Hotels make no attempt to hide the fact that they charge "foreign guests" a few dollars more for a room.

Panda Inn (Xióngmāo Shānzhuāng)   More upscale than Shāwān's hotels, this pleasant inn has close connections with the Giant Panda Breeding Center, conveniently nearby. Rooms are well maintained and clean, and pleasant views through picture windows make up for the bland interiors. Although there's no town to explore, tour groups are better-managed here than in Shāwān, and the inn has the best restaurant in town.

Hétáo Píng (next to the Panda Breeding Station). © 0837/624-3028. Fax 0837/624-3014. 53 units. ¥320 ($40). 30%–50% discounts. No credit cards. **Amenities:** Restaurant; limited room service. *In room:* TV, 24-hr. hot water.

Wòlóng Shānzhuāng (Wòlóng Hotel)   Situated in the Wòlóng Nature Reserve, this expansive hotel is a nice escape from the town. The view from your window will give you the sense of getting back to nature. The rooms are fairly small and simply appointed, but also have a rustic and cozy feel to them. Although the main driveway into the hotel suggests delusions of grandeur, it is a reasonable alternative to the Panda Inn.

Wòlóng Zìrán Bǎohù Qū (Wòlóng Nature Reserve). © 0837/624-6888. Fax 0837/624-6111. 323 units. ¥280–¥350 ($34–$43) standard room. No credit cards. **Amenities:** Restaurant; limited room service. *In room:* TV.

WHERE TO DINE

The **Wòlóng Hotel** prepares good, simple dishes, but the Panda Inn offers a greater variety. There are also a couple of small restaurants and stands on Shāwān's main street.

6 Jiŭzhài Gōu (Valley of Nine Villages)

Sìchuān Province, 450km (280 miles) N of Chéngdū, 102km (63 miles) NE of Sōngpān

Photographs of this World Heritage nature site look retouched. The lakes are too "jewel-like," the pools too "limpid," the fall colors too "flaming." Surprisingly, the brochures aren't lying; they aren't even exaggerating. For sheer scenic beauty and variety, Jiŭzhài Gōu has it all: dense forest, green meadow, rivers, rapids, ribbon lakes in various shades of blue and green, chalky shoals, and waterfalls of every kind—long and narrow, short and wide, terraced, rushing, and cascading. Of cultural interest are the six remaining Tibetan villages of the original nine from which this valley gets its name. Some 1,000 Tibetans, of 130 families, live within the site. And to facilitate sightseeing, so-called "green buses" run along special highways within the valley delivering passengers to various scenic spots. Another aid to tourism is a network of raised plank paths and wooden pavilions that afford visitors a proximity to natural wonders that would otherwise be unapproachable.

That said, you may lose your will to visit just getting to Jiŭzhài Gōu from Chéngdū; you must then face the honking, belching traffic along the strip of hotels outside the main gate, not to mention the contagion of avarice that seems to have infected the town. Cabbies are in cahoots with the hotels; hotel managers beg bribes; the PSB is on the take; the place claims to be "green," but the air is polluted. It's not a pretty sight.

Jiŭzhài Gōu gets three stars for its scenery and is docked four for everything else. But despite the cons, few places on earth have prettier scenery, and except for a few phototaking forays, the majority of tourists stay on the bus, so it's not hard to find solitude along the plank paths. In the end, as much as I loathed the 12-hour ride on a smoke-filled bus and the tacky town outside the gate, the 2 days spent inside the reserve were absolutely worth it. Jiŭzhài Gōu can be seen in 1 day, but 2 days is optimal.

The best time to go is from July to October, before the weather cools down significantly. Even at the height of summer, have a jacket on hand for rain and sudden temperature drops. To avoid crowds and get the best hotel discounts, come midweek. Busy times are Chinese New Year, Labor Day week (first week of May), and National Day week (first week of Oct). Some hotels close between November and March. *Note:* For Chinese translations of selected establishments listed in this section, please turn to appendix A.

ESSENTIALS

GETTING THERE   The newly opened **Jiŭhuáng Airport,** just northeast of Jiŭzhài Gōu, has greatly increased the park's accessibility, putting the park within striking distance of tourists from all neighboring provinces. However, the most convenient launching point is still likely to be Chéngdū, and ¥1,100 ($135) will get you a round-trip ticket for the 45-minute flight. From the airport, you can take a bus to Jiŭzhài Gōu (1½ hr.; ¥30/$3.75).

Air-conditioned **buses** (¥198/$25) depart Chéngdū every hour from 7am to 9am from the Xīn Nán Mén Bus Station and arrive approximately 12 hours later in Zhāngzhá Zhèn at the Long-Distance Bus Station (Chángtú Qìchē Kèyùn Zhàn) behind the Jiŭtōng Bīnguǎn—leaving you the evening to check into a hotel and have dinner. Two return buses leave at 7am and 8am for ¥195 ($24). Buy tickets at least a day in advance. A bus leaves Chéngdū from the less convenient Chádiànzi Kèyùn Zhàn west of the city center at 8:40am and drops passengers near the Jiŭzhài Gōu entrance for ¥192 ($24).

GETTING AROUND   Jiŭzhài Gōu's five designated scenic zones run along a Y-shaped route. Over 200 **shuttle buses** travel the 58km (36-mile) route from 7am until 6pm. The best sights and most of the plank paths are along the right branch, so if you haven't time to trace the entire route, go to the right first. If you're tempted to walk the full length, bear in mind that the distance from the entrance to the last scenic spot on this route—Yuánshǐ Sēnlín (Primeval Forest)—is about 32km (20 miles). For the best views, take the bus to the end and walk back. You can reboard at bus stops along the way. Very useful bilingual **tourist maps** are available for ¥5 (65¢) at the **Tourist's Center (Yóukè Zhōngxīn)** near the ticket office.

Note: Be sure to carry RMB. Only the five-star hotels accept credit cards. None accept traveler's checks, and only a few change U.S. dollars.

EXPLORING THE VALLEYS

With 2 days, using a combination of shuttle bus and walking, you can see all five scenic zones. For a more relaxed pace or extended walking, add a third day. Of the scenic zones, the two with the highest concentration of natural wonders are **Shùzhèng Jǐngqū** and **Rìzé Jǐngqū.** Each zone covers several miles and has wooden planks or stone paths that lead the visitor right up to waterfalls, across shoals, or to the edge of turquoise waters. These can be done in a day if that's all you have, or they can be spread over 2 days, leaving half of each day for wandering in the less-visited areas beyond **Panda Lake (Xióngmāo Hǎi)** to the right or beyond **Wǔcǎi Chí (Five-color Pool)** to the left. Admission to Jiŭzhài Gōu, which is open from 7am to 6pm, is ¥145 ($18) per person, and is only good for 1 day. The shuttle bus costs ¥90 ($11) per day.

WHERE TO STAY

For now, officials who say that tourists may not stay inside the park seem to be winning their battle with villagers who offer basic beds for around ¥20 ($2.50), and simple meals for ¥10 to ¥25 ($1.25–$3). Rooms have limited plumbing and no hot water, but some are in Tibetan style with brightly painted tables and window frames. If that appeals, inquire at the Zhārú Sì and at villages on the west side of the main road. You'll probably be asked to arrive after 6pm and leave before 7am, to avoid problems with officials.

Most visitors stay in one of the many hotels lining the 11km (7-mile) stretch of road outside Jiŭzhài Gōu Gōukǒu (Jiŭzhài Gōu Entrance), identified on the map as Zhāngzhā Town.

EXPENSIVE

Jiŭzhài Gōu Xīláidēng Dàjiŭdiàn (Sheraton Jiŭzhài Gōu Resort) ⨂   This huge complex is arguably the best five-star option in Jiŭzhài Gōu. The rooms are elegantly appointed and infused with a Tibetan quality, all the more notable considering the Chinese propensity for reducing minority cultures into kitsch. The hotel has more restaurants and amenities than any other in town and, for now, is the only one with a swimming pool and sauna. The grounds include a 500-seat theater with revolving stage for nightly Tibetan song and dance performances.

Jiŭzhài Gōu Scenic Area (1.5km/1mile from entrance to Jiŭzhài Gōu). ⓒ **0837/773-9988.** Fax 0837/773-9666. www.sheraton.com/jiuzhaigou. 482 units. ¥1,000–¥1,200 ($125–$150) standard room. 20%–40% discounts, depending on occupancy. Some rates include breakfast. 15% service charge. AE, DC, MC, V. **Amenities:** 5 restaurants; bar; indoor pool; gym; sauna; electronic game room; airline, train, and bus ticketing; business center; limited forex; limited room service; dry cleaning/laundry; Internet bar. *In room:* A/C, satellite TV, dataport, minibar, fridge, hair dryer, safe.

Xīngyǔ Guójì Dàjiǔdiàn (Xīngyǔ International Hotel)   This perfectly comfortable four-star hotel opened in 2001 but already shows signs of wear. There are a few Tibetan touches, but for the most part, the rooms, lobby, and restaurants hold no surprises. Discounted prices are reasonable, and staff is friendly and professional. For the comfort of a pricier hotel (but without some of the five-star luxuries), this hotel serves well.

Jiǔzhài Gōu Scenic Area (under 1.5km/1mile from entrance to Jiǔzhài Gōu). ℂ **0837/773-9222.** Fax 0837/773-9773. xingyuhotel@scxingyu.com. 193 units. ¥980 ($120) standard room; ¥2,100–¥2,800 ($256–$350) suite. Rates include breakfast. 20%–40% discounts. 15% service charge. No credit cards. Closed Nov–Dec. **Amenities:** 2 restaurants; airline, train, and bus ticketing; business center; limited room service; dry cleaning/laundry. *In room:* A/C, TV, fridge in some rooms.

INEXPENSIVE

Jiǔlǚ Dàjiǔdiàn   Proximity to the Jiǔzhài Gōu entrance, reasonable rates with hefty discounts, and friendly staff are the best reasons to stay in this otherwise average three-star hotel. There are also a few standard rooms that have larger bathrooms outfitted with a Jacuzzi for very little extra. Rooms were renovated in 2005 and are pleasantly decorated with Tibetan fabrics and patterns. Avoid rooms that are not in the main building—they tend to be dark and damp. There are limited hours for hot water. Chéngdū's Jiāotōng Bīnguǎn (Traffic Hotel) has connections with this hotel, and can make reservations for you.

Jiǔzhài Gōu Scenic Area (300m/984 ft. from Jiǔzhài Gōu entrance). ℂ **0837/773-9599.** Fax 0837/773-9939. 153 units. ¥280 ($35) standard room; ¥880 ($111) suite. 50%–60% discounts. Rates include breakfast. No credit cards. Closed roughly Dec–Mar, but dates vary. **Amenities:** Restaurant; airline and train ticketing; limited room service; dry cleaning/laundry. *In room:* A/C, TV.

Yínyuàn Bīnguǎn   Renovated in 2002, this small, few-frills hotel used to be Jiǔzhài Gōu's best—which says lots about how much building has taken place here in the last few years. Clean, good value, and staffed with cordial, conscientious people, it still doesn't come close to being the best anymore. Still, with only 60 rooms, it feels homier than most. Limited hours for hot water.

Jiǔzhài Gōu Scenic Area (150m/492 ft. from Jiǔzhài Gōu entrance). ℂ **0837/773-4890.** Fax 0837/773-4114. 60 units. ¥260–¥480 ($32–$60) standard room; ¥1,880 ($229) suite. 20%–50% discounts, depending on occupancy. No credit cards. **Amenities:** Restaurant; airline, train, and bus ticketing; limited room service; dry cleaning/laundry. *In room:* A/C, TV.

WHERE TO DINE

Except for hotel restaurants, there aren't lots of dining choices. For inexpensive (but still overpriced) local food, try one of the several identical *huǒguō* (hot pot) restaurants on the main street of Zhāngzhā Town. Another option is to pay ¥160 ($20) for dinner and a performance of Qiāng and Tibetan folk entertainment, which includes dancing, singing, and audience participation. Tibetan-style barbecued mutton, Tibetan tea, and a ritual welcoming liqueur are included in the ticket price. The **Gésānglā Art Troupe (Gésānglā Yìshù Tuán)** performs nightly at 7:30pm at Jiǔxīn Shānzhuāng (Jiǔxīn Mountain Villa), on the hotel strip 1km (½ mile) east of the Jiǔzhài Gōu entrance. For information, call ℂ **0837/773-9588.**

A snack bar selling kabobs, watermelon juice, pearl milk tea, and tofu on a stick is outside the Jiǔzhài Gōu entrance, next to the tourist center. Snacks are also sold inside the reserve, but they're overpriced and not very good.

7 Chóngqìng

Chóngqìng Municipality, 334km (208 miles) SE of Chéngdū, 1,346km (836 miles) S of Xī'ān, 1,000km (620 miles) upstream of Three Gorges Dam

If other major cities in China are undergoing face-lifts, Chóngqìng is having radical reconstructive surgery: In 1997, it became the fourth city to achieve the status of municipality (after Běijīng, Tiānjīn, and Shànghǎi). With summers so hot it's been dubbed one of China's Three Furnaces, and streets so steep that no one rides a bike, terrain and weather were once its chief claims to fame. Now, this cliff-side city over-looking the confluence of the Cháng and Jiālíng rivers has much to boast about. Chóngqìng is the biggest metropolitan area in the world (surpassing Tokyo); it's got the world's biggest dam site downriver; and it's in the midst of building the world's tallest skyscraper (the Chóngqìng Tower). But whether all this development is a boom or a binge is yet to be seen.

As recently as the 19th century, Chóngqìng was a remote walled city. Even after the steam engine eased passage through the Three Gorges, few easterners had any reason or desire to make the trip. That all changed in 1938, when Hànkǒu fell to the Japan-ese and downriver residents made a mass exodus up the Cháng Jiāng (Yángzǐ River). Chóngqìng became China's last wartime capital, and after withstanding 3 years of Japanese bombing, the city never looked back. Very few of the old ramshackle neigh-borhoods rebuilt after the war have survived "urban improvement," and except for an old prison complex and a few small museums and memorials there is little evidence of earlier eras.

Most travelers come to Chóngqìng because it's the first or last stop on a Three Gorges cruise. But until recently, levels of sulfur dioxide and suspended air particles were so high that visitors couldn't wait to leave. As the city implements pollution con-trol programs, that seems to be gradually changing. Chóngqìng's pleasures are mod-est, but there's enough here to make a 2- or 3-day stay enjoyable. The city is also just a 2-hour bus ride from the Buddhist Grottoes at Dàzú. *Note:* For Chinese translations of selected establishments listed in this section, please turn to appendix A.

ESSENTIALS

GETTING THERE   **Jiāngběi Airport** is 25km (15 miles) north of Chóngqìng, and 30 minutes by taxi (around ¥65/$8). It offers daily domestic service to Běijīng, Chéngdū, Guìlín, Hong Kong, Kūnmíng, Shànghǎi, and Xī'ān; it offers service to Lhasa twice a week. International destinations include Tokyo, Seoul, Bangkok, and Düssel-dorf. The Mínháng (CAAC) **airport shuttle bus** (© 023/6386-5824) leaves every half-hour from 6am to 6pm from Shàngqīng Sì for ¥15 ($1.90). Domestic and international air tickets are also on sale here from 7:30am to 6:30pm. **Dragonair** has offices in the Metropolis Building (Dàdūhuì Shāngshà), Zōuróng Lù 68 (© 023/6372-9900).

The **Main Railway Station** and **Long-Distance Bus Station** are next to each other on Nánqū Lù, near the Yángzǐ River. **Trains** from Shànghǎi and Běijīng take approx-imately 39 and 34 hours, respectively. Trains to Chéngdū take approximately 10 hours. The overnight, leaving at 9:06pm and arriving the next morning at 7:29am, saves you the cost of a hotel for a night. Official reports claim that a new railway line scheduled to open in 2005 will cut the trip between Chóngqìng and Chéngdū to just 3 hours. The soft-seat waiting lounge is on the far right of the station complex.

Luxury **buses** with a uniformed attendant and bathroom onboard connect Chóngqìng to Chéngdū; the 4-hour trip costs ¥121 ($15). The bus makes two stops in Chóngqìng: the first, at Chénjiā Píng, for those going to the wharf; the second, at the Fùyuàn Bīnguǎn, next to the Long-Distance Bus Station. As you exit, ignore the throng of private drivers vying to overcharge you. Walk across the parking lot to the taxi queue in front of the railway station. Insist on using the meter. The ride to any of the major hotels is ¥5 to ¥10 (65¢–$1.25). Large Volvo and Mercedes buses leave the Long-Distance Bus Station for Chéngdū every half-hour throughout the day for ¥110 ($14). Buses to Lè Shān leave from the Jiěfàng Bēi Qìchē Kèyùn Zhàn (Liberation Monument Bus Station) at Línjiāng Lù 60. (For Yángzǐ River travel, see section 9, "Middle Reaches of the Cháng Jiāng.")

GETTING AROUND   There are three types of **taxis.** Rates for midrange Xiàlì are ¥5 (75¢) for 3km (2 miles), then ¥1.80 (20¢) per kilometer thereafter. The rate increases to ¥2.30 (30¢) from 10pm to 7am. In addition to the 10 bridges that span the Jiālíng and Yángzǐ rivers, there is a cable car line across each river. Leave from Xīnhuá Lù to cross the Yángzǐ for ¥2 (25¢), or leave from Cāngbái Lù to cross the Jiālíng for ¥1.50 (20¢). Cable cars run from 6:30am to 10:30pm. **Buses/trolleys** serve all parts of the city. Rides with air-conditioning are ¥1.50 to ¥2.50 (20¢–30¢); rides without are ¥1 to ¥1.50 (15¢–20¢). Cable cars and some buses/trolleys have attendants.

VISITOR INFORMATION   CITS is located near the People's Square (Rénmín Guǎngchǎng). This branch, at 120 Zǎozi Lányá Zhèng Jiē, second floor (© **023/6385-0693;** fax 023/6385-0196; citscq@cta.cq.cn.), is particularly helpful.

FAST FACTS
Banks, Foreign Exchange & ATMs   The main branch of **Bank of China** (open Mon–Fri 9am–noon and 2–5:30pm), north of Liberation Monument on the north side of Mínzú Lù, has full foreign-exchange services and an ATM. The branch catty-corner from Harbour Plaza Hotel, Zōuróng Lù at Bāyī Lù, has a 24-hour ATM and offers foreign-exchange service, although limited to cash and U.S. dollar travelers checks.

Consulates   Both the Canadian and United Kingdom consulates are in the Metropolitan Plaza building (Dàdūhuì Shāngshà) on Wǔyī Lù, and are open Monday through Friday from 8:30am to 5:30pm. The **Canadian Consulate** is in Suite 1705 (© **023/6373-8007;** chonq@dfait-acci.gc.ca), and the **United Kingdom Consulate** is in Suite 2802 (© **023/6381-0321**). Take bus no. 306, 402, 413, or 601 to the Jiěfàng Bēi stop. From there, walk southeast on Zōuróng Lù to Wǔyī Lù. Metropolitan Plaza is next to the Harbour Plaza Hotel.

Internet Access   The area around Liberation Monument has lots of Internet bars, including **Reader's Club (Dúzhě Jùlèbù),** open 24 hours and located on the third floor of the Xīnhuá Bookstore at Mínshēng Lù 181 (opposite Nǚrén Guǎngchǎng; © 023/6371-6364). Rates are ¥2 (25¢) per hour; less with membership card. Coffee and tea are served. Enter from Xīnhuá Shūdiàn or from the side door of the adjacent bank. Dial-up is © **163.**

Post Office   The main post office is near Jiěfàng Bēi (Liberation Monument), at Mínquán Lù 3.

Visa Extensions   The **Administrative Division of Exit-Entry (Chūrùjìng Guǎnlǐ Chù)** processes visa extensions in five working days. Located at Wǔsì Lù 48, Fù 1 (© **028/8640-7067;** open Mon–Fri 9–11:30am and 2–5pm), it's next to the Municipal PSB; enter on Shùnchéng Dàjiē. Take bus no. 16 or 64 to the Rénmín Zhōng Lù and Wénwǔ Lù junction.

Chóngqìng

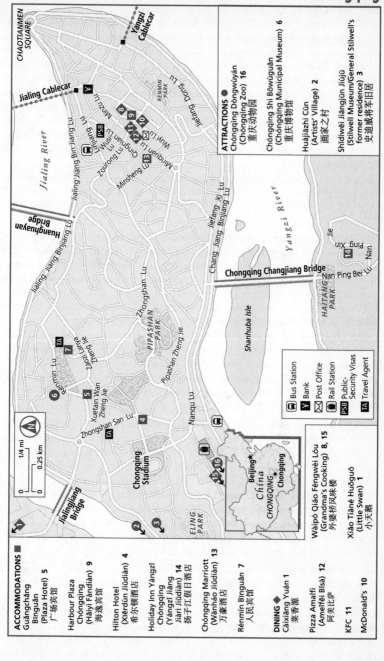

CHAOTIANMEN SQUARE

Yángzi Cablecar

Jialing Cablecar

Jialing River

Huanghuayan Bridge

RENMIN PARK

Yangzi River

Chongqing Changjiang Bridge

Nan Ping Bei Lu

Nan Ping Xin Jie

HAITANG PARK

Shanhuba Isle

PIPASHAN PARK

Zhongshan Sì Lu

Zhongshan San Lu

Nanqu Lu

Chongqing Stadium

Jialingjiang Bridge

ELING PARK

Beijing★
China
CHONGQING,
Chongqing

ATTRACTIONS ●

Chóngqìng Dòngwùyuán
(Chóngqìng Zoo) 16
重庆动物园

Chóngqìng Shì Bówùguǎn
(Chóngqìng Municipal Museum) 6
重庆博物馆

Huàjiāzhī Cūn
(Artists' Village) 2
画家之村

Shídìwēi Jiāngjūn Jiùjū
(Stilwell Museum/General Stilwell's
former residence) 3
史迪威将军旧居

Symbols

- Bus Station
- ¥ Bank
- ⊠ Post Office
- ▤ Rail Station
- PSB Public-
   Security Visas
- TA Travel Agent

ACCOMMODATIONS ■

Guǎngchǎng
Bīnguǎn
(Plaza Hotel) 5
广场宾馆

Harbour Plaza
Chóngqìng
(Hǎiyì Fàndiàn) 9
海逸宾馆

Hilton Hotel
(Xī'ěrdùn Jiǔdiàn) 4
希尔顿酒店

Holiday Inn Yángzǐ
Chóngqìng
(Yángzǐ Jiāng
Jiàrì Jiǔdiàn) 14
扬子江假日酒店

Chóngqìng Marriott
(Wànháo Jiǔdiàn) 13
万豪酒店

Rénmín Bīnguǎn 7
人民宾馆

DINING ◆

Càixiāng Yuán 1
菜香源

Pizza Amalfi
(Āmèifēi Bǐsà) 12
阿美菲比萨

KFC 11

McDonald's 10

Wàipó Qiáo Fēngwèi Lóu
(Grandma's Cooking) 8, 15
外婆桥风味楼

Xiǎo Tiāné Huǒguō
(Little Swan) 1
小天鹅

EXPLORING CHÓNGQÌNG

Artists' Village (Huàjiā Zhī Cūn) Seventeen state-sponsored artists—some of them renowned—live in this complex of cottages overlooking the Jiālíng River. This sight is a favorite with tour groups who roll in for a quick buying frenzy before or after their Three Gorges tour. Even if you're not prepared to spend lots of money, the vine-covered studios and residences, connected by stone walkways and surrounded by small gardens, provide a more interesting respite from the traffic than just another city park. Each artist has a small studio, and visitors roam the grounds from one to the next. The colony dates from the days when the function of art was to serve the state. There are few other places where the casual traveler can rub elbows with people who were part of that movement. Look for Niú Wén's pre- and post-1949 woodblock prints, which are rare finds.

Huàlóng Qiáo Jiē, Huá Cūn 24 (south bank of Jiālíng River near Huá Cūn bus stop; look for English sign at bus stop). ⓒ 023/6331-3735. 9am–6pm. Bus: no. 104, 215, or 261 to Huá Cūn. Taxi from People's Square about ¥10 ($1.25). You will have to go through a guarded gate, so have the characters (from the map key, p. 697) ready to show the guard.

Chóngqìng Zoo (Chóngqìng Dòngwùyuán) If you're going to Chéngdū and have time to visit one of the panda breeding centers (in the northern suburbs or at Wòlóng), then don't bother with the Chóngqìng Zoo. But if this is your only chance to see pandas, consider spending part of a morning at the giant panda and red panda enclosures. To get to the red pandas, go to the left of the English introduction board and down the stairs. The outdoor enclosure has a half-dozen extremely active small red pandas. Don't bother with the rest of the zoo; it will only depress you.

Tip: The best chance of seeing pandas is during feeding—between 8:30 and 10:30am. If the pandas aren't out, poke your head in the office behind the English introduction board and ask the zoo warden if he'll feed them. Sometimes that's all it takes.

Jiŭlóng Pō Qū, Xījiāo Yī Cūn 1, in city's southeast quadrant. ⓒ 023/6843-3494. Admission ¥20 ($2.50). Zoo summer 6:30am–9pm; winter 7am–9pm. Panda enclosures 8:30–10:30am and 3:30–4:30pm. Bus: no. 341 or 416 to Dòngwùyuán.

Cíqíkŏu ⋒ This small neighborhood with cobblestone streets in the Shāpíng District is becoming popular with travelers who have a few days in Chóngqìng; as yet, it hasn't turned into a theme park. The two main streets—lined with modest eastern Sìchuān–style buildings—form a T from the entrance. Shops on the first street sell paintings, batik clothing, and other items geared mainly for tourists.

At the top of the T, a right turn leads to the wharf. Along the way are several tea-houses and restaurants. One teahouse, Qīngdài Mínjū, has a nice courtyard just off the main thoroughfare where you can enjoy performances on traditional Chinese instruments. Farther along at Língyùn Mínyuè in another tearoom, a small ensemble of musicians gathers most days to play traditional music.

Gēlè Shān/Báigōng Guǎn/SACO (Gēlè Hill) Standing in a lovely setting with trees, shrubs, stone walkways, and a babbling brook, Báigōng Guǎn was originally a Sìchuān warlord's pied-à-terre, but it was taken over by the notoriously brutal Dài Lì—head of the Nationalist (KMT) secret police and guerrilla forces—and turned into a prison in 1939. Two years later, the U.S. spy agency SACO (Sino-American Cooperation Organization), which trained secret agents for the KMT, housed its servicemen here. It reverted to a prison in 1945, and it was here that the KMT slaughtered several hundred Communists and dissidents before retreating to Táiwān in

1949. The incident is known as the Bloodbath of 11/27, and many locals still come here to pay homage on that date.

The wooden buildings that were used as a prison are open to visitors. Photos of prisoners are displayed on the walls with poems and excerpts from letters—some in English translation—reflecting the political idealism of an earlier age.

Shāpíngbà Qū (3.2km/2 miles west of Hóngyán Cūn). Admission ¥5 (65¢); 2 prisons ¥10 ($1.25); 2 prisons and Hóngyán Hún Chénliè Guǎn ¥15 ($2). 8:30am–7pm. Bus: no. 210.

Sānxiá Bówùguǎn (Three Gorges Museum) Originally called the Chóngqìng Municipal Museum, this museum moved to its more modern and spacious location mid-2005. While still lacking a certain charisma, several items in this museum make the trip worthwhile. First is its lovely collection of Táng and Sòng heads carved out of stone. Most are of Buddha, Guānyīn, and various bodhisattvas, but what distinguishes them are their human rather than heavenly miens. A fine collection of terra-cotta sculptures from an Eastern Hàn tomb is also on the display. Discovered in Chóngqìng north of the Yángzǐ, they are small, whimsical figurines of musicians, dancers, singers, and storytellers—a lively group to spend eternity with. The museum also boasts collections that go back in time as far as the Shāng dynasty (ca. 1600–1045 B.C.). Of particular interest are the paulownia-wood "boat coffins" of the ancient Bā culture.

Rénmín Lù, north side of the People's Square (Rénmín Guǎngchǎng). Admission ¥10 ($1.25). 8:30am–5pm. Bus: no. 129, 215, 22, 111, 103, or 104.

Stilwell Museum/Former Residence of General Stilwell (Shǐdíwēi Jiāngjūn Jiùjū) After Pearl Harbor, then-U.S. President Roosevelt sent Gen. Joseph Stilwell (1883–1946) to Chóngqìng as commander-in-chief of Allied forces in the China-Burma-India theater of the war. Unfortunately, "Vinegar Joe" and the KMT general he was supposed to advise—Chiang Kai-shek—had rather different agendas, not to mention temperaments, and in 1944, at Chiang's urging, Stilwell was relieved of his post. Nonetheless, his contribution to the Burma Road campaign was significant—reason enough for the local government to continue to maintain a museum honoring him. His disdain for Chiang must also have endeared him to the party. The museum, housed in Stilwell's Chóngqìng residence, has a collection of newspaper clippings, photographs, letters, and Stilwell's personal belongings. A video tells the Chinese version of Stilwell's tour of duty and includes rare clips. Explanations are in English and Chinese. The Stilwell and Flying Tiger T-shirts sold here make unique gifts.

Jiālíng Xīn Cūn 63. ✆ 023/6387-2794. Admission ¥5 (65¢). No regular hours; doorman always on duty (or so it's claimed). Bus: no. 104, 215, or 261 to Lǐzìbà stop.

SHOPPING

Carrefour Supermarket (Jiālèfú Chāoshì) is inside the Xīn Chóngqìng Building. It's open from 9am to 10:30pm; take bus no. 111 or 166 to the Xiǎo Shízì stop. The supermarket is absolutely crammed with customers because you can get anything here—and cheaply. **KFC** is inside the same building. A **Watson** drugstore is on the first floor of Metropolitan Plaza (Dàdūhuì Guǎngchǎng), next to the Harbour Plaza on Wǔyī Lù, 1 block southeast of Jiěfàng Bēi. This seven-floor indoor mall has restaurants, upscale and international clothing stores, and even an ice-skating rink on the sixth floor.

WHERE TO STAY

EXPENSIVE

Chóngqìng Marriott (Wànháo Jiǔdiàn)   With its high-ceilinged lobby flanked by two sweeping staircases, palm trees, a steakhouse overlooking the rivers, and a Japanese restaurant with traditional architecture and decor, the Marriott is the most elegant choice in town. Ask for one of the rooms above the 19th floor, which are slightly bigger and have separate bathroom and shower. Rooms with walk-in closets and bathroom window are an extra ¥80 ($10).

Qīngnián Lù 77 (corner of Qīngnián Lù and Mínshēng Lù). ✆ 023/6388-8888. Fax 023/6388-8777. www.marriott hotels.com. 514 units. ¥1,480–¥1,780 ($180–$215) standard room; ¥1,780–¥2,580 ($215–$310) suite. 50%–60% discounts year-round; 15% service charge. AE, DC, MC, V. Bus: no. 306, 402, 413, or 601 to Jiěfàng Bēi. **Amenities:** 4 restaurants; 4 bars; indoor pool; health club; airline, train, and bus ticketing; business center; forex; 24-hr. room service; dry cleaning/laundry. *In room:* A/C, TV w/satellite channels, dataport, minibar, fridge, hair dryer, safe.

Harbour Plaza Chóngqìng (Hǎiyì Fàndiàn)   This five-star luxury hotel has a convenient downtown location (next to deluxe shopping on the city's pedestrian mall) that's catty-corner to a 24-hour ATM. The new, enlarged reception area is open and airy. Guest rooms are decorated in rich blues and golds, and most have views of the cityscape. Bathrooms are spacious and most have separate bath and shower. Though less glamorous than the Marriott, the Harbour Plaza still meets international standards in every way.

Wǔyì Lù (at Zōuróng Lù, 1 block southeast of Liberation Monument). ✆ 023/6370-0888. Fax 023/6372-6230. www. harbour-plaza.com/hpcq. 390 units. ¥1,330–¥1,450 ($160–$175) standard room; ¥1,660–¥2,000 ($200–$240) suite. 50%–65% discounts year-round; 15% service charge. AE, DC, MC, V. Bus: no. 306, 402, 413, or 601 to Jiěfàng Bēi. **Amenities:** 2 restaurants; 4 bars; indoor pool; health club; airline and train ticketing; business center; forex; 24-hr. room service; dry cleaning/laundry. *In room:* A/C, TV w/satellite channels, IDD, dataport, minibar, fridge, hair dryer, safe.

Hilton (Xīěrdùn Jiǔdiàn) ✎   Opened in 2002, this five-star hotel is one of Chóngqìng's finest, and highly recommended. Views are of the rivers and the Dàtiánwān Sport Stadium; rooms are attractively decorated. The hotel is well located near the business district and less than 3km (2 miles) from the railway station. It's also a short, interesting walk from Pípa Shān Gōngyuán and the City Museum.

Zhōngshān Sān Lù 139 (near Dàtiánwān Sport Stadium). ✆ 800/820-0600 or 023/6903-9999. Fax 023/6903-8738. www.hilton.com. 443 units. ¥1,440–¥1,680 ($180–$210) standard room; ¥2,160–¥3,280 ($270–$410) suite. 65% discounts year-round; 15% service charge. AE, DC, MC, V. Bus: no. 224, 368, 402, 411, or 605 to Liǎng Lùkǒu stop. **Amenities:** 2 restaurants; 2 bars; indoor pool; health club; sauna; airline, train, and bus ticketing; business center; forex; 24-hr. room service; dry cleaning/laundry. *In room:* A/C, satellite TV, dataport, minibar, fridge, hair dryer, safe.

Holiday Inn Yángzī Chóngqing (Yángzī Jiāng Jiàrì Fàndiàn)   Compared to the five-star Harbour, Hilton, and Marriott properties, this four-star isn't nearly as posh, nor can it boast a central location. But it does have beautiful views all around—on one side, the Cháng Jiāng, on the other, mountains. To compensate for the inconvenient location, a free shuttle service runs several times a day between the hotel and the French supermarket, Carrefour. The rooms are clean but slightly run down; bathrooms are small. The hotel feels like a Western budget inn, but even with the standard 50% discount, the rates aren't much better than those of a five-star property.

Nánpíng Běi Lù 15 (in Nán'ān District south of the Yángzī). ✆ 023/6280-3380. Fax 023/6280-0884. www.holiday-inn.com/hotels/chgch. 424 units. ¥1,080–¥1,120 ($135–$140) standard room; ¥1,480–¥1,760 ($185–$220) suite. Additional ¥40 ($5) for rooms with Cháng Jiāng views. Most rates include breakfast. 50% discounts year-round; 15% service charge. AE, DC, MC, V. Bus: no. 304, 306, 402, 428, 901, or 902. **Amenities:** 4 restaurants; bar; indoor pool; health club; airline, train, and bus ticketing; business center; forex; ATM; 24-hr. room service; dry cleaning/laundry. *In room:* A/C, satellite TV, dataport, minibar, fridge, hair dryer, safe.

MODERATE TO INEXPENSIVE

Guǎngchǎng Bīnguǎn (Plaza Hotel)   Located opposite Rénmín Guǎngchǎng, this midsize three-star hotel is particularly good value for three people traveling together, even without the hefty discounts that are standard. Despite renovations in 2004, prices have remained unchanged and, with the discounts, all rooms are very reasonably priced. Room decor and furnishings are standard and forgettable, but the staff, outfitted in crisp uniforms, are warm and welcoming, despite (or perhaps, due to) the fact that few foreigners have discovered this hotel. There are two standard room types—A and B. "A" rooms are slightly bigger and the bathroom ceilings slightly higher, but standard "B" rooms are perfectly acceptable. The difference isn't enough to warrant the additional $17 for an "A" room. The location puts guests within walking distance of the Municipal Museum, People's Square, People's Auditorium, and CITS.

Xuétiánwān Zhèng Jiē 2. ✆ **023/6355-8989.** Fax 023/6355-9000. 130 units. ¥328–¥468 ($41–$58) standard room; ¥788–¥888 ($98–$111) suite; ¥450 ($56) triple. 20% discounts year-round. AE, DC, MC, V. Bus: no. 103, 162, 181, or 261. **Amenities:** 2 restaurants; bar; airline, train, and bus ticketing; small business center; forex; room service; dry cleaning/laundry. *In room:* A/C, TV, minibar/fridge (suites only).

Rénmín Bīnguǎn   Directly connected to the People's Auditorium, this midrange hotel has a four-star east wing and a three-star south wing that isn't quite as plush, but is a good value for the price. The hotel has a central downtown location; a friendly, helpful staff; and a 1950s Russian architecture that offers a change from the usual. The south wing has several sizes of standards for different rates, so ask to see each option. The one room with the lowest rate (¥200/$25) is clean, but small and slightly mildewed. For ¥320 ($40) you get a bigger, airier room. But the east wing rooms are better still—with larger rooms and balconies in some units—and worth the extra money.

Rénmín Lù 175 400015. ✆ **023/6356-6351.** 197 units. East wing ¥320–¥620 ($40–$77) standard room; south wing ¥198–¥320 ($25–$40) standard room; ¥360 ($45) large 2-room suite with balcony and large bathroom. Some rates include breakfast. 30% discount is standard. AE, DC, MC, V. Bus: no. 16, 19, or 72. Minibus: no. 5. **Amenities:** 3 restaurants; bar; exercise room; airline, train, and bus ticketing; business center; forex; 24-hr. room service; dry cleaning/laundry. *In room:* A/C, TV, minibar, fridge.

WHERE TO DINE

One of the dishes most identified with Sìchuān cooking (though it may have come from Mongolia) is hot pot or *huǒguō* (fire pot). It is so popular here that a block of Wǔyī Lù (just off Mínzú Lù) is called **Huǒguō Jiē (Hot Pot Street)**. Street stalls and small restaurants serving this dish line the street, recognizable by their dining tables, the centers of which have a cooking pot with boiling broth and hot oil. Diners add meat, fish, sprouts, scallions, and any other ingredients they like to the pot. Once the submerged meat or vegetables are cooked, diners pluck pieces out with chopsticks and eat them plain or with a spicy dipping sauce. By tradition in both Sìchuān and Inner Mongolia, locals favor organ meats, intestines, brains, and chicken feet for this poorman's stew, but these days, in restaurants, choices abound. Like the best meals, the best hot pots use ingredients that combine a variety of tastes, textures, shapes, and colors.

Near Liberation Monument there's a **McDonald's** on the corner of Zōuróng Lù and Wǔyī Lù, cater-cornered from Harbour Plaza, and a **KFC** on Mínquán Lù at Jiěfàng Bēi.

Càixiāng Yuán 𝕬 SÌCHUĀN   Very popular with locals, this place serves traditional and nouveau Sìchuān. Strange-flavored duck *(guàiwèi Yāzi)*, with its perfect blend of salty, sweet, tingling, hot, sour, savory, and fragrant flavors, is a favorite here, and for good reason.

Building C-4 Jiāzhōu Huāyuán (Jiāzhōu Garden in Yúbĕi District). ☎ **023/6762-9325.** Meal for 2 ¥20–¥52 ($2.50–$6.50). No credit cards. 11:30am–2:30pm and 5:30–10pm. Bus: no. 465 or 602 to Jiāzhōu Huāyuán.

Pizza Amalfi (Āmĕifēi Bǐsà) PIZZA   Though some might find the act of topping pizza with raisins and oranges sacrilegious, the menu here is varied enough to please every palate. Highly recommended, though, is pizza topped with goat cheese.

Mínquán 3, 3rd floor, opposite the Liberation Monument, above the ground floor Unicom store. ☎ **023/6381-7868.** Meal for 2 ¥40–¥80 ($5–$10). No credit cards. 9am–10:30pm.

Wàipó Qiáo Fēngwèi Lóu (Grandma's Cooking) ⭐⭐ SÌCHUĀN   This extremely popular restaurant, now with two locations, is more evidence that nostalgia is selling well in China. One manager, lumping over 500 years together, defined the cuisine as "Míng-Qīng," and a real *wàipó* (grandmother), dressed in simple garb, greets customers. The larger restaurant, in the Metropolitan Plaza, has a separate hot pot dining room next door that does an equally rousing business. Three of the best entrees in the main restaurant are *tiĕbǎn shāo zhī yínxuĕyú* (silver snow fish cooked on an iron plate), serves six; the slightly hot *qīngjiāo bào zǐjī* (baby chicken quick-fried with green pepper); and *guōbā ròupiàn* (pork with bamboo shoots over crispy rice). Faintly sweet corn cakes *(yùmǐ bǐng)* complement the latter two dishes well.

Two locations: Zōuróng Lù 68, Dàdùhuì Guǎngchǎng 7 lóu (Metropolitan Plaza, 7th floor near Jiĕfàng Bēi and next to Harbour Plaza Hotel). ☎ **023/6383-5988.** Bus: no. 306, 413, or 601 to Jiĕfàng Bēi. 2nd location: Táodū Chéng-shì Jiŭdiàn èr Lóu (Táodū City Hotel, 2nd floor) Yángjiāpíng, Xījiào Lù 21 (near the zoo). ☎ **023/6878-1818.** Bus: no. 413 or 148. Meal for 2 ¥100 ($13). The Metropolitan Plaza location has an English menu. Reservations accepted either location. No credit cards. 10:30am–2pm and 5–9pm.

Xiǎo Tiān'é Huǒguō (Little Swan) ⭐⭐ HOT POT   One of the most popular hot pot restaurants in Sìchuān and beyond is a chain of 126 stores, the first of which opened over 20 years ago in Chóngqìng. Little Swan continues to be one of the best in town. This self-serve restaurant gives patrons a choice of hot or mild broth, and its buffet table of ingredients allows non-Mandarin speakers more control than usual over what goes into the pot.

Jiànxīn Bĕi Lù 78 ☎ **023/6785-5328.** Meal for 2 ¥30–¥80 ($3.50–$10). No credit cards. 11am–10pm. Bus: no. 181, 411, 601, or 902 to Hǎiguān.

8 Dàzú (Dàzú Buddhist Grottoes) ⭐⭐⭐

Chóngqìng Municipality, 83km (52 miles) W of Chóngqìng, 251km (156 miles) SE of Chéngdū

Among the most impressive and affecting artistic monuments that have survived through the ages are the extensive Buddhist cave paintings, sculptures, and carvings of Dàtóng, Luòyáng, Dūnhuáng, and Dàzú. Of the four sites, **Dàzú's stone carvings,** executed between 892 and 1249, are among the subtlest and most sophisticated, and worth going out of your way to see.

An unusual aspect of Dàzú is that in addition to Buddhist images, it contains Daoist and Confucian statues and themes—not only in separate areas but, in rare instances, in the same cave. Initiated outside the monastic establishment, the Dàzú carvings also commemorate historical figures as well as the project's benefactors, including commoners, warriors, monks, and nuns. In addition to what these carvings reveal about artistic advances made from the late Táng to the late Sòng, the garments and ornaments, along with garden and architectural settings, shed much light on everyday life in ancient China.

Of the six largest sites scattered around the county seat of Dàzú, two are most worth a visit—**Běi Shān,** completed in the late Táng dynasty (618–907); and **Bǎodǐng Shān,** started and completed in the Sòng dynasty (960–1279). If you have time or interest for only one, make it Bǎodǐng Shān.

ESSENTIALS

GETTING THERE   Buses leave Chóngqìng for Dàzú from the Long-Distance Bus Station (next to the railway station) every 30 minutes. The earliest bus is at 5:30am; the last return bus is scheduled to leave at 6pm. It's best to be at the Dàzú bus station by 5pm for the return trip to Chóngqìng. The 2-hour drive from Chóngqìng to Dàzú Xiàn Bus Station costs ¥31 to ¥39 ($3.85–$4.60). From the Dàzú Bus Station, catch a **minibus** for Bǎodǐng Shān. Buses depart every half-hour. The half-hour ride costs ¥3.50 to ¥4.50 (40¢–65¢) each way. Buses also depart from the small bus station in the north part of town for ¥4.50 (60¢). A **taxi** from Dàzú Xiàn to Bǎodǐng Shān is about ¥30 ($3.75).

Taking the **train** to Dàzú is slow and requires first going to Yóutíng; from Yóutíng, transfer to a bus going to the bus station. From the station, transfer to another bus to the grottoes. Whether coming from Chéngdū or Chóngqìng, the bus is considerably faster and more convenient.

TOURS & GUIDES   Guided trips to Bǎodǐng Shān can be arranged at Chóngqìng **CITS,** Zǎozi Lányá Zhèng Jiē 120, second floor (© **023/6385-0693;** fax 023/6385-0196; citscq@cta.cq.cn). The ¥1,300 ($162) fee for one or two people includes admission to Bǎodǐng and Běi Shān, a guide, transportation, and lunch. Alternately, English-language books give brief explanations of the more important carvings.

FAST FACTS

There are no useful services for visitors in Dàzú. Exchange money before you leave Chóngqìng.

EXPLORING DÀZÚ

Video cameras are permitted for a fee of ¥100 ($13), plus a ¥50 ($6.25) deposit for a permit. Plainclothes guards are stationed throughout the grotto area, so don't be tempted to tape without a permit. Still photography is allowed inside the grottoes except where signs indicate otherwise.

Bǎodǐng Shān ✿✿✿   Carvings of the cliff-side grottoes known as Dà Fó Wān (Big Buddha Cove) were initiated and directed by Zhào Zhìfèng, a self-styled Buddhist monk whose brand of Esoteric Buddhism incorporated current religious ideas and popular beliefs. Beginning in 1178 with the construction of Shèngshòu Temple at Xiǎo Fó Wān (Little Buddha Cove)—just north of Dà Fó Wān—the Bǎodǐng Shān project continued for 71 years, possibly halted by the Mongol offensive in Sìchuān. If Zhào lived that long (he'd have been 90) it would explain the unity of design and absence of repetition that mark Bǎodǐng Shān. The carvings are a series of instructive and cautionary scriptural stories arranged in order around a U-shaped cove with interludes of inscriptions and caves devoted to Buddhist deities. At the bottom curve of the U is a massive carving of a reclining **Sakyamuni Buddha** as he enters Nirvana (no. 11). It is just one of the many imposing sculptures at Bǎodǐng Shān. Others that should be noted include the stories of **parental devotion** (no. 15) and **Sakyamuni's filial piety** (no. 17). Local guides usually say these attest to the merging of Confucianism and Buddhism during the Sòng. But scholars see their inclusion as either a concession to Confucianism—when you want government endorsement, there's no point alienating folks—or, possibly, an answer to it from Buddhist scriptures. (In the parental devotion story, look for the nursing boy at the far right wearing the same split pants Chinese toddlers still wear today instead of diapers.) The gruesome **Hell of Knee-Chopping** (no. 20) captures the many faces of drunkenness (none flattering) without crossing the line into kitsch. These carvings are first and foremost works of art. The last story in the cove (no. 30) depicts the taming of a water buffalo and is meant to be a metaphor for taming the mind in meditation. One of the most accomplished carvings in this cove is no. 8, the **Thousand-arm Avalokitesvara** (aka Guānyīn), said to be the only Thousand-arm Avalokitesvara that really has a thousand arms (1,007, actually). Remarkably, each of its hands is in a different pose. Expect to spend 1½ to 2 hours if you're exploring on your own, another hour if you've hired a guide.

Tip: The greatest obstacle to enjoying these caves is the crowds. The best time to visit Bǎodǐng Shān is at noon, when they go to lunch. Go to Běi Shān (below) anytime—tours usually skip it.

15km (9 miles) northeast of the town of Lónggāng Zhèn (often called Dàzú Xiàn). It's about .5km (¼ mile) from the drop-off point (where the restaurants and souvenir stands are) to the entrance. Mini-trolley shuttle between parking lot and entrance ¥2 (25¢) one-way; ¥3 (35¢) round-trip. There's a private pay bathroom by the parking lot (5 máo/5¢) and another, cleaner restroom halfway to the entrance. No restrooms inside. Admission ¥80 ($10). Combination ticket for Bǎodǐng Shān and Běi Shān ¥120 ($15). 8:30am–6pm.

Běi Shān ⓕ   The problem with visiting Běi Shān after Bǎodǐng Shán is that it's a bit of a letdown. If you visit it first, though, you risk being glutted before properly feasting on the best. That said, Fó Wān (Buddha Cove), the cove at the top of Běi Shān, offers a fine series of religious and commemorative carvings, if somewhat less dazzling than the Sòng carvings. In 892, Wéi Jūnjìng, a military commander and imperial envoy, began carving Buddha images in what, at that time, was his encampment atop Běi Shān. That started a 250-year trend that resulted in the completion of nearly 10,000 statues scattered over the county by the end of the Sòng dynasty. Highlights of Běi Shān include the story of **Amitabha Buddha and his Pure Land** in Cave 245, which contains exquisite carved heads that look remarkably alive. Another is the statue of the **Bodhisattva Manjusri** in the largest cave at Fó Wān (no. 136). He appears high-minded and lofty, but it's the touch of self-satisfaction in his expression that captures his humanity and sets this statue apart.

2km (1¼ miles) north of the town of Lónggāng Zhèn (often called Dàzú Xiàn). Admission ¥60 ($6.50). Combination ticket for Běi Shān and Bǎodǐng Shān ¥85 ($11). 8:30am–6pm. Buses leave regularly from Dàzú Bus Station for ¥1 (15¢). A taxi from Dàzú Xiàn to Běi Shān is about ¥5 (65¢).

WHERE TO STAY

Dàzú Bīnguǎn   This hotel and the Běi Shā Bīnguǎn accept foreign visitors, but the Dàzú, with comparable rates, is so far superior (and cleaner) that it's the only recommendation I'll make. Rooms are decorated without imagination and contain the usual twin beds with cheap colored bedspreads, but there is a range of rooms for two, making this hotel affordable for most. Rooms in the back wing are small and show wear; bigger, more recently renovated standards are in the front. Both have bathrooms with combined bathroom and shower.

In the town of Lónggāng Zhèn, Dàzú County, Gōng Lóng Lù 47. From the Dàzú Bus Station, turn left (north) as you exit the station; cross the bridge over the Lài Xī River to its junction with Gōng Lóng Lù. Turn right (east). The hotel is about 275m (900 ft.) ahead on the right. ⓒ 023/4372-1888. Fax 023/4372-2967. 122 units. ¥298–¥498 ($36–$57) standard room. Rates include breakfast. No credit cards. **Amenities:** Restaurant; room service. *In room:* A/C, TV.

WHERE TO DINE

The tourist town of Bǎodǐng Shān outside the entrance gate has a number of small restaurants, noodle shops, and kabob stands serving good, simple dishes at inflated (but still inexpensive) prices. It's usually the Qīngdǎo or imported beer that hikes the bill up; unless you ask for local, that's what you'll get.

9 Middle Reaches of the Cháng Jiāng ⟨★⟩

THE THREE GORGES DAM (SĀNXIÁ BÀ)

The dream of constructing an enormous dam to harness and utilize the power of the Cháng Jiāng (Yàngzǐ River) originally belonged to Sun Yat-sen in the early 1920s, but every Chinese leader since—including Máo and Dèng Xiǎopíng—has shared it. The appeal of this massive project to premiers and presidents may have more to do with classical Chinese flood myths than engineering logic. The most enduring is the story of Yǔ, who was born out of the belly of his father's corpse. Through superhuman feats of repositioning mountains and changing the courses of rivers, Yǔ quelled the great flood of the world and restored natural order. Selfless and moral, his efforts left his body half-withered, yet he went on to found the (semi-mythical) Xià dynasty (ca. 21st–16th c. B.C.). There are also historical models of men who tamed rivers: Shǔ governor Lǐ Bīng supervised ancient China's largest irrigation project (256 B.C.) and is still admired for it; and the Suí Yángdì emperor (reigned 604–617) completed the building of the Grand Canal linking the north and south. Latest to see himself in the role of a new Yǔ out to suppress floods is the former premier Lǐ Péng (best remembered for suppressing the student democracy movement), who pushed approval of the dam through the National People's Congress in 1992, and with whom the dam is most identified, though he no longer holds office.

If all goes according to plan, the massive project will be finished in 2009, but whether it ensures Lǐ's fame or infamy is yet to be seen. It breaks so many records in terms of size, manpower utilized in its construction, volume of building materials (including 10 million lb. of cement), and projected energy output (equal to "10 nuclear power stations"), that there is no real precedent by which to assess the short-term, let alone long-term, effects. But that hasn't stopped pundits (and non-pundits) from trying.

The chief aims of the dam are flood control, power generation, safer navigation, and increased river shipping, but critics of the project cite more than a few concerns, such as the resettlement of one to two million people; the destruction of wildlife habitats, archaeological sites, and historical relics; and the environmental threat of trapped sewage and industrial waste.

DAM EFFECTS ALONG THE THREE GORGES ROUTE

Following are some of the immediate effects the 135m (443-ft.) water level is expected to have on sites along the Three Gorges route:

- The residents of Fēngdū have already been moved to the new city built across the river on higher ground. The mountain and kitsch, ghoulish temple complex with its sculptures of bug-eyed demons and "scenes of hell" will remain, but the mountain will be a semi-island.
- The town of Shíbǎo Zhài will be submerged and the water level will reach the base of the fortress. Excursions will still be possible, but the intriguing old town is gone.

The River by Any Other Name

The name "Yangtze" is troublesome. English dictionaries usually give it two or three accepted pronunciations and an equal number of ways to spell it: Yangtze, Yangtse, Yángzĭ. The irony of it is that Chinese almost never use that name. As far back as the Zhōu dynasty (1045 B.C.–246 B.C.), China's longest river was simply called Jiāng, meaning "River." ("Hé," also meaning "River," was used to refer to the Yellow River, China's other great waterway.) Sometime in the 3rd century, Chinese started calling it the Cháng Jiāng (meaning "Long River"), and that's what it's called today. Theories abound on how the name Yángzĭ came about. Some say it came from Cantonese; others that it was a Western invention. In fact, in the 6th century the name Yángzĭ Jiāng started showing up in poetry to refer to a short stretch of the river near Yángzhōu. By the 19th century the name was applied to the whole river; and for a time, under the Republic, Yángzĭ Jiāng was even the official name. But it returned to Cháng Jiāng under the People's Republic, and that is the river's proper name.

- Zhāngfēi Temple will be moved to higher ground across the river. The temple commemorates the upright Shǔ warrior who was beheaded by two dastardly commanders in his own army. The bulk of the temple and its collection were destroyed during the Cultural Revolution. What stands is the restored building.
- Báidì Chéng (White Emperor City) will be half-submerged. Trackers' paths carved into the cliffs of Qūtáng Gorge will be submerged.
- Three-quarters of Wàn Xiàn will be inundated. The last quarter, renovated and developed, has become the new downtown.
- Fúlíng (site of ancient royal tombs of the Bā Kingdom and the port town of 150,000 people that is the setting of *River Town,* Peter Hessler's fine personal account) will be inundated. Excavation of the tombs is underway.
- There was talk of building an underwater viewing chamber for the ancient stone carvings at White Crane Ridge, said to be the world's oldest hydrological records. The talk has shifted to carving reproductions of the originals instead. Moving them has also been discussed.
- The Dàníng and Shénnóng gorges will be slightly diminished, but naturally not enough to stop tours. Boats will be able to venture farther into these narrow gorges and provide a closer look at the ancient hanging coffins—among them a cluster of 24.
- The western part of Xīlíng Gorge will be submerged.
- The population of Bādōng has been moved upstream to the opposite side of the river. Landslide-prevention projects veil the nearby slopes.

TO CRUISE OR NOT TO CRUISE

Debate rages around the question of whether the **Three Gorges cruise** is the thrill of a lifetime or an overrated, overpriced yawn. Members of tour groups invariably rave about their luxury trip. The boats are plusher than they expected; the cabins roomier; the food better. If the scenery comes as a bit of a letdown—well, they weren't expecting *A Single Pebble.* And if the excursions aren't all they're cracked up to be, at least they're short. Perhaps one reason tour members find their Three Gorges cruise so delightful is that it puts a halt to the mania of touring for a few days.

While it's true that other parts of China have better scenery, prettiness isn't everything. The best part of these cruises is watching life on the river as it is today—in flux. A new city springs up on high, and a few hundred meters below it, the old city sits like a sloughed-off shell. If you choose to take an excursion, as most do, see "The Top Excursions," below, for the very best.

If you'd like to take the excursion but can't afford the steep cruise prices, cheaper tourist ferries and dirt-cheap passenger boats also make the trip. There are boats that sail all the way to Shànghǎi, but unless you're fanatical about river travel, limit your journey to the stretch between Chóngqìng and Yíchāng/Wǔhàn. From there eastward, the river widens and the scenery becomes decidedly prosaic, and train, bus, or plane is preferable.

The best times to go are September and October. In terms of weather, May, early June, and early November are risky, but they can be lovely. Summer is the rainy season, and winter is usually dry but quite cold. Fewer ships sail off season, and schedules are less reliable.

CRUISING INDUSTRY BE DAMMED?

No one, including cruise directors and travel agents, is entirely sure how the flooding of the Three Gorges all the way upstream to Chóngqìng will affect the Yángzǐ cruising industry—although, the fact that cruise lines such as Viking (see below) are adding the Three Gorges to their cruise roster suggests a certain optimism for the time being. June 2003 marked the end of Phase Two in construction and witnessed a rise in water level by 40m (85 ft.); at the end of the third and final phase in 2009 the expected rise will be an additional 50m (106 ft.). As a result, the peaks towering above the river are not as high, nor is bottom of the ravine as narrow. The ghost towns that now dot the banks of the Yángzǐ, evacuated in anticipation of the rising water level, make for an novel if unintended tourist curiosity, but the majesty of the Gorges themselves has definitely been compromised. In the meantime the Gorges might still be worth a visit, but 2009 will likely mark the end of the love affair.

THE CRUISE LINES

The following liners have the best English-speaking guides and the best ships. And after years of experience with foreign passengers, most have removed from their itineraries excursions that require a thorough familiarity with characters and events of the Three Kingdoms in order to enjoy them. Take advantage of off-season rates; book and buy in China; compare prices; bargain; and ask what the excursions are. The prices quoted here are rack rates, but 50% discounts are standard even during high season.

The cruising high seasons are April, May, September, and October. Shoulder seasons are late March, June, July, August, November, and early December. Some cruise ships offer specials in December, January, February, and March.

Orient Royal Cruises   Until the appearance of Viking River Cruises (below), Orient's *East King* and *East Queen* were arguably the plushest ships on the Yángzǐ—built to five-star standards and tied with the *Yellow Crane* (see Presidential Cruises, below) for the best food. Their cruise directors, both from the Philippines, do a superior job of attending to passenger needs and special requests, and their Chinese river guides deliver expert commentary in well-spoken English. Standard cabins have twin beds, a desk, and small fridge. Orient Royal offers one route, between Chóngqìng and Yíchāng, for 4 days.

Orient Royal Cruise, Wǔhàn office. Xīnhuá Lù 316, 14th floor, E Zuǒ (Block E), Liángyóu Bldg. ✆ **888/664-4888** or 027/8576-9988. Fax 027/8576-6688. www.orientroyalcruise.com. 80 cabins. ¥6,230–¥6,720 ($760–$820) per person, standard cabin; ¥13,500 ($1,640) per person largest suite. Shore excursions ¥560 ($70) per person. 50%–60% discounts year-round. AE, DC, MC, V. **Amenities:** 2 restaurants; 2 bars; exercise room; salon; massage; laundry. *In room:* A/C, closed-circuit TV, minibar/fridge, hair dryer on request.

Presidential Cruises

Presidential, run by CITS, has six ships currently operating on the Yángzǐ, imaginatively named MV1, MV2, and so on. The *Yellow Crane* (aka MV2) is built to China's four-star standard, and its cabins aren't as spacious as those of Viking and Orient Royal, but the ship is attractively appointed and well-staffed with an English-speaking crew. While the *Yellow Crane* lacks the slick promotion of Victoria and Orient Royal, the ship itself serves better food, is more luxurious than Victoria's ships, and very nearly meets the five-star standard of the *East King* and *East Queen*. Standard rooms are comparable in size and furnishing to those in Victoria Cruises' fleet.

The *Yellow Crane* travels between Chóngqìng and Yíchāng (3 days downriver, 4 days upriver). CITS in Wǔhàn and Chóngqìng usually offer great savings on these tours; see contact information below under "Lower-Cost Cruise Alternatives: Local Passenger Boats & Tourist Ferries."

Contact Wǔhàn Empress Travel, 15 Huìjì Lù, 7th floor Chángháng Dàjiǔdiàn, Wǔhàn. ✆ **027/8286-5977**. Fax 027/8286-6351. www.cits.net/travel/travel/river/river.jsp. 77 cabins. ¥2,740–¥3,120 ($335–$385) per person, standard cabin. 50% discounts. AE, DC, MC, V. **Amenities:** 2 restaurants; bar; exercise room; forex; salon; massage; laundry. *In room:* A/C, closed-circuit TV, hair dryer on request.

Victoria Cruises

Based in New York, this is one of the few Western-managed lines. At one time, Victoria had the most luxurious liners on the Yángzǐ. While they still offer first-rate cruises with some of the best English-speaking cruise directors and river guides, other cruise lines equal or surpass their ships' cabins, kitchen, and facilities, and are equally well-staffed. Standard cabins have twin beds and writing desk, but are slightly smaller than Orient Royal's *East King* and *East Queen*.

Victoria offers two routes: between Chóngqìng and Yíchāng (downriver 4 days, upriver 6 days); and between Chóngqìng and Shànghǎi (downriver 7 days, upriver 9 days).

57–08 39th Ave., Woodside, NY 11377. ✆ **800/348-8084** or 212/818-1680. Fax 212/818-9889. www.victoriacruises.com. 74–87 cabins. Cruise between Chóngqìng and Yíchāng: ¥6,000–¥6,400 ($775–$820) per person, standard cabin; ¥16,000 ($2,000) per person largest suite. Shore excursion ¥680 ($80) per person. Cruise between Chóngqìng and Shànghǎi: ¥11,480–¥12,300 ($1,400–$1,500) per person, standard cabin; ¥26,240–¥29,520 ($3,200–$3,600) per person largest suite. Shore excursion ¥1,845 ($225) per person. 50%–60% discounts year-round. AE, DC, MC, V. **Amenities:** Restaurant; bar; exercise room; forex; salon; massage; acupuncture; laundry. *In room:* A/C, closed-circuit TV, hair dryer on request.

Viking River Cruises

Not only the most recent cruise line to start plying the Three Gorges, Viking's two liners, the *Viking Century Sky* and the *Viking Century Star*, comfortably float above the competition as the top way to see the river. Effortlessly five-star, every room is spacious and tastefully appointed with blond woods. The food is excellent and plentiful—to the extent that it sometimes feels as though you are living from meal to meal—and the staff has a working grasp of English and is extremely friendly. Although the Viking's main route runs between Chóngqìng and Yíchāng (3–4 nights), the company also offers trips that go all the way to Shànghǎi (9 nights). The cost of the cruise covers daily (but optional) shore visits, including the Three Gorges Dam, the Lesser Three Gorges, and Shí Bǎo Zhài Temple. However, the day trips are little more than a distraction from the cruise itself. Viking cruises are usually sold as part of package tours visiting China's other key tourist meccas: Xī'ān, Běijīng, Hong Kong, and Shànghǎi. Prices vary according to package, time of year, and type of cabin you choose, so check the website for current rates.

Viking River Cruises, Inc., 5700 Canoga Ave., Suite 200, Woodland Hills, California 91367. ✆ 818/227-1234. www. vikingrivercruises.com. 153 cabins *(Century Sky)*, 93 cabins *(Century Star)*. Check website for current rates. AE, DC, MC, V. **Amenities:** Restaurant; 2 bars; exercise room; gym; sauna; salon; massage; laundry; Internet access. *In room:* A/C, closed-circuit/satellite TV, minibar, fridge, hair dryer.

The Top Excursions

One of the best excursions is to **Shí Bǎo Zhāi (Stone Treasure Fortress).** This square-edged **red pagoda** built in the 18th century hugs the cliff and is an elegant vision from the river. The climb up its 12 narrow staircases is only difficult when other tour groups are pressing from behind or blocking the way in front. Since the descent is down a back staircase, just let them all go ahead. Inside, look for the two "magic" holes. The first is the **Hole of the Greedy Monk.** As the story goes, when monks lived in the tower, the hole spouted just enough rice for their daily rations. One monk, thinking he'd like rations to sell in the market, tried to make the hole bigger. His avarice shut the source for good. Of the second hole, it is said that if you drop a duck down it **(Duck Tossing Hole),** within seconds you'll see the duck floating far below on the river.

Close to the top of the pagoda, if you peek under the **arched bridge** (which is meant to be crossed in three steps or less), you'll get a good look at a *wāwa yú*—the **giant Chinese salamander** that supposedly cries like a baby. This one has been here for years—how it survives is a mystery.

For impressive scenery, the half-day trip up **Shénnóng Stream** (near Bādōng) is the best of the excursions. Cruise passengers board a ferry that takes you to Shénnóng Xī. There, you climb into "peapod" boats that are rowed and pulled upstream by trackers (in shorts and handmade sandals), most of whom are farmers in the off season. Each boat has a female guide whose English isn't always up to the task, but she makes up for it by singing a Tǔjiā minority song for the group on the return trip. If the trackers are in the mood, one or two will join in. The scenery on this narrow stream is probably closer to what most travelers expect of the Three Gorges. **Towering cliffs** rise on either bank, and the water is crystal clear. On rare occasions, passengers catch sight of **monkeys** along the cliffs. The trackers used to go only far enough to glimpse the first **hanging coffin,** but now that the water level has risen, they may continue farther (though time is a factor, too). Depending on the ship and water conditions, you may go instead to the small gorges of the **Dàníng River** (near Wū Shān), where the scenery is equally beautiful and monkeys are more often sighted.

Whether or not you have any interest in engineering or construction, the sheer immensity of the **Three Gorges Dam Site** at **Sān Dǒu Píng** makes this worth a visit. Not only is it a unique photo opportunity, its monumental size lends it the visual (if not yet the historical) power of the Great Wall or Xī'ān's Terra-Cotta Warriors. The luxury cruise ships usually include it on their itineraries, while local tourist ferries don't. Before booking, make sure it's included. Its absence from the itinerary is reason enough to look elsewhere.

LOWER-COST CRUISE ALTERNATIVES: LOCAL PASSENGER BOATS & TOURIST FERRIES

Yángzǐ River supercheap **passenger boats** depart from Wǔhàn (for upriver trips) and from Chóngqìng (for downriver trips) year-round, but their facilities are foul, and so is the food. Their raison d'être is transport, not tourism, so they make no effort to go through the gorges in the light of day, and naturally there are no tourist excursions.

Numerous Chinese **tourist ferries** operate on the Yángzĭ, some of them with quite comfortable cabins and facilities. Management and staff are not used to foreign travelers and they rarely speak English, but the price, even for first class, is considerably less than the price on a luxury ship. These boats will invariably only take you as far as Yíchāng. The remaining leg on to Wǔhàn is best accomplished on the air-conditioned buses that travel the recently completed freeway that connects the two cities; in fact, the option to sail to Wǔhàn is becoming less available. Fourth-class passage from **Chóngqìng to Yíchāng** starts at ¥202 ($25) and isn't much better than ferry accommodations—a bunk in an eight-person dorm with a filthy toilet down the hall. Prices for first-class passage (two-bed cabin with private shower/toilet), excluding meals and excursions, start at ¥1,027 ($125) per person. Since you can pay on board or at the site for excursions, make sure they're *not* included in your ticket price, giving you more flexibility. Typically, excursions are to Fēngdū, Shí Bǎo Zhāi, and the Little Three Gorges, but these ships do not stop at the Three Gorges Dam construction site. Tickets can be booked in Chóngqìng inside the Navigation Office Building at Cháotiān Mén near the Cháotiān Mén Hotel, but you probably won't find an English speaker. Beware of so-called "government-run tour agencies" along the wharf; they are likely to charge much higher fees than the actual ticket cost. And be sure to ask which pier your boat will depart from.

In this instance, the better way to book is through **China International Travel Service (CITS)** in Wǔhàn, Táiběi Yī Lù 26, seventh floor, Xiǎo Nán Hú Building (© **027-8578-4100;** fax 027-8578-4089; citswuh@public.wh.hb.cn). In Chóngqìng, CITS is at Zǎozi Lányā Zhèng Jiē 120 (© **023-6385-0693;** fax 023-6385-0196; citscq@cta.cq.cn). The booking fee of ¥50 ($6.25) is worth every cent. The agents in the international division of both these offices are unusually well informed and helpful, and speak excellent English.

10 Wǔhàn

Húběi Province, 1,125km (699 miles) W of Shànghǎi, 1,354km (841 miles) E of Chóngqìng, 1,047km (650 miles) SE of Xī'ān

Wǔhàn is primarily an industrial and business center. Were it not for the fact that many of the Three Gorges tours traditionally begin or terminate in Wǔhàn, few Western tourists would ever make it here. However, trisected by the Yángzĭ River and its longest tributary, the Hànshuǐ, and dotted with a hundred-plus lakes and scores of parks, this city of 4.8 million urban residents is an agreeable place to spend a couple of days. Three districts—Wǔchāng, Hànyáng, and Hànkǒu—which used to be separate cities, comprise present-day Wǔhàn. Avoid summers when the city inevitably lives up to its reputation as one of China's Three Furnaces.

Wǔhàn is also the gateway to the Daoist mountain Wǔdāng Shān.

ESSENTIALS

GETTING THERE   **Tiānhé Airport** is 26km (16 miles) northwest of Wǔhàn. Destinations include Běijīng (six or seven flights daily); Guǎngzhōu (at least seven flights daily); Hong Kong (one flight daily); Shànghǎi (seven flights daily); Chéngdū (four or five flights daily); Chóngqìng (four or five flights daily); and Fukuoka and Tokyo (two flights weekly).

Wǔhàn

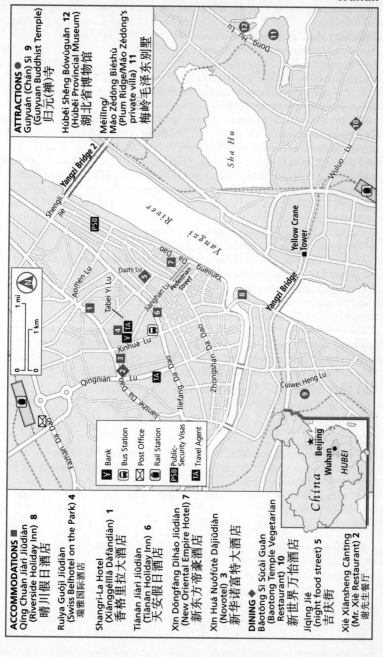

Yangzi Bridge 2

Shengli Jie

PSB

Aomen Lu

Dazhi Lu

Tabei Yi Lu

Xinhua Lu

Qingnian Lu

Fazhan Da Dao

Yanjiang Da Dao

Jianghan Lu

Pedestrian Street

Zhongshan Da Dao

Jiefang Da Dao

Jianshe Da Dao

Yangzi River

Sha Hu

Dong Hu Lu

Wuluo Lu

Cuiwei Heng Lu

Yellow Crane Tower

Yangzi Bridge

N

1 mi

1 km

0

0

China

★ Beijing

Wuhan

HUBEI

¥ Bank
🚌 Bus Station
✉ Post Office
🚉 Rail Station
PSB Public-Security Visas
TA Travel Agent

An **airport coach** between the airport and Hànkǒu Railway Station departs when full; board near the airport entrance. The trip takes 1 hour and costs ¥25 ($3). **Complimentary shuttle buses** to the airport leave from the China Southern (Nánfāng Hángkōng Gōngsī) office on Hángkōng Lù 2 hours before their flights. Buses from the airport to town leave 1 to 2 hours after China Southern arrivals. The trip takes 30 minutes. A **taxi** to Hànkǒu should be ¥50 to ¥70 ($6.25–$8.75), plus a ¥15 ($1.85) toll. Stand in the taxi queue and use the meter. Ignore independent drivers who will offer to drive you for hundreds of *yuán*.

Wǔhàn has a number of **railway stations,** but the two major terminals are **Hànkǒu Huǒchēzhàn** (mostly northbound) and **Wǔchāng Huǒchēzhàn** (mostly southbound). Major connections from Wǔchāng Station are Běijīng (T79/T80; 10 hr.; hard sleeper ¥280/$35); Guǎngzhōu (2269/2270; 10½ hr.; hard sleeper ¥280/$35); Kūnmíng (K109/K110; 32 hr.; hard sleeper ¥320/$39); and Shànghǎi (K122/123; 19 hr.; hard sleeper ¥201/$25). Major connections with Hànkǒu Station are fewer: Běijīng (T77/T78; 12 hr.; hard sleeper ¥281/$35); and Chóngqìng (T257/T258; 15 hr.; hard sleeper ¥272/$33).

Tickets can be booked 3 days in advance at the respective stations. Hotels and CITS will book tickets for a ¥50 ($6.25) fee.

The two main **long-distance bus stations** are the **Hànkǒu Chángtú Qìchēzhàn** on Jiěfàng Dà Dào at the Yǒuyì Lù intersection (mostly northbound), and the **Wǔchāng Chángtú Qìchēzhàn,** northeast of the railway station on Wǔluò Lù (mostly southbound). Buses for Shànghǎi leave from both stations (15½ hr.; ¥360/$43). It's best to buy tickets a day in advance.

The newest addition to Wǔhàn's transport infrastructure is a **light rail** line that began operating at the end of 2004. It is currently exclusive to Hànkǒu but is being extended to Wǔchāng. It runs along the old rail line on Jīng-Hàn Dà Dào, making stops every kilometer. It is operational between 6:30am and 9:30pm, and tickets cost ¥3 (40¢)

GETTING AROUND   Standard **taxi** rates are ¥8 ($1) for 3km (2 miles), then ¥1.40 (20¢) for each additional kilometer up to 7km. Above 7km (4⅓ miles), add 50% per kilometer.

FAST FACTS

Banks, Foreign Exchange & ATMS   There's a large **Bank of China** just off the pedestrian street at Zhōngshān Dà Dào 593 (at the junction with Jiānghàn Lù; look for a stately old European concession building near the overhead walkway) and it has an ATM out the front. Foreign exchange is Monday through Friday from 8:30am to noon and 1:30 to 5pm.

Internet Access   Dial-up is ⓒ **163.**

Post Office   A useful post office is at the west side of the railway station opposite the city bus terminal. There's another one on Jiānghàn Dà Dào Pedestrian Street, no. 134, which is open from 8:30am to 10pm.

Tours   China International Travel Service (CITS) is exceptionally helpful and straightforward about prices. They book flights, train rides, and cruises, and arrange guided tours. CITS is located at Zhōngshān Dà Dào 909, near the intersection with Yīyuàn Lù (ⓒ **027/8277-0344;** fax 027/8284-5833; citswuh@public.wh.hb.cn).

Visa Extensions   Applications are available at the **Gōngānjú Wàishì Kē (PSB Department of Foreign Affairs)** at Zhāng Zìzhōng Lù (ⓒ **027/8539-5394),** which is open Monday through Friday from 9 to noon and 2 to 5pm. The process takes three working days.

EXPLORING WŬHÀN

Guīyuán (Chán) Sì (Guīyuán Buddhist Temple)   Best known for its hall of 500 gilded *luóhàn* (enlightened disciples), each in a different posture and having distinct features, this temple was founded in the mid–17th century by the monk Bái Guāng. The present buildings date from the late Qīng dynasty to the beginning of the Republican era (1911–49), but the *luóhàn* were sculpted between 1822 and 1831. Men proceed to the left and women to the right, counting one *luóhàn* until the number equals their age. They note the number that designates that statue and, on their way out, for ¥3 (35¢) they buy the corresponding "*luóhàn* card," which tells their fortune. In the sutra library at the far end of the complex is a pretty jade Buddha with Indian influence that dates from the Northern Wèi dynasty (4th–5th c.).

Cuìwēi Héng Lù no. 20. ⓒ 027/8243-5212. Admission ¥10 ($1.25). 8am–4:30pm. Bus: no. 401 is the only bus that can enter the narrow Cuìwēi Héng Lù, but bus nos. 6 and 528 run along Yīngwǔ Dà Dào, which intersects Cuìwēi Héng Lù. From this intersection, it's a short walk to Guīyuán.

Húběi Shěng Bówùguǎn (Húběi Provincial Museum) 𝕲𝕲   "When the Master was in Qí he heard the Sháo [ceremonial music] and for three months was oblivious to the taste of food. He marveled, 'I never expected music to do this to me'" (from *The Analects,* Confucius).

Since no musical notations survive from the time of Confucius (ca. 551–479 B.C.), there's no way of knowing what the music he refers to above sounded like, but thanks to the excavation in 1978 of the intact tomb of Marquis Yǐ of Zēng (d. ca. 433 B.C.), visitors to this museum can see some of the actual instruments on which the music was played. In addition to an ensemble of ancient musical instruments, the tomb included coffins, gold and jade decorative items, weapons, and impressive bronze- and lacquerware from China's Warring States period (474–221 B.C.). The centerpiece of the exhibition is a huge set of 65 bronze chime bells, said to be the heaviest and possibly oldest extant musical instrument in the world. Inscriptions on the bells and hooks that hold them constitute the earliest known work on musicology. To give visitors an idea of how the bells were played and how their pentatonic scale sounded, musicians give an excellent 20-minute performance on classical instruments, which include replicas of the bronze bells. Two performances are scheduled each day. At press time, a major renovation, including the addition of two new halls, was underway and was scheduled for completion in early 2006. The new halls will feature Bronze Age artifacts and additional items from the Warring States period.

Wǔchāng, Dōng Hú Lù no. 188. ⓒ 027/8679-4127. Admission ¥30 ($3.75). 9–11:30am and 1:30–4:30pm. Bus: no. 14 or 578.

Méilǐng/Máo Zédōng Biéshù ("Plum Ridge"/Máo Zédōng's Private Villa)   If you have an extra hour or so after visiting the Provincial Museum (above), Máo's second-favorite pied-à-terre (after Běidài Hé) is a pleasant 10-minute walk from the museum. Built in 1958 as one of Máo's several private retreats, it was here that he hosted notables as diverse as labor activist Anna Louise Strong and U.S. president Richard Nixon. There are no English signs or explanations, but they're not necessary. The separate bedrooms of Máo and his wife Jiāng Qīng are as interesting for their plainness as Máo's private swimming pool is noted for its excessive size. Personal effects, such as Máo's blood-pressure gauge and his cherry-red house slippers, speak for themselves. However, those who don't read Chinese will miss such tidbits as what the chairman liked to eat (coarse multigrains and local snacks) and what Jiāng Qīng's hobbies were (photography, and that favored pastime of ambitious First Ladies—amassing shoes). Off the porch outside Jiāng Qīng's bedroom is an unmarked vault-door leading to the dank underground tunnels that would have sheltered Máo and his entourage in an emergency.

Wǔchāng, Dōng hú Lù no. 56. ⓒ 027/8679-6106. Admission ¥20 ($1.25). 8am–5pm. Bus: no. 578, 709, 14, or 701; get off at the Provincial Museum, then follow the tree-lined drive behind the old museum building several hundred meters (a 10- to 15-min. walk). Alternately enter by the main entrance on Dōng Hú Lù, a 10-min. walk to the left of the museum. The entrance is mark by a uniformed soldier. Follow the signs for Méilíng Yī Hào through the grounds.

SHOPPING & STROLLING

A few years ago, a half-mile stretch of **Jiānghàn Street** (between Jiānghàn Dà Dào and the wharf) was closed to motor traffic, and old stores were replaced with trendy new ones.

The street is a popular place to stroll, especially on hot summer evenings. If you walk south from Jiānghàn Street to the wharf, you'll get to the Customs Building and the former **foreign concession** area of Hànkǒu, which under the Treaty of Tiānjīn was forced open to British trade in 1859. The dozen or so remaining buildings in the European style of the 1920s and 1930s are spread along the wharf on **Yánjiāng Dà Dào** (a left turn off the pedestrian street). A number of the buildings (which include the Russian police station, the former German and U.S. consulates, several banks, businesses, and living quarters) are identified by signs in English. In efforts to entice foreign investors, Wǔhàn's mayor has invited overseas businesses to set up offices in these historical buildings.

The **Xīn Shìjiè Bǎihuò Shāngchǎng (New World Department Store)** on Jiànshè Dà Dào (around the corner from Novotel Hotel) has a large supermarket on the basement level. There is also a Carrefour in each of the three districts of Wǔhàn. The one in Hànkǒu is on Wǔshēng Lù.

WHERE TO STAY

EXPENSIVE

Shangri-La Hotel (Xiānggélǐlā Dàfàndiàn) Whatever the time of day, the lobby and cafe of this international hotel are abuzz with businesspeople and tourists. The Shangri-La's guest rooms are large, comfortable, and attractive—but nothing out of the ordinary for this level of hotel. Bathrooms are large and well designed, with separate shower cubicles.

Jiànshè Dà Dào 700. ⓒ 027/8580-6868. Fax 027/8577-6868. www.shangri-la.com/eng/hotel/14. 507 units. ¥1,066–¥1,164 ($130–$142) standard room. Rates include breakfast. 20%-40% discount available; 15% service charge. AE, DC, MC, V. Bus: no. 509 from railway station. **Amenities:** 2 restaurants; 2 bars; indoor pool; health club; sauna; airline, train, and bus ticketing; business center; forex; 24-hr. room service; dry cleaning/laundry. *In room:* A/C, satellite TV, dataport, minibar, fridge, hair dryer, safe.

MODERATE

Qíng Chuān Jiàrì Jiǔdiàn (Riverside Holiday Inn) *Kids* Perched on the west bank of the Yángzǐ River across from the Yellow Crane Tower—emblem of Wǔhàn—this four-star hotel has the best views in the city. The rooms themselves are immaculate and comfortably appointed even if the decor isn't inspired. Hefty discounts, a children's center, weekend barbecues by the river, and a Western buffet breakfast make this a good choice for families. Rooms overlooking the Yellow Crane Tower are slightly more expensive, but all rooms have comparable river views. One possible disadvantage of the Riverside's location is that it's across the Hàn River from Hànkǒu; but the actual distance to the city center is only about 4km (2½ miles).

Xǐmǎ Cháng Jiē 88 (next to Qíng Chuān Pavilion). © 027/8471-6688. Fax 027/8471-6181. www.sixcontinentshotels. com/h/d/hi/rates. 336 units. ¥828 ($100) standard room; ¥918 ($110) standard room with river view; ¥1,328 ($160) business suite. Most rates include breakfast. 50% discount standard, with higher discounts possible; 15% service charge. AE, DC, MC, V. Bus: no. 568, 559, 411, or 206. **Amenities:** 2 restaurants; 3 bars; tennis court; exercise room; sauna; reflexology center; children's center; airline, train, and bus ticketing; business center; forex; limited room service; dry cleaning/laundry. *In room:* A/C, satellite TV, fax (in some rooms), dataport, minibar, fridge, coffeemaker, hair dryer, safe.

Ruìyǎ Guójì Jiǔdiàn (Swiss Belhotel on the Park) *Value*
Situated on a relatively sleepy lane in the center of Hànkǒu, the Swiss Belhotel (formerly the New World Courtyard) is within walking distance of major shops and parks. The staff is used to repeat and extended-stay business guests, which may account for the genuine and universal warmth with which they treat even short-term guests. The Swiss Belhotel meets many of the standards of a much pricier hotel with amenities such as English TV programming and a Western-style breakfast buffet. Yet while the rooms are pleasant enough and very well maintained, they're not large, and the beds and furniture show wear. At $40 or $50 a night (standard room with a 50%-plus discount), this is the best bargain in town, but its popularity makes reservations advised. Call ahead from within China. An English speaker is always on duty.

Táiběi Yī Lù 9 (between Táiběi Lù and Xīnhuá Lù). © 027/6885-1888. Fax 027/6885-1988. www.swiss-belhotel. com. 137 units. ¥925 ($109) standard room; ¥2,020–¥2,210 ($238–$260) suite. Most rates include breakfast. 50% discount standard, higher discounts possible; 15% service charge. AE, DC, MC, V. Bus: no. 9 or 519 from railway station. Cab from airport ¥65 ($8.10). **Amenities:** 2 restaurants; bar; exercise room; sauna; airline, train, and bus ticketing; business center; forex; limited room service; dry cleaning/laundry. *In room:* A/C, satellite TV, minibar, fridge, hair dryer.

Tiān'ān Jiàrì Jiǔdiàn (Tiān'ān Holiday Inn)
If you'd prefer a central location (northwest end of Wǔhàn's pedestrian street, Jiānghàn Lù) and a spiffier decor (renovated in 2004) over terrific river views, pick this Holiday Inn over the Riverside. Otherwise, the two properties are very similar.

Jiěfàng Dà Dào 868. © 027/8586-7888. Fax 027/8584-5353. www.china.ichotelsgroup.com. 355 units. ¥458 ($55) standard room; ¥1,328 ($160) business suite. Most rates include breakfast. No standard discounts; 15% service charge. AE, DC, MC, V. Bus: no. 532 or 549. **Amenities:** 3 restaurants; deli; 2 bars; exercise room, sauna; children's center; business center; forex; limited room service; dry cleaning/laundry. *In room:* A/C, satellite TV, fax in some rooms, dataport, minibar, fridge, coffeemaker, hair dryer, safe.

Xīn Dōngfāng Dìháo Jiǔdiàn (New Oriental Empire Hotel)
The Swiss Belhotel is a better value, but this is a good choice if you want to be on the wharf. The staff is friendly and the royal blue carpets in the guest rooms haven't been damaged yet by cigarette burns and discarded tea leaves. Rooms are the standard model, but the view makes the difference. Try for a corner room, which overlooks the street and has two windows instead of one. Avoid rooms at the back, which face the back of a dark building and smell of mold. The price is the same, so it's only a matter of asking.

Yánjiāng Dà Dào 136 (between Shànghǎi Jiē and Nánjīng Lù; opposite Wǔhàn Port). © 027/8221-1881. Fax 027/ 8277-5912. hbxdf@Elong.com. 69 units. ¥358–¥458 ($42–$54) standard room; ¥558–¥888 ($66–$108) suite. Rates include breakfast. 30% discount available. No credit cards. Bus: no. 9 from railway station; another dozen city buses start and terminate from the bus station opposite the hotel. **Amenities:** 2 restaurants; bar; business center; forex; limited room service; dry cleaning/laundry. *In room:* A/C, TV.

Xīnhuá Nuòfùtè Dàjiǔdiàn (Novotel) Touted as bringing "the European touch" to Wǔhàn, this new French joint-venture (part of the Accor group) distinguishes itself from the pack of four-star hotels with its creative decor. In the guest rooms, cone-shaped bed lamps are set against blonde wood; the look is smart and streamlined. Though standard rooms are on the small side, they still feel light and airy. And small-ish bathrooms are made to feel roomier by a black marble counter that is big enough to accommodate a travel case and toiletries and looks elegant against white tiled walls. Novotel's central location between the concession area and the Hànkǒu railway station is convenient for both shopping and sightseeing.

Jiànshè Dà Dào 558 (next to New World Department Store Xīn Shìjiè Bǎihuò Shāngchǎng). ⓒ **800/221-4542** in the U.S. and Canada, or 027/8555-1188. Fax 027/8555-1177. www.accorhotels.com/asia. 303 units. ¥1,079 ($134) standard room; ¥1,162 ($145) deluxe standard room; ¥1,328–¥1,494 ($166–$186) suite. 20%–40% discount; 15% service charge. AE, DC, MC, V. Bus: no. 509 from railway station. Cab from airport ¥65 ($8.15). **Amenities:** 2 restaurants; bar; health club; sauna; business center; forex; 24-hr. room service; dry cleaning/laundry; executive floors. *In room:* A/C, satellite TV, fax in some executive rooms, dataport, minibar, fridge, hair dryer, safe.

WHERE TO DINE

If you're after a meal that's *not* Chinese, the coffee shop at the Shangri-La hotel serves the best **Western buffet breakfast** in town (¥128/$16). The **deli** at Tiānhé Holiday Inn sells European cheeses, French bread, and good hard rolls. **Pizza Hut, McDonald's,** and **KFC** are all concentrated on the same intersection on Jiānghàn Lù 1 block northwest of the overhead walkway at the Zhōngshān Dà Dào intersection. As you continue south, on the right side of the street, just before the Chinese Customs Building at Jiānghàn Lù 3, is the huge bakery **Huángguān Dàn'gāo,** which sells Western and Chinese cakes, cookies, and breads. It's open from 5am to midnight.

Bǎotōng Sì Sùcài Guǎn (Bǎotōng Temple Vegetarian Restaurant) ✿ BUD-DHIST VEGETARIAN Almost as popular with nonvegetarians, this restaurant prepares *zhāicài* (Buddhist cuisine) in the temple tradition, specializing in faux meat, fish, and fowl dishes. A delicious appetizer is *wǔxiāng niúròu* (faux beef with blended spices). Made from *dòufu pí* (the top, most nutritious layer of the tofu), this cold dish is served with hot sesame oil and soy sauce. Another *dòufu pí* main dish is *hóngshāo fǔzhú* (braised *dòufu pí* rolls with bamboo shoots and green pepper). Two dishes that don't pretend to be anything else are *quánjiāfú* (several kinds of mushroom sautéed with dates) and sautéed *yóumàicài*, which is a dark-green leafy vegetable similar to spinach. Both dishes are delicate and tasty.

Wǔluò Lù no. 289 (next to the temple entrance). No phone. Meal for 2 ¥100 ($13). No credit cards. 9am–8pm. Bus: no. 18, 25, 518, 519, 577, or 710 to Hóng Shān Gōngyuán stop.

Jíqìng Jiē (night food street) ✿ 𝒱𝑎𝑙𝑢𝑒 HÚBĚI Locals come in groups to this ren-ovated half-block of outdoor restaurants and make an evening of dining and enjoying roving singers, musicians, sketch artists, flower sellers, photographers, and shoe shin-ers. Customers who don't want to be disturbed request a "quiet plaque" (*jìngyīn tái);* if they're still approached, they hold up the sign and interlopers retreat (at least they did a week after the reopening). For those who want to be serenaded, there are plenty of choices, from Běijīng opera to modern pop songs. Customers order from a song menu with a price list. For around ¥10 ($1.25), a male opera singer of female roles (in the tradition of Méi Lánfāng, China's most famous Peking opera singer, who special-ized in female roles) will sing you an aria. A shoeshine costs ¥1 to ¥2 (15¢–25¢). Eat-ing here, you'll see people from all walks of life. Even those who aren't dining come to hear the music, and nobody seems to mind when bystanders (usually neighborhood seniors) decide to sing along.

All the restaurants on this street serve similar fare, which is generally quite good. Fish is a specialty, and one of the best is braised yellow fish (*hóngshǎo huángyú*). Served whole, it's only about 5 inches in length and bony, but the reward is tender, tasty flakes of saltwater fish. Like Sìchuān cuisine, Húběi dishes incorporate a lot of pepper—but not all the dishes are fiery *dànbái shāo gǔpái*, or pork ribs braised in egg white, is one such specialty that is succulent, flavorful, and *mild*. If you can stand the heat, a local favorite is *qiān biān méi* or deep-fried *dòufu* with garlic, red pepper, and Sìchuān pepper. These tender rounds of slightly fermented *dòufu*, curled up like cinnamon rolls, are delicious. A meal consisting of six dishes easily feeds four. Add three large beers and the cost is ¥84 ($11), or about $2.60 per person.

Jíqìng Jiē starting from Dàzhì Jiē. No English menu. Meal for 2 ¥40–¥60 ($5–$7). No credit cards. From 6:30pm until everyone goes home; liveliest time is after 10pm.

Xiè Xiānsheng Cāntīng (Mr. Xiè Restaurant) ✿✿ ⓥ*alue* VARIOUS CHINESE
This franchise, with three locations, makes for one of Wǔhàn's more popular nights out. Nearly always packed, the restaurants don't claim to offer any particular type of Chinese cuisine, although Húnán and Húběi dishes feature prominently. A couple to watch for include *xiǎomǐ páigǔ* (steamed spareribs and millet) and *jiānjiāo kòu wǔbǎo* (sautéed baby turnip greens with dried red peppers). In any case, the picture menu will help you order. The readily accessible Mr. Xiè is about a 10-minute walk from the Novotel and it's difficult to miss: The two-story building has big windows letting you see into the white-tiled interior, replete with gold gilded stairwell. But if you are willing to brave the decor, the food is worth the effort, as is the lively ambience of the Chinese indulging in their favorite pastime: eating.

Jiànshè Dà Dào 548 (10-min. walk west from the Novotel). ⓒ 027/8577-7188. Photo menu. Meal for 2 ¥50–¥100 ($6–$12). No credit cards. 11am–9:30pm. Also at Wǔchāng, Péngliúcháng Lù 249 (ⓒ 027/8891-8828) and Jiěfàng Dà Dào 910 (ⓒ 027/8577-7188).

11 Wǔdāng Shān

Húběi Province, 500km (311 miles) NW of Wǔhàn

In the hierarchy of sacred Daoist mountains, Wǔdāng is number one because of its association with the popular god Zhēnwǔ (Perfected Warrior). In the 7th century, a cult developed around him, and his popularity continued to grow for the next 7 centuries. By the Míng dynasty, Zhēnwǔ was considered the 82nd transformation of Lǎozǐ, and even supplanted the deified Lǎozǐ as the most important of the Daoist gods. Visitors to Wǔdāng have the Perfected Warrior to thank for many of the monasteries and temples that still stand on the mountain. It was in his honor that the Yǒnglè emperor ordered a massive building campaign on Wǔdāng Shān in 1412. Several of the extant buildings date back to that time.

Unlike Éméi Shān, Qīngchéng Shān, and Nán Yuè Héng Shān, Wǔdāng receives relatively few tourists, and it has preserved its temples and its Daoist tradition more successfully than the less-remote mountains. The price of preservation for the traveler is a longer journey and less-comfortable lodging. However, the mountain's rugged peaks covered in old-growth forest, along with its ancient monasteries—some built to fit the contours of the cliffs, others to mirror them—are well worth the sacrifice.

Another name associated with these mountains is Zhāng Sānfēng, the Daoist Immortal credited with inventing the discipline of *tàijíquán* in the late 14th century. Though less well known overseas, Wǔdāng's "internal" form of *wǔshù* (martial arts) is as highly regarded as Shàolín Temple's "external" form (p. 331). Students come from all parts of China to study at the many martial arts schools in town and on the mountain. The famous swords used in the Wǔdāng style are for sale everywhere.

The best times to visit are April through June and September through October, when the leaves turn as red as the gorgeous temple walls.

Note: For Chinese translations of selected establishments listed in this section, please turn to appendix A.

ESSENTIALS

GETTING THERE   The **train** from Wǔchāng to Shíyàn stops in Wǔdāng Shān village at 5:30am (K782/783, K784/781; 7 hr.; hard sleeper ¥127/$15). Unless you're staying more than a few days, buy your return ticket as soon as you arrive. The return train leaves at 11pm each day. Only hard-seat tickets are available at the ticket office but you can upgrade once on board.

Less convenient, **buses** from Wǔhàn go to Shíyàn (11 hr.), where you transfer to a minibus to Wǔdāng Shān. Buses wait for passengers in front of the railway station and depart when full. The ride takes 30 to 45 minutes and costs ¥10 ($1.25).

EXPLORING THE MOUNTAIN

The entrance to the mountain is less than a mile east of Wǔdāng Shān village. From there to the main temples and trail head is another 12km (7 miles). **Taxi vans** ply this stretch picking up passengers and dropping them at the base where hotels, shops, and the post office are located (¥10–¥15/$1.25–$2). At the time of writing, however, movement was underfoot to ban the freelance vans and other private vehicles and replace them with tour buses, complete with guides.

The peak can be reached **on foot** in 2½ hours up stone stairs. The views are magnificent. Save energy for the final very steep leg to the peak. Round-trip by **sedan chair** is ¥120 ($15). A **cable car,** which starts a short way up the mountain, goes to Tàihé Sì (near the peak). The 25-minute trip costs ¥70 ($5.65) one-way, ¥80 ($10) round-trip.

Best preserved from the Míng dynasty building boom is Wǔdāng Shān's **Zǐxiāo Gōng (Purple Mist Palace),** located on **Zhǎnqí Peak** (below the cliff Tàizǐ Yán). This large, still very active monastery was built in 1413. Its striking red halls often bustle with priests and pilgrims. You may also come upon a *tàijíquán* class practicing on one of the open terraces. Famous among its relics is a series of statues of Zhēnwǔ at various stages of his life.

The most dramatic of the existing temples, **Nányán Gōng (Southern Cliff Palace),** is built into the side of a sheer cliff, recalling Northern Héng Shān's Xuánkōng Sì—another Daoist temple that seems to defy gravity (p. 212). From Zǐxiāo Gōng, follow the trail up the mountain (southwest) to Wūyā Lǐng (about 2.5km/1½ miles); Nányán is just after Nántiān Mén. **Jīn Diàn (Golden Hall),** which sits on **Tiānzhù Fēng,** highest of Wǔdāng's 72 peaks (1,612m/1 mile high), is part of the 15th-century **Tàihé Gōng (Palace of Supreme Harmony)** complex. Its two-tiered roof, covered in gilded bronze, is, naturally, best viewed on a clear day when it sparkles. To reach Jīn Diàn from Nányán Gōng, continue up the path to Huánglóng Dòng (Yellow Dragon

Cave). From here, both ascending paths lead to the Golden Hall. The steeper route is to the right through the three "Heaven Gates."

Admission to the scenic area is ¥130 ($16); the fee includes admission to the mountain, transportation from the entrance to main temples, and entrance to all but three of the temples, which may be visited for an extra ¥10 ($1.25) each. Check your ticket to determine which temples require the extra fee.

WHERE TO STAY & DINE

The best two places to stay are on the mountain near Tiānzhù Peak. **Tàihé Gōng** offers very basic accommodations in their **Daoist Association Hostel (Dàojiào Xiéhuì Zhāodàisuǒ).** The cost of ¥200 ($10) for two includes a room with twin beds, shared bathroom, and limited hot water. The **Jīndǐng Lǚguǎn,** just below the Jīn Diàn, has comparable accommodations at similar rates. Both are clean and have restaurants. The **Jīnguì Jiǔdiàn** just down the hill from the Wǔyā Lǐng parking lot is basic and satisfactory, and costs ¥280 ($34) for a standard room, with discounts of up to 40% available. None of the hotels in Wǔdāng Shān have the charm, views, or quiet of the mountain. The **Wǔdāng Shān Bīnguǎn** (Wǔdāng Shān Zhèn Yǒnglè Lù 33) is the most comfortable and cleanest. Furniture and bedspreads show wear, and the bathroom sink is a bit dingy but acceptable. There's a Chinese restaurant on the premises. The price of a standard room ranges from ¥120 to ¥200 ($15–$25).

12 Chángshā

Húnán Province, 1,419km (882 miles) SE of Chóngqìng, 707km (440 miles) N of Guǎngzhōu

Chángshā is another hazy, congested, modern Chinese city hurrying to divest itself of any architectural trace of its past. But it is the capital of Húnán Province and gateway to one of the Five Sacred Mountains of Daoism and the gorgeous scenic area of the World Heritage Site, Wǔ Líng Yuán. It is also home to one of the most exciting tomb collections in China—the Mǎwáng Duī, which dates from the Western Hàn dynasty.

The city itself—most often associated with Máo and the model worker Léi Fēng—receives few foreign tourists. While Western visitors are fairly common, most come here not to see sights, but to research dissertations or adopt babies from Chángshā's orphanage. In the international hotels, it's not unusual to see a large table of wide-eyed European couples, each cradling a new Chinese baby girl.

ESSENTIALS

GETTING THERE   The **Chángshā Airport** is 34km (21 miles) east of town. Destinations include Běijīng (six or more flights daily); Guǎngzhōu (five flights daily); Hong Kong (irregular); Kūnmíng (six flights daily); Chéngdū (four flights daily); Shànghǎi (five or more flights daily); and Xī'ān (two or three flights daily). An **airport shuttle** from Mínháng Dàjiǔdiàn (Mínháng Hotel) at Wǔyī Dà Dào 5 (cross street Cháoyáng Lù) (© **0731/417-0288**) takes about 40 minutes and costs ¥15 ($1.85); it departs the hotel every half-hour. A taxi to the airport is around ¥100 ($13). **Chángshā Huǒchēzhàn (Chángshā Railway Station)** is at the east end of Wǔyī Dà Dào. The city is on the Běijīng–Guǎngzhōu railway line. Major connections include Běijīng (T1, T2; 15½ hr.; hard sleeper ¥345/$43); Guǎngzhōu (5361, 5362; 10½ hr.; hard sleeper ¥108/$13); and Kūnmíng (T61, T62; 24 hr.; hard sleeper ¥207/$26). Chángshā has three main **bus stations: Qìchē Nán Zhàn (South Station), Qìchē Dōng Zhàn (East Station),** and **Qìchē Xī Zhàn (West Station).** Buses to Nán Yuè

Héng Shān, Sháo Shān, Xiàmén, and Guìlín leave from the South Station. Buses to Hànkǒu (Wǔhàn), Guǎngzhōu, and Nánjīng leave from the East Station. Buses to Zhāng Jiā Jiè and Yíchāng leave from the West Station.

GETTING AROUND   Air-conditioned **public buses** cost ¥2 (25¢); non-air-conditioned buses cost ¥1 (15¢). Standard **taxi** rates are ¥8 ($1) for 3km (2 miles), then ¥1.80 (20¢) per kilometer up to 10km (6 miles). Beyond that, add 50% per kilometer.

FAST FACTS

Banks, Foreign Exchange & ATMs   The main **Bank of China** is at Fúróng Lù 593, near Bā Yī Qiáo (8-1 Bridge) and opposite Carrefour. It has full foreign-exchange services Monday through Friday from 8:30am to noon and 2 to 5pm, and an ATM. It also gives cash advances on credit cards. There's an **ATM** in the lobby of Huátiān Dàjiǔdiàn.

Internet Access   Internet cafes are fairly prolific between along the stretch of Zhongshan Lù, near the corner of Huangguang Lù, conveniently located to most of the hotels listed in this section. Alternately Shān Nán Lù, near Húnán University, has inexpensive Internet cafes on every block, but getting there requires crossing the Xiāng River. Dial-ups are ⓒ **163,** 165, or 169.

Post Office   The main post office is on the east side of the pedestrian block of Huángxìng Lù. Another is just north of the railway on Zhōng Běi Lù. It's open from 8am to noon and 2:30 to 5:30pm.

EXPLORING CHÁNGSHĀ

"Watered by the Yangtze and the Hàn, Chǔ is a land of lakes and rivers, of well-forested mountains. . . . The people live on fish and rice. Because there is always enough to eat, they are a lazy and improvident folk. . . . They believe in the power of shamans and spirits and are much addicted to lewd religious rites."
                    —1st-century historian Bān Gǔ concluding his survey of Chǔ history.

Húnán Shěng Bówùguǎn (Húnán Provincial Museum) ⚔   Between 1972 and 1974, the family plot of the chancellor to the prince of Chángshā (which was in the Chǔ Kingdom) was excavated at **Mǎwáng Duī** in the eastern suburbs of Chángshā. Of the three tombs—one each for the husband, wife, and son—only wife Xīn Zhuī's tomb was left undisturbed. Inside her tomb and her son's tomb (the chancellor's was looted) were thousands of funeral objects and hitherto lost classics copied on silk. Among them are the earliest known text of the Zhōu *Book of Changes* and two important versions of the *Dàodé Jīng (The Lǎozǐ)*. But the bulk of the manuscripts concern the quest for immortality through meditation, exercises, sexual practices, drugs, and alchemy. These rare records attesting to one family's search for the Dào are invaluable for what they reveal about the actual practice of religion in the early Hàn dynasty.

Perhaps the most astonishing object discovered in the tombs was the well-preserved corpse of Xīn Zhuī herself—who, after all, did achieve immortality of a kind. At the time of her death, she was 50 years old, stood 1.5m (5 ft.) tall, and weighed 75 pounds. She suffered from a variety of illnesses and ailments that included tuberculosis, hardening of the arteries, and lead poisoning; and her death was probably from a heart attack induced by an acute episode of gallstones. Reading her litany of ailments and looking at the intact corpse, it would appear that 50 years of life took a far greater toll on her body than did 2,100 years of death.

A massive renovation of the museum was completed in 2005, including the completion of a new wing for temporary exhibitions. As well, English guides are now available if you book in advance; call ⓒ **0731/451-3123.**

Chángshā

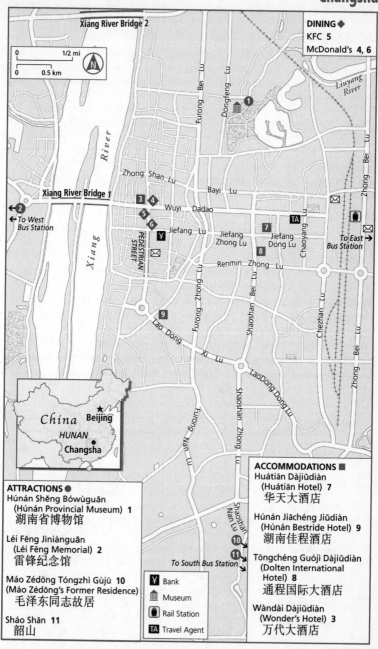

Xiang River Bridge 2

0   1/2 mi
0   0.5 km

DINING◆
KFC **5**
McDonald's **4, 6**

Liuyang River

Xiang River

Furong Bei Lu

Dongfeng Lu

Zhong Shan Lu

Bayi Lu

Xiang River Bridge 1

← **2**
← *To West Bus Station*

Wuyi Dadao

Jiefang Lu

Jiefang Zhong Lu

Jiefang Dong Lu

Chaoyang Lu

Zhong Bei Lu

To East Bus Station

PEDESTRIAN STREET

Renmin Zhong Lu

Furong Zhong Lu

Shaoshan Bei Lu

Chezhan Lu

Zhong Bei Lu

Lao Dong

9

Lao Dong Xi Lu

LaoDong Dong Lu

Shaoshan Zhong Lu

Furong Nan Lu

Shaoshan Nan Lu

10
11

To South Bus Station

China
★ Beijing
HUNAN
● Changsha

ATTRACTIONS ●

Húnán Shěng Bówùguǎn
(Húnán Provincial Museum) **1**
湖南省博物馆

Léi Fēng Jìniànguǎn
(Léi Fēng Memorial) **2**
雷锋纪念馆

Máo Zédōng Tóngzhì Gùjū **10**
(Máo Zédōng's Former Residence)
毛泽东同志故居

Sháo Shān **11**
韶山

¥   Bank
🏛   Museum
Ⓡ   Rail Station
TA   Travel Agent

ACCOMMODATIONS ■

Huátiān Dàjiǔdiàn
(Huátiān Hotel) **7**
华天大酒店

Húnán Jiāchéng Jiǔdiàn
(Húnán Bestride Hotel) **9**
湖南佳程酒店

Tōngchéng Guójì Dàjiǔdiàn
(Dolten International Hotel) **8**
通程国际大酒店

Wàndài Dàjiǔdiàn
(Wonder's Hotel) **3**
万代大酒店

Dōngfēng Lù 28. ✆ 0731/451-4630. Admission: Main exhibition ¥50 ($6); temporary exhibition ¥30 ($3.60). July–Sept Mon–Sat 8am–7pm; Oct–June Mon–Sat 8am–5:30pm. Sun and holidays 8:30am–6pm. (Hours will change with the new museum.) Last ticket sold 45 min. before closing. Bus: no. 113 or 303.

Léi Fēng Jìniànguǎn (Léi Fēng Memorial)   Those looking for a trace of Máo's China will find it here. The selfless soldier whose only ambition was to be "a little screw that would never rust in the revolutionary machinery" ended up getting a whole memorial to himself, not to mention the Léi Fēng Hospital, the Léi Fēng Hotel, and the big statue of Léi Fēng that flanks the street to the museum. Unfortunately, there are no English signs in this monument to a past era, but much of the collection is self-explanatory. It includes propaganda posters that trace the life of Léi Fēng and his family members, some obviously retouched photographs, and a number of Léi Fēng's personal effects. Give yourself about 45 minutes to an hour here.

Léi Fēng Zhèn 9, across Xiāng River, about 10km (6 miles) beyond the West Bus Station. ✆ 0731/810-7918. Admission ¥16 ($2). 8am–6pm. Bus: no. 12 or 15 to terminus; museum is a short walk north.

SHÁO SHĀN

In 1893, Máo Zédōng was born in this village 98km (60 miles) south of Chángshā. Beginning with the frenzied early years of the Cultural Revolution (1966–76) and continuing into the early 1990s, Sháo Shān was a mecca of sorts to millions of Chinese who made the pilgrimage here for reasons that changed over the years—from revolutionary zeal to coercion to, finally, nostalgia. Today the crowds have thinned out considerably, though they increase on holidays and on Máo's birthday, December 6. The sights include the house Máo grew up in, a memorial exhibition, the Máo Library, and the family ancestral home, but the latter two will be of little interest without knowledge of written Chinese. This is an easy day trip from Chángshā.

Máo Zédōng Tóngzhì Gùjū (Comrade Máo Zédōng's Former Residence)   Best of the two main sights, Máo's former home doesn't look that different from some

---

Máo's Roots

Máo's father was a poor peasant compelled out of poverty to join the army. Years later he returned to Sháo Shān with ambitions of bettering his lot. When Máo was born, his father owned 15 hectares (37 acres) of land and was a "middle peasant." By the time Máo was a teenager, his father had 22 hectares (55 acres) and the status of "rich peasant." Máo spent his childhood in Sháo Shān working in his father's rice paddies and, from age 8, studying the Confucian *Analects* and *The Five Classics*—meaning the most modern of his textbooks (the *Analects*) was from the 3rd century B.C.

In his interviews with Edgar Snow, Máo described a strict upbringing by a father he perceived as oppressive. What isn't often mentioned is that his mother was a devout Buddhist who raised her children in the religion. It wasn't until Máo broadened his reading that he lost his religious faith. Though Máo's family never went hungry, it was in Sháo Shān that he witnessed famine and the oppression of the poor. He claimed that such incidences and a natural rebelliousness inclined him toward revolution.

of the present farmhouses in Húnán and Sìchuān. The spartan but attractive brick buildings with curved wooden shingles have signs in Chinese and English that identify each room and contain a variety of intriguing implements, such as a large wok in the kitchen, grain-milling bowls, and equipment for hulling rice. Photos of Máo's family grace the walls. The barn is part of the house, and the bedroom of Máo's brother, Zétán, is right next to the pig pen. Give yourself 45 minutes to see the house and stroll the bucolic grounds.

Free admission. 8am–5pm. Buses (Iveco) between Chángshā's South Station (Nán Zhàn) and Sháo Shān leave both places every half-hour 8am–5pm for ¥24 ($3); the ride takes 1 hr. 40 min. The ride from Sháo Shān Bus Station to Máo's old home is 6km (3¾ miles). By motorcycle the trip costs ¥5 (65¢); by bus ¥1 (15¢).

Sháo Shān Máo Zédōng Tóngzhì Jìniànguǎn (Sháo Shān Máo Zédōng Museum)   Built in 2003, the highlight of the museum is undoubtedly the third-floor collection of items used by Máo during his life. The museum replaces a more extensive, stand-alone exhibition of Máo's personal items that was on the same site, but it still offers an interesting insight into the idiosyncrasies of the Great Helmsman, such as the bed that permanently slants to one side. The rest of the exhibition is concerned with Máo's exploits until liberation.

Admission ¥30 ($3.50). Summer 7:30am–5:30pm; winter 8am–5pm. From Máo's former residence, follow the path past the souvenir stands; to the left is the gravesite of Máo's parents; turn right and walk through long, narrow, dank tunnel. At the end go up to the right (pond on your left); at bottom of drive, Máo Library will be to the left; walk to street and turn right, then left through parking lot.

WHERE TO STAY
EXPENSIVE

Huátiān Dàjiǔdiàn   This newly renovated and upgraded (to five-star) hotel is Chángshā's biggest and most luxurious. It's also one of the most expensive, but with the 40%-to-50% discounts that are standard here, the rates become reasonable. Conformity usually defines hotel design in China, but the bold-colored fresco behind the reception counter of this hotel sets a tone of originality that carries throughout. For example, on the way to the elevator, guests cross a glass bridge that spans a fishpond full of goldfish. The guest rooms, too, have original touches. Bathroom sinks look like elegant glass bowls. In plusher rooms, a walk-in closet connects with both the bathroom and the bedroom. Business suites have huge bathrooms with bidets and very attractive separate shower and tub.

Jiěfàng Dōng Lù 300. ⓒ 0731/444-2888. Fax 0731/444-2270. www.huatian-hotel.com. 660 units. ¥660–¥780 ($82–$97) standard room; ¥1,080–¥1,380 ($135–$172) suite. Rates include breakfast. 40%–50% discount is standard. AE, DC, MC, V. Bus: no. 7 or 12 from railway. **Amenities:** 4 restaurants; bar; indoor pool; health club, airline, train, and bus ticketing; business center; forex; ATM; 24-hr. room service; dry cleaning/laundry. *In room:* A/C, satellite TV, dataport, broadband Internet access, minibar, fridge, hair dryer, safe.

Húnán Jiāchéng Jiǔdiàn (Húnán Bestride Hotel)   The competent staff and management of this midsize, Hong Kong–managed hotel go out of their way to make guests feel comfortable and appreciated. While it lacks some of the facilities of a five-star hotel, such as a pool and full-scale gym, the hotel is one of the best in town in terms of service, furnishings, upkeep, and comfort. Guest rooms were renovated in 2001 and still look well maintained. The rooms are airy and clean and have views of the city, which by night are stunning. The Chinese restaurant on the fourth floor serves outstanding food.

Láodòng Xī Lù 386. ⓒ 0731/511-8888. Fax 0731/511-1888. www.hnbrhotel.com. 238 units. ¥580–¥820 ($70–$99) standard room; ¥1,080–¥1,480 ($170–$208) suite. Rates include breakfast. 35%–50% discount is standard. 15%

service charge. AE, DC, MC, V. Bus: no. 139 from railway, 202, or 314. **Amenities:** 4 restaurants; 2 bars; spa; airline, train, and bus ticketing; business center; forex; 24-hr. room service; therapeutic massage; dry cleaning/laundry. *In room:* A/C, TV w/pay movies, broadband Internet access, minibar, fridge, hair dryer, safe.

Tōngchéng Guójì Dàjiǔdiàn (Dolten International Hotel) This popular hotel competes with the Huátiān for the title of Chángshā's plushest; yet despite its recent renovations late in 2004 it still comes in second. The guest rooms are spacious, the bedspreads and furnishings are tasteful. Service is efficient and this staff is friendly and professional—nothing is missing here. But there's nothing extra, either. The Dolten is a standard five-star hotel, and for that it can be counted on.

Sháo Shān Běi Lù 159. **℡** 0731/416-8888. Fax 0731/412-6688. www.dolton-hotel.com. 450 units. ¥918–¥1,118 ($115–$140) standard room; ¥1,380–¥1,688 ($170–$208) suite. Rates include breakfast. 35% discount is standard. 15% service charge. AE, DC, MC, V. Bus: no. 7 or 139 from railway. **Amenities:** 2 restaurants; 3 bars; gym; indoor pool; airline, train, and bus ticketing; business center; forex; 24-hr. room service; dry cleaning/laundry. *In room:* A/C, satellite TV, dataport, broadband Internet access, safe, minibar, fridge, hair dryer.

MODERATE

Wàndài Dàjiǔdiàn This pleasant four-star hotel, which opened in 2002, occupies floors 7 to 15 in an office building. Guest rooms frame the indoor garden plaza, but the best views are on the east side, overlooking Wǔyī Square, and on the west side, facing the river. Each standard room is clean and comfortable, with a Japanese-inspired wooden screen between the bed and the living area that gives the illusion of two rooms.

Huángxìng Zhōng Lù 101 (at Wǔyī Dà Dào; reception on 7th floor). **℡** 0731/488-2333. Fax 0731/488-2111. 321 units. ¥328–¥428 ($41–$53) standard room; ¥1,280–¥2,800 ($160–$350) suite. Rates include breakfast. 15%–20% discount is standard. AE, DC, MC, V. Bus: no. 132 from railway to Wǔyī Guǎngchǎng stop. **Amenities:** 2 restaurants; bar; exercise room; airline, train, and bus ticketing; business center; limited forex; 24-hr. room service; dry cleaning/laundry. *In room:* A/C, TV, dataport, hair dryer.

WHERE TO DINE

In the vicinity of Wǔyī Lù and Huángxìng Zhōng Lù, there's a **KFC** on the southwest corner of that intersection. A large **McDonald's** is on the northeast corner of Wǔyī Guǎngchǎng; in fact, McDonald's has reached near saturation point in Chángshā, making it all too easy to get your fix. A **Pizza Hut** has also appeared on Huángxìng Lù between Zhōngshān Lù and Jiěfàng Lù. The **Shénnóng Dàjiǔdiàn (Grand Sun City Hotel) coffee shop** and **City Pub** both serve plausible Western fare.

Xiāng Garden HÚNÁN The head chef of this fine restaurant on the fourth floor of the Bestride Hotel (Jiāchéng Jiǔdiàn) was once a chef in China's embassy in Germany. Here his kitchen puts out perfectly executed dishes that are beautifully presented and delicious. A few of the delicacies are *língjiǎo* (water chestnuts); *hóng zǎozi* (red dates); *qiàng qíncài xiàguǒ* (baby celery and pearl onions sautéed with macadamia nuts); *qīngjiāo qiézi* (eggplant sautéed with green pepper); and *mǐtāng sīguā* (rice soup with silk gourd).

Láodòng Xī Lù 386, Jiāchéng Jiǔdiàn (Bestride Hotel), 3rd floor. **℡** 0731/511-8888. Meal for 2 ¥50–¥160 ($6–$20). AE, DC, MC, V. 11:30am–3pm and 5–11pm. Bus: no. 139 from railway, 202, or 314.

13 Nán Yuè Héng Shān

Húnán Province, 137km (85 miles) S of Chángshā

> *"Those who mix medicines, who are avoiding political turmoil, or who seek quietude in order to practice the Way, have always gone into the mountains."*
> —*from* The Master Who Embraces Simplicity, *Gé Hóng (283–343)*

Located on the southwestern bank of the Xiāng River in the middle of Húnán Province, Nán Yuè Héng Shān—known locally as Nán Yuè (Southern Mountain) *or* Héng Shān—is one of the five sacred peaks (symbolizing the four directions and the center) of Daoism. It was believed that these peaks were supernatural channels connecting heaven and earth. For Daoists, mountains were the sites where *qì* (cosmic energy) was at its most refined; herbs and minerals—the ingredients of health and longevity elixirs—were found on mountains; and it was on mountains and in mountain caverns that seekers were most likely to find transcendent beings.

As far back as the 6th century, Nán Yuè was also a place of Buddhist worship; and it is the birthplace of the Nán Yuè school of Southern Chán (Zen) Buddhism, which got its start here in the 8th century.

Late summer and fall are the best times to visit. Locals warn visitors to resist the temptation of shortcuts on overgrown and little-used paths, where you're likely to encounter snakes.

ESSENTIALS

GETTING THERE   Direct **buses** (Iveco or Turbo) depart from Chángshā's South Bus Station every half-hour from 6:30am to 6pm for the 2¼-hour drive; the fare is ¥38 ($4.50). Buses leave the station when they're full. Return buses leave every 20 minutes from the same drop-off point in the town of Nán Yuè. If you take an early bus, it is possible to make this a day trip. You'll have time to enjoy the mountain and its temples if you combine hiking with cable car, bus, or motorcycle taxi. A **train** also runs between Chángshā and Nán Yuè Railway Station, but the trip takes 3 hours, plus another 30 to 40 minutes from the railway station to the town of Nán Yuè.

GETTING AROUND   The bus from Chángshā drops passengers off at the south end of town. To get to the mountain, walk north on the same road (Zhùróng Lù). The memorial archway *(páifang)* is straight ahead. Inside the archway, **minibuses** take passengers to the entrance for ¥1 (15¢). If the bus is slow to fill up, you can pay a bit more to be taxied there alone. Price is negotiable, but ¥5 (65¢) is about right. The distance is 1.5km (just under a mile). The **mountain park entrance** is at the north end of the village. Admission is ¥80 ($5) and covers entrance to all the sites and temples on the mountain. **Buses** charging ¥12 ($1.40) to the midsection of the mountain depart every 10 minutes from the park entrance. Another bus for ¥10 ($1.30) from the midway station goes to the top. A mile-long **cable car** also operates from the midway point. The ride to **Nántiān Mén,** three-quarters of the way to the summit, takes 7 minutes; the round-trip costs ¥100 ($13). From Nántiān Mén, **minibuses** go to the summit. The footpath from bottom to top is 14km (9 miles) long and takes about 4 hours to walk at a comfortable but steady clip. Private drivers with motorcycles take people to the summit for around ¥50 ($6).

NÁN YUÈ SIGHTS

The best preserved and most famous of the mountain temples is **Nán Yuè Dà Miào** at the southern foot of the mountain. Originally built in the Táng dynasty (618–907), it was destroyed by fire a number of times. The present temple dates to the Qīng dynasty (1644–1911). The main hall is noteworthy for its double roof, which is supported by 72 columns representing the inevitable 72 peaks of Nán Yuè. Halfway up the mountain, past the cable car entrance, is the Daoist monastery Xuándū Guàn. Here, worshippers light firecrackers, kowtow in front of the white marble statues of three Daoist Celestial Masters, or cast their fortunes by throwing two halves of a wooden oval on the ground. Eleven Daoist priests live in this monastery. Lodging is available for up to 3 days here. There is also a vegetarian restaurant.

Daoist and Buddhist monasteries and temples are scattered over the mountain. Most are small and worth a peek, but they don't need lots of time. **Zhùróng Hall** is at Nán Yuè's highest peak, **Zhùróng Fēng** (1,290m/4,232 ft.), where the views are magnificent.

WHERE TO STAY & DINE

Lodging can be found at the summit near Zhùróng Diàn and midway up the mountain just above the bus parking lot, in the vicinity of the cable car. Directly opposite the Xuándū Guàn (Xuándū Monastery) is the **Bàn Shān Tíng Shānzhuāng (Bàn Shān Tíng Mountain Inn; ℂ 0734/567-6239)**. Rooms are basic but very clean, and those on the south side have views of the mountain. The front-desk and kitchen staffs are friendly and eager to make guests comfortable. Guest rooms have private bathrooms, 24-hour hot water, and TV. A standard room costs ¥208 ($26); a room with older furniture and fixtures costs ¥148 ($18). Forty-percent discounts are standard, even in high season, but not during holidays.

The best accommodations on the mountain are at the **Cáifù Mountain Villa (Cáifù Shānzhuāng)**, built in 2000. To date, its primary claim to fame is that Jiāng Zémín stayed here while visiting the mountain in 2003. With the unimaginatively furnished standard rooms going for ¥998 ($121), even with its standard 20% to 30% discounts, Cáifù Mountain is no bargain—but it does offer the most comfortable stay on the mountain by far.

At the summit, the **Fúróng Shānzhuāng (ℂ 0734/566-3013)** has clean standard rooms with stunning views for ¥280 ($34). Discounts of 40% to 50% are often available. There is no air-conditioning, but electric blankets are available to take the chill off during winter.

In the summertime, it is also possible to stay in monasteries on the mountain for only a few dollars.

All of the inns on the mountain have small dining rooms and kitchens. Since there are no English menus, you may have to go to the kitchen and point to your order. Settle on a price in advance or you may end up getting the most expensive dish on the menu—or the largest serving. On average, each dish should cost about ¥5 to ¥10 (65¢–$1.25). In town, Dēng Shān Lù, running from the memorial archway through the center of town, has lots of restaurants serving local food.

14 Wǔ Líng Yuán/ Zhāng Jiā Jiè ⊛

Húnán Province, 269km (167 miles) NW of Chángshā, 480km (298 miles) SW of Wǔhàn

"O soul, go not to the south! In the south are a hundred leagues of flaming fire and coiling cobras; the mountains rise sheer and steep; tigers and leopards slink; the cow-fish is there, and the spit-sand, and the rearing python. O soul, go not to the south! There are monsters there that will harm you."
—*from the 3rd-century poem "Great Summons,"* Songs of Chŭ

Wǔ Líng Yuán's landscape might well have inspired the shamanistic poems of the classic collection *Songs of Chŭ*. Unlike most famous sights in China, the area remained remote and little visited until relatively late. To the ancients, that part of northwestern Húnán (at the southern periphery of the Chŭ Kingdom) was an inhospitable wilderness—mountainous terrain populated by wild animals. And unlike the sacred Buddhist and Daoist mountains, it did not draw pilgrims.

But that's all changed. Wǔ Líng Yuán Scenic and Historic Interest Area (also called Zhāng Jiā Jiè) became China's first National Forest Park in 1983, and in 1992, its core zone was inscribed as a World Heritage Site. Prior to that, whatever damage humans inadvertently spared this wild region over the centuries, they undid in a few decades of poaching, land clearing, tree felling, and polluting. Despite that, the natural beauty of the region—dominated by quartzite sandstone peaks and pillars—remains stunning and unusual; and opportunities to see rare plants and insects in this dense, subtropical forest still abound. What's more, restrictions on construction and pollution, as well as a total fire ban, are just a few of the measures now in place to protect this singular environment.

ESSENTIALS

GETTING THERE   Chángshā is the gateway city to Zhāng Jiā Jiè. In early 2005, train travel was faster and more convenient than the bus, but that should change with a new expressway slated for completion by the end of 2005. **Héhuā Airport** is 5km (3 miles) from Zhāng Jiā Jiè City (formerly called Dàyōng) and 37km (23 miles) from Zhāng Jiā Jiè National Forest Park. It has flights connecting with many major cities in China, including Běijīng, Shànghǎi, Guǎngzhōu, and Wǔhàn. It also has air service from Hong Kong. If you arrive by plane, there's no reason to bother with charmless Zhāng Jiā Jiè City (Zhāng Jiā Jiè Shì). Go directly to **Zhāng Jiā Jiè Village (Zhāng Jiā Jiè Cūn),** which is located just outside the entrance to the national park. By taxi, it's ¥70 ($8.75).

The **Zhāng Jiā Jiè Railway Station** is 8km (5 miles) southeast of town. Short of flying, the overnight train from Chángshā is the most comfortable choice. The K525/K528 leaves Chángshā at 7:28pm and arrives in Zhāng Jiā Jiè City the next morning at 9:35am; the K526/527 leaves Zhāng Jiā Jiè City at 5:05pm and arrives in Chángshā at 6:49am the next morning. Hard and soft sleepers cost ¥150 to ¥240 ($19–$30). The express K552/553, leaving Chángshā at 8:20am and arriving in Zhāng Jiā Jiè City at 2pm, is also convenient, though the return train (K554/551), with an evening arrival of 8:31pm, is less so. The railway station is also 45km (28 miles) southeast of Zhāng Jiā Jiè Village, which is at the main park entrance and is the best place to find lodging. As you exit the station, taxi drivers, porters, and kids selling maps will pounce, but just keep walking. A bus from the railway station to Zhāng Jiā Jiè Village departs from the square when it's full (an hour-plus wait sometimes). An alternative is a bus for ¥1 (15¢) leaving from the middle of the railway square to the bus station in town. From there, catch one of the many buses for the 1-hour trip to the village; the fare is ¥6 (75¢). Or you can take a taxi directly to Zhāng Jiā Jiè Cūn (Village) for about ¥90 ($11). As you exit, go to the **taxi stand** at the left end of the railway square. Taxi rates are ¥5 (65¢) for 3km (2 miles), then ¥1.50 (20¢) per kilometer. After 10km (6 miles), add 50% per kilometer.

By the time you read this the new expressway between Chángshā and Zhāng Jiā Jiè should be open, cutting the current 7-hour bus ride (at minimum) to 3½ hours. (At the time of writing, however, the train was still the superior option for comfort and convenience.) Bus fare at time of writing was ¥83 ($10) and three buses traveled each way at 6am, 10am, and 1pm, departing Chángshā from the terminal opposite the railway station.

GETTING AROUND   Vehicular and hiking paths provide access to some 240 designated scenic spots within Wǔ Líng Yuán. The scenic area comprises the three adjoining parklands of **Zhāng Jiā Jiè National Forest Park** to the south, **Tiānzǐ Shān Nature Reserve** to the north, and **Suǒ Xī Yù Nature Reserve** to the east. **Cable cars** for ¥48 ($6) lead to viewing platforms from Huángshí Zhài in the Zhāng Jiā Jiè forest area and from the eastern edge of Tiānzǐ Shān. A local **bus** connects Suǒ Xī Yù Village, located at the southeast entrance to the park, and Zhāng Jiā Jiè City Bus Station. The 32km (20-mile) trip costs ¥5 (65¢). Once inside the park, free buses will take you between designated stops, allowing you the freedom to alternate between walking and taking a ride.

In terms of lodging and proximity to the most sights, **Zhāng Jiā Jiè Village** makes the best base. The village has one main street, Jīnbiān Dà Dào , which is lined with hotels and leads to the National Forest Park entrance. As you approach the park, you'll see a small street to the left; it leads to the Xiāngdiàn Mountain Villa and a few restaurants and Internet cafes.

TOURS   For most of the sightseeing within the park, there's no need for a guide. But you must join a tour to go river rafting or to visit Huánglóng Cave (Huánglóng Dòng) in Suǒ Xī Yù. These can be organized by **Zhāng Jiā Jiè National Forest Park Travel Service,** which is conveniently located and much more customer-oriented than the CITS branches in either Zhāng Jiā Jiè City or Village. Their office is in Zhāng Jiā Jiè City and they are willing to either meet you at the train, or come out to the park (© 0744/822-7088; fax 0744/822-8488).

The freelance guides near the park entrance charge considerably less than the travel agencies, but you need to bargain. Price depends on the season and where you go, but generally, the asking price for an English-speaking guide starts at ¥100 ($13) a day. Be sure the person you hire has a guide's license; otherwise, you'll have to pay their entry fee.

HIKING   Exploring the mountain means following stone paths through spectacular forests of bamboo, oak, and pine to scenic spots and terraces that afford breathtaking views. Since every tour group takes these paths, you won't be alone, but the crowds can be part of the fun. For solitude, take the less-traveled paths, where the setting and scenery can be as dramatic as the popular sights. Admission is ¥245 ($30), good for 2 days.

FAST FACTS
Internet Access   Zhāng Jiā Jiè Village has several Internet cafes on the side street near the park. Turn left off the main street just before the park. The cafes usually charge ¥2 (25¢) per hour. Dial-up is © 163.

TOP SPOTS IN THE THREE PARKLANDS
In Zhāng Jiā Jiè National Forest Park: Huángshí Zhài. At the first fork after the entrance to the park, take the left road; hike 2 hours to this former mountain stronghold that is 1,080m (4,542 ft.) high and affords a panoramic view of forested peaks and jagged sandstone pillars. A cable car also goes to the plateau (see "Getting Around," above). Another path that leads through beautiful jade-green forest and passes a tight cluster of sandstone columns is reached by taking the right road at the first fork. Follow the path along Jīnbiān Stream. At the next fork, either take the left to Míhún Tái (and return the same way), or take the more traveled right-hand path to Zǐcǎo Tán. From there, take the right-hand path at the next two forks to return to the entrance.

In Tiānzǐ Shān Nature Reserve: Located just southeast of the cable car platform at Tiānzǐ Shān, **Yùbǐ Fēng** and **Tiānzǐ Gé** are two of the most famous spots for their imposing views of forested peaks and jutting sandstone pillars.

In Suǒ Xī Yù Nature Reserve: Bǎofēng Hú (Bǎofēng Lake). A boat ride on this lovely clear lake surrounded by lush forest is included in the admission fee of ¥62 ($7.75).

Huánglóng Dòng (Huánglóng Cave): The colored lights that illuminate famous Chinese caves are an acquired taste, but they shouldn't get in the way of appreciating this 11km-long (7-mile) cave that contains spectacular calcite deposits as well as a waterfall 50m (164 ft.) high. Entrance is ¥65 ($8) A guide is required (see "Tours," above). Most hotels can also arrange a guide.

WHERE TO STAY

In Zhāng Jiā Jiè City, the only four-star hotel is the **Dragon International Hotel (Xiānglóng Guójì Dàjiǔdiàn),** Jiěfàng Lù 46 (© **0744/571-2999;** fax 0744/571-2266). Standard rooms are ¥630 ($75). Although the Dragon is the best the town has to offer, it doesn't deserve its rating—for facilities or services—but the rooms are clean. Hotels in Zhāng Jiā Jiè Village are attractive and close to the park, and room rates are the most reasonable in the area.

Pípa Xī Bīnguǎn   This hotel and the Xiāngdiàn Mountain Villa are the best in Zhāng Jiā Jiè Village. The majority of guests are with tour groups, and at holidays it's been so full here that latecomers have had to sleep in the dining room and lobby. Rooms are clean but unadorned, and most have picture windows overlooking gardens and/or mountains. Some standard rooms have balconies. Buildings 1 and 2 were renovated in 2002; unrenovated building 3 should be your last choice. From the hotel, it's a 7-minute walk along the main street (Jīnbiān Dà Dào) to the park entrance. Manager Táng Míng speaks English and takes reservations on his mobile phone or by e-mail. Whether you call first or just turn up, do negotiate for a substantial discount.

Jīnbiān Dà Dào. © 137/0744-5536. www.pipaxi-hotel.com. 191 units. ¥548–¥648 ($67–$79) standard room. Rates include breakfast. 20% discounts. AE, DC, MC, V. **Amenities:** 2 restaurants; business center; limited forex; laundry. *In room:* A/C, TV, minibar, fridge, hair dryer.

Xiāngdiàn Shānzhuāng (Xiāngdiàn Mountain Villa) ⚐   Visiting dignitaries usually stay at the Pípa Xī Hotel (above), but that should change now that this hotel has upgraded to four-star. Rooms are simple, but pleasant and bright. Bathrooms combine tub and shower in a small, spotless space. The grounds have been beautifully landscaped and include lawns, a pond, and a pagoda; classical Chinese music plays faintly in the background—all to wonderful effect. Many of the rooms have close-up views of the mountains.

As you approach the park on the main street, turn left on the small lane just before you reach the park. The hotel is about 300m (984 ft.) ahead. © 0744/571-2266. Fax 0744/571-2172. 156 units. ¥400 ($50) standard room. Rates include breakfast. 20%–30% discounts. AE, DC, MC, V. **Amenities:** Restaurant; business center; limited forex; dry cleaning/laundry. *In room:* A/C, TV, minibar, fridge, hair dryer in some rooms, safe.

WHERE TO DINE

Zhāng Jiā Jiè City and Village, Tiānzǐ Shān, and Suǒ Xī Yù all have inexpensive restaurants featuring spicy Húnán dishes, but the food is not outstanding, nor are English-language menus available. Small restaurants serving Tǔjiā dishes can be found all along the main street of Zhāng Jiā Jiè Village. Tǔjiā cuisine specializes in fresh game (such as rabbit and various guinea-pig and weasel-like mammals), reptiles (including poisonous snakes), crayfish, eel, and crab, so if you're feeling adventurous, point to the creature that interests you, and they'll cook it for you. Settle on a price, first, though; these dishes can be expensive. The hotels have restaurants that are more accessible to foreign travelers, but the food is mediocre. The best I found was inside **Xiāngdiàn Shānzhuāng.** For a simple repast, on the main street about 150m (500 ft.) before the entrance to the park, across the stream, there's a row of small **noodle restaurants.** You can sit outside, watch the stream, and eat a bowl of noodles for under a dollar.

14

The Tibetan World

by Jen Lin-Liu

Less than half of the world's Tibetans reside in the **Tibetan Autonomous Region (TAR),** whose boundaries were established in 1965. Tibetans form the majority in large regions of neighboring Nepal, India, Sikkim, and Bhutan, as well as in the adjacent provinces of **Qīnghǎi, Gānsù, Sìchuān,** and **Yúnnán.** Disagreement over where Tibet begins and ends is an ongoing stumbling block in negotiations between the Tibetan government-in-exile, based in Dharamsala (in India), and the Chinese government.

For this guide, **Qīnghǎi** has been included, as it is part of the Tibetan plateau, and most of its area—which covers much of **Amdo** (northern Tibet) and **Kham** (eastern Tibet)—is culturally and ethnically Tibetan. In many ways a better destination than the TAR, it has yet to be overwhelmed by Hàn migration, and restrictions on both locals and travelers are less onerous.

Tibet became the "roof of the world" only recently, formed by the collision of the Indian subcontinent with the Eurasian landmass. Until 35 million years ago, the Himalayas formed the seabed of the Tethys Sea. Mollusks may still be found throughout the region.

Tibet is dominated by the vast, dry Tibetan plateau, a region roughly the size of western Europe, with an average elevation of 4,700m (15,400 ft.). Ringed by vast mountain ranges, such as the **Kūnlūn range** to the north and the **Himalayas** to the south, the plateau's west side features high plains, and the north is dominated by the deserts of the **Changtang** and the **Tsaidam Basin.** China's great rivers—the Yellow River and the Yángzǐ—rise in the east, carving out steep gorges. The greatest diversity in landscape, vegetation, and wildlife is found in the broad and fertile valleys of the Himalayas, but most of the border regions are closed to individual travel.

Most Tibetans still look back to the "heroic age" (7th–9th c.) of their history, when their armies dominated the Silk Routes and much of western China, assimilating the culture and technology of these regions. At the same time, Buddhism was introduced to Tibet from northern India. With the disappearance of Buddhism from India around the 13th century, Tibet became the new bearer of a complex faith, which combined a strict monastic code with Tantric Buddhism (with a strong emphasis on ritual). It is often characterized as "complete Buddhism."

The Tibetans went on to convert an entire people—the Mongols—despite being weakened by civil war and fighting between different schools of Tibetan Buddhism.

Just as China was often characterized as "closed" until it was "opened" by the West, the idea of Tibet as an inherently inward-looking Shangri-la is a longstanding myth. Isolationism was encouraged by the Manchu rulers from the 18th century onward, with some success. Regents backed by the Manchus held

Tips Dealing with Altitude Sickness

It's likely that you'll suffer from a headache and shortness of breath upon your arrival in Tibet—they are both common signs of altitude sickness. Other visitors have complained of sleeplessness, fatigue, and even vomiting. So take it easy, and let yourself get acclimated to the altitude your first days in Tibet, certainly before you venture to any higher altitudes. Altitude sickness pills called Diamox (acetazolamide) can also help; they can be taken a few hours before your arrival in Tibet. In Lhasa, you can pick up a Chinese medicine alternative called Hongjingpian at the local pharmacies. Oxygen canisters are available at most hotels, and there is also a doctor on duty 24 hours at the Lhasa Hotel in case you're really having trouble.

Most visitors to Tibet get through the trip with just a few minor symptoms, and cases of altitude sickness typically go away after a couple of days. There are a few danger signs, however, such as a deep liquidlike cough accompanied by a fever, that you should watch out for that may indicate your case is more serious. For more information, go to www.high-altitude-medicine.com.

---

sway over young Dalai Lamas who often died mysteriously before they were old enough to rule.

Dalai Lama XIII (1876–1934) tried to reverse the policy of isolation, but encountered resistance from the conservative monastic hierarchy. Troubled by the destruction of Mongolia by Russian Communists during the 1920s, he prophesied, "The officers of the state, ecclesiastical and secular, will find their lands seized and their other property confiscated, and they themselves forced to serve their enemies, or wander about the country as beggars do. All beings will be sunk in great hardship and in overpowering fear."

In 1951, Chinese Communist armies entered Lhasa, and the prophecy began to unfold. A revolt against Chinese rule rose in Kham (eastern Tibet) 5 years later, and Dalai Lama XIV (b. 1935) fled for India in March 1959, soon after the **Great Prayer (Monlam)** was celebrated in Lhasa. Tibet's darkest hour was the Cultural Revolution (1966–76), known to the Tibetans as the time when "the sky fell to earth." Monks and nuns were tortured, executed, and

imprisoned. Monasteries were looted and razed, and a vast body of Tibetan art was lost. Adding to the pain is the fact that many Tibetans, either willingly or coerced, participated in the destruction.

A revival of Tibetan culture and religion throughout the 1980s was checked after pro-independence protests, led by monks from **Drepung Monastery,** resulted in the declaration of martial law in March 1989, signed by chief of the local Communist Party Hú Jǐntāo, now president of China.

Travel in Tibet should not be taken lightly. There are wide variations in temperature throughout the day, and many visitors experience altitude sickness (see box below), particularly those who fly directly to Lhasa. The northern and western regions of Tibet are cold and arid, with an annual average temperature of about 32°F (0°C), while southern and eastern regions are warmer and wetter. Peak season runs from May to mid-October. Winter in Lhasa is cozy, but transport out can be difficult to arrange—the Friendship Highway from Nepal to Lhasa is effectively closed for the winter

Tibet

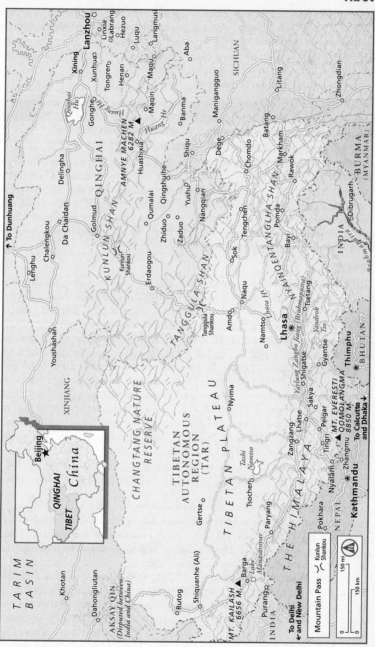

months. The last half of this chapter, from the section on Shiagtse onward, covers towns on the Friendship Highway, a loose way of describing the dusty road built from Lhasa, passing near the Himalayas and Mt. Everest, to the Nepali border. The trip has become a popular one among foreign travelers in recent years. *Note:* Unless otherwise noted, hours listed for attractions and restaurants are daily.

1 Xīníng

232km (144 miles) W of Lánzhōu, 781km (484 miles) E of Golmud. Altitude: 2,300m (7,544 ft.)

Once a key trading post on the southern Silk Route, Xīníng is perched on the northern edge of the Tibetan plateau and boasts a sizable Muslim population. Tibetan and Mongol monks and pilgrims may still be spied, drawn by **Kumbum (Tǎ'ěr Sì)** ✿ monastery to the south. A recent boom in the economy from the discovery of oil reserves and the city's attempt to market itself as a "summer resort" with its cooler than average temperatures has increased the supply of hotels and amenities the city has to offer. Still, there's little of interest in the city itself, but it's a useful base for exploring the **Amdo** and **Kham** regions to the south.

ESSENTIALS

GETTING THERE The **airport** is 29km (18 miles) east of Xīníng. An airport bus runs to the **CAAC** ticket office, Bāyī Lù 34 (© **0971/813-3333**). The bus trip from the airport takes a half-hour and costs ¥16 ($2). From the bus drop-off point, the Zhōngfǎyuán Bīnguǎn is a 15-minute walk west; or take bus no. 28 from Bāyī Lù to the railway and bus stations. CAAC delivers tickets free of charge. Oddly, discounts are possible during the peak season, but not in the off season. Other ticket offices are at the Qīnghǎi Bīnguǎn (© **0971/614-4888,** ext. 2473) and at the Wǔsì Dàjiē Shòupiào Chù (© **0971/612-2555**). There are flights to Běijīng, Shànghǎi, Lhasa, Kūnmíng, Ürümqi, Chéngdū, Dūnhuáng, Golmud, and Xī'ān.

The **railway station** (© **0971/719-2222**) is at the north end of town, at the junction of Jiànguó Lù and Hùzhù Xī Lù. Counters 1 to 5 are for normal ticket sales. Trains connect with Lánzhōu (3 hr.) at 12:12am (T654) and at 7:23pm (T656). Trains also connect with Běijīng (T152; 25 hr.) at 11:26am; Shànghǎi (K378; 33 hr.) at 8:49pm; Yínchuān (N902; 13 hr.) at 6:06pm; and Golmud (N909; 13 hr.) at 5:49pm. An express to Golmud (N903; 12 hr.) originates in Lánzhōu, passing through Xīníng at 9:46pm.

The railway station only sells tickets for the day of travel. You're better off purchasing tickets from the **Huǒchē Fēijī Shòupiào Chù** (open 8am–noon and 2–6pm) at Wǔsì Dàjiē 40 (© **0971/614-5555**). A ¥5 (60¢) commission is charged. Train tickets can be purchased up to 5 days in advance, and airline tickets are also sold. Take bus no. 9 from the railway station to Shāngyè Xiàng.

The **Long-Distance Bus Station** (© **0971/814-9611**) is just south of the railway station. Buses service Lánzhōu (5 hr.; ¥27/$3.40) every half-hour between 7am and 6:20pm; Tóngrén (4 hr.; ¥23/$2.90) roughly every hour between 7:30am and 5pm; Línxià via Xúnhuà (9 hr.; ¥37/$4.70) or via Liújiā Xiá (11 hr.; ¥36/$4.60) every 15 minutes between 7:15am and 9:15am; Hézuò (11 hr.; ¥43/$5.30) at 7:45am; Liújiā Xiá (3 hr.; ¥30/$3.80) at 10am, 10:30am, and 11am; Golmud (18 hr.; ¥80/¥85 [$10/$11] upper/lower berth) at 4pm—*take the train instead;* Tiānshuǐ (20 hr.; ¥105/$13)

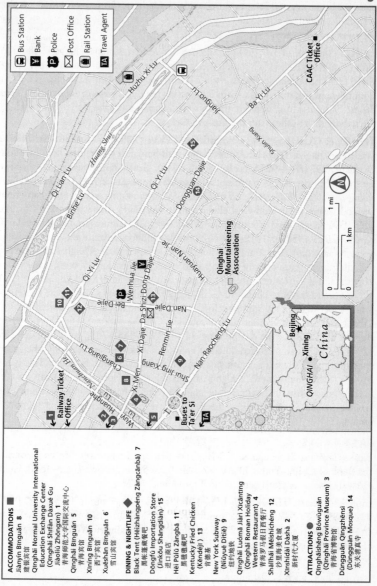

at 5pm and 6pm; Dūnhuáng (26 hr.; ¥164/¥189 [$21/$24] upper/lower berth) at 10:15am; Mǎqìn (14 hr.; ¥64/$8 seat, ¥90/$11 sleeper) at 7:30am (seat) and at 5 and 6pm (sleeper); Bānmǎ (26 hr.; ¥89/$11 seat, ¥125/$16 sleeper) at 9:45am; Yùshù (24 hr.; ¥94/$12 seat, ¥133/$17 sleeper) at 11am and 3pm (seat), and at 5 and 6pm (sleeper)—take the newer Nángqiān bus if you can; Nángqiān (30 hr.; ¥166/$21) on odd-numbered days at 5pm; and the wilds of Qūmálái (26 hr.; ¥100/$13 seat) on even-numbered days at 8:45am.

GETTING AROUND   Taxis come in two varieties. The Xiàlì taxi costs ¥6 (75¢) for 3km (2 miles), ¥1.10 (15¢) per kilometer thereafter. Santanas charge ¥7 (85¢) for 3km (2 miles), ¥1.20 (15¢) per kilometer thereafter. From 10pm to 5am they charge ¥1.40 (20¢) per kilometer. **Buses** require you to pop ¥1 (15¢) in a box. Bus no. 1 runs from the railway station to the main intersection *(dà shízi)*, passing the Bank of China. Bus no. 9 departs from opposite the railway station, passing the Hǎiyí Holiday Hotel, the railway ticket office, and the Boronia Cafe.

TOURS & GUIDES   The main office of **CITS** (© 0971/614-4888, ext. 2439) is inside the Qīnghǎi Bīnguǎn. A more competent branch is on the first floor of Xīníng Dàshà (© 0971/814-9254; fax 0971/812-9842). Get far more reliable info and service from the refreshingly professional **Qīnghǎi Mountaineering Association,** Tǐyù Xiàng 7 (© 0971/823-8922; fax 0971/823-8933; www.qma.org.cn; open 8am–noon and 2:30–6pm, May–mid-Oct; closed winter weekends). Take bus no. 33 to Nán Mén Tǐyùchǎng. Tashi Phuntsok of Wind Horse Adventure Tours (Jiěfàng Lu 4; © 0971/613-1358 or 1319-579-7628; www.windhorseadventuretours.com; windhorse@email.com) can arrange customized trekking trips in Qīnghǎi and the surrounding areas. He's a former monk who lived in India for 10 years, speaks great English, and is a great resource for any questions about Tibet and Qīnghǎi.

For onward travel to Lhasa, Air China has 2 flights per week during the winter and 3 flights per week in the summer. To buy such a plane ticket, you will need to buy a Tibet travel permit and "tour" unless you are a Chinese national. The **Tibet Tourism Bureau of Xīníng** at the Xīníng Bīnguǎn (© 0971/845-8701, ext. 2106, or 1389/725-9919; qxhotel@public.cn.qh.cn or xnhotel@sina.com) can help you arrange this annoying and costly bureaucratic nonsense. A permit and tour, both mandatory, cost ¥1,440 ($180) and include 3 nights' stay at the Kerry Hotel (Jírì Fàndiàn), a ramshackle guesthouse, in Lhasa, a tour guide for the sights, and transportation. After arriving in Lhasa and staying at the Kerry Hotel for 1 night, the rest of the tour is optional.

FAST FACTS

Banks, Foreign Exchange & ATMs   Traveler's checks and cash may be changed at the **Bank of China,** Yínmǎ Jiē 23 (Mon–Fri 9am–5pm; Sat–Sun 10am–4pm). Credit cards are also accepted. There are no international ATMs.

Internet Access   The 24-hour **Mǎn Jiāhóng Wǎngbā,** Rénmín Jiē 3–6 (© 0971/822-3199), is a 5-minute walk south from Dà Shízi. In the west of town, **Wǎngchóng Jùlèbù** is at Shènglì Lù 25. Near the station, **Liúxīngyǔ Wǎngbā** is downstairs at Zhàn Dōng Xiàng 9. Dial-up is © 165.

Post Office   The main post office is on the southwest corner of the main crossroads (second floor; open 8:30am–6pm).

Visa Extensions   The **PSB** at Běi Dàjiē 35 (© 0971/825-1758; Mon–Fri 8:30am–noon and 2:30–6pm) will arrange visa extensions in a couple of days.

AROUND XĪNÍNG
Dōngguān Qīngzhēnsì (Dōngguān Mosque)   Located in the center of a bustling
Muslim district, this is where some of Qīnghǎi's 800,000 Muslims gather for the call

to prayer. The buildings here aren't much to look at, but if you come during prayer times, you'll get an interesting glimpse into the lives of Chinese Muslims. During other times, elderly men sit in the square and gossip. Behind the mosque, there's a crowded produce market and next to the mosque are stores selling Muslim wares. On Dōngguān Dàjiē. Admission ¥10 ($1.25). 8am–9pm.

Kumbum (Tǎ'ěr Sì) ⌖ Jesuit missionary Emmanuel Huc, who visited in 1860, recorded, "On either side of the ravine, and up the edges of the mountains, rise, in amphitheatrical form, the white dwellings of the Lamas, each with its little white terrace and wall of enclosure, adorned only by cleanliness, while here and there tower far above them the Buddhist temples, with their gilt roofs glittering with a thousand colours and surrounded by elegant peristyles . . ."

One of the six largest **Geluk (Yellow Hat)** monasteries, Kumbum was established in 1560 to mark the birthplace of **Tsongkapa (Zōngkābā)**, founder of the Geluk School (described later in this chapter). The image of Tsongkapa is easily recognized by his pointed cap with long earflaps. Guides charging ¥50 ($6) cluster around the entrance, but as there are English signs, a guide is not essential. Facing away from the ticket office, a path leads up the hill from the left side of a row of eight white *chorten* (Tibetan stupas). Keep your ticket: It will be punched by bored monks lounging around the major temples. Shrill guides, huge Chinese tour groups, and glassed-in relics lend Kumbum the feel of a museum, but Hàn visitors are more respectful than in the past.

The most striking building is **Serdong Chenmo (Dà Jīnwǎ Diàn)** ⌖, at the heart of the complex, with its aquamarine tiles. The original structure is said to have been built by Tsongkapa's mother, around a sandalwood tree that sprouted from Tsongkapa's fertile placenta. The **Butter Sculpture Exhibition (Sūyóuhuā Zhǎnlǎn-guǎn),** farther up the slope, is popular with the locals. These sculptures were once only made for festivals, after which they would be destroyed.

Festivals are held the 8th to the 15th of the first **(Monlam)** and fourth **(Saka Dawa)** lunar months, as well as the third to eighth of the sixth lunar month, and the 20th to the 26th of the ninth lunar month, which celebrates **Tsongkapa's birthday.** Call ahead to check exact dates. Religious dancing, mass chanting, and "sunning the

Tsongkapa: Tibet's First Catholic?

While many portray **Tsongkapa** as a reformer or even revolutionary, in the history of Tibetan Buddhism he was actually a conservative who appealed to existing (but neglected) monastic precepts. Drawing on his prodigious knowledge of the Mahayana Buddhist canon, Tsongkapa emphasized monastic discipline, insisting on abstinence from sex and intoxicants. The Jesuit missionary Emmanuel Huc believed he saw a touch of Catholicism about the man, and hypothesized that "a premature death did not permit the Catholic missionary to complete the religious education of his disciple [Tsongkapa], who himself, when afterwards he became an apostle, merely applied himself . . . to the introduction of a new Buddhist liturgy."

Buddha" can be seen, as well as crowds of Tibetans who, in missionary Huc's day, "sang till they were fairly out of breath; they danced; they pushed each other about; they tumbled head over heels: and shouted till one might have thought that they had all gone crazy." Current festivals may be tamer.

(✆ 0971/223-2357. Admission ¥35 ($4.20). 8:30am–5:30pm. Buses (28km/17 miles; 1 hr.; ¥4/50¢) have their destination marked as HUÁNGZHŌNG, and depart after 6am from south of Kūnlún Qiáo (bus no. 3 from station). The last bus returns at 7:30pm. A round-trip taxi ride from the city center to the temple should cost no more than ¥100 ($13).

Qīnghǎi Shěng Bówùguǎn (Qīnghǎi Province Museum) 🐟   If you don't have much time to travel the rural parts of Qīnghǎi, this recently opened museum is definitely worth a visit for its collection of relics that includes Mongolian pottery, Tibetan *mani* stones (stones carved with religious script and images), and bronze coins from the Hàn dynasty. The permanent exhibition also features a display of traditional clothing and architecture from minority ethnic groups in Qīnghǎi, including Tibetans, Mongolians, and Huí, and the lesser-known groups like the Tǔ and Sālā. English descriptions are decent, though the explanations do little to explain each group's religious beliefs and cultural habits. Still, the museum far exceeds the quality of most of its provincial counterparts.

Xīníng Guǎngchǎng. Admission ¥15 ($1.80). 9am–4pm.

Qīnghǎi Hú (Lake Kokonor)   Large, high, salty, and stunningly blue, the lake that gave Qīnghǎi (Blue Lake) Province its name provides little reason to visit, unless you are there between April and early July. Over 100,000 birds migrate from the Indian Ocean to feed on spawn of Lake Kokonor's one variety of fish, the slow-growing scaly carp *(huángyú)*, which swims up the Bùkà Hé each spring. The fattened birds crowd onto tiny **Niǎo Dǎo (Bird Island)**, situated on the northwest side of the lake. Tibetans consider this island as the plug for the lake. In 2005, a bird flu scare closed down the lake for several weeks, when hundreds of migratory birds were found dead near the shore.

All hotels in Xīníng offer tours to Lake Kokonor, starting from ¥100 ($13). Be clear about what your tour includes. Bird-watchers should head for **Niǎo Dǎo Bīnguǎn** (✆ 0970/865-2447) on Bird Island, which has all levels of accommodations.

A better way to do Qīnghǎi Hú, if you're up for a hike and an overnight stay, is to hire a taxi for ¥100 ($13) to the **Tibetan Tent Guesthouse** (Zàngfáng Bīnguǎn; ✆ 0974/851-9688; fax 0974/851-9658) on the east side of the lake. This three-star guesthouse has decent accommodations in tents for ¥280 ($35). You can stay here for a night or have a meal before hiking around a small inlet of the lake, which should take at least half a day.

Admission to Bird Island Sanctuary ¥45 ($5.60) plus ¥5 (65¢) for the electric car from the entrance. 8:30am–5:30pm. Closed Nov–Feb.

SHOPPING

The **Dōngfú Importation Store** on Gònghé Lù, between Qīyī Lù and Dōngguān Dàjiē, has a small selection of hard-to-find Western goods including cheese, Pop-Tarts, cereal, and granola bars. Food supplies may also be picked up from the basement level of the **Wàntōng Guòwù Guǎngchǎng,** which features a huge assortment of grocery items and toiletries. One of Qīnghǎi's special exports is caterpillar fungus, called *dōngchóngxiàcǎo,* which can be soaked in vodka like a worm in tequila or brewed with soup. You can purchase the fungus at the stores to the right of the gate of **Xīníng Bīnguǎn,** with prices ranging from ¥100 to ¥1,000 ($12–$120).

WHERE TO STAY

For a city of its size, Xīníng has a wide choice of hotels. A 20% to 30% discount is standard at most establishments.

EXPENSIVE

By the time you arrive, the Yínlóng Bīnguǎn, Xīníng's first five-star hotel, should have opened its doors.

Jiànyín Bīnguǎn   This hotel, owned by the China Construction Bank, used to be one of the few places that allowed foreign tourists; unfortunately, it has suffered from neglect in recent years. Still, its central location makes it a decent choice. Once the tallest building in town, the Jiànyín is now overshadowed by a building across the street. The furniture in the rooms is worn, as are the bathrooms. Twin beds are larger and more comfortable than usual. A revolving restaurant on the 28th floor with Western food is popular with Chinese businessmen and tourists.

Xī Dàjiē 55. ✆ 0971/826-1886. 100 units. ¥328–¥398 ($41–$50) standard room; ¥498–¥1,080 ($62–$130) suite. AE, DC, MC, V. **Amenities:** 2 restaurants; business center; conference center; exercise room; bowling; sauna; travel agent. *In room:* A/C, TV.

Qīnghǎi Bīnguǎn ✵   Popular with tour groups, this four-star hotel recently underwent extensive renovations on its upper floors, which offer some of the most comfortable rooms and the best views in the city. Rooms on the 13th through 20th floors have been redone in simple wood tones and have large, clean bathrooms, while rooms on the 12th floor and below are shabby, with frayed carpets and stains on the walls—avoid these rooms at all costs.

Huánghé Lù 20. ✆ 0971/614-4888. Fax 0971/614-4145. 423 units. ¥324–¥618 ($41–$77) single; ¥459–¥658 ($57–$82) standard room; ¥609–¥1,298 ($76–$162) suite. Rates include breakfast. 20% discount. AE, DC, MC, V. **Amenities:** 4 restaurants; teahouse; concierge; business center; same-day dry cleaning/laundry; safe. *In room:* A/C, TV, fridge.

MODERATE

Xīníng Bīnguǎn ✵   Located on pleasant grounds away from the bustle of the city traffic, this hotel boasts better-than-average service for a three-star state-owned hotel. The Soviet-style architecture adds character, and the high ceilings and recent room renovations make for an enjoyable stay. Furnishings in the rooms match the dark, albeit fake, redwood floors; the bathrooms are spotless. The single rooms, while somewhat cramped, feature a larger than average twin bed and are ideal if you're traveling alone. Skip the Chinese breakfast buffet, unless you want last night's leftovers.

Qīyī Lù 348. ✆ 0971/845-8701. Fax 0971/845-0798. 327 units. ¥240–¥468 ($30–$55) standard room; ¥580–¥880 ($70–$107) suite. 20% discount possible. AE, DC, MC, V. **Amenities:** Restaurant; salon, business center, and travel agency; concierge; dry cleaning/laundry. *In room:* TV, broadband, water filter.

INEXPENSIVE

Qīnghǎi Normal University International Education Exchange Center (Qīnghǎi Shīfàn Dàxué Guójì Jiàoliú Zhōngxīn) *Finds*   Located on the campus of one of Qīnghǎi's biggest universities, this hotel offers a quiet environment away from the bustle of city traffic. You'll have to drag your bags a few hundred feet to the entrance of the guesthouse (taxis aren't allowed on campus), but the cheap rates and clean rooms and bathrooms make the effort worthwhile.

Qīnghǎi Shīfàn Dàxué Zhèngmén. ✆ 0971/630-3779. 20 units ¥120 ($15) standard room; ¥280 ($35) suite. No credit cards. *In room:* TV.

Xuěshān Bīnguǎn *(Value)* This hotel isn't much different from the usual two-star hotel, but its remarkable service and good price make it a standout. After check-in, a housekeeper comes around to ask if you need any laundry done—free of charge. The room includes a fruit bowl that is refreshed every day, and broadband Internet access for ¥10 ($1.25) for the entire day.

Jiěfàng Lù 24. ✆ 0971/823-1010. 32 units. ¥120 ($14) standard room. No credit cards. **Amenities:** Free laundry. *In room:* TV, broadband Internet access, water cooler.

WHERE TO DINE

Black Tent NEPALESE/TIBETAN This recent addition to Xīníng's restaurant scene was an instant hit with Tibetans and the foreign community (consisting of English teachers, nongovernmental organization workers, and missionaries). Unfortunately, the restaurant's Nepalese chef left the day before we visited, leaving a Tibetan understudy to feed a starving throng of diners. Hopefully, they'll have their kitchen staff in order by the time you visit. Despite a long wait for our food to arrive, the lentil soup and vegetable pakora were tasty.

Jiěfàng Lù 12. ✆ 0971/823-4029. Meal for 2 less than ¥100 ($13). English menu. No credit cards. 9:30am–midnight. Bus: no. 102.

Hēi Pǔlǔ Zhàngbā *(★★)* *(Finds)* TIBETAN Located a few steps away from the Xīníng Bīnguǎn, this charming and unpretentious teahouse and bar staffed with friendly Tibetans is quickly building up a solid clientele of monks and prominent Tibetans. The Tibetan furnishings are comfortable enough that you could while away hours here. Customers play games like darts and Chinese checkers upstairs. The menu includes a range of snacks, including Amdo steamed buns, lamb steak, and yogurt. We are especially enamored by this place because we left a valuable camera here accidentally, and came back to find that it had been safely placed behind the counter, waiting for us to return to claim it!

Qīyī Lù. ✆ 0971/845-9471. Meal for 2 less than ¥80 ($10). English menu. No credit cards. 11:30am–midnight. Bus: no. 102, 35, 14, or 15.

Qīnghǎi Luómǎ Jiàrì Xīcāntīng (Qīnghǎi Roman Holiday Western Restaurant) WESTERN If you've been on the road for a while, craving that Western-style sandwich or steak, this is your best option. Centrally located on the fifth floor of the Xīníng Sports Stadium (Xīníng Tǐyùguǎn), this establishment boasts a nice view of the city. Hopefully, the view and the chew (the steaks are rumored to be the best in town) will keep you distracted from the gaudy interior, which features cast-iron chairs and origami hung from the ceiling. Upstairs from the restaurant is a teahouse featuring a gigantic chessboard with human-size movable pieces.

Chángjiāng Lù, Xīníng Tǐyùguǎn, 5th floor. ✆ 0971/491-5288. Meal for 2 less than ¥200 ($25). English menu. No credit cards. 9am–2am. Bus: no. 15 or 80.

Shālǐhǎi Měishíchéng *(★)* *(Value)* MUSLIM/SICHUAN It might take a slight adjustment to appreciate the noisy and fluorescent-lit dining room, but the food keeps this place packed nearly 24 hours a day. The *chǎo miànpiàn*, small pieces of noodles stir-fried with green squash, beef, and peppers, is a steal at ¥3 (40¢) a bowl and incredibly satisfying—kind of like a spicy Chinese version of pasta primavera (with meat). After 6pm, the chefs fire up the front grill to serve *yángròuchuàn* (lamb skewers).

Běi Dàjiē 4. ✆ 0971-823-2039. Meal for 2 less than ¥100 ($13). No English menu. No credit cards. Open 24 hr. Bus: no. 102, 35, 14, or 15.

XĪNÍNG AFTER DARK

In the summer months, one of the most popular things to do at night is to eat on one of Xīníng's renowned **"eat streets."** The biggest one is on **Dàxīn Jiē,** where touts sell everything from barbecued fish to fried dumplings. *Warning:* This isn't the most hygienic environment; make sure you use disposable chopsticks.

You'll have to walk down a flight of stairs to get to the subterranean **New York Subway (Niǔyuē Dìtiě),** on Nánguān Jiē 57 (© 0971/369-5441 or 1370-974-9167), Xīníng's hippest nightclub. Jointly owned by an American and a friendly Xīníng native named Jack, the venue features a DJ spinning decent Western techno music while young women in tight bikini bottoms and bra tops dance around a stage. Another popular nighttime activity is a visit to a Tibetan *nangma,* a variety show with singing and dancing. One of the most popular, for both Tibetan and Hàn Chinese, is at the **Xīnshídài Dàshà,** seventh floor (© 0971/610-8758). The entertainment runs nightly from 9:30pm to 1:30am. For a little less flash, **Hēipǔlǔ Zàngbā** keeps its doors open until midnight and serves Huánghé Píjiǔ, a local beer; on a memorable Saturday night when I visited, waiters moved from table to table, serenading patrons, toasting them with beer, and wrapping white scarves around their necks. The scarf, or kata, is a sign of auspiciousness, or good thoughts.

2 Tóngrén (Rebkong)

181km (112 miles) S of Xīníng, 107km (66 miles) NW of Xiàhé. Altitude: 2,400m (4,872 ft.)

Tóngrén is at the center of a major revival in Tibetan art, particularly in sculpture and the painting of appliquéd *thangkas* (silk paintings). Although viewed by both Lhasa and Běijīng as being on the periphery of the Tibetan world, the locals remember their crucial role in the Sino-Tibetan peace treaty, signed in 822. This is still marked by the **Lurol Festival,** held in the middle of the sixth lunar month. With fertility dances and body piercing, it has a pagan feel. Monks are *not* allowed to attend. The major **Buddhist festival** is held from the 5th to the 12th days of the first lunar month, with debates, religious dancing, and the unveiling of large *thangkas* moving between the main temples of **Sengeshong Gompa, Gomar Gompa,** and **Rongpo Gompa.** The town itself is drab; nearly all the sites of interest are located several miles north.

ESSENTIALS

GETTING THERE   The **Tóngrén Bus Station** (© 0973/872-2014) connects Tóngrén with Xīníng (14 buses; 4 hr.; ¥23/$2.90) between 7:20am and 4pm; with Lánzhōu (9 hr.; ¥45/$5.60) at 6:50am; with Xiàhé (5 hr.; ¥18/$2.20) at 8am; with Liùjiā Xiá (3 hr.; ¥14/$1.70) at 9am and 11am; with Línxià (7 hr.; ¥27/$3.40) at 7:30am; and with the Mongolian town of Hénán (5 hr.; ¥21/$2.60) at 7:30am. Uphill from the bus station is a large roundabout with a statue of a horse. To the right is Zhōngshān Lù, the main street, which runs west to Tuánjié Lù, marked by an obelisk.

TOURS & GUIDES   The **Rebgong Cultural Center** (Fèngwǔ Zhōnglù 217; © 0973/879-7138; rebgonglibrary@yahoo.com), the town's new community center that features a library of Tibetan, Chinese, and English books, English-language lessons, and art classes, can help arrange an English-speaking tour guide. Sherab, the director, is a jolly ex-monk who knows everyone in town.

FAST FACTS

Banks, Foreign Exchange & ATMs   None available.

Internet Access Immediately east of the entrance to the Telecom Hotel is the non-smoking **Huángnán Diànxìn Fēngōngsī Wǎngbā** (© 0941/872-4196; open 10am–11pm). Dial-up is © 165.

Post Office The main post office is located on Tuánjié Nán Lù, diagonally across from the Huángnán Dàjiǔdiàn.

EXPLORING THE REGION

The main Geluk monastery of the region, **Rongpo Gompa (Lóngwù Sì;** ¥18/$2.25), is to the south of town. But the most popular outing for those interested in Tibetan art is a visit to the villages of **Shàng Wǔtún (Upper Wǔtún)** and **Xià Wǔtún (Lower Wǔtún)**, located 6.4km (4 miles) north of Tóngrén. The villages are filled with monks and laypeople turning out masses of Buddhist art for temples as far away as western Tibet; each village charges a ¥10 ($1.25) admission. The monks from **Sengeshong Yagotsang** (© 0973/872-9227; ¥10/$1.25) in the upper village are exceptionally friendly, and happy to show their work. Thangkhas can be purchased for ¥80 to ¥3,000 ($10–$280), depending on the size of the piece, how intricately drawn the art-work is, and how much gold paint is used. Don't be afraid to bargain, even if you are buying from a monk. The most celebrated painter of this village is **Shawu Tsering** (© 0973/872-5032), who is very sprightly for an octogenarian.

Minivans charging ¥3 (40¢) depart when full for **Shàng Wǔtún** and **Xià Wǔtún** from the roundabout near the Tóngrén bus station, or hail a three-wheeler for ¥10 ($1.25). You can hire a taxi to make the round trip for around ¥20 ($2.50). Directly across the river (Lóngwù Hé) is **Gomar Gompa (Guōmárì Sì;** ¥10/$1.25), marked by a spectacular five-tiered chorten (stupa). The climb to the top of the 38m (125-ft.) structure is a nervy one, as the ledges get narrower closer to the apex. The reward is a spectacular view down the valley. The monks are Tǔ, not Tibetan—even those fluent in the Amdo dialect won't understand a word they say.

WHERE TO STAY

Unfortunately, Tóngrén lacks any fashionable guesthouses; they're run of the muck in this town.

Diànxìn Bīnguǎn (Telecom Hotel) If there is any truth in the rumor that CCP leaders get kickbacks on the sale of titanium dioxide, then they cleaned up with this white-tiled edifice that can only be viewed with eye protection under the midday sun. Inside are simple, functionally furnished rooms; clean, blue bathrooms; and refreshingly efficient service.

Zhōngshān Lù 2 (on the north side, halfway down the main road). © 0973/872-6888. 33 units (shower only). ¥136 ($17) standard room; ¥260 ($32) suite. No credit cards. **Amenities:** Restaurant; bowling alley; same-day laundry. *In room:* TV.

Huángnán Bīnguǎn Slightly cheaper than the Telecom Hotel, this establishment located across the street, is your average 1½-star hotel. Avoid the front building rooms with squat toilets and televisions that are relics from the 1950s. Stay in the back wing for a few more dollars, as the rooms are a significant improvement. The hotel's restaurant is a good choice for an authentic Tibetan meal (see below).

Zhōngshān Lù 8. © 0973/872-2293. 100 units. ¥80–¥120 ($10–$15) standard room; ¥288 ($35) suite. No credit cards. **Amenities:** Restaurant. *In room:* TV.

WHERE TO DINE

Homeland of Rebkong Artist Restaurant (Règòng Yìshùkè) ✿ TIBETAN

The ambience doesn't get better than this at one of Tóngrén's few Tibetan restaurants. Monks and Tibetan government officials stroll in to sip yak butter tea and eat *momos* (yak dumplings). Try the *chǎo yángròu* (stir-fried mutton), the *tsampa* (barley flour mixed with yak butter, tea, and sugar), and the *rénshēnguǒ mǐfàn* (ginseng rice). It's also a good place to relax with a cup of tea or a beer.

Zhōngshān Lù 8 (1st floor of the Huángnán Bīnguǎn). ✆ 0973/831-4585. Meal for 2 ¥40 ($5). No credit cards. 7:30am–8:30pm.

Tàishān Miànshíguǎn ✿ *Value* MUSLIM

Popular with the few foreigners who live in town and the local community alike, this recommended restaurant serves an excellent *chǎo miànpiàn* (stir-fried noodle pieces with squash, beef, and onions). You can opt for the *qīngtāng miànpiàn*, which is a variation of the dish with soup. A counter with a variety of cold dishes sits at the front of the restaurant, including spicy cauliflower and cold seaweed. All you have to do is point to what you want.

On Zhōngshān Lù, a few doors away from the Huángnán Bīnguǎn. ✆ 0973/872-4504 or 139/0973-0206. Meal for 2 ¥20 ($2.50). No credit cards. 10am–11pm.

TÓNGRÉN AFTER DARK

Weekend nights, the most happening place in town is **Měinàxià** (Xiàzhòng Lù 37; ✆ 0973/831-4973), a Tibetan *nangma,* or nightclub. Entering via a fire escape on the side of the building felt like going to a club on New York's Lower East Side. Inside, young men in black sleeveless T-shirts take over the dance floor, grooving to a Chinese version of Kylie Minogue only to be edged out by couples (straight and gay) slow dancing to sappy love songs. For me, the highlight of the night was watching the performance of dancers in slinky off-the-shoulder dresses made of colorful wool shimmying to traditional Tibetan music.

3 Yùshù (Jyekundo) ✿✿

819km (508 miles) SW of Xīníng. Altitude: 3,200m (10,496 ft)

Because the Kham region inside the **Tibetan Autonomous Region (TAR)** is closed to individual travel, **Yùshù** is your best opportunity to visit a large, thriving Khampa town. Though named for the **Jyekundo Gompa,** which looms above the town, Yùshù has always been more trading center than monastic town.

The fierce reputation of the Khampas keeps Hàn migration down (aside from the odd Sìchuān restaurant). Housing has improved, and locals are extremely friendly; strangers may rise and grasp your hand before you join them for a meal. The spectacular **Horse Festival** is free of the vagaries of the lunar calendar and commences on July 25, on a grassy plain south of town.

ESSENTIALS

GETTING THERE   Locals dismiss talk of an **airport,** which government officials hope to build southeast of Yùshù. However, a Xīníng–Yùshù–Lhasa flight is a definite future possibility with the recent investment of ¥500 million ($63 million) from the national government, allegedly for an airport. Check with CAAC in Xīníng for the latest details.

The normal **bus** trip should take around 20 hours, though if your bus breaks down, it could take 40 hours! The road climbs steeply out of Xīníng, passing through **Yuèrì Shān** into vast grassland country. There are few towns along the way; take plenty of provisions. After **Măduō,** you enter an expanse of alpine lakes and gradually ascend to a pass at 5,082m (16,670 ft.). If you aren't overcome by altitude sickness, stop for fresh yogurt and perhaps some filling *tsampa* (roasted barley flour mixed with tea) in grasslands south of Qīngshuǐ Hé. The last major town, 48km (30 miles) before Yùshù, is **Xiēwū,** where a dirt road branches east to **Shíqú** (95km/60 miles) and **Mǎnígāngē** in Sìchuān. If several passengers for Sìchuān disembark, a minibus can be arranged at the Xiēwū crossroads.

The bus station is on Shènglì Lù. Turning left (north) as you exit the station, you pass the post office on your left; it's a 10-minute walk from there to the main T-junction with Mínzhǔ Lù, which runs left (west) towards the Yùshù Hotel and Zhìduō, and east towards Xīwū and Xīníng. Jiēgǔ Sì commands a hill northeast of the T-junction.

Xīníng buses offer either separate hard seat (not recommended) or sleeper service. Hard-seat buses, ¥96 ($12), depart 8:30am and 9am. Newer sleeper buses, ¥139 ($17) depart noon and 1pm. Book your ticket well in advance—you *don't* want to be stuck at the back of the bus. A minivan to Shíqú can be negotiated for ¥300 ($37), but most drivers are reluctant to go farther. The cheapest option is to get up early and hitch a lift on a truck to Shíqú (¥30/$3.70) or Gānzǐ (¥70/$8.70). The trucks depart from near the large yak statue, just west of the main T-junction.

FAST FACTS

Banks, Foreign Exchange & ATMs   None available.

Internet Access   **Qīngzàng Wǎngbā** is two storefronts east of the Yùshù Hotel (open 24 hr.; ¥3/40¢ per hour). The **Dōngwángjiāo Wǎngbā,** located next to the Jiégǔ Hotel, offers similar 24-hour service for the same rate. Dial-up is **16300.**

Post Office   The main post office (© **0976/8825024;** open Mon–Fri 9:30am–5:30pm, Sat–Sun 11am–4pm) is just north of the bus station. Overseas calls can be made from the **Diànxìnjú,** west of Yùshù Bīnguǎn on the south side of the street.

EXPLORING YÙSHÙ

At the **market** *(shāngchǎng)* ✦ on the southwest corner of the main T-junction, you can enjoy some of the sights, gestures, and attitudes described by Dutch missionary Susie Rijnhart, one of Tibet's earliest and most astute observers: "The men are mainly dressed in *pulu,* or colored drilling, have their hair mainly done in a great queue about which they adorn with bright rings and twist about their heads. . . .The women often wear a large disk of silver on their forehead and sometimes on the back of their head, and both sexes carry from their girdles silver needle cases, flint and steel boxes and occasionally an embroidered cloth case for their *tsamba* bowl. . . . "

Religious paraphernalia, including bells, prayer wheels, incense, and chanting tapes are sold alongside knives, snuff from India, and bundles of tea wrapped in bamboo. Prayer flags *(tar-choks)* handmade by printers from Dégé, and tailor-made *chubas* (Tibetan jackets), make excellent purchases. Kham is renowned for its richly colored carpets, but many are inferior weaves from Sìchuān. Better carpets are usually Nepalese imports, but the craft is being revived locally; a **carpet factory** (www.khadenrugs.com) opened in 2003. A huge **open-air local crafts market,** 100m (330 ft.) southeast of the T-junction, is under construction and slated to open sometime in 2006.

Jiégǔ Sì (Jyekundo Gompa)   The striking red, gray, and deep-blue walls of this monastery dominate Yùshù. Built in the characteristic tapering farmhouse style of Tibetan architecture, it was established in 1398 by the Sakya School on the site of a small Bon temple. It still houses some very dedicated practitioners. One monk housed adjacent to the temple has yet to see the light of day, and is well into his forties. So keep the noise down! Evening chanting sessions are regularly held in the golden-roofed red temple. *Note:* Remove your shoes before entering. The *dzong* (fortress), whose ruins lie above the temple, once commanded an unassailable position, looking out over river valleys to the east, west, and south. A stroll beyond the ruins up the ridge gives you a stunning panorama of Yùshù, and eventually of the surrounding peaks.

Free admission. Minivan ¥10 ($1.25), or walk up along the river east of the Dragon King Hotel.

Mǎní Shí Chéng ⟪⟨★⟩⟫   *Mani* stones *(mǎní shí)* usually carry the most popular Buddhist mantra, *om mane padme hum,* while others are more intricate, containing entire scriptures carved with gold lettering. Tibet's largest collection of *mani* stones stands 5km (3 miles) west of Yùshù. In 1955, there were optimistically estimated to be over two billion stones surrounding the temple, and although some now grace toilets in the area, the site has been resanctified and the pile is growing once more. The mass of stones and prayer flags towers over pilgrims who circumambulate the 1-sq.-km (½-sq.-mile) complex. It's a prodigious symbol of faith, especially when you consider that the temple is believed to have been established a little over 800 years ago. Stones were placed here by thankful pilgrims and traders from Sìchuān, Lhasa, and Xīníng, who would rest in Yùshù for several weeks. If you forgot to bring a *mani* stone, you can purchase one from some women of remarkable antiquity and persistence. On the road back to Yùshù, you may notice other stones by the side of the road, which have a less holy purpose and reflect the strength of Bon animistic traditions in the region. "Mouth stones" have the character for "mouth" inscribed one hundred times in a spiral pattern to seal the curse (usually against a business rival) on the reverse side. Understandably, these stones are carved and placed covertly.

Free admission. Open daylight hours. Minivan ¥10 ($1.25).

Vairocana Temple or Wénchéng Gōngzhǔ Miào (Temple of Princess Wénchéng)   Situated 20km (12 miles) south of town, just to the left (east) of the road to Nángqiān, lies a temple associated with Princess Wénchéng, who married King Songtsen Ganpo in a bid to halt Tibetan raids. Hàn commentators credit her with bringing all manner of spiritual and agricultural advancements to the Tibetans. On her way to Lhasa, the princess stopped with her retinue for a month in this remote gorge, and carved statues of **Vairocana Buddha** (one of the five transcendent or Tathagata Buddhas, said to transform delusion and ignorance) and the eight bodhisattvas into the naked rock. Some commentators suggest the delay was due to a miscarriage, and that Wénchéng's child is housed within the central effigy. The hall sheltering the images was added in 710 by the next Táng princess, Jīnchéng. These political marriages were to no avail: The Tibetans sacked Cháng'ān in 763. Behind the temple is a great deal of Tibetan and Chinese script, but the passage of time makes it difficult to decipher. A spectacular view of the temple is gained by climbing the hill opposite, but the climb is a steep 2 hours.

Admission ¥15 ($2). Open daylight hours. Return trip by minivan ¥50 ($6).

WHERE TO STAY

Yùshù lacks quality accommodations, and prices at all establishments tend to double during the Horse Festival, when it is best to book in advance (with a firm agreement on the price). If you are without a bathroom, both the **Hóngwèi Lù Línyù,** east of the T-junction and next to the Lóngwáng Hotel, and the Jié Shuānglín, opposite the Lābù Sì Hotel, are recommended. The price at each should be ¥5 (65¢). *Warning:* Some bathhouses offer "extra services."

Lóngwáng Bīnguǎn ⚔ This recently opened gem sits at the foot of the Jiégǔ Monastery, at the top of Hóngwèi Lù, and to the east of the T-junction. Limited to 20 rooms, the service is exceptional and many of the attendants speak impressive English. The Lóngwáng boasts clean rooms, double-paned windows, and a second-floor snack shop. The downsides? A lack of reliable hot water (though the neighboring Hóngwèi Bathhouse [see above] can meet this need) and the absence of private toilets, though there is one on premises.

Hóngwèi Lù. ✆ 0976/881-0222 or 0976/864-7233. 20 units (4 with bathroom). ¥80 ($10) single without bathroom; ¥150 ($19) single with bathroom. No credit cards. *In room:* TV.

Yùshù Bīnguǎn Lying about 200m (654 ft.) west of the main T-junction, on the right (north) side of the road, is Yùshù's best two-star lodgings. Beds can be spongy, and some of the staff are so rude you wonder if they should seek psychiatric help. Rooms on the north side are quieter. This is the best place in town with better-than-average rooms and decent English service. The hotel is building a new wing, which may be done by the time you get here.

Mínzhǔ Lù 12. ✆ 0976/882-2999. Fax 0976/882-2428. 89 units (41 without bathroom). ¥15 ($1.90) dorm bed; ¥160 ($20) standard room; ¥480 ($60) suite. No credit cards. **Amenities:** Restaurant; tour desk; sauna (¥25/$3). *In room:* TV.

WHERE TO DINE

Xiǎo Hóngniú Měishí Chéng ⚔ SÌCHUĀN Dining in Jyekundo's most upmarket eatery is done in private rooms—not really suited to the solo traveler. But those with a few friends will enjoy lavishly painted rooms, friendly service, and (if you wish) karaoke. A famished tour group might try tackling the *hǎo kǎo quányáng* (roast lamb) at ¥350 ($44), or perhaps would just settle for a *kǎo yángtuǐ* (roast leg of lamb) for ¥80 ($10). Other local favorites include the *suānlà fěntiáo* (sour and spicy vermicelli), *yángpái* (rack of lamb), and *huáyú* (a river fish).

400m (1,312 ft.) west of the Yùshù Bīnguǎn. ✆ 0976/882-4822. Meal for 2 ¥80–¥160 ($10–$20). No credit cards. 8am–11pm.

Yā Fànguǎn ⚔ *Finds* MUSLIM Noodles are the specialty of this perpetually full Huí-run establishment, found east of the main T-junction, just up the hill on the left (north) side. Easily identifiable by the yellow sign boasting two yaks, this strictly meat-and-pasta affair offers good value with such dishes as cold mutton and beef ribs, ¥18 ($2.25) and ¥20 ($2.50) per half-kilo (1.1 lb.) respectively. The delicious *pàozhang* and *gānbàn* are similar spaghetti-like dishes, both covered in a beef-and-vegetable sauce. Local traders taking a break from the nearby caterpillar fungus market frequently stop in, offering you an excellent chance to observe the art of Kham debate up close and loud.

Hóngwèi Lù 7. ✆ 0976/882-7568. Meal for 2 less than ¥20 ($2.50). No credit cards. 8am–10pm.

AROUND YÙSHÙ

Travel to areas around Yùshù—**Nángqiān, Záduō, Zhìduō,** and **Qūmálái**—no longer requires a permit. Thriving monasteries, remote nature reserves, and bumpy roads await the intrepid. The **Yùshù Bīnguǎn** (see "Where to Stay," above) rents Běijīng jeeps for 1-day trips for ¥200 ($16), but more extensive tours are best arranged through the **Qīnghǎi Mountaineering Association** (p. 736) in Xīníng. Unlike other operators, they are willing to arrange tours to Lhasa via Yùshù, following the traditional trade route along riverbeds for much of the way. Give them at least 2 weeks' notice.

4 Măqìn (Dàwŭ)

552km (342 miles) S of Xīníng, 525km (326 miles) NW of Aba. Altitude: 4,000m (13,120 ft.)

Few capital cities are one-street towns, but **Măqìn,** the capital of Golok Tibetan Autonomous Prefecture, is just that. Efforts to "settle" nomads are rarely successful (see below), and the town has a Wild West ambience. Nomads wander around for a few hours, and then amble out again. North of town is a picturesque **Mani temple,** choked with *tar-choks* (prayer flags), and the bustling **market** to the left of the bus station is worth a look. But the main reason to come here is to visit **Amnye Machen,** Amdo's holiest mountain. *Warning:* Măqìn is the coldest town in Qīnghǎi . . . and Qīnghǎi is a cold place.

ESSENTIALS

GETTING THERE   Compared to the trek out to Tibet's other renowned holy mountain, Kailash, getting to Amnye Machen is straightforward. The **bus** from Xīníng passes **Lājiā Sì,** a charming Geluk monastery on the upper reaches of the Yellow River, at daybreak, and arrives at Măqìn mid-morning. The **bus station** at Tuánjié Lù 137 (© **0975/838-2665**), open from 7am to 5:30pm, has services to Xīníng (14 hr.; ¥68/$8.50 seat or ¥93/$13 sleeper) at 8am (seat) and 4pm (sleeper). To continue south, you will need to arrange permits in Xīníng. There are buses for Dári

The Panchen Lama's Letter

The Great Leap Forward (1959–61) killed an estimated 30 million Chinese, but the horror of Qīnghǎi was unparalleled. The leftist policies of the city's radical governor, Gāo Fēng, are said to have wiped out up to half the population. Starvation claimed most lives, while the PLA's policy of "fighting the rebellion on a broad front" *(píngpàn kuòdà)* saw countless monks and nuns murdered. The Panchen Lama, viewed as a puppet of Běijīng, was sent to Qīnghǎi on a fact-finding mission in 1962. Upon his return, he penned a 70,000-word tract—*The Panchen Lama's Letter*—which implied genocide: "The population of [greater] Tibet has been seriously reduced. . . . it poses a grave danger to the very existence of the Tibetan race and could even push the Tibetans to the last breath." Máo was enraged, the "puppet" was put under house arrest, and he was only rehabilitated by the Party in 1988. Ending nomadism, of which Marxism takes a dim view, is still official government policy.

(4 hr.; ¥25/$3) at 7:30am; and on odd-numbered dates for Bānmǎ (10 hr.; ¥46/$5.70) and thence to Aba (1½ days; ¥80/$10) in Sìchuān, departing at 8am. Hiring a Běijīng **jeep** through CITS, you can connect directly with Mǎduō (¥1,000/$125), Aba (¥1,500/$187), and Yùshù (¥2,000/$250). Facing out from the bus station, you are on Tuánjié Lù. As major streets go, that's it. The direction to your left is roughly north.

TOURS & GUIDES CITS (© 0975/838-3368; fax 0975/838-3431; akitsgl@public.xn.qh.cn) is in the lobby of **Xuě Shān Bīnguǎn,** and goes by the name Amdo & Kham International Travel Service (open 9am–noon and 3–5:30pm). While they are friendly enough, you're better off arranging the trip through the Qīnghǎi Mountaineering Association in Xīníng. If want to tackle the *kora* (circuit) around Amnye Machen independently, avoid the Xuě Shān altogether. CITS keeps an eye out for foreigners, and will try to extract an "entrance ticket" of ¥100 ($13) and up, and an "environmental protection fee" of ¥30 ($3.70) per person per day. When asked what environmental projects this fee supports, they volunteer that there's an annual tourism fair in Hong Kong that they like to attend. They also rent Běijīng jeeps for ¥500 ($62) per day.

FAST FACTS

Banks, Foreign Exchange & ATMs   None available.

Internet Access   Hóng Niú Wǎngbā (© 0975/838-4994) is across the road, just north of the bus station, on the second floor of a music shop (open 10am–10pm; ¥4/50¢ per hour). Dial-up is © 16300.

Post Office   The main post office (Mon–Fri 9:30am–5:30pm; Sat–Sun 10:30am–4:30pm) is a 5-minute walk north of the bus station.

WHERE TO STAY

Xuě Shān Bīnguǎn   Located just south (right) of the bus station, this is Mǎqìn's premier hotel. That's not a big claim. Midsize rooms in building 2 *(èr lóu)* are sunny, beds are comfy, and there are new electric showers for the grubby tubs. The reception staff is so indolent that they will ask *you* to go tell the maid to check your room, rather than pick up the phone in front of them. Bargaining is fruitless.

Tuánjié Lù 109. © 0975/838-2142. 58 units (40 without bathroom). ¥12–¥28 ($1.50–$3.50) dorm bed; ¥96 ($12) standard; ¥144–¥388 ($18–$48) suite. No credit cards. **Amenities:** Restaurant; tour desk. *In room:* TV.

Xuěyù Bīnguǎn   To the left of the bus station, on the first corner, is this white-tiled, blue-glass monolith. Relatively new, it's the best choice if you want to avoid CITS. Guest rooms are narrow, but bathrooms are spacious with deep tubs, reversing the usual formula. Diagonally opposite is the **Diànxìn Bīnguǎn,** a similar property with dingier bathrooms.

Tuánjié Lù. © 0975/838-1889. 78 units (54 without bathroom). ¥20–¥26 ($2.50–$3.20) dorm bed; ¥96 ($12) twin. 20% discount possible. No credit cards. **Amenities:** Restaurant. *In room:* TV.

WHERE TO DINE

Both hotels listed above offer decent dining. Stock up on food supplies in town if you're heading out for a hike.

A NEARBY HOLY MOUNTAIN

About 86km (53 miles) from Mǎqìn stands **Amnye Machen (Mǎjī Gāngrì)** ✿✿✿. In 1929, American botanist Joseph Rock incorrectly measured its height at over 9,000m (30,000 ft.), making it (for a while) the world's highest peak. It actually comes in well short, at 6,282m (20,605 ft.), but it was unconquered until 1981 (partly because an earlier Chinese expedition climbed the wrong peak). One of the first Western visitors was the French adventurer Grenard, who was impressed by "a prodigious and resplendent mass of snow and ice, which strikes any man, however accustomed to mountains, with admiration and astonishment." The protector deity who resides in the mountain, **Machen Pomra,** is popular with Bonpos (followers of the Bon faith) and is also revered by Buddhists.

Many pilgrims start the trek from **Sānchàkǒu (Tselnak Khamdo),** where the road meets the pilgrimage circuit. Farther down the motor road is **Báitǎ (Chuwarna),** the traditional starting point for the trek where yaks and horses may be hired from ¥50 ($6) per day. The full circuit is a hefty 132km (82 miles), and there is no way of retracing your steps without incurring the wrath of Machen Pomra. Young folks whiz around in 4 days, carrying all their gear, but it's best to hire a yak or two to carry your gear and take 7 to 10 days. Riding on horseback should take no more than 3 days. The atmosphere of the *kora* is pious and social. Entire villages or families make the trip, coming from all corners of the Tibetan world for a pilgrimage that is equal to Kailash in significance. The scenery is unsurpassed.

A tent, a sleeping bag, food and fuel, and a spare pair of light shoes or sandals for the numerous stream crossings are essential. A sturdy water filter would also be an idea—there is a lot of glacial silt in the streams. Most pilgrims abstain from meat during the *kora*—a real sacrifice for the meat-loving Tibetans. May and June are the best months, when the snow is still on the peaks, after the deadly cold of winter and before the summer rains. September and October are also fine.

A **pilgrim bus** to Sānchàkǒu and Báitǎ crawls by at 8am, but a **Běijīng jeep** (2½ hr.; ¥20/$2.50 per person) is quicker. *Warning:* The road is rough—windows are often broken from the *inside.*

5 Golmud (Gé'ěrmù)

1165km (722 miles) N of Lhasa, 781km (484 miles) W of Xīníng, 524km (325 miles) S of Dūnhuáng. Altitude: 3,000m (9,840 ft.)

Unless you plan to travel overland to Lhasa, or unless potash plants and oil refineries excite you, there is no reason to visit this blot on the wild and gloomy landscape of the **Tsaidam Basin.** For the overland journey to Lhasa, it's CITS Golmud or nothing (see "Highway Robbery," below, for details). *Note:* For Chinese translations of selected establishments listed in this section, please turn to appendix A.

ESSENTIALS

GETTING THERE   The **airport** is 20km (12 miles) west of Golmud. A bus making the 30-minute trip for ¥10 ($1.25) connects with the **CAAC** office, just east of the PSB, at Cháidámù Lù 66 (© **0979/842-3333,** ext. 8808). The one flight connects with Xīníng, Xī'ān, and Qīngdǎo. Golmud is connected by **rail** to Xīníng (12½ hr., N904, 9:05pm; N910, 6:24pm) and Lánzhōu (17 hr.) by the N904, which leaves at 9:05pm. The left-luggage room is to the right (east). The **Golmud Bus Station** (© **0979/845-3688**) is directly opposite, with buses to Dūnhuáng (11 hr.; ¥55/$6.90 seat, ¥90/$11 sleeper) at 8am and 6pm; and to Xīníng (15 hr.; ¥70/$8.70) at 4pm. Buses for Tibet leave from the **Tibet Bus Station** at Yánqiáo Lù Zhōngduàn 15 (© **0979/848-2265**); CITS is waiting here.

GETTING AROUND   Taxis charge ¥5 to ¥6 (65¢–75¢). **Buses** cost ¥1 (15¢), paid to the conductor. The key bus is no. 2, which runs from the railway station to the center of town.

FAST FACTS
Banks, Foreign Exchange & ATMs   The **Bank of China** (Mon–Fri 8:30am–6:30pm; Sat–Sun 9:30am–4pm), Cháidámù Lù 19, changes cash and traveler's checks only.

Internet Access   "**Ài wǒ ba**" **Wǎngbā** (© 0979/845-7871; open 9am–midnight) is above a grocery store, on the corner of Xī Shìchǎng Sān Lù and Zhànqián Èr Lù. Dial-up is © 165.

Post Office   The main post office (open 9am–6pm summer; 9am–5pm winter) is on the northeast corner of Kūnlún Lù and Cháidámù Lù.

Visa Extensions   The **PSB** (open Mon–Fri, 8:30am–noon and 2:30–6pm) at Cháidámù Lù 68 (© 0979/844-2550) grants 1-month extensions in 2 days. Permits for closed areas of the Tsaidam Basin are arranged here.

WHERE TO STAY
Foreigners were once forced to stay at the **Gé'ěrmù Bīnguǎn** (© 0979/842-4288), and officially that is still the case, though no one cares to check. Rather than "Hello," the standard greeting is "Passport." They will photocopy it for CITS, who lurk upstairs. This is a cheap enough option at ¥50 ($6) for a bed, if you can stand the surly service. Discounts of 20% are standard at other establishments.

Wēi'ěrshì Dàjiǔdiàn   Tucked in a quiet location between town and railway station, this two-star hotel was thoroughly renovated in 2002. The comfortably furnished rooms are kept spotlessly clean; service is efficient and unobtrusive. Well-scrubbed dormitory rooms are at the back *(hòu lóu)*, but there are no common showers.

Highway Robbery

The only official way to reach Lhasa (28–50 hr.) overland is through CITS. You will be charged ¥1,700 ($212) for a trip that costs the locals ¥200 ($25). For ¥50 ($6) more, you can fly from Chéngdū. CITS proudly declares that the bus ticket costs exactly the same for foreigners, but when asked to itemize the remaining ¥1,500 ($187), they become vague and defensive. A tour of Lhasa and dormitory accommodations you don't want is included in the price. If being robbed isn't enough, you'll have to listen to unctuous apologies, such as, "Tibet is an autonomous region, there's nothing we can do," mixed with threats such as "You *must* go on the tour and stay at the Kirey Hotel."

Touts, whose vehicles always have three Americans waiting to leave, offer the unofficial option at the bus and railway stations. The asking price is ¥500 ($62), and while there is a risk (some have been deported), drivers are more generous with the police than CITS, so most get through. Inspect the vehicle first, and don't pay the balance until you reach Lhasa.

Railway on the Roof of the World

Golmud Railway Station staff is coy if asked when China's most ambitious railway link will open, but foundations have already been laid for over half of the track, and steel stretches far south of Golmud. Engineering challenges are substantial. The planned route will cross a 5,072m (16,636-ft.) pass through permanently frozen, earthquake-prone country. The central government is investing vast sums in this megaproject, and signs along the way, such as CONQUER NATURE and NEVER ADMIT DEFEAT, revisit the 1960s. Tibetans in Lhasa, already inundated by waves of Hàn migration that have made them a minority in their capital, are less excited by the project. One monk from Sera simply shrugged and sighed, "There's nothing we can do, but it will be the end for Tibet. The Chinese will come in, and our minerals will go out." A jaded CCP member admits, "There's going to be trouble, lots of unrest." He nods in the direction of an army barracks. "They're planning for it right now."

Jiāngyuán Nán Lù 26. ✆ 0979/843-1208. Fax 0979/842-4888. 64 units (12 without bathroom). ¥148 ($19) single; ¥158 ($20) standard room; ¥388 ($48) suite; ¥30–¥45 ($3.70–$5.60) dorm bed. Rates include breakfast. No credit cards. **Amenities:** Restaurant; concierge; business center; same-day laundry/dry cleaning. *In room:* TV.

Yóuzhèng Bīnguǎn (Post Hotel)   This clean and friendly three-star establishment opened in 2002. Rooms vary in size; a larger room is worth paying more for. The friendly travel agency will provide free information, but it isn't allowed to arrange your trip to Lhasa.

Yíngbīn Lù (directly opposite railway station). ✆ 0979/845-7001. Fax 0979/845-7020. 59 units (51 with shower only). ¥80 ($10) bed in a shared standard room; ¥128–¥168 ($16–$21) single; ¥128 ($16) standard room; ¥388 ($48) suite. No credit cards. **Amenities:** Restaurant; bike rental; concierge; tour desk; business center; same-day laundry/dry cleaning. *In room:* TV.

WHERE TO DINE

Liúyi Shǒu HOT POT   If you don't speak Chinese, a waiter will lead you straight to the kitchen, where you can select all the meat and vegetables you want. Two broths, spicy and nonspicy, are then brought to your table so that you can do the cooking yourself. As an added bonus, you get a bib to protect your shirt from any unforeseen splashes of spicy soup.

Cháidámù Lù 59. ✆ 0979/841-5333. Meal for 2 ¥50–¥80 ($6–$10). No credit cards. 9:30am–11pm.

6 Lhasa (Lāsà)

1,165km (722 miles) S of Golmud, 278km (172 miles) E of Shigatse. Altitude: 3,600m (11,808 ft.)

The religious and political heart of the Tibetan world, Lhasa sits on the north bank of the Kyi Chu, surrounded by colossal mountain ranges to the north and south. The first hint that you are entering the traditional capital of Tibet is the red and white palaces of the **Potala** 🌸🌸, home to Tibet's spiritual and temporal leaders, the Dalai Lamas, since the 17th century. Most Western visitors, however, are disillusioned to find a Chinese city. The Dalai Lama, the other enduring symbol of Tibetan purity and

Lhasa

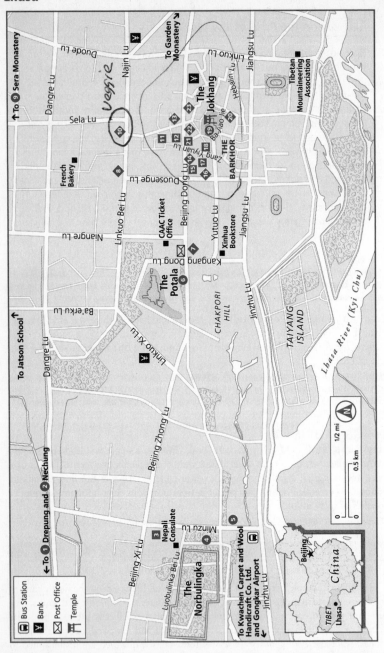

Legend:
- Bus Station
- Bank
- Post Office
- Temple

Map labels:

To 9 Sera Monastery
To Garden Monastery
Duode Lu
Najin Lu
Dangre Lu
Linkuo Lu
Jiangsu Lu
Tibetan Mountaineering Association
Veggie
Sela Lu
The Jokhang
Hebalin Lu
Ba'jiao Jie
THE BARKHOR
French Bakery
Linkuo Bei Lu
Duosenge Lu
Beijing Dong Lu
Zang Yiyuan Lu
Yutuo Lu
Niangre Lu
CAAC Ticket Office
Xinhua Bookstore
Jiangsu Lu
Kangang Dong Lu
The Potala
CHAKPORI HILL
Jinzhu Lu
TAIYANG ISLAND
Ba'erku Lu
Linkuo Xi Lu
Lhasa River (Kyi Chu)
Dangre Lu
To Jatson School
Beijing Zhong Lu
To 1 Drepung and 2 Nechung
Beijing Xi Lu
Luobulinka Bei Lu
The Norbulingka
Nepali Consulate
Minzu Lu
To Kwachen Carpet and Wool Handicraft Co. Ltd. and Gongkar Airport
Jinzhu Lu

Inset map:
Beijing
China
TIBET
Lhasa

Scale:
1/2 mi
0.5 km

ACCOMMODATIONS ■
Dhod Gu Hotel
(Dūngù Bīnguǎn) **22**
敦固宾馆
Kerry Hotel
(Jírì Fàndiàn) **23**
吉日饭店
Kyichu Hotel
(Jíqū Fàndiàn) **15**
吉曲饭店
Lhasa Hotel
(Lāsà Fàndiàn) **3**
拉萨饭店
Oh Dan Guesthouse
(Ōudān Bīnguǎn) **11**
欧丹宾馆
Pentoc Guesthouse
(Pānduō Bīnguǎn) **17**
攀多宾馆
Yak Hotel
(Yǎkè Bīnguǎn) **12**
亚宾馆

DINING ◆
Alu Cang Restaurant
(Ā'uócāng Cāntīng) **16**
阿罗仓餐厅
Dunya Restaurant
and Bar
(Dūnyà Jiǔbā) **13**
敦亚酒吧

Holy Land Vegetarian
Restaurant
(Gāoyuánhóng
Shūcàiguǎn) **10**
高原红蔬菜馆
Mayke Ame
(Mǎjí Ā'mǐ) **20**
玛吉阿米
Naga Restaurant
(Naga Xī Cāntīng) **14**
西餐厅
Niúwěi **8**
牛尾
Shānchéng Míng
Xiǎochī **21**
山城名小吃
Shangrila Restaurant
(Xiānggélǐlā Zàngshí) **23**
香格里拉藏食
Snowlands Restaurant
(Xuěyù Cāntīng) **18**
雪域餐厅
Xīnshìjì Bīnguǎn **7**
新世纪宾馆

ATTRACTIONS ●
Drepung Monastery
(Zhébàng Sì) **1**
哲蚌寺
Jokhang Temple
(Dàzhāo Sì) **19**
大昭寺

Nechung Monastery
(Nǎiqióng Sì) **2**
乃琼寺
Norbulingka
(Luóbùlínkǎ) **4**
罗布林卡
Potala Palace
(Bùdálā Gōng) **6**
布达拉宫
Sera Monastery
(Sèlā Sì) **9**
色拉寺
Tibet Museum
(Xīzàng
Bówùguǎn) **5**
西藏博物馆

mystery, fled the grounds of his summer residence, the **Norbulingka,** more than 40 years ago.

Nowhere is the grip of Chinese rule tighter. The effects of martial law, declared in March 1989, are still felt in Lhasa, particularly in the nearby Geluk monasteries of **Drepung** ⚔ and **Sera.** Hú Yàobāng, general secretary of the CCP during the early 1980s, compared Chinese policies and attitudes in Tibet to colonialism, and this feeling is still hard to shake. Since the 1980s, waves of Hàn migration from poor neighboring provinces have made Tibetans a minority in their own capital. Ironically, Hú Yàobāng's policy of opening Tibet to migration and trade led to this influx of Hàn migrants, which most Tibetans consider the most odious aspect of Chinese rule.

All Tibetan Buddhists aim to visit Lhasa at least once in their lives, drawn by the sacred **Jokhang Temple** ⚔⚔⚔, which forms the heart of the Tibetan quarter. It is recommended that you spend most of your time exploring this captivating neighborhood, also known as the **Barkhor District.**

ESSENTIALS

GETTING THERE   Previously, visitors to Tibet needed a group of five to constitute a tour group and thus obtain a Tibet Tourism Bureau (TTB) permit, which allows entry to the TAR. Now you can be a group of one. Those arriving by **air** from Kathmandu can obtain a standard 1-month tourist (L) visa and a TTB permit only by joining a group tour through a travel agency. Two good choices are **Royal Mt. Trekking,** P.O. Box 10798, Durbar Marg, Kathmandu (© **977-1/424-1452;** fax 977-1/424-5318; www.royal-mt-trek.com); and **Green Hill Tours & Treks,** P.O. Box 5072, Kathmandu (© **977-1/441-4803;** fax 977-1/441-9985; www.greenhilltours.com). **Gongkar Airport** is 97km (60 miles) southeast of Lhasa. Buses (1½ hr.; ¥35/$4.40) connect the airport with the **CAAC** ticket office in Lhasa at Niángrè Lù 1 (© **0891/683-3446**). The buses depart the office for the airport about 3 hours before flights. Check when purchasing your ticket, or call © **0891/682-6282.**

For tickets, fill out a form obtained from the information desk to the left, join a long line to book your flight, swap your passport for an invoice which you pay at the counter to the right, and finally pick up the ticket from the front of the original line. There are daily flights to Běijīng and Chéngdū; to Xī'ān (Mon, Wed, Thurs, and Sun) via Xīníng; to Guǎngzhōu (Tues) via Chóngqìng; and to Zhōngdiàn (Wed). Flights from Chéngdū and Xīníng connect to most destinations in China.

Tickets for international connections with Kathmandu (Tues and Sat) and Hong Kong (Thurs) are purchased from the **International Tickets Desk** to the right. *Tip:* When lines are long and you're purchasing a domestic ticket, buy it from the international counter.

The **bus station** (© **0891/682-4469**) is at the south end of town. Those arriving from the overland trek from Golmud will find that purchasing a ticket back to Golmud is considerably less expensive. A direct bus to Golmud (1,165km/722 miles; 28–50 hr.; ¥210/$24, sleeper) leaves at 8:30am; buses to Xīníng (1,947km/1,207 miles, ¥340/$41, sleeper) leave at 11:30am. Buses to Lánzhōu (2,216km/1,374 miles) leave at 1:30pm and also pass through Golmud. Buses connect with Shigatse (6 hr.; ¥38/$4.70) every half-hour from 8:30am; and buses for Tsedang (4 hr.; ¥27–¥40/$3.40–$5) depart at 9am, 10am, and 1pm. A new direct bus to Kathmandu leaves every Friday for ¥580 ($73); the ride takes 20 to 30 hours, depending on road conditions.

GETTING AROUND   **Taxis** within town are ¥10 ($1.25) for any destination. **Minibuses** charging ¥2 (25¢) and **buses** (with conductors) charging ¥1 (15¢) are plentiful.

TOURS & GUIDES   If you arrive in Lhasa without a tour arranged, and you wish to visit **closed areas** beyond Shigatse in the west, Tsetang in the east, Naqu in the north, and the region immediately south of Lhasa, you will need an **Aliens' Travel Permit.** This can only be obtained by joining a tour through **Foreign Individual Traveler (FIT)** branches in the Snowland Hotel at Zàng Yīyuàn Lù 4 (© **0891/634-9239;** fax 0891/634-3854) and in the Banak Shol Hotel at Běijīng Zhōng Lù 8 (©/fax **0891/634-4397**). The latter currently enjoys the better reputation. FIT will also organize private transportation within Tibet. Restrictions on travel tend to increase around certain dates, particularly the Monlam Festival (sometime mid-Jan to mid-Feb), the Saka Dawa Festival (sometime mid-May to mid-June), and the Dalai Lama's birthday on July 6. Those planning extensive trips should organize your tours through other agencies well before you arrive. Of the Lhasa-based tour operators, **Shigatse Travels,** located inside the Yak Hotel (© **0891/633-0489;** fax 0891/633-0482; ststad@public.ls.xz.cn), is highly recommended.

For journeys to **open areas,** and for a direct trip to the Nepali border, an Aliens' Travel Permit is not required. You may be able to rely on public transport for certain parts of the journey, but it's fraught with difficulties, ranging from lax bus drivers who don't care about schedules, a very bumpy ride, and patchy transit lines between smaller towns. It's much, much better to proceed through independent drivers or tour operators. The most popular ways for tourists to get around Tibet is to hire a Land Cruiser; a 5- to 6-day tour from Lhasa to Zhāngmù, the Nepali border, should cost between ¥3,000 and ¥4,000 ($375–$490); meals and accommodations are extra. The car should comfortably seat four passengers. If you're looking to share a ride with other passengers, check out the bulletin-board postings at Snowlands, the Pentoc, and the Kerry Hotel. Be sure to draw up a contract with the driver stating where you will visit and how long the trip will last; make a deposit and try to negotiate withholding the balance (ideally 25%) until your tour is completed—many travelers have been left stranded. Also be sure to check out the vehicle before you embark on your trip—you may even want to take the car and driver on a test drive on the streets of Lhasa to see how the car performs before agreeing to embark into the wilderness. Once you do arrive at your destination, and if you're happy with the service, tip your driver ¥50 to ¥100 ($6–$12). Gifts of music cassettes are also highly appreciated.

Those planning mountaineering expeditions must obtain permits from the **Tibetan Mountaineering Association** (© **0891/633-3720**), housed in a building immediately north of the Himalaya Hotel. Whatever difficulties you face, you won't be the first traveler in Tibet to have his or her way blocked by the authorities.

FAST FACTS

Banks, Foreign Exchange & ATMs The main branch of the **Bank of China,** west of the Potala Palace at Línkuò Xī Lù 28, accepts traveler's checks and credit cards at counters 5 and 6. There is an international ATM. Summer hours are weekdays from 9am to 1pm and 3:30 to 6pm; weekends 10am to 5pm. Winter hours are weekdays from 9:30am to 1:30pm and 3:30 to 6pm; weekends from 10:30am to 4:30pm. A branch of the bank on the northeast side of town, at Nàjīn Lù 188, exchanges cash and traveler's checks at counter 1, open weekdays from 9am to 1pm and 3:30 to 6pm; weekends from 10am to 5pm. Another branch that deals only in cash and traveler's checks is just west of the Banak Shol Hotel on Běijīng Dōng Lù. It's open weekdays from 9:30am to 1pm and 3 to 6pm.

Consulates North of the Norbulinka Palace, the **Nepalese Consulate-General** at Luóbùlínkǎ Běi Lù 13 (© **0891/682-2881;** fax 0891/683-6890) is open from 10am to 12:30pm on weekdays. Visas are processed in 1 day. Your first Nepalese visa for the year is valid for 60 days, and costs ¥255 ($32). If it's your second visa for the year, it's only valid for 30 days. Non-Chinese nationals can arrange their visas at the border (Zhāngmù). You can get a transit visa for free if you're only staying in Nepal for three days or less. Consular officials joke that this may be the only example of preferential treatment for foreigners in the TAR.

Internet Access The 24-hour **100M Wǎngbā,** Běijīng Zhōng Lù 155 (© **0891/ 633-3633**), offers broadband Internet access for ¥5 (65¢) per hour. The **Snowlands Guesthouse** (© **0891/633-7323**) has several computer terminals that also cost ¥5 (65¢) per hour. You can get your digital pictures downloaded onto a CD here, too. East of the post office is **Yóuzhèng Wǎngbā** (© **0891/624-1431**). The **Yak Hotel** at

Běijīng Zhōng Lù 100 (© **0891/632-3496**) has several computers, and stays open until 4am. Dial-up is © **165.**

Post Office The main post office is at Běijīng Dōng Lù 33. Summer hours are from 9am to 8pm; winter hours are from 9:30am to 6:30pm. The counter to the far left designated INTERNATIONAL POST BUSINESS is efficient; it's open from 9am to noon and 3:30 to 5:30pm.

Visa Extensions Here, travelers face the most feared **PSB** in China, at Běijīng Dōng Lù 4 (© **0891/632-4528**). At the entrance, a notice board instructs employees in the usage of polite language. Unfortunately, it's in Chinese. Visa officers spit out the term "individual traveler" as through it's a disfiguring and contagious affliction. They offer extensions of up to 5 days, usually processed in half a day. Hours are weekdays from 9am to 12:30pm and 3:30 to 6pm. Longer extensions are possible if you have an onward air ticket or have already arranged a tour. Extend your visa in Shigatse.

EXPLORING LHASA
Drepung Monastery (Zhébàng Sì)
Founded in 1416 by Tsongkapa's disciple Jamyang Choeje, Drepung was once Tibet's largest and most influential monastery, with over 10,000 monks. The seat of the Dalai Lamas before the "Great Fifth" Dalai Lama built the Potala Palace, many buildings survived the Cultural Revolution, but the order now pays a price for its prominent role in the pro-independence demonstrations of 1987. On September 27, 1987, about 20 Drepung monks unfurled banners and the Tibetan flag, and marched around the Barkhor before being arrested in front of the TAR Government HQ. This politicization of the monks is remarkable, as they were once loyal to their college first, and country second. Monks at Loseling College fought *against* Tibetan independence after the fall of the Qīng. The effects of a program of political indoctrination undertaken in 1996 are still felt. A PSB compound sits below the monastery, and "cadre monks" keep a close eye on day-to-day activities.

A circuit of the monastery begins with **Ganden Podrang (Ganden Palace),** and continues on to **Tsokchen (Assembly Hall), Ngakpa Tratsang (College of Tantric Studies), Jamyang Drubpuk** (Jamyang Choeje's **meditation cave,** attached to the east wall of the Assembly Hall), **Loseling Tratsang (College of Dialectics),** and **Tashi Gomang Tratsang.** The pilgrimage trail continues southeast down to the shadowy and enthralling **Nechung Monastery (Nǎiqióng Sì)** , home of the Nechung Oracle, who is consulted by the Dalai Lama on important matters of state. Separate admission to Nechung is ¥10 ($1.25).

To the left (west) of Drepung's Assembly Hall is the **kitchen,** where butter tea is prepared in huge wooden vats. Make much-needed donations to the monastery here. With the passing of the charismatic teacher Gen Lamrim in 1997, Drepung lost a major source of income. This master's lectures once drew devotees from all over the Tibetan world. The first floor of the **Assembly Hall** holds a striking statue of Dalai Lama XIII, magnificently lit by filtered sunshine and pungent yak butter lamps. Readings of the scriptures are often held at midday; hopefully you will be able to enjoy the spectacle of novices tumbling over one another in the race to fetch tea from the kitchen for their elders. Also popular with pilgrims is a chapel to the north of the second floor, which houses a mirror said to cure the facial diseases of those who gaze into it. The most revered image is a 15m-tall (49-ft.) statue of the 8-year-old **Maitreya Buddha,** designed by Tsongkapa and housed in the northwest section of the building, usually viewed from the third floor. You will be offered holy water: Cup your right hand above your left, take a quick sip, and splash the rest on your head.

© 0891/686-3149. Admission ¥55 ($7). 9am–4:30pm. Morning buses (10km/6¼ miles; 30 min.; ¥3/40¢) depart from west of the Jokhang. Returning to Lhasa, take bus no. 302 from Nechung Monastery, or bus no. 301 from the bottom of the hill.

Jokhang Temple (Dàzhāo Sì)   To fully explore Tibet's spiritual heart, visit this temple twice. From 8am, pilgrims line up to enter the Jokhang. You'll have no trouble singling the eager out-of-towners from the more detached city folk. In the morning, the rooms are unlocked, allowing pilgrims to rub their foreheads furiously against the sacred images. Your visit can be a painfully slow shuffle, lasting up to 2 hours, but it can be a moving experience.

Don't miss the image of **Palden Lhamo** on the third floor. The fierce protector of both Lhasa and the Dalai Lama, she is said to have murdered her own child to bring her husband and king to his senses and put an end to his endless military campaigns. Note the exquisite **deer and wheel motifs** on the roof. Both symbols allude to Sakyamuni's first sermon, "Turning the Wheel of the Doctrine," delivered in a deer park in Benares. Sakyamuni was initially reluctant to expound his teachings, believing they would be incomprehensible to most, but the god Brahma intervened. The deer and the wheel hark back to a time when believers respectfully avoided depicting the Buddha. A bodhi tree and a solitary footprint were also common symbols.

In the afternoon, a gate to the right of the main entrance admits tourists, and gives you an opportunity to view the ancient statuary and woodwork in relative peace, strident Chinese tour guides notwithstanding. The most revered object in Tibet is **Jowo Rinpoche**, a 1.5m (5-ft.) image of the young Buddha, which originated in India and was brought with Princess Wénchéng as dowry. Many credit her with selecting the temple's location according to the principles of geomancy (fēngshuǐ). Without the bustle of the morning crowd, take time to appreciate the ancient Newari door frames, columns, and finials (7th and 8th c.). Note the more recent yab-yum images of sexual union in a chapel to the south. Many mistakenly believe tantric practice has no place in the "reformed" Geluk School, but Tsongkapa simply restated the principle that only advanced practitioners should engage in tantric sex.

© 0891/633-6858. Admission ¥70 ($9). 8am–6:30pm.

Norbulingka (Luóbùlínkǎ)   Whatever traits the various manifestations of the Dalai Lama share, architectural taste is not one of them. The manicured gardens of the summer residence are pleasant—especially on weekends when locals gather for picnics—but the buildings, added by the 7th (who choose the site for its medicinal springs), 8th, 13th, and 14th incarnations, do not sit well together. The most interesting is **Takten Podrang,** commissioned by Dalai Lama XIV in 1954, 5 years before he fled to India. As at the Potala Palace, the lack of luxuries is striking. On the second floor is a fascinating **mural** depicting the history of Tibet, from the legendary union of a wild ogress with a monkey (an emanation of Avalokiteshvara), to the final frame of the young Dalai and Panchen Lamas meeting with Máo Zédōng and Zhōu Ēnlái. Duck under the rope to get a good look.

© 0891/682-6274. Admission ¥70 ($9). Mon–Sat 9am–1pm and 2:30–5:30pm; Sun 10am–1pm and 4–5:30pm.

Potala Palace (Bùdálā Gōng)   Commissioned by Dalai Lama V (17th c.), the Potala was built around the fortress of King Songtsen Gampo, which had stood usually viewed from the third floor. You will be offered holy water: Cup your right hand above your left, take a quick sip, and splash the rest on your head.

(**©** 0891/686-3149. Admission ¥55 ($7). 9am–4:30pm. Morning buses (10km/6¼ miles; 30 min.; ¥3/40¢) depart from west of the Jokhang. Returning to Lhasa, take bus no. 302 from Nechung Monastery, or bus no. 301 from the bottom of the hill.

Jokhang Temple (Dàzhāo Sì) ✿✿✿   To fully explore Tibet's spiritual heart, visit this temple twice. From 8am, pilgrims line up to enter the Jokhang. You'll have no trouble singling the eager out-of-towners from the more detached city folk. In the morning, the rooms are unlocked, allowing pilgrims to rub their foreheads furiously against the sacred images. Your visit can be a painfully slow shuffle, lasting up to 2 hours, but it can be a moving experience.

Don't miss the image of **Palden Lhamo** ✿ on the third floor. The fierce protector of both Lhasa and the Dalai Lama, she is said to have murdered her own child to bring her husband and king to his senses and put an end to his endless military campaigns. Note the exquisite **deer and wheel motifs** on the roof. Both symbols allude to Sakyamuni's first sermon, "Turning the Wheel of the Doctrine," delivered in a deer park in Benares. Sakyamuni was initially reluctant to expound his teachings, believing they would be incomprehensible to most, but the god Brahma intervened. The deer and the wheel hark back to a time when believers respectfully avoided depicting the Buddha. A bodhi tree and a solitary footprint were also common symbols.

In the afternoon, a gate to the right of the main entrance admits tourists, and gives you an opportunity to view the ancient statuary and woodwork in relative peace, strident Chinese tour guides notwithstanding. The most revered object in Tibet is **Jowo Rinpoche** ✿✿✿, a 1.5m (5-ft.) image of the young Buddha, which originated in India and was brought with Princess Wénchéng as dowry. Many credit her with selecting the temple's location according to the principles of geomancy *(fēngshuǐ)*. Without the bustle of the morning crowd, take time to appreciate the ancient Newari door frames, columns, and finials (7th and 8th c.). Note the more recent *yab-yum* images of sexual union in a chapel to the south. Many mistakenly believe tantric practice has no place in the "reformed" Geluk School, but Tsongkapa simply restated the principle that only advanced practitioners should engage in tantric sex.

(**©** 0891/633-6858. Admission ¥70 ($9). 8am–6:30pm.

Norbulingka (Luóbùlínkǎ)   Whatever traits the various manifestations of the Dalai Lama share, architectural taste is not one of them. The manicured gardens of the summer residence are pleasant—especially on weekends when locals gather for picnics—but the buildings, added by the 7th (who choose the site for its medicinal springs), 8th, 13th, and 14th incarnations, do not sit well together. The most interesting is **Takten Podrang,** commissioned by Dalai Lama XIV in 1954, 5 years before he fled to India. As at the Potala Palace, the lack of luxuries is striking. On the second floor is a fascinating **mural** ✿ depicting the history of Tibet, from the legendary union of a wild ogress with a monkey (an emanation of Avalokiteshvara), to the final frame of the young Dalai and Panchen Lamas meeting with Máo Zédōng and Zhōu Ēnlái. Duck under the rope to get a good look.

(**©** 0891/682-6274. Admission ¥70 ($9). Mon–Sat 9am–1pm and 2:30–5:30pm; Sun 10am–1pm and 4–5:30pm.

Potala Palace (Bùdálā Gōng) ✿✿   Commissioned by Dalai Lama V (17th c.), the Potala was built around the fortress of King Songtsen Gampo, which had stood on **Mount Mapori** for a millennium. "Potala" refers to a mountain in south India, the abode of Tibet's patron deity, Avalokiteshvara (Chenresik). Both the ancient kings and the Dalai Lamas are said to be manifestations of this bodhisattva, feminized in the Chinese Buddhist pantheon as Guānyīn, the goddess of mercy. A monastery, a palace, and a prison, it symbolizes the fusion of secular and religious power in Tibet. Early Tibetan temples, such as Samye Monastery, followed the Indian practice of modest locations, allowing temples to adhere to a mandala design. The Great Fifth, the last significant Dalai Lama before Dalai Lama XIII, was fond of imposing hilltop locations, making adherence to the mandala pattern impossible. Tibetologist Guiseppe Tucci saw the Potala as an "outgrowth of the rock underlying it, as irregular and whimsical as nature's work," and it was not a simple project. **Podrang Marpo (Red Palace)** was completed under the regent Desi Sangye Gyatso, 15 years after the then–Dalai Lama's death in 1682, and involved over 8,000 workers and artisans.

Most visitors enter the palace via the central staircase up to the **Eastern Courtyard (Deyang Shar).** Buildings are denoted numerically. You first reach the **Eastern Apartments** of the Dalai Lama XIV (3). Portraits of Dalai Lamas XIV and XIII once hung above the entrance, but they were removed in 1996. Inside the entrance is a splendid mural of Wǔtái Shān in northeast China, the earthly Pure Land of Manjusri, a bodhisattva who symbolizes wisdom. The simplicity of the present Dalai Lama's personal chambers, with prayer beads still resting by the bed, is moving, particularly for those who have met His Holiness. You next enter the **Red Palace,** the spiritual center and home to the remains of all the Dalai Lamas (except Dalai Lama VI, who was fonder of wenches than worship, and was eventually chased into exile by the Mongols). The throne room of Dalai Lama VII, **Sasum Lhakang** (6), contains an exquisite silver statue of Avalokiteshvara and an inscription on the north wall, dated 1722, wishing that the Chinese emperor would reign for ten thousand years. The Kāngxī emperor died in 1722. The most sacred chapel is **Phakpa Lhakang** ⚝ (10), part of the original 7th-century palace and housing a "self-arising" image of Avalokiteshvara. Even Chinese visitors are awed. As Tucci observed in the 1950s, "The crowds of pilgrims daily ascending the stairs of the Potala were a tangible proof of devotion. Rich or poor, dignitaries or peasants, they kneeled before each image: faith and ecstasy could be read on their faces. Holding copper pitchers full of clarified butter, they went to feed the temple lamps."

A meditation cave, **Chogyel Drupuk** (17), contains an image of Songtsen Gampo, with his Nepali and Chinese wives; it dates from the 7th or 8th century. The Dalai Lama V's death was kept secret for 12 years; his reliquary stupa is the most magnificent structure in the palace, containing over 3,000 kilograms (6,600 lb.) of gold, encrusted in jewels, and disappearing into the darkness of **Serdung Lhakang** (21).

Warning: Visits to the Potala are best made *after* you are accustomed to the altitude.

Běijīng Zhōng Lù. ✆ 0891/683-4362. Admission ¥100 ($13). You must make a reservation a few hours to 1 day in advance; at the ticket counter you will be assigned a time to return for entry. Admission to relics museum and roof additional ¥10 ($1.25) each. 9am–3pm.

Sera Monastery (Sèlā Sì)

This major Geluk monastery was founded in the early 15th century by Sakya Yeshe, a disciple of Tsongkapa. A pilgrimage circuit of the complex passes the colleges **Sera Me Tratsang, Ngakpa Tratsang,** and **Sera Je Tratsang** before reaching **Tsokchen,** the huge assembly hall (ca. 18th c.), which houses an image of Sakya Yeshe. The path continues up to **Sera Utse,** a hermitage that predates the monastery, a stiff 1½-hour hike up the mountain. Most visitors are drawn to Sera by the lively **debates** ☺☺☺ held in the Sera Je Tratsang Courtyard Monday to Saturday from 3 to 5pm.

Debates provide an opportunity for monks to demonstrate their scholarship and rise through the ranks. A prodigious body of religious literature must be digested before a monk can become a useful sophist. Visitors usually are struck by the physicality of the debates, with one monk sitting down, biding his time, while the other launches a verbal and physical attack. One monk noted that they were instructed that "the foot must come down so strongly that the door of hell may be broken open; and that the hands must make so great a noise that the voice of knowledge may frighten the devils all the world over."

© 0891/638-3639. Admission ¥60 ($7.50). 9am–4:30pm. Bus: no. 5 from northwest corner of Běijīng Dōng Lù and Duǒsēngé Lù.

Tibet Museum (Xīzàng Bówùguǎn)   While the Communist Party's propaganda ranges from laughable to downright offensive in this museum, it's still worth a visit for its extensive displays of *thangkas* (Tibetan scrolls), instruments, and gold copper statues of Buddhas. The museum also houses the gold seal of the vaunted 5th Dalai Lama, who is credited with unifying Tibet in the 17th century (though this isn't mentioned in the museum). A spiffy audio tour is included in the price of admission. The third floor isn't worth visiting, unless you like stuffed animal dioramas. Be sure to pick up the free pamphlet issued by the Information Office of the State Council, which recalls "the four glorious decades of regional ethnic autonomy in Tibet."

Admission ¥35 ($4.40). 9am–6:30pm.

SHOPPING

Just east of the Lhasa Hotel, **Téngwáng Pīfā Gòuwù Zhōngxīn** at Běijīng Zhōng Lù 71 (© **0891/681-8025**) is a well-stocked supermarket (open 9am–11:30pm). **Sàikāng Dàshà** is a fancy department store, 1 block east of the post office, open from 10am to 9pm. The **French Bakery** in Tuánjié Xīncūn (© **0891/634-9279;** Mon–Sat 11am–9pm) has wonderful *gâteaux.*

Thangka shops seem to be all over Lhasa now. In many storefront windows you'll see an artist hard at work at a canvas, painting the tiny details onto the Tibetan scroll that is used for meditation. Prices can range from several dollars to several thousand. The **Tibet Thangka Art House** (Zàng Yīyuàn Lù 75; © **0891/671-5338** or 1364-898-2836; riverintibet@sina.com.cn), **Eizhi Exquisite Tangka Shop** (Jírì Yīxiāng; © **0891/656-2509**), and **Dropenling** (listed below) are a few shops worth checking out.

Dropenling ☺ *(Finds)*   Taking its name from a Tibetan word that means "giving back for the betterment of all mankind," this store, tucked away near the Muslim quarter of Lhasa, gives all its profits back to the Tibetan artisans who make the store's handicrafts in an attempt to help Tibetan artisans compete with the Nepalese, whose goods have flooded Tibetan markets in recent years. The emphasis here is on quality—from fine-woven rugs to handbags and jewelry, which also comes with a hefty price tag. The store's goods have inspired pirates to make knockoffs for sale on the pilgrim's circuit of Johkong, but they aren't of the same quality.

Chak Tsal Gang Rd. 11 (just north of the Lhasa Mosque, about a 10-min. walk from Johkong Monastery.) © 0891/636-0558. www.tibetcraft.com. AE, DC, MC, V. 10am–8pm.

Jatson School (Cǎiquán Fúlì Tèshū Xuéxiào) *(Finds) (Kids)*   By shopping here, you are helping Tibet's handicrafts tradition to survive, and giving poor, orphaned, and disabled children a shot at life. They don't receive a *fēn* from the government, so your support is valued. Shopping doesn't have to be a guilty pleasure. The store, tucked away to the right of the entrance, sells traditional Tibetan clothing, paper, incense, mandala *thangkas*, yak-hide boots, dolls, door hangings, and more. Prices are more than fair, and you'll probably want to give more. The quality of work is astounding, and as nearly everything is made on-site, you can watch how it's done. Store hours are Monday to Saturday from 9:30am to 5:30pm.

Xuě Xīn Èr Cūn, 101 Xīnxiāng. ⓒ 0891/682-2130. Bus: no. 97 to Xuě Sāncūn; walk south, and the school is on the right-hand (west) side.

Khawachen Carpet and Wool Handicraft Co. Ltd (Kāwājiān Dìtǎn Hé Yángmáo Gōngyìpǐn Yǒuxiàn Gōngsī) *Value*   The hardy sheep of the Changtang produce wool that is ideal for carpet making. Unfortunately, most new Tibetan carpets or Hàn-inspired rugs use frightening themes or colors. This U.S.-Tibetan joint venture in the west of town gets it right: rich but tasteful shades woven into delightful traditional patterns. See the designs at www.innerasiarugs.com. You'll be able to pick them up a lot cheaper here than from the New York headquarters or the Lufthansa Center in Běijīng. Carpets can be made to order; allow a week for an average-size carpet. You're free to inspect the entire process from dyeing and drying to weaving and cutting. Unlike Lhasa's main Hàn-run factory (where 14-hr. shifts are common), conditions here are excellent. A courtesy car to the factory is provided for visitors, credit cards are accepted, and shipping can be arranged. Hours are Monday to Saturday from 9am to 1pm and 3 to 7pm.

Jīnzhū Xī Lù 103. ⓒ 0891/683-3257.

WHERE TO STAY
From December to March, Lhasa sees very few tourists, and most hoteliers halve their prices.

VERY EXPENSIVE
Lhasa Hotel (Lāsà Fàndiàn)   Situated in the Hàn part of town, north of the Norbulinka Palace, the former Holiday Inn Lhasa is no longer a well-run property. Many well-trained staff remain, but the enormous block-shaped hotel is disintegrating, from the stained carpets to the overgrown grounds, and you run the risk of dying a slow death waiting for service. The Tibetan-style rooms are more appealing and tend to be heavily booked. Aside from the older north wing *(běi lóu)*, all rooms have piped-in oxygen.

Mínzú Lù 1. ⓒ 0891/683-2221. Fax 0891/683-5796. 456 units. ¥1,020–¥1,555 ($127–$194) single or standard; from ¥2,058 ($257) suite. Rates include breakfast. 30% discounts; 15% service charge. AE, DC, MC, V. **Amenities:** 5 restaurants; bar; cafe; health club; concierge; tour desk; business center; forex (8am–10pm); shopping arcade; 24-hr. room service; same-day dry cleaning/laundry. *In room:* A/C, satellite TV, hair dryer.

MODERATE
Dhod Gu Hotel ⓡ   A Nepalese-owned venture, this hotel gets rave reviews from American tourists. It's conveniently located in the Tibetan quarter, the staff speaks English, and the rooms are very comfortable. Furnished with a sensory overload of tasteful Tibetan decorations, each room is uniquely designed, though lighting could be better. Bathrooms, though a bit worn, are squeaky clean. The big drawback here is the price, which is a little higher than some of its competitors.

Xiàlāsù Lù19. ⓒ 0891/632-2555. Fax 0891/632-3555. www.dhodghuhotel.com. 62 units. ¥400–¥640 ($50–$80) standard room; ¥1,050 ($125) suite. AE, DC, MC, V. **Amenities:** 3 restaurants; bakery; business center; laundry service; doctor on call; safe deposit; travel agent; forex. *In room:* A/C, satellite TV.

Kyichu Hotel (Jíqǔ Fàndiàn) 🏆🏆   Located in the Tibetan quarter, the Kyichu combines Western comfort with a welcoming Tibetan atmosphere. Rooms in the new south wing opened in 2001. Overlooking an incongruous lawn with white outdoor furniture, these midsize rooms boast clean wooden floors, simple furnishings, and spotless bathrooms with deep tubs. Tourists rave about the excellent service here, saying that the staff members are the nicest people in all of Tibet. The solar-heated hot water can be unreliable. The restaurant on the first floor prepares a superb buffet breakfast for ¥30 ($3.70).

Běijīng Dōng Lù 149. ⓒ 0891/633-1347. Fax 0891/632-0234. www.hotelkyichu.com. 52 units (22 with shower only). ¥230–¥320 ($29–$40) standard room. 20% discounts. AE, DC, MC, V. **Amenities:** Restaurant; bike rental; concierge; business center; same-day laundry. *In room:* TV.

Yak Hotel (Yǎkè Bīnguǎn)   Popular with both tour groups and individual travelers, this hotel is several notches up from some of the decrepit guesthouses that line Běijīng Dōng Lù. Individual rooms are decorated with Tibetan furnishings while the dorm rooms are plain and functional. Both the Yak and the Pentoc (listed below) are often considered "hubs" where tourists gather and share information. The bathrooms are very clean and showers are inviting. Next door is the ever-popular Dunya restaurant. The staff here is decent, though unwilling to give much of a discount as the place is often booked. Reserve ahead of time.

Běijīng Dōng Lù 100. ⓒ 0891/632-3496. 100 units. ¥30 ($4) dorm bed; ¥380 ($50) standard room. No credit cards. **Amenities:** Restaurant; travel agent; business center; same-day laundry. *In room:* A/C, TV.

INEXPENSIVE

Oh Dan Guesthouse (Ōudān Bīnguǎn) 🏆 *Finds*   Tucked away on a street that runs past Ramonche Monastery just north of Běijīng Dōng Lù, this new entry on the guesthouse scene offers immaculately clean and fresh rooms and bathrooms. It's near enough to the Barkhor but its location on a typical Tibetan street is so far devoid of the trappings of backpacker development. The rooftop patio offers stunning view of Potala Palace. The guesthouse has a rotating program of activities nightly, from *thangka* workshops to *momo* (dumpling) making to movie night.

Xiǎozhāo Sì Lù 15. ⓒ 0891/634-4999. Fax 0891/636-3992. 40 units. ohdan_guesthouse@yahoo.com. ¥45 ($5.20) dorm bed; ¥188 ($24) standard room without bathroom; ¥288 ($36) standard room with bathroom. Up to 30% discount. No credit cards. **Amenities:** Restaurant; travel agent; business center; laundry. *In room:* TV.

Pentoc Guesthouse (Pāduō Bīnguǎn) 🏆 *Value*   This guesthouse, once my favorite haunt in Lhasa, has suffered from its huge popularity (book ahead). Its constantly sold-out rooms, none of which have private bathrooms, are now showing sign of age. The staff is apathetic and moody on a bad day and enthusiastic on a good day, and the common showers are equally temperamental. Still, if you like a college dormitory atmosphere, enjoy meeting people, and don't have a lot of cash to spend on accommodations, this is a great place to stay. The hostel, Swiss-owned with Christian leanings, is ideally situated from exploring the Tibetan heart of Lhasa, located right next to the Barkhor Square District. The second-floor restaurant offers an ideal space, decorated with a Tibetan tent, to trade travel tips; it serves a good breakfast, too (but the good-looking baked goods always turn out a bit dry and flavorless). Movies are shown each night at 8pm.

Zàng Yīyuàn Dōng Lù 5. © 0891/632-6686. Fax 0891/633-0700. pentoc@public.ls.xz.cn. 24 units (no bathrooms). ¥40 ($5) dorm bed; ¥80 ($10) standard room. No credit cards. **Amenities:** Restaurant; bike rental; business center; 24-hr. forex; next-day laundry. *In room:* No phone.

WHERE TO DINE

Alu Cang Restaurant (Ā'luócāng Cāntīng) ⋇ TIBETAN
On the western edge of the Tibetan quarter, this restaurant is a longtime favorite with locals, who appreciate its unpretentious style and hearty cuisine. The second floor is packed at most hours. The English menu is unreliable, with beef and lamb often translated as yak. Specialties include radish with yak meat (lamb) and fried mutton spareribs. The simple curry rice is an excellent choice for those on the run. Notice the boycott of the Hàn-owned Lhasa Beer—Tibetans who can afford it drink Budweiser or Blue Label.

Duòsēngé Lù 21–32. © 0891/633-8826. Meal for 2 ¥30–¥70 ($3.70–$8.70). No credit cards. 9am–10pm.

Dunya Restaurant and Bar ⋇ WESTERN
Located on the east side of the Yak Hotel, Dunya serves decent if uninspired Western cuisine that's enhanced a lively atmosphere. The menu offers pizza, pasta, and a range of Asian dishes, from Malaysian noodles to vegetable dumplings. If you've just landed in Lhasa, get the "altitude relax tea." Who knows if it actually works, but it tastes good. The convivial bar upstairs, open late, is a favorite with Lhasa's growing expat community, and the kitchen is supposedly one of the cleanest in town.

Běijīng Dōng Lù 100. © 0891/633-3374. Reservations recommended. Main courses ¥10–¥45 ($1.25–$5.60). No credit cards. Apr–Oct only: 8am–10pm. Bar open noon–2am.

Holy Land Vegetarian Restaurant ⋇⋇ (Finds) VEGETARIAN/SÌCHUĀN
Not far from the dreaded PSB, this new restaurant, opened by a local monk, may not be a "find" for long, given just how good the food is. Waitresses greet you with a light tea and a watermelon slice, and then the gluttony begins. Fake meats tend to creep some people out, but the wheat gluten and tofu replicas of chicken, sausage, and even intestines, are more delicious than the real thing. Try to *gōngbào jīdǐng* (kung pao chicken), *qīngchǎo máodòu* (beans with soy beef), *gānbiān sùcháng* (soy pork slices with green pepper), *sōngrén yùmǐ* (pine nuts, carrots, and sweet corn), and the *cháng xiāngsū* (sliced soy-pork sausages). If you prefer less spicy dishes, let the kitchen know. The restaurant, simply decorated with wooden tables, is popular with health-conscious Tibetans.

Línkuò Běi Lù Wàibànshāng Píngfáng 10. © 0891/636-3851. Meal for 2 ¥60–¥80 ($8–$10). No credit cards. 10am–10pm.

Mayke Ame (Mǎjí Ā'mǐ) ⋇ NEPALI/TIBETAN
On the southeast corner of the Barkhor circuit stands Lhasa's most enchanting eatery. This may be the first Tibetan chain restaurant—they have outlets in Běijīng and Kūnmíng. If it's chilly, take a seat on the second floor, with its comfy sofas and relaxing Tibetan folk music. On a sunny day, soak up the spectacle of the *kora* (circuit) from the third-floor balcony. The manners of the staff are strained by the Hàn clientele—the most popular Chinese guidebook lists one restaurant, and this is it. There are many excellent vegetarian choices, including spinach-tofu ravioli, and the vegetable curry set with delicious dal.

Bājiǎo Jiē Dōngnán Jiǎo. © 0891/632-4455. Main courses ¥15–¥35 ($1.90–$4.40). No credit cards. 10am–11:30pm.

Naga Restaurant ⚔ TIBETAN/NEPALI/CONTINENTAL   Located on what's become the main backpacker drag of Lhasa, this quiet and cozy restaurant where diners sit cross-legged on the floor at low tables offers a quiet, subtle environment to enjoy a variety of dishes from French ratatouille to Nepalese paneer curry. There's a selection of international magazines including the *New Yorker* for browsing while you sip the delicious masala tea. It's rumored that the restaurant is undergoing some management changes, but it is hoped they'll maintain the quality of the food. Service can be lackadaisical.

Zàng Yīyuàn Dōng Lù. ⚭ 0891/632-7509. puntso12@hotmail.com. English menu. Meal for 2 ¥50–¥100 ($6–$12). No credit cards. 8am–11pm.

Shānchéng Míng Xiǎochī ⚔ Ⓥ𝘢𝘭𝘶𝘦 SÌCHUĀN   Most of Lhasa's best Chinese restaurants are located in the gaudy bathroom-tiled part of town, but why make the effort when you can get delicious Sichuanese food right next to Barkhor Square? Popular with Tibetan pilgrims and backpackers, this unassuming joint with stools and grubby tables serves spicy, juicy dumplings in soup and a good twice-cooked pork. The steamed buns with pork *(bāozi)* deserve a special mention.

Zàng Yīyuàn Lù 9. ⚭ 0891/699-3167. English menu. Meal for 2 ¥20 ($2.50). No credit cards. 8am–11pm.

Snowland Restaurant ⚔ INTERNATIONAL/TIBETAN   With the feel of a New York diner that's frequented by the Tibetan elite and international travelers, Snowland has emerged as the most competent kitchen in town. You're not going to get earth-shattering fare here, but the variety of options, from Japanese teriyaki to Indian curries, is at least decent if not pretty good. The Yak pepper steak, nan, dumplings, and crêpes suzette are all recommended.

Zàng Yīyuàn Lù (near Barkhor Square). ⚭ 0891/633-7323. English menu. Meal for 2 ¥100 ($13). No credit cards. 7:30am–11:30pm.

LHASA AFTER DARK

It's doubtful whether the tongue-in-cheek performance offered by the **Shangrila Restaurant (Xiānggélǐlā Zàngshí)** inside the Kirey Hotel (⚭ 0891/636-3880) qualifies as art, but it's certainly entertainment—and kids love it! The campy pantomime is held nearly every night, and without giving away too much, watch out for the yak! The restaurant is open from 7:30am to 10:30pm, and the performance starts at 8pm. Reservations are recommended from July to September. An excellent Tibetan buffet can be enjoyed for ¥40 ($5).

The hottest *nangma* (Tibetan nightclub) around is **Niúwěi** (Línkǒu Běi Lù 13; ⚭ 0891/655-8383), where booths of Tibetans down beers and groove to Tibetan singers that perform on a stage with a picture backdrop of Potala Palace. Another hot spot is the karaoke-cum-disco on the second floor of **Xīnshìjì Bīngguǎn** at Běijīng Zhōng Lù 155 (⚭ 0891/633-4895). A placard in the foyer announces that it is also the home of the Cadre Training Center. It's open nightly from 10pm to 3am. The Dunya restaurant and bar (see above) is open until 2am and is a meeting ground for expats.

AROUND LHASA

Ganden Monastery (Gāndān Sì)   Shelled by the Chinese army during the peaceful liberation of Tibet, the most significant monastery of the **Geluk School** is slowly undergoing a revival. Perched on a mountain east of Lhasa, to the south of the Kyi Chu, it was built in 1409 by **Tsongkapa.** Drawing on support from monks of the older schools, as well as laypeople, the school rapidly expanded, with disciples opening Drepung and Sera monasteries in 1416 and 1419 respectively. Mongol support during the 17th century eventually assured their status as the preeminent school of Tibetan Buddhism, and more than 3,000 monks lived here prior to 1950.

Food and lodging at Ganden are basic, and both are provided by the guesthouse to the left (west) of the parking lot. In front of this decaying two-story building, peddlers hawk yak butter and fragrant grass *(sang)* to pilgrims. The **Meditation Hall (Nga-chokhang)** ⚑, to the right (east) of the path beyond the bus stop, is atmospheric. Tsongkapa instructed his first disciples here. Chanting and the creation of *torma* (butter sculptures) take place throughout the day. Inside, to the left, is one of several dark and gruesome protector deity shrines that are off-limits to women. Other notable buildings are the **Assembly Hall,** behind and to the right of a prominent white chorten, where a jolly monk is likely to thwack you on the head with the shoes and hat of Tsongkapa. On the opposite side of a courtyard is a printing house, and above it stands **Tsongkapa's Reliquary (Serdung Lhakang),** which was devastated during the Cultural Revolution. Tsongkapa's tooth remains. Pilgrims waste little time in undertaking a spectacular *lingkhor* **(pilgrimage circuit)** ⚑⚑. The pilgrimage path commences from a tangle of *tar-choks* (prayer flags) to the left of the monastery. Allow at least an hour—you are above 4,000m (13,120 ft.). For the fit and acclimatized, the peak to the west offers spectacular views of the lush surrounding countryside.

ⓒ **0891/614-2077.** Admission ¥45 ($5.50). Photography ¥20–¥30 ($2.50–$3.70). Buses for Ganden depart from west of Barkor Sq. 6am or 6:30am (45km/28 miles; 2 hr.; ¥20/$2.50 round-trip, ¥10/$1.25 one-way). Bus returns at 2pm.

Samye Monastery (Sāngyē Sì) ⚑⚑
About 39km (24 miles) west of Tsetang, on the northern banks of the **Yarlung Tsangpo (Brahmaputra River),** stands Tibet's first monastery (late 8th c.), famous for its striking mandala design and as the site of the "Great Debate" (792–94) between the Indian Mahayanists and Chán (Japanese: Zen) Buddhists from China. This intriguing and protracted religious debate, held in the **Western Temple (Jampa Ling),** ended in victory for the Mahayanists. A predictable result, as Tibet was at war with China on several fronts. Chinese records claim that they won the theological battle, but the numerous Chinese monks and translators were nonetheless expelled from Tibet, and Mahayanist orthodoxy was established. Although Samye has been razed several times, the mandala symmetry is intact. The main temple, **Samye Utse,** symbolizes Mount Meru, the center of the universe, surrounded by the four temples of the continents, the eight temples of each subcontinent, and the sun (south, ruined) and moon (north) temples. The best view is gained from **Hepo-Ri** to the east of Samye, where Padmasambhava (Guru Rinpoche) is said to have subdued the local demons, making the site safe for construction. The secular support of King Trisong Detsen, who proclaimed Buddhism the state religion in 779, was perhaps more crucial.

Samye Utse (¥40/$5; open 8am–5:30pm) demonstrates the classic principles of Tibetan architecture. A solid barnlike first floor tapers to refined and intricate upper tiers. To left of the entrance is an original 5m-tall (16-ft.) obelisk that proclaims Buddhism to be the state religion and urges future generations to obey Buddhist law and support the temple. Many of the murals on the first and second floors are original, but the lighting is poor, so bring a flashlight.

Basic accommodations are available at the **Samye Monastery Guesthouse** (ⓒ **0891/736-2086**) for ¥20 to ¥35 ($2.40–$4.20). Adequate fare is offered in the restaurant, which has an English menu.

From Lhasa, buses for Samye Crossing, or *dùkŏu* in Chinese; depart beginning at 7:30am for the 3½-hour trip (¥25/$3), just south of the New Mandala restaurant. After a nippy crossing of the Brahmaputra in an open, flat-bottomed boat (1 hr.; ¥10/$1.25), tractors (40 min.; ¥3/40¢) connect with the monastery. Buses leave the monastery for Lhasa (6 hr.; ¥40/$5) via Tsetang at 8:30am. A rented car and driver can take a carload of four round-trip for ¥1,000 ($125).

Chimpu Caves (Qīngpŭ Shāndòng) The Chimpu retreat caves gave monks relief from constant study, but were also crucial in maintaining Buddhist traditions during periods of persecution, and in transmitting teachings before formal monasteries were established.

A warren of caves set in a lush U-shaped valley, Chimpu boasts some of the most sacred pilgrimage destinations in Tibet, including the cave where Guru Rinpoche first instructed his Tibetan disciples. Below is **Guruta Rock,** where Guru Rinpoche displayed his yogic prowess by leaving an enormous footprint. Above and to the left is the **meditation cave of Vairocana,** where the master translator dwelt for 12 years, eating the naked rock and thus solving the twin dilemmas of food and shelter. Grains and beans are appreciated as gifts by less-gifted retreat ants; to understand why, imagine subsisting on *tsampa* for a year. It is possible to camp here (far from PSB checkpoints), and there is a small store.

Northeast of Samye Monastery. Free admission. A truck (15km/9¼ miles; 1 hr.; ¥10/$1.25) departs Samye Monastery Guesthouse about 8am, and returns early afternoon. The walk takes 4 hr.

A TRIP TO A NEARBY LAKE

Namtso Lake ✿✿ can be done as a 2- or 3-day trip, depending on how much peace and nature you want. The crystal blue waters surrounded by snowcapped mountains are stunning and a nice change from the (relatively) bustling pace of Lhasa. The best

Where Is the Panchen Lama?

In 1995, the world was stunned to learn that China's Marxist leaders were authorities on Tibetan Buddhism. Shortly after the Panchen Lama's death in 1989, then-premier Lǐ Péng declared that "outsiders" would not be allowed "to meddle with the selection process." It was clear Běijīng was keen to minimize the Dalai Lama's role in the selection of the child who will eventually become the teacher of the next Dalai Lama. The list of candidates was leaked to Dharamsala and the Dalai Lama announced his choice in May, catching the Chinese authorities by surprise. Predictably, the 6-year-old candidate disappeared a month later and has not been seen since. Gyaltsen Norbu, the "official" Panchen Lama XI, was chosen in a clandestine ceremony held in the **Jokhang** in November 1995, and recently made his first public appearance at **Tashilhunpo Monastery.** Tibet's religious leaders, with a few brave exceptions, recognize Gyaltsen as the Panchen Lama. But Běijīng wasn't the only side playing politics with a young boy's life. As one of the few level-headed commentators on this tragedy noted, "The two protagonists in the dispute were clearly swayed by their eagerness to use the issue to gain maximum propaganda value."

way to get there is to hire a Land Cruiser, which costs ¥1,500 ($190) and can take up to four travelers. It's a 5-hour journey from Lhasa, and at an altitude of 4,700m (15,416 ft.), you should definitely acclimatize in Lhasa for a few days before attempting the journey here. Admission to the lake is ¥40 ($5); save your ticket, it may be checked during your stay. Stay at the **Nàmùcuò Kèzhàn** (© 0891/651-1390; no credit cards) which offers basic dorm beds for ¥50 ($6) each. Rooms come in an array of sizes from standards to quads. The restaurant serves decent Sìchuān fare.

7 Shigatse (Rikāzé)

278km (172 miles) W of Lhasa, 91km (56 miles) NW of Gyantse. Altitude: 3,900m (12,792 ft.)

Set to the south of the confluence of the Brahmaputra River and the Nyang Chu, the second-largest town in Tibet is considerably smaller than Lhasa, its ancient rival for political power. For a period between the 16th and 17th centuries, **Shigatse** was the capital of Tibet, and even after the capital shifted to Lhasa, it maintained influence both as the center of the **Tsang region** and as the home of the **Panchen Lama,** who traditionally resides in **Tashilhunpo Monastery.** Unfortunately, Chinese-style development has taken over the town and the Tibetan quarter is rather small and touristy. *Note:* For Chinese translations of selected establishments listed in this section, please turn to appendix A.

ESSENTIALS

GETTING THERE   Air tickets may be purchased from the **CAAC** office inside the Bank of China on Zhūfēng Lù (© 0892/882-4252), open from 4 to 5pm. The **bus station** is on Shànghǎi Lù (© 0892/882-2903), just north of the Shigatse Hotel. Buses connect with Lhasa (6 hr.; ¥38/$4.70) at 8am and 9:30am, and minibuses depart throughout the morning. Buses to Gyantse (1½ hr.; ¥20–¥25/$2.50–$3) depart every 2 hours from 9:30am to 5:30pm; to Sakya Monastery (6 hr.; ¥32/$4) every other day at 8am; to Lhatse (4 hr.; ¥30/$3.70) at 9am; and to Shelkar (Dìngrì; 6½ hr.; ¥65/$8.10) at 8:30am. An office just south of the bus station (© 0892/ 882-7222) has minibuses to Zhāngmù (12 hr.; ¥300/$37) which depart at 6am. *Note:* Your chances of boarding a bus to Gyantse are slim, as police impose heavy fines on drivers who harbor foreigners.

FAST FACTS

Banks, Foreign Exchange & ATMs   Cash and traveler's checks may be changed at counter 5 of the **Bank of China,** immediately south of the Shigatse Hotel, at Shànghǎi Lù 7. Credit card advances can also be made (open weekdays 9am–1pm and 3:30–6:30pm, weekends 10am–5pm).

Internet Access   *Avoid* China Telecom, with their WELCOME TO INTERNET sign. The welcome involves being fleeced. Continue north to **Guāngsù Zàixiàn Wǎngbā** at Shànghǎi Zhōng Lù 41, where you'll pay the same price the locals do (Yen)4/50¢ per hour) and enjoy a cup of jasmine tea. Dial-up is © 165.

Post Office   The main post office (open 9am–7pm) is at Zhūfēng Xī Lù 12.

Visa Extensions   The **PSB** at Jījílángkǎ Lù 3 (© 0892/882-2241) offers 1-month extensions a week before expiry (open 9am–1pm and 4–7pm summer; 10am–1pm and 3–6:30pm winter). Due to a recent visit from the TTC (Tibet Tourist Corporation), they are not issuing travel permits. The situation may change.

EXPLORING SHIGATSE

When Tibetologist Guiseppe Tucci visited, he found the *dzong* (fortress) in the north of town (a model for the Potala) to be "huge and dreary," but he needn't have worried. A few years later, PLA artillery did a thorough job: It is difficult to discern any structures, and the *dzong* does not appear on Chinese maps. The ruins are honeycombed with secret tunnels, but killjoys have barred up most of these.

Tashilhunpo Monastery (Zhāshílúnbù Sì)   This vast monastery of the **Geluk School** was established by the first Dalai Lama in 1447. The monastery gained standing when Panchen Lama IV, head abbot of Tashilhunpo and teacher of Dalai Lama V, was accepted as the personification of Amitabha Buddha, the Buddha of Longevity, thus becoming the "number two" lama in Tibet. The Mongols, Hàn, and British have exploited this division to good effect. Due to the size of the complex, start early in the morning, as all the temples are locked at midday. In the afternoon, you are more likely to enjoy chanting in the ancient **Assembly Hall (Dukhang).**

The pilgrimage circuit begins at **Jamkhang Chenmo,** at the west end of the complex, which houses a massive 26m (85-ft.) Maitreya (ca. 1914), a mass of gold around a wood and metal core. It was built by hand; around 900 artisans dedicated 4 years of their lives to it. But from an artistic perspective, Tashilhunpo is mediocre. As Tucci noted, "Everything was new and garish here. The collected composure of the primitives had been succeeded by baroque pomposity." Some composure remains in the gorgeous murals of Tsongkapa and his disciples that surround the reliquary stupa of Panchen Lama IV **(Kundung Lhakhang),** in the narrow cobblestone paths, and in the Assembly Hall, erected around an ancient sky-burial slab. The adjacent courtyard, with its striking flagpole, is the heart of the temple and the focus of religious dances.

A small new museum has opened on the grounds of Tashilhunpo, but houses little more than a few black-and-white photos taken at the monastery and a small display of thangkas and costumes. Admission to the museum is ¥5 (60¢).

Admission ¥55 ($7). Mon–Sat, summer 9am–12:30pm and 3:30–6:30pm; winter 10am–noon and 3–6pm.

SHOPPING

Shigatse bazaar stands in the shadow of the ruins, and aside from catering to the tourists, it has changed little. Khampa and Huí vendors hawk large knives, wooden tea bowls, prayer wheels, "bronze" statues, "ancient" coins, Tibetan medicine, incense from Calcutta, and cowboy hats and boots. The best-stocked supermarket is **Sìfāng Cháoshì** on Zhūfēng Lù (© **0892/883-7012**), open from 9am to 11pm.

WHERE TO STAY

Shénhú Jiǔdiàn (Hotel Manasarovar)   Despite its close involvement with FIT, this hotel, owned by the manager of the Yak Hotel, is tidy and well run. Staff is well trained and foreigner friendly. Simple and functionally furnished rooms have polished wooden floors and even sport potted plants. While the dormitories and communal showers are the cleanest in Tibet, the asking price is ludicrous. The breakfast and lunch buffets in the attached Nepali restaurant are recommended.

Qīngdǎo Dōng Lù 20. © **0892/883-2085.** Fax 0892/882-8111. www.hotelmanasarovartibet.com. 49 units (35 with bathroom). ¥350 ($44) single; ¥888 ($111) suite; ¥80–¥95 ($10–$12) dorm bed. 40% discount. No credit cards. **Amenities:** 2 restaurants; cafe; nightclub; concierge; business center; same-day laundry/dry cleaning. *In room:* A/C, TV.

Tenzin Hotel (Dàn Zēng Bīnguǎn)   *Value*   This recently refurbished guesthouse offers some of the best standard rooms in town, for less than half the cost rooms at the ugly three-star Chinese hotels in town. Rooms are nicely decorated with Tibetan furnishings and the bathrooms are very clean. Service is better than average. The only minor annoyance is the flies that buzz around in the hallways and some of the dorm rooms, which are popular with backpackers.

Bāng Jiā Líng 8. © 0892/882-2018. Fax 0892/883-1565. 30 units. ¥35 ($4.40) dorm bed; ¥160 ($20) standard room with bathroom. No credit cards. **Amenities:** Restaurant; laundry. *In room:* TV.

Wūzī Dàjiǔdiàn (Wutse Hotel) Located in a quiet Tibetan residential area to the southeast, this three-star hotel, run by the owners of the Wutse Hotel in Gyantse, is the newest in Shigatse. The competent, English-speaking staff works long hours. Spacious rooms are functionally furnished, the bathrooms are immaculate, but the hot water takes a while to warm up. A new wing will be open when you arrive, with dorm rooms and more dining options.

Sìchuān Nán Lù. © 0892/883-8666, ext. 8888. 60 units. ¥320 ($40) single; ¥260 ($32) standard room; ¥580 ($72) suite. 20% discounts. No credit cards. **Amenities:** Restaurant; bar; concierge; business center; same-day laundry. *In room:* TV, minibar.

WHERE TO DINE

Following FIT's lead, many restaurants in Shigatse, such as Shigatse Kitchen, have separate Chinese and English menus, with rather different prices.

Lǎoyǒu Lèyuán NOODLES ⋆ 𝘝𝘢𝘭𝘶𝘦 Wedged in between furniture stores on the pedestrian street *(bùxíng jiē)* that leads to the Tashilhunpo, this unassuming noodle shop run by a family from coastal Zhèjiāng province might be a bit hard to spot, but it's worth the effort. With little decor to speak of—just plastic blue-and-white chairs and tables that are nailed to the ground—and no menu, there's little to look at other than the food. But that seems to suit the diners just fine—just specify what you'd like from the three-dish menu: *miàn tiáo* (noodles with pork), *bāozi* (steamed buns with pork), or *jiǎozi* (dumplings in soup). Noodles and dumplings can be prepared spicy *(là)* or not *(búlà)*, with vinegar *(cù)* or without *(búyào cù)*. We ordered all three of the items and our bill came to a whopping ¥10 ($1.25)!

Bùxíng Jiē. No phone. Meal for 2 ¥10 ($1.25). No credit cards. 7am–11pm.

Yak Head Restaurant (Niútóu Zàngcān) TIBETAN You'd think a picture menu would help in most restaurants, but in this restaurant's case, it does more to hinder the ordering process with its obscenely blurry photos tucked neatly into an album. But no worries, a plucky waitress will do her best to explain what each photo is in broken English. Try the potato dumplings, the *rénshēnguǒ* (fried ginseng), or if you're feeling particularly adventurous, the yak head for a mere ¥30 ($4). The ambience can't be beat—a comfy outdoor patio beckons on warm afternoons while the cramped and cozy main room feels like a living room for monks, who hang out and watch TV at all hours of the day.

Bùxíng Jiē. © 0892/883-7186 or 1398/992-1574. Picture menu. Meal for 2 ¥30–¥60 ($4–$8). No credit cards. 8:30am–midnight.

Yǎlǔ Zàng Cāntīng ⋆ TIBETAN/CHINESE The dilemma that many travelers encounter when in Tibet is wanting to support Tibetan establishments, though the taste of tsampa and yak butter tea tends to drive them away. Yǎlǔzàng offers a happy solution: delicious Chinese food in a Tibetan-owned restaurant. Unfortunately, the Chinese dishes only appear on the Chinese menu, and the English menu is full of the standard backpacker fare. Ask for *chǎo bōcài* (stir-fried spinach), *tiěbǎn niúròu* (iron plate beef), *chǎo miànpiàn* (stir-fried noodle pieces), *qīngjiāo niúròu* (green peppers and beef), and *gāli tǔdòu* (curry potatoes). The environment is traditional Tibetan, which means benches covered with wool carpets and low tables. Be patient with the slow service.

Shāndōng Lù. ✆ 0892/883-3638. Meal for 2 ¥40–¥80 ($5–$10). No credit cards. 10am–midnight.

SHIGATSE AFTER DARK

If you haven't had a chance to hit a *nangma* yet in Tibet, Shigatse gives you an opportunity with **Huáiyù Mínzú Biǎoyì Zhōngxīn** (on Shànghǎi Lù just south of Zhūfēng Lù; ✆ 1398/902-2888). A lively performance with dancers dressed in yak costumes leaping on stage to techno-Tibetan music begins at 11pm.

8 Gyantse (Jiāngzī) ✶✶✶

67km (42 miles) SE of Shigatse, 255km (158 miles) SW of Lhasa. Altitude: 3,900m (11,700 ft.)

Presided over by the spectacular **Gyantse Dzong,** and once the third-largest town in Tibet, **Gyantse** is the only substantial settlement in the TAR to retain its vernacular architecture of sturdy two- and three-story farmhouses. Offering a rare and beautiful glimpse of Tibetan rural life, Gyantse should not be missed by any visitor to the TAR. Historically, it was a trading town for goods from Nepal, Sikkim, and Bhutan, and the closure of the border at Dromo (Yàdōng) has saved Gyantse from the ravages of development and Hàn colonization. Most members of Tibet's current generation of political leaders hail from Gyantse.

ESSENTIALS

GETTING THERE   Shigatse **buses** arrive and depart from the main roundabout, but you'll need to persuade the driver to risk a large fine. The 91km (56-mile) journey takes 1½ hours and costs ¥20 to ¥25 ($2.50–$3). If you've hired a Land Cruiser, the journey from Lhasa takes about 7 hours; from Shigatse, the journey is 2 hours.

FAST FACTS

Banks, Foreign Exchange & ATMs   None available.

Internet Access   The fastest connection is at the **Dàshìjiè Wǎngbā** (✆ 0892/898-2258). Located next to the Gyantse Hotel, they're open from 9:30am to midnight and charge ¥5 (60¢) per hour. Dial-up is ✆ 165.

Post Office   The main post office (open 9am–12:30pm and 3:30–7pm) is a few minutes' walk east of the main intersection on the corner of Wèiguó Lù and Jiānghóng Lù.

Visitor Information   The tourism bureau complaint number is ✆ 0892/899-6667 or 1390/892-2542.

EXPLORING GYANTSE

Gyantse Dzong (Jiāngzī Zōng Shān)   Towering above the settlement, this awesome fortress (ca. 13th c.) catches your eye as you approach Gyantse. It's a stiff hike up, but views of Pelkhor Chode, the ancient alleyways, and the jagged surrounding peaks are breathtaking. The **Hall of Anti-British** provides entertainment for fans of the Chinese practice of "using the past to serve the present." Pick your favorite saying, though it's hard to beat "They [the British] tried to occupy the fertile land of Tibet" (so why did they leave?). Another says that the Tibetan troops were fighting for the unity of the [Chinese] motherland, of which "Tibet has always been an inseparable part." The Tibetans drove disunited Chinese forces out of Tibet less than 10 years later, and the Seventeen-Point Agreement signed in 1951 provides recognition that Tibet had strayed from the fold of the motherland. Beyond the crude propaganda, a photo of Tibetan soldiers clasping spears and clad in medieval armor shows why they were butchered by the poorly conceived Younghusband expedition. Next is an exhibit of the torture methods of "Old Tibet," said to include tearing out a man's intestines and forcing him to eat them. In New Tibet, more sophisticated methods, such as the electric baton, are preferred.

Admission ¥30 ($3.70). Generally open 9am–5:30pm, though somewhat dependent on the whim of the ticket takers. Closed Nov–Mar.

Pelkhor Choede (Báijū Sì)   The once-mighty temple complex of Gyantse (ca. 1418) used to house several different orders under the one roof. While restoration is ongoing, only the **main temple,** a huge *thangka* **wall,** and **Gyantse Kumbum** stand intact. Many of the chapels in the main temple are locked; if you persist, one of the 30 remaining monks may open them. The different orders bequeathed different artistic styles, shown in the chapels of the second floor. To the right (east) is the bizarre **Neten Lhakhang,** decorated in Chinese style with leaping tigers and dragons, floating clouds, and pagodas, representing Manjusri's Pure Land in Wǔtái Shān.

The nine-story **Kumbum** ✿✿✿, the largest chorten in Tibet, towers to a height of 42m (140 ft.). The first five floors are four-sided, while the upper floors are circular, forming a huge three-dimensional mandala. Kumbum means "the hundred thousand images," and while the actual number of Buddhist images is around one-third of that estimate, even the most dedicated pilgrim won't have time to properly inspect all the chapels. They house the finest art preserved in Tibet. Vibrant color and a lively, naturalistic style characterize the murals, while the broad faces of the statues point to Chinese influence. The mandalas of the upper levels are exquisite, though an extra fee may be required to gain access to the seventh through ninth floors. Bring a flashlight.

Admission ¥40 ($5). Photography ¥10 ($1.25). 9am–1pm and 3–7pm.

SHOPPING

Gyantse is famous for its carpets. **The Carpet Factory** (© 0892/817-2004; open Mon–Sat, 9am–1pm and 3–7:30pm) is tucked away on the north side of Gyantse Dzong. The sales room is to the left of the entrance, but garish designs are prevalent. Near the factory, many people weave at home; you may be treated to a cup of sweet tea and a quick exhibition.

WHERE TO STAY

Look for rooms away from the road; mangy curs and nervous Hàn soldiers bark through the night. Discounts of 50% are negotiable, and prices seem to have come down in the past few years.

Jiāngzī Bīnguǎn (Gyantse Hotel) ✿   This hotel offers Gyantse's best accommodations, though the competition in the town isn't that stiff. You have your choice of three-star Western-style or Tibetan rooms. Opt for the Tibetan one if you'd like more character; they're outfitted with colorful furniture and *thangkas* on the walls. The one drawback is that the beds in the Tibetan rooms aren't as comfortable as those in the Western rooms. Bathrooms in either style are shiny and welcoming and include amenities like a hair dryer and a magnifying mirror, which you won't find elsewhere in town.

Yīngxióng Nán Lù 8. ⓒ 0892/817-2222. Fax 0892/817-2366. 106 units. ¥460 ($58) twin. 20% discounts possible. AC, DC, MC, V. **Amenities:** 2 restaurants; cafe; business center; salon; massage; fitness center; bike rental; doctor's clinic. *In room:* Satellite TV, hair dryer.

Jiàn Zàng Fàndiàn Just south of the Wutse Hotel, this small, orderly guesthouse was recently opened by a genial Tibetan doctor, Jiàn Zàng. His pharmacy still operates north of the hostel. Rooms are well lit and the beds are comfortable, but bathrooms are showing signs of decay. The dorms here are popular with backpackers, and additional dormitories and single rooms should be available when you arrive.

Yīngxióng Lù. ⓒ 0892/817-2324. Fax 0892/817-3910. 17 units. ¥40 ($5) dorm bed; ¥150 ($19) twin. No credit cards. **Amenities:** Restaurant; TV; next-day laundry. *In room:* TV.

Wūzī Fàndiàn (Wutse Hotel) Just south of the main intersection, this guesthouse has the feel of a Motel 6 (evidenced in the balconies), but is a notch up in terms of comfort from Jiàn Zàng's rooms. Rooms were recently renovated but bathrooms still suffer from sporadic hot water. The restaurant on the first floor serves decent banana pancakes and masala tea. A buffet dinner is served nightly.

Yīngxióng Nán Lù 8. ⓒ 0892/817-2888. Fax 0892/817-2880. wutse_deji888@yahoo.com.cn. 48 units (40 with bathroom). ¥40 ($5) dorm bed; ¥260 ($32) single; ¥220 ($27) standard room. No credit cards. **Amenities:** Restaurant; next-day laundry. *In room:* TV, hair dryer.

WHERE TO DINE

Tashi's (Zhāxī Zàngcān) ⚘ NEPALI/WESTERN   Located on the northwest side of the main intersection, at the foot of Gyantse Dzong, the final outpost of a Tibetan restaurant chain based in Lhasa. If the restaurant is quiet, ask the chef to show off and prepare something off the menu. Chicken Whitehouse, crumbed chicken breast stuffed with lamb mince, mushroom, ginger, and garlic, is his specialty. On the menu, the filling chicken curry set, creamy dal, and fresh flavored lassi are recommended.

Báijū Lù. ⓒ 0892/882-7512. Meal for 2 ¥50–¥130 ($6–$16). No credit cards. 7am–11pm. Closed Nov 20–Mar 1.

Zhuāng Yuán Restaurant ⚘ CHINESE   Mr. Zhuāng is one of the few restaurateurs in all of Tibet that gets the importance of customer service. He and his brother greeted us with an unpushy "hello" and beckoned us with a smile; they further tempted us with a look inside their fridge, stocked with fresh veggies. The food is not particularly authentic or stunning (one of his best-selling dishes is sweet-and-sour chicken, though, and the owner will invite you into the kitchen to watch flames shoot high into the air), and prices are aimed at foreigners. But Mr. Zhuāng's congeniality and fresh manners won us over anyway.

Yīngxióng Nán Lù. ⓒ 1367/802-0792. Meal for 2 ¥80 ($10). No credit cards. 7am–11pm.

9 Sakya (Sàjiā)

150km (93 miles) SW of Shigatse, 55km (34 miles) SE of Lhatse. Altitude: 4,200m (13,776 ft.)

This remote Tibetan township boasts one of the most magnificent and best-preserved monasteries in the TAR, and is the home of the **Sakya** school of Buddhism. Founded by Konchok Gyalpo in 1073, it is similar to the Kagyu order in being heavily influenced by Indian Tantric Buddhism, but it differs in that its lineage is hereditary, passed down through the **Khon family.** In 1247, Kodan Khan offered the head lama, Sakya Pandita, absolute power to rule over Tibet, in exchange for submission to Mongol rule. Mindful of the fate of the Xīxià Kingdom to the north of Tibet, annihilated 20 years previously by the hordes of Genghis Khan, Sakya Pandita readily agreed. At this point, theocratic rule in Tibet was born, and the concept of "priest and patron," used to this day to justify Chinese rule in Tibet, was developed. Marco Polo noted that the magical powers of the Sakya lamas were highly regarded, and it is said they won over Kublai Khan when they triumphed in a battle of supernatural powers with Daoists and Nestorian Christians. You wonder what Sakyamuni would have made of this. He once reprimanded a follower who levitated above a crowd, likening him to a prostitute showing herself for a few coins. While the influence of Sakya faded with the Mongols, they produced stunning religious paintings during the 15th and 16th centuries, and the monastery houses some remarkable statuary.

GETTING THERE   **Buses** from Lhatse or Shigatse stop at the Sakya Monastery Guesthouse. *Before* you get off the bus, buy a ticket for the following day's ride at 11am to either Shigatse (6 hr.; ¥32/$4) or to the intersection with the Friendship Highway (1½ hr.; ¥10/$1.25), if you are continuing west. Otherwise, you're here for 3 days. Land Cruisers make the trip from Latse, 50km (31 miles) away, in 1½ hours; a trip from Shigatse, 130km (81 miles) away, takes 4 to 5 hours.

GETTING AROUND   There are no street addresses in the simple two-street town of Sakya, but everything is easy enough to locate.

A 13TH-CENTURY MONASTERY

Sakya Monastery (Sàjiā Sì) 🏵🏵   The massive 35m (115-ft.) windowless gray walls of **Lhakhang Chenmo** tower above the village and fields on the southern bank of the Trum Chu. Completed in 1274, this monastery fort was largely funded by Kublai Khan, and unlike the older temples of north Sakya, it survived the Cultural Revolution. Little was left standing on the north side of the river, although a **nunnery** to the northeast is being revived.

Unlike the rich and confusing pantheon seen in most Geluk temples, most images in the **Assembly Hall (Dukhang)** 🏵🏵 are of the historical Buddha, Sakyamuni. You'll need a flashlight to see the exquisite statuary and murals. Look for a striking 11th-century image of the **"speaking" Buddha,** third from the left on the back wall, with its cheeky grin. Other great works include an image of the bodhisattva **Manjushri,** second from the right on the back wall, leaning gently to one side, suggesting a sympathetic ear to believers. Walk around the monastery's walls, which offer fantastic views of the surrounding areas. Only 170 monks remain, but they're a young, friendly bunch. They may show you the monastery's greatest treasure—a white **conch shell,** said to have housed a very early incarnation of Sakyamuni. Mountains of white *kata* (silk cloths) give away its location. Just south of the monastery stands a new modern-looking museum that should be open by the time you arrive.

📞 **0892/884-2428.** Admission ¥45 ($5.50). 8am–4pm.

WHERE TO STAY

Sakya Family Hotel (Lǔwǎ Sàjiā Bīnguǎn)   Run by a friendly Tibetan family, this cozy guesthouse has great atmosphere and nice budget rooms. A labyrinth of hallways will lead to the family's living room, where they'll invite you for a cup of tea. Toilets are of the pit kind and there are no showers, but if you can do without the amenities, choose this place over the Sakya Manasarovar Hotel and the rest of the shabby guesthouses in town.

© **0892/890-4555.** 20 beds. ¥30 ($4) dorm bed; ¥60 ($8) standard room (just 1 in the guesthouse). No credit cards. *In room:* TV, no phone.

Sakya Manasarovar Hotel (Shénhú Sàjiā Bīnguǎn) As you push out farther into the hinterlands of Tibet, modern amenities like hot water and flush toilets become harder to find. This hotel has the illusion of having those things, but bad plumbing means that the toilets give off a stench that wafts into all areas of the high-ceilinged floors; the solar heating system means that hot water is only available in daylight, when it's sunny. Still, if you're after such amenities, this is your best option in town. Rooms are new, beds are comfortable, and if you keep your door closed, you'll be saved from the smell of septic tanks. For the budget conscious, there are three common rooms with dorm beds, one of which has an attached bath. The restaurant serves decent Nepalese food, including nan and chicken tikka masala, and a good Tibetan noodle soup.

© **0892/824-2222.** 30 units. ¥25 ($3) dorm bed without bathroom; ¥35 ($4.40) dorm bed with bathroom; ¥160 ($20) standard room. No credit cards. **Amenities:** Restaurant. *In room:* TV, no phone.

WHERE TO DINE

The **Sakya Manasarovar Hotel** and the **Sakya Monastery Restaurant** serve decent cuisine. For Sichuanese, go to **Gāoyuán Chuāncài,** 1 block south and east of the Sakya Monastery Guesthouse (*©* **0892/824-2479;** meal for two ¥30–¥60/$3.70–$7.50; 8am–10pm). Dishes to try include *mápó dòufu* (spicy tofu with chopped meat), *yúxiāng qiézi* (eggplant in garlic sauce), and *gōngbào jīdīng* (spicy chicken with cashews).

10 Lhatse (Lāzī)

148km (92 miles) W of Shigatse, 325km (202 miles) NE of Zhāngmù. Altitude: 4,000m (13,120 ft.)

Stretching for a mile along the Friendship Highway, **Lhatse** is the jumping-off point for trips to **Mount Kailash** (p. 776) and **Ali,** or it can be an overnight stop between Lhasa and the Nepali border.

ESSENTIALS

GETTING THERE The **bus** will stop at Lhatse's only intersection. There is a bus to Shigatse (4 hr.; ¥30/$3.70) and the Sakya junction (40 min.; ¥5/60¢) at around 10am. A bus for Shelkar (81km/50 miles; 2½ hr.; ¥35/$4.40) passes through mid-morning, but a seat is not guaranteed. Sleeper buses for Ali (2–4 days; ¥650–¥750/$81–$94) pass by at 8am, and tickets for Ali are arranged by the **Yuèchuān Càiguǎn** (*©* **0892/832-2929**). Hitchhikers may need to walk about 6km (3¾ miles) west past the PSB checkpoint to increase your chances. Here, the road branches off south (left) toward Shelkar and west towards Mount Kailash and Ali. If you're traveling by Land Cruiser, the journey from Shigatse, 80km (50 miles) away, should take about 3 hours (if the road conditions are normal, that is). The journey to Pelbar, 90km (56 miles) away, also takes about 3 hours.

FAST FACTS

Banks, Foreign Exchange & ATMs None available.

Internet Access   Sitong Wǎngbā (② 0892/832-3528 or 0/1364-892-4982), on the main drag, charges ¥5 (60¢) per hour for a good connection. It's open from 11am until midnight. Dial-up is ② 165.

Post Office   The post office is located east of the intersection, on the south side.

WHERE TO STAY

If you're staying at a hotel without running hot water (read: no showers), Dà Shànghǎi Yùshì (② 0892/832-2868), north of the intersection, will let you take a hot shower for ¥8 ($1).

Lāzī Bīnguǎn (Lazi Hotel)   This is one of the nicer accommodations in Lhatse, which really isn't saying much. Rooms are clean enough, but there's only a common pit toilet (like everywhere else in Lhatse) and no showers. A restaurant called Tashi 2, which has no relation to the other Tashi restaurants in Tibet, adjoins the hotel; you can get decent backpacker fare and Chinese food here.

No formal address. ② 0892/832-2208. 14 units (no bathroom). ¥35 ($4.50) dorm room; ¥80 ($10) single or standard room; ¥105 ($13) triple room. No credit cards. *In room:* TV, no phone.

Nóngmín Yúlè Lǚguǎn (Tibetan Farmer's Adventure Hotel)   A 5-minute walk east of the main intersection on the north side of the highway, this Tibetan-run place is fly-infested and a little grubby, but still manages to offer a decent atmosphere. Set around a sunny courtyard, this hotel offers your last shot at a warm shower if you are bound for the Kailash region. The restaurant serves decent yak-fried noodles and other simple dishes, and you might have a chance to meet Tenzin, a friendly, blind employee who speaks fantastic English. He asked us to choose an English name for him, so we named him Daniel.

Zhōngní Lù 8. ② 0892/832-2333. 38 units (with shared bathroom). ¥35–¥60 ($4.40–$7.50) dorm bed. **Amenities:** Restaurant; bike rental; limited room service. *In room:* TV, no phone.

WHERE TO DINE

For Chinese food, try **Yuèchuān Càiguǎn** (no formal address; ② 0892/832-2929; May–Oct 7:30am–11:30pm), which offers Cantonese specialities like vermicelli clay pot *(zāchá fěnsī bāo)*, beef fried rice *(niúròu chǎofàn)*, and salty chicken *(chǐyóu jī)*. The Tibetan Farmer's guesthouse does a decent yak-fried noodles.

11 Pelbar (Dìngrì)

228km (141 miles) SW of Shigatse, 255km (158 miles) NE of Zhāngmù. Altitude: 4,000m (13,120 ft.)

Confusingly, there are three towns known as **Dìngrì**. The county capital town of **Shelkar,** 7km (4⅓ miles) farther west from **Pelbar (Dìngrì),** is referred to as **Xīn Dìngrì (New Tingri). Tingri,** the other base for treks in the Everest region, 60km (37 miles) farther west, is called **Lǎo Dìngrì (Old Tingri).** Other than dodging children peddling mollusks and demanding pens—will the idiots who give them away *please* do something more useful with their consciences and money?—there is little of interest in Pelbar. Pick up your permit for the **Qomolangma Nature Reserve** (see "Everest Trekking," p. 778) at the Qomolangma Service Center, on your right, set off the road, just after the turnoff. It's open 24 hours, and has the cleanest bathroom in a thousand-kilometer radius.

GETTING THERE   The **bus** from Shigatse will drop you at the Shelkar turnoff. There is no public transport between here and Zhāngmù. Heading east, a bus to Shigatse (6½

Wild China: Mount Kailash & Lake Manasarovar

Worshipped by the followers of no less than four religions—Tibetan Buddhists, Bonpos, Hindus, and Jains—**Mount Kailash (Gangdise)** draws pilgrims from the Tibetan world and beyond. For Tibetan Buddhists, it is Mount Meru, the center of the universe, and many aim to circumambulate the mountain 108 times, thus attaining Buddhahood in this lifetime. For Hindu pilgrims, who are allowed to cross the border at **Purang (Pŭlán)**, it is the abode of Shiva, one of the three supreme gods. The beauty of the 6,714m (22,028-ft.) peak, jutting up from the surrounding arid plain, is astounding, and the sight of **Lake Manasarovar** under a full moon is enough to have even the most cynical visitor believing in supernatural possibilities.

The **Saka Dawa Festival,** the traditional pilgrimage holiday held from late May to early June, is the most spectacular time to visit, but access (even for prebooked tours) is often restricted during this festival. Regardless, try to time your visit to coincide with the full moon.

Most Western visitors reach Mount Kailash with a tour. This is the most reliable option. Short tours, from either Lhasa or Kathmandu, last 14 days. More extensive tours of the region run for 21 days. The cost of a 21-day trip from Lhasa costs ¥16,000 ($2,000) and can be split between four travelers. Check out the FIT branches at the Kirey Hotel (© **0891/632-3462**) or the Snowlands Guesthouse (© **0891/632-3687**) in Lhasa. Beyond Zhongba (Zhòngbā, the road is in poor shape. Inspect your vehicle before you leave. The trip is not feasible from November to mid-April.

Sleeper buses (2–3 days; ¥750–¥900/$94–$112) connect Lhasa, Lhatse, and Ālǐ, though you take the chance of being turned back—permits are required. Bus services are seasonal, and usually take the northern route (*běi xiàn*) to Ālǐ, making it necessary to double back, as Ālǐis a 2-day drive northwest of Mount Kailash. Inquire at the **Ālǐ Bànshìchù** in Lhasa (© **0891/681-1577**), the **Yuèchuān Càiguăn** in Lhatse (© **0892/832-2929**), or the **Ālǐ Bus Station** (© **0897/282-1527**).

Accommodations along the route are usually ¥30 ($3.75) per bed. Even basic amenities, such as hot showers, are usually unavailable. Dishes at restaurants tend to cost more than they would in Lhasa, so figure that you'll spend around ¥80 ($10) per day on food, unless you're okay with instant noodles. Hitching is difficult, as few drivers are willing to risk a large fine, and most travel to Ālǐ via the bleak northern route.

hr.; ¥65/$8.10) originating in Shelkar passes through town around 9am. Those looking to hitch towards Nepal have to walk 6km (3¾ miles) past the PSB checkpoint, which inspects all vehicles. From Lhatse to Dìngrì, you'll drive past the Gyantsola Pass at 5,200m (17,056 ft.), a great place for your first view of the Himalayas. If there's road construction going on, the 90km (56-mile) drive may take up to 8 hours!

The traditional gateway to the mountain is the village of **Darchen (Dàjīn),** which sits on the southern edge of the pilgrimage circuit, although you can't see the mountain from here. Admission to the Kailash area is ¥50 ($6), collected at a checkpoint at the entrance to town. Foreigners must register with the PSB in Darchen upon arrival. Accommodations range in price from ¥25 ($3) to ¥80 ($10) for a dorm bed, and popular places include the Yak Hotel and the Darchen Guesthouse. At the **Gāngdǐsī Bīnguǎn** private standard rooms and triples with decent bathrooms go for ¥240 ($30) and ¥300 ($38) respectively. Some travelers have attempted to camp in the courtyard of some hotels, but they are often wake up covered with human feces and broken glass. The nearest bearable site to camp is a 1½-hour walk on the kora at Darpoche (marked with a flagpole). Outside the eastern entrance of the Gāngdǐsī Bīnguǎn is the **Lhasa Restaurant,** run by a charming retired teacher from Tsetang.

Most people take 3 days to complete the 53km (33-mile) circuit. Buddhists undertake the journey in a clockwise direction, while a handful of Bonpos walk counterclockwise. Stick with the majority. Do *not* count on finding accommodations in monasteries along the route—bring a tent! Waterproof hiking boots are a must, as there are numerous small river crossings. Bring all the food you think you'll need, as you'll only find instant noodles and a few other snacks for sale on the circuit. Even if you intend to hire porters or yaks at ¥60 ($7.50) per day, you should be very fit, as the trek is above 4,500m (14,760 ft.), rising to over 5,600m (18,370 ft.) on the second day.

Hor Qū (Huǒ'ěr Qū), 39km (24 miles) southeast of Darchen, is the most common jumping-off point for **Lake Manasarovar** (4,560m/14,957 ft.). Here you can enjoy unparalleled views of the Himalayas across turquoise waters which freeze over in winter, visit monasteries carved from the naked rock of the lakeshore, and even attempt the 90km (56-mile) circuit of the lake. **Chiu Gompa,** 35km (22 miles) south of Darchen and 8km (5 miles) south of the main road, has a few unmarked guesthouses that will rent you a bed for ¥40 ($5). A wash in the bathhouse that has unlimited hot-springs water costs ¥20 ($2.50). Entrance to the Chiu Monastery is free, and its setting, on a crag facing Lake Manasarovar, is the perfect place to relax and enjoy the view. If you go to Chiu Gompa, bring food from Darchen or Hor Qū. The **Indian Pilgrims Resthouse** by the lakeshore, where you can spend the night for ¥100 ($13), serves a few minimal dishes like egg-fried rice.

VISITOR INFORMATION   The **tourism complaint hot line** is 🕾 0/1388-902-**0366** or 0892/8262-2142.

WHERE TO STAY & DINE
Xuěyù Fàndiàn (Snowlands Hotel)   Located at the turnoff to Shelkar, this is the best of several grimy budget options. Unadorned and relatively clean rooms are set

Everest Trekking

The trek out to **Everest Base Camp** follows two main routes—from **Pelbar** via the wretchedly poor village of Chay, and from **Tingri** via Lungjiang. The former route (113km/70 miles) is usually traveled by 4WD in 3 hours along a much-improved road. The latter is a tough 3- to 4-day journey, and the path is hard to follow in places. Gary McCue's *Trekking in Tibet* is a reliable guide for this route and for other hikes in the Qomolangma Nature Preserve. A permit costs ¥65 ($8.10) per person and ¥405 ($51) per vehicle, purchased at Pelbar, Tingri or Chay. Accommodations are available in tents at **Base Camp** (¥20/$2.50) at an elevation of 5,150m (16,890 ft.). The "real" Base Camp with real expeditions and mountaineers is a couple of kilometers farther on. There are also basic rooms at **Rongbuk Monastery** (¥40/$5) at an elevation of 4,980m (16,330 ft.). *Warning:* There have been accounts of "wandering fingers" in this guesthouse. Watch your valuables.

The height of Mount Everest was recently fixed at 8,846m (29,015 ft.), somewhat lower than first believed, but on a clear day it presents an astounding vista, particularly from Pang La and Lamma La. Insistence on the use of Qomolangma (Zhūmùlǎngmǎ) rather than Mount Everest to label the world's highest peak would have pleased Sir George Everest, who staunchly believed in using local place-names.

around a sun-drenched courtyard, but the pit toilets are diabolical. The cozy attached restaurant has an English menu, and the staff is incredibly gracious and helpful.

C 0892/826-2848. 15 units. ¥20 ($2.50) dorm bed. No credit cards. **Amenities:** Restaurant. *In room:* No phone.

Zhūfēng Zōnghé Fúwù Zhōngxīn (Qomolangma Service Center)   Set off the road on your right, just after the turnoff, the service center, where you get your permit for the nature reserve, offers the best-priced rooms in town. Get a suite here, which is a bargain, and you'll be relaxing in a room with a lounge, two beds, and a mahjong table. The standard rooms are much smaller and only a tiny bit less in price. Bathrooms (private ones!) are clean and have flush toilets, something you won't take for granted after spending time in Tibet.

C 0892/826-2833. 30 units. ¥100 ($13) standard room; ¥120 ($15) suite. No credit cards. **Amenities:** Restaurant; bar; business center. *In room:* TV.

12 Tingri (Lǎo Dìngrì)

289km (179 miles) SW of Shigatse, 184km (114 miles) NE of Zhāngmù. Altitude: 4,300m (14,104 ft.)

An impoverished settlement with a breathtaking view of the world's highest peaks, **Tingri** is the favored starting point for those wishing to walk to **Everest Base Camp,** and a common overnight stop between Kathmandu and Lhasa. A row of white-tiled houses and shops under construction to the west of town suggests that a Hàn influx is planned. Magnificent views of Everest may be gained from the ruins of the late-18th-century **Tingri Dzong,** spread across a hill south of town.

WHERE TO STAY & DINE

Be forewarned: All the guesthouses in town are dumps, and look like truck stops, so bringing a sleeping bag to put over your bed is highly recommended and keep your expectations low on the cleanliness, plumbing, and electricity fronts. That said, the honest and shabby **Lhasa Fàndiàn (Lhasa Hotel;** ✆ **0892/826-2703),** with its pleasant staff, has rooms that are a tiny bit grubby; the cost of your dorm bed (¥25–¥45/$3–$5.50) depends on the quality of mattress you sleep on. A much-needed hot shower costs ¥10 ($1.25). **The Xuěbào Fàndiàn (Everest Snow Leopard Hotel;** ✆ **0892/826-2775)** offers what are marginally the best accommodations in town, but the price is expensive (¥40/$5 dorm bed), compared to other local guesthouses, and the service staff is rude. Hot water runs from 7 to 11pm, and showers are clean. For those en route to Everest Base Camp, you can get your permit for the Qomolangma Nature Reserve here. The **Amdo Restaurant,** located on the north side of the road in the middle of town, is popular with locals and has an English-language menu.

13 Zhāngmù (Dram)

473km (293 miles) SW of Shigatse. Altitude: 1,900m (6,232 ft.)

The Friendship Highway drops 1,400m (4,600 ft.) during the treacherous 30km (19 miles) of dirt road between **Nyalam** and the border town of **Zhāngmù.** The arid Tibetan plateau gives way to lush greenery and deliciously damp air. Nepalis complain about the cold, but you'll be shedding layers if you've arrived from Lhasa. A tiny collection of wooden houses before the border opened in 1980, Zhāngmù is now one of the wealthiest towns in Tibet, due to licit and illicit trade in gold, clothing, and footwear. Zhāngmù stretches for several miles through a series of switchbacks towards the border. Buildings are referred to in this section as though you are facing downhill.

ESSENTIALS

GETTING THERE   There is no public transport into Zhāngmù from Tibet. In a Land Cruiser, the drive from Tingri to Zhāngmù, 180km (112 miles), takes about 6 hours. At present, arriving overland from Nepal involves arranging a "group visa" of 15 to 20 days through a travel agency in Kathmandu. You are, however, not obliged to stay with the group, and can extend the visa elsewhere in China.

The border is open from 9:30am to 6:30pm on the Chinese side, and from 10am to 6pm on the Nepali side, with a time difference of 2½ hours. If you've hired a vehi-

Appendix A:
The Chinese Language

Chinese is not as difficult a language to learn as it may first appear to be—at least not once you've decided what kind of Chinese to learn. There are six major languages called Chinese. Speakers of each are unintelligible to speakers of the others, and there are, in addition, a host of dialects. The Chinese you are likely to hear spoken in your local Chinatown, in your local Chinese restaurant, or used by your friends of Chinese descent when they speak to their parents, is more than likely to be Cantonese, which is the version of Chinese used in Hong Kong and in much of southern China. But the official national language of China is **Mandarin (Pǔtōnghuà**—"common speech"), sometimes called Modern Standard Chinese, and viewed in mainland China as the language of administration, of the classics, and of the educated. While throughout much of mainland China people speak their own local flavor of Chinese for everyday communication, they've all been educated in Mandarin which, in general terms, is the language of Běijīng and the north. Mandarin is less well known in Hong Kong and Macau, but is also spoken in Táiwān and Singapore, and among growing communities of recent immigrants to North America and Europe.

Chinese grammar is considerably more straightforward than that of English or other European languages, even Spanish or Italian. There are no genders, so there is no need to remember long lists of endings for adjectives and to make them agree, with variations according to case. There are no equivalents for the definite and indefinite articles ("the," "a," "an"), so there is no need to make those agree either. Singular and plural nouns are the same. Best of all, verbs cannot be declined. The verb "to be" is *shì*. The same sound also covers "am," "are," "is," "was," "will be," and so on, since there are also no tenses. Instead of past, present, and future, Chinese is more concerned with whether an action is continuing or has been completed, and with the order in which events take place. To make matters of time clear, Chinese depends on simple expressions such as "yesterday," "before," "originally," "next year," and the like. "Tomorrow I go New York," is clear enough, as is "Yesterday I go New York." It's a little more complicated than these brief notes can suggest, but not much.

There are a few sounds in Mandarin that are not used in English (see the rough pronunciation guide below), but the main difficulty for foreigners lies in tones. Most sounds in Mandarin begin with a consonant and end in a vowel (or -n, or -ng), which leaves the language with very few distinct noises compared to English. Originally, one sound equaled one idea and one word. Even now, each of these monosyllables is represented by a single character, but often words have been made by putting two characters together, sometimes both of the same meaning, thus reinforcing one another. The solution to this phonetic poverty is to multiply the available sounds by making them tonal—speaking them at different pitches, thereby giving them different meanings. *Mā* spoken on a high level tone (first tone) offers a set of possible meanings different to those of *má* spoken with a rising tone (second tone), *mǎ* with a dipping then rising tone (third tone), or *mà* with an abruptly falling tone (fourth tone). There's also a different meaning for the neutral, toneless *ma*.

In the average sentence, context is your friend (there are not many occasions in which the third-tone *mǎ* or "horse" might be mistaken for the fourth-tone *mà* or "grasshopper," for instance), but, without tone, there is essentially no meaning. The novice best sing his or her Mandarin very clearly, as Chinese children do—a chanted singsong can be heard emerging from the windows of primary schools across China. With experience, the student learns to give particular emphasis to the tones on words essential to a sentence's meaning, and to treat the others more lightly. Sadly, most books using modern Romanized Chinese, called *Hànyǔ pīnyīn* ("Hàn language spell-the-sounds"), do not mark the tones, nor do these appear on **pīnyīn** signs in China. But in this book, the authors, most of whom speak Mandarin, have added tones to every Mandarin expression, so you can have a go at saying them for yourself. Where tones do not appear, that's usually because the name of a person or place is already familiar to many readers in an older form of Romanized Chinese, such as Wade-Giles, or Post Office (in which Běijīng was written misleadingly as Peking); or because it is better known in Cantonese: Sun Yat-sen, or Canton, for instance.

Cantonese has *eight* tones plus the neutral, but its grammatical structure is largely the same, as is that of all versions of Chinese. Even Chinese people who can barely understand each other's speech can at least write to each other, since written forms are similar. Mainland China, with the aim of increasing literacy (or perhaps of distancing the supposedly now thoroughly modern and socialist population from its Confucian heritage), instituted a ham-fisted simplification program in the 1950s, which reduced some characters originally taking 14 strokes of the brush, for instance, to as few as three strokes. Hong Kong, separated from the mainland and under British control until 1997, went its own way, kept the original full-form characters, and invented lots of new ones, too. Nevertheless, many characters remain the same, and some of the simplified forms are merely familiar shorthands for the full-form ones. But however many different meanings for each tone of *ma* there may be, for each meaning there's a different character. This makes the written form a far more successful communication medium than the spoken one, which leads to misunderstandings even between native speakers, who can often be seen sketching characters on their palms during conversation to confirm which one is meant.

The thought of learning 3,000 to 5,000 individual characters (at least 2,500 are needed to read a newspaper) also daunts many beginners. But look carefully at the ones below, and you'll notice many common elements. In fact, a rather limited number of smaller shapes are combined in different ways, much as we combine letters to make words. Admittedly, the characters only offer general hints as to their pronunciation, and that's often misleading—the system is not a phonetic one, so each new Mandarin word has to be learned as both a sound and a shape (or a group of them). But soon it's the similarities among the characters, not their differences, which begin to bother the student. English, a far more subtle language with a far larger vocabulary, and with so many pointless inconsistencies and exceptions to what are laughingly called its rules, is much more of a struggle for the Chinese than Mandarin should be for us.

But no knowledge of the language is needed to get around China, and it's almost a plus that Chinese take it for granted that outlandish foreigners (that's you and me unless you're of Chinese descent) can speak not a word (poor things) and must use whatever other limited means we have to communicate—this book and a phrase book, for instance. For help with navigation to sights, simply point to the characters below. When leaving your hotel, take one of its cards with you, and show it to the taxi driver when you want to return. At the end of this section, there's a limited list of useful words and phrases, which is best supplemented with a proper phrase book. If you have a Mandarin-speaking friend from the north (Cantonese speakers who know Mandarin as a second language tend to have fairly heavy accents), ask him or her to pronounce the greetings and words of thanks from the list below, so you can repeat after him and practice. While you are as much likely to be laughed *at* as *with* in China, such efforts are always appreciated.

1 A Guide to Pīnyīn Pronunciation

Letters in pīnyīn mostly have the values any English speaker would expect, with the following exceptions:

c ts as in bits

q *ch* as in *ch*in, but much harder and more forward, made with tongue and teeth

r has no true equivalent in English, but the *r* of *r*eed is close, although the tip of the tongue should be near the top of the mouth, and the teeth together

x also has no true equivalent, but is nearest to the *sh* of *sh*eep, although the tongue should be parallel to the roof of the mouth and the teeth together

zh is a soft j, like the *dge* in ju*dge*

The vowels are pronounced roughly as follows:

a as in f*a*ther

e as in *e*rr (*leng* is pronounced as English "lung")

i is pronounced *ee* after most consonants, but after c, ch, r, s, sh, z, and zh is a buzz at the front of the mouth behind the closed teeth

o as in s*o*ng

u as in t*oo*

ü is the purer, lips-pursed u of French t*u* and German *ü*. Confusingly, u after j, x, q, and y is always ü, but in these cases the accent over "ü" does not appear.

ai sounds like *eye*

ao as in *ou*ch

ei as in h*ay*

ia as in *ya*k

ian sounds like *yen*

iang sounds like *yang*

iu sounds like *you*

ou as in t*oe*

ua as in g*ua*va

ui sounds like *way*

uo sounds like *or*, but is more abrupt

Note that when two or more third-tone "ˇ" sounds follow one another, they should all, except the last, be pronounced as second-tone "ˊ."

2 Mandarin Bare Essentials

GREETINGS & INTRODUCTIONS

ENGLISH	PINYIN	CHINESE
Hello	Nǐ hǎo	你好
How are you?	Nǐ hǎo ma?	你好吗?
Fine. And you?	Wǒ hěn hǎo. Nǐ ne?	我很好你

ENGLISH	PINYIN	CHINESE
I'm not too well/things aren't going well	Bù hǎo	不好
What is your name? (very polite)	Nín guì xìng?	您贵姓
My (family) name is . . .	Wǒ xìng . . .	我姓 . . .
I'm known as (family, then given name)	Wǒ jiào . . .	我叫 . . .
I'm [American]	Wǒ shì [Měiguó] rén	我是美国人
[Australian]	[Àodàlìyà]	澳大利亚
[British]	[Yīngguó]	英国
[Canadian]	[Jiānádà]	加拿大
[Irish]	[Àiěrlán]	爱尔兰
[New Zealander]	[Xīnxīlán]	新西兰
I'm from [America]	Wǒ shì cóng [Měiguó] lái de	我是从美国来的
Excuse me/I'm sorry	Duìbùqǐ	对不起
I don't understand	Wǒ tīng bù dǒng	我听不懂
Thank you	Xièxie nǐ	谢谢你
Correct (yes)	Duì	对
Not correct	Bú duì	不对
No, I don't want	Wǒ bú yào	我不要
Not acceptable	Bù xíng	不行

BASIC QUESTIONS & PROBLEMS

ENGLISH	PINYIN	CHINESE
Excuse me/I'd like to ask	Qǐng wènyíxià	请问一下
Where is . . . ?	. . . zài nǎr?	在哪儿
How much is . . . ?	. . . duōshǎo qián?	多少钱
. . . this one?	Zhèi/Zhè ge . . .	这个 . . .
. . . that one?	Nèi/Nà ge . . .	那个 . . .
Do you have . . . ?	Nǐ yǒu méi yǒu	你有没有 . . .
What time does/is . . . ?	. . . jǐ diǎn?	. . . 几点?
What time is it now?	Xiànzài jǐ diǎn?	现在几点?
When is . . . ?	. . . shénme shíhou?	. . . 什么时候?
Why?	Wèishénme?	为什么?
Who?	Shéi?	谁?
Is that okay?	Xíng bù xíng?	行不行?
I'm feeling ill	Wǒ shēng bìng le	我生病了

TRAVEL

ENGLISH	PINYIN	CHINESE
luxury (bus, hotel rooms)	háohuá	豪华
high speed (buses, expressways)	gāosù	高速
air-conditioned	kōngtiáo	空调

NUMBERS

Note that more complicated forms of numbers are often used on official documents and receipts to prevent fraud—see how easily one can be changed to 2, 3, or even 10. Familiar Arabic numerals appear on bank notes, most signs, taxi meters, and other places. Be particularly careful with *4* and *10*, which sound very alike in many regions—hold up fingers to make sure. Note, too, that *yī,* meaning "one," tends to change its tone all the time depending on what it precedes. Don't worry about this—once you've started talking about money, almost any kind of squeak for "one" will do. Finally note that "two" alters when being used with expressions of quantity.

ENGLISH	PINYIN	CHINESE
0	líng	零
1	yī	一
2	èr	二
2 (of them)	liǎng ge	两个
3	sān	三
4	sì	四
5	wǔ	五
6	liù	六
7	qī	七
8	bā	八
9	jiǔ	九
10	shí	十
11	shí yī	十一
12	shí èr	十二
21	èr shí yī	二十一
22	èr shí èr	二十二
51	wǔ shí yī	五十一
100	yì bǎi	一百
101	yì bǎi líng yī	一百零一
110	yì bǎi yī (shí)	一百一（十）
111	yì bǎi yī shí yī	一百一十一
1,000	yì qiān	一千
1,500	yì qiān wǔ (bǎi)	一千五百
5,678	wǔ qiān liù bǎi qī shí bāi	五千六百七十八
10,000	yí wàn	一万

MONEY

The word *yuán* (¥) is rarely spoken, nor is *jiǎo,* the written form for ⅒th of a *yuán,* equivalent to 10 *fēn* (there are 100 *fēn* in a *yuán*). Instead, the Chinese speak of "pieces of money," *kuài qián,* usually abbreviated just to *kuài,* and they speak of *máo* for ⅒th of a *kuài. Fēn* have been overtaken by inflation and are almost useless. Often all zeros after the last whole number are simply omitted, along with *kuài qián,* which is taken as read, especially in direct reply to the question *duōshǎo qián*—"How much?"

ENGLISH	PINYIN	CHINESE
¥1	yí kuài qián	一块钱
¥2	liǎng kuài qián	两块钱

ENGLISH	PINYIN	CHINESE
¥0.30	sān máo qián	三毛钱
¥5.05	wǔ kuài líng wǔ fēn	五块零五分
¥5.50	wǔ kuài wǔ	五块五
¥550	wǔ bǎi wǔ shí kuài	五百五十块
¥5,500	wǔ qiān wǔ bǎi kuài	五千五百块
Small change	língqián	零钱

BANKING & SHOPPING

ENGLISH	PINYIN	CHINESE
I want to change money (foreign exchange)	Wǒ xiǎng huàn qián	我想换钱
credit card	Xìnyòngkǎ	信用卡
traveler's check	lǚxíng zhīpiào	旅行支票
department store	bǎihuò shāngdiàn	百货商店
	gòuwù zhōngxīn	购物中心
convenience store	xiǎomàibù	小卖部
market	shìchǎng	市场
May I have a look?	Wǒ Kànyíxia, hǎo ma?	我看一下，好吗？
I want to buy . . .	Wǒ xiǎng mǎi . . .	我想买。。。
How many do you want?	Nǐ yào jǐ ge?	你要几个？
Two of them	liǎng ge	两个
Three of them	sān ge	三个
1 kilo (2.2 lb.)	yì gōngjīn	一公斤
Half a kilo	yì jīn	一斤
or	bàn gōngjīn	公斤
1 meter (3¼ ft.)	yì mǐ	一米
Too expensive!	Tài guì le!	太贵了
Do you have change?	Yǒu língqián ma?	有零钱吗

TIME

ENGLISH	PINYIN	CHINESE
morning	shàngwǔ	上午
afternoon	xiàwǔ	下午
evening	wǎnshang	晚上
8:20am	shàngwǔ bā diǎn èr shí fēn	上午八点二十分
9:30am	shàngwǔ jiǔ diǎn bàn	上午九点半
noon	zhōngwǔ	中午
4:15pm	xiàwǔ sì diǎn yí kè	下午四点一刻
midnight	wǔ yè	午夜
1 hour	yí ge xiǎoshí	一个小时
8 hours	bā ge xiǎoshí	八个小时

ENGLISH	PINYIN	CHINESE
today	jīntiān	今天
yesterday	zuótiān	昨天
tomorrow	míngtiān	明天
Monday	Xīngqī yī	星期一
Tuesday	Xīngqī èr	星期二
Wednesday	Xīngqī sān	星期三
Thursday	Xīngqī sì	星期四
Friday	Xīngqī wǔ	星期五
Saturday	Xīngqī liù	星期六
Sunday	Xīngqī tiān	星期天

TRANSPORT

ENGLISH	PINYIN	CHINESE
I want to go to . . .	Wǒ xiǎng qù . . .	我想去。。。
plane	fēijī	飞机
train	huǒchē	火车
bus	gōnggòng qìchē	公共汽车
long-distance bus	chángtú qìchē	长途汽车
taxi	chūzū chē	出租车
airport	fēijīchǎng	飞机场
stop or station (bus or train)	zhàn	站
(plane/train/bus) ticket	piào	票

NAVIGATION

ENGLISH	PINYIN	CHINESE
north	Běi	北
south	Nán	南
east	Dōng	东
west	Xī	西
Turn left	zuǒ guǎi	左拐
Turn right	yòu guǎi	右拐
Go straight on	yìzhí zǒu	一直走
crossroads	shízì lùkǒu	十字路口
10 kilometers	shí gōnglǐ	十公里
I'm lost	Wǒ diū le	我丢了

HOTEL

ENGLISH	PINYIN	CHINESE
How many days?	Zhù jǐ tiān?	住几天？
standard room (twin or double with private bathroom)	biāozhǔn jiān	标准间

ENGLISH	PINYIN	CHINESE
passport	hùzhào	护照
deposit	yājīn	押金
I want to check out	Wǒ tuì fáng	我退房

RESTAURANT

ENGLISH	PINYIN	CHINESE
How many people?	Jǐ wèi?	几位
waiter/waitress	fúwùyuán	服务员
menu	càidān	菜单
I'm vegetarian	Wǒ shì chī sù de	我是吃素的
Do you have . . . ?	Yǒu méi yǒu . . . ?	有没有。。。?
Please bring a portion of . . .	Qǐng lái yí fènr . . .	请来一份儿。。。
beer	píjiǔ	啤酒
mineral water	kuàngquán shuǐ	矿泉水
Bill, please	jiézhàng	结帐

SIGNS

Here's a list of common signs and notices to help you identify what you are looking for, from restaurants to condiments, and to help you choose the right door at the public toilets. These are the simplified characters in everyday use in China, but note that it's increasingly fashionable for larger businesses, and those with a long history, to use more complicated traditional characters, so not all may match what's below. Hong Kong and Macau also use traditional characters, and sometimes use different terms altogether, especially for modern inventions. Also, very old restaurants and temples across China tend to write their signs from right to left.

ENGLISH	PINYIN	CHINESE
hotel	bīnguǎn	宾馆
	dàjiǔdiàn	大酒店
	jiǔdiàn	酒店
	fàndiàn	饭店
restaurant	fànguǎn	饭馆
	jiǔdiàn	酒店
	jiǔjiā	酒家
vinegar	cù	醋
soya sauce	Jiàngyóu	酱油
bar	jiǔbā	酒吧
Internet bar	wǎngbā	网吧
cafe	kāfēiguǎn	咖啡馆
teahouse	cháguǎn	茶馆
department store	bǎihuò shāngdiàn	百货商店
	gòuwù zhōngxīn	购物中心
market	shìchǎng	市场

ENGLISH	PINYIN	CHINESE
bookstore	shūdiàn	书店
police (Public Security Bureau)	gōng'ānjú	公安局
Bank of China	Zhōngguó Yínháng	中国银行
public . . .	gōngyòng	公用
. . . telephone	diànhuà	电话
. . . toilet	cèsuǒ	厕所
public telephone	gōngyòng diànhuà	公用电话
public toilet	gōngyòng cèsuǒ	公用厕所
male	nán	男
female	nǚ	女
entrance	rùkǒu	入口
exit	chūkǒu	出口
bus stop/station	qìchē zhàn	汽车站
long-distance bus station	chángtú qìchē zhàn	长途汽车站
luxury	háohuá	豪华
using highway	gāosù	高速
railway station	huǒchēzhàn	火车站
hard seat	yìng zuò	硬座
soft seat	ruǎn zuò	软座
hard sleeper	yìng wò	硬卧
soft sleeper	ruǎn wò	软卧
metro/subway station	dìtiězhàn	地铁站
airport	fēijīchǎng	飞机场
dock/wharf	mǎtóu	码头
passenger terminal (bus, boat, and so on)	kèyùn zhàn	客运站
up/get on	shàng	上
down/get off	xià	下
ticket hall	shòupiào tīng	售票厅
ticket office	shòupiào chù	售票处
left-luggage office	xíngli jìcún chù	行李寄存处
temple	sì	寺
	miào	庙
museum	bówùguǎn	博物馆
memorial hall	jìniànguǎn	纪念馆
park	gōngyuán	公园
hospital	yīyuàn	医院
clinic	zhěnsuǒ	诊所
pharmacy	yàofáng/yàodiàn	药房/药店
travel agency	lǚxíngshè	旅行社

3 Selected Destinations by City

Following are some translations for destinations not covered in maps in this book. Just point to the characters when asking a cab driver to take you to the specific destination.

BĚIJĪNG & HÉBĚI (CHAPTER 4)
SHĀNHĂI GUĀN 山海关
Accommodations & Dining

Jīguān Zhāodàisuǒ	机关招待所
Lónghuá Dàjiǔdiàn	龙华大酒店
Sì Tiáo Bāoziguǎn	四条包子馆
Wàng Yáng Lóu Fànzhuāng	望洋楼饭庄
Yìhé Jiǔdiàn (Friendly Cooperate Hotel)	谊合酒店

Attractions

Jiǎo Shān	角山
Lǎo Lóng Tóu	老龙头
Mèngjiāngnǚ Miào	孟姜女庙
Tiānxià Dìyī Guān	天下第一关
Wáng Jiā Dàyuàn	王家大院

SHÍJIĀZHUĀNG
Accommodations & Dining

Héběi Century Hotel (Héběi Shìjì Dàfàndiàn)	河北世纪大饭店
Huìwén Jiǔdiàn	汇文酒店
Quánjùdé	全聚德
Shāo'ézǎi	烧鹅仔
World Trade Plaza Hotel (Shìmào Guǎngchǎng Jiǔdiàn)	世贸广场酒店
Yànchūn Garden Hotel (Yànchūn Huāyuán Jiǔdiàn)	燕春花园酒店

Attractions

Bǎilín Sì	柏林寺
Cāngyán Shān	苍岩山
Zhàozhōu Qiáo	赵州桥
Zhèngdìng	正定

THE NORTHEAST (CHAPTER 5)
CHÁNGBÁI SHĀN 长白山
Accommodations

Xìndá Bīnguǎn	信达宾馆
Fúbǎi Bīnguǎn	福柏宾馆
Athlete's Village (Yùndòngyuán Cūn)	运动员村
Chángbái Shān International Hotel (Chángbái Shān Guójì Bīnguǎn)	长白山国际宾馆
Chángbái Shān Daewoo (Chángbái Shān Dàyǔ Fàndiàn)	长白山大宇饭店

Attractions

Tiān Chí (Heavenly Lake)	天池
Èrdào Bái Hé (Bái Hé for short), north shore (běi pō)	二道白河 北坡
Wēnquán Yù	温泉峪
Dìxià Sēnlín (Underground Forest)	地下森林

Měirén Sōng Sēnlín (Sylvan Pine Forest) 美人松森林
Sōngjiāng Hé 松江河
The Xī Pō Shān Mén (West Slope Mountain Gate) 西坡山门
Sōngjiāng Hé Bīnguǎn 松江河宾馆

ALONG THE YELLOW RIVER (CHAPTER 6)
YÁN'ĀN 延安
Accommodations

Yán'ān Bīnguǎn 延安宾馆
Yàshèng Dàjiǔdiàn 亚圣大酒店
Yínhǎi Guójì Dàjiǔdiàn 银海国际大酒店
Wúqǐ Dàjiǔdiàn 吴起大酒店

Attractions

Fènghuáng Shān (Phoenix Hill) 凤凰山
Wángjiāpíng Gémìng Jiùzhǐ (Former Revolutionary 王家坪革命旧址
    Headquarters at Wángjiāpíng)
Gémìng Jìniànguǎn (Revolutionary Memorial 革命纪念馆
    Hall/Museum)
Yángjiālǐng Jiùzhǐ (Yángjiālǐng Revolutionary 杨家岭旧址
    Headquarters)
Bǎotǎ (Baǒ Pagoda) 宝塔

PÍNGYÁO 平遥
Accommodations

Déjū Yuán 德居源
Tiān Yuán Kuí 天元魁

Attractions

Shì Lóu (Market Building) 市楼
ancient city wall (gǔ chéngqiáng) 古城墙
Rìshēng Chāng 日升昌
Bǎi Chuān Tōng 百川通
Chénghuáng Miào, Cáishén Miào 城隍庙, 财神庙
Zàojūn Miào 灶君庙
Xiànyá Shǔ (or Yámen) 县衙署, 衙门
Léi Lǚ Tài Gùjū 雷履泰故居
Zhènguó Sì 镇国寺
Qiáo Jiā Dàyuàn 乔家大院
Shuānglín Sì 双林寺
Wáng Family Courtyard (Wáng Jiā Dàyuàn) 王家大院
Yí Yuán (Grace Vineyard) 怡园

WǓTÁI SHĀN 五台山
Accommodations & Dining

Fúrén Jū Jiǔlóu 福仁居酒楼
Jìngxīn Zhāi 精心斋
Liángchéng Bīnguǎn 凉城宾馆
Nèiměnggǔ Jiēdàichù 内蒙古接待处
Qīxiángé Bīnguǎn 栖贤阁宾馆

Yínhǎi Shānzhuāng 银海山庄
Yīzhǎn Míngdēng Quánsùzhāi 一盏明灯全素斋

Attractions
Dàilóu Peak 代娄峰
Wǔtái Shān Tour Taxi Ticket Office 五台山旅游车出租
(Wǔtái Shān Lǔyóu Chē Chūzū)
Fēiyǔ Diànnǎo 飞宇电脑
Xiǎntōng Sì 显通寺
Tǎyuàn Sì 塔院寺
Nán Shān Sì 南山寺
Lóngquán Sì 龙泉寺
Nánchán Sì 南禅寺
Fóguāng Sì 佛光寺

THE SILK ROUTES (CHAPTER 7)
TIĀNSHUǏ 天水
Accommodations & Dining
Jiāotōng Bīnguǎn 交通宾馆
Kùchē Bīnguǎn 库车宾馆
Kùchē Fàndiàn 库车饭店
Qiūcí Bīnguǎn 龟兹宾馆
Wúmǎi'ěrhóng Měishí Chéng (Omarjan 吴买尔洪美食城
Muhammed Food City)
Wūqià Guǒyuán Cāntīng (Uqa Bhag Resturant) 乌恰果园餐厅

Attractions
Běidào Qū (long-distance bus station) 北道区长途汽车站
Gōnghuì Dàshà 工会大厦
Màijī Shān Shíkū 麦积山石窟

XIÀHÉ (LABRANG) 夏河
Accommodations
Lābùléng Bīnguǎn (Labrang Hotel) 拉不楞宾馆
Overseas Tibetan Hotel (Huáqiáo Fàndiàn) 华侨饭店
Tara Guesthouse (Zhuómǎ Lǔshè) 卓玛旅社

Attractions
Lābùléng Sì (Labrang Monastery) 拉不楞寺
Sāngkē 桑科

KUQA (KÙCHĒ) 库车
Accommodations & Dining
Jiāotōng Bīnguǎn 交通宾馆
Kùchē Bīnguǎn 库车宾馆
Kùchē Fàndiàn 库车饭店
Qiūcí Bīnguǎn 龟兹宾馆
Wúmǎi'ěrhóng Měishí Chéng (Omarjan 吴买尔洪美食城
Muhammed Food City)
Wūqià Guǒyuán Cāntīng (Uqa Bhag Resturant) 乌恰果园餐厅

Attractions

Kèzī'ěr Qiān Fó Dòng (Kizil Thousand Buddha Caves) 克孜尔千佛洞
Kùchē Dà Sì (Kuqa Grand Mosque) 库车大寺
Sūbāshí Gǔchéng (Jarakol Temple) 苏巴什古城
Xīngqīwǔ Dàshìchǎng (Friday Bazaar) 星期五大市场

KHOTAN (HÉTIÁN)   和田
Accommodations & Dining

Gāoyáng Kǎoròu Kuàicāndiàn 羔羊烤肉快餐店
Hétián Yíngbīnguǎn 和田迎宾馆
Huāyuán Bīnguǎn 花园宾馆
Tiānhǎi Bīnguǎn 天海宾馆

Attractions

Carpet Factory (Dìtǎn Chǎng) 地毯厂
Jade Factory (Gōngyì Měishù Yǒuxiàn Gōngsī) 工艺美术有限公司
Silk and Mulberry Research Center (Sīsāng Yánjiūsuǒ) 丝桑研究所
Sunday Market (Xīngqītiān Dàshìchǎng) 星期天大市场

EASTERN CENTRAL CHINA (CHAPTER 8)
AROUND ZHÈNGZHŌU

Gǒngyì 巩义
Běi Sòng Huánglíng (Imperial Tombs of 北宋皇陵
   the Northern Sòng Dynasty)
Shíkū Sì 石窟寺

DĒNGFĒNG & SŌNG SHĀN   登封
Accommodations & Dining

Fēngyuán Dàjiǔdiàn 丰源大酒店
Jīnguàn Miànbāo Xīdiǎn Fáng 京冠面包西点坊
Shàolín Guójì Dàjiǔdiàn (Shàolín International Hotel) 少林国际大酒店
Sìjì Chūn 四季春
Xiāngjī Wáng 香鸡王

Attractions

Guólǚ Dàlóu 国旅大楼
West Bus Station (Xī Kè Zhàn) 西客站
Tàishì Shān 太室山
Jùnjí Féng 峻极峰
Shàoshì Shān 少室山
Sōngyáng Suǒdào 嵩阳索道
Sōng Shān Diào Qiáo 嵩山吊桥
Sānhuáng Xínggōng (Sānhuáng Palace) 三皇行宫
Shàolín Sì (Shàolín Monastery) 少林寺
Shàolín Wǔshù Guǎn (Martial Arts Training Center) 少林武术馆
Shàolín Sì Tǎgōu Wǔshù Xuéxiào 少林寺塔沟武术学校
   (Shàolín Monastery Wǔshù Institute at Tǎgōu)
Sōngyuè Tǎ (Sōngyuè Pagoda) 嵩岳塔
Zhōngyuè Miào 中岳庙
Gàochéng Guānxīng Tái 告成观星台

LUÒYÁNG
洛阳

Accommodations
Bǎo Húlu 宝葫芦
Huáyáng Guǎngchǎng Guójì Dàjiǔdiàn 华阳广场国际大
  (Huáyáng Plaza Hotel) 酒店
Lǎo Jiē Dìyī Lóu 老街第一楼
Lǎo Jiē (Old Street) 老街
Luòyáng Peony Hotel (Luòyáng Mǔdān Dàjiǔdiàn) 洛阳牡丹大酒店
Míngyuàn Dàjiǔdiàn (Míngyuàn Hotel) 明苑大酒店
Mǔdān Chéng Bīnguǎn (Peony Plaza) 牡丹城宾馆
Xīn Yǒuyì Bīnguǎn (New Friendship Hotel) 新友谊宾馆

Attractions
Yī Xiàn 黟县
Huīzhōu District 徽州区
Shè Xiàn 歙县
Xīdì, Hóngcūn, and Nánpíng 西递 红村, 南平
Qiānkǒu, and Chéngkǎn 潜口呈坎

JÌ'NÁN
济南

Accommodations
Crowne Plaza Guìhé Jì'nán (Guìhé Huángguān Jiǔdiàn) 贵和皇冠酒店
Sofitel Silver Plaza Jì'nán (Suǒfēitè Yínzuò Dàfàndiàn) 索菲特银座大饭店
Qílǔ Bīnguǎn 齐鲁宾馆
Silver Plaza Quán Chéng Hotel (Yínzuò 银座泉城大酒
  Quánchéng Dàjiǔdiàn)
Guì Dū Dàjiǔdiàn 贵都大酒店
Jì'nán Tiědào Dàjiǔdiàn 济南铁道大酒店

Attractions
Bàotū Quán (Bàotū Spring) 趵突泉
Dà Míng Hú Gōngyuán (Dà Míng Hú Park) 大明湖公园

Dining
Xīn Lán Bái (Blue & White) 新蓝白
Lǎo Hángzhōu Jiǔ Wǎn Bàn 老杭州九碗拌

Other
long-distance bus station (chángtú qìchēzhàn) 长途汽车站
China Shāndōng Travel Service (Zhōngguó 中国山东旅行社
  Shāndōng Lǚxíngshè)

QŪFŪ
曲阜

Accommodations & Dining
Kǒng Fǔ Dàjiǔdiàn 孔府大酒店
Kǒng Fǔ Jiā Yán Táng 孔府家严堂
Quèlǐ Bīnshè (Quèlǐ Hotel) 阙里宾舍
Qūfǔ Yóuzhèng Bīnguǎn (Qūfǔ Post Hotel) 曲阜邮政宾馆
Yù Lóng Dàjiǔdiàn (Yù Lóng Hotel) 裕隆大酒店

Attractions

Kǒng Miào (Confucius Temple)   孔庙
Kǒng Fǔ (Confucian Mansion)   孔府
Kǒng Lín (Confucian Forest & Cemetery)   孔林
Kǒngzǐ Yánjiūyuàn (Confucius Academy)   孔子研究院
Shào Hào Lín (Tomb of Emperor Shào Hào)   少昊林

WÚXĪ   无锡
Accommodations & Dining

Hángyùn Dàshà (Ferry Building)   航运大厦
Húbīn Fàndiàn   湖滨饭店
New World Courtyard Wúxī (Wúxī Xīnshìjiè   无锡新世界万怡
   Wànyí Jiǔdiàn)   酒店
Sheraton Wúxī Hotel & Towers (Xǐláidēng Dàfàndiàn)   喜来登无锡大饭店
Tài Hú Fàndiàn   太湖饭店
Wúxī Qìchēzhàn (Wúxī Bus Station)   无锡汽车站

Attractions

Tài Hú (Lake Tài)   太湖
Yuántóuzhǔ (Turtle Head Isle)   鼋头渚
Xīhuì Gōngyuán   锡惠公园

YÍXĪNG   宜兴

Huì shān Clay Figurine Factory   惠山泥人厂
Yíxīng Táocí Bówùguǎn   宜兴陶瓷博物馆
Shànjuǎn Dòng   扇卷洞
Yíxīng Bus Station (Shěng Qìchēzhàn)   宜兴汽车站
Yíxīng Guójì Fàndiàn (Yíxīng International Hotel)   宜兴国际饭店

HÉFÉI   合肥
Accommodations & Dining

Holiday Inn Héféi (Héféi Gǔjǐng Jiàrì Jiǔdiàn)   合肥古井假日酒店
Huáqiáo Fàndiàn (Overseas Chinese Hotel)   华侨饭店
Jīn Mǎn Lóu Huāyuán Jiǔdiàn   金满楼花园酒店
Lǎo Xiè Lóngxiā   老谢龙虾
Noodles in Chopsticks (24 Xiǎoshí Miàn)   小时面
Novotel Héféi (Héféi Nuòfùtè Qíyún Shānzhuāng)   合肥诺富特齐云山庄

Attractions

Bāo Hé Gōngyuán   包河公园
Bāo Gōng Mù Yuán (Lord Bāo's Tomb)   包公墓园
Xiāoyáojīn Gōngyuán   逍遥津公园
Shāngyè Bùxíngjiē   商业步行街
Lǐ Hóngzhāng Gùjū   李鸿章故居
Ānhuī Shěng Bówùguǎn (Ānhuī Provincial Museum)   安徽省博物馆

TÚNXĪ   屯溪
Accommodations & Dining

Bǎo Húlu   宝葫芦
Huáng Shān Guójì Dàjiǔdiàn (Huáng Shān   黄山国际大酒店
   International Hotel)

Huáng Shān Guómài Dàjiǔdiàn	黄山国脉大酒店
Huáng Shān Huāxī Fàndiàn	黄山花溪饭店
Jiànguó Shāngwù Jiǔdiàn (Jiànguó Garden Hotel)	建国商务酒店
Lǎo Jiē Dìyī Lóu	老街第一楼
Lǎo Jiē (Old Street)	老街

Attractions

Bǎolún Gé (Bǎolún Hall)	宝纶阁
Chéngkǎn	呈坎
Dòushān Jiē	斗山街
Hóng Cūn	宏村
Huāshān Míkū (Mysterious Caves of Flower Mountain)	花山谜窟
Huīzhōu District	徽州区
Nánpíng	南屏
Qiánkǒu	潜口
Shè Xiàn	歙县
Xīdì	西递
Tángyuè Páifang Qún (Tángyuè Memorial Arches)	棠樾牌坊群
Xǔguó Shífáng (Xúgúo Stone Archway)	许国石坊
Yī Xiàn	黟县

SHÀNGHǍI (CHAPTER 9)
SŪZHŌU 苏州
Accommodations & Dining

Gloria Plaza Hotel Sūzhōu (Kǎilái Dàjiǔdiàn)	凯莱大酒店
Scholars Inn (Shūxiāng Méndì Shāngwù Jiǔdiàn)	书香门第商务酒店
Sheraton Sūzhōu Hotel & Tower (Sūzhōu Wúgōng Xǐláidēng Dàjiǔdiàn)	苏州吴宫喜来登大酒店
Sōng Hè Lóu (Pine and Crane Restaurant)	松鹤楼

Attractions

Forest of Lions Garden (Shī Zi Lín Yuán)	狮子林园
Gūsū Yuán (Gūsū Garden)	姑苏园
Humble Administrator's Garden (Zhuō Zhèng Yuán)	拙政园
Lingering Garden (Liú Yuán)	留园
Master of the Nets Garden (Wǎng Shī Yuán)	网师园
Pán Mén (Pán Gate)	盘门
Ruìguāng Tǎ	瑞光塔
Sūzhōu Cìxiù Yánjiūsuǒ (Sūzhōu Embroidery Research Institute)	苏州刺绣研究所
Sūzhōu Silk Museum (Sūzhōu Sīchóu Bówùguǎn)	苏州丝绸博物馆
Tiger Hill (Hǔ Qiū Shān)	虎丘山
Wúmén Qiáo	无门桥

HÁNGZHŌU 杭洲
Accommodations & Dining

Lóu Wài Lóu	楼外楼
Shangri-La Hotel Hángzhōu (Hángzhōu Xiānggélǐla Fàndiàn)	杭州香格里拉饭店

Sofitel Westlake Hángzhou (Hángzhōu Suǒfēitè Xīhú Dàjiǔdiàn) 杭州索菲特西湖大酒店

Xī Hú Tiāndì (West Lake Heaven and Earth) 西湖天地

Attractions

Bái Causeway (Bái Dī) 白堤
Duàn Qiáo (Broken Bridge) 断桥
Fēilái Fēng (Peak That Flew from Afar) 飞来峰
Léi Fēng Tǎ (Léi Fēng Pagoda) 雷峰塔
Língyǐn Sì (Língyǐn Temple) 灵隐寺
Lóngjǐng Wēnchá (Dragon Well Tea Village) 龙井温茶
Sān Tán Yìn Yuè (Three Pools Mirroring The Moon) 三潭印月
Solitary Island (Gūshān Dǎo) 孤山岛
Sū Causeway (Sū Dī) 苏堤
West Lake (Xī Hú) 西湖
Xiǎo Yíng Zhōu (Island of Small Seas) 小瀛洲
Zhèjiāng Provincial Museum (Zhèjiāng Bówùguǎn) 浙江博物馆
Zhōngguó Cháyè Bówùguǎn (Chinese Tea Museum) 中国茶叶博物馆
Zhōngguó Sīchóu Bówùguǎn (China Silk Museum) 中国丝绸博物馆

THE SOUTHEAST (CHAPTER 10)
NÍNGBŌ 宁波
Accommodations & Dining

Jīngāng Dàjiǔdiàn (Golden Port Hotel) 金港酒店
Shàngdǎo Kāfēi 上岛咖啡
Wénchāng Dàjiǔdiàn (Mandarin Prosperous Hotel) 文昌大酒店
Xīng bā kè (Starbucks) 星巴克

Attractions

Bǎoguó Sì 保国寺
Sān Jiāng Kǒu 三江口
Tiān Yī Gé Bówùguǎn 天一阁博物馆

WĒNZHŌU 温州
Accommodations & Dining

Fruit Restaurant (Chún Sōng Láng Shuǐguǒ Fáng) 莼淞郎水果坊
Fán Dōng Bīnguǎn 繁东宾馆
Hǎigǎng Měishí Fáng 海港美食舫
Jiāngxīn Liáoyǎngyuàn 江心疗养院
Jīnwàng Jiào Dàjiǔdiàn 金旺教大酒店
Shàngdǎo Kāfēi 上岛咖啡

Attractions

Jiāngxīn Gū Yǔ 江心孤屿
Wǔ Mǎ Jiē 五马街

TÀISHÙN COUNTY 泰顺县
Accommodations

Ā Guó Fàndiàn 阿国饭店
Tàishùn Guójì Dàjiǔdiàn 泰顺国际大酒店
Zhōulǐng Xiāng Lǚshè 洲岭乡旅社

Attractions

Běi Jiàn Qiáo	北涧桥
Dōng Yáng Qiáo	东洋桥
Liúzhái Qiáo	刘宅桥
Mù Gǒng Lángqiáo	木拱廊桥
Sān Tiáo Qiáo	三条桥
Wénxīng Qiáo	文兴桥
Xiānjū Qiáo	仙居桥
Xuēzhái Qiáo	薛宅桥
Yùwén Qiáo	毓文桥

FÚZHŌU
福州

Accommodations & Dining

Golden Resources International Hotel (Jīnyuán Guójì Dàjiǔdiàn)	金源国际大酒店
Fúzhōu Xiānggélǐlā Dàjiǔdiàn	福州香格里拉大酒店
Ā Bō Luó Dàjiǔdiàn	阿波罗大酒店
Ramada Plaza (Měilún Huáměidá Guǎngchǎng Dàjiǔdiàn)	美伦华美达广场大酒店

Attractions

Xī Hú Gōngyuán	西湖公园
Yāntái Shān Gōngyuán	烟台山公园
Yú Shān	于山

WǓYÍ SHĀN
武夷山

Accommodations & Dining

Bǎodǎo Dàjiǔdiàn	宝岛大酒店
Jīn Gǔ Yuán Dàjiǔdiàn	金谷园大酒店
Wǔyí Shānzhuāng (Wǔyí Mountain Villa)	武夷山庄

Attractions

Dà Hóng Pào	大红袍
Dà Wáng Fēng	大王峰
Tiānyóu Shān	天游山
Wǔyí Gōng	天游山
Xīng Cūn	兴村
Yuánshǐ Sēnlín Gōngyuán	原始森林公园

JǏNGDÉ ZHÈN
景德镇

Accommodations & Dining

Jīnshèng Bīnguǎn	金盛宾馆
Jīnyè Dàjiǔdiàn	金叶大酒店

Attractions

Sān Bǎo Shuǐduì (Water-powered Hammers)	三宝水碓
Táocí Bówùguǎn (Museum of Porcelain)	陶瓷博物馆
Táocí Lìshǐ Bówùguǎn (Ceramic Historical Exhibition Area)	陶瓷历史博物馆

SHĒNZHÈN   深圳
Accommodations & Dining
  Bàn Xī Jiǔdiàn   半溪酒店
  Guǎngxìn Jiǔdiàn   广信酒店
  Shangri-La (Xiānggélǐla Dàjiǔdiàn)   香格里拉大酒店
Attractions
  Luó Hú Shāngyè Chéng (Luó Hú Commercial City)   罗湖商业成
  Minsk World (Míngsīkè Hángmǔ Shìjiè)   明思克航母世界

THE SOUTHWEST (CHAPTER 12)
LÍ RIVER   漓江
  Buddha Cave   菩萨洞
  Gǔróng Gōngyuán   古榕公园
  Huángbù Dǎoyǐng   黄布倒影
  Jiǔmǎ Huàshān (Nine Horses Fresco Hill)   九马画山
  Moon Mountain   月亮山
  Water Cave   水岩
  Yáng Dī   杨堤
  Zhújiāng Pier   竹江码头

AROUND YÁNGSHUÒ
  Báishā   白沙
  Fúlì   福利
  Liú Gōng   留公
  Xīngpíng   兴坪
  Yángshuò Shèngdì   阳朔胜地
  Yú Cūn   渔村
  Yùlóng Hé   遇龙河

AROUND GUÌYÁNG
  Huángguǒshù Pùbù (Huángguǒshù Falls)   黄果树瀑布
  Lónggōng Dòng (Dragon Palace Caves)   龙宫洞
  Shítou Zhài (Stone Village)   石头寨
  Tiānlóng Túnbǎo   天龙屯堡
  Xīn Huángguǒshù Bīnguǎn   新黄国树宾馆

KǍILǏ   凯里
  Guótài Dàjiǔdiàn   国泰大酒店
  Kǎilǐ Lántiān Dàjiǔdiàn   凯里蓝天大酒店
  Màidéshì   麦德士
  Minorities Museum (Zhōu Mínzú Bówùguǎn)   州民族博物馆
  Shāngmào Jiē   商贸街

MIÁO/DÒNG AREAS
  Róngjiāng Bīnguǎn   榕江宾馆
  Yuèliàng Shān Bīnguǎn   月亮山宾馆
  Zhàoxìng   肇兴
  Lulu's Homestay (Fēngqíng Lǚyóu Shèwài   风情旅游涉外民居
    Mínjū Lǚguǎn)   旅馆
  Wénhuàzhàn Zhāodàisuǒ   文化站招待所

Bāshā 岜沙
Cóng Jiāng 从江
Dìpíng 地坪
Fǎnpái 反排
Huángpíng 黄平
Xī Jiāng 西江
Jìtáng 纪堂
Lángdé 郎德
Mátáng 麻塘
Róng Jiāng 榕江
Tái Jiāng 台江
Zhàoxìng 肇兴
Zhōuxī 舟溪

AROUND DÀLĬ

Ěr Hǎi Lake 洱海湖
Cāng Shān (Green Mountains) 苍山
Fèngyǎn Dòng (Phoenix Cave) 凤眼洞
Gǎntōng Sì 感通寺
Guānyīn Gé (Guānyīn Pavilion) 观音阁
Jīnsuō Dǎo 金梭岛
Pǔtuó Dǎo 普陀岛
Qīngbì Xī 清碧溪
Shāpíng 沙坪
Xǐ Zhōu 喜州
Zhōnghé Sì 中和寺
Zhōu Chéng 周城

AROUND LÌ JIĀNG

Báishā 白沙
Bīngchuān Gōngyuán (Glacier Park) 冰川公园
Chángjiāng Dìyī Wān (First Bend of the Yángzǐ) 长江第一湾
Lúgū Hú (Lúgū Lake) 泸沽湖
Máoniú Píng (Yak Meadow) 牦牛坪
Shí Gǔ 石鼓
Shù Hé 束河
Tiger Leaping Gorge (Hǔ Tiào Xiá) 虎跳峡
Yùfēng Sì (Yùfēng Temple) 玉峰寺
Yù Hú (Nguluko) 玉湖
Yùlóng Xuěshān (Jade Dragon Snow Mountain) 玉龙雪山
Yúnshān Píng (Spruce Meadow) 云杉坪

XIĀNGGÉLĬLĀ (ZHŌNGDIÀN)
Accommodations & Dining

香格里拉 （中甸）

Lóngfèng Xiáng Dàjiǔdiàn (Holy Palace Hotel) 龙凤祥大酒店
Snowland Café 雪域咖啡厅
Tiānjiè Shénchuān Dàjiǔdiàn (Paradise Hotel) 天界神川大酒店
Tibet Café 西藏咖啡馆

Attractions
Báishuǐ Tái (White Water Terraces) 白水台
Bìtǎ Hǎi (Bìtǎ Lake) 碧塔海
Ganden Sumtseling Gompa (Sōngzànlín Sì) 松赞林寺
Old town 古城
Old Town Scripture Chamber (Gǔchéng Zàngjīng Táng) 古城藏经堂

JĪNGHÓNG（景洪）& XĪSHUĀNGBĂNNÀ （西双版纳）
Accommodations & Dining
Bǎnnà Bīnguǎn 版纳宾馆
Cái Chūn Qīng 财春青
Dǎijiā Měishí Cūn 傣家美食村
Dǎiyuán Dàjiǔdiàn (Tai Garden Hotel) 傣园大酒店
Dōngguān Jiǎozǐ Guǎn 东关饺子馆
Měi Měi Café 美美咖啡
Mekong Café (Méigōng Kāfēiguǎ) 湄公咖啡馆
Xīshuāngbǎnnà Guānguāng Jiǔdiàn 西双版纳观光酒店

Attractions
Màntīng Gōngyuán 曼听公园
Mínzú Fēngqíng Yuán 民族风情园
Tropical Flower and Plants Garden (Rèdài Huāhuìyuán) 热带花卉园

AROUND JĪNGHÓNG
Bǎnnà Rainforest Valley (Bǎnnà Yǔlín Gǔ) 版纳雨林谷
Banna Wild Elephant Valley (Bǎnnà Yěxiàng Gǔ) 版纳野象谷
Dǎi Minority Folk Customs Park (Dǎi Zú Yuán) 傣族园
Gǎnlǎnbà (Měnghǎn) 橄榄坝 (勐罕)
Jīnuò Folk Custom Village (Jīnuò Mínsú Shānzhài) 基诺民俗山寨
Měnglà 勐腊
Měnglún 勐仑
Měngyǎng 勐养
Móhān 磨憨
Sānchàhé Nature Reserve (Sānchàhé Zìrán Bǎohùqū) 三岔河自然保护区
Xīshuāngbǎnnà Rèdài Zhíwùyuán 西双版纳热带植物园

Xiàngxíng Róngshù 象形榕树

YÁNGZǏ & BEYOND (CHAPTER 13)
ÉMÉI SHĀN 峨眉山
Accommodations
Éméi Shān Fàndiàn 峨眉山饭店
Hóngzhū Shān Bīnguǎn 红珠山宾馆
Jīn Dǐng Dàjiǔdiàn (Golden Summit Hotel) 金顶大酒店

Attractions
Bàoguó Sì 报国寺
Fúhǔ Sì 伏虎寺
Hóngchūn Píng 洪椿坪
Jīn Dǐng (Golden Peak) 金顶

Jiēyǐn Diàn (Jiēyǐn Hall)	接引殿
Jiǔlǎo Dòng (Jiǔlǎo Cave)	九老洞
Léidòng Píng (Léidòng Terrace)	雷洞坪
Niúxīn Tíng (Niúxīn Pavilion)	牛心亭
Qīngyīn Gé	清音阁
Qiānfó Dǐng (Qiānfó Peak)	千佛顶
Shèshēn Yán (Shèshēn Cliff)	摄身岩
Tourist Center (Lǚrén Zhōngxīn)	旅人中心
Wànfó Dǐng (Wànfó Peak)	万佛顶
Wànnián Sì (Wànnián Monastery)	万年寺
Wànnián Cable Car Station (Wànnián Chēchǎng)	万年车场
Xǐ Xiàng Chí (Elephant Bathing Pool)	洗象池
Xiānfēng Sì (Xiānfēng Monastery)	先峰寺

LÈ SHĀN — 乐山
Accommodations

Jífēng Lóu Bīnguǎn	集风楼宾馆
Jiā Zhōu Bīnguǎn	嘉州宾馆

Attractions

Dà Fó (Great Buddha)	大佛
Jiǔqǔ Zhàndào (Path of Nine Switchbacks)	九曲栈道
Wūyóu Shān (Wūyóu Mountain)	乌尤山

WÒLÓNG — 卧龙
Towns

Hétao Píng	核桃坪
Shāwān	沙湾

Accommodations

Panda Inn (Xióngmāo Shānzhuāng)	熊猫山庄
Sìtōng Bīnguǎn	四通宾馆

Attractions

Distillery	酒厂

JIǓZHÀI GŌU — 九寨沟
Accommodations

Jīnxīn Bīnguǎn (Jīnxīn Hotel)	金鑫宾馆
Jiǔzhài Gōu Dàjiǔdiàn (Jiǔzhài Gōu International Hotel)	九寨沟大酒店
Xīngyǔ Guójì Dàjiǔdiàn (Xīngyǔ International Hotel)	星宇国际大酒店
Yínyuàn Bīnguǎn (Yínyuàn Hotel)	银苑宾馆

CHÓNGQÌNG — 重庆
Accommodations

Guǎngchǎng Bīnguǎn (Plaza Hotel)	广场宾馆
Harbour Plaza (Hǎi Yì Fàndiàn)	海逸饭店
Hilton Hotel (Xīěrdùn Jiǔdiàn)	希尔顿酒店
Holiday Inn (Yángzǐ Jiāng Jiàrì Jiǔdiàn)	扬子江假日酒店
Marriott Hotel (Wànháo Jiǔdiàn)	万豪酒店
Rénmín Bīnguǎn	人民宾馆

Attractions

Chóngqìng Dòngwùyuán (Chóngqìng Zoo) 重庆动物园
Chóngqìng Shì Bówùguǎn (Chóngqìng Municipal Museum) 重庆博物馆
Huàjiā Zhī Cūn (Artists' Village) 画家之村
Shǐdíwēi Jiāngjūn Jiùjū (Stilwell Museum/ 史迪威将军旧居
   General Stilwell's former residence)

WÙLÍNG YUÁN/ZHĀNG JIĀ JIÈ   武陵源/张家界
Accommodations

Dragon International Hotel (Xiānglóng Guójì Dàjiǔdiàn) 湘龙国际大酒店
Mínsú Shānzhuāng (Mínsú Mountain Villa) 民俗山庄
Pípa Xī Bīnguǎn 琵琶溪宾馆
Xiāngdiàn Shānzhuāng (Xiāngdiàn Mountain Villa) 湘电山庄

THE TIBETAN WORLD (CHAPTER 14)
GOLMUD (GÉ'ĚRMÙ)   格尔木
Accommodations & Dining

Gé'ěrmù Bīnguǎn 格尔木宾馆
Wēi'ěrshì Dàjiǔdiàn 威尔士大酒店
Yóuzhèng Bīnguǎn (Post Hotel) 邮政宾馆
Liúyi Shǒu 留一手

SHIGATSE (RÌKĀZÉ)   日喀则
Accommodations & Dining

Huáiyù Mínzú Biǎoyì Zhōngxīn 怀玉民族表艺中心
Lǎoyǒu Lèyuán 老友乐园
Tenzin Hotel (Dàn Zēng Bīnguǎn) 旦增宾馆
Shénhú Jiǔdiàn (Hotel Manasarovar) 神湖酒店
Wūzī Dàjiǔdiàn (Wutse Hotel) 乌孜大酒店
Yak Head Restaurant (Niútóu Zàngcān) 牛头藏餐
Yǎlǔ Zàng Cāntīng 雅鲁藏餐厅

Attractions

Rìkāzé zhōngchéngbǎo 日喀则中城堡
Tashilhunpo Monastery (Zhāshílúnbù Sì) 扎什伦布寺
Shigatse bazaar jímào shìchǎng 集贸市场
Sìfāng Chāoshì 四方超市

Appendix B:
The Chinese Menu

One of the best things about any visit to China is the food, at least for the independent traveler. Tour groups are often treated to a relentless series of cheap, bland dishes designed to cause no complaints, and to keep the costs down for the Chinese operator, so do everything you can to escape and order some of the local specialties we've described for you in each chapter. Here they are again, listed alphabetically under the cities in which they are mentioned, and with characters you can show your waiter or waitress (but check back to the review first, as some of the dishes are unique to certain restaurants). Widely available Chinese standards are together at the top, so check there if the recommended dish isn't listed under its city heading.

Supplement this list by bringing along the bilingual menu from your local Chinese restaurant at home. The characters will not be quite the same as those used on the mainland (more similar to those used in Hong Kong and Macau), but they will be understood. Don't expect the dishes to be the same, however. Expect them to be *better*.

Any mainstream nonspecialty restaurant can and will make any common Chinese dish, whether it's on the menu or not. But ask for a spicy Sìchuān dish in a Cantonese restaurant in Guǎngzhōu, and you'll be sorely disappointed.

Outside Hong Kong and big hotels and expat cafe ghettos on the mainland, few restaurants have English menus. If, near your five-star hotel, you see restaurants with signs saying ENGLISH MENU, there's a fair chance you are going to be cheated with double prices, and you should eat elsewhere (unless it's an obvious backpacker hangout).

Menus generally open with *liáng cài* (cold dishes). For hygiene reasons in mainland China, except in top-class Sino-foreign joint-venture restaurants, you are strongly advised to avoid these cold dishes, especially if you're on a short trip. The restaurant's specialties also come early in the menü, often easily spotted by their significantly higher prices, and if you dither, the waitress will recommend them, saying, "I hear this one's good." Waitresses always recommend ¥180 ($23) dishes, never ¥18 ($2.25) ones. Occasionally, some of these may be made from creatures you would regard as pets or zoo creatures (or best in the wild), may be made from parts you consider inedible, or may contain an odd material like swallow saliva (the main ingredient of bird's nest soup, a rather bland and uninteresting Cantonese delicacy).

Main dishes come next, various meats and fish before vegetables and *dòufu* (tofu), and drinks at the end. There are rarely desserts, although Guǎngdōng (Cantonese) food has absorbed the tradition of eating something sweet at the end of the meal from across the border in Hong Kong, where all restaurants have something to offer of this kind, if only sliced fruit.

Soup is usually eaten last, although dishes arrive in a rather haphazard order. Outside Guǎngdōng Province, Hong Kong, and Macau, rice usually arrives toward the end, and if you want it with your meal you must ask (point at the characters for rice, below, when the first dish arrives).

There is no tipping. Tea, chopsticks, and napkins should be free, although if a wrapped packet of tissues arrives, there may be a small fee. Service charges do not exist outside of major hotels, and there are no cover charges or taxes. If you are asked what tea you would like, then you are going to receive something above average and will be charged. You should be careful, since some varieties of tea may cost more than the meal itself.

Most Chinese food is not designed to be eaten solo, but if you do find yourself on your own, ask for small portions *(xiǎo pán)*.

xiǎo pán   small portion   小盘

These are usually about 70% the size of a full dish and about 70% the price, but they enable you to sample the menu properly without too much waste.

POPULAR DISHES & SNACKS

PINYIN	ENGLISH	CHINESE
bābǎo zhōu	rice porridge with nuts and berries	八宝粥
bāozi	stuffed steamed buns	包子
bīngqílín	ice cream	冰淇淋
chǎofàn	fried rice	炒饭
chǎomiàn	fried noodles	炒面
cōng bào niúròu	quick-fried beef and onions	葱爆牛肉
diǎnxin	dim sum (snacks)	点心
gānbiān sìjìdòu	sautéed string beans	干煸四季豆
gōngbào jīdīng	spicy diced chicken with cashews	宫爆鸡丁
guōtiē	fried dumplings/potstickers	锅贴
hóngshāo fǔzhú	braised tofu	红烧腐竹
hóngshāo huángyú	braised yellow fish	红烧黄鱼
huíguō ròu	twice-cooked pork	回锅肉
huǒguō	hot pot	火锅
jiǎozi	dumplings/Chinese ravioli	饺子
jīngjiàng ròusī	shredded pork in soy sauce	京酱肉丝
mápó dòufu	spicy tofu with chopped meat	麻婆豆腐
miàntiáo	noodles	面条
mǐfàn	rice	米饭
mù xū ròu	sliced pork with fungus (mushu pork)	木须肉
niúròu miàn	beef noodles	牛肉面
ròu chuàn	kabobs	肉串
sānxiān	"three flavors" (usually prawn, mushroom, pork)	三鲜
shuǐjiǎo	boiled dumplings	水饺
suānlà báicài	hot-and-sour cabbage	酸辣白菜
suānlà tāng	hot-and-sour soup	酸辣汤
sù shíjǐn	mixed vegetables	素什锦
tángcù lǐji	sweet-and-sour pork tenderloin	糖醋里脊
tǔdòu dùn niúròu	stewed beef and potato	土豆炖牛肉
xīhóngshì chǎo jīdàn	tomatoes with eggs	西红柿炒鸡蛋
yóutiáo	fried salty doughnut	油条

PINYIN	ENGLISH	CHINESE
yúxiāng qiézi	eggplant in garlic sauce	鱼香茄子
yúxiāng ròusī	shredded pork in garlic sauce	鱼香肉丝
zhēngjiǎo	steamed dumplings	蒸饺
zhōu	rice porridge	粥

ORDERING HOT POT
Types of Hot Pot

yuānyang huǒguō	half spicy, half regular soup	锅底种类 鸳鸯火锅
qīngtāng huǒguō	chicken soup hot pot	清汤火锅
hóngwèi huǒguō	only spicy hot pot	红味火锅
yútóu huǒguō	fish head soup	鱼头火锅

shūcaì lèi	vegetables	蔬菜类
tǔdoù	potato	土豆
dòufu	tofu	豆腐
dòufu pí	tofu skin	豆腐皮
dòng dòufu	cold tofu	冻豆腐
dōngguā	Chinese melon	冬瓜
qīngsǔn	lettuce shoots	青笋
bái luób	fresh white radish	白罗卜
ǒupiàn	sliced lotus	藕片
fěnsī	glass noodles	粉丝
huángdòuyá	bean sprouts	黄豆芽
bōcaì	green spinach	菠菜
xiāngcaì	caraway seeds	香菜
dōngsǔn	bamboo shoots	冬笋
mùěr	black agaric mushroom	木耳
pínggū	flat mushrooms	平菇
jīnzhēngū	noodle mushrooms	金针菇
xiānggū	straw mushrooms	香菇
niángāo	Chinese rice cake	年糕

roù lei	meats	肉类
zhūròu piàn	sliced pork	猪肉片
niúròu piàn	sliced beef	牛肉片
jīròu piàn	sliced chicken	鸡肉片
féi niú	fatty hot pot beef	肥牛
féi yáng	lamb	肥羊
huǒtuǐ	ham	火腿
niúròu wán	beef balls	牛肉丸
ròu wánzi	meatballs	肉丸子
xiajiao	shrimp dumplings	虾饺

PINYIN	ENGLISH	CHINESE
dànjiǎo	egg dumplings	蛋饺
ānchun dàn	quail's eggs	鹌鹑蛋
yā cháng	duck's intestines	鸭肠
yā xuě	duck's blood	鸭血
yú tóu	fish head	鱼头
shànyú piàn	sliced eel	鳝鱼片
níqiu	loach	泥鳅
zhū nǎo	pig brains	猪脑

haǐxiān	**seafood**	鲜
xiā	shrimps	虾
yú piàn	sliced fish	鱼片
yú wán	fish balls	鱼丸
mòyú piàn	black carp strips	墨鱼片
yóuyú piàn	fish strips	鱿鱼片

tiáoliào	**seasoning**	选调料
làjiāo jiàng	chili hot sauce	辣椒酱
làyóu	chili oil	辣油
xiāngyóu	sesame oil	香油
huāshēng jiàng	peanut paste	花生酱
shāchá jiàng	barbeque sauce	沙茶酱
zhīma jiàng	sesame paste	芝麻酱
dà suàn	garlic	大蒜
xiāngcài	cilantro	香菜
cù	vinegar	醋

Useful Phrases		
Qǐng lái yī bēi bīng píjiǔ!	May I have a cold beer, please!	请来一杯冰啤酒！
Qǐng bǎ huǒ guān xiǎo yīdiǎn!	Could you turn the fire down a little, please?	请把火关小一点！
Qǐng bǎ huǒ kāi dà yīdiǎn!	Could you turn the fire up a little, please?	请把火开大一点！
Qǐng bāng wǒmen jiā yīdiǎn tāng!	Could you add some more water, please?	请帮我们加一点汤！

Běijīng		北京
chénpí lǎoyā shānzhēn bāo	duck, mandarin peel and mushroom soup	陈皮老鸭山珍煲
cuìpí qiézi	sweet-and-sour battered eggplant	脆皮茄子
dà lāpí	cold noodles in sesame and vinegar sauce	大拉皮
dà pán jī	diced chicken and noodles in tomato sauce	大盘鸡
guòqiáo mǐxiàn	crossing-the-bridge rice noodles	过桥米线

PINYIN	ENGLISH	CHINESE
huángdì sǔn shāo wánzi	imperial bamboo shoots and vegetarian meatballs	皇帝笋烧丸子
jiāoliū wánzi	crisp-fried pork balls	焦熘丸子
jīnpái tiáoliào	"gold label" sesame sauce (for Mongolian hot pot)	金牌调料
jīngjiàng ròusī	shredded pork with green onion rolled in tofu skin	京酱肉丝
jiǔxiāng yúgān	dried fish in wine sauce	酒香鱼干
juébā chǎo làròu	bacon stir-fried with bracken leaves	蕨粑炒腊肉
làbā cù	garlic-infused vinegar	腊八醋
láncài sìjīdòu	green beans stir-fried with salty vegetable	榄菜四季豆
lǎogānmā shāojī	spicy diced chicken with bamboo and ginger	老干妈烧鸡
làròu dòuyá juǎnbǐng	spicy bacon and bean sprouts in pancakes	腊肉豆芽卷饼
làwèi huájī bǎozǎifàn	chicken and sweet sausage on rice in clay pot	腊味滑鸡煲仔饭
liángbàn zǐ lúsǔn	purple asparagus salad	凉拌紫芦笋
málà tiánluó	field snails stewed in chili and Sìchuān pepper	麻辣田螺
mǎtí niúliǔ	stir-fried beef with broccoli, water chestnuts and tofu rolls	马蹄牛柳
mìzhì zhǐbāo lúyú	paper-wrapped perch and onions on sizzling iron plate	秘制纸包鲈鱼
niúròu wán shuǐjiǎo	beef ball dumplings	牛肉丸水饺
ròudīng báicài xiànbǐng	meat cabbage pie	肉丁白菜馅饼
rúyì hǎitái juǎn	vegetarian sushi rolls	如意海苔卷
sānbēi jī	chicken reduced in rice wine, sesame oil, and soy sauce	三杯鸡
sānxiān làohé	seafood and garlic chive buns	三鲜烙合
shāchá niúròu	beef sautéed with Taiwanese barbecue sauce	沙茶牛肉
shānyào gēng	yam broth with mushrooms	山药羹
shǒuzhuā fàn	Uighur-style rice with carrot and mutton	手抓饭
shǒuzhuā yáng pái	lamb chops roasted with cumin and chili	手抓羊排
shuǐzhǔ yú	boiled fish in spicy broth with numbing peppercorns	水煮鱼
suànxiāng jīchì	garlic paper-wrapped chicken wings	蒜香鸡翅
sǔngān lǎoyā bāo	stewed duck with dried bamboo shoots	笋干老鸭煲
Táiwān dòufu bāo	Taiwanese tofu and vegetables clay pot	台湾豆腐煲
tǔtāng shícài	clear soup with seasonal leafy greens	土汤时菜
Xībèi dà bàncài	Xībèi salad	西贝大拌菜

PINYIN	ENGLISH	CHINESE
xièsānxiān shuǐjiǎo	boiled crab dumplings with shrimp and mushrooms	蟹三鲜水饺
yángròu chuàn	spicy mutton skewers with cumin	羊肉串
yángyóu mádòufu	mashed soybean with lamb oil	洋油麻豆腐
yánjúxiā	shrimp skewers in rock salt	盐局虾
yè niúròu juǎn	grilled beef roll	叶牛肉卷
yóumiàn wōwo	steamed oatmeal noodles	莜面窝窝
yóutiáo niúròu	sliced beef with fried dough in savory sauce	油条牛肉
zhá guàncháng	taro chips with garlic sauce	炸灌肠
zhāngchá yā	crispy smoked duck with plum sauce	樟茶鸭
zhǐjícǎo kǎo niúpái	lotus-leaf-wrapped roast beef with mountain herbs	枳机草烤牛排
zhūròu báicài bāozi	steamed bun stuffed with pork and cabbage	猪肉白菜包子
zhúsūn qìguōjī	mushroom and mountain herbs chicken soup	竹荪气锅鸡
zhútǒng páigǔ	spicy stewed pork with mint	竹筒排骨

Chángchūn 长春

dà páigu	big ribs	大排骨
jiǎozi	dumplings/Chinese ravioli	饺子
jiājīdùnzhēnmó	tender pieces of chicken stewed with mushrooms in a dark savory sauce	家鸡炖榛蘑
Mǎnzhōu jiǎozi	Manchurian dumplings/ravioli	满洲饺子
yuānyang jiǎozi	meat and vegetable dumplings/ravioli	鸳鸯饺子

Chángshā 长沙

hóng zǎozi	red dates	红枣子
língjiǎo	water chestnuts	菱角
mǐtāng sīguā	rice soup with silk gourd	米汤丝瓜
qiàng qíncài xiàguǒ	baby celery and pearl onions sautéed with macadamia nuts	炝芹菜夏果
qīngjiāo qiézi	eggplant sautéed with green pepper	青椒茄子

Chéngdé 承德

cōng shāo yězhū ròu	wild boar cooked with onions	葱烧野猪肉
lùròu chǎo zhēnmó	venison stir-fried with hazel mushrooms	鹿肉炒榛磨
lǔròu dàcōng shuǐjiǎo	dumplings stuffed with donkey meat and onions	驴肉大葱水饺
quècháo shānjī piàn	"sparrow's nest" pheasant slices	雀巢山鸡片
zhēnmó shānjī dīng	nuggets of pheasant with local mushrooms	榛磨山鸡丁

PINYIN	ENGLISH	CHINESE
Chéngdū		成都
báitāng lǔ	plain broth	白汤卤
Càigēn Xiāng páigu	Càigēn Xiāng spareribs	菜根香排骨
cuìpí shàngsù	crispy vegetarian duck	脆皮上素
dòufu jìyú	tofu and golden carp	豆腐鲫鱼
gōngbào jīdīng	spicy diced chicken	宫爆鸡丁
huíguō hòupícài	twice-cooked thick-skinned greens	回锅厚皮菜
jiāozǐ zhēng guìyú	king crab steamed with peppercorns	椒子蒸桂鱼
Jiāróng suāncài kǎo bǐng	Jiāróng bread stuffed with cabbage and barbecued pork	嘉绒酸菜烤饼
jiāzhōu niúròu miàn	California beef noodles	加州牛肉面
lóngyǎn bāozi	dragon eye bāozi	龙眼包子
máoniú ròubāo	yak meat bāozi	牦牛肉包
pào cài	pickled vegetables	泡菜
pàocài jiāyú	fish with pickled vegetables	泡菜佳鱼
pàojiāo mòyúzǎi	pickled pepper with baby squid	泡椒墨鱼仔
suān luóbo chǎo máoniúròu	pickled cabbage with fried yak meat	酸萝卜炒牦牛肉
sūpí niúliǔ	crispy beef tenderloin	酥皮牛柳
yěcài bā	steamed rice bread with wild vegetable wrapped in corn husks	野菜粑
Yìndù gāli chǎocài	Indian vegetable curry	印度咖喱炒菜
yùer shāo jiǎyú	green turtle stewed with taro	芋儿烧甲鱼
Chóngqìng		重庆
guàiwèi yāzi	special flavored duck	怪味鸭子
guōbā ròupiàn	pork with bamboo shoots over crispy rice	锅巴肉片
qīngjiāo bào zǐjī	baby chicken quick-fried with green pepper	青椒爆仔鸡
tiěbǎn shāo zhī yínxuěyú	silver snow fish cooked on an iron plate	铁板烧汁银雪鱼
yùmǐ bǐng	corn cakes	玉米饼
Dàlǐ		大理
ěr kuài	stuffed rice dough	饵块
mùguā jī	fried chicken Bái style	木瓜鸡
rǔshàn	milk fan	乳扇
shāguō yú	stewed fish casserole	砂锅鱼
shuǐzhǔ ròupiàn	pork and vegetable in spicy broth	水煮肉片
Dàlián		大连
bāyú shuǐ jiǎo	fish dumplings	白鱼水饺
buōcài bàn máoxiàn	spinach with mussels	菠菜拌毛蚬
gōngbào yúdīng	kung pao fish	宫爆鱼丁

PINYIN	ENGLISH	CHINESE
nòngtáng zhūdǔ wáwacài	pig stomach cabbage soup	弄堂猪肚娃娃菜
wénchóng gé tāng	soup made with local clams and bok choy	文虫蛤汤
xiānggū guīshēn wēi tǔjī	chicken and mushrooms	香菇归参煨土鸡
yánzéng huánghuāyú	salt-dried yellow fish	盐噌黄花鱼
yùmǐmiàn bǐng	corn cakes	玉米面饼

Dāndōng
丹东

huǒguō	hot pot	火锅
lěngmiàn	cold noodles	冷面
shíguō bànfan	stone pot rice	石锅拌饭
shēngbàn niúròu	raw beef	生拌牛肉
xiānglà gǒuròu	spicy dog meat	香辣狗肉

Dàtóng
大同

chǎo lāmiàn	fried wheat noodles with ground mutton and spring onions	炒拉面
jiǎozi	dumplings	饺子
shāo qiézi	stewed eggplant	烧茄子
sōngrén yùmǐ	corn with pinenuts	松仁玉米

Dēngfēng & Sōng Shān
登封 嵩山

dāoxiāo miàn	knife-sliced noodles	刀削面

Dūnhuáng
敦煌

lǚròu huángmiàn	donkey meat yellow noodles	驴肉黄面
mulberry wine	sāngshèn jiǔ	桑椹酒
xìngpíshuǐ	dried apricot juice	杏皮水
yángpái	lamb chops	羊排

Fúzhōu
福州

Fó tiào qiáng	Buddha jumping over the wall	佛跳墙
guō biān hú	oyster-flavored rice powder soup	锅边糊
yóubǐng	fried dough cake	油饼

Golmud (Gé'ěrmù)
格尔木

huángmèn yángròu	lamb stew	黄焖羊肉
xiānggū càixīn	mushrooms and Chinese greens	香菇菜心
xiāngsū jī	crispy chicken	香酥鸡

Guǎngzhōu
广州

báizzhuó héxiā	Cantonese-style shrimp	白灼河虾
fěnsī zhēng shànbèi	steamed scallops with glass noodles	粉丝蒸扇贝
huādiāo zhù jī	chicken cooked in yellow wine	花雕住鸡

PINYIN	ENGLISH	CHINESE
liǔlián xuěgāo	durian ice cream	榴莲雪糕
jiǔhuáng ròusī	sliced pork with yellow chives	韭黄肉丝
mǎtí xiè	horseshoe crab	马碲蟹
qīngzhēng huāxiè	steamed crab	清蒸花蟹
tángcù sūròu	sweet-and-sour pork	糖醋酥肉
xiāngū xiān xiāwán	stir-fried fresh shrimp with straw mushrooms	鲜菇鲜虾丸
xīníng júròu pái	baked sparerib in lemon sauce	西宁肉排
yóu zhá chòu dòufu	fried stinky tofu	油炸臭豆腐
wǔ shé bāo lǎo jī	boiled five snakes and old chicken in soup	五蛇煲老鸡
zhīshì niúyóu jú hǎixiān dòufu	baked seafood and bean curd	芝士牛油局海鲜豆腐

Guìlín 桂林

dāndān miàn	noodles in spicy peanut sauce	担担面
Guìlín mǐfěn	Guìlín rice noodles	桂林米粉
mǎròu	horse meat	马肉
shāncūn làròu zhēng yúpiàn	steamed taro with smoked meat	山村腊肉蒸芋片
shāncūn tǔjī	free-range chicken	山村土鸡
shuǐzhǔ niúròu	beef and vegetables in a chili sauce	水煮牛肉
tángcù cuìpí yú	crispy sweet-and-sour fish	糖醋脆皮鱼
záliáng zhútǒng fàn	bamboo cooked rice	杂粮竹筒饭

Guìyáng 贵阳

báizhuó xiā	fresh blanched prawns	白灼虾
máo tái	Maotai rice wine	茅台
Miáojiā ānyú	Miáo sour fish	苗家胺鱼
Miáojiā tǔdòu piàn	Miáo deep-fried potato coins	苗家土豆片
Miáowèi páigǔ	spicy Miáo spareribs	苗味排骨
qīngzhēng yú	steamed fish	清蒸鱼
ròusī chǎomiàn	stir-fried noodles with pork	肉丝炒面
xián dànhuáng jìn qīngguā	salted eggs on a bed of cucumber	咸蛋皇浸青瓜
xiān huáishān kòu lǔròu	braised pork and vegetables	鲜淮山扣卤肉
yáng làjiāo	fried hot peppers	阳辣椒

Hángzhōu 杭州

Dōngpō ròu	a soya sauce pork dish named after the poet	东坡肉
Hángzhōu jiàohuà jī	"beggar's chicken"—baked in clay	杭州叫化鸡
lóngjǐng xiārén	shelled shrimp sprinkled with lóngjǐng tea	龙井虾仁

PINYIN	ENGLISH	CHINESE
Harbin		哈尔滨
dànhuáng jūnánguā	fried crepes with vegetables and egg	蛋黄（火局）南瓜
huǒguō	hot pot	火锅
jiācháng tǔdòu ní	homestyle mashed potatoes	家常土豆泥
jiànggǔ	pork ribs	酱骨
pá yáng ròu tiáo	lamb braised in soy-and-garlic sauce	扒盐肉条
sānxiān shuǐjiǎo	three flavor dumplings/ravioli	三鲜水饺
sōngrén yùmǐ shuǐjiǎo	corn and pine nut dumplings/ravioli	松仁玉米水饺
yīpǐn jūntāng	four-mushroom soup	一品菌汤
Héféi		合肥
dāndān miàn	spicy noodles with meat sauce	担担面
lóngxiā yī tiáo lù	lobster street	龙虾一条路
lóngxiā	Chinese-style crayfish	龙虾
Hétián		和田
jiànkāng chá	"healthy" tea	健康茶
Hohhot (Hūhéhàotè)		呼和浩特
chǎo fěn	millet granules	炒粉
chǎo miàn	fried noodles	炒面
dùndun	husked-wheat pancakes	钝钝
guǒtiáo	crisp fried dough	果条
guōzǎi	stew	锅仔
guōzǎi suāncài yáng zásuì	pickled vegetables and sheep organ stew	锅仔酸菜羊杂碎
jiācháng dòufu	home-style tofu	家常豆腐
lā miàn	pulled noodles	拉面
liángfěn	cold translucent noodles with sauce	凉粉
nǎichá	milk tea	奶茶
nǎi pízi	milk skin	奶皮子
shénxiān báicài tāng	Immortals' cabbage soup	神仙白菜汤
shǒubā ròu	mutton eaten with hands	手扒肉
sù hézi	fried vegetable pie	素合子
suāncài ròu chǎo fěn	wheat noodles with shredded pork	酸菜肉炒粉
tèsè kǎo rǔniú	barbecued marinated veal	特色烤乳牛
wō bǐng	corn cakes	窝饼
wōwo	husked wheat pasta in steamer	窝窝
Huáng Shān		黄山
huángshān èrdōng	stir-fried winter mushrooms and bamboo shoots	黄山二冬

PINYIN	ENGLISH	CHINESE
Jiāyùguān		嘉峪关
Jiāngnán qiánjiāng ròu	lightly battered chicken in sweet-and-sour sauce	江南钱江肉
kǎo yángpái	grilled rack of lamb	烤羊排
xīqín bǎihé chǎo xiān yóu	fresh squid on a bed of celery	西芹百合炒鲜鱿
yángròu chuàn	lamb skewers	羊肉串
Jílín		吉林
dà bàn shuǐ lāpí	cold mung-bean flour noodles with cilantro, peanuts, pork, and cucumbers with a spicy sesame sauce	大拌水拉皮
shǒusī yángròu,	tender shreds of lamb	手撕羊肉
zhēn bù tóng tánròu	pieces of fatty pork braised in a homemade beer-based sauce	真不同坛肉
Jìnán		济南
mǎ pópo mèn shuāngsǔn	steamed bamboo and asparagus	马婆婆焖双笋
Jǐngdé Zhèn		景德镇
sāngná niúròu	"sauna" beef	桑拿牛肉
jǐnggāng lǎobiǎo sǔn	peppery bamboo shoots with dried tofu	井岗老表笋
Jǐnghóng		景洪
kǎo sǔnzi	grilled bamboo shoots	烤笋子
kǎo yú	grilled fish	烤鱼
suānsǔn zhǔ jī	chicken cooked with pickled bamboo	酸笋煮鸡
suānsǔn zhǔ yú	fish boiled with sour bamboo shoots	酸笋煮鱼
xiāngzhú fàn	fragrant rice cooked in bamboo	香竹饭
zhútǒng fàn	glutinous rice cooked in bamboo	竹筒饭
Jiǔjiāng		九江
xiāng jiān mǐfěn ròu	minced pork in rice floor	香煎米粉肉
Kāifēng		开封
huāshēng gāo	peanut cake	花生糕
wǔxiāng shāobing	five-spice roasted bread	五香烧饼
xiǎolóng bāo	pork dumplings	小笼包
xìngrén chá	almond tea	杏仁茶
yángròu chuàn	spicy lamb kabob	羊肉串
zhīma duōwèi tāng	sesame soup	芝麻多味汤
Kǎilǐ		凯里
gǒuròu	dog meat	狗肉

PINYIN	ENGLISH	CHINESE
Kashgar (Kāshí)		喀什
bāchǔ mógu	field mushrooms steamed with bok choy, ginger, and garlic	巴楚蘑菇
bàn sān sī	capsicum, onion, carrot, and cucumber noodle salad	拌三丝
chǎokǎo ròu	beef stir-fry	炒烤肉
gānbiān tóngzǐjī	dry-fried spring chicken	干煸童子鸡
lāmiàn	"pulled" noodles	拉面
lǔ gēzi	whole pigeon soup	卤鸽子
wánzimiàn	beef ball noodles	丸子面
zhuā fàn	pilaf	抓饭
Kūnmíng		昆明
cuìpí rúyì yú	crispy vegetarian fish in a sweet-and-sour sauce	脆皮如意鱼
cuìpí yā	crispy fried vegetarian duck	脆皮鸭
guòqiáo mǐxiàn	crossing-the-bridge noodles	过桥米线
hóngshāo niúròu miàn	spicy beef noodles	红烧牛肉面
hóngshāo shīziqiú	vegetarian mushroom ball	红烧狮子球
hùnhé chǎo	fried mixed vegetables	混合炒
huǒshāo gānbā	barbecue dried beef	火烧干巴
jīnbì yān huóxiā	spicy prawn sashimi	金碧腌活虾
qìguō jī	steamed chicken	汽锅鸡
shāo yú	baked duck	烧鸭
shànyú miàn	noodles with eel	鳝鱼面
sūpí guànguàn jī	chicken soup with puff pastry	酥皮罐罐鸡
yēzi qìguō jī	coconut chicken	椰子汽锅鸡
yìndù gāli jī miàn	curry chicken noodles	印度咖喱鸡面
zhēng lǎo nánguā	steamed pumpkin	蒸老南瓜
zhútǒng ròu	pork cooked in bamboo	竹筒肉
Kuqa (Kùchē)		库车
dàpán jī	big-plate chicken	大盘鸡
gānzhá niúròu tiáo	spicy beef strips	干炸牛肉条
lǎohǔ cài	spicy salad	老虎菜
tángbàn huángguā	sweet cucumber	糖拌黄瓜
Lánzhōu		兰州
báobǐng yángròu	deep-fried lamb and green pepper pancake	薄饼羊肉
kǎo yángtuǐ	roast leg of lamb with walnuts	烤羊腿
měnggǔ yángpái	Mongolian lamb	蒙古羊排
niúròu miàn	beef noodles	牛肉面

PINYIN	ENGLISH	CHINESE
sùshí jīnjú bǎihé	sweet vegetarian lilies	素食金橘百合
shǒuzhuā ròu	meat to be eaten by hand	手抓肉

Lhasa (Lāsà)
拉萨

bāozi	steamed buns with pork	包子
cháng xiāngsī	sliced soy-pork sausages	长相思
gānbiān sùcháng	soy-pork slices with green pepper	干煸素肠
gōngbào jīdīng	kung pao chicken	宫爆鸡丁
ròusī miàntiáo	noodles with pork	肉丝面条
qīngchǎo máodòu	beans with soy beef	清炒毛豆
sōngrén yùmǐ	pine nuts, carrots, and sweet corn	松仁玉米

Lhatse (Lāzī)
拉孜

Zāchá fěnsī bāo	vermicelli clay pot	咂茶粉丝煲
niúròu chǎofàn	beef fried rice	牛肉炒饭
shǐyóu jī	salty chicken	豉油鸡

Lì Jiāng
丽江

fēngwèi cān	special Nàxī meal	风味餐
guòqiáo mǐxiàn	crossing-the-bridge noodles	过桥米线
jīdòu chǎo mǐfàn	fried rice with soya bean	鸡豆炒米饭
kǎoyú	barbecue fish	烤鱼
Lì Jiāng bābā	Lìjiāng baked pastry	丽江粑粑
Lì Jiāng dàguōcài	vegetables in broth	丽江大锅菜
Nàxī sāndiéshuǐ	Nàxī 36-dish special	纳西三叠水
qìguō jī	stewed chicken	汽锅鸡
shùwā	frog skin fungus	树蛙
zhá rǔbǐng	fried goat cheese	炸乳饼

Lóngshèng
龙胜

làròu	smoked pork	腊肉
zhútǒng fàn	fragrant rice cooked in bamboo	竹筒饭

Luòyáng
洛阳

Luòyáng Shuǐxí	Luòyáng water banquet	洛阳水席
mìzhī tǔdòu	sweet potato fries in syrup	蜜汁土豆
tángcù lǐji	sweet-and-sour fish	糖醋里脊
zhájiàngmiàn	noodles with bean sauce	炸酱面
zhēnyāncài	ham, radish, mushroom, and egg soup	珍腌菜

Mǎnzhōulǐ
满洲里

sānxiān fàn	three-flavor rice	三鲜饭
shuàn yángròu	mutton hot pot	涮羊肉

PINYIN	ENGLISH	CHINESE
sūbā tāng	beef, potato, and carrot in creamy tomato broth	苏巴汤
qīngshuǐ guōdǐ	vegetarian hot pot	清水锅底
Nánchāng		南昌
Jiāngxī zá cài	spicy mixed vegetables	江西杂菜
yútóu dòufu	fish head tofu	鱼头豆腐
Nánjīng		南京
pánsī yú	deep-fried fish-tail filets in sweet-and-sour sauce	盘丝鱼
shuǐjīng xiārén	tender sautéed shrimp	水晶虾仁
tiānmùhú yútóu	white fish head soup	天目湖鱼头
yāxuě fěnsī	duck-blood vermicelli	鸭血粉丝
Nánníng		南宁
fēngwèi niúzá	special seasoned tripe	风味牛杂
jiāoyán yā xiàba	spicy duck's tongue	椒盐鸭下巴
jiǔcài héxiā	river shrimp with chives	韭菜河虾
Píngyáo		平遥
jiàohuà jī	beggar's chicken	叫化鸡
lǎolao yóumiàn	husked oat pasta	栳栳莜面
māo ěrduo	cats' ears pasta	猫耳朵
tǔdòu shāo niúròu	corned beef with potatoes	土豆烧牛肉
xiāngsū jī	crispy aromatic chicken	香酥鸡
yóuzhá gāo	crispy puff with date and red bean paste	油炸糕
Qīngdǎo		青岛
gōngzhǔ yú	princess fish cooked in oil and steamed	公主鱼
jīngjiàng ròusī	shredded pork Peking style	京酱肉丝
shāo èrdōng	sautéed mushrooms with asparagus	烧二东
sōngshǔ guìyú	deep-fried sweet-and-sour fish	松鼠桂鱼
suànxiāng gǔ	fried pork chop with garlic	蒜香骨
tiěbǎn hélí kǎo dàn	iron plate clams with scrambled eggs	铁板河蜊烤蛋
xiāng sū jī	fragrant chicken	香酥鸡
yóubào hǎiluó	fried sea snails	油爆海螺
yóubā gǔfǎ zhēng qiézi	steamed eggplant	油粑古法蒸茄子
Quánzhōu		泉州
huǒtuǐ	ham	火腿
jiǎyú guī	mock turtle	甲鱼龟
níngméng jīpiàn	lemon chicken	柠檬鸡片
niúpái	beefsteak	牛排

PINYIN	ENGLISH	CHINESE
sùshí	vegetarian food	素食
shuǐguǒ shālā	fruit salad	水果沙拉
Xiàmén hǎilì jiān	Xiàmén-style baby oysters	厦门海蛎煎

Qūfǔ 曲阜

PINYIN	ENGLISH	CHINESE
dàizi shàngcháo	stewed pork, chicken, chestnuts, and ginseng	带子上朝
shénxiān yāzi	Immortals duck	神仙鸭子
shīlǐ yínxìng	sweet ginkgo	诗礼银杏
yángguān sāndié	chicken, vegetables, and egg folded together like a fan	阳关三叠

Sakya 萨迦

PINYIN	ENGLISH	CHINESE
gōngbào jīdīng	spicy chicken with cashews	宫爆鸡丁
mápó dòufu	spicy tofu with chopped meat	麻婆豆腐
yúxiāng qiézi	eggplant in garlic sauce	鱼香茄子

Shànghǎi 上海

PINYIN	ENGLISH	CHINESE
báopí yángròu juǎn	minced lamb wrapped in pancakes	薄皮羊肉卷
cōngyóu bǐng	scallion pancakes	葱油饼
dāndān miàn	noodles in spicy peanut sauce	担担面
dàzhá xiè	hairy crab	大闸蟹
duòjiāo yútóu	fish head steamed with red chili	剁椒鱼头
gānbiān tǔdòu bā	fried potato pancake	干煸土豆粑
gānguōjī guōzi	spicy chicken with peppers	干锅鸡锅子
huíguōròu jiābǐng	twice-cooked lamb wrapped in pancakes	回锅肉夹饼
huǒyán niúròu	beef with red and green peppers	火焰牛肉
kǎo quányáng	roast lamb	烤全羊
kǎo yángròu	barbecue lamb skewers	烤羊肉
lǎohǔ cài	Xīnjiāng salad	老虎菜
làzi jīdīng	spicy chicken nuggets	辣子鸡丁
mízhī huǒfǎng	pork and taro in candied sauce	蜜汁火舫
Nánxiáng xiǎolóng bāo	Nánxiáng crabmeat and pork dumplings	南翔小龙包
qīngzhēng dòuní	creamy mashed beans	青蒸豆泥
qícài dōngsǔn	winter shoots with local greens	荠菜冬笋
sānsī méimao sū	pork, bamboo, and mushroom-stuffed crisp	三丝眉毛酥
shīzi tóu	lion's head meatballs	狮子头
shuǐzhǔ yú	fish slices and vegetables in spicy broth	水煮鱼
shuǐjīng xiārén	stir-fried shrimp	水晶虾仁
sōngshǔ lúyú	sweet-and-sour fried perch	松鼠鲈鱼
suān dòujiǎo ròuní	diced sour beans with minced pork	酸豆角肉泥

PINYIN	ENGLISH	CHINESE
suān jiāngdòu làròu	sour long beans with chilies and bacon	酸豇豆腊肉
sùjī	vegetarian chicken	素鸡
sùyā	vegetarian duck	素鸭
xiǎolóng bāo	pork-stuffed steamed bread dumplings	小笼包
xiāngwèi hóngshǔ bō	fragrant sweet potato in monk's pot	香味红薯钵
xièfěn huì zhēnjūn	braised mushroom with crabmeat	蟹粉烩珍菌
xièfěn xiáolóng	pork and powdered crabmeat dumplings	蟹粉小笼

Shàoxīng
绍兴

jiǔniàng zāo sǔn	drunken bamboo shoots	酒酿糟笋
luóbo sī jiān dàiyú	shredded radish pan-fried with local fish	萝卜丝煎带鱼
méi qiān zhāng zhēng ròu bǐng	dried stinky tofu steamed with mincemeat	霉千张蒸肉饼
qīng zhēng chòu dòufu	steamed stinky tofu	清蒸臭豆腐
ròu tiáo mèn cài	pork strips with vegetables	肉条焖菜
Xiāo Shān luóbo gān	shredded radish	萧山萝卜干
yóu zhá chòu dòufu	fried stinky tofu	油炸臭豆腐
Yuèzhōu zāo jī	drunken chicken	越州糟鸡
zāo xiāng yuè jī	chicken marinated in local wine	糟香越鸡

Shěnyáng
沈阳

chuántǒng	Shàomiàn traditional steamed open-top dumplings	传统哨面
jiǎozi	dumplings/Chinese ravioli	饺子
biānxiàn sānxiān	three flavor	边馅三鲜
zhūròu báicài	pork and cabbage	猪肉白菜
shāomài	steamed open-top dumplings	烧麦
yùcuì shāomài	jade green steamed open-top dumplings	玉翠烧麦

Shigatse   Rikāzé
日喀则

chǎo buōcài	stir-fried spinach	炒菠菜
chǎo miànpiàn	stir-fried noodle pieces	炒面片
gāli tǔdòu	curry potatoes	咖喱土豆
tāng jiǎo	dumplings/ravioli in soup	汤饺
máoniú tóu	yak's head	牦牛头
qīngjiāo niúròu	green peppers and beef	青椒牛肉
rénshēnguǒ	fried ginseng	人参果
tiěbǎn niúròu	iron plate beef	铁板牛肉
tǔdòu jiǎozi	potato dumplings/ravioli	土豆饺子

Sūzhōu
苏州

gūsū lǔyā	marinated duck	姑苏卤鸭
huángmèn hémàn	braised river eel	黄焖河鳗

PINYIN	ENGLISH	CHINESE
sōngshǔ guìyú	sweet-and-sour deep-fried fish	松鼠桂鱼
zuìjī	drunken chicken	醉鸡
Tàiyuán		太原
cù	vinegar	醋
cuō jiāner	twisted points pasta	搓尖儿
guòyóuròu	pork "passed through oil"	过油肉
huoguo	hot pot	火锅
liángfěn	potato-flour noodle	凉粉
māo ěrduō	cat's ears pasta	猫耳朵
tóunǎo	mutton soup	头脑
xiǎobǐng	flat bread	小饼
Téngchōng		腾冲
dàjiùjià	rice-flour pastry stir-fried with ham, mushrooms, and vegetables	大救架
fèngyuán dòufu	tofu deep-fried in milk with eggs and coconut	凤园豆腐
gōngbǎo tiánjī	kung pao frogs' legs	宫保田鸡
sānsè yángyúsī	potato with red and green peppers	三色洋芋丝
shāguō máng mèn jībraised	chicken casserole	砂锅芒焖鸡
Téngchōng suānsǔn yú	Téngchōng sour fish with bamboo	腾冲酸笋鱼
Tiānshuǐ		天水
chǎo miàn	stir-fried noodles	炒面
niúròu miàn	beef noodles	牛肉面
shāguō jīkuài	chicken clay pot	砂锅鸡块
Tónglǐ		同里
mín bǐng	sweet glutinous rice pastry	闵饼
xiǎo xūnyú	smoked fish	小熏鱼
zhuàngyuán tí	braised pigs' trotters	状元蹄
Tóngrén		同
chǎo miànpiàn	stir-fried noodle pieces with squash, beef, and onions	炒面片
chǎo yángròu	stir-fried mutton	炒羊肉
qīngtāng miànpiàn	noodle pieces in soup	清汤面片
rénshēnguǒ mǐfàn	ginseng rice	人参果米饭
Tsetang (Zédāng)		泽当
cuìpí xiāngjiāo	banana fritters	脆皮香蕉
hóngshǔ bǐng	sweet-potato cakes	红薯饼

PINYIN	ENGLISH	CHINESE
Túnxī		屯溪
chòu dòufu	stinky tofu	臭豆腐
huángshān sùwèi yuán	stir-fried mountain vegetables, tofu, and herbs	黄山素味园
wǔcǎi shànsī	stir-fried eel with peppers, mushrooms, and bamboo shoots	五彩鳝丝
Yángzhōu chǎofàn	Yángzhōu fried rice	扬州炒饭
Turpan (Tǔlǔfān)		吐鲁番
kǎo bāozi	samsa	烤包子
sāngshèn jiǔ	mulberry wine	桑椹酒
Ürümqi (Wūlǔmùqí)		乌鲁木齐
bàobīng	ice frosty	爆冰
hóngshāo ròu	braised pork	红烧肉
Wēnzhōu		温州
wāròu mángguǒ chǎofàn	stir-fried rice with mango and frogs' legs	蛙肉芒果 炒饭
niúpái mùguā zhī	steak set with papaya sauce	牛排木瓜汁
qíyì guǒ jiā níngméngzhī	kiwi and lemon juice	奇异果加柠檬汁
yángtiáozhī	star fruit juice	杨桃汁
mùguāzhī	papaya fruit juice	木瓜汁
Wǔhàn		武汉
dànbái shāo gǔpái	pork ribs braised in egg white	蛋白烧骨排
dòufu pí	tofu skin	豆腐皮
Fáng Xiàn huāgū	flowering mushrooms from Fáng County	房县花菇
jiānjiāo luóboyè	sautéed baby turnip greens with dried red peppers	尖椒萝卜叶
miànwō	rice bread	面窝
qiān biān méi	deep-fried fermented tofu	千煸霉
quánjiāfú	mushrooms sautéed with dates	全家福
shuǐguǒ xiāngfàn	sticky rice with watermelon, pineapple, and melon	水果香饭
wǔxiāng niúròu	faux beef with blended spices	五香牛肉
xiǎomǐ zhútǒng páigǔ	spareribs and millet	小米竹筒排骨
yóumàicài	sautéed Chinese lettuce stalk	油麦菜
Wǔtái Shān		五台山
báiguǒ nánguā bāo	ginkgo nut with pumpkin	白果南瓜煲
huākāi xiànfó	mock ham with braised tofu	花开献佛
jǐnshàng tiānhuā	yuxiang shredded "pork"	锦上天(添)花

PINYIN	ENGLISH	CHINESE
lăncài ròumò sìjìdòu	olive leaf fried with string beans	榄菜肉末四季豆
luóhànzhāi	mixed vegetables fried with bean-starched noodles	罗汉斋
sùpái	deep-fried "meat" in brown sauce	素排
tiěbǎn hēijiāo níupái	grilled "steak" with black pepper sauce	铁板黑椒牛排
xǐqì yángyáng	"chicken" cubes fried with dried red peppers	喜气洋洋

Wúxī 无锡

miànjīn	fried balls of flour shredded and stir-fried with meat and vegetables	面筋
páigǔ	Chinese-style baby back ribs	排骨
Tàihú yínyú	deep-fried Lake Tài fish	太湖银鱼
Wúxī xiǎolóng	Wúxī dumplings	无锡小笼
xièfěn xiǎolóng	crab-meat and pork dumplings	蟹粉小笼
xiānròu húntun	pork wontons	虾肉馄饨

Wúyí Shān 武夷山

yóuzhá	pan-fried street snacks	油炸
nánguā bǐng	pumpkin cake	南瓜饼
qié zhī zhá xiāngjiāo	fried banana with tomato sauce	茄汁炸香蕉

Xiàmén 厦门

biánshí	Xiamen style mini wonton soup	扁食
bàn miàn	Xiamen style noodles with peanut sauce	拌面
dāngguī miànjīn tāng	Chinese angelica and gluten soup	当归面筋汤
gālí xiān yóu	curried squid	咖喱鲜鱿
hǎilì jiān	pan-fried oysters	海蛎煎
huáng zé hé	peanut soup	黄则和
luóhàn zhāi	stew of pine nuts, cabbage, cucumber, corn, mushrooms, and fresh coriander	罗汉斋
lúsǔn dòufu tāng	asparagus and tofu soup	芦笋豆腐汤
wāng jì xiànbǐng	small pastries stuffed with a variety of different sweet fillings	汪记馅饼
xiāng ní cáng zhēn	vegetables mashed into a paste	香泥藏珍

Xī'ān 西安

bābǎo tián xīfàn	eight-treasure sweet rice porridge	八宝甜稀饭
bìlǜ zá shuāng gū	bok choy with mushrooms	碧绿杂双菇
fěnzhēng yángròu	lamb between two steamed buns	粉蒸羊肉
guàntāng bāozi	specialty buns	灌汤包子
hóngshāo niúwěi	stewed oxtail	红烧牛尾
ròu jiā mó	shredded pork in a bun	肉夹摸
shǎn nán xiāngyù bǐng	sweet-potato pancake	陕南香芋饼

PINYIN	ENGLISH	CHINESE
suāntāng shuǐjiǎo	lamb dumplings	酸汤水饺
wōtóu	corn bun	窝头
xiǎochī	small snacks	小吃
yángròu pàomó	lamb soup with torn pieces of bun	羊肉泡馍
yōuzhì	local bun	优质
Xīníng		西宁
chǎo miànpiàn	noodle pieces stir-fried with green squash, beef, and peppers	炒面片
kǎo dàbǐng	roasted scones	烤大饼
liángpí	cold noodles with chili tofu	凉皮
Xúnhuà		循化
bàochǎo yějī	quick-fried pheasant	爆炒野鸡
hóngshāo niúwěi	oxtail braised in soy sauce	红烧牛尾
miàn piàn	flat noodle soup	面片
Yán'ān		延安
chǎomiàn hélè	pressed buckwheat noodles with vinaigrette dressing	炒面何勒
dāoxiāo miàn	dāoxiāo noodles	刀削面
huángmó	sweet steamed millet cake	黄馍
kǔcài tǔdòu	mashed potatoes with wild vegetables	苦菜土豆
mǐjiǔ	millet wine	米酒
niúròu liángfěn	bean-starched noodles fried with beef	牛肉凉粉
yángròu pàomó	mutton soup	羊肉泡馍
yóu mómo	fried doughnut made of millet	油
Yánbiān		边
lěngmiàn	cold noodles in vinegar broth	冷面
Yángshuò		阳朔
bàochǎo tiánluó	Lí River snails stuffed with pork	爆炒田螺
dàocáo zá ròu	Yao-style braised pork wrapped in rice stalks	稻草杂肉
hóngshǔ téng	sweet potato shoots	红薯藤
luósī fěn	spicy snail noodles	螺丝粉
píjiǔ yú	fish cooked in beer and spices	啤酒鱼
Yángzhōu		扬州
bāozi	steamed buns	包子
jiǎozi	dumplings/Chinese ravioli	饺子
Yánjí		延吉
lěngmiàn	cold noodles in vinegar broth	冷面

PINYIN	ENGLISH	CHINESE
Yínchuān		银川
bābǎozhōu	eight treasures soup	八宝粥
guàntāng bāozi	unleavened bāozi (steamed buns)	灌汤包子
hézi	savory pies	盒子
suānlà tǔdòu sī	shredded potatoes	酸辣土豆丝
Yīníng		伊宁
dàpán jī	whole chicken with vegetables and noodles	大盘鸡
náng bāo ròu	lamb and vegetable stew on a wheat pancake	馕包肉
Nàrén	roasted horse meat served on thick noodles with a side serving of nan and a salad of tomato, cucumber, and onion	纳仁
niúnǎi	yogurt	牛奶
yībǎzhuā	samosa with three fingerprints in each bun	一把抓
yóu tǎzi	steamed dumplings	油塔子
Yùshù		玉树
hǎo kǎo quányáng	roast lamb	好烤全羊
huáyú	a river fish	滑鱼
kǎo yángtuǐ	roast leg of lamb	烤羊腿
suānlà fěntiáo	sour-and-spicy vermicelli	酸辣粉条
yángpái	rack of lamb	羊排
Zhèngzhōu		郑州
bāsù shíjǐn	mushrooms, seasonal greens, and bamboo shoots	八素什锦
guōtiē dòufu	tofu casserole	锅贴豆腐
tèyōu huìmiàn	house specialty noodles	特优烩面
xiāngmá shāobǐng jiā niúròu	beef sandwiched between steamed buns	香麻烧饼夹牛肉
Miscellaneous		
Spicy	là	辣
or not	búlà	不辣
vinegar	cù	醋
without	búyào cù	不要醋
small bowl	xiǎo wǎn	小碗
large bowl	dà wǎn	大碗

Index

A Guide for Every Type of Traveler

FROMMER'S® COMPLETE GUIDES

For independent leisure or business travelers who value complete coverage, candid advice, and lots of choices in all price ranges.

These are the most complete, up-to-date guides you can buy. Count on Frommer's for exact prices, savvy trip planning, sight-seeing advice, dozens of detailed maps, and candid reviews of hotels and restaurants in every price range. All Complete Guides offer special icons to point you to great finds, excellent values, and more. Every hotel, restaurant, and attraction is rated from zero to three stars to help you make the best choices.

UNOFFICIAL GUIDES®

For honeymooners, families, business travelers, and anyone else who values no-nonsense, *Consumer Reports*–style advice.

Unofficial Guides are ideal for those who want to know the pros and cons of the places they are visiting and make informed decisions. The guides rank and rate every hotel, restaurant, and attraction, with evaluations based on reader surveys and critiques compiled by a team of unbiased inspectors.

FROMMER'S® IRREVERENT GUIDES

For experienced, sophisticated travelers looking for a fresh, candid perspective on a destination.

This unique series is perfect for anyone who wants a cutting-edge perspective on the hottest destinations. Covering all major cities around the globe, these guides are unabashedly honest and down-right hilarious. Decked out with a retro-savvy feel, each book features new photos, maps, and neighborhood references.

FROMMER'S® WITH KIDS GUIDES

For families traveling with children ages 2 to 14.

Here are the ultimate guides for a successful family vacation. Written by parents, they're packed with information on museums, outdoor activities, attractions, great drives and strolls, incredible parks, the liveliest places to stay and eat, and more.

Visit Frommers.com

WILEY

Now you know.

A Guide for Every Type of Traveler

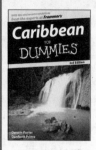

FOR DUMMIES® TRAVEL GUIDES

For curious, independent travelers.

The ultimate user-friendly trip planners, combining the broad appeal and time-tested features of the For Dummies guides with Frommer's accurate, up-to-date information and travel expertise. Written in a personal, conversational voice, For Dummies Travel Guides put the fun back into travel planning. They offer savvy, focused content on destinations and popular types of travel, with current and extensive coverage of hotels, restaurants, and attractions.

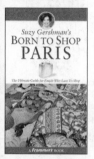

SUZY GERSHMAN'S BORN TO SHOP GUIDES

For avid shoppers seeking the best places to shop worldwide.

These savvy, opinionated guides, all personally researched and written by shopping guru Suzy Gershman, provide detailed descriptions of shopping neighborhoods, listings of conveniently located hotels and restaurants, easy-to-follow shopping tours, accurate maps, size conversion charts, and practical information about shipping, customs, VAT laws, and bargaining. The handy pocket size makes it easy to carry them in your purse while you shop 'til you drop.

FROMMER'S® DOLLAR-A-DAY GUIDES

For independent travelers who want the very best for their money without sacrificing comfort or style.

The renowned series of guides that gave Frommer's its start is the only budget travel series for grown-ups—travelers with limited funds who still want to travel in comfort and style. The $-a-Day Guides are for travelers who want the very best values, but who also want to eat well and stay in comfortable hotels with modern amenities. Each guide is tailored to a specific daily budget and is filled with money-saving advice and detailed maps, plus comprehensive information on sightseeing, shopping, nightlife, and outdoor activities.

FROMMER'S® PORTABLE GUIDES

For short-term travelers who insist on value and a lightweight guide, including weekenders and convention-goers.

Frommer's inexpensive, pocket-sized Portable Guides offer travelers the very best of each destination so that they can make the best use of their limited time. The guides include all the detailed information and insider advice for which Frommer's is famous, but in a more concise, easy-to-carry format.

Visit Frommers.com

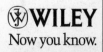

WILEY
Now you know.

Frommer's® Complete Guides

The only guide independent travelers need to make smart choices, avoid rip-offs, get the most for their money, and travel like a pro.

Available at bookstores everywhere.

Destinations in a Nutshell

FROMMER'S® COMPLETE TRAVEL GUIDES

Alaska
Amalfi Coast
American Southwest
Amsterdam
Argentina & Chile
Arizona
Atlanta
Australia
Austria
Bahamas
Barcelona
Beijing
Belgium, Holland & Luxembourg
Belize
Bermuda
Boston
Brazil
British Columbia & the Canadian
  Rockies
Brussels & Bruges
Budapest & the Best of Hungary
Buenos Aires
Calgary
California
Canada
Cancún, Cozumel & the Yucatán
Cape Cod, Nantucket & Martha's
  Vineyard
Caribbean
Caribbean Ports of Call
Carolinas & Georgia
Chicago
China
Colorado
Costa Rica
Croatia
Cuba
Denmark
Denver, Boulder & Colorado Springs
Edinburgh & Glasgow
England
Europe
Europe by Rail

Florence, Tuscany & Umbria
Florida
France
Germany
Greece
Greek Islands
Hawaii
Hong Kong
Honolulu, Waikiki & Oahu
India
Ireland
Italy
Jamaica
Japan
Kauai
Las Vegas
London
Los Angeles
Los Cabos & Baja
Madrid
Maine Coast
Maryland & Delaware
Maui
Mexico
Montana & Wyoming
Montréal & Québec City
Moscow & St. Petersburg
Munich & the Bavarian Alps
Nashville & Memphis
New England
Newfoundland & Labrador
New Mexico
New Orleans
New York City
New York State
New Zealand
Northern Italy
Norway
Nova Scotia, New Brunswick &
  Prince Edward Island
Oregon
Paris
Peru

Philadelphia & the Amish Country
Portugal
Prague & the Best of the Czech
  Republic
Provence & the Riviera
Puerto Rico
Rome
San Antonio & Austin
San Diego
San Francisco
Santa Fe, Taos & Albuquerque
Scandinavia
Scotland
Seattle
Seville, Granada & the Best of
  Andalusia
Shanghai
Sicily
Singapore & Malaysia
South Africa
South America
South Florida
South Pacific
Southeast Asia
Spain
Sweden
Switzerland
Texas
Thailand
Tokyo
Toronto
Turkey
USA
Utah
Vancouver & Victoria
Vermont, New Hampshire & Maine
Vienna & the Danube Valley
Vietnam
Virgin Islands
Virginia
Walt Disney World® & Orlando
Washington, D.C.
Washington State

FROMMER'S® DOLLAR-A-DAY GUIDES

Australia from $60 a Day
California from $70 a Day
England from $75 a Day
Europe from $85 a Day
Florida from $70 a Day

Hawaii from $80 a Day
Ireland from $90 a Day
Italy from $90 a Day
London from $95 a Day

New York City from $90 a Day
Paris from $95 a Day
San Francisco from $70 a Day
Washington, D.C. from $80 a Day

FROMMER'S® PORTABLE GUIDES

Acapulco, Ixtapa & Zihuatanejo
Amsterdam
Aruba
Australia's Great Barrier Reef
Bahamas
Berlin
Big Island of Hawaii
Boston
California Wine Country
Cancún
Cayman Islands
Charleston
Chicago

Disneyland®
Dominican Republic
Dublin
Florence
Las Vegas
Las Vegas for Non-Gamblers
London
Los Angeles
Maui
Nantucket & Martha's Vineyard
New Orleans
New York City
Paris

Portland
Puerto Rico
Puerto Vallarta, Manzanillo &
  Guadalajara
Rio de Janeiro
San Diego
San Francisco
Savannah
Vancouver
Venice
Virgin Islands
Washington, D.C.
Whistler

FROMMER'S® CRUISE GUIDES

Alaska Cruises & Ports of Call

Cruises & Ports of Call

European Cruises & Ports of Call

FROMMER'S® DAY BY DAY GUIDES

Amsterdam	London	Rome
Chicago	New York City	San Francisco
Florence & Tuscany	Paris	Venice

FROMMER'S® NATIONAL PARK GUIDES

Algonquin Provincial Park	National Parks of the American West	Yosemite and Sequoia & Kings
Banff & Jasper	Rocky Mountain	Canyon
Grand Canyon	Yellowstone & Grand Teton	Zion & Bryce Canyon

FROMMER'S® MEMORABLE WALKS

Chicago	New York	Rome
London	Paris	San Francisco

FROMMER'S® WITH KIDS GUIDES

Chicago	National Parks	Toronto
Hawaii	New York City	Walt Disney World® & Orlando
Las Vegas	San Francisco	Washington, D.C.
London		

SUZY GERSHMAN'S BORN TO SHOP GUIDES

Born to Shop: France	Born to Shop: Italy	Born to Shop: New York
Born to Shop: Hong Kong, Shanghai & Beijing	Born to Shop: London	Born to Shop: Paris

FROMMER'S® IRREVERENT GUIDES

Amsterdam	Los Angeles	Rome
Boston	Manhattan	San Francisco
Chicago	New Orleans	Walt Disney World®
Las Vegas	Paris	Washington, D.C.
London		

FROMMER'S® BEST-LOVED DRIVING TOURS

Austria	Germany	Northern Italy
Britain	Ireland	Scotland
California	Italy	Spain
France	New England	Tuscany & Umbria

THE UNOFFICIAL GUIDES®

Adventure Travel in Alaska	Hawaii	Paris
Beyond Disney	Ireland	San Francisco
California with Kids	Las Vegas	South Florida including Miami & the Keys
Central Italy	London	Walt Disney World®
Chicago	Maui	Walt Disney World® for Grown-ups
Cruises	Mexico's Best Beach Resorts	Walt Disney World® with Kids
Disneyland®	Mini Las Vegas	Washington, D.C.
England	Mini Mickey	
Florida	New Orleans	
Florida with Kids	New York City	

SPECIAL-INTEREST TITLES

Athens Past & Present	Frommer's Exploring America by RV
Cities Ranked & Rated	Frommer's NYC Free & Dirt Cheap
Frommer's Best Day Trips from London	Frommer's Road Atlas Europe
Frommer's Best RV & Tent Campgrounds in the U.S.A.	Frommer's Road Atlas Ireland
	Retirement Places Rated

FROMMER'S® PHRASEFINDER DICTIONARY GUIDES

French	Italian	Spanish

THE NEW TRAVELOCITY GUARANTEE

EVERYTHING YOU BOOK WILL BE RIGHT, OR WE'LL WORK WITH OUR TRAVEL PARTNERS TO MAKE IT RIGHT, RIGHT AWAY.

*To drive home the point,
we're going to use the word "right" in every single sentence.*

Let's get right to it. Right to the meat! Only Travelocity guarantees everything about your booking will be right, or we'll work with our travel partners to make it right, right away. Right on!

Here's a picture taken smack dab right in the middle of Antigua, where the guarantee also covers you.

The guarantee covers all but one of the items pictured to the right.

For example, what if the ocean view you booked actually looks out at a downright ugly parking lot? You'd be right to call – we're there for you. And no one in their right mind would be pleased to learn the rental car place has closed and left them stranded. Call Travelocity and we'll help get you back on the right track.

Now, you may be thinking, "Yeah, right, I'm so sure." That's OK; you have the right to remain skeptical. That is until we mention help is always right around the corner. Call us right off the bat, knowing that our customer service reps are there for you 24/7. Righting wrongs. Left and right.

Now if you're guessing there are some things we can't control, like the weather, well you're right. But we can help you with most things – to get all the details in righting,* visit **travelocity.com/guarantee**.

*Sorry, spelling things right is one of the few things not covered under the guarantee.

I'd give my right arm for a guarantee like this, although I'm glad I don't have to.

travelocity

You'll never roam alone.

IF YOU BOOK IT, IT SHOULD BE THERE.

Only Travelocity guarantees it will be, or we'll work with our travel partners to make it right, right away. So if you're missing a balcony or anything else you booked, just call us 24/7. **1-888-TRAVELOCITY.**

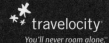

travelocity

You'll never roam alone.